TENNESSEE SOCIAL STUDIES

# WORLD
## HISTORY & GEOGRAPHY

### THE INDUSTRIAL REVOLUTION TO THE PRESENT

Jackson J. Spielvogel, Ph.D.

McGraw Hill

**About the Cover:** The images shown on the front cover show top to bottom: i) Ancient Chinese architecture, Beijing; ii) Magnifying glass and ancient map; iii) Arc de Triomphe du carrousel; iv) The Angel of Independence, Mexico City; v) New South African Fifty Rand banknote featuring Nelson Mandela portrait

**Cover:** hxdyl/iStock/Getty Images; Andrey Burmakin/Shutterstock; TonyBaggett/iStock/Getty Images; Moment Open/Getty Images; Sergio Mendoza Hochmann/Moment RF/Getty Images; Don Bayley/E+/Getty Images

mheducation.com/prek-12

Mc Graw Hill



Send all inquiries to:
McGraw-Hill Education
8787 Orion Place
Columbus, OH 43240

ISBN: 978-007-687170-4
MHID: 0-07-687170-3

Printed in the United States of America.

2 3 4 5 6 7 8 9 10 QVS 23 22 21 20 19

# AUTHORS

**Jackson Spielvogel, Ph.D.,** is associate professor emeritus of history at the Pennsylvania State University. He received his Ph.D. from The Ohio State University, where he specialized in Reformation history under Harold J. Grimm. His articles and reviews have been published in several scholarly publications. He is coauthor (with William Duiker) of *World History,* published in 1994 (8th edition, 2016). Professor Spielvogel has won five major university-wide awards, and in 2000, he became the first winner of the Schreyer Institute's Student Choice Award for innovative and inspired teaching.

**Contributing Author**

**Jay McTighe** has published articles in a number of leading educational journals and has coauthored 10 books, including the best-selling *Understanding by Design* series with Grant Wiggins. McTighe also has an extensive background in professional development and is a featured speaker at national, state, and district conferences and workshops. He received his undergraduate degree from The College of William and Mary, earned a Masters degree from The University of Maryland, and completed post-graduate studies at The Johns Hopkins University.

# ACADEMIC CONSULTANTS

**Gerardo V. Aldana, Ph.D.**
Professor, Department of Chicano Studies
Associate Dean, College of Creative Studies
University of California at Santa Barbara
Santa Barbara, California

**Karl E. Baughman, Ph.D.**
Assistant Professor
Department of History
Prairie View A&M University
Prairie View, Texas

**Brian N. Becker, Ph.D.**
Associate Professor
The Division of Social Sciences and History
Delta State University
Cleveland, Mississippi

**David Berger, Ph.D.**
Ruth and I. Lewis Gordon Professor of Jewish History
Dean, Bernard Revel Graduate School
Yeshiva University
New York, New York

**Michael C. Brose, Ph.D.**
Director, East Asian Studies Center and Pan Asia Institute
Indiana University
Bloomington, Indiana

**Tom Daccord**
Educational Technology Specialist
Co-Director, EdTechTeacher
Boston, Massachusetts

**Carolyn Gallaher, Ph.D.**
Associate Professor
School of International Service
American University
Washington, D.C.

**Jamie Goodall, Ph.D.**
Assistant Professor
Department of Public History
Stevenson University
Stevenson, Maryland

**Farid Mahdavi, Ph.D.**
Lecturer
Department of History
San Diego State University
San Diego, California

**Justin Pfeifer, Ph.D.**
Assistant Professor
Department of History
Peru State College
Peru, Nebraska

**Justin Reich**
Educational Technology Specialist
Co-Director, EdTechTeacher
Boston, Massachusetts

**Guy R. Welbon, Ph.D.**
Associate Professor Emeritus
South Asia Studies and Religious Studies
University of Pennsylvania
Philadelphia, Pennsylvania

# CONTENTS

Sotheby/akg-images

Division [LC-USZ62-64309]

# CONTENTS

Scala/White Images/Art Resource, NY

©Christie's Images/Corbis

# CONTENTS

©Sarin Images/Granger, NYC

Bettmann/Corbis

CONTENTS

Pictures From History/The Image Works

Rue des Archives/Granger, NYC -- All rights reserved.

# CONTENTS

Heinrich Hoffmann/Time & Life Pictures/ Getty Images

Wallace Kirkland/The LIFE Picture Collection/Getty Images

# CONTENTS

## World War II and the Holocaust (1939–1945) ........ 375

### Essential Questions

*Why do political actions often lead to war? • How does war impact society and the environment?*

## The Cold War (1945–1989) ........ 417

### Essential Question

*How does conflict influence political relationships?*

# CONTENTS

Gallo Images/Alamy

Bettmann/Corbis

## CONTENTS

# CONTENTS

# FEATURES

## POINTS OF VIEW



## THE WORLD'S LITERATURE



## BIOGRAPHY

# FEATURES

## MAKING CONNECTIONS



## CITIZENSHIP

# MAPS, CHARTS, AND GRAPHS

# MAPS, CHARTS, AND GRAPHS

# MAPS, CHARTS, AND GRAPHS

# PRIMARY SOURCES

# PRIMARY SOURCES



### CHAPTER 5



### CHAPTER 6

# PRIMARY SOURCES



**CHAPTER 7**



**CHAPTER 8**



**CHAPTER 9**

# PRIMARY SOURCES



**CHAPTER 10**



**CHAPTER 11**

# PRIMARY SOURCES



## CHAPTER 12



## CHAPTER 13



## CHAPTER 14

# PRIMARY SOURCES



### CHAPTER 15



### CHAPTER 16

# CONTENTS

SKILLBUILDER

# Reading and Creating a Thematic Map

## Why Learn This Skill?

You will often encounter thematic maps when studying history. Knowing how to read and create a thematic map will help you understand the information this type of map presents.

## Learning the Skill

A thematic map takes data about a region and puts it on a map using colors and symbols that show how the data connects to geographical features. Thematic maps can help you identify the physical and human systems of a geographic area. These maps can portray the politics, economy, society, culture, climate, or history of that area or any combination of those characteristics.

A land-use map is an example of a thematic map. It uses colors and symbols to show things such as where crops are grown, where mines are located, or the population density. Another example is a historical map that uses symbols, arrows, and colors to show the routes followed by explorers or how borders change over time.

## When reading a thematic map,

- **read the title.** This will help you understand the map's theme, location, time period, and type of data being shown.
- **read the map key.** Thematic maps use symbols and colors to convey information. Sometimes the symbols change size to indicate if more or less of something exists at that point on the map.
- **study the map and draw conclusions.** Look for patterns on the map. They reveal how the data presented by the thematic symbols and colors relates to the geographic features.

## When creating a thematic map,

- **identify the data you want to present.**
- **decide what kind of map you need.** What region do you want to show? What geographic features have to be included? This decision is usually based on the patterns you want to show.
- **decide what scale and units of measurement you will use.** Make sure your map is large enough to show the area you are concerned with but small enough that your data is readable. Make sure you use the correct units of measurement and include a map scale.
- **decide what symbols and colors best present the data.** Should the symbols change size or color for different sets of data? Does the map need to show things changing over time?
- **prepare your map key carefully.**

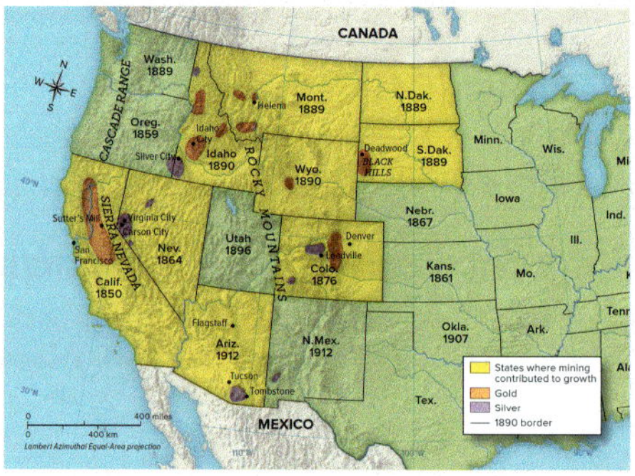


## Practicing the Skill

Analyze the thematic map "Mining Helps Build a Nation," then answer the following questions.

1. What part of the United States does the map show?
2. What symbols are used to depict mining activities?
3. What other information does the map provide?
4. Use the patterns on the map to list the states in order of their gold and silver discoveries. Explain why you put them in the order you did.

### Applying the Skill

Create your own thematic map. Research where different types of crops were grown in the American West from 1870 to 1900. Use the thematic map to show key events and the geographic patterns that resulted from farming and ranching in the West.

SKILLBUILDER

# Sequencing and Using a Time Line

## Why Learn This Skill?

Have you ever complained that history is just a bunch of dates that you have to memorize? Actually, history is a series of causes and effects that happen over time in a sequence. If you want to know what caused an event or what effect it had, you must know the sequence of events.

## Learning the Skill

Sequencing is simply putting things in the correct order. Putting historical events in the correct sequence will often reveal a possible relationship between them. Sequencing involves two types of chronology. **Absolute chronology** is the specific time and date something happened. **Relative chronology** tells when something happened compared to something else.

A time line presents a sequence of related historical events on a historical or vertical line. It lists events that occurred between specific dates in order, often with captions to give a quick summary of what happened. The number of years between these dates is called the time span. Time lines are usually divided into smaller segments, or time intervals.

## Practicing the Skill

Look at the time line of key events of nationalist movements in the Middle East, and then answer the questions that follow.

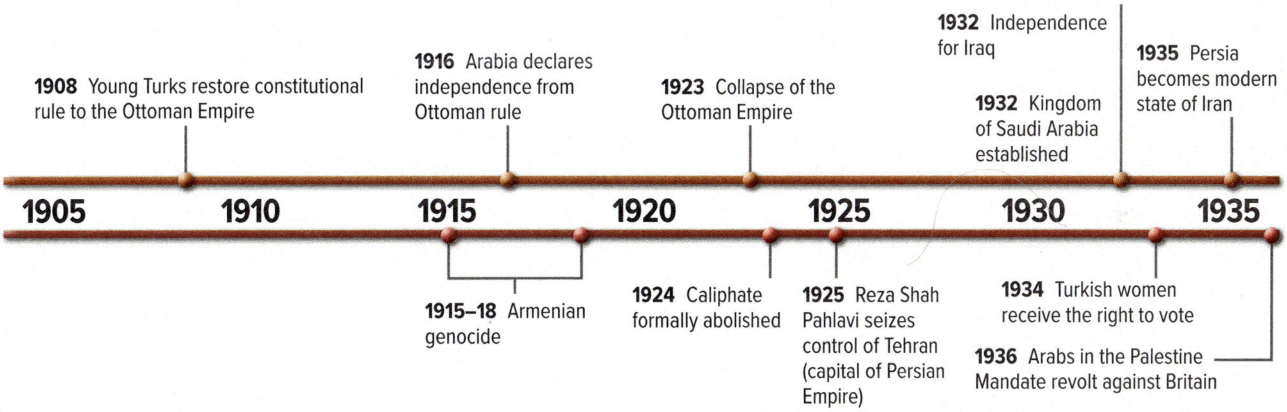


1. What is the time span of this time line?
2. What intervals is the time line using?
3. In what year did Iraq receive independence?
4. Use the time line to put these people and events in the correct relative chronology: Reza Shah Pahlavi, Armenian genocide, Young Turks, woman suffrage in Turkey.
5. What two major events happened in 1932? What relationship exists between the two events?
6. What possible cause-and-effect sequence does the time line show between the collapse of the Ottoman Empire and independence movements in the Middle East?

### Applying the Skill

Keeping in mind what you have learned, read through Chapter 10, Lesson 4: "Nationalism in Latin America." Create a time line sequencing the events of the nationalist movement from 1916 to 1940. Be sure to include dates and brief, one-sentence captions identifying key events and individuals.

SKILLBUILDER

# Understanding How Historians Interpret the Past

## Why Learn This Skill?

By now, you have probably realized that historians do not always agree about how historical events happened or how events affected things that happened later. When you study history, it is easy to become confused unless you have some idea of how historians interpret the past and the different approaches they use. Understanding how historians interpret events of the past will allow you to practice their methods within your textbook.

## Learning the Skill

The study of how historians approach history is called historiography. Historians must answer three big questions: *causation* (why a historical event happened), *outcome* (what happened as a result of the event) and *meaning* (why the event matters). Historians approach answering these questions in one of three ways:

- *Intentionalism* (or *volitionalism*): focuses on leaders and the choices they made
- *Structuralism*: focuses on the way things were organized, such as the rules and structure of the political system, the economy, and society
- *Intellectualism*: focuses on ideas, ideology, culture, and people's perceptions to understand the cause of an event

## Practicing the Skill

Read the following paragraphs about the causes of World War I, and then answer the questions that follow.

*"The system of nation-states that emerged in Europe in the last half of the nineteenth century led not to cooperation but rather to competition. Each European nation-state regarded itself as subject to no higher interest or authority. Each state was guided by its own self-interests and success. Furthermore, most leaders thought that war was an acceptable way to preserve the power of their national states. These attitudes made war an ever-present possibility.*

*"The imperialist expansion of the last half of the nineteenth century also played a role in the coming of war. The competition for lands abroad, especially in Africa, led to conflict and heightened the existing rivalries among European states."*

1. What would a structuralist emphasize in trying to understand the causes of World War I?
2. What theories about the causes of World War I would intellectual historians favor?
3. Underline a sentence or two in the passage in which historians practice a volitional, or intentionalist, approach to World War I.

## Applying the Skill

Using what you have learned, conduct your own inquiry into some aspect of World War I or the Russian Revolution. Identify and write a question about these topics you would like to answer. Then go online to find several sources that talk about the history related to your question. (Remember to include both primary and secondary sources.) After familiarizing yourself with your sources, write a hypothesis, or possible explanation, for your original question. Then ask yourself whether you are taking an intentional, structural, or intellectual approach to the question. Put together a short report presenting your conclusions.

# Analyzing Historical Evidence

## Why Learn This Skill?

As you learn about history from this textbook and other sources, it is important to understand where this information comes from and how we have come to understand events and ideas that happened long ago. Archaeologists, anthropologists, and historians analyze evidence in the field, and that work relates directly to what you learn in the classroom.

## Learning the Skill

Historians, archaeologists, and anthropologists collect evidence in a variety of ways to piece together the story of the past. Archaeologists look at past societies by analyzing what people have left behind. Anthropologists look at human life and culture, whether in the past or present. And historians work with both disciplines to help create a larger picture of the political, economic, and cultural aspects of a particular place and time. All may make field observations and conduct landscape analysis to better understand and analyze evidence and draw conclusions.

When gathering evidence about ancient societies, writings can be difficult to find or nonexistent, and so we have to piece together how ancient peoples lived, what they valued, and how they related to each other on the basis of artifacts left behind. Technology is also used to understand an artifact's date and function.

When analyzing artifacts, it is helpful to use the basic questions of who, what, when, where, how, and why:

- Who created this artifact?
- What was it used for or what does it represent?
- When was it made?
- Where did this artifact originate?
- How was it made or used?
- Why was it created or what was its purpose?

Sometimes, not all of these questions can be answered, and some may overlap, but any part that can provide answers will establish new information about a period in time.

## Practicing the Skill

Read the following excerpt and fill in the table below.

*"The Chauvet cave discovered in southern France in 1994 contained more than 300 paintings of lions, oxen, owls, panthers, and other animals. Most of these are animals that Paleolithic peoples did not hunt, which indicates that they were painted for religious or decorative purposes.*

*"Using stone lamps filled with animal fat to light the caves, early artists painted with fingers and twigs and even blew paint through hollow reeds. They mixed mineral ores with animal fat to make red, yellow, and black paint. A variety of realistically painted animals covers the caves. Few humans appear in these paintings, and when they do appear, they are drawn as sticklike figures."*

| | |
|---|---|
| **Who** | |
| **What** | |
| **When** | |
| **Where** | |
| **How/Why** | |

## Applying the Skill

Locate an artifact either in this textbook or on the Internet on an archaeology site. As a class, go through the points of the table to better understand how that artifact fits into its particular time period. Also identify the methods used by archaeologists, anthropologists, or historians to analyze evidence.

# SKILLBUILDER

## Interpreting Graphs

### Why Learn This Skill?

Using graphs is a good method of illustrating dates, facts, and figures. With a graph, you can easily compare change, progressions, and differences.

### Learning the Skill

There are basically three types of graphs:

- **Circle graphs:** They look like a pizza that has been divided into different-sized slices. They are useful for comparisons and percentages.
- **Bar graphs:** Individual bars are drawn for each item being graphed. The lengths of the bars easily illustrate differences or changes over time.
- **Line graphs:** Each item is indicated by a point on the graph. The points are then connected by a line. You can tell how values have changed by whether the line goes up or down.

Most graphs also have titles and labels that include extra information. If the title is named "Maria's Weekly Clothing Expenses," then it is plotting how much Maria spends on clothes every week. Labels indicate when and how much Maria spent on clothes. The viewer can determine relationships among different numbers in the graph with a simple glance. If it is a bar graph, the bars representing different numbers are different lengths.

### Practicing the Skill

Look closely at the bar graph on this page comparing the nuclear weapons stockpiles of the United States and the USSR from 1945 to 1985.

Graphs use a guide called a key to indicate what different bars, patterns, and colors represent. The key for this graph shows you which color bars represent the countries of the United States and the USSR. If there were more countries represented by bars in the graph, the key would include more colors for those countries, too. When other graphs are used in your lessons, pay close attention to the key and what it tells you. As the name suggests, it is your tool for unlocking the information in the graph.

### Skills Assessment

Study the bar graph and answer the following questions.

1. According to the graph, in what year did the United States have the greatest stockpile of nuclear weapons?
2. How many nuclear weapons did the USSR have in the year 1975?
3. In what year did the nuclear weapons stockpile of the USSR surpass that of the United States?
4. Using the graph, describe the trends you notice in the size of each nation's nuclear stockpile over the course of the Cold War.
5. Based on the graph, can you draw any conclusions about the relationship between the two superpowers during this time period?

### Applying the Skill

Study the bar graph on this page closely and write a paragraph summarizing how key events of the Cold War affected the nuclear weapons buildup of the two superpowers. Remember, a graph does not just present individual facts—it also presents relationships among those facts.

**NUCLEAR WEAPONS STOCKPILES, 1945–1985**

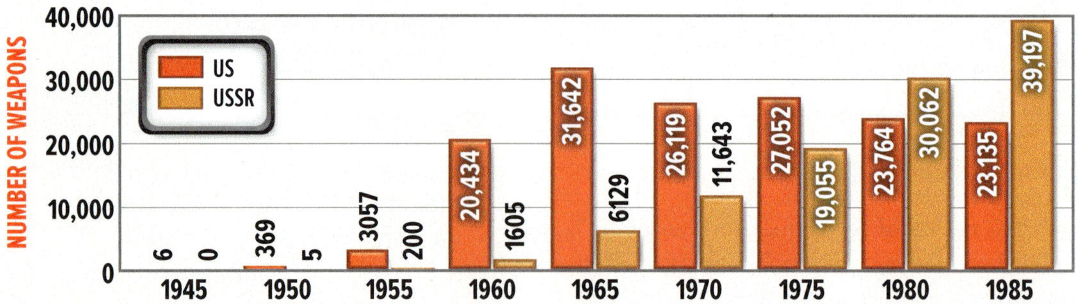


**Source:** Natural Resources Defense Council, "Archive of Nuclear Data," nrdc.org

SKILLBUILDER

# Analyzing Primary Sources

## Why Learn This Skill?

Did you ever witness or experience an event, only to discover that another witness remembers the same event differently than you do? An eyewitness account of a place or event is a primary source. The advantage of a primary source is that it contains firsthand knowledge. Understanding the information primary sources present is a key skill in understanding and interpreting historical events.

Primary sources may include diaries, letters, memoirs, interviews with eyewitnesses, images, photographs, news articles, and even legal documents. Today, older digital items such as email and even certain web pages could be considered primary sources. Often, primary sources provide detailed accounts of events but reflect only one perspective. For this reason, you must examine as many sources as possible before drawing any conclusions.

## Learning the Skill

Follow these steps to analyze a primary source:

1. Identify the author of the source. This may take a bit of research. Understanding who the author is will allow you to note any biases or opinions expressed by the author or creator of the source.
2. Identify when and where the document was written. Understanding the time period the primary source is from will help you better understand the perspective it presents.
3. Read the document for its content and answer the five "W" questions:
    - Who is it about?
    - What is it about?
    - When did it happen?
    - Where did it happen?
    - Why did it happen?
4. Determine what kind of information may be missing from the primary source. Having a second primary source to use as a comparison will help you.

## Practicing the Skill

Read the following excerpts below about the United States in Hawaii, and answer the questions that follow.

*"The United States had manifested towards the Hawaiians a spirit of goodwill, and had maintained an attitude of neighborly respect in all official relations. The visits of their naval vessels had been generally helpful and encouraging; the purposes of their immigrants had been generally civilizing and progressive."*

—The Blount Report on Affairs in Hawaii, 1894–95

*"MY GREAT AND GOOD FRIEND: It is with deep regret that I address you on this occasion. Some of my subjects, aided by aliens, have renounced their loyalty and revolted against the constitutional government of my Kingdom. They have attempted to depose me and to establish a provisional government, in direct conflict with the organic law of this Kingdom. Upon receiving incontestable proof that his excellency the minister plenipotentiary of the United States, aided and abetted their unlawful movements and caused United States troops to be landed for that purpose, I submitted to force, believing that he would not have acted in that manner unless by the authority of the Government which he represents."*

—Letter from Ex-Queen Liliuokalani to President Benjamin Harrison, February 1893

1. How do the two passages differ in their views on the annexation of Hawaii by the United States?
2. Which source did you find more believable, or valid? Why?

## Applying the Skill

Working with a partner, choose a recent current event in the news and locate two firsthand accounts of the event. In what ways do the accounts support each other? In what ways do they differ? Use what you have learned to evaluate the validity and usefulness of each source you have found. Then write a short paragraph describing which account you found to be more believable, and why.

(t)_______. 1895. Foreign Relations of the United States - 1894. Appendix II: Affairs in Hawaii. Washington: Government Printing Office; (b) Liliuokalani R. 1893. Letter to President Benjamin Harrison. Reprinted 1894. Hawaiian Islands - Report of the Committee on Foreign Relations, United States Senate. Vol. II. Washington: Government Printing Office.

SKILLBUILDER

# Using Secondary Sources

## Why Learn This Skill?

Recently you have learned about how to analyze primary sources. Now you will have the opportunity to learn how to make use of a similar type of item—secondary sources. Secondary sources are similar to primary sources. A secondary source is a kind of source that comments on or analyzes primary sources.

Unlike primary sources, secondary sources are often limited to documents or recordings. These items are created long after the event has occurred and offer an interpretation but not an eyewitness account of that event. This textbook, for instance, is a kind of secondary source.

Like primary sources, learning to use secondary sources will help you figure out whether these sources are presenting a complete and actual picture of a topic or event and whether you can rely on the information they present.

## Learning the Skill

Follow these steps when using a secondary source to determine what an author's main idea or argument is, and whether you agree with it:

1. Ask: Who is the author? What are his or her credentials? Is he or she trustworthy?
2. Who published the secondary source? Is there any indication of bias?
3. When was the source written?
4. Does the source have footnotes or endnotes and a bibliography in which the author lists the sources of evidence used to prepare the work?
5. Does the author use primary sources or mostly other secondary sources?
6. Are the primary sources used by the author reliable? Do you notice any weaknesses or biases?
7. Figure out the author's argument. What are the major questions or issues the author is trying to explain?
8. Do the author's conclusions make sense to you? What kind of evidence could be used to disprove them?

## Practicing the Skill

Recall that your textbook is a kind of secondary source. Take this opportunity to evaluate this textbook as a secondary source. Analyze your textbook by answering the following questions:

1. Can the textbook be used to analyze and answer historical questions?
2. Who are the authors of this program? What are their credentials?
3. Who published your textbook? Is there likely to be a bias in what they publish?
4. Does the textbook use primary sources? What kinds?
5. Does your textbook focus on one single argument or issue? Why or why not?
6. Pick one chapter from your textbook and analyze it as a secondary source. Try to identify its main argument and how it analyzes and explains the historical questions of the time period the chapter covers.

## Applying the Skill

Using the Internet, locate two secondary sources about the Boxer Rebellion (remember to look for sources that present ideas about the Boxer Rebellion, not just ones that list dates and information). Write a paragraph analyzing each of the sources. Remember to address the following questions: What is the author's opinion on the Boxer Rebellion? What evidence is used to support this position? Based on what you have learned, which of these two sources do you find more believable, and why?

# SKILLBUILDER

## Determining Cause and Effect

### Why Learn This Skill?

Why do we study history? We know things have happened in the past that have shaped the world we live in today. There are many things we appreciate and other things we think are wrong. The purpose of history, perhaps more than anything else, is to explain why things happened and what changed as a result. In short, understanding history requires you to identify cause-and-effect relationships.

### Learning the Skill

Determining cause and effect involves considering why an event occurred. A cause is an action, an event, a condition, or a decision that makes something else happen. What happens is the effect.

There are three kinds of causes. Necessary causes are causes that you must have or the event cannot happen. A sufficient cause is a cause that all by itself can cause an event, but it is not the only possible cause. Contributory causes cannot by themselves cause an event, but they can help shape the conditions under which it happens.

To determine cause and effect, follow these seven steps:

1. Ask why an event happened. List possible reasons for the event.
2. Look at the list. Which causes are necessary? Are they all necessary? Which ones might be sufficient but not needed to explain the event? Which causes only contributed to shaping the event?
3. Look at the timing of the causes. Which ones established conditions far in the past? These are long-range causes. Which ones helped trigger an event after conditions were in place? These are short-term or immediate causes.
4. To determine effects, ask, "What happened because of this?" or "What were the results of this?"
5. Examine which effects happened immediately and which ones developed only slowly over time. These are short- and long-range effects.
6. Be sure you have causes and events in the correct sequence.
7. Make sure there is a logical or reasonable connection between the causes and effects you have identified. Sometimes things happen close together, but that does not mean one caused the other. Writing history is all about explaining why your evidence proves a cause-and-effect relationship.

### Practicing the Skill

Open to the lesson "The Cold War Begins." Read the section entitled "The Division of Germany and the Berlin Airlift" and answer these questions.

1. What event is being explained in this section?
2. What causes are said to have explained the event?
3. Which causes are long-range causes? Which causes are short-term causes?
4. Which causes are necessary? Which are contributory?
5. What were the effects of these causes?

### Applying the Skill

Open to the lesson "The Cold War Begins." Reread the lesson and apply your skills at determining cause and effect. Write a brief essay describing the causes of the Cold War. Be sure to identify short-term and long-term causes, and point out which causes led to effects that in turn led to even more causes that intensified the Cold War. Identify which causes were necessary to the Cold War and which ones were contributory.

# Identifying Bias and Points of View

## Why Learn This Skill?

Every day, social media, talk shows, blog posts, text messages, and email flood us with opinions and commentary. To understand and assess what we see, hear, and read and then to make good decisions and choices, we must be able to detect bias and a source's point of view. Understanding bias and point of view is especially useful when using primary sources to understand a historical era and interpret events.

## Learning the Skill

Everyone has bias—or tendency to look at information based on their own experiences, knowledge, prejudices, and emotional reactions. People's biases and points of view are based on many factors, including age, gender, race, ethnic background, economic class, religion, education, location, occupation, relationships, and personal experiences. All these things need to be taken into account when looking for bias in a point of view.

**To determine a point of view and to detect bias in written, oral, and visual materials, follow these steps:**

1. **What argument is being made?** What are you being asked to think, to do, to feel, or to believe? This is the point of view.
2. **Gather information about the author.** Is there anything that would cause the author to have a particular bias?
3. **Assess motivation.** Will the author benefit from people adopting his or her point of view? Who will benefit?
4. **Determine the context.** What was going on when the argument was made?
5. **Examine the language or visual imagery being used.** Is it emotional? Do the words or pictures have positive or negative overtones? Are facts included that can be verified? Does the author use a lot of metaphors or analogies? Does the author use terms that may have different connotations because of when he or she wrote them or where they originated?
6. **Apply prior knowledge about the subject.** Does the point of view match other sources? If necessary, research other sources on the subject and compare them to the author's viewpoint. How might the author's bias affect how he or she interprets events, and how might others, with different biases, interpret the same events differently?

## Practicing the Skill

Examine the cartoon by Winsor McCay, published in 1931, found in Chapter 11 of this book.

1. How would you describe the image's emotional content?
2. Winsor McCay often depicted European nations as hoping to take advantage of the United States in foreign affairs. What might that suggest about his point of view regarding the League of Nations?
3. Based on your knowledge of the period between the two world wars, what bias and point of view is being depicted in this cartoon?

### Applying the Skill

**Detecting Bias in Oral Material** Go to the Points of View feature in the chapter on World War I. Read the excerpts from the speeches presented there. What points of view do the speeches reveal? What biases do you detect? Research both speakers and write a paragraph explaining their points of view.

SKILLBUILDER

# Locating Turning Points in History

## Why Learn This Skill?

Geographic factors are crucial to understanding major events in history. If we cannot put together time and place, we cannot get the full picture of an event's significance.

## Learning the Skill

Turning points in history occur when major periods of change or events change the way people live or look at the world. Turning points can include the following:

- revolutions
- exploration
- discoveries
- the rise and fall of empires
- social and religious change, such as disease, urbanization, industrialization, the introduction of new religions, and new technology

Location is an influential and motivating factor when it comes to turning points in history, as these events or ideas can affect a particular region or a larger part of the world. When attempting to locate places of historical significance in which turning points occurred, ask yourself these questions:

- In what area of the world did the turning point occur? Was it in one particular region, or was it widespread?
- What is special or different about the geography of the location the turning point occurred?
- Can you recognize a pattern between different turning points that occurred in the same area?

## Practicing the Skill

Examine this map of Europe and the Mediterranean world, noting the various cities included on it. Each city holds historical significance by being a part of at least one turning point in history.

1. Most of the cities on the map are located around seas or major rivers. What general conclusion can you reach about the role of access to major waterways and turning points in history?
2. On the basis of your answer to Question 1, how might seas and rivers affect turning points in history?
3. After examining this map, use areas called out to identify at least two turning points in history that could be illustrated on this map.

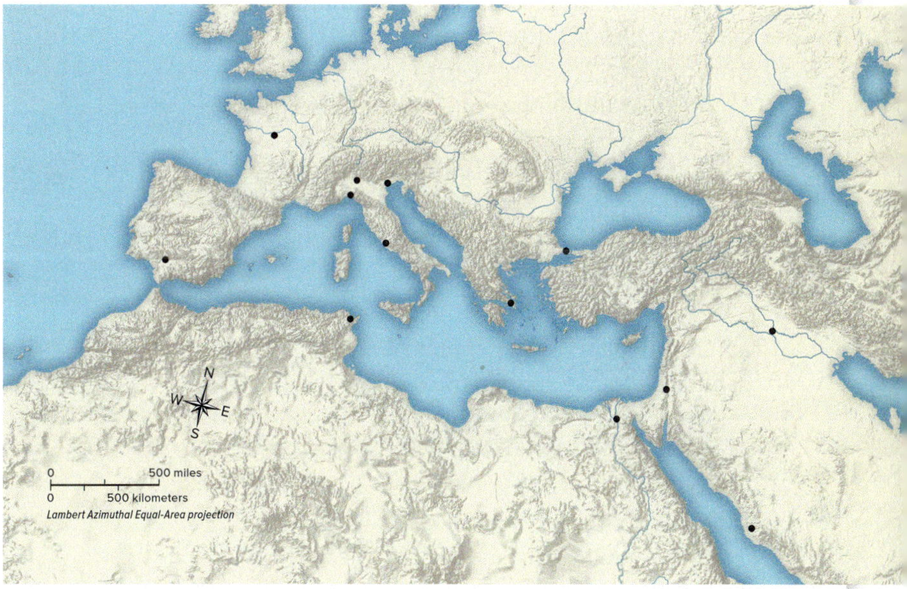


## Applying the Skill

Using your knowledge of current events, select a region of the world and a significant current event happening there. Write a paragraph explaining how that significant event could become a turning point in history for students reading about it in the future. Be sure to explain how location plays a role in a turning point in history. Use the examples included in the bulleted list under "Learning the Skill" for guidance, if needed.

# Making Generalizations

## Why Learn This Skill?

Have you heard statements such as "Only tall people play basketball well" and "Dogs make better pets than cats"? Do you accept these statements at face value, or do you stop and consider whether they are valid?

## Learning the Skill

The statements listed above are called generalizations. A generalization is a broad statement about a topic. A generalization takes facts from specific cases and then makes an inference that certain general conclusions can be derived from those facts. At a minimum, to be valid, a generalization must be based on accurate information.

Let's examine the generalization "Only tall people play basketball well." We can find many examples of tall basketball players, but many shorter players also excel at this sport. In other words, we can find facts that disprove the generalization.

Suppose you want to make a generalization about the relative danger of airplane travel compared to automobile travel. First, you would collect accident statistics involving airplanes and cars. Your next step would be to classify the information into categories. Then you would look for relationships between these categories. For example, you might put the airplane and automobile statistics in separate categories. You might also categorize the number of accidents and the number of fatalities. Finally, you should make a generalization that is consistent with most of the facts you gathered.

To make and test generalizations, follow these four steps:

1. First collect information about a topic. This information must consist of facts, not opinions.
2. Compare and contrast what those facts are telling you.
3. Look for a conclusion or common element that fits all the facts. Make a generalization from these common elements.
4. Test your generalization to see whether you can falsify it. Look for facts to support or disprove it.

## Practicing the Skill

Reread the lesson "The Emergence of Mass Society" while examining the above photo of immigrants in New York in the early 1900s. Then answer these questions:

1. What class divisions arose during this period of time?
2. A progressive muckraker, Jacob Riis, took the photo above. What kinds of issues is he trying to show in the photo?
3. What are the problems that urban reformers tried to solve during this period?
4. What changes did urban reformers favor when trying to resolve problems?
5. What generalizations can you make about these reformers and the types of reforms they wanted?

### Applying the Skill

**Making Generalizations** Read the passage "Self Help" from the lesson "The Emergence of Mass Society." Based on the passage, write a generalization about the author that describes his beliefs.

# Making Inferences and Drawing Conclusions

## Why Learn This Skill?

While driving, you hear a news report about a fire downtown. As you approach downtown, traffic is heavy. You cannot see any smoke, but you infer that the traffic is caused by the fire.

*Infer* means "to evaluate information and to arrive at a conclusion." When you make inferences, you draw conclusions that are not stated directly.

## Learning the Skill

Follow the steps below to help make inferences and draw conclusions.

1. Read carefully to determine the main facts and ideas.
2. Write the important facts.
3. Consider any information you know that relates to this topic.
4. Determine how your own knowledge adds to or changes the material.
5. What inferences can you make about the material that are not stated in the facts that you gathered from your reading?
6. Use your knowledge and reason to develop conclusions about the facts.
7. If possible, find specific information that proves or disproves your inference.

bpk, Berlin/Museum fuer Asiatische Kunst, Staatliche Museen, Berlin, Germany/Art Resource, NY

## Practicing the Skill

Read the passage below, then answer the questions that follow.

*"In 1511, the Portuguese seized Melaka and soon occupied the Moluccas. Known to Europeans as the Spice Islands, the Moluccas were the chief source of the spices that had originally attracted the Portuguese to the Indian Ocean.*

*"The Portuguese, however, lacked the military and financial resources to impose their authority over broad areas. Instead, they set up small settlements along the coast, which they used as trading posts or as way stations en route to the Spice Islands.*

*"The situation changed with the arrival of the English and Dutch traders, who were better financed than were the Portuguese. The shift in power began in the early 1600s, when the Dutch seized a Portuguese fort in the Moluccas and drove out the Portuguese.*

*"During the next fifty years, the Dutch occupied most of the Portuguese coastal forts along the trade routes throughout the Indian Ocean. The aggressive Dutch traders also drove the English traders out of the spice market, reducing the English influence to a single port on the southern coast of Sumatra."*

1. What events does the writer describe?
2. What facts are presented?
3. What can you infer about the Dutch traders during this period?
4. What conclusion can you make about the spice market, other than those specifically stated by the author?

## Applying the Skill

Locate a political cartoon from a news source or magazine. Share the cartoon with the class by cutting it out, printing a copy, or creating a whiteboard projection. List three valid inferences based on the work.

# A Guide for Students and Parents

Welcome to World History & Geography: *The Industrial Revolution to the Present.* This program provides an overview of human history from the rise of absolutism to the challenges faced by modern nations today. World History & Geography: *The Industrial Revolution to the Present* focuses on the study of significant people, events, and issues during this time. You will explore the economic, political, social, and cultural origins of the nations of the world today. You will view and interpret history from a variety of perspectives, including geographic, historical, political, economic, social, and cultural. These multiple perspectives will aid your study of history as you will analyze information from people who lived at the time or experts who have studied the period.

The importance of the knowledge and skills you gain this year extends well beyond your classroom. As Americans, we study history not only to learn about important people and events, but also to be prepared to live in a complex, interdependent world. Learning about the economic, political, social, and cultural origins of the nations of the world today helps us develop critical thinking skills and become more informed citizens. It helps us understand our own values and institutions, such as patriotism and government. We hope this program will help you succeed as a student and as a valuable member of your community.

### The Tennessee Social Studies State Standards and Practices

On the following pages, you will find the Tennessee Social Studies State Standards and Practices. These are the concepts and skills you should learn and demonstrate as you work through the World History & Geography: *The Industrial Revolution to the Present* program. You may wish to review these standards during the year as you work your way through the program.

▼ *Hernando de Soto Bridge over the Mississippi River, Memphis*

JUPITERIMAGES/Thinkstock/Alamy

## Age of Revolution (1750–1850)

**Overview:** Students will analyze English efforts to limit the power of monarchs, the Age of Enlightenment, the American Revolution, and the French Revolution and discuss their enduring effects on political expectations for self-government and individual liberty.

W. 01 Describe the concept of the divine right of kings as well as the features, strengths, and weaknesses of European absolutism, including: Louis XIV, Versailles, and Peter the Great.

W.02 Compare documents that establish limits on government in response to absolute monarchy(e.g., the Magna Carta and the English Bill of Rights).

W.03 Compare the major ideas of philosophers during the Age of Enlightenment, such as Charles-Louis de Montesquieu, Thomas Hobbes, John Locke, and Jean-Jacques Rousseau.

W.04 Examine the causes and consequences of the English Civil War.

W.05 Identify the major causes of the French Revolution, including the impact of:
- The American Revolution
- Conflicting social classes
- Economic factors
- Enlightenment political thought
- Government corruption and weakness

W.06 Summarize the major events of the French Revolution (e.g., storming of the Bastille, execution of Louis XVI, reign of terror), and trace the evolution of France's government from constitutional monarchy to democratic despotism to the Napoleonic Empire.

W.07 Analyze the geographic, political, and social factors that contributed to the rise and fall of Napoleon Bonaparte's empire.

W.08 Identify how the ideas of the Enlightenment inspired Thomas Jefferson and the Declaration of Independence, and compare the American Revolution with the French Revolution.

W.09 Explain the effects of the French Revolution on Europe and the world, including the influence of:
- • the Napoleonic Code
- the Concert of Europe
- the Haitian Revolution

## The Industrial Revolution (1750s–1900s)

**Overview:** Students will analyze the emergence of the Industrial Revolution in Europe and the geographic, economic, political, and social implications of the changes that resulted from it.

W.10 Explain how the Agricultural Revolution, mechanization, and the "enclosure movement" led to rapid population growth, rural to urban migration, and the growth of major cities in Europe and North America.

W.11 Explain the geographic and economic reasons why the Industrial Revolution began in England, including:
- natural resources
- entrepreneurship
- labor
- access to capital.

W.12 Analyze how geographic and cultural features were an advantage or disadvantage to the diffusion of the Industrial Revolution.

W.13 Describe the geographic scale, trade routes, and conditions of the forced migration of Africans to the Western Hemisphere, including connections between slave labor and the growth of industrial economies.

W.14 Explain how scientific and technological innovations (e.g., the steam engine, new textile technology, steel processing, medical advances, electricity, and new methods of transportation) led to massive social, economic, cultural, and demographic changes.

W.15 Evaluate the industrialization of Europe in terms of:
- Social benefits (e.g., increases in productivity and life expectancy)
- Social costs (e.g., harsh working and living conditions, pollution, child labor, and income inequality)
- Attempts to address these costs (e.g., political reform, urban planning, philanthropy, labor unionism, education reform, and public health and sanitation)

▲ *Union Battery Before the 'Peach Orchard' at Shiloh National Military Park*

W.16 Compare and contrast the rise of the following economic theories as a result of industrialization:
- capitalism
- communism
- socialism

## Nationalism and Imperialism (1850–1914)

**Overview:** Students will analyze patterns of European nationalism and imperialism, including the cultural, geographic, and political effects on colonized regions.

W.17 Define nationalism, and explain how nationalism, cultural geography, and physical geography contributed to the unification of nations, such as Germany and Italy.

Library of Congress

W.18 Describe the rise of anti-Semitism in Europe during this time period.

W.19 Define imperialism, and analyze reasons for 19th century imperialism, including:
- competition between empires
- cultural justifications
- the search for natural resources and new markets in response to rapid industrialization.

W.20 Describe the natural resources and geographic features of Africa, their role in attracting European economic interests, and their impact on global trade.

W.21 Analyze the outcomes of the Berlin Conference and the impact of superimposed boundaries on African indigenous populations, and compare the geographic progression of imperialistic claims on the African continent by European empires.

W.22 Describe successful (e.g., Ethiopia) and unsuccessful (e.g., Zulu Wars and Ashanti Wars) examples of African resistance to European imperialism.

W.23 Describe the importance of India to the British Empire, the Suez Canal as a connection between Great Britain and India, and India's reaction to British rule.

W.24 Explain the growing influence of western powers on China from the Opium Wars through the Boxer Rebellion.

W.25 Explain cultural diffusion, and describe the diffusion of cultures between Europe, Africa, and Asia as a result of European imperialism.

W.26 Analyze Japan's abandonment of isolationism, its embrace of technological and political changes, and its consequent rise as an imperial power in the late 19th century.

W.27 Describe the natural resources and geographic features of Central and South America, their role in attracting American and European economic interests, and their impact on global trade.

W.28 Compare and contrast the impact of economic imperialism on Central and South America with the impact of imperialism on other parts of the world.

## World War I through the Depression (1910s–1930s)

**Overview:** Students will analyze the causes and course of World War I, the military, economic, and political effects of the war, and the causes and consequences of the global depression of the 1930s.

W.29 Explain how tensions between nations and states contributed to regional conflicts of the era.

W.30 Explain how the rise of militarism, alliances, imperialistic rivalries, and growing nationalism led to the outbreak of World War I.

W.31 Describe how trench warfare, the resulting stalemate, war of attrition, and advances in weaponry (e.g., chemical weapons, machine guns, submarines, tanks) affected the course and outcome of World War I.

W.32 Analyze the importance of geographic factors in military decision-making, and determine the principal theaters and significance of major battles in World War I (e.g., Battles of the Marne, Verdun, the Somme, etc.).

W.33 Explain how the entrance of the United States and the exit of Russia affected the course and outcome of World War I.

W.34 Define total war, and describe its effect on European civilian populations, including:
- Food shortages
- Industrial production of war materials
- Naval/submarine blockades
- Women as war workers

W.35 Describe the effects of World War I, including the significance of:
- Armenian Genocide
- Collapse of major empires
- Economic losses
- Environmental changes
- Loss of human life
- Movement of populations
- Spread of disease

W.36 Compare the goals of leading nations (i.e., U.S., France, Great Britain, Italy, and Japan) at the Paris Peace Conference with the outcomes of the Treaty of Versailles and its impact on Germany.

▼ *View of fog in the Smokies from Clingman's Dome Observation Tower, in Great Smoky Mountains National Park, Tennessee.*

Jon Bilous/Shutterstock

W.37 Analyze the shifts in geopolitical boundaries post-World War I resulting from the Treaty of Versailles and the League of Nations mandate system.

W.38 Determine the causes and consequences of the Bolshevik Revolution and Russian Civil War.

W.39 Analyze the cultural, economic, and intellectual trends of the 1920s.

W.40 Describe the collapse of international economies in 1929 that led to the Great Depression, including the significance of:
- Overproduction
- Unemployment
- Inflation
- Restrictive trade policies
- Post-war economic relationships between the U.S. and Europe

## Rise of Totalitarianism and World War II (1930s–1945)

**Overview:** Students will analyze the rise of fascism and totalitarianism after World War I, the causes and course of World War II, and the military, economic, and political effects of the war.

W.41 Explain how economic instability, nationalism, and political disillusionment in Germany and Japan led to the rise of totalitarian regimes.

W.42 Compare and contrast the rise to power, goals, and characteristics of Adolf Hitler, Benito Mussolini, and Joseph Stalin's totalitarian regimes.

W.43 Analyze the role of geographic features and natural resources in increasing tensions prior to and during World War II.

W.44 Compare the Italian, German, and Japanese efforts to expand their empires in the 1930s, including:
- the invasion of Ethiopia
- German militarism
- atrocities in China.

W.45 Explain the role of military alliances, appeasement, isolationism, and the domestic distractions in Europe and the U.S. prior to the outbreak of World War II.

W.46 Describe how geography and technology (e.g., airplanes, advanced medicine, propaganda, radar) influenced wartime strategies, including:
- blitzkrieg
- "island hopping"
- kamikaze
- strategic bombing.

W.47 Describe the geography and outcomes of major battles and turning points of World War II in both the European and Pacific theaters, including:
- Battle of Britain
- Battle of Midway
- Battle of Stalingrad
- Battle of Normandy
- Battle of the Bulge

W.48 Describe the roles of leaders during World War II, including the significance of:
- Winston Churchill
- Adolf Hitler
- Benito Mussolini
- President Franklin D. Roosevelt
- Joseph Stalin
- Hideki Tojo
- President Harry S. Truman

W.49 Describe the persecution of Jews and other targeted groups in Europe leading up to World War II, and explain why many people were unable to leave and their efforts to resist persecution.

W.50 Explain the state-sponsored mass murder of the Jews in Nazi-controlled lands, and describe the varied experiences of Holocaust survivors and victims.

W.51 Explain the decisions made in the Atlantic Charter and at the Tehran, Yalta, and Potsdam Conferences.

▲ *World's Fair Park in Knoxville Tennessee*

W.52 Describe the development of atomic bombs, and evaluate both the decisions to use them and the impact of their use.

W.53 Describe the cultural, economic, geographic, and political effects of World War II, including:
- Casualties of the war (military and civilian)
- Changes to geopolitical boundaries
- Creation of the United Nations
- Destruction of cultural heritage
- Division of Germany
- Impact of the Nuremberg trials
- Refugees and displaced populations

W.54 Summarize the nature of reconstruction in Europe after 1945, including both the economic and political purposes of the Marshall Plan.

W.55 Explain the origins and significance of the establishment of the State of Israel, and describe the reactions by surrounding Arab countries to the United Nations' decision to establish Israel.

W.56 Describe the economic and military power shift at the end of World War II, such as Soviet control over Eastern Europe and the economic recoveries of Germany and Japan.

## Cold War (1945–1991)

**Overview:** Students will analyze events and changes that resulted from the post-World War II rivalry between communist and democratic governments.

W.57 Analyze the rise of communism and Mao Zedong in China, as well as the related political, social, and economic impacts on China.

W.58 Describe the characteristics of the Cold War, and explain reasons for the rising tensions between the Soviet Union and former Allied powers.

W.59 Summarize the functions of the Warsaw Pact and NATO, including their roles in organizing postwar Europe.

W.60 Describe methods of Soviet control in Eastern Europe and the role of Berlin as a focal point in escalating Cold War tensions.

W.61 Explain the role of the nuclear arms race, mutual assured destruction, and arms control agreements within the context of rising tensions between the Soviet Union and U.S.

W.62 Describe examples of national uprisings against the Soviet Union (e.g., Hungary and Czechoslovakia), and explain why they were unsuccessful.

W.63 Describe the competition in Asia between the Soviet Union and U.S., including the wars in Koreaand Vietnam as examples of proxy wars.

W.64 Explain reasons for the rapid decline of communist systems in the late 1980s, including:
- Economic inefficiency
- Unsustainable military spending
- Mikhail Gorbachev's reforms
- Mass protests in Eastern Europe and China
- 1991 Soviet coup d'état

W.65 Analyze the political, economic, social, and geographic consequences of the collapse of communist governments in the Soviet Union and Eastern Europe.

## Creation of New States and Decolonization (1940s–1980s)

**Overview:** Students will analyze the development of new states that resulted from post-World War II decolonization, migration, political change, economic development, and ideological conflict.

W.66 Explain the push and pull factors of migration.

W.67 Explain the reasons for and the effects of the partition of the Indian subcontinent into India and Pakistan in 1947.

W.68 Explain the factors that led to the creation of a lasting democratic government in India as well as the roles of political leaders (e.g., Mohandas Gandhi, Jawaharlal Nehru, Indira Gandhi).

W.69 Describe the development, goals, and outcomes of nationalist movements in Africa, including the ideas and roles of nationalist leaders (e.g., Jomo Kenyatta, Patrice Lumumba, and Gamal Abdel Nasser).

W.70 Explain the fight against and dismantling of the apartheid system in South Africa, including the roles of Nelson Mandela and the African National Congress.

W.71 Analyze the political, economic, ethnic, and military challenges faced by newly-created countries in post-imperial Africa (e.g., civil war, genocide, corruption).

▼ *Aerial view of the Nashville skyline and the Cumberland River at sunset, Nashville-Davidson, Tennessee, USA*

Malcolm MacGregor/Moment Open/Getty Images

W.72 Explain how ideological conflicts between capitalism and communism led to armed insurgencies, revolutions, and military dictatorships in Latin American nations, including:
- Argentina
- Colombia
- Cuba
- Nicaragua.

W.73 Describe how competing national, ethnic, and religious interests led to conflict and the establishment of new countries in the Balkans.

W.74 Compare and contrast the causes and effects of modern genocide, including in:
- Cambodia
- Rwanda
- the former Yugoslavia.

W.75 Explain the causes and effects of German reunification on both West and East Germany.

W.76 Analyze the response of Arab countries to the creation of the State of Israel and the peace processes in the Middle East, including the Camp David and Oslo Accords.

▲ *Tennessee State Capitol building in Nashville, TN in the evening*

## Understanding the Contemporary World (1980s- present)

**Overview:** Students will analyze the major developments and globalization in the world since the end of the Cold War.

W.77 Analyze the demographic changes of countries in post-World War II regions, using population pyramids and census data.

W.78 Explain the challenges of rapid population growth on developing countries (e.g., China and India) and of population decline in developed countries (e.g., Germany, Japan, and Sweden), and give examples of policies implemented to both slow and increase population growth.

W.79 Describe the cultural, economic, geographic, and political effects of significant technological, ideological, medical, and scientific developments and breakthroughs of the era.

W.80 Evaluate the impact of geospatial technologies (such as GPS and GIS) on retail, military, transportation, city planning, and communication.

Andriy Kravchenko/Alamy Stock Photo

W.81 Analyze the economic, political, and social impacts of drug and human trafficking in the contemporary era.

W.82 Analyze how technology has intensified patterns of globalization and led to the idea of space-time compression, containerization, and computer technology.

W.83 Explain the goals and consequences of trade organizations and treaties and how they have played a role in the growing global economic system.

W.84 Identify examples of supranational organizations, and discuss the benefits and drawbacks of membership.

W.85 Analyze the causes and effects of an increased role of South and East Asian countries in the global economy.

W.86 Describe the international importance and rapid economic development of the oil-rich Persian Gulf states.

W.87 Explain implications of the transition from the use of fossil fuels to alternative and renewable energy sources.

W.88 Describe governing ideologies, conflicts among nations (e.g., Persian Gulf War), and popular religious or democratic movements in the Middle East/North Africa.

W.89 Analyze the causes and consequences of terrorism and international efforts to counteract it.



▼ *Downtown Chattanooga*

# Tennessee Social Studies Practices, Grades 9-12

**SSP.01 Collect data and information from a variety of primary and secondary sources, including:**
- Printed materials (e.g., literary texts, newspapers, political cartoons, autobiographies, speeches, letters, personal journals)
- Graphic representations (e.g., maps, timelines, charts, photographs, artwork)
- Artifacts
- Media and technology sources

**SSP.02 Critically examine a primary or secondary source in order to:**
- Extract and paraphrase significant ideas
- Discern differences between evidence and assertion
- Draw inferences and conclusions
- Recognize author's purpose, point of view, and potential bias
- Assess the strengths and limitations of arguments

**SSP.03 Synthesize data from a variety of sources in order to:**
- Establish accuracy and validity by comparing sources to each other
- Recognize disparities among multiple accounts
- Frame appropriate questions for further investigation

**SSP.04 Construct and communicate arguments citing supporting evidence to:**
- Demonstrate and defend an understanding of ideas
- Compare and contrast viewpoints
- Illustrate cause and effect
- Predict likely outcomes
- Devise new outcomes or solutions

**SSP.05 Develop historical awareness by:**
- Recognizing how and why historical accounts change over time
- Perceiving and presenting past events and issues as they might have been experienced by the people of the time, with historical empathy rather than present-mindedness
- Evaluating how unique circumstances of time and place create context and contribute to action and reaction
- Identifying patterns of continuity and change over time, making connections to the present

**SSP.06 Develop geographic awareness by:**
- Using the geographic perspective to analyze relationships, patterns, and diffusion across space at multiple scales (e.g., local, national, global)
- Analyzing and determining the use of diverse types of maps based on the origin, authority, structure, context, and validity
- Analyzing locations, conditions, and connections of places and using maps to investigate spatial associations among phenomena
- Examining how geographers use regions and how perceptions of regions are fluid across time and space
- Analyzing interaction between humans and the physical environment

# SCAVENGER HUNT

**World History and Geography** contains a wealth of information. The trick is to know where to look to access all the information in the book. If you complete this scavenger hunt exercise with your teachers or parents, you will see how the textbook is organized and how to get the most out of your reading and study time. Let's get started!

1. **How many chapters and lessons are in this book?**
2. **Where do you find the glossary and the index? What is the difference between them?**
3. **Where can you find primary sources in the textbook?**
4. **If you want to quickly find all the maps, charts, and graphs about World War II, where do you look?**
5. **How can you find information about Nelson Mandela?**
6. **Where can you find a graphic organizer that lists the causes of the French Revolution discussed in Chapter 3?**
7. **Where and how do you find the vocabulary for Chapter 16, Lesson 3?**
8. **Who is the subject of the biography in Chapter 15, Lesson 1?**
9. **You want to read about the Mexican Revolution. How will you find it?**
10. **What time period does Chapter 2 cover? How do you know?**

◀ *Painted in 1677, years before Mary became queen, court painter Sir Peter Lely's portrait of her already conveys a regal pride and self-assurance.*

1550 — 1715

# Conflict and Absolutism in Europe

## CHAPTER 1



**GO DIGITAL**
*It's All Online!*

## ASKING ESSENTIAL QUESTIONS

***What effect might social, economic, and religious conflicts have on a country? How would the exercise of absolute power affect a country?***

**What Will You Learn?** You will learn about political and religious conflicts in Europe and the resulting impact on European cultural and political thought.

**Why Does This Matter?** Absolute monarchies dominated most of Europe during the 18th century. Some states, such as England, rejected absolutism and began to institute systems of representative government to set limitations on their monarchs. These transformations gave rise to hearty debates about the role of the state, natural rights, freedom, and equality. These ideas gave shape to the world we still live in, and they remain perceptible in documents we still venerate today, such as the Declaration of Independence.

**How Will You Know That You Learned It?** You will be able to identify what caused the political and religious conflicts in Europe and explain how these conflicts affected the political thought and cultural patterns of Europe.

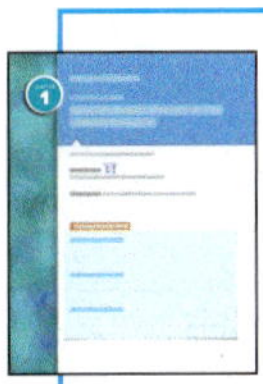

**Using Your Inquiry Journal** As you read this chapter and examine the primary sources, use your Inquiry Journal to help you make notes and expand your list of questions. As you gather information, think about how you will answer the Essential Questions above.

Sotheby/akg-images

# PLACE & TIME Europe 1550–1715

During the sixteenth and seventeenth centuries, Europe was the scene of conflicts fueled by religious differences, along with political and economic rivalries. In some European nations, these conflicts led to the absolute power of a single ruler; in others, a constitutional monarchy developed.

## STEP INTO THE PLACE

Read the quotations from the English Bill of Rights and the Duc de Saint-Simon and look at the information presented on the map of Europe in 1650.

1. **SPATIAL THINKING** Based on the map, why might the Holy Roman Empire have faced challenges in keeping its territory under control?

2. **RELATING EVENTS** Explain why Parliament would be threatened if the king of England took actions like those attributed to Louis XIV.

“Whereas the late King James the Second, by the assistance of diverse evil counselors, judges and ministers employed by him, did endeavor to subvert and extirpate the Protestant religion and the laws and liberties of this kingdom;... That the freedom of speech and debates or proceedings in Parliament ought not to be impeached or questioned in any court or place out of Parliament;. . .”

—from the English Bill of Rights, 1689

“Louis XIV took great pains to be well informed of all that passed everywhere; in the public places, in the private houses, in society and familiar intercourse. His spies and tell-tales were infinite. He had them of all species; many who were ignorant that their information reached him; others who knew it; others who wrote to him direct, sending their letters through channels he indicated; and all these letters were seen by him alone, and always before everything else; others who sometimes spoke to him secretly in his cabinet, entering by the back stairs.”

—Duc de Saint-Simon, from *Memoirs*, 1694–1723



## STEP INTO THE TIME

**EVALUATING** Choose an event from the European portion of the time line and predict its long-term political, social, or cultural consequences.

### EUROPE

- **1555** Peace of Augsburg divides Christianity in Germany
- **1562** French Wars of Religion begin
- **1588** England defeats the Spanish Armada
- **1598** Henry IV issues the Edict of Nantes; ends Wars of Religion
- **1618** Start of the Thirty Years' War

**1550** — **1575** — **1600**

### WORLD EVENTS

- **1566** Ottoman Sultan Süleyman I dies
- **1588** Shāh ʻAbbās becomes ruler of Persian Ṣafavid dynasty
- **1598** Rurik dynasty ends in Russia; Romanovs succeed in 1613
- **1603** Tokugawa shogunate begins in Japan

**1623** Shakespeare's *First Folio* is published

**1630** English found Massachusetts Bay Colony

**1644** China's Ming dynasty is overthrown; Qing dynasty succeeds

**1661** Louis XIV begins absolutist rule in France

**1680** Pueblo Rebellion temporarily overthrows Spanish rule in New Mexico

**1682** La Salle claims Mississippi Valley for France

**1690** John Locke publishes *Two Treatises of Government*

**1697–1698** Peter the Great visits the West

**1707** Death of Aurangzeb, last great Mogul emperor

**1715** Louis XIV dies

1625 — 1650 — 1675 — 1700 — 1725

## ESSENTIAL QUESTION

- *What effect might social, economic, and religious conflicts have on a country?*

# THE STORY BEGINS...

LESSON 1

# Europe in Crisis

In the Act of Supremacy, Queen Elizabeth I of England required anyone taking public or church office to swear an oath recognizing her as the governor both of the country and of the Church of England:

> "I, [the archbishop], do utterly testify and declare in my conscience, that the queen's highness is the only supreme governor of this realm, and of all other her highness's dominions and countries, as well in all spiritual or ecclesiastical things or causes, as temporal, and that no foreign prince, person, prelate, state or potentate, has, or ought to have, any jurisdiction, power, superiority, preeminence, or authority ecclesiastical or spiritual, within this realm; and therefore I do utterly renounce and forsake all foreign jurisdictions, powers, superiorities, and authorities, and do promise that from henceforth I shall bear faith and true allegiance to the queen's highness, her heirs and lawful successors, and to my power shall assist and defend all jurisdictions, pre-eminences, privileges, and authorities granted or belonging to the queen's highness, her heirs and successors, or united and annexed to the imperial crown of this realm. So help me God, and by the contents of this book."

—*Act of Supremacy,* 1559

The law was a victory for Protestants and a bitter defeat for Catholics during a time of fierce struggle between the two forms of Christianity. It was a struggle that had engulfed not only England but most of Europe during the sixteenth and seventeenth centuries.

*The painting depicts the gathering of the Spanish Armada in 1588 as it prepares for an assault on England.* ▶

| | Spain | England | France |
|---|---|---|---|
| Government | | | |
| Religion | | | |
| Conflicts | | | |

**ANALYZING KEY IDEAS AND DETAILS**

**CITING TEXT EVIDENCE** Read closely to identify the government, religion, and conflicts in Spain, England, and France. Make sure to note any significant events and dates. Record these details in a graphic organizer like this one.

# SPAIN'S CONFLICTS

**GUIDING QUESTION** *What were the outcomes of the religious conflicts in France and Spain?*

By 1560, Calvinism and Catholicism had become highly militant, or combative, religions. They were aggressive in winning converts and in eliminating each other's authority. Their struggle was the chief cause of the religious wars that plagued Europe in the sixteenth century. However, economic, social, and political forces also played an important role in these conflicts.

## SPAIN'S MILITANT CATHOLICISM

The greatest supporter of militant Catholicism in the second half of the 1500s was King Philip II. He was the son of Charles V—the Holy Roman Emperor, King of Spain, and Archduke of Austria. Charles V's brother, Ferdinand I, succeeded him as Holy Roman Emperor. Philip II inherited from Charles V the kingdoms of Milan, Naples, Sicily, the Netherlands, and Spain and its empire in the Americas. Philip, who reigned from 1556 to 1598, ushered in an age of Spanish greatness. To strengthen his control, Philip insisted on strict conformity to Catholicism and strong monarchal authority. He also had the powerful Spanish navy at his command.

Around 1500, Catholic kingdoms in Spain had reconquered Muslim areas there and expelled Spanish Jews. Muslims were forced to convert or to go into exile. Spain saw itself as a nation chosen by God to save Catholic Christianity from Protestant **heretics**. Philip II, the "Most Catholic King," championed Catholic causes. His actions led to spectacular victories and defeats. Spain's leadership of a Holy League against the Turks resulted in a stunning victory over the Turkish fleet in the Battle of Lepanto in 1571. Philip was not so fortunate in his other **conflicts**.

## RESISTANCE FROM THE NETHERLANDS

One of the richest parts of Philip's empire, the Spanish Netherlands, consisted of 17 provinces (modern-day Netherlands and Belgium). Philip's attempts to strengthen his control in this region caused resentment and opposition from the nobles of the Netherlands. Philip also tried to crush Calvinism in the Netherlands. When violence erupted in 1566, Philip sent 10,000 troops to crush the rebellion.

Philip faced growing resistance from the Dutch in the northern provinces led by William the Silent, the prince of Orange. The struggle dragged on until 1609 when a 12-year truce finally ended the war. The northern provinces began to call themselves the United Provinces of the Netherlands and became the core of the modern Dutch state. In fact, the seventeenth century has often been called the golden age of the Dutch Republic by scholars because the United Provinces held center stage as one of Europe's great powers.

**ANALYZING KEY IDEAS AND DETAILS**

1. **SUMMARIZING** Summarize the rise and fall of the Spanish Empire under Philip II's reign.
2. **DETERMINING CENTRAL IDEAS** Reread the subsection "Protestantism in England." What part of this section suggests that Queen Elizabeth was on a collision course with Spain?

**DETERMINING MEANING**

From what you know about the meaning of the word **heretic**, create a definition for the word *heresy*. Use a dictionary or an online reference to check your definition.

## PROTESTANTISM IN ENGLAND

Elizabeth Tudor ascended the English throne in 1558. During her reign, the small island kingdom became the leader of the Protestant nations of Europe and laid the foundations for a world empire.

Intelligent, careful, and self-confident, Elizabeth moved quickly to solve the difficult religious problem she inherited from her Catholic half-sister, Queen Mary Tudor. Elizabeth repealed the laws favoring Catholics. A new Act of Supremacy named Elizabeth as "the only supreme governor" of both church and state. The Church of England under Queen Elizabeth I followed a moderate Protestantism that kept most people satisfied.

Elizabeth was also moderate in her foreign **policy**. She tried to keep Spain and France from becoming too powerful by balancing power. If one nation seemed to be gaining in power, England would support the weaker nation. The queen feared that war would be disastrous for England and for her own rule; however, she could not escape a conflict with Spain.

## DEFEAT OF THE SPANISH ARMADA

In 1588, Philip II made preparations to send an **armada**—a fleet of warships—to invade England. A successful invasion of England would mean the overthrow of Protestantism. The fleet that set sail had neither the ships nor the manpower that Philip had planned to send.

The hoped-for victory never came. The armada was battered by the faster English ships and sailed back to Spain by a northern route around Scotland and Ireland where it was pounded by storms.

**DETERMINING MEANING**

Read the text of the paragraph that contains the word **armada**. Which branch of the U.S. military do you think *armada* is synonymous with? How do you know?

**GEOGRAPHIC REASONING**

Spain's Philip II ruled the world's largest empire at the time.

1. **HUMAN-ENVIRONMENT INTERACTION** How might the distribution of Philip's empire have made it difficult to administer?
2. **SPATIAL THINKING** Based on the map, is the argument that Philip's relationship with the Holy Roman Emperor was important valid? Explain.

### HEIGHT OF SPANISH POWER UNDER PHILIP II 1560

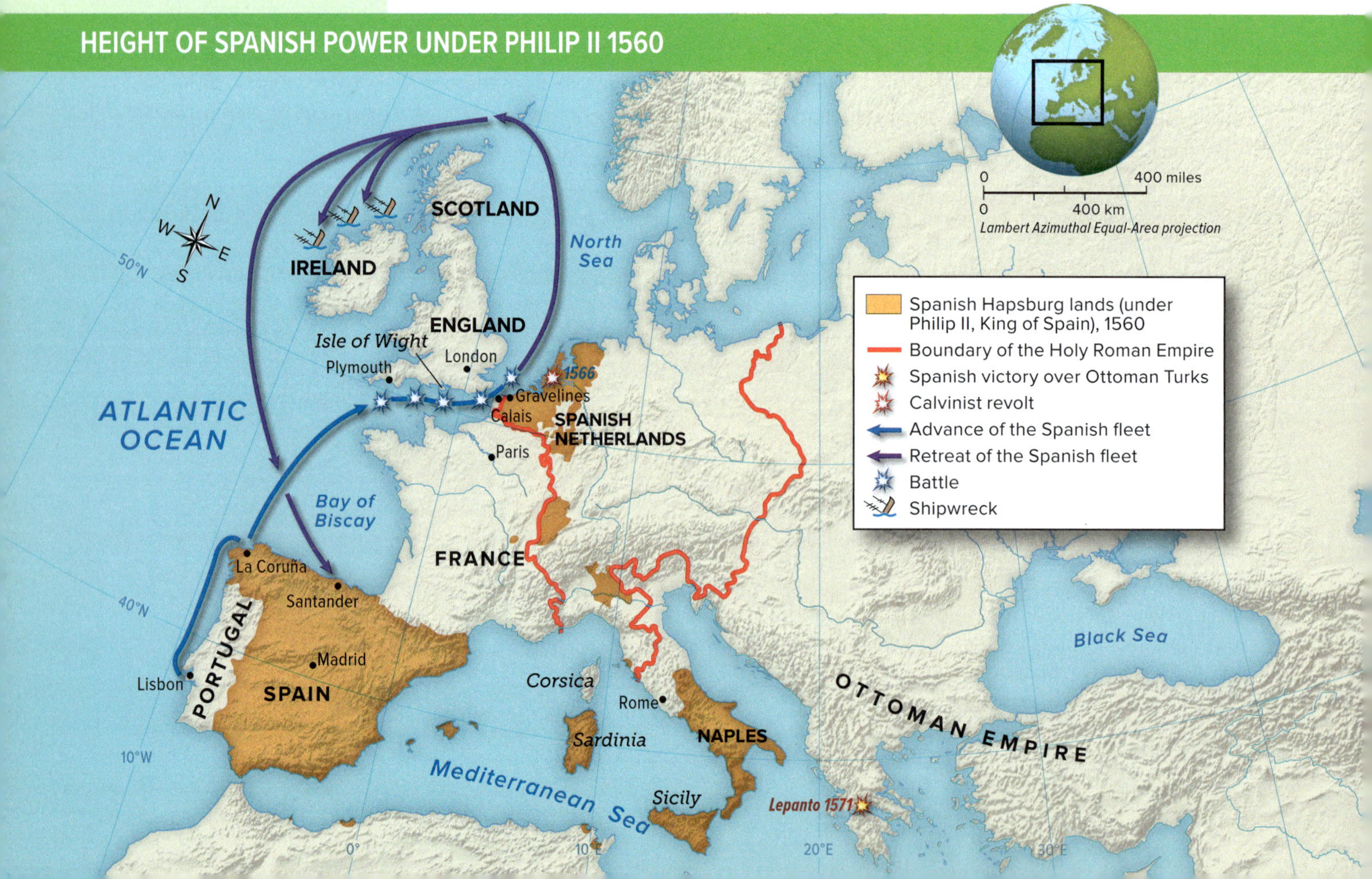

By the end of Philip's reign in 1598, Spain was not the great power that it appeared to be. Spain was the most populous empire in the world, but it was bankrupt. Philip II had spent too much on war. His successor spent too much on his court. The armed forces were out of date, and the government was inefficient. Spain continued to play the role of a great power, but the real power in Europe had shifted to England and France.

### ✓ CHECKING FOR UNDERSTANDING

1. **SUMMARIZING** What were the outcomes of the religious conflicts in France and Spain?
2. **IDENTIFYING EFFECTS** What was the effect of Philip's efforts to strengthen control in the Netherlands and crush Calvinism?
3. **UNDERSTANDING CONTEXT** Why might the overthrow of Protestantism in England have been important to Philip II?

*Queen Elizabeth I of England*



## THE FRENCH WARS OF RELIGION

**GUIDING QUESTION** *What fueled the French civil wars of the sixteenth century?*

Of the sixteenth-century religious wars, none was more shattering than the French civil wars known as the French Wars of Religion (1562–1598). Religious conflict was at the center of these wars. The Catholic French kings persecuted Protestants throughout the country, but the persecution did little to stop the spread of Protestantism.

### UNDERSTANDING CRAFT AND STRUCTURE

1. **ANALYZING TEXT** Why did the writer use the word *shattering* in the text? How does this word help you to understand the significance of the wars?
2. **DETERMINING MEANING** The text states, "To solve the religious problem, Henry IV issued the Edict of Nantes in 1598." What does the word *edict* mean in this context?

### HUGUENOTS

Huguenots (HYOO • guh • nahts) were French Protestants influenced by John Calvin. They made up only about 7 percent of the total French population, but 40 to 50 percent of the nobility became Huguenots. This made the Huguenots a powerful political threat to the Crown.

An extreme Catholic party—known as the ultra-Catholics—strongly opposed the Huguenots. Having the loyalty of parts of northern and northwestern France, they could pay for and recruit large armies.

Religion was the most important issue, but other factors played a role in the ensuing French civil wars. Towns and provinces were willing to assist the nobles in weakening the growing power of the French monarchy.

### HENRY IV AND THE EDICT OF NANTES

For 30 years, battles raged in France between the Catholics and the Huguenots. In 1589, Henry of Navarre, the Huguenot political leader, succeeded to the throne as Henry IV. He realized that as a Protestant he would never be accepted by Catholic France. Therefore, he converted to Catholicism. When Henry IV was crowned king in 1594, the fighting in France finally came to an end.

To solve the religious problem, Henry IV issued the Edict of Nantes in 1598. The edict recognized Catholicism as the official religion of France. It also gave the Huguenots the right to worship and to enjoy all political privileges such as holding public offices. This edict appeased both Catholics and Huguenots.

> "III. We ordain that the Catholic Apostolic and Roman religion shall be restored and reestablished in all places and localities of this our kingdom and countries subject to our sway, where the exercise of the same has been interrupted, in order that it may be peaceably and freely exercised, without any trouble or hindrance . . .
>
> VI. And in order to leave no occasion for troubles or differences between our subjects, we have permitted, and herewith permit, those of the said religion called Reformed to live and abide in all the cities and places of this our kingdom and countries of our sway, without being annoyed, molested, or compelled to do anything in the matter of religion contrary to their consciences . . .
>
> VII. It is permitted to all lords, gentlemen, and other persons making profession of the said religion called Reformed, holding the right of high justice [or a certain feudal tenure], to exercise the said religion in their houses. . . ."

—*Edict of Nantes* 1598

**ANALYZING PRIMARY SOURCES**

1. **DETERMINING CENTRAL IDEAS** What conditions does the Edict of Nantes put on practicing Protestantism?
2. **CITING TEXT EVIDENCE** What language in the text suggests that the edict is intended to bring about peace?

### ☑ CHECKING FOR UNDERSTANDING

1. **SUMMARIZING** What fueled the French civil wars of the sixteenth century?
2. **EVALUATING EVIDENCE** What might have happened in France if Henry IV had not issued the Edict of Nantes?
3. **EVALUATING EVIDENCE** What evidence from the text best explains why Henry IV had to convert to Catholicism to be accepted as a leader? Explain.

## CRISES IN EUROPE

**GUIDING QUESTION** *How was Europe affected by social and economic crises in the seventeenth century?*

In addition to political upheaval and religious warfare, severe economic and social crises plagued Europe in the sixteenth and seventeenth centuries. One major economic problem was **inflation**, or rising prices. A growing population in the sixteenth century increased the demand for land and food and drove up prices for both.

### ECONOMIC AND SOCIAL CRISES

By 1600, an economic slowdown had begun in parts of Europe. Spain's economy, grown dependent on imported silver, was failing by the 1640s. Its mines were producing less silver. Its fleets were subject to pirate attacks. Also, the loss of Muslim and Jewish artisans and merchants hurt the economy. Italy, the financial center of Europe in the Renaissance, was also declining economically.

Population figures in the 1500s and 1600s reveal Europe's worsening conditions. The 1500s was a period of growing population, possibly due to a warmer climate and increased food supplies. Europe's population probably increased from 60 million in 1500 to 85 million by 1600. By 1620, the population had leveled off. It had begun to decline by 1650, especially in central and southern Europe. Warfare, plague, and famine all contributed to the population decline and to the creation of social tensions. One source of tension involved the witchcraft trials.

**INTEGRATING KNOWLEDGE AND IDEAS**

1. **ASSESSING** The text states that the problems Europe faced in this period were "severe." Does the evidence in this section support this idea? Explain.
2. **ANALYZING INFORMATION** What information does the painting of the accused witches provide that the text does not?

**DETERMINING MEANING**

Reread the paragraph that includes the word **inflation**. Would inflation help or harm most people?

TEXT:Excerpt from Edict of Nantes, 1598. From Readings in European History, Volume II: From the Opening of the Protestant Revolt to the Present Day by James Harvey Robinson. London: Ginn & Company, 1906.

## THE WITCHCRAFT TRIALS

A belief in witchcraft, or magic, had been part of traditional village culture for centuries. The religious zeal that led to the Inquisition and the hunt for heretics was extended to concern about witchcraft. During the sixteenth and seventeenth centuries, an intense hysteria affected the lives of many Europeans. Perhaps more than a hundred thousand people were charged with witchcraft. As more and more people were brought to trial, the fear of witches grew, as did the fear of being accused of witchcraft.

Common people—usually the poor and those without property—were the ones most often accused of witchcraft. More than 75 percent of those accused were women. Most of them were single or widowed and over 50 years old.

*A public execution of accused witches in England*

Under intense torture, accused witches usually confessed to a number of practices. For instance, many said that they had sworn allegiance to the devil and attended sabbats, nightly gatherings at which they feasted and danced. Others admitted to casting evil spells.

By 1650, the witchcraft hysteria had begun to lessen. As governments grew stronger, fewer officials were willing to disrupt their societies with trials of witches. In addition, attitudes were changing. People found it unreasonable to believe in the old view of a world haunted by evil spirits.

### ✓ CHECKING FOR UNDERSTANDING

1. **DETERMINING CONTEXT** How was Europe affected by social and economic crises in the seventeenth century?
2. **IDENTIFYING CAUSES** What led to inflation during the sixteenth and seventeenth centuries?
3. **IDENTIFYING CONNECTIONS** How did the growth of stronger governments lead to the end of the witchcraft hysteria?

**CITIZENSHIP**

### INNOCENT UNTIL PROVEN GUILTY

The witchcraft trials of the sixteenth and seventeenth centuries put the burden of proof on the accused, forcing them to prove that they were not witches. This was often an impossible task. Making matters worse, the interrogation techniques included torture and depriving the accused of food and sleep and other methods that would lead to wrongful confessions. Ancient Roman law included the concept "presumption of innocence," or what is more commonly known as "innocence until proven guilty." This principle was largely revived during the Enlightenment and is a central premise of the legal system in the United States today.

**CITING TEXT EVIDENCE** Why might innocent people have confessed to witchcraft?

# THE THIRTY YEARS' WAR

**GUIDING QUESTION** *What were the causes and effects of the Thirty Years' War?*

Religious disputes continued in Germany after the Peace of Augsburg in 1555. One reason for the disputes was that the peace settlement had not recognized Calvinism. By the 1600s, Calvinism had spread through Europe.

The Thirty Years' War is considered the "last of the religious wars" in Europe. Beginning in 1618 in the Holy Roman Empire, the war first involved the struggle between Catholic forces, led by the Holy Roman emperors, and Protestant nobles in Bohemia. As Denmark, Sweden, France, and Spain entered the war, the conflict became more political. For instance, the conclusion of the war would largely be a struggle between the Catholic nations of France, directed by the Catholic Cardinal Richelieu, and the Holy Roman Empire and Spain in an attempt to gain European leadership and dominance.

**ANALYZING KEY IDEAS AND DETAILS**

1. **CITING TEXT EVIDENCE** Was religion the only factor that contributed to the outbreak of the Thirty Years' War? Cite specific words in the text that support your answer.
2. **ANALYZING IDEAS** The text states the Peace of Westphalia "firmly established the concept of national sovereignty." Find one sentence in the text that supports this claim.

An Execution of Witches in England (engraving), English School, (17th century (after)/Private Collection/The Stapleton Collection/Bridgeman Images

*A villager is attacked by a soldier during the Thirty Years' War.*

All major European powers except England were involved in the plundering and destruction of Germany during the Thirty Years' War. The Peace of Westphalia officially ended the war in 1648 and gave Sweden, France, and their allies new territories. The treaty firmly established the concept of **national sovereignty** and is regarded by many scholars to herald the rise of the modern state system in Europe.

Sweden's acquisitions in the Baltic Sea region increased its power in northern Europe. The peace settlement also divided the more than 300 states of the Holy Roman Empire into independent states, each with the freedom to determine their own religion and to conduct foreign policy. The Holy Roman Empire ceased to be a political entity. Another 200 years would pass before German unification.

**DETERMINING MEANING**

To better understand **national sovereignty**, break down the phrase. *National* refers to something related to a nation. *Sovereign* means "having an independent government." What would it mean for a country to have national sovereignty?

### ✓ CHECKING FOR UNDERSTANDING

1. **EXPLAINING CAUSE AND EFFECT** What were the causes and effects of the Thirty Years' War?
2. **COMPARING AND CONTRASTING** How was the Holy Roman Empire different at the end of the Thirty Years' War?
3. **DISTINGUISHING FACT FROM OPINION** The original motivation for the Thirty Years' War was political. Is this statement true or false? Explain.



## LESSON 1 REVIEW

### Time and Place

1. **ANALYZING CHANGE** Explain how the rise of national sovereignty in Europe might have impacted relations among European states.

### Building History-Social Science Analysis Skills

2. **EVALUATING** How did Philip II's support of militant Catholicism contribute to the decline of the Spanish Empire during the sixteenth century?

3. **SUMMARIZING** How did the French resolve their religious conflict after the French Wars of Religion? Why did the French resolution leave the nation stronger than Philip's failed campaigns left Spain?

4. **INTERPRETING** Although the fear of witchcraft had been a part of European culture for centuries, what factors during the sixteenth and seventeenth centuries contributed to the intense hysteria and fear surrounding the practice of witchcraft?

### Writing About History

5. **ARGUMENTATIVE WRITING** Write an argumentative essay supporting or refuting the following claim: Philip II was justified in attempting to return Europe to a state of religious unity under the spiritual authority of the Catholic Church. Be sure to cite specific ideas and examples from the text in your response.

### Collaborating

6. **COLLABORATING** With a partner, discuss the similarities and differences between Queen Elizabeth I of England and King Philip II of Spain in terms of their personalities as rulers, their relationships to religion, and their foreign policies.

## ESSENTIAL QUESTION

- *What effect might social, economic, and religious conflicts have on a country?*

LESSON 2

# War and Revolution in England

## THE STORY BEGINS...

Having defeated King Charles I in the English Civil War, Lord Protector Oliver Cromwell was now finding it difficult to work with what remained of the British Parliament. In a move similar to that of the kings who preceded him, Cromwell dismissed Parliament entirely with the following speech:

> “It is not fit that you should sit here any longer! You have sat too long here for any good you have been doing lately. You shall now give place to better men!. . . You call yourselves a Parliament; I say you are no Parliament! Some of you are drunkards . . . some of you are . . . living in open contempt of God's Commandments. Following your own greedy appetites, and the Devil's Commandments. Corrupt unjust persons ... scandalous to the profession of the Gospel: how can you be a Parliament for God's People? Depart, I say; and let us have done with you. In the name of God,—go!”

—speech by Oliver Cromwell, 1653

This struggle among Cromwell, the monarchy, and Parliament would dominate seventeenth-century England. The consequences would impact English government and political thought in ways that still affect the modern world.

*Charles I (center, on horseback) leads the Royalist forces against Parliamentarians in the English Civil War.* ▶

| Conflict | Summary |
|---|---|
| | |
| | |

**ANALYZING KEY IDEAS AND DETAILS**

**Determining Central Ideas** Read closely to determine the central ideas about the conflicts in England that were prompted by religious concerns. Summarize these conflicts and their results in a graphic organizer like this one.

# REVOLUTIONS IN ENGLAND

**ANALYZING KEY IDEAS AND DETAILS**

1. **SUMMARIZING** Write a brief summary of the events that led to civil war in England in 1642.
2. **ANALYZING EVENTS** What was the main purpose of the Glorious Revolution?

**GUIDING QUESTIONS** *How did disagreements over rule between the Stuarts and Parliament lead to the English Civil War? What were the causes and effects of the Glorious Revolution?*

In addition to the Thirty Years' War, a series of rebellions and civil wars rocked Europe in the seventeenth century. By far the most famous struggle was the civil war in England known as the English Revolution. The war was between king and Parliament to determine what role each should play in governing England. It would take another revolution later in the century to finally reach a resolution.

## THE STUARTS AND DIVINE RIGHT

The Tudor dynasty ended with the death of Queen Elizabeth I in 1603. The Stuart line of rulers began when the king of Scotland, Elizabeth's cousin, ascended the English throne and became James I.

James believed that he received his power from and was only responsible to God. This is called the **divine right of kings**. Parliament did not think much of the divine right of kings. It had come to assume that the monarch and Parliament ruled England together.

Religion was an issue as well. The **Puritans**—Protestants in England inspired by Calvinist ideas—did not like the king's strong defense of the Church of England. While they were members of the Church of England, the Puritans wished to remove any remaining resemblances to Catholicism from their church. Many of England's gentry, mostly well-to-do landowners, had become Puritans. The Puritan gentry formed an important part of the House of Commons, the lower house of Parliament. It was not wise to alienate them.

The conflict that began during the reign of James came to a head during the reign of his son, Charles I. Charles, like his father, believed in the divine right of kings. In 1628, Parliament passed a Petition of Right. The petition placed limits on the king's ability to tax, imprison citizens without cause, quarter troops, and institute martial law. Although Charles initially accepted this petition, he later ignored it after realizing the limits it put on his power.

Charles also tried to impose more ritual on the Church of England. Thousands of Puritans went to America rather than accept his policy. Thus the struggles of the English Reformation influenced American history.

## CIVIL WAR AND COMMONWEALTH

Complaints grew until England slipped into a civil war in 1642 between the supporters of the king (the **Cavaliers**, or Royalists) and the parliamentary forces (called the **Roundheads**). Parliament proved victorious, due largely to the New Model Army of Oliver Cromwell, who was a military genius.

The New Model Army chiefly consisted of more extreme Puritans, known as the Independents. These men believed they were doing battle for God. As Cromwell wrote, "This is none other but the hand of God; and to Him alone belongs the glory." Some credit is due to Cromwell. His soldiers were well-disciplined and trained in the new military tactics of the 1600s.

The victorious New Model Army lost no time in taking control. Cromwell purged Parliament of any members who had not supported him. What was left—the so-called Rump Parliament—had Charles I executed on January 30, 1649. The execution of the king horrified much of Europe. Parliament next abolished the monarchy and the House of Lords and declared England a **commonwealth**, a type of republic.

Cromwell found it difficult to work with the Rump Parliament and finally dispersed it by force, exclaiming, "I have been forced to do this. I have sought the Lord, night and day, that He would slay me, than put upon me the doing of this work." After destroying both king and Parliament, Cromwell set up a military dictatorship.

## THE RESTORATION

Cromwell ruled until his death in 1658. The army, realizing how unpopular it had become, restored the monarchy in 1660 in the person of Charles II, the son of Charles I.

The **restoration** of the Stuart monarchy, known as the Restoration period, did not mean, however, that the work of the English Revolution was undone. Parliament kept much of the power it had won and continued to play an important role in government. The principle that Parliament must give its consent to taxation was also accepted. Charles, however, continued to push his own ideas, some of which were clearly out of step with many of the English people.

Charles was sympathetic to Catholicism. Moreover, his brother James, heir to the throne, did not hide the fact that he was a Catholic. Parliament's suspicions about their Catholic leanings were therefore aroused when Charles took the bold step of suspending the laws that Parliament had passed against Catholics and Puritans after the restoration of the monarchy. Parliament would have none of it and forced the king to back down. Driven by a strong anti-Catholic sentiment, Parliament then passed a Test Act, specifying that only Anglicans (members of the Church of England) could hold military and civil offices.

Arousing more suspicion, on his deathbed, Charles II had decided to **convert** to Catholicism. After Charles died without a son, James II became king in 1685. James was an open and devout Catholic. He named Catholics to high positions in the government, army, navy, and universities. Religion once more became a cause of conflict between king and Parliament.

Parliament objected to James's policies but stopped short of rebellion. Members knew he was an old man and his Protestant daughters, Mary and

### DETERMINING MEANING

Following the civil war, Parliament declared England to be a **commonwealth**. How is a commonwealth different from a monarchy?

### DETERMINING MEANING

The word *restore* means to "bring something back to its original condition." Based on this definition, why might the period following the death of Oliver Cromwell be referred to as the **Restoration** period?

### DETERMINING MEANING

Read the paragraph that contains the word **convert**. Using context clues, write a definition of the word *convert*. Use a dictionary or an online reference to check your definition.

*Oliver Cromwell, Lord Protector of England during the Commonwealth*

Anne, born to his first wife, would succeed him. However, in 1688, James and his second wife, a Catholic, had a son. Now the possibility of a Catholic monarchy loomed large.

## A GLORIOUS REVOLUTION

A group of English nobles invited the Dutch leader, William of Orange, to invade England. In their invitation, they informed William that most of the kingdom's people wanted a change. The invitation put William and his wife Mary, the daughter of James II, in a difficult position. It would be appalling for Mary to rise up against her father. However, William, a foe of France's Catholic king Louis XIV, welcomed this opportunity to fight France with England's resources.

William began making preparations to invade England in early 1688. It was not until early October that James realized William's intentions. In November 1688, William's forces landed at Torbay and began their march toward London. James responded by sending forward his army. Following the desertion of many of his soldiers and the defection of his daughter Anne and her husband, James retreated to London. There he made plans for his wife and son to flee to France where James later joined them.

With almost no bloodshed, England had undergone a "Glorious Revolution." The issue was not if there would be a monarchy but who would be monarch.

In January 1689, Parliament offered the throne to William and Mary. They accepted it, along with a Bill of Rights, which contained many of the same ideas as the Petition of Right. The Bill of Rights set forth Parliament's right to make laws and to levy taxes. It also made it impossible for kings to oppose or to do without Parliament by stating that standing armies could be raised only with Parliament's consent. The rights of citizens to keep arms and to have a jury trial were also confirmed.

## THE ENGLISH BILL OF RIGHTS

The English Bill of Rights also helped create a system of government based on the **rule of law** and a freely elected Parliament. The rule of law holds that all people are subject to the same laws, even someone such as a king or queen. It limits the power of monarchs and forces them to make decisions that obey the laws of their state. Under the rule of law, the monarch's power was no longer absolute. This idea was a dramatic break from most political thought in Europe's past. This bill laid the foundation for a limited, or constitutional, monarchy.

**ANALYZING PRIMARY SOURCES**

**IDENTIFYING CONNECTIONS** This document states James II abdicated the government. What does this mean, and how do the events of the Glorious Revolution support or not support this statement?

> "...King James the Second having abdicated the government and the throne being thereby vacant, his Highness the prince of Orange (who it hath pleased Almighty God to make the glorious instrument of delivering this kingdom from popery and arbitrary power) did (by the advice of the Lords Spiritual and Temporal and divers principal persons of the Commons) cause letters to be written to the Lords Spiritual and Temporal . . . in order to such an establishment as that their religion, laws and liberties might not again be in danger of being subverted. . . ."

—from the English Bill of Rights

Another important action of Parliament was the Toleration Act of 1689. This act granted Puritans, but not Catholics, the right of free public worship. It did mark a turning point in English history because few English citizens would ever again be persecuted for religion.

By deposing one king and establishing another, Parliament had destroyed the divine-right theory of kingship. William was, after all, king by the grace of Parliament, not by the grace of God. Parliament had asserted its right to be part of the government. Parliament did not have complete control of the government, but it now had the right to participate in affairs of state. Over the next century, Parliament would gradually prove to be the real authority in the English system of constitutional monarchy.

### ☑ CHECKING FOR UNDERSTANDING

1. **EXPLAINING CAUSE AND EFFECT** How did disagreements over rule between the Stuarts and Parliament lead to the English Civil War? What were the causes and effects of the Glorious Revolution?

2. **INTERPRETING** Why would King James I favor the concept of the divine right of kings? Why might Parliament have opposed this idea?

3. **COMPARING AND CONTRASTING** In what important way was the monarchy of William and Mary different from the previous Stuart monarchy?

## LEGAL AND POLITICAL THOUGHT

**GUIDING QUESTION** *How did the English Revolution influence political thought?*

Concerns with order and power were reflected in English legal and political thought. William Blackstone, a judge and professor of law, wrote *Commentaries on the Laws of England*, arguing that political stability could be achieved by a revived emphasis on English common law. Two English political thinkers, Thomas Hobbes and John Locke, provided their own responses to the English revolutions of the seventeenth century.

Thomas Hobbes was alarmed by the revolutionary upheavals in England. In 1651, he published the political work *Leviathan* to try to deal with the problem of disorder. Hobbes argued that before organized society, humans were guided not by reason and moral ideals but by a ruthless struggle for self-preservation. To save themselves from destroying one another, people made a social contract and agreed to form a state. Hobbes called the state "that great LEVIATHAN . . . to which we owe . . . our peace and defense." People in the state agreed to be governed by an absolute ruler with unlimited power to suppress rebellion and to preserve order.

> “The only way to erect such a Common Power, as may be able to defend them from the invasion of [Foreigners], and the injuries of one another, and thereby to secure them in such sort, as that by their [own industry], and by the [fruits] of the Earth, they may nourish themselves and live contentedly; is, to [confer] all their power and strength upon one Man, or upon one Assembly of men, that may reduce all their Wills, by plurality of voices, unto one Will. . . .”
>
> —Thomas Hobbes, *Leviathan,* 1651

**UNDERSTANDING CRAFT AND STRUCTURE**

1. **ANALYZING TEXT** What technique does the author use to describe legal and political thought in England during the seventeenth century?

2. **ANALYZING TEXT** The text in the second paragraph states, "Thomas Hobbes was alarmed by the revolutionary upheavals in England." Why did the writer use the word *alarmed* here?

**ANALYZING PRIMARY SOURCES**

1. **DETERMINING POINT OF VIEW** What is Hobbes's point of view about how society should function?

2. **ANALYZING IDEAS** According to Hobbes, how does this type of society show unity?

Hobbes, Thomas. 1886. Leviathan or The Matter, Forme and Power of a Common Wealth Ecclesiastical and Civil. George Routledge and Sons; Hobbes, Thomas. 1651. Leviathan or the Matter, Forme, & Power of a Common-Wealth Ecclesiastical and Civill. London: Andrew Crooke

*Title page from* Leviathan, *by Thomas Hobbes, 1651*

North Wind Picture Archives

John Locke viewed the exercise of political power quite differently. His *Two Treatises of Government*, published in 1690, argued against the absolute rule of one person. Unlike Hobbes, Locke believed that before society was organized, humans lived in a state of equality and freedom rather than in a state of war. As a result, all humans had certain **natural rights**—rights with which they were born. These included rights to life, liberty, and property. These ideas were a dramatic break from traditional European political thought.

Like Hobbes, however, Locke believed people found it difficult to protect their natural rights. Thus, they agreed to establish a government to ensure the protection of their rights and to judge those who violated them. Government would protect the rights of the people, and the people would act reasonably. However, if a government broke the contract—for example, if a monarch failed to protect citizens' natural rights—the people would be within their rights to alter or remove the government and to form a new government.

To Locke, *people* meant the landholding aristocracy. He was not an advocate of democracy, but his ideas proved important in the eighteenth century. These ideas were used to support demands for constitutional government, the rule of law, and the protection of rights. Locke's ideas can be found in both the American Declaration of Independence and the United States Constitution.

**DETERMINING MEANING**

Read the paragraph that contains the term **natural rights**. Name three examples of natural rights you can find in the text. From where do natural rights come?

## ✓ CHECKING FOR UNDERSTANDING

1. **IDENTIFYING CONNECTIONS** How did the English Revolution influence political thought?
2. **ANALYZING CHANGE** Why did people such as Hobbes and Locke write about the relationships between governed people and ruling powers?
3. **SUMMARIZING** Did Hobbes or Locke have more trust in self-governance? Why?

## LESSON 2 REVIEW

### Time and Place

1. **EXPLAINING CAUSES** Explain how religious issues contributed to political unrest in England in the 17th century.

### Building History-Social Science Analysis Skills

2. **COMPARING AND CONTRASTING** What was the main difference between the Roundheads and the Cavaliers?
3. **SUMMARIZING** What was the impact of Oliver Cromwell's involvement in the civil war of 1642?
4. **COMPARING AND CONTRASTING** How were the ideas of Hobbes and Locke similar? How were they different?

### Writing About History

5. **ARGUMENTATIVE WRITING** Write a paragraph arguing either Locke's or Hobbes's position. Be sure to include specific ideas. Use material in the chapter to illustrate your argument.

### Collaborating

6. **EVALUATING POINT OF VIEW** Debate the conflict between the king and Parliament in England. One partner should take the position of the king; the other should argue for Parliament.

ESSENTIAL QUESTION

- *How does the exercise of absolute power affect a country?*

LESSON 3

# Absolutism in Europe

## THE STORY BEGINS...

King Louis XIV of France wanted to rule his kingdom however he saw fit. This put him at odds with noblemen, one of whom described him as follows:

> "Louis XIV's vanity was without limit or restraint; it colored everything and convinced him that no one even approached him in military talents, in plans and enterprises, in government. Hence those pictures and inscriptions in the gallery at Versailles which disgust every foreigner; those opera prologues that he himself tried to sing; that flood of prose and verse in his praise for which his appetite was insatiable; those dedications of statues copied from pagan sculpture, and the insipid and sickening compliments that were continually offered to him in person and which he swallowed with unfailing relish; hence his distaste for all merit, intelligence, education, and, most of all, for all independence of character and sentiment in others; his mistakes of judgment in matters of importance; his familiarity and favor reserved entirely for those to whom he felt himself superior in acquirements and ability; and, above everything else, a jealousy of his own authority which determined and took precedence of every other sort of justice, reason, and consideration whatever."

—Louis de Rouvroy, duc de Saint-Simon, 1746

Louis XIV shared these traits and attitudes with many of his fellow monarchs. During the eighteenth century, absolute rule spread across the courts of Europe.

*Among Louis XIV's numerous building programs was a series of new warships and coastal forts.* ▶

PHOTO:Heritage Image Partnership Ltd/Alamy Stock Photo; TEXT:Robinson, James Harvey. 1906. Readings in European History - Volume II. Boston: Ginn and Company.

| Leader | Accomplishments |
|---|---|
| Louis XIV | |
| Frederick William | |
| Peter the Great | |

**ANALYZING KEY IDEAS AND DETAILS**

**SUMMARIZING** Read closely to determine the accomplishments of the European leaders discussed in this lesson. Summarize these accomplishments in a graphic organizer like this one.

# FRANCE UNDER LOUIS XIV

**GUIDING QUESTION** *Why is the reign of Louis XIV regarded as the best example of absolutism in the seventeenth century?*

One response to the crises of the seventeenth century was to seek more **stability** by increasing the power of the monarch. The result was what historians have called absolutism.

**Absolutism** is a system in which a ruler holds total power. In seventeenth-century Europe, absolutism was tied to the idea of the divine right of kings. This means that absolute monarchs supposedly received their power from God and were responsible to no one except God. They had the ability to make laws, to levy taxes, to administer justice, to control officials, and to determine foreign policy.

The reign of Louis XIV is considered the best example of absolutism in the seventeenth century. French culture, language, and manners reached into all levels of European society. French diplomacy and wars dominated the political affairs of Europe. The court of Louis XIV was imitated throughout Europe.

**ANALYZING KEY IDEAS AND DETAILS**

1. **SUMMARIZING** Summarize the reign of Louis XIV.
2. **CITING TEXT EVIDENCE** What were the roles of Cardinals Richelieu and Mazarin in French politics?

**DETERMINING MEANING**

Based on what you know about the meaning of *stable* and the role of a king or queen, what might it mean for a monarchy to achieve "stability" in the age of absolutism?

## RICHELIEU

French history for the 50 years before Louis XIV was a period of struggle as governments fought to avoid the breakdown of the state. Louis XIII and Louis XIV were only boys when they came to the throne. The government was left in the hands of royal ministers. In France, two ministers, Cardinal Richelieu with Louis XIII and Cardinal Mazarin with Louis XIV, played important roles in preserving the **authority** of the monarchy.

Cardinal Richelieu (RIH • shuh • loo), Louis XIII's chief minister, strengthened the monarchy's power. Because the Huguenots were seen as a threat to the king, Richelieu took away their political and military rights. He did preserve their religious rights. Richelieu also set up a network of spies to uncover and crush conspiracies by nobles, executing the conspirators. Near the end of his career, Richelieu wrote about the accomplishments of himself and his king:

> "When your Majesty resolved to admit me to his council and to a share in his confidence, I can say with truth that the Huguenots divided the State with the monarchy, that the nobles behaved as if they were not subjects, and that the chief governors of provinces acted as if they had been independent sovereigns. . . . I then undertook to employ all my energy and all the authority that you were pleased to give me to ruin the Huguenot faction, to humble the pride of the nobles, to reduce all your subjects to their duty, and to exalt your name to its proper position among foreign nations."
>
> —Cardinal Richelieu

**DETERMINING MEANING**

*Absolute* means "total." Based on this, write a definition for the political system known as **absolutism**. Use a dictionary or an online reference to check your definition.

TEXT:Lodge, Sir Richard. 1903. The Life of Cardinal Richelieu - with Explanatory Notes by Henry Ketcham. New York: A.L. Burt.

## LOUIS IN POWER

After his minister Cardinal Mazarin died in 1661, Louis XIV took over supreme power. The new king, at the age of 23, stated his desire to be a real king and the sole ruler of France.

> "[Up] to this moment I have been pleased to entrust the government of my affairs to the late Cardinal. It is now time that I govern them myself. You [secretaries and ministers of state] will assist me with your counsels when I ask for them... . I request and order you to seal no orders except by my command... . I order you not to sign anything, not even a passport . . . without my command; to render account to me personally each day and to favour no one."
>
> —Louis XIV, quoted in *Princes and Peoples*

**ANALYZING PRIMARY SOURCES**

1. **ANALYZING IDEAS** How do Louis XIV's instructions to his chancellor exemplify absolutism?
2. **DETERMINING POINT OF VIEW** What does this excerpt reveal about Louis XIV's view of his place in French society?

Well aware of her son's love of fun and games and his affairs with the maids, Louis's mother laughed at him. Louis was serious, however. He kept a strict routine and also fostered the myth of himself as the Sun King—the source of light for all his people.

One key to Louis's power was his control of the central policy-making machinery of government. The royal court that Louis established at Versailles (vuhr • SY) served three purposes. The royal council was the personal household of the king. In addition, the chief offices of the state were located there. Finally, Versailles was the place powerful subjects came to find favors and offices for themselves.

The greatest danger to Louis's rule came from the highest nobles and royal princes. They believed they should play a role in the government. Instead, Louis removed them from the royal council. It was the king's chief administrative body, which supervised the government. At the same time, Louis enticed the nobles and royal princes to come to his court, where he kept them busy with court life and out of politics.

Louis's government ministers were to obey his every wish. Said Louis, "I had no intention of sharing my authority with them." Thus, Louis had complete authority over the traditional areas of royal power: foreign policy, the church, and taxes. Although Louis had absolute power over nationwide policy making, his power was limited at the local level. Nobles, local officials, and town councils had more influence than the king in the daily operation of local governments. As a result, the king bribed important people in the provinces to see that his policies were carried out.

Desiring to maintain religious harmony as part of the monarchal power in France, Louis pursued an anti-Protestant policy aimed at converting the Huguenots to Catholicism. Early in his reign, Louis ordered the destruction of Huguenot churches and the closing of their schools. As many as 200,000 Huguenots fled to England, the United Provinces, and the German states.

The cost of building palaces, maintaining his court, and pursuing his wars made finances a crucial issue for Louis XIV. He was most fortunate in having the services of Jean-Baptiste Colbert (kohl • BEHR) as controller-general of finances.

**MAKING CONNECTIONS TO TECHNOLOGY**

### CANALS

Under Louis XIV, Jean-Baptiste Colbert initiated many efforts to improve France's finances, including the building of canals. Canals are artificial waterways. People build canals for several reasons, including to transport goods. The origins of canal building are ancient. In the seventh century B.C.E., the Assyrians built a stone-lined canal that was 50 miles long. For Europe, the eighteenth century was a golden age of canal building. Advances in technology—for example, the types of locks and gates used to regulate the flow of water—allowed Colbert to build a canal 149 miles long. Despite revolutionary changes in transportation that occurred over the last two centuries, canals are still important. Modern canals include such technology as boat lifts and inclined planes to more easily transport vehicles. Canals such as the Suez Canal in Egypt and the Panama Canal in Central America are important lines of communication that allow the flow of goods, people, and money to move smoothly around the world.

**CITING TEXT EVIDENCE** How did technological advances improve canals?

*Triumph of King Louis XIV of France driving the Chariot of the Sun preceded by Aurora,* by Joseph Werner

Giraudon/Bridgeman Art Library

Colbert sought to increase France's wealth and power by following mercantilism. To decrease imports and increase exports, he granted subsidies to new industries. To improve communications and the transportation of goods within France, he built roads and canals. To decrease imports directly, Colbert raised tariffs on foreign goods and created a merchant marine to carry French goods.

To increase his royal power, Louis developed a standing army numbering 400,000 in time of war. He wished to achieve the military glory befitting the Sun King and ensure that his Bourbon dynasty dominated Europe. To achieve his goals, Louis waged four wars between 1667 and 1713. Many nations formed coalitions to prevent him from dominating Europe. Through his wars, Louis added some territory and set up a member of his own dynasty on the throne of Spain.

## LEGACY OF LOUIS XIV

In 1715, the Sun King died. He left France surrounded by enemies and many of the French people in poverty. On his deathbed, the 76-year-old monarch seemed remorseful when he told his successor (his great-grandson), "You are about to become a great king. Do not imitate me either in my taste for building or in my love of war. Live in peace with the nations. . . . Strive to relieve the burdens of your people in which I have been so unfortunate as to fail."

Did Louis mean it? We do not know. In any event, his successor probably did not remember this advice; Louis's great-grandson was only five years old.

### ✓ CHECKING FOR UNDERSTANDING

1. **SUMMARIZING** Why is the reign of Louis XIV regarded as the best example of absolutism in the seventeenth century?
2. **IDENTIFYING STEPS** Why did Louis XIV advise his great-grandson not to imitate the ways of the Sun King?
3. **DETERMINING CONTEXT** How was the monarchy of Louis XIV characteristic of absolutism?

# THE SPREAD OF ABSOLUTISM

GUIDING QUESTION *How did Prussia and Austria emerge as great powers in seventeenth- and eighteenth-century Europe?*

Although absolutism largely failed in Spain, it was more successful in central and eastern Europe. After the Thirty Years' War, there were more than 300 German states. Of these, Prussia and Austria **emerged** in the seventeenth and eighteenth centuries as two great European powers.

## THE DECLINE OF SPAIN

At the beginning of the seventeenth century, Spain was the most populous empire in the world. To most Europeans, Spain seemed the greatest power of the age. Reality was quite different, however.

**UNDERSTANDING CRAFT AND STRUCTURE**

1. **ANALYZING TEXT** How does the text present the topic of the spread of absolutism? How does the way this text is organized help you to understand the information?
2. **DETERMINING MEANING** What does the word *populous* mean in the context in which it is used in the text?

The reign of Philip IV came closest to the practice of absolute monarchy. A program of political reform sought to centralize the government of Spain in the hands of the monarchy. However, unlike Louis XIV in France, the king was unable to curtail the power of the Spanish nobles. Expensive military campaigns led to revolts and the decline of Spain as a great power.

## THE EMERGENCE OF PRUSSIA

Frederick William the Great Elector laid the foundation for the Prussian state. Realizing that Prussia was a small, open territory with no natural frontiers for defense, Frederick William built a large and efficient standing army. He had a force of 40,000 men, which made the Prussian army the fourth-largest in Europe.

To maintain the army and his own power, Frederick William set up the General War Commissariat to levy taxes for the army and oversee its growth. The Commissariat soon became an agency for civil government as well. The new bureaucratic machine became the elector's chief instrument to govern the state. Many of its officials were members of the Prussian landed aristocracy, or the Junkers, who also served as officers in the army.

In 1701, Frederick William's son Frederick officially gained the title of king. Elector Frederick III became King Frederick I.

### DETERMINING MEANING

What does the use of the word "**emerged**" tell you about the states of Prussia and Austria before the seventeenth century?

## THE NEW AUSTRIAN EMPIRE

The Austrian Hapsburgs had long played a significant role in European politics as emperors in the Holy Roman Empire. By the end of the Thirty Years' War, their hopes of creating an empire in Germany had been dashed. In the seventeenth century, however, the Hapsburgs created a new empire in eastern and southeastern Europe.

## EXPANSION OF PRUSSIA AND AUSTRIA TO 1713

### GEOGRAPHIC REASONING

Prussia and Austria emerged as great European powers during the seventeenth and eighteenth centuries.

1. **EXPLORING PLACE** What geographical features might account for Austria's decision to expand to the north and east?
2. **HUMAN-ENVIRONMENT INTERACTION** What problems might Prussia have encountered in governing its territories?

The core of the new Austrian Empire was the traditional Austrian lands in present-day Austria, the Czech Republic, and Hungary. After the defeat of the Turks at Vienna in 1683, Austria took control of all Hungary, Transylvania, Croatia, and Slavonia. By 1700, the Austrian Hapsburgs had gained a sizable new empire.

Over the course of the eighteenth century, various Austrian monarchs would attempt to strengthen their control over the state. Maria Theresa, the only Austrian empress, made several reforms to reinforce the monarch's power. Her son, the emperor Joseph II, also attempted to rule as an absolute monarch. Despite these attempts, the Austrian monarchy never became a highly centralized absolutist state, such as France. This was largely because the Austrian Empire remained a collection of territories held together by the person of the Hapsburg emperor, who was archduke of Austria and king of Hungary, Bohemia, and Croatia. Each of these areas were populated by their own national groups with their own traditions and laws. No common sentiment tied the regions together other than the ideal of service to the Hapsburgs.

### ☑ CHECKING FOR UNDERSTANDING

1. **ANALYZING CHANGE** How did Prussia and Austria emerge as great powers in seventeenth- and eighteenth-century Europe?
2. **SUMMARIZING** Summarize the events that led to the decline of Spain as a great power.
3. **EVALUATING** How was the role of the military significant in Prussia and Austria?

**ANALYZING KEY IDEAS AND DETAILS**

1. **DETERMINING CENTRAL IDEAS** What is the central idea of this section?
2. **CITING TEXT EVIDENCE** What evidence does the text give to support the idea that Peter was "determined" to Westernize Russia?

**DETERMINING MEANING**

Ivan IV became the first Russian ruler to take the title of **czar**. The word *czar* is a Russian transliteration of the Roman title Caesar. What does this suggest about the powers of a czar?

## PETER THE GREAT

**GUIDING QUESTION** *How did Russia emerge as a powerful state under Peter the Great?*

A powerful Russian state emerged in the fifteenth century under the principality of Muscovy and its rulers known as grand dukes. In the sixteenth century, one of these grand dukes, Ivan IV, became the first ruler to take the title of **czar**, the Russian word for *caesar*. Muscovy would now be known as the state of Russia.

Ivan expanded the territories of Russia eastward. He also crushed the power of the Russian nobility, or **boyars**. He was known as Ivan the Terrible because of his ruthless deeds, including stabbing his son to death in a heated argument. When Ivan's dynasty ended in 1598, a period of anarchy, the Time of Troubles, followed. This period ended when the *zemsky sobor*, or national assembly, chose Michael Romanov as the new czar in 1613.

The Romanov dynasty lasted until 1917. One of its most prominent members was Peter the Great, who became czar in 1689. Like other Romanov czars who preceded him, Peter was an absolute monarch who claimed the divine right to rule.

After becoming czar, Peter visited the West. Determined to Westernize Russia, he was eager to borrow European technology. Modernization of the army and navy was crucial to make Russia a great power. Peter employed Russians and Europeans as officers. He drafted peasants for 25-year stints of service to build a standing army of 210,000 soldiers. By Peter's death in 1725, Russia was a great military power and an important European state.

Peter began to introduce Western customs, practices, and manners into Russia. He ordered the first Russian book of etiquette to teach Western manners. Men had to shave their beards and shorten their coats. Upper-class women were allowed to remove their traditional face-covering veils.

Along with making Russia into a great state and military power, Peter wanted to open a "window to the West," meaning a port with ready access to Europe. This could be achieved only on the Baltic Sea, which Sweden, the most important power in northern Europe, controlled. Peter acquired the lands he sought after a long war with Sweden. On the Baltic in 1703, Peter began construction of a new city, St. Petersburg, a base for the new Russian navy and a window to the West. St. Petersburg became Russia's most important port and remained the Russian capital until 1918.

To impose the rule of the central government more effectively, Peter divided Russia into provinces. He hoped to create a "police state," a well-ordered community governed by law. However, few bureaucrats shared his concept of honest service and duty to the state. Peter's personality created an atmosphere of fear. He wrote to one administrator, "According to these orders act, act, act. I won't write more, but you will pay with your head if you interpret orders again." Peter wanted the impossible—that his administrators be slaves and free persons at the same time.

### ☑ CHECKING FOR UNDERSTANDING

1. **IDENTIFYING CONNECTIONS** How did Russia emerge as a powerful state under Peter the Great?
2. **INFERRING** Why was Peter the Great determined to control the Baltic Sea?
3. **IDENTIFYING CONNECTIONS** In what ways did Peter the Great modernize both the culture and the military of Russia?

**BIOGRAPHY**

### PETER THE GREAT
**(1672–1725)**

As czar, Peter protected the interests of Russia's ruling class by creating a Table of Ranks, which modified the status of nobility. He also changed the rules so that the property of all landowners became hereditary instead of dependent on their service to the czar. In his appointments, Peter chose the most talented candidates, regardless of their level in society.

**DRAWING CONCLUSIONS** How might Peter's policy make those he appointed more loyal to him?

PHOTO:Hulton Archive/Getty Images; TEXT:Peter the Great and the Emergence of Russia by Benedict Humphrey Sumner. London: English Universities Press, 1956.

## LESSON 3 REVIEW

### Time and Place

1. **ANALYZING CHANGE** Write a paragraph that relates the term *czar* to the term *absolutism* by giving two examples of czars and telling how they ruled absolutely.

### Building History-Social Science Analysis Skills

2. **EVALUATING** What were the geographical and financial consequences of the rise of absolutism in Europe in the seventeenth century?
3. **EXPLAINING CAUSES** Why were the highest nobles and royal princes in France the greatest danger to Louis's rule? What does this danger suggest about how absolutism arises?
4. **INTERPRETING** What kept the Austrian Empire from having a fully centralized absolutist state?

### Writing About History

5. **ARGUMENTATIVE WRITING** Write a paragraph that addresses the following question: Was absolutism an effective method of governing a state?

### Collaborating

6. **PRESENTING** In a small group, select one of the absolutist rulers discussed in this lesson. Together, create a presentation summarizing his rule, focusing on the reforms he attempted. Share your findings with the class.

# WHAT ROLE DID HOBBES AND LOCKE PLAY IN GOVERNMENT?

During the struggle for power that dominated English life in the 1600s, the differing political views of Thomas Hobbes and John Locke played significant roles in reinforcing, as well as inflaming, the attitudes of the two sides of the conflict: the monarchy and Parliament.

At the heart of the issue was the ongoing dispute over what kind of monarchy would rule England. Simply put, Hobbes supported an absolute monarchy, in which the king had complete and sole power. Locke believed in a limited monarchy, in which the king and Parliament shared power. These different views of government and the political conflicts that resulted from them were very complicated, but the eventual outcome of the dispute was clear and uncomplicated. With the ascension of William and Mary to the throne in 1689, supporters of a limited monarchy had won a permanent victory.

### VOCABULARY

*commonwealth:* an independent country

*sovereign:* politically independent

*beholding:* indebted

*subjection:* the act of being forced under one's control

*usurp:* to seize and hold by force or without the right to do so

*unalienable:* not able to be taken away

PRIMARY SOURCE: DOCUMENT

## EXCERPT FROM *LEVIATHAN*

Thomas Hobbes's best known work, *Leviathan*, was published in 1651. This excerpt discusses the nature of laws.

> "There is a sixth doctrine, plainly, and directly against the essence of a **commonwealth**, and 'tis this, that the **sovereign** power may be divided. For what is it to divide the power of a commonwealth, but to dissolve it? for powers divided mutually destroy each other. And for these doctrines, men are chiefly **beholding** to some of those, that making profession of the laws, endeavour to make them depend upon their own learning, and not upon the legislative power. Lastly, when in a warre (forraign, or intestine,) the enemies got a final Victory; so as (the forces of the Common-wealth keeping the field no longer) there is no farther protection of Subjects in their loyalty; then is the Common-wealth DISSOLVED, and every man at liberty to protect himself by such courses as his own discretion shall suggest unto him. For the Soveraign, is the publique Soule, giving Life and Motion to the Common-wealth; which expiring, the Members are governed by it no more, than the Carcasse of a man, by his departed (though Immortal) Soule."

### ANALYZE THE TEXT

1. **ANALYZING CENTRAL IDEAS** Why does Hobbes believe that power in a commonwealth should not be divided?
2. **DETERMINING POINT OF VIEW** According to Hobbes, what do people assume when they advocate that a division of powers is good for a commonwealth? Does he agree with this assumption?

PRIMARY SOURCE: DOCUMENT

## EXCERPT FROM *TWO TREATISES OF GOVERNMENT*

This passage from Locke's *Two Treatises of Government*, published in 1690, addresses the laws and the authority to create them.

> "People have not appointed so to do, they make Laws, whom the People have not appointed so to do, they make Laws without Authority, which the People are not therefore bound to obey; by which means they come again to be out of **subjection**, and may constitute to themselves a new Legislative, as they think best, being in full liberty to resist the force of those, who without Authority would impose any thing upon them. Everyone is at the disposure of his own Will, when those who had by the delegation of the Society, the declaring of the publick [sic] Will, are excluded from it, and others **usurp** the place who have no such Authority or Delegation. . . . When such a single Person or Prince sets up his own Arbitrary Will in place of the Laws, which are the Will of the Society, declared by the Legislative, then the Legislative is changed."

### ANALYZE THE TEXT

1. **DETERMINING MEANING** What does Locke mean when he states that "others usurp the place who have no such Authority or Delegation"?
2. **ANALYZING CENTRAL IDEAS** When Locke says that people are not obligated to obey laws that are made without their authority, what is he implying about government?

PRIMARY SOURCE: DOCUMENT

## EXCERPT FROM THE DECLARATION OF INDEPENDENCE

This excerpt from the American Declaration of Independence, which was written in 1776, draws directly on the conventions of Locke's theories of government.

> "We hold these truths to be self-evident, that all men are created equal, that they are endowed by their Creator with certain **unalienable** Rights, that among these are Life, Liberty and the pursuit of Happiness.—That to secure these rights, Governments are instituted among Men, deriving their just powers from the consent of the governed, —That whenever any Form of Government becomes destructive of these ends, it is the Right of the People to alter or to abolish it, and to institute new Government, laying its foundation on such principles and organizing its powers in such form, as to them shall seem most likely to effect their Safety and Happiness."

### ANALYZE THE TEXT

1. **ANALYZING TEXTS** According to the Declaration of Independence, what duty does mankind have to fulfill when faced with a tyrannical government? Cite evidence from the text to support your answer.
2. **ANALYZING TEXTS** In the Declaration of Independence, how does the concept of "unalienable rights" connect to government?

Declaration of Independence. July 4, 1776. Records of the Continental and Confederation Congresses and the Constitutional Convention 1774–1789. Record Group 360, National Archives.

### MULTIPLE PERSPECTIVES

1. **COMPARING AND CONTRASTING** When Hobbes uses the term *legislative power*, to whom is he referring? To whom is Locke referring when he uses the term *Legislative*?
2. **IDENTIFYING CONNECTIONS** Locke's views on government influenced some of the ideas in the U.S. Declaration of Independence and the U.S. Constitution. What ideas in the excerpt from *Two Treatises* can you find in the Declaration of Independence to support this statement?
3. **COMPARING AND CONTRASTING** How are Locke's and Hobbes's views similar? How are they different? Write a paragraph comparing the philosophies of the two thinkers. List one specific example of a similarity and a difference in your response. Be sure to use proper grammar, spelling, capitalization, and punctuation in your response.

# STUDY GUIDE

## EUROPE IN CRISIS
### LESSON 1

**THE THIRTY YEARS' WAR**

- Begun in 1618, the conflict was at first a war between Protestants and Catholics.
- After 10 years, the forces of the Catholic Holy Roman Emperor had crushed the Protestants.
- Fearing a powerful emperor, Denmark, France, and Sweden entered the war.
- With Catholic France fighting the Catholic emperor, the war was now political rather than religious.
- Ended in 1648 with the Treaty of Westphalia, reducing the power of the emperor and empowering German princes.

## REVOLUTIONS IN ENGLAND
### LESSON 2

**The Stuarts and Divine Right**

King James I of the Stuart Dynasty believed he received his power from and was responsible only to God.

**Civil War and Commonwealth**

A civil war erupted in 1642 between the supporters of the King Charles I (Cavaliers) and supporters of Parliament (Roundheads).

**The Restoration**

Although the Stuart dynasty was restored with Charles II in 1660, Parliament kept much of the power it had won in the civil war.

**Glorious Revolution**

Nervous about the Catholicism of King James II, Parliament invited his Protestant daughter Mary and her husband William of Orange to invade and to take the throne.

## ABSOLUTISM IN EUROPE
### LESSON 3

Absolutism is a system in which a ruler holds absolute power. In seventeenth-century Europe, this power was believed to be received from God (divine right of kings). These leaders claimed the divine right to rule.

- **France** Louis XIV
- **Prussia** Frederick the Great
- **Austria** Joseph II
- **Russia** Peter the Great

# CHAPTER 1 Assessment

**Directions: On a separate sheet of paper, answer the questions below. Make sure you read carefully and answer all parts of the questions.**

## Short Answer

❶ **RELATING EVENTS** What was the religion of King Philip II of Spain? How did Philip's political actions show his religious beliefs?

❷ **EXPLAINING CAUSE AND EFFECT** How did the number of people in Europe fluctuate in the sixteenth and seventeenth centuries? What effect did the change in population have on societies and their economies?

❸ **UNDERSTANDING CONTEXT** What did the Petition of Right limit? Who was responsible for it?

❹ **SUMMARIZING** How did Thomas Hobbes and John Locke differ in the kind of government they thought would be best?

❺ **IDENTIFYING CONNECTIONS** What steps did Louis XIV take to increase his royal power? What effects did his actions have on his country and his people?

❻ **IDENTIFYING CONNECTIONS** What inspired Frederick William to build a large standing army in Prussia?

❼ **SUMMARIZING** How was Louis XIV's power limited at the local level and how did he address the issue?

❽ **IDENTIFYING CONNECTIONS** What led to the decline of Spain as a great power?

❾ **RELATING EVENTS** With respect to religious harmony in their countries, compare Elizabeth I's decisions when she took the throne in England to Henry IV's actions in France when he took the throne in France.

❿ **INTERPRETING** Speculate on the strength of the arguments against many women accused of witchcraft during the Inquisition in the sixteenth and seventeenth centuries.

⓫ **IDENTIFYING CONNECTIONS** What factors kept the Austrian Empire from becoming a centralized, absolutist state?

⓬ **UNDERSTANDING CONTEXT** What were the roles of the English nobility, Parliament, and religion in the Glorious Revolution?

⓭ **EXPLAINING CAUSE AND EFFECT** What impact did Peter the Great have on Russia?

## History and Social-Science Analysis

⓮ **INTEGRATING INFORMATION** Working with a partner, use posterboard to create a large chart that lists social, economic, and religious conflicts in at least four European countries during the sixteenth and seventeenth centuries; the chart should also show the effects of those conflicts on each country and its culture. Include visuals such as sketches, maps, and photos of art.

⓯ **IDENTIFYING CONNECTIONS** How did the religious wars of the sixteenth and seventeenth centuries affect Europe? How did the concept of heresy contribute to the issues being fought over?

## Analyzing Visuals

Use the image to answer the following question.

⓰ **INTERPRETING** How does the painting, *Triumph of King Louis XIV of France Driving the Chariot of the Sun Preceded by Aurora,* in which Louis XIV is depicted as a combination of Helios the bringer of day and Apollo, the god of light and culture, illustrate his reign?



**Need Extra Help?**

| If You've Missed Question | ❶ | ❷ | ❸ | ❹ | ❺ | ❻ | ❼ | ❽ | ❾ | ❿ | ⓫ | ⓬ | ⓭ | ⓮ | ⓯ | ⓰ |
|---|---|---|---|---|---|---|---|---|---|---|---|---|---|---|---|---|
| Review Lesson | 1 | 1 | 2 | 2 | 3 | 3 | 3 | 3 | 1 | 1 | 3 | 2 | 3 | 1 | 1 | 3 |

## Research and Presentation

**17** **ARGUMENTATIVE WRITING** Select the war or rebellion in England during the time period that you feel had the greatest impact on England's future government. Conduct additional research about the events leading up to and the outcomes of the conflict. Then write an argument using the information which supports your point of view.

**18** **IDENTIFYING CONNECTIONS** Contrast absolute monarchies and constitutional, or limited, monarchies. What are the differences between each type of monarchy? How did the type of monarchy that a country had affect the satisfaction of its people? Use information gathered from primary and secondary sources to provide examples to support your answer. Create a graphic organization to record your response.

**19** **SUMMARIZING** Create a graph to show the percentages of Catholics and Protestants in France during the French Wars of Religion. Create a second graph showing the percentages of Catholic and Protestant nobility in France at the time. Use spreadsheet software or another digital tool to create your graph. Be sure to include a title and a key. What conclusions can you draw from your graph?

## Reading and Analyzing Primary Sources

Use the document to answer the following questions.

In 1589, King James I of England wrote, anonymously, a book in which he defended the divine right of kings to absolute power.

> "And as ye see it manifest that the king is over-lord of the whole land, so is he master over every person that inhabiteth the same, having power over the life and death of every one of them; for although a just prince will not take the life of any of his subjects without a clear law, yet the same laws whereby he taketh them are made by himself or his predecessors; and so the power flows always from himself. . . ."

—from *True Law of Free Monarchies*

**20** **INTERPRETING** Which position does James I take on whether subjects have protection against execution by their ruler?

**A.** He claims that they are protected by laws that are passed by Parliament.
**B.** He claims that they are protected by the laws of nature.
**C.** He claims that they are protected by precedent.
**D.** He claims that they have no such protection.

**21** **UNDERSTANDING CONTEXT** Why does the king say that all kings are overlords of their whole lands?

**A.** He believes that Parliament has given the king absolute authority.
**B.** He believes that all law comes from the king.
**C.** He believes that the people have agreed to be ruled by the king.
**D.** He believes that kings take power by defeating other kings.

**22** **IDENTIFYING CONNECTIONS** From where does James I believe the king's authority comes?

**A.** He believes the king's authority comes from God.
**B.** He believes the king's authority comes from himself.
**C.** He believes the king's authority comes from Parliament.
**D.** He believes the king's authority comes from the people.

## Writing About History

**23** **DRAWING CONCLUSIONS** During their rule, monarchs can either strengthen or weaken their countries. Craft a one-page essay explaining which monarch described in this chapter you most admire and which monarch you least admire for how he or she governed. Support your answer with examples of actions taken by each monarch.

## Speaking and Listening About History

**24** **EVALUATING** Meet in a small group to discuss the following questions: How did the English Civil War transform the political front in England? How did it lay part of the groundwork for the development of democratic systems of government? Have one member of your group serve as a moderator for the group discussion.

**Need Extra Help?**

| If You've Missed Question | 17 | 18 | 19 | 20 | 21 | 22 | 23 | 24 |
|---|---|---|---|---|---|---|---|---|
| Review Lesson | 1 | 3 | 1 | 2 | 2 | 2 | 1–3 | 2 |

◀ *This engraving is based on a portrait of Mary Wollstonecraft by John Opie. Wollstonecraft advocated for equal rights for women based on the ideal of reason that was the foundation of the Enlightenment.*

Library of Congress, Prints & Photographs Division [LC-USZ62-64309]

1550 — 1800

# The Enlightenment and Revolutions

CHAPTER 2



**GO DIGITAL**
*It's All Online!*

## ASKING ESSENTIAL QUESTIONS

***Why do new ideas often spark change? How do new ways of thinking affect the way people respond to their surroundings?***

**What Will You Learn?** You will learn how new scientific and political ideas sowed seeds of change in Europe and North America.

**Why Does This Matter?** The scientific and political ideas Enlightenment scientists, political thinkers, and others developed in this period continue to shape the way we understand natural phenomena, to inform our expectations of government, and to form the basis for a wide variety of technological innovations that we now take for granted.

**How Will You Know That You Learned It?** You will be able to identify significant scientific and political ideas that arose during the Scientific Revolution and the Enlightenment and explain how these ideas represented a fundamental break with Europe's past.

**Using Your Inquiry Journal** As you read this chapter and examine the primary sources, use your Inquiry Journal to help you make notes and expand your list of questions. As you gather information, think about how you will answer the Essential Questions above.

# PLACE & TIME Europe and the World 1550 to 1800

The seventeenth and eighteenth centuries witnessed the Scientific Revolution and the Enlightenment. Philosophers and scientists produced new theories about the structure of the universe and humankind's relationship to it. As European powers explored the world and expanded their colonial empires, conflicts erupted. This first age of global warfare culminated in the Seven Years' War, fought in Europe, North America, and India.

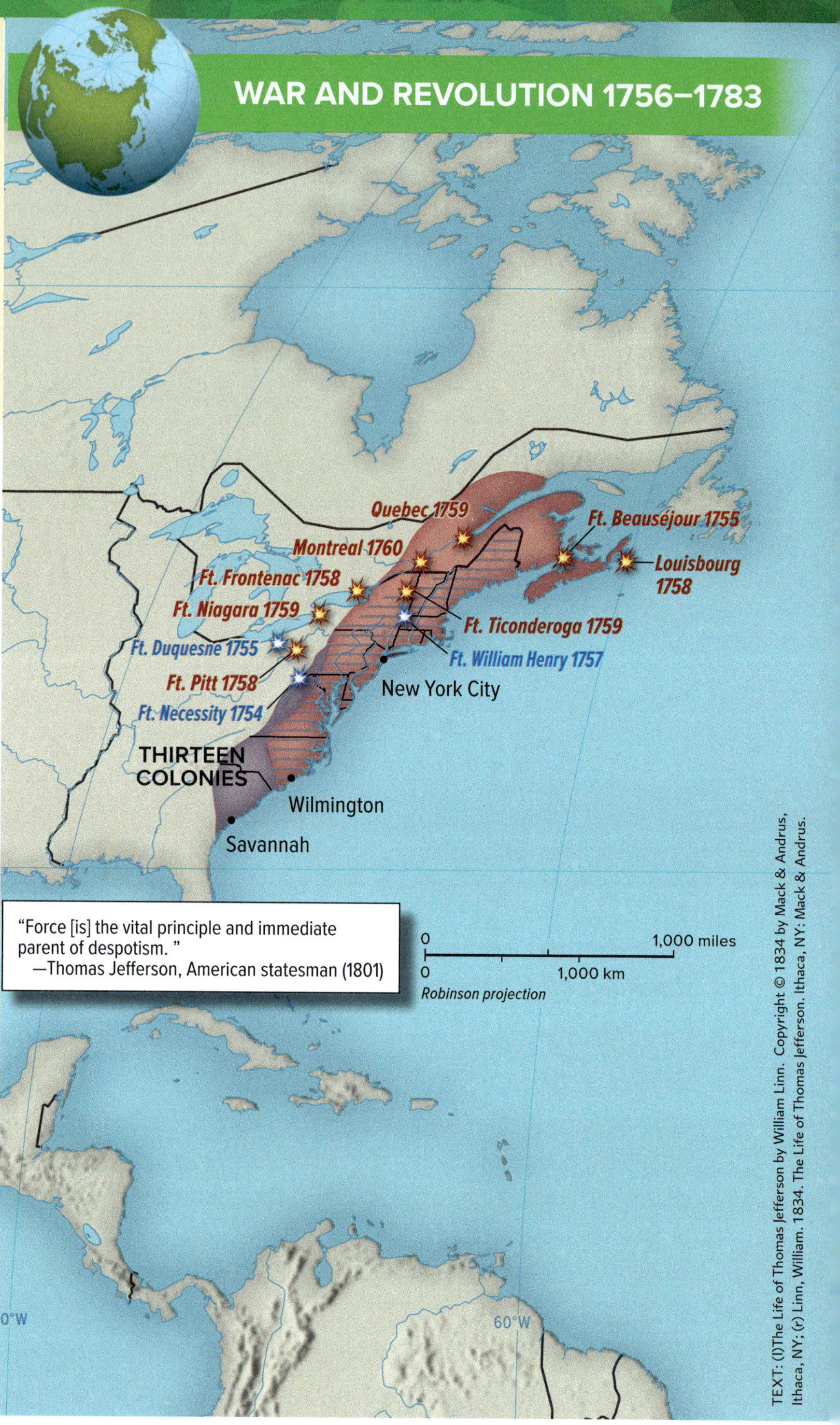


## STEP INTO THE PLACE

Read the quote below and look at the information presented on the map.

1. **SPATIAL THINKING** Based on the map, what conclusions can you draw about the size and scope of the Seven Years' War?
2. **DETERMINING CONTEXT** How does Locke's attitude toward war reflect the ideas of Enlightenment thinkers?

> "Though . . . politics [cannot] be founded on any thing but the consent of the people . . . in the noise of war, which makes so great a part of the history of mankind, this consent is little taken notice of: and therefore many have mistaken the force of arms for the consent of the people, and reckon conquest as one of the originals of government. But conquest is as far from setting up any government, as demolishing an [sic] house is from building a new one in the place. . . . Without the consent of the people, [one] can never erect a new one."
>
> —John Locke, from *Two Treatises of Government*, 1690

## STEP INTO THE TIME

**CHRONOLOGICAL THINKING**

How do the events on the time line reflect on the intellectual breakthroughs that took place in Europe during this era?

## EUROPE

**1610** Galileo Galilei publishes *The Starry Messenger*

**1637** René Descartes publishes *Discourse on Method*

**1550** — **1600** — **1650**

## WORLD EVENTS

**1562** Beginning of Akbar's reign in India

**1588** Shāh 'Abbās comes to power in Persia

**1603** Tokugawa shogunate begins in Japan

**1607** Founding of Jamestown Colony in Virginia

**1632–53** Construction of Taj Mahal

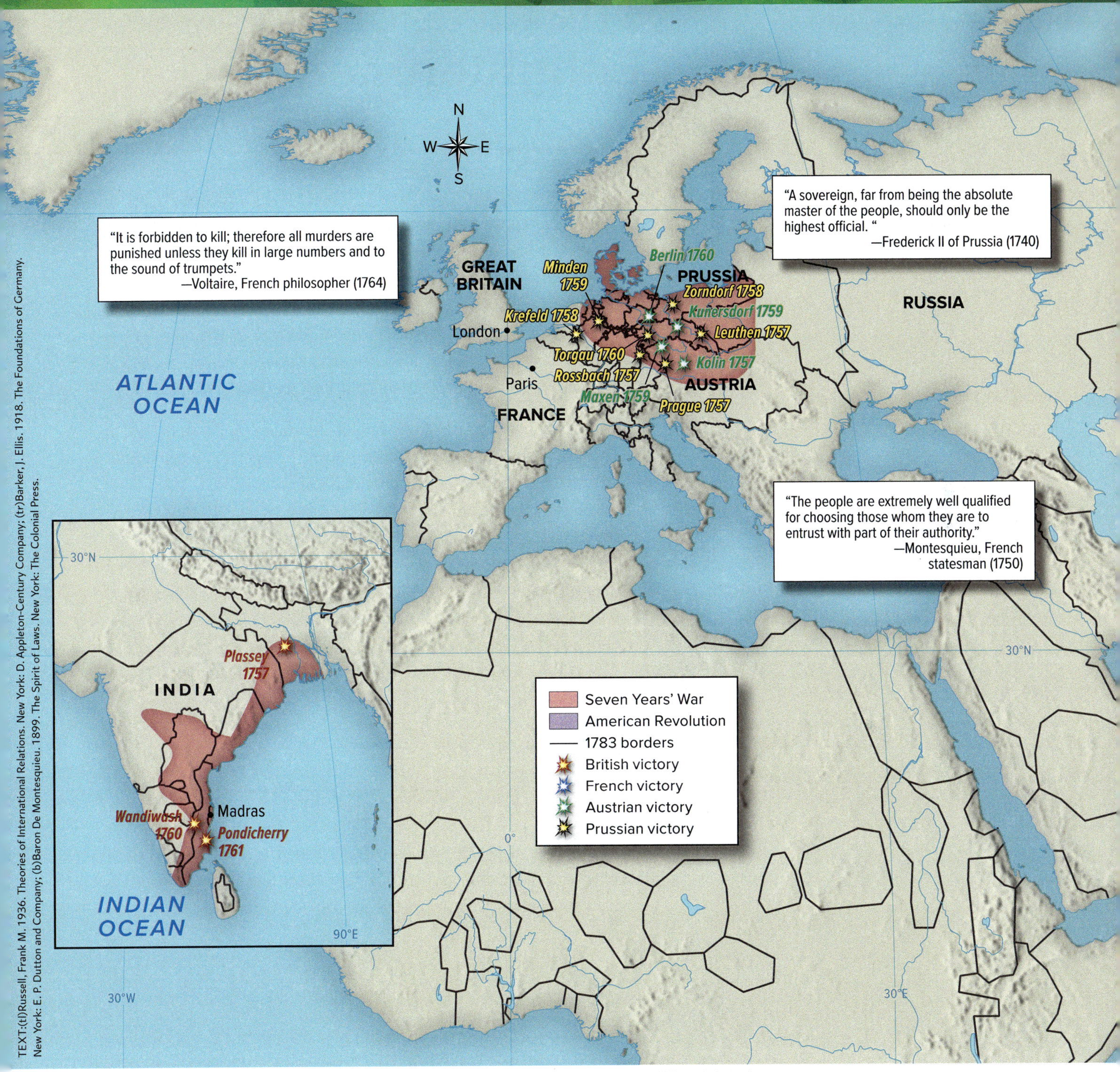


"It is forbidden to kill; therefore all murders are punished unless they kill in large numbers and to the sound of trumpets."
—Voltaire, French philosopher (1764)

"A sovereign, far from being the absolute master of the people, should only be the highest official."
—Frederick II of Prussia (1740)

"The people are extremely well qualified for choosing those whom they are to entrust with part of their authority."
—Montesquieu, French statesman (1750)

TEXT:(t)Russell, Frank M. 1936. Theories of International Relations. New York: D. Appleton-Century Company; (tr)Barker, J. Ellis. 1918. The Foundations of Germany. New York: E. P. Dutton and Company; (b)Baron De Montesquieu. 1899. The Spirit of Laws. New York: The Colonial Press.

**1700** **1750** **1800**

- **1661** Kangxi, the greatest Qing emperor, comes to the throne
- **1690** John Locke publishes *Two Treatises of Government*
- **1691** Sor Juana Inés de la Cruz writes her self-defense
- **1728** Vitus Bering explores sea between Siberia and North America
- **1740** War of Austrian Succession begins
- **1751** Denis Diderot begins to publish *Encyclopedia*
- **1756** Seven Years' War breaks out in North America, Europe, and India
- **1762** Jean-Jacques Rousseau publishes *The Social Contract*
- **1763** War in Europe and War in India ends
- **1776** Adam Smith publishes *The Wealth of Nations*
- **1786** Reign of Frederick the Great of Prussia ends
- **1787** Zulu ruler Shaka is born
- **1788** U.S. Constitution is ratified
- **1796** Reign of Catherine the Great of Russia ends

ESSENTIAL QUESTIONS

- *Why do new ideas often spark change?*
- *How do new ways of thinking affect the way people respond to their surroundings?*

# THE STORY BEGINS...

LESSON 1

# The Ideas of the Enlightenment

Prior to the Enlightenment, knowledge was something acquired through careful study of the works of Classical thinkers, like Plato and Aristotle. But as the foundations of science and the scientific method began to take shape in the Early Modern period, philosophers began to recognize the value of observation and experience. Thinking about learning in this way, as the seventeenth-century British philosopher John Locke does in the excerpt below, transformed how people understood the very concept of knowledge:

> "Let us then suppose the mind to be, as we say, white paper, void of all characters, without any ideas:—How comes it to be furnished? Whence comes it by that vast store which the busy and boundless fancy of man has painted on it with an almost endless variety? Whence has it all the MATERIALS of reason and knowledge? To this I answer, in one word, from EXPERIENCE. In that all our knowledge is founded; and from that it ultimately derives itself. Our observation employed either, about external sensible objects, or about the internal operations of our minds perceived and reflected on by ourselves, is that which supplies our understandings with all the MATERIALS of thinking. These two are the fountains of knowledge, from whence all the ideas we have, or can naturally have, do spring."

—*An Essay Concerning Human Understanding,* John Locke, 1689

The key to understanding knowledge was "experience," Locke argued. Such thoughts held out the alluring possibility that through learning and experience humanity might actually create a better society.

*Enlightenment ideas were often shared person to person in the drawing rooms of the wealthy known as "salons."* ▶

| Ideas of the Enlightenment | |
|---|---|
| John Locke | Isaac Newton |
| | |
| | |
| | |

**ANALYZING KEY IDEAS AND DETAILS**

**CITING TEXT EVIDENCE** Read closely to identify the key ideas of John Locke and Isaac Newton in a graphic organizer like this one.

# PHILOSOPHY AND REASON

**GUIDING QUESTION** *How did the Scientific Revolution change people's worldview?*

New concepts of the universe brought about by the Scientific Revolution strongly influenced the Western view of humankind and played a crucial role in the Enlightenment.

## DESCARTES AND RATIONALISM

Nowhere is this more evident than in the work of the seventeenth-century French philosopher René Descartes (day • KAHRT), who brought a philosophical perspective to the natural sciences. He began by considering the doubt and uncertainty that seemed to be everywhere in the confusion of the seventeenth century. He ended with a philosophy that largely dominated Western thought until the twentieth century.

The starting point for Descartes's new system was doubt. In his most famous work, *Discourse on Method,* written in 1637, Descartes decided to set aside all he had learned and to begin again. One fact seemed to him to be beyond doubt—his own existence. Descartes emphasized the importance of his own mind, accepting only those things his reason said were true. From his first principle—"I think, therefore I am"—Descartes used his reason to arrive at a second principle. He argued that because "the mind cannot be doubted but the body and material world can, the two must be radically different."

From this idea came the principle of the separation of mind and matter (and of mind and body). Descartes's idea that mind and matter were completely separate allowed scientists to view matter as dead or inert. That is, matter was something that was totally detached from the mind and that could be investigated independently by reason. Descartes has rightly been called the father of modern **rationalism**. This system of thought is based on the belief that reason is the chief source of knowledge.

## BACON AND THE SCIENTIFIC METHOD

During the Scientific Revolution, people became concerned about how they could best understand the physical world. The result was the creation of the **scientific method**—a systematic procedure for collecting and analyzing evidence. The scientific method was crucial to the evolution of science in the modern world.

**INTEGRATING KNOWLEDGE AND IDEAS**

1. **INTEGRATING INFORMATION** How do Descartes's ideas support the formation of rationalism?
2. Why was the scientific method crucial to the evolution of science?

The person who developed the scientific method was not a scientist, but an English philosopher with few scientific credentials. Francis Bacon believed that scientists should not rely on the ideas of ancient authorities. Instead, they should learn about nature by using **inductive reasoning**—proceeding from the particular concepts to general concepts. Bacon also practiced the theory of **empiricism**. This theory says knowledge is achieved through observation. Empiricism, coupled with experimentation and inductive reasoning, would ultimately lead philosophers and scientists to a greater understanding of the natural world.

Before beginning this reasoning, scientists try to free their minds of opinions that might distort the truth. Then they start with detailed facts and proceed toward general principles. From observing natural events, scientists propose hypotheses, or possible explanations, for the events. Then systematic observations and carefully organized experiments to test the hypotheses would lead to correct general principles.

Bacon, concerned with practical matters as well as science, firmly believed in his scientific method. He stated that "the true and lawful goal of the sciences is none other than this: that human life be endowed with new discoveries and powers." Bacon wanted science to benefit industry, agriculture, and trade. He said, "I am laboring to lay the foundation, not of any sect or doctrine, but of human utility and power."

Bacon believed this "human power" could be used to "conquer nature in action." The control and domination of nature became an important concern of science and the technology that accompanied it.

### ✓ CHECKING FOR UNDERSTANDING

1. **IDENTIFYING CONNECTIONS** How did the Scientific Revolution change people's worldview?
2. **COMPARING AND CONTRASTING** How are the ideas of Descartes and Bacon similar? How are their ideas different from systems of thought from earlier time periods?
3. **IDENTIFYING CONNECTIONS** How can the scientific method be used to benefit agriculture?

## IDEAS OF THE PHILOSOPHES

**ANALYZING KEY IDEAS AND DETAILS**

1. **DETERMINING CENTRAL IDEAS** How were the ideas of Montesquieu, Voltaire, and Diderot similar?
2. **SUMMARIZING** Write a brief summary of this section in your own words.

**GUIDING QUESTIONS** *What role did philosophes play in the Enlightenment? How did the belief in logic and reason promote the beginnings of the social sciences?*

The Enlightenment was an eighteenth-century philosophical movement of intellectuals who were greatly impressed with the achievements of the Scientific Revolution. One of the favorite words of these intellectuals was *reason*. Scholars have come to call this period the "Age of Reason." By *reason,* these intellectuals meant the application of the scientific method to an understanding of all life. The ideas of the Enlightenment thinkers were a break from the superstitions of the medieval period and Renaissance before them. They hoped that by using the scientific method, they could make progress toward a better society than the one they had inherited. *Reason, natural law, hope, progress*—these were common words to the thinkers of the Enlightenment. The ideas of the Enlightenment would become a force for reform and eventually revolution.

The intellectuals of the Enlightenment were especially influenced by the ideas of two seventeenth-century Englishmen—John Locke and Isaac Newton. In his *Essay Concerning Human Understanding,* Locke argued that every person was born with a tabula rasa, or blank mind. Locke's ideas suggested that people were molded by the experiences that came through their senses from the surrounding world. Enlightenment thinkers began to believe that if environments were changed and people were exposed to the correct influences, they could be changed to create a new—and better—society.

The ideas of Isaac Newton also influenced eighteenth-century intellectuals. Newton believed the physical world and everything in it was like a giant "world machine," operating according to natural laws that could be uncovered through systematic investigation.

**DETERMINING MEANING**

Based on what you know about the word *system*, write a definition of the word *systematic*. Use a dictionary or an online reference to check your definition.

The Enlightenment thinkers reasoned that if Newton was able to discover the natural laws that governed the physical world, then by applying his scientific methods, they would be able to discover the natural laws that governed human society. If all institutions would then follow these natural laws, the result would be an ideal society.

## THE ROLE OF PHILOSOPHY

The intellectuals of the Enlightenment were known by the French word **philosophe** (FEE • luh • ZAWF), meaning "philosopher." Not all philosophers were French, however, and few were philosophers in the strict sense of the term. They were writers, professors, journalists, economists, and, above all, social reformers. They came chiefly from the nobility and the middle class.

Most leaders of the Enlightenment were French, although the English had provided the philosophical inspiration for the movement. It was the French philosophes who affected intellectuals elsewhere and created a movement that influenced the entire Western world.

To the philosophes, the role of philosophy was to change the world. The use of reason and a spirit of rational criticism were to be applied to everything, including religion and politics. In the first half of the eighteenth century, three individuals dominated the intellectual landscape—Montesquieu (MAHN • tuhs • KYOO), Voltaire, and Diderot (dee • DROH).

## MONTESQUIEU

Charles-Louis de Secondat, the baron de Montesquieu, was a French noble. His famous work *The Spirit of the Laws* (1748) was a study of governments. In it, Montesquieu tried to find the natural laws that govern the social and political relationships of human beings.

Montesquieu stated that England's government had three branches: the executive (the monarch), the legislative (Parliament), and the judicial (the courts of law). The government functioned through a **separation of powers**. In this separation, the executive, legislative, and judicial powers of the government limit and control each other in a system of checks and balances. By preventing any one person or group from gaining too much power, this system provides the greatest freedom and security for the state.

**ANALYZING PRIMARY SOURCES**

1. **DETERMINING POINT OF VIEW** What does Montesquieu fear will happen to citizens if the three powers of government are not separated?
2. **ANALYZING IDEAS** How do the ideas in the first two paragraphs support the ideas in the third paragraph?

The system of checks and balances through separation of powers was Montesquieu's most lasting contribution to political thought. Translation of his work into English made it available to American philosophes, who worked his principles into the United States Constitution.

> "When legislative power is united with executive power in a single person or in a single body of the magistracy, there is no liberty, because one can fear that the same monarch or senate that makes tyrannical laws will execute them tyrannically.
>
> Nor is there liberty if the power of judging is not separate from legislative power and from executive power. If it were joined to legislative power, the power over the life and liberty of the citizens would be arbitrary, for the judge would be the legislator. If it were joined to executive power, the judge could have the force of an oppressor.
>
> All would be lost if the same man or the same body of principal men, either of nobles, or of the people, exercised these three powers: that of making the laws, that of executing public resolutions, and that of judging the crimes or the disputes of individuals."
>
> —Baron de Montesquieu, *The Spirit of the Laws* 1748

*Voltaire helped spread Enlightenment ideas through his writings.*

## VOLTAIRE

The greatest figure of the Enlightenment was François-Marie Arouet, known simply as Voltaire. A Parisian, Voltaire came from a prosperous middle-class family. His numerous writings during the eighteenth century brought him both fame and wealth.

Voltaire was well known for his criticism of Christianity. He often challenged the actions of the Church, one of the most powerful institutions of the time. He had a strong belief in religious toleration, fighting against religious intolerance in France. Voltaire championed **deism**, an eighteenth-century religious philosophy based on reason and natural law. Deism built on the idea of the Newtonian world machine. In the deists' view, a mechanic (God) had created the universe. To Voltaire and most other philosophes, the universe was like a clock. God, the clockmaker, had created it, set it in motion, and allowed it to run without his interference and according to its own natural laws.

*The press room of a print shop, from Diderot's* Encyclopedia, *1751*

**CITING TEXT EVIDENCE** How did both printing and the *Encyclopedia* contribute to the promotion of Enlightenment ideas?

## DIDEROT

Denis Diderot went to the University of Paris. His father hoped Denis would pursue a career in law or the Church. He did neither. Instead, he became a writer, covering many subjects. Diderot's most famous contribution to the Enlightenment was the *Encyclopedia, or Classified Dictionary of the Sciences, Arts, and Trades,* a 28-volume collection of knowledge that he edited. Published between 1751 and 1772, the purpose of the *Encyclopedia,* according to Diderot, was to "change the general way of thinking."

The *Encyclopedia* became a weapon against the old French society. Many of its articles attacked religious superstition and supported religious toleration. Others called for social, legal, and political reforms. Sold to doctors, clergymen, teachers, and lawyers, the *Encyclopedia* spread Enlightenment ideas.

## ✓ CHECKING FOR UNDERSTANDING

1. **DETERMINING CONTEXT** What role did philosophes play in the Enlightenment? How did the belief in logic and reason promote the beginnings of the social sciences?
2. **IDENTIFYING CONNECTIONS** How did the achievements of the Scientific Revolution influence the ideas of the Enlightenment?
3. **RELATING EVENTS** How are Montesquieu's ideas still in use today?

# NEW SOCIAL SCIENCES

**GUIDING QUESTION** *How did the belief in logic and reason promote the beginnings of the social sciences?*

The philosophes, as we have seen, believed that Newton's methods could be used to discover the natural laws underlying all areas of human life. This led to what we would call the social sciences—areas such as economics and political science.

The Physiocrats and Scottish philosopher Adam Smith have been viewed as the founders of the modern social science of economics. The Physiocrats, a French group, were interested in identifying the natural economic laws that governed human society. They maintained that if individuals were free to pursue their own economic self-interests, all society would benefit. The state, then, should not interrupt the free play of natural economic forces by imposing regulations on the economy. Instead, the state should leave the economy alone. This doctrine became known by its French name, **laissez-faire** (LEH • SAY • FEHR), meaning "to let (people) do (what they want)."

The clearest statement on laissez-faire was made in 1776 by Adam Smith in his famous work, *The Wealth of Nations*. Like the Physiocrats, Smith believed that the state should not interfere in economic matters. This idea is the foundation of what is today called a market economy. In a market economy, the pricing of goods and services are guided solely by the interactions between people and businesses. According to this idea, there should be little government intervention in economics. Indeed, Smith gave to government only three basic roles. First, it should protect society from invasion (the function of the army). Second, the government should defend individuals and their property from injustice (the function of the police). And finally, it should keep up certain public works that private individuals alone could not afford—roads and canals, for example—but which are necessary for social interaction and trade.

### ANALYZING KEY IDEAS AND DETAILS

1. **DETERMINING CENTRAL IDEAS** What is the central idea of this section? How does the text present and develop this idea?
2. **CITING TEXT EVIDENCE** What evidence in the text supports the idea that Adam Smith supported the doctrine of laissez-faire?

## ✓ CHECKING FOR UNDERSTANDING

1. **IDENTIFYING CONNECTIONS** How did the belief in logic and reason promote the beginnings of the social sciences?
2. **IDENTIFYING CONNECTIONS** How was Adam Smith influenced by Isaac Newton?
3. **ANALYZING CHANGE** What impact did Adam Smith and the doctrine of laissez-faire have on political thought? How did this compare to political ideas of earlier times?

# POLITICAL THOUGHT IN THE ENLIGHTENMENT

**UNDERSTANDING CRAFT AND STRUCTURE**

1. **ANALYZING TEXT PRESENTATION** How does the writer introduce the topic of political thought in the Enlightenment? How does the writer develop this topic from the beginning to the end of this section?
2. **DETERMINING MEANING** The text states that "individuals give up certain natural rights to their government in return for benefits shared by everyone. . . ." What does the word *natural* mean in this context? What are natural rights?

**GUIDING QUESTION** *How did the political ideas of the Enlightenment represent a break with the ideas of Europe's past?*

Enlightenment political thinkers of the eighteenth century were inspired by seventeenth-century English political thinkers such as John Locke and Thomas Hobbes and their emphasis on natural rights. They also found inspiration in the English Bill of Rights, which firmly established the concept of the rule of law. These ideas, together with Europe's Judeo-Christian culture and the rediscovery of Greco-Roman philosophy, would influence Enlightenment thought on democracy, representation, and good governance.

## NEW POLITICAL IDEAS

During the Enlightenment, ideas such as divine right of kings and the unquestionable status of nobles and clergy had been the foundation of government for centuries. These methods of governing are authoritarian and promoted strict obedience to rulers at the expense of personal freedoms. **Authoritarian** institutions and ideas governed almost every state and empire in the world at this time. However, during the Enlightenment, authoritarian ideas began to be challenged. Some thinkers embraced ideas of natural rights, the rule of law, and representative government.

Some of the political ideals of the Enlightenment had their origins in Judeo-Christian culture and Greco-Roman philosophy. Jewish and Christian scriptures had promoted ideas of kindness, fairness, and equality. Ideas of the ancient Greeks and Romans, rediscovered during the Renaissance, also inspired the political thought of the Enlightenment. The works of many ancient Greek philosophers such as Plato and Aristotle held up the concept of the rule of law as essential to preventing the rise of a tyrannical government. The rule of law holds that all people, both those who govern and the people they govern, are equal under the law. Enlightenment thinkers also adopted

1. **DETERMINING CONTEXT** What view did the U.S. Founders take of the Magna Carta?
2. **IDENTIFYING CONNECTIONS** What do the Magna Carta and the English Bill of Rights have in common?

**CITIZENSHIP**

### THE MAGNA CARTA'S INFLUENCE

The Magna Carta arose out of a dispute between English nobles and the king. At the time, neither group considered the document of importance to the lower classes. The principles in the Magna Carta, however, had an influence on the development of future documents, such as the English Bill of Rights, which, along with the Magna Carta, influenced the U.S. Constitution and U.S. Bill of Rights.

The Magna Carta was initially intended as a document to reaffirm the feudal system and to allow nobles more rights. However, in the creation of the English Bill of Rights and the U.S. Constitution, the view of the Magna Carta as an assertion of the rights of the common man against authoritarian rulers played a crucial role. Both the Magna Carta and the English Bill of Rights placed limits on the monarchy and established individual rights. In turn, many early U.S. state constitutions—upon which the U.S. Constitution is partially based—provided for the rights of citizens, listing protections they had from the government. The U.S. Bill of Rights was also born under such an influence. When interpreted broadly, the Magna Carta can be seen as limiting a monarch's power and influencing Enlightenment thought about democracy and governance.

Greco-Roman ideas of **citizenship**, which viewed public service as necessary for a government to maintain its authority.

Enlightenment thinkers found inspiration in ancient forms of government such as the democracy of ancient Athens, in which male citizens had an equal vote. The republican form of government used in ancient Rome, in which administrative officials were elected to represent the interests of their community, was highly valued as well. Enlightenment thinkers came to believe these forms of representative government, which depended on participation of the governed, better reflected the will of its citizens.

## THE SOCIAL CONTRACT

One of the most famous philosophers of the later Enlightenment was Jean-Jacques Rousseau (ru • SOH). In his *Discourse on the Origins of the Inequality of Mankind*, Rousseau argued that people had adopted laws and government in order to preserve their private property. In the process, they had become enslaved by government and needed to regain their freedom.

In his major work *The Social Contract*, published in 1762, Rousseau presented his concept of the **social contract**. Through a social contract, an entire society agrees to be governed by its general will. Individuals who wish instead to follow their own self-interests must be forced to abide by the general will. "This means nothing less than that [they] will be forced to be free," said Rousseau. Thus, liberty is achieved by being forced to follow what is best for "the general will" because the general will represents what is best for the entire community. In other words, individuals give up certain natural rights to their government in return for benefits shared by everyone in society, such as security, fair regulations, and the accomplishment of greater goals that benefit all people.

The concept of a social contract became important to Enlightenment political thought. It reinforced the idea that the people, rather than kings or queens, form the foundation of that state's government. Furthermore, Enlightenment thinkers argued that governments exist to protect the people's natural rights and their right to life and liberty. However, earlier political thinkers such as Locke and Hobbes believed these rights belonged only to elite members of society. By the middle of the eighteenth century, this idea had begun to change. Some philosophers now began to argue that all people, regardless of their social class, shared the same rights and that all people were equal before the law. For some Europeans, these ideas were new and became revolutionary.

## REVOLUTIONARY IDEAS

Ultimately, Enlightenment thinkers saw governments that did not respect the social contract as **illegitimate**. The people, they argued, were free to overthrow such a government and to create a new one that would better reflect the will of the people. This included all forms of government that did not protect an individual's natural rights, from absolutist monarchies to representative republics and democracies.

Enlightenment political ideals would become more popular at the end of the eighteenth century, when they inspired revolutions in America and France. They continue to influence much of the world, inspiring those who continue to champion individual freedom and representative government in the modern period.

**DETERMINING MEANING**

From what you know about the meaning of the word *legitimate*, write a definition of the word **illegitimate**. Use a dictionary or an online reference to check your definition.

## ☑ CHECKING FOR UNDERSTANDING

1. **DETERMINING CONTEXT** How did the political ideas of the Enlightenment represent a break with the ideas of Europe's past?
2. **IDENTIFYING CONNECTIONS** How were European political thinkers of the Enlightenment influenced by ideas from other cultures?
3. **RELATING EVENTS** How might the ideas behind the "social contract" have affected the lives of ordinary people during the Age of Reason?

CITIZENSHIP

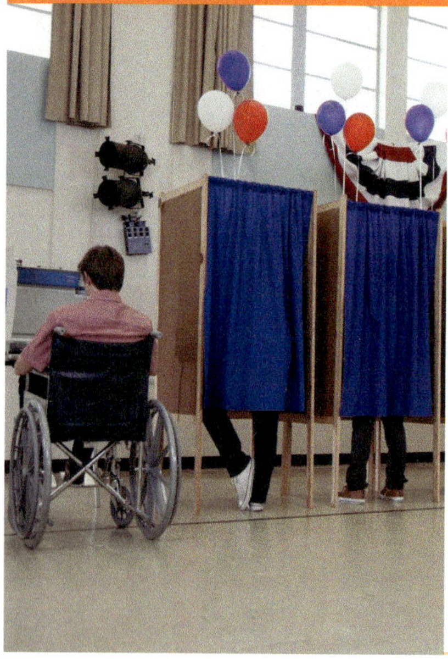

### WHAT IS A REPRESENTATIVE GOVERNMENT?

A representative government is one in which citizens elect a leader or group of leaders to represent them in government. The United States uses a representative government system as part of the democratic process. When the "Founding Fathers" of the United States first structured the country's government, they knew the nation would be too large for all citizens to make political decisions collectively. So they established a system in which citizens would vote for leaders to make those decisions. This allowed the government to act more quickly and efficiently while ensuring that all citizens would still get a voice in government. Elected leaders serve at all levels of government: federal (including the president and members of Congress), state (including a governor and state representatives), and local (including a mayor and council members).

1. **COMPARING AND CONTRASTING** How is a representative government different from an authoritarian government?
2. **IDENTIFYING CONNECTIONS** How is the idea of representative government related to ideas of the Enlightenment?

# THE SPREAD OF IDEAS

**GUIDING QUESTION** *How did the Enlightenment ideas influence society and culture?*

By the late 1760s, a new **generation** of philosophes had come to maturity. Ideas about liberty and the condition of women were spread through an increasingly literate society.

## WOMEN'S RIGHTS

For centuries, male intellectuals argued that the nature of women made them inferior to men and made male domination of women necessary. However, by the eighteenth century, female thinkers began to express their ideas about improving the condition of women. Mary Wollstonecraft, an English writer, advanced the strongest statement for the rights of women. Many see her as the founder of the modern European and American movements for women's rights.

In *A Vindication of the Rights of Woman*, Wollstonecraft identified two problems with the views of many Enlightenment thinkers. She noted that the same people who argued that women must obey men also said that government based on the **arbitrary** power of monarchs over their subjects was wrong. Wollstonecraft pointed out that the power of men over women was equally wrong.

### ANALYZING KEY IDEAS AND DETAILS

1. **ANALYZING CENTRAL IDEAS** Summarize this section in two or three sentences, and explain how ideas spread during the Enlightenment.
2. **CITING TEXT EVIDENCE** In the section "The Growth of Reading," which text supports the idea that women were beginning to be taken more seriously in the intellectual community?

Hill Street Studios/Getty Images

Wollstonecraft further argued that the Enlightenment was based on an ideal of reason in all human beings. Therefore, because women have reason, they are entitled to the same rights as men. Women, Wollstonecraft declared, should have equal rights in education, as well as in economic and political life.

*Mary Wollstonecraft was an advocate of women's rights.*

## THE GROWTH OF READING

Of great importance to the Enlightenment was the spread of its ideas to the literate elite of European society. The growth of both publishing and the reading public during the eighteenth century was noticeable. Books had previously been aimed at small groups of the educated elite. Now many books were directed at the new reading public of the middle classes, which included women and urban artisans. Especially appealing to these readers were the works of novelists who began to use realistic social themes. The English writer Henry Fielding wrote novels about people without morals who survive by their wits. Fielding's best-known work is *The History of Tom Jones, a Foundling*, which describes the adventures of a young scoundrel.

An important aspect of the growth of publishing and reading in the eighteenth century was the development of magazines and newspapers for the general public. The first daily newspaper was printed in London in 1702. Newspapers were relatively cheap and were even provided free in many coffeehouses. Coffeehouses also served as gathering places for the exchange of ideas.

**DETERMINING MEANING**

Enlightenment thinkers argued in favor of government based on reason, and against the **arbitrary** power of monarchs. Based on this, what definition can you infer for the word *arbitrary*?

Enlightenment ideas were also spread through the salon. **Salons** were the elegant drawing rooms of the wealthy upper class's great urban houses. Invited guests gathered in these salons and took part in conversations that were often centered on the new ideas of the philosophes. The salons brought writers and artists together with aristocrats, government officials, and wealthy middle-class people. Aristocratic women who hosted the salons were in a position to sway political opinion and to help spread the ideas of the Enlightenment.

**INTEGRATING INFORMATION** Do the coffeehouses of today serve the same purpose as early ones did? Why or why not?

## RELIGION IN THE ENLIGHTENMENT

Although many philosophes attacked the Christian churches, most Europeans in the eighteenth century were still Christians. People also sought a deeper personal devotion to God. For instance, the desire of ordinary Protestants for greater depths of religious experience led to the development of new religious movements in Protestantism.

In England, the most famous new religious and evangelical movement—Methodism—was the work of John Wesley, an Anglican minister. Wesley had a mystical experience in which "the gift of God's grace" assured him of salvation. This experience led him to become a missionary to the English people to bring them the "glad tidings" of salvation. Wesley often preached two or three times a day.

His sermons often caused people to have emotional conversion experiences. Many converts then joined Methodist societies to do good works. One notable reform they influenced was the abolition of the slave trade in the early 1800s. After Wesley's death, Methodism became a separate Protestant group.

*An eighteenth-century coffeehouse in London*

## ✓ CHECKING FOR UNDERSTANDING

1. **IDENTIFYING CONNECTIONS** How did the Enlightenment ideas influence society and culture?
2. **INTERPRETING** Why did Mary Wollstonecraft argue in favor of women's rights? How were her ideas interpreted at the time?
3. **UNDERSTANDING CHANGE** How did ideas circulate among the literate elite of European society? What changes allowed these ideas to reach more people than ever before?

# ENLIGHTENMENT AND THE ARTS

**GUIDING QUESTION** *How did Enlightenment ideas influence society and culture?*

The ideas of the Enlightenment also had an impact on the world of culture. Eighteenth-century Europe witnessed both traditional practices and important changes in art, music, and literature.

## ARCHITECTURE AND ART

The palace of Louis XIV at Versailles, in France, had made an enormous impact on Europe. Other European rulers followed Louis XIV's lead and also built grand residences. These palaces were modeled more on the Italian baroque style of the 1500s and 1600s than on the late seventeenth-century French classical style of Versailles.

One of the greatest architects of the eighteenth century was Balthasar Neumann. Neumann's two masterpieces are the Church of the Fourteen Saints in southern Germany and the Residence, the palace of the prince bishop of Würzburg. In these buildings, secular and spiritual become one, as lavish and fanciful ornament, light, bright colors, and elaborate detail greet the visitor. The baroque and neoclassical styles that had dominated seventeenth-century art continued into the eighteenth century. By the 1730s, however, a new artistic style, known as **rococo**, had spread all over Europe. Unlike the baroque style, which stressed grandeur and power, rococo emphasized grace, charm, and gentle action. Rococo made use of delicate designs colored in gold with graceful curves. The rococo style was highly secular. Its lightness and charm spoke of the pursuit of pleasure, happiness, and love.

Rococo's appeal is evident in the work of Antoine Watteau. In his paintings, gentlemen and ladies in elegant dress reveal a world of upper-class pleasure and joy. Underneath that exterior, however, is an element of sadness. The artist suggests such sadness in his paintings by depicting the fragility and passing nature of pleasure, love, and life. One of his masterpieces, the *Embarkation for Cythera*, shows French rococo at its peak.

**INTEGRATING KNOWLEDGE AND IDEAS**

1. **INTEGRATING INFORMATION** After reading the section "Architecture and Art," study the painting *The Swing*, by Fragonard. Does the painting support the text's description of rococo art? Explain.
2. **EVALUATING TEXT EVIDENCE** What text evidence supports the claim that Enlightenment ideas influenced the arts?

*The Swing,* by Jean-Honore Fragonard, 1767

## MUSIC

Eighteenth-century Europe produced some of the world's most enduring music. Two geniuses of the second half of the eighteenth century, Franz Joseph Haydn and Wolfgang Amadeus Mozart, were innovators who wrote classical music rather than the baroque music of Bach and Handel. Haydn spent most of his adult life as musical director for wealthy Hungarian princes. Visits to England introduced him to a world in which musicians wrote for public concerts rather than princely patrons. This "liberty," as he called it, led him to write two great works, *The Creation* and *The Seasons*.

Mozart was truly a child prodigy. He gave his first harpsichord concert at age six and wrote his first opera at twelve. His failure to get a regular patron to support him financially made his life miserable. Nevertheless, he wrote music passionately. His works *The Marriage of Figaro*, *The Magic Flute*, and *Don Giovanni* are three of the world's greatest operas. Haydn remarked to Mozart's father, "Your son is the greatest composer known to me. . . . "



### ✓ CHECKING FOR UNDERSTANDING

1. **IDENTIFYING CONNECTIONS** How did Enlightenment ideas influence society and culture?
2. **ANALYZING CHANGE** How was rococo a departure from the earlier baroque style?
3. **RELATING EVENTS** How was music impacted by the Enlightenment? How has this impact affected music today?

## LESSON 1 REVIEW

### Time and Place

1. **DETERMINING MEANING** Write a paragraph explaining what Montesquieu meant by the phrase *separation of powers* and where he saw this principle applied.

### Building History-Social Science Analysis Skills

2. **IDENTIFYING CONNECTIONS** How did Enlightenment thinkers use the ideas of the Scientific Revolution?
3. **ANALYZING CHANGE** Why did Enlightenment ideas spread more rapidly among the wealthy, educated, and middle class than among the poor?
4. **EXPLAINING CAUSE AND EFFECT** How did religious ideas during the Enlightenment build on sixteenth-century religious ideas?

### Writing About History

5. **ARGUMENTATIVE WRITING** Write a paragraph about the most important idea discussed in this lesson. Explain why you feel that idea is the most important in the lesson. Be sure to give specific details to support your claim, including how that idea is still influential today.

### Collaborating

6. **USING MULTIMEDIA** In a small group, discuss the social contract and how it reflects a break with Europe's past. Assume the role of either an aristocrat, a merchant, or a peasant from the Age of Reason. Discuss how the social contract applies to your group. Create a political cartoon, a skit, or collaborate on a short fictional story to illustrate the components of the social contract and how it impacts your life.

# Candide, or Optimism

**by Voltaire**

**PURPOSE:** To explore how a writer uses satire to highlight religious and political corruption and oppression during the Enlightenment in Europe

**BACKGROUND INFORMATION** Voltaire was born François-Marie Arouet on November 21, 1694. He assumed the pen name "Voltaire" in 1718. Voltaire was a critical and satiric writer who used his wit to attack both church and state. *Candide*, a satire of French life before the revolution, is one of Voltaire's most brilliant and well-known works. In it, Voltaire points out the Enlightenment ideals of freedom of thought, social justice, and religious tolerance—and how life at the time fell far short of these ideals. This excerpt is based on Voltaire's own experience with the Prussian court and army.

## Explore the Text

**The Scene:** As the narrative begins, Candide has just been cast out of a castle owned by the Baron and away from his love, Miss Cunégonde, the Baron's daughter. He meets army recruiters for the king of the Bulgars (Frederick the Great, king of Prussia, who was at war with the French when Voltaire wrote *Candide*). He is then pressed into service of the Prussian army against his will. After drilling with the army for two days, and misunderstanding the rules of army life, he leaves his barracks and sets out on a walk.

**The Characters:** Candide, the protagonist, is a naïve young man who all too often trusts the wrong people and fails to think for himself. Dr. Pangloss is Candide's overly optimistic mentor who believes that everything—even evil—happens for the best and cannot be changed. Jacques is a member of the Anabaptists, who held "radical" views on property and religious discipline and who believed in delaying baptism until adulthood.

**The Plot:** Candide has been taught that "everything is for the best in this best of all possible worlds." He often repeats this phrase to reassure himself. However, his adventures usually prove the opposite—pointing out the disconnection between some ideas of the Enlightenment and reality.

*Candide s'enfuit au plus vite dans un autre village.*

Candide, Ch. III.

Promptly they slip irons on his legs and lead him to the regiment. There they cause him to right face, left face, present arms, order arms, aim, fire, doubletime, and they give him thirty strokes of the rod. Next day he does the drill a little less awkwardly and gets only twenty strokes; the third day, they give him only ten, and he is regarded by his comrades as a prodigy.

Candide, quite thunderstruck[1], did not yet understand very clearly how he was a hero. One fine spring morning he took it into his head to go for a walk, stepping straight out as if it were a privilege of the human race, as of animals in general, to use his legs as he chose. He had scarcely covered two leagues when four other heroes [Prussian soldiers], each six feet tall, overtook him, bound him, and threw him into a dungeon. At the court-martial they asked which he preferred, to be flogged thirty-six times by the entire regiment or to receive summarily[2] a dozen bullets in the brain. In vain did he argue that the human will is free and insist that he preferred neither alternative; he had to choose; by virtue of the divine gift called "liberty" he decided to run the gauntlet thirty-six times, and actually endured two floggings.

The regiment was composed of two thousand men. That made four thousand strokes, which laid open every muscle and nerve from his nape to his butt. As they were preparing for the third beating, Candide, who could endure no more, begged as a special favor that they would have the goodness to smash his head. His plea was granted; they bandaged his eyes and made him kneel down. The King of the Bulgars [Frederick the Great, King of Prussia], passing by at this moment, was told of the culprit's crime; and as this king had a rare genius, he understood, from everything they told him of Candide, that this was a young metaphysician[3], extremely ignorant of the ways of the world, so he granted his royal pardon, with a generosity which will be praised in every newspaper in every age. A worthy surgeon cured Candide in three weeks with the ointments described by Dioscorides[4]. He already had a bit of skin back and was able to walk when the King of the Bulgars went to war with the King of the Abares [the French].

Nothing could have been so fine, so brisk, so brilliant, so well-drilled as the two armies. The trumpets, the fifes, the oboes, the drums, and the cannon produced such a harmony as was never heard in hell. First the cannons battered down about six thousand men on each side; then volleys of musket

#### DETERMINING MEANING

The name *Candide* is French for *candid*, which means "honest, sincere, and open." What can you infer is the significance of Voltaire using this name for the protagonist?

#### UNDERSTANDING CRAFT AND STRUCTURE

How does Voltaire's use of repetition and the words he selects for the following sentence convey a sense of military action? "Nothing could have been so fine, so brisk, so brilliant, so well-drilled as the two armies."

---

[1] **thunderstruck:** stunned or surprised

[2] **summarily:** done without delay or formality

[3] **metaphysician:** philosopher

[4] **Dioscorides:** Greek physician and pharmacist who compiled a five-volume reference book on medicinal herbs in the first century C.E.

*Voltaire helped spread Enlightenment ideas through his writings.*

fire removed from the best of worlds about nine or ten thousand rascals who were cluttering up its surface. The bayonet[5] was a sufficient reason for the demise of several thousand others. Total casualties might well amount to thirty thousand men or so. Candide, who was trembling like a philosopher, hid himself as best he could while this heroic butchery was going on. . . .

Candide fled as fast as he could to another village; this one belonged to the Bulgars, and the heroes of the Abare cause had given it the same treatment. Climbing over ruins and stumbling over corpses, Candide finally made his way out of the war area, carrying a little food in his knapsack[6] and never ceasing to dream of Miss Cunégonde. His supplies gave out when he reached Holland; but having heard that everyone in that country was rich and a Christian, he felt confident of being treated as well as he had been in the castle of the Baron before he was kicked out for the love of Miss Cunégonde.

He asked alms of several grave personages, who all told him that if he continued to beg, he would be shut up in a house of correction and set to hard labor.

Finally he approached a man who had just been talking to a large crowd for an hour on end; the topic was charity. Looking doubtfully at him, the orator[7] demanded:

—What are you doing here? Are you here to serve the good cause?

—There is no effect without a cause, said Candide modestly; all events are linked by the chain of necessity and arranged for the best. I had to be driven away from Miss Cunégonde, I had to run the gauntlet[8], I have to beg my bread until I can earn it; none of this could have happened otherwise.

—Look here, friend, said the orator, do you think the Pope is Antichrist?

—I haven't considered the matter, said Candide; but whether he is or not, I'm in need of bread.

**UNDERSTANDING CRAFT AND STRUCTURE**

A statement of paradox is a statement of two things in which both are true, but both seemingly cannot be true at the same time. In what way does the term "heroic butchery" convey a paradox?

[5] **bayonet:** blade that may be fixed to the muzzle of a rifle for use in hand-to-hand fighting

[6] **knapsack:** small bag, similar to a backpack

[7] **orator:** public speaker

[8] **run the gauntlet:** to go through a dangerous experience in order to reach a goal

—You don't deserve any, said the other; away with you, you rascal, you rogue, never come near me as long as you live.

Meanwhile, the orator's wife had put her head out of the window, and, seeing a man who was not sure the Pope was Antichrist, emptied over his head a pot full of —— Scandalous! The excesses into which women are led by religious zeal!

A man who had never been baptized, a good Anabaptist named Jacques, saw this cruel and heartless treatment being inflicted on one of his fellow creatures, a featherless biped possessing a soul; he took Candide home with him, washed him off, gave him bread and beer, presented him with two florins, and even undertook to give him a job in his Persian-rug factory—for these items are widely manufactured in Holland. Candide, in an ecstasy of gratitude, cried out:

—Master Pangloss was right indeed when he told me everything is for the best in this world; for I am touched by your kindness far more than by the harshness of that black-coated gentleman and his wife.

**DETERMINING MEANING**

When the woman in the window heard Candide refuse to say that the pope was the Antichrist, she emptied her chamber pot (a pot used in homes before there were toilets) over his head. Voltaire notes that this was an example of "religious zeal." What does this context suggest about the meaning of the word *zeal*?

**UNDERSTANDING CRAFT AND STRUCTURE**

How does Voltaire give Candide a chance to be optimistic?

## Text-Based Discussion

1. **ANALYZING LITERATURE** What is the significance of Jacques being described as unbaptized while also described as "good"? What is the irony in these descriptions?
2. **DETERMINING MEANING** What is the meaning of Master Pangloss's phrase "everything is for the best in this world"?
3. **ANALYZING LITERATURE** What is Voltaire satirizing in the following lines and in Candide's subsequent punishment? How does this relate to the philosophy of the Enlightenment?

   "One fine spring morning he took it into his head to go for a walk, stepping straight out as if it were a privilege of the human race, as of animals in general, to use his legs as he chose. He had scarcely covered two leagues when four other heroes [Prussian soldiers], each six feet tall, overtook him, bound him, and threw him into a dungeon."
4. **DETERMINING CENTRAL IDEAS** What does the episode with the king of the Bulgars suggest about Voltaire's opinion on criminal justice?
5. **CITING TEXT EVIDENCE** How does Voltaire characterize religious leaders? What evidence from the narrative can you cite to support these characteristics?

## ESSENTIAL QUESTIONS

- *Why do new ideas often spark change?*
- *How do new ways of thinking affect the way people respond to their surroundings?*

LESSON 2

# Enlightened Absolutism and the Balance of Power

## THE STORY BEGINS...

Louis XIV of France fancied himself the "Sun King," the source of light for all his people. All of France was there to support him and his reign. As the eighteenth century wore on, however, the concepts of the Enlightenment began to eat away at this kind of absolutism. Read, for example, what the great Prussian King of the eighteenth century, Frederick II, had to say about the role of royalty:

> "Princes, sovereigns, and kings have not been given supreme authority in order to live in luxurious self-indulgence and debauchery. They have not been elevated by their fellow-men to enable them to strut about and to insult with their pride the simple-mannered, the poor, and the suffering. They have not been placed at the head of the State to keep around themselves a crowd of idle loafers whose uselessness drives them towards vice. The bad administration which may be found in monarchies springs from many different causes, but their principal cause lies in the character of the sovereign."
>
> —*"Forms of Government and the Duties of Rulers,"* Frederick II ("the Great"), 1777

The model Frederick is proposing in this excerpt is the model of the enlightened absolutist. That is, he was only "the first servant of the state," who was restrained by his responsibilities to his subjects.

*Frederick II of Prussia attempted to govern his realm by Enlightenment principles.* ▶

PHOTO: Chronicle/Alamy Stock Photo; TEXT:Dorwart, Reinhold August. 1953. The Administrative Reforms of Frederick William I of Prussia. Harvard University Press.

| Enlightened Absolutism | | | |
|---|---|---|---|
| Country/State | Prussia | Austria | Russia |
| Ruler | Frederick II | Joseph II | Catherine the Great |
| Philosophy | | | |
| Actions | | | |

**ANALYZING KEY IDEAS AND DETAILS**

**CITING TEXT EVIDENCE** Read closely to identify the philosophies and actions of European rulers during the Enlightenment in a graphic organizer like this one.

# ENLIGHTENMENT AND ABSOLUTISM

**GUIDING QUESTION** *How were European rulers guided by Enlightenment thought?*

Enlightenment thought influenced European politics in the eighteenth century. The philosophes believed in natural rights for all people. These rights included equality before the law; freedom of religious worship; freedom of speech; freedom of the press; and the rights to assemble, to hold property, and to pursue happiness. To establish and preserve these natural rights, most philosophes believed that people must be governed by enlightened rulers. Enlightened rulers must allow natural rights and nurture the arts, sciences, and education. Above all, they must obey and enforce the laws fairly for all subjects. Only strong monarchs could bring about the enlightened reforms society needed.

In the later eighteenth century, a new type of monarchy, **enlightened absolutism**, emerged. In this system, rulers tried to govern by Enlightenment principles while maintaining their royal powers. Did Europe's rulers actually follow the advice of the philosophes and become enlightened? To answer this question, we examine three states—Prussia, Austria, and Russia.

Two able Prussian kings, Frederick William I and Frederick II, made Prussia a major European power in the eighteenth century. Frederick William I maintained a highly efficient bureaucracy of civil service workers.

They observed the supreme values of obedience, honor, and, above all, service to the king. As Frederick William asserted: "One must serve the king with life and limb, . . . and surrender everything except salvation. The latter is reserved for God. But everything else must be mine."

Frederick William's other major concern was the army. By the end of his reign in 1740, he had doubled the army's size. Although Prussia was a small state, it had the fourth-largest army after France, Russia, and Austria. The Prussian army, because of its size and its good reputation, was the most important institution in the state.

Members of the nobility, who owned large landed estates with many serfs, were the officers in the Prussian army. These officers, too, had a strong sense of service to the king or state. As Prussian nobles, they believed in duty, obedience, and sacrifice.

Frederick II, or Frederick the Great, who ruled from 1740 to 1786, was one of the best educated monarchs of the time. He was well versed in Enlightenment ideas and exchanged letters with the French philosopher and writer Voltaire. Frederick was also a dedicated ruler. He, too, enlarged the Prussian army by actively recruiting the nobility into civil service.

**ANALYZING KEY IDEAS AND DETAILS**

1. **DETERMINING CENTRAL IDEAS** What is the central idea of this section? How does the text present and develop this idea?

2. **CITING TEXT EVIDENCE** What evidence in the text supports the idea that Frederick II ruled according to Enlightenment principles?

**ANALYZING PRIMARY SOURCES**

1. **DETERMINING POINT OF VIEW** Why does Voltaire think Frederick the Great will be a strong ruler?
2. **DETERMINING MEANING** What does the phrase "hater of superstition" suggest about how Frederick differs from the rulers who came before him?

Frederick kept a strict watch over the bureaucracy.

> "Your great mind estimates metaphysics very highly . . . You can hardly understand, sir, what a consolation it is for Mme. du Chatelet and myself to find you so true a philosopher, and so good a hater of superstition. . . .
>
> My only misfortune is that my health is so feeble that I shall most likely never be a personal witness of the good you do and the great example you set. Happy they who will see those great days, who with their own eyes will witness the reign of glory and prosperity! But I shall at least have enjoyed the favours of the philosopher-prince, and the first-fruits of his soul."
>
> —Voltaire, in a letter to Frederick the Great

For a time, Frederick seemed quite willing to make enlightened reforms. He abolished the use of torture except in treason and murder cases. He also granted limited freedom of speech and press, as well as greater religious toleration. However, Frederick kept Prussia's serfdom and rigid social structure intact and avoided any additional reforms.

The Austrian Empire had become one of the great European states by the start of the eighteenth century. It was hard to rule, however, because it was a sprawling empire composed of many nationalities, languages, religions, and cultures. Empress Maria Theresa, who inherited the throne in 1740, worked to centralize and strengthen the state. Although not open to the philosophes' calls for reform, she did work to improve the condition of the serfs.

**DETERMINING MEANING**
The word **successor** has the same root as the word *succeed*. One definition of *succeed* is "to follow after another in order." Based on this information, write a definition of the word *successor*. Use a dictionary or an online reference to check your definition.

Her son, Joseph II, believed in the need to sweep away anything standing in the path of reason: "I have made Philosophy the lawmaker of my empire." Joseph abolished serfdom and eliminated the death penalty. He established the principle of equality of all before the law and enacted religious reforms, including religious toleration.

Joseph's reform program largely failed, however. He alienated the nobles by freeing the serfs. He alienated the Catholic Church with his religious reforms. Even the serfs were unhappy because they could not understand the drastic changes. Joseph realized his failure when he wrote his own epitaph for his gravestone: "Here lies Joseph II who was unfortunate in all his enterprises." His **successors** undid almost all of Joseph II's reforms.

*Maria Theresa, empress of Austria, and some of her children*

In Russia, Peter the Great was followed by six weak successors who were often put in power and deposed by the palace guard. A group of nobles murdered the last of these six successors, Peter III. His German wife emerged as ruler of all the Russians.

Catherine II, or Catherine the Great, ruled Russia from 1762 to 1796. She was an intelligent woman who was familiar with the works of the philosophes and seemed to favor enlightened reforms. She considered the idea of a new law code that would recognize the principle of equality of all people in the eyes of the law.

In the end, however, Catherine did nothing because she knew that her success depended on the support of the Russian nobility. Her policy of favoring the landed nobility led to worse conditions for the Russian peasants and **eventually** to rebellion. Led by an illiterate Cossack (a Russian warrior), Yemelyan Pugachov, the rebellion spread across southern Russia but soon collapsed. Catherine took stronger measures against the peasants. Rural reform was halted, and serfdom was expanded into newer parts of the empire.

Catherine proved to be a worthy successor to Peter the Great in her policies of territorial expansion. Russia spread southward to the Black Sea by defeating the Turks under Catherine's rule. To the west, Russia gained about 50 percent of Poland's territory, with the remainder split between Prussia and Austria. The Polish state disappeared until after World War I.

Of the rulers under discussion, only Joseph II sought truly radical changes based on Enlightenment ideas. Both Frederick II and Catherine II liked to talk about enlightened reforms. They even attempted some, but their priority was maintaining the existing system.

In fact, all three of these enlightened absolutists—Frederick, Joseph, and Catherine—were guided primarily by their interest in the power and welfare of their states. When they did manage to strengthen their positions as rulers, they did not undertake enlightened reforms to benefit their subjects. Rather, their power was used to collect more taxes and thus to create armies, to wage wars, and to gain even more power.

*Catherine II (Catherine the Great) was a strong Russian ruler.*

The philosophes **condemned** war as a foolish waste of life and resources. Despite their words, the rivalry among states that led to costly struggles remained unchanged in eighteenth-century Europe. Europe's states were chiefly guided by their rulers' self-interest.

The eighteenth-century monarchs were concerned with the balance of power. This concept meant that states should have equal power to prevent any one from dominating the others. Large armies created to defend a state's security, however, were often used to conquer new lands as well. As Frederick II of Prussia said, "The fundamental rule of governments is the principle of extending their territories." This rule led to two major wars in the eighteenth century.

**DETERMINING MEANING**

When a house is condemned it is deemed unfit to live in. Based on this knowledge, write a definition of the word **condemned.** Check your definition against a dictionary or online reference.

### ☑ CHECKING FOR UNDERSTANDING

1. **DETERMINING CONTEXT** How were European rulers guided by Enlightenment thought?
2. **ANALYZING CHANGE** What obstacles did European rulers face when making new reforms based on Enlightenment principles?
3. **UNDERSTANDING CONTEXT** Although Catherine recognized Enlightenment principles, she did not make many reforms. Why? What outcome might have been different if she had made some enlightened reforms?

## THE SEVEN YEARS' WAR

**GUIDING QUESTION** *How did changing alliances in Europe lead to the Seven Years' War and how was the war carried out on a global scale?*

The stage was set for the Seven Years' War when, in 1740, a major war broke out over the succession to the Austrian throne. When the Austrian emperor Charles VI died without a male heir, his daughter, Maria Theresa, succeeded him. King Frederick II of Prussia took advantage of the confusion surrounding the succession of a woman to the throne by invading Austrian Silesia, a piece of land that he hoped to add to Prussia. By this action, Frederick refused to

**UNDERSTANDING CRAFT AND STRUCTURE**

**ANALYZING TEXT** In what order does the text present the facts about the war? Does the way the text is organized help you better understand the information?

## THE SEVEN YEARS' WAR IN EUROPE 1756–1763

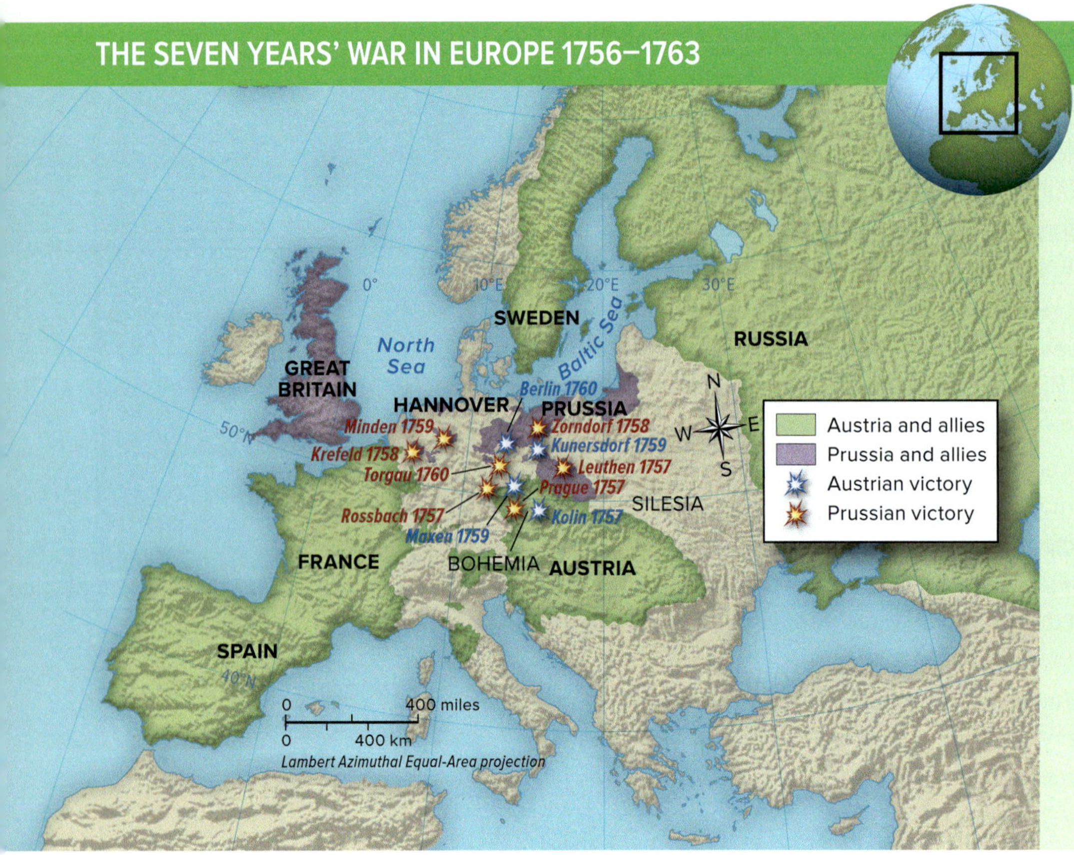


### GEOGRAPHIC REASONING

Changing alliances led to the Seven Years' War in Europe.

1. **EXPLORING PLACE** Identify the countries that belonged to each of the two European alliances.
2. **EXPLORING REGIONS** Is the following argument valid? *The map shows that Austria most likely won the Seven Years' War.* Explain.

**DETERMINING MEANING**

Something that is *legitimate* is done according to accepted rules and standards. How does knowing the meaning of *legitimate* help you determine what it means that Frederick refused to recognize the legitimacy of Maria Theresa as the empress of Austria?

recognize the legitimacy of the empress of Austria. France then entered the war against Austria, its traditional enemy. In turn, Maria Theresa allied with Great Britain.

The War of the Austrian Succession (1740–1748) was fought in three areas of the world. In Europe, Prussia seized Silesia while France occupied some Austrian territory. In Asia, France took Madras (today called Chennai) in India from the British. In North America, the British captured the French fortress of Louisbourg at the entrance of the St. Lawrence River.

By 1748, all parties were exhausted and agreed to the Treaty of Aix-la-Chapelle. The treaty guaranteed the return of all occupied territories but Silesia to their original owners. Prussia's refusal to return Silesia meant yet another war, for Maria Theresa refused to accept the loss. She rebuilt her army while working diplomatically to separate Prussia from its chief ally, France. In 1756 Maria Theresa achieved what was soon labeled a diplomatic revolution.

## THE WAR IN EUROPE

**DETERMINING MEANING**

Reread the first paragraph of "The War in Europe." What is a **rivalry**? Which context clues help you to determine the meaning of *rivalry*?

French-Austrian **rivalry** had been a fact of European diplomacy since the late sixteenth century. However, two new rivalries now replaced the old one: the rivalry of Britain and France over colonial empires and the rivalry of Austria and Prussia over Silesia.

France abandoned Prussia and formed an alliance with Austria. Russia, which saw Prussia as a major threat to Russian goals in central Europe, joined the new alliance with France and Austria. In turn, Britain allied with Prussia. This diplomatic revolution of 1756 led to another worldwide war. The war had three major areas of conflict: Europe, India, and North America.

Europe witnessed the clash of the two major alliances: the British and Prussians against the Austrians, Russians, and French. The superb army and military skill of Frederick the Great of Prussia enabled him at first to defeat the Austrian, French, and Russian armies. Under attack from three different directions, however, his forces were gradually worn down.

Frederick faced disaster until Peter III, a new Russian czar who greatly admired Frederick, withdrew Russian troops from the conflict. This withdrawal created a stalemate and led to the desire for peace. The European war ended in 1763. All occupied territories were returned to their original owners, except Silesia. Austria officially recognized Prussia's permanent control of Silesia.

## THE WAR IN INDIA

The struggle between Britain and France that took place in the rest of the world had more decisive results. Known as the Great War for Empire, it was fought in India and North America. The French had returned Madras to Britain after the War of the Austrian Succession, but the struggle in India continued. The British ultimately won out, not because they had better forces but because they were more persistent. With the Treaty of Paris in 1763, the French withdrew and left India to the British.

## THE WAR IN NORTH AMERICA

The greatest conflicts of the Seven Years' War took place in North America. On the North American continent, the French and British colonies were set up differently. The French government administered French North America (Canada and Louisiana) as a vast trading area. It was valuable for its fur, leather, fish, and timber, but its colonies were thinly populated.

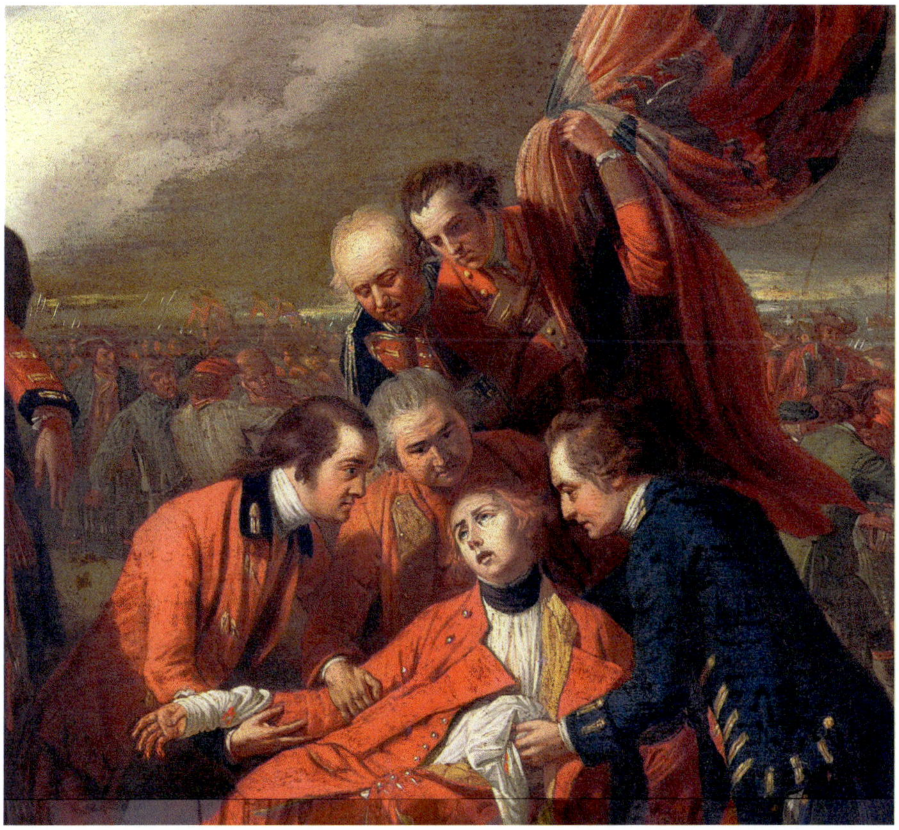

*This painting by Benjamin West shows the death of the British General James Wolfe.*

British North America consisted of thirteen prosperous colonies on the eastern coast of what is now the United States. Unlike the French colonies, the British colonies were more populated, containing more than 1 million people by 1750.

The British and French fought over two main areas in North America. One consisted of the waterways of the Gulf of St. Lawrence, which were protected by the fortress of Louisbourg and by forts that guarded French Quebec. The other area they fought over was the unsettled Ohio River valley. The French scored a number of victories at first. British fortunes were revived, however, by the efforts of William Pitt the Elder, Britain's prime minister. Pitt was convinced that the French colonial empire would have to be destroyed for Britain to create its own colonial empire.

A series of British victories soon followed. In 1759 British forces under General Wolfe defeated the French under General Montcalm on the Plains of Abraham, outside Quebec. Both generals died in the battle. The British went on to seize Montreal, the Great Lakes area, and the Ohio River valley. The French were forced to make peace. By the Treaty of Paris, the French transferred Canada and the lands east of the Mississippi to England. Spain, an ally of the French, transferred Spanish Florida to British control. In return, the French gave their Louisiana territory to the Spanish. By 1763, Great Britain had become the world's greatest colonial power.

### ✓ CHECKING FOR UNDERSTANDING

1. **IDENTIFYING CONNECTIONS** How did changing alliances in Europe lead to the Seven Years' War and how was the war carried out on a global scale?

2. **EXPLAINING CAUSE AND EFFECT** Why were there conflicts on three continents (Europe, North America, and Asia)?

3. **USING MAPS** Based on the map, why was Russia's involvement influential to the outcome of the Seven Years' War?

## LESSON 2 REVIEW

### Time and Place

1. **IDENTIFYING CONNECTIONS** Explain how the European quest to build empires led to global conflict.

### Building History-Social Science Analysis Skills

2. **DETERMINING CONTEXT** Define the term *enlightened absolutism*. Discuss one example of an eighteenth-century monarch and explain how he or she fulfilled or failed to fulfill this ideal.

3. **INTERPRETING** What was the significance of Silesia during the Seven Years' War in Europe? What was the outcome of this conflict?

4. **SUMMARIZING** What triggered the Seven Years' War in North America? What was the outcome?

### Writing About History

5. **NARRATIVE WRITING** Narrate a series of events that helps tell the story of both the War of the Austrian Succession and the Seven Years' War. Use transitional words and phrases to show a clear sequence.

### Collaborating

6. **COLLABORATING** With a partner, select one of the following monarchs: Frederick II, Joseph II, or Catherine II. Create a short presentation discussing how they embraced Enlightenment ideas.

## ESSENTIAL QUESTIONS

- *Why do new ideas often spark change?*
- *How do new ways of thinking affect the way people respond to their surroundings?*

LESSON 3

# The American Revolution

## THE STORY BEGINS...

The great transformations that occurred across Europe as a result of the Enlightenment came to the American colonies, too. Many in Britain's thirteen colonies were especially receptive to these ideas. These colonists were reluctant to accept burdens from the British crown without greater representation in government. Consider, for example, what colonists had to say about a burdensome tax imposed from the heart of the empire:

> "The Stamp Act, therefore, is to be regarded only as an EXPERIMENT OF YOUR DISPOSITION. If you quietly bend your Necks to that Yoke, you prove yourselves ready to receive any Bondage to which your *Lords* and *Masters* shall please to subject you. Some Persons perhaps may fondly hope, it will be as easy to obtain a Repeal of the Stamp Act after it is put in Execution, as if the Execution of it is avoided. But be not deceived. The late Ministry publickly declared, "that it was *intended* to establish the Power of *Great-Britain* to tax the colonies." Can we imagine then, that when so great a Point is carried, and *we have tamely submitted*, that any other Ministry will venture to propose, or that the Parliament will consent to pass, an Act to renounce this Advantage? No! Power is of a tenacious Nature: What it seizes it will retain."

—John Dickinson, *"Address on Stamp Act,"* 1765

The strong language in this excerpt shows the extent to which the colonists guarded themselves against the grasping power of a monarch. In attempting to strengthen its hold on its empire, Great Britain had actually weakened it.

*The "Boston Tea Party," done in defiance of the Tea Act of 1773, was a prelude to the American Revolution.* ▶

| Influences on the American Revolution | |
|---|---|
| Cause | Effect |
| The English Bill of Rights affirmed Parliament's right to make laws. | |
| Governments of England and Scotland were united. | |
| | A new dynasty was established, with George I as king. |
| Trade and industry thrived. | |

### ANALYZING KEY IDEAS AND DETAILS

**CITING TEXT EVIDENCE** Read closely to identify the causes and effects that influenced the American Revolution. Record them in a graphic organizer like this one.

# BRITAIN AND THE AMERICAN REVOLUTION

**ANALYZING KEY IDEAS AND DETAILS**

1. **DETERMINING CENTRAL IDEAS** What is the central idea of the section "Common Sense"? How does the text present and develop this idea?
2. **SUMMARIZING** Write a brief summary of the section "British Defeat."

**GUIDING QUESTION** *What were the causes of and influences on the American Revolution?*

In 1688 the Glorious Revolution resulted in a document called the English Bill of Rights that affirmed Parliament's right to make laws. As a result of this, the monarch of Great Britain and Parliament shared power. The monarch chose ministers, who were responsible to the Crown. These ministers then set policy for governing the country, and they also guided Parliament. Parliament's power to make laws, to levy taxes, and to pass the budget indirectly influenced the monarch's ministers.

The United Kingdom of Great Britain came into existence in 1707, when the governments of England and Scotland were united. Joined since the early 1600s in a personal union under the Stuart dynasty, both England and Scotland operated with their own distinct governments while sharing the same monarch. Following the union of 1707, the term *British* came to refer to both the English and the Scots.

In 1714 a new dynasty was established when the last Stuart ruler, Queen Anne, died without an heir. The crown was offered to her nearest relatives, Protestant rulers of the German state of Hannover. The first Hanoverian king, George I, did not speak English. In addition, neither George I nor George II knew the British system of government well, so their chief ministers were allowed to deal with Parliament.

In the meantime, growing trade and industry led to an ever-increasing middle class. This group strongly favored the expansion of trade and of Britain's world empire. They found a spokesman in William Pitt the Elder, who became head of cabinet in 1757. He expanded the British Empire by acquiring Canada and India in the Seven Years' War.

In North America, then, Britain controlled Canada as well as the 13 colonies on the eastern coast of what is now the United States. The British colonies were well populated, containing more than 1 million people by 1750. They were also prosperous.

In theory, the British Board of Trade, the Royal Council, and Parliament controlled the colonies. In actuality, the colonies had legislatures that often acted independently of these groups. Merchants in port cities such as Charleston, New York, and Boston did not want the British government running their affairs.

## THE AMERICAN REVOLUTION BEGINS

After the Seven Years' War, British leaders wanted to get new colonial revenues from the colonies. These revenues would then be used to cover war costs. These would also pay for the expenses of maintaining an army to defend the colonies.

In 1765 Parliament imposed the Stamp Act on the colonies. The act required certain printed materials, such as legal documents and newspapers, to carry a stamp showing that a tax had been paid to Britain. Opposition was widespread and often violent. The act was repealed in 1766, ending the immediate crisis, but the cause of the dispute was not resolved.

Crisis followed crisis in the 1770s. To counteract British actions, the colonies organized the First Continental Congress, which met in Philadelphia in September 1774. Members urged colonists to take up arms and to organize militias.

Fighting finally erupted between colonists and the British army in April 1775 in Lexington and Concord, Massachusetts. Meeting soon afterward, the Second Continental Congress set up an army, called the Continental Army. George Washington served as its commander in chief.

## *COMMON SENSE*

Although the revolution had begun, the colonies had yet to declare their independence. Many patriots believed most colonists were still loyal to the king. However, in January 1776, public opinion began to change when Thomas Paine published a persuasive pamphlet called *Common Sense*. Born in England, Paine strongly believed in the rights of people to govern their own affairs and to separate from the rule of a monarch. In *Common Sense*, Paine argued that monarchies had been set up by seizing power from the people. King George III was a tyrant, he argued, and it was time for the colonists to declare independence. George Washington noted that "*Common Sense* is working a powerful change in the minds of men." Within three months, *Common Sense* had sold 100,000 copies.

> "The powers of governing still remaining in the hands of the king, he will have a negative over the whole legislation of this continent. And as he hath shewn himself such an inveterate enemy to liberty, and discovered such a thirst for arbitrary power; is he, or is he not, a proper man to say to these colonies, "*You shall make no laws but what I please*." And is there any inhabitant in America so ignorant, as not to know, that according to what is called the *present constitution*, that this continent can make no laws but what the king gives leave to; and is there any man so unwise, as not to see, that (considering what has happened) he will suffer no law to be made here, but such as suit his purpose. We may be as effectually enslaved by the want of laws in America, as by submitting to laws made for us in England. After matters are made up (as it is called) can there be any doubt, but the whole power of the crown will be exerted, to keep this continent as low and humble as possible?"
>
> —Thomas Paine, *Common Sense*, 1776

**ANALYZING PRIMARY SOURCES**

1. **ANALYZING TEXTS** Why does Paine object to the idea of being ruled by a monarch?
2. **DETERMINING POINT OF VIEW** What does Paine fear will happen if Britain continues to rule the colonies?

One by one, the provincial congresses and legislatures told their representatives at the Continental Congress to vote for independence. On July 4, 1776, the Second Continental Congress approved the Declaration of Independence written by Thomas Jefferson. With this stirring political document, the American Revolution had formally begun.

TEXT:Paine, Thomas. 1776. Common Sense. Philadelphia: W. & T. Bradford

## THE DECLARATION OF INDEPENDENCE

The Declaration of Independence contains important legal and political ideas. It states that ". . . all men are created equal, that they are endowed by their Creator with certain unalienable Rights, that among these are Life, Liberty and the pursuit of Happiness." In simple terms, this forms a legal foundation for the principles of equality before the law and individual rights. The impact of these legal ideas is immense. Unlike later governing documents of the United States, the Declaration of Independence includes broad statements supporting equality and human rights. Today, the Declaration of Independence continues to influence human and property rights movements all over the world.

*Painting depicting the signing of the Declaration of Independence*

**INTEGRATING INFORMATION**
What does this painting reveal about the process that led to the colonial break with Great Britain?

In its opening line, the Declaration of Independence spelled out that the United States was a new nation, ready to interact with other nations on an equal footing. Politically, the writers of the Declaration of Independence were asserting that a government existed only because of **popular sovereignty**—or the right to govern through the consent of the people. Additionally, the Declaration firmly states that a government that fails to uphold the ideals of liberty could be justifiably overthrown by the people. These political ideas expressed in the Declaration of Independence inspired revolutionaries in Latin America, France, and other parts of Europe just decades after the American Revolution. Today they continue to influence revolutionaries and political reformers across the globe.

**DETERMINING MEANING**

To better understand **popular sovereignty**, break down the phrase. *Popular* refers to something that has the approval of a majority of people. *Sovereign* means "having an independent government." What would it mean for a country to have *popular sovereignty*?

## THOMAS JEFFERSON

Thomas Jefferson, the author of the Declaration of Independence, was an American revolutionary, Founder, and politician. He was heavily influenced by Enlightenment thinkers John Locke, Francis Bacon, and Isaac Newton. As a supporter of the Enlightenment, Jefferson distrusted a strong central government, favoring republicanism and having a strong belief in religious freedom and the separation of church and state. Jefferson authored the Virginia Statute for Religious Freedom in 1777, which the Virginia legislature adopted as law in 1786. Jefferson's republican political principles and his views on religious freedom would profoundly influence the formation of the U.S. Constitution in 1787.

As a Founder of the United States, Jefferson's popularity carried him from governor of Virginia to secretary of state, vice president, and eventually the third president of the United States (1801–1809). Although a strong presidential figure instrumental in doubling the size of the United States with the Louisiana Purchase in 1803, Jefferson also set a standard of presidency that emphasized a weak executive power. Thomas Jefferson's political writings continue to influence American politics today.

## BRITISH DEFEAT

Support from foreign countries was important to the colonies' cause. These nations were eager to gain revenge for earlier defeats at the hands of the British. The French supplied arms and money to the rebels. French officers and soldiers also served in Washington's army. In February 1778, following a British defeat, the French granted diplomatic recognition to the new United States. When Spain and the Dutch Republic entered the war, the British faced war with the Europeans as well as the Americans.

When General Cornwallis was forced to surrender to the American and French forces under Washington at Yorktown in 1781, the British decided to end the war. In 1783 the Treaty of Paris recognized the independence of the American colonies. The treaty also granted the Americans control of the western territory from the Appalachians to the Mississippi River.

### ✓ CHECKING FOR UNDERSTANDING

1. **IDENTIFYING CAUSES** What were the causes of and influences on the American Revolution?
2. **IDENTIFYING CONNECTIONS** How did England's Glorious Revolution influence the ideas of the American Revolution?

**ANALYZING PRIMARY SOURCES**

### DECLARATION OF INDEPENDENCE

"We hold these truths to be self-evident; that all men are created equal; that they are endowed by their Creator with certain inalienable rights; that among these are life, liberty and the pursuit of happiness; that to secure these rights, governments are instituted among men, deriving their just powers from the consent of the governed . . ."

—from the Declaration of Independence

**DETERMINING MEANING** Rewrite the excerpt from the Declaration of Independence in your own words.

# THE BIRTH OF A NEW NATION

**GUIDING QUESTIONS** *What were the effects of the American Revolution? Why did intellectuals believe the formation of the United States carried out Enlightenment thought?*

After overthrowing British rule, the former colonies feared the power of a strong central government. The states' first constitution, the Articles of Confederation (1781), created a weak central government that lacked the power to deal with the nation's problems. In 1787 delegates met in Philadelphia at the Constitutional Convention to revise the Articles of Confederation. The delegates decided to plan for an entirely new government.

## THE CONSTITUTION

The proposed Constitution created a **federal system** in which the national government and the state governments shared power. Based on Montesquieu's ideas, the national, or federal, government was separated into three branches: executive, legislative, and judicial. Each branch had power to check, or restrain, acts of the other branches.

A president served as the head of the executive branch, which is why it may be referred to as a presidential democracy. The legislative branch consisted of elected representatives in two houses—the Senate and the House

**UNDERSTANDING CRAFT AND STRUCTURE**

**ANALYZING TEXT PRESENTATION** Reread the section "Significance of the Revolution." What part of this paragraph states an *effect* of the American Revolution? What words signal that this is an effect?

**DETERMINING MEANING**

To better understand the term **federal system**, break down the phrase. *Federal* refers to a central government. A *system* is a set of connected ideas or actions. What would it mean for a country to have a *federal system*? What did this mean for the United States?

TEXT:Declaration of Independence, July 4, 1776, transcript, The Charters of Freedom, National Archives and Records Administration [http://www.archives.gov/exhibits/charters/declaration_transcript.html].

CITIZENSHIP

## CHECKS AND BALANCES IN GOVERNMENT

The U.S. government consists of three branches: the executive, legislative, and judicial branches. Not only does each branch have a different function in government, but it also has specific powers that help it keep the other branches in check. The judicial branch has the power to review the actions of the executive and legislative branches to ensure they are constitutional. The executive branch has the power to veto laws created by the legislative branch. The legislative branch can override a president's veto with a two-thirds vote, and it can also bring impeachment charges against the executive or judicial branch. This system of checks and balances was created by the writers of the U.S. Constitution and remains in place today.

1. **DETERMINING CENTRAL IDEAS** What is the main purpose of the checks and balances system?
2. **IDENTIFYING CONNECTIONS** How might the colonists' experience under British rule have affected their decision to include checks and balances in the U.S. Constitution?

of Representatives. The Supreme Court and other courts formed the judicial branch. After ratification by 9 of the 13 states, the Constitution took effect.

## JAMES MADISON

Although many individuals contributed to the framing of the U.S. Constitution, the master builder was James Madison. He believed that power should be divided among the national government, state governments, and the people. The Virginia Plan presented at the Constitutional Convention was a reflection of this idea. The Virginia Plan, which was primarily the work of Madison, proposed that the government be divided into three branches with equal power: the legislative, executive, and judicial branches.

Madison's idea of a "division of powers" contributed greatly to the federal system currently in operation in the United States today. Madison thought dividing power in such a way would result in a more representative government that was less likely to be tyrannical. This system has inspired the creation of other federal systems of government throughout the world today.

**DETERMINING MEANING**

To *amend* something is to change it. From what you know about the meaning of the word *amend*, write a definition of the word **amendment**. Use a dictionary or an online reference to check your definition.

## THE BILL OF RIGHTS

As promised during ratification negotiations, the new Congress proposed 12 **amendments** to the Constitution. The states approved 10 of the amendments. Together, these amendments became known as the Bill of Rights. The Glorious Revolution of 1688 in England had also resulted in a Bill of Rights.

These 10 amendments **guaranteed** freedom of religion, speech, press, petition, and assembly. They gave Americans the right to bear arms and to be protected against unreasonable searches and arrests. They guaranteed trial by jury, due process of law, and the protection of property rights. Many of the rights in the Bill of Rights were derived from the natural rights proposed by the eighteenth-century philosophes and John Locke.

**DETERMINING MEANING**

Read the paragraph that begins, "These 10 amendments **guaranteed** freedom of religion, speech, press, petition, and assembly." What does it mean to *guarantee* freedom of speech?

*On July 26, 1788, New Yorkers celebrated the ratification of the Constitution.*



## SIGNIFICANCE OF THE REVOLUTION

The American Revolution was not the first time in history a people overthrew a tyrannical monarch or broke free from an oppressive nation. However, the ideas that inspired the revolution and the new government it created were unique. It was the first large, successful revolt that was driven by Enlightenment ideals. Natural rights, individual liberties, and popular sovereignty, among others, were all ideas of the Enlightenment that inspired a revolt against the British government. These ideas also formed a foundation for the government the Americans created after their successful revolution.

European intellectuals saw the American Revolution as the confirmation of the premises of the Enlightenment. For many it confirmed that a new age and a better world could be achieved. The revolution would soon inspire popular revolts in parts of Europe and Latin America. Indeed, many popular revolts over the past 240 years looked to the American Revolution as a model to be followed. Many activists across the globe continue to draw inspiration from the American Revolution and its commitment to the Enlightenment ideals of liberty for all people.

### ✓ CHECKING FOR UNDERSTANDING

1. **IDENTIFYING EFFECTS** What were the effects of the American Revolution? Why did intellectuals believe the formation of the United States carried out Enlightenment thought?
2. **IDENTIFYING CAUSES** Why did delegates meet to revise the Articles of Confederation?
3. **INTERPRETING** What is meant by "division of powers," and how was this idea important to the creation of a new government?

**MAKING CONNECTIONS TO TODAY**

### CONSTITUTIONAL AMENDMENTS

The framers of the Constitution designed it to be updated. Article V states that the Constitution can be amended by a two-thirds majority vote of each house of Congress or by a national convention. From the time it was ratified through today, the Constitution has been amended 27 times. In addition to the Bill of Rights, there have been many other important amendments. One of the most important was the Thirteenth, which was ratified in 1865 after the Civil War. It abolished slavery. Another was the Nineteenth, in 1920, which gave women the right to vote.

1. **CITING TEXT EVIDENCE** Why might the framers of the Constitution have designed it to be updated?
2. **CITING TEXT EVIDENCE** Why might the framers have required a two-thirds majority of Congress to make amendments?

## LESSON 3 REVIEW

### Time and Place

1. **IDENTIFYING CONNECTIONS** How did the Seven Years' War harm Britain's interests during the American Revolution?

### Building History-Social Science Analysis Skills

2. **IDENTIFYING CONNECTIONS** How did Montesquieu's ideas influence the creation of the government of the United States?
3. **DETERMINING CONTEXT** How did Enlightenment ideas influence the writing of the Declaration of Independence?
4. **RELATING EVENTS** How did the outcome of the American Revolution have a lasting impact on global politics? What might have happened if the outcome had been different?

### Writing About History

5. **INFORMATIVE WRITING** Write an essay discussing the influence of Enlightenment philosophy on the American Revolution, the Declaration of Independence, and the U.S. Constitution.

### Collaborating

6. **COLLABORATING** With a partner, discuss important elements of the government created by the American colonists.

# COMPARING THE U.S. BILL OF RIGHTS AND THE ENGLISH BILL OF RIGHTS

The Scientific Revolution and the Enlightenment drove many changes around the world in the seventeenth and eighteenth centuries. The Glorious Revolution in England brought about the English Bill of Rights, which acknowledged Parliament's right to make laws and to limit royal interference. The Enlightenment also played a role in the American Revolution that led to the U.S. Constitution and Bill of Rights. Many natural rights put forth by seventeenth- and eighteenth-century French and English philosophers are reflected in these documents.

**VOCABULARY**

*misconstruction:* failure to understand; misinterpretation

*abridging:* lessening or curtailing

*redress:* to correct or make right through compensation

*temporal (temporall):* relating to worldly affairs

*subverted:* undermined or overturned something

*aforesaid:* said or mentioned before

*auntient:* ancient

**PRIMARY SOURCE: DOCUMENT**

## THE U.S. BILL OF RIGHTS

The U.S. Bill of Rights, written in 1791, contains the first 10 amendments to the U.S. Constitution. The excerpt below includes the introduction and three amendments.

> "THE Conventions of a number of the States, having at the time of their adopting the Constitution, expressed a desire, in order to prevent **misconstruction** or abuse of its powers, that further declaratory and restrictive clauses should be added: And as extending the ground of public confidence in the Government, will best ensure the beneficent ends of its institution.
>
> RESOLVED by the Senate and House of Representatives of the United States of America, in Congress assembled, two thirds of both Houses concurring, that the following Articles be proposed to the Legislatures of the several States, as amendments to the Constitution of the United States, all, or any of which Articles, when ratified by three fourths of the said Legislatures, to be valid to all intents and purposes, as part of the said Constitution; viz.
>
> Amendment I Congress shall make no law respecting an establishment of religion, or prohibiting the free exercise thereof; or **abridging** the freedom of speech, or of the press; or the right of the people peaceably to assemble, and to petition the Government for a **redress** of grievances.
>
> Amendment II A well regulated Militia, being necessary to the security of a free State, the right of the people to keep and bear Arms, shall not be infringed.
>
> Amendment VIII Excessive bail shall not be required, nor excessive fines imposed, nor cruel and unusual punishments inflicted."

**ANALYZE THE TEXT**

1. **ANALYZING TEXT** What does the U.S. Bill of Rights say about the right to bear arms? What events in U.S. history might account for this?
2. **ANALYZING TEXT** What body or bodies does the U.S. Bill of Rights identify as the authority for issuing the Bill of Rights? Why does it specify these bodies?

PRIMARY SOURCE: DOCUMENT

## THE ENGLISH BILL OF RIGHTS

Created in 1689 after the Glorious Revolution, the English Bill of Rights established many political principles that would inspire later Enlightenment thinkers and even the crafters of the U.S. Bill of Rights.

> "And whereas the said late King James the Second haveing Abdicated the Government and the Throne being thereby Vacant His Hignesse the Prince of Orange (whome it hath pleased Almighty God to make the glorious Instrument of Delivering this Kingdome from Popery and Arbitrary Power) did (by the Advice of the Lords Spirituall and **Temporall** and diverse principall Persons of the Commons) cause Letters to be written to the Lords Spirituall and Temporall being Protestants and other Letters to the severall Countyes Cityes Universities Burroughs and Cinque Ports for the Choosing of such Persons to represent them as were of right to be sent to Parlyament to meete and sitt at Westminster upon the two and twentyeth day of January in this Yeare one thousand six hundred eighty and eight in order to such an Establishment as that their Religion Lawes and Liberties might not againe be in danger of being **Subverted**, Upon which Letters Elections haveing beene accordingly made.
>
> **The Subject's Rights.**
>
> And thereupon the said Lords Spirituall and Temporall and Commons pursuant to their respective Letters and Elections being now assembled in a full and free Representative of this Nation takeing into their most serious Consideration the best meanes for attaining the Ends **aforesaid** Doe in the first place (as their Auncestors in like Case have usually done) for the Vindicating and Asserting their **auntient** Rights and Liberties, Declare.
>
> **Right to petition.**
>
> That it is the Right of the Subjects to petition the King and all Commitments and Prosecutions for such Petitioning are Illegall.
>
> **Subjects' Arms.**
>
> That the Subjects which are Protestants may have Arms for their Defence suitable to their Conditions and as allowed by Law.
>
> **Freedom of Speech.**
>
> That the Freedome of Speech and Debates or Proceedings in Parlyament ought not to be impeached or questioned in any Court or Place out of Parlyament.
>
> **Excessive Bail.**
>
> That excessive Baile ought not to be required nor excessive Fines imposed nor cruell and unusuall Punishments inflicted."

### ANALYZE THE TEXT

1. **CITING TEXT EVIDENCE** What does the English Bill of Rights say about the right to petition? Why is this important? Is this reflected in the U.S. Bill of Rights?

2. **DETERMINING MEANING** What does the phrase "it hath pleased Almighty God" in the preamble suggest about the English Bill of Rights?

### MULTIPLE PERSPECTIVES

1. **IDENTIFYING CONNECTIONS** How are Locke's ideas about human rights reflected in the other three documents you read?

2. **IDENTIFYING CAUSES** What reasons do the excerpts provide for the creation of the Declaration of the Rights of Man, the U.S. Bill of Rights, and the English Bill of Rights?

3. **COMPARING AND CONTRASTING** Compare and contrast the treatment of freedom of speech in the Declaration of the Rights of Man, the U.S. Bill of Rights, and the English Bill of Rights.

# STUDY GUIDE

## IDEAS OF THE ENLIGHTENMENT
LESSON 1

**Montesquieu**

Attempted to find the natural laws that govern the social and political relationships of human beings

**Voltaire**

Believed in deism, which holds that God created the universe, set it in motion, and allowed it to run without interference according to its natural laws

**Adam Smith**

Promoted the idea of laissez-faire economics, which holds that the state should not interfere in economic matters

**Mary Wollstonecraft**

Advocated for women's rights by claiming that because the Enlightenment was based on an ideal of reason in all human beings, women should have the same rights as men

## THE SEVEN YEARS' WAR
LESSON 2

**The Seven Years' War was fought in three areas of the world.**

**Europe**

Prussia seized Silesia while France invaded Austrian territory. In 1763 Austria officially recognized Prussia's permanent control of Silesia.

**Asia**

France took Madras in India from the British. After the Treaty of Paris in 1763, the French withdrew and left India to the British.

**North America**

The British captured the French fortress of Louisbourg at the entrance of the St. Lawrence River. By the Treaty of Paris, the French transferred Canada and the lands east of the Mississippi to England. Spain transferred Spanish Florida to British control, and in return, France gave its Louisiana territory to the Spanish.

## EVENTS OF THE AMERICAN REVOLUTION
LESSON 3

- **1765** - Colonists revolt against British taxes they think are unfair
- **1774** - The First Continental Congress convenes and urges colonists to form private armies to fight the British
- **1776** - The colonies officially declare their independence from Britain
- **1781** - The British surrender
- **1783** - The Treaty of Paris, which recognized the independence of the colonies, is signed
- **1787** - The U.S. Constitution is approved, forming the government that rules today

# CHAPTER 2 Assessment

**Directions: On a separate sheet of paper, answer the questions below. Make sure you read carefully and answer all parts of the questions.**

## Short Answer

1. **SUMMARIZING** Explain the influence of Descartes on Enlightenment thought.

2. **UNDERSTANDING CONTEXT** How did Bacon's ideas about inductive reasoning and empiricism influence philosophers and scientists?

3. **SUMMARIZING** What were the effects of the Scientific Revolution? Explain the Scientific Revolution's impact on the Enlightenment.

4. **IDENTIFYING CONNECTIONS** Explain how the changes during the Scientific Revolution affected not only technology but values and beliefs.

5. **UNDERSTANDING CHANGE** What was the goal of the philosophes? Did their movement have an impact on our lives today?

6. **SUMMARIZING** In Adam Smith's *The Wealth of Nations,* what three roles does Smith argue government should have?

7. **UNDERSTANDING CONTEXT** Describe Jean-Jacques Rousseau's political philosophy, as explained in his work *The Social Contract.*

8. **INTERPRETING** Identify the characteristics of an enlightened absolute monarchy. Then answer this question: Was Catherine the Great an enlightened ruler? Why or why not?

9. **IDENTIFYING CONNECTIONS** What were the causes of the Seven Years' War? Why was it fought in three different areas of the world?

10. **IDENTIFYING CONNECTIONS** How did the Seven Years' War set the stage for the American Revolution?

11. **DETERMINING CONTEXT** What was unique about the U.S. Declaration of Independence? What did it have in common with documents and ideas from other countries?

12. **IDENTIFYING CONNECTIONS** What countries helped the American colonists win their independence from Great Britain, and why?

13. **IDENTIFYING CAUSES** How did the U.S. Constitution attempt to balance concerns over a strong central government and the weaknesses of the Articles of Confederation?

## History and Social-Science Analysis

14. **DESCRIBING** Create a chart demonstrating the alliances formed during the Seven Years' War. Considering the relationship between geography and the development of a nation, why did countries create their particular alliances?

15. **ANALYZING CHANGE** Francis Bacon's ideas about opinions, reasons, facts, and observations resulted in the new practice of following a scientific method. What does this new method, with its emphasis on thought processes and the collection of knowledge, lead you to conclude about previous thought processes and methods for collecting knowledge?

16. **DRAWING CONCLUSIONS** Use the image to answer the following question.

    Consider the viewpoints of leaders of women's rights during the Enlightenment period, such as Mary Wollstonecraft. How might Wollstonecraft have responded to the depiction of the woman in this painting? What scenes might she have suggested an artist should depict?

**Need Extra Help?**

| If You've Missed Question | 1 | 2 | 3 | 4 | 5 | 6 | 7 | 8 | 9 | 10 | 11 | 12 | 13 | 14 | 15 | 16 |
|---|---|---|---|---|---|---|---|---|---|---|---|---|---|---|---|---|
| Review Lesson | 1 | 1 | 1 | 1 | 1 | 1 | 1 | 2 | 2 | 2 | 3 | 3 | 3 | 2 | 1 | 1 |

# CHAPTER 2 Assessment, continued

## Research and Presentation

**17** **ANALYZING CHANGE** Work with a partner to create a word web showing how the Enlightenment changed ways of thinking. Start with a circle labeled "Enlightenment." Draw three circles beyond it labeled "politics," "religion," and "the arts." Add circles to these three describing changes in attitudes and behaviors. To the side, place a circle labeled "Scientific Revolution." Draw circles beyond it labeled "natural laws," "rational criticism," and "rights for all." Add lines connecting circles where the values of the Scientific Revolution overlap with those of the Enlightenment. You may include artwork, maps, and primary sources in your web.

**18** **INTERPRETING** Choose an example of art, architecture, and music from the Enlightenment period. Create a multimedia presentation that discusses the characteristics of each piece, including how it reflects the culture in which it was produced. Make a claim arguing what it is about these pieces that allow them to remain popular today.

**19** **COMPARING AND CONTRASTING** Reread the excerpt from the Declaration of Independence in the chapter. Compare and contrast the rights described in this excerpt as they are understood in the United States today with the way they were understood when the document was written.

## Reading and Analyzing Primary Sources

Use the document to answer the following questions.

> "To understand political Power right, and derive it from its Original, we must consider, what State all Men are naturally in, and that is, a State of perfect Freedom to order their Actions, and dispose of their Possessions, and Persons as they think fit, within the Bounds of the Law of Nature, without asking Leave, or depending upon the Will of any other Man. A State also of Equality wherein all the Power and Jurisdiction is Reciprocal, no one having more than another; there being nothing more evident, than that the Creatures of the same Species and Rank, promiscuously born to all the same advantages of Nature, and the use of the same Faculties, should also be equal one amongst another without Subordination or Subjection, unless the Lord and Master of them all should by any Manifest Declaration of his Will set one above another, and confer on him, by an evident and clear Appointment, an undoubted Right to Dominion and Sovereignty. But though this be a State of Liberty yet it is not a State of License; though Man in that State have an uncontroulable Liberty, to dispose of his Person or Possessions. . ."

—from John Locke's *Two Treatises of Government*

**20** **UNDERSTANDING CONTEXT** What does Locke consider true freedom?

**A.** The ability to act as one sees fit without permission from anyone else

**B.** The condition of one person having more power than anyone else

**C.** The right of one person to be the leader over all others

**D.** A condition that comes from government rather than nature

**21** **INTERPRETING** What is Locke's opinion of the kings making laws? Where did he acquire his distrust of rulers with absolute power?

**A.** The king should be able to make any laws he sees fit; the American system of democracy.

**B.** The king should make laws that put certain citizens in charge of others; the abuses of English noblemen.

**C.** The king should make only laws that protect the rights of citizens; the abuses of English monarchs.

**D.** The king should make only laws that constrain the rights of citizens; the abuses of French Huguenots.

**22** **UNDERSTANDING CONTEXT** What reaction do you think this treatise received from those who first read it, and why?

**A.** Many people likely found it boring because it is similar to many previous political treatises.

**B.** Many people likely found it shocking because it was such a dramatic break with previous political thought.

**C.** Many people likely found it upsetting because it expressed their concerns in a way that depressed them.

**D.** Many people likely found it incomprehensible because it expresses ideas in a way they could not understand.

## Writing About History

**23** **IDENTIFYING CONNECTIONS** Trace the belief in natural rights from its origins to 1776.

## Speaking and Listening About History

**24** **ANALYZING CHANGE** Meet in a small group to discuss the following questions: How did Mary Wollstonecraft contribute to the changing roles of women during the Enlightenment? How is the influence of these changes felt in today's society? Have one member of your group serve as a moderator of the group discussion.

### Need Extra Help?

| If You've Missed Question | 17 | 18 | 19 | 20 | 21 | 22 | 23 | 24 |
|---|---|---|---|---|---|---|---|---|
| Review Lesson | 1 | 1 | 3 | 1 | 1 | 1 | 2 | 1 |

◀ This detail from *Portrait of Napoleon Bonaparte in the Garb of the King of Italy*, by Andrea Appiani, shows Napoleon wearing a laurel wreath, a classical symbol of triumph

1789 — 1815

# The French Revolution and Napoleon

## CHAPTER 3



**GO DIGITAL**
*It's All online!*

## ASKING ESSENTIAL QUESTIONS

***What causes revolution? How does revolution change society?***

**What Will You Learn?** You will learn which events and circumstances led to the French Revolution and how this major turning point in French history led to the rise of Napoleon Bonaparte.

**Why Does This Matter?** France would create a short-lived republic after a brutal revolution. The general Napoleon Bonaparte would use the weakness of the new French government to his advantage, take control of the country, and crown himself Emperor. Napoleon would then lead a war of conquest across Europe, and in doing so spread the ideas of the Enlightenment and the spirit of the revolution across the continent. Napoleon would fall, but his actions would inspire revolutionary movements up to the present day.

**How Will You Know That You Learned It?** You will be able to identify the causes and effects of the French Revolution, the impact of Napoleon's rule in post-Revolutionary France, and the influence of these events on further independence movements.

**Using Your Inquiry Journal** As you read the story of the French Revolution and Napoleon in this chapter and examine the primary sources, use your Inquiry Journal to help you make notes and expand your list of questions. As you gather information, think about how you will answer the Essential Questions above.

# PLACE & TIME France 1785 – 1815

The political, economic, and social conflicts that led to the French Revolution changed the role of citizens and the structure of political systems in France. However, it was not the only conflict of the latter eighteenth century. Countries around the world engaged in conflict over territories, resources, and independence. This resulted in sweeping social and cultural change.

## STEP INTO THE PLACE

Read the quotes and look at the information presented on the map.

1. **SPATIAL THINKING** What were the types of government that existed in Europe in 1789?
2. **DETERMINING CONTEXT** What were the concerns addressed by de Calonne and Rousseau? How do these concerns correspond to the types of governments in Europe on the eve of the French Revolution?

"[A country] where certain areas are totally freed from burdens of which others bear the full weight, where the richest class contributes least, where privileges destroy all balance, where it is impossible to have either a constant rule or a common will, is necessarily a very imperfect kingdom, brimming with abuses, and one that is impossible to govern well."

—Charles Alexandre de Calonne, France's finance minister, from a memorandum on reform to Louis XVI, 1786

"I conceive that there are two kinds of inequality among the human species; one, which I call natural or physical, because it is established by nature, and consists in a difference of age, health, bodily strength, and the qualities of the mind or of the soul: and another, which may be called moral or political inequality, because it depends on a kind of convention, and is established, or at least authorized by the consent of men. This latter consists of the different privileges, which some men enjoy to the prejudice of others; such as that of being more rich, more honoured, more powerful or even in a position to exact obedience."

—Jean-Jacques Rousseau, from *A Dissertation on the Origin and Foundation of the Inequality of Mankind,* 1755

## STEP INTO THE TIME

**CHRONOLOGICAL THINKING**

Choose an event from the France portion of the time line and write a paragraph predicting the general social, political, or economic consequence that event might have on the world.

### FRANCE

- **July 14, 1789** The Storming of the Bastille
- **August 26, 1789** The Declaration of the Rights of Man and the Citizen is approved
- **January 21, 1793** Louis XVI, King of France, is executed
- **September 1793** Reign of Terror begins
- **November 1795** The Directory heads French government

**1785** **1790** **1795**

### WORLD EVENTS

- **1789** George Washington inaugurated as first U.S. president
- **1792** Mary Wollstonecraft writes *A Vindication of the Rights of Woman*
- **1794** Eli Whitney patents the cotton gin
- **1794** Persia's Qājār dynasty begins

PHOTO:(t)Kean Collection/Getty Images; (b)Stock Montage/Archive Photos/Getty Images; TEXT:(t)Koenigsberger, Helmut Georg. 1987. Early Modern Europe 1500-1789. Longman an imprint of Pearson Education; (b)Rousseau, Jean Jacques. 1913, 1916, 1920. The Social Contract & Discourses. E. P. Dutton & Co.

**November 9, 1799**
Napoleon overthrows the French government

**December 2, 1804**
Napoleon crowns himself emperor

**June–December 1812**
Napoleon Bonaparte invades Russia and retreats in defeat

**April 6, 1814**
Napoleon abdicates as emperor

**June 18, 1815**
Allies defeat Napoleon at the Battle of Waterloo

**1800** **1805** **1810** **1815**

**1803**
United States purchases Louisiana Territory from France

**1804**
Francois-Dominique Toussaint-Louverture's leadership leads to Haitian independence

**1806**
Abdication of Emperor Francis II ends the Holy Roman Empire

**1810**
Miguel Hidalgo leads Mexican independence movement

**1814**
Congress of Vienna in Austria

## ESSENTIAL QUESTIONS

- *What causes revolution?*
- *How does revolution change society?*

LESSON 1

# The French Revolution Begins

## THE STORY BEGINS...

The storming and destruction of the Bastille, Paris's great prison and a hated symbol of the monarchy, was one of the pivotal events of the French Revolution. An Englishman named Mr. Jenkinson, who was in Paris at the time, wrote the following eyewitness account of the event:

> "The Bastille made some Resistance but was taken yesterday Evening. The Governor and sub-Governor had their Heads cut off, which were carried in Triumph around the City. . . . the King was at first very resolute. The thoughts however of the Danger he was in have this Evening induced him to recant all his former words & to submit in everything. Deputies have arrived this afternoon from Versailles with this goodnews, and it is reported that the King will be here himself tomorrow, but I own I very much doubt it. The Consternation that has prevailed in Paris for the last two days, is beyond all power of description. Few People have gone out of their doors, & all Public Amusement for the first time have been stopped. I however have seen every thing of importance from the first Enterance of the Troops to the taking of the Bastille which I was present at yesterday Evening & indeed the whole sight has been such, that nothing would have . . . tempted me to miss it."

—a letter from English visitor Mr. Jenkinson in Paris, dated July 15, 1789

Today the anniversary of the storming of the Bastille is celebrated each year as France's independence day holiday. The storming of the Bastille kicked off a series of events that would change France, Europe, and the wider world.

*In this painting, the governor of the Bastille, Bernard René Jourdan, is arrested as his prison is stormed.* ▶

| The French Revolution | |
|---|---|
| Long-Range | Immediate |
| | |
| | |

**ANALYZING KEY IDEAS AND DETAILS**

**IDENTIFYING CAUSES** Read closely to identify the long-range and immediate causes of the French Revolution. Record each cause in a graphic organizer like this one.

# CAUSES OF THE FRENCH REVOLUTION

**GUIDING QUESTIONS** *How did the structure of social classes in France lead to discontent? How did the economic crises in France lead to the meeting of the Estates-General?*

The French Revolution has often been seen as a major turning point in European history. The institutions of the Old Regime were destroyed. A new order emerged, based on individual rights, representative institutions, and a concept of loyalty to the nation rather than the monarch.

The long-range causes of the French Revolution are to be found in the condition of French society. Before the Revolution, French society was based on inequality. Since the Middle Ages, France's population was divided into three orders, or **estates**.

The First Estate, or clergy, numbered about 130,000 (out of a total population of 27 million) and owned about 10 percent of the land. The clergy were radically divided. The higher clergy—cardinals, bishops, and heads of monasteries—were from noble families and shared their outlook and interests. The parish priests were often poor and from the class of commoners.

The Second Estate, or nobility, numbered about 350,000 and owned about 25 to 30 percent of the land. They played a crucial role in society in the 1700s. They held leading positions in the government, the military, the law courts, and the Roman Catholic Church. Despite controlling most of the wealth, neither the clergy nor the nobles had to pay the **taille** (TAH • yuh), France's chief tax.

Unlike the First and Second Estates, the Third Estate was divided by vast differences in occupation, level of education, and wealth. Peasants made up 75 to 80 percent of the Third Estate and owned about 35 to 40 percent of the land. Middle-class members of the Third Estate owned the rest. At least half the peasants had little or no land on which to live.

Peasants owed certain duties to the nobles, which were a holdover from medieval times when serfdom was widespread. For example, a peasant had to pay a fee to grind his or her flour or to press his or her grapes because the local lord controlled the flour mill and wine press. When the harvest time came, the peasant had to work a certain number of days harvesting the noble's crop. Peasants fiercely resented these duties.

Another part of the Third Estate consisted of urban craftspeople, shopkeepers, and workers. These people were also struggling to survive. In the 1700s, the price of **consumer** goods increased much faster than wages, which left these urban groups with decreased buying power.

**ANALYZING KEY IDEAS AND DETAILS**

**DETERMINING CENTRAL IDEAS**
What is the central idea of this section?

**DETERMINING MEANING**

The word **estate** comes from the Latin word *stare*, which means "to stand." How does the origin of the word *estate* apply to its use in this section?

**DETERMINING MEANING**

The word **taille** is a French word meaning "cut." How does the meaning of this word better help the reader understand its meaning in pre-Revolutionary France?

**DETERMINING MEANING**

The word **bourgeoisie** contains the word *bourg*, which was the name given to French market towns. How might being familiar with this root help a person determine the meaning of *bourgeoisie*?

The **bourgeoisie** (burzh • wah • ZEE), or middle class, was another part of the Third Estate. This group included about 8 percent of the population, or more than 2 million people. They owned about 20 to 25 percent of the land. The bourgeoisie included merchants, bankers, and industrialists, as well as professional people—lawyers, holders of public offices, doctors, and writers.

The middle class was unhappy with the privileges held by nobles. They did not want to abolish the nobility, however, but to better their own position. Some bourgeoisie had managed to become nobles by being appointed to public offices that conferred noble status. About 6,500 new nobles had been created by appointment during the 1700s.

The bourgeoisie also shared certain goals with the nobles. Both groups were increasingly upset with a monarchal system resting on privileges and on an old and rigid social order. Both were also drawn to the new political ideas of the Enlightenment.

Increased criticism of the old order of society had been part of the eighteenth-century Enlightenment. The philosophes did not advocate revolution. Their ideas, however, were widely spread among the literate middle class and noble elites of France. When the revolution began, revolutionary leaders often quoted Enlightenment writers, especially Rousseau.

Social conditions and Enlightenment ideas, then, formed an underlying background to the French Revolution. The immediate cause of the revolution was the near collapse of the French budget. Although the economy had been expanding for 50 years, there were periodic crises. Bad harvests in 1787 and 1788 and a slowdown in manufacturing led to food shortages, rising prices for food, and unemployment.

On the eve of the revolution, the French economy was in crisis. Despite these problems, the French king and his ministers continued to spend enormous sums of money on wars and court luxuries. The queen, Marie Antoinette, was especially known for her extravagance and this too caused

**POLITICAL CARTOON**

## THE THREE ESTATES

This French political cartoon depicts the Three Estates. The circular object that pushes down on the middle figure represents the monarchy, who is burdening the people with taxes. The armored figure on the left side of the cartoon represents the nobility, the Second Estate. The robed figure on the right side of the cartoon represents the clergy, the First Estate. The crouched figure in the middle of the cartoon represents the commoners in France, the Third Estate.

**INTEGRATING INFORMATION** How does this visual depiction of the Three Estates demonstrate the roles they held in society?

Library of Congress, Prints & Photographs Division [LC-USZC2-3604]

CITIZENSHIP

## AN EARLY LEGISLATURE: THE ESTATES-GENERAL

The Estates-General was the name of the pre-Revolutionary French assembly. It was similar to the British Parliament but, in practice, much weaker. The king of France appointed its members, each of whom represented one of the three estates in French society. The absolutist nature of France's monarchy meant the Estates-General were very infrequently consulted by the king. By design, the Third Estate represented nearly 97 percent of France's population. In spite of this, it had only twice as many members as the other two. Additionally, each of the three estates had the same amount of voting power, even if they were not the same size. Through this system, a small minority could easily outvote the majority of the people. Today the Estates-General serves as an example of a representative body that poorly reflects the interests of those it is called on to represent.

1. **COMPARING AND CONTRASTING** How was the Estates-General different from a modern representative government?
2. **IDENTIFYING CONNECTIONS** Was the Estates-General consistent with the Enlightenment's ideals of representative government?

popular resentment. When the government decided to spend huge sums to help the American colonists against Britain, the budget went into total crisis.

With France on the verge of financial collapse, Louis XVI was forced to call a meeting of the Estates-General. This was the French parliament, and it had not met since 1614.

### ✓ CHECKING FOR UNDERSTANDING

1. **IDENTIFYING CAUSE AND EFFECT** How were economic problems a contributing cause of the French Revolution?
2. **IDENTIFYING CONNECTIONS** How did Enlightenment ideas influence members of the Third Estate?
3. **UNDERSTANDING CONTEXT** What reasons did the peasants in France have to resent the nobility?

# THE NATIONAL ASSEMBLY

**GUIDING QUESTIONS** *Why did the Third Estate declare itself to be the National Assembly? What were the French peasants reacting to in their rebellions of 1789?*

Louis XVI called a meeting of the Estates-General at Versailles on May 5, 1789. In the Estates-General, the First and Second Estates each had about 300 representatives. The Third Estate had almost 600 representatives. Most of the Third Estate wanted to set up a constitutional government that would make the clergy and nobility pay taxes, too.

From the start, there were arguments about voting. Traditionally, each estate had one vote—the First and Second Estates could outvote the Third Estate two to one. The Third Estate demanded instead that each deputy have one vote. Under this new system, with the help of a few nobles and clerics, the Third Estate would then have a majority vote. The king, however, stated that he favored the current system.

### UNDERSTANDING CRAFT AND STRUCTURE

1. **ANALYZING TEXT** How does the text present the information about the National Assembly? Does the way the text is organized help you better understand the information?
2. **DETERMINING MEANING** What is the difference between the terms *revolt* and *revolution* as they are used in the text?

*The Oath of the Tennis Court, June 20, 1789,* by Jacques-Louis David

**IDENTIFYING BIAS** The artist was a member of the Third Estate. Do you think an artist belonging to one of the other two estates might paint this scene differently?

On June 17, 1789, the Third Estate boldly declared that it was the National Assembly and would draft a constitution. Three days later, on June 20, its deputies arrived at their meeting place, only to find the doors had been locked. They then moved to a nearby indoor tennis court and swore that they would continue meeting until they had a new constitution. The oath they swore became known as the Tennis Court Oath.

> “The National Assembly, considering that it has been summoned to determine the Constitution of the kingdom, to effect the regeneration of public order, to maintain the true principles of monarchy; that nothing can prevent it from continuing its deliberations in whatever place it may be forced to establish itself, and lastly, that wherever its members meet together, there is the National Assembly,
>
> Decrees that all the members of this Assembly shall immediately take a solemn oath never to separate, and to reassemble wherever circumstances shall require, until the constitution of the kingdom shall be established and consolidated upon firm foundations; and that, the said oath being taken, all the members and each of them individually shall ratify by their signatures this steadfast resolution.”
>
> —The Tennis Court Oath, June 20, 1789

### ANALYZING PRIMARY SOURCES

1. **DETERMINING CENTRAL IDEAS** What does this oath state?
2. **ANALYZING IDEAS** How was this oath important to the French Revolution?

Louis XVI prepared to use force against the Third Estate. On July 14, 1789, about 900 Parisians gathered in the courtyard of the Bastille (ba • STEEL)—an old fortress used as a prison and armory. They stormed the Bastille, and after four hours of fighting, the prison warden surrendered. The rebels cut off the warden's head and demolished the Bastille brick by brick. Paris was abandoned to the rebels.

When King Louis XVI returned to his palace at Versailles after a day of hunting, the duc de la Rochefoucauld-Liancourt told him about the fall of the Bastille. Louis is said to have exclaimed, “Why, this is a revolt.” “No, Sire,” replied the duke. “It is a revolution.”

Louis XVI was informed that he could no longer trust royal troops to shoot at the mob. The king's authority had collapsed in Paris. Meanwhile, all over France, revolts were breaking out. Popular hatred of the entire landholding system, with its fees and obligations, had finally spilled over into action.

Peasant rebellions became part of the vast panic known as the Great Fear. Rumors spread from village to village that foreign troops were on the way to put down the revolution. The peasants reacted by breaking into the houses of the lords to destroy the records of their obligations.

### ✓ CHECKING FOR UNDERSTANDING

1. **IDENTIFYING CONNECTIONS** Why did the Third Estate declare itself to be the National Assembly? What were the French peasants reacting to in their rebellions of 1789?
2. **IDENTIFYING CONNECTIONS** What effect did the early events of the French Revolution have on the old social order?
3. **COMPARING AND CONTRASTING** How did Louis XVI's opinions concerning a French constitution differ from those of the members of the Third Estate?

## END OF THE OLD REGIME

**GUIDING QUESTION** *How did the French Revolution enter a new phase after the storming of the Bastille?*

The National Assembly reacted to news of peasant rebellions and rumors of a possible foreign invasion. It reacted swiftly and moved against elements of the old regime in France. On August 4, 1789, the National Assembly voted to abolish all legal privileges of the nobles and clergy.

### DECLARATION OF THE RIGHTS OF MAN

On August 26, the National Assembly adopted the Declaration of the Rights of Man and the Citizen. Inspired by the English Bill of Rights of 1689 and by the American Declaration of Independence and Constitution, this charter of basic liberties began with "the natural and imprescriptible rights of man" to "liberty, property, security, and resistance to oppression."

Reflecting Enlightenment thought, the declaration proclaimed that all men were free and equal before the law, that appointment to public office should be based on talent, and that no group should be exempt from taxation. Freedom of speech and of the press were affirmed. The declaration raised an important issue: Should equal rights include women? Many deputies agreed, provided that, as one man said, "women do not [hope] to exercise political rights and functions." One writer, Olympe de Gouges, refused to accept this **exclusion** of women. Echoing the words of the official declaration, she wrote:

> "Believing that ignorance, omission, or scorn for the rights of woman are the only causes of public misfortunes and of the corruption of governments, the women have resolved to set forth in a solemn declaration the natural, inalienable, and sacred rights of woman in order that this declaration, constantly exposed before all the members of the society, will ceaselessly remind them of their rights and duties."

—from *Declaration of the Rights of Woman and the Female Citizen,* 1791

### THE KING CONCEDES

In the meantime, Louis XVI remained quiet at Versailles. He refused to accept the National Assembly's decrees. On October 5, thousands of Parisian women

**INTEGRATING KNOWLEDGE AND IDEAS**

1. **INTEGRATING INFORMATION** How does the excerpt from the *Declaration of the Rights of Woman and the Female Citizen* support the descriptions in the text?
2. **INTEGRATING INFORMATION** Based on the information in the text, why did one observer describe France as being "on a volcano ready to spout flames"?

(t to b)Beik, Paul Harold. 1970. The French Revolution. Harper and Row; Duiker, William J. and Spielvogel, Jackson J. 2008. The Essential World History: Volume II: Since 1500. Thomson Wadsworth; Levy, Darline Gay; Applewhite, Harriet Branson; Johnson, Mary Durham. 1979. Women in Revolutionary Paris 1789-1795, Selected Documents with Notes and Commentary. The Board of Trustees at the University of Illinois.

**ANALYZING PRIMARY SOURCES**

**DECLARATION OF THE RIGHTS OF MAN AND THE CITIZEN**

"1. Men are born and remain free and equal in rights; social distinctions can be established only for the common benefit.

7. No man can be accused, arrested, or detained except in cases determined by the law, and according to the forms which it has prescribed . . .

10. No one may be disturbed because of his opinions, even religious, provided that their public demonstration does not disturb the public order established by law."

—from the Declaration of the Rights of Man and the Citizen, 1789

**CITING TEXT EVIDENCE** How does this document reflect Enlightenment thought?

armed with broomsticks, pitchforks, pistols, and other weapons marched to Versailles. Some of the women then met with the king. They told him their children were starving because there was no bread. These women forced Louis to accept the new decrees.

The crowd insisted that the royal family return to Paris. On October 6, they did so. As a goodwill gesture, they carried wagonloads of flour from the palace storehouse. They were escorted by women who chanted: "We are bringing back the baker, the baker's wife, and the baker's boy." The king, the queen, and their son were now virtual prisoners in Paris.

## CHURCH REFORMS

Under the old regime, the Catholic Church had been an important pillar of the old order. The revolutionaries believed they had to reform it, too. The new revolutionary government had another serious motivation, however: the need for money. By seizing and selling off Church lands, the National Assembly was able to increase the state's revenues.

Finally, the Church was formally brought under the control of the state. A new Civil Constitution of the Clergy said that bishops and priests were to be elected by the people, not appointed by the pope and the Church hierarchy. The state would also pay the salaries of the bishops and priests. Because of these changes, many Catholics became enemies of the revolution.

## NEW CONSTITUTION AND NEW FEARS

The new Constitution of 1791 set up a limited monarchy. There was still a king, but a Legislative Assembly would make the laws. All men were given the right to vote, regardless of social status. The Legislative Assembly, however, was to consist of 745 representatives chosen in such a way that only the more affluent members of society would be elected. Some wanted to go further and grant broader rights to women and enslaved people. Political radicals wanted even more reforms. Infighting, royal resistance, and threats of invasion would put an end to these hopes.

The king detested the new order and his loss of absolute power. In June 1791, the royal family attempted to flee France in disguise. They almost succeeded but were recognized, captured, and brought back to Paris. In this unsettled situation, the new Legislative Assembly first met in October 1791. France's relations with the rest of Europe soon led to the king's downfall.

*The arrest of Louis XVI and his family at Varennes, July 1791*

**UNDERSTANDING CONTEXT** What events prompted the royal family to try to escape France?

## WAR WITH AUSTRIA

Over time, some European leaders began to fear that revolution would spread to their countries. The kings of Austria and Prussia even threatened to use force to restore Louis XVI to full power. Insulted by this threat and fearing attack, the Legislative Assembly decided to strike first, declaring war on Austria in the spring of 1792. The French fared badly in the initial fighting. A frantic search for scapegoats began. One observer in France noted:

> "Everywhere you hear the cry that the king is betraying us, the generals are betraying us, that nobody is to be trusted; . . . that Paris will be taken in six weeks by the Austrians. . . . We are on a volcano ready to spout flames."

—quoted in *The Oxford History of the French Revolution*

## RISE OF THE PARIS COMMUNE

In the spring of 1792, angry citizens demonstrated to protest food shortages and defeats in the war. In August, Paris radicals again decided the fate of the revolution. They declared themselves a commune—a popularly run city council—and attacked the royal palace and Legislative Assembly.

The French Revolution was entering a more radical and violent stage. Members of the new Paris Commune took the king captive. They forced the Legislative Assembly to suspend the monarchy and to call for a National Convention. This time they wanted a more radical change. All the representatives who would decide the nation's future would be elected through universal male suffrage, in which all adult males had the right to vote. This would broaden the group of voters to include men who did not meet the initial standards for citizenship established by the Assembly.

Many members of the Paris Commune proudly called themselves **sans-culottes**, meaning "without breeches." Wearing long trousers, not the knee-length breeches of the nobles, they identified themselves as ordinary patriots. Often, sans-culottes are depicted as poor workers, but many were merchants or artisans—the elite of their neighborhoods.

**DETERMINING MEANING**

Read the text of the paragraph that contains the word **sans-culottes**. How does the description of the people who are identified under this term in the paragraph go along with its meaning?

### ☑ CHECKING FOR UNDERSTANDING

1. **RELATING EVENTS** How did the French Revolution enter a new phase after the storming of the Bastille?
2. **IDENTIFYING CONNECTIONS** What was the connection between the revolutionaries taking Louis XVI prisoner and the war with Austria?
3. **EXPLAINING CAUSE AND EFFECT** How did the war with Austria lead to the suspension of the French monarchy?

## LESSON 1 REVIEW

### Time and Place

1. **UNDERSTANDING CONTEXT** List and describe all of the types of people who made up the French bourgeoisie. What different points of view did people within this class have about the French government, and how did these points of view reflect the events and beliefs of this time period?

### Building History-Social Science Analysis Skills

2. **EXPLAINING CAUSES** Use your notes on the long-range and immediate causes of the French Revolution to compare and contrast one distant and one immediate cause of the French Revolution.
3. **IDENTIFYING EFFECTS** Describe how the structure of social classes in France led to discontent. How did the different classes feel about their government at the start of the revolution?
4. **RELATING EVENTS** Describe the nature of the economic crises that the French experienced before the revolution. How did these crises lead to the meeting of the Estates-General?

### Writing About History

5. **INFORMATIVE WRITING** Write an essay exploring the influences on the Declaration of the Rights of Man and the Citizen. Be sure to include a discussion of influential documents from other countries. Also discuss influences specific to France, identifying cultural, political, and economic concerns the authors wanted to address.

### Collaborating

6. **PRESENTING** Work in a small group to describe the three French estates. As a group, select one estate and design a poster illustrating the role it played in French society.

POINTS OF VIEW

# When Can Society Rightfully Break the Social Contract?

In a famous debate, two Englishmen, Edmund Burke and Thomas Paine, answer this question very differently. Burke, horrified by revolutionary violence, emphasized that people should be cautious before breaking with tradition. Paine, a fervent supporter of the American Revolution, argued for great freedom in establishing a new government.

"Society is indeed a contract. Subordinate contracts for objects of mere occasional interest may be dissolved at pleasure—but the State ought not to be considered as nothing better than a partnership agreement in a trade of pepper and coffee . . . or some other such low concern, to be taken up for a little temporary interest, and to be dissolved by the **fancy** of the parties. It is to be looked on with other **reverence**; because it is not a partnership of a temporary and perishable nature. It is a partnership in all science; a partnership in all art; a partnership in every virtue, and in all perfection. As the ends of such a partnership cannot be obtained in many generations, it becomes a partnership not only between those who are living, but between those who are living, those who are dead, and those who are to be born. Each contract of each particular State is but a clause in the great **primaeval** contact [contract] of eternal society, linking the lower with the high natures, connecting the visible and invisible world, according to a fixed compact sanctioned by the **inviolable** oath which holds all physical and all moral natures, each in their appointed place. This law is not subject to the will of those, who by an obligation above them, and the infinitely superior, are bound to submit their will to that law"

—Edmund Burke, Reflections on the Revolution in France, and on the Proceedings in Certain Societies in London Relative to that Event, 1789

**VOCABULARY**

*fancy:* notion or whim

*reverence:* honor or respect

*primaeval:* [primeval] from the earliest times of the world

*inviolable:* unable to be attacked; unassailable

PHOTO:image courtesy National Gallery of Art; TEXT:Bliss, William D. P. Edited 1897. The Encyclopedia of Social Reform, page 1286. New York and London: Funk & Wagnalls Company.

"Every age and generation must be as free to act for itself in all cases as the age and generations which preceded it. The **vanity** and presumption of governing beyond the grave is the most ridiculous and insolent of all the **tyrannies**. Man has no property in man; neither has any generation a property in the generations which are to follow. The Parliament or the people of 1688, or of any other period, had no more right to dispose of the people of the present day, or to bind or to control them in any shape whatever, than the parliament or the people of the present day have to dispose of, bind, or control those who are to live a hundred or a thousand years hence. Every generation is, and must be, competent to all the purposes which its occasions require. It is the living, and not the dead, that are to be accommodated. When man ceases to be, his power and his wants **cease** with him; having no longer any participation in the concerns of this world, he has no longer any authority in directing who shall be its governors, or how its government shall be organized, or how administered."

—Thomas Paine, *The Rights of Man*, 1792

---

**VOCABULARY**

*vanity:* quality of having too much pride

*tyrannies:* oppressive powers

*cease:* to stop

## What Do YOU Think?

1. **CITING TEXT EVIDENCE** What language does Burke use to contrast the social contract with other types of contracts? Why does he make this comparison?

2. **DETERMINING CENTRAL IDEAS** What does the term *property* mean in this sentence? "Man has no property in man; neither has any generation a property in the generations which are to follow."

3. **DETERMINING POINT OF VIEW** Burke and Paine reference people who should be considered part of the social contract. Who does Burke include? Who does Paine include? Why are these distinctions significant?

4. **EVALUATING ARGUMENTS** Which groups in France during the revolutionary period would have likely agreed with the arguments made by Burke? Which groups would have likely agreed with Paine? Explain.

5. **COLLABORATING** Meet with a partner in a think-pair-share. One student should take the role of Edmund Burke, and the other should take the role of Thomas Paine. Paraphrase each excerpt, using present-day language. Then read your paraphrase of the excerpt aloud. Conclude by taking turns discussing with which of these arguments you agree. Give evidence and reasons for your decision.

PHOTO:Library of Congress Prints & Photographs Division: TEXT: Paine, Thomas. 1894. The Writings of Thomas Paine. G.P. Putnam's Sons.

## ESSENTIAL QUESTIONS

- *What causes revolution?*
- *How does revolution change society?*

# THE STORY BEGINS...

LESSON 2

# Radical Revolution and Reaction

The French Revolution was being consumed by chaos. War, food shortages, and royal plots led to resentment and fear. Some believed violent clampdowns were the only way to bring an end to this chaos and to create a stable republican government. Was such violence necessary? One revolutionary, Maximilien Robespierre, argued that it was:

> “If virtue be the spring of a popular government in times of peace, the spring of that government during a revolution is virtue combined with terror: virtue, without which terror is destructive; terror, without which virtue is impotent. Terror is only justice prompt, severe and inflexible; it is then an emanation of virtue; it is less a distinct principle than a natural consequence of the general principle of democracy, applied to the most pressing wants of the country . . . The government in a revolution is the despotism of liberty against tyranny.”

— Maximilien Robespierre, *On the Principles of Political Morality,* February 1794

Robespierre's vision would soon become a reality. It would also result in stability, but not as he had planned.

*Public executions became a common occurrence during a period of the French Revolution known as the Terror.* ▶

PHOTO:Pierre-Antoine Demachy/Getty Images; TEXT:Robespierre, M. 1794. Report Upon the Principles of Political Morality Which Are to Form the Basis of the Administration of the Interior Concerns of the Republic. Philadelphia.

| Actions Taken by the National Convention |
|---|
| |
| |
| |
| |

**ANALYZING KEY IDEAS AND DETAILS**

**SUMMARIZING** Read closely to identify the actions taken by the National Convention during the French Revolution. Record each action in a graphic organizer like this one.

# THE MOVE TO RADICALISM

**GUIDING QUESTION** *Why did the French Revolution become more radical?*

In September 1792, the newly elected National Convention began meeting. The Convention had been called to draft a new constitution, but it also served as the ruling body of France. It was dominated by lawyers, professionals, and property owners. Two-thirds of its deputies were under the age of 45, but most had some political experience as a result of the revolution. Almost all distrusted the king. It was therefore no surprise that the National Convention's first major step on September 21 was to abolish the monarchy and to establish a republic.

After 1789, citizens had formed political clubs of varying social and political views. Many deputies belonged to these clubs. The Girondins (juh • RAHN • duhns) tended to represent areas outside Paris. They feared the radical mobs of Paris. The Mountain represented the interests of radicals in Paris, and many belonged to the Jacobin (JA • kuh • buhn) club. Increasingly they felt the king needed to be executed to ensure he was not a rallying point for opponents of the republic.

> "I judge you by your past conduct; I judge you for yourself. Tell me, what confidence would we have in the word, in the protestations, in the oaths of a king who had summoned the nation only to engage it to fill the abyss dug by the wastefulness of his ministers, of the household princes, of his favorites, and of the other scoundrels of his court; of a king who tried to dissolve the National Assembly as soon as he found some opposition to his wishes; of a king who worked six weeks, and quite cold-bloodedly, at the execution of a terrible plan to put the capital to fire and sword, in order to punish its unfortunate inhabitants for the generous support that they seemed to promise the representatives of the nation against the attacks of despotism . . ."
>
> —From Jean-Paul Marat, *L'Ami du Peuple,* December 29, 1790

**UNDERSTANDING CRAFT AND STRUCTURE**

1. **ANALYZING TEXT** What does the name "the Mountain" tell you about the radical group in the French Revolution? How do you think they earned this name?
2. **COMPARING POINTS OF VIEW** What do the actions of Austria, Prussia, Spain, Portugal, Britain, and the Dutch Republic after the execution of Louis XVI indicate about how they viewed his execution?

**ANALYZING PRIMARY SOURCES**

1. **DETERMINING CENTRAL IDEAS** What does Marat accuse King Louis XVI of?
2. **ANALYZING IDEAS** How does Marat's views of the king reflect those of the radicals in the French Revolution?

In early 1793, the Mountain convinced the Convention to pass a decree condemning Louis XVI to death. On January 21, the king was beheaded on the guillotine. Revolutionaries had adopted this machine because it killed quickly and, they thought, humanely. The king's execution created new enemies for the revolution, both at home and abroad. A new crisis was at hand.

The execution of King Louis XVI reinforced the trend toward a new radical phase. The local government in Paris—the Commune—had a number of working-class leaders who wanted radical change. Led by Georges Danton, it put constant pressure on the National Convention to adopt more radical measures. Moreover, the National Convention itself still did not rule all of France.

Gilchrist, J. and Murray, W. J. 1971. The Press in the French Revolution: A Selection of Documents taken from the Press of the Revolution for the years 1789-1794. New York: Ginn & Company Ltd.

*This print by Faucher-Gudin depicts Louis XVI's execution on January 21, 1793.*

**INTERPRETING** Why did the guillotine replace previous execution methods during the Revolution?

Peasants in western France, as well as many people in France's major cities, refused to accept the authority of the Convention.

A foreign crisis also loomed large. After Louis XVI was executed, a coalition of Austria, Prussia, Spain, Portugal, Britain, and the Dutch Republic took up arms against France. The French armies began to fall back. By late spring 1793, the coalition was poised to invade. It seemed possible that the revolution would be destroyed and the old regime reestablished.

### ✓ CHECKING FOR UNDERSTANDING

1. **SUMMARIZING** What radical steps did the National Convention take?
2. **DETERMINING CONTEXT** Why did the French Revolution become more radical?

## THE REIGN OF TERROR

**GUIDING QUESTION** *How did the new French government deal with crises?*

To meet these crises, the National Convention gave broad powers to a special committee of 12 known as the Committee of Public Safety. This led to democratic despotism, where democratically elected leaders began to act as dictators or tyrants. For instance, the Committee came to be dominated by the radical Jacobin Maximilien Robespierre. For approximately a year during 1793 and 1794, the Committee of Public Safety took control of the government. To defend France from **domestic** threats, the Committee adopted policies that became known as the Reign of Terror.

As a temporary measure, revolutionary courts were set up to prosecute counterrevolutionaries and traitors. Almost 40,000 people were killed during the French Reign of Terror. Of those, 16,000 people, including Marie Antoinette and Olympe de Gouges, died by the guillotine. Most executions occurred in towns that had openly rebelled against the Convention.

Revolutionary armies were set up to bring rebellious cities under the control of the Convention. The Committee of Public Safety decided to make an example of Lyon, a city that rebelled during a time when the Republic was in peril, and 1,880 citizens of Lyon were executed. When guillotining proved too slow, the condemned were shot with grapeshot (a cluster of small iron balls) into open graves. A foreign witness wrote:

> "Whole ranges of houses, always the most handsome, burnt. The churches, convents, and all the dwellings of the former patricians were in ruins. When I came to the guillotine, the blood of those who had been executed a few hours beforehand was still running in the street . . . I said to a group of sans-culottes. . . that it would be decent to clear away all this human blood.— Why should it be cleared? one of them said to me. It's the blood of aristocrats and rebels. The dogs should lick it up."

—quoted in *The Oxford History of the French Revolution*

**ANALYZING KEY IDEAS AND DETAILS**

1. **CITING TEXT EVIDENCE** Based on the information in the text, what types of people suffered under the Reign of Terror?
2. **ANALYZING IDEAS** What is meant by the phrase "Reign of Terror"? What effect does referring to this period in history by this name create?

**DETERMINING MEANING**

The word **domestic** comes from the Latin word *domus*, which means "house." How does the origin of the word *domestic* help you to better understand its meaning?

In western France, too, revolutionary armies were brutal and merciless in defeating rebels. Perhaps the most notorious violence occurred in the city of Nantes, where victims were executed by being loaded onto and then sunk in barges in the Loire River.

People from all classes were killed during the Terror. Clergy and nobles made up about 15 **percent** of the victims, while the rest were from the Third Estate. The Committee of Public Safety held that all this bloodletting was only temporary. When the war and domestic crisis were over, the true "Republic of Virtue" would follow, and the Declaration of the Rights of Man and the Citizen would be realized.

**DETERMINING MEANING**

The word **percent** comes from the phrase *per centum,* which is Latin for "by the hundred." How might knowing the meaning of this phrase help a person determine the meaning of *percent*?

In addition to the Terror, the Committee of Public Safety took other steps to control and shape a French society. Robespierre called this new order the Republic of Virtue—a democratic republic composed of good citizens. As outward signs of support for the republic, the titles "citizen" and "citizeness" were to replace "mister" and "madame." Women wore long dresses inspired by the clothing worn in the ancient Roman Republic.

Good citizens would be formed by good education. A law aimed at primary education for all was passed but not widely implemented. Another law abolished slavery in French colonies.

Because people were alarmed about high inflation, the Committee tried to control the prices of essential goods such as food, fuel, and clothing. The controls did not work well because the government had no way to enforce them.

From the beginning, women had been active participants in the revolution, although they had no official power. During the radical stage of the revolution, women observed sessions of the National Convention and were not shy about making their demands.

In 1793, two women founded the Society for Revolutionary Republican Women in Paris. Most members were working-class women who asserted that they were ready to defend the republic. Most men, however, believed that women should not participate in either politics or the military.

*Parade in Paris ridiculing Christianity and the Church, 1793*

**DETERMINING CONTEXT** Why, by 1793, would some Parisians hold a parade mocking the Church?

*The Battle of Valmy was a victory for the French over the Austrians.*

The Convention also pursued a policy of de-Christianization. Its members believed that the Catholic religion encouraged superstition rather than the use of reason. The word *saint* was removed from street names, churches were looted and closed by revolutionary armies, and priests were encouraged to marry. In Paris, the cathedral of Notre Dame, the center of the Catholic religion in France, was designated a "temple of reason." In November 1793, a public ceremony dedicated to the worship of reason was held in the former cathedral. Patriotic young girls dressed in white dresses paraded before a temple of reason where the high altar had once stood.

Another example of de-Christianization was the adoption of a new calendar. Years would no longer be numbered from the birth of Jesus but from September 22, 1792—the first day of the French Republic. The calendar contained 12 months. Each month consisted of three 10-day weeks, with the tenth day of each week a day of rest.

These changes in the calendar had a significant effect on religion in France, eliminating Sundays, Sunday worship services, and church holidays. Robespierre came to realize, however, that most French people would not accept these efforts at de-Christianization. France was still overwhelmingly Catholic.

**IDENTIFYING CONNECTIONS**
How did the execution of Louis XVI lead to the foreign crisis of 1793?

### ✓ CHECKING FOR UNDERSTANDING

1. **INTERPRETING** Why did the French government use force against its own people?
2. **EXPLAINING EFFECTS** How did the new French government deal with crises?
3. **SUMMARIZING** What was the desired effect of the Reign of Terror?

## A NATION IN ARMS

**GUIDING QUESTION** *How did the new French government deal with crises?*

As foreign troops gathered on its borders, the revolution seemed to be in danger. To save the republic, the Committee of Public Safety issued a decree to raise an army:

> "Young men will fight, young men are called to conquer. Married men will forge arms, transport military baggage and guns and will prepare food supplies. Women, who at long last are to take their rightful place in the revolution and follow their true destiny, will forget their futile tasks: their delicate hands will work at making clothes for soldiers; they will make tents and they will extend their tender care to shelters where the defenders of the *Patrie* [homeland] will receive the help that their wounds require. Children will make lint of old cloth. It is for them that we are fighting: children, those beings destined to gather all the fruits of the revolution, will raise their pure hands toward the skies. And old men, performing their missions again, as of yore, will be guided to the public squares of the cities where they will kindle the courage of young warriors and preach the doctrines of hate for kings and the unity of the Republic."
>
> —from the mobilization decree, August 23, 1793

**ANALYZING KEY IDEAS AND DETAILS**

1. **CITING TEXT EVIDENCE** How does the excerpt from the mobilization decree of August 23, 1793, support the text?
2. **SUMMARIZING** How did the French deal with the pressures they faced at this stage in the revolution?

In less than a year, the new French government had raised a huge army—by September 1794, it had more than a million soldiers. It was the largest army ever seen in Europe, and it pushed the invaders back across the Rhine. It even conquered the Austrian Netherlands. In earlier times, wars were the business of rulers who fought rivals with professional soldiers. The new French army was created by a people's government. Its wars were now people's wars.

By the summer of 1794, the French had largely defeated their foreign foes. There was less need for the Reign of Terror, but it continued nonetheless. Robespierre was obsessed with ridding France of all the corrupt elements. Many in the National Convention who feared Robespierre decided to act, lest they be the next victims. They gathered enough votes to condemn him, and Robespierre was guillotined on July 28, 1794.

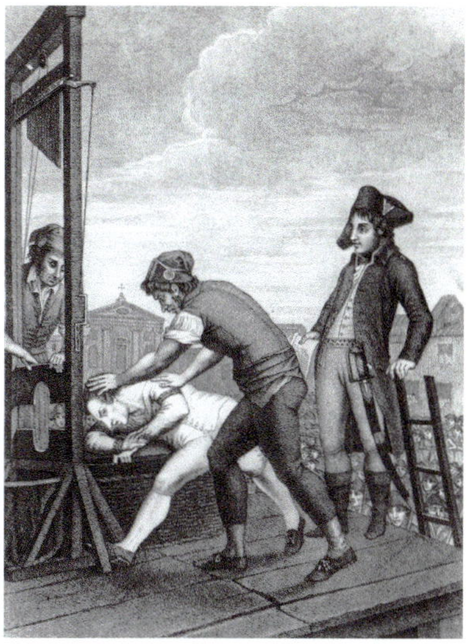

▲ *Execution of Robespierre on July 28, 1794*

## ✓ CHECKING FOR UNDERSTANDING

1. **IDENTIFYING CONNECTIONS** How did the French army become the people's army?
2. **IDENTIFYING EFFECTS** What did the new French army accomplish?
3. **EXPLAINING CAUSES** Why did the National Convention choose to execute Robespierre in 1794?

# THE DIRECTORY

**GUIDING QUESTION** *How did the constant transition within the French government influence its effectiveness?*

After the death of Robespierre, a reaction set in as more moderate middle-class leaders took control. The Reign of Terror came to a halt. The National Convention reduced the power of the Committee of Public Safety. Churches were allowed to reopen. Finally, the Constitution of 1791 was scrapped and a new constitution was created.

The Constitution of 1795 set up two legislative houses. A lower house, the Council of 500, drafted laws. An upper house of 250, the Council of Elders, accepted or rejected proposed laws. Members of both houses were chosen by **electors,** or qualified voters. Only those who owned or rented property worth a certain amount could be electors—only 30,000 people in the whole nation qualified. This was a significant change from the universal male suffrage the Paris Commune had demanded.

Under the new constitution, the executive was a committee of five called the Directory, chosen by the Council of Elders. The Directory, which lasted from 1795 to 1799, became known mainly for corruption. People reacted against the sufferings and sacrifices that had been demanded in the Reign of Terror. Some people made fortunes from government contracts or by loaning the government money at very high interest rates. They took advantage of the government's severe money problems during these difficult times.

At the same time, the government of the Directory faced political enemies from both conservatives and radicals. Some people wanted to bring back the monarchy, while others plotted to create a more radical regime like Robespierre's. Likewise, economic problems continued with no solution in sight. Finally, France was still conducting expensive wars against foreign enemies.

### UNDERSTANDING CRAFT AND STRUCTURE

1. **ANALYZING TEXT** The text in the third paragraph describes the character of the government that followed the Reign of Terror. What does this description suggest about further reactions within France?
2. **DETERMINING MEANING** The text states that Napoleon "toppled" the Directory. What might the word *topple* mean in this context? What other elements of the text help support this meaning?

### DETERMINING MEANING

The word **elector** means "chooser" in Latin. How does this word origin help the reader better understand the role of the electors in Revolutionary France?

To stay in power, the Directory began to rely on the military, but one military leader turned on the government. In 1799 the successful and popular general Napoleon Bonaparte toppled the Directory in a **coup d'état** (KOO day • TAH), a sudden overthrow of the government. Napoleon then seized power.

## COMPARING TWO REVOLUTIONS

The American Revolution and the French Revolution had many causes in common. The impulses for both revolutions grew out of Enlightenment ideas about personal freedom and the power of the state. In the American colonies, these ideas appeared in the writings of Thomas Paine and Thomas Jefferson. In France, they appeared in the works of Jean-Jacques Rousseau.

Although both revolutions had similar inspirations, their outcomes were quite different. American colonists gained independence, but the monarchy remained intact in Great Britain. In France, however, revolutionaries overthrew the monarchy quickly and violently, executing the king.

Participants of both revolutions were quick to organize new governments based on Enlightenment principles. The Constitution in America was formed through heated debate and several compromises, but little violence. The French Revolution ended quite differently. Although the monarchy was ended, the new democratic government soon gave way to despotic figures such as Robespierre and Napoleon. The horrific violence of the Terror, too, darkened the outcome of the French Revolution. Despite these bleak periods, the French people remained committed to Enlightenment ideas, and the spirit of "Liberty, Equality, and Fraternity" continues to inspire French government and social life.

### ✓ CHECKING FOR UNDERSTANDING

1. **EXPLAINING EFFECTS** Did the transition from the Committee of Public Safety to the Directory help respond to the French people's needs?

2. **IDENTIFYING CONNECTIONS** How was the Directory a response to the abuses of the Terror?

## LESSON 2 REVIEW

### Time and Place

1. **UNDERSTANDING CONTEXT** Explain how the coup d'état in which Napoleon took part differed from other transitions in the revolutionary French government.

### Building History-Social Science Analysis Skills

2. **SUMMARIZING** Use your notes to write a paragraph describing the actions taken by the National Convention and some of the consequences of these actions.

3. **RELATING EVENTS** Consider the changes that occurred during the French Revolution. Why did the French Revolution become more radical? How did this change reflect changes in French values?

4. **DETERMINING CONTEXT** How did the monarchy deal with crises? How did the new French government react differently?

### Writing About History

5. **EXPLANATORY WRITING** Write an essay tracing the changes in the French government between the Constitution of 1791 and the Constitution of 1795. Include defining characteristics of each new form of government and how it led to the next change in leadership.

### Collaborating

6. **INTEGRATING INFORMATION** With a partner, list the different French governments that followed the fall of the monarchy. How did this lack of stability influence the government's effectiveness?

## ESSENTIAL QUESTIONS

- *What causes revolution?*
- *How does revolution change society?*

LESSON 3

# The Rise of Napoleon and the Napoleonic Wars

## THE STORY BEGINS...

After the years of chaos in revolutionary France, Napoleon Bonaparte was a very different type of figure. He inspired fear and respect but also brought stability to France. After seizing control of the government, Napoleon gave this account of the event in his own words:

> "Each party in turn came to me, confided to me their designs, imparted their secrets, and requested my support. I refused to be the man of a party....
>
> The factions, intimidated, dispersed and fled. The majority, freed from their assaults, returned freely and peaceably into the hall; listened to the propositions made for the public safety, deliberated, and drew up the salutary resolution which will become the new and provisional law of the Republic.
>
> Frenchmen, you doubtless recognise in this conduct the zeal of a soldier of liberty, of a citizen devoted to the Republic. Conservative, tutelary, and liberal ideas resumed their authority upon the dispersion of the factions, who domineered in the Councils, and who, in rendering themselves the most odious of men, did not cease to be the most contemptible."

—*Napoleon's Account of his Coup d'État,* September 10, 1799

Napoleon was an impressive warrior and a careful politician. He appealed to the virtues of the Republic and its citizens. His true loyalties rested with himself and with power.

*Napoleon Bonaparte gained fame with his military skill. As Emperor of France, he would conquer much of Europe.* ▶

| Achievements of Napoleon's Rule |
| --- |
| |
| |
| |
| |

**ANALYZING KEY IDEAS AND DETAILS**

**SUMMARIZING** Read closely to identify the actions taken by the National Convention during the French Revolution. Record each action in a graphic organizer like this one.

# THE RISE OF NAPOLEON

**ANALYZING KEY IDEAS AND DETAILS**

1. **CITING TEXT EVIDENCE** What evidence from the text suggests that Napoleon knew how to run a powerful state like France?
2. **SUMMARIZING** Briefly summarize in your own words the information in "The Rise of Napoleon" section.

**GUIDING QUESTION** *How did instability in the French government create an opportunity for Napoleon to take power?*

Napoleon Bonaparte's role in the French Revolution is complex. In one sense, he brought it to an end when he came to power in 1799. Yet he was a product of the revolution as well. Without it, he would never have risen to power, and he himself never failed to remind the French that he had preserved the best parts of the revolution during his reign as emperor.

## EARLY LIFE

Napoleon was born in 1769 in Corsica, an island in the Mediterranean, only a few months after France had annexed the island. His father came from minor nobility in Italy, but the family was not rich. Napoleon was talented, however, and won a scholarship to a famous military school.

When he completed his studies, Napoleon was commissioned as a lieutenant in the French army. Although he became one of the world's greatest generals and a man beloved by his soldiers, there were few signs of his future success at this stage. He spoke with an Italian accent and was not popular with his fellow officers.

Napoleon devoted himself to his goals. He read what French philosophers had to say about reason, and he studied famous military campaigns. When revolution and war with Europe came about, there were many opportunities for Napoleon to use his knowledge and skills.

## MILITARY SUCCESSES

Napoleon rose quickly through the ranks. In 1792 he became a captain. Two years later, at age 24, the Committee of Public Safety made him a brigadier general. In 1796 he became commander of the French armies in Italy. There Napoleon won a series of battles with speed, surprise, and decisive action. He also defeated the armies of the Papal States and their Austrian allies. These victories gave France control of northern Italy.

Throughout the Italian campaigns, Napoleon's energy and initiative earned him the devotion of his troops. His personal qualities and his charisma allowed him to win the support of those around him. In 1797 he returned to France as a beloved hero. He was given command of an army in training to invade Britain, a constant enemy of France. Napoleon knew, however, that the French could not carry out that invasion. Instead, Napoleon suggested striking indirectly at Britain by taking Egypt.

*The Coronation of the Emperor Napoleon I* by Jacques-Louis David

**INTERPRETING** How does David want his viewer to see Napoleon in this painting?

Jacques Louis David/Getty Images

Egypt lay on the route to India, one of Britain's most important colonies and a major source of its wealth. The British were a great sea power and controlled the Mediterranean. By 1799, the British had defeated the French naval forces supporting Napoleon's army in Egypt. Seeing certain defeat, Napoleon abandoned his army and returned to Paris.

## CONSUL AND EMPEROR

In Paris, Napoleon took part in the coup d'état of 1799 that overthrew the Directory and set up a new government, the **consulate**. In theory, it was a republic, but, in fact, Napoleon held absolute power. Napoleon was called first consul, a title borrowed from ancient Rome. He appointed officials, controlled the army, conducted foreign affairs, and influenced the legislature. In 1802 Napoleon was made consul for life. Two years later, he crowned himself Emperor Napoleon I.

**DETERMINING MEANING**

The word **consulate** comes from the Latin root meaning "to take counsel." How does knowing its root help you understand this post-revolutionary government?

## PEACE WITH THE CHURCH

One of Napoleon's first moves at home was to establish peace with the Catholic Church. In matters of religion, Napoleon was a man of the Enlightenment. He believed in reason and felt religion was at most a social convenience. However, because most of France was Catholic, it was a good idea to mend relations with the Church.

In 1801 Napoleon came to an agreement with the pope, which recognized Catholicism as the religion of a majority of the French people. In return, the pope would not ask for the return of the Church lands seized in the revolution.

> "In consequence, after this mutual recognition, as well for the benefit of religion as for the maintenance of internal tranquility, they [The French Republic and the Vatican] have agreed as follows:

**ANALYZING PRIMARY SOURCES**

1. **DETERMINING CENTRAL IDEAS** What is the core of the agreement made in the text of this document?
2. **ANALYZING IDEAS** What did this agreement change in France? How did it help the government establish peace with the Catholic Church?

> 1. The catholic, apostolic and Roman religion shall be freely exercised in France: its worship shall be public, and in conformity with the police regulations which the government shall deem necessary for the public tranquility . . . .
>
> 6. Before entering upon their functions, the bishops shall take directly, at the hands of the First Consul, the oath of fidelity which was in use before the change of government, expressed in the following terms: 'I swear and promise to God, upon the holy scriptures, to remain in obedience and fidelity to the government established by the constitution of the French Republic. I also promise not to have any intercourse, nor to assist by any council, nor to support any league, either within or without, which is inimical to the public tranquility; and if, within my diocese or elsewhere, I learn that anything to the prejudice of the state is being contrived, I will make it known to the government.' ”
>
> —From *Concordat with Pope Pius VII,* 1801–1802

With this agreement, the Catholic Church was no longer an enemy of the French government. It also meant that people who had acquired Church lands in the revolution became avid supporters of Napoleon.

**MAKING CONNECTIONS**

### THE INFLUENCE OF THE NAPOLEONIC CODE

The Napoleonic Code had a substantial and lasting influence in many countries around the world. The Code was implemented in many European and Latin American countries throughout the nineteenth century forming the foundation for civil law systems in countries such as Spain, Italy, Portugal, Belgium, Poland, and the Netherlands as well as Haiti, the Dominican Republic, Chile, Bolivia, Ecuador, Colombia, Uruguay, and Argentina. While the influence of the Code lessened in the twentieth century as some countries introduced new civil codes, these new codes continued to be influenced in part by the Napoleonic Code.

## CODIFICATION OF THE LAWS

Napoleon's most famous domestic achievement was to codify the laws. Before the revolution, France had almost 300 different legal systems. During the revolution, efforts were made to prepare a single law code for the nation. However, the work was not completed until Napoleon's reign.

Seven law codes were created, but the most important was the Civil Code, or Napoleonic Code, introduced in 1804. It preserved many of the principles the revolutionaries had fought for: equality of all citizens before the law, the right of the individual to choose a profession, religious toleration, and the abolition of serfdom and all feudal obligations.

For women and children, the Civil Code was a step back. During the radical stage of the revolution, new laws had made divorce easier and allowed children, even daughters, to inherit property on an equal basis. The Civil Code undid these laws. Women were now "less equal than men." When they married, they lost control over any property they had. They could not testify in court, and it became more difficult for them to begin divorce proceedings. In general, the code treated women like children, who needed protection and who did not have a public role.

## A NEW BUREAUCRACY

Napoleon also developed a powerful, centralized administrative machine. He focused on developing a bureaucracy of **capable** officials. Early on, the regime showed that it did not care about rank or birth. Public officials and military officers alike were promoted based on their ability. Opening careers to men of talent was a reform that the middle class had clamored for before the revolution.

Napoleon also created a new aristocracy based on meritorious service to the nation. Between 1808 and 1814, Napoleon created about 3,200 nobles. Nearly 60 percent were military officers, while the rest were civil service or state and local officials. Socially, only 22 percent of this new aristocracy were from noble families of the old regime; about 60 percent were middle class in origin.

Anderson, Frank Maloy. 1904. The Constitutions and Other Select Documents Illustrative of the History of France 1789-1901. Minneapolis: The H. W. Wilson Company.

## PRESERVER OF THE REVOLUTION?

In his domestic policies, then, Napoleon did keep some major reforms of the French Revolution. Under the Civil Code, all citizens were equal before the law. The concept of opening government careers to more people was another gain of the revolution that he retained.

On the other hand, Napoleon destroyed some revolutionary ideals. Liberty was replaced by a despotism that grew increasingly arbitrary, in spite of protests by such citizens as the prominent writer Anne-Louise-Germaine de Staël. Napoleon shut down 60 of France's 73 newspapers and banned books, including de Staël's. He insisted that all manuscripts be subjected to government scrutiny before they were published. Even the mail was opened by government police.

### ✓ CHECKING FOR UNDERSTANDING

1. **EXPLAINING EFFECTS** How did Napoleon's Civil Code address the problems with the French legal system that had existed since before the Revolution?
2. **IDENTIFYING CONNECTIONS** How did instability in the French government create an opportunity for Napoleon to take power?
3. **SUMMARIZING** How did relations between the government and the Catholic Church change under Napoleon?

**ANALYZING PRIMARY SOURCES**

**NAPOLEON'S REIGN**

"What is the throne?—a bit of wood gilded and covered with velvet—I am the state—I alone am here the representative of the people. Even if I had done wrong you should not have reproached me in public—people wash their dirty linen at home. France has more need of me than I of France."

—Napoleon, quoted in *The History of Napoleon Buonaparte*

**DRAWING CONCLUSIONS** How did Napoleon understand his role as leader of the French people?

# NAPOLEON'S EMPIRE

**GUIDING QUESTIONS** *Why would changes in France cause concern in other European countries? How did Napoleon's military background shape his perspective?*

Napoleon is, of course, known less for his domestic policies than for his military leadership. His conquests began soon after he rose to power.

## BUILDING THE EMPIRE

When Napoleon became consul in 1799, France was at war with a European coalition of Russia, Great Britain, and Austria. Napoleon realized the need for a pause in the war. "The French Revolution is not finished," he said, "so long as the scourge of war lasts . . . . I want peace, as much to settle the present French government, as to save the world from chaos." In 1802 a peace treaty was signed, but it did not last long. War with Britain broke out again in 1803. Gradually, Britain was joined by Austria, Russia, Sweden, and Prussia. In a series of battles at Ulm, Austerlitz, Jena, and Eylau from 1805 to 1807, Napoleon's Grand Army defeated the Austrian, Prussian, and Russian armies.

From 1807 to 1812, Napoleon was the master of Europe. His Grand Empire was composed of three major parts: the French Empire, dependent states, and allied states. The French Empire was the inner core of the Grand Empire. It consisted of an enlarged France extending to the Rhine in the east and including the western half of Italy north of Rome.

Dependent states were kingdoms ruled by relatives of Napoleon. Eventually these included Spain, Holland, the kingdom of Italy, the Swiss Republic, the Grand Duchy of Warsaw, and the Confederation of the Rhine—a union of all German states except Austria and Prussia. Allied states were countries defeated by Napoleon and then forced to join his struggle against Britain. These states included Prussia, Austria, Russia, and Sweden.

**UNDERSTANDING CRAFT AND STRUCTURE**

1. **ANALYZING TEXT PRESENTATION** Read the sub-section "Building the Empire." What is being emphasized by the phrase, "From 1807 to 1812, Napoleon was the master of Europe"?
2. **ANALYZING TEXT** What clue does the phrase "the nobility and the clergy...lost their special privileges" tell you about the values Napoleon wished to spread across Europe?

Doyle, William. 1989. The Oxford History of the French Revolution. Oxford University Press.

## NAPOLEONIC EUROPE 1799–1812

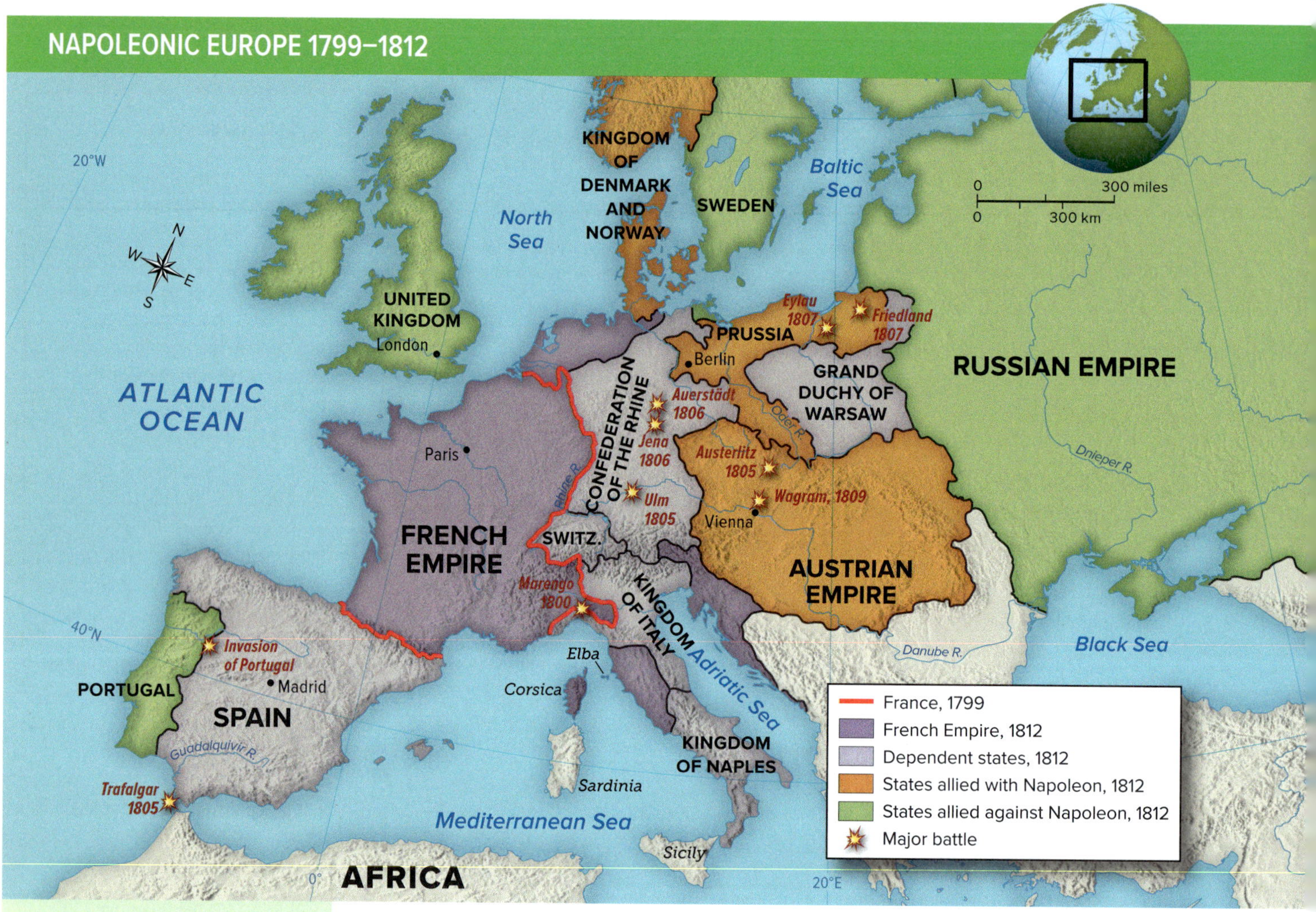


### GEOGRAPHIC REASONING

Napoleon's Grand Empire spread over much of Europe.

1. **SPATIAL THINKING** Why might Napoleon have chosen to ally with states instead of taking them over?
2. **EXPLORING PLACE** What role did the physical geography of Europe play in the rise and spread of Napoleon's empire?

## SPREADING THE PRINCIPLES OF THE REVOLUTION

Within his empire, Napoleon sought to spread some of the principles of the French Revolution, including legal equality, religious toleration, and economic freedom. In the inner core and dependent states of his Grand Empire, Napoleon tried to destroy the old order. The nobility and the clergy everywhere in these states lost their special privileges. Napoleon decreed equality of opportunity with offices open to those with ability, equality before the law, and religious toleration. The spread of French revolutionary principles was an important factor in the development of **liberal** traditions in many of these countries.

Napoleon hoped that his Grand Empire would last for centuries, but his empire collapsed almost as rapidly as it was formed. Two major reasons help explain this collapse: Britain's ability to resist Napoleon and the rise of a new force known as nationalism.

### DETERMINING MEANING

The word **liberal** has the same root as the word *liberated*. Something or someone that is *liberated* is free. How might knowing the meaning of *liberated* help a person determine the meaning of *liberal*?

## BRITISH RESISTANCE

In spite of his military genius and powerful army, Napoleon was never able to conquer Great Britain. Great Britain was able to hold Napoleon at bay due to its sea power, which made it almost invulnerable. Napoleon hoped to invade Britain, but the British defeated the combined French-Spanish fleet at Trafalgar off the coast of Spain in 1805. This battle permanently weakened his navy and ended any plans Napoleon might have had for an invasion.

Unable to beat Great Britain at sea, Napoleon then turned to his "Continental System" in an effort to defeat the island nation. The aim of the Continental System was to stop British goods from reaching the European continent to be sold there. By weakening Britain economically, Napoleon would destroy its ability to wage war.

The Continental System also failed. Allied states resented being told by Napoleon that they could not trade with the British. Some began to cheat. Others resisted. Furthermore, new markets in the Middle East and in Latin America gave Britain new outlets for its goods. Indeed, by 1810, British overseas exports were at near-record highs.

## A NEW FORCE

A second significant factor in the defeat of Napoleon was **nationalism**. One of the most important forces of the nineteenth century, nationalism is the sense of unique identity of a people based on common language, religion, and national symbols. A new era was born when the French people decided that they were the nation.

Napoleon marched his armies through the German states, Spain, Italy, and Poland, arousing new ideas of nationalism in two ways. First, the conquered peoples became united in their hatred of the invaders, and they banded together to resist their conquerors. Second, the conquered peoples saw the power and strength of national feeling. It was a lesson not lost on them or their rulers.

**DETERMINING MEANING**

Read the text of the paragraph that contains the word **nationalism**. Which words in the paragraph provide context clues you can use to determine the meaning of *nationalism*?

### ✓ CHECKING FOR UNDERSTANDING

1. **IDENTIFYING EFFECTS** What were the consequences for a country conquered by Napoleon's Grand Army?
2. **UNDERSTANDING CONTEXT** Why would changes in France cause concern in other European countries? How did Napoleon's military background shape his perspective?
3. **IDENTIFYING CAUSES** How did nationalism contribute to the defeat of Napoleon?

## LESSON 3 REVIEW

### Time and Place

1. **UNDERSTANDING CHANGE** Explain how instability in the French government allowed Napoleon the chance to take power.
2. **DETERMINING CONTEXT** What does the origin of the word *consul* suggest about why Napoleon chose to use the Roman term to describe his new government?

### Building History-Social Science Analysis Skills

3. **EXPLAINING ISSUES** Explain what nationalism is and describe the role it played in Napoleon's fall from power.
4. **COMPARING** What were some of Napoleon's achievements, and how did they compare to those of the revolutionary government? Compare the achievements of Napoleon to those of the French government during the Reign of Terror.

### Writing About History

5. **ARGUMENTATIVE WRITING** Write an essay analyzing whether or not Napoleon preserved the ideals of the French Revolution through his domestic and foreign policies. Choose one side using support from the text.

### Collaborating

6. **EVALUATING** With a partner, list ways in which Napoleon's military background shaped his perspective on leadership and government.

ESSENTIAL QUESTIONS

- *What causes revolution?*
- *How does revolution change society?*

LESSON 4

# The Fall of Napoleon and the European Reaction

## THE STORY BEGINS...

Toward the end of his reign, it became clear to many people in France that Napoleon Bonaparte's ideals were at odds with those of the Revolution. One of his critics, French writer and political activist Benjamin Constant, wrote the following about him when the then-former ruler was in exile:

> "When he first arrived here, alone, out of poverty and obscurity, and until he was twenty-four, his greedy gaze wandering over the country around him, why did we show him a country in which any religious idea was the object of irony? When he listened to what was professed in our circles, why did serious thinkers tell him that man had no other motivation than his own interest? If he discovered easily enough that all the subtle interpretations through which, once the principle had been stated, we sought to elude its implications, were illusory, it was because his instinct was sound and his judgment quick. As I never attributed to him virtues which he did not possess, I am not obliged to deny him the faculties which he did. If in the heart of man there is nothing but interest, tyranny has only to frighten or to seduce him in order to dominate him."
>
> —Benjamin Constant, from *The Spirit of Conquest and Usurpation,* 1814

Though he remained a hero to much of France, most of Europe had come to see Napoleon as a tyrant.

*After being sentenced to exile in 1814, Napoleon says an emotional good-bye to his Imperial Guard.* ▶

| Napoleon's Downfall | Europe's Response |
|---|---|
| | |
| | |
| | |

**ANALYZING KEY IDEAS AND DETAILS**

**SUMMARIZING** Read closely to identify the actions and events that led to Napoleon's downfall and how Europe responded. Record each action in a graphic organizer like this one.

# THE FALL OF NAPOLEON

**GUIDING QUESTION** *How did Napoleon lose his empire?*

Napoleon's downfall began in 1812 when he decided to invade Russia. Within only a few years, his fall was complete.

The Russians had refused to remain in the Continental System, leaving Napoleon with little choice but to invade. He knew the risks in invading such a large country, but he also knew that if he did not punish the Russians for ignoring the Continental System, other nations would follow suit.

In June 1812, a Grand Army of more than 600,000 men entered Russia. Napoleon's hopes depended on a quick victory over the Russians, but they refused to do battle. Instead they retreated for hundreds of miles. As they retreated, they burned their own villages and countryside to keep Napoleon's army from finding food. When the Russians did fight at Borodino, Napoleon's forces won an indecisive victory, which cost many lives.

Finally reaching Moscow, the Grand Army found the city ablaze. With no food or supplies for his army, Napoleon abandoned the Russian capital in late October. As the winter snows began, Napoleon led the "Great Retreat" west across Russia. Thousands of soldiers starved and froze along the way. Fewer than 40,000 of the original 600,000 soldiers arrived back in Poland in January 1813.

This military disaster led other European states to rise up and attack the crippled French army. Paris was captured in March 1814. Napoleon was soon sent into exile on the island of Elba, off the northwest coast of Italy. The victorious powers restored monarchy to France in the person of Louis XVIII, brother of the executed king, Louis XVI.

The new king had little support, and the French people were not ready to surrender the glory of empire. Nor was Napoleon ready to give up. Restless in exile, he left the island of Elba and slipped back into France. The new king sent troops to capture Napoleon, who opened his coat and addressed them: "Soldiers of the 5th regiment, I am your Emperor. . . . If there is a man among you [who] would kill his Emperor, here I am!"

No one fired a shot. Shouting "Long live the Emperor!" the troops went over to his side. On March 20, 1815, Napoleon entered Paris in triumph.

Russia, Great Britain, Austria, and Prussia again pledged to defeat the man they called the "Enemy and Disturber of the Tranquility of the World." Meanwhile, Napoleon raised another French army of devoted veterans who rallied from all over France. He then readied an attack on the allied troops stationed across the border in Belgium.

**ANALYZING KEY IDEAS AND DETAILS**

1. **CITING TEXT EVIDENCE** Identify text evidence that supports the claim that Napoleon's decision to invade Russia was a mistake that threatened his control of Europe.
2. **ANALYZING CENTRAL IDEAS** Explain how the central idea explains the section's title, "The Fall of Napoleon."

(t)Schom, Alan M. 1997. Napoleon Bonaparte. HarperCollins Publishers; (b)Conner, Susan P. 2004. The Age of Napoleon. Greenwood Press.

▲ *The burning of Moscow in October of 1812*

At Waterloo in Belgium on June 18, 1815, Napoleon met a combined British and Prussian army under the Duke of Wellington and suffered a bloody defeat. This time, the victorious allies exiled him to St. Helena, a small island in the south Atlantic. Napoleon remained in exile until his death in 1821, but his memory haunted French political life for many decades.

### ☑ CHECKING FOR UNDERSTANDING

1. **IDENTIFYING EFFECTS** How did Napoleon's disaster in Russia affect both his Grand Army and his nation?
2. **UNDERSTANDING CONTEXT** Why was Louis XVIII's reign not successful when the monarchy was restored in France?
3. **IDENTIFYING CONNECTIONS** What role did physical geography play in the loss of Napoleon's empire?

**ANALYZING KEY IDEAS AND DETAILS**

1. **ANALYZING EVENTS** Reread the paragraph that begins, "The haughty Austrian foreign minister . . . ." What part of this paragraph indicates that the monarchies of Europe believed it was possible to go back to a pre-Revolutionary status?
2. **DETERMINING CENTRAL IDEAS** What is the central idea of this section of the text?

## EUROPEAN REACTION

**GUIDING QUESTION** *Why did the turmoil of the French revolutionary years result in a conservative European reaction?*

After the defeat of Napoleon, European rulers moved to restore the old order. This was the goal of the victors—Great Britain, Austria, Prussia, and Russia—when they met at the Congress of Vienna in September 1814 to arrange a final peace settlement.

The haughty Austrian foreign minister, Prince Klemens von Metternich (MEH • tuhr • nihk), was the most influential leader at that meeting in Vienna. Metternich claimed that the principle of legitimacy guided him. He meant that lawful monarchs from the royal families who had ruled before Napoleon would be restored to their positions of power. This, they believed, would ensure peace and stability in Europe. The victorious powers had already restored the Bourbon king to the French throne in 1814.

Practical considerations of power were addressed at the Congress of Vienna. The great powers rearranged territories in Europe, believing this would form a new balance of power. The powers at Vienna wanted to keep any one country from dominating Europe. This meant balancing political and military forces that guaranteed the independence of the great powers. To balance Russian territorial gains, for example, new territories were given to Prussia and Austria.

The Second Treaty of Paris, signed on November 20, 1815, came after the final defeat of Napoleon. Among other things, it reset the borders of France to match those from 1790. It also required France to pay a heavy fine to the Allied nations. The Allied nations also set plans for the occupation of France and set rules on the future French military:

**ANALYZING PRIMARY SOURCES**

**DETERMINING CENTRAL IDEAS** Why did the treaty call for the occupation of France by Allied troops? Why do you think the language in this section of the treaty is so well chosen?

> "... .it has been judged indispensable to occupy, during a fixed time, by a corps of Allied Troops certain military positions along the frontiers of France, under the express reserve, that such occupation shall in no way prejudice the Sovereignty of His Most Christian Majesty, nor the state of possession, such as it is recognized and confirmed by the present Treaty. The number of these troops shall not exceed 150,000 men. . ."
>
> —from the Second Treaty of Paris, 1815

## EUROPE AFTER THE CONGRESS OF VIENNA 1815

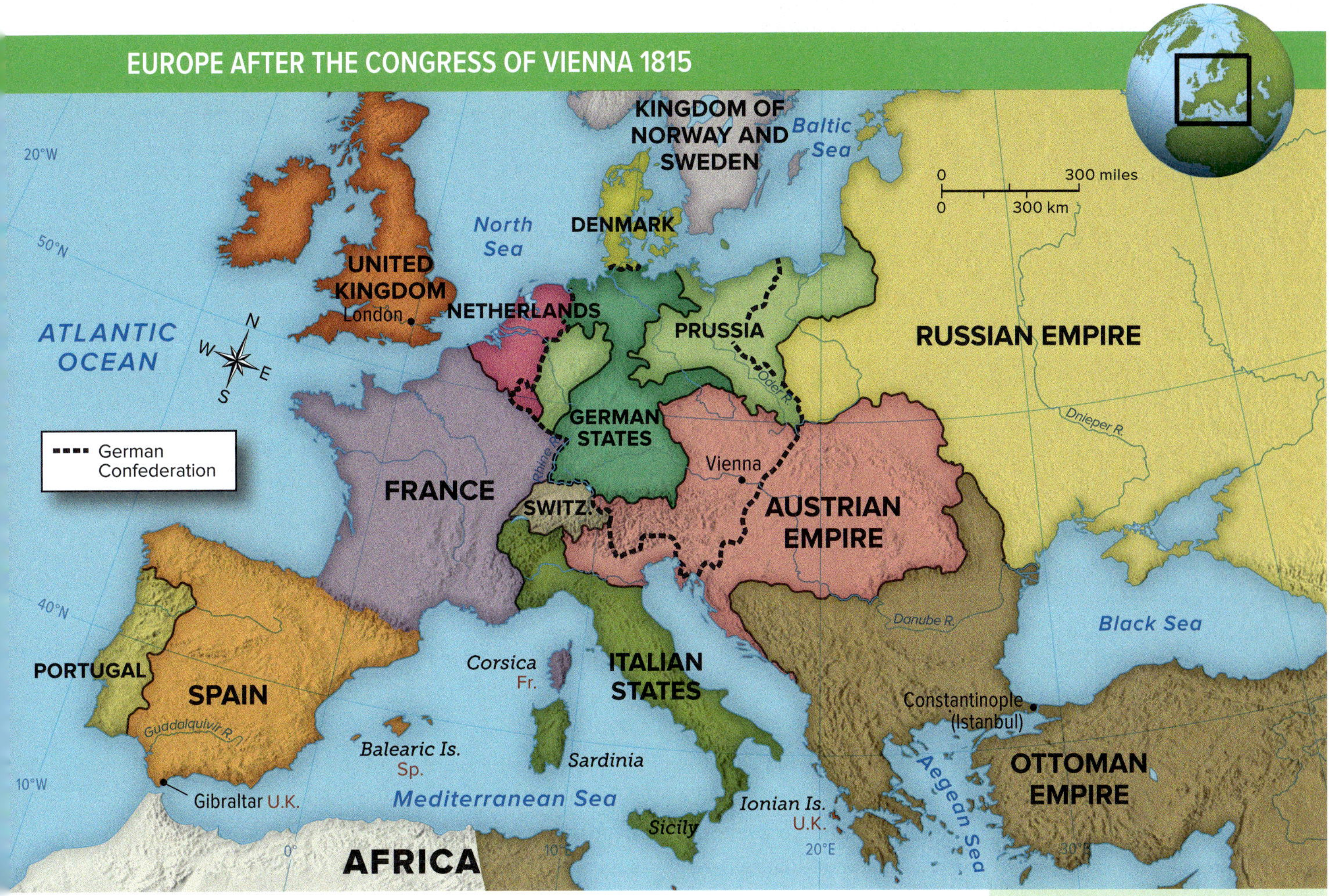


The arrangements worked out at the Congress of Vienna were a victory for rulers who wanted to contain the forces of change that the French Revolution had unleashed. These rulers, such as Metternich, believed in the political philosophy known as **conservatism**.

Most conservatives at that time favored obedience to political authority. They also believed that religion was crucial to keep order in society. Conservatives hated revolutions and were unwilling to accept demands from people who wanted either individual rights or representative governments.

To maintain the new balance of power, Great Britain, Russia, Prussia, and Austria (and later France) agreed to meet in conferences to discuss their common interests and to maintain peace in Europe. These meetings came to be called the Concert of Europe.

The great powers adopted a **principle of intervention**. According to this principle, they had the right to send armies into countries in order to restore legitimate monarchs to their thrones. Britain argued that they should not interfere in the internal affairs of other states. However, the other great powers used military force to end revolutions in Spain and Italy.

### ✓ CHECKING FOR UNDERSTANDING

1. **IDENTIFYING CONNECTIONS** Why did the turmoil of the French revolutionary years result in a conservative European reaction?

2. **INTERPRETING** What was the underlying goal of the Congress of Vienna?

### GEOGRAPHIC REASONING

The Congress of Vienna rearranged territories to maintain a balance of power.

1. **SPATIAL THINKING** Within what political boundaries is Vienna located?

2. **PATTERNS AND MOVEMENT** Compare this map to the map of Napoleonic Europe in Lesson 3. What countries gained territory from France after the Congress of Vienna?

### DETERMINING MEANING

The word **conservative** has the same root as the word *conserve*. To *conserve* something is to protect it from harm or destruction. How might knowing the meaning of *conserve* help a person determine the meaning of *conservative*?

# FORCES OF CHANGE

**GUIDING QUESTION** *What happened to revolutionary ideas after the Revolution?*

Between 1815 and 1830, conservative governments throughout Europe worked to maintain the old order. However, powerful forces for change—known as liberalism and nationalism—were also at work.

**ANALYZING KEY IDEAS AND DETAILS**

1. **DETERMINING CENTRAL IDEAS** What is the central idea of this section, and how does the development of the concepts of "liberalism" and "nationalism" help emphasize the central idea of this section?
2. **ANALYZING CENTRAL IDEAS** To what end does the author of this section reference the "American Bill of Rights"?

## LIBERALISM

Liberalism is a political philosophy that grew out of the Enlightenment. During the Enlightenment, a loose group of European and American intellectuals were part of what came to be called a "republic of letters." Most Enlightenment political thinkers are considered to have taken part in this informal group and it includes such names as the French philosophe Voltaire and the American Founder Benjamin Franklin. These thinkers wrote back and forth, exchanging Enlightenment ideas on the failures of monarchy, inequality in society, and the need for government reform. In this way, the revolutionary ideas of liberalism spread across Europe and America.

**DETERMINING MEANING**

Read the text of the paragraph that contains the word **liberalism**. Which words in the paragraph provide context clues you can use to determine the meaning of *liberalism*?

**Liberalism** held that people should be as free as possible from government restraint. Liberal beliefs included the protection of **civil** liberties, the basic rights of all people. Civil liberties included equality before the law and freedom of assembly, speech, and the press. Liberals believed that freedoms should be guaranteed by a document such as the American Bill of Rights.

**DETERMINING MEANING**

The word **civil** comes from the Latin word *civis*, which means "citizen." How does knowing its root help you determine the meaning of *civil*?

Many liberals favored a government ruled by a **constitution**—a concept called constitutionalism. For example, in a constitutional monarchy, a king or queen must follow the laws of the constitution. Liberals believed that written documents would help guarantee people's rights.

**DETERMINING MEANING**

To better understanding the meaning of the word **constitution**, consider its origin: *Constituere* is a Latin word that means "to establish" or "to appoint." Based on this information, write a definition of *constitution*. Use a dictionary or an online reference to check your definition.

Most liberals wanted religious toleration for all, as well as separation of church and state. Liberals also demanded the right of peaceful opposition to the government. They believed that a representative assembly (legislature) elected by qualified voters should make laws. These liberal ideals were similar to republicanism, the belief that a government's power comes from the rule of law and the citizens who are allowed to vote.

Liberals took their new and revolutionary ideas only so far. For instance, liberals believed the right to vote and to hold office should be open only to men of property. In different locations, certain groups of people, such as enslaved people in the United States, were denied citizenship or rights entirely. Liberalism was tied to middle-class men who wanted voting rights for themselves so they could share power with the landowning classes. The liberals feared mob rule and had little desire to let the lower classes share power.

The republican governments created by the American and French revolutionaries served as models of liberal ideas in action. For instance, a revolt led by military leaders enforced a liberal constitution in Spain in 1820. That same year, an uprising began in neighboring Portugal that resulted in the creation of a liberal constitution and government. Across the Atlantic, the people of Latin America and the Caribbean were also emboldened by revolutionary ideas. Most of the colonies in this region would fight for and gain their independence in the 1820s. Although they met with limited success, each new state arising from these revolutions would attempt to create a new republican government founded on liberal ideas.

## NATIONALISM

Nationalism arose when people began to identify themselves as part of a community—a nation—defined by a distinctive language, common institutions, customs, and in some cases religion. In earlier centuries, people's loyalty belonged to a king or queen or to their town or region. In the nineteenth century, people began to believe that their chief loyalty was to the nation.

Nationalism did not become a popular force for change until the French Revolution. From then on, nationalists came to believe that each nationality should have its own government. Thus, the Germans, who were separated into many principalities, wanted national unity under one central government in a newly united German state. Subject peoples, such as the Hungarians, wanted the right to establish their own governments.

Nationalism was a threat to the existing order. A united Germany would upset the balance of power set up at the Congress of Vienna in 1815. An independent Hungarian state would mean the breakup of the Austrian Empire. Conservatives feared such change and tried to repress nationalism.

Nationalism found a strong ally in liberalism. Most liberals believed that freedom could be possible only in people who ruled themselves. They now believed each group of people should have its own nation-state.

### ✓ CHECKING FOR UNDERSTANDING

1. **DETERMINING CONTEXT** Why did nationalism become popular after the French Revolution?
2. **ANALYZING CHANGE** What happened to revolutionary ideas after the French Revolution was over?
3. **IDENTIFYING CONNECTIONS** How were liberalism and republicanism connected?

**CITIZENSHIP**

### CONSTITUTIONS

A constitution is more than a simple list of rules or a code of laws. Constitutions include laws and basic principles under which a state is governed. Not only do they establish a framework for a government but they often guarantee the rights of the citizens who are governed by it. The oldest written constitution in the world belongs to the United States of America. Enshrining Enlightenment principles such as the separation of powers, representative government, and religious liberty, it has become a model for democratic and republican forms of government across the world.

1. **EVALUATING** Why is it important that a nation's laws be written?
2. **DETERMINING CONTEXT** Why would a supporter of Enlightenment ideals also support a constitution? How would a constitution help create a more stable, long-lasting government?

## LESSON 4 REVIEW

### Time and Place

1. **SUMMARIZING** In your own words, describe Napoleon's downfall and the various European responses to his downfall.
2. **EVALUATING** Explain why the turmoil of the French revolutionary years resulted in a conservative European reaction.

### Building History-Social Science Analysis Skills

3. **IDENTIFYING CONNECTIONS** Explain how the principle of interventionism is an idea based on conservatism.
4. **DRAWING CONCLUSIONS** How did Napoleon lose his empire?

### Writing About History

5. **EXPLANATORY WRITING** Using the narrative and outside research, write an essay describing Napoleon's invasion of Russia. Include his motivations for invasion, the logistical difficulties in carrying out the invasion, Russia's response, and the economic, political, and human toll of Napoleon's retreat.

### Collaborating

6. **EVALUATING POINT OF VIEW** With a partner, discuss how revolutionary ideas evolved after Napoleon's rule.

# WHO SHOULD BE A CITIZEN?

One definition of a citizen is a free person who owes loyalty to a nation and who receives protection, rights, and privileges in return. In France, the Declaration of the Rights of Man and the Citizen addressed social distinctions, but opinions differed on how to interpret the document. Read the excerpts from Robespierre and d'Aelders and study Fragonard's painting to see how they viewed citizenship and the continuing struggle for rights.

### VOCABULARY

*sovereignty:* power; authority

*equivalent:* same, of equal force

*decrees:* authoritative decisions; declarations

*enlightened:* knowledgeable, comprehending

*consecrate:* make sacred

*cantankerous:* having a bad disposition; quarrelsome

PRIMARY SOURCE: SPEECH

## CONDITIONS OF ELIGIBILITY

In 1789, Maximilien Robespierre stated his view on property requirements for holding office and voting.

> "Nothing is more in line with your declaration of rights, according to which all privileges, all distinctions, all exceptions must disappear. The Constitution establishes that **sovereignty** resides in the people, in all the individuals of the people. Each individual therefore has the right to participate in making the law which governs him and in the administration of the public good which is his own. If not, it is not true that all men are equal in rights, that every man is a citizen. If he who only pays a tax **equivalent** to a day of work has fewer rights than he who pays the equivalent to three days of work, and he who pays at the level of ten days has more rights than he whose tax only equals that value of three, then he who enjoys 100,000 livres [French pounds] of revenue has 100 times as many rights as he who only has 1,000 livres of revenue. It follows from all your **decrees** that every citizen has the right to participate in making the law and consequently that of being an elector or eligible for office without the distinction of wealth."

ANALYZE THE TEXT

1. **IDENTIFYING BIAS** What does Robespierre think about basing citizenship on whether a person has property or pays taxes?
2. **CITING TEXT EVIDENCE** What elements indicate Robespierre fears the current system could devolve into a new social order where some people have great power and others have none?

PRIMARY SOURCE: DOCUMENT

## THE INJUSTICES OF THE LAWS

D'Aelders expressed her opinions on the inequality of the sexes in 1790:

> ". . . justice must be the first virtue of free men, and justice demands that the laws be the same for all beings, like the air and the sun. And yet everywhere, the laws favor men at the expense of women, because everywhere power is in your hands. What! Will free men, an **enlightened** people living in a century of enlightenment and philosophy, will they **consecrate** what has been the abuse of power in a century of ignorance? . . . The prejudices with which our sex has been surrounded—supported by unjust laws which only accord us a secondary existence in society and which often force us into the humiliating necessity of winning over the **cantankerous** and ferocious character of a man, who, by the greed of those close to us has become our master—those prejudices have changed what was for us the sweetest and most saintly of duties, those of wife and mother, into a painful and terrible slavery. . . . Oh! Gentlemen, if you wish us to be enthusiastic about the happy constitution that gives back men their rights, then begin by being just toward us. From now on we should be your voluntary companions and not your slaves. Let us merit your attachment!"

ANALYZE THE TEXT

1. **ANALYZING IDEAS** What does d'Aelders mean by women's "secondary existence in society"?
2. **CITING TEXT EVIDENCE** What aspect of the d'Aelders excerpt suggests that she believes the Revolution has finally brought about a new way of thinking about the relationship between men and women?

Hunt, Lynn. Translated and edited 1996. The French Revolution and Human Rights: A Brief Documentary History. Boston/New York: Bedford/St. Martin's.

SECONDARY SOURCE: PAINTING

## "BOISSY D'ANGLAS SALUTES THE HEAD OF THE DEPUTY FERAUD, MAY 20, 1795," BY ALEXANDRE FRAGONARD

On May 20, 1795, an angry mob in the Convention hacked off the head of deputy Feraud and presented it to the chairman, Boissy d'Anglas, who saluted the head. After this incident, d'Anglas presented measures to take precautions against anarchy. Usually the crowds in the balcony were merely rowdy, insulting and threatening the deputies. At times like the one in the painting, they became a mob, invading the chamber and killing deputies with whom they disagreed.

▲ *Boissy d'Anglas salutes the head of the deputy Feraud, May 20, 1795,* by Alexandre Fragonard

### ANALYZE THE SOURCE

1. **UNDERSTANDING CONTEXT** What do you think Fragonard's opinion might have been of universal suffrage—the right of all citizens to vote?
2. **IDENTIFYING BIAS** Considering the date the painting was completed in 1831, what might we conclude about Fragonard's attitude to this more radical period of the Revolution?

### MULTIPLE PERSPECTIVES

1. **COMPARING AND CONTRASTING** Although Robespierre was not a supporter of equal rights for women, list some similarities between his and d'Aelders's arguments.
2. **ANALYZING TEXTS** How does d'Aelders's portrayal of women compare and contrast with Fragonard's?
3. **EVALUATING** How would you answer the question "Who should be a citizen?" Which source has a position most like your own? Which is most unlike your own? Why?

# STUDY GUIDE

## THE THREE ESTATES IN FRANCE
**LESSON 1**

### FIRST ESTATE
**CLERGY**
- 130,000 people, 0.5% of the population
- Owned 10% of the land
- Did not have to pay the taille

### SECOND ESTATE
**NOBILITY**
- 350,000 people, 2% of the population
- Owned 25 to 30% of the land
- Did not have to pay the taille

### THIRD ESTATE
**PEASANTS, WORKERS, BOURGEOISIE (MIDDLE CLASS)**
- More than 26 million people, 97% of the population
- Owned about 60% of the land
- Paid the taille

## CAUSES OF THE FRENCH REVOLUTION
**LESSON 2**

- Dissension among the three estates
- Social inequality
- Political ideas of the Enlightenment
- Financial excess led to near collapse of government

→ FRENCH REVOLUTION

## THE FRENCH REVOLUTION
**LESSON 3**

- **1789** JULY 14 — The Storming of the Bastille
- **1793** JANUARY 21 — Louis XVI, King of France, Executed
- **1793** SEPTEMBER — Reign of Terror Begins
- **1794** JULY — Robespierre arrested and executed; Reign of Terror ends
- **1795** NOVEMBER — The Directory heads the French government

## RISE AND FALL OF NAPOLEON LESSON 4

- Napoleon conquered most of Europe and built empire
- Napoleon created Civil Code
- Napoleon made peace with the Catholic Church
- Napoleon took power from the Directory

- Napoleon is defeated in Russia
- European powers make war on France
- European powers capture Paris, and Napoleon is sent into exile
- Napoleon returns to France but is defeated at Waterloo in 1815
- Napoleon returns to exile

# CHAPTER 3 Assessment

**Directions:** On a separate sheet of paper, answer the questions below. Make sure you read carefully and answer all parts of the questions.

## Short Answer

1. **SUMMARIZING** What was the Declaration of the Rights of Man and the Citizen?

2. **DESCRIBING** What was the significance of the meeting of the Estates-General in 1789?

3. **IDENTIFYING CONNECTIONS** What was the Great Fear? How did peasant actions reflect the system of estates under which they had lived?

4. **SUMMARIZING** What was the Reign of Terror, and how did it end?

5. **RELATING EVENTS** Under the National Convention, what efforts were made to de-Christianize France?

6. **IDENTIFYING EFFECTS** What effect did the Constitution of 1795 have?

7. **DETERMINING CENTRAL ISSUES** What were four major principles that were reflected in the Napoleonic Civil Code?

8. **SUMMARIZING** What powers did Napoleon exercise as First Consul in France?

9. **IDENTIFYING CONNECTIONS** How did the idea of nationalism rise from the Napoleonic Wars?

10. **EXPLAINING CAUSE AND EFFECT** What was the Continental System, and was it effective? Explain.

11. **IDENTIFYING STEPS** Describe the events that led to the fall of Napoleon.

12. **EXPLAINING CAUSE AND EFFECT** What was the significance of the Congress of Vienna?

13. **RELATING EVENTS** How did the great powers maintain the balance of power in Europe?

14. **IDENTIFYING CAUSES** What was the role of physical geography in Napoleon's first significant defeat?

15. **RELATING EVENTS** How did the ideologies of liberalism and conservatism differ?

## History and Social-Science Analysis

16. **INFORMATIVE WRITING** Create a chart showing Napoleon's successes and failures in respect to the French Revolution. What would the revolutionaries that came before him have considered his successes? What would they have considered to be his failures?

| Successes | Failures |
|---|---|
| | |

17. **DRAWING CONCLUSIONS** Use this image to answer the following question.

This painting shows Napoleon's armies during their retreat from Moscow. What does it say about this event in Napoleon's reign? Does this appear to be a realistic portrayal? Why or why not?

18. **ANALYZING SOURCES** Use the image to answer the following question.

This editorial cartoon shows the Estates-General forging a new constitution. What opinion is the cartoonist expressing? Who does the person in the middle represent, and how can you tell?

**Need Extra Help?**

| If You've Missed Question | 1 | 2 | 3 | 4 | 5 | 6 | 7 | 8 | 9 | 10 | 11 | 12 | 13 | 14 | 15 | 16 | 17 | 18 |
|---|---|---|---|---|---|---|---|---|---|---|---|---|---|---|---|---|---|---|
| Review Lesson | 1 | 1 | 1 | 1 | 2 | 2 | 2 | 3 | 3 | 3 | 4 | 4 | 4 | 3 | 1 | 2 | 4 | 2 |

(t) Art Collection 2/Alamy Stock Photo; (b) The Granger Collection, New York

## Research and Presentation

19 **EVALUATING** Research more about the storming of the Bastille on July 14, 1789, and the national holiday in France that commemorates this date and the events of July 14, 1790. Create a multimedia presentation that explains the customs tied to Bastille Day.

20 **EVALUATING EVIDENCE** Explain how the ideas of the French Revolution changed the government in France. Write a one-page summary describing how France progressed from an absolute monarchy to a constitutional monarchy to a republic to democratic despotism and then to the Napoleonic Empire.

## Reading and Analyzing Primary Sources

Use the document to answer the following questions.

> "What the peoples of Germany desire most impatiently is that talented commoners should have the same right to your esteem and to public employments as the nobles, that any trace of serfdom and of an intermediate hierarchy between the sovereign and the lowest class of the people should be completely abolished. The benefits of the Code Napoléon, the publicity of judicial procedure, the creation of juries must be so many distinguishing marks of your monarchy."
>
> —Napoleon, in a letter to the king of Westphalia, 1807

21 **CITING TEXT EVIDENCE** How does Napoleon believe civil and military workers should be hired?

- **A.** They should be chosen only from the lower classes.
- **B.** They should be promoted based on previous service.
- **C.** They should be chosen only from the highest classes.
- **D.** They should be chosen based on merit and nothing else.

22 **CITING TEXT EVIDENCE** What is Napoleon saying in addressing "the peoples of Germany"?

- **A.** He is writing a letter meant to be read by all Germans.
- **B.** He is writing from the perspective of a German person.
- **C.** He is suggesting that his reader focus on the well-being of his subjects.
- **D.** He is suggesting that his reader's subjects should be subdued however possible.

23 **DETERMINING CENTRAL IDEAS** What does Napoleon believe that the king of Westphalia should do to improve his country's justice system?

- **A.** He should change the social order so that more people have more opportunities.
- **B.** He should abolish the posts of judges and juries and have his own ministers rule on cases.
- **C.** He should draft a national constitution and appoint legislators to represent the people.
- **D.** He should make the laws much more strict and severely punish those who break them.

## Writing About History

24 **INFORMATIVE WRITING** Using information you have learned in this chapter and previous chapters, compare and contrast the French Revolution with the Glorious Revolution in England and the American Revolution. Discuss their political, economic, and social causes and their long-term effects.

## Speaking and Listening About History

25 **COLLABORATING** Meet in a small group to discuss the following questions: How did the ideas of the Enlightenment help cause the French Revolution? How closely did the various factions of revolutionaries follow Enlightenment beliefs? How closely did Napoleon follow Enlightenment beliefs when he ruled France? Have one member of your group serve as a moderator of the group discussion.

**Need Extra Help?**

| If You've Missed Question | 19 | 20 | 21 | 22 | 23 | 24 | 25 |
|---|---|---|---|---|---|---|---|
| Review Lesson | 1 | 2 | 3 | 3 | 3 | 2 | 4 |

◄ *Painted in about 1829 by Antonio Salas, this portrait of Bolívar, showing him as a dramatic figure posed against a dark background, presents the nationalist as a triumphant military leader.*

1800 — 1870

# Industrialization and Nationalism

## CHAPTER 4



**GO DIGITAL**
*It's All online!*

## ASKING ESSENTIAL QUESTIONS

***How can innovation affect ways of life? How does revolution bring about political and economic change?***

**What Will You Learn?** You will learn how the Industrial Revolution transformed the nature of labor and economics in much of Europe and how nationalism led to revolutions and independence movements throughout Europe and the Americas.

**Why Does This Matter?** Today changes and innovations come rapidly and there are noticeable changes over just the course of a generation. This process of swift change began in the early 1800s, with the Industrial Revolution. Governments, too, began to change. Democracies and representative governments began to spread across Europe and the Americas as the forces of liberalism and nationalism, freed by decades of war and revolution, could no longer be easily quieted.

**How Will You Know That You Learned It?** You will be able to identify the industrial innovations and political movements that influenced economic development and political reform and revolution.

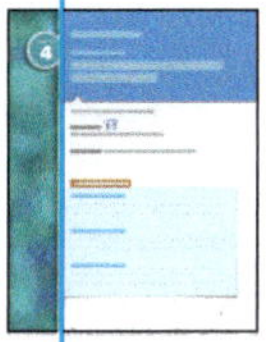

**Using Your Inquiry Journal** As you read this chapter and examine the primary sources, use your Inquiry Journal to help you make notes and expand your list of questions. As you gather information, think about how you will answer the Essential Questions above.

# PLACE & TIME Europe 1800–1880

The people of the nineteenth century witnessed the dramatic rise and fall of governments, the explosion of war and changing borders, and the rise of liberal economics and nationalist politics. The British government's support for free trade and its willingness to make political compromises to the middle classes helped it avoid the fate of many European nations in which citizens took up arms for national identity in 1848. There were many causes of the revolutions of 1848, including nationalism, the repressive nature of governments, and famines. The men and women of the middle classes and the urban working classes were discontented with their leaders.

## STEP INTO THE PLACE

Read the quotes and look at the information presented on the map.

**1. PATTERNS AND MOVEMENT** What do the plotted occurrences of the revolutions of the 1830s and 1840s on the map suggest about the revolutions themselves?

**2. DRAWING CONCLUSIONS** Compare the lines from Shelley's poem to the excerpt from Macaulay's speech, focusing on their views of revolution. Use the map to draw a conclusion about which viewpoint dominated British politics in the nineteenth century.

"Men of England, wherefore plough
For the lords who lay ye low?
Wherefore weave with toil and care
The rich robes your tyrants wear? . . .

Sow seed,—but let no tyrant reap:
Find wealth,—let no imposter heap;
Weave robes,—let not the idle wear;
Forge arms,—in your defence to bear . . ."

—Percy Bysshe Shelley, from "A Song: 'Men of England,'" 1819

"For the sake, therefore, of the whole society, for the sake of the labouring classes themselves, I hold it to be clearly expedient that, in a country like this, the right of suffrage should depend on a pecuniary [monetary] qualification ... I am opposed to Universal Suffrage, because I think that it would produce a destructive revolution. I support this plan [electoral reform], because I am sure that it is our best security against a revolution."

—Thomas Babington Macaulay, from a speech in Parliament, March 2, 1831

## STEP INTO THE TIME

**UNDERSTANDING CHRONOLOGY**

What does the time line suggest about the stability of France during the nineteenth century?

PHOTO:(t)©Image Asset Management Ltd./SuperStock; (b)Hulton Archive/Getty Images; TEXT:(t)Shelley, Percy. 1839. Edited by Mrs. Shelley, The Poetical Works of Percy Bysshe Shelley, Vol. III. Edward Moxon; (b)Lord Macaulay. 1860. "A Speech Delivered in The House of Commons on the 2nd of March, 1831" - From Speeches of Lord Macaulay. London: Longman, Green, Longman, and Roberts.

### EUROPE

**1804** Richard Trevithick's steam locomotive runs on an industrial rail line in Britain

**1807** Britain abolishes the slave trade

**1814** Congress of Vienna meets

**1830** French Revolution of 1830—Charles X flees the country to be replaced by the new constitutional monarchy of Louis-Philippe

**1800** — **1820**

### WORLD EVENTS

**1779–1807** Selim III reigns as sultan of the Ottoman Empire and attempts reform efforts

**1804** Haitians defeat French invasion and declare independence

**1810–1825** Wars of independence in Latin America

**1820** Mexico declares independence from Spain

# REVOLUTIONARY OUTBURSTS AND POLITICAL REVOLUTIONS 1830–1848

**1833** British Factory Act begins age of government regulations over factories

**1839** Opium War begins in China

**1840**

**1842** Treaty of Nanjing grants Hong Kong Island to Britain in perpetuity

**1848** Revolutions erupt in Europe, beginning with the overthrow of Louis-Philippe in France

**1850** Tai Ping Rebellion begins in China

**1852** A year after a coup d'état overthrows the French Republic, Second Empire is proclaimed in France

**1853–1856** Crimean War

**1860**

**1865** Confederate forces surrender, ending the American Civil War

**1867** French troops withdraw from Mexico

**1867** Dual monarchy of Austria-Hungary is created

**1868** Meiji Restoration in Japan

**1869** Opening of the Suez Canal, ending overland route and reducing shipping costs

**1871** German unification achieved under William I

**1880**

## ESSENTIAL QUESTIONS

- *What are the effects of political and economic expansion?*
- *How can innovation affect ways of life?*

# THE STORY BEGINS...

LESSON 1

# The First Global Economic Systems

As the number of European colonies grew in the 1500s and 1600s, the volume and area of European trade also grew, beginning a process that led to a world economy. An Atlantic slave trade brought as many as 10 million enslaved Africans to the Americas between 1500 and the late 1800s. King Afonso of Congo (Bakongo) attempted to describe the extent of the crisis in his country:

> "[W]e cannot reckon how great the damage is, since the [slave traders] are taking every day our natives, sons of the land and the sons of our noblemen and vassals and our relatives,... [S]o great, Sir, is the corruption and licentiousness that our country is being completely depopulated...."

—Afonso of Congo, from a letter to the king of Portugal, 1526

DEA/A. DAGLI ORTI/De Agostini Picture Library/Getty Images

*The growing demand for labor in the Americas fueled the slave trade in Africa. In this image, caravans of enslaved Africans are led by local slave traders.* ▶

| Europe, Africa, and Asia | | The Americas |
|---|---|---|
| | ⟷ | |

**ANALYZING KEY IDEAS AND DETAILS**

**IDENTIFYING** Use a graphic organizer like this one to note how plants, animals, and diseases moved between Europe, Africa, and Asia and the Americas as a result of the Columbian Exchange.

# THE COMMERCIAL REVOLUTION

**GUIDING QUESTION** *What economic theories were put into practice during the age of exploration?*

Many Italian city-states grew rich from trade during the early Renaissance. However, the Italians and Ottomans controlled key trade routes. In the 1400s, other European powers who also sought spices, silk, and other goods from Asia began to look for alternative trade routes. The resulting 300-year-long age of exploration reshaped the world economy. The economic impact of the Renaissance was so fundamental that it is called the Commercial Revolution. This economic revolution saw the rapid expansion of European economies and the building of vast international trading empires.

The economic factors that contributed to the Commercial Revolution included trade, exploration, colonization, and new financial practices. To find new trade routes, European states sent ships down the coast of Africa or across the Atlantic. These explorations opened European eyes to economic opportunities in faraway lands. New lands held new trade partners or valuable resources to exploit. Soon, European powers established colonies in every continent they visited. These colonies were the outposts of new trading networks that made European powers rich during the Commercial Revolution.

The flow of wealth was so great that new financial practices emerged to manage the money, including new kinds of banking, accounting, and insurance. Joint-stock companies, a financial practice which began in the Middle Ages, flourished in this period. A **joint-stock company** is a business where stocks, or a share of ownership in the company, can be bought and owned by shareholders. The practice of "buying in" to a company to purchase its stocks provided trade companies with a large pool of money they could use to fund overseas ventures.

The new economic principle of **mercantilism** also contributed to the success of the Commercial Revolution. Mercantilists believed that the prosperity of a nation depends on a large supply of bullion, or gold and silver. The fastest route to a large supply of gold and silver was to extract it from one's colonies. The other method was to earn the gold and silver through having a favorable balance of trade. The balance of trade is the difference in value between what a nation imports and what it exports over time. Imports are goods brought into a country; exports are goods shipped out of a country. When the balance is favorable, the exported goods are of greater value than the imported goods.

To encourage exports, governments stimulated the growth of industries and trade. They granted **subsidies** to new industries. Subsidies are payments made to support enterprises a government thinks are beneficial. Governments also

**ANALYZING KEY IDEAS AND DETAILS**

1. **DETERMINING CENTRAL IDEAS** What is the central idea of this section? How is this idea presented and developed?
2. **SUMMARIZING** In your own words, write a brief summary of this section.

improved transportation systems. They placed high taxes on foreign goods to keep the balance of trade favorable. Taxes make foreign goods less attractive because they raise the price of imports. Colonies were important as sources of raw materials and as markets for exports of manufactured goods.

### ✓ CHECKING FOR UNDERSTANDING

1. **EXPLAINING EFFECTS** How might mercantilism have encouraged colonial expansion abroad?
2. **ANALYZING CHANGE** What were the effects of European exploration on different parts of the world?

**INTEGRATING KNOWLEDGE AND IDEAS**

1. **ASSESSING** What information in the text supports the claim that a major goal of European exploration was to gain wealth?
2. **INTEGRATING INFORMATION** How did the exchange of plants and animals transform economic activity?

## THE COLUMBIAN EXCHANGE

**GUIDING QUESTION** *How did the Columbian Exchange affect the Americas and Europe?*

A major goal of European exploration was to gain wealth. European nations increased their wealth by exploiting sources of precious metals and raw materials in their colonies. They also increased exports of goods from producers at home to colonial markets overseas. All of this economic activity created an immense trade network. The resulting exchange of plants and animals between Europe and the Americas is known as the Columbian Exchange. This name recognizes the explorer Christopher Columbus's key role in bringing Europe into contact with the Americas. This complex process had far-reaching results on peoples around the world.

Colonization and trade drove the Columbian Exchange. Colonists established **plantations** to grow sugar, cotton, vanilla, and other crops introduced to the Americas. Colonists established ranches where they raised livestock brought from Europe. Much of what the colonists grew and raised was exported to Europe. Europeans brought such plants and animals as wheat, citrus fruit, honeybees, horses, and cattle to the Americas. Horses enabled Native Americans on the Great Plains to travel faster and over greater distances and made hunting more effective. Agricultural products native to the Americas, such as potatoes, cocoa, corn, tomatoes, and tobacco, were shipped to Europe.

The exchange of plants and animals between Europe and the Americas transformed economic activity on both sides of the Atlantic. Potatoes became a basic food staple in some areas of Europe. There was a rapid increase in population because potato plants produced more food per acre than foods that had been grown there before. New food crops from the Americas not only supported population growth, but also changed tastes and created new markets. For example, the export of American crops to China encouraged a population explosion during the Qing dynasty, which began in 1644.

Some aspects of the Columbian Exchange proved deadly. With no immunity to European diseases, the indigenous peoples of Mexico and Central and South America were ravaged by smallpox, measles, and typhus. Many of them died. Hispaniola had a population of 250,000 when Columbus arrived in 1492. By 1538, fewer than 500 indigenous people had survived. In Mexico, the population dropped from 25 million in 1500 to 1 million in 1630. Similar devastation occurred elsewhere in the region. In North America, entire communities of Native Americans died in epidemics of diseases brought by European settlers.

Colonization had other negative effects, such as the encomienda granted by Spain to Spanish settlers. This was the right to use indigenous peoples as

**GOLD IMPORTS TO SPAIN IN THE SIXTEENTH CENTURY**

| Period | Gold Imports (In grams) |
|---|---|
| 1503–1510 | 4,965,180 |
| 1511–1520 | 9,153,220 |
| 1521–1530 | 4,889,050 |
| 1531–1540 | 14,466,360 |
| 1541–1550 | 24,957,130 |
| 1551–1560 | 42,620,080 |
| 1561–1570 | 11,530,940 |
| 1571–1580 | 9,429,140 |
| 1581–1590 | 12,101,650 |
| 1591–1600 | 19,451,420 |
| Total | 153,564,170 |

**Source:** Earl J. Hamilton, *American Treasure and the Price Revolution in Spain, 1501–1650*

1. **INTERPRETING** About how many times greater were gold imports in 1551-1560 than they had been at the beginning of the century?
2. **INTEGRATING INFORMATION** How does this pattern of change illustrate mercantilist goals?

laborers on plantations. The holders of an encomienda were supposed to protect the indigenous peoples, but they often abused them.

### ✓ CHECKING FOR UNDERSTANDING

1. **IDENTIFYING CONNECTIONS** How did the Columbian Exchange contribute to population growth?
2. **EXPLAINING EFFECTS** What were the negative effects of the Columbian Exchange?

## EUROPEAN RIVALS IN THE EAST

**GUIDING QUESTION** *How did the nature of European exploration change by the seventeenth century?*

The Spanish and Portuguese were not the only European trading powers. The Dutch, English, and French also expanded their activities into Asia. The first Dutch fleet had arrived in India in 1595 and formed the East India Company, pushing the Portuguese out of the spice trade in Southeast Asia. The Dutch domination of the spice trade led to massive profits for merchants and made the seventeenth century a Golden Age for the Dutch as they surpassed the Spanish and Portuguese in world trade.

The English soon followed. During the first half of the seventeenth century, the English presence in India steadily increased. By 1650, the British had established a number of trading posts. From them, English ships carried Indian-made cotton goods to the East Indies. There they were bartered for spices, which were shipped back to England.

English success in India attracted rivals. While the Dutch focused on the spice trade, the French established forts along the coast of India. British efforts, however, limited the French, who were soon restricted to a handful of small territories on the southeastern coast of the subcontinent. During the Seven Years' War, the British forced the French to withdraw completely from India. The British East India Company then began to expand, ultimately giving it complete control of India.

**UNDERSTANDING CRAFT AND STRUCTURE**

1. **ANALYZING TEXT PRESENTATION** Why is the seventeenth century referred to as a "Golden Age" for the Dutch?
2. **ANALYZING TEXT** What clue does the text provide to indicate future conflicts among European countries?

### ✓ CHECKING FOR UNDERSTANDING

1. **INTERPRETING** How was the Dutch form of mercantilism different from that of Portugal or Spain?
2. **SUMMARIZING** How did the British East India Company establish dominance in India?

## THE ATLANTIC SLAVE TRADE

**GUIDING QUESTION** *How did European expansion affect Africa and the slave trade?*

European expansion led to a dramatic increase in the slave trade. Traffic in enslaved people was not new. As in other areas of the world, slavery had been practiced in Africa since ancient times. However, the demand for enslaved Africans increased with the European settlement of the Americas in the 1490s and the planting of sugarcane there.

Europeans established plantations in the 1500s along the coast of Brazil and on Caribbean islands to grow sugarcane. Growing sugarcane was very labor intensive. Early on, Europeans enslaved indigenous peoples and forced them to work these fields. However, European diseases quickly devastated the

**ANALYZING KEY IDEAS AND DETAILS**

1. **DETERMINING CENTRAL IDEAS** What is the central idea of this section, and how does the text develop and present this idea?
2. **CITING TEXT EVIDENCE** What were the effects of the slave trade? Cite specific words from the text that support your answer.

indigenous population, resulting in a shortage of labor. In response, Europeans enslaved people from Africa and forcibly transported them to the Americas to toil on these plantations.

In 1518 a Spanish ship carried the first enslaved Africans directly from Africa to the Americas. During the next two centuries, the trade in enslaved people grew dramatically. It became part of the triangular trade that connected Europe, Africa, and the Americas.

The triangular trade functioned as follows: European merchant ships carried European manufactured goods, such as guns and cloth, to Africa where they were traded for enslaved people. The enslaved Africans were then sent to the Americas and sold. European merchants then bought tobacco, molasses, sugar, and raw cotton in the Americas and shipped them back to Europe.

As a result of this triangular trade, as many as 10 million enslaved Africans were brought to the Americas between the early sixteenth century and the late nineteenth century. Their journey from Africa to the Americas became known as the **Middle Passage,** the middle portion of the triangular trade route. Many enslaved Africans died on the journey. Those who survived often died from diseases to which they had little or no immunity.

Death rates were higher for newly arrived enslaved Africans than for those born and reared in the Americas. The new generation developed at least a partial immunity to many diseases. Slaveholders rarely encouraged enslaved people to have children as many believed that buying a new enslaved person was less expensive than rearing a child from birth to working age.

Before Europeans arrived in the fifteenth century, most enslaved persons in Africa were prisoners of war. Europeans first bought enslaved people from African merchants at slave markets in return for gold, guns, or other European goods. Local slave traders first obtained their supplies of enslaved persons

**GEOGRAPHIC REASONING**

1. **PATTERNS AND MOVEMENT** Which part of Africa was the greatest source of enslaved people? Why?
2. **GLOBAL INTERCONNECTIONS** What is the connection between the slave trade and the triangular trade?

## ATLANTIC SLAVE TRADE 1500S AND 1600S

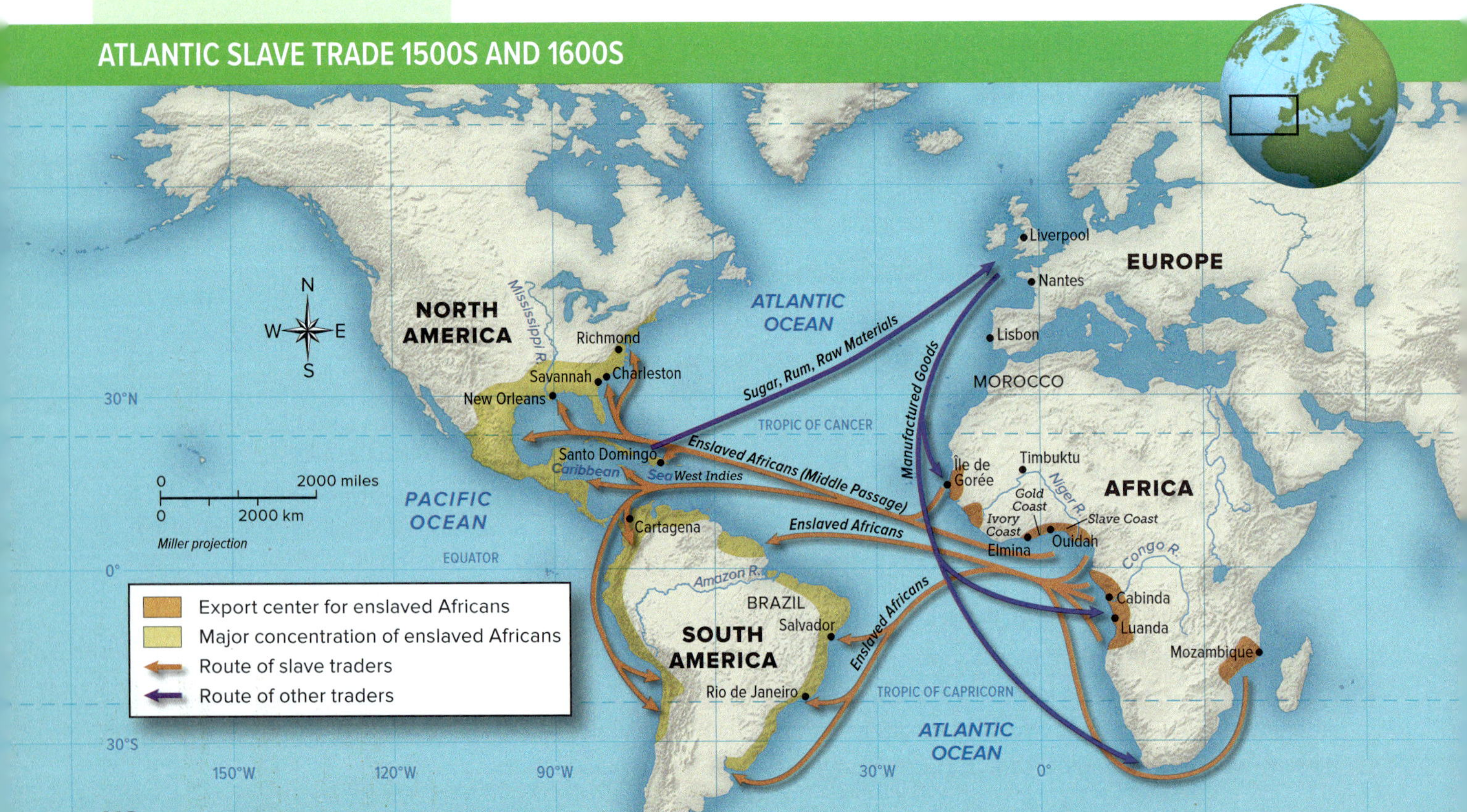

from nearby coastal regions. As demand grew, they had to move farther inland to find their victims. Local rulers became concerned about the impact of the slave trade on their societies and spoke out against the slave trade. Europeans and other Africans, however, generally ignored such protests. Local rulers who traded in enslaved people viewed the slave trade as a source of income. Many sent raiders into defenseless villages.

## EFFECTS OF THE ATLANTIC SLAVE TRADE

The slave trade was a tragedy for the victims and their families. Its broader effects varied from region to region. The slave trade depopulated some areas and deprived many African communities of their youngest and strongest men and women. The desire of slave traders to provide a constant supply of enslaved persons increased warfare in Africa. Coastal or near-coastal African chiefs and their followers, armed with guns acquired from the trade in enslaved people, increased raids and wars on neighboring peoples. The slave trade had a devastating effect on some African states. Benin, located in West Africa, was a dynamic society in the sixteenth century. Benin was pulled into the slave trade, and the population declined and warfare increased. The people of Benin lost faith in their gods, their art deteriorated, and human sacrifice became more common. A corrupt and brutal place, it took years to discover the brilliance of the earlier culture that was destroyed by slavery. The use of enslaved Africans remained largely acceptable to European society. Europeans continued to view Africans as inferior beings fit chiefly for slave labor. Not until the Society of Friends, known as the Quakers, began to condemn slavery in the 1770s did feelings against slavery begin to build in Europe. Even then, it was not until the French Revolution in the 1790s that the French abolished slavery. The British ended the slave trade in 1807 and abolished slavery throughout the empire in 1833. Despite these reforms, slavery continued in the newly formed United States until the Civil War of the 1860s.

### ✓ CHECKING FOR UNDERSTANDING

1. **EXPLAINING CAUSE AND EFFECT** How did epidemics among the indigenous populations contribute to an increase in the trade of enslaved Africans?

2. **SUMMARIZING** What led to the increased demand for enslaved Africans?

## LESSON 1 REVIEW

### Time and Place

1. **IDENTIFYING CONNECTIONS** Write a paragraph explaining the function of colonies in increasing the wealth of European nations.

### Building History-Social Science Analysis Skills

2. **EVALUATING** Which economic theory was put into practice during the age of exploration?

3. **ANALYZING CHANGE** How did the Columbian Exchange affect the Americas and Europe?

4. **INTERPRETING** How did European exploration change by the seventeenth century?

5. **EXPLAINING EFFECTS** How did the European expansion affect Africa and the slave trade?

### Writing About History

6. **INFORMATIVE WRITING** Write a paragraph describing the effects, both positive and negative, of European trade on the Americas. Be sure to refer to specific ideas and events in your paragraph.

## ESSENTIAL QUESTIONS

- *How can innovation affect ways of life?*
- *How does revolution bring about political and economic change?*

# THE STORY BEGINS...

*The Industrial Revolution changed how people work, where they live, and how they travel, as seen in this image of an early subway train.* ▼

LESSON 2

# The Industrial Revolution

Productivity in Britain in the early 1800s was booming. Industrialization and the movement of work into factories full of fast-moving machines was nothing short of a revolution. However, there was a human cost. In 1832, British Parliament investigated the working conditions in textile factories. In this account, a man describes the damage done by repetitive movements to children working at the mills:

> *"At the top to the spindle there is a fly goes across, and the child takes hold of the fly by the ball of his left hand, and he throws the left shoulder up and the right knee inward; he has the thread to get with the right hand, and he has to stoop his head down to see what he is doing; they throw the right knee inward in that way, and all the children I have seen, that bend in the right knee. I knew a family, the whole of whom were bent outwards as a family complaint, and one of those boys was sent to a worsted-mill, and first he became straight in his right knee, and then he became crooked in it the other way."*

—a witness account from
"The Life of the Industrial Worker in Nineteenth-Century England," 1832

Investigations like these eventually led to hearings and child labor legislation. Industrialization meant the nature of work and patterns of life were swiftly changing.

| Cause | Effect |
| --- | --- |
| | |
| | |
| | |
| | |

**ANALYZING KEY IDEAS AND DETAILS**

**IDENTIFYING EFFECTS** Read closely to identify the causes and effects of the Industrial Revolution in England. Record the information in a graphic organizer like this one.

# THE INDUSTRIAL REVOLUTION IN GREAT BRITAIN

**GUIDING QUESTIONS** *What was the significance of the Agricultural Revolution in Great Britain? Why did the Industrial Revolution start in Great Britain?*

The Industrial Revolution began in Great Britain in the 1760s. However, it took decades to spread to other Western nations. Several factors contributed to make Great Britain the starting place.

First, an Agricultural Revolution beginning in the eighteenth century changed agricultural practices. Expansion of farmland, improvements in crop storage and transportation, innovations in fertilizers, and new crops such as the potato dramatically increased the food supply. More people could be fed at lower prices with less **labor**. Now even ordinary British families could use some of their income to buy manufactured goods.

Second, with the increased food supply, fewer people faced starvation, and the population grew. Access to more easily obtained and a broader variety of foodstuffs also resulted in a healthier population. When Parliament passed enclosure movement laws in the eighteenth century, landowners fenced off common lands. This forced many peasants to move to towns, creating a labor supply for factories.

Third, Britain had a ready supply of money, or **capital**, to invest in new machines and factories. **Entrepreneurs** found new business opportunities and new ways to make profits.

Fourth, natural resources were plentiful in Britain. The country's rivers provided water power for the new factories and a means for transporting raw materials and finished products. Britain also had abundant supplies of coal and iron ore.

Finally, a supply of markets gave British manufacturers a ready outlet for their goods. Britain had a vast colonial empire, and British ships could transport goods anywhere in the world. Also, because of population growth and cheaper food at home, domestic markets increased. A growing demand for cotton cloth led British manufacturers to look for ways to increase production.

## COTTON PRODUCTION AND NEW FACTORIES

In the eighteenth century, Great Britain had surged far ahead in the production of inexpensive cotton goods. The manufacture of cotton cloth was a two-step process. First, spinners made cotton thread from raw cotton. Then, weavers wove the cotton thread into cloth on looms. In the eighteenth century,

**ANALYZING KEY IDEAS AND DETAILS**

1. **SUMMARIZING** Write a brief summary in your own words of the section "Cotton Production and New Factories."
2. **ANALYZING EVENTS** Why might the development of steam-powered rail transport have helped advance the Industrial Revolution?

**DETERMINING MEANING**

The word **capital** is a multiple-meaning word. What clues from the context of the text help you determine which meaning for *capital* the author intends?

MAKING CONNECTIONS TO PERSPECTIVES

## WHY AN INDUSTRIAL "REVOLUTION"?

A revolution is a dramatic and wide-reaching change in the way something works or is organized. Many historians argue the change brought by the Industrial Revolution was not sudden but gradual and uneven. Does this mean that calling this period a "revolution" is inaccurate? Not necessarily. What historians have come to realize is the Industrial Revolution was a period of successive waves of innovations that brought about persistent economic growth. This growth led to social, economic, and even cultural changes. The Industrial Revolution separated work and home life, led to the growth of cities, and even led to changes in the food we eat and the clothing we wear. It has led to the usage of vast quantities of fossil fuels and competition for these resources among nations. The Industrial Revolution dramatically transformed our world and helped create the global environmental crisis we now face.

**CITING TEXT EVIDENCE** Why is this period of innovation and change ultimately called a revolution? Is the label appropriate?

**DETERMINING MEANING**

The term **cottage industry** describes a method of production. How does the definition of *cottage industry* help explain the changes in cotton production that occurred during the Industrial Revolution?

individuals did these tasks in their rural cottages. This production method was thus called a **cottage industry**.

A series of technological advances during this time made the cottage industry inefficient. In 1764 James Hargreaves had invented a machine called the spinning jenny, which made the spinning process much faster. In fact, spinners produced thread faster than weavers could use it.

The invention of a water-powered loom by Edmund Cartwright in 1787 made it possible for the weaving of cloth to catch up with the spinning of thread. It was now more efficient to bring workers to the new machines and to have them work in factories near streams and rivers, which were used to power many of these early machines.

**ANALYZING PRIMARY SOURCES**

1. **DETERMINING CENTRAL IDEAS** What is Radcliffe's central idea in this excerpt?
2. **ANALYZING IDEAS** How does the excerpt show that the Industrial Revolution provided a good opportunity for entrepreneurship?

> "... I shall confine myself to the families in my own neighbourhood. These families, up to the time I have been speaking of, whether as cottagers or small farmers, had supported themselves by the different occupations I have mentioned in spinning and manufacturing, as their progenitors from the earliest institutions of society had done before them. But the mule-twist now coming into vogue, for the warp, as well as weft, added to the water-twist and common jenny yarns, with an increasing demand for every fabric the loom could produce, put all hands in request of every age and description. The fabrics made from wool or linen vanished, while the old loom-shops being insufficient, every lumber-room, even old barns, cart-houses, and outbuildings of any description were repaired, windows broke through the old blank walls, and all fitted up for loom-shops. ..."

—William Radcliffe, *Origin of the New System of Manufacture, Commonly Called Power Loom Weaving,* 1828

The cotton industry became even more productive when the steam engine was improved in the 1760s by James Watt, a Scottish engineer. In 1782 Watt made changes that enabled the engine to drive machinery. Steam power could now be used to spin and weave cotton. Before long, cotton mills using steam engines could be found throughout Britain. Because steam engines were fired by coal, not powered by water, they did not need to be located near rivers.

Radcliffe, William. 1828. Origin of the New System of Manufacture, Commonly Called "Power-Loom Weaving". Stockport: James Lomax, Advertiser-Office.

British cotton cloth production increased dramatically. In 1760 Britain had imported 2.5 million pounds (1.14 million kg) of raw cotton, which was used to produce cloth in cottage industries. By 1840, 366 million pounds (166 million kg) of cotton were imported each year. By this time, cotton cloth was Britain's most valuable product. Sold around the world, British cotton goods were produced mainly in factories.

The factory was another important element in the Industrial Revolution. From its beginning, the factory created a new labor system. Factory owners wanted to use their new machines constantly. So workers were forced to work in shifts to keep the machines producing at a steady rate. This was a change from the way work was performed in the cottage industry and all preindustrial societies. Formerly, the activities of work and home were performed in the same location. For the first time, the two became separate locations.

*Titled* Carding, Drawing, and Roving, *this print shows girls and women working in an English cotton mill.*

**UNDERSTANDING CONTEXT**
What does this image suggest about how industrialization proceeded during the era of the early factories?

Early factory workers came from rural areas where they were used to periods of hectic work, such as harvest time, followed by periods of inactivity. Early factory owners therefore disciplined workers to a system of regular hours and repetitive tasks. For example, adult workers were fined for being late and were dismissed for more serious misconduct, especially being drunk. Child workers were often beaten with a rod or whipped to keep them at work. One early industrialist said that his aim was "to make such machines of the Men as cannot err."

On the conditions of child factory workers:

> "Provided a child should be drowsy, the overlooker walks round the room . . . and he touches the child on the shoulder, and says, 'Come here.' In the corner of the room there is an iron cistern; it is filled with water . . . he takes this boy, and holding him up by the legs, dips him over head in the cistern, and sends him to work for the remainder of the day. . . ."
>
> —from a British Parliament report, quoted in *The History of the Factory Movement, Vol I,* 1857

**ANALYZING PRIMARY SOURCES**

1. **ANALYZING TEXT** Why might the British Parliament have examined the conditions of child factory workers?
2. **EVALUATING TEXT EVIDENCE** What impact might child labor have had on families in industrial Britain?

## COAL, IRON, AND RAILROADS

Prior to the Industrial Revolution, people relied on wood as a cheap source of energy and as a resource for buildings, ships, and tools. In Great Britain, a rapidly growing population resulted in an overreliance on wood that resulted in deforestation by the mid-1500s. To resolve this problem, the British turned to coal, a **fossil fuel**, which seemed then to be unlimited in quantity. Throughout the 1600s and 1700s, this resulted in the creation of machinery powered by coal instead of wood, which in turn led to the creation of a system of factory production and innovations in transportation, such as the steam engine.

The steam engine was crucial to Britain's Industrial Revolution. The success of the steam engine increased the need for coal and led to an expansion in coal production. New processes using coal aided the transformation of another industry—the iron industry.

Britain's natural resources included large supplies of iron ore. A better quality of iron was produced in the 1780s when Henry Cort developed a process called **puddling**. In this process, coke, which was derived from coal, was used to burn away impurities in crude iron, called pig iron, and to produce iron of high quality.

**DETERMINING MEANING**
The word **puddling**, as it is used in context, is a noun. How can the word be a noun if the *-ing* ending indicates an action?

The British iron industry boomed. In 1740 Britain had produced 17,000 tons (15,419 metric tons, or t) of iron. After Cort's process came into use in the 1780s, production jumped to nearly 70,000 tons (63,490 t). In 1852 Britain produced almost 3 million tons (2.7 million t)—more iron than was produced by the rest of the world combined. High-quality iron was used to build new machines, especially trains.

In the eighteenth century, more efficient means of moving resources and goods developed. Railroads were particularly important to the success of the Industrial Revolution. Richard Trevithick, an English engineer, built the first steam locomotive. In 1804 Trevithick's locomotive ran on an industrial rail line in Britain. It pulled 10 tons (9 t) of ore and 70 people at 5 miles (8.05 km) per hour. Better locomotives soon followed. One called the *Rocket* was used on the first public railway line, which opened in 1830 and extended 32 miles (51.5 km) from the cotton-manufacturing town of Manchester to the thriving port of Liverpool.

▲ *The* Rocket *locomotive*

The *Rocket* sped along at 16 miles (25.7 km) per hour while pulling a 40-ton (36-t) train. Within 20 years, locomotives were able to reach 50 miles (80.5 km) per hour, an incredible speed. In 1840 Britain had almost 2,000 miles (3,218 km) of railroads. In 1850 more than 6,000 miles (9,654 km) of railroad track crisscrossed much of the country.

Building railroads created new jobs for farm laborers and peasants. Railroads, too, led to a revolution in transportation. Arrival and departure schedules for trains led to a standardization of time, resulting in the synchronization of clocks across regions. Less expensive transportation led to lower-priced goods, thus creating larger markets. More sales meant more demand and the need for more factories and more repetitive-motion machinery. Business owners could reinvest their profits in new equipment, adding to the growth of the economy and the need to expand into new markets. This type of regular, ongoing economic growth became a basic feature of the new industrial economy.

### ✓ CHECKING FOR UNDERSTANDING

1. **EXPLAINING CAUSE AND EFFECT** What was the significance of the Agricultural Revolution in Great Britain? Why did the Industrial Revolution start in Great Britain?
2. **EXPLAINING EFFECTS** How did Britain's extra supply of money lead to entrepreneurial opportunities for British businesses?
3. **UNDERSTANDING CONTEXT** What effect did the change in railroads have on the Industrial Revolution?

**ANALYZING KEY IDEAS AND DETAILS**

1. **DESCRIBING** Based on the map and the text, why do you think major railway lines were located near major ports?
2. **DETERMINING CENTRAL IDEAS** What is the central idea of this section? How does the text present and develop this idea?

## THE SPREAD OF INDUSTRIALIZATION

**GUIDING QUESTION** *What factors fed the spread of industrialization in Europe and North America?*

By the mid-nineteenth century, Great Britain had become the world's first industrial nation. It had also become the world's richest nation. Great Britain produced one-half of the world's coal and manufactured goods. Its cotton industry alone in 1850 was equal in size to the industries of all other European countries combined.

The Industrial Revolution spread to the rest of Europe at different times and at different speeds. France was one of the first states to be industrialized in continental Europe. Industrialization there was a slow process. The French economy was hindered by political instability in the late eighteenth and early nineteenth century. France also did not have a good source of coal, which was an important resource for industrial development. In contrast to the heavy mechanization in Britain during this period, many goods produced in France were still handmade. There was also some resistance to the mechanization of these traditional industries and the government protected them. In the late nineteenth century the French government began to play a major role in the industrialization of France. Roads were improved and the French rail system was expanded.

The Industrial Revolution in the German states took place in the mid-nineteenth century. The German state of Prussia was especially rich in iron and coal resources and its government assisted in the development of iron, steel, and chemical manufacturing companies. The unification of the German state in 1870 led to rapid industrial growth. Unification, too, made the development of railroad transportation much easier than before. By the early twentieth century, Germany was a great industrial power.

An Industrial Revolution also occurred in the United States during the first half of the nineteenth century. In 1800 more than 5 million people lived in the United States, and nearly 6 out of every 7 American workers were farmers.

## INDUSTRY IN GREAT BRITAIN 1850

### GEOGRAPHIC REASONING

By 1850, Great Britain was an industrial nation.

1. **PATTERNS AND MOVEMENT** Which major ports are located along coalfields?
2. **SPATIAL THINKING** What geographical factors help explain why industrialization began in Great Britain?

No city had more than 100,000 people. In contrast, the U.S. population had grown to more than 30 million people by 1860. Many of these people moved into the cities. Eight cities had populations of more than 100,000, and only about 50 percent of American workers were farmers.

A large country, the United States needed a good transportation system to move goods across the nation. Thousands of miles of roads and canals were built to link east and west. Robert Fulton built the first paddle-wheel steamboat, the *Clermont*, in 1807. Steamboats made transportation easier on the waterways of the United States.

Most important in the development of an American transportation system was the railroad. By 1860, about 30,000 miles (48,270 km) of railroad track covered the continental United States. The railroad soon turned the United States into a single massive market for the manufactured goods produced in the Northeast.

Labor for the growing number of factories in the Northeast came chiefly from the farm population. Women and girls made up a large majority of the workers in large textile (cotton and wool) factories.

### ☑ CHECKING FOR UNDERSTANDING

1. **UNDERSTANDING CONTEXT** What factors fed the spread of industrialization in Europe and North America?
2. **UNDERSTANDING CHANGE** Why was France slower to become industrialized than Britain?
3. **RELATING EVENTS** What changed in the United States that allowed for an Industrial Revolution?

## THE IMPACT OF INDUSTRIALIZATION

**GUIDING QUESTION** *What was the impact of industrialization in Europe?*

The Industrial Revolution led to innovations in the way people worked, traveled, and produced goods. It drastically changed society in Britain, France, Germany, and other parts of Europe. In the first half of the nineteenth century, cities grew, and two new social classes—the middle class and the working class—emerged. People also began to struggle with the consequences industrialization had on their environment.

**UNDERSTANDING CRAFT AND STRUCTURE**

1. **DETERMINING POINT OF VIEW** This section describes the work of Robert Owen. Based on what you know of industrialization and what Owen did, what can you infer about his reaction to industrialization?
2. **ANALYZING TEXT PRESENTATION** How does the way the text is organized help you understand the reason for the rise of socialism?

### POPULATION GROWTH AND URBANIZATION

European population stood at an estimated 140 million in 1750. By 1850, the population had almost doubled to 266 million. The key to this growth was a decline in death rates, wars, and major epidemic diseases, such as smallpox and plague. Because of an increase in the food supply, people were better fed and more resistant to disease.

Famine and poverty were two factors that impacted global migration and urbanization. More than 1 million people died during the Irish potato famine, and poverty led a million more to migrate to the Americas. Industrialization also spurred urbanization, as large numbers of people migrated from the countryside to cities to work in factories.

In 1800 Great Britain had one major city, London, with a population of about 1 million. Six cities had populations between 50,000 and 100,000. By 1850, London's population had swelled to about 2.5 million. Nine cities had populations of more than 100,000. Also, more than 50 percent of the population lived in towns and cities.

The rapid growth of cities in the first half of the nineteenth century led to pitiful living conditions for many, leading urban reformers to call on local governments to clean up their cities. Reform would be undertaken in the second half of the nineteenth century.

## NEW SOCIAL CLASSES

The Middle Ages saw the rise of commercial capitalism, an economic system based on trade. **Industrial capitalism**, an economic system based on industrial production, rose during the Industrial Revolution. This system produced a new middle-class group—the industrial middle class.

In the Middle Ages, the bourgeois, or middle-class person, was the burgher, or town dweller. The bourgeois were merchants, officials, artisans, lawyers, and intellectuals. Later, the term *bourgeois* came to include people involved in industry and banking, as well as lawyers, teachers, and doctors. The new industrial middle class that emerged during the Industrial Revolution was made of the people who built the factories, bought the machines, and developed the markets. They had initiative, vision, ambition, and often greed. One said, "Getting of money . . . is the main business of the life of Man. . . ."

The Industrial Revolution also created an industrial working class that faced wretched working conditions. Work hours ranged from 12 to 16 hours

**DETERMINING MEANING**

To better understand the meaning of the phrase **industrial capitalism**, consider its component parts. Based on what you know of its parts, write a definition of the phrase. Use a dictionary or an online reference to check your definition.

**CITIZENSHIP**

### WORKPLACE SAFETY REGULATIONS

Industrial work can be dangerous today, but it was an especially dangerous business in the late 1700s and early 1800s. Coal mines were prone to collapse. New machines, especially power looms in textile mills, were swift moving and hazardous. Accidents, even deaths, became commonplace in mines and factories. In the early Industrial Revolution, there were no rules or regulations meant to protect workers in the event of an accident.

As the risks involved in industrialized workplaces became more widely known, governments began to step in and to create laws meant to protect industrial workers. Beginning in 1802 in Great Britain, a series of Factory Acts were gradually passed to establish processes for factory inspections and safety standards. Although this process was slow, it resulted in laws that made factories, mines, and other industrial locations safer places to work. Due to these and other efforts, accidents and deaths were gradually reduced.

Lawmakers' attempts to regulate safety in the workplace did not stop in the 1800s. Today the Occupational Safety and Health Administration, a division of the United States Department of Labor, continues to monitor places of employment to ensure proper rules and regulations for the safety of workers are followed. Modern efforts have proved successful. In the United States, deaths in the workplace decreased by 80 percent from 1913 to 2013.

**DRAWING CONCLUSIONS** Why might governments have had an interest in creating workplace safety rules and regulations?

▲ *Children and women working in an English coal mine*

each day, 6 days per week. There was no security of employment, and there was no minimum wage.

Conditions in the coal mines were harsh. Steam-powered engines lifted the coal from the mines to the top, but the men inside the mines dug out the coal. Dangerous conditions, including cave-ins, explosions, and gas fumes, were a way of life. The cramped conditions in the mines and their constant dampness led to workers' deformed bodies and ruined lungs.

The worst conditions were in the cotton mills, which were also dirty, dusty, dangerous, and unhealthy. In Britain, women and children made up two-thirds of the cotton industry's workforce by 1830. However, the number of child laborers declined after the Factory Act of 1833. This act set nine as the minimum age for employment and limited hours for older children. After this, women came to make up 50 percent of the British labor force in textile factories. They were paid half or less than half of what men received. When the work hours of children and women were limited, a new pattern of work emerged. Men now earned most of the family income by working outside the home. Women took over daily care of the family and performed low-paying jobs that could be done at home.

> "The spirit of self-help, as exhibited in the energetic action of individuals, has in all times been a marked feature in the English character, and furnishes the true measure of our power as a nation. Rising above the heads of the mass, there were always to be found a series of individuals distinguished beyond others, who commanded the public homage. But our progress has also been owing to multitudes of smaller and less known men. Though only the generals' names may be remembered in the history of any great campaign, it has been in a great measure through the individual valour and heroism of the privates that victories have been won."
>
> —Samuel Smiles, *Self Help,* 1882

**ANALYZING PRIMARY SOURCES**

1. **ANALYZING IDEAS** According to Smiles, how did industrialization impact the average family?
2. **ANALYZING IDEAS** What other interpretation of the impact of the Industrial Revolution on the family does Smiles challenge?

## EARLY SOCIALISM

In the first half of the nineteenth century, the pitiful conditions created by the Industrial Revolution gave rise to a movement known as **socialism**. In this economic system, society—usually in the form of the government—owns and controls some means of production, such as factories and utilities. Socialists generally favor policies that benefit the working classes in their societies.

Early socialism was largely the idea of intellectuals. To later socialists, especially the followers of Karl Marx, such ideas were impractical dreams. They contemptuously labeled the earlier reformers utopian socialists, a term that has lasted to this day. Robert Owen, a British cotton manufacturer, was one utopian socialist. He believed that humans would show their natural goodness if they lived in a cooperative environment. Owen transformed the squalid factory town of New Lanark, Scotland, into a flourishing community. He created a similar community at New Harmony, Indiana, in the United States in the 1820s, which failed.

In the 1880s, the Chancellor of Germany, Otto von Bismarck, responded to the development of the socialist movement by creating old-age pensions, accident insurance, medical care, and unemployment insurance. Beginning in the 1890s, the government of France slowly began to adopt these same measures. These moves formed the basis of the modern European welfare state.

**DETERMINING MEANING**

To better understanding the meaning of the word **socialism**, consider its suffix: *-ism* means "denoting a system, principle, or movement of ideology." Based on the meaning of its parts, write a definition of *socialism*. Use a dictionary or an online reference to check your definition.

## ENVIRONMENTAL CONSEQUENCES

The shift from an agrarian society to an industrial society during the Industrial Revolution changed the pressures society put on its natural resources. A dramatic increase in the use of coal as an energy source and iron as a building material led to a slow depletion of these resources that were once considered inexhaustible. Discarded rock and waste materials from mining processes were also not controlled and often polluted nearby groundwater, streams, and vegetation.

As the number of factories and railroads increased, their impact on the environment also became difficult to ignore. Vast movements of earth moved to create canals, railroads, and new road systems forever changed the landscape. As with mines, there were no laws to regulate industrial waste from factories. Perhaps the greatest environmental problem with factories during the Industrial Revolution was the smog and soot produced by the countless machines burning coal. As factories and railroad hubs were most often in urban centers, this resulted in serious health issues for the rapidly growing populations of these cities.

### ✓ CHECKING FOR UNDERSTANDING

1. **DRAWING CONCLUSIONS** What was the impact of industrialization in Europe?
2. **EVALUATING** How did people's lives improve during the population growth of the 1800s, and then decline?
3. **IDENTIFYING EFFECTS** What actions did the British government take in response to the Industrial Revolution?

## LESSON 2 REVIEW

### Time and Place

1. **ANALYZING CHANGE** Explain how the Industrial Revolution in Great Britain was similar to and different from technological revolutions we have seen more recently in the digital world.

### Building History-Social Science Analysis Skills

2. **SUMMARIZING** Why does it help for an industrialized nation to have a good supply of natural resources?
3. **EVALUATING** How did France's resistance to manufactured goods affect its economy?
4. **INTERPRETING** How was the middle class different during the Industrial Revolution from what it was during the Middle Ages, and how did that difference affect the society as a whole?

### Writing About History

5. **INFORMATIVE WRITING** Write an informative essay explaining how the ideas of the Industrial Revolution changed Europe during the nineteenth century and how those changes still impact our lives today. Be sure to cite specific ideas about the Industrial Revolution in your response.

### Collaborating

6. **PRESENTING** Working with a partner, create a multimedia presentation about one invention from the early industrial age. Presentations should address who the inventor was, how it works, the problem it solves, and any products that were developed as a result of this invention. Present your multimedia presentation to the class, and answer any questions.

# THE INDUSTRIAL REVOLUTION IN GREAT BRITAIN

Review the sources below on industrial production, population growth, and railroad development to better understand how Great Britain became a leading nation in economic output during the Industrial Revolution.

SECONDARY SOURCE: GRAPH

## INDUSTRIAL PRODUCTION IN GREAT BRITAIN BETWEEN 1830 AND 1850

This graph charts the production of coal, cotton, and pig iron. These were three very important metrics for understanding the growth of Great Britain during the Industrial Revolution.

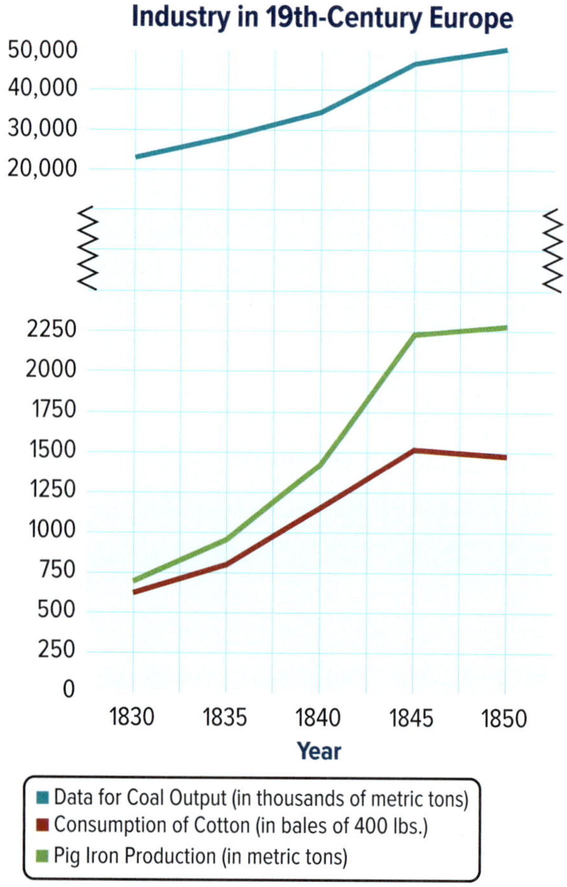


### ANALYZE THE SOURCE

**DETERMINING CONTEXT** What does the increase in the consumption of cotton, pig iron, and coal suggest about the role of these goods in the industrialization of Great Britain? Why might the output of coal be much higher than the other two resources?

SECONDARY SOURCE: GRAPH

## POPULATION GROWTH IN INDUSTRIALIZING LONDON

This bar graph shows the rate at which industrializing London grew compared to cities where the pace of industrialization was slower.

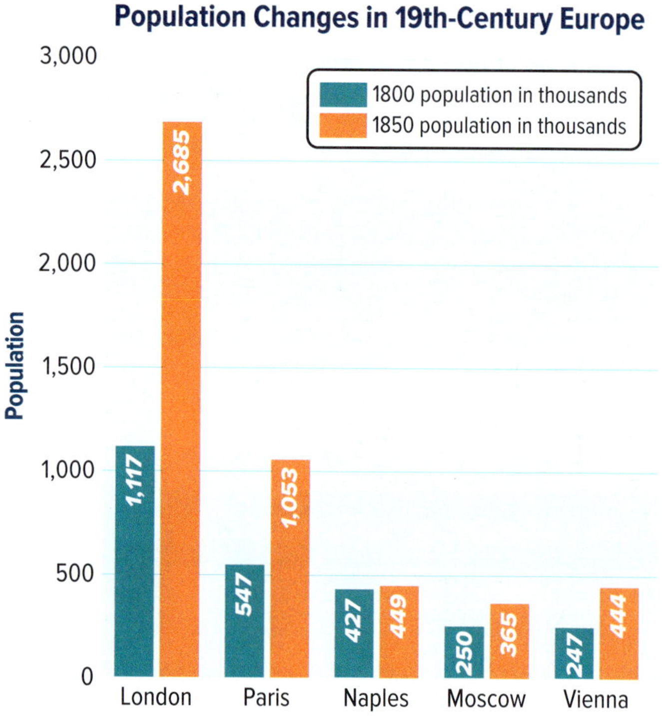


**Source:** European Historical Statistics, 1750-1970

### ANALYZE THE SOURCE

1. **IDENTIFYING CONNECTIONS** Given the information in the population graph, what connections can you make between the industrialization and population growth?
2. **EXPLAINING CAUSE AND EFFECT** Considering the relation between population growth and industrialization what might we conclude about the amount of industrialization occurring in Naples between the years 1800 and 1850?

SECONDARY SOURCE: MAP

## RAILWAY NETWORKS IN 1850 EUROPE

This map shows the extent of rail transport networks in Europe in the year 1850.

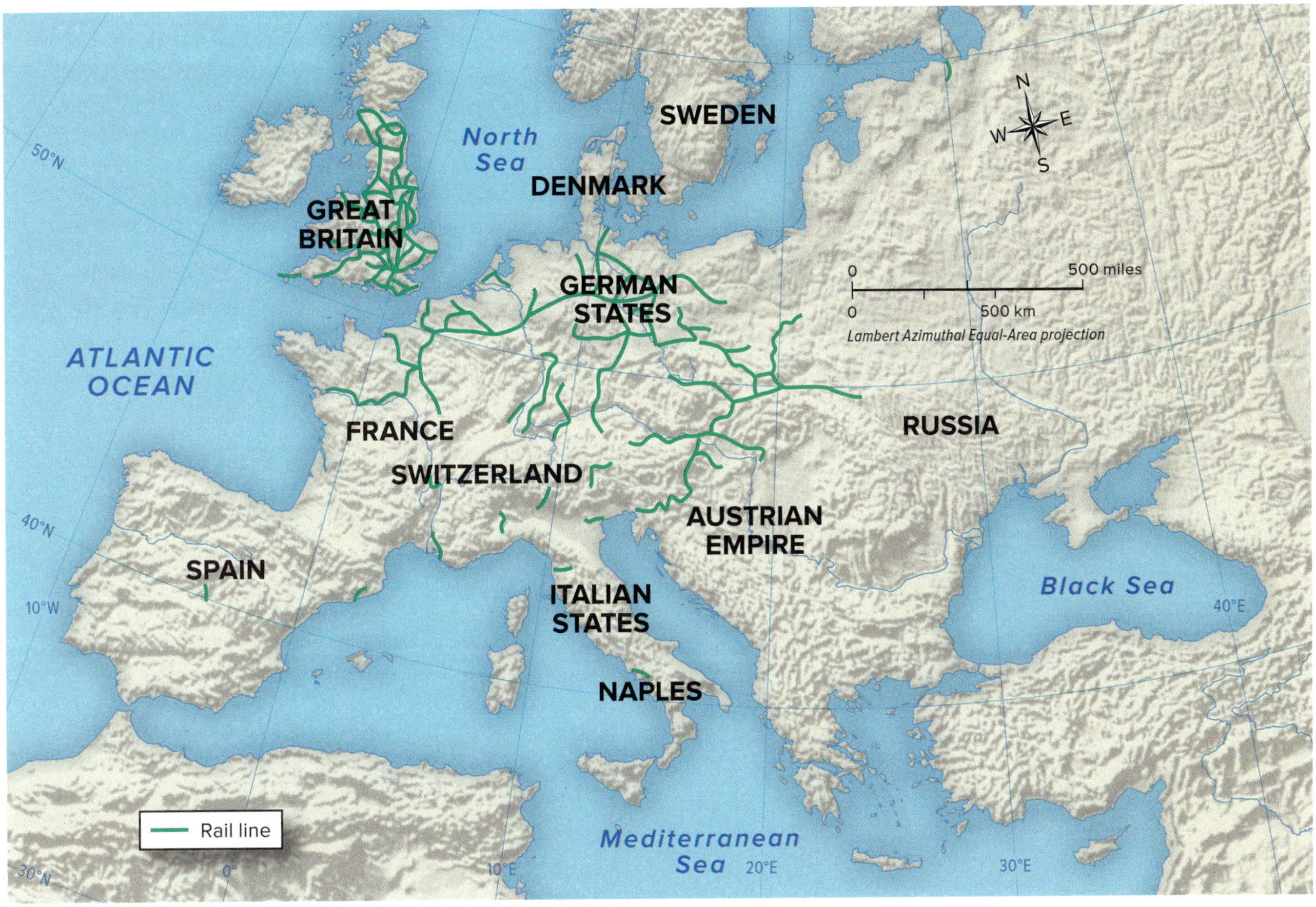


### ANALYZE THE SOURCE

1. **USING MAPS** Considering the railroad map from 1850, what might one conclude about the relationship between railroad construction and the process of industrialization?
2. **UNDERSTANDING CONTEXT** If we accept that there is a positive relationship between railroad construction and industrialization, what can one conclude about the process of industrialization in the German states versus that process in France?

### MULTIPLE PERSPECTIVES

1. **ANALYZING SOURCES** In what ways might the development of railroads in Europe during the nineteenth century have been both a product of industrialization and something that perpetuated that industrializing process? Use multiple sources to support your answer.
2. **UNDERSTANDING CHANGE** Based on the data in the graphs and map, in what way might a worker in Europe and a wealthy capitalist have experienced the Industrial Revolution differently? Use multiple sources to support your answer.

## ESSENTIAL QUESTIONS

- *How can innovation affect ways of life?*
- *How does revolution bring about political and economic change?*

LESSON 3

# Nationalism and Political Revolutions

## THE STORY BEGINS...

On February 23rd, 1848, revolts in Paris, France, grew increasingly destructive as citizens rebelled against the constitutional monarch that had been put in place just a decade earlier:

> “About a quarter past ten, while on my way, by another route, to the boulevards, I suddenly, with others, was startled by the aspect of a gentleman who, without his hat, ran madly into the middle of the street, and began to harangue the passersby. “To arms!” he cried, “we are betrayed. The soldiers have slaughtered a hundred unarmed citizens by the Hôtel des Capucines. Vengeance!” and having given the details of the affair, he hurried to carry the intelligence to other quarters. The effect was electric; each man shook his neighbor by the hand, and far and wide the word was given that the whole system must fall.”

—Percy B. St. John, *The French Revolution of 1848: The Three Days of February,* 1848

The revolutions of 1848 would spark change not only in France but across Europe.

*Protests and revolts across France in February of 1848 culminated at the Town Hall of Paris on February 25.* ▶

PHOTO:Bridgeman Art Library - London/Superstock; TEXT: St. John, Percy B. 1848. French Revolution in 1848 - The Three Days of February, 1848. New York: Geo. P. Putnam.

| | | | | |
|---|---|---|---|---|
| | | | | |
| | | | | |
| | | | | |
| | | | | |

**ANALYZING KEY IDEAS AND DETAILS**

**IDENTIFYING CONNECTIONS** Read closely to identify facts about the revolutions of 1830 and 1848. Use a chart like this one to compare and contrast the revolutions.

# THE REVOLUTIONS OF THE 1830S

**GUIDING QUESTION** *How did liberalism and nationalism present a challenge to conservatism in Europe during the 1830s and 1840s?*

Governments in Europe attempted to maintain the old order during the early decades of the nineteenth century. Beginning in 1830, however, the forces of change—liberalism and nationalism—began to break through the conservative domination of Europe.

In France the king was the Bourbon monarch Charles X. Brother to previous kings Louis XVI and Louis XVIII, he was a determined reactionary. Charles X rejected ideas for liberal reforms. He attempted to censor the press and to take away voting rights from much of the middle class. In response, liberals overthrew Charles X in 1830 and established a constitutional monarchy. Louis-Philippe, a distant cousin of Charles X, took the throne. Political support for the new monarch came from the upper-middle class.

In the same year, three more revolutions occurred in Europe. Nationalism was the chief force in all three of them. The southern states of the United Kingdom of the Netherlands had been incorporated into the kingdom in 1815, during the Congress of Vienna. Never happy under the rule of the Dutch king, these states rebelled in 1830, creating the independent state of Belgium.

Both Poland and Italy, which were ruled by foreign powers, made efforts to break free during this period. These efforts, however, were less successful. Poland had been granted some autonomy as a client state of Napoleon's empire, but during the Congress of Vienna, the Poles were placed back under the rule of Prussia, Austria, and Russia. An uprising was attempted in 1830, but Russian troops crushed this attempt to establish an independent Polish nation.

Italy during this period was ruled by a collection of small kingdoms and aristocratic states. Much of the northern part of the peninsula was governed by the Austrian Empire. These areas broke out in open revolt in 1830. However, Austrian troops marched south in 1831 and put down revolts, one by one.

**UNDERSTANDING CRAFT AND STRUCTURE**

1. **DETERMINING POINT OF VIEW** What type of emotional language does the writer use in this section to show the importance of the liberalism view to those who fought for it?
2. **ANALYZING TEXT PRESENTATION** How does the text present information about the challenges to conservatism in the 1830s? Does the way the text is organized help you better understand the information?

## ✓ CHECKING FOR UNDERSTANDING

1. **UNDERSTANDING CONTEXT** How did liberalism and nationalism present a challenge to conservatism in Europe during the 1830s and 1840s?
2. **EXPLAINING CAUSE AND EFFECT** How did the concept of nationalism affect the revolutions that occurred throughout Europe in the 1830s?
3. **UNDERSTANDING CONTEXT** How were the concepts of liberalism and nationalism related in the 1830s?

# THE REVOLUTIONS OF 1848

**GUIDING QUESTIONS** *How did liberalism and nationalism present a challenge to conservatism in Europe during the 1830s and 1840s? What were the results of the revolutionary uprisings that occurred throughout Europe in 1848?*

Despite liberal and nationalist successes in France and Belgium, the conservative order still dominated much of Europe as the midpoint of the nineteenth century approached. However, the forces of liberalism and nationalism continued to grow. These forces of change erupted once more in the revolutions of 1848.

## ANOTHER FRENCH REVOLUTION

Revolution in France was again the spark for revolution in other countries. Severe economic problems beginning in 1846 brought untold hardship in France to the lower middle class, workers, and peasants. At the same time, members of the middle class clamored for the right to vote. The government of Louis-Philippe refused to make changes, and opposition grew.

The monarchy was finally overthrown in 1848. A group of moderate and **radical** republicans set up a provisional, or **temporary**, government. The republicans were people who wanted France to return to a government of elected leaders and representatives. The memory of the French Revolution and of the early attempts at creating a republic remained strong.

*Burning the French throne at the Place de la Bastille, 1848*

Bibliotheque Nationale, Paris/Bridgeman Art Library

The provisional government called for the election of representatives to a Constituent Assembly that would draw up a new constitution. Election would be determined by **universal male suffrage,** meaning all adult men could vote. The provisional government also set up national workshops to provide work for the unemployed. From March to June, the number of unemployed enrolled in the national workshops rose from about 66,000 to almost 120,000. This emptied the treasury and frightened the moderates, who reacted by closing the workshops on June 21, 1848.

### ANALYZING KEY IDEAS AND DETAILS

1. **ANALYZING IDEAS** Based on the illustration and text, what effect did the continued growth of liberalism and nationalism have on French society?
2. **DETERMINING CENTRAL IDEAS** What is the central idea of the section "Revolt in the German States"? How does the text present and develop this idea?

### DETERMINING MEANING

The text states that both moderate and **radical** republicans helped set up the temporary French government. How can you compare the terms used to describe these two groups of republicans?

### DETERMINING MEANING

The word **temporary**, comes from the Latin root *tempus* or *tempor-*, meaning "time." As described in the text, how does a *temporary* government relate to the idea of "time"?

### DETERMINING MEANING

The term **universal male suffrage** describes how the French provisional government would be elected. How does this differ from the way elections are held today?

MAKING CONNECTIONS TO TODAY

## PUBLIC PROTESTS

John Locke and certain political thinkers of the Enlightenment established the idea that a government is meant to protect the rights and liberties of its citizens. The government of the United States and the governments of many nations around the world are products of this idea. But what happens when citizens' rights are not protected? In the Europe of the 1830s and 1840s, people around the European continent took to the streets to protest and make demands on the state. These patterns still persist even today. When certain groups feel that the official avenues of political change are not sufficient, they often organize peaceful public protests in an attempt to attract the attention of officials who can make that change happen.

1. **COMPARING AND CONTRASTING** How are modern protests similar to and different from the ones that occurred throughout Europe in the 1830s and 1840s?
2. **RELATING EVENTS** When would you become involved in a protest of government action?

*Taiwanese citizens protest a controversial China-Taiwan trade pact in 2014.*

The workers refused to accept this decision to close down the workshops. They poured into the streets in protest. In four days of bitter and bloody fighting, government forces crushed this working-class revolt. Thousands were killed and thousands more were sent to the French prison colony of Algeria, across the Mediterranean Sea in northern Africa.

The new French constitution, ratified on November 4, 1848, set up a republic called the Second Republic. The Second Republic had a single legislature elected by universal male suffrage. A president, also chosen by universal male suffrage, served for four years. In the elections for the presidency held in December 1848, Charles Louis Napoleon Bonaparte (called Louis-Napoleon), the nephew of the famous French ruler, won a resounding victory.

*The National Guard breaks up a labor uprising in Vienna, 1848.*

**INTEGRATING INFORMATION**
How does this image illustrate the chaos and level of participation in the 1848 revolts?

## REVOLT IN THE GERMAN STATES

News of the 1848 revolution in France led to upheaval in other parts of Europe. The Congress of Vienna, which lasted from 1814 to 1815, had recognized the existence of 38 independent German states (called the German Confederation). Of these, Austria and Prussia were the two great powers. The other states varied in size.

In 1848 cries for change led many German rulers to promise constitutions, a free press, jury trials, and other liberal reforms. In May 1848, an all-German parliament, called the Frankfurt Assembly, was held to fulfill a liberal and nationalist dream—the preparation of a constitution for a new united Germany. The Frankfurt Assembly's proposed constitution provided for a German state with a parliamentary government and a hereditary emperor ruling under a limited monarchy. The constitution also allowed for direct election of deputies to the parliament by universal male suffrage.

Ultimately, however, the Frankfurt Assembly failed to gain the support needed to achieve its goal. Frederick William IV of Prussia, to whom the throne was offered, refused to accept the crown from a popularly elected assembly. Thus, the assembly members had no real means of forcing the German rulers to accept their drafted constitution. German unification was not achieved.

**DETERMINING MEANING**

How can you use the individual word parts of the phrase **multinational empire** to come up with your own definition of the term?

## REVOLUTIONS IN CENTRAL EUROPE

The Austrian Empire also had its problems. It was a **multinational empire**—a collection of different peoples, including Germans, Czechs, Magyars (Hungarians), Slovaks, Romanians, Slovenes, Poles, Croats, Serbs, Ruthenians (Ukrainians), and Italians. Only the German-speaking Hapsburg dynasty held the empire together. The Germans, although only a quarter of the population, played a leading role in governing the Austrian Empire.

In March 1848, demonstrations erupted in the major cities. To calm the demonstrators, the Hapsburg court dismissed Metternich, the Austrian foreign minister, who fled to England. In Vienna, revolutionary forces took control of the capital and demanded a liberal constitution. To appease the revolutionaries, the government gave Hungary its own legislature. In Bohemia, the Czechs clamored for their own government.

Austrian officials had made concessions to appease the revolutionaries but were determined to reestablish their control over the empire. In June 1848, Austrian military forces crushed the Czech rebels in Prague. By the end of October, the rebels in Vienna had been defeated as well. With the help of a Russian army of 140,000 men, the Hungarian revolutionaries were finally subdued in 1849. The revolutions in the Austrian Empire had failed.

**MAKING CONNECTIONS ACROSS CULTURES**

### MULTINATIONAL EMPIRES

Up until very recently, most states in Europe were not nation-states, but large multiethnic empires. For example, the Austrian Empire in the mid-nineteenth century controlled vast territories. These territories included various ethnic groups with their own unique cultural histories and languages. Austria's empire included Hungarians, Poles, Italians, Czechs, Slovaks, and many others. As nationalism became a driving force in Europe, these ethnic groups came to demand their own independent states. This circumstance is not unknown today. Modern Spain, for instance, includes Catalans, Galicians, and Basques, each with their own cultural histories. This has resulted in tensions and independence movements, especially amongst the Catalans and Basques.

**UNDERSTANDING CHANGE** Give a possible example of ways citizens can overcome language barriers in a multinational empire.

## REVOLTS IN THE ITALIAN STATES

The Congress of Vienna had set up nine states in Italy, which were divided among the European powers. These states included the Kingdom of Piedmont in the north; the Two Sicilies (Naples and Sicily); the Papal States; a handful of small states; and the northern provinces of Lombardy and Venetia, which were now part of the Austrian Empire.

In 1848 a revolt broke out against the Austrians in Lombardy and Venetia. Revolutionaries in other Italian states also took up arms and sought to create liberal constitutions and a unified Italy. By 1849, however, the Austrians had reestablished complete control over Lombardy and Venetia. The old order also prevailed in the rest of Italy.

## THE FAILURES OF 1848

Throughout Europe in 1848, popular revolts started upheavals that led to liberal constitutions and liberal governments. But how could so many successes in 1848 soon be followed by so many failures? Two particular reasons stand out.

The unity of the revolutionaries had made the revolutions possible. However, moderate liberals and more radical revolutionaries were soon divided over their goals; therefore, conservative rule was reestablished.

In 1848 nationalities everywhere had also revolted in pursuit of self-government. However, little was achieved as divisions among nationalities proved disastrous. The Hungarians, for example, sought their freedom from the Austrians. At the same time, they refused the same to their minorities—the Slovenes, Croats, and Serbs. Instead of joining together to fight the old empire, minorities fought each other. The old order prevailed. Even with the reestablishment of conservative governments, however, the forces of nationalism and liberalism continued to influence political events.

### ✓ CHECKING FOR UNDERSTANDING

1. **UNDERSTANDING CONTEXT** How did liberalism and nationalism present a challenge to conservatism in Europe during the 1830s and 1840s? What were the results of the revolutionary uprisings that occurred throughout Europe in 1848?
2. **COMPARING AND CONTRASTING** How was the revolution in France in 1848 similar to and different from the revolutions of the 1830s?
3. **IDENTIFYING CONNECTIONS** What argument could Slovaks, Romanians, and Poles make in support of a nationalist uprising against the Austrian Empire?

### ANALYZING PRIMARY SOURCES

**GIUSEPPE MAZZINI ON YOUNG ITALY**

"Young Italy is a brotherhood of Italians who believe in a law of *Progress* and *Duty*, and are convinced that Italy is destined to become one nation. . .

Young Italy is *Unitarian*.

Because, without unity, there is no true nation.

Because without unity, there is no real strength; and Italy, surrounded as she is by powerful, united, and jealous nations, has need of strength before all things. . . . "

—Giuseppe Mazzini, from *General Instructions for the Members of Young Italy*, 1832

**INFERRING** Why would Italy's history have convinced Mazzini of the need for national unity?

Mazzini, Guiseppe. 1890. Life and Writings of Joseph Mazzini, Vol I. Smith, Elder & Co.

## LESSON 3 REVIEW

### Time and Place

1. **ANALYZING CHANGE** Explain how popular political thought throughout Europe changed from 1830 through the 1840s.

### Building History-Social Science Analysis Skills

2. **SUMMARIZING** How were the uprisings in France different from those in the German states?
3. **UNDERSTANDING CONTEXT** Were the nationalism and liberalism movements of the 1830s and 1840s a complete failure? Explain.
4. **INTERPRETING** Why did the Italian states fail to become unified after they were divided by revolts in 1848?

### Writing About History

5. **INFORMATIVE WRITING** Write an informative essay explaining the positive and negative effects of revolution on a society. Be sure to cite specific ideas about the nationalism and political movements throughout Europe in the 1830s and 1840s.

### Collaborating

6. **DETERMINING CONTEXT** With a partner, list reasons most of the rebellions of the 1830s and 1840s were unsuccessful.

ESSENTIAL QUESTIONS

- *How can innovation affect ways of life?*
- *How does revolution bring about political and economic change?*

THE STORY BEGINS...

LESSON 4

# Nationalism, Unification, and Reform

After winning the Franco-Prussian War, William I of Prussia was proclaimed emperor of the Second German Empire. In this letter to Count Otto von Bismarck, the new emperor showered his praise on his subject:

> "The brilliant position now occupied by my country has been attained through an unexpectedly rapid sequence of great events during the past six years. The work to which I called you ten years ago falls within this time. How you have justified the confidence with which I then summoned you, lies open to the world. It is to your counsel, your circumspection, your unwearying activity that Prussia and Germany owe the world-historical occurrence which is embodied in my capital to-day."

—William I of Prussia, from a letter dated March 21, 1871

Germany, through unification, had now harnessed its industrial and military resources to become the strongest state in Europe. Although the revolutions of 1848 had been defeated, nationalism and liberalism remained powerful forces.

PHOTO:DEA/G. DAGLI ORTI/Getty Images; TEXT:William I. 1903. Translated by J. A. Ford. The Correspondence of William I. & Bismarck with Other Letters from and to Prince Bismarck. New York: Frederick A. Stokes Company.

*King William I of Prussia is proclaimed the new emperor of Germany in the palace of Versailles.* ▶

| Great Britain | France | Austrian Empire | Russia |
|---|---|---|---|
| | | | |
| | | | |
| | | | |

**ANALYZING KEY IDEAS AND DETAILS**

**SUMMARIZING** Read closely to identify the changes that took place in the countries of Europe in the nineteenth century. Summarize these changes in a graphic organizer like this one.

# TOWARD NATIONAL UNIFICATION

GUIDING QUESTION *What led to the unification of Italy and Germany after the revolutions of 1848?*

The revolutions of 1848 had failed. By 1871, however, both Germany and Italy would be unified. Nation-states were rapidly becoming the most common form of political organization.

## BREAKDOWN OF THE CONCERT OF EUROPE

The Ottoman Empire had long controlled most of the Balkans in southeastern Europe. By 1800, however, the Ottoman Empire was in decline. Russia was interested in expanding its power into Ottoman lands in the Balkans. This expansion would allow Russian ships to sail through the Dardanelles, the straits between the Black Sea and the Mediterranean Sea. If Russia could achieve this goal, it would become the major power in eastern Europe and challenge British naval control of the eastern Mediterranean. Other European nations feared Russian ambition and had their own interest in the decline of the Ottoman Empire.

In 1853 the Russians invaded the Turkish Balkan provinces of Moldavia and Walachia. In response, the Ottoman Turks declared war on Russia. Great Britain and France, fearful of Russian gains in this war, declared war on Russia the following year. This conflict came to be called the Crimean War. The Crimean War was poorly planned and poorly fought. Eventually, heavy losses caused the Russians to seek peace. By the Treaty of Paris, signed in March 1856, Russia agreed to allow Moldavia and Walachia to be placed under the protection of all the great powers.

The effect of the Crimean War was to destroy the Concert of Europe. Austria and Russia, the chief powers maintaining the status quo before the 1850s, were now enemies. Austria, with its own interests in the Balkans, had refused to support Russia in the Crimean War. A defeated and humiliated Russia withdrew from European affairs for the next 20 years. Austria was now without friends among the great powers. This situation opened the door to the **unification** of Italy and Germany.

## ITALIAN UNIFICATION

In 1850 Austria was still the dominant power on the Italian Peninsula. After the failure of the revolution of 1848, Italian nationalists began to look to the northern Italian state of Piedmont for leadership in achieving the unification of

**UNDERSTANDING CRAFT AND STRUCTURE**

1. **ANALYZING TEXT PRESENTATION** In what order does the text present the facts that led to the unification of Italy and Germany? Does the way the text is organized help you better understand the information?
2. **DETERMINING MEANING** The text states that the loss of Alsace and Lorraine left France "burning for revenge." Using context clues, can you explain why the author would use this expression?

**DETERMINING MEANING**

The word **unification** contains the Latin root *uni-*, which means "one." The root *uni-* is found in the words *unique, union*, and *united*. How might knowing the meaning of the Latin root help a person determine the meaning of *unification*?

## UNIFICATION ITALY 1859–1870

## UNIFICATION GERMANY 1866–1871

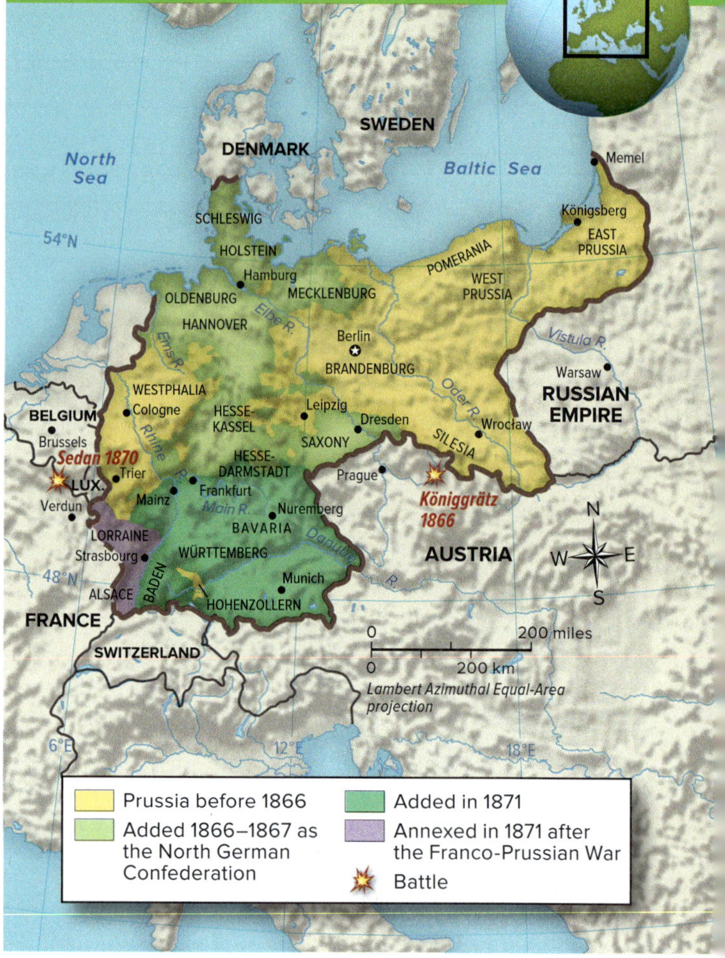


### GEOGRAPHIC REASONING

By 1871 Italy and Germany had unified.

1. **SPATIAL REASONING** Explain how the physical geography of Italy and Germany contributed to unification.
2. **EXPLORING REGIONS** Considering the provinces Germany won in the Franco-Prussian War, how might this have affected its relationship with France?

Italy. The royal house of Savoy ruled the Kingdom of Piedmont. Included in the kingdom were the island of Sardinia, and small regions in the northwest of Italy known as Piedmont, Nice, and Savoy. The ruler of the kingdom, beginning in 1849, was King Victor Emmanuel II.

The king named Camillo di Cavour his prime minister in 1852. As prime minister, Cavour pursued a policy of economic growth in order to equip a large army. Cavour, however, knew that Piedmont's army was not strong enough to defeat the Austrians. So he made an alliance with the French emperor Louis-Napoleon. Cavour then provoked the Austrians into declaring war in 1859.

Following that conflict, a peace settlement gave Nice and Savoy to the French. Lombardy, which had been under Austrian control, was given to Piedmont. Austria retained control of Venetia. Cavour's success caused nationalists in other Italian states (Parma, Modena, and Tuscany) to overthrow their governments and join their states to Piedmont.

Meanwhile, in southern Italy, a new Italian leader had arisen. Giuseppe Garibaldi, a dedicated patriot, raised an army of a thousand volunteers. A branch of the Bourbon dynasty ruled the Two Sicilies (Sicily and Naples), and a revolt had broken out in Sicily against the king. Garibaldi's forces landed in Sicily and, by the end of July 1860, controlled most of the island. In August, Garibaldi's forces crossed over to the mainland and began a victorious march up the Italian Peninsula. The entire Kingdom of the Two Sicilies fell in early September.

Garibaldi chose to turn over his conquests to Piedmont. On March 17, 1861, a new state of Italy was proclaimed under King Victor Emmanuel II. The task of unification was not yet complete, however. Austria still held Venetia in the north; and Rome was under the control of the pope, supported by French troops.

The Italians gained control of Venetia as a result of supporting Prussia in a war between Austria and Prussia. In 1870, during the Franco-Prussian War, French troops withdrew from Rome. Their withdrawal enabled the Italian army to annex Rome on September 20, 1870. Rome became Italy's new capital.

## GERMAN UNIFICATION

After the Frankfurt Assembly failed to achieve German unification in 1848 and 1849, Germans looked to Prussia for leadership in the cause of German unification. In the course of the nineteenth century, Prussia had become a strong, prosperous, and authoritarian state. The Prussian king had firm control over the government and the army. Prussia was also known for its **militarism**, or reliance on military strength.

In the 1860s, King William I tried to enlarge the Prussian army. When the Prussian legislature refused to levy new taxes for the proposed changes, William I appointed a new prime minister, Count Otto von Bismarck.

Bismarck has often been seen as the foremost nineteenth-century practitioner of realpolitik—the "politics of reality." In other words, this is politics based on practical matters rather than on ethics. Bismarck openly voiced his strong dislike for anyone who opposed him. After his appointment, Bismarck ignored the legislative opposition to the military reforms. He proceeded to collect taxes and to strengthen the army. From 1862 to 1866, Bismarck governed Prussia without approval of the parliament. In the meantime, he followed an active foreign policy, which soon led to war.

After defeating Denmark with Austrian help in 1864, Prussia gained control of the duchies of Schleswig and Holstein. Bismarck then goaded the Austrians into a war on June 14, 1866. The Austrians, no match for the well-disciplined Prussian army, were defeated on July 3.

Prussia now organized the German states north of the Main River into the North German Confederation. The southern German states, which were largely Catholic, feared Protestant Prussia. However, they also feared France, their western neighbor. As a result, they agreed to sign military alliances with Prussia for protection against France.

Prussia now dominated all of northern Germany, and the growing power and military might of Prussia worried France. In 1870 Prussia and France became embroiled in a dispute over the candidacy of a relative of the Prussian king for the throne of Spain. Taking advantage of the situation, Bismarck pushed the French into declaring war on Prussia on July 19, 1870—a conflict called the Franco-Prussian War.

Prussian armies advanced into France. At Sedan, on September 2, 1870, an entire French army and the French ruler, Napoleon III, were captured. Paris finally surrendered on January 28, 1871. An official peace treaty was signed in May. France had to pay 5 billion francs (about $1 billion) and give up the provinces of Alsace and Lorraine to the new German state. The loss of these territories left the French burning for revenge.

**DETERMINING MEANING**

The word **militarism** has the same root as the word *military*. *Military* means "related to soldiers or war." How might knowing the meaning of *military* help a person determine the meaning of *militarism*?

**BIOGRAPHY**

### OTTO VON BISMARCK (1815–1898)

Otto von Bismarck came from the class of aristocratic Prussian landowners known as Junkers. Under his leadership, Prussia won a series of European wars outside Germany. These victories compelled the other German states to unite in a single empire under Prussian rule. Bismarck became a national hero. In 1871, when King William I of Prussia was proclaimed the German kaiser, Bismarck became chancellor of this new German empire.

**CONTRASTING** How did Bismarck's method of unifying Germany differ from Garibaldi's method of unifying Italy?

**DETERMINING MEANING**

Read the paragraph that contains the word **kaiser**. This word is a Germanic transliteration of the word *Caesar*, a title adopted by the Roman Empire after the reign of Caesar Augustus for all its emperors. What does this background suggest about the meaning and use of *kaiser*?

Even before the war had ended, the southern German states had agreed to enter the North German Confederation. On January 18, 1871, Bismarck and 600 German princes, nobles, and generals filled the Hall of Mirrors in the palace of Versailles, 12 miles (19.3 km) outside Paris. William I of Prussia was proclaimed **kaiser**, or emperor, of the Second German Empire (the first was the medieval Holy Roman Empire).

The Prussian monarchy and the Prussian army had achieved German unity. The authoritarian and militaristic values of Prussia were triumphant in the new German state. With its industrial resources and military might, Germany had become the strongest power in Europe.

### ✓ CHECKING FOR UNDERSTANDING

1. **IDENTIFYING CAUSES** What led to the unification of Italy and Germany after the revolutions of 1848?
2. **USING MAPS** How did the unification of the German states change the balance of power in Europe?
3. **SUMMARIZING** How did the Crimean War destroy the Concert of Europe?

**UNDERSTANDING CRAFT AND STRUCTURE**

1. **ANALYZING TEXT PRESENTATION** How has the author organized the section called "Russia"?
2. **DETERMINING MEANING** Why does the author describe the Hungarians as "fiercely nationalistic"?

## NATIONALISM AND REFORM IN EUROPE

**GUIDING QUESTION** *What were the political climates in Great Britain, France, Austria, and Russia?*

While Italy and Germany were being unified, other states in Europe were also experiencing changes. These states include Great Britain, France, the Austrian Empire, and the Russian Empire.

### GREAT BRITAIN

Great Britain managed to avoid the revolutionary upheavals of the first half of the nineteenth century. In 1815 aristocratic landowning classes, which dominated both houses of Parliament, governed Great Britain. In 1832 Parliament passed a bill that increased the number of male voters. The new voters were chiefly members of the industrial middle class.

By giving the industrial middle class a direct interest in the process of ruling and government, Britain avoided revolution in 1848. In the 1850s and 1860s, Parliament also made social and political reforms that relieved some internal stresses and helped the country remain stable. Another reason for Britain's stability was its continuing economic growth. By 1850, industrialization and growth in trade had brought prosperity to the British middle class. After 1850, the real wages of many workers also rose significantly.

One key reform in Great Britain was the Slavery Abolition Act of 1833, which abolished slavery in most parts of the British Empire. Though this was inspired by the work of many in Great Britain's abolition movement, in many ways it was a consequence of the Industrial Revolution. Machines produced goods more efficiently than human beings, making slavery unprofitable. However, the British still depended heavily on trade with states that continued to engage in slavery, such as the United States.

*Great Britain's Queen Victoria in her coronation robes, 1838*

Popperfoto/Getty Images

Queen Victoria, whose reign from 1837 to 1901 was the longest in English history, reflected perfectly the national pride of the British. Her sense of duty and moral respectability came to define the values and attitudes of her age, which was later called the Victorian Age.

## FRANCE

In France, events after the revolution of 1848 moved toward the restoration of the monarchy. Four years after his election as president in 1848, Louis-Napoleon returned to the people to ask for the restoration of the empire. In this **plebiscite**, or popular vote, 97 percent responded with a yes vote. On December 2, 1852, Louis-Napoleon assumed the title of Emperor Napoleon III (Napoleon II was the son of Napoleon Bonaparte, but he never ruled France). The Second Empire had begun.

The government of Napoleon III was clearly authoritarian. As chief of state, Napoleon III controlled the armed forces, police, and civil service. Only he could introduce legislation and declare war. The Legislative Corps gave an appearance of representative government, because the members of the group were elected by universal male suffrage for six-year terms. However, they could neither initiate legislation nor affect the budget.

Napoleon III completely controlled the government and limited civil liberties. To distract the public from their loss of political freedom, he focused on expanding the economy. Government subsidies helped foster the rapid construction of railroads, harbors, roads, and canals.

In the midst of this economic expansion, Napoleon III also carried out a vast rebuilding of the city of Paris. The old Paris of narrow streets and walls was replaced by a modern Paris of broad boulevards, spacious buildings, public squares, an underground sewage system, a new public water supply system, and gaslights.

In the 1860s, opposition to some of Napoleon III's economic and governmental policies arose. In response, Napoleon III began to liberalize his **regime**. For example, he gave the legislature more power. After the French were defeated in the Franco-Prussian War in 1870, however, the Second Empire fell.

**DETERMINING MEANING**

To better understand the meaning of the word **regime**, consider its root. This word comes from the Latin word *regimen,* which means "rule."

## THE AUSTRIAN EMPIRE

Nationalism was a major force in nineteenth-century Europe. However, one of Europe's most powerful states—the Austrian Empire—was a multinational empire that had been able to frustrate the desire of its ethnic groups for independence.

After the Hapsburg rulers crushed the revolutions of 1848 and 1849, they restored centralized, autocratic government to the empire. Austria's defeat at the hands of the Prussians in 1866, however, forced the Austrians to make concessions to the fiercely nationalistic Hungarians.

The result was the Compromise of 1867, which created the dual monarchy of Austria-Hungary. Each of these two components of the empire now had its own constitution, legislature, government bureaucracy, and capital (Vienna for Austria and Budapest for Hungary). Holding the two states together were a single monarch—Francis Joseph was emperor of Austria and king of Hungary—and a common army, foreign policy, and system of finances.

**DETERMINING MEANING**

Read the paragraph that contains the word **emancipation**. Which words provide context clues you can use to determine the meaning of *emancipation*?

**ANALYZING PRIMARY SOURCES**

1. **CITING TEXT EVIDENCE** Why does Alexander say he is issuing this edict? Cite evidence from the text to support your response.
2. **ANALYZING EVENTS** What steps does Alexander state that the newly freed serfs must take to own the land on which they live?

## RUSSIA

At the beginning of the nineteenth century, Russia was still rural, agricultural, and autocratic. The Russian czar was regarded as a divine-right monarch with unlimited power. In 1856, however, the Russians suffered a humiliating defeat in the Crimean War. Even conservatives realized Russia was falling behind the western European states. Czar Alexander II decided to make some reforms.

Serfdom was the largest problem in czarist Russia. On March 3, 1861, Alexander issued an **emancipation** edict, which freed the serfs. Peasants could now own property. The government provided land for the peasants by buying it from the landlords. A portion of Alexander's edict reads:

> "In considering the various classes and conditions of which the State is composed we came to the conviction that the legislation of the empire having wisely provided for the organization of the upper and middle classes . . . has not attained the same degree of efficiency as regards the peasants attached to the soil [serfs]. . .
>
> These facts had already attracted the notice of our predecessors of glorious memory, and they had taken measures for improving the conditions of the peasants; but among those measures some were not stringent enough . . . and others . . . have been restricted to certain localities or simply adopted as an experiment. We thus came to the conviction that the work of a serious improvement of the condition of the peasants was a sacred inheritance bequeathed to us by our ancestors, a mission which, in the course of events Divine Providence called upon us to fulfill. . . .
>
> In virtue of the new dispositions above mentioned, the peasants attached to the soil will be invested within a term fixed by the law with all the rights of free cultivators. . . ."
>
> —Alexander II, *Emancipation Manifesto,* 1861

The new land system, however, was not very helpful to the peasants. The landowners often kept the best lands for themselves. The newly freed Russian peasants had little good land to support themselves. Emancipation, then, led not to a free, landowning peasantry but to an unhappy, land-starved peasantry that followed old ways of farming.

Alexander II attempted further reforms meant to help Russia catch up with the more industrialized nations of Europe. Russia's railway system was improved. The Russian government also sponsored some industrialization programs. Many foreign investors were also allowed to provide funds for Russian industry. Although it did not catch up with many other European powers, by 1900, Russia had made a great leap in industrialization.

In the end, however, Alexander's reforms pleased no one. Reformers wanted more changes, but conservatives thought the Czar was destroying Russia's basic institutions. When radicals assassinated Alexander II in 1881, his son, Alexander III, turned against most social reform programs.

▾ *Russian peasants in the late nineteenth century*

**ANALYZING INFORMATION** How does this image convey the possible living conditions of Russian peasants?

### ☑ CHECKING FOR UNDERSTANDING

1. **DETERMINING CONTEXT** What were the political climates in Great Britain, France, Austria, and Russia?
2. **IDENTIFYING CONNECTIONS** How did Great Britain avoid the major political changes other European powers experienced in 1830 and 1848?



PHOTO:Private Collection/The Stapleton Collection/Bridgeman Images; TEXT:Alexander II. 1862. Emancipation Manifesto. Reported in The Annual Register Or A View Of The History And Politics Of The Year 1861. London: J. & F. H. Rivington.

# NATIONALISM IN THE UNITED STATES

**GUIDING QUESTION** *How did nationalism influence events in the United States during the 1800s?*

The U.S. Constitution committed the nation to liberalism and nationalism. Yet unity did not come easily. By the mid-nineteenth century, disagreements about slavery threatened to tear the United States apart.

The South's economy was based on growing cotton on plantations, chiefly by slave labor. Four million enslaved African Americans were in the South by 1860, compared with one million in 1800. The South was determined to maintain the cotton economy and plantation-based slavery. **Abolitionism**, a movement to end slavery, arose in the North and directly challenged the Southern way of life.

As opinions over slavery grew more divided, compromise became less possible. Abraham Lincoln said in a speech in 1858 that "this government cannot endure, permanently half slave and half free." When Lincoln was elected president in November 1860, war became certain. In April, fighting erupted between North and South.

The American Civil War (1861–1865) was a bloody struggle. Lincoln's Emancipation Proclamation declared most of the nation's enslaved people "forever free." The Confederate forces surrendered on April 9, 1865. The United States remained united, "one nation, indivisible."

**UNDERSTANDING CRAFT AND STRUCTURE**

**ANALYZING TEXT PRESENTATION** What text structure does the author use to present the topic of nationalism in the United States?

**MAKING CONNECTIONS TO TECHNOLOGY**

### THE COTTON GIN

In 1793, an American named Eli Whitney invented the cotton gin. This machine automatically pulled cotton through wire teeth, easily removing the seeds. As a result, cotton became much easier to process and more profitable than other crops. The tragic consequence of Whitney's invention, however, was that it also made the institution of slavery indispensable in the American South. As cotton became more profitable, Southern planters relied more and more on the forced labor of enslaved people to plant, grow, and pick this crop.

### ✓ CHECKING FOR UNDERSTANDING

1. **IDENTIFYING CONNECTIONS** How did nationalism influence events in the United States during the 1800s?
2. **INTERPRETING** Why did the North and South have different views about slavery?
3. **UNDERSTANDING CONTEXT** What issues divided Americans in the 1800s?

## LESSON 4 REVIEW

### Time and Place

1. **IDENTIFYING CONNECTIONS** Write a paragraph about the American Civil War in which you define the terms *emancipation* and *abolitionism*. Indicate relationships between these terms.

### Building History-Social Science Analysis Skills

2. **COMPARING AND CONTRASTING** How were the wars in nineteenth-century Europe similar to and different from the Civil War in the United States?
3. **INTERPRETING** How were the economic changes in Great Britain, France, and Russia a reflection of the political conditions at the time?
4. **SUMMARIZING** Why were the Hapsburgs forced to compromise with the Hungarians? What was the outcome?

### Writing About History

5. **EXPLANATORY WRITING** Write an essay evaluating the nineteenth-century social reforms that took place in Great Britain, Russia, and the United States. Were the reforms successful? Did they contribute to the stability of these nations?

### Collaborating

6. **COLLABORATING** With a partner, use a graphic organizer to describe the changes and conflicts that took place in Great Britain, France, the Austrian Empire, and Russia during the nineteenth century.

## ESSENTIAL QUESTIONS

- *How can innovation affect ways of life?*
- *How does revolution bring about political and economic change?*

# THE STORY BEGINS...

LESSON 5

# Nation Building in Latin America

Spain and Portugal lost control of their Latin American empires in the early 1800s. Simón Bolívar, one of the leaders of the independence movement in Latin America, was elected president of Gran Colombia at the Congress of Angostura in 1819. Here he gave an address:

> "America, on becoming separated from the Spanish monarchy, found itself like the Roman Empire, when that enormous mass fell to pieces in the midst of the ancient world. Each dismembered portion formed then an independent nation in accordance with its situation or its interests, the difference being that those members established anew their former associations. We do not even preserve the vestiges of what we once were; we are not Europeans; we are not Indians, but an intermediate species between the aborigines and the Spaniards—Americans by birth and Europeans in right, we are placed in the dilemma of disputing with the natives our titles of possession and maintaining ourselves in the country where we were born, against the opposition of the invaders. Thus ours is a most extraordinary and complicated case. Moreover, our part has always been a purely passive one; our political existence has always been null, and we find ourselves in greater difficulties in attaining our liberty than we ever had when we lived on a plane lower than servitude, because we had been robbed not only of our liberty but also of active and domestic tyranny."

—Simón Bolívar, *Address at the Congress of Angostura,* 1819

Bolivar, Simon. 1919. Translated by Francisco Javier Yanes. An Address of Bolivar at the Congress of Angostura (February 15, 1819). Washington, DC: Press of B.S. Adams.

| Place | Leader | Outcome |
|---|---|---|
| | | |
| | | |
| | | |

**ANALYZING KEY IDEAS AND DETAILS**

**SUMMARIZING** Read closely to identify the revolts described in this lesson. List the leaders and summarize the outcomes of these revolts in a graphic organizer like this one.

# NATIONALIST REVOLTS

**GUIDING QUESTION** *How were nationalist revolts in Latin America influenced by the French and American Revolutions?*

By the end of the eighteenth century, the new political ideals stemming from the successful American Revolution were beginning to influence the creole elites. **Creoles** were the descendants of Europeans who had permanently settled in Latin America. They controlled land and business and were attracted to the principles of equality of all people in the eyes of the law, free trade, and a free press. The creoles especially disliked the domination of their trade by Spain and Portugal.

The creole elites soon began to use their new ideas to denounce the rule of the Spanish and Portuguese monarchs and their ***peninsulares*** (Spanish and Portuguese officials who resided temporarily in Latin America for political and economic gain and then returned to their homeland). The creole elites resented the *peninsulares*, who dominated Latin America and drained the region of its wealth.

At the beginning of the nineteenth century, Napoleon's wars provided the creoles with an opportunity for change. When Napoleon overthrew the monarchies of Spain and Portugal, the authority of the Spaniards and Portuguese in their colonial empires was weakened. Then, between 1807 and 1825, a series of revolts enabled most of Latin America to gain independence from their European rulers.

**ANALYZING KEY IDEAS AND DETAILS**

1. **DETERMINING CENTRAL IDEAS** What is the central idea of this section? How does the text present and develop this idea?
2. **CITING TEXT EVIDENCE** What evidence in the text supports the idea that the British played an important role in the movement toward Latin American independence?

## REVOLT IN HAITI

An unusual revolution occurred before the independence movements in Central and South America. Saint Domingue—on the island of Hispaniola in the Caribbean Sea—was a French sugar colony. Life for the enslaved people forced to work on this French sugar colony was difficult, and many plantation owners were unforgiving. In 1791, as the French monarchy was falling, François-Dominique Toussaint Louverture (too • SAN • loo • VUHR • TYUR) led the more than 100,000 enslaved people on Haiti in an uprising.

The Haitian Revolution found inspiration in the American and French Revolutions that came before it. The cause for the revolution was strengthened by the Enlightenment principle of the equality of all men. This idea, they argued, applied to enslaved peoples as much as it applied to the peasants in France. During a thirteen-year uprising, the Haitian revolutionaries seized control of the island of Hispaniola. On January 1, 1804, the western part of Hispaniola, now called Haiti, became the first independent state in Latin America.

The leader of the Haitian Revolution, Toussaint Louverture, was eventually captured by the French. Sent to a prison in France, he would die there in 1803, less than a year before Haiti would gain its independence. While in prison, he wrote a memoir defending his revolt against France. In this memoir, he discussed his role in developing a constitution for the new nation. His notes recall a warning given to the assembly:

> "When this assembly met, I represented to its members that they had an arduous and responsible task before them; that they were to make laws adapted to the country, advantageous to the Government, and beneficial to all, — laws suited to the localities, to the character and customs of the inhabitants. The Constitution must be submitted for the sanction of the Government, which alone had the right to adopt or reject it. Therefore, as soon as the Constitution was decided upon and its laws fixed, I sent the whole, by a member of the assembly, to the Government, to obtain its sanction."
>
> —Toussaint Louverture, *Memoir of the Life of General Toussaint Louverture,* 1802

**ANALYZING PRIMARY SOURCES**

1. **DETERMINING CENTRAL IDEAS** What is Toussaint Louverture's central idea in this paragraph?
2. **CITING TEXT EVIDENCE** Why does Louverture say he should not be held at fault for the constitution? Cite evidence from the text to support your response.

**MAKING CONNECTIONS ACROSS CULTURES**

### THE AMERICAN, FRENCH, AND HAITIAN REVOLUTIONS

Within a span of about 30 years, revolutions erupted in the thirteen colonies in North America, in France, and in the French colony of Saint Domingue (Haiti). Each revolution found its inspiration in the ideas of the Enlightenment, and these principles of freedom and equality were at the heart of all three revolutions. However, when each revolution was over, these principles were applied differently. In the United States and France, natural rights were not applied equally and were withheld from women and from men who did not own property. In the United States, too, Enlightenment ideas of freedom and equality were not extended to enslaved people. Haiti was different. In a colony largely populated by enslaved people, these revolutionary principles meant the total abolition of slavery. Haiti was the first colonial territory to abolish slavery. France would abolish slavery in its colonies in 1848. And in the United States, the abolition of slavery would come only after a brutal civil war in the 1860s.

1. **IDENTIFYING CONNECTIONS** How were these revolutions inspired by the Enlightenment?
2. **RELATING EVENTS** How was the Haitian Revolution different from the American and French Revolutions?

## REVOLT IN MEXICO

Beginning in 1810, Mexico also experienced a revolt. The first real hero of Mexican independence was Miguel Hidalgo. A parish priest, Hidalgo lived in a village about 100 miles (160 km) from Mexico City.

Hidalgo had studied the French Revolution. He roused the local indigenous people and **mestizos**, people of mixed European and indigenous descent, to free themselves from the Spanish: "Will you be free? Will you make the effort to recover from the hated Spaniards the lands stolen from your forefathers, three hundred years ago?"

On September 16, 1810, Hidalgo led this ill-equipped army of thousands of indigenous people and mestizos in an attack against the Spaniards. His forces were soon crushed, and a military court later sentenced Hidalgo to death. However, his memory lives on even today. In fact, September 16, the first day of the uprising, is Mexico's Independence Day.

**DETERMINING MEANING**

Using context clues, write a definition of the word **mestizo**. Use a dictionary or online reference to check your definition.

(t)Beard, John Relly. 1863. Toussaint L'Ouverture: A Biography and Autobiography. Boston: James Redpath, Publisher; (b)Bancroft, Hubert Howe. 1885. The Works of Hubert Howe Bancroft, Volume XII, History of Mexico, Vol. IV, 1804-1824. A. L. Bancroft & Company.

The role of indigenous people and mestizos in Mexico's revolt against Spanish control frightened the creoles and the *peninsulares*. Afraid of the masses, they cooperated in defeating the revolutionary forces. Creoles and *peninsulares* then decided to overthrow Spanish rule. These conservative elites wanted an independent nation ruled by a monarch. They selected a creole military leader, Agustín de Iturbide (EE • tur • BEE • thay), to set up a new government. In 1821 Mexico declared its independence from Spain. Iturbide named himself emperor in 1822 but was deposed in 1823. Mexico then became a republic.

## REVOLTS IN SOUTH AMERICA

José de San Martín of Argentina and Simón Bolívar of Venezuela, both members of the creole elite, were hailed as the "Liberators of South America." Bolívar began the struggle for Venezuelan independence in 1810. He also led revolts in New Granada (Colombia) and Ecuador. By 1819, these countries had formed Gran Colombia.

By 1810, the forces of San Martín had liberated Argentina from Spanish authority. In January 1817, San Martín led his forces over the Andes Mountains to attack the Spanish in Chile. The journey was an amazing feat. Two-thirds of the pack mules and horses died during the trip. Soldiers suffered from lack of oxygen and severe cold while crossing mountain passes more than two miles (3.2 km) above sea level.

The arrival of San Martín's forces in Chile completely surprised the Spanish forces there. As a result, they were badly defeated at the Battle of Chacabuco on February 12, 1817. Chile declared its independence in 1818. In 1821 San Martín advanced on Lima, Peru, the center of Spanish authority.

San Martín was convinced that he could not complete the liberation of Peru alone. He welcomed Simón Bolívar and his forces. Bolívar, the "Liberator of Venezuela," took on the task of crushing the last significant Spanish army at Ayacucho on December 9, 1824.

By the end of 1824, Peru, Uruguay, Paraguay, Colombia, Venezuela, Argentina, Bolivia, and Chile had become free of Spain. Earlier, in 1822, the prince regent of Brazil had declared Brazil's independence from Portugal. The Central American states had become independent in 1823. In 1838 and 1839, they divided into five republics: Guatemala, El Salvador, Honduras, Costa Rica, and Nicaragua.

## THREATS TO INDEPENDENCE

In the early 1820s, one major threat remained to the newly won independence of the Latin American states. Members of the Concert of Europe favored using troops to restore Spanish control in Latin America. The British, who wished to trade with Latin America, disagreed. They proposed joint action with the United States against any European moves against Latin America.

Distrustful of British motives, James Monroe, the president of the United States, acted alone in 1823. In the Monroe Doctrine, he declared that the Americas were off limits for any colonizational efforts, and strongly warned against any European **intervention** in the Americas.

**DETERMINING MEANING**

The word **intervention** has the same prefix as the word *interfere*. How might knowing the meaning of *interfere* help a person determine the meaning of *intervention*?

▼ *General San Martín after crossing the Andes in 1817*

More important to Latin American independence than American words, however, was the British navy. Other European powers feared the power of the British navy, which stood between Latin America and any planned European invasion force.

## ✓ CHECKING FOR UNDERSTANDING

1. **ANALYZING CAUSES** How were nationalist revolts in Latin America influenced by the French and American Revolutions?
2. **UNDERSTANDING CONTEXT** How might the post-revolution government of Mexico have been different if Hidalgo's revolt had succeeded?
3. **IDENTIFYING CONNECTIONS** What do Hidalgo, José de San Martín, and Simón Bolívar have in common?

# NATION BUILDING

**UNDERSTANDING CRAFT AND STRUCTURE**

1. **ANALYZING TEXT PRESENTATION** How has the author organized this section to present key points about nation building?
2. **ANALYZING TEXT** What words or phrases in the text describe the experiences of Latin American nations in negative terms? How do these words and phrases affect the tone of the text?

**GUIDING QUESTIONS** *What difficulties did newly independent Latin American countries face? How did economic dependence on foreign investment influence Latin America through the mid-1800s?*

The new Latin American nations faced a number of serious problems between 1830 and 1870. The wars for independence had resulted in a staggering loss of people, property, and livestock. During the course of the nineteenth century, the new Latin American nations would become economically dependent on Western nations once again.

## RULE OF THE CAUDILLOS AND INEQUALITY

**DETERMINING MEANING**

What words in the text suggest that the rule of the **caudillos** was problematic for the masses of Latin America?

Most of the new nations of Latin America began with republican governments, but they had no experience in self-rule. Soon after independence, strong leaders known as **caudillos** gained power.

Caudillos ruled chiefly by military force and were usually supported by the landed elites. Many kept the new national states together. Some were also modernizers who built roads and canals, ports, and schools. Others were destructive.

Mexican General Antonio López de Santa Anna, for example, ruled Mexico from 1833 to 1855. He misused state funds, halted reforms, and created chaos. In 1835 American settlers in the Mexican state of Texas revolted against Santa Anna's rule. Texas gained its independence in 1836 and U.S. statehood in 1845. War between Mexico and the United States soon followed (1846–1848). Mexico was defeated and lost almost one-half of its territory to the United States.

Fortunately for Mexico, Santa Anna's disastrous rule was followed by a period of reform from 1855 to 1876. This era was dominated by Benito Juárez, a Mexican national hero. The son of Zapotec peasants, President Juárez brought liberal reforms to Mexico, including separation of church and state, land distribution to the poor, and an educational system for all of Mexico.

Other caudillos, such as Juan Manuel de Rosas in Argentina, were supported by the masses. These caudillos became extremely popular and brought about radical change. Unfortunately, the caudillo's authority depended on his personal power. When he died or lost power, civil wars for control of the country often **erupted**.

A fundamental problem for all the new Latin American nations was the domination of society by the landed elites. Large estates remained a way of life in Latin America. By 1848, for example, the Sánchez Navarro family in Mexico possessed 17 estates made of 16 million acres (6,480,000 ha).

Land remained the basis of wealth, social prestige, and political power throughout the nineteenth century. Landed elites ran governments, controlled courts, and kept a system of inexpensive labor. These landowners made enormous profits by growing single **cash crops**, such as coffee, for export. Most of the population had no land to grow basic food crops. As a result, the masses experienced dire poverty.

▲ *Mexican General Antonio López de Santa Anna*



## IMPERIALISM AND ECONOMIC DEPENDENCE

Political independence brought economic independence, but old patterns were quickly reestablished. Instead of Spain and Portugal, Great Britain now dominated the Latin American economy. British merchants moved into Latin America, and British investors poured in funds. Old trade relationships soon reemerged.

Latin America continued to serve as a source of raw materials and foodstuffs for the industrial nations of Europe and the United States. Exports included wheat, tobacco, wool, sugar, coffee, and hides. At the same time, Latin American countries imported finished consumer goods, especially textiles, and had limited industry.

The emphasis on exporting raw materials and importing finished products ensured the ongoing domination of the Latin American economy by foreigners. Latin American countries remained economically dependent on Western nations, even though they were no longer colonies.

**DETERMINING MEANING**

Landowners made large profits from growing **cash crops** such as coffee. Based on the text, do you think the landowners grew cash crops for personal use or to sell?

### ☑ CHECKING FOR UNDERSTANDING

1. **IDENTIFYING CONNECTIONS** What difficulties did newly independent Latin American countries face? How did economic dependence on foreign investment influence Latin America through the mid-1800s?

2. **DETERMINING CONTEXT** How did caudillos come to power in so many new Latin American nations?

3. **IDENTIFYING CAUSES** Why did Latin American countries continue to experience economic dependence after achieving political independence?

## LESSON 5 REVIEW

### Time and Place

1. **INTERPRETING** Give examples of three cash crops that were grown in Latin America and explain why they were cash crops.

### Building History-Social Science Analysis Skills

2. **DETERMINING CONTEXT** Why did the creoles oppose the presence of the *peninsulares*?
3. **EXPLAINING EFFECTS** How did Napoleon influence the outcome of political events in Latin America?
4. **SUMMARIZING** What were some of the consequences of Santa Anna's rule?

### Writing About History

5. **NARRATIVE WRITING** Write a diary entry from the perspective of a creole leader in Mexico at the time Miguel Hidalgo is rousing the indigenous people and mestizos or leading them into battle. Be sure to include reactions to the events taking place at this time.

### Collaborating

6. **COLLABORATING** With a partner, discuss the revolts in Latin America. Make a generalization about the success or failure of the various revolutions. Give examples to support your conclusions.

# STUDY GUIDE

## THE FIRST GLOBAL ECONOMIC SYSTEMS
**LESSON 1**

**Commercial Revolution**

Mercantilism, which was the belief that the prosperity of a nation depended on its supply of bullion (gold and silver) contributed to the success of the Commercial Revolution.

**The Columbian Exchange**

The exchange of plants, animals, and even things like diseases between Europe and the Americas was a part of the Columbian Exchange.

## THE INDUSTRIAL REVOLUTION
**LESSON 2**

**Changes during the Industrial Revolution**

- Cotton production became more efficient
- Improvements to iron production
- Development of factories
- Growth of cities
- Development of the industrial middle class and the working class

## THE REVOLUTIONS OF THE 1840S
**LESSON 3**

**France:** The monarchy was overthrown by moderate, radical republicans and a new French constitution was ratified, changing France to a republic and electing a president.

**Germany:** Liberalism and nationalism led the Frankfurt Assembly to call for a parliamentary government.

**Central Europe:** Czech and Hungarian revolutionaries demanded liberal constitutions and their own governments; the Austrian military defeated the Hungarian revolutionaries.

**Italian States:** A revolt broke out against the Austrians in Lombardy and Venetia in 1848. By 1849, however, the Austrians had reestablished complete control over Lombardy and Venetia.

## ITALIAN AND GERMAN UNIFICATION
**LESSON 4**

| Italy | Germany |
|---|---|
| United under the rule of King Victor Emmanuel II by Cavour (in the north) and Garibaldi (in the south) | United with the help of the Prussians and the Emperor of Prussia, William I |

## INDEPENDENCE IN LATIN AMERICA
**LESSON 5**

- Hispaniola west, now Haiti (1804)
- Mexico (1821)
- Brazil (1823)
- Chile (1818)
- Argentina (1810)
- Central American States (1823)
- Peru, Uruguay, Paraguay, Colombia, Venezuela, Bolivia (by the end of 1824)

# CHAPTER 4 Assessment

**Directions: On a separate sheet of paper, answer the questions below. Make sure you read carefully and answer all parts of the questions.**

## Short Answer

1. **UNDERSTANDING CONTEXT** Explain the shift in the British textile manufacturing from the eighteenth to the nineteenth century helping initiate the Industrial Revolution. What key inventions and inventors led the way?

2. **EXPLAINING CAUSES** How might the working conditions in mines and mills have led the new industrial working class to support socialism?

3. **INTERPRETING** What do the actions of the Austrian government in response to the revolts of 1848 suggest about its interest and relationship to reform?

4. **UNDERSTANDING CONTEXT** How did the ideas of liberalism influence political revolutions?

5. **SUMMARIZING** Summarize the key events that led Italy to ultimately unify. Emphasize how this process involved a chain of events.

6. **EXPLAINING CAUSE AND EFFECT** What can you conclude about the relationship between Britain's economic transformations and its political stability?

7. **IDENTIFYING CONNECTIONS** What were the influences of Central and South American revolutionaries, including Simón Bolívar?

8. **EXPLAINING CAUSE AND EFFECT** How did the domination of large estates that produced cash crops affect a majority of the Latin American population—the non-landowning population?

9. **DESCRIBING** What is the theory of mercantilism?

10. **SUMMARIZING** What did the governments of European nations do to encourage exports and favorable trade balances?

11. **ANALYZING CHANGE** In what way did the governments of the earliest industrialized countries encourage the process of industrialization?

12. **ANALYZING ISSUES** What benefits did foreign investors provide to newly independent Latin American countries? What were the drawbacks of foreign investment?

13. **SUMMARIZING** Summarize the relationship between the scientific developments of the nineteenth century and the cultural movements that resulted.

## History and Social-Science Analysis

14. **INTERPRETING** Working with a partner, create a large chart that lists social and economic transformations that brought about, perpetuated, and resulted from the Industrial Revolution.

15. **IDENTIFYING BIAS** We live in a world created by the Industrial Revolution. How does this affect your views about industrialization? Are those views reflected in the text?

16. **ANALYZING CHANGE** Explain the origin and the outcomes of Europe's Commercial Revolution. What factors contributed to its development? Present your answers along with supporting reasons and evidence in the form of an essay.

**Need Extra Help?**

| If You've Missed Question | 1 | 2 | 3 | 4 | 5 | 6 | 7 | 8 | 9 | 10 | 11 | 12 | 13 | 14 | 15 | 16 |
|---|---|---|---|---|---|---|---|---|---|---|---|---|---|---|---|---|
| Review Lesson | 2 | 2 | 3 | 3 | 4 | 4 | 5 | 5 | 1 | 1 | 2 | 5 | 2 | 2 | 2 | 1 |

# Assessment, continued

## Research and Presentation

**17** **RELATING EVENTS** Create a map that shows the expanse of the Austrian Empire in the 1840s. Label the nations of people it encompassed. Include an inset of modern Europe today that shows a comparison of the past to present-day national borders.

**18** **RESEARCHING FOR INQUIRY** Read one or two chapters from Mary Shelley's *Frankenstein*. Then write an essay answering the following question: To what extent is this book a reflection of the costs of industrialization and scientific advancement? Create a graphic organizer to present your argument.

**19** **USING EVIDENCE** Review the text on the various revolutions in Latin America. Then draft an essay explaining the most significant causes of revolution at this time generally. Be sure to point to particular cases. But you should concentrate on looking at larger themes that show relationships across different contexts. Create a graphic organizer to present your conclusions.

## Reading and Analyzing Primary Sources

Use the document to answer the following questions.

In 1832, Italian nationalist Giuseppe Mazzini wrote the following about the political movement for Italian unification, Young Italy.

> "Young Italy is a brotherhood of Italians who believe in a law of Progress and Duty, and are convinced that Italy is destined to become one nation. . . Young Italy is Unitarian. Because, without unity, there is no true nation. Because without unity, there is no real strength; and Italy, surrounded as she is by powerful, united, and jealous nations, has need of strength before all things. . . ."
>
> —Giuseppe Mazzini, from *General Instructions for the Members of Young Italy,* 1832

**20** **DETERMINING CENTRAL IDEAS** Based on the excerpt above, which of the following positions would Mazzini likely support about Italy's future?

**A.** He would accept a federal state that recognizes regional differences.
**B.** He would reject the call for war to unify Italy.
**C.** He would propose special protections for non-Italians.
**D.** He would prefer a single Italian state with one government.

**21** **CITING TEXT EVIDENCE** Which line from the excerpt supports the conclusion that Mazzini thinks war with others in Europe is the likely price to pay for unification?

**A.** "Young Italy is a brotherhood of Italians who believe in a law of Progress and Duty, and are convinced that Italy is destined to become one nation . . ."
**B.** ". . . Italy, surrounded as she is by powerful, united, and jealous nations . . ."
**C.** "Because without unity, there is no real strength;"
**D.** "Young Italy is Unitarian."

**22** **ANALYZING CENTRAL IDEAS** What does the reference to Italians believing in "a law of Progress and Duty" suggest about Mazzini's ideas on nationalism?

**A.** He believes nationalism is the natural result of progress.
**B.** He believes nationalism requires great sacrifice.
**C.** He believes nationalism is a challenge to the natural order.
**D.** He believes nations are destined to expand and to conquer.

## Writing About History

**23** **USING EVIDENCE** How did the Industrial Revolution affect the formation of new economic and political systems in Europe? How did these systems compare with the absolutist and agricultural societies of the previous era?

## Speaking and Listening About History

**24** **COLLABORATING** Meet in a small group to discuss the following question: How might the Industrial Revolution have contributed to the challenges newly independent Latin American states faced? Have one member of your group serve as a moderator for the group discussion.

**Need Extra Help?**

| If You've Missed Question | 17 | 18 | 19 | 20 | 21 | 22 | 23 | 24 |
|---|---|---|---|---|---|---|---|---|
| Review Lesson | 2 | 2 | 5 | 3 | 3 | 3 | 1–5 | 2, 5 |

Mazzini, Guiseppe. 1890. Life and Writings of Joseph Mazzini, Vol I. Smith, Elder & Co.

◀ *By applying research in electromagnetic waves, Marconi invented the wireless telegraph. Marconi is shown here with his invention, which became the basis of modern radio.*

1870 — 1914

# Mass Society and Democracy

## CHAPTER 5



**GO DIGITAL**
*It's All online!*

## ASKING ESSENTIAL QUESTIONS

***How can industrialization affect a country's economy?***
***How are political and social structures influenced by economic changes?***

**What Will You Learn?** You will learn how ongoing technological innovation in the late 19th and early 20th centuries provoked economic, social, political and cultural changes in Europe and North America.

**Why Does This Matter?** Much of modern society was shaped during the Second Industrial Revolution. Technological advances in the late 1800s expanded global trade, spurred urbanization, and increased social stratification. They also empowered unions, women, and many others to demand higher standards of living and more rights and protections.

**How Will You Know That You Learned It?** You will be able to identify significant technological innovations from the Second Industrial Revolution and to explain how those innovations contributed to pivotal economic, social, political, and cultural changes in Europe and North America.

**Using Your Inquiry Journal** As you read this chapter and examine the primary sources, use your Inquiry Journal to help you make notes and expand your list of questions. As you gather information, think about how you will answer the Essential Questions above.

# PLACE & TIME Europe 1870–1914

In the late 1800s, the European population increased in industrial areas. Workers migrated from the countryside to find employment in coal mines, factories, domestic service, and offices. Working-class families crowded into urban areas, where they struggled with insufficient housing and services. Urbanization often caused poverty, unemployment, the spread of disease, and political unrest. Between 1870 and 1914, Great Britain, France, and Germany gradually responded to the needs of their growing populace.

## STEP INTO THE PLACE

Read the quotes and look at the information presented on the map.

**1. PATTERNS AND MOVEMENT** Based on the map, in what parts of Europe would you expect to find the highest rates of urbanization in 1900? Near what physical features are these areas concentrated?

**2. IDENTIFYING CONNECTIONS** What do the sources suggest about the lives and status of working-class women during the Second Industrial Revolution?

“For the next three months I was nearer to starvation than any time since. I learned the bitterness of a hopeless search for work. . . . The best plan was to visit the wholesale firms in the City and get information about vacancies from the commercial travellers, and then journey as fast as the old horse buses allowed—perhaps right across London—only to find a queue of 150 to 200 applicants already there.”

—Margaret Bondfield, from *A Life's Work*, on her unemployment before becoming one of the first female members of Parliament in Britain

“It is like this in working-class families. The man, the one who after all has to work (*sic*), consumes the largest share of the available food. The children too have as much as possible. In most cases the mother is left out—she has to be satisfied with one or two mouthfuls if there is not enough to go round, and lives on bread, coffee, and potatoes. A working man's wife makes daily sacrifices for her family. She is happy if nobody shouts for more, even is [sic] she is still hungry herself.”

—from Union of Construction Workers, Hamburg, Germany, 1908

## STEP INTO THE TIME

**CHRONOLOGICAL THINKING**

Based on the time line, what types of change were taking place in Europe and other parts of the world during the Second Industrial Revolution? How would you describe the pace of that change?



**EUROPE**

- **1870** Women in Great Britain win the right to own some property
- **1875** German Social Democratic Party emerges
- **1876** Alexander Graham Bell invents telephone
- **1884** British Reform Act increases the number of adult male voters

1870 — 1875 — 1880 — 1885

**WORLD EVENTS**

- **1876** Ottoman Empire's first Constitution
- **1884** Berlin West Africa conference opens
- **1885** Indian National Congress forms

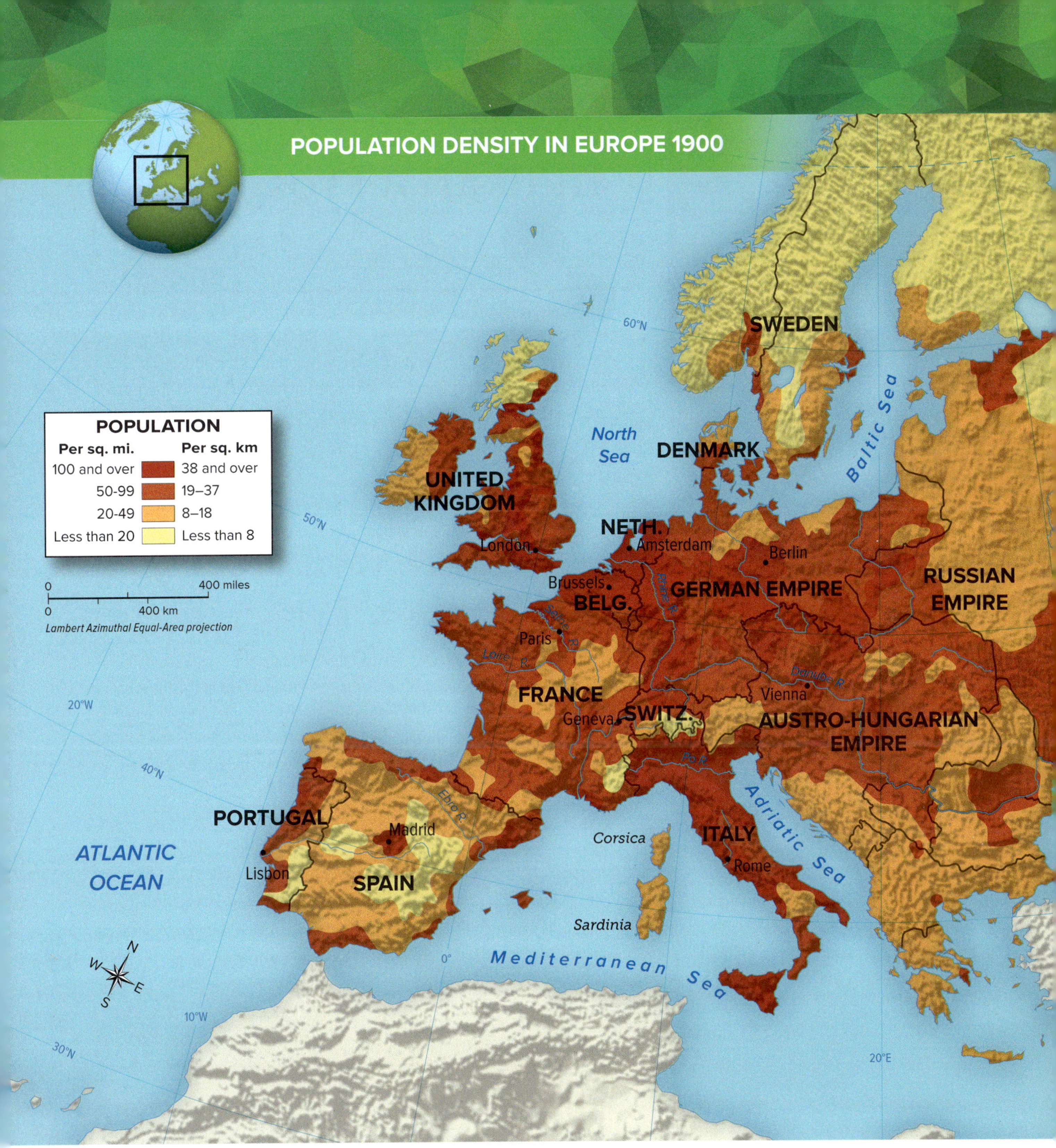


- **1888** Abolition of slavery in Brazil
- **1890** Emperor William II fires Otto von Bismarck
- **1894** Czar Nicholas II begins reign over Russian Empire
- **1894** China and Japan go to war over Korea
- **1899** South African War (Boer War) begins
- **1900** Labour Party forms in Great Britain
- **1900** Boxer Rebellion in China
- **1903** Emmeline Pankhurst and her daughters found the Women's Social and Political Union
- **1908** Congo annexed by Belgium
- **1910** Mexican revolution begins
- **1912** Universal male suffrage begins in Italy
- **1912** African National Congress forms
- **1914** Panama Canal opens

1890 1895 1900 1905 1910 1914

ESSENTIAL QUESTIONS

- *How can industrialization affect a country's economy?*
- *How are political and social structures influenced by economic changes?*

LESSON 1

# The Growth of Industrial Prosperity

## THE STORY BEGINS...

On November 15, 1884, *Scientific American* reported on the 400 men from the Edison Electric Lighting Company who wore lightbulbs on their heads as they marched through New York City. Wires ran from the bulbs, down their sleeves, to a steam generator.

> "That an electric lighting plant, complete in every detail, and in full operation, can be moved at the uneven pace of a procession over the rough paving of a street, without interrupting the current or in any degree changing the brilliancy and steadiness of the light, is a fact which, while of interest to the scientific world, clearly shows the perfection to which electric lighting machinery has been brought. . . . Upon the first and last part of the line of march every part of the plant worked most admirably, and the illumination was intense and beautiful, the light flooding every nook and cranny in the streets passed through. But in the intervening distance, . . . this portion of the parade was conspicuous solely on account of the darkness that pervaded it. This interruption was caused by mud from the water tanks clogging the hose leading to the pump. All went well after the hose had been cleaned."

—*Scientific American,* November 15, 1884

Little did the magazine's readers know that they were observing a revolution not only in lighting but also in production, transportation, and communication that would power the modern world.

*The assembly line, seen here in action at a Ford automobile factory, revolutionized industrial production.* ▶

| The Second Industrial Revolution | |
|---|---|
| Technologies and Innovations | Effects |
| | |
| | |
| | |
| | |
| | |

**ANALYZING KEY IDEAS AND DETAILS**

**DESCRIBING** Read closely to identify the effects of technologies and innovations from the Second Industrial Revolution. Record these effects in a graphic organizer like this one.

# THE SECOND INDUSTRIAL REVOLUTION

**GUIDING QUESTION** *What were the causes and effects of the Second Industrial Revolution in Western Europe?*

The first Industrial Revolution had given rise to textiles, railroads, and iron. Use of fossil fuels such as coal and then petroleum and natural gas resulted in revolutionary changes in energy usage, both in factories and homes. In the Second Industrial Revolution, steel, chemicals, and electricity led the way to new industrial frontiers.

## STEEL, ELECTRICITY, AND A NEW ENGINE

In 1855 Sir Henry Bessemer patented a new process for making high-quality steel efficiently and cheaply known as the Bessemer process. Steel soon replaced iron and was used in the building of lighter, smaller, and faster machines and engines. It was also used in railways, ships, and weapons. In 1860 Great Britain, France, Germany, and Belgium produced 125,000 tons (112,500 t) of steel. By 1913, the total was an astounding 32 million tons (29 million t).

Electricity was a valuable new form of energy. It was converted into other energy forms, such as heat, light, and motion, and moved easily through wires. In the 1870s, the first practical generators of electrical current were developed. By 1910, hydroelectric power stations and coal-fired, steam-generating plants connected homes and factories to a common source of power.

Electricity gave birth to a series of inventions. Homes and cities began to have electric lights when Thomas Edison in the United States and Joseph Swan in Great Britain created the lightbulb. A revolution in communications also began. Alexander Graham Bell invented the telephone in 1876. Guglielmo Marconi sent the first radio waves across the Atlantic Ocean in 1901.

By the 1880s, streetcars and subways powered by electricity had appeared in major European cities. Electricity transformed the factory as well. Conveyor belts, cranes, and machines could all be powered by electricity. With electric lights, factories could remain open 24 hours a day.

The development of the internal-combustion engine, fired by oil and gasoline, provided a new source of power in transportation. This engine gave rise to ocean liners with oil-fired engines, as well as to the airplane and the automobile. In 1903 Orville and Wilbur Wright made the first flight in a fixed-wing plane at Kitty Hawk, North Carolina. In 1919 the first regular passenger air service was established.

**UNDERSTANDING CRAFT AND STRUCTURE**

1. **ANALYZING TEXT** How does the text structure suggest a cause-and-effect relationship between industrial technologies and broader economic changes?
2. **DETERMINING MEANING** Why does the author describe the amount of steel produced in 1913 as "astounding"? How does the word *astounding* shape the overall meaning or tone of this section?

**MAKING CONNECTIONS TO TODAY**

### COAL AND OIL

Both the First and Second Industrial Revolution depended on vast imports of raw materials such as cotton (for textile manufacturing) and copper wire (for electricity). A source of energy to fuel new machines was important, too. At first, this was wood, but as the Industrial Revolutions progressed, this turned to fuels such as coal. With the invention of the internal combustion engine, petroleum became this necessary fuel source. The legacy of the Second Industrial Revolution is today's dependence on a global trade in oil.

## NEW PATTERNS AND PRODUCTS

Industrial production grew at rapid pace in large part because of greatly increased sales of manufactured goods. Europeans could afford to buy more of these consumer products for several reasons. Wages for workers increased after 1870. In addition, prices for manufactured goods were lower because of an increase in supply and reduced transportation costs. Goods were being produced more quickly and with greater efficiency. One of the biggest reasons for more efficient production was the **assembly line**, a new manufacturing method pioneered by Henry Ford in 1913. The assembly line allowed for a much more efficient **mass production** of goods.

In the cities, the first department stores began to sell a new range of consumer goods. These goods—clocks, bicycles, electric lights, and typewriters, for example—were made possible by the steel and electrical industries. A consumer culture, where manufacturers focused on creating and selling inexpensive, standardized goods to consumers, was formed.

The assembly line and mass production led to the creation of a process called "division of labor" where larger assembly tasks were divided into smaller processes in order to improve efficiency. However, while division of labor allowed workers to become more specialized it also meant that the tasks factory workers performed became increasingly repetitive. Work schedules became regimented and standardized, based around a shift system. Specialized teams of workers would end their work day and be replaced by another team of equally specialized workers. Factory workers could go home, but production would never cease.

### DETERMINING MEANING

To better understand **assembly line**, consider that *assembly* contains the root *assemble*, which means "to put together the parts of something." With this in mind, write your own definition of *assembly line*. Use a dictionary or an online reference to check your definition.

### DETERMINING MEANING

The word *mass* refers to a large quantity or number. How does this meaning help you understand the phrase **mass production**?

### GEOGRAPHIC REASONING

1. **EXPLORING REGIONS** What industries were important to Central Europe? What about the United Kingdom?

## INDUSTRIALIZATION IN EUROPE 1914

## UNEVEN INDUSTRIALIZATION

Not everyone enjoyed the benefits from the Second Industrial Revolution. By 1900, Europe was divided into two economic zones. Great Britain, Belgium, France, the Netherlands, Germany, the western part of the Austro-Hungarian Empire, and northern Italy made up an advanced industrialized core. These nations had a high standard of living and adequate systems of transportation. Southern Italy, most of Austria-Hungary, Spain, Portugal, the Balkan territories, and Russia remained largely agricultural economies. These areas provided food and raw materials for the industrial countries and had a much lower standard of living than the rest of Europe.

*In a Ford plant, each worker in the assembly line repeats one task over and over to build Model T automobiles.*

**INTEGRATING INFORMATION** How did the assembly line transform the car industry?

©Culver Pictures, Inc./SuperStock

## THE CORPORATION

**Corporations** grew in number and wealth during the Second Industrial Revolution. Corporations were not new by the time of the Industrial Revolution. However, the growth in wealth during this era saw them rise to a prominence not previously seen. As they competed against one another for profits, these corporations continued to grow as they sponsored new innovations in consumer goods and refinements in systems of production. Many corporations that came into existence during the Second Industrial Revolution continue to exist today.

**DETERMINING MEANING**

What context clues in the paragraph help you determine the meaning of **corporation**?

## TOWARD A WORLD ECONOMY

The Second Industrial Revolution, combined with the growth of transportation by steamship and railroad, fostered a true world economy. Industrial production changed the lives of those who worked in and out of factories. Raw materials from across the world became essential to the creation of European manufactured goods. By 1900, Europeans were receiving beef and wool from Argentina and Australia, coffee from Brazil, iron ore from Algeria, and sugar from Java. Despite this increase in global trade, most of the world's people continued to depend on subsistence agriculture to meet their everyday needs.

European capital was invested abroad to develop railways, mines, electrical power plants, and banks. Of course, foreign countries also provided markets for Europe's manufactured goods. Standards of living rose, but for the most part, wealth became increasingly concentrated in an investor class that resided largely in Europe and North America. With its capital, industries, and military might, Europe dominated the world economy by 1900.

### ✓ CHECKING FOR UNDERSTANDING

1. **EXPLAINING CAUSE AND EFFECT** What were the causes and effects of the Second Industrial Revolution in Western Europe?

2. **IDENTIFYING CONNECTIONS** How did inventions such as electricity and steel work together to revolutionize transportation?

3. **USING MAPS** How does the map support conclusions about industrialization made in the text?

# ORGANIZING THE WORKING CLASSES

**ANALYZING KEY IDEAS AND DETAILS**

**CITING TEXT EVIDENCE** What evidence supports the conclusion that socialism developed as a response to industrialization?

**GUIDING QUESTION** *How was socialism a response to industrialization?*

By the time of the Second Industrial Revolution, the economic system of industrial capitalism had become the dominant economic system. However, the **transition** to an industrialized society was hard on workers. The desire to improve their working and living conditions led many industrial workers to form socialist political parties and socialist trade unions. The theory on which they were based had been developed by Karl Marx. One form of Marxist socialism was eventually called communism.

## MARX'S THEORY

In 1848 *The Communist Manifesto* was published. It was written by two Germans, Karl Marx and Friedrich Engels, who were appalled at the horrible conditions in the industrial factories. They blamed the system of industrial capitalism for these conditions.

Marx believed that all world history was a "history of class struggles." According to Marx, oppressor and oppressed have always "stood in constant opposition to one another." One group—the oppressors—owned the means of production, such as land, raw materials, and money. They controlled government and society. The other group—the oppressed—owned nothing and depended on the owners of the means of production.

**DETERMINING MEANING**

Read the text of the paragraph that contains the words **bourgeoisie** and **proletariat**. Which context clues help you understand the meanings of these words?

Marx believed he saw a society that was "more and more splitting up into two great hostile camps, into two great classes directly facing each other: Bourgeoisie and Proletariat." The **bourgeoisie**—the middle class—were the oppressors. The **proletariat** (PROH • luh • TEHR • ee • uht)—the working class—were the oppressed.

Marx predicted that the struggle between the two groups would finally lead to a revolution. The proletariat would violently overthrow the bourgeoisie. After their victory, the proletariat would form a dictatorship to organize the means of production. However, because the proletariat victory would essentially abolish the economic differences that create separate social classes, Marx believed the final revolution would ultimately produce a classless society. The state itself, which had been a tool of the bourgeoisie, would wither away.

## SOCIALIST PARTIES

In time, working-class leaders formed socialist parties based on Marx's ideas. Most important was the German Social Democratic Party (SPD), which emerged in 1875. Under the direction of its Marxist leaders, the SPD advocated revolution while organizing itself into a mass political party that competed in elections for the German parliament. When in parliament, SPD delegates worked to pass laws that would improve conditions for the working class. In spite of government efforts to destroy it, in 1912 the SPD became the largest single party in Germany.

Socialist parties also emerged in other European states. In 1889 leaders of the various socialist parties joined together and formed the Second International. This was an association of national socialist groups that would fight against capitalism worldwide.

Marx, Karl and Engels, Frederick. 1906. Translated by Frederick Engels. Manifesto of the Communist Party. Charles H. Kerr & Company.

Marxist parties were divided over their goals. Pure Marxists thought that capitalism could be defeated only by a violent revolution. Other Marxists, called **revisionists**, rejected the revolutionary approach. This ideology came to be called social democracy. Social democrats argued that workers could work within the capitalist system to gain necessary economic and social reforms beneficial to the working class. Social democrats continued to organize in political parties and worked with other parties to gain reforms. As workers received the vote, they could achieve their aims by working within democratic systems.

## TRADE UNIONS

Another force working for evolutionary, rather than revolutionary, socialism was the trade union, or labor union. Industrial workers became dissatisfied with the rigid time-discipline and dangerous conditions associated with work in a factory. To protest these conditions and fight for improvements workers organized in a union and began strikes. In a strike, a union calls on its members to stop work in order to pressure employers to meet their demands for higher wages or improved factory safety. Gaining the right to strike became an important part of the trade union and labor movements.

At first, laws were passed that made strikes illegal under any circumstances. Capitalists, conservative politicians, and even some liberals saw strikes as a threat to society and law and order. As a consequence, many early strikes were crushed. However, in Great Britain, unions won the right to strike in the 1870s. By 1914, there were almost 4 million workers in British trade unions. In the rest of Europe and in the United States, trade unions had varying degrees of success in helping workers achieve a better life.

### ✓ CHECKING FOR UNDERSTANDING

1. **EXPLAINING CAUSE AND EFFECT** How was socialism a response to industrialization?
2. **EVALUATING** How did socialist parties differ from one another and from Karl Marx?
3. **IDENTIFYING CONNECTIONS** How did trade unions reflect socialist ideas?

*This 1904 German Social Democratic Party poster translates, "Proletarians of the World, Unite!"*

**IDENTIFYING CONNECTIONS** How did Marx's ideas represent a threat to nation-states and their governments?

**DETERMINING MEANING**

The suffix *-ist* means "one who does or makes." The word *revision* comes from the root word *revise*, meaning "to change." How do these word parts help you understand the word **revisionist**?



## LESSON 1 REVIEW

### Time and Place

1. **ANALYZING CHANGE** Explain what social and economic changes resulted from use of the assembly line and mass production.

### Building History-Social Science Analysis Skills

2. **ANALYZING CHANGE** How did change brought on by the Second Industrial Revolution affect parts of Europe in different ways?
3. **PREDICTING** What were the likely geographic and environmental effects of rapid industrialization in parts of Europe?
4. **UNDERSTANDING CONTEXT** How did the Second Industrial Revolution signal the start of the modern age? Cite evidence from the text to support your ideas.

### Writing About History

5. **EXPLANATORY WRITING** Write a paragraph explaining the obstacles that socialist parties likely faced in achieving socialist economic and political reforms. Be sure to cite evidence from the text to support your conclusions.

### Collaborating

6. **DETERMINING CONTEXT** Identify one invention from the Second Industrial Revolution, and explain why it was revolutionary.

ESSENTIAL QUESTIONS

- *How can industrialization affect a country's economy?*
- *How are political and social structures influenced by economic changes?*

# THE STORY BEGINS...

LESSON 2

# The Emergence of Mass Society

Florence Nightingale worked not only to care for the sick and injured but also to improve medical training for women as nurses and to win respect for women as professional nurses, teachers, and other workers. She also wanted to achieve social reforms to improve public health and relieve the plight of the working and impoverished classes.

> "In these days of investigation and statistics, ... we seem to think figures will do instead of facts, and calculation instead of action. We remember the policeman who watched his burglar enter the house, and waited to make quite sure whether he was going to commit robbery with violence or without, before interfering with his operations. So as we read such an account as this we seem to be watching, not robbery, but murder going on, and to be waiting for the rates of mortality to go up before we interfere; we wait to see how many of the children playing round the houses shall be stricken down. We wait to see whether the filth will really trickle into the well, and whether the foul water really will poison the family, and how many will die of it. And then, when enough have died, we think it time to spend some money and some trouble to stop the murders going further, and we enter the results of our 'masterly inactivity' neatly in tables; but we do not analyse and tabulate the saddened lives of those who remain, and the desolate homes in our 'sanitary districts.'"

—Florence Nightingale, *Rural Hygiene, Official Report of the Central Conference of Women Workers,* 1894

*Urbanization rapidly increased during the late 1800s and poor sanitation saw a rise in health problems for many city dwellers.* ▶

PHOTO:Heritage Image Partnership Ltd/Alamy Stock Photo; TEXT: Nightingale, Florence. 1894. Rural Hygiene, Official Report of the Central Conference of Women Workers. In Selected Writings of Florence Nightingale, edited 1954 by Lucy Ridgley Seymer. New York: The Macmillan Co.

| Changes During Second Industrial Revolution | | |
|---|---|---|
| Elite Class | Middle Class | Working Class |
| | | |
| | | |

**ANALYZING KEY IDEAS AND DETAILS**

**SUMMARIZING** Read closely to identify changes experienced by men, women, and children in each social class. Summarize these changes in a graphic organizer like this one.

# THE NEW URBAN ENVIRONMENT

**GUIDING QUESTION** *Why did European cities grow so quickly in the nineteenth century?*

With the emergence of a mass society, governments now had to consider how to appeal to the masses, rather than just to the wealthier citizens. Housing and public sanitation in the cities were two areas of great concern.

With few jobs available in the countryside, people from rural areas migrated to cities to find work in the factories. As a result, more and more people lived in cities. In the 1850s, urban dwellers made up about 40 percent of the English population, 15 percent in France, 10 percent in Prussia (Prussia was the largest German state), and 5 percent in Russia. By 1890, urban dwellers had increased to about 60 percent in England, 25 percent in France, 30 percent in Prussia, and 10 percent in Russia. In industrialized nations, cities grew tremendously. Between 1800 and 1900, the population in London grew from 960,000 to 6,500,000.

Cities also grew faster in the second half of the nineteenth century because of improvements in public health and sanitation. Improvements came in the 1840s after a number of urban reformers urged local governments to do something about the filthy living conditions that caused deadly **epidemic diseases** in the cities. Cholera (KAH • luh • ruh), for example, had ravaged Europe in the early 1830s and 1840s.

On the advice of reformers, city governments created boards of health to improve housing quality. City medical officers and building inspectors were authorized to inspect dwellings for public health hazards. Regulations required running water and internal drainage systems for new buildings.

Clean water and an effective sewage system were critical to public health. The need for freshwater was met by a system of dams and reservoirs. Tunnels and aqueducts then carried water from the countryside to the city and into homes. Gas and electric heaters made regular hot baths possible. The treatment of sewage was improved by building underground pipes that carried raw sewage far from the city for disposal. A public campaign in Frankfurt, Germany, featured the slogan "from the toilet to the river in half an hour."

**ANALYZING KEY IDEAS AND DETAILS**

1. **DETERMINING CENTRAL IDEAS** What is the central idea of this section?
2. **CITING TEXT EVIDENCE** Cite specific evidence from the text that describes the steps the government took to address the challenges of the new urban environments.

**DETERMINING MEANING**

To better understand what an **epidemic disease** is, consider the origin of each word. *Epidemic* comes from the Greek *epi*, meaning "among," and *demos*, meaning "people." *Disease* comes from a French word meaning "sickness." Use these word origins to write a definition for *epidemic disease*.

## ☑ CHECKING FOR UNDERSTANDING

1. **EXPLAINING CAUSE AND EFFECT** Why did European cities grow so quickly in the nineteenth century?
2. **EVALUATING** How do concerns faced by many modern cities resemble concerns experienced by growing cities in the industrial era?

# SOCIAL STRUCTURE OF MASS SOCIETY

**UNDERSTANDING CRAFT AND STRUCTURE**

1. **ANALYZING TEXT** How do the heading and subheadings in this section organize information for easier understanding?
2. **DETERMINING MEANING** The text states that immigrants "reshaped the social fabric of America." What is the meaning of the expression "the social fabric of America"?

**GUIDING QUESTION** *How did class divisions in Europe change during the nineteenth century?*

After 1871, most people enjoyed a higher standard of living. Still, the disparity between the wealthiest and the poorest members of society grew. Between the few who were rich and the many who were poor existed several middle-class groups.

## THE NEW ELITE

At the top of European society stood a wealthy elite. This group made up only 5 percent of the population but controlled from 30 to 40 percent of the wealth. During the 1800s, the most successful industrialists, bankers, and merchants—the wealthy upper-middle class—had joined with the landed aristocracy—the upper class—to form this new elite. Whether aristocratic or upper-middle class in background, members of the elite became leaders in the government and military.

## THE DIVERSE MIDDLE CLASSES

Although some members of the upper-middle class became part of the new elite, the rest of the middle class consisted of several groups at varying economic and social levels. Below the upper-middle class was a middle group that included lawyers, doctors, members of the civil service, business managers, engineers, architects, accountants, and chemists. Beneath this solid and comfortable middle group was a lower-middle class of small shopkeepers, traders, and prosperous farmers.

The Second Industrial Revolution produced a new group of white-collar workers between the lower-middle class and the lower classes. This group included traveling salespeople, bookkeepers, telephone operators, department store salespeople, and secretaries. Although not highly paid, these white-collar workers were often committed to middle-class ideals.

The middle classes shared a certain lifestyle with values that dominated much of nineteenth-century society. The European middle classes believed in hard work, which was open to everyone and guaranteed positive results. Outward appearances were also important to the middle classes. The etiquette book *The Habits of Good Society* was a best seller.

## THE WORKING CLASSES

Below the middle classes on the social scale were the working classes—also referred to as the lower classes—which made up almost 80 percent of the European population. Many in the working class had found employment as wage laborers in factories, mills, and other industrial centers. As industrial machinery became more complex and expensive to purchase and to maintain, wage labor often remained the only reasonable employment option for the vast majority of the urban working class. This resulted in greater inequality as factory owners benefitted from larger and larger profits while continuing to pay low wages to their employees.

*In 1886, these women and girls worked as domestic servants in British households.*

**ANALYZING INFORMATION** What job would you expect to find these women and girls doing? How did their social standing and lives most likely differ from those of their employers?

Popperfoto/Getty Images

The urban working class consisted of many different groups. They might be skilled artisans or semiskilled laborers, but many were unskilled day laborers or domestic servants. In Britain in 1900, one out of every seven employed persons was a domestic servant. Most servants were women.

After 1870, workers in urban areas began to live more comfortably. Reforms created better living conditions in cities. In addition, a rise in wages, along with a decline in many consumer costs, made it possible for workers to buy extra clothes or to pay to entertain themselves in their few leisure hours. Many of these gains had come through the efforts of strikes and labor organizing. With these methods, many workers had won better wages, a 10-hour workday, and a Saturday afternoon off.

The benefits of industrial society, electricity, sanitation, and the use of powered machinery were mostly unknown to the rural working classes. These classes included landholding peasants, farm laborers, and sharecroppers. Human and animal energy, usually from draft animals such as horses or oxen, remained the primary means of production for these working-class farmers. Wealthy landowners could most often afford newer machinery powered by coal or gas, and they reaped the benefit of greater efficiency and larger crop yields. Most poor farmers, focusing on subsistence agriculture and unable to afford these new machines, could not compete. The result was increasing inequality between these two classes of rural society.

## SAMUEL SMILES AND *SELF-HELP*

As industrialization slowly transformed society, many struggled with the resulting inequalities and poverty that could result. Some, like Scottish doctor, political thinker, and author Samuel Smiles, argued that industrial-era poverty was not a matter of inequality, but the result of irresponsible habits. His book *Self-Help*, first published in 1859, encouraged British citizens to work hard to improve their lot in life rather than to look to government to uplift them through aid and other measures:

> "The spirit of self-help, as exhibited in the energetic action of individuals, has in all times been a marked feature in the English character, and furnishes the true measure of our power as a nation. Rising above the heads of the mass, there were always to be found a series of individuals distinguished beyond others, who commanded the public homage. But our progress has also been owing to multitudes of smaller and less known men. Though only the generals' names may be remembered in the history of any great campaign, it has been in a great measure through the individual valour and heroism of the privates that victories have been won. And life, too, is "a soldiers' battle,"—men in the ranks having in all times been amongst the greatest of workers. . . . Daily experience shows that it is energetic individualism which produces the most powerful effects upon the life and action of others, and really constitutes the best practical education. Schools, academies, and colleges, give but the merest beginnings of culture in comparison with it. Far more influential is the life-education daily given in our homes, in the streets, behind counters, in workshops, at the loom and the plough, in counting-houses and manufactories, and in the busy haunts of men."
>
> —Samuel Smiles, *Self-Help*, 1882

Although not everyone agreed with Smiles's perspective, *Self-Help* became a best-selling book and made Smiles a celebrity in Victorian Great Britain.

**MAKING CONNECTIONS TO TODAY**

### URBANIZATION

Estimates suggest that just 3 percent of the world's population lived in cities in 1800. Only one city, Beijing, China, had a population of more than 1 million. A century later, in the year 1900, that percentage increased to 14 percent. Then, just 12 cities had populations topping 1 million. Most of those cities were in Europe and the United States. Today, more than half the world's population is urban. The top 30 cities have populations larger than London had in 1900. Of those, the 10 largest cities have populations above 14 million. None of those cities lies in Europe, and just one, New York City, is in the United States.

1. **ANALYZING CHANGE** Why did changes in population take place at different rates in different places?
2. **ASSESSING** What evidence supports the conclusions that the pace of urbanization has shifted geographically?

**ANALYZING PRIMARY SOURCES**

1. **IDENTIFYING BIAS** What political bias does Smiles express in this excerpt? How does this bias shape his central idea?
2. **ASSESSING** What evidence does Smiles offer to support his ideas?

TEXT:Smiles, Samuel. 1882. Self-Help. London: John Murray.

## IMMIGRATION TO THE UNITED STATES

The industrial era witnessed unprecedented levels of global migration, much of it from Europe and Asia to the United States. Between 1880 and 1920, more than 20 million immigrants came to the United States, the majority of them from Central, Eastern, and Southern Europe and some from China and Japan. These immigrants left their homes to escape poverty, war, religious persecution, and restrictions on their social classes. Some were skilled in a trade they continued to practice when they arrived in the United States. Most were unskilled and found work in America's industrial cities such as New York, Chicago, and San Francisco.

Immigrants worked for low wages and endured harsh working conditions. In spite of these hardships, the economic and social opportunities they found encouraged further immigration to the United States. Immigration provided a steady supply of labor for the United States and allowed for a broad expansion of industry and infrastructure. Immigrants also reshaped the social fabric of America and, by the 1890s, made up a large percentage of the population of many of its major cities. They left a cultural imprint in these places in the form of native-language newspapers, social clubs, churches, and synagogues.

### ✓ CHECKING FOR UNDERSTANDING

1. **SUMMARIZING** How did class divisions in Europe change during the nineteenth century?
2. **INTERPRETING** Does the text provide data to support the conclusion that wealth was evenly distributed among social classes in the late 19th century? Explain.
3. **UNDERSTANDING CONTEXT** Read the third paragraph under the subheading "The Diverse Middle Classes." What words and phrases help you understand the meaning of *etiquette*? Why would etiquette have been important to emergent professionals?

# WOMEN'S EXPERIENCES

**GUIDING QUESTION** *How did the Second Industrial Revolution influence women's roles in society?*

In 1800 women were mainly defined by their families and household roles. In the nineteenth century, women struggled to change their status.

## NEW JOB OPPORTUNITIES

During much of the nineteenth century, working-class groups maintained the belief that women should remain at home to bear and nurture children. Middle-class women were not allowed to enter the industrial workforce.

The Second Industrial Revolution opened the door to new jobs for women. There were not enough men to fill the relatively low-paid, white-collar jobs that were being created. A "white-collar" job is one typically done in an office setting as opposed to blue-collar jobs, which are most often jobs on a factory floor. Both industrial plants and retail shops hired women as clerks, typists, secretaries, and salesclerks.

The expansion of government services also created job opportunities for women. Many of these tasks were white-collar jobs like many of the new jobs in private industry. Women took jobs in education, health, and social services. Some middle-class women held these jobs, but they were mainly filled by the working class.

**UNDERSTANDING CRAFT AND STRUCTURE**

1. **DETERMINING MEANING** What words and phrases provide context clues to the meaning of *advocated*? Write a sentence in which you use the word to explain an important idea from the text.
2. **ANALYZING TEXT** How does the author develop the claim that many women in the working class had access to new types of jobs during the Second Industrial Revolution?

## MARRIAGE AND THE FAMILY

As the chief family wage earners, men worked outside the home. Women were left to care for the family. Throughout the 1800s, marriage remained almost the only honorable and available career for most women. The number of children born to the average woman began to decline—the most significant development in the modern family. This decline was tied to improved economic conditions and increased use of birth control.

The family was the central institution of middle-class life. With fewer children in the family, mothers could devote more time to child care and domestic leisure. Middle-class women were discouraged from finding paid labor or work outside the home. The home for middle-class families became a kind of refuge from the dangers of the industrial world. The middle-class family fostered an ideal of togetherness. The Victorians in Britain created the family Christmas with its Yule log, tree, songs, and exchange of gifts.

The lives of working-class women were different from those of their middle-class counterparts. Most working-class women had to earn money to help support their families. Their contributions made a big difference in the economic survival of their families. For the children of the working classes, childhood was over by the age of 9 or 10. By this age, children often became apprentices or were employed in odd jobs.

Between 1890 and 1914, family patterns among the working class began to change. Higher-paying jobs in heavy industry and improvements in the standard of living made it possible for working-class families to depend on the incomes of husbands alone. By the early twentieth century, some working-class mothers could afford to stay at home, following the pattern of middle-class women. At the same time, working-class families aspired to buy new consumer products such as sewing machines and cast-iron stoves.

## WOMEN'S RIGHTS

Modern **feminism**, or the movement for women's rights, had its beginnings during the Enlightenment. At this time, some women **advocated** equality for women based on the doctrine of natural rights.

In the 1830s, a number of women in the United States and Europe argued for the right of women to own property. By law, a husband had almost total control over his wife's property. These early efforts were not very successful, however. Married women did not win the right to own some property until 1870 in Great Britain, 1900 in Germany, and 1907 in France.

The fight for property rights was only the beginning of the women's movement. Some middle- and upper-middle-class women fought for and gained access to universities. Others sought entry into occupations dominated by men. Although training to become doctors was largely closed to women, some entered the medical field by becoming nurses. The efforts of the British nurse Florence Nightingale, combined with those of Clara Barton in the U.S. Civil War, transformed nursing into a profession of trained, middle-class "women in white."

**ANALYZING PRIMARY SOURCES**

### EMMELINE PANKHURST ON MILITANCY

"Be militant in your own way. Those of you who can express your militancy by going to the House of Commons and refusing to leave without satisfaction, as we did in the early days—do so. . . . Those of you who can express your militancy by joining us in our anti-Government by-election policy—do so. Those of you who can break windows—do so (great applause). . . ."

—Emmeline Pankhurst, from a speech on October 17, 1912

**DETERMINING MEANING**

Use the word parts of **feminism** to break down the meaning of the word. The suffix *-ism* refers to a practice, system, or set of ideas for doing something. The root word comes from the Latin *femina*, meaning "woman." How do the word parts help you understand *feminism*?

*On May 21, 1914, Emmeline Pankhurst was arrested while trying to enter Buckingham Palace to petition the King of England for women's rights.*

**ANALYZING INFORMATION** What does the image suggest about the tactics of Pankhurst and other suffragettes and about the official response to those tactics?

**DETERMINING MEANING**

*Suffragette* and *suffragist* are related words for **suffrage**. All three words come from the Latin *suffragari*, meaning "to vote for someone." Use all three words in a sentence that explains their meanings.

By the 1840s and 1850s, the movement for women's rights expanded as women called for equal political rights. They believed that **suffrage**, the right to vote, was the key to improving their overall position. Members of the women's movement, called suffragists, had one basic aim: the right of women to full citizenship in the nation-state.

The British women's movement was the most active in Europe. The Women's Social and Political Union, founded in 1903 by Emmeline Pankhurst and her daughters, used unusual publicity stunts to call attention to its demands. Its members pelted government officials with eggs, chained themselves to lampposts, and smashed department store windows. British police answered with arrests and brutal treatment of leading activists.

Before 1914, women had the right to vote in only a few nations, such as Norway and Finland, along with some American states. It took the upheaval of World War I to make governments give in on this basic issue.

### ✓ CHECKING FOR UNDERSTANDING

1. **IDENTIFYING CONNECTIONS** How did the Second Industrial Revolution influence women's roles in society?
2. **UNDERSTANDING CHANGE** List the order in which the women's movement generally gained more rights for women.

**ANALYZING KEY IDEAS AND DETAILS**

1. **ANALYZING EVENTS** How did societies establish and expand universal public education during the industrial era?
2. **SUMMARIZING** How did a culture of leisure develop during the Second Industrial Revolution?

## EDUCATION AND LEISURE

**GUIDING QUESTION** *How did society change as a result of urbanization and industrialization?*

Universal education was a product of the mass society of the late nineteenth and early twentieth centuries. Before that time, education was reserved mostly for the elite and the wealthier middle class. Between 1870 and 1914, most Western governments began to finance a system of primary education. Boys and girls between the ages of 6 and 12 were required to attend these schools.

**CITIZENSHIP**

### PUBLIC EDUCATION

When compulsory education first emerged in eighteenth-century Prussia, it had two aims: to educate the population for a modern economy and to create effective citizens. The system proved to be effective at achieving these two goals—so effective, in fact, that when the United States created a public education system of its own, its builders looked to the Prussian system as a model. This model became the foundation for the public education system still active in the United States today.

The goal of creating effective citizens remains a centerpiece of American public education today. Civics and Government courses remain central to the curriculum of most states. Many other districts, too, have begun to include public service projects as a portion of the curriculum as well.

1. **DETERMINING CENTRAL IDEAS** Why are public schools important? How might societies be different without public education?
2. **EVALUATING** How might the idea of public education today differ from the idea of public education in the industrial era?

Hero Images/Getty Images

Why did Western nations make this commitment to public education? One reason was industrialization. In the first Industrial Revolution, workers without training or experience were able to meet factory needs. The new firms of the Second Industrial Revolution needed trained, skilled workers.

The chief motive for public education was political. Giving more people the right to vote created a need for better-educated voters. Even more importantly, primary schools instilled patriotism.

Compulsory elementary education created a demand for teachers, and most of them were women. Many men saw teaching as a part of women's "natural role" as nurturers of children. Women were also paid lower salaries than men, which in itself was a strong incentive for states to set up teacher-training schools for women.

The Second Industrial Revolution allowed people to pursue new forms of leisure. Popular mass leisure both entertained large crowds and distracted them from the realities of work lives. Leisure came to be viewed as what people do for fun after work. The industrial system gave people new times—evening hours, weekends, and a week or two in the summer—to indulge in leisure activities. Amusement parks, dance halls, and organized team sports became enjoyable ways for people to spend their leisure hours.

*In the 1870s, electricity helped make Blackpool by the Sea a popular resort town as people in Britain sought to spend more time on leisure and entertainment at beaches, amusement parks, and more.*

**EVALUATING** How does Blackpool by the Sea compare with modern ideas about leisure and entertainment?



## ✓ CHECKING FOR UNDERSTANDING

1. **EXPLAINING CAUSE AND EFFECT** How did society change because of urbanization and industrialization?
2. **UNDERSTANDING CHANGE** What does the text suggest about education before the development of mass society in the late nineteenth century? What conclusions can you draw about how that education was provided?
3. **IDENTIFYING CONNECTIONS** What evidence supports the idea that compulsory public education served an economic benefit for society?

# LESSON 2 REVIEW

## Time and Place

1. **ANALYZING CHANGE** Why did European cities grow so quickly in the nineteenth century compared with the rate of urbanization in earlier centuries?

## Building History-Social Science Analysis Skills

2. **INTERPRETING** Industrialization in Europe and North America led to a mass society in which traditional social roles and ties began to break down. Individuals became members of the masses, subject to rule by impersonal governments and employed by impersonal business entities. What evidence supports this reasoning?

3. **ANALYZING INFORMATION** How did urbanization change the physical and human landscape of Europe and North America in the late nineteenth century? What environmental challenges resulted?

4. **COMPARING AND CONTRASTING** How do modern ideas about education and leisure in Europe and North America compare and contrast with those of the nineteenth century?

## Writing About History

5. **NARRATIVE WRITING** Write a paragraph explaining how industrialization and urbanization helped the women's movement.

## Collaborating

6. **PRESENTING** With a small group, create an advertisement for an amusement park or dance hall of the era. Be sure to include information, such as the hours of operation, that is based on your research.

# THE LIVES OF WOMEN IN A MODERNIZING WORLD

The most prominent women's rights movement of the industrial era called for women's suffrage. Women had been striving to gain the vote since some countries had first granted male citizens that right. In the late 19th century, however, the movement intensified and spread, especially in the United States and Britain. Still, not all women agreed on the need for suffrage. Opposition mounted as suffragists pressed their case.

**VOCABULARY**

*laborious:* requiring considerable effort or time

*despotic:* tyrannical; arbitrary

*purdah:* a curtain screening women

*sedan chairs:* portable chairs placed on poles

**PRIMARY SOURCE: DOCUMENT**

## MARY AUGUSTA ARNOLD WARD ON WOMEN'S SUFFRAGE

Signed by 104 other women, this article argues against suffrage. Ward founded the Anti-Suffrage League in 1908.

> "1. While desiring the fullest possible development of the powers, energies, and the education of women, we believe that their work for the State, and their responsibilities towards it, must always differ essentially from those of men, and that therefore their share in the working of the State machinery should be different from that assigned to men. . . . To men belong the struggle of debate and legislation in Parliament; the hard and exhausting labour implied in the administration of the national resources and powers; the conduct of England's relations towards the external world; the working of the army and navy; all the heavy, **laborious**, fundamental industries of the State. . . . In all these spheres women's direct participation is made impossible either by the disabilities of sex, or by strong formations of custom and habit resting ultimately upon physical difference, against which it is useless to contend. . . .
>
> 2. . . . For whatever may be the duty and privilege of the parliamentary vote for men, we hold that citizenship is not dependent upon or identical with the possession of the suffrage. Citizenship lies in the participation of each individual in effort for the good of the community. And we believe that women will be more valuable citizens, will contribute more precious elements to the national life without the vote than with it."

**ANALYZE THE TEXT**

1. **DETERMINING CENTRAL IDEAS** What is the central argument of Ward's article?
2. **ASSESSING** What evidence does Ward offer to justify her position? What assumptions does she make?

**PRIMARY SOURCE: SPEECH**

## EMMELINE PANKHURST ON WOMEN'S SUFFRAGE

Here Pankhurst argues Britain's government will not be truly representative until women have the right to vote.

> "What, then, is the vote that we are hearing so much about just now, so much more than people have heard in discussion at least, for a great many years? I think we may give the vote a threefold description. We may describe the vote as, first of all, a symbol, secondly, a safeguard, and thirdly, an instrument. It is a symbol of freedom, a symbol of citizenship, a symbol of liberty. It is a safeguard of all those liberties which it symbolizes. And in these later days it has come to be regarded more than anything else as an instrument, something with which you can get a great many more things than our forefathers who fought for the vote ever realised as possible to get with it. . . .
>
> Wherever masses of people are gathered together there must be government. Government without the vote is more or less a form of tyranny. Government with the vote is more or less representative according to the extent to which the vote is given. In this country they tell us we have representative government. So far as women are concerned, while you have representative government for men, you have **despotic** government for women. So it is in order that the government of the country may be made really representative, may represent not only all classes of the community, but both sexes of the community, that this struggle for the vote is going on on the part of women."

**ANALYZE THE TEXT**

1. **DETERMINING MEANING** What does Pankhurst mean by a representative government exists for men in Great Britain, while women live under a despotic government?
2. **DETERMINING MEANING** How does Pankhurst use metaphor to support her argument? Is it an effective metaphor? Explain.

(l)Knowles, James. 1889. The Nineteenth Century - A Monthly Review Vol. XXV - January-June 1889. London: Kegan Paul, Trench, & Co.; (r)Pankhurst, Emmeline G.

PRIMARY SOURCE: SPEECH

## CARRIE CHAPMAN CATT ON WOMEN'S SUFFRAGE

In 1913, American women's suffrage leader Carrie Chapman Catt delivered an address about what she had observed on a trip to various countries around the world.

> "We held public meetings in many of the towns and cities of four continents, of four large islands, and on ships of three oceans, and had representatives of all the great races and nationalities in our audiences. We are now in touch with the most advanced development of the women's movement in Egypt, Palestine, India, Burma, China, Japan, Java, and the Philippine and Hawaiian Islands. . . .
>
> Behind the **purdah** in India, . . . behind veils and barred doors and closed **sedan chairs** there has been rebellion in the hearts of women all down the centuries. . . . We spoke with many women all over the East who had never heard of a "women's movement," yet isolated and alone, they had thought out the entire program of woman's emancipation. . . . We must give aid to these sisters. . . . When I review the slow, tragic struggle upward of the women in the West, I am overwhelmed with the awfulness of the task these Eastern women have assumed. . . . I would that we could put a protecting arm around these heroic women and save them from the cruel blows that they are certain to receive. . . . For every woman of every tribe and nation, every race and continent . . . we must demand deliverance."

### ANALYZE THE TEXT

1. **ANALYZING TEXT** What purpose does the first paragraph serve? How does it support her central argument?
2. **DETERMINING MEANING** What does Catt mean when she says women must demand deliverance? How do you know?

PRIMARY SOURCE: PHOTOGRAPH

## SUFFRAGETTE ARRESTED

*Police lead a suffragette to jail.*

### ANALYZE THE SOURCE

1. **EVALUATING** Were public arrests, as illustrated here, beneficial or detrimental to the suffrage movement? How would you determine their impact?
2. **DETERMINING CONTEXT** Does this image appear typical of the treatment of suffragists by officials at the time? How were suffragists treated by the public?

### MULTIPLE PERSPECTIVES

1. **DIFFERENTIATING** How might Pankhurst respond to Ward's claim that women can be citizens without the vote?
2. **COMPARING POINTS OF VIEW** Compare and contrast Ward's and Pankhurst's descriptions of voting. Would Catt most likely agree with Ward or Pankhurst? Use details from the sources to support your response.
3. **ASSESSING** Does Ward or Pankhurst make a more effective argument? Explain how the reasoning in one source makes a more persuasive case than the reasoning in the other source.

## ESSENTIAL QUESTION

- *How are political and social structures influenced by economic changes?*

LESSON 3

# The National State and Democracy

# THE STORY BEGINS...

In response to ongoing civil unrest that threatened to unravel his rule entirely, Czar Nicholas II issued what came to be called the October Manifesto, extending limited freedoms to the Russian people, including the right to organize a people's assembly.

> "We have therefore ordered the government to take the following measures in fulfilment of our unbending will:
>
> 1. Fundamental civil freedoms will be granted to the population, including real personal inviolability, freedom of conscience, speech, assembly and association.
> 2. Participation in the Duma will be granted to those classes of the population which are at present deprived of voting powers, insofar as is possible in the short period before the convocation of the Duma, and this will lead to the development of a universal franchise.
> 3. There will be no delay to the Duma elections which have already been organized. It is established as an unshakeable rule that no law can come into force without its approval by the State Duma and representatives of the people will be given the opportunity to take real part in the supervision of the legality of government bodies."

—Czar Nicholas II, *Manifesto of October 17, 1905*

Russia was one of several empires that experienced dramatic political change, brought on in part by the rise of mass society. Such changes would also shake the scales in the global balance of power.

*Thousands of striking workers and their families marched to the Winter Palace of Czar Nicholas II in St. Petersburg, Russia, to petition for better working conditions and higher wages.* ▶

| Nation | Changes to Government |
|---|---|
| Great Britain | |
| France | |
| Italy | |
| Germany | |
| Austria-Hungary | |
| Russia | |
| United States | |

**ANALYZING KEY IDEAS AND DETAILS**

**DESCRIBING** Read closely to identify key changes to government in the nations listed. Record one to two events, with the year in which they occurred, for each nation.

# WESTERN EUROPE: POLITICAL DEMOCRACY

**GUIDING QUESTION** *What happened with democracy in Western Europe in the late nineteenth century?*

By the late nineteenth century there were many signs that political democracy was expanding in Western Europe. First, universal male suffrage laws were passed. Second, the prime minister was responsible to the popularly elected legislative body, not to a king or president. This principle is called **ministerial responsibility** and is crucial for democracy. Third, mass political parties formed.

Great Britain had long had a working two-party parliamentary system. In a parliamentary system, the party with the greatest representation in parliament forms the government, the leader of which is the prime minister. The two parties—the Liberals and Conservatives—competed to pass laws that expanded the right to vote. Reform acts in 1867 and 1884 increased the number of adult male voters. By 1918, males over 21 and women over 30 could vote.

At the beginning of the twentieth century, then, political democracy was becoming well established in Britain. Social reforms for the working class soon followed. In 1900, a new Labour Party emerged and dedicated itself to the interests of workers. To retain the workers' support, the Liberals voted for social reforms, such as unemployment benefits and old-age pensions.

In France, the collapse of Louis-Napoleon's Second Empire left the country in confusion. Finally, in 1875, the Third Republic gained a republican constitution. The new government had a president and a two-house legislature. The upper house, or Senate, was elected by high-ranking officials. All adult males voted for members of the lower house, the Chamber of Deputies. A premier (or prime minister), who led the government, was responsible to the Chamber of Deputies.

France failed to develop a strong parliamentary system. The existence of a dozen political parties forced the premier to depend on a coalition of parties to stay in power. Nevertheless, by 1914, the Third Republic had the loyalty of most voters.

Italy had emerged by 1870 as a united state. However, there was little national unity because of the gulf between the poverty-stricken south and the industrialized north. Turmoil between labor and industry weakened the social fabric of the nation. Even universal male suffrage, granted in 1912, did little to halt the widespread government corruption and weakness.

**ANALYZING KEY IDEAS AND DETAILS**

1. **CITING TEXT EVIDENCE** Cite specific text evidence to support the idea that nations in Western Europe were becoming more democratic.

2. **ANALYZING IDEAS** How does the text explain that democratization developed and stalled in France?

**DETERMINING MEANING**

*Responsibility* means being answerable or accountable to someone else for one's actions. Which sentence helps you understand the meaning of **ministerial responsibility**? Explain how this phrase signaled democratization in Western Europe.

## ☑ CHECKING FOR UNDERSTANDING

1. **SUMMARIZING** What happened with democracy in Western Europe in the late nineteenth century?
2. **ANALYZING CHANGE** Why did France and Italy have a harder time than Britain developing strong democratic governments?
3. **DETERMINING CONTEXT** The related words *parliament* and *parliamentary* come from a French word meaning "to speak, to talk." Why was the concept of talking in a body such as the parliament important to the spread of democracy in Western Europe?

# CENTRAL AND EASTERN EUROPE: THE OLD ORDER

**UNDERSTANDING CRAFT AND STRUCTURE**

1. **ANALYZING TEXT** How does the main heading preview the main idea in the text that follows? How does it set up a contrast with the previous section and its heading?
2. **ANALYZING TEXT PRESENTATION** What structure does the author use to develop the topic of late-nineteenth-century politics in Central and Eastern Europe?

**GUIDING QUESTION** *What political developments did Central and Eastern Europe experience in the late nineteenth century?*

Unlike the republics and constitutional monarchies of many Western European states, Central and Eastern Europe had more conservative governments. In Germany, the Austro-Hungarian Empire, the Ottoman Empire, and Russia, the position of the monarch remained much stronger. In all these states, too, the old ruling groups continued to dominate politics.

## GERMANY

The constitution of the new imperial Germany that Otto von Bismarck began in 1871 set up a two-house legislature. The lower house, called the Reichstag, was elected on the basis of universal male suffrage. Ministers of government, however, were responsible not to the parliament but to the person of the emperor, who controlled the armed forces, foreign policy, and the bureaucracy. As chancellor (prime minister), Bismarck worked to keep Germany from becoming a democracy.

**MAKING CONNECTIONS TO PERSPECTIVES**

### INDUSTRIALIZATION AND COMPETITION

The Second Industrial Revolution ramped up competition among nation-states. In the 1800s, the British Empire had dominated world trade and politics. However, by the end of the century, Germany was catching up. Across the Atlantic Ocean, the United States, too, benefited from technological advances in transportation that enabled it to compete. Industrialization also empowered other nations. Although none reached the expanse of the British Empire at its height, several of these nations expanded their territory, resources, and wealth. The ongoing need for resources to fuel economic growth inspired Kaiser William II's *Weltpolitik*, or world policy, by which Germany sought to establish its own colonial empire and to achieve political, economic, and military power.

1. **SUMMARIZING** How did industrialization help the United States become more competitive with European nations?
2. **DETERMINING CENTRAL IDEAS** Why did Germany so aggressively pursue *Weltpolitik* under Kaiser William II?

## GEOGRAPHIC REASONING

In 1871 Europe was mostly controlled by large empires.

1. **EXPLORING REGIONS** On what continent(s) did each empire have territory?
2. **SPATIAL THINKING** Study a modern map of the region shown. What do you think happened between the time of this map and today?

By the reign of William II, kaiser from 1888 to 1918, Germany had become the strongest military and industrial power in Europe. With the expansion of industry and cities came demands for democracy. Conservative forces—especially the nobility and big industrialists—tried to thwart the movement for democracy by supporting a strong foreign policy. They believed that expansion abroad would increase their profits and would also divert people from pursuing democratic reforms.

## AUSTRIA-HUNGARY

After the creation of the dual monarchy of Austria-Hungary in 1867, Austria adopted a constitution that, in theory, set up a parliamentary system with ministerial responsibility. In reality, the emperor, Francis Joseph, largely ignored this system. He appointed and dismissed his own ministers and issued decrees when the parliament was not in session.

The empire remained troubled by conflicts among its ethnic groups. A German minority governed Austria but felt increasingly threatened by Czechs, Poles, Italians, and other Slavic groups within the empire. Representatives of these groups in the new parliament agitated for their freedom, which encouraged the autocratic emperor to ignore the parliament and govern by imperial decrees.

Unlike Austria, Hungary had a parliament that worked. It was controlled by landowners who dominated the peasants and ethnic groups.

*At the beginning of his rule, Czar Nicholas II said, "I shall maintain the principle of autocracy just as firmly and unflinchingly as did my unforgettable father."*

## RUSSIA

In Russia, Nicholas II began his rule in 1894 believing that the absolute power of the czars should be preserved. Conditions were changing, however. By 1900, Russia had become the fourth-largest producer of steel. With industrialization came factories, an industrial working class, and pitiful working and living conditions. Socialist parties developed, but government repression forced them underground.

Growing discontent and opposition to the czarist regime finally exploded. On January 22, 1905, a massive procession of workers went to the Winter Palace in St. Petersburg to present a petition of grievances to the czar. Troops opened fire on the peaceful demonstration, killing hundreds. This "Bloody Sunday" caused workers throughout Russia to strike.

Nicholas II was eventually forced to grant civil liberties and to create a legislative assembly, the **Duma**. By 1907, the czar curtailed the power of the Duma and again used the army and bureaucracy to rule Russia.

**DETERMINING MEANING**

Consider the origins of **Duma**. It comes from an old Russian word meaning "council." This word, in turn, has Germanic roots meaning "thought, or judgment." Use these meanings to write a definition for **Duma** in your own words. Use a dictionary or online resource to check your definition.

## THE OTTOMAN EMPIRE

The Ottoman Empire, with its capital of Istanbul in Europe's far southeastern edge, was beset by problems in the 1800s. Beginning in the 1600s, the empire had lost much of its economic power. The opening of the Americas to trade greatly reduced trade that passed through the empire's lands. This result was the creation of a trade imbalance between the empire and the rest of Europe.

Beginning in the 1800s, the Ottoman Sultans attempted to industrialize the empire's economy. However, strict price regulations and the influence of European empires and corporations meant their industries could not compete with much cheaper manufactured goods from elsewhere. By the middle of the 1800s, the economy of the Ottoman Empire was in serious decline.

The empire's economic peril meant there was little money in the treasury to modernize its economy, government, or military. By the mid-1800s, some European leaders would take to calling the Ottoman Empire the "sick man of Europe." In the late 1800s, it would lose most of its territory in Europe to nationalist revolts and uprisings.

### ☑ CHECKING FOR UNDERSTANDING

1. **UNDERSTANDING CHANGE** What political developments did Central and Eastern Europe experience in the late nineteenth century?
2. **DETERMINING CONTEXT** Why do you think Bismarck wanted to prevent democratization of Germany?

**ANALYZING KEY IDEAS AND DETAILS**

1. **DETERMINING CENTRAL IDEAS** What is the main idea of the first paragraph in the section, and why does this matter?
2. **ANALYZING IDEAS** What is significant about the ideas and the placement of the final paragraph in the section?

# THE UNITED STATES

**GUIDING QUESTION** *How did the Second Industrial Revolution affect the United States?*

Four years of civil war had preserved the American nation, but the Old South had been destroyed. In 1865 the Thirteenth Amendment to the Constitution was passed, abolishing slavery. Later, the Fourteenth and Fifteenth Amendments gave citizenship to African Americans and the right to vote to African American males. New state laws in the South, however, soon stripped African Americans of the right to vote. By 1880, supporters of white supremacy were back in power everywhere in the South.

Between 1860 and 1914, the United States shifted from a farm-based economy to an industrial economy. American steel and iron production was the best in the world in 1900. Industrialization led to urbanization. By 1900, the United States had three cities with populations of more than 1 million, with New York reaching 4 million.

In 1900 the United States was the world's richest nation, but the richest 9 percent of Americans owned 71 percent of the wealth. Many workers labored in unsafe factories, and devastating cycles of unemployment made them **insecure**. Many tried to organize unions, but the American Federation of Labor represented only 8.4 percent of the labor force.

**DETERMINING MEANING**

The word *supremacy* comes from the root word *supreme*. Synonyms for the word include *primacy* and *superiority*. What does *white supremacy* mean? What can you conclude about supporters of white supremacy?

## NEW TERRITORY ABROAD

In the late 1800s, the United States began to expand abroad. The Samoan Islands in the Pacific were the first important U.S. colony. By 1887, Americans controlled the sugar industry on the Hawaiian Islands. As more Americans settled in Hawaii, they wanted political power. When Queen Liliuokalani (lih • LEE • uh • woh • kuh • LAH • nee) tried to strengthen the monarchy to keep the islands under her people's control, the United States sent military forces to the islands. The queen was deposed and the United States annexed Hawaii in 1898. In 1898 the United States defeated Spain in the Spanish-American War. As a result, the United States acquired the former Spanish possessions of Puerto Rico, Guam, and the Philippines.

### ✓ CHECKING FOR UNDERSTANDING

1. **IDENTIFYING CONNECTIONS** How did the Second Industrial Revolution affect the United States?
2. **DETERMINING CONTEXT** Why did the United States annex Hawaii despite opposition from Hawaii's native ruler and people?
3. **EVALUATING** How has the United States changed since the post-Civil War period? What lessons do you think can be learned from the political challenges of the late 19th century?

# INTERNATIONAL RIVALRIES

**GUIDING QUESTION** *How did international rivalries push Europe close to war?*

Otto von Bismarck realized that Germany's emergence in 1871 as the most powerful state in continental Europe had upset the balance of power established at Vienna in 1815. Fearing that France intended to create an anti-German alliance, Bismarck made a defensive alliance with Austria-Hungary in 1879. In 1882 Italy joined this alliance.

This Triple Alliance thus united the powers of Germany, Austria-Hungary, and Italy in a defensive alliance against France. At the same time, Bismarck maintained a separate treaty with Russia. Bismarck was aware that Germany's position in the center of Europe made it strategically vulnerable. He greatly feared Germany being forced to fight a war on two fronts, its east and its west. A German alliance with Russia would put these fears to rest.

**ANALYZING KEY IDEAS AND DETAILS**

1. **ANALYZING IDEAS** How did William II influence Germany's foreign policy?
2. **ANALYZING EVENTS** How does the text explain the causes of World War I?

*In this political cartoon, Kaiser William II (seated) dismisses Otto von Bismarck (standing), while Germany, represented by the figure in the background, looks on.*

1. **INTEGRATING INFORMATION** What does Kaiser William II's throne suggest about his rule?
2. **INTEGRATING INFORMATION** How does the cartoonist suggest that Bismarck's firing will affect Germany?

## NEW DIRECTIONS: WILLIAM II

In 1890 Kaiser William II fired Bismarck and took control of Germany's foreign policy. The kaiser embarked on an activist policy dedicated to enhancing German power. He craved international prestige and wanted, as he put it, to find Germany's rightful "place in the sun."

One of the changes William made in foreign policy was to drop the treaty with Russia. Almost immediately, in 1894, France formed an alliance with Russia. Germany thus had a hostile power on her western border and on her eastern border—exactly the situation Bismarck had feared. Over the next decade, German policies caused the British to draw closer to France. By 1907, an alliance of Great Britain, France, and Russia—the Triple Entente—stood opposed to the Triple Alliance. Europe was now dangerously divided into two opposing camps unwilling to compromise.

## CRISES IN THE BALKANS

In the late 1800s, the Ottoman Empire began to fall apart. Most of its Balkan provinces gained their freedom. As this was happening, two Great Powers—Austria-Hungary and Russia—saw their chance to gain influence in the Balkans. Their rivalry over the Balkans was one of the causes of World War I.

By 1878, Greece, Serbia, Romania, and Montenegro had become independent. Bulgaria was not independent but was allowed to operate autonomously under Russian protection. The Balkan territories of Bosnia and Herzegovina were placed under the protection of Austria-Hungary.

Bettmann/Corbis

In 1908 Austria-Hungary took the drastic step of annexing Bosnia and Herzegovina. Serbia was outraged. The annexation of Bosnia and Herzegovina, two Slavic-speaking territories, led to an international **controversy** and dashed the Serbians' hopes of creating a large Serbian kingdom that would include most of the southern Slavs.

The Russians, self-appointed protectors of their fellow Slavs, supported the Serbs and opposed the annexation. Backed by the Russians, the Serbs prepared for war against Austria-Hungary. At this point, Kaiser William II of Germany demanded that the Russians accept Austria-Hungary's annexation of Bosnia and Herzegovina or face war with Germany.

Weakened from their defeat in the Russo-Japanese War in 1905, the Russians backed down but vowed revenge. Two wars between Balkan states in 1912 and 1913 further embittered the inhabitants and created more tensions among the Great Powers.

Austria-Hungary was convinced that Serbian nationalism was a threat to its empire and that Serbia must be crushed. Serbia, too, blamed Austria-Hungary for its failure to create a large Serbian kingdom. Serbia's chief supporter, Russia, was determined not to back down again in the event of another confrontation with Austria-Hungary or Germany in the Balkans. Finally, the allies of Austria-Hungary and Russia were determined to support their respective allies more strongly in another crisis. By the beginning of 1914, these countries viewed each other with suspicion. Europe was on the verge of war.

| Triple Alliance, 1882 |
| --- |
| • Germany |
| • Austria-Hungary |
| • Italy |
| **Triple Entente, 1907** |
| • Great Britain |
| • France |
| • Russia |

1. **INTEGRATING INFORMATION** Draw and shade a political map that shows the Triple Alliance and the Triple Entente.
2. **INTERPRETING** How do the chart and your map show that the formation of the two alliances might lead to military conflict?

### ✓ CHECKING FOR UNDERSTANDING

1. **IDENTIFYING CAUSES** How did international rivalries push Europe close to war?
2. **INTERPRETING** What did Kaiser William II mean when he said that he wanted Germany to find its rightful "place in the sun"? How do you know?
3. **RELATING EVENTS** How might events in Europe have unfolded differently had the Ottoman Empire had a strong government able to hold onto its empire?

**DETERMINING MEANING**

The word *controversy* comes from the prefix *contra-*, meaning "against," and the word *vertere*, meaning "to turn." How do these word parts help you understand the meaning of *controversy*?

## LESSON 3 REVIEW

### Time and Place

1. **ANALYZING CHANGE** Explain the political changes that took place in Western Europe during the late nineteenth century. How did the extent of change vary in different countries?

### Building History-Social Science Analysis Skills

2. **EXPLAINING CAUSE AND EFFECT** Did industrialization in Russia undermine the power of Czar Nicholas II? Explain.

3. **INTEGRATING INFORMATION** Draw two circle graphs showing the distribution of wealth in the United States in the late nineteenth century. How equitable, or inequitable, was that distribution? Explain how your graphs support your reasoning.

4. **IDENTIFYING CONNECTIONS** How did international rivalries push Europe close to war?

### Writing About History

5. **INFORMATIVE WRITING** Write a paragraph about the impact of labor issues on government in Britain and Russia. Be sure to cite evidence from the text to support your ideas.

### Collaborating

6. **USING MAPS** With a partner, study the Europe 1871 map in the lesson. Together, come up with explanations as to why the Balkans became a natural source of conflict as Ottoman control over the region weakened.

ESSENTIAL QUESTION

- *How are political and social structures influenced by economic changes?*

THE STORY BEGINS...

LESSON 4

# Modern Ideas and Uncertainty

When American author Mark Twain returned from Europe in 1900, he told several New York newspapers he opposed the United States' territorial acquisition overseas:

> "I left these shores, at Vancouver, a red-hot imperialist. I wanted the American eagle to go screaming into the Pacific. . . . Why not spread its wings over the Phillippines, I asked myself? . . . I said to myself, here are a people who have suffered for three centuries. We can make them as free as ourselves, give them a government and country of their own, put a miniature of the American constitution afloat in the Pacific, start a brand new republic to take its place among the free nations of the world. It seemed to me a great task to which [we] had addressed ourselves. But I have thought some more, since then, and I have read carefully the treaty of Paris, and I have seen that we do not intend to free, but to subjugate the people of the Phillippines. We have gone there to conquer, not to redeem . . . It should, it seems to me, be our pleasure and duty to make those people free, and let them deal with their own domestic questions in their own way. And so I am an anti-imperialist. I am opposed to having the eagle put its talons on any other land."

—Mark Twain, *New York Herald*, October 15, 1900

Imperialism was one of many subjects Twain explored in his writings. At the end of the nineteenth century and the start of the twentieth century, authors and artists served as mirrors for events in the world and often became powerful voices for change.

◀ *Doubts about the direction of modern society can be seen in the artistic and literary movements of the late 1800s and early 1900s.*

| Modernism | |
|---|---|
| Literature | |
| Art | |
| Science | |

**ANALYZING KEY IDEAS AND DETAILS**

**DETERMINING CENTRAL IDEAS** Read closely to identify ways in which literature, art, and science reflected a culture of modernity in the late nineteenth and early twentieth centuries. List notable movements, styles, and achievements of authors, artists, and scientists during this era in a graphic organizer like this one.

# THE CULTURE OF MODERNITY

**GUIDING QUESTION** *How did innovation change literature, the visual arts, and music in the late 1800s and early 1900s?*

Between 1870 and 1914, many writers and artists rebelled against the traditional literary and artistic styles that had dominated European cultural life since the Renaissance. The changes they produced have since been called **modernism**.

## LITERATURE

Western novelists and poets who followed the naturalist style believed that literature should be realistic and address social problems. Naturalist authors such as Henrik Ibsen and Émile Zola explored the role of women in society, alcoholism, and urban slums in their work.

In the United States, writers and journalists who focused on these issues came to be called muckrakers. Muckrakers included authors such as Upton Sinclair and Theodore Dreiser. Upton Sinclair's (1878–1968) novellas and short stories were meant to bring attention to ill treatment of the working class. His most famous work, *The Jungle*, brought attention to the plight of workers in Chicago's stockyards and also to the poor sanitary conditions found there.

> "There would be meat stored in great piles in rooms; and the water from leaky roofs would drip over it, and thousands of rats would race about on it. . . . [A] man could run his hand over these piles of meat and sweep off handfuls of the dried dung of rats. . . .
>
> Such were the new surroundings in which Elzbieta was placed, and such was the work she was compelled to do. It was stupefying, brutalizing work; it left her no time to think, no strength for anything. She was part of the machine she tended, and every faculty that was not needed for the machine was doomed to be crushed out of existence. . . ."
>
> —Upton Sinclair, *The Jungle,* 1906

Theodore Dreiser (1871–1945) was a more traditional naturalist author. His most famous novel, *Sister Carrie*, depicts a young woman who sets out to find opportunity in the city and instead learns about the hardship of urban life.

> "The place smelled of the oil of the machines and the new leather—a combination which, added to the stale odours of the building, was not pleasant even in cold weather. The floor, though regularly swept every evening, presented a littered surface. Not the slightest provision had been made for the comfort of the employees, the idea being that something was gained by giving them as little and making the work as hard and unremunerative as possible. . . ."
>
> —Theodore Dreiser, *Sister Carrie,* 1900

**ANALYZING KEY IDEAS AND DETAILS**

1. **DETERMINING CENTRAL IDEAS** How did modernism in architecture, art, music, and literature reflect changes brought on by industrialization?
2. **SUMMARIZING** Write a one-sentence summary of the section "Music."

**DETERMINING MEANING**

*Modern* describes something in the present time or in the most recent past. How was **modernism** modern?

**ANALYZING PRIMARY SOURCES**

**COMPARING AND CONTRASTING** How does Dreiser's *Sister Carrie* and its themes resemble and differ from Sinclair's *The Jungle*?

(t)Sinclair, Upton. 1906. The Jungle. Project Gutenberg Ebook #140; (b)Dreiser, Theodore. 1900. Sister Carrie. New York: Doubleday, Page & Co.

Claude Monet, *Haystacks,* 1891

Pablo Picasso, *Houses on the Hill,* 1909

## PAINTING AND ARCHITECTURE

Since the Renaissance, Western artists had tried to represent reality with accuracy. By the late 1800s, artists were seeking new forms of expression to reflect their changing worldviews. Impressionism was a movement that began in France in the 1870s, when a group of artists rejected indoor studios and went to the countryside to paint nature directly. One important impressionist was Claude Monet (moh • NAY), who painted pictures that captured the interplay of light, water, and sky.

In the 1880s, a new movement, postimpressionism, arose in France and soon spread. For Vincent van Gogh, art was a spiritual experience. He was especially interested in color and believed that it could act as its own form of language. Van Gogh maintained that artists should paint what they feel.

By the early 1900s, artists were no longer convinced that their main goal was to represent reality. This was especially true in the visual arts. One reason for the decline of realism in painting was photography, which became popular after George Eastman created the Kodak camera in 1888.

Artists tended to focus less on mirroring reality, which the camera could do, and more on creating reality. Painters and sculptors looked for meaning in individual consciousness. Between 1905 and 1914, this search for expression created modern art. Pablo Picasso was an important figure in modern art. Picasso created a new artistic style—cubism. Cubism used geometric designs to re-create reality in the viewer's mind.

**Abstract** painting emerged around 1910. Wassily Kandinsky, a Russian, was one of the first to use an abstract style. Kandinsky sought to avoid visual reality altogether. He believed that art should speak directly to the soul. To do so, it must use only line and color.

Modernism in the arts revolutionized architecture and gave rise to functionalism. Functionalism was the idea that buildings, like the products of machines, should be functional, or useful. All unnecessary ornamentation should be stripped away. Architects, led by Louis H. Sullivan, used reinforced concrete, steel frames, and electric elevators to build skyscrapers virtually free of ornamentation.

### IMPRESSIONISM AND CUBISM: MONET AND PICASSO

Contrast these two landscape paintings by impressionist Claude Monet (top) and cubist Pablo Picasso (bottom). Impressionists presented their impressions of scenes at specific moments in time. Cubist painters built on the abstraction of impressionist art and took it considerably further, often by reducing scenes to their underlying geometric shapes.

1. **INTEGRATING INFORMATION** How did impressionism and cubism each represent a departure from traditional painting techniques? Refer to these two paintings to defend your claims.
2. **INTEGRATING INFORMATION** In what ways are impressionism and cubism similar? In what ways are they different? Refer to these two paintings to defend your claims.

## MUSIC

At the beginning of the twentieth century, developments in music paralleled those in painting. The music of the Russian composer Igor Stravinsky exploited expressive sounds and bold rhythms. Stravinsky's ballet *The Rite of Spring* revolutionized music. When it was performed in Paris in 1913, the sounds and rhythms of the music and dance caused a near riot by an outraged audience.

### ✓ CHECKING FOR UNDERSTANDING

1. **UNDERSTANDING CHANGE** How did innovation change literature, the visual arts, and music in the late 1800s and early 1900s?
2. **IDENTIFYING CONNECTIONS** Why might some journalists and authors of the late nineteenth century have been called muckrakers?

# UNCERTAINTY GROWS

**GUIDING QUESTION** *How did scientific discoveries in the late 1800s impact the way people saw themselves and their world?*

Science was one of the chief pillars supporting the worldview of many Westerners in the nineteenth century. Many believed that by applying scientific laws, humans could understand the physical world and reality.

## CURIE AND THE ATOM

Throughout much of the 1800s, Westerners believed in a mechanical concept of the universe that was based on the ideas of Isaac Newton. The universe was viewed as a giant machine. Time, space, and matter were objective realities existing independently of those observing them. Matter was thought to be made of solid material bodies called atoms.

These views were seriously questioned at the end of the nineteenth century. The French scientist Marie Curie discovered that an element called radium gave off energy, or radiation, that apparently came from within the atom itself. Atoms were not just material bodies but small active worlds.

## EINSTEIN AND RELATIVITY

In the early twentieth century, Albert Einstein, a German-born scientist, provided a new view of the universe. His special theory of relativity stated that space and time are not absolute but are relative to the observer.

According to this theory, neither space nor time has an existence independent of human experience. Moreover, matter and energy reflect the relativity of time and space. Einstein concluded that matter is just another form of energy. The vast energies contained within the atom were explained. To some, however, a relative universe was one without certainty.

## FREUD AND PSYCHOANALYSIS

Sigmund Freud (FROYD), a doctor from Vienna, proposed theories regarding the nature of the human mind. His major theories were published in 1900 in *The Interpretation of Dreams*.

According to Freud, human behavior was strongly determined by past experiences and internal forces of which people were largely unaware. Repression of such experiences began in childhood, so he devised a method—known as **psychoanalysis**—by which a therapist could probe deeply into the patient's memory. In this way, the patient could retrace the repressed thoughts all the way back to his or her childhood origins. If the patient's conscious mind could be made aware of the unconscious and its repressed contents, the patient could be healed.

### ☑ CHECKING FOR UNDERSTANDING

1. **IDENTIFYING CONNECTIONS** How did scientific discoveries in the late 1800s impact the way people saw themselves and their world?
2. **EVALUATING** How does the work of scientists Marie Curie and Albert Einstein remain important today?

**UNDERSTANDING CRAFT AND STRUCTURE**

1. **ANALYZING TEXT** How does the text organize information to help you understand its main ideas?
2. **DETERMINING MEANING** Freud developed a therapy to work with a patient's repressed thoughts. What is a repressed thought?

*Marie Curie was the first woman to win a Nobel Prize. In 1903, she and her husband together were awarded half the Nobel Prize for Physics for their study in radiation. The other half went to Antoine Henri Becquerel for his studies in radioactivity.*

**INTERPRETING** How does this photograph signal a remarkable shift in social as well as scientific norms during the industrial era?

# EXTREME NATIONALISM

**UNDERSTANDING CRAFT AND STRUCTURE**

**ANALYZING CENTRAL IDEAS**
How did Social Darwinism use the idea of natural selection to justify nationalism and racism?

**GUIDING QUESTION** *What role did nationalism play in the late 1800s?*

Nationalism and the idea of the nation-state strengthened in the decades following the Napoleonic Wars. The cultural, technical, and governmental innovations and developments of the industrial era also helped these ideas flourish. Increases in literacy and the development of popular print media in the form of newspapers and widely read books led to a national literary culture. The development of national rail systems and road networks made travelling longer distances easier, faster, and cheaper. Central governments gained in power, reducing the power and independence of regional and local governments. As a result of these changes, it had become natural for the people of a nation-state to picture themselves as part of a larger national community by the late 1800s.

As a consequence of these developments, nationalism became more intense in many countries in the late 1800s. In addition to focusing on who could be included as a citizen of a nation, some began to focus on who should be excluded. Many made use of **Social Darwinism**, which was the radical belief that Darwin's theory of natural selection could be applied to modern human societies. A British philosopher, Herbert Spencer, argued that social progress came from "the survival of the fittest"—that is, the strong advanced while the weak declined. This kind of thinking allowed some people to reject the idea they should take care of the less fortunate.

Extreme nationalists also used Social Darwinism. They said that nations, too, were engaged in a "struggle for existence" in which only the fittest nations would survive. This idea was also used to justify racism, or the belief that some peoples were superior to others.

**CITIZENSHIP**

## INDIVIDUAL RIGHTS VERSUS THE NEEDS OF GOVERNMENT

The quick conviction of Alfred Dreyfus, followed by the discovery of his innocence, led many to doubt whether the French government respected the rights of its citizens. Indeed the French government's use of anti-Semitism to scapegoat a French citizen, to protect itself from embarrassment and scandal, revealed that the state was willing to ignore the rights of an individual for the sake of what it saw as its own needs. This tension between the needs of the state and the rights of the individual persists today. For instance, should a government have the ability to ignore the rights of individual citizens if it believes that in doing so it protects society as a whole? This problem is a difficult one, and it will continue to feature in court cases and political discussions as long as governments struggle with their own needs and the rights of their citizens.

Al Bello/Getty Images Sport/Getty Images

1. **IDENTIFYING CAUSES** Cite specific reasons from the text for why the French state was so eager to trample Dreyfus's rights.
2. **EVALUATING ARGUMENTS** Outside the examples given in the text, name an individual right that is in competition with the needs of the state. What do you support in your example: the needs of the state or the rights of individuals? Cite evidence to support your position.

The growth of extreme nationalism and racism also led to the growth of anti-Semitism, or hostility toward and discrimination against Jews. The **intensity** of anti-Semitism was evident from the Dreyfus affair in France. In 1894, a military court, meeting in an atmosphere of public, vehement expressions of anti-Jewish hostility, found Alfred Dreyfus, a Jewish captain in the French general staff, guilty of selling army secrets. After the trial, evidence emerged that proved Dreyfus innocent. Despite this, the country remained deeply divided over the issue for years, and it was not until 1899 that the government felt compelled to pardon Dreyfus.

The Dreyfus affair led many Jews in France to feel as though they were not seen as French and were instead seen as outsiders. Many Jews in France, and indeed in Europe as a whole were beginning to see that the Enlightenment principles of equality and citizenship were not being applied to them.

The worst treatment of Jews at the turn of the century occurred in Russia. Persecutions and **pogroms**, or organized attacks, were widespread. Hundreds of thousands of Jews decided to emigrate to escape the persecution. Some Jews, probably about 25,000, immigrated to Palestine in the Ottoman Empire, which became home for a Jewish nationalist movement called **Zionism**.

For many Jews, the land of ancient Israel had long been the land of their dreams. A key figure in the growth of political Zionism was Theodor Herzl, who stated in his book *The Jewish State* (1896), "The Jews who wish it will have their state." Settlement in the Palestine region was difficult, however, because it was then part of the Ottoman Empire, which was opposed to Jewish immigration. Although 3,000 Jews went annually to Palestine between 1904 and 1914, the Zionist desire for a homeland remained only a dream on the eve of World War I.

**DETERMINING MEANING**

The Yiddish word **pogrom** derives from the Russian *pogromu*, meaning "devastation, or destruction." How does the word's origin help you understand its meaning?

**DETERMINING MEANING**

In the late nineteenth century, *Zion* came to mean "the Jewish people" or "the Jewish homeland." The name *Zion* has historical roots. In the Jewish Bible, *Zion* refers to a fortress in Canaan captured by King David, and called the "City of David." Why is **Zionism** an appropriate name for the Jewish nationalist movement that emerged in the late nineteenth century?

### ✓ CHECKING FOR UNDERSTANDING

1. **IDENTIFYING CONNECTIONS** What role did nationalism play in the late 1800s?

2. **DETERMINING CONTEXT** What evidence suggests that anti-Semitism was on the rise in Europe in the late nineteenth century?



## LESSON 4 REVIEW

### Time and Place

1. **ANALYZING CHANGE** How did scientific discoveries in the late nineteenth century change ideas about time and space?

### Building History-Social Science Analysis Skills

2. **ANALYZING CHANGE** How did innovation change literature, the visual arts, and music in the late 1800s?

3. **INTERPRETING** What purpose did Herbert Spencer have in interpreting Charles Darwin's theory of natural selection as "survival of the fittest"?

4. **IDENTIFYING CONNECTIONS** How did nationalism in France and Russia lead to a Jewish nationalist movement?

### Writing About History

5. **EXPLANATORY WRITING** Write a paragraph explaining how artistic and scientific ideas of the present day could lead to uncertainty. Discuss at least one artist and a scientist.

### Collaborating

6. **EVALUATING POINT OF VIEW** In small groups, discuss the modernism movement in art. What was this movement a reaction against? How did technology influence this movement?

# STUDY GUIDE

## CHANGES DURING THE SECOND INDUSTRIAL REVOLUTION
### LESSON 1

Electricity led to the lightbulb, telephone, radio, subways, and machines and lights in factories.

A new way to make steel, the Bessemer process, allowed for improved machines, engines, and weapons.

The internal-combustion engine led to the inventions of ocean liners, airplanes, and automobiles.

Production was more efficient due to the assembly line, which was pioneered by Henry Ford in 1913.

## THE SOCIAL STRUCTURE IN MASS SOCIETY
### LESSON 2

**The New Elite**

5% of the population but controlled 30–40% of the wealth (industrialists, bankers, merchants, and the aristocracy)

**Diverse Middle Class**

**Middle group below upper-middle class** (lawyers, doctors, members of the civil service, business managers, engineers, architects, accountants, and chemists)

**Lower-middle class** (small shopkeepers, traders, and prosperous farmers)

**New white-collar worker group** (traveling salespeople, bookkeepers, telephone operators, department store salespeople, and secretaries)

**Working Class or Lower Class**

Made up almost 80% of the European population (peasants, farm laborers, skilled artisans, domestic servants, and the urban working class)

## THE SPREAD OF DEMOCRACY IN EUROPE
### LESSON 3

**Western Europe**

**Great Britain**
Strong parliamentary system and well-established democracy

**France**
Third Republic with a president and parliament; weak but still supported by most voters

**Italy**
National state without unity and with a corrupt and weak government

## MODERN IDEAS AND THE ARTS
### LESSON 4

**Functionalism**
The idea that buildings, like the products of machines, should be functional or useful

**Symbolism**
The idea that the external world is only a collection of symbols reflecting true reality

**Impressionism**
Rejects indoor studios to paint pictures that capture the interplay of light, water, and sky, reflecting the natural world

**Cubism**
Uses geometric designs to re-create reality in the viewer's mind

**Abstract**
Avoids visual reality and lets art speak directly to the soul through line and color only

**Naturalism**
The idea that literature should address social problems

# CHAPTER 5 Assessment

**Directions: On a separate sheet of paper, answer the questions below. Make sure you read carefully and answer all parts of the questions.**

## Short Answer

1. **UNDERSTANDING CHANGE** How did the assembly line improve industrial production?

2. **DETERMINING CENTRAL IDEAS** Why did socialism appeal to and mobilize the working class?

3. **IDENTIFYING CONNECTIONS** Explain how rapid urbanization led to problems, and describe city governments' responses.

4. **ANALYZING CHANGE** When did public education become widespread, and why had it not happened earlier?

5. **IDENTIFYING CONNECTIONS** How did ministerial responsibility relate to how power was distributed in Central Europe?

6. **IDENTIFYING EFFECTS** How did industrialization impact the wealth of the United States in the late nineteenth century?

7. **SUMMARIZING** Describe two painting styles that became popular in the late nineteenth or early twentieth century.

8. **DETERMINING CENTRAL IDEAS** What was Sigmund Freud's purpose in writing *The Interpretation of Dreams*? What larger goal did his work have?

9. **ANALYZING EVENTS** What did the First Industrial Revolution and the Second Industrial Revolution have in common? How did they differ?

10. **IDENTIFYING CONNECTIONS** What conclusions can you draw about the quality of life and lifestyle of urban workers in the 1870s (the period that followed labor reforms) such as 10-hour workdays, the six-day work week, and increased wages?

11. **DETERMINING CONTEXT** How might extreme nationalists' perceptions of themselves have led them to believe in Social Darwinism?

12. **EXPLAINING CAUSE AND EFFECT** What were some of the signs that democracy was expanding in the late nineteenth century? What were some reasons for that expansion?

## History and Social-Science Analysis

13. **IDENTIFYING CONNECTIONS** Make a word web with the word "Industrialization" in the center circle. Draw arrows to two radiating circles, labeled "Strong Economy" and "Weak Economy." Draw another layer of radiating circles from each of these circles to show which political and social structures were influenced by economic changes from 1870 to 1914. Explain each of the connections.

14. **EVALUATING ARGUMENTS** Evaluate Karl Marx's reasoning that European society in the late 1800s was divided into two distinct, and opposed, classes: the proletariat and the bourgeoisie. Do you agree or disagree? Why or why not?

## Analyzing Visuals

15. **DETERMINING POINT OF VIEW** The image reads "Proletarians of the World, Unite!" What point of view does this poster reflect? Do you think a nationalist would approve of its message? Explain.

16. **UNDERSTANDING CONTEXT** How does the poster use symbolism to support its message and to persuade viewers?



**Need Extra Help?**

| If You've Missed Question | 1 | 2 | 3 | 4 | 5 | 6 | 7 | 8 | 9 | 10 | 11 | 12 | 13 | 14 | 15 | 16 |
|---|---|---|---|---|---|---|---|---|---|---|---|---|---|---|---|---|
| Review Lesson | 1 | 1 | 2 | 2 | 3 | 3 | 4 | 4 | 1 | 2 | 4 | 3 | 1 | 2 | 2 | 2 |

## Research and Presentation

**17** **SUMMARIZING** Choose one of the figures that impacted scientific thinking in the late 1800s, such as Marie Curie, Albert Einstein, and Sigmund Freud, and summarize the shift in thinking that resulted from his or her work. How did this shift in thinking reflect other trends brought on by industrialization? Share and discuss your conclusions in a small group.

**18** **PRESENTING** Choose one example each of art, architecture, literature, and music from the Second Industrial Revolution in Europe and North America. Prepare a multimedia presentation that identifies each piece and its makers, and discusses the innovative characteristics of each piece, including how it reflects the trend toward modernism in the late nineteenth and early twentieth centuries. Take a position on how these pieces remain relevant today.

**19** **RELATING EVENTS** Work with a partner to make a concept web to show how government changed in Europe in the late nineteenth and early twentieth centuries. Start with a circle labeled "Government in Europe." Draw lines connecting the center oval to ovals around it. Record details about government changes in Austria-Hungary, Britain, France, Germany, Italy, and Russia. With your partner, discuss how industrialization influenced changes in government in each country.

## Reading and Analyzing Primary Sources

Use the document to answer the following questions.

Emmeline Pankhurst explained in a 1913 speech why it was so important for women to have a voice in their government.

> "I wonder that women have the courage to take upon themselves the responsibilities of marriage and motherhood when I see how little protection the law of my country affords them. I wonder that a woman will face the ordeal of childbirth with the knowledge that after she has risked her life to bring a child into the world she has absolutely no parental rights over the future of that child."
>
> — quoted in *Sources of the Western Tradition, Volume II: From the Renaissance to the Present*

**20** **IDENTIFYING BIAS** What biographical information helps you identify Pankhurst's bias?

**A.** She worked as a teacher and a social worker.
**B.** She grew up in an urban working-class family.
**C.** She was a leader in the women's rights movement.
**D.** She served in several important positions in government.

**21** **DETERMINING POINT OF VIEW** Based on the excerpt, with which argument would Pankhurst most likely agree?

**A.** Women should not have to work in factories.
**B.** Women have an obligation to take care of their families.
**C.** Women deserve equal rights and protections from government.
**D.** Women can best serve their communities as teachers and activists.

**22** **DISTINGUISHING FACT FROM OPINION** Which statement can most easily be verified as fact?

**A.** "women have the courage to take upon themselves the responsibilities of marriage and motherhood"
**B.** "I see how little protection the law of my country affords them"
**C.** "that a woman will face the ordeal of childbirth"
**D.** "she has absolutely no parental rights over the future of that child"

## Writing About History

**23** **EXPLANATORY WRITING** How do the living conditions of the masses of people affect how a nation is ruled? How does a move toward democracy affect the living conditions of the masses?

## Speaking and Listening About History

**24** **COLLABORATING** In a small group, identify one event, innovation, movement, or other change from each lesson. Discuss how the four changes relate to one another. Do any of the changes have a causal relationship? How do you know?

**Need Extra Help?**

| If You've Missed Question | 17 | 18 | 19 | 20 | 21 | 22 | 23 | 24 |
|---|---|---|---|---|---|---|---|---|
| Review Lesson | 4 | 4 | 3 | 2 | 2 | 2 | 2 | 1–4 |

TEXT:Perry, Marvin; Peden, Joseph R.; and Von Laue, Theodore H. 1999. Sources of the Western Tradition: Volume II, From the Renaissance to the Present. Houghton Mifflin Company.

◄ *This photograph shows Tagore in 1929, when he was nearly 70. Although a passionate nationalist, he nevertheless strove for a balance between modern Western influence and ancient Indian traditions. One expression of this effort was his habit of writing his poetry first in Bengali and then translating it into English.*

1800 — 1914

# The Reach of Imperialism

## CHAPTER 6

**LESSON 1**
Colonial Rule in Southeast Asia

**ANALYZING SOURCES**
Explaining Imperialism

**LESSON 2**
Empire Building in Africa

**POINTS OF VIEW**
Two Perspectives on Imperialism

**LESSON 3**
British Rule in India

**LESSON 4**
Imperialism in Latin America

**GO DIGITAL**
*It's All online!*

## ASKING ESSENTIAL QUESTIONS

***What are the causes and effects of imperialism?***
***How do some groups resist control by others?***

**What Will You Learn?** You will learn about the causes and effects of European and American imperialism in Africa, India, Latin America, and Southeast Asia and how some groups resisted colonial rule.

**Why Does this Matter?** After 1870, the industrialized nations of Europe acquired a large number of colonies in Africa and Asia. This led to resentment and nationalist movements, which would begin a slow struggle for independence. The effects of imperialism persist today. Many of the once-colonized nations were left with colonial borders that have led to continuing ethnic, religious, and political conflicts.

**How Will You Know That You Learned It?** You will be able to identify the causes and effects of the "new imperialism" and explain how groups resisted the control of colonial powers.

**Using Your Inquiry Journal** As you read this chapter and examine the primary sources, use your Inquiry Journal to help you make notes and expand your list of questions. As you gather information, think about how you will answer the Essential Questions above.

Bettmann/Corbis

## PLACE & TIME Asia and Africa 1800–1914

The nineteenth century was known for a new wave of imperialism as European powers, Japan, and the United States seized control of new territories and conquered peoples in Asia and Africa. The race for new colonies was fueled by competition among the European powers, nationalism, demand for raw materials, superior technology, and a belief in racial hierarchies. In Latin America, independence movements struggling to throw off Spanish authority succeeded by the mid-nineteenth century.

### STEP INTO THE PLACE

Read the quotes and look at the information presented on the map.

1. **SPATIAL THINKING** What does the map reflect about the competitiveness of European colonial powers?

2. **IDENTIFYING CONNECTIONS** In 1893, Frederick Lugard was arguing for more funding for African colonies, while journalists such as Edmund Morel argued against the practice. What were the central motivations for imperialism, and what were the perceived costs to conquered peoples?

“We owe to the instincts of colonial expansion of our ancestors, those vast and noble dependencies which are our pride and the outlets of our trade to-day; and we are accountable to posterity that opportunities which now present themselves of extending the sphere of our industrial enterprise are not neglected, for the opportunities now offered will never recur again.”

—Frederick Lugard, British colonial administrator, from *The Rise of Our East African Empire,* 1893

“What the partial occupation of his soil by the white man has failed to do; what the mapping out of European political ‘spheres of influence’ has failed to do; what the maxim and the rifle, the slave gang, labour in the bowels of the earth and the lash, have failed to do; what imported [diseases] have failed to do; what even the oversea slave trade failed to do, the power of modern capitalistic exploitation, assisted by modern engines of destruction, may yet succeed in accomplishing. For from the evils of the latter, scientifically applied and enforced, there is no escape for the African.”

—Edmund D. Morel, British author, from *The Black Man's Burden,* 1920

### STEP INTO THE TIME

**CHRONOLOGICAL THINKING**

How do the events on the time line show resistance to European colonialism?

## AFRICA, ASIA, AND LATIN AMERICA

**1819** Great Britain sends Sir Thomas Raffles to Singapore

**1830** French take over Algeria

**1830** Belgium creates an independent state

**1841** Explorer David Livingstone arrives in Africa

1800 — 1815 — 1830

## WORLD EVENTS

**1807** Slave trade to British colonies outlawed

**1812** Napoleon invades Russia

PHOTO:(t)Pictorial Press Ltd/Alamy; (b)Library of Congress, Prints & Photographs Division [LC-USZ62-130451]; TEXT:(t)Captain F. D. Lugard, D.S.O. 1893. The Rise of Our East African Empire,

## THE SPREAD OF EUROPEAN COLONIALISM BY 1914

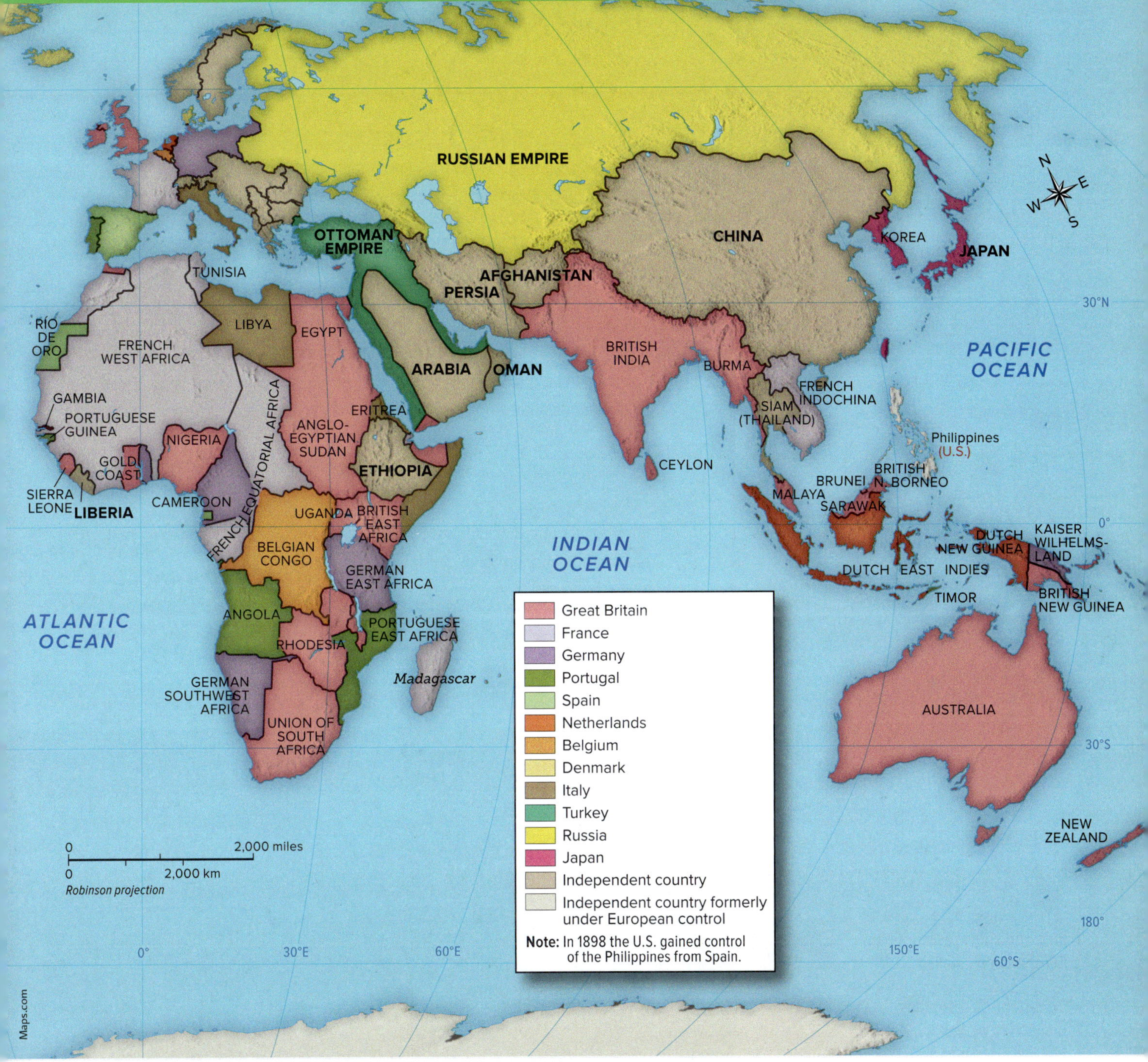


**1845**

**1848** Demonstrations erupt in the Austrian Empire

**1857** Great Rebellion begins in India

**1860**

**1861** Jefferson Davis leads Confederacy as U.S. Civil War begins

**1874** Great Britain annexes west coastal states of Africa

**1875**

**1877** "Jim Crow" laws enforce segregation in southern United States

**1890**

**1893** Union of French Indochina formed

**1896** Ethiopians defeat Italian army at Adwa

**1900** Most of Southeast Asia under Western rule

**1905**

**1907** France, Great Britain, and Russia create Triple Entente

**1914** Panama Canal opens

**1914** Assassination of Archduke Francis Ferdinand

**1914**

## ESSENTIAL QUESTIONS

- *What are the causes and effects of imperialism?*
- *How do some groups resist control by others?*

# THE STORY BEGINS...

LESSON 1

# Colonial Rule in Southeast Asia

Sir Thomas Stamford Raffles traveled to Singapore in 1819 to found a British colony. He described it as follows:

> "I am happy to inform you that everything is going on well here. It bids fair to be the next port to Calcutta; all we want now is, the certainty of permanent possession, and this, of course, depends on authorities beyond our control. You may take my word for it, this is by far the most important station in the East; and, as far as naval superiority and commercial interests are concerned, of much higher value than whole continents of territory."

—letter from Sir Thomas Stamford Raffles, 1819

Raffles's assessment would prove correct, and Singapore would open up new areas of trade and further expansion into Asia for Great Britain.

*Singapore under British rule during the late 1800s* ▶

| Region | Political Status |
|---|---|
| Burma | |
| Singapore | |
| Vietnam | |
| Thailand | |
| Philippines | |

**ANALYZING KEY IDEAS AND DETAILS**

**CITING TEXT EVIDENCE** Read closely to identify the political status of various regions of Southeast Asia. Record each status in a graphic organizer like this one.

# THE NEW IMPERIALISM

**GUIDING QUESTION** *What were the motivations for the new imperialism?*

In the nineteenth century, a new phase of Western expansion began. European nations began to view Asian and African societies as a source of industrial raw materials and a market for Western manufactured goods.

In the 1880s, European states began an intense scramble for overseas territory. **Imperialism**, the extension of a nation's power over other lands, was not new. Europeans had set up colonies and trading posts in North America, South America, and Africa by the sixteenth century.

However, the imperialism of the late nineteenth century, called the "new imperialism" by some historians, was different. Earlier, European states had been content, especially in the case of Africa and Asia, to set up a few trading posts where they could carry on trade and perhaps some missionary activity. Now they sought nothing less than direct control over vast territories.

## MOTIVES FOR IMPERIALISM

Why did Westerners begin to increase their search for colonies after 1880? There was a strong economic motive. Capitalist states in the West were looking for both markets and raw materials such as tea, coffee, rubber, oil, and tin. These resources were quickly becoming essential for the creation of many commodities European industries produced. The issue was not simply an economic one, however. European nation-states were involved in heated rivalries. They acquired colonies abroad in order to gain a strategic and economic advantage over their rivals. Colonies were also a source of national prestige. To some people, in fact, a nation could not be great without colonies.

In addition, imperialism was tied to Social Darwinism and racism. Social Darwinists believed that in the struggle between nations, the fit are victorious. **Racism** is the belief that race determines traits and capabilities. Racists erroneously believe that particular races are superior or inferior.

Imperial ambitions and conquests strengthened European nationalism and led some colonizers to view colonized people as inferior "others." Some Europeans, however, took a more religious and humanitarian approach to imperialism. They believed Europeans had a moral responsibility to civilize those they considered primitive people. They called this responsibility the "white man's burden." To some, this meant bringing the Christian message to the "heathen masses." To others, it meant bringing the benefits of Western democracy and capitalism to these societies.

**ANALYZING KEY IDEAS AND DETAILS**

1. **SUMMARIZING** Write a brief summary of "new imperialism."
2. **IDENTIFYING STEPS** What evidence in the text supports the idea that new technologies helped to advance imperialism?

**MAKING CONNECTIONS**

### IMPERIALISM AND THE DIFFUSION OF CULTURES

Cultural diffusion is the spread of culture traits, both material and non-material, from one culture to another. Cultural diffusion has influenced cultural change since the dawn of human history. As European states pushed beyond trading posts to establish colonies in Africa and Asia, European ideas and practices spread. European states set up government and legal systems in these colonies that changed how societies were governed. Educational systems, often missionary-established schools, furthered the spread of Christianity as well as the language of the colonizers. The colonies became not only a source of raw materials but a market for exports, spreading European agricultural and material goods throughout the areas. Economic systems also reflected European influence.

MAKING CONNECTIONS TO SCIENCE

### THE ROLE OF QUININE

The disease malaria is especially devastating in tropical and subtropical regions, which offer good conditions for the mosquitoes that carry and spread it. By 1850, European doctors had learned how to treat malaria with quinine, a drug that greatly reduced the death rate from the disease. Quinine is obtained from the bark of the cinchona tree, which is native to South America. Indigenous people of Peru were the first people to use this bark to treat malaria. With the use of quinine, everyone in these tropical and subtropical regions now had a defense against a devastating disease.

1. **CITING TEXT EVIDENCE** Why did malaria keep Europeans from colonizing Africa before 1850?
2. **CITING TEXT EVIDENCE** How did quinine allow for European colonization of Africa?

## NEW TECHNOLOGIES AND IMPERIALISM

Nineteenth-century technological developments were also important in the development and growth of imperialism. New military weapons, such as the machine gun, gave Europeans a superior military force, enabling them in pitched battles to defeat those who resisted a takeover of their lands. Military superiority also gave European nations a huge advantage in diplomacy with these new territories. European nations could often get what they wanted from Asian and African societies with only the presence of a powerful advanced navy, a process referred to as **gunboat diplomacy**.

New forms of transportation, a direct result of the Industrial Revolution in Europe, helped advance imperialism as well. Technological developments in railroad and steam power allowed Europeans to travel faster and more easily. These advances also helped Europeans remove resources from colonies more easily and allowed European missionaries to travel to more remote locations.

New forms of communication also advanced imperialism. The telegraph, for example, allowed colonial regimes to communicate with Europe faster than ever before, giving European nations a high degree of control over their colonies. And advances in print technology helped Christian missionaries spread their religion and better organize new colonial churches.

Medical advancements also served to further imperialist adventures. Long journeys and tropical climates took a heavy toll on European conquerors. New medicines, such as the use of quinine to combat malaria, made it possible for Europeans to live in difficult climates. Thus, larger numbers of Europeans could now survive in Africa and Asia.

### ☑ CHECKING FOR UNDERSTANDING

1. **INTERPRETING** What were the motivations for the new imperialism?
2. **IDENTIFYING CONNECTIONS** What is the relationship between religion and imperialism?
3. **UNDERSTANDING CONTEXT** How did Europeans justify imperialism?

# COLONIAL TAKEOVER

**GUIDING QUESTION** *What led to Western dominance in Southeast Asia?*

The new imperialism was evident in Southeast Asia. The region had long been known for its consumable resources such as sugar, tea, and various spices. In 1800 the Europeans had two established colonies in the region: the Spanish Philippines and the Dutch East Indies. By 1900 virtually the entire area was under Western rule.

**UNDERSTANDING CRAFT AND STRUCTURE**

1. **ANALYZING TEXT** How has the author organized the text describing the colonial takeover of Southeast Asia?
2. **DETERMINING MEANING** The text states that in the Philippines, "President McKinley had his stepping-stone to the rich markets of China." Look at the map of Southeast Asia. Why might the United States have considered the Philippines to be a "stepping-stone"?

## GREAT BRITAIN

The process of colonial expansion began with Great Britain. In 1819 Great Britain sent Sir Thomas Stamford Raffles to found a new colony on a small island at the tip of the Malay Peninsula. A strategic location overlooking a high-traffic shipping lane, it was called Singapore or "city of the lion." In the new age of steamships, it soon became a major stopping point for traffic traveling to or from China.

During the next few decades, the British advance into Southeast Asia continued. Next to fall was the kingdom of Burma (modern Myanmar). Britain wanted control of Burma in order to protect its possessions in India. It also sought a land route through Burma into southern China. Although the difficult terrain along the frontier between Burma and China caused this effort to fail, British activities in Burma led to the collapse of the Burmese monarchy. Britain soon established control over the entire country.

## FRANCE

France, which had some missionaries operating in Vietnam, nervously watched the British advance into Burma. The local Vietnamese authorities, who viewed Christianity as a threat to Confucian doctrine, persecuted the French missionaries. However, Vietnam failed to stop the Christian missionaries. Vietnamese internal rivalries divided the country into two separate governments—the north and the south.

France was especially alarmed by British attempts to monopolize trade. To stop any British movement into Vietnam, the French government decided in 1857 to force the Vietnamese to accept French protection.

The French eventually succeeded in making the Vietnamese ruler give up territories in the Mekong River delta. The French occupied the city of Saigon and, during the next 30 years, extended their control over the rest of the country. In 1883 France seized the city of Hanoi and later made the Vietnamese empire a French **protectorate**.

In the 1880s, France extended its control over neighboring Cambodia, Annam, Tonkin, and Laos. By 1887 France included all its new possessions in a new Union of French Indochina.

**DETERMINING MEANING**

The word **protectorate** contains the same root word as the words *protection, protected,* and *protector*. How does this help you understand what a *protectorate* is?

**GEOGRAPHIC REASONING**

European countries used Southeast Asia as a source for raw materials.

1. **GLOBAL INTERCONNECTIONS** Which territory was the primary source of spices?
2. **HUMAN-ENVIRONMENT INTERACTION** Which raw materials did the United States have access to in Southeast Asia?

### IMPERIALISM IN SOUTHEAST ASIA 1900

## THAILAND—THE EXCEPTION

After the French conquest of Indochina, Thailand (then called Siam) was the only remaining free state in Southeast Asia. But the rivalry between the British and the French threatened to place Thailand under colonial rule, too.

Two remarkable rulers were able to prevent that from happening. One was King Mongkut (known to theatergoers as the king in *The King and I*), and the other was his son, King Chulalongkorn. Both promoted Western learning and maintained friendly relations with the major European powers. In 1896 Britain and France agreed to maintain Thailand as an independent buffer state between their possessions in Southeast Asia.

*Filipinos mount an insurrection against the Americans in Manila in February 1899.*

**IDENTIFYING BIAS** Contrast the depiction of the Filipinos with that of the American soldiers.

## THE UNITED STATES

In 1898 during the Spanish-American War, U.S. naval forces under Commodore George Dewey defeated the Spanish fleet in Manila Bay in the Philippines. Believing it was his moral obligation to "civilize" other parts of the world, President William McKinley decided to turn the Philippines, which had been under Spanish control, into an American colony. This action would also prevent the area from falling into the hands of the Japanese. The islands gave the United States convenient access to trade with China.

Many Filipinos did not wish to be under American control. Emilio Aguinaldo (AH • gee • NAHL • doh) was the leader of a movement for independence in the Philippines. He began his revolt against the Spanish and went into exile in 1898. When the United States acquired the Philippines, Aguinaldo continued the revolt and set himself up as the president of the Republic of the Philippines. Led by Aguinaldo, the guerrilla forces fought bitterly against the U.S. troops to establish their independence.

Many in the U.S. government, however, were unwilling to give up the advantages gained by possession of the Philippines. One senator said:

**ANALYZING PRIMARY SOURCES**

**UNDERSTANDING CONTEXT** How does Beveridge's statement reflect a mixture of moral idealism and a desire for profit?

> "Mr. President, the times call for candor. The Philippines are ours forever. And just beyond the Philippines are China's illimitable markets. We will not retreat from either. We will not abandon an opportunity in [Asia]. We will not renounce our part in the mission of our race, trustee, under God, of the civilization of the world."
>
> —Senator Albert Beveridge, from a speech before the U.S. Senate, January 9, 1900

The fight for Philippine independence resulted in three years of bloody warfare. However, the United States eventually defeated the guerrilla forces, and President McKinley had his stepping-stone to the rich markets of China.

### ✓ CHECKING FOR UNDERSTANDING

1. **EXPLAINING EFFECTS** What led to Western dominance in Southeast Asia?
2. **EVALUATING** Why was Thailand "the exception"? How did Thailand manage to be an exception?

# COLONIAL REGIMES

GUIDING QUESTION *How did colonial powers govern their colonies?*

Western powers governed their new colonial empires by either indirect or direct rule. Their chief goals were to **exploit** the natural resources of the lands and to open up markets for their own manufactured goods.

## INDIRECT AND DIRECT RULE

Sometimes a colonial power could realize its goals by cooperating with local political elites. For example, the Dutch East India Company used **indirect rule** in the Dutch East Indies. Under indirect rule, local rulers were allowed to keep their authority and status in a new colonial setting. This made access to the region's natural resources easier. Indirect rule was cheaper because fewer officials had to be trained. It also affected local culture less.

However, indirect rule was not always possible. Some local elites resisted foreign conquest. In these cases, the local elites were replaced with Western officials. This system was called **direct rule**. Great Britain administered Burma directly through its colonial government in India. In Indochina, France used both systems. It imposed direct rule in southern Vietnam but ruled indirectly through the emperor in northern Vietnam.

To justify their conquests, Western powers spoke of bringing the "blessings" of Western civilization to their colonial subjects. They imposed their cultural norms to their colonies such as European marriage practices and Western styles of dress. They also attempted to alter the role of women in colonial societies to more closely match the roles of European women. And while they promised to bring the practice of representative government to their colonial subjects, many Westerners came to fear the idea of Southeast Asian peoples and people in their colonies elsewhere being allowed political rights.

## COLONIAL ECONOMIES

The colonial powers did not want their colonists to develop their own industries. Thus, colonial policy stressed the **export** of raw materials. This policy often led to the development of plantation agriculture. In this system, peasants worked as wage laborers on the foreign-owned plantations. Plantation owners kept wages at poverty levels to increase profits. Conditions on plantations were often so unhealthful that thousands died. Also, peasants bore the burden of high taxes.

Nevertheless, colonial rule did bring some benefits to Southeast Asia. A modern economic system began there. Colonial governments built railroads, highways, and other structures that benefited Southeast Asian peoples as well as colonials. The development of an export market helped create an entrepreneurial class in rural areas. In the Dutch East Indies, for example, small growers of rubber, palm oil, coffee, tea, and spices began to share in the profits of the colonial enterprise. Most of the profits, however, were taken back to the colonizing country.

### ANALYZING KEY IDEAS AND DETAILS

1. **DETERMINING CENTRAL IDEAS** What is the central idea of the section "Indirect and Direct Rule"?
2. **CITING TEXT EVIDENCE** What evidence suggests that colonial rule was not beneficial for peasants in Southeast Asia?

### DETERMINING MEANING

Read the paragraph that contains the word **exploit**. Using context clues, write a definition of the word *exploit*. Use a dictionary or an online resource to check your definition.

### DETERMINING MEANING

To *rule* is to govern. What is the difference between **direct rule** and **indirect rule**? Use context clues in the text to inform your response.

### DETERMINING MEANING

To *import* is to bring goods into a country. What does it mean to **export** raw materials?

*A group of Vietnamese children poses with locally made baskets in southern Vietnam.*

## INFORMAL EMPIRES

Industrialized nations came to have an economic edge over nonindustrialized nations. Goods produced in factories could be made faster, cheaper, and in much larger quantities than goods made in traditional and largely manual ways in nonindustrialized nations. Over the course of the late nineteenth and early twentieth centuries, the production of goods stagnated or decreased in places such as India, China, and Latin America but increased in parts of Europe and in the United States.

Many nonindustrialized nations became increasingly dependent on industrialized nations. This resulted in a relationship that some scholars describe as an "informal empire." In an "informal empire," nonindustrialized nations, although not formally colonized, became increasingly dependent on industrialized nations. These nations would then sometimes threaten violence in order to obtain economic or other agreements that usually benefited them alone.

### ✓ CHECKING FOR UNDERSTANDING

1. **SUMMARIZING** How did colonial powers govern their colonies?
2. **USING MAPS** According to the map, what raw materials did the Dutch have access to by controlling the Dutch East Indies?
3. **DESCRIBING** What kind of economic system did colonial rulers establish?

## RESISTANCE TO COLONIAL RULE

**GUIDING QUESTION** *How did indigenous people in Southeast Asia respond to colonial rule?*

Many subject peoples in Southeast Asia resented colonization. At first, resistance came from the existing ruling class. In Burma, for example, the monarch himself fought Western domination. By contrast, in Vietnam, after the emperor had agreed to French control of his country, a number of government officials set up an organization called Can Vuong ("Save the King"). They fought against the French without the emperor's help.

Meanwhile in the Philippines, a revolutionary group called the Katipunan, led by Emilio Aguinaldo, formed in 1892. They first fought against their Spanish rulers. When Spain yielded control of the Philippines to the United States, the Katipunan fought the Americans for independence as well. Aguinaldo wrote the following about the struggle against colonial rule:

> "Oh, dear Philippines! Blame your wealth, your beauty for the stupendous disgrace that rests upon your faithful sons.
>
> You have aroused the ambition of the Imperialists and Expansionists of North America and both have placed their sharp claws upon your entrails!
>
> Loved mother, sweet mother, we are here to defend your liberty and independence to the death! We do not want war; on the contrary, we wish for peace; but honourable peace, which does not make you blush nor stain your forehead with shame and confusion. And we swear to you and promise that while America with all her power and wealth could possibly vanquish us; killing all of us; but enslave us, never!!!"

—Emilio Aguinaldo, *True Version of the Philippine Revolution,* 1899

**UNDERSTANDING CRAFT AND STRUCTURE**

1. **ANALYZING TEXT** How does the writer introduce the topic of resistance to colonial rule in Southeast Asia? How does the writer develop this topic from the beginning to the end of this section?
2. **DETERMINING MEANING** The text states that a new class of Westernized intellectuals was the first generation of Asians to "embrace" Western ideas and values. What does it mean to *embrace* an idea?

**ANALYZING PRIMARY SOURCES**

1. **DETERMINING MEANING** What does Aguinaldo mean by "blame your wealth, your beauty for the stupendous disgrace"?
2. **CITING TEXT EVIDENCE** How does this excerpt display Aguinaldo's patriotism? Cite specific evidence from the text.

Aguinaldo y Famy, Don Emilio. 1899. True Version of the Philippine Revolution. Project Gutenberg Ebook 12996.

Sometimes resistance to Western control took the form of peasant revolts. Peasants were often driven off the land to make way for plantation agriculture. Angry peasants then vented their anger at the foreign invaders. For example, in Burma in 1930, the Buddhist monk Saya San led a peasant uprising against the British colonial regime.

This 1874 engraving depicts the government palace at Saigon, which the French constructed to administer Indochina.

Private Collection/Archives Charmet/The Bridgeman Art Library

Early resistance movements failed. They were overcome by Western powers. In the early 1900s, however, a new kind of resistance emerged that was based on nationalism. The leaders were often from a new class that the colonial rule had created: Westernized intellectuals in the cities. They were the first generation of Asians to embrace the institutions and values of the West. Many were educated in the West, spoke Western languages, and worked in jobs connected with the colonial regimes.

At first, many of the leaders of these movements did not focus clearly on the idea of nationhood. Instead, they simply tried to defend the economic interests or religious beliefs of the Southeast Asian peoples. In Burma, for example, students at the University of Rangoon formed an organization to protest against official persecution of the Buddhist religion and British lack of respect for local religious traditions. They protested against British arrogance and failure to observe local customs in Buddhist temples. Not until the 1930s, however, did these resistance movements, such as those begun in Burma, begin to demand national independence.

### ✓ CHECKING FOR UNDERSTANDING

1. **EVALUATING** How did indigenous peoples in Southeast Asia respond to colonial rule?
2. **INTERPRETING** How was colonial rule a threat to Southeast Asian culture?
3. **IDENTIFYING CONNECTIONS** Why were resistance movements often led by Southeast Asian people who had been educated in the West?

## LESSON 1 REVIEW

### Time and Place

1. **DESCRIBING** Write a paragraph describing different forms of colonial rule. Be sure to define *protectorate, direct rule,* and *indirect rule* and to discuss specific examples.

### Building History-Social Science Analysis Skills

2. **SUMMARIZING** Write a paragraph summarizing the political situation of the regions of Southeast Asia by 1900.
3. **IDENTIFYING CONNECTIONS** How did conflicts in Europe affect the colonization of Southeast Asia?
4. **DESCRIBING** What is an informal empire?

### Writing About History

5. **EXPLANATORY WRITING** Write an essay discussing the effects of colonial rule on the countries that were colonized. Be sure to discuss at least two specific examples.

### Collaborating

6. **EVALUATING** With a partner, select a colonial nation from this period. Write a report for the colonial government describing the relationship between an industrial and colonial nation, considering the perspectives of both groups from the time.

# EXPLAINING IMPERIALISM

Imperialism has been explained in many different ways. A Social Darwinist, a Presbyterian missionary, a colonial administrator, and a novelist account for differing viewpoints of the system in the excerpts below.

**VOCABULARY**

*stagnate:* to stop moving

*venerable:* worthy of great respect

PRIMARY SOURCE: LECTURE

## THE STANDPOINT OF A SOCIAL DARWINIST

"If you bring the white man into contact with the black, you too often suspend the very process of natural selection on which the evolution of a higher type depends. You get superior and inferior races living on the same soil, and that coexistence is demoralizing for both. They naturally sink into the position of master and servant, if not admittedly or covertly into that of slave-owner and slave. Frequently they inter-cross, and if the bad stock be raised the good is lowered. . . . Thus it comes about that when a struggle for existence between races is suspended, the solution of great problems may be unnaturally postponed; instead of the slow, stern processes of evolution, cataclysmal solutions are prepared for the future. . . .

You may say: Let us cease to struggle; let us leave the lands of the world to the races that cannot profit by them to the full; let us cease to compete in the markets of the world. Well, we could do it, if we were a small nation living off the produce of our own soil, and a soil so worthless that no other race envied it and sought to appropriate it. We should cease to advance; but then we should naturally give up progress as a good which comes through suffering. I say it is impossible for a small rural community to stand apart from the world-contest and to **stagnate**, if no more powerful nation wants its possessions."

—*lecture from British mathematician Karl Pearson*, 1900

### ANALYZE THE TEXT

1. **CITING TEXT EVIDENCE** Cite specific statements from "The Standpoint of a Social Darwinist" that reflect Karl Pearson's belief that some races are naturally dominant over others.
2. **DETERMINING POINT OF VIEW** What does Pearson fear would happen if countries attempted to coexist peacefully instead of one dominating the other?

PRIMARY SOURCE: LETTER

## A PRESBYTERIAN MISSIONARY ON BRITISH IMPERIALISM

"4. All the men and all the money (over £140,000) used in civilizing and Christianizing the New Hebrides, have been British. Now fourteen missionaries, and the "Dayspring" mission ship, and about 150 native evangelists and teachers are employed in the above work on this group, in which over £6,000 yearly of British and British-colonial money is expended, and certainly it would be unwise to let any other power now take possession and reap the fruits of all this British outlay.

8. The thirteen islands of this group on which life and property are now comparatively safe, the 8,000 professed Christians on the group, and all the churches formed from among them are, by God's blessing, the fruits of the labors of British missionaries, who, at great toil, expense, and loss of life have translated, got printed, and taught the natives to read the Bible in part or in whole in nine different languages of this group, while 70,000 at least are longing and ready for the Gospel. On this group twenty-one members of the mission family died or were murdered by the savages in beginning God's work among them, not including good Bishop Patteson, of the Meiauesian Mission, and we fear all this good work would be lost if the New Hebrides fall into other than British Hands.

For the above reasons, and others that might be given, we sincerely hope and pray that you will do all possible to get Victoria and the other colonial governments to help and unite in urging Great Britain at once to take possession of the New Hebrides group. Whether looked at in the interests of humanity, or of Christianity, or commercially, or politically, sure it is most desirable that they should at once be British possessions. . . ."

—letter from Presbyterian missionary John Paton to the British government, 1900

### ANALYZE THE TEXT

1. **DETERMINING CENTRAL IDEAS** How does John Paton justify Great Britain's right to take possession of the New Hebrides islands?
2. **IDENTIFYING CONNECTIONS** What does Paton's letter indicate about the role of religion in European imperialism?



TEXT:(l)Pearson, Karl. 1905. National Life From the Standpoint of Science - Second Edition. London: Adam and Charles Black.;(r)__________, 1884.

## PRIMARY SOURCE: DOCUMENT

# A BRIT DEFENDS IMPERIALISM

"The control of the Nile sources, with the significance which that control bears to Egypt and to the commerce which finds its outlet on the Red Sea ports. Here, again, it is necessary to realise not only the advantage to ourselves, but the alternative disadvantage of seeing the Nile basin in the hands of a foreign Power. . . .

It is sufficient to reiterate here, that as long as our policy is one of free trade, we are compelled to seek new markets; for old ones are being closed to us by hostile tariffs, and our great dependencies, which formerly were the consumers of our goods, are now becoming our commercial rivals. It is inherent in a great colonial and commercial empire like ours that we go forward or go backward. To allow other nations to develop new fields, and to refuse to do so ourselves, is to go backward; and this is the more deplorable, seeing that we have proved ourselves notably capable of dealing with native races, and of developing new countries at a less expense than other nations."

—Frederick Lugard, *The Rise of Our East African Empire,* 1893

## PRIMARY SOURCE: NOVEL

# A NOVELIST EXPLORES BELGIAN ATROCITIES

"We looked at the **venerable** stream not in the vivid flush of a short day that comes and departs for ever, but in the august light of abiding memories. And indeed nothing is easier for a man who has, as the phrase goes, "followed the sea" with reverence and affection, than to evoke the great spirit of the past upon the lower reaches of the Thames. The tidal current runs to and fro in its unceasing service, crowded with memories of men and ships it had borne to the rest of home or to the battles of the sea. It had known and served all the men of whom the nation is proud, from Sir Francis Drake to Sir John Franklin, knights all, titled and untitled—the great knights-errant of the sea. . . . They had sailed from Deptford, from Greenwich, from Erith—the adventurers and the settlers; kings' ships and the ships of men on 'Change; captains, admirals, the dark "interlopers" of the Eastern trade, and the commissioned "generals" of East India fleets. Hunters for gold or pursuers of fame, they all had gone out on that stream, bearing the sword, and often the torch, messengers of the might within the land, bearers of a spark from the sacred fire. What greatness had not floated on the ebb of that river into the mystery of an unknown earth! . . . The dreams of men, the seed of commonwealths, the germs of empires."

—Joseph Conrad, *Heart of Darkness*, 1899

### ANALYZE THE TEXT

1. **DETERMINING CENTRAL IDEAS** According to Frederick Lugard, what made the Nile basin particularly attractive to Europeans?
2. **DETERMINING CONTEXT** Based on the Lugard excerpt, how was competition a factor in European imperialism?

### ANALYZE THE TEXT

1. **CITING TEXT EVIDENCE** What does the excerpt from *Heart of Darkness* suggest about how European citizens felt about imperialists? Cite evidence from the text.
2. **DETERMINING MEANING** What does the phrase "the germs of empires" suggest about the explorers in *Heart of Darkness*?

### MULTIPLE PERSPECTIVES

1. **COMPARING POINTS OF VIEW** How do Pearson and Paton justify imperialism as being in the best interest of the groups taken over?
2. **COMPARING AND CONTRASTING** How is Lugard's point of view about imperialism similar to and different from those of Pearson and Paton?

and London: William Blackwood and Sons.;(r)Conrad, Joseph. 1899. Heart of Darkness. Project Gutenberg Ebook #219.

## ESSENTIAL QUESTIONS

- *What are the causes and effects of imperialism?*
- *How do some groups resist control by others?*

LESSON 2

# Empire Building in Africa

## THE STORY BEGINS...

Cecil Rhodes, a British businessman, held a view of non-Europeans in Africa that was common during this time period:

> “The natives know nothing about the politics of the country. They have told me time after time that they do not understand these politics. ‘Leave us alone, but let us try and deal with some of our little local questions.’ That is the common statement they have made to me. . . . I feel, too, that if the people desire it the canteens should be removed from their midst. Further, it is our duty as a Government to remove these poor children from this life of sloth and laziness, and to give them some gentle stimulus to come forth and find out the dignity of labour.”
>
> —speech by Cecil Rhodes, 1894

Rhodes's condescension toward Africans was typical of colonial powers, against which resentment would build among the non-Europeans.

*A scene from British rule in East Africa* ▶

| Western Power | Area of Africa |
|---|---|
| Belgium | |
| Britain | |
| France | |
| Germany | |

**ANALYZING KEY IDEAS AND DETAILS**

**DETERMINING CENTRAL IDEAS** Read closely to identify which countries controlled different parts of Africa. Record each status in a graphic organizer like this one.

# WEST AFRICA AND NORTH AFRICA

**GUIDING QUESTION** *Why were European countries interested in West Africa and North Africa?*

Before 1880, Europeans were content to let African rulers and merchants represent European interests. Between 1880 and 1900, however, Great Britain, France, Germany, Belgium, Italy, Spain, and Portugal, spurred by intense rivalries among themselves, placed virtually all Africa under European rule.

**UNDERSTANDING CRAFT AND STRUCTURE**

**ANALYZING TEXT** What is the purpose of dividing this section into the subsections "West Africa" and "North Africa"?

**DETERMINING MEANING**

The word **annex** comes from the Latin root *annect-*, which means "connected." How does knowing the meaning of the Latin root help you understand what it means to *annex* a country?

## WEST AFRICA

Europeans had a keen interest in Africa's raw materials, especially those of West Africa, such as peanuts, timber, hides, and palm oil. Earlier in the nineteenth century, Europeans had profited from the slave trade in this region of Africa. By the late 1800s, however, trade in enslaved people had virtually ended. As the slave trade declined, Europe's interest in other forms of trade increased. The growing European presence in West Africa led to increasing tensions.

For a long time, most African states maintained their independence. However, in 1874 Great Britain **annexed** the western coastal states and established a protectorate in Nigeria. By 1900, France had added the huge area of French West Africa to its colonial empire. This left France in control of the largest part of West Africa. In addition, Germany controlled Togo, Cameroon, German Southwest Africa, and German East Africa.

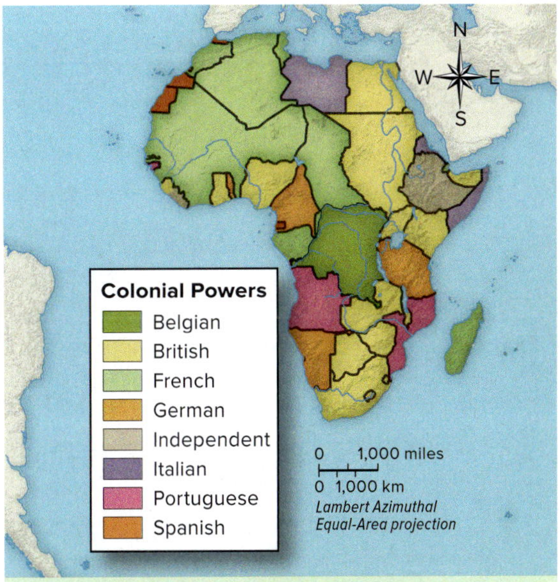


**GEOGRAPHIC REASONING**

**SPATIAL THINKING** Which colonial power controlled most of West Africa?

## NORTH AFRICA

In 1805 an officer of the Ottoman army named Muhammad Ali seized power and created an independent Egyptian state. Muhammad Ali introduced a series of reforms to bring Egypt into the modern world. He modernized the army, set up a public school system, and helped create small industries that refined sugar, produced textiles and munitions, and built ships.

The growing economic importance of the Nile Valley in Egypt, along with the development of steamships, gave Europeans the desire to build a canal east of Cairo to connect the Mediterranean and Red Seas. Such a canal would allow transport between Europe and Asia, without traveling around Africa. In 1854 a French entrepreneur, Ferdinand de Lesseps, signed a contract to begin building the Suez Canal. The canal was completed in 1869.

BIOGRAPHY

### MENELIK II
**(1844–1913)**

Born in Ethiopia in 1844, Menelik II endured great difficulty as a youth. His father was killed during an invasion, and Menelik was taken prisoner. Ten years later, he escaped, led a revolt, and was crowned emperor of Ethiopia in 1889.

During Menelik's reign, Italy invaded Ethiopia. Menelik's defeat of the Italian troops at the Battle of Adwa on March 1, 1896 made him one of the most well-respected leaders in the world. Ethiopia was one of only two African countries, along with Liberia, to remain independent from European control during this time.

In addition to his military victories, Menelik pursued modernization in Ethiopia in the form of building railroads, bridges, a telephone network, and a modern school system.

**ANALYZING IDEAS** How was Ethiopia able to stay independent throughout the era of European colonization?

The British took an active interest in Egypt after the Suez Canal was opened. Believing that the canal was its "lifeline to India," Great Britain tried to gain as much control as possible over the canal area. In 1875 Britain bought Egypt's share in the Suez Canal. When an Egyptian army revolt against foreign influence broke out in 1881, Britain suppressed the revolt. Egypt became a British protectorate in 1914.

The British believed they should also control Sudan, south of Egypt, to protect their interests in Egypt and the Suez Canal. In 1881 Muslim cleric Muhammad Ahmad, known as the Mahdi (in Arabic, "the rightly guided one"), launched a revolt that brought much of Sudan under his control. Britain sent a military force under General Charles Gordon to restore Egyptian authority over Sudan. However, Muhammad Ahmad's troops wiped out Gordon's army at Khartoum in 1885. General Gordon himself died in the battle. Not until 1898 were British troops able to seize Sudan.

The French also had colonies in North Africa. In 1879 after about 150,000 French people had settled in the region of Algeria, the French government established control there. Two years later, France imposed a protectorate on neighboring Tunisia. In 1912 France established a protectorate over much of Morocco.

Italy joined the competition for colonies in North Africa by attempting to take over Ethiopia. In 1896, however, the Italian invading forces were defeated by the Ethiopian army led by Emperor Menelik II. Italy now was the only European state defeated by an African state. This humbling loss led Italy to try again in 1911. Italy invaded and seized Turkish Tripoli, which it renamed Libya.

### ☑ CHECKING FOR UNDERSTANDING

1. **INTERPRETING** Why were European countries interested in West Africa and North Africa?
2. **IDENTIFYING CONNECTIONS** In what way did the construction of a canal in Egypt further the imperial interests of the British in South Asia?
3. **IDENTIFYING CAUSES** In what way did the decline in the slave trade in West Africa trigger an increase in colonial expansion in the region?

## CENTRAL AND EAST AFRICA

**GUIDING QUESTION** *Why did European countries compete for colonies in Central Africa and East Africa?*

### CENTRAL AFRICA

As with North and Western Africa, various Central African territories were soon added to the list of European colonies. Reports from European explorers venturing into the region aroused popular interest in the dense tropical jungles of Central Africa.

David Livingstone was one such explorer. He arrived in Africa in 1841 as a 27-year-old medical missionary. During the 30 years he spent in Africa, Livingstone trekked through regions **uncharted** by Europeans. He sometimes traveled by canoe, but mostly Livingstone walked and spent much of his time exploring the interior of the continent.

**ANALYZING KEY IDEAS AND DETAILS**

1. **ANALYZING EVENTS** Reread the paragraphs that discuss the activities of David Livingstone. For what purpose does the writer recount these events?
2. **CITING TEXT EVIDENCE** The text in this section explains that Germany felt it important to establish colonies overseas. What text evidence supports the claim that the German people were eager to establish colonies?

During his travels through Africa, Livingstone made detailed notes of his discoveries. He sent this information back to London whenever he could. The maps of Africa were often redrawn based on Livingstone's eyewitness accounts and reports. A major goal of Livingstone's explorations was to find a navigable river that would open Central Africa to European commerce and Christian missionaries.

Deep within the African interior, it was not uncommon for Livingstone's communications with Europe to be infrequent. When Livingstone disappeared for a while, an American newspaper, the *New York Herald,* hired a young journalist, Henry Stanley, to find the explorer. Stanley did find him, on the eastern shore of Lake Tanganyika. Overwhelmed by finding Livingstone alive if not well, Stanley greeted the explorer with these now-famous words, "Dr. Livingstone, I presume?"

After Livingstone's death in 1873, Stanley decided to carry on the great explorer's work. Unlike Livingstone, however, Henry Stanley had a strong dislike of Africa. He once said, "I detest the land most heartily."

In the 1870s, Stanley explored the Congo River in Central Africa and sailed down it to the Atlantic Ocean. Soon, he was encouraging the British to send settlers to the Congo River basin. When Britain refused, Stanley turned to King Leopold II of Belgium.

King Leopold II was the real driving force behind the colonization of Central Africa. He rushed enthusiastically into the pursuit of an empire in Africa. "To open to civilization," he said, "the only part of our globe where it has yet to penetrate, to pierce the darkness which envelops whole populations, it is, I dare to say, a crusade worthy of this century of progress." Profit, however, was equally important to Leopold. In 1877 he hired Henry Stanley to set up Belgian settlements in the Congo.

Leopold's claim to the vast territories of the Congo aroused widespread concern among other European states. France, in particular, rushed to plant its flag in the heart of Africa. Leopold ended up with the territories around the Congo River. France occupied the areas farther north. Leopold governed the Congo more as a personal estate than as a colony. His rule of the Congo would become notorious for the brutal treatment of the Congolese people.

*This 1872 British illustration depicts the meeting between Stanley and Livingstone on November 19, 1872.*

**EXPLAINING CAUSES** Why did the phrase "Dr. Livingstone, I presume?" become so famous?

## EAST AFRICA

By 1885 Britain and Germany had become the chief rivals in East Africa. Germany had come late to the ranks of the imperialist powers. At first, the German chancellor Otto von Bismarck downplayed the importance of colonies. As more and more Germans called for a German empire, however, Bismarck relented and became a convert to colonialism. As he expressed it, "All this colonial business is a sham, but we need it for the elections."

In addition to its West African holdings, Germany tried to develop colonies in East Africa. Most of East Africa had not yet been claimed by any other power. However, the British were also interested in the area because control of East Africa would connect the British Empire in Africa from South Africa to Egypt. Portugal, France, Italy, and Belgium also claimed parts of East Africa. Many began to worry that this "Scramble for Africa" would lead to conflict among the European powers.

ANALYZING PRIMARY SOURCES

1. **ANALYZING TEXT** How does Lugard develop his claims that colonial expansion is advantageous?
2. **DETERMINING POINT OF VIEW** What do the words *duty* and *responsibilities* indicate about Lugard's point of view?

The British offical Frederick Lugard described the contest as follows:

> "The 'Scramble for Africa' by the nations of Europe — an incident without parallel in the history of the world — was due to the growing commercial rivalry, which brought home to civilised nations the vital necessity of securing the only remaining fields for industrial enterprise and expansion. It is well, then, to realise that it is for our advantage — and not alone at the dictates of duty — that we have undertaken responsibilities in East Africa. It is in order to foster the growth of the trade of this country, and to find an outlet for our manufactures and our surplus energy, that our far-seeing statesmen and our commercial men advocate colonial expansion."
>
> —Frederick Lugard, *The Rise of Our East African Empire*, 1893

**MAKING CONNECTIONS TO TODAY**

### THE BERLIN CONFERENCE

European rulers knew little about Africa's political and social systems, and no Africans participated at the Berlin Conference. As a result, Europeans created colonial boundaries that often cut across cultural, religious, ethnic, and traditional boundaries, which forced peoples of very different backgrounds and beliefs to occupy the same areas. The introduction of Christianity added to the tension. Religious and ethnic tensions set African peoples against one another and strengthened European rule. The ill-conceived boundaries drawn by the colonial powers continue to contribute to conflict in the region today.

To settle conflicting claims, European countries met at the Berlin Conference in 1884 and 1885. The conference officially recognized both British and German claims for territory in East Africa. Portugal received a clear claim on Mozambique. No African delegates, however, were present at this conference.

### ✓ CHECKING FOR UNDERSTANDING

1. **INTERPRETING** Why did European countries compete for colonies in Central Africa and East Africa?
2. **COMPARING AND CONTRASTING** How were David Livingstone and Henry Stanley similar in their attitudes toward Africa? How were they different?
3. **EXPLAINING CAUSES** How did Leopold's actions lead to the "Scramble for Africa"?

## SOUTH AFRICA

**GUIDING QUESTION** *How was European dominance different in South Africa?*

Nowhere in Africa did the European presence grow more rapidly than in the south. By 1865 the total white population of South Africa had risen to nearly 200,000 people. The Boers, or Afrikaners—as the descendants of the original Dutch settlers were called—had occupied Cape Town and surrounding areas in South Africa since the seventeenth century. During the Napoleonic Wars, however, the British seized these lands from the Dutch. South Africa included vast resources of gold and diamonds to be mined. These would provide great wealth for the British and capital for industrial investment. The British realized the strategic and economic value of South Africa and encouraged settlers to come to what they now called the Cape Colony.

### THE BOER REPUBLICS

In the 1830s, disgusted with British rule, the Boers moved from the coastal lands and headed northward on the Great Trek. Altogether one out of every five Dutch-speaking South Africans joined the trek. Their parties eventually settled in the region between the Orange and Vaal (VAHL) Rivers and in the region north of the Vaal River. In these areas, the Boers formed two independent republics—the Orange Free State and the Transvaal (later called the South African Republic).

ANALYZING KEY IDEAS AND DETAILS

1. **DETERMINING CENTRAL IDEAS** What is the central idea of the section?
2. **ANALYZING INDIVIDUALS** What is the connection between Cecil Rhodes and British imperialism in Africa?

Captain F. D. Lugard, DSO. 1893. The Rise of Our East African Empire - Early Efforts in Nyasaland and Uganda. In Two Volumes - Vol. II. Edinburgh and London: William Blackwood and Sons.

The Boers believed that white superiority was ordained by God. They denied non-Europeans any place in their society, other than as laborers or servants. As they settled the lands, the Boers put many of the **indigenous** peoples, those native to a region, in these areas on reservations.

The Boers had frequently battled the indigenous Zulu people. In the early 1800s, the Zulu, under a ruler named Shaka, had carved out their own empire. The Zulu remained powerful and assembled an army in 1879 of at least 40,000 to resist the British in what was known as the Anglo-Zulu War. While initially successful, the Zulu were defeated after the British government launched a full-scale military campaign.

## CECIL RHODES

In the 1880s, British policy in South Africa was influenced by Cecil Rhodes. Rhodes had founded diamond and gold mining companies that had made him a fortune. Rhodes was a great champion of British expansion. He said once, "I think what [God] would like me to do is to paint as much of Africa British red as possible." One of Rhodes's goals was to create a series of British colonies "from the Cape to Cairo"—all linked by a railroad.

When gold and diamonds were discovered in the Transvaal, British settlers swarmed in looking to make their fortunes. The Boer residents resented the settlers and they were sometimes mistreated.

Rhodes then secretly backed a raid that was meant to spark an uprising among British settlers against the Transvaal government. The raid failed, and the British government forced Rhodes to resign as head of the Cape Colony. This action was too late, however, to prevent a war between the British and the Boers.

## THE BOER WAR

This war, called the Boer War, dragged on from 1899 to 1902. Fierce guerrilla resistance by the Boers angered the British. They responded by burning crops and forcing about 120,000 Boer women and children into detention camps, where lack of food caused some 20,000 deaths. Eventually, the vastly larger British army won. A peace treaty was signed in 1902.

In 1910 the British created an independent Union of South Africa, which combined the old Cape Colony and the Boer republics. The new state would be a self-governing nation within the British Empire. To appease the Boers, the British agreed that only whites, with a few propertied Africans, would vote.

### ✓ CHECKING FOR UNDERSTANDING

1. **ANALYZING CHANGE** How was European dominance different in South Africa?
2. **EXPLAINING CAUSES** What were the events that led to the Boer War?
3. **DETERMINING CONTEXT** What role did Cecil Rhodes play in promoting British imperialism in South Africa

**MAKING CONNECTIONS**

### AFRICAN RESISTANCE

In the eighteenth and nineteenth centuries, the Asante, or Ashanti, state occupied what is currently southern Ghana. The Asante had a successful trade empire with strong rulers who effectively resisted British forces in the early 1800s. However, by the 1870s the British took control of what became known as the Gold Coast colony, including Elmina, which the Asante also claimed. The Asante sent troops to occupy the Gold Coast, but they were unable to hold off the British who eventually made it to the capital. The war ended when the Treaty of Fomena was signed in 1874.

*In 1881 Cecil Rhodes formed the De Beers Mining Company, which still dominates the world diamond market.*

PHOTO:FPG/Getty Images; TEXT: Rhodes, Cecil. 1899. Quoted in The American Monthly Review of Reviews, Volume 20. Edited by Albert Shaw. The Review of Reviews Company.

INTEGRATING KNOWLEDGE AND IDEAS

1. **EVALUATING ARGUMENTS** What evidence does the author present that supports the conclusion that indirect rule was "basically a fraud"?

2. **INTEGRATING INFORMATION** The information in this section explains that the British were not always honest in their colonial dealings. How does the excerpt of the letter from Lobengula to Queen Victoria support the argument that the British used deceit to further their colonial interests?

**DETERMINING MEANING**

Read the paragraph that contains the word **traditions**. Using context clues, write a definition of *tradition*. Use a dictionary or an online reference to check your definition.

*The Zulu chief Cetewayo surrendered to the British after they captured the city of Ulundi in July 1879.*

**EXPLAINING CAUSES** Why was Zulu chief Cetewayo unable to maintain power?

# EFFECTS OF IMPERIALISM IN AFRICA

**GUIDING QUESTION** *How did European governance lead to African nationalism?*

By 1914 Great Britain, France, Germany, Belgium, Italy, Spain, and Portugal had divided up Africa. Only Liberia, which had been created as a homeland for the formerly enslaved persons of the United States, and Ethiopia remained free states. African peoples who dared to resist were devastated by the Europeans' superior military force.

## COLONIAL RULE IN AFRICA

As was true in Southeast Asia, most European governments ruled their new territories in Africa with the least effort and expense possible. Indirect rule meant relying on existing political elites and institutions. The British especially followed this approach. At first, in some areas, the British simply asked a local ruler to accept British authority and to fly the British flag over official buildings.

The concept of indirect rule was introduced in the Islamic state of Sokoto, in northern Nigeria, beginning in 1903. This system of indirect rule in Sokoto had one good feature: It did not disrupt local customs and institutions. However, it did have some unfortunate consequences. The system of indirect rule was basically a fraud because British administrators made all major decisions. The local African authorities served chiefly to enforce those decisions.

Another problem was that the policy of indirect rule kept the old African elite in power. Such a policy provided few opportunities for ambitious and talented young Africans from outside the old elite. In this way British indirect rule sowed the seeds for class and ethnic tensions, which erupted after independence came in the twentieth century.

Most other European nations governed their African possessions through a form of direct rule. This was true in the French colonies. At the top was a French official, usually known as a governor-general. He was appointed from Paris and governed with the aid of a bureaucracy in the capital city of the colony.

The French ideal was to assimilate African subjects into French culture rather than preserve indigenous **traditions**. Africans were eligible to run for office and even serve in the French National Assembly in Paris. A few were also appointed to high-powered positions in the colonial administration.

## RISE OF AFRICAN NATIONALISM

A new class of leaders emerged in Africa by the beginning of the twentieth century. Exposed to the colonial norms by colonizing nations, and educated in colonial schools or in Western nations, they were the first generation of Africans to know a great deal about the West.

The members of this new class admired Western culture and sometimes disliked the ways of their own countries. They were eager to introduce Western cultural norms, ideas, and institutions into their societies. Still, many of these new leaders came to resent the foreigners and their contempt for African peoples. These intellectuals recognized the gap between theory and practice in colonial policy. Westerners had exalted the Enlightenment ideas of democracy, equality, and political freedom but did not apply these values in the colonies.

There were few democratic institutions. African peoples could have only low-paying jobs in the colonial bureaucracy. To many Africans, colonialism had meant losing their farmlands or working on plantations or in factories run by foreigners. Some African leaders lost even more, such as the rights to mine the natural resources in their countries.

Middle-class Africans did not suffer as much as poor African peasants. However, members of the middle class also had complaints. They usually qualified only for menial jobs in the government or business. Even then, their salaries were lower than those of Europeans in similar jobs.

Europeans expressed their assumed superiority over Africans in other ways. Segregated clubs, schools, and churches were set up as more European officials brought their wives and began to raise families. Europeans were also condescending in their relationships with Africans. For instance, Europeans had a habit of addressing Africans by their first names.

Such conditions led many members of the new urban educated class to feel great confusion toward their colonial rulers and the civilization the colonists represented. Some educated Africans found aspects of Western culture to be more attractive than their own. However, these intellectuals fiercely hated colonial rule and were determined to assert their own nationality and cultural destiny. Out of this mixture of hopes and resentments emerged the first stirrings of modern nationalism in Africa.

During the first quarter of the twentieth century, resentment turned to action. Across Africa, indigenous peoples began to organize political parties and movements seeking the end of foreign rule. They wanted to be independent and self-governing.

**ANALYZING PRIMARY SOURCES**

**IMPERIALISM IN AFRICA**

"Some time ago a party of men came to my country, the principal one appearing to be a man called Rudd. They asked me for a place to dig for gold, and said they would give me certain things for the right to do so. I told them to bring what they could give and I would show them what I would give. A document was written and presented to me for signature. I asked what it contained, and was told that in it were my words and the words of those men. I put my hand to it. About three months afterwards I heard from other sources that I had given by the document the right to all the minerals of my country."

—Lobengula, a southern African king, in a letter to Queen Victoria, quoted in *The Imperialism Reader*

### ✓ CHECKING FOR UNDERSTANDING

1. **EXPLAINING EFFECTS** How did European governance lead to African nationalism?
2. **COMPARING AND CONTRASTING** In what way did the different colonial style of the French allow elite colonial subjects to benefit from colonialism?
3. **INTERPRETING** In what ways were Western nations hypocritical in their treatment of their colonies?

## LESSON 2 REVIEW

### Time and Place

1. **DESCRIBING** Identify the predominant areas of Africa controlled by various European nations.

### Building History-Social Science Analysis Skills

2. **ANALYZING CHANGE** What major trend can you identify in the progress of African colonialism over the course of the nineteenth century?
3. **EXPLAINING EFFECTS** What was one consequence of Rhodes's meddling into the affairs of the Transvaal government?
4. **UNDERSTANDING CONTEXT** What role did the Italian defeat in 1896 play in encouraging later Italian colonial pursuits in Africa?

### Writing About History

5. **INFORMATIVE WRITING** In one or two paragraphs, explain the effects of the Berlin conference of 1884–1885 on the scramble for Africa.

### Collaborating

6. **IDENTIFYING CONNECTIONS** With a partner, discuss how the traditions of indigenous Africans influenced their relations with Europeans.

# Two Perspectives on Imperialism

In the last decades of the nineteenth century, commenters frequently noted that the sun never set on the British Empire. But while there was wide agreement about its size and power, there was no such consensus on the role it should play in the world. Rudyard Kipling supported British imperialism and in his 1899 poem "The White Man's Burden," he called for the United States to join Britain in bringing the light of civilization to the far corners of the world. His words appear shocking to modern audiences, and were not shared by everyone in his own time. One individual who disagreed with Kipling's assessment was E. D. Morel, a British journalist. In 1900 he began a campaign against slavery in Belgium's Congo Free State. Morel disagreed with Kipling's assessment of European imperialism and wrote "The Black Man's Burden" in 1920 as a response to Kipling's poem.

"Take up the White Man's burden
Send forth the best ye breed
Go bind your sons to exile
To serve your captives' need;
To wait in heavy harness,
On fluttered folk and wild
Your new-caught, sullen peoples,
Half-devil and half child.

Take up the White Man's burden
The **savage** wars of peace
Fill full the mouth of Famine
And bid the sickness cease;
And when your goal is nearest
The end for others sought,
Watch Sloth and **heathen** Folly
Bring all your hope to naught.

Take up the White Man's burden
No **tawdry** rule of kings,
But toil of serf and sweeper
The tale of common things.
The ports ye shall not enter,
The roads ye shall not tread,
Go make them with your living,
And mark them with your dead.

Take up the White Man's burden
And reap his old reward;
The blame of those ye better,
The hate of those ye guard
The cry of hosts ye humour
(Ah, slowly!) toward the light:
"Why brought ye us from bondage,
Our loved Egyptian night?"

---

**VOCABULARY**

*savage:* uncivilized
*heathen:* uncultured
*tawdry:* low or mean

PHOTO:duncan1890/iStock/Getty Images; TEXT:Kipling, Rudyard. 1899. The White Man's Burden. From The Riverside Literature Series: Kipling Stories and Poems Every Child Should Know - Book II. Edited by Mary E. Burt and W. T. Chapin. April 1909. Cambridge, Massachusetts: The Riverside Press.

"It is [the Africans] who carry the 'Black man's burden. . .' In **hewing** out for himself a fixed abode in Africa, the white man has massacred the African in heaps. . .

What the partial occupation of his soil by the white man has failed to do; . . . what the [machine gun] and the rifle, the slave gang, labour in the **bowels** of the earth and the lash, have failed to do; what imported measles, smallpox and syphilis have failed to do; whatever the overseas slave trade failed to do; the power of modern capitalistic exploitation, assisted by modern engines of destruction, may yet succeed in accomplishing. . .

For from the evils of the latter, scientifically applied and enforced, there is no escape for the African. Its destructive effects are not **spasmodic**: they are permanent. In its permanence resides its fatal consequences. It kills not the body merely, but the soul. It breaks the spirit. It attacks the African at every turn, from every point of vantage. It wrecks his polity, uproots him from the land, invades his family life, destroys his natural pursuits and occupations, claims his whole time, enslaves him in his own home. . . .

Thus the African is really helpless against the material gods of the white man, as embodied in the trinity of imperialism, capitalistic exploitation, and militarism."

---

**VOCABULARY**

*hewing:* making, shaping, or smoothing with cutting blows

*bowels:* the inward or interior parts

*spasmodic:* occuring in brief bursts

## What Do YOU Think?

1. **DETERMINING MEANING** What was the impact of imperialism on the colonized territories in Africa, according to Morel?
2. **CITING TEXT EVIDENCE** Quote lines in Rudyard Kipling's poem that reflect his view of colonized peoples. What values did Kipling assume his readers shared with him?
3. **INTERPRETING** What was Morel implying so many things "failed to do" that "the power of modern capitalistic exploitation..." might succeed in doing? Was this accomplished?
4. **IDENTIFYING CONNECTIONS** Do you think Kipling is urging the reader to "Take up the White Man's burden" sarcastically, or was he being genuine? How did you arrive at your answer?
5. **UNDERSTANDING CONTEXT** What is Morel comparing imperialism, capitalism, and militarism to when he refers to them as a "trinity"? What is he saying in making this comparison?
6. **DETERMINING CONTEXT** Kipling writes as if he believes imperialism brought betterment to the lives of those colonized. What improvements does he claim, and how do they conflict with the conditions described by Morel?

PHOTO:Library of Congress Prints and Photographs Division [LC-USZ62-130451]; TEXT: Morel, E. D. 1920. The Black Man's Burden. New York: B. W. Huebsch, Inc.

## ESSENTIAL QUESTIONS

- *What are the causes and effects of imperialism?*
- *How do some groups resist control by others?*

# THE STORY BEGINS...

LESSON 3

# British Rule in India

Mohandas Gandhi wrote a great deal about how to win and protect independence for India:

> "Freedom is a priceless thing. But it is a stable possession only when it is acquired by a nation's strenuous effort. What is not by chance or outward circumstance, or given by the generous impulse of a tyrant prince or people is not a reality. A nation will truly enjoy freedom only when in the process of winning or defending its freedom, it has been purified and consolidated through and through, until liberty has become a part of its very soul. Otherwise it would be but a change of the form of government, which might please the fancy of politicians, or satisfy the classes in power, but could never emancipate a people. An Act of Parliament can never create citizens in Hindustan. The strength, spirit, and happiness of a people who have fought and won their liberty cannot be got by Reform Acts. Effort and sacrifice are the necessary conditions of real stable emancipation. Liberty unacquired, merely found, will on the test fail like the Dead-Sea-apple or the magician's plenty."

—Mohandas Gandhi, *Freedom's Battle,* 1922

The Indian independence movement would gain traction throughout the early 1900s.

*A British commander leads a unit of Burmese troops in south Asia.* ▶

| Causes | Effects |
|---|---|
| British manufactured goods | |
| Cotton crops | |
| School system | |

### ANALYZING KEY IDEAS AND DETAILS

**DESCRIBING** Read closely to determine the causes and effects of British influence on India. Record the effects in a graphic organizer like this one.

# THE GREAT REBELLION

**GUIDING QUESTION** *What was the source of conflict between the British and the Indian people?*

Over the course of the eighteenth century, British power in India had increased while the power of the Mogul rulers had declined. The British government gave a trading company, the British East India Company, power to become actively involved in India's political and military affairs. To rule India, the British East India Company had its own soldiers and forts. It also hired Indian soldiers, known as **sepoys**, to protect the company's interests in the region.

### ANALYZING KEY IDEAS AND DETAILS

1. **SUMMARIZING** Write a 2–3 sentence summary of the Great Rebellion and the events that led to it.
2. **DETERMINING CENTRAL IDEAS** What is the central idea of the section "Effects of the Rebellion"? How does the author develop this idea?

## EVENTS LEADING TO REBELLION

In 1857 a growing Indian distrust of the British led to a revolt. The British call the revolt the Sepoy Mutiny. Mutiny means an open rebellion against authorities. Indians, however, call it the First War of Independence. Neutral observers label it the Great Rebellion.

The major immediate cause of the revolt was a rumor that the troops' new rifle cartridges were greased with cow and pig fat. The cow was sacred to Hindus. The pig was taboo to Muslims. To load a rifle at that time, soldiers had to bite off the end of the cartridge. To the sepoys, both Hindus and Muslims, touching these greased cartridges to their lips would mean that they themselves were polluted.

### DETERMINING MEANING

What is the difference between a **rebellion** and a **mutiny**? What context clues helped you to understand this?

*This engraving of the Battle of Kanpur (Cawnpore) shows sepoys on horseback fighting British soldiers.*

**EXPLAINING CAUSES** Which side had the military advantage in this battle? Why?

A group of sepoys at an army post in Meerut, near Delhi, refused to load their rifles with the cartridges. The British charged them with mutiny, publicly humiliated them, and put them in prison. This treatment of their comrades enraged the sepoy troops in Meerut. They went on a rampage, killing 50 European men, women, and children. Soon other Indians joined the revolt, including princes whose land the British had taken.

Within a year, however, Indian troops loyal to the British and fresh British troops had crushed the rebellion. Although Indian troops fought bravely and outnumbered the British by about 230,000 to 45,000, they were not well organized. Rivalries between Hindus and Muslims kept the Indians from working together.

Atrocities were terrible on both sides. At Kanpur (Cawnpore), Indians massacred 200 defenseless women and children in a building known as the House of the Ladies. Recapturing Kanpur, the British took their revenge before executing the Indians.

## EFFECTS OF THE REBELLION

As a result of the uprising, the British Parliament transferred the powers of the East India Company directly to the British government. In 1876 Britain's Queen Victoria took the title Empress of India. The people of India were now her directly governed colonial subjects, and India became the "jewel" in her imperial crown.

Although the rebellion failed, it helped fuel Indian nationalism. The rebellion marked the first significant attempt by the people of South Asia to throw off British Raj (rule). Later, a new generation of Indian leaders would take up the cause of independence.

### ✓ CHECKING FOR UNDERSTANDING

1. **INTERPRETING** What was the source of conflict between the British and the Indian people?
2. **DETERMINING CONTEXT** What do Indians call the "Sepoy Mutiny"? Why might the British and the Indians have different names for this event?
3. **EXPLAINING EFFECTS** What were the effects of the Great Rebellion in India?

# BRITISH COLONIAL RULE

**GUIDING QUESTION** *What were the consequences of British rule in India?*

After the Great Rebellion, the British government began to rule India directly. They appointed a British official known as a **viceroy** (a governor who ruled as a representative of a monarch). A British **civil** service staff assisted the viceroy. This staff of about 3,500 officials ruled almost 300 million people, the largest colonial population in the world. British rule involved benefits that would come at a cost for Indians.

British rule in India had several benefits for colonial subjects. It brought order and stability to a society badly divided into many states with different, and sometimes opposing, political systems. It also led to a fairly honest, efficient government.

**ANALYZING KEY IDEAS AND DETAILS**

1. **CITING TEXT EVIDENCE** What evidence in the text supports the claim that "British rule in India had several benefits for colonial subjects"?
2. **ANALYZING IDEAS** What were the negative consequences of British rule in India?

**DETERMINING MEANING**

What was the role of a **viceroy** in India?

**DETERMINING MEANING**

The word **civil** contains the same Latin root as the words *civilization, civilian,* and *civic*. How does knowing the meanings of these words help a person understand the role of a *civil* service staff?

Through the efforts of the British administrator and historian Lord Thomas Macaulay, a new school system was set up. The new system used the English language, as Macaulay explained:

> "What then shall [the language of education] be? [Some] maintain that it should be the English. The other half strongly recommend the Arabic and Sanskrit. The whole question seems to me to be, which language is the best worth knowing? . . . It is, I believe, no exaggeration to say that all the historical information which has been collected from all the books written in the Sanskrit language is less valuable [than] what may be found in [short textbooks] used at preparatory schools in England."
>
> —Lord Macaulay, from speech to Parliament, February 2, 1835

The goal of the new school system was to train Indian children to serve in the government and army. The new system served only elite, upper-class Indians, however. Ninety percent of the population remained relatively uneducated and illiterate.

The British hired Indians and built roads, canals, universities, and medical centers. A postal service was introduced shortly after it appeared in Great Britain. India's first rail network, beginning in Bombay, opened in 1853. By 1900, 25,000 miles (40,225 km) of railroads crisscrossed India. Health and sanitation conditions were also improved.

The Indian people paid a high price for the peace and stability brought by British rule. Perhaps the greatest cost was economic. British entrepreneurs and a small number of Indians reaped financial benefits from British rule, but it brought hardship to millions of others in both the cities and the countryside. British manufactured goods destroyed local industries. British textiles put thousands of women out of work and severely damaged the Indian textile industry.

In rural areas, the British sent the zamindars to collect taxes. The British believed that using these local officials would make it easier to collect taxes from the peasants. However, the zamindars in India took advantage of their new authority. They increased taxes and forced the less fortunate peasants to become tenants or to lose their land entirely. Peasant unrest grew.

The British also encouraged many Indian farmers to switch from growing food to growing cotton. As a consequence, food supplies could not keep up with the growing population. Between 1800 and 1900, 30 million Indians died of starvation.

Finally, British rule was degrading, even for the newly educated upper classes who benefited the most from it. The best jobs and the best housing were reserved for Britons. Although many British colonial officials sincerely tried to improve the lot of the people in India, British arrogance and racial attitudes cut deeply into the pride of many Indians and led to the rise of an Indian nationalist movement.

## ✓ CHECKING FOR UNDERSTANDING

1. **EXPLAINING EFFECTS** What were the consequences of British rule in India?
2. **IDENTIFYING BIAS** What does Macaulay's bias in favor of English indicate about the consequences of British colonialism in India?

**MAKING CONNECTIONS TO SPORTS**

### COMMONWEALTH GAMES

One legacy of imperialism is evident in the Commonwealth Games. Participation in the games is limited to amateur athletes who come from one of the countries of the British Commonwealth, the free association of states that includes many former parts of the British Empire. A more recent addition to the games is cricket, which the British brought to their colonies. Cricket is especially popular in India.

TEXT: Excerpt from "Lord Macaulay's Minute, 2nd February, 1835" by Thomas Babington Macaulay. London: Williams and Norgate, 1871.

# INDIAN NATIONALISTS

**ANALYZING KEY IDEAS AND DETAILS**

1. **DETERMINING CENTRAL IDEAS** What is the central idea of this section? How does the text present and develop this idea?
2. **ANALYZING EVENTS** What is the connection between Gandhi and Indian nationalism?

**GUIDING QUESTION** *What led to an Indian independence movement?*

The first Indian nationalists were upper-class and English-educated. Many of them were from urban areas, such as Bombay (Mumbai), Madras (Chennai), and Calcutta (Kolkata). Some were trained in British law and were members of the civil service.

At first, many Indian nationalists preferred reform to revolution. However, the slow pace of reform convinced many that relying on British goodwill was futile. In 1885 a small group of Indians met in Bombay to form the Indian National Congress (INC). The INC did not demand immediate independence. Instead, the group called for a share in the governing process.

The INC had difficulties because of religious differences. The INC sought independence for all Indians, regardless of class or religious background. However, many of its leaders were Hindu and reflected Hindu concerns. Later, Muslims called for the creation of a separate group called the Muslim League. Such a league would represent the interests of the millions of Muslims in Indian society.

In 1914 the return of a young Hindu from South Africa brought new life to India's struggle for independence. Mohandas Gandhi was born in 1869 in Gujarat, in western India. He studied in London and became a lawyer. In 1893 Gandhi went to South Africa to work in a law firm serving Indian workers there. He soon learned of the racial exploitation of Indians living in British-controlled South Africa.

On his return to India, Gandhi became active in the independence movement. Using his experience in South Africa, he began a movement based on nonviolent resistance. Its aim was to force the British to improve the lot of the poor and to grant independence to India. Ultimately, Gandhi's movement led to Indian independence. In 1922, he wrote:

**ANALYZING PRIMARY SOURCES**

1. **DETERMINING CENTRAL IDEAS** According to Gandhi, what is the most effective method for India to rebel against foreign masters? What methods does he reject?
2. **DETERMINING POINT OF VIEW** Why is Gandhi opposed to the idea of violent resistance?

> "Violence may rid a nation of its foreign masters but will only enslave it from inside. No nation can really be free which is at the mercy of its army and its military heroes. If a people rely for freedom on its soldiers, the soldiers will rule the country, not the people. Till the recent awakening of the workers of Europe, this was the only freedom which the powers of Europe really enjoyed. True freedom can exist only when those who produce, not those who destroy or know only to live on other's labour, are the masters. . . .
>
> Submission or withdrawal of co-operation is the real and only alternative before India. Submission to injustice puts on the tempting garb of peace and, gradual progress, but there is no surer way to death than submission to wrong."

—Mohandas Gandhi, *Freedom's Battle,* 1922

## ☑ CHECKING FOR UNDERSTANDING

1. **IDENTIFYING CAUSES** What led to an Indian independence movement?
2. **INTERPRETING** How did Gandhi's experience in South Africa inform his decisions in India?
3. **DESCRIBING** Explain what led to the creation of the Muslim League.

TEXT: Gandhi, Mahatma. 1922. Freedom's Battle - Being a Comprehensive Collection of Writings and Speeches on the Present Situation. Second Edition. Project Gutenberg Ebook #10366.

# COLONIAL INDIAN CULTURE

**GUIDING QUESTION** *How did British rule influence Indian culture?*

From the beginning of their rule, the British imposed their own cultural norms on India and they often showed disrespect for India's cultural heritage. The Taj Mahal, for example, was built as a tomb for the beloved wife of an Indian ruler. The British used it as a favorite site for weddings and parties. Many partygoers even brought hammers to chip off pieces as souvenirs.

The tension in India that arose from British domination led to a cultural awakening as well. The cultural revival began in the early nineteenth century with the creation of a British college in Calcutta (Kolkata). A local publishing house was opened. It issued textbooks on a variety of subjects, including the sciences, Sanskrit, and Western literature. The publisher also printed grammars and dictionaries in various Indian languages.

This revival soon spread to other regions of India. It led to a search for a new national identity and literary expression. Indian novelists and poets began writing historical romances and epics. Some wrote in English, but most were uncomfortable doing so. They preferred to use their own regional languages.

Printed in the various regional Indian languages, newspapers were a common medium used to arouse mass support for nationalist causes. These newspapers reached the lower-middle-class populations—tens of thousands of Indians who had never learned a word of English. In his newspaper *Kesari* ("The Lion"), journalist Balwantrao Gangadhar Tilak used innuendo (suggestion) to convey negative feelings about the British without ever writing anything that could have been seen as disloyal by the British government or colonial officials.

Indian religious traditions were also affected by the technological changes happening in the subcontinent. As parts of India were better connected by the creation of a rail system, religious traditions from once-isolated Indian regions spread out into the subcontinent. These traditions left their mark on the larger religious traditions of the subcontinent, while retaining their regional identities.

**ANALYZING KEY IDEAS AND DETAILS**

1. **ANALYZING IDEAS** How did printed texts influence Indian culture?
2. **ANALYZING EVENTS** What is the connection between Rabindranath Tagore and Indian nationalism?

## RABINDRANATH TAGORE

The most famous Indian author was Rabindranath Tagore, winner of the Nobel Prize in Literature in 1913. A great writer and poet, Tagore had many talents. He was also a social reformer, spiritual leader, educator, philosopher, singer, painter, and international spokesperson for the moral concerns of his age. Tagore liked to invite the great thinkers of the time to his expansive country home, or **estate**. There he set up a school that became an international university.

> "The conditions which have prevailed in India from a remote antiquity have guided its history along a particular channel, which does not and cannot coincide with the lines of evolution taken by other countries under different sets of influences. It would be a sad misreading of the lessons of the past to tread too closely in the footsteps of any other nation, however successful in its own career.
>
> I feel strongly that our country has been entrusted with a message which is not a mere echo of the living voices that resound from western shores . . ."

—Rabindranath Tagore from a letter, January 4, 1909

**DETERMINING MEANING**

Read the text of the paragraph that contains the word **estate**. Which words provide context clues you can use to determine the meaning of *estate*?

**ANALYZING PRIMARY SOURCES**

**DRAWING CONCLUSIONS** What attitude would Tagore have had toward the opinion expressed by Macaulay about the use of English to educate Indians?

TEXT: Tagore, Rabindranath. 1909. Edited 1997 by Krishna Dutta and Andrew Robinson. Selected Letters of Rabindranath Tagore. Cambridge University Press.

Tagore's life mission was to promote pride in a national Indian consciousness in the face of British domination. He wrote a widely read novel in which he portrayed the love-hate relationship of India toward its colonial mentor. The novel reflected an Indian people who admired and imitated the British but who agonized over how to establish their own national identity.

Rabindranath Tagore, however, was more than an Indian nationalist. His life's work was one long prayer for human dignity, world peace, and the mutual understanding and union of East and West. As Tagore once said,

> "It is my conviction that my countrymen will truly gain their India by fighting against the education that teaches them that a country is greater than the ideals of humanity."
>
> —Rabindranath Tagore, from *Nationalism*

*Many Indians worked as domestic servants in the homes of British colonialists.*

**IDENTIFYING CONNECTIONS**
Why might Indian domestic servants have become resentful of British rule?

## ✓ CHECKING FOR UNDERSTANDING

1. **EVALUATING** How did British rule influence Indian culture?
2. **UNDERSTANDING CONTEXT** What does the emergence of a cultural awakening in India indicate about the role of nationalism in the process of decolonization?
3. **IDENTIFYING CONNECTIONS** How did newspapers and literature help shape the nationalist movement?

PHOTO:©Underwood & Underwood/Corbis; TEXT:Tagore, Sir Rabindra Nath. "Nationalism in India", 1919. From India's Nation Builders, by D.N. Bannerja. New York: Brentano's.

# LESSON 3 REVIEW

## Time and Place

1. **IDENTIFYING CAUSES** Why did British Parliament transfer power from the British East India Company to Queen Victoria?

## Building History-Social Science Analysis Skills

2. **IDENTIFYING EFFECTS** What were the consequences of the major British modernization projects such as railroads and canals for the Indian people? Cite examples from text.
3. **RELATING EVENTS** What was the source of conflict between the British and the Indian people?
4. **EXPLAINING EFFECTS** What part did Indian artistic and literary expression play in pushing India toward decolonization?

## Writing About History

5. **EXPLANATORY WRITING** Write a short paragraph outlining the general British attitude toward the people of India and the consequences of that attitude. Pay careful attention to your usage of English grammar in your response.

## Collaborating

6. **USING MULTIMEDIA** In a small group, discuss British rule in India. Together, research the early independence movement in colonial India, focusing on the people involved, their grievances with the colonial government, and their early demands. Then, create a short multimedia presentation highlighting your research.

## ESSENTIAL QUESTIONS

- *What are the causes and effects of imperialism?*
- *How do some groups resist control by others?*

# THE STORY BEGINS...

LESSON 4

# Imperialism in Latin America

In order to build the Panama Canal, President Theodore Roosevelt supported a rebellion that allowed Panama to separate from Colombia. He defended this action in the following excerpt from his autobiography:

> "If Brazil, or the Argentine, or Chile, had been in possession of the Isthmus, doubtless the canal would have been built under the governmental control of the nation thus controlling the Isthmus, with the hearty acquiescence of the United States and of all other powers. But in the actual fact the canal would not have been built at all save for the action I took. If men choose to say that it would have been better not to build it, than to build it as the result of such action, their position, although foolish, is compatible with belief in their wrongheaded sincerity. But it is hypocrisy, alike odious and contemptible, for any man to say both that we ought to have built the canal and that we ought not to have acted in the way we did act."

—Theodore Roosevelt, *An Autobiography,* 1913

American interference in the affairs of Latin America, along with control of government by elites, would lead to growing resentment and, in some cases, revolution.

*American troops fighting in the Battle of San Juan Hill ▶*

| Problems | |
|---|---|
| Reforms | |

ANALYZING KEY IDEAS AND DETAILS

**DETERMINING CENTRAL IDEAS** Read closely to determine the problems faced by Mexico after 1870 and the reforms enacted in the constitution of 1917. Summarize these problems and reforms in a graphic organizer like this one.

# THE U.S. IN LATIN AMERICA

**GUIDING QUESTION** *What was the impact of U.S. involvement in Latin America in the early 1900s?*

In the late 1800s, the United States began to intervene in the affairs of its southern neighbors to secure its strategic interests and raw materials for its industries. In 1895 writer and journalist José Martí returned to Cuba after years of exile. Martí helped form the Cuban Revolutionary Party in 1892 and began organizing a rebellion against Spanish rule. He teamed up with a group of revolutionary generals and invaded Cuba in April 1895. Martí, though, was killed in battle by the Spanish the following month.

The brutality with which the Spanish crushed the rebellion shocked Americans and began a series of events that led the United States to declare war against Spain in 1898. As a result of the Spanish-American War, Cuba effectively became a protectorate of the United States. By the treaty that ended the war, Puerto Rico was also annexed to the United States.

In 1903 President Theodore Roosevelt supported a rebellion that allowed Panama to separate from Colombia and establish a new nation. In return, the United States was granted control of a 10-mile strip of land through the country. There the United States built the Panama Canal, which opened in 1914 and was one of the world's greatest engineering feats of its time. The canal connects the Atlantic and Pacific Oceans. On average, it takes a ship 8 to 10 hours to move through the canal passage.

In 1904 President Roosevelt further expanded American involvement in Latin America. At the time, European powers threatened to send warships to Santo Domingo in the Dominican Republic to collect debts owed to them. In a statement

ANALYZING KEY IDEAS AND DETAILS

**SUMMARIZING** Write a 2–3 sentence summary of the last three paragraphs of "The U.S. in Latin America" section.

**MAKING CONNECTIONS TO TECHNOLOGY**

## THE PANAMA CANAL

The Panama Canal is perhaps the greatest work of engineering in history. Decades before it was built, engineers argued over how it could be done. French diplomat Ferdinand de Lesseps proposed building the canal at sea level, eliminating the need for *locks*, which raise and lower ships. But engineer Adolphe Godin de Lépinay disagreed. He proposed to dam two rivers, creating artificial lakes above sea level. The canal would join those lakes together, and locks would connect them to the ocean on either side. When the canal was eventually built, it was Lépinay's proposal that was essentially followed.

*Workers wait along the railroad tracks during the construction of the Panama Canal.*



**INFERRING** Draw a map showing how ships traveled before the opening of the Panama Canal.

that became known as the Roosevelt Corollary to the Monroe Doctrine, Roosevelt claimed that the United States could intervene in any Latin American nation guilty of "chronic misconduct" (such as the inability to repay debts). The United States then took control of debt collection in the Dominican Republic.

American investments in Latin America soon expanded. In the early 1900s, the United States began to pursue "**dollar diplomacy**," extending its influence by investing in Latin American development. Although this policy appeared to be for the benefit of Latin American countries, it was also meant to secure control over the finances and raw materials of Latin America for the United States. The United States soon replaced Europe as the source of loans and investments. Direct U.S. investments reached $3.5 billion, out of a world total of $7.5 billion.

As American investments grew, so too did the resolve to protect those investments. U.S. military forces were sent to Cuba, Mexico, Guatemala, Honduras, Nicaragua, Panama, Colombia, Haiti, and the Dominican Republic to protect American interests. Some expeditions stayed for years. U.S. Marines were in Haiti from 1915 to 1934 and in Nicaragua from 1912 to 1933. Increasing numbers of Latin Americans began to resent this interference from the "big bully" to the north.

### ✓ CHECKING FOR UNDERSTANDING

1. **SUMMARIZING** What was the impact of U.S. involvement in Latin America in the early 1900s?
2. **RELATING EVENTS** How did the U.S. benefit from supporting the rebellion that led to Panama separating from Colombia?
3. **EVALUATING** In what ways were U.S. actions in Latin America during the early 1900s imperialist?

## REVOLUTION IN MEXICO

GUIDING QUESTION *What were the causes and effects of the Mexican Revolution?*

After 1870, large landowners in Latin America began to take a more direct interest in national politics and even in governing. In Argentina and Chile, for example, landholding elites controlled the governments. They adopted constitutions similar to those of the United States and European democracies. The ruling elites, however, limited voting rights.

In some countries, large landowners supported dictators who looked out for the interests of the ruling elite. Porfirio Díaz, who ruled Mexico between 1877 and 1911, created a conservative, centralized government. The army, foreign capitalists, large landowners, and the Catholic Church supported Díaz. All these groups benefited from their alliance with Díaz. However, growing forces for change in Mexico led to a revolution.

During Díaz's dictatorial reign, the wages of workers had declined. Ninety-five percent of the rural population owned no land, **whereas** about 1,000 families owned almost all Mexico. A large percentage of Mexico's land was also owned by foreign investors, most of them Americans. This was seen as unjust, especially by **tenant farmers** called *campesinos*. A moderate landowner, Francisco Madero, forced Díaz from power in 1911. The door to a wider revolution then opened.

**ANALYZING KEY IDEAS AND DETAILS**

1. **CITING TEXT EVIDENCE** What evidence in the text suggests that the majority of the Mexican population was unhappy under the leadership of Porfirio Díaz?
2. **ANALYZING CENTRAL IDEAS** How did Pancho Villa, Emiliano Zapata, and Venustiano Carranza influence revolution in Mexico?

**DETERMINING MEANING**

To better understand the term **tenant farmers**, break down the phrase. A *tenant* is a person who lives on land that is rented from a landowner. A *farmer* is a person who grows crops. Based on this, what is a *tenant farmer*?

## HUERTA'S COUP AND CIVIL WAR

Unpopular with both liberals and conservatives, Madero made a valiant effort to handle the revolutionary forces. He put some of the best officials in his administration, and he sought a balance in dealing with foreign interests. However, before his efforts could bear fruit, his government was overthrown by General Victoriano Huerta in 1913. Backed by the United States and by conservatives who wanted a return to the old order, Huerta's coup put an end to Madero's reforms.

This coup was deeply unpopular and resulted in a revolutionary uprising. Huerta was rapidly removed from power in 1914 by a coalition of revolutionary forces. However, these forces failed to agree on Mexico's future and the country erupted into a civil war. The three sides were led by Pancho Villa, Emiliano Zapata, and Venustiano Carranza.

Villa's center of power was located in Mexico's northern states. Villa generally favored reforms that benefited Mexico's working class, landless peasants. His army dominated the northern countryside and he even led an excursion into New Mexico, which angered the United States. Villa's ideas, such as a Mexico of citizen-soldiers, were radical:

> "We will put the army to work. In all parts of the Republic we will establish military colonies composed of the veterans of the Revolution. The State will give them grants of agricultural lands and establish big industrial enterprises to give them work. Three days a week they will work and work hard, because honest work is more important than fighting, and only honest work makes good citizens. And the other three days they will receive military instruction and go out and teach all the people how to fight. Then, when the Patria is invaded, we will just have to telephone from the palace at Mexico City, and in half a day all the Mexican people will rise from their fields and factories, fully armed, equipped and organized to defend their children and their homes."

—Pancho Villa, from *Insurgent Mexico,* 1914

**ANALYZING PRIMARY SOURCES**

1. **DETERMINING POINT OF VIEW** How might events in Mexico in the late 1800s and early 1900s have affected Villa's point of view on armies?
2. **ANALYZING IDEAS** How does Villa plan to change Mexican culture when he becomes the leader of the country?

*Revolutionary leaders, such as Pancho Villa (seated second from left) and Emiliano Zapata (seated second from right), raised armies from the masses of discontented poor to fight for land reform in Mexico.*

**INTERPRETING** What is the significance of this 1915 photograph of Mexican revolutionaries?

Emiliano Zapata led radical calls for reform and redistribution of land. He had also resisted Madero's government for not going far enough to ease the burdens of the campesinos. Centered in Mexico's southern states, Zapata had for years aroused the masses of campesinos and seized and redistributed the estates of wealthy landholders.

Emiliano Zapata and Pancho Villa were working for similar goals, although their centers of power were in opposite regions of Mexico. The two generals made natural, if somewhat reluctant, allies. From 1914 to 1915, they came together to resist the third general, a man named Venustiano Carranza.

Born into a wealthy family of landowners, Carranza was more politically moderate than Villa or Zapata. Carranza hoped to ease the sufferings of the poor in Mexico while at the same time to maintain the property rights of most landowners. Although his army was smaller than Villa's or Zapata's, Carranza was assisted by brilliant generals. Carranza defeated Villa's army in 1915, and Zapata's forces were steadily reduced and finally defeated in 1919. Carranza's forces were now the dominant army in Mexico. Carranza was victorious and would go on to head a new Mexican government.

Zapata would fight on and was ambushed and killed by forces loyal to Carranza in 1919. Villa would go on to lead a resistance to Carranza, only agreeing to lay down his arms in 1920. He was assassinated in 1923.

## A NEW CONSTITUTION

Following Carranza's victory, a new constitution was enacted in 1917, and Carranza was elected Mexico's president. This new constitution put in place many of the nonradical goals of the revolution. The constitution set up a government led by a president and elected by universal male suffrage. It also created land-reform policies, established limits on foreign investors, and set an agenda to help the workers. This agenda included the rights of workers to form unions, set a minimum wage, and limited working hours.

Between 1910 and 1920, the Mexican Revolution caused great damage to the Mexican economy. However, the revolution helped bring about a more democratic and politically stable Mexico. The Constitution of 1917 remains the governing document of Mexico today.

Ultimately, the Mexican Revolution was a conflict with social and economic roots. Inequality and excessive foreign influence resulted in resentments among Mexico's landless poor that bubbled over into a decades-long chaotic struggle for the soul of the nation. The revolution led to an awakening of nationalism and an outpouring of patriotism throughout Mexico. National pride was evident as intellectuals and artists sought to capture what was unique about Mexico with special emphasis on its past.

### ☑ CHECKING FOR UNDERSTANDING

1. **EXPLAINING CAUSE AND EFFECT** What were the causes and effects of the Mexican Revolution?
2. **UNDERSTANDING CHANGE** What were the circumstances that helped dislodge the Díaz dictatorship in 1911?
3. **ANALYZING CHANGE** How did Díaz, Madero, Villa, and Zapata help incite or prolong the Mexican Revolution?

**BIOGRAPHY**

### EMILIANO ZAPATA
**(1879–1919)**

The son of a farmer, Emiliano Zapata took an early interest in protecting the rights of Mexican landowners. Early in life, Zapata led protests against inequalities. Later, he assembled a guerrilla army of Mexican peasants that moved from city to city, forcibly taking land from wealthy owners and redistributing it to poor peasants.

Zapata's army helped force Mexican dictator Díaz from power and installed Madero as president. However, Madero rejected Zapata's radical land reform proposals and tried to disband his army. In turn, Zapata declared Madero unfit to rule.

After Madero's overthrow, Zapata was eventually defeated by the forces of his rival Venustiano Carranza. In 1919 Zapata was ambushed and killed by soldiers loyal to Carranza.

His dreams for land reforms unfulfilled, Zapata remains an inspiration for revolutionaries in southern Mexico today called "Zapatistas."

**DESCRIBING** How did Zapata's farm upbringing affect his later life as a soldier and politician?

# PROSPERITY AND SOCIAL CHANGE

**UNDERSTANDING CRAFT AND STRUCTURE**

1. **ANALYZING TEXT** How has the author organized the history of prosperity and social change in Latin America? Why is the text organized this way?
2. **DETERMINING MEANING** The text states that "Latin American export economies *boomed*." Why might the author use the word *boomed* instead of a less descriptive word, such as *grew*?

**GUIDING QUESTION** *How did prosperity change Latin America after 1870?*

After 1870, Latin America began an age of prosperity based to a large extent on the export of a few basic items and cash crops. These included wheat and beef from Argentina, coffee from Brazil, coffee and bananas from Central America, and sugar and silver from Peru. These foodstuffs and raw materials were largely exchanged for cheap finished goods—textiles, machines, and luxury items—from Europe and the United States. The abundance and low cost of these European and American goods often placed local Latin American industries at a disadvantage.

After 1900, Latin Americans looked to increase their own industrial capacity. They built factories to produce textiles, foods, and construction materials. Still, the growth of the Latin American economy remained mostly in the export of raw materials. As a result, Latin America remained economically dependent on Western nations and their foreign investment. Investment from the United States, especially, grew after 1900.

**DETERMINING MEANING**

What is the difference between *imports* and *exports*?

Despite its economic growth, Latin America was still an underdeveloped region of the world. Old patterns still largely prevailed in Latin American societies. Rural elites dominated their estates and their workers. Slavery had been abolished by 1888, but former enslaved people and their descendants were at the bottom of society. The indigenous peoples were still largely poverty stricken.

**DETERMINING MEANING**

The word **sector** has the same root as the word *section*. *Section* means "a smaller part of a whole." How might knowing the meaning of *section* help a person determine the meaning of *sector*?

## SHIFTS IN LATIN AMERICAN SOCIETY

One result of the prosperity of increased exports was growth in the middle **sectors** of Latin American society. Lawyers, merchants, shopkeepers, businesspeople, schoolteachers, professors, bureaucrats, and military officers increased in numbers. As in Europe and the United States, these groups were settled mostly in urban areas. São Paulo in Brazil, Mexico City in Mexico, and Lima in Peru began to grow and expand as these regions industrialized.

**CITIZENSHIP**

### PUERTO RICO AND THE UNITED STATES

Puerto Ricans have been U.S. citizens since 1917. But this does not mean the island gets to send electors to elect the president. It does get to send a representative to the U.S. House, but that representative does not get a vote. Puerto Rico could change this; it could decide to become a state. But since 1967, there have been four referenda in which Puerto Ricans rejected statehood. In June 2017, Puerto Rican voters overwhelmingly supported a referendum to start down the path of statehood. However, the U.S. Congress must determine that Puerto Rico is an incorporated territory in order for it to be eligible for statehood.

*A man holds a Puerto Rican flag at a rally.*

ROBERTO SCHMIDT/AFP/Getty Images

1. **EVALUATING** What are the historical reasons Puerto Rico has been in the unusual situation it has since 1898?
2. **ANALYZING CHANGE** What might Puerto Rico gain from statehood? What might it stand to gain from independence?

Regardless of the country in which they lived, middle-class Latin Americans shared some common characteristics. They lived in cities and sought education and decent incomes. They also saw the United States as a model, especially in regard to industrialization. The middle class sought liberal reform, not revolution. After they had the right to vote, they generally sided with the landholding elites.

As Latin American export economies boomed, the working class grew. So too did the labor unions, especially after 1914. Radical unions often advocated the use of the general strike as an instrument for change. By and large, the governing elites were able to stifle the political influence of the working class by limiting their right to vote.

The need for industrial workers also led Latin American countries to seek immigrants from Europe. For example, between 1880 and 1914, 3 million Europeans, primarily Italians and Spaniards, settled in Argentina.

As in Europe and the United States, in Latin America industrialization led to urbanization. Buenos Aires (called "the Paris of South America") had 750,000 inhabitants by 1900 and 2 million by 1914. By that time, 53 percent of Argentina's population lived in cities.

### ☑ CHECKING FOR UNDERSTANDING

1. **ANALYZING CHANGE** How did prosperity change Latin America after 1870?
2. **IDENTIFYING EFFECTS** What was an effect of industrialization in Latin America?
3. **UNDERSTANDING CHANGE** How did an increase in exports change Latin America after 1870?

**ANALYZING PRIMARY SOURCES**

**DETERMINING CAUSE AND EFFECT**

Historians look for patterns to determine causes and effects of important historical phenomena and events, such as industrialization. For example, economic imperialism, which occurs when an independent but less developed country is controlled economically by the businesses and investments of other countries, is often seen as an effect of industrialization in Latin America. Did the process of industrialization have the same effects on European countries as it did on Latin American countries? Use historical analysis skills to answer this question.

## LESSON 4 REVIEW

### Time and Place

1. **RELATING EVENTS** What were some positive and negative consequences of U.S. and European involvement in Latin America?

### Building History-Social Science Analysis Skills

2. **UNDERSTANDING CONTEXT** What role did the Roosevelt Corollary to the Monroe Doctrine play in continuing U.S. intervention in Latin America?
3. **INTERPRETING** What does the application of "dollar diplomacy" suggest about U.S. motives in Latin America in the early twentieth century?
4. **SUMMARIZING** Summarize the government of Porfirio Díaz in Mexico.

### Writing About History

5. **ARGUMENTATIVE WRITING** Write a paragraph that supports or argues against this point of view: The United States was right to do whatever was necessary to build the Panama Canal because it is such an important and strategic waterway. Be sure to use correct punctuation, spelling, and capitalization.

### Collaborating

6. **INTEGRATING INFORMATION** With a small group, imagine you are working on a new constitution for Mexico after the revolution. What provisions do you include in the new constitution? Create a short constitution outlining your plans. Alongside your constitution, include explanations for each provision you have created, detailing why you have included it. Be sure to consider the goals and expectations of all classes of Mexican society as you create your document.

# STUDY GUIDE

## WESTERN DOMINANCE IN SOUTHEAST ASIA
### LESSON 1

**New Imperialism in the late 1800s**

- **Great Britain** Singapore and Burma
- **France** Union of French Indochina Vietnam, Laos, Annam, Cambodia, Tonkin
- **United States** Philippines

## EMPIRE BUILDING IN AFRICA
### LESSON 2

Europeans became interested in Africa's raw materials after the slave trade ended in the late 1800s.

**West Africa**

- Great Britain annexed states on Africa's west coast.
- France added much of West Africa to its empire.
- Germany gained control of Togo, Cameroon, German Southwest Africa, and German East Africa.

**North Africa**

- Great Britain established a protectorate in Egypt in 1914.
- The British seized Sudan in 1898.
- France imposed a protectorate on Tunisia and Morocco.

## THE GREAT REBELLION
### LESSON 3

- Sepoys were Indian soldiers hired to protect the British East India Company's interests.
- The Great Rebellion occurred when a rumor started that rifle cartridges were greased with cow fat (sacred to Hindus) and pig fat (taboo to Muslims).
- The sepoys refused to load their rifles with the cartridges and so the British publicly humiliated and imprisoned them.
- This enraged a group of sepoys who rebelled, killing 50 European men, women, and children.
- The rebellion continued for a year until the British troops and Indian troops loyal to their empire were able to crush it.

## IMPERIALISM IN LATIN AMERICA
### LESSON 4

- **1898** After the Spanish-American War, Cuba and Puerto Rico were controlled by the United States.
- **early 1900s** The United States began investing in Latin America through "dollar diplomacy" and the military was sent to protect U.S. investment in Latin America.
- **1903** The United States supported Panama's rebellion against Colombia and got control of a strip of land where the Panama Canal was built.
- **1904** President Roosevelt declared that the United States could take over debt collection in Latin American nations.

# CHAPTER 6 Assessment

**Directions: On a separate sheet of paper, answer the questions below. Make sure you read carefully and answer all parts of the questions.**

## Short Answer

1. **EXPLAINING EFFECTS** What new class did colonial rule create? How did this eventually lead to the end of colonialism?

2. **EXPLAINING CAUSE AND EFFECT** For what reason did colonial powers mandate export of raw materials in colonies? What labor structure did this establish?

3. **IDENTIFYING CONNECTIONS** Compare and contrast the system of indirect colonial rule and direct colonial rule. What were the pros and cons for the people being ruled in each system?

4. **SUMMARIZING** What economic motivations led Europeans to seize control in West Africa? Describe which European nations gained control in West Africa.

5. **IDENTIFYING CAUSES** What was the social motivation that influenced European missionaries as they traveled to the rain forests of Central Africa?

6. **EXPLAINING EFFECTS** Who were the Boers? How did they influence the European presence in South Africa?

7. **UNDERSTANDING CONTEXT** Why did the British not set up universal public education in India?

8. **IDENTIFYING CAUSES** What was the spark for India's cultural revival? What are some examples of it?

9. **RELATING EVENTS** Within resistance movements in India, what area of focus came first, and what shifted in their focus and purpose beginning in the 1930s?

10. **DRAWING CONCLUSIONS** What can you deduce from the three different names for the rebellion of 1857 in India and the perspectives of the groups that use them?

11. **SUMMARIZING** What provisions did the Mexican Constitution of 1917 include?

12. **IDENTIFYING CONNECTIONS** What caused the increase in the number of Latin Americans in the middle class in the late nineteenth century?

13. **EXPLAINING CAUSE AND EFFECT** What were the major causes and the major effects of the revolution in Mexico?

## History and Social-Science Analysis

14. **GATHERING EVIDENCE** Work with a partner to create a time line showing at least three causes and three effects of imperialism, as well as three examples of resistance to imperialism (successful or unsuccessful) between 1800 and 1914. Include visuals such as photos, sketches, and maps. You may also include primary sources. Be prepared to explain any connections you find.

## Analyzing Visuals

Use the image to answer the following questions.

15. **DETERMINING CONTEXT** What evidence of Western influence can you identify in this photograph?

16. **CONSTRUCTING HYPOTHESES** Were there benefits to European imperialism in Cambodia? Use the photograph to make your argument.

## Research and Presentation

17. **USING MAPS** Create a map that shows the Suez Canal and the neighboring African and Mediterranean countries, key cities, and bodies of water. Include a key that reflects the accurate length of the canal.



**Need Extra Help?**

| If You've Missed Question | 1 | 2 | 3 | 4 | 5 | 6 | 7 | 8 | 9 | 10 | 11 | 12 | 13 | 14 | 15 | 16 | 17 |
|---|---|---|---|---|---|---|---|---|---|---|---|---|---|---|---|---|---|
| Review Lesson | 1 | 1 | 1 | 2 | 2 | 2 | 3 | 3 | 3 | 3 | 4 | 4 | 4 | 1 | 1 | 1 | 2 |

# CHAPTER 6 Assessment, continued

18 **EVALUATING** Choose one of the colonial regimes described in this chapter, such as French Indochina or British India, and research how today's independent nations of Vietnam and India, for example, have cultural traditions that are rooted in their colonial histories. Or, conversely, research how the countries European nations colonized impacted cultural practices at home. Areas of research could include food, art, music, games and sports, or other aspects of culture. Communicate your findings through writing and images, using computer software to publish your work.

## Reading and Analyzing Primary Sources

Use the document to answer the following questions.

In 1893, Captain F. D. Lugard presented a justification for Great Britain's indirect rule of East Africa.

> "There are some who say we have no right in Africa at all, that 'it belongs to the natives.' I hold that our right is the necessity that is upon us to provide for our ever-growing population—either by opening new fields for emigration, or by providing work. . . In Africa, moreover, there is among the people a natural inclination to submit to a higher authority. That intense detestation of control which animates our Teutonic races does not exist among the tribes of Africa, and if there is any authority that we replace, it is the authority of the Slavers and Arabs, or the intolerable tyranny of the 'dominant tribe'."
>
> —quoted in *Civilization Past & Present*

19 **SUMMARIZING** Which of the following is not a reason Captain Lugard gives to justify Great Britain's takeover of African nations?

**A.** Britain needs to provide for its growing population.
**B.** Africans have a natural inclination to submit to a higher authority.
**C.** Africa is full of natural resources that will be useful to the British people.
**D.** British rule is better than that of slavers, Arabs, or the dominant local tribe.

20 **EVALUATING** Why might Captain Lugard's arguments be less convincing today?

**A.** The idea that Britain needs to provide for its people would be seen as outdated.
**B.** The idea that Africans want to submit to a higher authority would be seen as unfounded.
**C.** The idea that Africa is full of natural resources would be seen as inaccurate.
**D.** The idea that African governments can be improved would be seen as lacking evidence.

21 **SUMMARIZING** What counterargument does Captain Lugard provide against his argument that Great Britain is justified in taking over African nations?

**A.** He says people claim Africa belongs to Africans.
**B.** He says people claim Britain has no need for African land.
**C.** He says people claim Africans would not want British rule.
**D.** He says people claim the current African governments are better than British rule.

## Writing About History

22 **SUMMARIZING** Craft a one-page essay comparing and contrasting the indigenous peoples' resistance to colonization in Southeast Asia, Africa, India, and Latin America. Discuss who resisted, the tactics they used, and their successes or failures.

## Speaking and Listening About History

23 **EVALUATING** Meet in a small group to discuss the characteristics of imperialism. Discuss two types of imperial rule. What was the impact of European imperialism in the late nineteenth century? Have one member of your group serve as a moderator of the group discussion.

24 **DETERMINING CONTEXT** Meet in a small group to debate the roles of military, transportation, communication, and medical technology in advancing imperialism in the nineteenth century. Make a claim as to which advancement had the greatest impact, using reasons and evidence to support your argument. Have one member of your group serve as a moderator of the group discussion.

**Need Extra Help?**

| If You've Missed Question | 18 | 19 | 20 | 21 | 22 | 23 | 24 |
|---|---|---|---|---|---|---|---|
| Review Lesson | 1–4 | 2 | 2 | 2 | 1 | 1 | 1 |

TEXT: Captain F. D. Lugard, D.S.O. 1893. The Rise of Our East African Empire, Volume I. William Blackwood and Sons.

Dowager Empress Cixi of the Qing Dynasty, seen here with representatives of the American diplomatic corps in the late 1890s. By this time, China had become powerless to stop the influence of Western powers on its internal affairs.

1800 — 1914

# Challenge and Transition in East Asia

## CHAPTER 7



**GO DIGITAL**
*It's All online!*

## ASKING ESSENTIAL QUESTIONS

***How can new ideas accelerate economic and political change?***
***How do cultures influence each other?***

**What Will You Learn?** You will learn how governments of nineteenth-century China and Japan reacted to the growing influence of Western empires in East Asia.

**Why Does this Matter?** Many goods people use today have been created in the factories of China. Before the nineteenth century, however, East Asian states such as China and Japan restricted trade with the West. During the nineteenth century, Western countries forced these countries to open their markets to merchants from the West. The Japanese government ultimately grew more powerful during this period. In contrast, the Chinese government became increasingly unstable, leading to the collapse of the Qing dynasty.

**How Will You Know That You Learned It?** You will be able to define major political events, figures, and cultural changes in East Asia in the nineteenth and early twentieth centuries. You will be able to explain how these developments shaped the transformation of China and Japan.

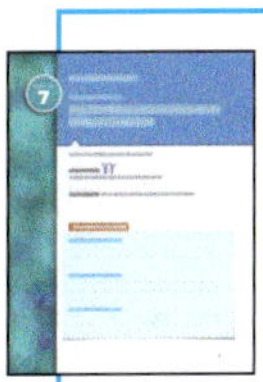

**Using Your Inquiry Journal** As you read this chapter and examine the primary sources, use your Inquiry Journal to help you make notes and expand your list of questions. As you gather information, think about how you will answer the Essential Questions above.

# PLACE & TIME East Asia 1800–1914

The centuries-old Qing dynasty, China's last, finally fell as a result of many factors, including foreign pressures, social unrest, and the resistance of the autocratic government to the introduction of reforms. By contrast, Japan's empire expanded as its leaders embraced industrial development and commerce, undertook educational and governmental reform, and used Western ideas, institutions, and technology to create a new national order. Important victories over China and Russia secured Japanese military leadership in East Asia.

## STEP INTO THE PLACE

Read the quotes and look at the information presented on the map.

1. **UNDERSTANDING CONTEXT** How might attitudes toward change in China and Japan have affected the two countries' histories during this period?
2. **EXPLORING PLACE** What does the map reveal about the factors that led to the fall of the Qing Dynasty?

## STEP INTO THE TIME

**UNDERSTANDING CHANGE**

Using the time line, compare the number of rebellions and revolutions in the East to the rest of the world. Were revolutions and rebellions common elsewhere during this period?

"Those who insist that there is no need for reform still say, 'Let us follow the ancients, follow the ancients.' They coldly sit and watch everything being laid to waste by following tradition, and there is no concern in their hearts. . . . Now there is a big mansion which has lasted a thousand years. The tiles and bricks are decayed and the beams and rafters are broken up, its fall is foredoomed. Yet the people in the house are still happily playing or soundly sleeping. Even some who have noted the danger know only how to weep bitterly, folding their arms and waiting for death without thinking of any remedy. . . . A nation is also like this."

—Liang Qichao, comments made in 1896 after China's defeat by Japan, quoted in *East Asia: A New History*

"I am willing to admit my pride in Japan's accomplishments [in rapid modernization]. The facts are these: It was not until the sixth year of Kaei (1853) that a steamship was seen for the first time. . . . by 1860, the science was sufficiently understood to enable us to sail a ship across the Pacific. . . . I think we can without undue pride boast before the world of this courage and skill. . . . I feel convinced that there is no other nation which has the ability or the courage to navigate a steamship across the Pacific after a period of five years of experience in navigation and engineering."

—Yukichi Fukuzawa, from his autobiography, 1898

**EAST ASIA**

- **1800** China prohibits trade in opium
- **1800** Qing dynasty at the height of its power
- **1804** Russian ambassador arrives in Nagasaki
- **1839** Opium War begins in China
- **185** Tai Ping Rebelli begins in Chi

**1800 — 1820 — 1840**

**WORLD EVENTS**

- **1804** Napoleon Bonaparte is crowned Emperor
- **1821** José de San Martín advances on Lima, Peru
- **1823** Monroe Doctrine is announced
- **1848** Nationalist and liberal revolutions erupt in Europe

**1853** U.S. asks Japan to open foreign relations

**1856** Second Opium War begins

**1860**

**1865** American Civil War ends

**1868** Japanese emperor Mutsuhito begins Meiji rule

**1879** Thomas Edison develops the electric lightbulb

**1880**

**1894** José Martí leads revolt against Spanish rule in Cuba

**1899** U.S. establishes Open Door Policy with China

**1900**

**1902** Afrikaners are defeated in the Boer War

**1905** Russia grants Liaodong Peninsula to Japan

**1910** Japan annexes Korea

**1911** Followers of Sun Yat-sen launch Chinese rebellion

**1914**

**1914** World War I begins

## ESSENTIAL QUESTIONS

- *How can new ideas accelerate economic and political change?*
- *How do cultures influence each other?*

LESSON 1

# The Decline of the Qing Dynasty

## THE STORY BEGINS...

In the nineteenth century, the European empires gradually spread their influence into China, weakening the ruling Qing dynasty. Once a powerful empire that refused to see any kingdom as its equal, the Qing emperors were now routinely humiliated by Europeans who could threaten with technologically advanced militaries. The British led the way in perpetrating these humiliations, with the goal of establishing a foothold in China and conducting trade. This was finally achieved after the First Opium War resulted in the Treaty of Nanjing:

> "It being obviously necessary and desirable that British subjects should have some port . . . His Majesty the Emperor of China cedes to Her Majesty the Queen of Great Britain, &c., the island of Hongkong, to be possessed in perpetuity by her Britannic Majesty, her heirs and successors, and to be governed by such laws and regulations as Her Majesty the Queen of Great Britain, &c., shall see fit to direct."
>
> —Article III of The Treaty of Nanjing, 1842

In addition to providing the British the island of Hong Kong, the treaty devastatingly forced the emperor of China to recognize "Her Majesty the Queen of Great Britain" as an equal, if not a superior monarch. These humiliations would not soon be forgotten.

*Resentful of the growing influence of Westerners in China, Chinese rebels called the Boxers, or the Society of Harmonious Fists, began an uprising and carried out attacks against Westerners. Here a group of Boxers are seen attacking a Chinese city.* ▶

PHOTO:Heritage Images/Hulton Fine Art Collection/Getty Images; TEXT:The Office of the Chinese Repository. 1844. The Treaty of Nanking, Signed August 29th, 1842. And the Supplementary Treaty, Signed October 8th, 1843. In the Chinese and English Languages. Macao: The Office of the Chinese Repository.

| Major Crises in China, 1800-1911 | | |
|---|---|---|
| Crises | Key Figures | Outcome |
| The First Opium War | | |
| The Tai Ping Rebellion | | |
| The One Hundred Days of Reform | | |
| The Boxer Rebellion | | |

**ANALYZING KEY IDEAS AND DETAILS**

**SUMMARIZING** Read closely to identify key figures and outcomes of major conflicts in China during this period. Record the key figures, and summarize the outcomes in a graphic organizer like this one.

# CAUSES OF DECLINE

**GUIDING QUESTION** *What factors influenced the decline of the Qing Empire?*

In the year 1800, after a long period of peace and prosperity, the Qing dynasty of the Manchus was at the height of its prestige and power. A little more than a century later, however, humiliated and harassed by the Western powers, the Qing dynasty collapsed.

One important reason for the abrupt decline and fall of the Qing dynasty was the intense external pressure that the Western imperial powers had applied to Chinese society. However, internal problems also played a major role in the dynasty's fall.

After an extended period of growth, the Qing dynasty began to suffer from corruption, peasant unrest, and incompetence. These weaknesses were made worse by rapid growth in the country's population. By 1900, there were 400 million people in China. Population growth created a serious food shortage. In the 1850s, one observer wrote, "Not a year passes in which a terrific number of persons do not perish of famine in some part or other of China."

The ships, guns, and ideas of foreigners **highlighted** the growing weakness of the Qing dynasty and probably hastened its end. By 1800, Europeans had been in contact with China for more than 200 years. Wanting to limit contact with outsiders, the Qing dynasty had restricted European merchants to a small trading outlet at Guangzhou (GWAHNG • JOH), or Canton. The merchants could deal with only a few Chinese firms. The British did not like this arrangement.

Britain had a trade deficit, or an unfavorable trade balance, with China. That is, it imported more goods from China than it exported to China. Qing dynasty regulations also meant that Britain had to pay China with silver for the difference between its imports—tea, silk, and porcelain—from China and its exports—Indian cotton—to China. At first, the British tried to negotiate with the Chinese to improve the trade imbalance. When negotiations failed, the British turned to trading opium.

## THE OPIUM WAR

Opium was grown in northern India under the sponsorship of the British East India Company and then shipped directly to Chinese markets. Demand for opium—a highly addictive drug—in South China jumped dramatically. Soon, silver was flowing out of China and into the pockets of the officials of the British East India Company.

**UNDERSTANDING CRAFT AND STRUCTURE**

1. **ANALYZING TEXT PRESENTATION** How does the text present information about the decline of the Qing dynasty? How does this argument further the historical argument presented?
2. **DETERMINING MEANING** The text states, "ideas of foreigners highlighted the growing weakness of the Qing dynasty." What does the word *highlighted* mean in this context?

**INTEGRATING INFORMATION** Use the information in the table to create a bar graph of the amount of opium imported into China.

| Opium Imported into China* | |
|---|---|
| Year | Number of Chests |
| 1729 | 200 |
| 1767 | 1,000 |
| 1830 | 10,000 |
| 1838 | 40,000 |

*(1 chest = approximately 135 pounds)

Huc, M. 1855. A Journey Through the Chinese Empire, Volume II. Harper & Brothers, Publishers.

MAKING CONNECTIONS TO TODAY

## HONG KONG

In 1898 Great Britain signed a 99-year lease on the island of Hong Kong. As a British colony, Hong Kong was influenced by the representative traditions of British government. It also gained an appreciation for capitalism at the same time China was becoming increasingly Communist. In the 1970s, for example, Hong Kong became a regional economic powerhouse based on high-tech industries. Then, in 1997 the British returned Hong Kong to the Chinese government. Hong Kong is today a part of modern China, an authoritarian state. However, present-day Hong Kong maintains much greater autonomy or independence than other Chinese cities. For example, Hong Kong has a capitalist economy, unlike the rest of China. Likewise, Hong Kong has a democratically elected leader, called the Chief Executive.

1. **DETERMINING CENTRAL IDEAS** In what way does the history of British rule in Hong Kong continue to influence Hong Kong today?
2. **DETERMINING MEANING** What context clues in the paragraph help you determine the meaning of "autonomy"?

**DETERMINING MEANING** Analyze the root words for **extraterritoriality**. *Extra* can be defined as "outside or beyond." *Territory* refers to "a geographic area under one government." How might knowing the definitions of *extra* and *territory* help when defining *extraterritoriality*?

The Chinese reacted strongly. They appealed to the British government on moral grounds to stop the traffic in opium. Lin Zexu, a Chinese government official, wrote to Queen Victoria:

> "Suppose there were people from another country who carried opium for sale to England and seduced your people into buying and smoking it; certainly your honorable ruler would deeply hate it and be bitterly aroused."
>
> —quoted in *The British Imperial Century,* 1815–1914

The British refused to halt their activity, however. As a result, the Chinese blockaded the foreign area in Guangzhou to force traders to surrender their opium. The British responded with force, starting the Opium War (1839–1842).

The Chinese were no match for the British. British warships destroyed Chinese coastal and river forts. When a British fleet sailed almost unopposed up the Chang Jiang (Yangtze River) to Nanjing, the Qing dynasty made peace.

In the Treaty of Nanjing in 1842, the Chinese agreed to open five coastal ports to British trade, to limit taxes on imported British goods, and pay for the costs of the war. China also agreed to give the British ownership of the island of Hong Kong. Nothing was said in the treaty about the opium trade. Moreover, in the five ports, Europeans lived in their own sections and were subject not to Chinese laws but to their own laws—a practice known as **extraterritoriality**.

The Opium War marked the beginning of the establishment of Western influence in China. For the time being, the Chinese dealt with the problem by pitting foreign countries against one another. Concessions granted to the British were offered to other Western nations, including the United States. Soon, thriving foreign areas were operating in the five treaty ports along the southern Chinese coast.

*This illustration by E. Duncan shows the British steamship* Nemesis *destroying Chinese war junks in Anson's Bay, 1841.*

PHOTO: World History Archive/Alamy; TEXT: Teng, Ssu-yu and Fairbank, John King. 1954. China's Response to the West: A Document Survey, 1839–1923. President and Fellows of Harvard College: Harvard University Press.

## THE TAI PING REBELLION

In the meantime, the failure of the Chinese government to deal with pressing internal economic problems led to a peasant revolt, known as the Tai Ping (TIE PING) Rebellion (1850–1864). It was led by Hong Xiuquan, a Christian convert who viewed himself as a younger brother of Jesus.

Hong was convinced that God had given him the mission of destroying the Qing dynasty. Joined by great crowds of peasants, Hong captured the town of Yongan and proclaimed a new dynasty, the Heavenly Kingdom of Great Peace (*Tai Ping Tianguo* in Chinese—hence the name of the rebellion.)

In March 1853, the rebels seized Nanjing, the second largest city of the empire, and massacred 25,000 men, women, and children. The revolt continued for 10 more years but gradually began to fall apart. Europeans came to the aid of the Qing dynasty when they realized the destructive nature of the Tai Ping forces. One British observer noted there was "no hope of any good ever coming of the rebel movement. They do nothing but burn, murder, and destroy."

In 1864 Chinese forces with European aid recaptured Nanjing and destroyed the rebels. The Tai Ping Rebellion was one of the most devastating civil wars in history. As many as 20 million people died during the 14-year struggle.

China's struggle with the West prevented the Qing dynasty from dealing effectively with internal unrest. Beginning in 1856, the British and the French applied force to gain greater trade privileges. As a result of the Treaty of Tianjin in 1858, the Chinese agreed to legalize the opium trade and to open new ports to foreign trade. They also surrendered the Kowloon Peninsula to Great Britain.

### GEOGRAPHIC REASONING

By 1900, parts of China were divided into separate spheres of influence.

1. **SPATIAL THINKING** After Russia, which country had the largest sphere of influence in China?
2. **GLOBAL INTERCONNECTIONS** Why were countries able to maintain ports in other countries' spheres of influence?

### SPHERES OF INFLUENCE IN CHINA 1900

## EFFORTS AT REFORM

By the late 1870s, the Qing dynasty was in decline. Unable to restore order themselves, government troops had relied on forces recruited by regional warlords to help fight the Tai Ping Rebellion. To finance their armies, the warlords had collected taxes from local people. After the revolt, many of these warlords kept their armies.

In its weakened state, the Qing court finally began to listen to the appeals of reform-minded officials. The reformers called for a new policy they called "**self-strengthening**." That is, China should adopt Western technology but keep its Confucian values and institutions.

**DETERMINING MEANING**

To define **self-strengthening**, examine its parts. *Self* refers to a person's, or in this case a nation's, "true character." To *strengthen* means "to increase in power or effectiveness." How might knowing the definitions of *self* and *strengthen* help when defining *self-strengthening*?

Some reformers wanted to change China's traditional political institutions by introducing democracy. However, such ideas were too radical for most reformers. During the last quarter of the nineteenth century, the Chinese government tried to modernize China's military forces and to build up industry without touching the basic elements of Chinese civilization. Railroads, weapons factories, and shipyards were built. However, the Chinese value system remained unchanged.

### ✓ CHECKING FOR UNDERSTANDING

1. **IDENTIFYING CAUSES** What factors influenced the decline of the Qing Empire?
2. **EXPLAINING CAUSE AND EFFECT** How did the Opium War contribute to the long-term decline of Chinese power?
3. **INTERPRETING** What concerns did the Qing dynasty have about contact with foreign nations?

**INTEGRATING KNOWLEDGE AND IDEAS**

1. **ANALYZING INFORMATION** How does the information in the biographical feature about Empress Ci Xi support and enhance the argument offered in the text that China was suffering from an "internal crisis"?
2. **ASSESSING** How does the information in the "Mounting Pressures" and the "Internal Crisis" sections work together to reinforce the argument proposed at the outset of this section that China was witnessing an "Advance of Imperialism"?

# THE ADVANCE OF IMPERIALISM

**GUIDING QUESTION** *Why were spheres of influence established in China?*

In the end, however, the changes did not help the Qing stay in power. The European advance into China continued during the last two decades of the nineteenth century. Internal conditions also continued to deteriorate.

## MOUNTING PRESSURES

In the north and northeast, Russia took advantage of the Qing dynasty's weakness to force China to give up territories north of the Amur River in Siberia. In Tibet, a struggle between Russia and Great Britain kept both powers from seizing the territory outright. This allowed Tibet to become free from Chinese influence.

Even more ominous changes were taking place in the Chinese heartland. European states began to create **spheres of influence**, areas in which the imperial powers had **exclusive** trading rights. After the Tai Ping Rebellion, warlords in the provinces began to negotiate directly with foreign nations. In return for money, the warlords granted these nations exclusive trading rights or railroad-building and mining privileges. In this way, Britain, France, Germany, Russia, and Japan all established spheres of influence in China.

**DETERMINING MEANING**

Read the paragraph that contains the phrase **spheres of influence**. Which words in the paragraph give context clues about the meaning of *spheres of influence*?

In 1894, another blow furthered the disintegration of the Qing dynasty. The Chinese went to war with Japan over Japanese inroads into Korea, a land that the Chinese had controlled for a long time. The Chinese were soundly defeated. Japan demanded and received the island of Taiwan and the Liaodong (LYOW • DOONG) Peninsula. Fearing Japan's growing power, however, the European powers forced Japan to give the Liaodong Peninsula back to China.

New pressures for Chinese territory soon arose. In 1897, Chinese rioters murdered two German missionaries. Germany used this incident as a pretext to demand territories in the Shandong (SHON • DOONG) Peninsula. When the Chinese government approved the demand, other European nations made new claims on Chinese territory.

## INTERNAL CRISIS

This latest scramble for territory took place at a time of internal crisis in China. In June 1898, the young emperor Guang Xu (GWANG SHYOO) launched a massive reform program based on changes in Japan. During the following weeks, known as the One Hundred Days of Reform, the emperor issued edicts calling for major political, administrative, and education reforms. With these reforms, Guang Xu intended to modernize government bureaucracy by following Western models; to adopt a new education system that would replace the traditional civil service examinations; and to adopt Western-style schools, banks, and a free press. Guang Xu also intended to train the military to use modern weapons and Western fighting techniques.

Many conservatives at court, however, opposed these reforms. They saw little advantage in copying the West. As one said, "An examination of the causes of success and failure in government reveals that . . . the adoption of foreignism leads to disorder." According to this conservative, traditional Chinese rules needed to be reformed and not rejected in favor of Western changes.

Most important, Empress Dowager Ci Xi (TSUH • SEE), the emperor's aunt, opposed the new reform program. Ci Xi became a dominant force at court and opposed the emperor's reforms. With the aid of the imperial army, she eventually imprisoned the emperor. Other supporters of the reforms were imprisoned, exiled, or prosecuted. These actions ended Guang Xu's reforms. Although Guang Xu's efforts aroused popular sympathy, they had limited support within Chinese society overall.

### ✓ CHECKING FOR UNDERSTANDING

1. **INTERPRETING** Why were spheres of influence established in China?

2. **EXPLAINING CAUSE AND EFFECT** What role did foreign countries play in causing internal crises in China? How did spheres of influence change the Qing's authority within their own borders?

3. **UNDERSTANDING CONTEXT** Why might conservatives in the Qing Dynasty oppose adopting Western reforms such as Western approaches to education, banking, and the military?

BIOGRAPHY

### CI XI (1835–1908)

Though never the official ruler of China, Ci Xi was the power behind the throne for 47 years. Ci Xi was appointed regent when her son, the emperor's only heir, became emperor at age six. After her son died, she ruled for her three-year-old nephew, Guang Xu. Ci Xi officially retired when Guang Xu came of age. Later, however, when he tried to institute reforms, Ci Xi had him imprisoned and resumed the regency. In 1899 she supported the Boxer Rebellion, which ultimately failed, and fled Beijing after China's defeat. She did not return to Beijing until 1902.

**DRAWING CONCLUSIONS** How did Ci Xi acquire and maintain power in a political system dominated by men?

PHOTO:Hu Weibiao/Panorama/The Image Works; TEXT:De Barry, Wm. Theodore; Chan, Wing-tsit; and Tan, Chester. 1960. Sources of Chinese Tradition, Volume II. Columbia University Press.

# RESPONSES TO IMPERIALISM

**GUIDING QUESTION** *What were the responses to imperialism in China?*

As foreign pressure on the Qing dynasty grew stronger, both Great Britain and the United States feared that other nations would overrun the country should the Chinese government collapse.

**ANALYZING KEY IDEAS AND DETAILS**

1. **DETERMINING CENTRAL IDEAS** What is the central idea of this section? How is this idea presented and developed?
2. **SUMMARIZING** In your own words, write a brief summary of this section.

## OPENING THE DOOR TO CHINA

In 1899, U.S. Secretary of State John Hay wrote a note to Britain, Russia, Germany, France, Italy, and Japan. Hay presented a proposal that ensured equal access to the Chinese market for all nations and preserved the unity of the Chinese empire. When none of the other imperialist governments expressed opposition to the idea, Hay proclaimed that all major states with economic interests in China had agreed that the country should have an Open Door policy.

> “Earnestly desirous to remove any cause of irritation and to insure at the same time to the commerce of all nations in China the undoubted benefits which should accrue from a formal recognition by the various powers claiming ‘spheres of interest’ that they shall enjoy perfect equality of treatment for their commerce and navigation within such ‘spheres,’ the Government of the United States would be pleased to see His German Majesty’s Government give formal Assurances, and lend its cooperation in securing like assurances from the other interested powers, that each, within its respective sphere of whatever influence.
>
> First. Will in no way interfere with any treaty port or any vested interest within any so-called ‘sphere of interest’ or leased territory it may have in China.”

–U.S. Secretary of State John Hay, *“First Open Door Note,”* 1899

**ANALYZING PRIMARY SOURCES**

**DETERMINING CENTRAL IDEAS** This note was sent to the other great powers with economic interests in China. What does this suggest about Hay’s central idea and intentions in this excerpt?

In part, the **Open Door policy** reflected American concern for the survival of China. However, it also reflected the interests of some U.S. trading companies. These companies wanted to operate in open markets and disliked the existing division of China into separate spheres of influence dominated by individual countries.

The Open Door policy did not end the system of spheres of influence. However, it did reduce restrictions on foreign imports imposed by the dominating power within each sphere. The Open Door policy also helped reduce imperialist hysteria over access to the China market. The policy lessened fears in Britain, France, Germany, and Russia that other powers would take advantage of China’s weakness and attempt to dominate the China market for themselves.

*This photograph, from around 1901, shows Chinese men who took part in the Boxer Rebellion. They were captured and imprisoned by the American forces at Tientsin, China.*

**CONSTRUCTING HYPOTHESES** Why do you think the foreign response to the Boxer Rebellion was “immediate and overwhelming”?

## THE BOXER REBELLION

The Open Door policy came too late to stop an uprising known as the Boxer Rebellion. "Boxer" was the popular name given to members of a secret organization called the Society of Harmonious Fists. Members of this group practiced a system of exercise—a form of shadowboxing, or boxing with an imaginary opponent—that they thought would protect them from bullets.

PHOTO:Library of Congress Prints & Photographs Division [LC-USZ62-68811]; TEXT:Moore, Gregory. 2015. Defining and Defending the Open Door Policy - Theodore Roosevelt and China, 1901-1909. Lanham, Maryland: Lexington Books.

The Boxers were upset by economic distress and the foreign takeover of Chinese lands. Viewing foreign governments and their people as responsible for the problems in Chinese society, their ultimate goal was to push all foreigners out of China. Their slogan was "Support the Qing government and destroy the foreigner." They especially disliked Christian missionaries and Chinese converts to Christianity who seemed to threaten Chinese traditions. At the beginning of 1900, Boxer bands roamed the countryside and slaughtered foreign missionaries and Chinese Christians. Foreign business people and the German envoy to Beijing were also victims.

Response to the killings from foreign governments was immediate and overwhelming. An allied army consisting of 20,000 British, French, German, Russian, American, and Japanese troops attacked Beijing in August 1900. The army restored order and demanded more concessions from the Chinese government. The Chinese government was forced to pay a heavy **indemnity** to the powers that had crushed the uprising. The imperial government was now weaker than ever.

### ✓ CHECKING FOR UNDERSTANDING

1. **ANALYZING CHANGE** What were the responses to imperialism in China?
2. **DRAWING CONCLUSIONS** Did the Boxer Rebellion lead to any reduction in the foreign presence in China? Explain your answer.
3. **RELATING EVENTS** What did John Hay and the U.S. government hope the Open Door Policy would accomplish?

CITIZENSHIP

### FREE-TRADE AGREEMENTS

Modern-day international trade agreements such as the Association of Southeast Asian Nations (ASEAN) and the proposed Trans Pacific Partnership (TPP) establish specific trading rules among the member states. Nonmembers follow different rules and pay different tariffs. These trade deals are popular for some because they increase the flow of trade among member nations. Critics argue that these deals drive down wages and flood home markets with cheaper goods from other countries. Some have argued for doing away with these trade agreements, while others hope to find a more balanced approach.

**EVALUATING** In what way are criticisms of modern free-trade agreements similar to criticisms of trade relations with foreign powers expressed by some in nineteenth-century Chinese society?

## LESSON 1 REVIEW

### Time and Place

1. **ANALYZING CHANGE** What changes took place in China during this period that led to the decline of the Qing dynasty?

### Building History-Social Science Skills

2. **UNDERSTANDING CHANGE** How did losing the Opium War change how China interacted with other nations?
3. **IDENTIFYING CAUSES** What was the policy of "self-strengthening"? Did it succeed? Why or why not?
4. **IDENTIFYING CONNECTIONS** What were some issues that emerged from the establishment of spheres of influence? How did the Open Door Policy intend to fix these problems?

### Writing About History

5. **INFORMATIVE WRITING** Write an informative essay explaining how the events of the nineteenth century changed China and how these problems may relate to contemporary political issues in the world today. You must cite specific people, places, and events in your response.

### Collaborating

6. **COLLABORATING** In a small group, discuss the consequences behind industrializing or not industrializing for a state such as China. Discuss the following: What are the costs of industrializing? What are the benefits? How do these costs and benefits for China differ from those faced by European states?

# Ode for Youth

by An Unknown Member of the Tai Ping Rebellion

**PURPOSE:** To understand how the Tai Ping rebellion incorporated many ideas from Christianity and traditional Chinese ideas into their movement to overthrow the Qing dynasty

**BACKGROUND INFORMATION** The Tai Ping rebellion was led by Hong Xiuquan (hung she-o chew-on), a convert to Christianity, who believed he was Jesus Christ's younger brother. Xiuquan was a leader and founder of an organization called the "God Worshipping Society." Members of this group adopted a kind of Christianity. They declared a "Tai Ping Heavenly Kingdom" with Hong Xiuquan as their king. The Tai Ping rebellion lasted fourteen years (1850-1864), and even though the Tai Ping lost, they had numerous victories over Qing forces. At times, the Tai Ping occupied the city of Nanjing, and they almost captured the Qing's capital in Beijing. By the early 1860s, however, the Tai Ping rebels were nearing defeat. The final blow came in the form of Hong Xiuquan's death on June 1, 1864.

## Explore the Text

**The Scene:** In the southern Chinese province of Guanxi, a new religious sect is growing called the God Worshipping Society. This new religious sect is rooted in a rough interpretation of Christianity. With China in seeming decline, the sect is attracting large numbers of converts and gobbling up territory at a frightening rate.

**Key Historical Actors:** The author of this poem is unknown, but he was clearly familiar with the Tai Ping Rebellion and its fundamental principles governing family relationships. Hong Xiuquan was the leader of the Tai Ping rebellion, and he believed that members of the Qing dynasty were demons. Hong Xiuquan thought that it was his duty to rid them from China. During this period, the Qing dynasty was trying to manage the growing influence of the Western powers in China.

**Key Ideas:** The text demonstrates the influence of Christianity but also of traditional Chinese culture on the ideas of the Tai Ping Rebellion. This text highlights the importance of traditional family roles for the Tai Ping rebels. While the Tai Ping wished to overthrow the Qing dynasty, they did not wish to end traditional ideas about the role of women in Chinese society.

**On Reverence For Parents**

As grain is stored against a day of need,
So men bring up children to tend their old age.
A filial son begets filial children;
The reward here is truly wonderful.

**On The Fathers' Way**

When the ridgepole is straight, nothing will be irregular below;
When the father is strict, the Way will be formed.
Let him not provoke his children to wrath,
And the whole dwelling will be filled with harmony.

**On The Mothers' Way**

Mothers, beware of **partiality**;
Tenderly instruct your children in virtue.
When a mother's **demeanor** is worthy of her daughter-in-law's imitation,
The happy feeling will reach high heaven.

**On The Sons' Way**

Sons, be patterns to your wives;
Obedience to parents is your natural duty.
To the tattle of women never listen,
And you will not be estranged from your own flesh.

---

**partiality: unfair bias or favoritism**

**demeanor: behavior**

**DETERMINING CENTRAL IDEAS**

What does the central idea of this passage suggest about the author's attitude about the roles people should play in their families?

**DETERMINING MEANING**

Read the text of the section that contains the word ***dwelling***. Which words in the section give context clues about the meaning of *dwelling*?

Library of Congress Prints and Photographs Division [LC-DIG-det-4a05589]

**CITING TEXT EVIDENCE**

Cite evidence from the text that shows that the author expected women to be subservient to men.

**On The Daughters-In-Law's Way**

You who are married into other families,
Be gentle and yielding, and your duty will be fulfilled.
Do not quarrel with your sisters-in-law
Or quarrel and **vex** the father-in-law and mother-in-law.

**On The Elder Brothers' Way**

Elder brothers, instruct your younger brothers;
Remember always your common parentage.
Should the younger brother commit some trifling fault,
Bear with it and be **indulgent**.

**On The Younger Brothers' Way**

That there should be old and young is ordered by Heaven;
The way to follow elder brothers lies in respect.
When younger brothers understand Heaven's manifest principles,
Happiness and honor will be their portion.

**On The Elder Sisters' Way**

Elder sisters, instruct your younger brothers and sisters;
Refine the good that you may turn to Heaven.
Should there be reason to return to your parents' home,
Gather the younger ones and tell them what is wrong and right.

---

**vex:** to make someone feel annoyed, frustrated, or worried

**indulgent:** to be overly generous to or lenient with someone

Niday Picture Library/Alamy Stock Photo

**On The Younger Sisters' Way**

Girls, obey your elder brothers and sisters;
By obliging and avoid a high display.
With careful diligence cultivate the upright,
And mind and keep the Ten Heavenly Commandments.

**On The Husbands' Way**

The husband's way is based on firmness;
Love for a wife should be qualified by prudence.
And should the lioness east of the river roar,
Let not the heart be filled with terror.

**On The Wives' Way**

The wife's way lies in the three obediences;
Do not disobey your husband.
If hens crow in the morning,
There will be self-sought misery for the family

—from *Tai Ping Rebellion: History and Documents,* by Franz Michael and Chung-Li Chang (Seattle: University of Washington Press, 1971)

#### EVALUATING TEXT EVIDENCE

What can we conclude about the fact that the poem's reference to family roles and relationships appears to borrow from the ancient and influential Chinese philosophers, such as Confucius?

#### ANALYZING TEXT PRESENTATION

How does the text present information about family roles in Chinese society? Do you find the text's organization clear and logical?



## Text-Based Discussion

1. **IDENTIFYING CONNECTIONS** What are some larger changes occurring in China during this period that are reflected in the Tai Ping Rebellion?
2. **SUMMARIZING** In a few sentences, summarize the key points within the passage.
3. **ANALYZING POINTS OF VIEW** Based on the text, what can you determine about the author[s] point of view?
4. **COMPARING AND CONTRASTING** List similarities and differences between the Tai Ping and the Boxer Rebellions.
5. **ANALYZING CHANGE** Based on this text, can we infer that the influence of Western ideas in China helped women obtain greater rights during this period?

## ESSENTIAL QUESTIONS

- *How can new ideas accelerate economic and political change?*
- *How do cultures influence each other?*

LESSON 2

# Revolution in China

## THE STORY BEGINS...

After the failure of the Boxer Rebellion in China, the Qing dynasty made a desperate move to institute reforms. These reforms came far too late. When the Empress Ci Xi died in 1908, the country slipped into a period of revolution. The Qing dynasty finally collapsed in early 1912, and China fell into civil war. The general Sun Yat-sen and his Nationalist Party fought to turn China into a republic. A few years later he wrote the following words about his country's future:

> "China therefore needs a republican government just as a boy needs school. As a schoolboy must have good teachers and helpful friends, so the Chinese people, being for the first time under republican rule, must have a farsighted revolutionary government for their training. This calls for the period of political tutelage, which is a necessary transitional stage from monarchy to republicanism."

—Sun Yat-sen, *"The Three Stages of Revolution,"* 1918

Sun Yat-sen's support for representative government demonstrated the growing influence of Western ideas in China and set the stage for a period of traumatic modernization.

PHOTO:Art Collection 2/Alamy Stock Photo; TEXT:Yat-Sen, Sun. 1918. Selections From a Program of National Reconstruction: "The Three Stages of Revolution". Quoted by de Bary, Wm. Theodore and Lufrano, Richard. 2000. In Sources of Chinese Tradition, Second Edition. Volume II - From 1600 Through the Twentieth Century. New York: Columbia University Press.

*Sun Yat-sen became a central figure in the post-Qing dynasty Chinese republic.* ▶

| The Chinese Civil War | |
|---|---|
| Causes | Key Figures |
| | |
| | |
| | |

**ANALYZING KEY IDEAS AND DETAILS**

**DESCRIBING** Read closely to identify causes and key figures that contributed to the Chinese Civil War. Record each cause in a graphic organizer similar to this one.

# THE FALL OF THE QING

**GUIDING QUESTION** *What led to the fall of the Qing dynasty?*

After the Boxer Rebellion, the Qing dynasty in China tried desperately to reform itself. Ci Xi, who had long resisted suggestions from her advisers for change, now embraced a number of reforms.

A new education system based on the Western model was adopted, and the civil service examination system was dropped. In 1909 legislative assemblies were formed at the **provincial**, or local, level. Elections for a national assembly were held in 1910.

The emerging new elite, composed of merchants, professionals, and reform-minded gentry, soon became impatient with the slow pace of political change. They were angry when they discovered that the new assemblies were not allowed to pass laws but could only give advice to the ruler. Moreover, the recent reforms had done nothing for the peasants, artisans, and miners, whose living conditions were getting worse as taxes increased. Unrest grew in the countryside as the dynasty continued to ignore deep-seated resentments.

**ANALYZING KEY IDEAS AND DETAILS**

1. **DETERMINING CENTRAL IDEAS** What is the central idea of this section? Describe how the section presents and advances this idea.
2. **SUMMARIZING** In your own words, summarize this section.

**DETERMINING MEANING**

In order to understand the word **provincial**, consider its similarity to the word *province*, which refers to a district or region in a country. How does knowing the meaning of *province* help a reader determine the meaning of *provincial*?

## THE RISE OF SUN YAT-SEN

The first signs of revolution appeared during the 1890s when the young radical Sun Yat-sen formed the Revive China Society.

Sun Yat-sen believed that the Qing dynasty was in a state of decay and could no longer govern the country. Unless the Chinese were united under a strong government, they would remain at the mercy of other countries. Although Sun believed that China should follow the pattern of Western countries, he also knew that the Chinese people were hardly ready for democracy.

Sun instead developed a three-stage reform process. The first stage would be a military takeover. In the second stage, a transitional **phase**, Sun's own revolutionary party would prepare the people for democratic rule. The final stage called for establishment of a constitutional democracy.

At a convention in Tokyo in 1905, Sun united members of radical groups from across China and formed the Revolutionary Alliance, which eventually became the Nationalist Party. In presenting his program, Sun Yat-sen called for the following changes:

**DETERMINING MEANING**

Read the text of the paragraph that contains the word **phase**. Which words in the paragraph provide context clues you can use to determine the meaning of *phase*?

> “Establish the Republic: Now our revolution is based on equality, in order to establish a republican government. All our people are equal and all enjoy political rights. . . . Equalize land ownership: The good fortune of civilization is to be shared equally by all the people of the nation. . . . Its [the land’s] present price shall be received by the owner . . . after the revolution [it] shall belong to the state.”

— quoted in *Sources of Chinese Tradition*, 1960

Sun’s new organization advocated his Three People’s Principles, which promoted nationalism, democracy, and the right for people to pursue their own livelihoods. Although the new organization was small, it benefited from the rising discontent generated by the Qing dynasty’s failure to improve conditions in China.

**BIOGRAPHY**

## SUN YAT-SEN (1866–1925)

**Chinese Revolutionary**

Sun Yat-sen was the leader of the revolutionary movement that overthrew the Qing dynasty. Sun was born to a peasant family in the south and was educated in Hawaii. He returned to China to practice medicine but soon began to use his earnings to finance revolutionary activities.

A failed rebellion forced Sun to flee to Japan and later to the United States and London. He raised money and recruited Chinese exiles to carry out his revolutionary plans. After the Qing government collapsed in 1911, he returned to China. Sun decided to back General Yuan Shigai as president in 1912. He was afraid that more fighting would lead only to chaos and foreign intervention.

Sun never realized his dream of leading a new Chinese republic, but both the Republic of China on Taiwan and the People’s Republic of China honor him as the founder of modern China.

1. **IDENTIFYING CONNECTIONS** How do Sun Yat-sen’s Western education and embrace of liberal ideals reflect larger changes in China at the turn of the twentieth century?
2. **ANALYZING IDEAS** Why do you think both the Republic of China on Taiwan and the People’s Republic of China honor Sun Yat-sen?

**THINKING LIKE A HISTORIAN**

### CLASSIFICATION AND REVOLUTIONS

Historians look for general characteristics and particular patterns to classify events. Political revolutions are important phenomena that historians analyze. For example, a historian might classify one event as a revolution while another as an uprising. The author of this textbook notes that “the events of 1911 were less a revolution than a collapse of the old order.” In other words, the revolution of 1911 was not really a revolution. Think about other revolutions you have learned about in your textbook and why this might be so.

## THE REVOLUTION OF 1911

The Qing dynasty was near its end. In 1908, Empress Dowager Ci Xi died. Her nephew Guang Xu, a prisoner in the palace, died one day before his aunt. The throne was now occupied by China’s “last emperor,” the infant Henry Pu Yi.

In October 1911, followers of Sun Yat-sen launched an uprising in central China. At the time, Sun was traveling in the United States. Thus, the revolt had no leader, but the government was too weak to react. The Qing dynasty collapsed, opening the way for new political forces.

Sun’s party had neither the military nor the political strength to form a new government. The party was forced to turn to a member of the old order, General Yuan Shigai (YOO • AHN SHUR • GIE), who controlled the army.

PHOTO:Ivan Vdovin/Alamy Stock Photo; TEXT:Teng, Ssu-yu; Fairbank, John K.; Sun, E-tu Zen; Fang, Chaoying; et al. 1954. China’s Response to the West - A Documentary Survey 1839-1923. Cambridge, Massachusetts: Harvard University Press.

Yuan was a prominent figure in military circles. He had been placed in charge of the imperial army sent to suppress the rebellion. However, he abandoned the government and negotiated with members of Sun Yat-sen's party. General Yuan agreed to serve as president of a new Chinese republic and to allow the election of a legislature. Sun arrived in China in January 1912, after reading about the revolution in a Denver, Colorado newspaper. He and Yuan exchanged telegrams:

> "I beg to call the attention of Premier Yuan in Peking to the fact that when I reached Shanghai two days ago my comrade entrusted me with the responsibility of organizing a provisional government. . . . Although I have accepted this position for the time being, it is actually waiting for you, and my offer will eventually be made clear to the World. I hope that you will decide to accept this offer."

—telegram from Sun Yat-sen to Yuan Shigai, January 1, 1911, quoted in *The Political History of China, 1840–1928*

> "I have received your telegram of the first. The choice between monarchism and republicanism in the political system is to be decided by public opinion and there is no way to predict what the decision will be. I dare not participate in the provisional government. You have been kind to offer me such great honor, but I am sorry to say that I dare not accept it; I hope I shall be excused from doing so."

—telegram from Yuan Shigai to Sun Yat-sen, January 2, 1911, quoted in *The Political History of China, 1840–1928*

**ANALYZING PRIMARY SOURCES**

1. **SUMMARIZING** In your own words, summarize the excerpts from the telegrams between Yuan Shigai and Sun Yat-sen.
2. **EXPLAINING CAUSES** What do you believe led Yuan Shigai to refuse Sun Yat-sen's offer?

In the eyes of Sun Yat-sen's party, the events of 1911 were a glorious revolution that ended 2,000 years of imperial rule. However, the 1911 uprising was hardly a revolution. It produced no new political or social order. Sun Yat-sen and his followers still had much to accomplish.

The Revolutionary Alliance was supported mainly by an emerging urban middle class, and its program was based largely on Western liberal democratic principles. However, the urban middle class in China was too small to support a new political order. Most of the Chinese people still lived on the land, and few peasants supported Sun Yat-sen's party. In effect, then, the events of 1911 were less a revolution than a collapse of the old order.

## AN ERA OF CIVIL WAR

After the collapse of the Qing dynasty, the military took over. Sun Yat-sen and his colleagues had accepted General Yuan Shigai as president of the new Chinese republic in 1911 because they lacked the military force to compete with his control over the army. Many feared that if the revolt lapsed into chaos, the Western powers would intervene. If that happened, the last shreds of Chinese independence would be lost. However, even the general's new allies distrusted his **motives**.

**DETERMINING MEANING**

Read the sentences before and after the sentence that contains the word **motives**. How do these sentences help you determine the meaning of *motive*?

Yuan understood little of the new ideas sweeping into China from the West. He ruled in a traditional manner and even tried to set up a new imperial dynasty. The reformers hated Yuan for using murder and terror to destroy the new democratic institutions. The traditionalists hated Yuan for being disloyal to the dynasty he had served.

Yuan's dictatorial efforts rapidly led to clashes with Sun's party, now renamed the ***Guomindang***, or Nationalist Party. When Yuan dissolved the new parliament, the Nationalists launched a rebellion. The rebellion failed, and Sun Yat-sen fled to Japan.

Yuan was strong enough to brush off the challenge from the revolutionary forces, but he could not turn back history. He died in 1916 and was succeeded by one of his officers. Over the next several years, China slipped into civil war as the power of the central government disintegrated and military warlords seized power in the provinces. Their soldiers caused massive destruction throughout China.

### ✓ CHECKING FOR UNDERSTANDING

1. **IDENTIFYING CAUSES** What led to the fall of the Qing dynasty?
2. **EXPLAINING CAUSES** Why did Yuan Shigai's inauguration as president of China in 1911 lead to a civil war?
3. **INTERPRETING** In the provisional government, why did Sun Yat-sen ask Yuan Shigai to serve as president, instead of taking on the job himself?

## CULTURAL CHANGES

**GUIDING QUESTION** *How did Western influences change Chinese society and culture?*

Western influences forced the Chinese to adapt to new ways of thinking and living. Early twentieth-century Chinese culture reflected the struggle between Confucian social ideas and those of the West.

**UNDERSTANDING CRAFT AND STRUCTURE**

1. **ANALYZING TEXT PRESENTATION** How does the section organize information about social and cultural changes taking place in China? Do you find this structuring of the information effective?
2. **DETERMINING MEANING** According to the text, Chinese society and culture were "in transition." What does it mean to be in *transition*?

*As part of the changes to the Chinese economy, trade increased between China and the West, as shown in this circa 1900 photograph of the New Market in Hong Kong.*

**INTERPRETING** Name an aspect from this image that shows the Western influence on Chinese society.

## SOCIETY IN TRANSITION

When European traders began to move into China in greater numbers in the mid-1800s, Chinese society was in a state of transition. The growth of industry and trade was especially noticeable in the cities, where a national market for **commodities** such as oil, copper, salt, and tea had appeared.

The Chinese economy had never been more productive. Faster and more reliable transportation and a better system of money and banking had begun to create the foundation for a money economy. Foreign investments in China grew rapidly, and the money went into modernizing the Chinese economy. New crops brought in from abroad increased food production and encouraged population growth.

The coming of Westerners to China affected the Chinese economy in three ways. Westerners introduced modern means of transportation and communications, created an export market, and integrated the Chinese market into the nineteenth-century world economy.

To some, these changes were beneficial. Shaking China out of its old ways quickened a process of change that had already begun. Western influences forced the Chinese to adopt new ways of thinking and acting, and Western ideas stimulated the desire to modernize. Westerners also provided something else to the Chinese. They gave them a model, funds, and the technical knowledge to modernize.

At the same time, China paid a heavy price for these new ways of living and conducting business. Imperialism imposed a state of dependence on China, and many Chinese were exploited. Imperialism condemned the country to a condition of underdevelopment. Its local industry was largely destroyed. Also, many of the profits in the new economy went to foreign countries rather than back into the Chinese economy.

## THE PACE OF CHANGE QUICKENS

During the first quarter of the twentieth century, the pace of change in China quickened even more. After World War I, which temporarily drew foreign investment out of the country, Chinese businesspeople began to develop new ventures. Shanghai became the bastion of the new bourgeoisie. People lived in Shanghai at the same rhythm they lived in other modern cities. Wuhan, Tianjin, and Guangzhou also became major industrial and commercial centers with a growing middle class and an industrial working class.

In 1800 daily life in China was the same as it had been for centuries. Most Chinese were farmers, living in one of thousands of villages near rice fields and on hillsides throughout the countryside. A farmer's life was governed by the harvest cycle, village custom, and family ritual. A few men were educated in the Confucian classics. Women worked in the home or worked out in the fields. All children were expected to obey their parents, and wives were expected to submit to the wishes of their husbands.

A visitor to China 125 years later would have seen a different society, although it would still have been recognizably Chinese. The changes were most striking in the cities, among the urban middle class. Here the educated and wealthy had been visibly affected by the growing Western cultural presence. Confucian social ideas were declining rapidly in influence.

**DETERMINING MEANING**

Read the paragraph that contains the word **commodities**. Which words in the paragraph provide context clues you can use to determine the meaning of *commodities*?

**MAKING CONNECTIONS TO TODAY**

### SHIFTS IN THE GLOBAL MARKETPLACE

Prior to the Industrial Revolution China, along with India, accounted for nearly half the world's manufacturing. In the year 1900, however, China was in a state of rapid decline and was losing control of its economy to Western Powers. Over a century later, China is in a very different situation. It is now a global center of manufacturing, producing electronics, clothing, plastics, and other consumer and industrial goods. It has a manufacturing output of over $1.5 trillion per year and its economy is steadily outpacing every other economy on the planet. Today, its contributions to the global economy are projected to surpass that of the U.S. in 2018. The center of the world economy that shifted to Europe and North America after the Industrial Revolution is slowly shifting back to Asia.

1. **DETERMINING CENTRAL IDEAS** What does the central idea of this passage indicate about the changes in the world economy since 1900?
2. **EVALUATING ARGUMENTS** It could be inferred that China's great size is a major contributor to its rise in economic power. Does this passage or the text provide sufficient evidence to support this inference?

## CULTURE IN TRANSITION

Nowhere in China was the struggle between old and new more visible than in the culture. Radical reformers wanted to eliminate traditional culture, condemning it as an instrument of oppression. They were interested in creating a new China that would be respected by the modern world.

The first changes in traditional culture came in the late nineteenth century. Intellectuals began to introduce Western books, art, and ideas to China. Soon, China was flooded by Western culture as intellectuals called for a new culture based on that of the modern West.

Western literature and art became popular in China, especially among the urban middle class. Traditional culture, however, remained popular, especially in rural areas. Most creative artists followed foreign trends, while traditionalists held on to Chinese culture. Literature in particular was influenced by foreign ideas. Western novels and short stories began to attract a larger audience. Although most Chinese novels written after World War I dealt with Chinese subjects, they reflected the Western tendency toward a realistic portrayal of society. Often, they dealt with the new Westernized middle class. Most of China's modern authors showed a clear contempt for the past.

Ba Jin, the author of numerous novels and short stories, was one of China's foremost writers of the twentieth century. Born in 1904, Ba Jin was well attuned to the rigors and expected obedience of Chinese family life. In his trilogy, *Family, Spring,* and *Autumn*, he describes the disintegration of traditional Confucian ways as the younger members of a family attempt to break away from their elders.

### ✓ CHECKING FOR UNDERSTANDING

1. **ANALYZING CHANGE** How did Western influences change Chinese society and culture?
2. **SUMMARIZING** What intellectual and cultural innovations took place in China following the revolution?
3. **EVALUATING** How did Western ideas and institutions help or hurt the Chinese economy? Be specific.

## LESSON 2 REVIEW

### Time and Place

1. **IDENTIFYING EFFECTS** Identify one significant effect of reforms taking place in China at the end of the Qing dynasty.

### Building History-Social Science Analysis Skills

2. **INFERRING** Analyze the telegrams between Sun Yat-sen and Yuan Shigai. Do you think Sun Yat-sen and Yuan Shigai shared the same motives for their support of the provisional government in 1911? Why or why not?
3. **EVALUATING** How did interactions with the West change Chinese literature? Can you find any parallels between how international relations changed Chinese culture and how similar forces affect popular culture in the present?
4. **COMPARING AND CONTRASTING** Compare and contrast the beliefs Yuan Shigai and Sun Yat-sen held about the type of government China should adopt after the Revolution of 1911.

### Writing About History

5. **EXPLANATORY WRITING** Write an essay explaining how the Revolution of 1911 resulted in a civil war. Be sure to cite specific people, events, and ideas from this section in your response.

### Collaborating

6. **INTEGRATING INFORMATION** With a partner, discuss the changes that took place in China during the nineteenth century. Take turns listing examples of how these changes affected not only its government but also its economy and culture.

## ESSENTIAL QUESTIONS

- *How can new ideas accelerate economic and political change?*
- *How do cultures influence each other?*

# THE STORY BEGINS...

LESSON 3

# The Rise of Modern Japan

In the early 1600s, Japan isolated itself from the rest of the world in a policy known as *Sakoku*. No one, especially Westerners, could enter, and no Japanese could leave. Japan's rulers were determined to protect their country from what they saw as harmful outside influences. By the mid-1800s, this policy proved impossible to maintain. As with China, Western powers pressured the Japanese to open their country and their markets. On July 8th, 1853, four American warships appeared outside the capital, Tokyo, in a display of strength that forced Japan to open itself to trade with the West. Recognizing the futility of resistance, a Japanese lord said the following:

> "We must construct new steamships, especially powerful warships, and these we will load with goods not needed in Japan. For a time we will have to employ Dutchmen as masters and mariners, but we will put on board with them Japanese of ability and integrity who must study the use of large guns, the handling of ships, and the rules of navigation. Openly these will be called merchant vessels, but they will in fact have the secret purpose of training a navy. As we increase the number of ships and our mastery of technique, Japanese will be able to sail the oceans freely and gain direct knowledge of conditions abroad without relying on the secret reports of the Dutch. Thus we will eventually complete the organization of a navy."

—*Observations of Ii Naosuke, Lord (daimyo) of Hakone,* 1853

Japan opened itself to trade and eagerly pursued a modernization program. Naosuke was unaware, but his suggestions would lead to a transformation of Japanese society.

*In the last quarter of the nineteenth century, the Japanese rapidly adopted Western industrial and military technologies.* ▶

PHOTO:World History Archive/Alamy Stock Photo; TEXT:Ii Naosuke. 1853. Quoted by Lu, David J. 1997. Japan: A Documentary History. Armonk, New York and London, England: M.E. Sharpe, Inc.

| Important Changes in Japan, 1853–1914 | | |
|---|---|---|
| Political | Cultural | Military |
| | | |
| | | |
| | | |

**ANALYZING KEY IDEAS AND DETAILS**

**CITING TEXT EVIDENCE** Read closely to identify important cultural, political, and technological changes taking place in Japan. Record each change in a graphic organizer such as this one.

# JAPAN RESPONDS TO FOREIGN PRESSURE

**UNDERSTANDING CRAFT AND STRUCTURE**

1. **ANALYZING TEXT PRESENTATION** Analyze how the text describes Japan's response to foreign pressures. What are some key events listed in the text?
2. **DETERMINING MEANING** The text states, "His forces collapsed, ending the shogunate system." What does the word *collapsed* mean in this context?

**DETERMINING MEANING**

Read the paragraph that contains the word **concessions**. Which phrase in the paragraph provides context clues you can use to determine the meaning of *concessions*?

**GUIDING QUESTION** *How did Japan respond to foreign pressure to end its isolationist policies?*

New technologies from Western Europe spread across the world at a rapid pace. The Japanese followed the example of Western nations and made use of the new knowledge and technology to emerge as a modern imperialist power by the end of the nineteenth century. However, they also worked diligently to preserve Japanese values.

By 1800, the Tokugawa shogunate had ruled Japan for 200 years. It had kept an isolationist policy, allowing only Dutch and Chinese merchants at its port at Nagasaki. Western nations wanted to end Japan's isolation, believing that the expansion of trade on a global basis would benefit all nations.

The first foreign power to succeed with Japan was the United States. In the summer of 1853, Commodore Matthew Perry arrived in Edo Bay (now Tokyo Bay) with an American fleet of four warships. Perry brought a letter from President Millard Fillmore, asking the Japanese for better treatment of sailors shipwrecked on the Japanese islands. (Foreign sailors shipwrecked in Japan were treated as criminals and exhibited in public cages.) He also asked to open foreign relations between the United States and Japan. Perry returned about six months later for an answer, this time with a larger fleet. Some shogunate officials recommended **concessions**, or political compromises. The guns of Perry's ships ultimately made Japan's decision.

Under military pressure, Japan agreed to the Treaty of Kanagawa with the United States. The treaty provided for the return of shipwrecked American sailors, the opening of two Japanese ports to Western traders, and the establishment of a U.S. consulate in Japan. In 1858 a more detailed treaty called for the opening of several new ports to U.S. trade and residence. Japan soon signed similar treaties with several European nations.

Resistance to opening foreign relations was especially strong among the samurai warriors in two southern territories, Satsuma and Choshu. In 1863 the Sat-Cho alliance (from Satsuma-Choshu) forced the shogun to promise to end relations with the West. In 1868, when the shogun refused, the Sat-Cho leaders attacked the shogun's palace in Kyōto. His forces collapsed, ending the shogunate system and beginning the Meiji Restoration.

## ✓ CHECKING FOR UNDERSTANDING

1. **SUMMARIZING** How did Japan respond to foreign pressure to end its isolationist policies?
2. **IDENTIFYING CONNECTIONS** Why would Western nations want Japan to end its isolation?
3. **UNDERSTANDING CHANGE** How did the guns of the U.S. Navy make "Japan's decision" to open foreign relations with the United States?

# THE MEIJI RESTORATION

**GUIDING QUESTION** *How did the Meiji Restoration change Japan?*

The Sat-Cho leaders had genuinely mistrusted the West, but they soon realized that Japan must change to survive. The new leaders embarked on a policy of reform that transformed Japan into a modern industrial nation. The symbol of the new era was the young emperor Mutsuhito. He called his reign the Meiji (MAY • jee), or "Enlightened Rule." This period has thus become known as the Meiji Restoration.

Of course, the Sat-Cho leaders controlled the Meiji ruler, just as the shogunate had controlled earlier emperors. In recognition of the real source of political power, the capital was moved from Kyōto to Edo (now named Tokyo), the location of the new leaders.

## TRANSFORMATION OF JAPANESE POLITICS

When in power, the new leaders moved to abolish the old order and to strengthen power in their hands. To undercut the power of the daimyo (the local nobles), the new leaders stripped them of their lands in 1871. In turn, the lords were named governors of the territories formerly under their control. The territories were now called **prefectures**.

The Meiji reformers set out to create a modern political system based on the Western model. During the next 20 years, the Meiji government carefully studied Western political systems. As the process evolved, two main factions appeared, the Liberals and the Progressives. The Liberals wanted political reform based on the Western liberal democratic model, which vested supreme authority in a parliament. The Progressives wanted power to be shared between the legislative and executive branches, with the executive branch having more control.

During the 1870s and 1880s, these factions fought for control. The Progressives won. The Meiji constitution, adopted in 1889, was modeled after that of Imperial Germany. It gave most authority to the executive branch.

In theory, the emperor exercised all executive authority, but in practice, he was a figurehead. Real executive authority rested in the prime minister and his cabinet of ministers chosen by the Meiji leaders. The upper house included royal appointees and elected nobles, while the lower house was elected. The two houses were to have equal legislative powers.

The final result was a political system that was democratic in form but authoritarian in practice. Although modern in external appearance, it was still traditional because power remained in the hands of a ruling oligarchy (the Sat-Cho leaders). The system allowed the traditional ruling class to keep its influence and economic power.

### ANALYZING KEY IDEAS AND DETAILS

1. **ANALYZING CENTRAL IDEAS** Explain how the central idea of this section explains the section's title, "The Meiji Restoration."
2. **CITING TEXT EVIDENCE** Identify text evidence that supports the following claim made in this section: "The Meiji reformers set out to create a modern political system based on the Western model."

### DETERMINING MEANING

The word **prefecture** has the same root as the word *prefect*. *Prefect* is a noun referring to the government official in charge of a local territory or region, similar to a governor in the United States. How might knowing the meaning of *prefect* help a person determine the meaning of *prefecture*?

*Japanese artist Hiroshige III created this woodblock print of the Tokyo-Yokohama railway just years after the Meiji Restoration opened the door to Western trade and ideas.*

**IDENTIFYING BIAS** Do you think the artist was biased in his depiction of the railway? Why or why not?

Asian Art & Archaeology, Inc./Corbis

*These woodblock prints are part of a series called "Famous Places on the Tokaido: A Record of the Process of Reform" (1875).*

**UNDERSTANDING CHANGE** What are some modern technologies depicted in these prints, and how do they show the effects of reform?

**DETERMINING MEANING**

Analyze the paragraph that contains the word **subsidies**. Which words in the paragraph provide the context clues you can use to determine the meaning of *subsidies*?

## MEIJI ECONOMICS

The Meiji leaders also set up a land reform program, which made the traditional lands of the daimyo the private property of the peasants. The daimyo were compensated with government bonds. The Meiji leaders then levied a new land tax, which was set at an annual rate of 3 percent of the estimated value of the land. The new tax was a great source of revenue for the government but a burden for farmers.

Under the old system, farmers had paid a fixed percentage of their harvest to the landowners. In bad harvest years, they had owed little or nothing. Under the new system, the farmers had to pay the land tax every year, regardless of the quality of the harvest. As a result, in bad years, many peasants were unable to pay their taxes. This forced them to sell their lands to wealthy neighbors and to become tenant farmers who paid rent to the new owners. By the end of the nineteenth century, about 40 percent of all farmers were tenants.

With its budget needs met by the land tax, the government turned to the promotion of industry. The Meiji government gave **subsidies** to needy industries, provided training and foreign advisers, and improved transportation and communications. By 1890, the country had more than 1,400 miles of railroad, and telegraph lines linked all major cities. These modernizations were aided by the spread of Western science and technology. Japan's industrial sector was beginning to grow. By 1900, key industries included tea, silk, weapons, and shipbuilding.

From the start, a unique feature of the Meiji model of industrial development was the close relationship between government and private business. The government encouraged new industries by giving businesspeople money and privileges. This process was aided by the adoption of a European-style banking system. After an industry was on its feet, it was turned over entirely to private ownership.

## MODERN INSTITUTIONS AND SOCIAL STRUCTURES

The Meiji reformers also transformed other institutions. A new imperial army based on compulsory military service was formed in 1871. All Japanese men now served for three years. The new army was well equipped with modern weapons.

Education also changed. The Meiji leaders realized the need for universal education. In 1871 a new ministry of education adopted the American model of elementary schools, secondary schools, and universities. It brought foreign specialists to Japan to teach, and it sent students to study abroad.

Before the Meiji reforms, the lives of all Japanese people were determined by their membership in families, villages, and social classes. Japanese society was highly hierarchal. Belonging to a particular social class determined a person's occupation and social relationships. Women were especially limited by the "three obediences": child to father, wife to husband, and widow to son. Husbands could obtain a divorce; wives could not. Marriages were arranged, and the average marital age of females was 16 years. Females did not share inheritance rights with males. Few received any education outside the family.

The Meiji Restoration had a marked effect on the traditional social system in Japan. Special privileges for the aristocracy were abolished. For the first time, women were allowed to seek an education. As the economy shifted from an agricultural to an industrial base, many Japanese began to get new jobs and to establish new social relationships.

Western fashions and culture became the rage. A new generation began to imitate the clothing styles, eating habits, and social practices of Westerners. The game of baseball was imported from the United States.

The social changes brought about by the Meiji Restoration also had a less attractive side. Many commoners were ruthlessly exploited in the coal mines and textile mills. Workers labored up to 20 hours a day. Coal miners in some areas worked in temperatures up to 130 degrees Fahrenheit (54 degrees C). When they tried to escape, they were shot.

The transformation of Japan into a "modern society" did not detach the country entirely from its old values, however. Traditional values based on loyalty to the family and community were still taught in schools. Traditional Japanese values were also given a firm legal basis in the 1889 constitution, which limited the right to vote to men. The Civil Code of 1898 played down individual rights and placed women within the **context** of their family role.

### ✓ CHECKING FOR UNDERSTANDING

1. **ANALYZING CHANGE** How did the Meiji Restoration change Japan?
2. **UNDERSTANDING CONTEXT** The text explains that "the Sat-Cho leaders had genuinely mistrusted the West," but they still pursued Western reforms. Why?
3. **EXPLAINING CAUSE AND EFFECT** How did the new land tax in Japan affect small farmers?

## JAPANESE EXPANSION

**GUIDING QUESTION** *Why did Japan turn itself into an imperialist power?*

The Japanese soon copied Western imperialism. The Japanese knew that Western nations had amassed some of their wealth and power because of their colonies. Those colonies had provided sources of raw materials, inexpensive labor, and markets for manufactured products. To compete, Japan would also have to expand.

The Japanese began their program of territorial expansion close to home. In 1874 Japan claimed control of the Ryukyu (ree • YOO • kyoo) Islands, which belonged to the Chinese Empire. Two years later, Japan's navy forced the Koreans to open their ports to Japanese trade. The Chinese grew concerned by Japan's growing influence there.

In the 1880s, Chinese-Japanese rivalry over Korea intensified. In 1894, the two nations went to war, and Japan won. In the treaty ending the war, China recognized Korea's independence.

China also ceded Taiwan and the Liaodong Peninsula, with its strategic naval base at Port Arthur, to Japan. In time, the Japanese gave the Liaodong Peninsula back to China.

Rivalry with Russia over influence in Korea led to increasingly strained relations. The Russo-Japanese War began in 1904. Japan launched a surprise attack on the Russian naval base at Port Arthur, which Russia had taken from

CITIZENSHIP

### SOCIAL MOBILITY

The modernization process that occurred during the Meiji Restoration transformed Japanese society. Educational and economic reforms freed groups such as women and commoners to seek education and to contribute in ways previous generations could not. In short, it allowed for greater social mobility. In other words, your social status is determined by merit instead of the social status of your parents. In the United States, social mobility has always been a much prized characteristic of American civic life. The idea that children can hope to surpass their parents in social status is seen by many as a key to economic and political stability.

1. **ANALYZING IDEAS** Why might socially mobile societies have more stable democracies?
2. **INTERPRETING** How might the emergence of a form of social mobility because of the reforms during the Meiji Restoration have furthered the process of modernization at that time?

### INTEGRATING KNOWLEDGE AND IDEAS

1. **ANALYZING INFORMATION** What does the use of the word *expansion* in the heading of this section suggest about the content in the section?
2. **ASSESSING** What information in the text supports the claim that the Chinese grew concerned over Japan's influence?

## JAPANESE EXPANSION 1870–1918

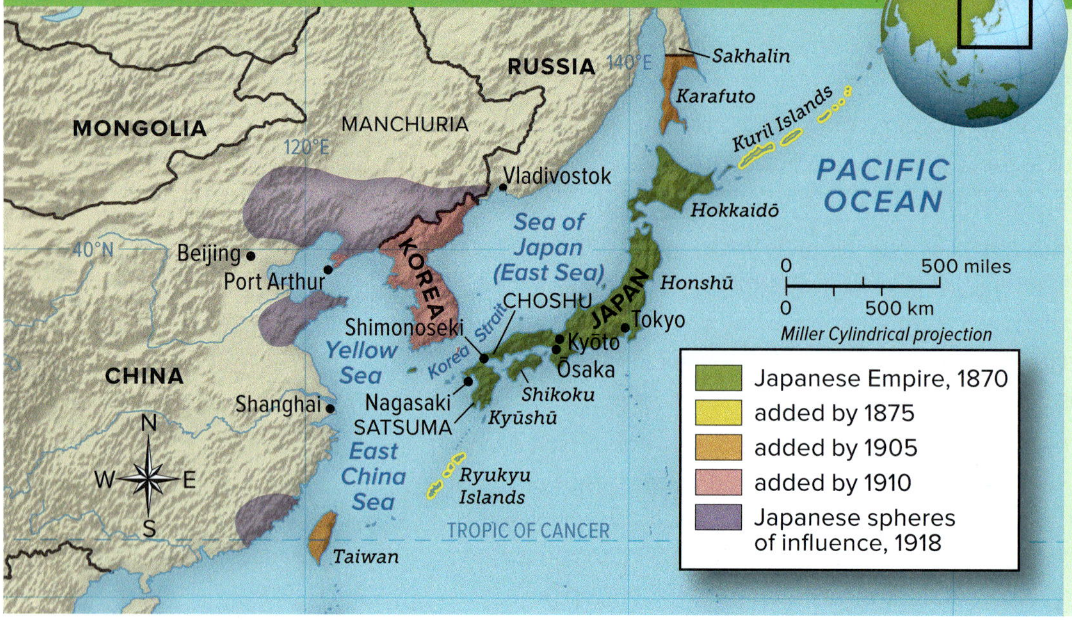


### GEOGRAPHIC REASONING

From 1870 to 1918 Japan expanded into Korea and China.

1. **PATTERNS AND MOVEMENT** What lands did Japan take by 1905?
2. **GLOBAL INTERCONNECTIONS** What countries did Japan come into conflict with as it expanded?

China in 1898. In the meantime, Russia had sent its Baltic fleet halfway around the world to East Asia, only to be defeated by the new Japanese navy off the coast of Japan. After their defeat, the Russians agreed to a humiliating peace, the Treaty of Portsmouth, in 1905.

> "**ARTICLE II.** The Imperial Russian Government, acknowledging that Japan possesses in Korea paramount political, military and economical interests, engages neither to obstruct nor interfere with measures for guidance, protection and control which the Imperial Government of Japan may find necessary to take in Korea. . . .
>
> **ARTICLE IX.** The Imperial Russian Government cedes to the Imperial Government of Japan in perpetuity and full sovereignty the southern portion of the Island of Saghalin and all the islands adjacent thereto and the public works and properties thereon."
>
> —The Treaty of Portsmouth, 1905

### ANALYZING PRIMARY SOURCES

1. **CITING TEXT EVIDENCE** What specific language in these articles makes it clear that Russia is the weaker party in the negotiations that resulted in the Treaty of Portsmouth? Cite specific details from the document.
2. **EXPLAINING EFFECTS** What do the guarantees created by the treaty suggest about Japan's interests in East Asian geopolitics at this stage?

Russia also gave the Liaodong Peninsula back to Japan, as well as the southern part of Sakhalin (SA • kuh • LEEN), an island north of Japan. The Japanese victory over Russia stunned the world. Japan had become one of the great powers.

After its victory, Japan established a sphere of influence in Korea. The United States recognized Japan's role there, and in return, Japan recognized American authority in the Philippines. In 1910 Japan annexed Korea outright.

Some Americans began to fear Japan's power in East Asia. In 1907 President Theodore Roosevelt made a "gentlemen's agreement" with Japan that essentially stopped Japanese immigration to the United States.

### ✓ CHECKING FOR UNDERSTANDING

1. **UNDERSTANDING CHANGE** Why did Japan turn itself into an imperialist power?
2. **UNDERSTANDING CONTEXT** Explain why the Japanese adopted Western-style imperialism.
3. **USING MAPS** Based on the map and text, list the dates and names of territories acquired by Japan during this period.

Tyler, Sydney. 1905. The Japan-Russia War - An Illustrated History of the War in the Far East - The Greatest Conflict of Modern Times. Harrisburg, PA.: The Minter Company.

# CULTURE IN AN ERA OF TRANSITION

**GUIDING QUESTION** *How did contact between Japan and the West influence culture?*

The wave of Western technology and ideas that entered Japan after 1850 greatly altered traditional Japanese culture. Dazzled by European literature, Japanese authors began imitating the imported models. They began to write novels that were patterned after the French tradition of realism. Japanese authors presented social conditions and the realities of war as objectively as possible.

Other aspects of Japanese culture were also changed. The Japanese invited engineers, architects, and artists from Europe and the United States to teach their "modern" skills to Japanese students. The Japanese copied Western architectural styles. Huge buildings of steel and reinforced concrete, adorned with Greek columns, appeared in many Japanese cities.

A national reaction had begun by the end of the 1800s, and many Japanese artists began to return to older techniques. In 1889 the Tokyo School of Fine Arts was established to promote traditional Japanese art.

These cultural exchanges were mutual. Japanese arts and crafts, porcelains, textiles, fans, folding screens, and woodblock prints became fashionable in Europe and North America. Japanese gardens, with their close attention to the positioning of rocks and falling water, became especially popular in the United States.

### ☑ CHECKING FOR UNDERSTANDING

1. **IDENTIFYING CAUSES** How did contact between Japan and the West influence culture?
2. **IDENTIFYING CONNECTIONS** What were some of the key features of Western literature that Japanese writers adopted?
3. **INFERRING** Why did the Japanese invite engineers, architects, and artists from the United States and Europe to visit Japan?

**ANALYZING KEY IDEAS AND DETAILS**

**CITING TEXT EVIDENCE** The text in this section explains that Japan adopted Western practices and then experienced a nationalist reaction to these adoptions. What text evidence supports the claim that Japan experienced a nationalist reaction to these adoptions?

*This Japanese garden and teahouse was showcased at the World's Fair in St. Louis, Missouri, in 1904.*

Buyenlarge/Archive Photos/Getty Images

## LESSON 3 REVIEW

### Time and Place

1. **IDENTIFYING CAUSES** Identify one major way Japan was transformed through the Meiji Restoration.

### Building History-Social Science Analysis Skills

2. **UNDERSTANDING CONTEXT** How did the prefecture system affect the daimyo?
3. **INFERRING** In your own words, summarize some instances when Japan rejected Western values and preserved traditional Japanese ideas about society.
4. **INTERPRETING** What challenges did women face in Meiji Japan?

### Writing About History

5. **EXPLANATORY WRITING** Write an essay explaining how foreign influence changed Japan, and discuss the continued relevance of the choice that Japan faced in the 1850s: isolation versus foreign trade in goods and culture. Be sure to cite specific evidence from the text.

### Collaborating

6. **USING MULTIMEDIA** With a small group, research cultural exchanges between the United States and Japan in the present day. Find three examples of Japanese art, music, film, or other popular media to share with the class.

# CONNECTING EAST AND WEST

Over the course of the nineteenth century, Western imperial powers focused their attention on East Asia. The following excerpts reveal the different perspectives on this process through the eyes of an American president, a Chinese politician, and a Japanese scholar. Read them to understand this period in Asian history.

**VOCABULARY**

*abstain:* to refrain; keep from

*dominions:* royal lands

*preserved:* maintained or kept

*armament:* military equipment

PRIMARY SOURCE: LETTER

## TRADE WITH JAPAN

This letter from the U.S. president was delivered by Matthew C. Perry to the emperor of Japan in July 1853.

> "I have directed Commodore Perry to assure your Imperial Majesty that I entertain the kindest feelings towards your Majesty's person and government; and that I have no other object in sending him to Japan, but to propose to your Imperial Majesty that the United States and Japan should live in friendship, and have [trade] with each other. . . . I have particularly charged Commodore Perry to **abstain** from any act, which could possibly disturb the peace of your Imperial Majesty's lands.
>
> The United States of America reaches from ocean to ocean, and our territory of Oregon and the state of California lie directly opposite to the **dominions** of your Imperial Majesty. Our steamships can go from California to Japan in eighteen days. Our great state of California produces about sixty millions of dollars in gold, every year, besides silver, quicksilver, precious stones, and many other valuable articles.
>
> Japan is also a rich and fertile country, and produces many very valuable articles. . . . our two countries should trade with each other, for the benefit both of Japan and the United States. We know that the ancient laws of your Imperial Majesty's government do not allow of foreign trade except with the Dutch. But as the state of the world changes, and new governments are formed, it seems to be wise from time to time to make new laws. . . ."

**ANALYZE THE TEXT**

1. **DETERMINING MEANING** Fillmore's letter states, "I particularly charged Commodore Perry to abstain from any act, which could possibly disturb the peace of your Imperial Majesty's lands." What does the word *abstain* mean in this context?

2. **CITING TEXT EVIDENCE** How is Fillmore's letter a combination of salesmanship and diplomacy? Cite evidence from the text.

PRIMARY SOURCE: MANUSCRIPT

## WESTERN INFLUENCE IN CHINA

In the early 1900s the Chinese politician and scholar Liang Qichao petitioned the Qing emperor to abolish the old exam system, to resist foreign domination, and to embrace Western technology.

> "Of course, we may laugh at those old folks among us who block their own road of advancement and claim that we Chinese have all that is found in Western learning. But should we not laugh even more at those who are drunk with Western ways and regard everything Chinese as worthless. . . . What we need to learn is the essential spirit of that system and not the conditions under which it was produced. . . . For example, Confucius said a great deal about ethics of an aristocratic nature, which is certainly not suitable today. But we should not take Confucius lightly simply because of this. Shall we cast Plato aside simply because he said that the slavery system should be **preserved**?
>
> I therefore hope that our dear young people will, first of all, have a sincere purpose of respecting and protecting our civilization; second, that they will apply Western methods to the study of our civilization and discover its true character; third, that they will put our own civilization in order and supplement it with others' so that it will be transformed and become a new civilization. . . ."

**ANALYZE THE TEXT**

1. **DETERMINING POINT OF VIEW** Does Liang Qichao believe the Chinese people should adopt Western ideas, traditional Chinese philosophy, or a mix of both?

2. **DETERMINING CENTRAL IDEAS** What does Liang Qichao mean when he says Chinese people should "apply Western methods to the study of our civilization and discover its true character"?



(l)Fillmore, Millard. 1852. Millard Fillmore to the Mikado of Japan, November 13, 1852. Edited by Frank H. Severance. 1907. From Millard Fillmore Papers, Volume X. Buffalo Historical Society; (r)De

SECONDARY SOURCE: AUTOBIOGRAPHY

## COMPARING THE WEST AND THE EAST

Yukichi Fukuzawa (1835–1901), from a low-ranking samurai family in Japan, traveled to the United States and to Europe. He wrote many influential books on how the Japanese could become strong and independent. His autobiography, from 1899, is excerpted below.

> "The final purpose of all my work was to create in Japan a civilized nation as well equipped in the arts of war and peace as those of the Western world. I acted as if I had become the sole functioning agent for the introduction of Western learning. It was natural that I should be disliked by the older type of Japanese as if I were working for the benefit of foreigners. . . .
>
> From my own observations in both [Western] and [Eastern] civilizations, I find that each has certain strong points and weak points. . . . But when I compare the two in a general way as to wealth, **armament**, and the greatest happiness for the greatest number, I have to put the Orient below the Occident. Granted that a nation's destiny depends upon the education of its people, there must be some fundamental differences in the education of Western and Eastern peoples.
>
> In the education of the East, so often saturated with Confucian teaching, I find two things lacking; that is to say, a lack of studies in number and reason in material culture, and a lack of the idea of independence in spiritual culture. But in the West I think I see why their statesmen are successful in managing their national affairs, and the businessmen in theirs. . . .
>
> And I reasoned that Chinese philosophy as the root of education was responsible for our obvious short- comings. . . . And I took every opportunity in public speech, in writing, and in casual conversations, to advocate my doctrine of independence. . . . During my endeavor I came to believe less than ever in the old Chinese teaching."

**ANALYZE THE TEXT**

1. **CITING TEXT EVIDENCE** Cite evidence from the Yukichi Fukuzawa text that supports the idea that he admires Western culture.
2. **ANALYZING IDEAS** What criticisms does Yukichi Fukuzawa have of Eastern society?

### MULTIPLE PERSPECTIVES

1. **COMPARING AND CONTRASTING** Compare and contrast Yukichi Fukuzawa's and Liang Qichao's opinions of Western and Eastern cultures.
2. **ANALYZING IDEAS** How do all three texts show the growing power of Western nations in the East?

# STUDY GUIDE

## THE QING DYNASTY

### LESSON 1

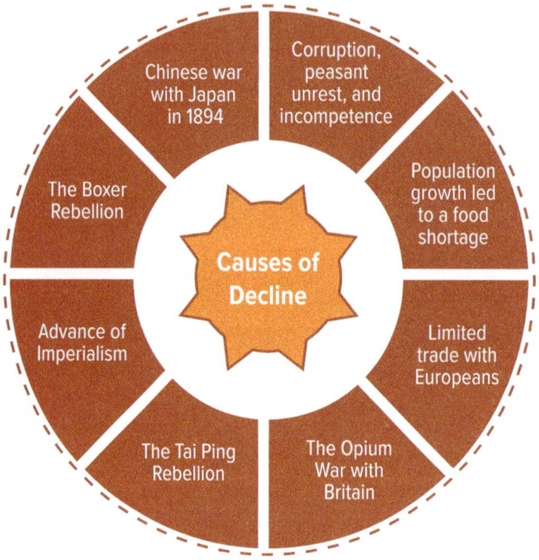


## WESTERN INFLUENCE IN CHINA

### LESSON 2

In the mid-1800s, the Chinese economy went through a period of transition when European traders moved into China in greater numbers. The economy was affected by the West in three ways.

## THE MEIJI RESTORATION

### LESSON 3

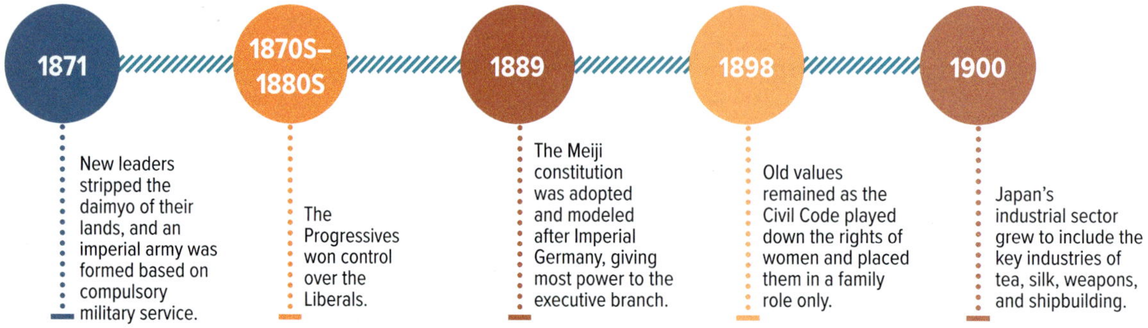

# CHAPTER 7 Assessment

**Directions: On a separate sheet of paper, answer the questions below. Make sure you read carefully and answer all parts of the questions.**

## Short Answer

1. **IDENTIFYING CAUSES** What were the main causes of the first Opium War?

2. **ANALYZING CHANGE** What were the goals of the Tai Ping Rebellion? Why do you think Western nations fought against the rebels?

3. **SUMMARIZING** What events led to the creation of the spheres of influence in China? What nations possessed these spheres of influence?

4. **UNDERSTANDING CONTEXT** Explain the relationship among China, Japan, and Korea during this period.

5. **SUMMARIZING** Why were the Qing reforms after the Boxer Rebellion unsuccessful?

6. **IDENTIFYING EFFECTS** List some of the immediate effects of the fall of the Qing dynasty.

7. **DESCRIBING** How did Western ideas influence Chinese authors?

8. **EXPLAINING EFFECTS** How did the Japanese react to the growing Western influence in East Asia? How was this different from the way the Chinese reacted?

9. **UNDERSTANDING CHANGE** Why did the Meiji government adopt many Western ideas and institutions after overthrowing the shogunate?

10. **CITING TEXT EVIDENCE** Cite evidence from the text showing how Western ideas influenced Japanese art and culture during the Meiji Restoration.

11. **ANALYZING CHANGE** Which Western values inspired Meiji reforms? Which values did the Meiji not copy?

12. **UNDERSTANDING CONTEXT** Why did Western nations want to end Japan's long-held isolationist policy?

## History and Social-Science Analysis

13. **CONSTRUCTING HYPOTHESES** List the nations with spheres of influence in China. Considering how many foreign nations had territory in China, why was the Open Door Policy necessary to prevent future conflicts?

14. **EXPLAINING EFFECTS** What were the effects of European imperialism in Asia and China?

15. **ANALYZING CHANGE** Why did the Japanese change at such a rapid pace during the Meiji Restoration?

16. **SUMMARIZING** What was Sun Yat-sen's vision for reform in China?

## Analyzing Visuals

*Use the image to answer the following questions.*

17. **ANALYZING SOURCES** How does this image depict Japanese culture during the Meiji Restoration?

18. **INTERPRETING** How does the painting show variation in economic status among different groups of people?

**Need Extra Help?**

| If You've Missed Question | 1 | 2 | 3 | 4 | 5 | 6 | 7 | 8 | 9 | 10 | 11 | 12 | 13 | 14 | 15 | 16 | 17 | 18 |
|---|---|---|---|---|---|---|---|---|---|---|---|---|---|---|---|---|---|---|
| Review Lesson | 1 | 1 | 1 | 1 | 2 | 2 | 2 | 2 | 3 | 3 | 3 | 3 | 1 | 2 | 3 | 2 | 3 | 3 |

# Assessment, continued

## Research and Presentation

**19** **INTEGRATING INFORMATION** Using maps, pictures, and quotes as sources, work together with a partner to examine and list the ways in which Japan both rejected and accepted Western influence.

**20** **PRESENTING** Conduct research on Confucianism, and create a presentation that explains some of its key principles and expressions. Explain how Westernized thinking began to change Confucianism. Cite specific evidence in your presentation.

## Reading and Analyzing Primary Sources

Use the document to answer the following questions. In 1868, after ending the shogunate, the Sat-Cho reformers insisted that the new emperor sign the Charter Oath below.

> "Article 1. Deliberative assemblies shall be widely established and all matters decided by public discussion.
>
> Article 2. All classes, high and low, shall unite in vigorously carrying out the administration of the affairs of state.
>
> Article 3. The common people, no less than the civil and military officials, shall each be allowed to pursue his own calling so that there may be no discontent.
>
> Article 4. Evil customs of the past shall be broken off and everything based upon the just laws of Nature.
>
> Article 5. Knowledge shall be sought throughout the world so as to strengthen the foundation of imperial rule."
>
> —Quoted in *East Asia: a New History*

**21** **ANALYZING CENTRAL IDEAS** Which article reflects the abandonment of isolation in Japan under the Meiji Restoration?

**A.** The article about creating assemblies
**B.** The article granting freedom of occupation to all classes
**C.** The article that prescribes abandoning rules not supported by the laws of nature
**D.** The article prescribing seeking knowledge around the world

**22** **DETERMINING CENTRAL IDEAS** What do these articles suggest that Japan should do to change?

**A.** Japan should consider its past for future policy.
**B.** Japan should look at the example of other traditional empires for reform.
**C.** Japan should emulate Western political ideas.
**D.** The emperor alone should decide Japan's future policies.

**23** **ANALYZING CENTRAL IDEAS** After years of isolation, how were other nations likely to react to these articles?

**A.** Many countries likely found these articles beneficial, so they could trade more with Japan.
**B.** Neighboring countries might have worried that Japan would adopt Western imperialism.
**C.** Some nations likely feared that they would not be able to trade with Japan.
**D.** Both A and B

## Writing About History

**24** **EXPLANATORY WRITING** How did Western culture affect China and Japan? How did Chinese and Japanese cultures affect Western nations?

## Speaking and Listening About History

**25** **COMPARING AND CONTRASTING** Using what you learned and additional research, meet in a small group to compare the life of a Chinese farmer in 1800 with the life of a middle-class person 125 years later. How might their beliefs, work, income, and politics differ? Have one member of your group serve as a moderator of the group discussion.

**Need Extra Help?**

| If You've Missed Question | 19 | 20 | 21 | 22 | 23 | 24 | 25 |
|---|---|---|---|---|---|---|---|
| Review Lesson | 3 | 1 | 3 | 3 | 3 | 1–3 | 1 |

McNelly, Theodore. 1963. Contemporary Government of Japan. Houghton Mifflin.

◄ A young French infantryman pauses for a photograph during World War I. In France, the troops of the enemy armies lived in trenches in the ground and faced each other across the barbed wire marking the limits of the narrow, deadly strip known as "no-man's-land."

1914 — 1919

# World War I and the Russian Revolution

## CHAPTER 8



**GO DIGITAL**
*It's All online!*

## ASKING ESSENTIAL QUESTIONS

***Why do politics often lead to war? How can technology impact war?***

**What Will You Learn?** You will learn about the impact of two major events of the 1910s, a war that shook the entire planet and a revolution that toppled the monarch of one of the world's largest empires.

**Why Does this Matter?** In 1914, the monarchies of Europe went to war with one another. France and the United States were the only representative governments among the combatants. By 1918, nearly everything had changed. The monarchies of Russia, Germany, and Austria-Hungary had fallen, and by 1922, the last Ottoman sultan would abdicate. Representative governments rose to take their place. Colonies around the world would feel emboldened to challenge European hegemony. World War I would be the crucible that would transform the old world into a world closer to the one we live in today.

**How Will You Know That You Learned It?** You will be able to identify the causes, major events, and outcome of World War I and of the Russian Revolution.

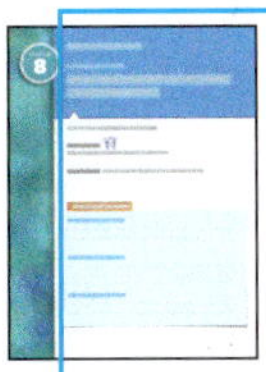

**Using Your Inquiry Journal** As you read this chapter and examine the primary sources, use your Inquiry Journal to help you make notes and expand your list of questions. As you gather information, think about how you will answer the Essential Questions above.

# PLACE & TIME Europe and Russia 1914–1919

In the years before World War I, European powers made use of the industrial innovations of the late nineteenth century to create new weapons. Most European nations also enlarged their armies. In 1882 Germany, Italy, and Austria-Hungary came together in the Triple Alliance, while in 1907 Great Britain, France, and Russia formed the Triple Entente. Retaliation against the 1914 assassination of Francis Ferdinand, Archduke of Austria-Hungary, tested those alliances and eventually drew Europe into World War I.

## STEP INTO THE PLACE

Read the quote and look at the information presented on the map.

1. **RELATING EVENTS** Why did the assassination of Archduke Francis Ferdinand spark World War I?

2. **SPATIAL REASONING** Consider the placement of Germany and Austria-Hungary in Europe. What challenges might this present these nations in a war against France, the United Kingdom, Italy, Russia, Serbia, and Romania?

"A note of genuine regret is that, deprived of the Archduke's strong personality, Austria inevitably will be more subject to German influence. Several journalists express the fear that the consequences will be sufficiently serious again to plunge the Balkans, if not Europe, into a conflict.

Apprehension lest the Sarajevo crime prove a dire blow to the stability of Europe almost overshadows the feeling of horror and reprobation over the assassination and deep sympathy for the aged Emperor in the comments of the morning papers."

—from a special cable from Paris to *The New York Times*, June 29, 1914

## STEP INTO THE TIME

**UNDERSTANDING CHRONOLOGY**

Which two events of 1917 resulted in a turning point in the war?

### EUROPE

**June 1914** Assassination of Archduke Francis Ferdinand sparks World War I

**August 1914** Germany is at war with Russia and France

**1916** Germany engages in unrestricted submarine warfare

**1914 — 1915 — 1916**

### WORLD EVENTS

**August 1914** Japan declares war on Germany

**1915** Ottoman Turks commit genocide against Armenians

**1916** Germans flee Cameroon for Spanish Guinea

## EUROPE 1914

**February-December 1916** German offensive at the Battle of Verdun

**1917** Russian Revolution begins

**December 1917** The peace conference at Brest-Litovsk opens

**1918** Germany agrees to truce

**November 11, 1918** Germany and Allies sign an armistice

**June 1919** Treaty of Versailles signed

**1917** **1918** **1919**

**1917** U.S. enters World War I

**October 1917** Brazil declares war on Germany

**1918** Worldwide influenza epidemic begins

**1919** U.S. president Woodrow Wilson helps form the League of Nations

**1919** Togo becomes a French mandate

## ESSENTIAL QUESTIONS

- *Why do politics often lead to war?*
- *How can technology impact war?*

# THE STORY BEGINS...

LESSON 1

# World War I Begins

During the first decade of the 1900s, aggressive tensions built up in the nations of Europe. The continent seemed ready to erupt into war; the only thing missing was a spark. In 1914, a young Serbian nationalist named Gavrilo Princip provided it when he assassinated the Austro-Hungarian archduke and his wife during a procession. Borijove Jevtic, another Serbian nationalist, was arrested along with Princip and gave this account of the assassination and arrest:

> "The cars sped to the Town Hall and the rest of the conspirators did not interfere with them. After the reception in the Town Hall General Potiorek, the Austrian Commander, pleaded with Francis Ferdinand to leave the city, as it was seething with rebellion. . . Here Princip had taken his stand.
>
> As the car came abreast he stepped forward from the kerb, drew his automatic pistol from his coat and fired two shots. . . [Francis Ferdinand] uttered only one word, 'Sofia' -- a call to his stricken wife. Then his head fell back and he collapsed. He died almost instantly."

—Borijove Jevtic, on the assassination of Francis Ferdinand, 1914

One month later to the day, Austria-Hungary declared war on Serbia. This set off a series of war declarations as these nations' allies entered the fray. Princip, too young to execute by the laws of the region, was put in prison, while Europe and much of the world descended into a kind of war that no one alive had ever seen.

PHOTO:Chronicle/Alamy Stock Photo; TEXT:Jevtic, Borijove. 1914. Quoted in Critical Perspectives on World War I. 2005. Edited by Tamra Orr. New York, NY: The Rosen Publishing Group, Inc.

*The great rivalries across Europe primed the continent for a decisive battle that would sort out the many problems with violence.* ►

| Events Leading to World War I |
|---|
| |
| |
| |
| |
| |

**ANALYZING KEY IDEAS AND DETAILS**

**IDENTIFYING STEPS** Read closely to identify the sequence of events leading to the outbreak of World War I. Record each event in a graphic organizer like this one.

# CAUSES OF THE WAR

GUIDING QUESTION *What factors contributed to the start of World War I?*

Nineteenth-century liberals believed that if European states were organized along national lines, these states would work together and create a peaceful Europe. They were very wrong.

## NATIONALISM, IMPERIALISM, MILITARISM, AND ALLIANCES

The system of nation-states that emerged in Europe in the last half of the nineteenth century led not to cooperation but rather to competition. Each European nation-state regarded itself as subject to no higher interest or authority. Each state was guided by its own self-interests and success. Furthermore, most leaders thought that war was an acceptable way to preserve the power of their national states. These attitudes made war an ever-present possibility.

The imperialist expansion of the last half of the nineteenth century also played a role in the coming of war. The competition for lands abroad, especially in Africa, led to conflict and heightened the existing rivalries among European states.

Nationalism, along with imperialism, had another serious result. Not all ethnic groups had become nations in Europe. Slavic minorities in the Balkans and the Austro-Hungarian Empire still dreamed of their own national states. The Irish in the British Empire and the Poles in the Russian Empire had similar dreams.

Industrialization offered new methods of shipbuilding and the use of iron, steel, and chemicals for new weapons. The growth of mass armies and navies after 1900 heightened tensions in Europe. It was obvious that if war did come, it would be highly destructive.

Most Western countries had established **conscription**, a **military** draft, as a regular practice before 1914. European armies doubled in size between 1890 and 1914. With its 1.3 million men, the Russian army had grown to be the largest. The French and German armies were not far behind, with 900,000 soldiers each. The British, Italian, and Austro-Hungarian armies numbered between 250,000 and 500,000 soldiers each.

Militarism—the aggressive preparation for war—was growing. As armies grew, so did the influence of military leaders. They drew up vast and **complex** plans for quickly mobilizing millions of soldiers and enormous quantities of supplies in the event of war.

**ANALYZING KEY IDEAS AND DETAILS**

1. **DETERMINING CENTRAL IDEAS** What is the central idea of this section, and how does the text present and develop this idea?
2. **CITING TEXT EVIDENCE** What evidence in the text supports the idea that the crisis in the Balkans helped to set the stage for a large scale war?

**DETERMINING MEANING**

The word **conscription** comes from the Latin roots *con-*, which means "together," and *scribere*, which means "to write." How does the origin of the word *conscription* help you to better understand its meaning?

**DETERMINING MEANING**

Read the text of the paragraph that contains the word **military**. As a noun, the word *military* means "the armed forces of a nation." How does this definition help the reader understand how *military* is used as an adjective?

**DETERMINING MEANING**

The word **complex** contains the Latin root *plex-*, which means "to weave." How might knowing the meaning of this root word help a person determine the meaning of *complex*?

Fearing that any changes would cause chaos in the armed forces, military leaders insisted that their plans could not be altered. This left European political leaders with little leeway. In 1914 they had to make decisions for military instead of political reasons.

At the same time, a system of alliances intensified the dangers of militarism. Europe's great powers had been divided into two loose political alliances. Germany, Austria-Hungary, and Italy formed the Triple Alliance in 1882. France, Great Britain, and Russia created the Triple Entente in 1907.

In the early years of the twentieth century, a series of crises tested these alliances. Especially troublesome were the crises in the Balkans between 1908 and 1913. At its height, the Ottoman Empire controlled most of southeastern Europe, parts of the Middle East, and areas of northern Africa. The Treaty of London that ended the First Balkan War in 1913 resulted in the Ottoman Empire losing nearly all its European possessions. Many of the victors, too, disagreed with portions of the treaty. These events left European states angry at each other and eager for revenge. By 1914, the major European states had come to believe that their allies were important. They were willing to use war to preserve their power and the power of their allies.

**GEOGRAPHIC REASONING**

In 1914 Europe was divided into the Triple Alliance and Triple Entente.

1. **SPATIAL THINKING** According to the map, which alliance had more territory?
2. **HUMAN POPULATION** Which alliance had more soldiers?

## ALLIANCES IN EUROPE 1914

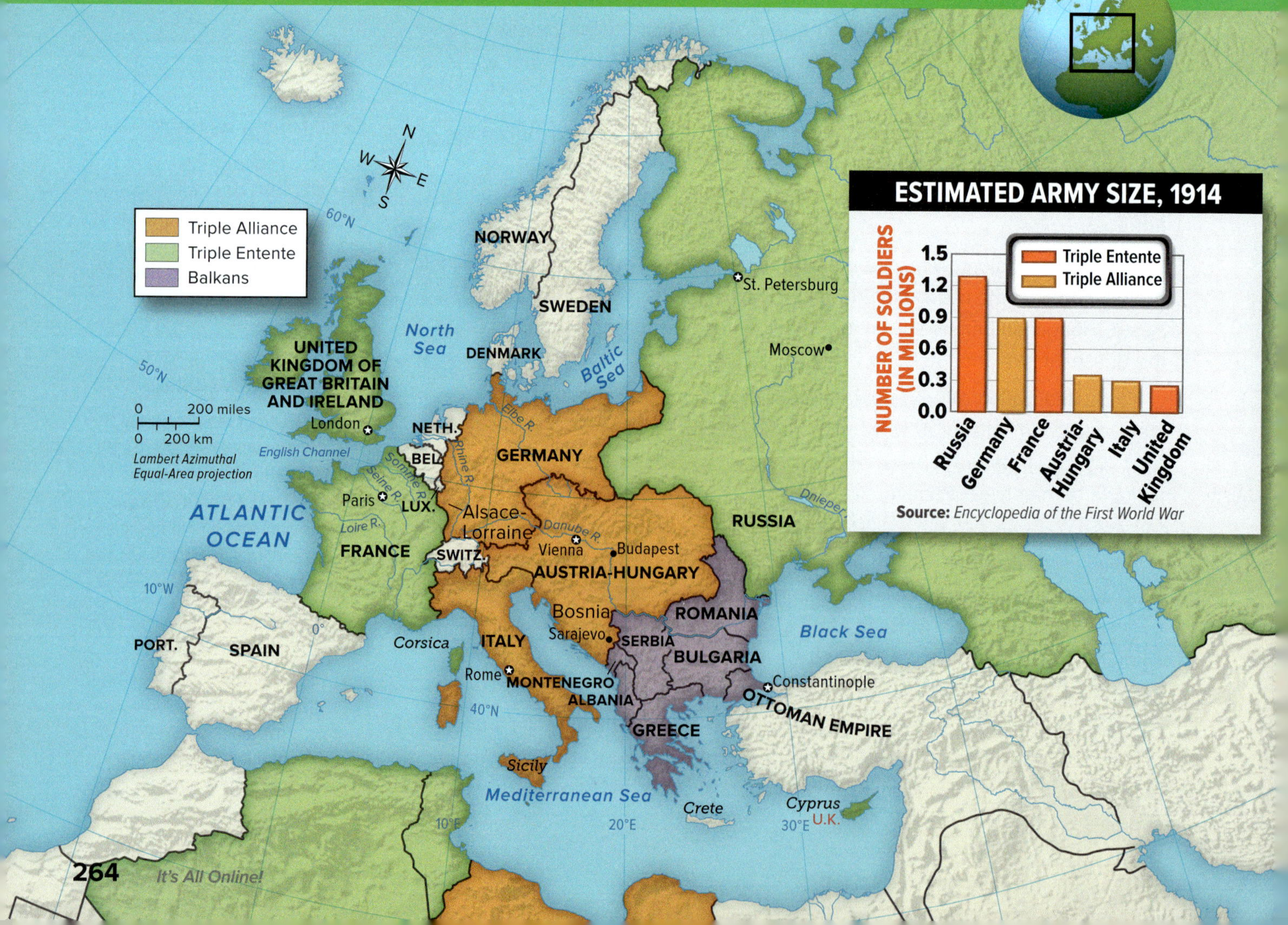

> "Article I. There will be from the date of the exchange of the ratifications of the present treaty, peace and friendship between His Majesty the Emperor of the Ottomans on the one part, and their Majesties the Allied Sovereigns on the other part, as well as between their heirs and successors, their States and respective subjects in perpetuity.
>
> Article II. His Majesty the Emperor of the Ottomans cedes to their Majesties the Allied Sovereigns all the territories of his Empire on the continent of Europe to the west of a line drawn from Enos on the Aegean Sea to Midia on the Black Sea with the exception of Albania. The exact line of the frontier from Enos to Midia will be determined by an international commission. . . .
>
> Article IV: His Majesty the Emperor of the Ottomans declares that he cedes to their Majesties the Allied Sovereigns the Isle of Crete, and that he renounces in their favour all the rights of sovereignty and other rights which he possessed on that Isle."
>
> —Treaty of London, 1913

**ANALYZING PRIMARY SOURCES**

1. **DETERMINING CENTRAL IDEAS** How did the Treaty of London contribute to the disintegration of the Ottoman Empire?
2. **IDENTIFYING CONNECTIONS** How might the Treaty of London have led to anger and resentment in the Ottoman Empire?

### INTERNAL DISSENT

National desires were not the only source of internal strife at the beginning of the twentieth century. Socialist labor movements also had grown more powerful. The Socialists were increasingly inclined to use strikes, even violent ones, to achieve their goals.

Some conservative leaders, alarmed at the increase in labor strife and class division, feared that European nations were on the verge of revolution. European leaders may have seen entry into the war in 1914 as a way to increase patriotism and to divert attention from the discontent at home.

### ✓ CHECKING FOR UNDERSTANDING

1. **IDENTIFYING CAUSES** What factors contributed to the start of World War I?
2. **RELATING EVENTS** How did militarism in Europe threaten peace on the continent?
3. **IDENTIFYING CAUSES** How could internal dissent have contributed to the outbreak of World War I?

## THE OUTBREAK OF WAR

**GUIDING QUESTION** *How did the assassination of Archduke Francis Ferdinand spark the outbreak of war?*

Nationalism and imperialism, militarism and alliances, and the desire to stifle internal dissent might all have played a role in starting World War I. However, it was the decisions that European leaders made in response to a crisis in the Balkans that led directly to the conflict.

### ASSASSINATION IN SARAJEVO AND RESPONSES

By 1914, Serbia, supported by Russia, was determined to create a large independent Slavic state in the Balkans. Austria-Hungary, which had its own Slavic minorities to contend with, was equally determined to prevent that from happening.

**ANALYZING KEY IDEAS AND DETAILS**

1. **CITING TEXT EVIDENCE** This section explains that Serbia had motives other than just seeking justice for the death of the Archduke when it became involved in war with Austria-Hungary. What evidence in the text supports this assertion?
2. **IDENTIFYING STEPS** The text indicates that there were a number of related steps that led to the outbreak of war. What were the steps Austria, Russia, and Germany took following the assassination of the archduke?

Oakes, Sir Augustus and Mowat, R. B. 1916. Select Treaties and Documents - To Illustrate the Development of the Modern European States System 1815-1916. Oxford: The Clarendon Press.

On June 28, 1914, Archduke Francis Ferdinand, the heir to the Hapsburg throne of Austria-Hungary, and his wife Sophia visited the city of Sarajevo (sar • uh • YAY • voh) in Bosnia. A group of conspirators waited there in the streets.

In that group was Gavrilo Princip, a 19-year-old Bosnian Serb. Princip was a member of the Black Hand, a Serbian terrorist organization that wanted Bosnia to be free of Austria-Hungary and to become part of a large Serbian kingdom. An assassination attempt earlier that morning by one of the conspirators had failed. Later that day, however, Princip succeeded in fatally shooting the archduke and his wife.

The Austro-Hungarian government did not know if the Serbian government was directly involved in the archduke's assassination, but it did not care. It saw an opportunity to "render Serbia innocuous once and for all by a display of force," as the Austrian foreign minister put it. Austrian leaders wanted to attack Serbia but feared that Russia would intervene on Serbia's behalf. So, they asked for—and received—the backing of their German allies. Emperor William II of Germany gave Austria-Hungary a "blank check," promising Germany's full support if war broke out between Russia and Austria-Hungary. On July 28, Austria-Hungary declared war on Serbia.

Russia was determined to support Serbia's cause. On July 28, Czar Nicholas II ordered partial mobilization of the Russian army against Austria-Hungary. **Mobilization** is the process of assembling troops and supplies for war. In 1914 mobilization was considered an act of war.

Leaders of the Russian army informed the czar that they could not partially mobilize. Their mobilization plans were based on a war against both Germany and Austria-Hungary. Mobilizing against only the one front of Austria-Hungary, they claimed, would create chaos in the army. Based on this claim, the czar ordered full mobilization of the Russian army on July 29, knowing that Germany would consider this order an act of war.

**DETERMINING MEANING**

The word **mobilization** includes the root *mobile*, which means "movable." How does knowing the meaning of this root word help a reader to better understand the meaning of the word *mobilization*?

*Men marched through the streets of downtown Berlin after receiving news of the call for the mobilization of German troops in World War I.*

**INTERPRETING** Based on the picture, how do you think these Berliners felt about the news they received concerning the mobilization for war?

## THE CONFLICT BROADENS

Indeed, Germany reacted quickly. The German government warned Russia that it must halt its mobilization within 12 hours. When Russia ignored this warning, Germany declared war on Russia on August 1.

Like the Russians, the Germans had a military plan. General Alfred von Schlieffen (SHLEE • fuhn) had helped draw up the plan, which was known as the Schlieffen Plan. It called for a two-front war with France and Russia because the two had formed a military alliance in 1894.

According to the Schlieffen Plan, Germany would conduct a small holding action against Russia while most of the German army would carry out a rapid invasion of France. This meant invading France by moving quickly along the level coastal area through Belgium. After France was defeated, the German invaders would move to the east against Russia.

Under the Schlieffen Plan, Germany could not mobilize its troops solely against Russia. Therefore, it declared war on France on August 3. At about the same time, it issued an ultimatum to Belgium demanding that German troops be allowed to pass through Belgian territory. Belgium, however, was a neutral nation.

On August 4, Great Britain declared war on Germany, officially for violating Belgian neutrality. In fact, Britain, which was allied with France and Russia, was concerned about maintaining its own world power. As one British diplomat put it, if Germany and Austria-Hungary won the war, "what would be the position of a friendless England?" By August 4, all the great powers of Europe were at war.

*The Schlieffen Plan had German troops attack France by quickly moving through Belgium.*

**EXPLORING REGIONS** What impact did the Schlieffen Plan have on the conflict in Europe?

### ✓ CHECKING FOR UNDERSTANDING

1. **EXPLAINING CAUSES** How did the assassination of Archduke Francis Ferdinand spark the outbreak of war?
2. **DETERMINING CONTEXT** What prompted Russia to enter the war in 1914?
3. **SUMMARIZING** How did the Schlieffen Plan impact the beginning of the war?

## LESSON 1 REVIEW

### Time and Place

1. **IDENTIFYING CONNECTIONS** What was the connection between nationalism and imperialism in early twentieth-century Europe?

### Building History-Social Science Analysis Skills

2. **UNDERSTANDING CONTEXT** How did alliances among European nation-states help lead to the start of World War I?
3. **EXPLAINING CAUSE AND EFFECT** What effect did the rise of nationalism in Europe have on the continent's stability?
4. **IDENTIFYING CAUSES** Describe the motivation behind the assassination of Archduke Francis Ferdinand. Was it done with the desire of starting a war?

### Writing About History

5. **NARRATIVE WRITING** Imagine you are a citizen of Germany. You have been reading the newspapers daily since the assassination of Francis Ferdinand, archduke of Austria. Write two or more journal entries on different days between the assassination on June 28, 1914, and August 4, 1914, reflecting on the events.

### Collaborating

6. **EVALUATING POINT OF VIEW** Break into two groups, one representing Serbia, the other representing Austria-Hungary. Debate reasons for and against the creation of an independent Slavic state in the Balkans.

## ESSENTIAL QUESTIONS

- *Why do politics often lead to war?*
- *How can technology impact war?*

LESSON 2

# World War I

## THE STORY BEGINS...

Young men across Europe, from London to St. Petersburg, greeted the arrival of war with great excitement. Many believed that this was an opportunity to demonstrate heroism on the battlefield and to bring honor to their nations. But as these men who became soldiers discovered the reality of the trenches, their dreams of glory turned into nightmares. Consider the description this British soldier sent his mother in a letter the year the war began:

> "The soldiers at the front need more rest. While in the trenches the water is over our knees most of the time. The war is going to last some time yet, and might be another twelve months before it is over. The war has only just begun and its going to be a war of exhaustion. After the regular armies have done their work it means that all the young lads at home being trained and disciplined and will take our place in the field. The sooner people understand this, the better, it will be for the nation."
>
> —letter from Private H. F. Leppard, December 19, 1914

The soldier's assessment would prove an understatement. The war would drag on in stalemate for several more years.

*Soldiers fighting in trenches across Europe lived in horrible conditions with mud floors, open skies. They were tormented by rats and fleas.* ▶

PHOTO:Neurdein/Roger Viollet/Getty Images; TEXT:Leppard, Private H. F. 1914.

| | Allied Powers | Central Powers |
|---|---|---|
| Pre-war name | | |
| Original members | | |
| Later additions | | |

**ANALYZING KEY IDEAS AND DETAILS**

**SUMMARIZING** Read closely to identify how alliances shifted during World War I. Record each shift in a graphic organizer like this one.

# 1914 TO 1915: ILLUSIONS AND STALEMATE

**GUIDING QUESTION** *How did the war on the Eastern Front differ from war on the Western Front?*

Before 1914, many political leaders believed war to be impractical because it involved so many political and economic risks. Others believed that their countries' diplomats could easily prevent war. In August 1914, both ideas were shattered. However, the new illusions that replaced them soon proved to be equally foolish.

Government **propaganda**—ideas that are spread to influence public opinion for or against a cause—had stirred national hatreds before the war. Now, in August 1914, the urgent pleas of European governments for defense against aggressors encouraged the civilian population to support total war. Most people seemed genuinely convinced that their nations' causes were right and just. By contrast, they also came to believe that the nations they opposed were wholly evil.

A new set of illusions also fed the enthusiasm for war. In August 1914, almost everyone believed the war would be over in a few weeks. After all, almost all European wars since 1815 had, in fact, ended in a matter of weeks. The soldiers who boarded the trains for the war front in August 1914 and the jubilant citizens who saw them off believed the warriors would be home by Christmas.

**UNDERSTANDING CRAFT AND STRUCTURE**

1. **ANALYZING TEXT PRESENTATION** How does the text present the information about conflict in Europe between 1914 and 1915? Why is this helpful?
2. **DETERMINING MEANING** Reread the first paragraph. Which words set the tone of this section? What is that tone?

**DETERMINING MEANING**

Read the text of the paragraph that contains the word **propaganda**. Consider that this word has the same root as *propagate*, which means "to multiply or transmit." How does the word *propaganda* as it is used in this lesson reflect this?

## THE WESTERN FRONT

German hopes for a quick end to the war rested on a military gamble. German plans for a war with both France and Russia—Otto von Bismarck's dreaded war on two fronts—hoped for an early defeat of France. The plan for France's defeat, called the Schlieffen Plan, called for the German army to make a vast encircling movement through Belgium into northern France. According to the plan, the German forces would sweep around Paris. This plan would allow the German army to avoid the forts on their border with France and to move their army into the broad plains of Belgium. Doing so would give them room to maneuver their army and to surround most of the French forces.

However, the German advance was halted a short distance from Paris at the First Battle of the Marne, which took place on September 5th through September 12th in 1914. Scrambling to stop the advancing Germans, French military leaders loaded 2,000 Parisian taxicabs with fresh troops and sent them to the front line.

**DETERMINING MEANING**

The word **trench** means "a deep furrow, ditch, or cut." From this definition, how might one describe *trench warfare*?

The war quickly turned into a stalemate as neither the Germans nor the French could dislodge each other from the trenches they had dug for shelter. Two lines of trenches soon reached from the English Channel to the frontiers of Switzerland. The Western Front had become bogged down in **trench warfare**. For three years, the Western Front moved only about three miles per year in any one direction.

**GEOGRAPHIC REASONING**

World War I took place along two main fronts.

1. **SPATIAL THINKING** What can be assumed about the course of the war from the dates of the victories of the Allied and Central Powers?
2. **HUMAN-ENVIRONMENT INTERACTION** Why does the farthest advance of the Allied and Central Powers change more on the Eastern Front than the Western Front?

## THE EASTERN FRONT

Unlike the Western Front, front lines covered a great distance and on the Eastern Front were marked by mobility. The cost in lives, however, was equally enormous. At the beginning of the war, the Russian army moved into eastern Germany but was decisively defeated at the Battle of Tannenberg on August 30. They were defeated again at the Battle of Masurian Lakes on September 15. After these defeats, the Russians were no longer seen as a serious threat to Germany.

Austria-Hungary, Germany's ally, fared less well at first. The Austrians had been defeated by the Russians in Galicia and thrown out of Serbia as well. To make matters worse, the Italians betrayed their German and Austrian allies in the Triple Alliance by attacking Austria in May 1915. Italy thus joined France, Great Britain, and Russia, who had previously been known as the Triple Entente but now were called the Allied Powers, or Allies.

**WORLD WAR I IN EUROPE 1914–1918**

By this time, the Germans had come to the aid of the Austrians. A German-Austrian army defeated the Russian army in Galicia and pushed the Russians far back into their own territory. Russian casualties stood at 2.5 million killed, captured, or wounded. The Russians were almost knocked out of the war.

Encouraged by their success against Russia, Germany and Austria-Hungary, joined by Bulgaria in September 1915, attacked and eliminated Serbia from the war. Their successes in the east would enable the German troops to move back to the offensive in the west.

A boy delivers a newspaper to men living in the trenches during World War I.

### ✓ CHECKING FOR UNDERSTANDING

1. **RELATING EVENTS** How did the war on the Eastern Front differ from war on the Western Front?
2. **UNDERSTANDING CONTEXT** Why was it believed the war would come to a close by the end of 1914?
3. **SUMMARIZING** Which side was ahead in the war at the end of 1915?

## TRENCH AND AIR WARFARE

**GUIDING QUESTION** *What made World War I more devastating than any previous wars?*

**SUMMARIZING** How was trench warfare different from previous forms of warfare?

On the Western Front, the trenches dug in 1914 had by 1916 become elaborate systems of defense. The Germans and the French each had hundreds of miles of trenches, which were protected by barbed-wire entanglements up to 5 feet (about 1.5 m) high and 30 yards (about 27 m) wide. Concrete machine-gun nests and other gun batteries, supported farther back by heavy artillery, protected the trenches. Troops lived in holes in the ground, separated from each other by a strip of territory known as no-man's-land.

Trench warfare baffled military leaders who had been trained to fight wars of movement and maneuver. At times, the high command on either side would order an offensive that would begin with an artillery barrage to flatten the enemy's barbed wire and to leave them in a state of shock. After "softening up" the enemy in this fashion, a mass of soldiers would climb out of their trenches with fixed bayonets and hope to work their way toward the enemy trenches.

The attacks rarely worked because men advancing unprotected across open fields could be fired at by the enemy's machine guns. In 1916 and 1917, millions of young men died in the search for the elusive breakthrough. In just 10 months at Verdun, France, 700,000 men lost their lives over a few miles of land. World War I had turned into a **war of attrition**, a war based on wearing down the other side with constant attacks and heavy losses. Machine guns, along with other technological advancements such as poison gas, aircraft, and high explosives, allowed for destruction of human life on a scale that was previously unknown.

**ANALYZING KEY IDEAS AND DETAILS**

1. **DETERMINING CENTRAL IDEAS** What is the central idea of this section? Write a brief summary of this section in your own words.
2. **ANALYZING IDEAS** What clues does the word *baffled* give the reader about the challenges of fighting World War I?

**DETERMINING MEANING**

The word **attrition** means "the process of wearing down." Based on this information, what would be the characteristics of a *war of attrition*?

Trench warfare created dangerous conditions for soldiers even out of combat. Rainfall could quickly fill a trench with water and mud. Soldiers standing in these cold, damp trenches for long periods of time often contracted a medical condition called "trench foot" that would require the amputation of the infected limb. Snowfall, too, brought deadly cold to trenches and resulted in many soldiers contracting frostbite. Deaths and injuries resulting from such conditions often proved just as harmful to most soldiers as did bullets and artillery shells. British poet Wilfred Owen wrote about the experience:

> "Bent double, like old beggars under sacks,
> Knock-kneed, coughing like hags, we cursed through sludge,
> Till on the haunting flares we turned our backs,
> And towards our distant rest began to trudge.
> Men marched asleep. Many had lost their boots,
> But limped on, blood-shod. All went lame; all blind;
> Drunk with fatigue; deaf even to the hoots
> Of gas-shells dropping softly behind.
>
> Gas! GAS! Quick, boys!—An ecstasy of fumbling
> Fitting the clumsy helmets just in time,
> But someone still was yelling out and stumbling
> And flound'ring like a man in fire or lime.—
> Dim through the misty panes and thick green light,
> As under a green sea, I saw him drowning."

—Wilfred Owen, *"Dulce et Decorum Est,"* 1917

**ANALYZING PRIMARY SOURCES**

1. **ANALYZING CENTRAL IDEAS** What is Owen writing about in this poem?
2. **ANALYZING THEMES** What view of war is Owen presenting in this poem?

## THE BIRTH OF AIR WARFARE

By the end of 1915, airplanes appeared on the battlefront for the first time in history. Planes were first used to spot the enemy's position. Soon, planes also began to attack ground **targets**, especially enemy communications. Fights for control of the air space occurred and then increased over time. At first, pilots fired at each other with handheld pistols. Later, machine guns were mounted on the noses of planes, which made the skies considerably more dangerous.

The Germans also used their giant airships—known as zeppelins—to bomb London and eastern England. Inaccurate and imprecise, these bombing campaigns caused little damage but frightened many people. Germany's enemies, however, soon found that zeppelins, which were filled with highly flammable hydrogen gas, quickly became raging infernos when hit by the fire of antiaircraft guns.

### ✓ CHECKING FOR UNDERSTANDING

1. **DETERMINING CONTEXT** What made World War I more devastating than previous wars?
2. **DETERMINING CONTEXT** Why is World War I described as a "war of attrition"?
3. **SUMMARIZING** How were airplanes first used in World War I?

# A WORLD WAR

**GUIDING QUESTION** *Why did the war widen to become a world conflict?*

Because of the stalemate on the Western Front, both sides sought to gain new allies. Each side hoped new allies would provide a winning advantage, as well as a new source of money and war goods.

## WIDENING OF THE WAR

Bulgaria entered the war on the side of the Central Powers, as Germany, Austria-Hungary, and the Ottoman Empire were called. Russia, Great Britain, and France—the Allied Powers—declared war on the Ottoman Empire. The Allies tried to open a Balkan front by landing forces at the Gallipoli (guh • LIH • puh • lee) Peninsula, southwest of Constantinople, in April 1915. Ultimately the rugged terrain of the peninsula proved treacherous for Allied forces. The front opened up by the Allies was also very small, which gave Ottoman troops an advantage. Ultimately, the campaign was a disaster, and the Allies withdrew.

By 1917, the war had truly become a world conflict. While stationed in the Middle East in 1917, a British officer known as Lawrence of Arabia urged Arab princes to revolt against their Ottoman overlords. In 1918 British forces from Egypt mobilized troops from India, Australia, and New Zealand and worked to destroy the Ottoman Empire in the Middle East. Keeping the Suez Canal open and in British hands was essential for transporting troops from these areas to the front. The Middle East would become another broad front in the war.

Africa, too, became another theater in the war. British, French, Italian, Belgian, and Portuguese colonial forces clashed with German forces in the last contest for control of Africa. Africa's tropical and desert climates and terrain made traditional European warfare here difficult. Waterways proved crucial for quickly moving troops. The Allies also took advantage of Germany's preoccupations in Europe and lack of naval strength to seize German colonies in the rest of the world. Japan, a British ally beginning in 1902, seized a number of German-held islands in the Pacific. Australia seized German New Guinea.

## THE ARMENIAN GENOCIDE

During the war, the Ottoman Turks further alienated the Allies with their policies toward minority subjects, especially the Armenians. The Armenians are an ethnic group whose historic homeland is in what is now eastern Turkey. At the time, the Christian Armenian minority had been pressing the Ottoman government for years to make reforms giving the Armenian people rights and protections. The Ottoman government refused and in 1915 accused the Armenians of supporting the Russians in the war. The Ottoman government then used those allegations to begin a **genocide** of the Armenian people. A genocide is the deliberate mass murder of a particular racial, political, or cultural group.

The Ottomans arrested Armenian community, political, and intellectual leaders and sent most to their deaths. The Ottoman government seized Armenian private property and land. Armenian men, women, and children were forced into concentration camps. Many Armenian men were also sent to work camps where they were forced to work until they died of exhaustion. Many were simply murdered. The remaining Armenians were deported. More than 500,000

**ANALYZING KEY IDEAS AND DETAILS**

1. **ANALYZING CENTRAL IDEAS** What is the central idea of the subsection "Widening of the War"? How does the title of this subsection reflect the central idea?
2. **CITING TEXT EVIDENCE** What evidence in the text supports the idea that in 1915, Germany did not want to engage in war with the United States?

**MAKING CONNECTIONS TO PERSPECTIVES**

### HUMAN RIGHTS IN A TIME OF WAR

Today, most countries disapprove of actions in wartime that violate human rights. Such actions, however, were common during World War I. For instance, many citizens who openly opposed their country's entry into the war were imprisoned or silenced. Rights such as freedom of speech were limited in many cases for fear of dampening patriotism. Many countries also limited the rights of residents who were from or had family ties to enemy nations. For instance, many German-born residents of the United States were required to register with the government. A little more than 2,000 were placed into internment camps for the duration of the war. A similar action would occur in the United States during World War II with people of Japanese heritage. In that specific case, many of those forcibly placed into internment camps were American citizens.

**ANALYZING TEXT** Based on the text, what reasons did countries give for limiting freedom of speech during wartime?

innocent people were forced into exile during the period from 1915 to 1923. Sent through the desert and swamps of Syria and Mesopotamia, 400,000 died on this death march. Along the way, many were raped, tortured, or forced into starvation. Still others were kidnapped and forced to adopt Turkish customs and practice Islam against their will. One eyewitness to the deportation in 1915 said:

> "[She] saw vultures hovering over children who had fallen dead by the roadside. She saw beings crawling along, maimed, starving and begging for bread. . . . [S]he passed soldiers driving before them . . . whole families, men, women and children, shrieking, pleading, wailing . . . setting out for exile into the desert from which there was no return."
>
> —Anita Engle, from *The Nili Spies*

Between 1915 and 1923, more than 1.5 million Armenians, more than half of their population, were murdered. Russia, France, and Britain denounced the Turkish actions as being "crimes against humanity and civilization." Because of the war, however, the killings continued.

## ENTRY OF THE UNITED STATES

At first, the United States tried to remain neutral, but as the war dragged on, it became more difficult to do so. The immediate cause of the United States involvement grew out of the naval war between Germany and Great Britain.

Britain had used its superior navy to set up a blockade of Germany. The blockade kept war materials and other goods from reaching Germany by sea. Germany, in turn, set up its own blockade of Britain and enforced it with the use of **unrestricted** submarine warfare, including the sinking of passenger liners.

**DETERMINING MEANING**

The word **unrestricted** comes from the Latin word *restrictus*, which means "bound," and the root *un-*, which means "not." How does the origin of the word *unrestricted* help you better understand its meaning?

On May 7, 1915, German forces sank the British ship *Lusitania*. About 1,100 civilians, including more than 100 Americans, died. After strong protests from the United States, the German government suspended unrestricted submarine warfare in September 1915 to avoid antagonizing the United States further. Only once did the Germans and British engage in direct naval battle—at the Battle of Jutland on May 31, 1916; neither side won a conclusive victory.

*The sinking of the* Lusitania *made the front page of the* New York Herald. *Germany claimed the British passenger ship was a fair target because it carried 173 tons of ammunitions as cargo.*

**ANALYZING EVENTS** How did the sinking of the *Lusitania* help bring the United States into the war?

THE NEW YORK HERALD.

THE LUSITANIA IS SUNK; 1,000 PROBABLY ARE LOST

GERMANS TORPEDO THE GIANT STEAMSHIP AND SHE FOUNDERS EIGHT MILES FROM IRISH COAST

RESCUE VESSELS SPEED TO THE SCENE TO PICK UP SURVIVORS; ONLY 500 ARE ACCOUNTED FOR

George A. Kessler One of Those Saved, Cable Message to Cunard Office Says

By January 1917, however, the Germans were eager to break the deadlock in the war. German naval officers convinced Emperor William II that resuming the use of unrestricted submarine warfare could starve the British into submission within six months. When the emperor expressed concern about the United States, German Admiral Holtzendorf assured him: "I give your Majesty my word as an officer that not one American will land on the continent."

The German naval officers were quite wrong. The British were not forced to surrender. Further, the escalating human rights violations, including the German targeting of neutral vessels, rising civilian casualties, and the use of chemical weapons, helped bring the United States into the war in April 1917. U.S. troops did not arrive in large numbers in Europe until 1918. However, the entry of the United States into the war gave the Allied Powers a psychological boost and a major new source of money and war goods.

### ✓ CHECKING FOR UNDERSTANDING

1. **EXPLAINING CAUSE AND EFFECT** Why did the war widen to become a world conflict?
2. **EXPLAINING ISSUES** Why was the sinking of the *Lusitania* a major turning point in the war?
3. **SUMMARIZING** Summarize the events that led up to the Armenian Genocide.

# THE IMPACT OF TOTAL WAR

**GUIDING QUESTION** *What was the impact of total war?*

As World War I dragged on, it became a **total war**. Railways and modern naval ships transported soldiers from across the world to front lines far from their homelands. The use of industrial technology and scientific advancements mechanized warfare, which required the use of all available resources. The lives of all citizens in the warring countries, however far from the battlefields, were also affected. The home front was rapidly becoming a cause for as much effort as the war front.

## INCREASED GOVERNMENT POWERS

Most people had expected the war to be short. Little thought had been given to long-term wartime needs. Governments had to respond quickly, however, when the new war machines failed to achieve their goals. Many more men and supplies were needed to continue the war effort. To meet these needs, governments expanded their powers. Countries drafted tens of millions of young men, hoping for that elusive breakthrough to victory.

Wartime governments throughout Europe also expanded their power over their economies. Free-market capitalistic systems were temporarily put aside. Governments set up price, wage, and rent controls. They also rationed food supplies and materials, regulated imports and exports, and took over transportation systems and industries. In effect, to mobilize all the resources of their nations for the war effort, European nations set up **planned economies**.

As a result of total war mobilization, the differences between soldiers at war and civilians at home were narrowed. In the view of political leaders, all citizens were part of a national army that was dedicated to victory. Woodrow Wilson, president of the United States, said that the men and women "who remain to till the soil and man the factories are no less a part of the army than the men beneath the battle flags."

## MANIPULATION OF PUBLIC OPINION

Both military and civilian casualties resulted from a war that had many fronts, which helped weaken the patriotic enthusiasm that marked the early stages of the war. By 1916, signs indicated that civilian morale was beginning to crack. War governments, however, fought back against growing opposition to the war.

Authoritarian regimes, such as those of Germany, Russia, and Austria-Hungary, relied on force to subdue their populations. With the pressures of the war, however, even democratic states expanded their police powers to stop internal dissent. The British Parliament, for example, passed the Defence of the Realm Act (DORA). It allowed the government to arrest protesters as traitors. Newspapers were censored, and sometimes publication was suspended.

Wartime governments made active use of propaganda to increase enthusiasm for the war. As the war progressed and morale sagged, governments were forced to devise new techniques for motivating citizens.

**UNDERSTANDING CRAFT AND STRUCTURE**

1. **ANALYZING TEXT** How is the information in this section of the text organized?
2. **ANALYZING TEXT PRESENTATION** In what order does the writer present facts in the section "Total War and Society"? How does this shape the tone of the section?

*This British recruiting poster is an example of wartime propaganda.*

**ANALYZING IDEAS** What is the message of this poster, and how might it have encouraged support for the war?

CITIZENSHIP

## CIVIC DUTY IN TIMES OF EMERGENCY

The contributions of a nation's citizens during times of major upheaval, such as war or natural disaster, can often be the deciding factor as to how well that nation overcomes the challenge. This was the case on the home front of the United States during World War I. For instance, citizens grew produce in "victory gardens" on both public and private land to reduce pressure on the national food supply. This practice of civic duty remains a powerful motivator today, even outside the pressures of "total war." The ideals of patriotism, community and cooperation have spurred citizens to donate time, energy and resources during emergencies such as Hurricane Katrina in 2005. People from around the country sent resources or traveled to Louisiana, donating blood and mucking out storm-ravaged houses. When wildfires destroyed hundreds of thousands of acres in Kansas and Oklahoma in 2017, Midwestern farmers brought hay bales to feed surviving animals. In many cases, that feeling of civic duty is what drove them to take action.

## TOTAL WAR AND SOCIETY

By 1918, 16 million military personnel and civilians had died and millions more returned home wounded. In the fall of 1918, a deadly influenza struck, adding to the horrors of World War I. Probably spread by soldiers returning from the front, influenza became the deadliest epidemic in history. An estimated total of 50 million people died worldwide.

Total war also had a significant impact on European society. World War I created new roles for women. Because so many men left to fight at the front, women were asked to take over jobs that were not available to them before. Women found themselves employed in jobs that once were considered beyond their capacity. These jobs included civilian occupations such as chimney sweeps, truck drivers, farm laborers, and factory workers in heavy industry. For example, 38 percent of the workers in the Krupp Armaments works in Germany in 1918 were women.

The place of women in the workforce was far from secure, however. Both men and women seemed to expect that many of the new jobs for women were only temporary.

(t)Ken Hawkins/Alamy Stock Photo; (b)Library of Congress Prints and Photographs Division

*Heavy conscription in most combatant states resulted in labor shortages.*

At the end of the war, as men returned to the job market, governments quickly removed women from the jobs they were encouraged to take earlier. By 1919, 650,000 women in Great Britain were unemployed. Wages for the women who were still employed were lowered.

Nevertheless, in some countries, the roles women played in wartime economies had a positive impact on the women's movement for social and political emancipation. The most obvious gain was the right to vote, which was given to women in Germany, Austria, and the United States immediately after the war. British women over the age of 30 gained the right to vote, together with the right to stand for Parliament, in 1918.

Many upper- and middle-class women also gained new freedoms. In ever-increasing numbers, young women from these groups took jobs, lived in their own apartments, and relished their new independence.

**DETERMINING MEANING**

The prefix *dis* comes from Latin and means "apart" or "away." How does the meaning of this prefix help you better understand the meaning of the word "**displaced**"?

## FRONT LINE POPULATION DISPLACEMENT

During the course of the war, millions of civilians would be **displaced** from their homes due to the fighting. French and Belgian citizens along the Western Front, and German, Russian, Polish, and Serbian citizens, among others on the Eastern Front, would become refugees due to their homelands being turned into war zones. Many of these refugees would return home after the front lines had moved or the war came to a close. Some of these refugees, however, would not survive their ordeal.

### ✓ CHECKING FOR UNDERSTANDING

1. **IDENTIFYING EFFECTS** What was the impact of total war?
2. **EXPLAINING ISSUES** How was the concept of freedom of speech compromised in democratic countries during World War I?
3. **UNDERSTANDING CONTEXT** Why did some European countries set up planned economies during World War I?

## LESSON 2 REVIEW

### Time and Place

1. **UNDERSTANDING CONTEXT** How did European governments' power expand as a result of World War I?

### Building History-Social Science Analysis Skills

2. **DETERMINING CONTEXT** How was propaganda used by European governments before and during World War I?
3. **SUMMARIZING** Describe the steps that resulted in the development of trench warfare.
4. **EXPLAINING EFFECTS** What impact did the war have on the movement of populations?

### Writing About History

5. **EXPLANATORY WRITING** Write a paragraph discussing the role women played in World War I.

### Collaborating

6. **PRESENTING** Working as a group, come up with a clear and concise argument as to why the United States should have entered World War I (or why it should not have done so). Present your argument to the class, asking them to decide whether they agree with your group.

POINTS OF VIEW

# Who Caused World War I?

Immediately after World War I, historians began to assess which nation was most responsible for beginning the war. As these two selections from American historian Harry Elmer Barnes and German historian Fritz Fischer show, opinions have varied considerably.

"The Russian general mobilization, undertaken with full **connivance** of the French, was ordered at a time when diplomatic negotiations were moving rapidly toward a satisfactory settlement of the major problems in the crisis. Hence, the Russian general mobilization not only initiated military hostilities, but was also the sole reason for the failure of diplomatic efforts.

England was for peace provided France was not drawn into the conflict, but was determined to come into the War in case France was involved. As France decided from the beginning to stand with Russia for war, and as England refused to attempt to restrain either France or Russia, England was **inevitably** drawn away from her encouragement of the German efforts towards a diplomatic settlement of the crisis and into the support of the military aggression of France and Russia. . . .

In estimating the order of guilt of the various countries we may safely say that the only direct and immediate responsibility for the World War falls upon Serbia, France and Russia, with the guilt about equally distributed. Next in order-far below France and Russia-would come Austria, though she never desired a general European war. Finally, we should place Germany and England as tied for last place, both being opposed to war in the 1914 crisis. Probably the German public was somewhat more favorable to military activities than the English people, but, as we have amply explained above, the Kaiser made much more **strenuous** efforts to preserve the peace of Europe in 1914 than did Sir Edward Grey."

—Harry Elmer Barnes, *The Genesis of the World War*, 1927

**VOCABULARY**

*connivance:* willingness to secretly allow

*inevitably:* unavoidably

*strenuous:* requiring or using great effort

Barnes, Harry Elmer. 1927. The Genesis of the World War: An Introduction to the Problem of War Guilt. New York & London: Alfred A. Knopf.

“It is, however, not the purpose of this work to enter into the familiar controversy, on which whole libraries have been written, over the question of war guilt, to discuss exhaustively the responsibility of the individual statesmen and soldiers of all the European powers concerned, or to pass final judgment on them. We are concerned solely with the German leaders' objectives and with the policy actually followed by them in the July crisis, and that only in so far as their policy throws light on the **postulates** and origins of Germany's war aims.

It must be repeated: given the tenseness of the world situation in 1914-a condition for which Germany's world policy, which had already led to three dangerous crises (those of 1905, 1908 and 1911), was in no small measure responsible . . . . As Germany willed and coveted the Austro-Serbian war and, in her confidence in her military superiority, deliberately faced the risk of a conflict with Russia and France, her leaders must bear a substantial share of the historical responsibility for the outbreak of general war in 1914. This responsibility is not **diminished** by the fact that at the last moment Germany tried to arrest the march of destiny, for her efforts to influence Vienna were due exclusively to the threat of British intervention and, even so, they were half-hearted, **belated** and immediately revoked.”

—Fritz Fischer, *Germany's Aims in the First World War*, 1961

---

**VOCABULARY**

*postulates:* things suggested or assumed as true as the basis for discussion

*diminished:* made smaller or less

*belated:* coming or happening later than should have been the case

## What Do YOU Think?

1. **DETERMINING CENTRAL IDEAS** Which single sentence in Barnes's short history of the origins of the war most clearly states his central thesis?

2. **ANALYZING IDEAS** The Fischer excerpt notes, “It must be repeated: given the tenseness of the world situation in 1914 – a condition for which Germany's world policy, which had already led to three dangerous crises (those of 1905, 1908 and 1911), was in no small measure responsible. . . .” What does this sentence suggest about the evidence Fischer will likely use to support his claim about Germany's culpability?

3. **EXPLAINING ISSUES** Considering the details in each excerpt, what do both historians agree upon as to the larger context of the origins of the war?

4. **DIFFERENTIATING** How are these two historians' interpretations of Germany's role in the outbreak of World War I different? Support your answer by citing evidence from both excerpts.

5. **EVALUATING EVIDENCE** Based on the evidence in the text, whose opinion is better supported—Barnes's or Fischer's?

Fischer, Fritz. 1961. Germany's Aims in the First World War. New York: W. W. Norton & Company, Inc.

ESSENTIAL QUESTIONS

- *Why do politics often lead to war?*
- *How can technology impact war?*

LESSON 3

# The Russian Revolution

## THE STORY BEGINS...

The Romanov dynasty, which had ruled Russia for three centuries, fell from power in 1917 when Czar Nicholas II was forced to abdicate. Upon stepping down from the throne, Russia's last czar made the following statement:

> "By the Grace of God, We, Nicholas II, Emperor of All the Russias, Tzar of Poland, Grand Duke of Finland, etc., etc., make known to all our loyal subjects:
>
> In the days of the great struggle with the external enemy who for the last three years has been striving to enslave our country, it has pleased God to send to Russia a new and painful trial. Internal troubles threaten to have a fatal effect on the outcome of this hard-fought war. The destinies of Russia, the honor of our heroic army, the happiness of the people, the whole future of our dear country, demand that at any cost the war should be carried to a victorious close.
>
> Our bitter enemy has shot his bolt and the moment is near when our valiant army, in concert with our glorious allies, will finally crush him...
>
> May the Lord God help Russia."

—*Abdication of Nicholas II,* March 15, 1917

The collapse of the Russian monarchy would create a power vacuum that would be filled by Vladimir Lenin and the Bolsheviks.

*The worker struggle within Russia combined with the pressure of World War I brought about a powerful transformative revolution in Russia.* ▶

| Events |
| --- |
| |
| |
| |

**ANALYZING KEY IDEAS AND DETAILS**

**IDENTIFYING STEPS** Read closely to identify the events that led to Lenin's rise to power in 1917. Record each event in a graphic organizer like this one.

## BACKGROUND TO REVOLUTION

**GUIDING QUESTION** *What factors and events led to the Russian Revolution?*

After its defeat by Japan in 1905 and the Revolution of 1905, Russia was unprepared militarily and technologically for the total war of World War I. Russia had no competent military leaders. Even worse, Czar Nicholas II insisted on taking personal charge of the armed forces despite his lack of ability and training.

In addition, Russian industry was unable to produce the weapons needed for the army. Many soldiers trained using broomsticks. Others were sent to the front without rifles and told to pick up one from a dead comrade. Thus, it is not surprising that the Russian army suffered incredible losses. Two million soldiers were killed between 1914 and 1916, and another 4 to 6 million were wounded or captured. By 1917, the Russian will to fight had vanished.

An autocratic ruler, Czar Nicholas II relied on the army and bureaucracy to hold up his regime. He was further cut off from events when a man named Grigory Rasputin (ra • SPYOO • tuhn), known to be a mystic, began to influence the czar's wife, Alexandra. With the czar at the battlefront, it was rumored that Alexandra made all the important decisions after consulting Rasputin. Rasputin's influence made him an important power behind the throne.

As the leadership stumbled its way through a series of military and economic disasters, the Russian people grew more upset with the czarist regime. Even conservative aristocrats who supported the monarchy believed something needed to be done. They assassinated Rasputin in December 1916, but it was too late to save the monarchy.

At the beginning of March 1917, working-class women led a series of strikes in the capital city of Petrograd (formerly St. Petersburg), helping change Russian history. A few weeks earlier, the Russian government had started bread rationing in Petrograd after the price of bread skyrocketed. Many of the women who stood in the lines waiting for bread were also factory workers who worked 12-hour days. Exhausted from standing in line and distraught over their half-starving and sick children, the women finally revolted.

On March 8, about 10,000 women marched through the city of Petrograd demanding "Peace and Bread" and "Down with Autocracy." Soon the women were joined by other workers. Together they called for a general strike. The strike shut down all the factories in the city on March 10.

Alexandra wrote to her husband Nicholas II at the battlefront: "This is a hooligan movement. If the weather were very cold they would all probably stay at home." Nicholas ordered troops to break up the crowds by shooting them if

**ANALYZING KEY IDEAS AND DETAILS**

1. **SUMMARIZING** Summarize the actions that were taken by the Duma after it met in March of 1917.
2. **CITING TEXT EVIDENCE** What evidence in the text supports the claim that Russia was unprepared for war?

**THINKING LIKE A HISTORIAN**

### HOW IMPORTANT WAS RASPUTIN?

In the introduction to his best-selling book *Nicholas and Alexandra*, historian Robert Massie quotes Aleksandr Kerensky's observation, "If there had been no Rasputin, there would have been no Lenin." The role of Rasputin in the history of Russia is one debated by historians. Was he such an important figure or was his influence merely the stuff of legends? How much influence can one man have to effect historical change? Use the Internet to find reliable sources about how much Rasputin contributed to the fall of the Russian monarchy.

necessary. Soon, however, large numbers of the soldiers joined the demonstrators and refused to fire on the crowds.

The Duma, or legislative body, which the czar had tried to dissolve, met anyway. On March 12, it established the provisional government, which mainly consisted of middle-class representatives. It urged the czar to step down. Because he no longer had the support of the army or even the aristocrats, Nicholas II reluctantly agreed and stepped down on March 15, ending the 300-year-old Romanov dynasty.

The provisional government, headed by Aleksandr Kerensky (keh • REHN • skee), decided to carry on the war to preserve Russia's honor. This decision to remain in World War I was a major blunder. It satisfied neither the workers nor the peasants, who were tired and angry from years of suffering and wanted an end to the war.

**DETERMINING MEANING**

The word **soviet** comes from the Russian word *sovet,* which means "council." How does this word origin help the reader better understand the role of the soviets in the Russian Revolution?

The government also faced a challenge to its authority—the **soviets**. The soviets were councils comprised of representatives from the workers and soldiers. The soviet of Petrograd was formed in March 1917. At the same time, soviets sprang up in army units, factory towns, and rural areas. The soviets, largely made of Socialists, represented the more radical interests of the lower classes. One group—the Bolsheviks—came to play a crucial role.

### ☑ CHECKING FOR UNDERSTANDING

1. **IDENTIFYING CAUSES** What factors and events led to the Russian Revolution?
2. **SUMMARIZING** How was the Russian military unprepared for World War I?
3. **IDENTIFYING EFFECTS** What happened as a result of the workers' protests in Petrograd?

## LENIN AND THE BOLSHEVIKS

**GUIDING QUESTION** *How did Russia move from a czarist regime to a Communist regime?*

The Bolsheviks began as a small faction of a Marxist party called the Russian Social Democrats. The Bolsheviks came under the leadership of Vladimir Ilyich Ulyanov (ool • YAH • nuhf ), known to the world as V. I. Lenin. Under Lenin's direction, the Bolsheviks became a party dedicated to violent **revolution**. Lenin believed that only violent revolution could destroy the capitalist system. A "vanguard" (forefront) of activists, he said, must form a small party of well-disciplined, professional revolutionaries to accomplish the task.

**ANALYZING KEY IDEAS AND DETAILS**

1. **ANALYZING EVENTS** Reread the paragraph that begins, "At the same time. . . ." What part of this paragraph states an effect of the discontent of the Russian people prior to the Bolshevik Revolution?
2. **DETERMINING CENTRAL IDEAS** What did Lenin believe was necessary to create change in Russia?

Between the years 1900 and 1917, Lenin spent most of his time abroad. When the Russian provisional government was formed in March 1917, he saw an opportunity for the Bolsheviks to seize power. In April 1917, German military leaders, hoping to create disorder in Russia, shipped Lenin back to Russia. Lenin and his associates were sent in a sealed train to prevent their ideas from infecting Germany.

**DETERMINING MEANING**

The word **revolution** comes from the Latin word *revolvere*, which means "to turn or roll back." How does the origin of the word *revolution* help you better understand its meaning?

Lenin's arrival in Russia began a new phase of the Russian Revolution. Lenin maintained that the soviets of soldiers, workers, and peasants were ready-made instruments of power. He believed that the Bolsheviks should work toward gaining control of these groups and then use them to overthrow the provisional government.

At the same time, the Bolsheviks reflected the discontent of the people. They promised an end to the war. They also promised to redistribute all land to the peasants, to transfer factories and industries from capitalists to committees of workers, and to transfer government power from the provisional government to the soviets. Three simple slogans summed up the Bolshevik program: "Peace, Land, Bread," "Worker Control of Production," and "All Power to the Soviets."

### ✓ CHECKING FOR UNDERSTANDING

1. **RELATING EVENTS** How did Russia move from a czarist regime to a Communist regime?
2. **UNDERSTANDING CONTEXT** To what types of people did the Bolsheviks try to appeal?
3. **DESCRIBING** What happened after Lenin arrived in Russia from Germany?

## THE BOLSHEVIKS SEIZE POWER

**GUIDING QUESTION** *How did Russia move from a czarist regime to a Communist regime?*

By the end of October 1917, Bolsheviks made up a slight majority in the Petrograd and Moscow soviets. The number of party members had grown from 50,000 to 240,000. With Leon Trotsky as head of the Petrograd soviet, the Bolsheviks were in a position to claim power in the name of the soviets. Lenin wrote:

> "The situation is critical in the extreme. In fact it is now absolutely clear that to delay the uprising would be fatal. . . .
>
> History will not forgive revolutionaries for procrastinating when they could be victorious today (and they certainly will be victorious today), while they risk losing much tomorrow, in fact, they risk losing everything.
>
> If we seize power today, we seize it not in opposition to the Soviets but on their behalf. . . . The government is tottering. It must be given the death-blow at all costs."
>
> —Vladimir Lenin, "Call to Power," October 24, 1917

**ANALYZING KEY IDEAS AND DETAILS**

**SUMMARIZING** Write a brief summary of this section in your own words.

**ANALYZING PRIMARY SOURCES**

1. **DETERMINING CENTRAL IDEAS** What is Lenin urging in this call?
2. **ANALYZING IDEAS** How do Lenin's words reflect the views of the Bolshevik Revolution?

During the night of November 6, Bolshevik forces seized the Winter Palace, the seat of the provisional government. The government quickly collapsed with little bloodshed. This overthrow coincided with a meeting of the all-Russian Congress of Soviets, which represented local soviets countrywide. Outwardly, Lenin turned over the power of the provisional government to the Congress of Soviets. The real power, however, passed to a council headed by Lenin.

*This painting depicts the Bolshevik attack on the Winter Palace during the October Revolution.*

**EXPLAINING CAUSES** Why did the Bolsheviks attack the Winter Palace during the October Revolution?

The Bolsheviks, who soon renamed themselves the Communists, still had a long way to go. Lenin had promised peace, yet he realized delivering that would not be easy. It would mean the humiliating loss of much Russian territory, but there was no real choice.

On March 3, 1918, Lenin signed the Treaty of Brest-Litovsk with Germany and gave up eastern Poland, Ukraine, Finland, and the Baltic provinces. To his critics, Lenin argued that it made no difference. The spread of the socialist revolution throughout Europe would make the treaty largely irrelevant. In any case, he had promised peace to the Russian people. Real peace did not come, however, because the country soon sank into civil war.

### ✓ CHECKING FOR UNDERSTANDING

1. **UNDERSTANDING CONTEXT** Why was it difficult to achieve the peace that the Bolsheviks had promised?
2. **INTERPRETING** Why had the number of Bolsheviks increased so much by 1917?
3. **ANALYZING CHANGE** How was the outward appearance of the new government different from the reality?

## CIVIL WAR IN RUSSIA

**GUIDING QUESTION** *What forces opposed the Communist government?*

Many people were opposed to the new Bolshevik, or Communist, government. These people included not only groups that were loyal to the czar but also liberal and anti-Leninist socialists. They were joined by the Allies, who were concerned about the Communist takeover. The Allies sent troops to Russia in the hope of bringing Russia back into the war. The Allies rarely fought on Russian soil, but they gave material **aid** to anti-Communists.

Between 1918 and 1921, the Communist, or Red, Army fought on many fronts. The first serious threat to the Communists came from Siberia. An anti-Communist, or White, force attacked and advanced almost to the Volga River before being stopped. Attacks also came from the Ukrainians and from the Baltic regions. In mid-1919, White forces swept through Ukraine and advanced almost to Moscow before being pushed back.

By 1920, however, the major White forces had been defeated and Ukraine retaken. The next year, the Communist regime regained control over the independent nationalist governments in Georgia, Russian Armenia, and Azerbaijan.

The royal family was another victim of the civil war. After the czar **abdicated**, he, his wife, and their five children had been held as prisoners. In April 1918, they were moved to Yekaterinburg, a mining town in the Urals. On the night of July 16, members of the local soviet murdered the czar and his family and burned their bodies in a nearby mine shaft.

**UNDERSTANDING CRAFT AND STRUCTURE**

1. **ANALYZING TEXT** How does this section of the text use a chronological structure to organize ideas?
2. **ANALYZING TEXT PRESENTATION** Why does the author end this section with the death of the royal family?

**DETERMINING MEANING**

The word **abdicate** includes the root *ab-*, meaning "away," and *dicare*, or "declare." How might knowing the origin of the word *abdicate* help a person determine its meaning?

### ✓ CHECKING FOR UNDERSTANDING

1. **IDENTIFYING CONNECTIONS** What forces opposed the Communist government?
2. **DETERMINING CONTEXT** Why did the Allied forces support the anti-Communist forces in Russia?
3. **USING MAPS** Based on the map, where was most of the revolutionary activity?

# TRIUMPH OF THE COMMUNISTS

**GUIDING QUESTION** *What factors helped the Communists win the Russian civil war?*

How did Lenin and the Communists triumph in the civil war over such overwhelming forces? One reason was that the Red Army was a well-disciplined fighting force. This was largely due to the organizational genius of Leon Trotsky. As commissar of war, Trotsky reinstated the draft and insisted on rigid discipline. Soldiers who deserted or refused to obey orders were executed on the spot.

Furthermore, the disunity of the anti-Communist forces weakened their efforts. Political differences created distrust among the White Russians. Some White Russians insisted on restoring the czarist regime. Others, however, wanted a more liberal and democratic program. The White Russians, then, had no common goal.

The Communists, in contrast, had a single-minded sense of purpose. Inspired by their vision of a new socialist order, the Communists had revolutionary zeal and strong convictions. They also were able to translate their revolutionary faith into practical instruments of power. A policy of **war communism**, for example, was used to ensure regular supplies for the Red Army. War communism meant the government controlled the banks and most industries, seized grain from peasants, and centralized state administration under Communist control.

### GEOGRAPHIC REASONING

The events of the Russian Revolution led to a civil war.

1. **SPATIAL THINKING** Measure the distance from Russia's westernmost border in 1914 to the western border under Bolshevik control in October 1919.
2. **GLOBAL INTERCONNECTIONS** Why did so many attacks toward the Bolsheviks occur from outside of Russia?

### ANALYZING KEY IDEAS AND DETAILS

1. **SUMMARIZING** Summarize the main points in this section. In your summary note the causes of the Communist victory in the Russian Civil War.
2. **CITING TEXT EVIDENCE** What evidence in the text supports the claim that the Communists had triumphed in Russia by 1921?

**DETERMINING MEANING**

Read the text of the paragraph that contains the word **communism**. From what word do you think *communism* arose? Check your answer using a dictionary.

Another instrument was Communist revolutionary terror. A new Red secret police—known as the Cheka—began a Red Terror. Aimed at destroying all those who opposed the new regime, the Red Terror added an element of fear to the Communist regime.

Finally, foreign armies on Russian soil enabled the Communists to appeal to the powerful force of Russian patriotism. At one point, more than 100,000 foreign troops—mostly Japanese, British, American, and French—were stationed in Russia in support of anti-Communist forces. Their presence made it easy for the Communist government to call on patriotic Russians to fight foreign attempts to control the country.

By 1921, the Communists were in total command of Russia. The Communist regime had transformed Russia into a centralized state dominated by a single party. The state was also largely hostile to the Allied Powers, because the Allies had tried to help the Communists' enemies in the civil war.

### ✓ CHECKING FOR UNDERSTANDING

1. **DRAWING CONCLUSIONS** What factors helped the Communists win the Russian civil war?
2. **INTERPRETING** What role did the Cheka play in the Communist regime in Russia?
3. **SUMMARIZING** What advantages did the Bolsheviks have over the Whites in the Russian civil war?

## LESSON 3 REVIEW

### Time and Place

1. **UNDERSTANDING CONTEXT** What caused many Russians from across all levels of society to lose faith in Czar Nicholas II at the beginning of World War I?

### Building History-Social Science Analysis Skills

2. **EVALUATING** How was Rasputin influential in the events leading up to the Russian Revolution?
3. **ANALYZING CHANGE** How did Lenin start a new phase of the Russian Revolution?
4. **USING MAPS** Based on the map, what was the significance of the land lost by Russia in the Treaty of Brest-Litovsk?

### Writing About History

5. **ARGUMENTATIVE WRITING** Write a short paragraph arguing whether or not the Russian Revolution was a result of World War I.

### Collaborating

6. **INTEGRATING INFORMATION** With a partner, use the Internet or other sources to find and discuss examples of Bolshevik propaganda posters. Discuss how they reflected the discontent of the people or how they manipulated their emotions. How did propaganda support the Bolshevik slogan "Peace, Land, Bread"?

## ESSENTIAL QUESTIONS

- *Why do politics often lead to war?*
- *How can technology impact war?*

# THE STORY BEGINS...

*President Wilson, shown here with British Prime Minister David Lloyd George, Italian Premier Vittorio Orlando, and French Premier Georges Clemenceau, played a huge role in the efforts to secure peace after the end of the war.* ▶

LESSON 4

# World War I Ends

World War I was a devastating event that lasted much longer than had been expected. When the war ended, the conversation immediately turned to how such a calamity could be prevented in the future. U.S. President Woodrow Wilson had a plan to do just that. In 1918, he delivered the Fourteen Points to Congress:

> “We entered this war because violations of right had occurred which touched us to the quick and made the life of our own people impossible unless they were corrected and the world secure once for all against their recurrence. What we demand in this war, therefore, is nothing peculiar to ourselves. It is that the world be made fit and safe to live in; and particularly that it be made safe for every peace-loving nation which, like our own, wishes to live its own life, determine its own institutions, be assured of justice and fair dealing by the other peoples of the world as against force and selfish aggression. All the peoples of the world are in effect partners in this interest, and for our own part we see very clearly that unless justice be done to others it will not be done to us. . . .
>
> Unless this principle be made its foundation no part of the structure of international justice can stand. The people of the United States could act upon no other principle; and to the vindication of this principle they are ready to devote their lives, their honor, and everything they possess. The moral climax of this the culminating and final war for human liberty has come, and they are ready to put their own strength, their own highest purpose, their own integrity and devotion to the test.”

—from *The Fourteen Points,* Woodrow Wilson, January 8, 1918

Unfortunately, World War I would prove not to be the “final war.” The conditions in which it left Europe would only set the stage for an even greater conflict.

| France | Great Britain | United States |
| --- | --- | --- |
| | | |

**ANALYZING KEY IDEAS AND DETAILS**

**SUMMARIZING** Read closely to identify the central national interest of each Allied power in the Paris Peace Conference. Record each interest in a graphic organizer like this one.

# THE LAST YEAR OF THE WAR

**UNDERSTANDING CRAFT AND STRUCTURE**

1. **ANALYZING TEXT PRESENTATION** How does the text present the information about the last year of World War I? Does the way the text is organized help you better understand the information?
2. **DETERMINING MEANING** The text states that a group of "radical socialists" formed the German Communist Party. What does the word *radical* mean in this context?

**GUIDING QUESTION** *How did World War I come to an end?*

The year 1917 was not a good one for the Allies. Allied offensives on the Western Front had been badly defeated. The Russian Revolution, which began in November 1917, led to Russia's withdrawal from the war a few months later. On the positive side, however, the entry of the United States into the war in 1917 gave the Allies a much-needed **psychological** boost. The United States also provided fresh troops and supplies.

For Germany, the withdrawal of the Russians offered new hope for a successful end to the war. Germany was then free to concentrate entirely on the Western Front. Erich Ludendorff, who guided German military operations, decided to make one final military gamble—a grand offensive in the west.

The German attack was launched in March 1918. By April German troops were within about 50 miles (80 km) of Paris. However, the German advance was stopped at the Second Battle of the Marne on July 18. French, Moroccan, and American troops (140,000 fresh American troops had just arrived), supported by hundreds of tanks, pushed the Germans back over the Marne. Ludendorff's gamble had failed.

With more than a million American troops pouring into France, Allied forces began an advance toward Germany. On September 29, 1918, General Ludendorff told German leaders that the war was lost. He demanded that the government ask for peace at once.

*British cavalry pass the ruins of the Albert Cathedral. It was destroyed in the Second Battle of the Somme in France.*

**UNDERSTANDING CHANGE**
What does this photograph tell you about the changing nature of warfare in World War I?

## COLLAPSE AND ARMISTICE

German officials soon found that the Allies were unwilling to make peace with the autocratic imperial government of Germany. Reforms for a liberal government came too late for the tired, angry German people.

On November 3, 1918, sailors in the northern German town of Kiel mutinied. Within days, councils of workers and soldiers formed throughout northern Germany and took over civilian and military offices. Emperor William II gave in to public pressure and left the country on November 9. After his departure, the Social Democrats under Friedrich Ebert announced the creation of a democratic republic. Two days later, on November 11, 1918, the new German government signed an **armistice** to end the fighting.

**DETERMINING MEANING**

The word **psychological** comes from the Greek word *psyche*, which means "mind." How does the origin of the word *psychological* help you better understand its meaning?

**DETERMINING MEANING**

The word **armistice** comes from the Latin roots *arma* ("arms or weapons") and *stitium* ("to stop"). How might knowing the meanings of these roots help a person determine the meaning of *armistice*?

## REVOLUTIONARY FORCES

The war was over, but the revolutionary forces that had been set in motion in Germany were not yet exhausted. A group of radical socialists, unhappy with the Social Democrats' moderate policies, formed the German Communist Party in December 1918. A month later, the Communists tried to seize power in Berlin.

The new Social Democratic government, backed by regular army troops, crushed the rebels and murdered Rosa Luxemburg and Karl Liebknecht (LEEP • KNEHKT), leaders of the German Communists. A similar attempt at Communist revolution in the city of Munich, in southern Germany, was also crushed. The new German republic had been saved. The attempt at revolution, however, left the German middle class with a deep fear of communism.

Austria-Hungary also experienced disintegration and revolution. As the empire grew war weary, ethnic groups increasingly sought to achieve their independence. By the time World War I ended, the Austro-Hungarian Empire had ceased to exist. The empire was replaced by the independent republics of Austria, Hungary, and Czechoslovakia, along with the large monarchical state called Yugoslavia.

### ✓ CHECKING FOR UNDERSTANDING

1. **UNDERSTANDING CHANGE** How did World War I come to an end?
2. **IDENTIFYING CAUSES** What prompted the Germans to call for the emperor's abdication?
3. **IDENTIFYING EFFECTS** What effect did the United States' entry into World War I have on the Allied forces?

# THE PEACE SETTLEMENTS

**GUIDING QUESTION** *How was a final settlement of World War I established?*

In January 1919, representatives of 27 victorious Allied nations met in Paris to make a final settlement of World War I. Over the course of the war, the reasons for fighting World War I had changed dramatically. When European nations went to war in 1914, most simply sought territorial gains. By the beginning of 1918, however, they also were expressing more idealistic reasons for the war.

**ANALYZING KEY IDEAS AND DETAILS**

1. **DETERMINING CENTRAL IDEAS** What is the central idea of "Wilson's Proposals"? How does the text present and develop this idea?
2. **SUMMARIZING** Write a brief summary of the Treaty of Versailles.

## WILSON'S PROPOSALS

No one expressed these idealistic reasons for war better than the president of the United States, Woodrow Wilson. Even before the end of the war, Wilson outlined "Fourteen Points" to the U. S. Congress—his basis for a peace settlement that he believed justified the enormous military struggle being waged.

Wilson's proposals for a truly just and lasting peace included reaching the peace agreements openly rather than through secret diplomacy. His proposals also included reducing armaments (military forces or weapons) and ensuring self-determination (the right of each people to have their own nation).

Wilson portrayed World War I as a people's war against "absolutism and militarism." These two enemies of liberty, he argued, could be eliminated only by creating democratic governments and a "general association of nations." This association would guarantee "political independence and territorial integrity" to all states.

Wilson became the spokesperson for a new world order based on democracy and international **cooperation**. When he arrived in Europe for the peace conference, Wilson was cheered enthusiastically by many Europeans. President Wilson soon found, however, that more practical motives guided other states.

**DETERMINING MEANING**

Read the paragraph that contains the word **reparations**. Based on how it is used in this paragraph, what word do you think it is related to?

## THE PARIS PEACE CONFERENCE

Delegates met in Paris in early 1919 to determine the peace settlement. Complications soon arose at the Paris Peace Conference. For one thing, secret agreements that had been made before the war had raised the hopes of European nations for territorial gains. These hopes, however, conflicted with the principle of self-determination put forth by Wilson.

National interests also complicated the deliberations of the Paris Peace Conference. David Lloyd George, prime minister of Great Britain, had won a decisive victory in elections in December 1918. His platform was simple: make the Germans pay for this dreadful war.

France's approach to peace was chiefly guided by its desire for national security. To Georges Clemenceau (kleh • muhn • SOH), the premier of France, the French people had suffered the most from German aggression. The French desired security against future German attacks. Clemenceau wanted Germany stripped of all weapons, vast German payments—**reparations**—to cover the costs of the war, and a separate Rhineland as a buffer state between France and Germany.

The most important decisions at the Paris Peace Conference were made by Wilson, Clemenceau, and Lloyd George, acting on behalf of the United States, France, and Great Britain (who were called the Big Three). Germany was not invited to attend, and Russia could not be present because of its civil war.

In view of the conflicting demands that arose at the Paris Peace Conference, it was no surprise that the Big Three quarreled. Wilson wanted to create a world organization, the League of Nations, to prevent future wars. Clemenceau and Lloyd George wanted to punish Germany. In the end, only compromise made it possible to achieve a peace settlement.

Wilson's wish for the creation of an international peacekeeping organization to be the first order of business was granted. On

The Signing of Peace in the Hall of Mirrors, Versailles, 28th June 1919 *by Sir William Orpen depicts the major powers at Versailles. Wilson, Clemenceau, and Lloyd George (left to right) are seated at the table across from the German delegate.*

**UNDERSTANDING CONTEXT** Why are the members of the delegation seated in this order around the table?

Imperial War Museum/akg-images

January 25, 1919, the conference accepted the idea of a League of Nations. In return, Wilson agreed to make compromises on territorial arrangements among the countries. He did so because he believed that the League of Nations could later fix any unfair settlements.

Clemenceau also compromised to obtain some guarantees for French security. He gave up France's wish for a separate Rhineland and instead accepted a defensive alliance with Great Britain and the United States. However, the U.S. Senate refused to ratify this agreement, which weakened the Versailles peace settlement.

## THE TREATY OF VERSAILLES

The final peace settlement of Paris consisted of five separate treaties with the defeated nations of Germany, Austria, Hungary, Bulgaria, and Turkey. The Treaty of Versailles with Germany was by far the most important.

The Germans considered it a harsh peace. They were especially unhappy with Article 231, the so-called War Guilt Clause, which declared that Germany (and Austria) were responsible for starting the war. The treaty ordered Germany to pay reparations (financial compensation) for all damages that the Allied governments and their people had sustained as a result of the war.

The military and territorial provisions of the Treaty of Versailles also angered the Germans. Germany had to reduce its army to 100,000 men, cut back its navy, and eliminate its air force. Alsace and Lorraine, taken by the Germans from France in 1871, were returned. Sections of eastern Germany were awarded to a new Polish state.

German land along the Rhine River became a demilitarized zone, stripped of all weapons and fortifications. This, it was hoped, would serve as a barrier to any future German moves against France. Although outraged by the "dictated peace," Germany accepted the treaty.

**CITIZENSHIP**

### THE TREATY OF VERSAILLES AND THE LEAGUE OF NATIONS

U.S. President Woodrow Wilson was among the world leaders who negotiated the Treaty of Versailles, but when he returned to the United States and presented the treaty to the Senate for ratification, they refused. Why?

It was Wilson's own brainchild, the League of Nations, that many senators objected to. Article X of the treaty granted the League of Nations the authority to declare war without Congress's approval. Many senators feared this would weaken U.S. power. Many of Wilson's opponents in Congress prevented him from obtaining the necessary two-thirds majority necessary for ratification. Although the United States would later sign a separate peace treaty with Germany, it never ratified the Treaty of Versailles and did not join the League of Nations.

1. **DETERMINING CONTEXT** Why did most U.S. senators oppose the Treaty of Versailles?
2. **INTERPRETING** What role did previous U.S. policies toward foreign affairs play in the refusal to join the League of Nations?

## EUROPE AND THE MIDDLE EAST AFTER WORLD WAR I 1922

### GEOGRAPHIC REASONING

After World War I, new countries and mandates were formed in Europe and the Middle East.

1. **EXPLORING REGIONS** How did Europe change as a result of the Treaty of Versailles?
2. **HUMAN POPULATION** Why do you think East Prussia was separated from the rest of Germany?

## SELF-DETERMINATION AND THE MANDATE SYSTEM

The Treaty of Versailles and the separate peace treaties made with the other Central Powers redrew the map of Eastern Europe. Many of these changes had occurred by the end of the war. The German and Russian empires lost much of their territory in Eastern Europe. The Austro-Hungarian Empire disappeared.

New nation-states emerged from the lands of these three empires. These include Finland, Latvia, Estonia, Lithuania, Poland, Czechoslovakia, Austria, and Hungary. New territorial arrangements were also made in the Balkans. Romania acquired additional lands. Serbia formed the nucleus of a new state, called Yugoslavia, which combined populations of Serbs, Croats, and Slovenes.

The principle of self-determination supposedly guided the Paris Peace Conference. However, the mixtures of peoples in Eastern Europe made it impossible to draw boundaries along strict ethnic lines. As a result of compromises, almost every Eastern European state was left with ethnic minorities. Some states would begin population transfers, where ethnic minorities were forced to leave the countries in which they lived to settle in new states where they were among the majority. The problem of ethnic minorities within nations would lead to many conflicts later.

Yet another centuries-old empire—the Ottoman Empire—was broken up by the peace settlement. To gain Arab support against the Ottoman Turks during the war, the Western Allies had promised to recognize the independence of Arab states in the Ottoman Empire. When World War I was over, however, the Western nations changed their minds. France controlled the territory of Syria, and Britain controlled the territories of Iraq and Palestine. In addition to these

**DETERMINING MEANING**

The word **mandate** is similar to the Latin word *mandatum*, which means "to give in." How does this word origin help the reader better understand what the text means when it describes territories acquired after World War I as *mandates*?

transfers, Great Britain, France, Belgium, and Japan were given governing control over Germany's various colonies in Africa and the Pacific.

These acquisitions were officially called **mandates**. Woodrow Wilson opposed the outright annexation of colonial territories by the Allies. As a result, in the mandate system, a nation officially governed a territory on a temporary basis as a mandate on behalf of the League of Nations but did not own the territory.

World War I shattered the liberal, rational society that had existed in Europe at that time. The deaths of about 16 million people, as well as the incredible destruction caused by the war, undermined the whole idea of progress. Veterans often came home injured mentally and physically. These men, along with the millions who did not return home, served as a constant reminder of the horrors of modern warfare. Entire populations had participated in a devastating slaughter.

World War I was a total war—one that involved a complete mobilization of resources and people. As a result, the power of governments over the lives of their citizens increased. Freedom of the press and speech were limited in the name of national security. World War I made the practice of strong central authority a way of life.

The turmoil created by the war also seemed to open the door to even greater insecurity. Combat in Western Europe, Eastern Europe, and the Middle East left marks on these societies that were felt long after the fighting ended. Revolutions broke up old empires and created new states, which led to new problems. The hope that Europe and the rest of the world would return to normalcy was soon dashed.

### ✓ CHECKING FOR UNDERSTANDING

1. **SUMMARIZING** How was a final settlement of World War I established?
2. **INTERPRETING** On what issues did the French, British, and Americans disagree in the peace negotiations?
3. **EXPLAINING EFFECTS** What effect did the Treaty of Versailles have on population movement?

**MAKING CONNECTIONS TO TODAY**

### THE INFLUENZA PANDEMIC OF 2009

The pandemic of 1918 was caused by a type of the H1N1 influenza virus. A previously unknown strain of this virus appeared in 2009. First occurring in Mexico in February 2009, the disease spread rapidly across the world, presumably through air travel. In June, the World Health Organization, or WHO, declared that H1N1 had become a pandemic, or an outbreak affecting a large portion of the population over a wide geographic area. Unlike the 1918 outbreak, the H1N1 flu did not mutate into a more deadly form, and the death toll remained relatively low. In August 2010, the WHO announced that the H1N1 flu had moved into a postpandemic stage.

1. **COMPARING AND CONTRASTING** How were the pandemics of 1918 and 2009 similar and different?
2. **CITING TEXT EVIDENCE** What evidence from this passage suggests that there exists a health infrastructure now that did not exist during the 1918 pandemic? Cite evidence from the passage.

## LESSON 4 REVIEW

### Time and Place

1. **INTERPRETING** How did the geography of Europe change as a result of the end of World War I?

### Building History-Social Science Analysis Skills

2. **EVALUATING** Define the terms *armistice* and *reparations* and discuss their significance for Germany at the end of World War I.
3. **EVALUATING** In what ways was the last year of the war both good and bad for the Allied forces?
4. **SUMMARIZING** Based on the text, what did each of the Big Three nations hope to gain in the peace negotiations?

### Writing About History

5. **EXPLANATORY WRITING** Write an essay discussing the elements of the World War I peace settlement that seemed likely to lead to future conflict.

### Collaborating

6. **EVALUATING POINT OF VIEW** With a partner or as a group, discuss the national interests of Great Britain, France, and the United States as they entered the Paris Peace Conference. Discuss how the culmination of these interests in the Treaty of Versailles were viewed by Germany.

# VOICES OF THE GREAT WAR

Many writers and artists struggled to come to terms with the consequences of the war and the paradise that seemed to be lost. Read the following selections from artists struggling to capture the profound feelings of the war generation.

**VOCABULARY**

*hollow:* an unfilled space; empty

*cellar:* storage rooms underneath a building; basement

*ostracized:* shunned; excluded from a group

**PRIMARY SOURCE: POEM**

## "THE HOLLOW MEN" BY T. S. ELIOT

T. S. Eliot (1888–1965), an American-British poet, wrote "The Hollow Men" in 1925 to describe how the war affected the men who fought it.

> "We are the **hollow** men
> We are the stuffed men
> Leaning together
> Headpiece filled with straw. Alas!
> Our dried voices, when
> We whisper together
> Are quiet and meaningless
> As wind in dry grass
> Or rats' feet over broken glass
> In our dry **cellar**
> Shape without form, shade without colour,
> Paralysed force, gesture without motion;
> Those who have crossed
> With direct eyes, to death's other Kingdom
> Remember us—if at all—not as lost
> Violent souls, but only
> As the hollow men
> The stuffed men.
> . . . . . . . . . . . . . . . . . . . . . . . . .
> This is the way the world ends
> This is the way the world ends
> This is the way the world ends
> Not with a bang but a whimper."

**ANALYZE THE TEXT**

1. **ANALYZING THEMES** Eliot wrote the poem "The Hollow Men" after the war. How does the theme of this poem differ from attitudes in 1914?
2. **DETERMINING MEANING** What does the phrase "hollow men" refer to in Eliot's poem?

**PRIMARY SOURCE: NOVEL**

## *ALL QUIET ON THE WESTERN FRONT* BY ERICH MARIA REMARQUE

Erich Maria Remarque (1897–1970) served in the German army. The following is from his famous novel, *All Quiet on the Western Front*, published in 1929.

> "Kantorek had been our schoolmaster, a stern little man in grey tail-coat, with a face like a shrew-mouse. . . .
>
> During drill-time Kantorek gave us long lectures until the whole of our class went, under his shepherding, to the District Commandant and volunteered. . . .
>
> There was, indeed, one of us who hesitated and did not want to fall into line. That was Josef Behm, a plump, homely fellow. But he did allow himself to be persuaded, otherwise he would have been **ostracized**. . . . even one's parents were ready with the word "coward"; no one had the vaguest idea what we were in for. . . .
>
> Strange to say, Behm was one of the first to fall. He got hit in the eye during an attack, and we left him lying for dead. . . .
>
> Naturally we couldn't blame Kantorek for this. . . . There were thousands of Kantoreks, all of whom were convinced that they were acting for the best—in a way that cost them nothing. And that is why they let us down so badly. . . ."

**ANALYZE THE TEXT**

1. **INTERPRETING** What does *All Quiet on the Western Front* imply about the kind of pressures young men were under to go to war?
2. **DETERMINING MEANING** In *All Quiet on the Western Front*, what does the author mean by writing: "And that is why they let us down so badly"? Who are "they," and who are "us"?

(l)Eliot, T. S. 1925. "The Hollow Men". From Poems, 1909-1925. London: Faber & Faber Limited; (r)Remarque, Erich Maria. 1929. Translated from the German by A. W. Wheen. All Quiet On The Western Front. London: G. P. Putnam's Sons.

PRIMARY SOURCE: MEMOIR

## *OVER THE TOP* BY ARTHUR GUY EMPEY

Arthur Guy Empey (1883–1963) reflects upon his experiences during World War I in the trenches in France. This is an excerpt from his book *Over the Top*.

> "Suddenly, the earth seemed to shake and a thunderclap burst in my ears. I opened my eyes,—I was splashed all over with sticky mud, and men were picking themselves up from the bottom of the trench. The parapet on my left had toppled into the trench, completely blocking it with a wall of tossed-up earth. The man on my left lay still. . . . A German "Minnie" (trench mortar) had exploded in the [trench].
>
> . . . Stretcher-bearers came up the trench on the double. After a few minutes of digging, three still, muddy forms on stretchers were carried down the communication trench to the rear. Soon they would be resting "somewhere in France," with a little wooden cross over their heads. They had done their bit for King and Country, had died without firing a shot. . . . I was dazed and motionless. Suddenly a shovel was pushed into my hands, and a rough but kindly voice said: "Here, my lad, lend a hand clearing the trench, but keep your head down, and look out for snipers. . . .

> "Lying on my belly on the bottom of the trench, I filled sandbags with the sticky mud.
>
> . . . The harder I worked, the better I felt.
>
> Occasionally a bullet would crack overhead, and a machine gun would kick up the mud on the bashed-in parapet. At each crack I would duck and shield my face with my arm. One of the older men noticed this action of mine, and whispered: "Don't duck at the crack of a bullet, Yank; the danger has passed,— you never hear the one that wings you. Always remember that if you are going to get it, you'll get it, so never worry." . . . [Days later] we received the cheerful news that at four in the morning we were to go over the top and take the German frontline trench. My heart turned to lead."

### ANALYZE THE TEXT

1. **SUMMARIZING** What happens in the trench at the beginning of *Over the Top*? How do the soldiers respond?
2. **DETERMINING POINT OF VIEW** Why might cleaning the trench make the narrator of *Over the Top* feel better than before?

### MULTIPLE PERSPECTIVES

1. **DETERMINING CENTRAL IDEAS** What is the collective interpretation of the war when considering all of these sources together?
2. **COMPARING POINTS OF VIEW** How are the horrors of trench warfare depicted in *All Quiet on the Western Front* and *Over the Top*? How does each narrator react?

Empey, Arthur Guy. 1917. Over the Top. New York and London: G. P. Putnam's Sons.

# STUDY GUIDE

## THE CAUSES OF WORLD WAR I
**LESSON 1**

**NATIONALISM**

The system of nation-states led to competition as each state was guided by self-interest and most leaders saw war as an acceptable way to preserve power.

**IMPERIALISM**

The competition for lands abroad, especially in Africa, led to conflict and heightened the existing rivalries among European states.

**MILITARISM**

Most western countries had a military draft, called conscription, before 1914. Armies were growing, as was the influence of military leaders.

**ALLIANCES**

Europe's great powers had been divided into two loose political alliances. Germany, Austria-Hungary, and Italy formed the Triple Alliance in 1882. France, Great Britain, and Russia created the Triple Entente in 1907.

## DIFFERENT APPROACHES TO WAR
**LESSON 2**

**WESTERN FRONT**

The Germans and the French became stuck in trench warfare on the Western Front when neither could dislodge each other from the trenches they had dug for shelter.

**EASTERN FRONT**

More movement on the Eastern Front resulted in the Germans defeating the Russians, which allowed them to move back to the offensive in the West.

## THE RUSSIAN CIVIL WAR
**LESSON 3**

**FACTORS THAT HELPED THE COMMUNISTS WIN**

- The Red Army was a well-disciplined fighting force.
- The anti-Communist forces suffered from a lack of unity.
- The presence of foreign armies on Russian soil allowed the Communists to appeal to the force of Russian patriotism.
- The Cheka, a Red secret police, began a Red Terror that inspired fear in those who opposed the new regime.
- The war communism policy ensured regular supplies for the Red Army.

## THE TREATY OF VERSAILLES
**LESSON 4**

**The final peace settlement of Paris consisted of five separate treaties with defeated nations. The Treaty of Versailles with Germany was by far the most important. The Germans were unhappy with several parts of the settlement, but they accepted the treaty.**

- The so-called War Guilt Clause declared that Germany (and Austria) were responsible for starting the war. It required that Germany pay financial compensation for all damages that Allied governments and their people sustained as a result of the war.
- Germany had to reduce its army to 100,000 men, cut back its navy, and eliminate its air force.
- Alsace and Lorraine, taken by the Germans from France in 1871, were returned.
- Sections of eastern Germany were awarded to a new Polish state.
- German land along the Rhine River became a demilitarized zone, stripped of all weapons and fortifications.

# CHAPTER 8 Assessment

**Directions: On a separate sheet of paper, answer the questions below. Make sure you read carefully and answer all parts of the questions.**

## Short Answer

1. **IDENTIFYING CONNECTIONS** Why did Serbia want all Serbs to be united into a single state, and why did Austria-Hungary oppose this?

2. **UNDERSTANDING CONTEXT** What was the relationship between the creation of alliances between the European powers and the conflict between Serbia and Austria-Hungary developing into a major war?

3. **CONTRASTING** Why was the war on the Western Front less active than that of the Eastern Front?

4. **IDENTIFYING EFFECTS** How did World War I change the roles of women in European society?

5. **IDENTIFYING CAUSES** What was the main cause of the Russian Revolution of 1917?

6. **RELATING EVENTS** How did Lenin's return to Russia influence the outcome of the Russian Revolution?

7. **ANALYZING CHANGE** What events led to Germany's surrender in World War I?

8. **EXPLAINING EFFECTS** What does the nature of the League of Nations suggest about the problems it was designed to solve?

9. **IDENTIFYING CONNECTIONS** What was the connection between militarism and nationalism at the start of World War I in 1914?

10. **UNDERSTANDING CONTEXT** How did the European continent divide as World War I began to take shape?

11. **ANALYZING CHANGE** Describe the events that led to Germany signing an armistice on November 11, 1918.

12. **IDENTIFYING CONNECTIONS** What did the Treaty of Versailles require of the Germans?

13. **IDENTIFYING CAUSES** What circumstances created the situation that allowed the Bolsheviks to overthrow the provisional government?

14. **DETERMINING CONTEXT** How did trench warfare, machine guns, and airplanes characterize battle in World War I?

15. **EXPLAINING ISSUES** What made World War I a "total war"?

## History and Social-Science Analysis

16. **IDENTIFYING EFFECTS** Create a chart showing the results of the war for the Allied and Central Powers. What most likely resulted from the effects of this war?

17. **EXPLAINING CAUSES** Based on what you know about the origins of the war, why might the United States Senate have been reluctant to sign a treaty after fighting in World War I?

18. **ANALYZING SOURCES** This graph shows the estimated army size of each country in each alliance in 1914. Use the graph to answer the following question.

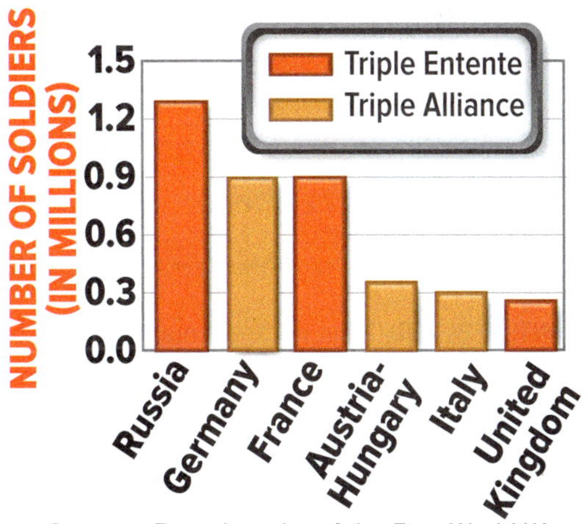


**Source:** *Encyclopedia of the First World War*

What geographical pattern do you find between the alliances and what might be the significance of this pattern?

**Need Extra Help?**

| If You've Missed Question | 1 | 2 | 3 | 4 | 5 | 6 | 7 | 8 | 9 | 10 | 11 | 12 | 13 | 14 | 15 | 16 | 17 | 18 |
|---|---|---|---|---|---|---|---|---|---|---|---|---|---|---|---|---|---|---|
| Review Lesson | 1 | 1 | 2 | 2 | 3 | 3 | 4 | 4 | 1 | 2 | 4 | 4 | 3 | 2 | 2 | 4 | 4 | 1 |

## Research and Presentation

**19** **USING MULTIMEDIA** Work with a partner to create a multimedia display of political motives and technological advances that contributed to the destructiveness of World War I. Provide a photograph, a drawing, or an artifact that symbolizes each contributing factor and an audio or a written explanation of the factor. You may also include primary sources.

**20** **USING MAPS** Create a pair of maps that show the historical and political boundaries in Europe before and after the Treaty of Versailles. Use hand-drawn illustrations or computer software to clearly show the changes. Explore the best method of presentation, perhaps through overlays or use of color. Provide data about the changes, such as number of independent states or population distribution.

## Reading and Analyzing Primary Sources

Use the document to answer the following questions. In the document, a nurse describes treating soldiers in World War I.

> "I wish those people who write so glibly about this being a holy war and the orators who talk so much about going on no matter how long the war lasts and what it may mean could see a case—to say nothing of ten cases—of mustard gas in its early stages—could see the poor things burnt and blistered all over with great mustard-coloured suppurating [oozing] blisters, with blind eyes . . . all sticky and stuck together, and always fighting for breath, with voices a mere whisper, saying that their throats are closing and they know they will choke."

—quoted in *Eye-Deep in Hell: Trench Warfare in World War I*

**21** **INTERPRETING** What words or phrases used by the nurse tell the reader how she feels about the war?

**A.** holy war
**B.** blind eyes
**C.** in its early stages
**D.** burnt and blistered

**22** **DRAWING CONCLUSIONS** What conclusions can you draw about the use of mustard gas as a weapon in the context of medical expertise and history?

**A.** Mustard gas caused great pain to its victims.
**B.** Victims of mustard gas were permanently harmed.
**C.** Mustard gas was very widely used during World War I.
**D.** Medical personnel in the war did not know how to deal with mustard gas.

**23** **IDENTIFYING BIAS** What does the nurse believe is making those who are in favor of the war ignore its human costs?

**A.** patriotic pride
**B.** a lack of awareness
**C.** greed and arrogance
**D.** disrespect for the war's victims

## Writing About History

**24** **EXPLANATORY WRITING** In what ways was World War I a bigger and more destructive conflict than any previous conflicts?

## Speaking and Listening About History

**25** **COLLABORATING** Meet in a small group to discuss the following questions: What effect did the Russian Revolution have on the outcome of the war? Would the war have been resolved any differently had Russia never left? If Russia had stayed in the war, would the Bolshevik Revolution have been as successful as it was? Have one member of your group serve as a moderator of the group discussion.

**Need Extra Help?**

| If You've Missed Question | 19 | 20 | 21 | 22 | 23 | 24 | 25 |
|---|---|---|---|---|---|---|---|
| Review Lesson | 2 | 4 | 2 | 2 | 2 | 2 | 3 |

Ellis, John. 1976. Eye-Deep in Hell: Trench Warfare in World War I. Croom Helm.

◄ Boys in the Hitler Youth participated in Nazi rallies and activities where they spent time with other children with minimal parental guidance. This photograph was taken circa 1939.

1919 — 1939

# The West Between the Wars

## CHAPTER 9



**GO DIGITAL**
*It's All online!*

## ASKING ESSENTIAL QUESTIONS

***What can cause economic instability? How might political change impact society?***

**What Will You Learn?** You will learn about economic instability in the years after World War I and how it and frustrations following World War I led to the rise of dictatorships, most notably in Nazi Germany.

**Why Does This Matter?** The dictators of interwar Europe used fear as a weapon. As these dictators spread their influence over the institutions of their respective states, they transformed these fears into grievances. Fueled by these grievances, angry masses could be counted on to violently enforce loyalty in their communities. In this way, these regimes accomplished the perfect insult. Fear, the emotion that once justified their existence, now rebuked any challenge to the order they represented.

**How Will You Know That You Learned It?** You will better understand the Great Depression and explain how this economic crisis led to the growth of authoritarian regimes in Europe.

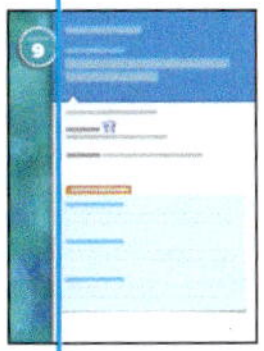

**Using Your Inquiry Journal** As you read this chapter and examine the primary sources, use your Inquiry Journal to help you make notes and expand your list of questions. As you gather information, think about how you will answer the Essential Questions above.

Heinrich Hoffmann/Time & Life Pictures/Getty Images

# PLACE & TIME Europe 1919–1939

At the end of the First World War, world leaders attempted to craft a lasting peace. However, the 1920s and 1930s witnessed severe economic crises that led to political instability. Authoritarian political leaders used widespread fear of disorder to gain power. When in power, they violently suppressed all opposition.

## STEP INTO THE PLACE

Read the quotes and look at the information presented on the map.

1. **COMPARING** Compare and contrast Hitler's and Stalin's ideas about the goal of government.

2. **GLOBAL INTERCONNECTIONS** Given the distribution of dictatorships shown on the map, what might we conclude about the pressures on the countries of Czechoslovakia and Austria during this period?

"[T]he Soviet power is a *new form* of state organization, different in principle from the old bourgeois-democratic and parliamentary form, a *new type* of state, adapted not to the task of exploiting and oppressing the labouring masses, but to the task of completely emancipating them from all oppression and exploitation, to the task facing the dictatorship of the proletariat."

—Stalin, from *Foundations of Leninism*, 1939

## STEP INTO THE TIME

**EVALUATING**

Examine the time line. What does the time line suggest about foreign relations in the interwar period?

"The state is a means to an end. Its end lies in the preservation and advancement of a community of physically and psychically homogeneous creatures. This preservation itself comprises first of all existence as a race and thereby permits the free development of all the forces dormant in this race. Of them a part will always primarily serve the preservation of physical life, and only the remaining part the promotion of a further spiritual development."

—Hitler, from *Mein Kampf*, 1925

PHOTO:(t)©RIA Novosti/TopFoto/The Image Works; (b)SuperStock/SuperStock; TEXT:(t) Stalin, Joseph. 1939. The Foundations of Leninism; (b)Hitler, Adolf. 1925. Mein Kampf. (Quoted by Boyler, John W. and Goldstein, Jan. 1987. Readings in Western Civilization Vol. 9: Twentieth-Century Europe. The University of Chicago.)

### EUROPE

- **1919** Treaty of Versailles
- **1922** Vladimir Lenin and the Communists create the USSR
- **1923** French and Belgian troops occupy the Ruhr Valley
- **1924** Joseph Stalin leads Soviet Union after Lenin's death
- **1926** Benito Mussolini establishes a Fascist dictatorship in Italy

**1919** — **1925**

### WORLD EVENTS

- **1920** First meeting of the League of Nations
- **1922** League of Nations confirms British Mandate for Palestine
- **1923** Mustafa Kemal, Atatürk, proclaims Republic of Turkey
- **1923** Nationalists and Communists are allies in China
- **1926** Fidel Castro, future president of Cuba, is born

## RISE OF DICTATORSHIPS IN EUROPE 1938

**1929** U.S. stock market crashes; Great Depression begins

**1930** Gandhi's civil disobedience movement begins in India

**1932** Terror Famine begins in Ukraine

**1932** Ibn Sa'ūd establishes the kingdom of Saudi Arabia

**1933** Paul von Hindenburg appoints Adolf Hitler as Chancellor

**1934** Beginning of the Long March by Chinese Communists

**1935** Nuremberg laws in Germany strip Jews of their citizenship

**1938** Japan passes military draft law

**April 1, 1939** Francisco Franco overthrows the Spanish Republic

1930 — 1935 — 1939

## ESSENTIAL QUESTIONS

- *What can cause economic instability?*
- *How might political change impact society?*

LESSON 1

# Instability After World War I

## THE STORY BEGINS...

German artist George Grosz described the effects of hyperinflation on shopping in Germany:

> "Lingering at the [shop] window was a luxury because shopping had to be done immediately. Even an additional minute meant an increase in price. One had to buy quickly because a rabbit, for example, might cost two million marks more by the time it took to walk into the store. A few million marks meant nothing, really. It was just that it meant more lugging. The packages of money needed to buy the smallest item had long since become too heavy for trouser pockets. They weighed many pounds. . . . People had to start carting their money around in wagons and knapsacks. I used a knapsack."

—George Grosz, *A Little Yes and a Big NO,* trans. L.S. Dorin (Dial, 1946), 124.

In 1914, a little over four German marks equaled one United States dollar. By 1923, four trillion marks equaled one United States dollar. Families saw their life savings disappear. People in Germany were losing hope. The Great Depression would spread this despair across Europe and the Americas.

*The Great Depression devastated American life in the 1930s as unemployment soared across the country.* ▼

| Causes of the Depression | Effects of the Depression |
|---|---|
| | |
| | |
| | |
| | |

**ANALYZING KEY IDEAS AND DETAILS**

**DESCRIBING** Read closely to identify causes and effects of the Great Depression. Record these causes and effects in a graphic organizer like this one.

# UNEASY PEACE, UNCERTAIN SECURITY

**GUIDING QUESTION** *What led to new problems in the years after World War I?*

From the beginning, the peace settlement at the end of World War I left nations unhappy. President Woodrow Wilson had realized that the peace settlement included provisions that could serve as new causes for conflict. He had placed many of his hopes for the future in the League of Nations. This organization, however, was not very effective in maintaining the peace.

One problem was the failure of the United States to join the League. Many American were **isolationists**, meaning they wanted to avoid involvement in European affairs. The U.S. Senate, in spite of President Wilson's wishes, refused to ratify, or approve, the Treaty of Versailles. That meant the United States could not join the League of Nations. Without the United States, the League of Nations' effectiveness was weakened.

Between 1919 and 1924, desire for security led the French government to demand strict enforcement of the Treaty of Versailles. This tough policy began with the issue of reparations (payments) that the Germans were supposed to make for the damage they had done in the war. In April 1921, the Allied Reparations Commission determined that Germany owed 132 billion German marks (33 billion U.S. dollars) for reparations, payable in **annual** installments of 2.5 billion marks.

The new German republic made its first payment in 1921. One year later, the German government faced a financial crisis and announced that it could not pay any more reparations. Outraged, France sent troops to occupy the Ruhr Valley, Germany's chief industrial and mining center. France planned to collect reparations by using the Ruhr mines and factories.

## INFLATION IN GERMANY

The German government adopted a policy of passive resistance to this French occupation. German workers went on strike. The German government mainly paid their salaries by printing more paper money. This only added to the inflation (rise in prices) that had already begun in Germany by the end of the war. The German mark soon became worthless. In 1914, 4.2 marks equaled 1 U.S. dollar. By the end of November 1923, the ratio had reached an incredible 4.2 trillion marks to equal 1 dollar.

Both France and Germany began to seek a way out of the disaster. In August 1924, an international commission adopted a new plan for reparations.

**ANALYZING KEY IDEAS AND DETAILS**

**DETERMINING CENTRAL IDEAS** Reread the paragraph that starts, "One problem was the failure . . ." What do the central ideas in this paragraph suggest about the march to war in Europe?

**DETERMINING MEANING**

The term **isolationist** contains the root word *isolate*, which means "to keep separate." Based on this, what can you infer about *isolationists'* beliefs regarding foreign policy?

*This woman uses German marks to light her stove during the Great Depression.*

**UNDERSTANDING CONTEXT** Why would this woman burn money during the Great Depression?

The Dawes Plan, named after the American banker who chaired the commission, first reduced reparations. It then coordinated Germany's annual payments with its ability to pay. The Dawes Plan also granted an initial $200 million loan for German recovery. This loan soon opened the door to heavy American investment in Europe. A brief period of European prosperity followed.

## THE TREATY OF LOCARNO

With prosperity came a new European diplomacy. The foreign ministers of Germany and France, Gustav Stresemann and Aristide Briand, fostered a spirit of cooperation. In 1925, they signed the Treaty of Locarno, which guaranteed Germany's new western borders with France and Belgium. Many viewed the Locarno pact as the beginning of a new era of European peace.

Three years later, the Kellogg-Briand Pact brought even more hope. Sixty-five nations signed this accord and pledged to "renounce [war] as an instrument of national policy." Nothing was said, however, about what would be done if anyone violated the pact.

### ✓ CHECKING FOR UNDERSTANDING

1. **EXPLAINING CAUSES** What led to new problems in the years after World War I?
2. **IDENTIFYING CONNECTIONS** What were German reparations supposed to accomplish?

# THE GREAT DEPRESSION

**GUIDING QUESTION** *What triggered the Great Depression?*

The brief period of prosperity that began in Europe in 1924 ended in an economic collapse that came to be known as the Great Depression. A **depression** is a period of low economic activity and rising unemployment.

Two factors played a major role in the start of the Depression. First was a series of downturns in the economies of individual nations in the second half of the 1920s. For example, prices for farm products, especially wheat, fell rapidly due to overproduction. As a result, rural consumers bought fewer goods, leading manufacturing countries to increase tariffs. International trade declined. An increase in the use of oil and hydroelectricity led to a slump in the coal industry.

The second trigger was an international financial crisis involving the U.S. stock market. Much of the European prosperity between 1924 and 1929 was built on U.S. bank loans to Germany. However, during the 1920s, the U.S. stock market boomed, and by 1928, American investors pulled money out of Germany to invest it in stocks. Then, in October 1929, the U.S. stock market crashed. Stock prices plunged.

In a panic, U.S. investors withdrew more funds from Germany and other European markets. By 1931 trade was slowing, industrial production was declining, and unemployment was rising.

### ✓ CHECKING FOR UNDERSTANDING

1. **IDENTIFYING CONNECTIONS** What triggered the Great Depression?
2. **RELATING EVENTS** Why was the U.S. market crash pivotal in triggering the Great Depression?

**INTEGRATING KNOWLEDGE AND IDEAS**

1. **INTEGRATING INFORMATION** The text indicates that Germany was vulnerable to the economic decline that triggered the Great Depression. How does the unemployment chart support and expand upon this idea?
2. **EVALUATING ARGUMENTS** This section argues that changes in the U.S. economy contributed to economic hardship in Germany. How does the author use evidence to support this argument?

**DETERMINING MEANING**

Read the paragraph that contains the word **depression**. What context clues help you understand the meaning of *depression*?

Shotwell, James T. 1929. War as an Instrument of National Policy and its Renunciation in the Pact of Paris. New York: Harcourt, Brace, and Company.

# RESPONSES TO THE DEPRESSION

**GUIDING QUESTION** *How did the Great Depression affect confidence in democracy?*

Financial crisis and economic depression were not new in Europe. However, the extent of the economic downturn after 1929 truly made this depression the Great Depression. During 1932, which was the worst year of the Depression, nearly 1 in every 4 British workers was unemployed. About 5.5 million Germans, or roughly 30 percent of the German labor force, had no jobs. In many of Germany's largest cities, the unemployed and homeless filled the streets.

Governments were unsure of how to deal with the severity of the crisis. Many governments decided to raise tariffs on imports in a hope to generate revenue and to exclude foreign goods from home markets. However, this worsened the crisis and had serious political effects.

One effect of the economic crisis was increased government activity in the economy. The Great Depression also led masses of people to follow political leaders who offered simple solutions to their problems in return for dictatorial powers. Everywhere in Europe, democracy seemed under threat or to be on the defensive.

In 1919, most European states, both major and minor, had democratic governments. In a number of states, women could now vote. Male political leaders had rewarded women for their contributions to the war effort by granting them voting rights. (However, women could not vote until 1944 in France, 1945 in Italy, and 1971 in Switzerland.) In the 1920s, maintaining these democratic governments was not easy.

### ANALYZING KEY IDEAS AND DETAILS

1. **CITING TEXT EVIDENCE** What evidence in the text suggests that Germany suffered greatly during the Depression? Cite evidence from the text to support your answer.
2. **ANALYZING EVENTS** Reread the final two paragraphs beginning with "The Roosevelt administration instituted. . . ." What parts of these paragraphs states an effect of the new U.S. policies? What words signal that this is an effect?

### UNEMPLOYMENT 1928–1938

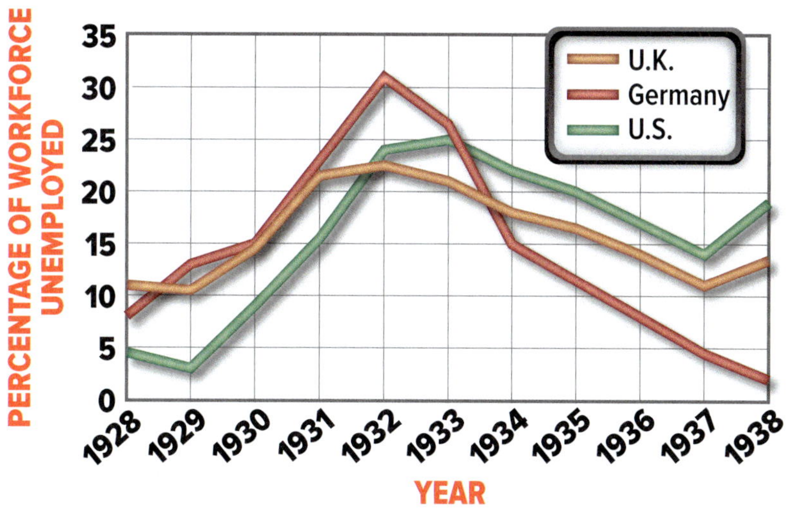


**Sources:** *European Historical Statistics, 1750–1970; Historical Statistics of the United States*

**ECONOMIC REASONING**

1. **GLOBAL ECONOMY** In which years was the height of the Great Depression?
2. **NATIONAL ECONOMIES** During the period from 1928 to 1938, which country experienced the largest rise in unemployment?

akg-images

MAKING CONNECTIONS TO TODAY

## RECESSION VERSUS DEPRESSION

A recession and a depression differ in severity. By definition, a recession is when the economy shrinks for two consecutive fiscal quarters. When the United States experienced a recession in 2008, people worried unemployment would reach Great Depression levels. But in studying unemployment numbers, economists discovered that, although the economic downturn was the worst since World War II, it was nowhere near as bad as the Great Depression. In 1933, unemployment had reached 29.4 percent. In December 2010, 9.4 percent of the U.S. population was unemployed.

1. **EVALUATING** Why might the recession of 2008 not have brought about the degree of extremism triggered by the Depression of the 1930s?
2. **UNDERSTANDING CHANGE** The Great Depression of the 1930s created the circumstances for the rise of Hitler in Germany. What does this suggest about the relationship between economic disruption and political disruption?

**DETERMINING MEANING**

The phrase **collective bargaining** combines the words *collective*, meaning "done by a group," and *bargaining*, meaning "negotiating terms." Based on these definitions, what is *collective bargaining*?

## GERMANY

Imperial Germany ended in 1918 with Germany's defeat in the war. A German state known as the Weimar (VY • mahr) Republic emerged. This new republic implemented a government with liberal democratic principles. The Weimar Republic, however, was plagued by serious economic problems. Germany experienced runaway inflation in 1922 and 1923. With it came serious social problems. Families on fixed incomes watched their life savings disappear.

To make matters worse, after a period of relative prosperity from 1924 to 1929, Germany was struck by the Great Depression. In 1930, unemployment had grown to 3 million people by March and to 4.38 million by December. The Depression paved the way for fear and the rise of extremist parties.

## FRANCE

France, too, suffered from financial problems after the war. Because it had a more balanced economy, France did not begin to feel the full effects of the Great Depression until 1932. The economic instability it then suffered soon had political effects. During a 19-month period in 1932 and 1933, six different cabinets were formed as France faced political chaos. Finally, in June 1936, a coalition of leftist parties—Communists, Socialists, and Radicals—formed the Popular Front government.

The Popular Front started a program for workers that some have called the French New Deal. This program was named after the New Deal in the United States. The French New Deal gave workers the right to **collective bargaining**, a 40-hour workweek in industry, and a minimum wage.

## GREAT BRITAIN

Although Britain experienced limited prosperity from 1925 to 1929, by 1929, it too faced the growing effects of the Great Depression. The Labour Party failed to solve the nation's economic problems and fell from power in 1931. A new government, led by the Conservatives, claimed credit for bringing Britain out of the worst stages of the Depression by using the traditional policies of balanced budgets and protective tariffs.

Political leaders in Britain largely ignored the new ideas of a British economist, John Maynard Keynes. Keynes argued that unemployment came from a decline in demand, not from overproduction. He believed governments could increase demand by creating jobs through **deficit spending**, or going into debt if necessary. Keynes's ideas differed from those who believed that depressions should be left to resolve themselves without government interference.

## THE UNITED STATES

After Germany, no Western nation was more affected by the Great Depression than the United States. All segments of society suffered. By 1932, U.S. industrial production fell by almost 50 percent from its 1929 level. By 1933, there were more than 12 million unemployed. Under these conditions, Democrat Franklin D. Roosevelt won the presidential election in 1932 by a landslide. Believing in free enterprise, Roosevelt believed capitalism must be reformed to save it. He pursued a policy of active governmental economic intervention known as the New Deal.

The New Deal included an increased program of public works. The Works Progress Administration (WPA), established in 1935, was a government organization employing about 3 million people at its peak. Workers built bridges, roads, post offices, and airports.

The Roosevelt administration instituted new social legislation that began the U.S. welfare system. In 1935, the Social Security Act created a system of old-age pensions, to be collected at age 65 by those no longer working. It also supplied unemployment insurance, or a temporary income to workers who had lost their jobs. Finally, this legislation also provided small welfare payments to others in need, including those with disabilities.

> "The civilization of the past hundred years, with its startling industrial changes, has tended more and more to make life insecure. Young people have come to wonder what would be their lot when they came to old age. The man with a job has wondered how long the job would last...
>
> This social security measure gives at least some protection to thirty millions of our citizens who will reap direct benefits through unemployment compensation, through old-age pensions and through increased services for the protection of children and the prevention of ill health...
>
> It is, in short, a law that will take care of human needs and at the same time provide for the United States an economic structure of vastly greater soundness."
>
> —President Roosevelt, statement on signing the Social Security Act, 1935

These reforms may have prevented a social revolution in the United States, but they did not solve the unemployment problems. In 1938, unemployment in the United States was more than 10 million. Only World War II and the growth of weapons industries brought U.S. workers back to full employment.

### ✓ CHECKING FOR UNDERSTANDING

1. **INTERPRETING** How did the Great Depression affect people's confidence in democracy?
2. **SUMMARIZING** How might collective bargaining have helped French workers?
3. **UNDERSTANDING CONTEXT** What were the intended outcomes of federally funded New Deal projects such as the WPA?

CITIZENSHIP

### A SAFETY NET FOR AMERICAN WORKERS

During the Great Depression, observers realized that the consequences of not providing social safety measures for workers in an industrial economy were disastrous. As a result, the U.S. Congress and Roosevelt created the Social Security Act of 1935, which created a federally run pension system and allowed for state-federal partnerships for unemployment insurance, which pays the unemployed a percentage of their former wages as they look for new jobs. The Depression is now long gone, but these provisions persist. Indeed, over the years, the government has worked to improve and strengthen both. These actions were proven prudent when the United States entered the recession of 2008. Millions lost their jobs and savings at this time. Congress reacted by repeatedly extending unemployment insurance for those who struggled to find work. Likewise, those who lost their savings could fall back on Social Security to help pay the bills.

**COMPARING AND CONTRASTING** What does the continuing need for programs such as Social Security and unemployment insurance suggest about the similarities and differences between the 1930s and the 2008 recession?

## ARTS AND SCIENCES

**GUIDING QUESTION** *How were the arts and sciences influenced by World War I?*

With political, economic, and social uncertainties came intellectual uncertainties. These were evident in the artistic and scientific achievements of the years following World War I. The shocks of World War I had left many authors and artists, such as F. Scott Fitzgerald and Pablo Picasso, with a sense of aimlessness when it was over. This led to the creation of countercultural art movements that challenged established styles. Writer Gertrude Stein coined the phrase "the lost generation" to describe the feeling of spiritual disorientation felt by many artists

**ANALYZING KEY IDEAS AND DETAILS**

**DETERMINING CENTRAL IDEAS** What is the central idea of this section? How does the text present and develop this idea? Write a brief summary of this section in your own words.

*The Persistence of Memory* (1931), a surrealist painting by Salvador Dalí

**DETERMINING MEANING**

The word *surreal* means "bizarre." Based on this, what is **surrealism**?

and authors. Author Ernest Hemingway's work *The Sun Also Rises*, a central work of this "lost generation," portrays many individuals psychologically damaged by the human losses of World War I.

After 1918, the prewar fascination with the absurd and the unconscious content of the mind seemed even more **appropriate** in light of the nightmares of World War I battlefronts. "The world does not make sense, so why should art?" was a common remark. This sentiment gave rise to Dadaism and surrealism.

The Dadaists were artists who were obsessed with the idea that life has no purpose. They tried to express the insanity of life in their art. A more important artistic movement than Dadaism was **surrealism**. By portraying the unconscious such as fantasies, dreams, and even nightmares, the surrealists sought to show the greater reality that exists beyond the physical world. One of the world's foremost surrealist painters, the Spaniard Salvador Dalí, placed recognizable objects in unrecognizable relationships, thus making the irrational visible.

The prewar physics revolution begun by Albert Einstein continued in the 1920s and 1930s. In fact, some have called the 1920s the "heroic age of physics." Newtonian physics had made people believe that all phenomena could be defined and predicted. In 1927, German physicist Werner Heisenberg's **uncertainty principle** shook this belief. Physicists knew that atoms were made of smaller parts, or subatomic particles. The uncertainty principle is based on the unpredictable behavior of these subatomic particles. Heisenberg's theory essentially suggests that all physical laws are based on uncertainty. This theory challenged Newtonian physics and represented a new worldview. The principle of uncertainty fit in well with the other uncertainties of the interwar years.

### ✓ CHECKING FOR UNDERSTANDING

1. **IDENTIFYING CONNECTIONS** How were the sciences influenced by World War I?
2. **UNDERSTANDING CONTEXT** How were Dadaism and surrealism a reaction to World War I?
3. **SUMMARIZING** Why is the term "lost generation" used to refer to those who came of age during the years following World War I?



## LESSON 1 REVIEW

### Time and Place

1. **DETERMINING CONTEXT** Identify one artist or writer from the postwar period and explain how his or her work reflects the mood of the time.

### Building History-Social Science Analysis Skills

2. **INFERRING** How did World War I change the physical landscape of Europe? How could that change have contributed to the Depression?
3. **UNDERSTANDING CONTEXT** The Great Depression economically overwhelmed an already exhausted continent. What might have occurred differently if the Great Depression did not happen?
4. **ANALYZING CHANGE** What economic problems were brought about by the Great Depression? How did these problems lead people to accept authoritarian governments?

### Writing About History

5. **EXPLANATORY WRITING** Write an essay explaining President Roosevelt's New Deal and its immediate and lasting effect on the U.S. economy.

### Collaborating

6. **EVALUATING** Select one nation discussed in the lesson while a partner selects a second nation. Compare and contrast the ways your selected nations were similar and different in their approach to the Depression.

## ESSENTIAL QUESTIONS

- *What can cause economic instability?*
- *How might political change impact society?*

LESSON 2

# The Rise of Dictatorial Regimes

## THE STORY BEGINS...

Shortly before Vladimir Lenin died in 1924, a power struggle began between Leon Trotsky and Joseph Stalin over who would succeed him as leader of the Soviet Union. Stalin had built his reputation as a dedicated Communist in the years leading up to the Russian Revolution. After the revolution, he bolstered his reputation through service to Lenin's government and with speeches such as this one:

> "Russia is so far the only country where the workers and peasants have seized power. The pre-condition for the seizure of power was the most profound revolution in the world, which was followed by the abolition of the old machinery of state power and the rise of a new one. The position in the old days was that the workers as a rule toiled for the masters, while the masters governed the country. This, in fact, explains why, before the revolution, all the experience in governing the country was concentrated in the ruling classes. But after the October Revolution, power was assumed by the workers and peasants, who had never governed before, who knew only how to work for others, and who had no adequate experience in governing the country."

—Joseph Stalin, speech at the Opening of the First All-Russian Conference of Responsible Personnel of the Workers' and Peasants' Inspection, October 15, 1920

Stalin would triumph in his power struggle against Trotsky. Like Mussolini in Italy, Hitler in Germany, and other dictators in states across Europe, Stalin would turn his country into an authoritarian state.

*Dictators such as Joseph Stalin made use of new forms of mass media, such as radio and film, to enhance their power, prestige, and public image.* ▶

PHOTO:Laski Diffusion/Getty Images; TEXT:Stalin, Joseph 1920. Speech at the Opening of the First All-Russian Conference of Responsible Personnel of the Workers' and Peasants' Inspection - October 15, 1920. Reprinted in 1953 J. V. Stalin Works Volume 4 - November 1917-1920. Moscow: Foreign Languages Publishing House.

| Emerging Dictatorial Leaders | | |
|---|---|---|
| Name | Party | Country |
| | | |
| | | |
| | | |

**ANALYZING KEY IDEAS AND DETAILS**

**DETERMINING CENTRAL IDEAS** Re-read the lesson closely, paying close attention to emerging dictators. Record each leader, nationality, and party in a graphic organizer like this one.

# THE RISE OF DICTATORS

**ANALYZING KEY IDEAS AND DETAILS**

1. **DETERMINING CENTRAL IDEAS** Read the two paragraphs that start with the sentence "By 1922, Mussolini's movement was growing quickly." What is the central idea of these two paragraphs? Does the last sentence, "By the end of the year, Mussolini ruled Italy as *Il Duce*, 'The Leader,'" first support or contradict the central idea?
2. **CITING TEXT EVIDENCE** The section titled "The Fascist State" begins with the sentence "Believing that the Fascist state should be totalitarian, Mussolini used various means to establish complete control over the Italian people." What evidence does the author provide to suggest that this goal was not achieved?

**DETERMINING MEANING**

Synonyms for **totalitarian** include *undemocratic, tyrannical, one-party, oppressive,* and *repressive*. What do these synonyms suggest about a *totalitarian* state?

**DETERMINING MEANING**

The word **fascism** comes from the Italian word *fascio,* meaning, among other things, "political group." In a *fascist* country, the strong central government controls the people and is more important than the individual. How might a *fascist* leader rule the people?

**GUIDING QUESTION** *How did Mussolini create a dictatorial state in Italy?*

By 1939, only two major European states—France and Great Britain—remained democratic. The Depression led to a loss of confidence in civic institutions and governments. Authoritarians took advantage of this disillusionment to gain political momentum and power. Italy, the Soviet Union, Germany, and many other European states adopted dictatorial regimes. These regimes took both old and new forms.

A new form of dictatorship was the modern totalitarian state. In a **totalitarian state**, the government aims to control the political, economic, social, intellectual, and cultural lives of its citizens. Totalitarian regimes pushed the central state's power far beyond what it had been in the past. These regimes wanted more than passive obedience; they wanted to conquer the minds and hearts of their subjects. They achieved this goal through mass propaganda techniques and modern communications.

The totalitarian states were led by a single leader and a single party. They rejected the ideal of limited government power and the guarantee of individual freedoms. Instead, individual freedom was subordinated to the collective will of the masses as determined by the leader. The masses were expected to be actively involved in achieving the state's goals.

## FASCISM IN ITALY

In the 1920s, Benito Mussolini (MOO • suh • LEE • nee) set up the first European fascist movement in Italy. Mussolini began his political career as a Socialist. In 1919, he created a new political group, the *Fascio di Combattimento*, or League of Combat. *Fascism* comes from that name.

As a political philosophy, **fascism** (FA • SHIH • zuhm) glorifies the state above the individual by emphasizing the need for a strong central government led by a dictatorial ruler. In a fascist state, the government controls the people and stifles any opposition.

By 1922, Mussolini's movement was growing quickly. The middle-class fear of socialism, communism, and disorder made the Fascists increasingly attractive to many people. Mussolini knew that many Italians were still angry over the failure to receive more land from the peace treaty. He knew nationalism was a powerful force and demanded more land for Italy. Mussolini converted thousands to the Fascist Party with his nationalistic appeals.

In 1922, Mussolini and the Fascists threatened to march on Rome if they were not given power. Victor Emmanuel III, the king of Italy, gave in and made

## POLITICS IN EUROPE 1930s

Mussolini prime minister. Mussolini used his position as prime minister to create a Fascist dictatorship. He was made head of the government with the power to make laws by decree. The police were given unrestricted authority to arrest and jail anyone for either political or nonpolitical crimes. In 1926, the Fascists outlawed all other political parties in Italy and set up a secret police, known as the OVRA. By the end of the year, Mussolini ruled Italy as *Il Duce* (eel DOO • chay), "The Leader."

## THE FASCIST STATE

Believing that the Fascist state should be totalitarian, Mussolini used various means to establish complete control over the Italian people. The OVRA watched citizens' political activities and enforced government policies. The Italian Fascists also tried to exercise control over the mass **media**, including newspapers, radio, and film. The media was used to spread propaganda. Simple slogans such as "Mussolini Is Always Right" were used to mold Italians into a single-minded Fascist community.

The Fascists also used organizations to promote the ideals of fascism. For example, by 1939, about 66 percent of the population between the ages of 8 and 18 were members of Fascist youth groups. These youth groups particularly focused on military activities and values.

### GEOGRAPHIC REASONING

1. **PATTERNS AND MOVEMENT** Where were authoritarian governments located?
2. **PATTERNS AND MOVEMENT** Determine which countries transitioned from democratic to non-democratic in the 1930s.

*Mussolini addressing a crowd of more than 500,000 people*

With these organizations, the Fascists hoped to create a nation of new Italians who were fit, disciplined, and war-loving. In practice, however, the Fascists largely maintained traditional social **attitudes**. This was especially evident in their policies on women. The Fascists portrayed the family as the pillar of the state. Seen as the foundation of the family, women were to be homemakers and mothers. According to Mussolini, these roles were "their natural and fundamental mission in life."

Mussolini attempted to place Italian industries and the economy under the control of the state. He also strengthened the Italian army and engaged in conflicts in Albania and in Libya and Ethiopia in Africa. However, Mussolini never achieved the degree of totalitarian control seen in Hitler's Germany or Stalin's Soviet Union. The Italian Fascist Party did not completely destroy the country's old power structure. Mussolini's compromise with the traditional institutions of Italy was evident in his dealings with the Catholic Church. In the Lateran Accords of February 1929, Mussolini's regime recognized the sovereign independence of a small area of 109 acres (about 44 hectares) within Rome known as Vatican City. The Church had claimed this area since Italian unification in 1870. Mussolini's regime also recognized Catholicism as the "sole religion of the State." In return, the Catholic Church urged Italians to support the Fascist regime.

### ✓ CHECKING FOR UNDERSTANDING

1. **EXPLAINING CAUSES** How did Mussolini create a dictatorial state in Italy?
2. **USING MAPS** Look at the map. Where were nondemocratic governments mostly concentrated?
3. **UNDERSTANDING CONTEXT** Why did so many Italian people find fascism acceptable?

## FROM RUSSIA TO THE USSR

**GUIDING QUESTION** *How did Stalin gain and maintain power in the USSR?*

During the civil war in Russia, Lenin had followed a policy of war communism. The government controlled most industries and seized grain from peasants to ensure supplies for the army. When the war was over, peasants began to sabotage the Communist program by hoarding food. Moreover, drought caused a terrible famine between 1920 and 1922. As many as 5 million died. With agricultural disaster came industrial collapse. By 1921, industrial output was only 20 percent of its 1913 level. Russia was exhausted. A peasant banner proclaimed, "Down with Lenin and horseflesh. Give us the Czar and pork." As Leon Trotsky said, "The country, and the government with it, were at the very edge of the abyss."

### LENIN'S NEW ECONOMIC POLICY

In March 1921, Lenin pulled Russia back from the abyss. He abandoned war communism in favor of his New Economic Policy (NEP). The NEP was a modified version of the old capitalist system. Peasants were allowed to sell their produce openly. Retail stores, as well as small industries that employed fewer than 20 workers, could be privately owned and operated. Heavy industry, banking, and mines, however, remained in the hands of the government.

#### ANALYZING KEY IDEAS AND DETAILS

1. **DETERMINING CENTRAL IDEAS** What is the central idea of the subsection titled "Costs of Stalin's Programs"? How does the text present and develop this idea? Write a brief summary of this section in your own words.
2. **CITING TEXT EVIDENCE** One key point related in this section is that Stalin gradually gained more power. What evidence from the text indicates that early on he had to contend with competing centers of power in the USSR?

PHOTO:©Jean, Baptiste, Greuz/Age Fotostock America; TEXT:(t to b)Mussolini, Benito. Quoted 2010 by Suanders, Francis Stonor in The Woman Who Shot Mussolini. Metropolitan Books, Henry Holt and Company; Knight, Patricia. 2003. The Lateran Pacts From Mussolini and Fascism. Routledge; ______. 1919. "Russia Under the Bolsheviki" from Current History: A Monthly Magazine of the New York Times. The New York Times Company; Trotsky, Leon. Translated 2004 by Eastman, Max. The Revolution Betrayed. Dover Publication.

## THE SOVIET UNION

In 1922, Lenin and the Communists formally created a new state called the Union of Soviet Socialist Republics. The state was also known as the USSR (its initials) or as the Soviet Union (its shortened form). By that time, a revived market and a good harvest had ended the famine. Soviet agricultural production climbed to 75 percent of its prewar level. Overall, the NEP saved the Soviet Union from complete economic disaster. Lenin, however, intended the NEP to be only a temporary retreat from the goals of communism.

Lenin died in 1924. A struggle for power began at once among the seven members of the Politburo (PAH • luht • BYUR • OH)—the Communist Party's main policy-making body. The Politburo was severely divided over the future direction of the Soviet Union.

One group, led by Leon Trotsky, wanted to end the NEP and to launch Russia on a path of rapid industrialization, chiefly at the expense of the peasants. This group also wanted to spread communism abroad. It believed that the revolution in Russia would survive only with new communist states.

Another group in the Politburo rejected the idea of worldwide communist revolution. Instead, it wanted to focus on building a socialist state in Russia and to continue Lenin's NEP. This group believed that rapid industrialization would harm the living standards of the peasants.

## STALIN AND HIS FIVE-YEAR PLANS

These divisions were further strained by an intense personal rivalry between Leon Trotsky and another Politburo member, Joseph Stalin. By 1927, Stalin had the upper hand. By this time, he had removed Trotsky and several other Bolsheviks from the Communist Party and the government. Trotsky fled the

### GEOGRAPHIC REASONING

By 1939, the Soviet Union was increasingly industrialized and collectivized.

1. **EXPLORING PLACE** What resource was most plentiful near the Caspian Sea?
2. **EXPLORING REGIONS** Why do you think the forced labor region was mostly located in the far east of Russia?

country and was murdered years later, most likely on Stalin's orders, in Mexico. With Trotsky and most of the old Bolsheviks out of the way, Stalin was free to establish a powerful dictatorship. He seized all power for himself and greatly curtailed the freedom of the press. Now no one could oppose him or speak out against his policies.

Stalin maintained a cult of personality by using media and propaganda to create a heroic, idealized image. The press presented Stalin as a powerful, all-knowing leader and as the father of the people of the USSR.

**ANALYZING PRIMARY SOURCES**

1. **UNDERSTANDING CONTEXT** Why might Avidenko have written this poem?
2. **INTERPRETING** What does this poem reveal about the image of Stalin and his cult of personality?
3. **IDENTIFYING BIAS** Do you think the author actually felt this strongly about Stalin? Why or why not?

> "Thank you, Stalin. Thank you because I am joyful. Thank you because I am well. No matter how old I become, I shall never forget how we received Stalin two days ago. Centuries will pass, and the generations still to come will regard us as the happiest of mortals, as the most fortunate of men, because we lived in the century of centuries, because we were privileged to see Stalin, our inspired leader. Yes, and we regard ourselves as the happiest of mortals because we are the contemporaries of a man who never had an equal in world history. . . .
>
> Everything belongs to thee, chief of our great country. And when the woman I love presents me with a child the first word it shall utter will be: Stalin."

—A. O. Avidenko, *Hymn to Stalin*

Stalin made a significant shift in economic policy in 1928 when he ended the NEP. That year he launched his First Five-Year Plan. The Five-Year Plans set economic goals for five-year periods. Their purpose was to transform Russia virtually overnight from an agricultural into an industrial country.

The First Five-Year Plan focused on production of military and capital goods (goods devoted to the production of other goods such as heavy machines). The plan quadrupled the production of heavy machinery and doubled oil production. Between 1928 and 1937, during the first two Five-Year Plans, steel production in Russia increased from 4 million to 18 million tons (3.6 to 16.3 million t) per year.

## COSTS OF STALIN'S PROGRAMS

The social and political costs of industrialization were enormous. The number of workers increased by millions between 1932 and 1940, but investment in housing actually declined after 1929. The result was that millions of workers and their families lived in miserable conditions. Real wages of industrial workers declined by 43 percent between 1928 and 1940.

**DETERMINING MEANING**

*Collective* can mean "done by a group." It can also mean "a political principle of centralized social or economic control." What do these definitions suggest about **collectivization** of farmland?

With rapid industrialization came equally rapid **collectivization** of agriculture, a system in which private farms were eliminated. Instead, the government owned all the land, and the peasants worked it. The peasants resisted by hoarding crops and killing livestock. In response, Stalin stepped up the program. By 1934, 26 million family farms had been collectivized into 250,000 units.

**DETERMINING MEANING**

**Authoritarian** comes from the word *authority,* which can mean "a person having control or influence over others." In a totalitarian government, leaders seek total control over their citizens to create a new social order. How might *authoritarian* and *totalitarian* systems differ?

Collectivization was done at tremendous cost. Hoarding food and slaughtering livestock led to widespread famine. The Ukraine region was the center of this famine. Estimates range from 2.4 to 7.5 million Ukrainian deaths out of 10 million total in the Soviet Union. Some scholars consider the famine a deliberate move by Stalin. This "Terror Famine" was meant to cripple the movement for Ukrainian independence.

Avidenko, A. O. 1935. Hymn to Stalin. Quoted 1983 by McCauley, Martin. Stalin and Stalinism. New York: Routledge.

Stalin's programs had other costs as well. To achieve his goals, Stalin strengthened his control over the party and freely violated human rights. Those who resisted were sent into forced labor camps, known as Gulags, in Siberia. During the time known as the Great Purge, Stalin expelled numerous people from all aspects of Soviet life. Many were publicly shamed in elaborate "show trials" that were meant to display assumed guilt rather than to determine innocence. Members of Soviet society affected by the purges included army officers, diplomats, union officials, intellectuals, artists, engineers, non-Russians, Jews, members of the Communist Party suspected of disloyalty, and even ordinary citizens. About 8 million were arrested and sent to the Gulags; they never returned. Others were executed.

The Stalin era also overturned permissive social legislation enacted in the early 1920s. To promote equal rights for women, the Communists had made the divorce process easier. After Stalin came to power, the family was praised as a small collective. Parents were responsible for teaching the values of hard work, duty, and discipline to their children.

### ✓ CHECKING FOR UNDERSTANDING

1. **SUMMARIZING** How did Stalin gain and maintain power in the USSR?
2. **UNDERSTANDING CHANGE** Explain how Joseph Stalin used his position in the Communist Party and other means to gain control over the USSR.
3. **SUMMARIZING** What was the Great Purge?

## AUTHORITARIAN STATES IN THE WEST

**GUIDING QUESTION** *What was the goal of authoritarian governments in the West?*

A number of governments in the Western world were not totalitarian but were **authoritarian**. These states adopted some of the features of totalitarian states, in particular, their use of police powers. However, these authoritarian governments did not want to create a new kind of mass society. Instead, they wanted to preserve the existing social order.

### EASTERN EUROPE

At first, it seemed that political democracy would become well established in Eastern Europe after World War I. Austria, Poland, Czechoslovakia, Yugoslavia (known as the kingdom of the Serbs, Croats, and Slovenes until 1929), Romania, Bulgaria, and Hungary all adopted parliamentary systems. However, authoritarian regimes soon replaced most of these systems.

Parliamentary systems failed in most Eastern European states for several reasons. These states had little tradition of political democracy. In addition, they were mostly rural and agrarian. Large landowners still dominated most of the land. Powerful landowners, the churches, and even some members of the small middle class feared land reform. They also feared communist upheaval and ethnic conflict. These groups looked to authoritarian governments to maintain the old system. Only Czechoslovakia, which had a large middle class, a liberal tradition, and a strong industrial base, maintained its political democracy.

**ANALYZING PRIMARY SOURCES**

**STALIN'S PURGE**

Poet Anna Andreyevna Gorenko, who wrote under the pseudonym Anna Akhmatova, was silenced during the Great Purge and watched as loved ones and fellow writers were imprisoned and disappeared. In 1942, her poem "Courage" appeared:

"We know that our fate in
the balance is cast
And we are the history makers.
The hour for courage has
sounded at last
And courage has never forsaken us.
We do not fear death where the
wild bullets screech,
Nor weep over homes that are
gutted,
For we shall preserve you our own
Russian speech,
The glorious language of Russia!
Your free and pure utterance we
shall convey
To new generations, unshackled
you'll stay
Forever!"

—quoted in *Anna Akhmatova and Her Circle*

**DRAWING CONCLUSIONS** According to this poem, what may be lost in the Great Purge that "we" must save?

**UNDERSTANDING CRAFT AND STRUCTURE**

1. **DETERMINING MEANING** The text introduces the term ***authoritarian*** and contrasts it with the term ***totalitarian***. What is that difference? What does this contrast suggest about the difference between the regimes discussed previously in the lesson and those that will be discussed in this section?
2. **DETERMINING POINT OF VIEW** Reread the subsection titled "Spain." Search this section for words that signal an opinion. Write the full sentence that contains the opinion, and explain how you identified it.

## SPAIN

In Spain, too, political democracy failed to survive. Led by General Francisco Franco, Spanish military forces revolted against the democratic government in 1936. A brutal and bloody civil war began.

Foreign intervention complicated the Spanish Civil War. The fascist regimes of Italy and Germany aided Franco's forces with arms, money, and soldiers. Hitler used the Spanish Civil War as an opportunity to test the new weapons of his revived air force. German bombers destroyed the city of Guernica in April 1937. The Spanish republican government was aided by 40,000 foreign volunteers. The Soviet Union sent in trucks, planes, tanks, and military advisers.

The Spanish Civil War came to an end when Franco's forces captured Madrid in 1939. Franco established a dictatorship that lasted until his death in 1975. Because Franco's dictatorship favored traditional groups and did not try to control every aspect of people's lives, it is an example of an authoritarian rather than a totalitarian regime. Nevertheless, his rule was harsh. He relied on special police forces, and opponents to the regime who had not fled into exile were imprisoned.

In his mural *Guernica* Spanish artist Pablo Picasso immortalized the horrible destruction of the city of Guernica in April 1937.

**INTEGRATING INFORMATION**
What one word best sums up the mood of *Guernica*? Use details from the painting to explain how the artist created this mood.

Art Archive/Reina Sofia Museum, Madrid

### ☑ CHECKING FOR UNDERSTANDING

1. **INTERPRETING** What was the goal of authoritarian governments in the West?
2. **DETERMINING CONTEXT** In what ways did Franco's government preserve the existing social order?
3. **UNDERSTANDING CHANGE** Why was Czechoslovakia able to maintain a political democracy when its neighbors did not?

## LESSON 2 REVIEW

### Time and Place

1. **USING MAPS** Examine the map "Politics in Europe," noting which countries were ruled by an authoritarian or fascist leader. Why might democratic nations be fearful?

### Building History-Social Science Analysis Skills

2. **UNDERSTANDING CONTEXT** Why would Mussolini choose a slogan such as "Mussolini is Always Right"?
3. **UNDERSTANDING CONTEXT** What was the goal of authoritarian governments in the West?
4. **ANALYZING CHANGE** Explain the changes that took place as a government transitioned from democratic to authoritarian.

### Writing About History

5. **USING EVIDENCE** In a short essay, describe the political structures of Italy in the 1930s. How did Mussolini gain control? How did he maintain his hold on the government?

### Collaborating

6. **EVALUATING POINT OF VIEW** In this lesson, the text makes a distinction between authoritarian regimes of the interwar period and totalitarian regimes of the interwar period. It puts Mussolini's Italy in the latter category. Hold a debate with one or more of your fellow students about whether his regime should be considered more totalitarian than authoritarian, and why it matters.

ESSENTIAL QUESTIONS

- *What can cause economic instability?*
- *How might political change impact society?*

THE STORY BEGINS...

LESSON 3

# Hitler and Nazi Germany

As a young Austrian serving in the Bavarian Army during World War I, Adolf Hitler saw action in Belgium and France. There he slogged through the trenches and witnessed his fellow soldiers decimated, although he received the news of Germany's defeat while in a hospital being treated after a gas attack. He never forgot the way he believed Germany was insulted by the peace terms it had to accept. A few years after the war, he gave the following speech in Munich:

> "The German people after twenty-five or thirty years, in consequence of the fact that it will never be able to pay all that is demanded of it, will have so gigantic a sum still owing that practically it will be forced to produce more than it does today. What will the end be? and the answer to that question is Pledging of our land, enslavement of our labor-strength. Therefore, in the economic sphere, November 1918 was in truth no achievement, but it was the beginning of our collapse. And in the political sphere we lost first our military prerogatives, and with that loss went the real sovereignty of our State, and then our financial independence, for there remained always the Reparations Commission so that practically we have no longer a politically independent German Reich, we are already a colony of the outside world. We have contributed to this because so far as possible we humiliated ourselves morally, we positively destroyed our own honor and helped to befoul, to besmirch, and to deny everything which we previously held as sacred."

—Adolf Hitler, *"Speech of April 12, 1922,"* Munich

Even as a young man, Hitler was skilled at inciting resentment. He used this skill to rise to power in Germany and to remake the state on his terms.

*Nazi leader Adolf Hitler rides through a parade in the Sudetenland region of Czechoslovakia, 1938.* ▶

| Adolf Hitler's Rise to Power |
| --- |
| |
| |
| |
| |
| |
| |

**ANALYZING KEY IDEAS AND DETAILS**

**IDENTIFYING STEPS** As you read, take note of the events that led to Adolf Hitler's rise to power. Record these events in a graphic organizer like this one.

# HITLER AND NAZISM

**ANALYZING KEY IDEAS AND DETAILS**

1. **DETERMINING CENTRAL IDEAS** What is the central idea of this section? How does the text present and develop this idea?
2. **ANALYZING EVENTS** Reread the section titled "Rise of Nazism." What part of this section states an effect of Hitler's arrest and imprisonment?

**DETERMINING MEANING**

The word **Nazi** comes from a shortened version of Hitler's party name: The National Socialist German Workers' Party, or NSDAP. What does the larger name suggest about Hitler's appeal?

**GUIDING QUESTION** *What was the basis of Adolf Hitler's ideas?*

Adolf Hitler was born in Austria in 1889. A failure in school, he traveled to Vienna to become an artist but was rejected by the academy. Here he developed his basic political ideas. At the core of Hitler's ideas was racism, especially anti-Semitism (hostility toward Jews). Hitler was also an extreme nationalist who knew how political parties could effectively use propaganda and terror.

After serving four years on the Western Front during World War I, Hitler remained in Germany and entered politics. In 1919, he joined the little-known German Workers' Party, one of several right-wing extreme nationalist parties in Munich.

By the summer of 1921, Hitler had taken total control of the party. By then the party had been renamed the National Socialist German Workers' Party (NSDAP, an abbreviation of the German name), or **Nazi**, for short. Within two years, party membership had grown to 55,000 people, with 15,000 in the party militia. The militia was variously known as the SA, the Storm Troops, or the Brownshirts, after the color of their uniforms.

An overconfident Hitler staged an armed uprising against the government in Munich in November 1923. This uprising, called the Beer Hall Putsch, was quickly crushed, and Hitler was sentenced to prison, where he wrote *Mein Kampf*, or *My Struggle,* an account of his movement and its basic ideas.

In *Mein Kampf*, Hitler links extreme German nationalism, strong anti-Semitism, and anticommunism together by a Social Darwinian theory of struggle. This theory emphasizes the right of "superior" nations to *Lebensraum* (LAY • buhnz • ROWM)—"living space"—through expansion. It also upholds the right of "superior" individuals to gain authoritarian leadership over the masses.

## RISE OF NAZISM

While in prison, Hitler came to the conclusion that the Nazis would have to attain power legally through elections, not by a violent overthrow of the Weimar Republic. This meant that the Nazi Party would have to be a mass party that could compete for votes.

When out of prison, Hitler expanded the Nazi Party in Germany. By 1929, it had a national party organization. Three years later, it had grown to over 800,000 members and had become the largest party in the Reichstag—the German parliament.

No doubt, Germany's economic difficulties were a crucial factor in the Nazis' rise to political power. Unemployment had risen dramatically, growing from 4.35 million in 1931 to about 5.5 million by the winter of 1932. Hitler also promised a new Germany that appealed to nationalism and militarism.

> "The National Government will therefore regard it as its first and foremost duty to reestablish the unity of spirit and will of our [people]. It will preserve and defend the foundations upon which the power of our nation rests. It will extend its strong, protecting hand over Christianity as the basis of our entire morality, and the family as the germ cell of the body of our [people] and State. It will reawaken in our [people], beyond the borders of rank and class, its sense of national and political unity and its resultant duties. It will establish reverence for our great past and pride in our old traditions as the basis for the education of our German youth."
>
> —Adolf Hitler, "Appeal to the German People" speech, 1933

**ANALYZING PRIMARY SOURCES**

1. **DETERMINING CENTRAL IDEAS** What is Hitler's main campaign promise in this excerpt?
2. **UNDERSTANDING CONTEXT** Why do you think this speech might have appealed to some Germans? Who might it have appealed to the most?

## THE NAZIS TAKE CONTROL

After 1930, the German government ruled by decree with the support of President Hindenburg. The Reichstag had little power. Increasingly, the right-wing elites of Germany—the industrial leaders, landed aristocrats, military officers, and higher bureaucrats—looked to Hitler for leadership. Under pressure, Hindenburg agreed to allow Hitler to become chancellor in 1933 and to create a new government.

Within two months, Hitler had laid the foundation for the Nazi Party's complete control over Germany. Hitler's "legal seizure" of power came on March 23, 1933, when a two-thirds vote of the Reichstag passed the Enabling Act. This law gave the government the power to ignore the constitution for four years while it issued laws to deal with the country's problems. It also gave Hitler's later actions a legal basis. He no longer needed the Reichstag or President Hindenburg. In effect, Hitler became a dictator appointed by the parliamentary body itself.

With their new power, the Nazis quickly brought all institutions under their control. They purged the civil service of democratic elements and of Jews—whom they blamed for Europe's economic woes. They set up prison camps called **concentration camps** for people who opposed them. All political parties except the Nazis were abolished.

By the end of the summer of 1933, only seven months after being appointed chancellor, Hitler had established the basis for a totalitarian state. When Hindenburg died in 1934, the office of president was abolished. Hitler became sole ruler of Germany. People took oaths of loyalty to their *Führer* (FYUR • uhr), or "Leader."

### ☑ CHECKING FOR UNDERSTANDING

1. **SUMMARIZING** What was the basis of Adolf Hitler's ideas?
2. **DETERMINING CONTEXT** What role did the Beer Hall Putsch play in Hitler's rise to power?
3. **IDENTIFYING CONNECTIONS** In what ways were economic difficulties a factor in the rise of the Nazis' political power?

Hitler, Adolf. 1933. The First Radio Broadcast of Adolf Hitler's Proclamation. Reprinted 1945 in Adolf Hitler Collection of Speeches 1922-1945.

# THE NAZI STATE, 1933–1939

**GUIDING QUESTION** *How did Hitler build a Nazi state?*

Hitler wanted to develop a totalitarian state. He had not simply sought power for power's sake. He had a larger goal—the development of an **Aryan** racial state that would dominate Europe and possibly the world for generations to come. (*Aryan* is a term used to identify people speaking Indo-European languages. The Nazis misused the term by treating it as a racial designation and identifying the Aryans with the ancient Greeks and Romans and twentieth-century Germans and Scandinavians.) The Nazis thought the Germans were the true descendants and leaders of the Aryans and would create an empire.

To achieve his goal, Hitler needed the active involvement of the German people. Hitler stated:

> "We must develop organizations in which an individual's entire life can take place. Then every activity and every need of every individual will be regulated by the collectivity represented by the party. There is no longer any arbitrary will, there are no longer any free realms in which the individual belongs to himself. . . . The time of personal happiness is over."
>
> —quoted in *Hitler,* 1973

The Nazis pursued the creation of the totalitarian state in several ways. For one thing, they used mass demonstrations and spectacles to make the German people an instrument of Hitler's policies. These meetings, especially the Nuremberg party rallies that were held every September, usually evoked mass enthusiasm and excitement.

### ANALYZING KEY IDEAS AND DETAILS

1. **CITING TEXT EVIDENCE** The text claims that Hitler used terror to control Germany. What evidence does the text provide to support this claim? Cite evidence from the text in your answer.
2. **ANALYZING EVENTS** Reread the paragraph that begins, "In September 1935, . . ." What part of this paragraph states an effect of the Nazi racial policies?

### DETERMINING MEANING

The word **Aryan** comes from a Sanskrit word meaning "noble." Why do you think Hitler would have been drawn to this word? How did he misuse the term?

*SS troops march through the streets of Berlin on Hitler's birthday in 1939.*

### UNDERSTANDING CONTEXT

How could marches, such as the one pictured, create allegiance to the Nazi state?

## THE STATE AND TERROR

As sole ruler of Nazi Germany, Hitler relied on instruments of terror to maintain control. The *Schutzstaffeln,* German for "Guard Squadrons," known in shorthand as the SS, were an important force for maintaining order. The SS was originally created as Hitler's personal bodyguard. Under the direction of Heinrich Himmler, the SS came to control not only the secret police forces that Himmler had set up but also the regular police forces across the German state.

The SS was based on two principles: terror and adherence to Nazi ideology. Terror included the instruments of repression and murder—secret police, criminal police, concentration camps, and later, execution squads and death camps, or concentration camps in which prisoners are killed. For Himmler, the chief goal of the SS was to further the "Aryan master race."

## ECONOMICS

In the economic sphere, Hitler used public works projects and grants to private construction firms to put people back to work and to end the Depression. A massive rearmament program, however, was the key to solving the unemployment problem. Unemployment, which had reached more than 5 million in 1932, dropped to less than 500,000 in 1937. The regime claimed full credit for solving Germany's economic woes. Its part in ending the Depression was an important factor in leading many Germans to accept Hitler and the Nazis.

*This Nazi propaganda poster features a mother with her children. It says, "Now we again have a happy future. For that, we thank the Führer on December 4."*

## WOMEN AND NAZISM

Women played a crucial role in the Aryan state as bearers of the children who, the Nazis believed, would bring about the triumph of the "Aryan race." The Nazis believed men were destined to be warriors and political leaders, while women were meant to be wives and mothers. In this way, each could best serve to maintain the entire community.

Nazi ideas determined employment opportunities for women. Jobs in heavy industry, the Nazis thought, might hinder women from bearing healthy children. Professions such as university teaching, medicine, and law were also considered unsuitable for women, especially married women. The Nazis instead encouraged women to pursue occupations such as social work and nursing. The Nazi regime pushed its campaign against working women with poster slogans such as "Get hold of pots and pans and broom and you'll sooner find a groom!"

## ANTI-SEMITIC POLICIES

From its beginning, the Nazi Party reflected the strong anti-Semitic beliefs of Adolf Hitler. When in power, the Nazis translated anti-Semitic ideas into anti-Semitic policies.

In September 1935, the Nazis announced new anti-Semitic laws at the annual party rally in Nuremberg. These Nuremberg laws defined who was considered a Jew—anyone with even one Jewish grandparent. They also stripped Jews of their German citizenship and civil rights and forbade marriages between Jews and German citizens. Eventually, German Jews were also **required** to wear yellow Stars of David and to carry identification cards saying they were Jewish.

A more violent phase of anti-Jewish activity began on the night of November 9, 1938—*Kristallnacht,* or the "night of shattered glass." In a destructive rampage, Nazis burned synagogues and destroyed some 7,000 Jewish businesses in Germany, Austria, and in the Sudetenland in Czechoslovakia. Thirty thousand Jewish males were arrested and sent to concentration camps. Jews were now barred from all public transportation and all public buildings, including schools and hospitals. They were **prohibited** from owning, managing, or working in any retail store. Finally, under the direction of the SS, Jews were encouraged to emigrate from Germany. The fortunate Jews were the ones who managed to escape from the country.

**DETERMINING MEANING**

Read the paragraph that contains the word **required**. Based on context clues, write a definition for the word *require*. Use a dictionary or online resource to check your definition.

**DETERMINING MEANING**

The text about Nazi anti-Semitic policies includes the following two sentences: "Jews were now barred from all public transportation and all public buildings, including schools and hospitals. They were prohibited from owning, managing, or working in any retail store." What does the word **prohibited** mean in this context?

## CULTURE AND LEISURE

A series of inventions in the late 1800s had led the way for a revolution in mass communications. Especially important was Marconi's discovery of wireless radio waves. By the end of the 1930s, there were 9 million radios in Great Britain. Full-length motion pictures appeared shortly before World War I. By 1939, about 40 percent of adults in the more developed countries were attending a movie once a week.

Of course, radio and the movies could be used for political purposes. Radio offered great opportunities for reaching the masses. The Nazi regime encouraged radio listening by urging manufacturers to produce inexpensive radios that could be bought on an installment plan.

Film, too, had propaganda potential, a fact not lost on Joseph Goebbels (GUHR • buhlz), the German propaganda minister. Believing that film was one of the "most modern and scientific means of influencing the masses," Goebbels created a special film division in his Propaganda Ministry. The film division supported the making of both feature films and documentaries—nonfiction films—that carried the Nazi message.

The Nazis also made use of the new mass leisure activities that had emerged by 1900. Mass leisure offered new ways for totalitarian states to

Director Leni Riefenstahl filming *Triumph of the Will* at the Luitpoldhain Arena in Nuremberg, 1934

MAKING CONNECTIONS TO SPORTS

## OLYMPIC GAMES IN BERLIN

Hitler had intended the 1936 Olympic Games in the capital of Germany, Berlin, to showcase for the world the extent to which he had rebuilt the country under his authority. The Olympics were also a perfect opportunity, Hitler believed, to showcase the German people's physical superiority. Germany's team was the largest to attend the games and included 348 athletes in total. The team from the United States, which included 18 African Americans, had the second largest. One of these African Americans, runner Jesse Owens, won four gold medals. Owens's victories ruined Hitler's plans for a display of Aryan superiority and brought the athlete fame in Germany and the United States.

1. **DRAWING CONCLUSIONS** Why do you think ordinary Germans might have been thrilled about hosting the Olympic Games in 1936?
2. **IDENTIFYING CONNECTIONS** Considering the desire for the Nazi regime to show off the physical abilities of the Aryan Germans, what can we assume about treatment of ethnic minority athletes in Germany at this time?

control the people. The Nazi regime adopted a program called *Kraft durch Freude* ("Strength through Joy"). The program offered a variety of leisure activities to amuse the working class. These activities included concerts, operas, films, guided tours, and sporting events. Hitler used sporting events such as the Olympic Games, which were held in Berlin in 1936, to show the world Germany's physical strength and prestige.

### ✓ CHECKING FOR UNDERSTANDING

1. **UNDERSTANDING CHANGE** How did Hitler build a Nazi state?
2. **IDENTIFYING CONNECTIONS** How do you think the Nazi control of media such as radio and film helped keep the regime in power?

## LESSON 3 REVIEW

### Time and Place

1. **UNDERSTANDING CONTEXT** Considering the value Nazis placed upon racial superiority, what role did the state-sponsored ridicule of minorities serve?

### Building History-Social Science Analysis Skills

2. **UNDERSTANDING CONTEXT** Use your notes to identify the anti-Semitic policies enforced by the Nazi Party.
3. **UNDERSTANDING CONTEXT** What was the basis of Adolf Hitler's ideas?
4. **DRAWING CONCLUSIONS** In what ways did Hitler and the Nazi Party seek to control every aspect of citizens' lives?

### Writing About History

5. **INFORMATIVE WRITING** Write a paragraph discussing how Hitler used the existing German political structure and the economic situation in Germany to rise to power.

### Collaborating

6. **EVALUATING** Working in a group, examine the photographs of the Nazi regime and army included in the lesson. Discuss what these photographs suggest about the Nazi regime and what it wanted to emphasize to the outside world.

# THREE SPEECHES ON REFORM

During the 1920s and 1930s, many world leaders attempted to make significant economic reforms in their countries. These three speeches from Britain, Germany, and the Soviet Union are examples of these calls to action.

**VOCABULARY**

*proletariat:* working-class people

**PRIMARY SOURCE: SPEECH**

## RAMSAY MACDONALD ON CAPITALISM

Ramsay MacDonald was prime minister of Britain's first two Labour governments. In this 1930 speech, he defends the government and argues for reforming capitalism.

> "It is not the Labour Government that is on trial; it is Capitalism that is being tried. We told you in those days that the time would come when finance would be more powerful than industry. That day has come. . . . We told you in those days that the time would come when the man who went into the workshop and into the factory, and his employer as well, would no longer be in the simple relationship of master and man, but that the master would become impersonal, and that powers that have nothing to do with industry would control industry—the powers of gambling with credit. That day has come. . . .
>
> So, my friends, we are not on trial; it is the system under which we live. It has broken down, not only in this little island, it has broken down in Europe, in Asia, in America; it has broken down everywhere, as it was bound to break down. And the cure, the new path, the new idea is organization—organization which will protect life, not property; organization which may protect property, but protect property in proper relation to life; organization which will see to it that when science discovers and inventors invent, the class that will be crushed down by reason of knowledge shall not be the working class, but the loafing class. This is the policy that we are going to pursue slowly, steadily, persistently, with knowledge and with our minds working upon a plan."

**ANALYZE THE TEXT**

1. **DETERMINING MEANING** What is MacDonald referring to when he says "the powers of gambling with credit" now control industry?
2. **DETERMINING CENTRAL IDEAS** According to MacDonald, in what ways will his new policies benefit the working class?

**PRIMARY SOURCE: SPEECH**

## JOSEPH STALIN ON INDUSTRIALIZATION

In this 1928 speech, Joseph Stalin describes his hopes to revolutionize Russia from the top down through rapid industrialization and collectivization.

> "The whole point is that we are behind Germany in this respect and are still far from having overtaken her technically and economically. The question of a fast rate of development of industry would not face us so acutely if we were not the only country but one of the countries of the dictatorship of the **proletariat**, if there were a proletarian dictatorship not only in our country but in other, more advanced countries as well, Germany and France, say.
>
> If that were the case, the capitalist encirclement could not be so serious a danger as it is now . . . we could receive from them machines for making our industry and agriculture more productive, supplying them in turn with raw materials and foodstuffs, and we could, consequently, expand our industry at a slower rate. But you know very well that that is not yet the case and that we are still the only country of the proletarian dictatorship and are surrounded by capitalist countries, many of which are far in advance of us technically and economically . . .
>
> What has to be done to end this contradiction? To end it, we must overtake and outstrip the advanced technology of the developed capitalist countries. . . . Either we do this, or we shall be forced to the wall."

**ANALYZE THE TEXT**

1. **DETERMINING POINT OF VIEW** Why does Stalin fear his capitalist neighbors, like Germany and France?
2. **ANALYZING TEXT PRESENTATION** How does Stalin emphasize the urgent need to modernize the nation?

(l)Weir, L. MacNeill. 1938. The Tragedy of Ramsay MacDonald: A Polticial Biography. Martin Secker and Warburg Ltd.; (r)Stalin, Josef. 1928. J. V. Stalin Works - Volume 11: 1928 - March 1929. Moscow: Foreign Languages Publishing House.

PRIMARY SOURCE: SPEECH

## HITLER ON GERMAN UNITY

In 1932, the Nazi Party was concerned about financing its election campaign. Hitler gave this speech to the Industry Club, outlining his plan to develop economic strength and unity.

> "Today we stand at the turning-point of Germany's destiny. If the present development continues, Germany will one day of necessity land in Bolshevist chaos, but if this development is broken, then our people must be taken into a school of iron discipline and gradually freed from the prejudices of both camps. A hard schooling, but one we cannot escape! . . .
>
> And so in contrast to our own official Government I cannot see any hope for the resurrection of Germany if we regard foreign politics of Germany as the primary factor: the primary necessity is the restoration of the sound national German body-politic armed to strike. In order to realize this end I founded thirteen years ago the National Socialist Movement: that Movement I have led during the last twelve years, and I hope that one day it will accomplish this task and that, as the fairest result of its struggle, it will leave behind it a German body-politic completely renewed internally, intolerant of anyone who sins against the nation and its interests, intolerant against anyone who will not acknowledge its vital interests, or who opposes them, intolerant and pitiless against anyone who shall attempt once more to destroy or disintegrate this body-politic, and yet ready for friendship and peace with anyone who has a wish for peace and friendship."

Hitler, Adolf. Quoted 2002. Stackelberg, Roderick and Winkle, Sally A. The Nazi Germany Sourcebook: An Anthology of Texts. New York: Routledge.

### ANALYZE THE TEXT

1. **DETERMINING CENTRAL IDEAS** What does Hitler view as a primary necessity in the "resurrection of Germany"?
2. **DETERMINING CONTEXT** Why might Hitler's National Socialist Movement have become more popular during this era in German history?
3. **ANALYZING TEXT PRESENTATION** How does Hitler's speech compare with those of MacDonald and Stalin? How would you describe the tone of this speech?

### MULTIPLE PERSPECTIVES

1. **CITING TEXT EVIDENCE** In crisis times, political leaders often raise people's fears about what will happen if they do not take action. Explain what specific fear each speaker calls up in his audience. Cite evidence from each text.
2. **DETERMINING CENTRAL IDEAS** Hitler and Stalin both worry that their countries will be ruined if change is not made. What do they want to do to stop it?

# STUDY GUIDE

## THE GREAT DEPRESSION
### LESSON 1

**GERMANY**
- Unemployment had grown to 3 million people by March 1930 and to 4.38 million by December.
- The Depression paved the way for fear and the rise of extremist parties.

**FRANCE**
- Suffered economic instability in 1932 that had political effects
- In June 1936 a coalition of leftist parties formed the Popular Front government, which started a program that gave workers the right to collective bargaining, a 40-hour workweek in industry, and a minimum wage.

**UNITED STATES**
- From 1929 to 1932, industrial production fell by 50 percent.
- Unemployment was at 25 percent in 1933.
- The New Deal set up Works Progress Administration, which hired 3 million people.
- Social Security Act and unemployment insurance were created.

**GREAT BRITAIN**
- The government changed from Labour Party to Conservative Party in 1931.
- The idea of deficit spending was introduced, but the British government did not follow it.

## THE RISE OF DICTATORIAL REGIMES
### LESSON 2

**TOTALITARIAN STATE**
A state in which the government aims to control the political, economic, social, intellectual, and cultural lives of its citizens

**FASCISM**
A political philosophy that glorifies the state above the individual by emphasizing the need for a strong central government led by a dictatorial ruler

**AUTHORITARIAN**
Favoring or enforcing strict obedience to authority, especially that of the government, at the expense of personal freedom

**COLLECTIVIZATION**
A system in which private farms are eliminated and peasants work land owned by the government

## THE NAZI PARTY IN GERMANY
### LESSON 3

Used mass demonstrations and spectacles to make the German people an instrument of Hitler's policies

Used instruments of terror such as secret police, criminal police, concentration camps, execution squads, and death camps

Were antifeminist and believed that women were best suited to be wives and mothers

Reflected the strong anti-Semitic beliefs of Adolf Hitler, announcing new anti-Semitic laws at Nuremberg in 1935

Used the new inventions of radio, film, and television to produce propaganda that carried the Nazi message

# CHAPTER 9 Assessment

**Directions:** On a separate sheet of paper, answer the questions below. Make sure you read carefully and answer all parts of the questions.

## Short Answer

1. **DESCRIBING** Identify two causes of the Great Depression and describe their impact.

2. **IDENTIFYING CONNECTIONS** What outlook did the arts and physics share in the 1920s? What was a root cause for this outlook?

3. **RELATING EVENTS** What effects did the U.S. Senate's refusal to ratify the Treaty of Versailles have?

4. **SUMMARIZING** Describe the situations that allowed authoritarian governments to flourish in the 1920s.

5. **COMPARING POINTS OF VIEW** How did leaders in the Soviet Union differ in their plans for the new country following Lenin's untimely death?

6. **IDENTIFYING CONNECTIONS** Why was Mussolini's movement appealing to many Italians, and through what means did Mussolini and the Fascists establish control over the Italian people?

7. **EVALUATING** How do you think Americans would react today to propaganda that said, "Our leader is always right"? Why would people react that way?

8. **DETERMINING MEANING** Explain the concept of *lebensraum* and how it applied to Nazi ideology.

9. **IDENTIFYING CONNECTIONS** How did Hitler's government respond to the Depression?

## History and Social-Science Analysis

Use the image to answer the following question.

*This painting,* The Persistence of Memory, *was painted by Salvador Dalí in 1931.*

10. **INTERPRETING** Why might some have suggested that Dalí was playing on Einstein's theory of relativity? How does this reflect the mood in Europe after World War I?

Use the image to answer the following question.

*This political cartoon by John Baer was published in 1932.*

11. **IDENTIFYING BIAS** What is happening in this cartoon? Who wants a new deal? Who is happy with the old deal? What does the cartoonist think?

12. **EVALUATING** Hitler, Mussolini, and Stalin monitored people's political activity and punished dissenters. How might a dictator monitor citizens' political activities today?

13. **EXPLAINING EFFECTS** How did agricultural collectivization impact Russian peasants?

14. **IDENTIFYING BIAS** Leni Riefenstahl claimed *Triumph of the Will* was a "documentary, not propaganda." Why might she have stated this?

15. **RELATING EVENTS** In what order did Hitler's actions against Jews happen? What does this chronology show about the effects of escalating hate speech and behavior?

**Need Extra Help?**

| If You've Missed Question | 1 | 2 | 3 | 4 | 5 | 6 | 7 | 8 | 9 | 10 | 11 | 12 | 13 | 14 | 15 |
|---|---|---|---|---|---|---|---|---|---|---|---|---|---|---|---|
| Review Lesson | 1 | 1 | 1 | 2 | 2 | 2 | 3 | 3 | 3 | 1 | 1 | 3 | 2 | 3 | 3 |

## Research and Presentation

16 **USING MULTIMEDIA** With the collapse of the capitalist market system that caused the Great Depression, political alternatives to liberal democracies emerged, particularly communism and fascism. Through the use of a graphic, compare and contrast how communist and fascist governments responded to the collapse of the capitalist system during the Great Depression.

17 **PRESENTING** Choose a piece of art, music, and propaganda from the 1920s, from the same country. Create a multimedia presentation that discusses each piece and how it reflects the culture in which it was created.

18 **ARGUMENTATIVE WRITING** Research the types of propaganda used by totalitarian governments, such as radio programs, rallies, posters, drama films, and documentaries, and analyze why they were effective forms of persuasion. Make a claim and use evidence to support your argument.

19 **RESEARCHING FOR INQUIRY** Research the political environments in Italy and Germany after World War I. How were these environments a consequence of World War I? How were these environments similar to and different from other countries in Europe? Include examples from several countries in your response, and make generalizations based upon the similarities you identify.

## Reading and Analyzing Primary Sources

Use the document to answer the following questions.

> "During the past two years widespread economic depression and consequent unemployment have brought instability and unrest not only at home but in many other countries of the Western Hemisphere. Since March, 1929, there have been revolutions in no less than seven Latin American republics, resulting in the forcible overthrow in six of them of the existing governments."

—Henry L. Stimson, Address by the Secretary of State before the Council on Foreign Relations, New York City, February 6, 1931

20 **SUMMARIZING** What is Henry Stimson saying in his address?

**A.** That the Depression has affected only countries in America and Europe
**B.** That the Depression should not worry Americans
**C.** That the solution to the Depression is a Fascist state
**D.** That the Depression should worry Americans, as it has led to revolutions in Latin America

21 **DESCRIBING** How did America react to the Depression as compared to many European nations?

**A.** America did nothing, while European countries took on major loans from Asian powers.
**B.** America implemented the New Deal policies, while many European nations turned to dictators.
**C.** America elected an authoritarian leader, whereas many European nations did not react at all.
**D.** No countries reacted to the Depression.

22 **DETERMINING CENTRAL IDEAS** Who is Stimson's message meant for?

**A.** American political leaders
**B.** Latin American political leaders
**C.** European leaders
**D.** Adolf Hitler

## Writing About History

23 **USING EVIDENCE** Explore the ways in which Mussolini, Stalin, and Hitler implemented totalitarian regimes. How were these authoritarian states similar? In which ways were they different? Examine the political structures from the Soviet Union, Italy, and Germany during the 1930s, listing two similarities and two differences. Be sure to explain your choices.

## Speaking and Listening About History

24 **COLLABORATING** In small groups, discuss the following questions: In what ways did war contribute to the Great Depression? How did Western nations and political leaders respond similarly and differently to the Depression? How is a depression today different from a depression in the 1920s? Have one member act as a moderator, and be prepared to present your ideas to the class.

**Need Extra Help?**

| If You've Missed Question | 16 | 17 | 18 | 19 | 20 | 21 | 22 | 23 | 24 |
|---|---|---|---|---|---|---|---|---|---|
| Review Lesson | 2, 3 | 1–3 | 2 | 2, 3 | 1 | 1 | 1 | 2 | 1 |

Stimson, Henry L. 1931. "Address by the Secretary of State Before the Council on Foreign Relations, New York City". February 6, 1931. Washington: Government Printing Office.

◀ *This photograph shows Gandhi in his characteristic white garb woven of homespun cloth that he wore as a sign of solidarity with India's poor and as a rejection of foreign-made goods.*

1919 — 1939

# Nationalism Around the World

## CHAPTER 10



**GO DIGITAL**
*It's All online!*

### ASKING ESSENTIAL QUESTIONS

***How can political control lead to nationalist movements?***
***How does economic exploitation lead to nationalist movements?***

**What Will You Learn?** You will learn about the rise of independence movements outside Europe and the factors that inspired them.

**Why Does This Matter?** After World War I, many revolutionary leaders in colonies drew upon Enlightenment ideas of representative government and on nationalism. These groups demanded that the governments of their respective countries reflect the national character and will of their people. Today, most states around the world are organized on principles of representation. For many, these early independence movements form the foundation of the representative governments they have today.

**How Will You Know That You Learned It?** You will be able to identify key nationalist leaders in Africa, Asia, and Latin America and explain how their leadership styles influenced the results of independence movements.

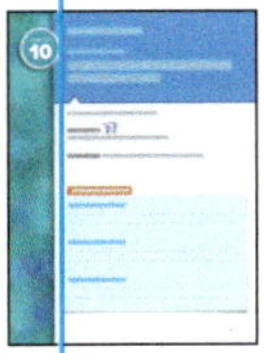

**Using Your Inquiry Journal** As you read this chapter and examine the primary sources, use your Inquiry Journal to help you make notes and expand your list of questions. As you gather information, think about how you will answer the Essential Questions above.

## PLACE & TIME Africa and Asia 1919–1939

In the 1920s and 1930s, independence movements, already present before World War I, strengthened in many parts of the world. The collapse of the Ottoman Empire led to the creation of Turkey, Iraq, and Saudi Arabia. In Africa, a new generation educated abroad and African veterans of World War I often led protests of colonial governments, but independence would not be achieved until after World War II. Asian nationalists, including Mohandas Gandhi in British India and Ho Chi Minh in French Indochina, struggled against colonial rule. In China, an alliance against imperialists between Nationalists and Communists broke down, leading to civil war.

### STEP INTO THE PLACE

Read the quotes and look at the information presented on the map.

1. **COMPARING POINTS OF VIEW** What political goal did nationalist movements have in common? How did Mao Zedong and Mohandas Gandhi approach their goals differently?

2. **EXPLORING PLACE** Based on the information in the map, what differences do you see between the independent nations and the colonies in terms of how power changed or was maintained?

"A revolution is not a dinner party, or writing an essay, or painting a picture, or doing embroidery; it cannot be so refined, so leisurely and gentle, so temperate, kind, courteous, restrained and magnanimous. A revolution is an insurrection, an act of violence by which one class overthrows another."

—Mao Zedong, from *Report on an Investigation of the Peasant Movement in Hunan*, 1927

"Passive resistance is a method of securing rights by personal suffering; it is the reverse of resistance by arms. When I refuse to do a thing that is repugnant to my conscience, I use soul-force ... If I do not obey the law and accept the penalty for its breach, I use soul-force... Everybody admits that sacrifice of self is infinitely superior to sacrifice of others."

—Mohandas Gandhi, from *Indian Home Rule*, 1909

### STEP INTO THE TIME

**SEQUENCING**

How do the events on the time line show the progression of political change in India during the interwar years?

## AFRICA AND ASIA

**1919** British massacre of unarmed Indian protesters at Amritsar

**1920–22** Mohandas Gandhi's Non-Cooperation Movement

**1921** Young Kikuyu Association protests British taxes in Africa

**1919** — **1924**

## WORLD EVENTS

**1919** League of Nations formed; League of Nations Mandates established

**1922** Independence of Egypt

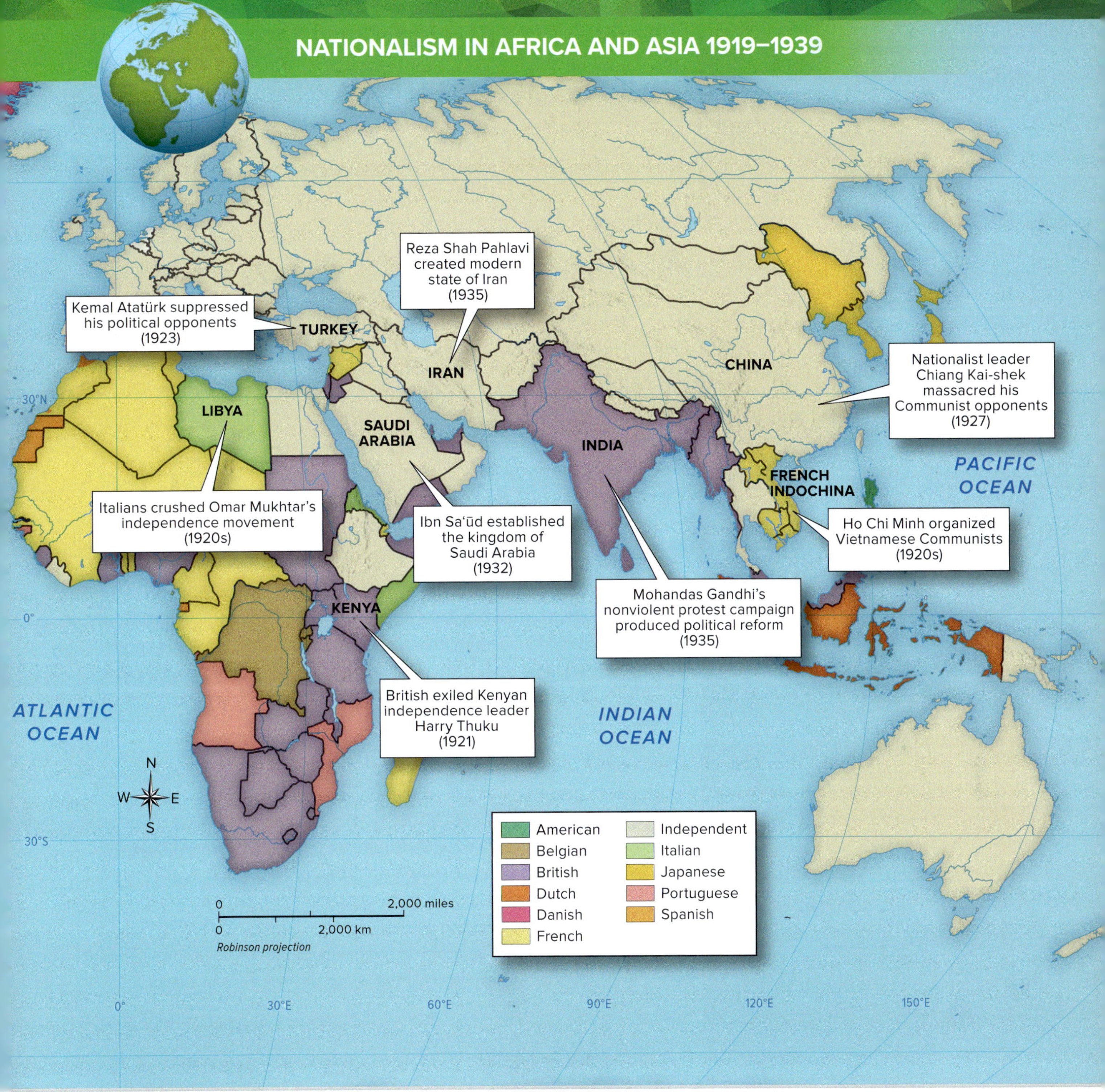


**1928** Chiang Kai-shek becomes head of the Nationalists in China

**1928** Jomo Kenyatta leads Kikuyu (Bantus) political association

**1929** Jawaharlal Nehru elected President of Indian National Congress

**1931** Japanese troops invade Manchuria following Mukden Incident

**1934–36** Mao Zedong leads Long March of Chinese Communists

**1929** — **1934** — **1939**

**1929** Great Depression begins

**1932** Independence for Iraq

**1933** FDR announces the Good Neighbor policy

**1938** Getúlio Vargas founds authoritarian state in Brazil

**1938** Lázaro Cárdenas seizes control of Mexican oil industry

**1939** World War II begins

**1939** British limit number of Jewish immigrants to Palestine

ESSENTIAL QUESTIONS

- *How can political control lead to nationalist movements?*
- *How does economic exploitation lead to nationalist movements?*

# THE STORY BEGINS...

LESSON 1

# Nationalism in the Middle East

In the beginning of the twentieth century, a group of reformers inside the Ottoman Empire calling themselves the Young Turks decided to come out of the shadows. Their goal was to take the empire, by force if necessary, into the modern era. This group issued the following proclamation in 1908. It included some of the following ideas:

> "7. The Turkish tongue will remain the official state language. Official correspondence and discussion will take place in Turkish. . . .
>
> 9. Every citizen will enjoy complete liberty and equality, regardless of nationality or religion, and be submitted to the same obligations. All Ottomans, being equal before the law as regards rights and duties relative to the State, are eligible for government posts, according to their individual capacity and their education. Non-Muslims will be equally liable to the military law. . . .
>
> 17. All schools will operate under the surveillance of the state. In order to obtain for Ottoman citizens an education of a homogenous and uniform character, the officials schools will be open, their instruction will be free, and all nationalities will be admitted. Instruction in Turkish will be obligatory in public schools."

—Young Turks, *Proclamation for the Ottoman Empire,* 1908

The demands of the young reformers, such as creating a national language and a national school system, were seen as necessary for transforming the empire into a modern nation state. How committed the Young Turks were to fairness and equality also remains in doubt. Regardless, modernization of the Turkish state would not truly be achieved until the defeat of the Ottoman Empire in World War I and the reforms of Mustafa Kemal, otherwise known as Atatürk.

*Atatürk (right) would modernize Turkey after the collapse of the Ottoman Empire.* ▶

| Ottoman Empire Successors | |
|---|---|
| Key Player | Results of Action |
| | |
| | |
| | |
| | |

**ANALYZING KEY IDEAS AND DETAILS**

**SUMMARIZING** Read closely to identify the key players in the restructuring of the land once ruled by the Ottomans. Record the names and summarize the accomplishments of these individuals in a graphic organizer like this one.

# DECLINE OF THE OTTOMAN EMPIRE

**GUIDING QUESTION** *What led to the final decline and fall of the Ottoman Empire?*

The Ottoman Empire—which once included parts of Eastern Europe, the Middle East, and North Africa—had been growing steadily weaker. The empire's size had decreased dramatically during the nineteenth century when it lost much of its European territory. Ottoman rule also ended in North Africa.

In 1876 Ottoman reformers seized control of the empire's government and adopted a constitution that set up a **legislature**. However, the sultan they placed on the throne, Abdülhamīd II, suspended the new constitution. Abdülhamīd paid a high price for his authoritarian actions, living in constant fear of assassination. He kept 1,000 loaded revolvers hidden throughout his guarded estate.

The suspended constitution became a symbol of change to a group of reformers named the Young Turks. This group forced the restoration of the constitution in 1908 and deposed the sultan the following year. However, the Young Turks lacked strong support for their government.

## IMPACT OF WORLD WAR I

The final blow to the old empire came from World War I. After the Ottoman government allied with Germany, the British sought to undermine Ottoman rule in the Arabian Peninsula by supporting Arab nationalist activities there. The nationalists were aided by the dashing British adventurer T. E. Lawrence, popularly known as Lawrence of Arabia.

In 1916 Arabia declared its independence from Ottoman rule. British troops advanced from Egypt and seized the Ottoman territories on the eastern coast of the Mediterranean Sea. After suffering more than 300,000 deaths during the war, the Ottoman Empire made peace with the Allies in October 1918.

## REACTION TO THE ARMENIAN GENOCIDE

The Armenian Genocide was begun in the middle of World War I. As a consequence, many outside nations were unable to come to the Armenians' aid, or refused to. Still, the genocide was not a secret. Count Wolff-Metternich, German Ambassador to the Ottomans, said in a cable to his government in 1916:

> "In its attempt to carry out its purpose to resolve the Armenian question by the destruction of the Armenian race, the Turkish government has refused to be deterred neither by our representations, nor by those of the American Embassy, nor by the delegate of the Pope, nor by the threats of the Allied Powers, nor in deference to the public opinion of the West representing one-half of the world."

**ANALYZING KEY IDEAS AND DETAILS**

1. **DETERMINING CENTRAL IDEAS** What is the central idea of the subsection titled "Impact of World War I"? How does the text present and develop this idea?
2. **CITING TEXT EVIDENCE** Identify text evidence that supports the claim that Ottoman reformers struggled to modernize the empire in the late nineteenth century.

**DETERMINING MEANING**

**Legislature** is made of the roots *legis*, meaning "law," and *latus*, meaning "propose." From what you know about the definitions of these root words, write a definition of *legislature*. Use a dictionary or online resource to check your definition.

Toriguian, Shavarsh. 1973. The Armenian Question and International Law. Hamaskaine Press.

The United States, not at war with the Ottoman Empire until 1917, had many diplomats stationed in embassies across the Ottoman Empire. Some of these American officials witnessed brutal acts committed against the Armenians. Most reported what they saw to Henry Morgenthau, Sr., the United States ambassador to the Ottoman Empire. He reported the event to the American government in 1915. After the war, Morgenthau recounted the deportations:

> "When the Turkish authorities gave the orders for these deportations, they were merely giving the death warrant to a whole race; they understood this well, and, in their conversations with me, they made no particular attempt to conceal the fact. . . . I am confident that the whole history of the human race contains no such horrible episode as this."

—from a report from Henry Morgenthau to the U.S. government

The Ottoman Sultanate collapsed and gave way to a Turkish Republic in 1923. This new government refused to acknowledge the genocide and has yet to acknowledge it today. The Armenian Genocide would become a prototype for other genocides yet to come. German officials would use Turkish concentration and work camps as models for their own camps during the Holocaust in the 1940s. Ethnic cleansing, a policy of killing or forcibly removing an ethnic group from its lands, is a similar practice to genocide. Ethnic cleansing would be used by Serbs against a Muslim minority in the Bosnian War of 1993–1996.

### ☑ CHECKING FOR UNDERSTANDING

1. **IDENTIFYING CAUSES** What led to the final decline and fall of the Ottoman Empire?
2. **SUMMARIZING** In what ways did the war effort affect the Ottoman government?
3. **EVALUATING** How did the outcomes of the Armenian petitions for independence vary from Arabia's declaration of independence, just one year later?

**MAKING CONNECTIONS TO TODAY**

### THE INTERNATIONAL RED CROSS

The humanitarian organization known as the International Red Cross was founded in Geneva, Switzerland, in 1863. Initially founded to provide aid to victims of war, it soon expanded its role to assist in emergencies and disasters. Chapters of the Red Cross came to the aid of refugees of the Armenian Genocide early on in the crisis. Members organized relief efforts to provide medical aid, clothing, and food to victims. They also performed other services such as helping reunite relatives who had lost one another during deportations. The actions of Red Cross members brought attention to the plight of the Armenian people early in the tragedy and brought aid when no other organization could. Chapters of the International Red Cross continue to provide aid and assistance to victims of war and disasters across the world today.

**ANALYZING KEY IDEAS AND DETAILS**

1. **DETERMINING CENTRAL IDEAS** Read the first two paragraphs under the heading "The Modernization of Turkey." What is the central idea of this section? Does the last sentence, "The Ottoman Empire had finally come to an end," support or contradict the central idea?
2. **ANALYZING IDEAS** This section of the text includes the sentence "Perhaps the most significant aspect of Atatürk's reform program was his attempt to break the power of the Islamic religion." What clue does this sentence give the reader about what Turkish reformers understood to be "modernization"?

## MIDDLE EAST CHANGES

**GUIDING QUESTION** *How did the Middle East change after the fall of the Ottoman Empire?*

As the Ottoman Empire crumbled, Turkey, Iran, and Saudi Arabia emerged as modern states. At the same time, tensions mounted between the Jewish and Muslim inhabitants in the Palestine Mandate.

Morgenthau, Henry. 1919. Ambassador Morgenthau's Story. Garden City and New York: Doubleday, Page & Company.

## THE MODERNIZATION OF TURKEY

At the end of World War I, the tottering Ottoman Empire collapsed. Great Britain and France made plans to divide Ottoman territories in the Middle East. Only the area of what is present-day Turkey remained under the control of the Ottoman government. Then, Greece invaded Turkey and seized the western parts of the Anatolian Peninsula.

The invasion alarmed key **elements** in Turkey, who were organized under the leadership of the war hero Colonel Mustafa Kemal. Kemal summoned a national congress calling for the creation of an elected government and a new Republic of Turkey. His forces drove the Greeks from the Anatolian Peninsula. In 1923 the last of the Ottoman sultans fled the country, which was then declared to be the new Turkish Republic. The Ottoman Empire had finally come to an end.

President Kemal was now popularly known as Atatürk (AT • uh • TUHRK), or "father Turk." Over the next several years, he tried to transform Turkey into a modern state. A democratic system was put in place, but Atatürk did not tolerate opposition and harshly suppressed his critics.

Atatürk's changes went beyond politics. Many Arabic elements were eliminated from the Turkish language, which was now written in the Roman alphabet. Popular education was introduced, and all Turkish citizens were forced to adopt family (last) names, in the European style.

Atatürk also took steps to modernize Turkey's economy. Factories were established, and a five-year plan provided for state direction over the economy. Atatürk also tried to modernize Turkey's agricultural production, although he had little effect on the nation's peasants.

Perhaps the most significant aspect of Atatürk's reform program was his attempt to break the power the Islamic religion had on Turkish government and on Turkish society. His ultimate goal was to transform Turkey into a secular state—a state that rejects religious influence on its policies. Atatürk said, "Religion is like a heavy blanket that keeps the people of Turkey asleep."

The **caliphate** was formally abolished in 1924. Men were forbidden to wear the fez, the brimless cap worn by Turkish Muslims. When Atatürk began wearing a Western panama hat, one of his critics remarked, "You cannot make a Turk into a Westerner by giving him a hat."

Women were strongly discouraged from wearing the veil, a traditional Islamic custom. New laws gave women marriage and inheritance rights equal to men's. In 1934 women received the right to vote. All citizens were also given the right to convert to other religions.

**DETERMINING MEANING**

Read the paragraph that contains the word **elements**. Using context clues, write a definition of *elements*. Use a dictionary or online resource to check your definition.

*The Young Turks rode through the streets of Turkey waving flags in 1908.*

**INTEGRATING INFORMATION**

What about this man's attire suggests the photo was taken before Atatürk's rule?

DETERMINING MEANING

**Caliphate** contains the root *caliph*, which is an Islamic ruler who traces his lineage and political power to the prophet Muhammad. What can this information tell you about the meaning of *caliphate*?

The legacy of Kemal Atatürk was enormous. In practice, not all of his reforms were widely accepted, especially by devout Muslims. However, most of the changes that he introduced were kept after his death in 1938. By and large, the Turkish Republic was the product of Atatürk's determined efforts.

## THE BEGINNINGS OF MODERN IRAN

A similar process of modernization was underway in Persia. Under the Qājār dynasty (1794–1925), the country had not been very successful in resolving its domestic problems. Increasingly, the dynasty turned to Russia and Great Britain to protect itself from its own people, which led to a growing foreign presence in Persia. The discovery of oil in the southern part of the country in 1908 attracted more foreign interest. Oil exports increased, and most of the profits went to British investors.

The growing foreign presence led to the rise of a native Persian nationalist movement. In 1921 Reza Khan, an officer in the Persian army, led a military mutiny that seized control of Tehran, the capital city. In 1925 Reza Khan established himself as shah, or king, and was called Reza Shah Pahlavi. The name of the new dynasty he created, Pahlavi, was the name of the ancient Persian language.

During the next few years, Reza Shah Pahlavi tried to follow the example of Kemal Atatürk in Turkey. Reza Shah Pahlavi hoped to reduce foreign influence in Iran. He worked to maintain or even increase Iran's political independence from foreign powers, especially Great Britain and the Soviet Union. He introduced a number of reforms to strengthen and modernize the government, the military, and the economic system. Persia became the modern state of Iran in 1935.

Unlike Atatürk, Reza Shah Pahlavi did not try to destroy the power of Islamic beliefs. However, he did encourage the creation of a Western-style educational system and forbade women to wear the veil in public.

Foreign powers continued to harass Iran. To free himself from Great Britain and the Soviet Union, Reza Shah Pahlavi drew closer to Nazi Germany. During World War II, the shah rejected the demands of Great Britain and the Soviet Union to expel a large number of Germans from Iran. He also rejected their requests to allow troops and supplies to move across Iran. In response, Great Britain and the Soviet Union sent troops into the country. Reza Shah Pahlavi resigned and was replaced by his son, Mohammad Reza Pahlavi.

## ARAB NATIONALISM

World War I offered the Arabs an excellent opportunity to escape from Ottoman rule. However, what would replace that rule? The Arabs did not have a nation-state, but they were united by their language and by the Islamic cultural and religious heritage that nearly all of them shared. However, efforts by generations of political leaders to create a single Arab nation have not found success.

Because Britain supported the efforts of Arab nationalists in 1916, the nationalists hoped this support would continue after the war. Instead, Britain agreed with France to create mandates in the area. These were former Ottoman territories that the new League of Nations now supervised. The

## MIDDLE EAST 1919–1935

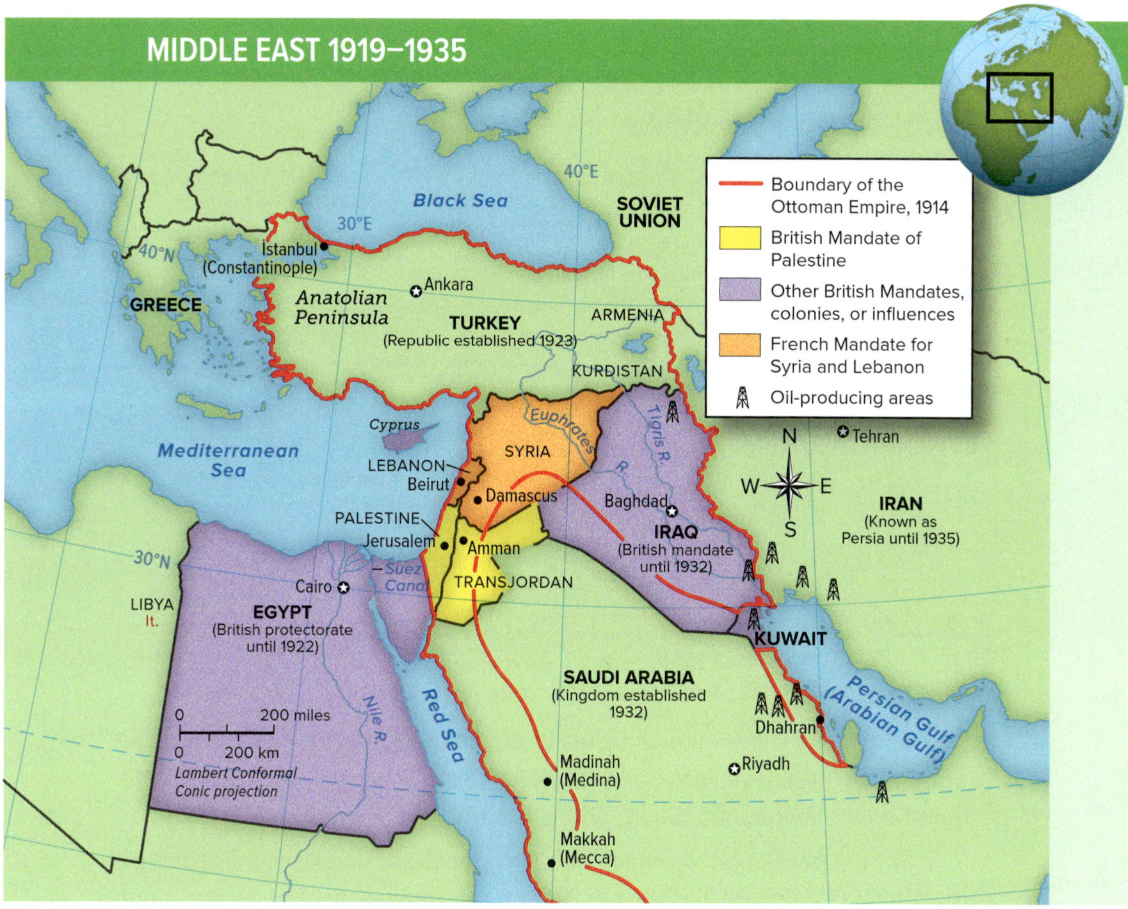


### GEOGRAPHIC REASONING

After the fall of the Ottoman Empire, mandates were established in the Middle East.

1. **PATTERNS AND MOVEMENT** How did the territories under the Ottoman Empire change after World War I?
2. **HUMAN-ENVIRONMENT INTERACTION** Which mandates and nations had access to oil?

league, in turn, granted its members the right to govern particular mandates. The Iraq and Palestine Mandates (which included Transjordan) were assigned to Great Britain; the Syria and Lebanon Mandates were assigned to France.

> "To those colonies and territories which as a consequence of the late war have ceased to be under the sovereignty of the states which formerly governed them and which are inhabited by peoples not yet able to stand by themselves under the strenuous conditions of the modern world, there should be applied the principle that the well-being and development of such peoples form a sacred trust of civilization and that securities for the performance of this trust should be embodied in this Covenant.
>
> The best method of giving practical effect to this principle is that the tutelage of such peoples should be entrusted to advanced nations who, by reason of their resources, their experience or their geographical position, can best undertake this responsibility, and who are willing to accept it, and that this tutelage should be exercised by them as mandatories on behalf of the League."
>
> —the Covenant of the League of Nations, Article 22, 1919

### ANALYZING PRIMARY SOURCES

1. **DETERMINING MEANING** What does *tutelage* mean in this context?
2. **ANALYZING IDEAS** How does this passage from Article 22 justify giving Europeans the power to oversee territories once controlled by the Ottoman Empire?

Through the mandate system established by the League of Nations following the war, Europeans created the modern map of the Middle East. The Europeans determined future borders and divided the peoples. In general, the people in these states had no strong identification with their designated country. However, a sense of Arab nationalism remained.

League to Enforce Peace (U.S.) 1919. The Paris Covenant for a League of Nations - Text of the Plan Adopted by the Paris Peace Conference April 28, 1919. New York: League to Enforce Peace.

MAKING CONNECTIONS TO TODAY

### WORLD OIL RESERVES

Saudi Arabia has the largest oil reserves in the world, possessing one-fifth of Earth's known supplies. The Saudi reserves are estimated to be more than 260 billion barrels. Saudi Arabia is also the location of the world's largest oil field, Al-Ghawār, which was discovered in 1948 and still holds 70 billion barrels after 60 years of production. For total proven oil reserves, however, Venezuela leads the pack. Following Venezuela in proven oil reserves are Saudi Arabia, Canada, Iran, Iraq, and Kuwait. The United States, with proven reserves of 36.5 billion barrels, ranks 11th, just behind Nigeria.

1. **CITING TEXT EVIDENCE** Considering what you have learned in this short passage, what can you deduce about the relationship between oil wealth and national wealth? Cite specific details from the text.
2. **EVALUATING** What can you assume about the national economy of Saudi Arabia based on the statistics in this short passage?

## SAUDI ARABIA

In the early 1920s, a reform leader, Ibn Sa'ūd, united Arabs in the northern part of the Arabian Peninsula. Devout and gifted, Ibn Sa'ūd won broad support. He established the kingdom of Saudi Arabia in 1932.

At first, the new kingdom, which consisted mostly of the vast central desert of the Arabian Peninsula, was desperately poor. Its main source of income came from the Muslim pilgrims who visited Makkah (Mecca) and Madinah (Medina). During the 1930s, however, U.S. prospectors began to explore for oil. Standard Oil made a successful strike at Dhahran, on the Persian Gulf, in 1938. Soon, the Arabian-American oil company Aramco was created. The isolated kingdom was suddenly flooded with Western oil industries that brought the promise of wealth.

## PALESTINE AND THE BALFOUR DECLARATION

The situation in the Palestine Mandate complicated matters in the Middle East even more. Although the land of Israel had been the home of the Jews in antiquity, some Jews were forced into exile in the first century C.E. A Jewish presence always remained, but Muslim Arabs made up about 80 percent of the region's population. In the Palestine Mandate, the nationalism of Jews and Arabs came into conflict because both groups viewed the area as a potential national state.

Since the 1890s, Zionists—Jewish nationalists—had advocated that a Jewish state be reestablished in the ancient Jewish homeland. Jews recalled that the ancient state of Israel was located there. Arabs pointed out that their ancestors also had lived in the region of Palestine for centuries. As a result of the Zionist movement and growing anti-Semitism in Europe, more Jews began to migrate to Palestine. Then during World War I, the British government, hoping to win Jewish support for the Allies, issued the Balfour Declaration. It expressed support for a national home for the Jews in Palestine and added that this goal should not undermine the rights of the non-Jewish peoples living there or the rights of Jews living in other countries. The League of Nations' British Mandate for Palestine (1922) incorporated the Balfour Declaration.

> "His Majesty's Government view with favour the establishment in Palestine of a national home for the Jewish people, and will use their best endeavors to facilitate the achievement of this object, it being clearly understood that nothing shall be done which may prejudice the civil and religious rights of existing non-Jewish communities in Palestine, or the rights and political status enjoyed by Jews in any other country."
>
> —from the Balfour Declaration

**ANALYZING PRIMARY SOURCES**

**DRAWING CONCLUSIONS** How does the Balfour Declaration simultaneously acknowledge the Zionist desire for a Jewish state and the challenges in the region?

The Balfour Declaration drew even more Jews to the Palestine Mandate. In 1933 the Nazi regime in Germany began policies that later led to the Holocaust and the murder of 6 million Jews. During the 1930s, many Jews fled to the Palestine Mandate. Violence flared between Arab and Jewish inhabitants.

In 1936, Arabs in the Palestine Mandate revolted, demanding both independence from Britain and an end to Jewish immigration. Trying to end the revolt, the British declared in 1939, on the eve of the Holocaust, that only 75,000 Jewish people would be allowed to immigrate to the mandate over the next five years; after that, no more Jews could do so. This decision, which closed one of the only escape routes for Jews in Nazi-occupied Europe, only intensified the tension and increased the bloodshed.

### ✓ CHECKING FOR UNDERSTANDING

1. **UNDERSTANDING CHANGE** How did the Middle East change after the fall of the Ottoman Empire?
2. **ANALYZING CHANGE** How did the leadership styles of Atatürk and Reza Shah Pahlavi change their countries?

Balfour, Arthur James. 1917. Excerpt of the Balfour Declaration. From The American War Congress and Zionism: Statements by Members of the American War Congress on the Jewish National Movement. New York: Zionist Organization of America.

## LESSON 1 REVIEW

### Time and Place

1. **UNDERSTANDING CHANGE** How did Reza Shah Pahlavi's attempts to free Iran from foreign intervention end up backfiring?

### Building History-Social Science Analysis Skills

2. **DETERMINING CONTEXT** Identify one nationalist leader in the Middle East and how his actions contributed to the success of the movement.
3. **EVALUATING** Explain some of the changes Atatürk instituted to the traditional clothing worn by the Turkish people. What do these changes reveal about the transformations experienced by Turkish society?
4. **IDENTIFYING CONNECTIONS** How might the similar occupations of Kemal Atatürk and Reza Shah Pahlavi have given them a shared outlook?

### Writing About History

5. **EXPLANATORY WRITING** Write an essay explaining the ways the Middle East changed in the years following World War I. How did various religious connections affect life in Ottoman territories after the empire collapsed? Include a discussion of the modernization movements in Turkey and Iran as well as the role of the League of Nations in changing the shape of everyday life.

### Collaborating

6. **PRESENTING** With a partner, use the Internet or other sources to find and discuss examples of news articles, editorials, or other items from the time period that bring attention to the Armenian Genocide. Share your findings with the class, explaining how your source brought attention to the Armenian Genocide to the United States.

# NATIONALIST MOVEMENTS AROUND THE WORLD

Different groups responded to the rise of nationalist self-determination around the world in different ways. As the following excerpts show, nationalism expresses a notion of national belonging determined by a set of characteristics. For some groups, these characteristics are religious; for others, they are ethnic.

**VOCABULARY**

*sovereign:* free from external control

*collectivity:* people as a whole

*civil disobedience:* refusal to obey government demands

*exploitation:* unfair use

*disarmament:* the reduction or elimination of weapons

*cosmopolitanism:* an international scope

PRIMARY SOURCE: DOCUMENT

## ARAB STUDENTS' DECLARATION

This manifesto was written by Arab students in Brussels in 1938, at the first Arab Students' Congress in Europe.

> "I. Our National Pact
>
> I am an Arab, and I believe that the Arabs constitute one nation. The sacred right of this nation is to be **sovereign** in the Arab homeland, to unite all its parts, and to found political, economic, and social institutions more sound and more compatible than the existing ones. . . .
>
> I pledge myself to God, that I will strive in this path to my utmost, putting the national interest above any other consideration.
>
> II. First Principles
>
> *Arab Nationalism:* It is the feeling for the necessity of independence and unity which the inhabitants of the Arab lands share. . . . It is based on the unity of the homeland, of language, culture, history, and a sense of the common good.
>
> *The Arab Movement:* . . . Its motive force is her glorious past, her remarkable vitality and the awareness of her present and future interests. This movement strives . . . to liberate and unite the Arab homeland, to found political, economic, and social organizations more sound than the existing ones, and to attempt afterward to work for the good of the human **collectivity** and its progress. These aims . . . will be realized without subscribing to any particular creed of the modern Western ones such as Fascism, Communism, or Democracy."

**ANALYZE THE TEXT**

1. **DETERMINING CENTRAL IDEAS** According to the Arab students in 1938, what were the goals of the Arab nationalist movement?
2. **UNDERSTANDING CONTEXT** What events during this period most likely prompted the Arab Students' Congress to call for nationalism?

PRIMARY SOURCE: DOCUMENT

## GANDHI TAKES THE PATH OF CIVIL DISOBEDIENCE

In this 1930 letter to the Viceroy Lord Irwin, Mohandas Gandhi explains why British rule in India must end.

> "Before embarking on **civil disobedience** and taking the risk I have dreaded to take all these years, I would fain approach you and find a way out.
>
> . . . Though I hold the British rule in India to be a curse, I do not, therefore, consider Englishmen in general to be worse than any other people on earth. I have the privilege of claiming many Englishmen as dearest friends. Indeed much that I have learned of the evil of British rule is due to the writings of frank and courageous Englishmen who have not hesitated to tell the truth about that rule.
>
> And why do I regard British rule as a curse? It has impoverished the ignorant millions by a system of progressive **exploitation** and by a ruinously expensive military and civil administration which the country can never afford.
>
> It has reduced us politically to serfdom. It has sapped the foundations of our culture. And, by the policy of cruel **disarmament**, it has degraded us spiritually. Lacking the inward strength, we have been reduced . . . to a state bordering on cowardly helplessness. . . ."

**ANALYZE THE TEXT**

1. **ANALYZING TEXT PRESENTATION** Why does Gandhi repeat the word *curse* and call the British government "evil" throughout his argument? What impact do these words have on his message?
2. **DETERMINING CONTEXT** Why does Gandhi defend individual Englishmen in the midst of his critique of the British government? How does this relate to his policy of civil disobedience?

(l)Haim, Sylvia G. 1962. First Arab Students' Congress. From Arab Nationalism: An Anthology. Berkeley: University of California Press; (r)Ghandi, Mohandas. Quoted 2014 by Frances Fell McDermott, Leonard

PRIMARY SOURCE: DOCUMENT

## A REVOLUTIONARY'S VISION

This passage is part of a lecture given on February 17, 1924, by the Chinese revolutionary Sun Yat-sen.

> "Now we want to revive China's lost nationalism and use the strength of our four hundred millions to fight for mankind against injustice; this is our divine mission. The Powers are afraid that we will have such thoughts and are setting forth a specious doctrine. They are now advocating **cosmopolitanism** to inflame us, declaring that, as the civilization of the world advances and as mankind's vision enlarges, nationalism becomes too narrow, unsuited to the present age, and hence that we should espouse cosmopolitanism. . . . But it is not a doctrine which wronged races should talk about. We, the wronged race, must first recover our position of national freedom and equality before we are fit to discuss cosmopolitanism . . .
>
> European superiority to China is not in political philosophy but altogether in the field of material civilization. . . . A few hundred years ago, Europe could not compare with China, so now if we want to learn from Europe we should learn what we ourselves lack—science—but not political philosophy. Europeans are still looking to China for the fundamentals of political philosophy. . . ."

*Sun Yat-sen, seen here with other Chinese republican officials*

### ANALYZE THE TEXT

1. **CITING TEXT EVIDENCE** What argument does Sun Yat-sen make for the Chinese to favor nationalism over cosmopolitanism? What is the relationship he establishes between the two views? Cite evidence from his text to illustrate his argument.
2. **DETERMINING MEANING** Who are "the Powers" that Sun Yat-sen refers to?



### MULTIPLE PERSPECTIVES

1. **DETERMINING CENTRAL IDEAS** All three excerpts discuss challenges that their groups face from foreign powers. Identify these challenges.
2. **COMPARING POINTS OF VIEW** How are the three excerpts similar in how they portray nationalism?

## ESSENTIAL QUESTIONS

- *How can political control lead to nationalist movements?*
- *How does economic exploitation lead to nationalist movements?*

# THE STORY BEGINS...

LESSON 2

# Nationalism in Africa and Asia

In 1931, France celebrated a century of rule in Algeria. The French proudly boasted of their policies in Algeria. It was not a colony, they claimed; it was part of France. Many Algerian nationalists, however, disagreed. In 1936, a group of nationalist Algerian scholars penned the following condemnation of French rule:

> "We the *oulema*, speaking in the name of the majority of natives of this country, say to those who claim to be French: 'You do not represent us! . . . the Muslim population of Algeria has its own history, religious unity, language, culture and traditions . . . This Muslim population is not part of France, cannot be part of France, and does not want to be part of France."

—"Clear Statement," *El oulema*, April 1936

Although Algeria would remain in French hands for nearly three more decades, the rest of colonial Africa would begin to crumble as African nationalist movements took the lead in championing independence.

*A statue of Jomo Kenyatta, the man considered to be the founding father of the state of Kenya, in Nairobi, Kenya.* ▶

PHOTO:dbimages/Alamy Stock Photo; TEXT:Ageron, Charles-Robert. 1964. Modern Algeria: A History from 1830 to the Present. Translated 1991 by Michael Brett. Trenton, New Jersey: Africa World Press, Inc.

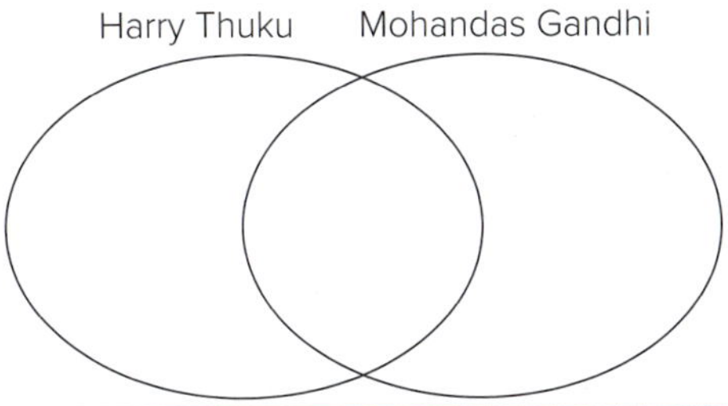


**ANALYZING KEY IDEAS AND DETAILS**

**DETERMINING CENTRAL IDEAS** Use a Venn diagram like this one to compare and contrast the background and accomplishments of Harry Thuku and Mohandas Gandhi.

## AFRICAN INDEPENDENCE MOVEMENTS

**GUIDING QUESTION** *What motivated African independence movements after World War I?*

Black Africans fought in World War I in British and French armies. Many Africans hoped that independence after the war would be their reward. As one newspaper in the Gold Coast argued, if African **volunteers** who fought on European battlefields were "good enough to fight and die in the Empire's cause, they were good enough to have a share in the government of their countries." Most European leaders were not ready to give up their colonies.

The peace settlement after World War I was a huge disappointment. Germany was stripped of its African colonies, but these colonies were awarded to Great Britain and France to be administered as mandates for the League of Nations. Britain and France now governed a vast portion of Africa.

### AFRICAN PROTESTS

After World War I, Africans became more active politically. The European colonizers that conquered and exploited Africa also introduced Western education. In educating Africans, the colonial system gave them visions of a world based on the ideals of liberty and equality. In Africa, the missionary schools taught these ideals to their pupils. The African students who studied abroad, especially in Britain and the United States, and the African soldiers who served in World War I learned new ideas about freedom and nationalism in the West. Many Africans in European colonial states expected to be given their independence after the war. When this did not occur it led to disappointment and frustration. As more Africans became aware of the enormous gulf between Western ideals and practices, they decided to seek reform.

Reform movements took different forms. One of the most important issues in Kenya concerned land redistribution. Large tracts of land were given to white settlers. Black Africans received little if any **compensation** for this land and became squatters on the land they believed was their own.

During the 1920s, moderate protest organizations, mostly founded by the Kikuyu, emerged in Kenya. The Kikuyu Association, founded in 1920 by farmers, was intent on blocking further land confiscation. This association was willing to work for reform within the existing colonial structure.

**ANALYZING KEY IDEAS AND DETAILS**

1. **CITING TEXT EVIDENCE** What evidence in the text supports the claim that the "peace settlement after World War I was a huge disappointment"?
2. **ANALYZING CENTRAL IDEAS** What is the central idea of "New Leaders"? How does the central idea explain the section's title?

**ANALYZING PRIMARY SOURCES**

**COLONIALISM IN AFRICA**

" By driving [the African] off his ancestral lands, the Europeans have . . . reduced him to a state of serfdom incompatible with human happiness. The African is conditioned, by the cultural and social institutions of centuries, to a freedom of which Europe has little conception, and it is not in his nature to accept serfdom for ever. He realizes that he must fight unceasingly for his own complete emancipation [freedom]."

—Jomo Kenyatta, from *Facing Mount Kenya*

**DRAWING CONCLUSIONS** Why does Kenyatta equate colonialism with serfdom?

## AFRICA 1939

### GEOGRAPHIC REASONING

In 1939 nationalist resistance to European rule spread across Africa.

1. **EXPLORING REGIONS** Which countries had active national resistance movements by 1939?
2. **EXPLORING PLACE** Which country had the earliest nationalist resistance movement according to the information on the map?

Some of the Kenyan protesters were more radical, however. The Young Kikuyu Association, organized by Harry Thuku in 1921, challenged European authority. Thuku, a telephone operator, protested against the high taxes levied by the British rulers. His message was simple:

> “Hearken, every day you pay . . . tax to the Europeans of Government. Where is it sent? It is their task to steal the property of the Kikuyu people.”
>
> —quoted in *Africa: History of a Continent*

Thuku was arrested. When an angry crowd stormed the jail and demanded his release, government authorities fired into the crowd and killed at least 20 people. Thuku was sent into exile.

Libya also struggled against foreign rule in the 1920s. Forces led by Omar Mukhtar used guerrilla warfare against the Italians and defeated them a number of times. The Italians reacted ferociously. They established concentration camps and used all available modern weapons to crush the revolt. Mukhtar's death ended the movement.

Although colonial powers typically responded to such movements with force, they also began to make some reforms. They made these reforms in an effort to satisfy African peoples. Reforms, however, were too few and too late. By the 1930s, an increasing number of African leaders were calling for independence, not reform.

Davidson, Basil. 1972. Africa: History of a Continent. Spring Books.

## NEW LEADERS

Calls for independence came from a new generation of young African leaders. Many had been educated abroad, in Europe, and the United States. Those who studied in the United States were especially influenced by the ideas of W. E. B. Du Bois and Marcus Garvey.

Du Bois, an African American who was educated at Harvard University, was the leader of a movement that tried to make all Africans aware of their own cultural heritage. Garvey, a Jamaican who lived in Harlem in New York City, stressed the need for the unity of all Africans, a movement known as **Pan-Africanism**. His *Declaration of the Rights of the Negro Peoples of the World*, issued in 1920, had a strong impact on later African leaders.

Leaders and movements in individual African nations also appeared. Educated in Great Britain, Jomo Kenyatta of Kenya argued in his book *Facing Mount Kenya* that British rule was destroying the traditional culture of the peoples of Africa.

Léopold Senghor, who studied in France and wrote poetry about African culture, organized an independence movement in Senegal. Nnamdi Azikiwe of Nigeria began a newspaper, *The West African Pilot*, in 1937 and urged nonviolence as a method of gaining independence. These are just a few of the leaders who worked to end colonial rule in Africa. Success, however, would not come until after World War II.

**DETERMINING MEANING**

**Pan-Africanism** contains the Greek prefix *pan*, which means "all." What does this tell a reader about the meaning of *pan-Africanism*? What else can you learn from the context of the text?

### ✓ CHECKING FOR UNDERSTANDING

1. **EVALUATING** What motivated African independence movements after World War I?
2. **UNDERSTANDING CONTEXT** Name four African leaders and discuss their motivations for African independence.
3. **DRAWING CONCLUSIONS** What role do you think nationalist newspapers, such as Nigeria's *The West African Pilot*, played in independence movements?

# REVOLUTION IN SOUTHEAST ASIA

**GUIDING QUESTION** *Why was communism more accepted in Asia after World War I?*

Before World War I, the Marxist doctrine of social revolution had no appeal for Asian intellectuals. After all, most Asian societies were still agricultural and hardly ready for revolution. That situation changed after the revolution in Russia in 1917. Lenin and the Bolsheviks showed that a revolutionary Marxist party could overturn an outdated system—even one that was not fully industrialized—and begin a new one.

In 1920 Lenin adopted a new revolutionary strategy aimed at societies outside the Western world. He spread the word of Karl Marx through the Communist International, or Comintern, a worldwide organization of Communist parties formed in 1919 to advance world revolution. Agents were trained in Moscow and then returned to their countries to form Marxist parties. By the end of the 1920s, almost every colonial society in Asia had a Communist party.

How successful were these new parties? In some countries, the local Communists established a cooperative relationship with nationalist parties to struggle against Western imperialism. This was true in French Indochina.

**ANALYZING KEY IDEAS AND DETAILS**

1. **DETERMINING CENTRAL IDEAS** What is the central idea of this passage? What does this central idea suggest about pre-World War I notions of the relationship between communism and industrialization?
2. **CITING TEXT EVIDENCE** What evidence in the text suggests that Lenin worked to change the perception of communism in non-Western nations?

Moscow-trained Ho Chi Minh organized the Vietnamese Communists in the 1920s. The strongest Communist-nationalist alliance was formed in China. In most colonial societies, though, Communist parties of the 1930s failed to gain support among the majority of the population.

### ☑ CHECKING FOR UNDERSTANDING

1. **EXPLAINING CAUSE AND EFFECT** Why was communism more accepted in Asia after World War I?
2. **DRAWING CONCLUSIONS** Why did Lenin have to reframe the message of communism for non-Western societies?
3. **IDENTIFYING CONNECTIONS** How did communism spread to Asia after World War I?

## INDIAN INDEPENDENCE

**ANALYZING KEY IDEAS AND DETAILS**

1. **ANALYZING EVENTS** Reread the paragraph that begins "Nonviolence was central to . . ." What part of this paragraph states an effect of the British policies in India? What words signal that this is an effect?
2. **ANALYZING IDEAS** Reread the paragraph that begins, "In the meantime, another problem . . ." What clue does this paragraph give the reader about the increasing complexity of Indian independence?

**DETERMINING MEANING**

Reread the section "Protest and Reform." Using context clues, write a definition for **civil disobedience**. Use a dictionary or online resource to check your definition.

**GUIDING QUESTION** *Who and what shaped India's independence movement?*

Mohandas Gandhi was active in the Indian National Congress and the movement for Indian self-rule before World War I. Like many in India, Gandhi was disheartened that India was not granted self-rule after the war. The Indian people began to refer to him as India's "Great Soul," or Mahatma. After the war, Gandhi remained an important figure, and new leaders also arose to respond to British colonialism.

### PROTEST AND REFORM

Gandhi left South Africa in 1914. When he returned to India, he organized mass protests against British laws. A believer in nonviolence, Gandhi used the methods of **civil disobedience** to push for Indian independence.

In 1919 British troops killed hundreds of unarmed protesters in Amritsar, in northwestern India. Horrified at the violence, Gandhi briefly retreated from active politics but was later arrested and imprisoned for his role in protests.

In 1935 Britain passed the Government of India Act, which expanded the role of Indians in governing. Before, the Legislative Council could give advice only to the British governor. Now, it became a two-house parliament, and two-thirds of its Indian members were to be elected. Five million Indians (still a small percentage of the total population) were given the right to vote.

### A PUSH FOR INDEPENDENCE

The Indian National Congress (INC), founded in 1885, sought reforms in Britain's government of India. Reforms, however, were no longer enough. Under its new leader, Motilal Nehru, the INC wanted to push for full independence from Britain.

Gandhi, now released from prison, returned to his earlier policy of civil disobedience. He worked hard to inform ordinary Indians of his beliefs and methods. It was wrong, he said, to harm any living being. He believed that hate could be overcome only by love, and love, rather than force, could win people over to one's position.

CITIZENSHIP

## NONVIOLENCE AND THE AMERICAN CIVIL RIGHTS MOVEMENT

In a democracy, when politicians refuse to heed the will of the people, majorities can vote them out of office. Not every system is a democracy, however; and even in a democracy, some do not have the right to vote or the privileges that enable them to be heard. This was the case in British India. To bring about change in this system, Gandhi used tactics that made it costly for the authorities to ignore his concerns. Civil rights leaders in the United States, such as Martin Luther King, Jr., recognized the potency of these tactics. King used bus boycotts, sit-ins, and mass marches to protest segregation. Frequently, his peaceful tactics were met with violence by authorities. The contrast between his nonviolence and their violence reached the wider public through film and photographs. The shock triggered by this contrast further helped undermine racial segregation in the United States.

**RELATING EVENTS** Why might U.S. civil rights figures such as Martin Luther King, Jr., have adopted the tactics of civil disobedience they observed in India?

Nonviolence was central to Gandhi's campaign of noncooperation and civil disobedience. To protest unjust British laws, Gandhi told his people: "Don't pay your taxes or send your children to an English-supported school. . . . Make your own cotton cloth by spinning the thread at home, and don't buy English-made goods. Provide yourselves with home-made salt, and do not buy government-made salt."

Britain had increased the salt tax and prohibited Indians from manufacturing or harvesting their own salt. In 1930 Gandhi led a protest. He walked to the sea with his supporters in what was called the Salt March. On reaching the coast, Gandhi picked up a pinch of salt. Thousands of Indians followed his act of civil disobedience. Gandhi and many other members of the INC were arrested.

## NEW LEADERS AND PROBLEMS

In the 1930s, Jawaharlal Nehru entered the movement. The son of Motilal Nehru, Jawaharlal studied law in Great Britain. He was a new kind of Indian politician—upper class and intellectual.

The INC drafted a resolution called Purna Swaraj to declare India's independence.

> "We believe that it is the incredible right of the Indian people, as of any other people, to have freedom to enjoy the fruits of their soil and have the necessities of life, so that they may have full opportunities of growth. We believe also that if any government deprives a people of these and oppress them, the people have a further right to alter or abolish it. The British Government in India has not only deprived the Indian people of their freedom but has based itself on the exploitation of the masses, and has ruined India . . ."

—*Declaration of Purna Swaraj*, 1930

### ANALYZING PRIMARY SOURCES

1. **DETERMINING CENTRAL IDEAS** According to the declaration, why should the Indian people become independent from British rule?
2. **DETERMINING MEANING** What does the phrase "enjoy the fruits of their soil" suggest about the Indian people?

The independence movement in India split into two paths. The one identified with Gandhi was religious, anti-Western, and traditional. The other, identified with Nehru, was secular, pro-Western, and modern. The two approaches created uncertainty about India's future path.

In the meantime, another problem arose in the independence movement. Hostility between Hindus and Muslims had existed for centuries. Muslims were dissatisfied with the Hindu dominance of the INC and they raised the cry "Islam is in danger."

By the 1930s, the Muslim League was under the leadership of Mohammed Ali Jinnah. The league believed in the creation of a separate Muslim state of Pakistan ("the land of the pure") in the northwest.

### ✓ CHECKING FOR UNDERSTANDING

1. **UNDERSTANDING CONTEXT** Who and what shaped India's independence movement?
2. **IDENTIFYING CONNECTIONS** How did Nehru differ from Gandhi? What was the result of having two prominent individuals working for India's independence but from different perspectives?
3. **SUMMARIZING** What solution did the Muslim League propose in response to the tension between Muslims and Hindus?

## A MILITARIST JAPAN

**GUIDING QUESTION** *What triggered the rise of militarism in Japan?*

Japanese society developed along a Western model. Meiji Era reforms led to increasing prosperity and a modern industrial and commercial sector.

### A *ZAIBATSU* ECONOMY

In the Japanese economy, various manufacturing processes were concentrated within a single enterprise called the ***zaibatsu***, a large financial and industrial corporation. These vast companies controlled major segments of the Japanese industrial sector. By 1937, the four largest *zaibatsu* (Mitsui, Mitsubishi, Sumitomo, and Yasuda) controlled 21 percent of the banking, 26 percent of the mining, 35 percent of the shipbuilding, and more than 60 percent of the paper manufacturing and insurance industries.

The concentration of wealth led to growing economic inequalities. City workers were poorly paid and housed. Economic crises added to this problem. After World War I, inflation in food prices led to food riots. A rapid increase in population led to food shortages. (The population of the Japanese islands increased from 43 million in 1900 to 73 million in 1940.) Later, when the Great Depression struck, workers and farmers suffered the most.

With hardships came calls for a return to traditional Japanese values. Traditionalists especially objected to the growing influence of Western ideas and values on Japanese educational and political systems. At the same time, many citizens denounced Japan's attempt to find security through cooperation with the Western powers. Instead, they demanded that Japan use its strength to dominate Asia.

**UNDERSTANDING CRAFT AND STRUCTURE**

1. **ANALYZING TEXT PRESENTATION** Reread the section under the subheading "The Rise of Militarism." How does the writer contrast the move toward democracy in the early twentieth century with the move toward authoritarianism decades later?
2. **DETERMINING MEANING** According to the text, "During the early 1930s, civilians formed extremist patriotic organizations such as the Black Dragon Society." What is an extremist organization?

**DETERMINING MEANING**

Read the paragraph containing the word ***zaibatsu***. What context clues tell you the meaning of this Japanese word?

*Japanese women at a silk factory in 1913 check the unreeling of raw silk.*

**DETERMINING CONTEXT**
Contrast the Japanese economy before and after World War I.

## JAPAN AND THE WEST

In the early twentieth century, Japan had difficulty finding sources of raw materials and foreign markets for its manufactured goods. Until World War I, Japan fulfilled these needs by seizing territories, such as Taiwan, Korea, and southern Manchuria. While the mandate system established by the League of Nations had given Japan the authorization to govern former German-held islands north of the Equator in the western Pacific, Japan's policy of seizing territories drew the concern of the other nations, especially the United States.

In 1922 the United States held a conference of nations with interests in the Pacific. This conference created a nine-power treaty that recognized the territorial integrity of China and the maintenance of the Open Door policy. Japan agreed, in return for recognition of its control of southern Manchuria. However, this agreement did not prove popular. Heavy industry, mining, and manufacture of appliances and automobiles require resources that are not found in abundance in Japan. The Japanese government came under pressure to find new sources for raw materials abroad.

**DETERMINING MEANING**
*Integrity* is derived from the Latin root *integer*, meaning "entire." How does knowing the meaning of the Latin root help a reader understand the meaning of *integrity* in this context?

## THE RISE OF MILITARISM

During the early 1900s, Japan had moved toward a more democratic government. The parliament and political parties grew stronger. The influence of the old ruling oligarchy, however, remained strong.

At the end of the 1920s, a militant group within the ruling party gained control of the political system. Some militants were civilians who were convinced that Western ideas had corrupted the parliamentary system. Others were military members who were angered by the cuts in military spending and the government's pacifist policies of the early 1920s.

During the early 1930s, civilians formed extremist patriotic organizations such as the Black Dragon Society. Members of the army and navy created similar societies. One group of middle-level army officers invaded Manchuria without

MAKING CONNECTIONS ACROSS CULTURES

## KOREAN INDEPENDENCE

On March 1, 1919, Korean nationalists gathered to read a declaration of independence from Japan. The declaration found inspiration in many of the political ideas of the Enlightenment. Two of these were the social contract, or the idea that citizens give certain rights to their government in exchange for fair leadership, and natural rights, or the inalienable rights such as life and liberty. Nearly two million Koreans participated in organized demonstrations throughout the territory. Although they were violently put down by Japan, they did inspire the creation of a provisional government in Shanghai. When Japan was forced out in 1945, that provisional government took over in the south. March 1st remains a holiday today in both North and South Korea.

1. **IDENTIFYING CONNECTIONS** What ideals of the March First Movement did the founders of the United States share?

2. **INTERPRETING** In what ways was the Empire of Japan in violation of the social contract with the Korean people?

government approval in 1931. Within a short time, all Manchuria had been conquered. The Japanese government opposed the conquest, but the people supported it. Unable to act, the government became dominated by the military.

Japanese society was put on wartime status. A military draft law was passed in 1938. Economic resources were placed under strict government control. All political parties were merged into the Imperial Rule Assistance Association, which called for Japanese expansion abroad. Labor unions were disbanded, and education and culture were purged of most Western ideas.

### ✓ CHECKING FOR UNDERSTANDING

1. **ANALYZING CHANGE** What triggered the rise of militarism in Japan?

2. **DETERMINING CONTEXT** What factors contributed to the growing backlash against Japan's Westernization?

3. **SUMMARIZING** How did organizations such as the Black Dragon Society come to dominate Japanese politics?

## LESSON 2 REVIEW

### Time and Place

1. **DETERMINING CONTEXT** How was the Italian response in Libya different from the British actions in Kenya and India?

### Building History-Social Science Skills

2. **IDENTIFYING CONNECTIONS** What did the works of Du Bois and Garvey contribute to nationalist movements in Africa?

3. **RELATING EVENTS** How did the Comintern strengthen certain Asian nationalist movements?

4. **IDENTIFYING EFFECTS** How did World War I affect the political environment of Africa?

### Writing About History

5. **EXPLANATORY WRITING** Write an essay explaining why Gandhi's single pinch of salt taken from the ocean was a significant act. What rhetorical point did the Salt March participants make that day? What were the larger issues at stake?

### Collaborating

6. **COLLABORATING** Several leaders of nationalist movements were educated in Western nations. With a partner, discuss how this experience influenced them. Discuss specific examples of individuals and their actions.

## ESSENTIAL QUESTIONS

- *How can political control lead to nationalist movements?*
- *How does economic exploitation lead to nationalist movements?*

LESSON 3

# Revolutionary Chaos in China

## THE STORY BEGINS...

He Zhen was a Chinese feminist who saw communism as a solution to inequality between the sexes. She published an article titled "What Women Should Know About Communism," in 1917, in a journal she and her husband published.

> "Those of us who are women suffer untold bitterness and untold wrongs in order to get hold of this rice bowl. . . I have a good idea that will exempt you from relying on others while still finding food naturally. How? By practicing communism. Think of all the things in the world. They were either produced by nature or by individual labor. Why can rich people buy them but poor people cannot? It is because the world trades with money... If every single woman understands that nothing is more evil than money, and they all unite together to cooperate with men to utterly overthrow the rich and powerful and then abolish money, then absolutely nothing will be allowed for individuals to own privately."
>
> —He Zhen, 1917

This was a period of change for China. Both the Nationalists and the Communists saw their movements as a way to liberate China from foreign influence and the Chinese people from oppression.

*Sun Yat-sen, considered by many to be the founding father of the Republic of China, seen here on a 100 Yuan banknote* ▶

PHOTO:Ivan Vdovin/Alamy Stock Photo; TEXT:Zhen, He. 1917. "What Women Should Know About Communism". Quoted by de Bary, Wm. Theodore. 2008. Sources of East Asia Tradition - Volume 2: The Modern Period. New York: Columbia University Press.

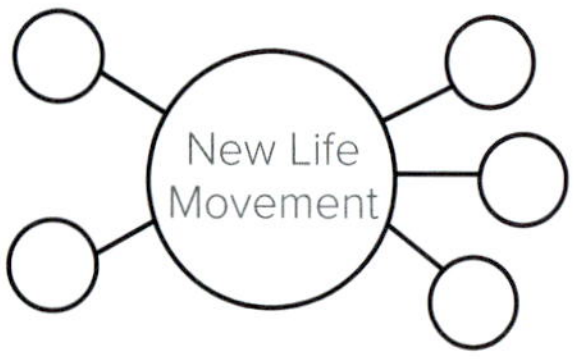


**ANALYZING KEY IDEAS AND DETAILS**

**DETERMINING CENTRAL IDEAS** Read closely to identify the Confucian values that Chiang Kai-shek appealed to in order to bring Western ideas to culturally conservative segments of the Chinese population. Record these values in a cluster diagram like this one.

**ANALYZING KEY IDEAS AND DETAILS**

1. **SUMMARIZING** Summarize the subsection titled "The Nationalist-Communist Alliance." What specific words and phrases in the text describe the motivations behind this alliance?
2. **CITING TEXT EVIDENCE** The text in the subsection "The Communists in Hiding" notes that Mao Zedong had different ideas about the role of communism in China. What evidence in the text supports this claim?

**DETERMINING MEANING**

Read the paragraph that contains the word **ceased**. Look for contextual evidence and write a definition for *ceased*. Check your definition against a dictionary or online resource.

**ANALYZING PRIMARY SOURCES**

1. **DETERMINING POINT OF VIEW** What does Sun Yat-sen think is the reason Chinese culture and society have not developed?
2. **ANALYZING TEXT PRESENTATION** Why does Sun compare Hong Kong to Xiangshan?

# NATIONALISTS AND COMMUNISTS

**GUIDING QUESTION** *How did the relationship between the Nationalists and the Communists evolve?*

Revolutionary Marxism had its greatest impact in China. By 1920, central authority had almost **ceased** to exist in China. Two different political forces began to emerge as competitors for the right to rule China: Sun Yat-sen's Nationalist Party, which had been driven from the political arena several years earlier, and the Chinese Communist Party.

## THE NATIONALIST-COMMUNIST ALLIANCE

In 1921 a group of young radicals, including several faculty and staff members from Beijing University, founded the Chinese Communist Party (CCP) in the commercial and industrial city of Shanghai. Comintern agents soon advised the new party to join with the more experienced Nationalist Party.

Sun Yat-sen, leader of the Nationalists, welcomed the cooperation. He needed the expertise and the diplomatic support that the Soviet Union could provide. His anti-imperialist words alienated many Western powers. One English-language newspaper in Shanghai wrote: "All his life, all his influence, all his energies are devoted to ideas that keep China in turmoil, and it is utterly undesirable and improper that he should be allowed to prosecute those aims here." In 1923 the Nationalists and Communists formed an alliance to oppose the warlords and to drive the imperialist powers out of China.

> "Hong Kong impressed me a great deal, because there was orderly calm, and because there was artistic work being done without interruption. I went to my home in Xiangshan twice a year and could immediately notice the great difference. There was disorder instead of order, insecurity instead of security. . . .
>
> Although they are only fifty miles apart, the differences impressed me so much that I began to wonder why it was that foreigners have done such marvellous things with this barren rock in only seventy or eighty years, whilst China with several thousand years of civilization has not even one place like Hong Kong. . . .
>
> We in China can imitate what has been done elsewhere, and the first thing to do is get a change of government so as to make everything else possible."

—Sun Yat-sen, address to the students of Hong Kong University, 1923

For more than three years, the two parties overlooked their mutual suspicions and worked together. They formed a revolutionary army to march north and to seize control over China. The so-called Northern Expedition began

Yat-sen, Sun. 1923. Address to the Students of Hong Kong University. February 20, 1923. Reprinted 1988 in Renditions: A Chinese-English Translation Magazine - Numbers 29 & 30 (Spring & Autumn 1988).

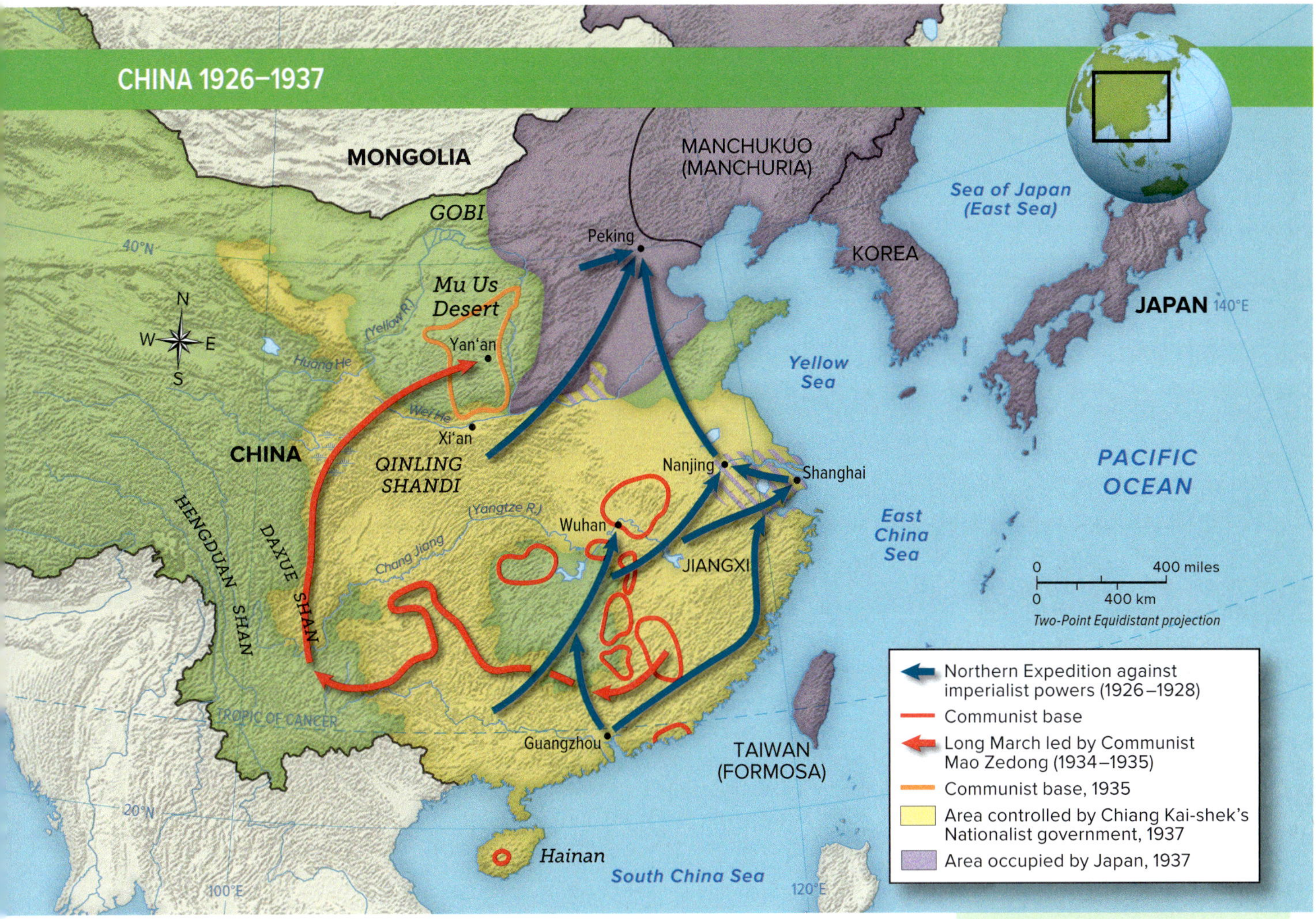


in the summer of 1926. By the following spring, revolutionary forces had taken control of all of China south of the Chang Jiang (Yangtze River), including the major river ports of Wuhan and Shanghai.

Tensions between the parties **eventually** rose to the surface. Sun Yat-sen died in 1925, and General Chiang Kai-shek (JYAHNG KY • SHEHK), his military subordinate, succeeded him as head of the Nationalist Party. Chiang pretended to support the alliance with the Communists but actually planned to destroy them. In April 1927, he struck against the Communists in Shanghai, killing thousands. After the Shanghai Massacre, the Nationalist-Communist alliance ceased to exist.

In 1928 Chiang Kai-shek founded a new Chinese republic at Nanjing. During the next three years, he worked to reunify China. Although Chiang saw Japan as a serious threat, he believed that the Communists were more dangerous. He once remarked that "the Japanese are like a disease of the skin, but the Communists are like a disease of the heart."

## THE COMMUNISTS IN HIDING

After the Shanghai Massacre of April 1927, most of the Communist leaders went into hiding in the city. There, they tried to revive the Communist movement in its traditional urban base among the working class. Shanghai was a rich recruiting ground for the party. People were discontented and looking for leadership.

**GEOGRAPHIC REASONING**

After World War I, China was torn among Nationalists, Communists, and Japan.

1. **GLOBAL INTERCONNECTIONS** Why would it be significant for the Nationalists to control Nanjing and Shanghai?
2. **HUMAN-ENVIRONMENT INTERACTION** What geographic features likely helped the Communists defend their 1935 base?

Some party members, however, fled to the mountainous Jiangxi (JYAHNG • SHEE) Province south of the Chang Jiang. They were led by the young Communist organizer Mao Zedong (MOW DZUH • DUNG). Unlike most other leading members of the Communist Party, Mao was convinced that a Chinese revolution would be driven by the poverty-stricken peasants in the countryside rather than by the urban working class. Mao, the son of a prosperous peasant, had helped organize a peasant movement in southern China during the early 1920s.

Chiang Kai-shek now tried to root the Communists out of their urban base in Shanghai and their rural base in Jiangxi Province. He succeeded in the first task in 1931. Most party leaders in Shanghai were forced to flee to Mao's base in southern China.

**BIOGRAPHY**

## MAO ZEDONG (1893–1976)

Mao Zedong was the founding chairman of the People's Republic of China. As a young Communist revolutionary, he went to his home in the countryside of Hunan, where he saw political unrest growing among the peasants. He realized that the Soviet-style communism that he and others were pursuing—focusing on factory workers in cities—was not a perfect fit for China. Instead, he decided to organize a revolution of rural peasants. Mao sought to adapt communism to fit the conditions, culture, and traditions of China. Mao was largely responsible for laying the groundwork for a modern, self-sufficient China, but at an extreme cost. Many of his later policies, such as the Great Leap Forward and the Cultural Revolution, brought enormous suffering and political repression.

1. **UNDERSTANDING CONTEXT** Why was it important that Mao focused on the revolutionary potential among the peasants in rural China rather than the factory workers in the cities?

2. **DETERMINING CENTRAL IDEAS** What effect did Mao's visit to his hometown have on his plans for the Communist Party in China?

**DETERMINING MEANING**

A *guerrilla* is a member of a small independent military group, typically that fights against a larger and more established group. Read the paragraph that contains the phrase **guerrilla tactics**. What does the definition of *guerrilla* tell you about this military strategy?

Chiang Kai-shek then turned his forces against Mao's stronghold in Jiangxi Province. Chiang's forces far outnumbered Mao's, but Mao made effective use of **guerrilla tactics**, using unexpected methods such as sabotage and deception to fight the enemy. Four slogans by Mao describe his methods:

> "When the enemy advances, we retreat! When the enemy halts and camps, we trouble them! When the enemy tries to avoid battle, we attack! When the enemy retreats, we pursue!"
>
> —quoted in *Red Star Over China*

## THE LONG MARCH

In 1934 Chiang's troops, with their superior military strength, surrounded the Communist base in Jiangxi and set up a blockade of the stronghold. With the villages behind Chiang's troops, no food or supplies could pass to the Communist base. Chiang even built small forts to prevent Communist raids. However, Mao's army, the People's Liberation Army (PLA), broke through the Nationalist lines and began its famous Long March.

PHOTO:©Dean Fox/SuperStock; TEXT:Snow, Egar. 1938. Red Star Over China.

Both Mao and Chiang knew that unless Mao's army could cross the Chang Jiang, it would be wiped out. Mao's army began a desperate race. Moving on foot through mountains, marshes, rivers, and deserts, the army traveled almost 6,000 miles (9,600 km), averaging 24 miles (38 km) each day, to reach the last surviving Communist base in northwest China. All along those miles, Mao's troops had to fight Chiang's army. Many of Mao's troops froze or starved. One survivor of the Long March remembered:

> "As the days went by, there was less and less to eat. After our grain was finished, we ate the horses and then we lived on wild vegetables. When even the wild vegetables were finished, we ate our leather belts. After that we had to march on empty stomachs."
>
> —quoted in *A Short History of China*

One year later, Mao's troops reached safety in the dusty hills of northern China. Of the 90,000 troops who had embarked on the journey, only 9,000 remained. In the course of the Long March, Mao Zedong had become the sole leader of the Chinese Communist Party. To people who lived at the time, it must have seemed that the Communist threat to the Nanjing regime was over. To the Communists, however, there remained hope for the future.

### ✓ CHECKING FOR UNDERSTANDING

1. **IDENTIFYING CONNECTIONS** How did the relationship between the Nationalists and Communists evolve?
2. **INTERPRETING** Why did the Nationalists and Communists form an alliance?
3. **ANALYZING CHANGE** What does the success of Chiang's military in 1931 indicate about Communist power in the years after this?

## THE NEW CHINA

**GUIDING QUESTION** *What characterized the new China?*

Even while trying to root out Mao's Communist forces, Chiang was trying to build a new Chinese nation. He publicly declared his commitment to Sun Yat-sen's plans for a republican government. But first, a transitional period would occur. In Sun's words:

> "China . . . needs a republican government just as a boy needs school. As a schoolboy must have good teachers and helpful friends, so the Chinese people, being for the first time under republican rule, must have a farsighted revolutionary government for their training. This calls for the period of political tutelage, which is a necessary transitional stage from monarchy to republicanism. Without this, disorder will be unavoidable."
>
> —quoted in *Sources of Chinese Tradition*

In keeping with Sun's program, Chiang announced a period of political tutelage (training) to prepare the Chinese people for a final stage of constitutional government. Even the humblest peasant would be given time to understand the country's problems and the new government. In the meantime, the Nationalists used their dictatorial power to carry out a land-reform program and the modernization of the urban industrial sector.

### ANALYZING KEY IDEAS AND DETAILS

1. **DETERMINING CENTRAL IDEAS** Read the paragraph that starts, "Meanwhile, a Westernized middle class began to form . . ." What is the central idea of this paragraph? Does the quote from the Chinese poet support or contradict the central idea?
2. **CITING TEXT EVIDENCE** The text notes that Chiang had a difficult time implementing reforms. What evidence does the writer present to support this claim?

### DETERMINING MEANING

*Tutelage* is derived from the Latin *tutela*, meaning "protection" or "guardian." How does knowing the meaning of the Latin root help a reader understand the meaning of *tutelage* in this context?

(t)Hookham, Hilda. 1970. A Short History of China. St. Martin's Press; (b)Yat-Sen, Sun. 1918. Selections From a Program of National Reconstruction: "The Three Stages of Revolution". Quoted by de Bary, Wm. Theodore and Lufrano, Richard. 2000. In Sources of Chinese Tradition, Second Edition. Volume II - From 1600 Through the Twentieth Century. New York: Columbia University Press.

**ANALYZING PRIMARY SOURCES**

**THE NEW LIFE MOVEMENT**

"The new life movement is based upon the preservation of these four virtues [courtesy, duty, honesty, and honor], and it aims to apply them to actual, existing conditions, in order that the moral character of the nation shall attain the highest possible standard."

—Madame Chiang Kai-shek, quoted in *War Messages and Other Selections*

**DRAWING CONCLUSIONS** What were the goals of the New Life Movement?

## A CLASS DIVIDE

It would take more than plans on paper to create a new China, however. Years of neglect and civil war had severely weakened the political, economic, and social fabric of the nation. Faint signs of an impending industrial revolution were appearing in the major urban centers. However, most of the people who lived in the countryside were drained by warfare and civil strife. Rural peasants—up to 80 percent of China's population—were still poor and overwhelmingly illiterate.

Meanwhile, a Westernized middle class began to form in the cities. It was here that the new Nanjing government found much of its support. However, the new Westernized elite were concerned with the middle-class Western values of individual advancement and material accumulation. They had few links with the peasants in the countryside or with the rickshaw (a small, two-wheeled cart that usually carried one passenger and was pulled by a person) driver, "running in this world of suffering," in the words of a Chinese poet. In the cities, observers would have believed that Chiang Kai-shek had lifted China into the modern world. Young people in cities wore European clothes; they went to the movies and listened to the radio.

PHOTO:Keystone-France/Gamma-Keystone/Getty Images; TEXT:Soong Chiang, May-Ling. 1938. War Messages and Other Selections. The China Information Committee.

*Rural peasants toil in the fields in 1930s China.*

**ANALYZING CHANGE** How does this image of life in rural China differ from the depiction of life in urban Nanjing in the 1930s?

## INNOVATIONS AND TRADITIONS

Chiang Kai-shek was aware of the problem of introducing foreign ideas into a population that was still culturally conservative. Thus, while attempting to build a modern industrial state, he tried to bring together modern Western innovations with traditional Confucian values of hard work and obedience. With his U.S.-educated wife Soong Mei-ling, Chiang set up a "New Life Movement." Its goal was to promote traditional Confucian social ethics, such as integrity, propriety, and righteousness. Four ancient Confucian virtues would serve as guides for living: Li (courtesy), I (duty), Lien (honesty), and Chih (honor). At the same time, it rejected what was viewed as the excessive individualism and material greed of Western capitalist values.

Unfortunately for Chiang Kai-Shek, Confucian ideas had been widely discredited when the traditional system failed to provide answers to China's decline. Moreover, Chiang Kai-shek faced a host of other problems. The Nanjing government had total control over only a handful of provinces in the Chang Jiang valley. Also, the Japanese threatened to gain control of northern China. The Great Depression also was having an ill effect on China's economy. All of these problems created difficulties for Chiang.

**MAKING CONNECTIONS TO TECHNOLOGY**

### INFRASTRUCTURE AND NATIONAL UNITY

Transportation systems, such as highways, railroads, and airports, known generally as "infrastructure," can serve as important tools of national unification. For instance, the ability to fly from Los Angeles to New York in a few hours means the business, cultural, and political connections between these two cities, and thus the east and west coasts of the United States, stay strong. Chiang Kai-shek understood this and sought to pull together China in a similar way. Despite his efforts at military unification in the 1920s, in the 1930s, he still had to contend with minor warlords in different parts of China. By overseeing the construction of 3,000 miles of railways and tens of thousands of miles of roads and creating a joint venture with American and German companies for a national airline, Chiang sought both modernization and political unification in the multiethnic, multilingual country of China.

1. **IDENTIFYING CONNECTIONS** How might these improvements in transportation infrastructure have benefited Chiang's political power?
2. **DRAWING CONCLUSIONS** Given what you have learned about nineteenth- and twentieth-century China, why might Chiang have believed it necessary to invest so heavily in transportation networks in China?

## LIMITED PROGRESS

In spite of these problems, Chiang did have some success. He undertook a massive road-building project and repaired and extended much of the country's railroad system as well. More than 50,000 miles (80,467 km) of highways were built around and through the coastal areas. New factories, most of which the Chinese owned, were opened. Through a series of agreements, the foreign powers ended many of their leases, gave up extraterritorial rights, and returned the customs service to Chinese control. Chiang established a national bank and improved the education system.

The government was also repressive. Fearing Communist influence, Chiang suppressed all opposition and censored free expression. In so doing, he alienated many intellectuals and political moderates. Because Chiang's support came from the rural landed gentry as well as the urban middle class, he did not push for programs that would lead to a **redistribution of wealth,** the shifting of

**DETERMINING MEANING**

Read the paragraph containing the phrase **redistribution of wealth**. What does the context tell you about the meaning of this policy?

wealth from a rich minority to a poor majority. A land-reform program was enacted in 1930, but it had little effect on the country. For the peasants and poor townspeople, no real improvement occurred under the Nanjing government. Sun Fo, Sun Yat-sen's son, expressed disapproval of the Nanjing government:

> "We must frankly admit the fact that in these twenty years the machinery and practice of the Kuomintang [Chinese Nationalist Party] have turned in a wrong direction, inconsistent with the party constitution drafted by Dr. Sun Yat-sen in 1923 and contrary to the spirit of democracy. The practice of the revolutionary party has subsequently become the same as that of a bureaucratic regime."

—quoted in *China,* 1946

Chiang Kai-shek's government had a little more success in promoting industrial development. Between 1927 and 1937, industrial growth in China averaged only about 1 percent per year. Much of the national wealth was in the hands of the so-called "four families," a group of senior officials and close subordinates of the ruling elite. Military expenses took up approximately half the budget. Little money was left for social and economic development.

The new government, then, had little success in dealing with the deep-seated economic and social problems that affected China during the interwar years. This was especially true when internal disintegration and foreign pressure were occurring during the virtual collapse of the global economic order during the Great Depression. In addition, militant political forces in Tokyo were determined to extend Japanese influence and power in an unstable China.



### ☑ CHECKING FOR UNDERSTANDING

1. **ANALYZING CHANGE** What characterized the new China?
2. **UNDERSTANDING CONTEXT** How were the goals of the New Life Movement presented as a continuation of Confucian values? How might these goals benefit industrialization efforts?
3. **INTERPRETING** Why did Chiang Kai-shek argue that a period of political tutelage was necessary for China?

## LESSON 3 REVIEW

### Time and Place

1. **CONSTRUCTING HYPOTHESES** Why was Chiang Kai-shek's strategy of enlisting Confucian values as a way to spread Western ideals a failure?
2. **INTERPRETING** How did the geography of China add difficulty to the People's Liberation Army's Long March?

### Building History-Social Science Analysis Skills

3. **EVALUATING** Why was Shanghai chosen as a key recruitment area for the Communist Party after the Shanghai Massacre?
4. **RELATING EVENTS** How did outside political and economic factors contribute to Sun Fo's criticism of the Nationalist Party and Chiang Kai-shek's leadership?

### Writing About History

5. **NARRATIVE WRITING** Imagine you are a young person living in Nanjing or another Chinese city. What does life look like for you under the new programs begun by Chiang Kai-shek? Are daily tasks easier for you now than they used to be? Use specific examples to make your argument.

### Collaborating

6. **EVALUATING POINT OF VIEW** Working as a group, come up with a clear and concise argument as to why the Nationalists should have worked with the Communists or why they should not have done so. Present your argument to the class, asking them to decide whether they agree with your group.

## ESSENTIAL QUESTIONS

- *How can political control lead to nationalist movements?*
- *How does economic exploitation lead to nationalist movements?*

LESSON 4

# Nationalism in Latin America

## THE STORY BEGINS...

Industrial workers in Argentina began to organize into unions and use labor strikes to improve working conditions. One newspaper reporter described the 1919 "Tragic Week" strikes that rocked the nation.

> "General Dellepine has assumed the dictatorship, giving as a reason the Government's inability to cope with the strike. Women and children have been warned off the streets in Buenos Aires by the Government, because the latter are unable to protect them. Newspapers were burned in the streets by mobs who would not permit their circulation, with the exception of the "Lavanguardia," a semi-Socialist journal. Russians were responsible for the strike. In some instances, the soldiers refused strike duty."

—*The Advertiser,* Jan. 14, 1919

While these workers saw the strikes as legitimate attempts to increase support for their cause and improve their condition, others saw the strikes as a sign of chaos. In the 1930s, this latter interpretation would become dominant in elite circles and would result in coups across Latin America.

*Protests in the city of Buenos Aires in the early 20th century* ▶

Bettmann/Getty Images

| Country | Industry |
|---|---|
| | |
| | |
| | |
| | |

### ANALYZING KEY IDEAS AND DETAILS

**SUMMARIZING** As you read, take note of which Latin American nations developed national industries. Record the name of each nation and industry in a graphic organizer like this one.

# THE LATIN AMERICAN ECONOMY

### ANALYZING KEY IDEAS AND DETAILS

1. **SUMMARIZING** Summarize the difference the writer identifies between American and British investments in Latin American industries.
2. **ANALYZING CENTRAL IDEAS** Reread the paragraph that starts with the sentence "The Great Depression, however, . . ." What clue does this paragraph provide readers about the state of domestic industrial development in Latin American countries prior to the Great Depression?

### DETERMINING MEANING

Read the paragraph that contains the word **investor**. What does the context tell you about the meaning of *investor*?

**GUIDING QUESTION** *What factors influenced the Latin American economy during the 1920s and 1930s?*

In the early twentieth century, the Latin American economy was based largely on the export of foodstuffs and raw materials. Some countries relied on only one or two products for sale abroad. Argentina, for example, exported beef and wheat; Chile, nitrates and copper; Brazil, coffee and cotton; Caribbean nations, such as Cuba, sugar; and Central America, bananas. A few reaped large profits from these exports. For most of the people, however, the returns were small.

## ROLE OF THE UNITED STATES

Beginning in the 1920s, the United States began to replace Great Britain as the major **investor** in Latin America. British investors had put money into stocks and other forms of investment that did not give them direct control of the companies. U.S. investors, however, put their funds directly into production facilities and ran companies themselves. In this way, large segments of Latin America's export industries fell into U.S. hands. A number of smaller Central American countries became independent republics, but their economies often depended on wealthy nations. The U.S.-owned United Fruit Company, for example, owned land, packing plants, and railroads in Central America. American firms also gained control of the copper-mining industry in Chile and Peru, as well as of the oil industry in Mexico, Peru, and Bolivia.

Many Latin Americans resented U.S. control of Latin American industries. A growing nationalist awareness led many of them to view the United States as an imperialist power. It was not difficult for Latin American nationalists to show that profits from U.S. businesses were sometimes used to keep ruthless dictators in power. In Venezuela, for example, U.S. oil companies had close ties to the dictator Juan Vicente Gómez.

The United States had always cast a large shadow over Latin America. It had intervened militarily in Latin American affairs for years. This was especially true in Central America and the Caribbean. Many Americans considered both regions vital to U.S. security.

The United States made some attempts to change its relationship with Latin America in the 1930s. In 1933 President Franklin D. Roosevelt announced the Good Neighbor policy, rejecting the use of U.S. military force in Latin America. The president then withdrew the last U.S. Marines from Haiti in 1934. For the first time in 30 years, no U.S. troops were stationed in Latin American countries.

> "In the field of world policy I would dedicate this Nation to the policy of the good neighbor—the neighbor who resolutely respects himself and, because he does so, respects the rights of others—the neighbor who respects his obligations and respects the sanctity of his agreements in and with a world of neighbors.
>
> If I read the temper of our people correctly, we now realize, as we have never realized before, our interdependence on each other; that we cannot merely take, but we must give as well; that if we are to go forward we must move as a trained and loyal army, willing to sacrifice for the good of a common discipline, because, without such discipline, no progress is made, no leadership becomes effective."
>
> —Franklin D. Roosevelt, *Inaugural Address*, 1933

**ANALYZING PRIMARY SOURCES**

1. **UNDERSTANDING CONTEXT** What is unusual about President Roosevelt's admonition to "respect the sanctity" of obligations and agreements?
2. **IDENTIFYING CONNECTIONS** How might President Roosevelt's reminder of the interdependence of neighbors resonate with Americans at this time?

## IMPACT OF THE GREAT DEPRESSION

The Great Depression was a disaster for Latin America's economy. Weak U.S. and European economies meant less demand for Latin American exports, especially coffee, sugar, metals, and meat. The total value of Latin American exports in 1930 was almost 50 percent below the figures for the years 1925 through 1929. The countries that depended on the export of only one product were especially hurt.

The Great Depression, however, had one positive effect on the Latin American economy. When exports declined, Latin American countries could no longer buy manufactured goods from abroad. Thus their governments began to encourage the development of new industries to produce manufactured goods. The hope was that industrial development would bring greater economic independence.

Often, however, individuals could not start new industries because capital was scarce in the private sector. Governments then invested in the new industries. This led to government-run steel industries in Chile and Brazil and government-run oil industries in Argentina and Mexico.

### ☑ CHECKING FOR UNDERSTANDING

1. **DETERMINING CONTEXT** What factors influenced the Latin American economy during the 1920s and 1930s?
2. **EXPLAINING CAUSE AND EFFECT** How did the changing demand for Latin American exports during the Great Depression affect the nations' economies?
3. **SUMMARIZING** How did the U.S. method of investing differ from that of Great Britain?

*Workers load bananas at a United Fruit Company farm in Central America.*

**CITING TEXT EVIDENCE** What text evidence tells you who benefited most from profits of the export of bananas harvested by these workers?

# AUTHORITARIAN RULE

**GUIDING QUESTION** *Who controlled politics in Latin America?*

Most Latin American countries had republican forms of government. In reality, however, a relatively small group of church officials, military leaders, and large landowners ruled each country. This elite group controlled the masses of people, who were mostly poor peasants. Military forces were crucial in keeping these special-interest groups in power. Indeed, military leaders often took control of the government.

This trend toward authoritarianism increased during the 1930s, largely because of the impact of the Great Depression. Domestic instability caused by economic crises led to the creation of many military dictatorships in the early 1930s. This trend was especially evident in Argentina, Brazil, and Mexico. Together, these nations possessed more than half of the land and wealth of Latin America.

### ANALYZING KEY IDEAS AND DETAILS

1. **CITING TEXT EVIDENCE** The writer claims that the actions of Lázaro Cárdenas brought him popular approval. Cite one sentence that supports this claim.
2. **DETERMINING CENTRAL IDEAS** Reread the paragraph that begins, "Most Latin American countries had . . ." What part of this paragraph states a cause of the rise of militarism in Latin American countries?

## ARGENTINA

Argentina was controlled by an **oligarchy**, a government in which a select group of people exercises control. This oligarchy of large landowners who had grown wealthy from the export of beef and wheat failed to realize the growing importance of industry and cities in their country. This group also ignored the growing middle class, which reacted by forming the Radical Party in 1890.

In 1916 Hipólito (ee · PAW · lee · TOH) Irigoyen (IHR • ih • GOH • YEHN), leader of the Radical Party, was elected president of Argentina. The Radical Party, however, feared the industrial workers, who were using strikes to improve their conditions. The party thus drew closer to the large landowners and became more corrupt.

The military also was concerned with the rising power of the industrial workers. In 1930 the Argentine army overthrew President Irigoyen and reestablished the power of the large landowners. Through this action, the military hoped to continue the old export economy and thus to stop the growth of working-class power that would come with more industrialization.

During World War II, restless military officers formed a new organization, the Group of United Officers (GOU). They were unhappy with the Argentinian government and overthrew it in June 1943.

### DETERMINING MEANING

The word **oligarchy** has the same root as the word *monarchy*, which is a type of government that is ruled by one individual. How might knowing the meaning of *monarchy* help a person determine the meaning of *oligarchy*? Check your definition by looking in a dictionary or online resource.

## BRAZIL

In 1889 the army overthrew the Brazilian monarchy and **established** a republic. It was controlled chiefly by the landed elites, who had become wealthy from large coffee plantations.

By 1900, three-fourths of the world's coffee was grown in Brazil. As long as coffee prices remained high, the ruling oligarchy was able to maintain its power. The oligarchy largely ignored the growth of urban industry and the working class that came with it.

The Great Depression devastated the coffee industry. By the end of 1929, coffee prices had hit a record low. In 1930 a military coup made Getúlio Vargas, a wealthy rancher, president of Brazil. Vargas ruled Brazil from 1930 to 1945. Early in his rule, he appealed to workers by establishing an eight-hour workday and a minimum wage.

### DETERMINING MEANING

**Establish** is derived from the Latin *stabilire*, which means "to make stable." How does this help someone understand the meaning of the word *establish* in this context?

Faced with strong opposition in 1937, Vargas made himself dictator. Beginning in 1938, he established his New State. It was basically an authoritarian state with some fascist-like features. Political parties were outlawed, and civil rights were restricted. Secret police silenced Vargas's opponents.

Vargas also pursued a policy of stimulating new industries. The government established the Brazilian steel industry and set up a company to explore for oil. By the end of World War II, Brazil had become Latin America's chief industrial power. In 1945 the army, fearing that Vargas might prolong his power illegally after calling for new elections, forced him to resign.

## MEXICO

Mexico was not an authoritarian state, but neither was it truly democratic. The Mexican Revolution of the early twentieth century was the first significant effort in Latin America to overturn the system of large landed estates and to raise the living standards of the masses. Out of the revolution emerged a relatively stable political order.

The government was democratic in form. However, the official political party of the Mexican Revolution, known as the Institutional Revolutionary Party, or PRI, controlled the major groups within Mexican society. Every six years, party bosses of the PRI chose the party's presidential candidate. That candidate was then dutifully elected by the people.

**CITIZENSHIP**

### GOVERNMENT CORRUPTION

Viana Photography/Alamy Stock Photo

Waiting in line at a local Department of Motor Vehicles for a license can be frustrating. But what if you had to pay a bribe just to get in the door? How frustrating would that be? For many around the world, this is not a rhetorical question; it is a reality. In many especially poorer countries such as Yemen, Sudan, and Venezuela, corruption is a part of life. Government workers there commonly use their authority to exact benefits such as bribes. Corruption such as this tends to contribute to the growing gap between rich and the poor, as the wealthy are able to make the corruption work for their benefit. This has a direct effect on representative democracy because average people tend to discount the actions of the state, assuming it works only to support the powerful. This is precisely the position the PRI found itself in during the mid-twentieth century. Mexicans knew it had become corrupt and that the elections were frauds. As a result, they believed change was out of their reach.

1. **IDENTIFYING CONNECTIONS** What is the likely relationship between the long rule of the PRI and the rise of corruption in Mexico?
2. **COMPARING AND CONTRASTING** Why might poorer countries have a more difficult time handling corruption than wealthier countries?

## ANALYZING PRIMARY SOURCES

### PRESIDENT CÁRDENAS ON OIL AND THE UNITED STATES

Cárdenas in his first report to Congress in 1935:

"The exploitation of oil in Mexico has, for many years, taken place in a way characteristic of foreign companies; that is to say, our country, though independent and enjoying advanced social ideas, permits the extraction of its wealth and natural resources by the foreigner without preserving for itself any permanent benefit."

—quoted in *Oil and Politics in Latin America: Nationalist Movements and State Companies*

**DETERMINING CONTEXT** How did Cárdenas attempt to address the injustice that he perceived in this relationship?

**DETERMINING MEANING**

Using context clues from the text, explain what oil *reserves* are.

**ANALYZING KEY IDEAS AND DETAILS**

1. **CITING TEXT EVIDENCE** The writer claims that art played an active role in the rise of nationalist movements of Latin America. What evidence does the writer present to support this claim?
2. **DETERMINING CENTRAL IDEAS** Read the three paragraphs under the heading "Culture in Latin America." Does the emphasis on the work of Diego Rivera support or contradict the central idea?

A new wave of change began with Lázaro Cárdenas (KAHR • duhn • AHS), president of Mexico from 1934 to 1940. He moved to fulfill some of the original goals of the revolution. His major step was to distribute 44 million acres (17.8 million ha) of land to landless Mexican peasants. This action made him enormously popular with the peasants.

President Cárdenas also took a strong stand with the United States over oil. By 1900, Mexico was known to have enormous oil reserves, especially in the Gulf of Mexico. Over the next 30 years, oil companies from Britain and, in particular, the United States, made large investments in the Mexican oil industry. After a dispute with the foreign-owned oil companies over workers' wages, the Cárdenas government seized control of the oil fields and the property of the foreign-owned oil companies.

The U.S. oil companies were furious and asked President Franklin D. Roosevelt to intervene. He refused, reminding them of his promise in the Good Neighbor policy not to send U.S. troops into Latin America. Mexicans cheered Cárdenas as the president who stood up to the United States.

Eventually, the Mexican government did pay the oil companies for their property. It then set up PEMEX, a national oil company, to run the oil industry. PEMEX did not do well at first, however, because exports fell. Still, for many, PEMEX was a symbol of Mexican independence.

### ☑ CHECKING FOR UNDERSTANDING

1. **SUMMARIZING** Who controlled politics in Latin America?
2. **ANALYZING CHANGE** Was any country successful in wresting control from the oligarchy?
3. **UNDERSTANDING CONTEXT** What authoritarian policies did Getúlio Vargas enact to hold on to the political power he had been given by a military coup?

# CULTURE IN LATIN AMERICA

**GUIDING QUESTION** *How was Latin American culture influenced by European art?*

During the early twentieth century, European artistic and literary movements began to penetrate Latin America. In major cities, such as Buenos Aires, Argentina, and São Paulo, Brazil, wealthy elites expressed interest in the work of modern artists.

Latin American artists went abroad to Europe and brought back modern techniques, which they often adapted to their American roots. Many artists and writers used their work to promote the emergence of a new national spirit. An example was the Mexican artist Diego Rivera. Rivera had studied in Europe, where he was especially influenced by fresco painting in Italy. After his return to Mexico, he developed a monumental style that filled wall after wall with murals. Rivera's wall paintings can be found in such diverse places as the Ministry of Education and the Social Security Hospital. His works were aimed at the masses of people, many of whom could not read.

Rivera sought to create a national art that would portray Mexico's past, especially its Aztec legends, as well as Mexican festivals and folk customs. His work also carried a political and social message. Rivera did not want people to forget the Mexican Revolution, which had overthrown the large landowners and the foreign interests that supported them.

*This detail from Diego Rivera's* The Conquest or Arrival of Hernán Cortés in Veracruz *is part of a series of frescoes on pre-Hispanic and colonial Mexico painted on the inner courtyard walls of the National Palace in Mexico City.*

**DETERMINING CENTRAL IDEAS** In what way is this painting a typical Diego Rivera work in terms of its subject matter and themes?



## ☑ CHECKING FOR UNDERSTANDING

1. **IDENTIFYING CONNECTIONS** How was Latin American culture influenced by European art?

2. **IDENTIFYING CONNECTIONS** What subjects did Diego Rivera use in his murals? How did he use his art to unify Mexicans and to create a national art style?

## LESSON 4 REVIEW

### Time and Place

1. **EVALUATING EVIDENCE** President Roosevelt's Good Neighbor policy ushered in a new era of foreign relations with Central and South America. What practices did Roosevelt seek to end? Did this end all American influence in the region?

### Building History-Social Science Skills

2. **IDENTIFYING CONNECTIONS** How did American investment of the early twentieth century support the oligarchies and elites in Argentina and Brazil? How might this support have been in opposition to the spirit of Roosevelt's Good Neighbor policy?

3. **RELATING EVENTS** Wealthy landowners in Argentina and Brazil held on to power and influence even when the government was purportedly democratic. How did conflict between social classes shape their involvement in regime changes?

4. **IDENTIFYING CONNECTIONS** How did American investment in Mexican oil companies have an effect on Mexican politics?

### Writing About History

5. **INFORMATIVE WRITING** How did U.S. and British companies influence the development of nationalism in Latin American countries?

### Collaborating

6. **COLLABORATING** With a partner, select one of the countries discussed in this lesson. Together, research the history of these countries between the two World Wars. Create a time line reflecting ten events in its history during this period. Be sure to include events relating to your country's political and economic history.

# The Postmaster

by Sir Rabindranath Tagore

**PURPOSE:** To explore how a nationalist Indian writer explores the social dynamics at play in 1930s British India.

**BACKGROUND INFORMATION** Sir Rabindranath Tagore was born in India at the height of British colonialism in South Asia. Over his life he saw India transform and modernize. He recognized the challenges that came with this transition. He was a creative novelist, short-story writer, and poet, becoming the first non-European to win the Nobel Prize in Literature in 1913. Tagore greatly resented British colonialism and frequently advocated for independence. Many of his stories, like the story *The Postmaster* here, draw on themes of sadness and hardship.

## Explore the Text

**The Scene:** As the narrative begins, the postmaster is reflecting upon his position in the small Indian outpost. He resents having to leave his home in the large city of Calcutta for this poor town. He looks around disapprovingly at the poverty and squalor he sees and wishes to escape from.

**The Characters:** The postmaster is a young man from the big city of Calcutta. He is clearly educated and likely from a middle-class Indian family. The other character is Ratan. She is a poor orphaned child living in the small village. She provides for herself by helping care for the postmaster.

The postmaster first took up his duties in the village of Ulapur. Though the village was a small one, there was an **indigo** factory near by, and the proprietor, an Englishman, had managed to get a post office established.

Our postmaster belonged to Calcutta. He felt like a fish out of water in this remote village. His office and living-room were in a dark thatched shed, not far from a green, slimy pond, surrounded on all sides by a dense growth.

The men employed in the indigo factory had no leisure; moreover, they were hardly desirable companions for decent folk. Nor is a Calcutta boy an adept in the art of associating with others. Among strangers he appears either proud or ill at ease. At any rate, the postmaster had but little company; nor had he much to do.

At times he tried his hand at writing a verse or two. That the movement of the leaves and the clouds of the sky were enough to fill life with joy—such were the sentiments to which he sought to give expression. But God knows that the poor fellow would have felt it as the gift of a new life, if some genie of the Arabian Nights had in one night swept away the trees, leaves and all, and replaced them with a **macadamised** road, hiding the clouds from view with rows of tall houses.

The postmaster's salary was small. He had to cook his own meals, which he used to share with Ratan, an orphan girl of the village, who did odd jobs for him.

When in the evening the smoke began to curl up from the village cowsheds, and the cicalas chirped in every bush; when the mendicants of the Baül sect sang their shrill songs in their daily meeting-place, when any poet, who had attempted to watch the movement of the leaves in the dense bamboo thickets, would have felt a ghostly shiver run down his back, the postmaster would light his little lamp, and call out "Ratan."

**DETERMINING MEANING**

Based on the text, what can you assume a cicala is?

Ratan would sit outside waiting for this call, and, instead of coming in at once, would reply, "Did you call me, sir?"

"What are you doing?" the postmaster would ask.

"I must be going to light the kitchen fire," would be the answer.

And the postmaster would say: "Oh, let the kitchen fire be for awhile; light me my pipe first."

At last Ratan would enter, with puffed-out cheeks, vigorously blowing into a flame a live coal to light the tobacco. This would give the postmaster an opportunity of conversing. "Well, Ratan," perhaps he would begin, "do you remember anything of your mother?" That was a fertile subject. Ratan partly remembered, and partly didn't. Her father had been fonder of her than her mother; him she recollected more vividly. He used to come home in the evening after his work, and one or two evenings stood out more clearly than

---

**indigo:** a dark-blue dye

**macadamised:** a type of road covering that uses layers of small stone others, like pictures in her memory. Ratan would sit on the floor near the postmaster's feet, as memories crowded in upon her. She called to mind a little brother that she had—and how on some bygone cloudy day she had played at fishing with him on the edge of the pond, with a twig for a make-believe fishing-rod. Such little incidents would drive out greater events from her mind. Thus, as they talked, it would often get very late, and the postmaster would feel too lazy to do any cooking at all. Ratan would then hastily light the fire, and toast some unleavened bread, which, with the cold remnants of the morning meal, was enough for their supper.

On some evenings, seated at his desk in the corner of the big empty shed, the postmaster too would call up memories of his own home, of his mother and his sister, of those for whom in his exile his heart was sad,—memories which were always haunting him, but which he could not talk about with the men of the factory, though he found himself naturally recalling them aloud in the presence of the simple little girl. And so it came about that the girl would allude to his people as mother, brother, and sister, as if she had known them all her life. In fact, she had a complete picture of each one of them painted in her little heart.

One noon, during a break in the rains, there was a cool soft breeze blowing; the smell of the damp grass and leaves in the hot sun felt like the warm breathing of the tired earth on one's body. A persistent bird went on all the afternoon repeating the burden of its one complaint in Nature's audience chamber.

The postmaster had nothing to do. The shimmer of the freshly washed leaves, and the banked-up remnants of the retreating rain-clouds were sights to see; and the postmaster was watching them and thinking to himself: "Oh, if only some kindred soul were near—just one loving human being whom I could hold near my heart!" This was exactly, he went on to think, what that bird was trying to say, and it was the same feeling which the murmuring leaves were striving to express. But no one knows, or would believe, that such an idea might also take possession of an ill-paid village postmaster in the deep, silent mid-day interval of his work.

**UNDERSTANDING CRAFT AND STRUCTURE**

**ANALYZING TEXT** Based on the preceding paragraphs, what can you infer has led the postmaster to pay attention to Ratan?

The postmaster sighed, and called out "Ratan." Ratan was then sprawling beneath the guava-tree, busily engaged in eating unripe guavas. At the voice of her master, she ran up breathlessly, saying: "Were you calling me, Dada?" "I was thinking," said the postmaster, "of teaching you to read." And then for the rest of the afternoon he taught her the alphabet.

Thus, in a very short time, Ratan had got as far as the double consonants.

It seemed as though the showers of the season would never end. Canals, ditches, and hollows were all overflowing with water. Day and night the patter of rain was heard, and the croaking of frogs. The village roads became impassable, and marketing had to be done in **punts**.

---

**punt:** a long, narrow, flat-bottomed boat

One heavily clouded morning, the postmaster's little pupil had been long waiting outside the door for her call, but, not hearing it as usual, she took up her dog-eared book, and slowly entered the room. She found her master stretched out on his bed, and, thinking that he was resting, she was about to **retire** on tip-toe, when she suddenly heard her name—"Ratan!" She turned at once and asked: "Were you sleeping, Dada?" The postmaster in a plaintive voice said: "I am not well. Feel my head; is it very hot?"

In the loneliness of his exile, and in the gloom of the rains, his ailing body needed a little tender nursing. He longed to remember the touch on the forehead of soft hands with tinkling bracelets, to imagine the presence of loving womanhood, the nearness of mother and sister. And the exile was not disappointed. Ratan ceased to be a little girl. She at once stepped into the post of mother, called in the village doctor, gave the patient his pills at the proper intervals, sat up all night by his pillow, cooked his gruel for him, and every now and then asked: "Are you feeling a little better, Dada?"

It was some time before the postmaster, with weakened body, was able to leave his sick-bed. "No more of this," said he with decision. "I must get a transfer." He at once wrote off to Calcutta an application for a transfer, on the ground of the unhealthiness of the place.

Relieved from her duties as nurse, Ratan again took up her old place outside the door. But she no longer heard the same old call. She would sometimes peep inside **furtively** to find the postmaster sitting on his chair, or stretched on his bed, and staring absent-mindedly into the air. While Ratan was awaiting her call, the postmaster was awaiting a reply to his application. The girl read her old lessons over and over again,—her great fear was lest, when the call came, she might be found wanting in the double consonants. At last, after a week, the call did come one evening. With an overflowing heart Ratan rushed into the room with her—"Were you calling me, Dada?"

The postmaster said: "I am going away to-morrow, Ratan."

"Where are you going, Dada?"

"I am going home."

"When will you come back?"

"I am not coming back."

Ratan asked no other question. The postmaster, of his own accord, went on to tell her that his application for a transfer had been rejected, so he had resigned his post and was going home.

For a long time neither of them spoke another word. The lamp went on dimly burning, and from a leak in one corner of the thatch water dripped steadily into an earthen vessel on the floor beneath it.

▲
*The author of* The Postmaster, *Sir Rabindranath Tagore*



---

**retire:** to leave or rest

**furtively:** secretly

▶ *A scene from Indian society, circa 1890*

After a while Ratan rose, and went off to the kitchen to prepare the meal; but she was not so quick about it as on other days. Many new things to think of had entered her little brain. When the postmaster had finished his supper, the girl suddenly asked him: "Dada, will you take me to your home?"

**DETERMINING MEANING**

What is Tagore trying to convey by explaining that the "whole night, in her waking and in her dreams, the postmaster's laughing reply haunted her—"'What an idea!'"?

The postmaster laughed. "What an idea!" said he; but he did not think it necessary to explain to the girl wherein lay the absurdity.

That whole night, in her waking and in her dreams, the postmaster's laughing reply haunted her—"What an idea!"

On getting up in the morning, the postmaster found his bath ready. He had stuck to his Calcutta habit of bathing in water drawn and kept in pitchers, instead of taking a plunge in the river as was the custom of the village. For some reason or other, the girl could not ask him about the time of his departure, so she had fetched the water from the river long before sunrise, that it should be ready as early as he might want it. After the bath came a call for Ratan. She entered noiselessly, and looked silently into her master's face for orders. The master said: "You need not be anxious about my going away, Ratan; I shall tell my successor to look after you." These words were kindly meant, no doubt: but **inscrutable** are the ways of a woman's heart!

Ratan had borne many a scolding from her master without complaint, but these kind words she could not bear. She burst out weeping, and said: "No, no, you need not tell anybody anything at all about me; I don't want to stay on here."

The postmaster was dumbfounded. He had never seen Ratan like this before.

The new incumbent duly arrived, and the postmaster, having given over charge, prepared to depart. Just before starting he called Ratan and said:

---

**inscrutable:** impossible to understand

"Here is something for you; I hope it will keep you for some little time." He brought out from his pocket the whole of his month's salary, retaining only a trifle for his travelling expenses. Then Ratan fell at his feet and cried: "Oh, Dada, I pray you, don't give me anything, don't in any way trouble about me," and then she ran away out of sight.

The postmaster heaved a sigh, took up his carpet bag, put his umbrella over his shoulder, and, accompanied by a man carrying his many-coloured tin trunk, he slowly made for the boat.

When he got in and the boat was under way, and the rain-swollen river, like a stream of tears welling up from the earth, swirled and sobbed at her bows, then he felt a pain at heart; the grief-stricken face of a village girl seemed to represent for him the great unspoken pervading grief of Mother Earth herself. At one time he had an impulse to go back, and bring away along with him that lonesome waif, forsaken of the world. But the wind had just filled the sails, the boat had got well into the middle of the turbulent current, and already the village was left behind, and its outlying burning-ground came in sight.

So the traveller, borne on the breast of the swift-flowing river, consoled himself with philosophical reflections on the numberless meetings and partings going on in the world—on death, the great parting, from which none returns.

But Ratan had no philosophy. She was wandering about the post office in a flood of tears. It may be that she had still a lurking hope in some corner of her heart that her Dada would return, and that is why she could not tear herself away. Alas for the foolish human heart!

**ANALYZING KEY IDEAS AND DETAILS**

**CITING TEXT EVIDENCE** As the postmaster is about to leave, he begins to feel different about Ratan. What evidence from the story indicates that his attitude is changing?

**ANALYZING THEMES** How does Tagore explore the concept of abandonment over the course of the story?

Tagore, Sir Rabindranath. 1918. 'The Postmaster'. From Mashi and Other Stories. London: Macmillan and Co., Limited.

## Text-Based Discussion

1. **CITING TEXT EVIDENCE** What was life like for an orphan such as Ratan in rural India? Include elements that are described explicitly and ones you can infer.
2. **ANALYZING TEXT** Why do you think Tagore chose to depict the postmaster having a change of heart at precisely the moment he was leaving?
3. **DETERMINING MEANING** What might it mean that Ratan begins to call the postmaster "Dada"?
4. **DETERMINING THEMES** The difficult transition of modernization was a common theme in Tagore's works. What does this story suggest about modernization in India?
5. **ANALYZING LITERATURE** Considering what you have learned about India and the challenges it faced in this period, what might it mean that Tagore never gives the postmaster his own name?

# STUDY GUIDE

## THE DECLINE OF THE OTTOMAN EMPIRE AND TURKEY'S MODERNIZATION

### LESSON 1

- **1876** Ottoman reformers set up a legislature and appoint a sultan
- **1908** Young Turks restore the constitution and depose the sultan
- **1915–1918** Armenian genocide occurs
- **1916** Arabia declares independence from Ottoman rule
- **1923** Turkey becomes a modern state after the last of the Ottoman sultans flee the country
- **1924** Ottoman Caliphate is formally abolished

## NATIONALISM IN AFRICA AND ASIA

### LESSON 2

- **INDIA** Gandhi led the independence movement.
- **AFRICA** Western ideas about liberty and equality spread.
- **ASIA** Communism spread after World War II.
- **JAPAN** Militarists gained control of the government.

## CHARACTERISTICS OF THE NEW CHINA

### LESSON 3

- Class division between rural peasants and a Westernized middle class
- Failed attempt by Chiang Kai-shek to instill Confucian ethics in the population
- Rejection of excessive individualism and material greed of Western capitalist values
- Lack of industrial growth due to the nation's wealth being controlled by senior officials and subordinates of the ruling elite
- Government suppressed all opposition and censored free expression
- New roads built, railroad system repaired and extended, and over 50,000 miles of coastal highway built

## THE UNITED STATES IN LATIN AMERICA

### LESSON 4

1. In the 1920s the United States started to become the major investor in Latin America.
2. Unlike the British, U.S. investors ran companies themselves by putting their funds directly into production facilities.
3. Many American companies gained control of the copper mining industry in Chile and Peru and the oil industry in Mexico, Peru, and Bolivia.
4. Many Latin Americans resented U.S. control over Latin American industries and began to view the United States as an imperialist power.
5. In the 1930s President Roosevelt introduced the Good Neighbor policy, which rejected the use of military force in Latin America.

# CHAPTER 10 Assessment

**Directions: On a separate sheet of paper, answer the questions below. Make sure you read carefully and answer all parts of the questions.**

## Short Answer

1. **SUMMARIZING** Identify two leaders of nationalist movements in the Middle East and how their leadership changed their nations.

2. **UNDERSTANDING CONTEXT** What might have happened differently if Arabs had been able to unite as one nation after the war?

3. **IDENTIFYING STEPS** Before World War I, the Young Turks were organizing for reforms in the Ottoman Empire. What four steps led to their organization and the achievement of independence after the war?

4. **SUMMARIZING** What was one of the motivating factors for the nationalists in Kenya to work for independence from Great Britain?

5. **EXPLAINING CAUSES** What led so many Africans to demand independence after World War I?

6. **INTERPRETING** What were the advantages and disadvantages of Gandhi's strategy for gaining independence for India?

7. **IDENTIFYING CAUSES** What factors led to an empowered Japanese military in the 1930s?

8. **SUMMARIZING** How did Japan's geography influence its imperialist agenda?

9. **IDENTIFYING CONNECTIONS** Why did the Nationalist Party and the Communist Party in China form an alliance, and what events occurred as a result?

10. **IDENTIFYING CAUSES** What efforts did Chiang Kai-shek make to modernize China during his rule?

11. **DETERMINING MEANING** Explain the significance of Chiang Kai-shek's statement that "the Japanese are like a disease of the skin, but the Communists are like a disease of the heart." What does this tell you about which opponent he saw as more dangerous?

12. **IDENTIFYING CONNECTIONS** What effect did the economic crises of the 1930s have on many Latin American countries?

13. **DESCRIBING** Describe the effect the Argentinian labor strikes had in 1930. Could they be considered successful?

14. **IDENTIFYING CONNECTIONS** What does the presence of Rivera's murals in the Ministry of Education and the Social Security Hospital reveal about the government's opinion of his nationalism?

15. **EXPLAINING CAUSE AND EFFECT** How did President Roosevelt's Good Neighbor policy result in the Mexican government's success in seizing the property of American oil businesses in Mexico?

16. **IDENTIFYING CONNECTIONS** How were the philosophies of Omar Mukhtar and Mao Zedong similar?

## History and Social-Science Analysis

17. **UNDERSTANDING CONTEXT** Assume the role of an indigenous resident in one of the following locations in 1921: Persia, Kenya, China, or Mexico. Describe how economic oppression led this person to support a nationalist movement.

18. **UNDERSTANDING CHANGE** Create a table listing the changes Atatürk instituted in Turkey, distinguishing between those directed at secularization and those directed at modernization.

| Secularizing | Modernizing |
|---|---|
| | |
| | |
| | |
| | |
| | |

19. **IDENTIFYING CONNECTIONS** How were the American Civil Rights Movement and Gandhi's Salt March similar?

**Need Extra Help?**

| If You've Missed Question | 1 | 2 | 3 | 4 | 5 | 6 | 7 | 8 | 9 | 10 | 11 | 12 | 13 | 14 | 15 | 16 | 17 | 18 | 19 |
|---|---|---|---|---|---|---|---|---|---|---|---|---|---|---|---|---|---|---|---|
| Review Lesson | 1 | 1 | 1 | 1 | 2 | 2 | 2 | 2 | 3 | 3 | 3 | 4 | 4 | 4 | 4 | 2, 3 | 1 | 1 | 2 |

## Analyzing Visuals

Use the image to answer the following question.
In this cartoon the man (left), John Bull (middle), and the woman represent the Ottoman Turks, England, and Armenians respectively.

**20** **IDENTIFYING BIAS** How is Armenia conveyed in the cartoon? Do you think the cartoonist supports the Armenians?

## Research and Presentation

**21** **USING TECHNOLOGY** Research one of the leaders of the African independence movement and explain his contributions, including any significant writing. Consider individuals such as Jomo Kenyatta and Léopold Senghor. Use the Internet to prepare a digital archive of your work and results to share with your class, including key pieces of information.

**22** **INTEGRATING INFORMATION** Conduct your own research on the Armenian Genocide, including primary and secondary sources, and include proper citations. Examine the effects of the genocide on the Armenian people and the ways in which it became a prototype of subsequent genocides.

## Reading and Analyzing Primary Sources

Use the document to answer the following questions.
This passage is part of a lecture given on February 17, 1924, by the Chinese revolutionary Sun Yat-sen.

> "Now we want to revive China's lost nationalism and use the strength of our four hundred millions to fight for mankind against injustice; this is our divine mission. The Powers are afraid that we will have such thoughts and are setting forth a specious doctrine. They are now advocating cosmopolitanism to inflame us, declaring that, as the civilization of the world advances and as mankind's vision enlarges, nationalism becomes too narrow, unsuited to the present age, and hence that we should espouse cosmopolitanism. . . . But it is not a doctrine which wronged races should talk about. We, the wronged race, must first recover our position of national freedom and equality before we are fit to discuss cosmopolitanism."

–Sun Yat-sen, 1924

**23** **DETERMINING CENTRAL IDEAS** What two concepts is Sun Yat-sen contrasting in this excerpt?

**A.** Cosmopolitanism and nationalism
**B.** Injustice and divinity
**C.** Europe and China
**D.** The present and the past

**24** **ASSESSING** Which best describes a reason given for why China needs to focus on nationalism presently?

**A.** Cosmopolitanism is an exclusively European concept.
**B.** China has been wronged as a race so must focus on nationalism now.
**C.** Cosmopolitanism is too narrow for the Chinese.
**D.** The notions behind cosmopolitanism hurt China's hopes for prosperity.

## Writing About History

**25** **EXPLANATORY WRITING** What was the purpose Lenin had for founding the Comintern?

## Speaking and Listening About History

**26** **COLLABORATING** In a small group, discuss militarism. How is it different from the application of military force in specific situations? Which nation experienced militarism in the years between World War I and World War II, and how did it shape society? Where can militarism be seen in various places today?

**Need Extra Help?**

| If You've Missed Question | 20 | 21 | 22 | 23 | 24 | 25 | 26 |
|---|---|---|---|---|---|---|---|
| Review Lesson | 1 | 2 | 1 | 3 | 3 | 2 | 2 |

◄ These prisoners at Auschwitz were liberated by the Soviets in January 1945. Victims of the Holocaust suffered cruelty at the hands of their Nazi captors. Those who survived were ill or dying of starvation and maltreatment.

1939 — 1945

# World War II and the Holocaust

## CHAPTER 11



**GO DIGITAL**
*It's All online!*

## ASKING ESSENTIAL QUESTIONS

***Why do political actions often lead to war?***
***How does war impact society and the environment?***

**What Will You Learn?** You will learn about the causes, effects, and events of World War II.

**Why Does This Matter?** World War II had a profound effect on Europe's population, as the Nazis essentially fought two wars: one against the military forces of Allies and another against the peoples of Europe they deemed inferior. For instance, by the time of the Allied liberation of the Nazi concentration camps in 1945, the Nazis had murdered nearly two-thirds of European Jews. Furthermore, the events of World War II and the war's ultimate resolution influenced relationships among countries that still resonate today. The alliances and enemies made during the Second World War influenced foreign relations in the tense nuclear era that followed it.

**How Will You Know That You Learned It?** You will be able to identify, describe, and explain the main events, concepts, and policies relating to World War II.

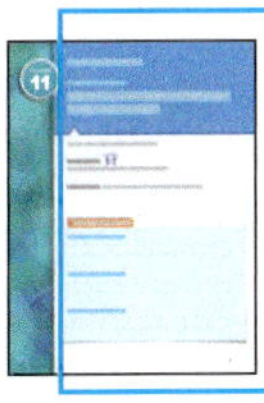

**Using Your Inquiry Journal** As you read this chapter and examine the primary sources, use your Inquiry Journal to help you make notes and expand your list of questions. As you gather information, think about how you will answer the Essential Questions above.

# PLACE & TIME Europe 1939–1945

World War II was the most devastating war in history. Germany and Japan achieved stunning territorial victories between 1939 and 1942. In 1941 the United States and the Soviet Union entered the war, turning the tide against fascist expansion. New military technology, such as aerial photography, informed the military strategies of both the Axis and Allied powers and changed the way the war was fought.

## STEP INTO THE PLACE

Read the quotes and look at the information presented on the map.

1. **SPATIAL THINKING** According to the map, what was particularly dangerous about the location of the Soviet Union during World War II?

2. **DETERMINING CENTRAL IDEAS** Based on the two sources, how did the Allies use aerial photographs for strategic purposes during the war in Europe?

"Aerial photos were the only solid, irrefutable evidence of where an enemy was, what he was doing and what he had with which to do it. Intelligence was a 'force multiplier,' permitting our side to put resources or air strikes on the most critical ground, and aerial photographic intelligence was the most reliable source."

—Colonel Roy M. Stanley, United States Air Force, *Asia from Above*

"These [36-inch cameras mounted on the belly of the aircraft] produced 3-D views of the areas being photographed, which were then examined by our intelligence people. Details as small as a golf ball were detectable. We also carried a smaller camera in the port side of the aircraft, and with this we could take oblique pictures. Some of the trips involved low-level photographs, and this required flying at tree-top level. On 15 May [1943] we were jumped by six Bf 109s [German fighter planes] while flying photo runs over Oslo...We were able to do ever decreasing turns and avoid their gunfire. We were also able to inch our way over to Sweden. The Swedes will never know how grateful we were to them as they opened up with every flak [anti-aircraft] battery on their coast."

—Flight Lieutenant Bill White, Royal Air Force, recalling a reconnaissance mission to find a German battleship harbored in Norway, quoted in *Mosquito Photo-Reconnaissance Units of World War 2*



## STEP INTO THE TIME

**CHRONOLOGICAL THINKING**

According to the time line, what was the major difference in the Allied offensives leading to the German and Japanese surrenders?

### EUROPEAN AND NORTH AFRICAN THEATER

- **September 1, 1939** German invasion of Poland
- **September 3, 1939** Britain and France declare war on Germany
- **June 1940** France falls to Germany
- **1941** Germany invades the Soviet Union

**1939** — **1940** — **1941**

### PACIFIC THEATER

- **1939** Japan shocked by signing of Nazi-Soviet Nonaggression Pact
- **1940** Japan demands rights to resources in French Indochina
- **1941** Japan acquires Chinese territory in Second Sino-Japanese War

# WORLD WAR II: DECEMBER 1942

**A** **Atlantic:** U-Boats damage U.S. shipping in Operation Drumbeat; Allies struggling to find a counter to the submarines.

**B** **African Front:** Allies invade North Africa November 8, beginning Operation Torch.

**C** **Russian Front:** Germans and Russians are engaged in the Battle of Stalingrad, regarded as the largest battle in the history of warfare.

**D** **China:** China, at war with Japan since 1937, joins Allies after attack on Pearl Harbor, declares war on Germany.

**E** **Pacific:** Japan expands, taking Singapore in February, but Allies win decisive victory at Midway.

**1942** **1943** **1944** **1945**

**December 7, 1941** Japanese attack Pearl Harbor

**1942–43** Allies and Germany battle for control over North Africa

**1942** Japanese conquer Thailand, Philippines, Malaya

**1942** United States Navy defeats Japanese at Battle of Midway Island

**May 1943** Japanese launch offensive in central China

**June 6, 1944** Allies under U.S. General Dwight D. Eisenhower launch D-Day invasion

**December 8, 1944** U.S. Air Force begins bombardment of Iwo Jima

**March 1945** Allies cross the Rhine after the Battle of the Bulge

**May 7, 1945** Germany surrenders

**August 1945** United States drops atomic bombs on Japan

**August 14, 1945** Japan surrenders

## ESSENTIAL QUESTIONS

- *Why do political actions often lead to war?*
- *How does war impact society and the environment?*

# THE STORY BEGINS...

LESSON 1

# World War II Begins

As Nazi Germany began to menace Europe, leaders of other countries debated the dangers of opposing or appeasing its leader. Winston Churchill believed Hitler must be confronted and made the following argument in the British Parliament after Germany's 1938 invasion of Czechoslovakia:

> "We are in the presence of a disaster of the first magnitude which has befallen Great Britain and France. Do not let us blind ourselves to that. It must now be accepted that all the countries of Central and Eastern Europe will make the best terms they can with the triumphant Nazi Power. The system of alliances in Central Europe upon which France has relied for her safety has been swept away, and I can see no means by which it can be reconstituted. The road down the Danube Valley to the Black Sea, the resources of corn and oil, the road which leads as far as Turkey, has been opened. In fact, if not in form, it seems to me that all those countries of Middle Europe, all those Danubian countries, will, one after another, be drawn into this vast system of power politics--not only power military politics but power economic politics--radiating from Berlin, and I believe this can be achieved quite smoothly and swiftly and will not necessarily entail the firing of a single shot."

—Winston Churchill, from a statement delivered to British Parliament, 1938

At the time, many Members of Parliament considered Churchill himself a dangerous alarmist. Continued German aggression in Europe would prove them wrong.

*A German soldier throws a grenade during the German invasion of Poland.* ▶

| European Reactions to Nazi Germany | |
|---|---|
| Germany's Actions | Immediate Reactions |
| | |
| | |
| | |
| | |

**ANALYZING KEY IDEAS AND DETAILS**

**IDENTIFYING EFFECTS** Read closely to identify the actions of Nazi Germany that led to World War II and the initial reactions of other European nations. Record these actions and reactions in a graphic organizer like this one.

# THE GERMAN PATH TO WAR

**GUIDING QUESTIONS** *What was Hitler's motivation for German expansion? What alliances and events contributed to the outbreak of World War II?*

World War II in Europe had its beginnings in the ideas of Adolf Hitler. He believed that Germans belonged to a so-called Aryan race that was superior to all other races and nationalities. Consequently, Hitler believed that Germany was capable of building a great civilization. To be a great power, however, he thought that Germany needed more land to support a larger population.

Already in the 1920s, Hitler had indicated that a Nazi regime would find this land to the east—in the Soviet Union. Germany therefore must prepare for war with the Soviet Union. After the Soviet Union had been conquered, according to Hitler, its land would be resettled by German peasants. The Slavic peoples could be used as slave labor to build an Aryan racial state that Hitler thought would **dominate** Europe for a thousand years.

## HITLER VIOLATES TREATY

After World War I, the Treaty of Versailles had limited Germany's military power. As chancellor, Hitler, posing as a man of peace, stressed that Germany wished to revise the unfair provisions of the treaty by peaceful means. Germany, he said, only wanted its rightful place among the European states.

On March 9, 1935, however, Hitler announced the creation of a new air force. One week later, he began a military draft that would expand Germany's army from 100,000 to 550,000 troops. These steps were in direct **violation** of the Treaty of Versailles. France, Great Britain, and Italy condemned Germany's actions and warned against future aggressive steps. In the midst of the Great Depression, distracted by internal problems, and with the terrors of World War I still fresh in their memories, these nations did nothing further.

Hitler was convinced that the Western states had no intention of using force to maintain the Treaty of Versailles. Hence, on March 7, 1936, he sent German troops into the Rhineland. The Rhineland was part of Germany, but, according to the Treaty of Versailles, it was a **demilitarized** area. That is, Germany was not allowed to have weapons or fortifications there. France had the right to use force against any violation of this provision but would not act without British support.

Great Britain did not support the use of force against Germany. The British government viewed the occupation of German territory by German troops as a reasonable action by a dissatisfied power. *The London Times* noted that the

**ANALYZING KEY IDEAS AND DETAILS**

1. **SUMMARIZING** Write a summary of the series of events that led to Britain and France declaring war on Germany.
2. **CITING TEXT EVIDENCE** Why do political actions often lead to war? Cite three pieces of text evidence from the lesson to support your response.

**DETERMINING MEANING**

To better understand **violation**, break down the term. *Violate* means "to fail to respect or comply with." The suffix *-ion* means "an action or condition." Who failed to respect whom in the context of the paragraph beginning "On March 9, 1935 . . ."?

**DETERMINING MEANING**

The root of the word **demilitarized** is *military*. *Military* means "related to armed forces." How does knowing the meaning of *military* help you determine the meaning of *demilitarized*?

**DETERMINING MEANING**

Read the paragraph that begins, "Great Britain did not support the use of force against Germany." How does the content of the paragraph help you figure out what **appeasement** means?

Germans were "only going into their own back garden." Great Britain thus began to practice a policy of **appeasement**. This policy was based on the belief that if European states satisfied the reasonable demands of dissatisfied powers, the dissatisfied powers would be content, and stability and peace would be achieved in Europe.

## NEW ALLIANCES

Meanwhile, Hitler gained new allies. Benito Mussolini of Italy had long dreamed of creating a new Roman Empire. In October 1935, Mussolini's forces invaded Ethiopia. Angered by French and British opposition to his invasion, Mussolini welcomed Hitler's support. He began to draw closer to the German dictator.

In 1936 both Germany and Italy sent troops to Spain to help General Francisco Franco in the Spanish Civil War. In October 1936, Mussolini and Hitler made an agreement recognizing their common interests. One month later, Mussolini spoke of the new alliance between Italy and Germany, called the Rome-Berlin Axis. Also in November, Germany and Japan signed the Anti-Comintern Pact, promising a common front against communism.

**GEOGRAPHIC REASONING**

Germany expanded its borders from 1935–1939.

1. **SPATIAL THINKING** Which countries did Germany occupy during this time?
2. **PATTERNS AND MOVEMENT** What was Germany's rationale for this initial expansion?

## UNION WITH AUSTRIA

By 1937, Germany was once more a "world power," as Hitler proclaimed. He was convinced that neither France nor Great Britain would provide much opposition to his plans. In 1938 he decided to pursue one of his goals: Anschluss (AHN • shloos), or union, with Austria, his native land. By threatening Austria with invasion, Hitler forced the Austrian chancellor to put Austrian Nazis in charge of the government. The new government promptly invited German troops to enter Austria and "help" in maintaining law and order. One day later, on March 13, 1938, after his triumphal return to his native land, Hitler annexed Austria to Germany.

**GERMAN EXPANSION 1935–1939**

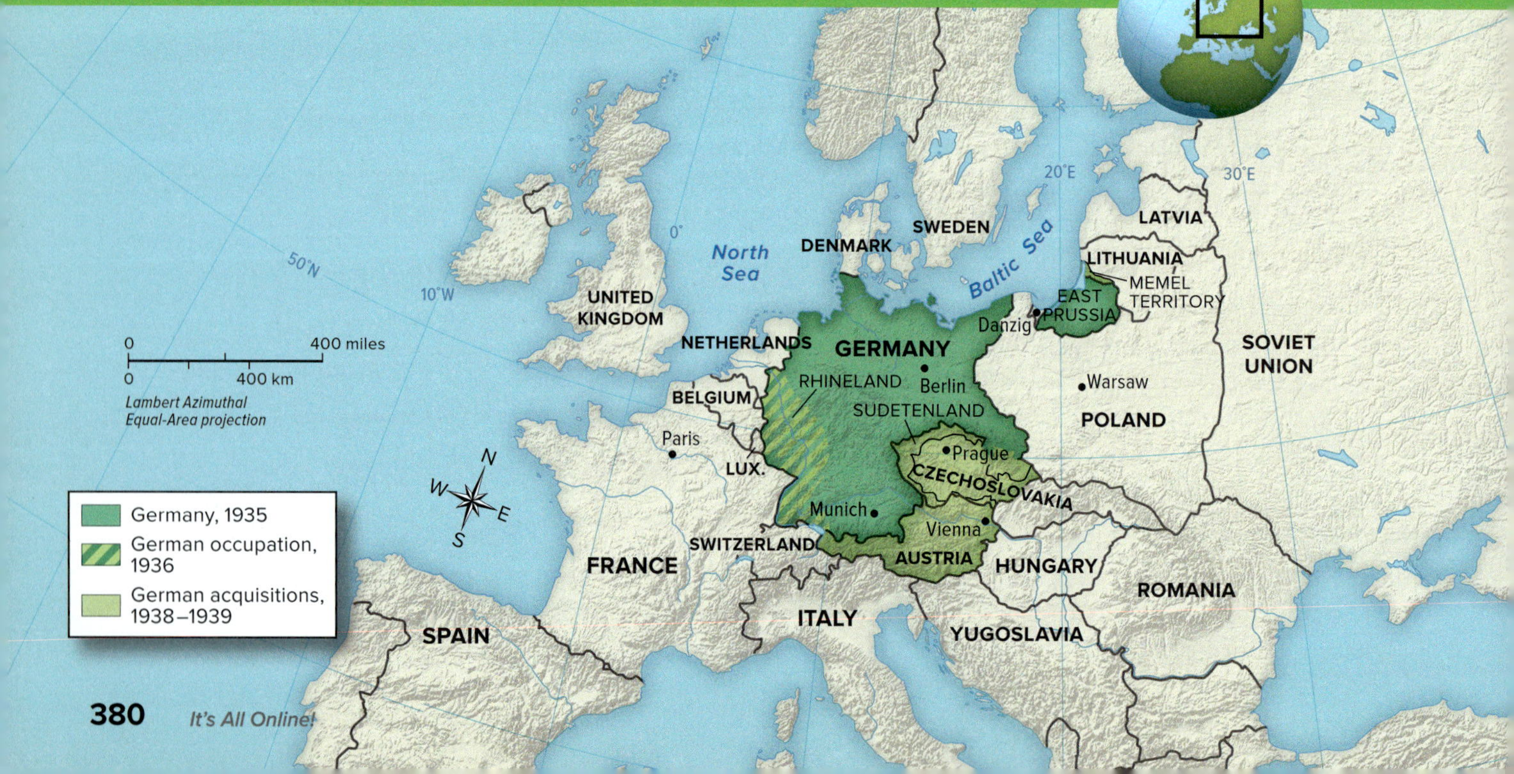

## DEMANDS AND APPEASEMENT

Hitler's next objective was the destruction of Czechoslovakia. On September 15, 1938, he demanded that Germany be given the Sudetenland, an area in northwestern Czechoslovakia that was inhabited largely by Germans. He was willing to risk "world war" to achieve his objective.

At a hastily arranged conference in Munich, British, French, German, and Italian representatives did not object to Hitler's plans but instead reached an agreement that met virtually all Hitler's demands. German troops were allowed to occupy the Sudetenland. The Czechs, abandoned by their Western allies, stood by helplessly.

*After the Munich Conference, Adolf Hitler, Nevile Henderson, Neville Chamberlain, and Joachim von Ribbentrop (left to right) at the Munich airport on September 29, 1938.*

**IDENTIFYING CONNECTIONS** What did the Munich Conference demonstrate about appeasement policies?

The Munich Conference was the high point of Western appeasement of Hitler. When Neville Chamberlain, the British prime minister, returned to England from Munich, he boasted that the agreement meant "peace for our time." One British statesman, Winston Churchill, warned instead that the settlement at Munich was "a disaster of the first magnitude." Hitler, however, had promised Chamberlain that he would make no more demands. Like many others, Chamberlain believed Hitler's promises.

In fact, Hitler was more convinced than ever that the Western democracies would not fight. Increasingly, he was sure that he could not make a mistake, and he had by no means been satisfied at Munich.

In March 1939, Hitler invaded and took control of Bohemia and Moravia in western Czechoslovakia. In the eastern part of the country, Slovakia became a puppet state controlled by Nazi Germany. On the evening of March 15, 1939, Hitler triumphantly declared in Prague that he would be known as the greatest German of them all.

At last, the Western states reacted to the Nazi threat. Hitler's aggression had made clear that his promises were worthless. When Hitler began to demand the Polish port of Danzig, Great Britain saw the danger and offered to protect Poland in the event of war. At the same time, both France and Britain realized that only the Soviet Union was powerful enough to help contain Nazi aggression. They began political and military negotiations with Joseph Stalin, the Soviet dictator, but these failed.

The United States, still suffering the effects of the Great Depression, continued on a path of nonintervention. Congress passed a series of laws stating the terms of neutrality to prevent the entry of the United States into any foreign wars. Known as neutrality acts, these laws also reflected the Americans' isolationist feelings. These feelings were so strong that Congress held investigations into possible harmful business interests that had led the country to enter World War I.

*This political cartoon depicts Adolf Hitler and Joseph Stalin as a newlywed couple after the signing of the Nazi-Soviet Nonaggression Pact.*

**INTERPRETING** What might be the inspiration for the sentiment shown here?

## HITLER AND THE SOVIETS

Meanwhile, Hitler continued to believe that the West would not fight over Poland. He now feared, however, that the West and the Soviet Union might make an alliance. Such an alliance could mean a two-front war for Germany. To prevent this, Hitler made his own agreement with Stalin.

On August 23, 1939, Germany and the Soviet Union signed the Nazi-Soviet Nonaggression Pact. In it, the two nations promised not to attack each other.

To get the nonaggression pact, Hitler offered Stalin control of eastern Poland and the Baltic states. Because he expected to fight the Soviet Union anyway, it did not matter to Hitler what he promised—he was accustomed to breaking promises.

Hitler shocked the world when he announced the treaty. Hitler was now free to attack Poland. He told his generals, "Now Poland is in the position in which I wanted her . . . . I am only afraid that at the last moment some swine will yet submit to me a plan for mediation."

Hitler need not have worried. On September 1, German forces invaded western Poland. British Prime Minister Neville Chamberlain admitted that Britain's previous policies of appeasement had to be amended. Two days later, Britain and France declared war on Germany.

**ANALYZING PRIMARY SOURCES**

**DETERMINING CENTRAL IDEAS** What does Neville Chamberlain's main point in this speech suggest about the future of Britain and the war?

> "It now only remains for us to set our teeth and to enter upon this struggle, which we ourselves earnestly endeavored to avoid, with determination to see it through to the end. We shall enter it with a clear conscience, with the support of the Dominions and the British Empire, and the moral approval of the greater part of the world. We have no quarrel with the German people, except that they allow themselves to be governed by a Nazi Government."
>
> —Neville Chamberlain, speech to Parliament, September 1, 1939

### ☑ CHECKING FOR UNDERSTANDING

1. **EXPLAINING CAUSES** What was Hitler's motivation for German expansion?
2. **UNDERSTANDING CONTEXT** What alliances and events contributed to the outbreak of World War II?
3. **RELATING EVENTS** How might the Treaty of Versailles have contributed to World War II?

## THE JAPANESE PATH TO WAR

**GUIDING QUESTION** *Why did Japan want to seize other countries?*

Japan, already an imperial power that had colonized Korea in 1910, undertook a plan to take control of all Manchuria in 1931. On the night of September 18, Japanese soldiers, disguised as Chinese soldiers, blew up a small section of the Manchurian Railway near the city of Mukden. Japan owned this area, and the Japanese soldiers wanted to blame the "Mukden incident" on the Chinese. The Japanese army used this incident to justify its taking all Manchuria in a series of rapid military advances.

Manchuria offered many resources the Japanese needed. After this conquest, the Japanese army became committed to an expansionist policy—a policy of enlarging the Japanese Empire.

By September 1932, the Japanese army had formed Manchuria into a separate state and renamed it Manchukuo. They placed a puppet ruler, Henry Pu Yi, on the throne. As an infant, Henry Pu Yi had been China's "last emperor." He had abdicated that throne, however, following the revolution of 1911 in China.

**ANALYZING KEY IDEAS AND DETAILS**

1. **SUMMARIZING** What events led to the Japanese eventually launching an attack on U.S. and European colonies?
2. **ANALYZING EVENTS** Reread the paragraph that begins, "When Germany signed the nonaggression pact. . . ." What part of this paragraph states an *effect* of the new pact? What words signal that this is an effect?

Chamberlain, Neville. 1939. On the Nazi Invasion of Poland. Reprinted by Whiticker, Alan J. 2007. Speeches That Shaped the Modern World - Concise Edition. New Holland Publishers (Australia).

Worldwide protests against the Japanese seizure of Manchuria led the League of Nations to send in investigators. When the investigators issued a report condemning the seizure, Japan withdrew from the league. The United States refused to recognize the Japanese takeover of Manchuria but was unwilling to threaten force.

*During the Second Sino-Japanese War, the Japanese air force bombed Shanghai.*

**UNDERSTANDING CONTEXT** What role did Japanese leaders hope to force the Chinese to play in the New Order in East Asia?

Over the next several years, Japan continued its expansion and established control over the eastern part of Inner Mongolia and areas in north China around Beijing. Japan was technically a constitutional monarchy, with Emperor Hirohito, grandson of Emperor Meiji, as head of state. Although Hirohito was aware of all strategic decisions and had approved each military action, neither he nor government leaders could control the army. In fact, it was the army that established Japanese foreign policy. By the mid-1930s, militants connected to the government and the armed forces had gained control of Japanese politics.

## WAR WITH CHINA

Chiang Kai-shek tried to avoid a conflict with Japan so that he could deal with what he considered the greater threat, the Chinese Communists. When clashes between Chinese and Japanese troops broke out, he sought to appease Japan by allowing it to govern areas in north China.

As Japan moved steadily southward, protests against Japanese aggression grew stronger in Chinese cities. In December 1936, Chiang ended his military efforts against the Communists and formed a new united front against the Japanese. In July 1937, Chinese and Japanese forces clashed south of Beijing and hostilities spread.

Although Japan had not planned to declare war on China, the 1937 incident turned into a major conflict. Japan seized the Chinese capital of Nanjing in December. The Japanese Army destroyed the city and massacred more than 100,000 civilians and prisoners of war. The event was so brutal it became known as the "Rape of Nanjing." Chiang Kai-shek refused to surrender and moved his government upriver, first to Hankou, then to Chongqing. Temporarily defeated, the Chinese continued to resist.

## THE NEW ASIAN ORDER

Japanese military leaders had hoped to force Chiang to agree to join a New Order in East Asia, comprising Japan, Manchuria, and China. Japan would attempt to establish a new system of control in Asia with Japan's guiding its Asian neighbors to prosperity.

Part of Japan's plan was to seize Soviet Siberia, with its rich resources. During the late 1930s, Japan began to cooperate with Nazi Germany. Japan assumed that the two countries would ultimately launch a joint attack on the Soviet Union and divide Soviet resources between them.

When Germany signed the nonaggression pact with the Soviets in August 1939, Japanese leaders had to rethink their goals. Because Japan lacked the resources to defeat the Soviet Union, it looked to South Asia for raw materials for its military machine.

**DETERMINING MEANING**

The text mentions the United States warned Japan it would apply economic **sanctions**. What does the word *sanctions* most likely mean in this context?

## JAPAN LAUNCHES ATTACK

A move southward would risk war with the European powers and the United States. Japan's attack on China had already aroused strong criticism, especially in the United States. Still, in the summer of 1940, Japan demanded the right to exploit economic resources in French Indochina.

The United States objected. It warned Japan it would apply economic **sanctions** unless Japan withdrew from the area and returned to its borders of 1931. Japan badly needed the oil and scrap iron it was getting from the United States. Should these resources be cut off, Japan would have to find them elsewhere. This would threaten Japan's long-term objectives.

Japan was now caught in a dilemma. To guarantee access to raw materials in Southeast Asia, Japan had to risk losing them from the United States. After much debate, Japan decided to launch a surprise attack on U.S. and European colonies in Southeast Asia.

### ✓ CHECKING FOR UNDERSTANDING

1. **DETERMINING CONTEXT** Why did Japan want to seize other countries?
2. **RELATING EVENTS** What was the relationship between the Second Sino-Japanese War and the Chinese Civil War?
3. **SUMMARIZING** What prompted Japanese attacks on U.S. and European colonies in Southeast Asia?

## LESSON 1 REVIEW

### Time and Place

1. **IDENTIFYING CONNECTIONS** What was the connection between Germany's and Japan's paths to war?

### Building History-Social Science Analysis Skills

2. **UNDERSTANDING CONTEXT** How did the Nazi-Soviet Nonaggression Pact benefit Hitler?
3. **EXPLAINING CAUSE AND EFFECT** What effect did the Munich Conference have on the spread of the Third Reich?
4. **IDENTIFYING CAUSES** Describe the motivation behind Britain's and France's ultimate declaration of war on Germany.

### Writing About History

5. **ARGUMENTATIVE WRITING** Write a paragraph that argues for or against the following statement: The British policy of appeasement was the main cause for Germany's aggressive actions. Use proper grammar and usage in your paragraph.

### Collaborating

6. **EVALUATING POINT OF VIEW** With a partner, discuss the importance of Czechoslovakia to Hitler's early plans for the domination of Europe. Write a brief explanation of your conclusions.

## ESSENTIAL QUESTIONS

- *Why do political actions often lead to war?*
- *How does war impact society and the environment?*

LESSON 2

# World War II

## THE STORY BEGINS...

Following the outbreak of war in late 1939, fighting spread throughout Europe and Africa. Japan remained at war with China and joined the Germans in their war against the Allies as well. The United States maintained an official policy of neutrality. As President Franklin D. Roosevelt stated to Congress, this policy ended when the Japanese bombed Pearl Harbor:

> "Yesterday, December 7, 1941—a date which will live in infamy—the United States was suddenly and deliberately attacked by naval and air forces of the Empire of Japan. [. . .] Hostilities exist. There is no blinking at the fact that our people, our territory, and our interests are in grave danger. With confidence in our armed forces—and the unbounding determination of our people—we will gain the inevitable triumph—so help us God. I ask that the Congress declare that since the unprovoked and dastardly attack by Japan on Sunday, December 7, 1941, a state of war has existed between the United States and the Japanese Empire."

—Franklin Delano Roosevelt, in a joint address to Congress leading to a declaration of war against Japan

Four days after Pearl Harbor, Hitler declared war on the United States. The war had truly become a worldwide struggle.

*An American soldier surveys a bombed-out section of a European city.* ▶

| Date of Entry into World War II | |
|---|---|
| Country | Year |
| | |
| | |
| | |
| | |
| | |
| | |

**ANALYZING KEY IDEAS AND DETAILS**

**CITING TEXT EVIDENCE** Read closely to identify when each country entered the war. Record these dates in a graphic organizer like this one.

# EUROPE AT WAR

**GUIDING QUESTION** *What were Germany's gains and losses during the early years of the war?*

Hitler stunned Europe with the speed and efficiency of the German attack on Poland. His **blitzkrieg**, or "lightning war," used armored columns, called panzer divisions, supported by airplanes. Each panzer division was a strike force of about 300 tanks with accompanying forces and supplies.

The forces of the blitzkrieg broke quickly through Polish lines and encircled the bewildered Polish troops. Regular infantry units then moved in to hold the newly conquered territory. Within four weeks, Poland had surrendered. On September 28, 1939, Germany and the Soviet Union divided Poland.

**ANALYZING KEY IDEAS AND DETAILS**

1. **ANALYZING EVENTS** Reread the paragraph that begins, "The forces of the blitzkrieg. . . ." What part of this paragraph states an *effect* of the blitzkrieg? What language signals this is an effect?
2. **CITING TEXT EVIDENCE** What did the blitzkrieg entail? Cite specific words in the text to support your answer.

**DETERMINING MEANING**

Read the paragraph that begins, "Hitler stunned Europe. . . ." How does the content of the paragraph help you figure out what **blitzkrieg** means?

## HITLER'S EARLY VICTORIES

After a winter of waiting, Hitler resumed the attack on April 9, 1940, with another blitzkrieg against Denmark and Norway. One month later, Germany launched an attack on the Netherlands, Belgium, and France. The main assault was through Luxembourg and the Ardennes Forest. German panzer divisions broke through weak French defensive positions there and raced across northern France.

French and British forces were taken by surprise. Anticipating a German attack, France had built a defense system, called the Maginot (MA • zhuh • NOH) Line, along its border with Germany. The line was a series of concrete and steel fortifications armed with heavy artillery. The Germans, however, decided not to cross the Maginot Line. Instead, they went around it and attacked France from its border with Belgium.

By going around the Maginot Line, the Germans split the Allied armies, trapping French troops and the entire British army on the beaches of Dunkirk. Only by the heroic efforts of the Royal Navy and civilians in private boats did the British manage to evacuate 338,000 Allied (mostly British) troops. An English skipper described the scene:

> "The soldiers were coming off the beach clinging to bits of wood and wreckage and anything that would float. As we got close enough we began . . . picking up as many as we could . . . [and taking] them off to one of the ships lying off in the deep water."

—quoted in *Blood, Tears and Folly,* 1993

**DETERMINING MEANING**

The root of the word **isolationism** is *isolate*. To *isolate* means "to be or make a person or place separate from others." How does knowing the origins of *isolate* help you determine the meaning of *isolationism*?

The French signed an armistice on June 22, 1940. German armies now occupied about three-fifths of France. An authoritarian regime under German control was set up over the remainder of the country. It was known as Vichy France and was led by an aged French hero of World War I, Marshal Henri Pétain. Germany was now in control of Western and Central Europe, but Britain had still not been defeated. In fact, after Dunkirk, the British **resolve** heightened. Especially helpful in rallying the British people were the stirring speeches of Winston Churchill, who had become prime minister in May 1940.

President Franklin D. Roosevelt denounced the aggressors, but domestic distractions such as the Great Depression helped direct the United States's strict policy of **isolationism**. A series of **neutrality** acts, passed in the 1930s, prevented the United States from taking sides or becoming involved in any European wars. Many Americans believed the United States had been drawn into World War I due to economic **involvement** in Europe, and they wanted to prevent a recurrence. Roosevelt was convinced that the neutrality acts actually encouraged Axis aggression and they were gradually relaxed as the United States supplied food, ships, planes, and weapons to Britain.

## THE BATTLE OF BRITAIN

Hitler realized that an amphibious (land-sea) invasion of Britain could succeed only if Germany gained control of the air. At the beginning of August 1940, the Luftwaffe (LOOFT • vah • fuh)—the German air force—launched a major offensive. German planes bombed British air and naval bases, harbors, communication centers, and war industries.

The British fought back with determination. They were supported by an effective radar system that gave them early warning of German attacks. Nevertheless, the British air force suffered critical losses.

In September, in retaliation for a British attack on Berlin, Hitler ordered a shift in strategy. Instead of bombing military targets, the Luftwaffe began massive bombing of British cities. Hitler hoped in this way to break British morale. Instead, because military targets were not being hit, the British were able to rebuild their air strength quickly. Soon, the British air force was inflicting major losses on Luftwaffe bombers. Hitler postponed the invasion of Britain indefinitely.

## ATTACK ON THE SOVIET UNION

Although he had no desire for a two-front war, Hitler became convinced that Britain was remaining in the war only because it expected Soviet support. If the Soviet Union were smashed, Britain's last hope would be eliminated. Moreover, Hitler had convinced himself the Soviet Union had a pitiful army and could be defeated quickly.

Hitler's invasion of the Soviet Union was scheduled for the spring of 1941, but the attack was delayed because of problems in the Balkans. Hitler had already gained the political cooperation of Hungary, Bulgaria, and Romania. However, the failure of Mussolini's invasion of Greece in 1940 had exposed Hitler's southern flank to British air bases in Greece. To secure his Balkan flank, Hitler seized both Greece and Yugoslavia in April.

Reassured, Hitler invaded the Soviet Union on June 22, 1941, betraying the Nazi-Soviet Nonaggression Pact signed in 1939. He believed the Russians could still be decisively defeated before the brutal winter weather set in. The

BIOGRAPHY

### FRANKLIN D. ROOSEVELT (1882–1945)

President Franklin D. Roosevelt was the only U.S. president elected to serve four terms in office. He led the United States during two major crises—the Great Depression and World War II. Before Pearl Harbor, President Roosevelt convinced the U.S. Congress to send "all aid short of war" to Britain and the Soviet Union to help fight the Nazis. The United States sent ships and guns in exchange for military bases in Britain. After the attack on Pearl Harbor, the United States entered the war in earnest. Roosevelt led the war effort until his death in office in 1945.

**EXPLAINING CAUSES** How did the Great Depression prepare Roosevelt for the war effort?

MAKING CONNECTIONS

### THE ATLANTIC CHARTER

By the middle of 1941, with Germany's invasion of the Soviet Union and increased fears that Japan would exploit the circumstances to seize European territories in Southeast Asia, the U.S. and Great Britain met to discuss common goals. A joint declaration, known as the Atlantic Charter, was issued in August 1941 that contained principles that both nations committed to including the restoration of self-governments, chosen by the people, for all countries occupied during the war. Roosevelt had hoped the declaration would increase American support for entry into the war, but it failed to do so. However, it did affirm U.S. and Great Britain's solidarity against Axis Powers' aggression and would be incorporated in the Declaration of the United Nations in 1942.

## WORLD WAR II IN EUROPE AND NORTH AFRICA 1939–1941

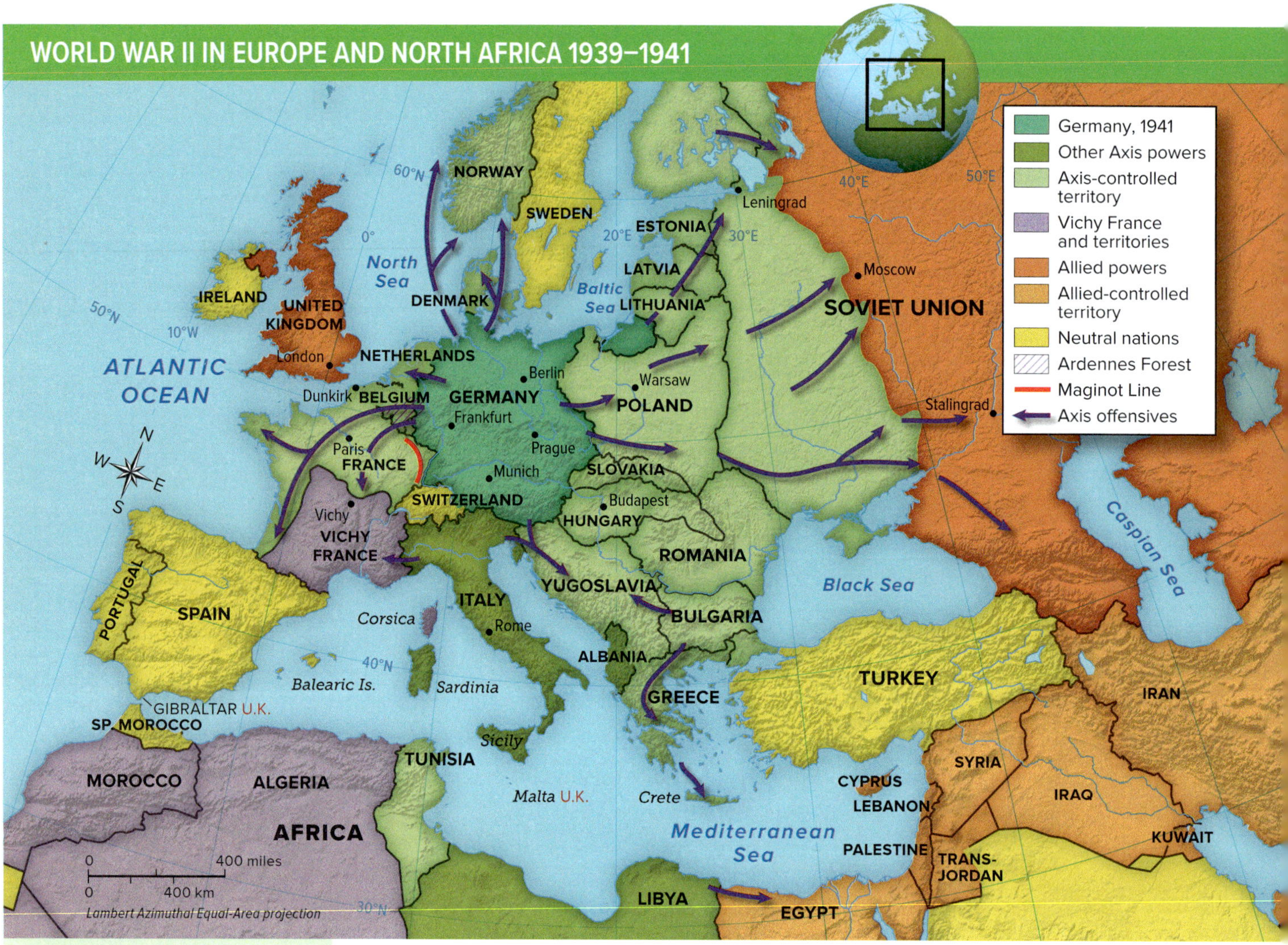


### GEOGRAPHIC REASONING

By 1941, Germany had conquered most of continental Europe.

1. **GLOBAL INTERCONNECTIONS** Why was it significant that Germany failed to occupy the Soviet Union?
2. **PATTERNS AND MOVEMENT** What did Axis Powers attempt in Africa?

massive attack stretched out along a front some 1,800 miles (about 2,900 km) long. German troops advanced rapidly, capturing 2 million Russian soldiers. By November, one German army group had swept through the Ukraine. A second army was besieging the city of Leningrad, while a third approached within 25 miles (about 40 km) of Moscow, the Soviet capital.

An early winter and fierce Soviet resistance, however, halted the German advance. Certain of quick victory, the Germans had not planned for winter uniforms. For the first time in the war, German armies had been stopped. Britain and the Soviet Union forced Iran to allow them to create an overland supply route in that country after a brief invasion in 1941. Iran's king was deposed and this route become critical to the Soviet war effort. A counterattack in December 1941 by a Soviet army came as an ominous ending to the year for the Germans.

### ✓ CHECKING FOR UNDERSTANDING

1. **DETERMINING CONTEXT** What were Germany's gains and losses during the early years of the war?
2. **IDENTIFYING CONNECTIONS** How did technology affect the Battle of Britain for both the Germans and the British?
3. **SUMMARIZING** What was Germany's military strategy in the early part of the war? Summarize in two to three sentences.

# JAPAN AT WAR

**GUIDING QUESTION** *What brought the United States into the war?*

Japan took advantage of Hitler's conquests in Western Europe to seize European colonies in Asia. However, it realized American power in the Pacific could block further conquests, which helped lead the Japanese to attack the U.S. naval base at Pearl Harbor in Hawaii on December 7, 1941. The surprise attack damaged or destroyed more than 350 aircraft, damaged or sunk 18 ships, and killed or wounded more than 3,500 Americans. The same day, the Japanese attacked the Philippines and advanced on Malaya. Later, they invaded the Dutch East Indies and occupied several islands in the Pacific Ocean. By the spring of 1942, almost all Southeast Asia and much of the western Pacific had fallen to the Japanese.

A triumphant Japan now declared the creation of a "community" of nations: the Greater East Asia Co-Prosperity Sphere. The entire region would now be under Japanese direction. Japan also announced its intention to liberate areas of Southeast Asia from Western colonial rule. For the moment, however, Japan needed the resources of the region for its war machine and treated the countries under its rule as conquered lands.

Japanese policy was now largely dictated by Prime Minister Hideki Tōjō—formerly a general—who in the course of the war became a virtual military dictator. Tōjō had hoped Japan's lightning strikes at American bases would destroy the U.S. fleet in the Pacific. The Roosevelt administration, he thought, would now accept Japanese domination of the Pacific.

But the Japanese miscalculated. The attack on Pearl Harbor unified American opinion about becoming involved in the war. The United States joined with European nations and Nationalist China in a combined effort to defeat Japan. Believing American **involvement** in the Pacific would make the United States ineffective in the European theater of war, Hitler declared war on the United States four days after Pearl Harbor. As in World War I, another European conflict had turned into a global war.

### ✓ CHECKING FOR UNDERSTANDING

1. **EXPLAINING CAUSES** What brought the United States into the war?
2. **UNDERSTANDING CONTEXT** What error did the Japanese make in their attack on Pearl Harbor, and how did this harm their ultimate military strategy?
3. **RELATING EVENTS** How did the Japanese approach to war compare to the German approach?

#### ANALYZING KEY IDEAS AND DETAILS

1. **ANALYZING CENTRAL IDEAS** What is the main idea of this section? Summarize "Japan at War" in two to three sentences, using your own words.
2. **CITING TEXT EVIDENCE** What words does the text use to signal the consequences of Japan's attacks on Pearl Harbor, Malaya, and other countries?

#### DETERMINING MEANING

Return to the paragraph beginning "But the Japanese miscalculated." How does this paragraph help you understand the meaning of the word **involvement** in this context?

# THE ALLIES ADVANCE

**GUIDING QUESTION** *How did the involvement of the United States change the war?*

The entry of the United States into the war created a new coalition, the Grand Alliance. To overcome mutual suspicions, the three major Allies—Great Britain, the United States, and the Soviet Union—agreed to stress military operations and to ignore political differences. At the beginning of 1943, the Allies agreed to fight until the Axis Powers—Germany, Italy, and Japan—surrendered unconditionally, which required the Axis nations to surrender without any favorable condition. This cemented the Grand Alliance by making it nearly impossible for Hitler to divide his foes.

#### ANALYZING KEY IDEAS AND DETAILS

1. **ANALYZING CENTRAL IDEAS** Summarize this section in two to three sentences. Then, explain how the central idea illustrates this section's title, "The Allies Advance."
2. **CITING TEXT EVIDENCE** The text in this section explains how the Grand Alliance formed. What text evidence shows the resolve of these countries in facing the Axis Powers?

## THE EUROPEAN THEATER

In spite of some minor setbacks, defeat was far from Hitler's mind at the beginning of 1942. As Japanese forces advanced into Southeast Asia and the Pacific, Hitler and his allies continued fighting the war in Europe against Britain and the Soviet Union.

Until late 1942, it seemed that the Germans might still find victory. In North Africa, German forces broke through the British defenses in Egypt and advanced toward the strategically important port city of Alexandria. The Suez Canal, so important to the Allied war effort, was under threat of capture. A renewed German offensive in the Soviet Union led to the capture of the entire Crimea in the spring of 1942. However, by the fall of 1942, the war had turned against the Germans.

**ANALYZING PRIMARY SOURCES**

**HITLER IN AUGUST 1942**

"As the next step, we are going to advance south of the Caucasus and then help the rebels in Iran and Iraq against the English. Another thrust will be directed along the Caspian Sea toward Afghanistan and India. Then the English will run out of oil. In two years we'll be on the borders of India. Twenty to thirty elite German divisions will do. Then the British Empire will collapse."

—quoted in *Spandau*, 1976

**EXPLAINING EFFECTS** Why was Hitler so optimistic after he captured the Crimea?

## THE TIDE TURNS

In North Africa, British forces had stopped General Erwin Rommel's troops at the battled of El Alamein in the summer of 1942. The Germans then retreated back across the desert. In November 1942, British and American forces invaded French North Africa. They forced the German and Italian troops there to surrender in May 1943.

On the Eastern Front, after the capture of the Crimea, Hitler's generals wanted him to concentrate on the Caucasus and its oil fields. Hitler, however, decided that Stalingrad, a major industrial center on the Volga River, should be taken first. In perhaps the most terrible and brutal battle of the war, between November 1942 and February 2, 1943, the Soviets launched a counterattack. German troops were stopped and then encircled, and supply lines were cut off, all in frigid winter conditions. The Germans were forced to surrender at Stalingrad. The entire German Sixth Army, considered the best of the German troops, was lost.

By February 1943, German forces in Russia were back to their positions of June 1942. By the spring, even Hitler knew that the Germans would not defeat the Soviet Union.

## THE ASIAN THEATER

In 1942 the tide of battle in the East also changed dramatically. In the Battle of the Coral Sea on May 7 and 8, 1942, American naval forces stopped the Japanese advance and saved Australia from being invaded.

The turning point of the war in Asia came on June 4, at the Battle of Midway Island. U.S. planes destroyed four attacking Japanese aircraft carriers. The United States defeated the Japanese navy and established naval superiority in the Pacific.

During World War II, soldiers throughout the world relied on military technology more than they had during World War I. They increased their use of tanks, airplanes, and submarines, which caused massive destruction of both military and civilian populations. In a radio address, President Roosevelt explained some of these changes.

**ANALYZING PRIMARY SOURCES**

1. **ANALYZING TEXT PRESENTATION** How does Roosevelt explain the changes in warfare to American civilians? How does he develop this topic from the beginning to the end of this section?
2. **ANALYZING TEXT** What words or phrases in the text describe Roosevelt's shifting view of the oceans' role in war? How do these words and phrases affect the tone of this excerpt?

Roosevelt, Franklin D. 1942. Fireside Chat #19 - Progress of the War. February 23, 1942. Franklin D. Roosevelt -- 'The Great Communicator'. The Master Speech Files, 1898, 1910-1945. Series 3: 'The Four Freedoms' and FDR in World War II. File No. 141-A.

> “This war is a new kind of war. It is different from all other wars of the past, not only in its methods and weapons but also in its geography. It is warfare in terms of every continent, every island, every sea, every air lane in the world. . . . The broad oceans which have been heralded in the past as our protection from attack have become endless battlefields on which we are constantly being challenged by our enemies.”
>
> —Franklin Delano Roosevelt, “Fireside Chat,” February 23, 1942

By the fall of 1942, Allied forces in Asia were gathering for two operations. One, commanded by U.S. General Douglas MacArthur, would move into the Philippines through New Guinea and the South Pacific Islands. The other would move across the Pacific with a combination of U.S. Army, Marine, and Navy attacks on Japanese-held islands. This strategic policy, called “island hopping,” was begun in an effort to capture some Japanese-held islands while bypassing others in an effort to more easily reach the islands of Japan. The policy began to bear fruit early in its use. After engagements near the Solomon Islands that lasted from August to November 1942, Japanese fortunes in the war began to fade.

### ✓ CHECKING FOR UNDERSTANDING

1. **EXPLAINING EFFECTS** How did the involvement of the United States change the war?
2. **RELATING EVENTS** How did the United States’s entry into the war differ from that of its European allies?
3. **SUMMARIZING** Summarize this section in two to three sentences, explaining the Allies’ early military strategy.

**BIOGRAPHY**

### DOUGLAS MACARTHUR (1880–1964)

Born to a military father, Douglas MacArthur attended West Point Military Academy. After graduation, he served in World War I. When Japan attacked Pearl Harbor in 1941, MacArthur was stationed in the Philippines. He planned a defense of the islands but was eventually ordered by President Roosevelt to retreat to Australia. MacArthur disapproved of the U.S. strategy to focus more on the war in Europe and urged a focus on the Pacific as well. MacArthur designed the “island hopping” strategy that proved effective in the Pacific Theater. He drove the Japanese out of New Guinea and the Solomon Islands.

In 1945, the president appointed him general, then commander of all American troops in the Pacific. In this role, MacArthur oversaw the Japanese surrender of 1945.

## LESSON 2 REVIEW

### Time and Place

1. **EXPLAINING EFFECTS** What is a blitzkrieg and what supplies and equipment did it require?

### Building History-Social Science Analysis Skills

2. **IDENTIFYING CONNECTIONS** How did World War II’s actors and their goals and strategies compare with those of World War I?

3. **INTERPRETING** The text states that the “turning point of the war in Asia” was the Battle of Midway Island. What textual evidence supports this claim?

4. **EVALUATING** Describe the policy of “island hopping.” Did it provide an advantage or disadvantage to those who used it, and how was it employed during World War II?

### Writing About History

5. **NARRATIVE WRITING** Research one of the battles described in this lesson. Then write a descriptive account of the battle from the perspective of a soldier fighting in that battle.

### Collaborating

6. **PRESENTING** With a partner, create a five-minute presentation in which you select one member of the Grand Alliance and the factors that led to that country’s joining.

# WHAT WERE THE CAUSES OF WORLD WAR II?

Just over two decades after the end of World War I, Great Britain and France declared war on Germany, marking the beginning of World War II. However, historians have long discussed the causes of World War II. In the following primary sources from the prewar and early war years, three authors take positions to argue what the main causes of the conflict were.

**VOCABULARY**

*impunity:* freedom from punishment

*capital ship:* large warship, such as a battleship

*Freikorps:* German guerrilla force that sought to add the Sudetenland region to Germany

*Four-power meeting:* meeting of Germany, Italy, France, and Britain to discuss Germany's claims to the Sudetenland

**PRIMARY SOURCE: ARTICLE**

## THE BREAKDOWN OF THE SYSTEM OF COLLECTIVE SECURITY

British historian Dr. G. P. Gooch addressed the threat of war in a 1938 article excerpted here.

> "Since the Allies declined to scale down their armaments to the German level, Germany was certain to climb towards theirs as soon as she felt strong enough to do so with **impunity**.
>
> The Disarmament Conference which opened at Geneva in February 1932 had taken years to prepare, and it met too late. Even the chance of a limited agreement was lost owing to the lack of a strong lead at the outset by a Great Power . . . Each country was virtuously ready for reductions in categories which were not of vital importance to itself, but stood out for those which it needed most. Thus Great Britain longed for the abolition of the submarine, which nearly starved us in 1917, while she clung to the **capital ship**. . . . When the Conference adjourned for the summer holidays in 1932, it was clear that it had failed. In the autumn Germany retired, but was brought back by a promise of equality of status. . . .
>
> Such a system proved unattainable, and a year later Hitler's Germany withdrew not only from the Conference but from the League [of Nations] itself. . . . Since that moment Germany has been re-arming at feverish speed, and Europe is back again in its pre-War mood when everyone was afraid of Berlin. Our own colossal re-armament programme is the measure of our alarm."

**ANALYZE THE TEXT**

1. **CITING TEXT EVIDENCE** Cite textual evidence that shows Gooch's opinion of the causes of World War II.
2. **IDENTIFYING CONNECTIONS** Based on what you have read in the previous lesson, critique Gooch's argument as it is presented here. What historical events and/or people does it overlook?

**PRIMARY SOURCE: DIARY**

## VICTOR KLEMPERER'S DIARY ENTRIES

The following passages are from 1938 diary entries of Victor Klemperer, a Jewish professor who lived in Nazi Germany.

> "The immense act of violence on the [German] annexation of Austria, the immense increase in [Germany's] power both internally and externally, the defenseless trembling fear of England, France, etc. We shall not live to see the end of the Third Reich. . . .
>
> The Third Reich will win again—whether by bluff or by force. . . . Chamberlain flies to Hitler for the second time tomorrow. England and France remain calm, in Dresden the Sudeten German "**Freikorps**" is almost ready to invade [Czechoslovakia]. And the populace here is convinced that the Czechs alone are to blame and that Hitler loves peace. . . .
>
> **Four-power meeting** today [September 29] at three in Munich. Czechoslovakia continues to exist, Germany gets the Sudetenland, probably a colony as well. . . . For the populace on the front pages of the German press it is of course the absolute success of Hitler, the prince of peace and brilliant diplomat. . . . No shot is fired, and the [German] troops have been marching in since yesterday. Wishes for peace and friendship have been exchanged with England and France, Russia is cowering and silent, a zero. Hitler is being acclaimed even more extravagantly than in the Austria business."

**ANALYZE THE TEXT**

1. **DETERMINING CENTRAL IDEAS** What does Klemperer believe were the main causes of World War II?
2. **RELATING EVENTS** Assess the events regarding Czechoslovakia that Klemperer references in the passage. Why were they of international importance?

(l)Gooch, Dr. G. P. Excerpt from "The Breakdown of the System of Collective Security." 1938. From Problems of Peace, Twelfth Series: Geneva and the Drift to War. By Geneva Institute of International

PRIMARY SOURCE: CARTOON

## LET SAM DO IT

*The weakness of the League of Nations is illustrated in this 1931 cartoon, "Let Sam Do It," by Winsor McCay.*

### ANALYZE THE SOURCE

1. **ANALYZING IDEAS** Analyze the main figures shown in the cartoon. Whom do they represent?
2. **INTERPRETING** What argument does this cartoon make about the origins of World War II?

### MULTIPLE PERSPECTIVES

1. **IDENTIFYING CAUSES** Each of the three authors presents a unique view on the causes of World War II. Differentiate among their main ideas in two to three sentences.
2. **COMPARING POINTS OF VIEW** Each source presents a different point of view. What connects the three sources? How are they similar?
3. **EXPLAINING ISSUES** Using your own knowledge of the origins of World War II from the chapter, critique the primary sources you have just read. Which, if any, provides a convincing explanation for the origins of World War II?

## ESSENTIAL QUESTION

- *How does war impact society and the environment?*

# LESSON 3
# The Home Front and Civilians

## THE STORY BEGINS...

American Meda Brendall worked as a welder during World War II, as American men went off to fight. In an interview, she described her experience as follows:

> “It's a good thing that the women went in. It's a good thing that they showed the world that they can do things, too. ‘Oh, it's dirty work.’ Well, making a pie can be a dirty work. And so I just looked at it—so I get dirty. There's soap.”
>
> —Meda Brendall

The mobilization of American women to take over traditionally “masculine” jobs was one of many effects the war had on civilians.

*Women testing artillery shells in an American munitions factory* ▶

PHOTO:Library of Congress Prints and Photographs Division [LC-USZ62-97395]; TEXT:Brendall, Meda. 2011. Video Interview: Meda Montana Hallyburton Brendall. Recorded October 26, 2011. Library of Congress - American Folklife Center - Veterans History Project.

| Civilian Life: Compare and Contrast | | | | |
|---|---|---|---|---|
| | Soviets | Germans | Americans | Japanese |
| Bombing | | | | |
| Access to Food and Shelter | | | | |

**ANALYZING KEY IDEAS AND DETAILS**

**DESCRIBING** Read closely to understand life on the home front for American, German, Soviet, and Japanese civilians. Compare and contrast the lives of civilians in these countries in a graphic organizer like this one.

# THE MOBILIZATION OF FOUR NATIONS

**GUIDING QUESTION** *How did countries mobilize for war?*

Even more than World War I, World War II was a total war. Fighting was much more **widespread** and covered most of the world. Economic **mobilization** was more extensive; so, too, was the mobilization of women. The number of civilians killed—almost 20 million—was far higher than those killed in World War I. Many of these victims were children.

World War II had an enormous impact on civilian life in the Soviet Union, the United States, Germany, and Japan. The mobilization efforts on these different fronts had greatly affected the outcome of the war.

**ANALYZING KEY IDEAS AND DETAILS**

**ANALYZING IDEAS** This section includes the sentence "Traditional habits of obedience and hierarchy were used to encourage citizens, . . ." What clue does this sentence give the reader about the public reactions of Japanese citizens to the war?

## THE SOVIET UNION

Known to the Soviets as the Great Patriotic War, the German-Soviet war witnessed the greatest land battles in history, as well as incredible ruthlessness. The initial military defeats suffered by the Soviet Union led to drastic emergency measures that affected the lives of the civilian population. The city of Leningrad (now St. Petersburg), for example, experienced 900 days of siege. Its inhabitants became so desperate for food that they even ate dogs, cats, and mice. Probably 1.5 million people died in the city.

As the German army made its rapid advance into Soviet territory, Soviet workers dismantled and shipped the factories in the western part of the Soviet Union to the interior—to the Urals, western Siberia, and the Volga regions. Machines were placed on the bare ground. As laborers began their work, walls went up around them.

Stalin called the widespread military and industrial mobilization of the nation a "battle of machines." The Soviets won, producing 78,000 tanks and 98,000 artillery pieces. In 1943, 55 percent of the Soviet national income went for war materials, compared with 15 percent in 1940. As a result of the emphasis on military goods, Soviet citizens experienced severe shortages of both food and housing.

Soviet women played a major role in the war effort. Women and girls worked in industries, mines, and railroads. Overall, the number of women working in industry increased almost 60 percent. Soviet women were also expected to dig antitank ditches and to work as air-raid wardens. Also, the Soviet Union was the only country in World War II to use women in battle. Soviet women served as snipers and in aircrews of bomber squadrons.

**DETERMINING MEANING**

The root of the word **mobilization** is *mobile*. *Mobile* means "able to move or be moved easily." How does knowing the meaning of *mobile* help you determine the meaning of *mobilization*?

## THE UNITED STATES

The home front in the United States was quite different from that of the other major powers. The United States was not fighting on its own territory. Eventually, the United States became the arsenal of the Allied Powers; it produced much of the military equipment the Allies needed. The height of war production came in November 1943. At that point, the country was building 6 ships a day and 96,000 planes per year.

Roosevelt emphasized total war and mobilization as part of U.S. aims and strategies.

> "Our national policy is this:
>
> First, by an impressive expression of the public will and without regard to partisanship, we are committed to all-inclusive national defense.
>
> Second . . . we are committed to full support of all those resolute peoples, everywhere, who are resisting aggression and are thereby keeping war away from our hemisphere. . . .
>
> Third . . . we are committed to the proposition that principles of morality and considerations for our own security will never permit us to acquiesce in a peace dictated by aggressors and sponsored by appeasers. . . .
>
> Therefore, the immediate need is a swift and driving increase in our armament production."

—Franklin Delano Roosevelt, "Four Freedoms Speech," 1941

**ANALYZING PRIMARY SOURCES**

1. **SUMMARIZING** Write a brief summary of America's war aims as described by Roosevelt.
2. **ANALYZING IDEAS** How does Roosevelt's use of numbered points help emphasize the central idea that the United States must ramp up its armaments production?

*An African-American woman works in a U.S. munitions factory during World War II.*

**IDENTIFYING EFFECTS** How did munitions factories such as the one shown here impact U.S. communities?

The mobilization of the American economy and workforce resulted in some social turmoil, however. The construction of new factories created boomtowns. Thousands came there to work but then faced a shortage of houses and schools. Sixteen million men and women were enrolled in the military and moved frequently. Another 16 million, mostly wives and girlfriends of servicemen or workers looking for jobs, also moved around the country.

More than a million African Americans moved from the rural South to the cities of the North and West looking for jobs in industry. The presence of African Americans in areas in which they had not lived before led to racial tensions and sometimes even racial riots. In Detroit in June 1943, for example, white mobs roamed the streets attacking African Americans. One million African Americans joined the military, where they served in segregated units. For some, this treatment later led to a fight for their civil rights.

Japanese Americans faced even more serious issues. On the West Coast, 110,000 Japanese Americans, 65 percent of whom had been born in the United States, were removed to camps surrounded by barbed wire and required to take loyalty oaths. Public officials claimed this policy was necessary for security reasons. California governor Culbert Olson expressed the racism in this policy:

CITIZENSHIP

## MILITARY CONSCRIPTION

As the U.S. mobilized for war, it conscripted millions of men into the armed forces. Conscription, sometimes called "the draft," is the process of compelling nonmilitary civilians to register for military service. In the First World War, for example, 24 million men were compelled to register for service. In World War II, that number increased to 50 million. Although not all those registered were actually called to serve, enough were called to create labor shortages. In World War II, many factories employed women to fill the positions of men called to serve. There was limited opposition to conscription during the world wars. This changed 20 years later, during the Vietnam conflict, as opposition to the draft grew along with opposition to that war. Military conscription was ended in the United States in 1973, two years before the end of the Vietnam War.

1. **EVALUATING** Why might World War II have required mass conscription although recent wars have not?
2. **IDENTIFYING CONNECTIONS** Why might the labor shortages created by conscription have helped further the cause of civil rights among some groups in the United States?

> "[W]hen I look out at a group of Americans of German or Italian descent, I can tell whether they're loyal or not. I can tell how they think and even perhaps what they are thinking. But it is impossible for me to do this with inscrutable Orientals, and particularly the Japanese."
>
> —quoted in *Japanese Americans: The Formation and Transformation of an Ethnic Group*

## GERMANY

In August 1914, Germans had enthusiastically cheered their soldiers marching off to war. In September 1939, the streets were quiet. Even worse for the Nazi regime, many feared disaster.

Hitler was well aware of the importance of the home front. He believed that the collapse of the home front in World War I had caused Germany's defeat. To avoid a repetition of that experience, he adopted economic policies that may have cost Germany the war.

To maintain the morale of the home front during the first two years of the war, Hitler refused to cut consumer goods production or to increase the production of armaments. Blitzkrieg gave the Germans quick victories and enabled them to plunder the food and raw materials of conquered countries. In this way, they could avoid taking away resources from the civilian economy. After German defeats on the Russian front and the American entry into the war, however, the economic situation in Germany changed.

Early in 1942, Hitler finally ordered a massive increase in armaments production and in the size of the army. Hitler's architect, Albert Speer, was made minister for armaments and munitions in 1942. Speer was able to triple the production of armaments between 1942 and 1943, in spite of Allied air raids.

A total mobilization of the economy was put into effect in July 1944. Schools, theaters, and cafés were closed. By that time, though, total war mobilization was too late to save Germany from defeat.

Nazi attitudes toward women changed over the course of the war. Before the war, the Nazis had worked to keep women out of the job market. As the war progressed and more and more men were called up for military service,

MAKING CONNECTIONS TO TODAY

## WOMEN IN THE U.S. MILITARY

During World War II, women participated in organizations such as the Women's Army Corps (WACs), where they served in administrative, noncombat positions. In 1948 President Harry S. Truman signed the Women's Armed Services Integration Act, which enabled women to become active members of all branches of the U.S. military. At that time, women made up 2 percent of the armed forces. Today, women make up 15 percent of the military, although they are often excluded from direct combat missions. In 2009 only 6 percent of the Marine Corps was made of women, while women accounted for 20 percent of the Air Force, 14 percent of the Army, and 15 percent of the Navy.

1. **COMPARING AND CONTRASTING** In what way has the modern military departed from and still retain aspects of World War II attitudes about women's participation in war?
2. **CITING TEXT EVIDENCE** The passage suggests that Truman's Women's Armed Services Integration Act was largely successful in achieving its goals. How does the passage support this claim?

this position no longer made sense. In spite of this change, the number of women working in industry, agriculture, commerce, and domestic service increased only slightly. The total number of employed women in September 1944 was 14.9 million, compared with 14.6 million in May 1939. Many women, especially those who belonged to the middle class, did not want jobs, particularly in factories.

## JAPAN

Wartime Japan was a highly mobilized society. To guarantee its control over all national resources, the government created a planning board to control prices, wages, labor, and resources. Traditional habits of obedience and hierarchy were used to encourage citizens to sacrifice their resources, and sometimes their lives, for the national cause.

**DETERMINING MEANING**

Read the paragraph that begins, "The calls for sacrifice..." How does the content of the paragraph help you figure out what **kamikaze** means?

The calls for sacrifice reached a high point in the final years of the war. Young Japanese were encouraged to volunteer to serve as pilots in suicide missions against U.S. fighting ships at sea. These pilots were known as **kamikaze**, or "divine wind."

Japan was reluctant to mobilize women on behalf of Japan's war effort. General Hideki Tōjō, prime minister from 1941 to 1944, opposed female employment. He argued in October 1943:

> "The weakening of the family system would be the weakening of the nation. . . . [W]e are able to do our duties . . . only because we have wives and mothers at home."

—quoted in *Valley of Darkness: The Japanese People and World War Two,* 1978

Female employment increased during the war but only in areas such as the textile industry and farming, in which women had traditionally worked. Instead of using women to meet labor shortages, the Japanese government brought in Korean and Chinese laborers.

### ☑ CHECKING FOR UNDERSTANDING

1. **RELATING EVENTS** How was the role of women similar in the United States and the U.S.S.R. during wartime?
2. **EXPLAINING CAUSE AND EFFECT** Why were Japanese leaders reluctant to employ women in roles traditionally filled by men during the war?

# THE BOMBING OF CITIES

**GUIDING QUESTION** *How did the bombing of cities impact the home front?*

**ANALYZING KEY IDEAS AND DETAILS**

1. **DETERMINING CENTRAL IDEAS** What is the central idea of this section? How does the text present and develop this idea?
2. **CITING TEXT EVIDENCE** What were the effects of bombing in Germany and Japan on their war efforts? Cite specific words in the text that support your answer.

Bombing was used in World War II against military targets, enemy troops, and civilian populations. Bombing made the home front a dangerous place.

Although a few bombing raids had been conducted in the last year of World War I, the aircraft of the time were limited by how far they could fly and by how much they could carry. The bombing of civilians had led to a public outcry, leading many leaders to believe that bombing civilian populations would force governments to make peace. As a result, European air forces began to develop long-range bombers that carried enormous payloads in the 1930s.

## BRITAIN

The first sustained use of civilian bombing began in early September 1940. Londoners took the first heavy blows. For months, the German air force bombed London nightly. Thousands of civilians were killed or injured, and enormous damage was done to the buildings of London. In spite of the extensive damage done to lives and property, Londoners' morale remained high.

The **blitz**, as the British called the German air raids, soon became a national experience. The blitz was carried to many other British cities and towns. The ability of Londoners to maintain their morale set the standard for the rest of the British population. The theory that the bombing of civilians would force peace was proved wrong.

Many children were evacuated from cities during the war to avoid the bombing. The British moved about 6 million children and their mothers in 1939. Some British parents even sent their children to Canada and the United States. This, too, could be dangerous. When the ocean liner *Arandora Star* was hit by a German torpedo, it had 77 British children on board. They never made it to Canada.

*The blitz leveled buildings in England. A man stands amid the rubble of what was the Coventry Cathedral in November 1940.*

**EXPLAINING EFFECTS** What effects did the blitz have on both the British landscape and British morale?

## GERMANY

The British failed to learn from their own experience, however. Churchill and his advisers believed that destroying German communities would break civilian morale and bring victory. Major bombing raids on German cities began in 1942. On May 31, 1942, Cologne became the first German city to be attacked by 1,000 bombers.

Bombing raids added an element of terror to the dire **circumstances** caused by growing shortages of food, clothing, and fuel. The Germans, too, sought to protect their children from the bombings by evacuating them from the cities. They had a program that created about 9,000 camps for children in the countryside. Especially fearful to the Germans were the incendiary bombs, which created firestorms that swept through cities. The ferocious bombing of Dresden from February 13 to 15, 1945, created a firestorm that may have killed as many as 35,000 inhabitants and refugees.

Germany suffered enormously from the Allied bombing raids. Millions of buildings were destroyed; half a million civilians died. Nevertheless, it is highly unlikely that Allied bombing sapped the German morale. Instead, Germans, whether pro-Nazi or anti-Nazi, fought on stubbornly, often driven simply by a desire to live. At times, even young people were expected to fight in the war. In the last years of the war, Hitler Youth members, often only 14 or 15 years old, served in the front lines.

**DETERMINING MEANING**

The text about the **blitz** begins "The first sustained use of civilian bombing. . ." How does the context help you to understand the implications of the term *blitz*?

**DETERMINING MEANING**

To better understand **widespread**, break down the word. *Wide* means "including a great variety of." *Spread* means "to distribute." What does it mean for something to be *widespread*?

Nor did the bombing destroy Germany's industrial capacity. Production of war materials actually increased between 1942 and 1944, in spite of the bombing. However, the **widespread** destruction of transportation systems and fuel supplies made it extremely difficult for the new materials to reach the German military.

## JAPAN

Japan was open to air raids toward the end of the war because its air force had almost been destroyed. Moreover, its crowded cities were built of flimsy materials that were especially vulnerable to fire.

B-29 Superfortresses fly over Mount Fuji en route to Tokyo.



Attacks on Japanese cities by the new U.S. B-29 Superfortresses, the biggest bombers of the war, had begun on November 24, 1944. By the summer of 1945, many of Japan's industries had been destroyed, along with one-fourth of its dwellings. To add to the strength of its regular army, the Japanese government decreed the mobilization of all people between the ages of 13 and 60 into a People's Volunteer Corps.

In Japan, the bombing of civilians reached a new level with the use of the first atomic bomb. Fearing high U.S. casualties in a land invasion of Japan, President Truman and his advisers decided to drop atomic bombs in August 1945. The result was the deaths of thousands of Japanese civilians.

### ✓ CHECKING FOR UNDERSTANDING

1. **EXPLAINING EFFECTS** How did the bombing of cities impact the home front?
2. **DETERMINING CONTEXT** How did the blitz differ from World War I bombings?
3. **IDENTIFYING EFFECTS** What was the impact of bombings in Germany and Britain on the environment in Europe?

## LESSON 3 REVIEW

### Time and Place

1. **UNDERSTANDING CHANGE** Describe the social effects of U.S. mobilization for World War II.

### Building History-Social Science Analysis Skills

2. **UNDERSTANDING CONTEXT** How was World War II a total war?
3. **EXPLAINING CAUSES** What effect did bombings such as the British bombing of Dresden create in Germany?
4. **INTERPRETING** Evaluate Roosevelt's point of view and reasoning in the "Four Freedoms" speech. What does he advocate? What evidence does he provide?

### Writing About History

5. **INFORMATIVE WRITING** Do research to find out more about the blitz in London or another city in Great Britain. In paragraph form, present a detailed sequence of steps or events that would typically occur for average citizens in their homes from the time planes were sighted until the "all clear" signal. Use transitional words and phrases, and list your source or sources.

### Collaborating

6. **INTEGRATING INFORMATION** Discuss in a small group the following question: How did the use of bombs during World War II prolong or shorten the conflict? Debate their strategic usefulness, giving reasons for your support or opposition.

## ESSENTIAL QUESTIONS

- *Why do political actions often lead to war?*
- *How does war impact society and the environment?*

LESSON 4

# The New Order and the Holocaust

## THE STORY BEGINS...

As Germany fought the Allied nations, Adolf Hitler's racial prejudices resulted in acts of severe violence against Jews in the Third Reich. These prejudices were long-standing. As early as 1932, Hitler had proclaimed:

> "The word Aryan . . . stands for work, nobility and unselfishness, while the name Jew means lack of self-sacrifice. . . . The most important cause of Germany's collapse is a lack of appreciation of the race problem, and especially, of the Jewish menace."

—Adolf Hitler, 1932

During World War II, the Nazis carried out a terrifying, large-scale genocide against European Jews, whom they subjected to death squads and death camps. Other disadvantaged groups, such as Gypsies and homosexuals, also became targets. This program of mass killings eventually became known as the Holocaust.

*Concentration camp prisoners lined up for a daily inspection. Holocaust victims were subjected to cruel and dehumanizing treatment by the Nazis.* ▶

| The German and Japanese New Order | |
|---|---|
| Events and Programs | Causes |
| The colonization of Eastern Europe | |
| The creation of the *Einsatzgruppen* | |
| The creation of death camps | |
| Japanese invasions of Southeast Asia | |

### ANALYZING KEY IDEAS AND DETAILS

**IDENTIFYING CAUSES** Read closely to identify the causes of the given events and programs under the German and Japanese New Orders. Note that each event or program may have more than one cause. Record these causes in a graphic organizer like this one.

# THE NEW ORDER IN EUROPE

### ANALYZING KEY IDEAS AND DETAILS

**SUMMARIZING** Summarize the main points of this section in two to three sentences. What were the key components of the New Order in Europe?

**GUIDING QUESTION** *How did Germany establish a New Order in Europe?*

In 1942 the Nazi regime stretched across continental Europe from the English Channel in the west to the outskirts of Moscow in the east. Nazi-occupied Europe was largely organized in one of two ways. Nazi Germany directly annexed some areas, such as western Poland, and made them into German provinces. Most of occupied Europe, however, was run by German military or civilian officials with help from local people who collaborated with the Nazis.

Nazi administration in the conquered lands to the east was especially ruthless. Seen as the "living space" for German expansion, these lands were populated, Nazis thought, by racially inferior Slavic peoples. Hitler's plans for an Aryan racial empire were so important to him that the Nazis began to put their racial program into effect soon after the conquest of Poland. Hitler recalled the genocide of the Armenians in his plans saying, "Who, after all, speaks today of the annihilation of the Armenians?"

### DETERMINING MEANING

Read the paragraph that begins, "Heinrich Himmler, . . ." Based on the context of this paragraph, what does **ethnic** mean?

Heinrich Himmler, the leader of the SS, was in charge of German resettlement plans in the east. Himmler's task was to move the Slavic peoples out and to replace them with Germans. Slavic peoples included Czech, Polish, Serbo-Croatian, Slovene, and Ukrainian people. One million Poles were uprooted and moved to southern Poland. Hundreds of thousands of **ethnic** Germans were brought in to colonize the German provinces in Poland.

The invasion of the Soviet Union made the Nazis even more excited about German colonization. Hitler planned a colossal project of social engineering after the war. Poles, Ukrainians, and Russians would be removed and become slave labor. German peasants would settle on the abandoned lands and "Germanize" them.

### DETERMINING MEANING

The text about forced labor by the Germans states that it led "more and more people to resist the Nazi **occupation** forces." What does the word *occupation* mean in this context?

By the summer of 1944, more than 7 million European workers labored in Germany. They made up approximately 20 percent of Germany's labor force. Another 7 million workers were forced to labor for the Nazis in their own countries on farms, in industries, and in military camps.

The use of forced labor caused many problems for Germany. Sending so many workers to Germany disrupted industrial production in the occupied countries. Then, too, the brutal way in which Germany recruited foreign workers led more and more people to resist the Nazi **occupation** forces.

Hitler, Adolf. 1939. Quoted 1996 by U.S. Congress & House. The History of the Armenian Genocide: Hearing Before the Committee on International Relations, 104th Congress, Second Session, May 15, 1996.

## ✓ CHECKING FOR UNDERSTANDING

1. **SUMMARIZING** How did Germany establish a New Order in Europe?
2. **IDENTIFYING CAUSES** What did German leaders hope to accomplish by invading the Soviet Union?
3. **ANALYZING CHANGE** What were the differences between Nazi-annexed territories and Nazi-occupied territories?

# THE HOLOCAUST

**GUIDING QUESTION** *How did Adolf Hitler's views on race influence the New Order?*

No aspect of the Nazi New Order was more terrifying than the deliberate attempt to exterminate the Jews. Racial struggle was a key element in Hitler's world of ideas. He saw it as a clearly defined conflict of opposites. On one side were the Aryans, who were the creators of human cultural development, according to Hitler. On the other side were the Jews, whom Hitler blamed for Germany's defeat in World War I and the Depression.

Himmler and the SS closely shared Hitler's racial ideas. The SS was given responsibility for what the Nazis called their Final Solution to the Jewish problem. The Final Solution was **genocide** of the Jewish people.

## THE *EINSATZGRUPPEN*

Reinhard Heydrich, head of the SS's Security Service, had the task of administering the Final Solution. Heydrich created special strike forces, called *Einsatzgruppen*, to carry out Nazi plans. After the defeat of Poland, these forces rounded up all Polish Jews and put them in ghettos set up in many Polish cities. Conditions in the ghettos were horrible. Families were crowded together in unsanitary housing. The Nazis tried to starve residents by allowing only minimal amounts of food. In spite of their suffering, residents carried on.

Some residents organized resistance against the Nazis, such as the Warsaw Ghetto Uprising. As Nazis shipped Jews from the Warsaw ghetto to the death camp at Treblinka, the residents formed a resistance group. When more deportations were ordered in January 1943, the Jews fought back. The Germans suspended deportations until April 19, the first day of Passover. Against overwhelming odds, the Jewish resistance in the ghetto fought German deportation to the death camps until May 16 when Germans finally took the ghetto and dynamited the Great Synagogue of Warsaw.

In June 1941, the *Einsatzgruppen* were given the new job of acting as mobile killing units. These SS death squads followed the regular army's advance into the Soviet Union. Their job was to round up Jews in their villages, to execute them, and to bury them in mass graves.

## THE DEATH CAMPS

The *Einsatzgruppen* probably killed more than 1 million Jews. As appalling as that sounds, it was too slow by Nazi standards. They decided to kill the European Jews in specially built death camps.

### DETERMINING MEANING

The word **genocide** is made of the ancient Greek word *genos,* meaning "tribe," and the Latin *cide,* which means "killing." Based on these word parts, what is genocide?

### ANALYZING KEY IDEAS AND DETAILS

1. **DETERMINING CENTRAL IDEAS** What is the central idea of this section, and how does the text present and develop this idea?
2. **ANALYZING IDEAS** This section of the text includes the statement that the Nazis were responsible for the deaths of as many as 9 to 10 million non-Jewish people during the Holocaust. What clue does this sentence give the reader about the scale of Nazi atrocities?

### ANALYZING PRIMARY SOURCES

**NAZI DEATH SQUADS**

"The unit selected for this task would enter a village or city and order the prominent Jewish citizens to call together all Jews for the purpose of resettlement. They were requested to hand over their valuables to the leaders of the unit, and shortly before the execution to surrender their outer clothing. The men, women, and children were led to a place of execution which in most cases was located next to a more deeply excavated anti-tank ditch. Then they were shot, kneeling or standing, and the corpses thrown into the ditch."

—from *Nazi Conspiracy and Aggression,* Vol. 5, 1946

**DETERMINING MEANING** How do the actions described above exemplify genocide?

## MAJOR NAZI DEATH CAMPS

### GEOGRAPHIC REASONING

During the war, Germany created prison and death camps around Europe.

1. **SPATIAL THINKING** Where did Germany locate the death camps?
2. **EXPLORING PLACE** What advantage did the *Einsatzgruppen* gain by operating in Eastern Europe and the Soviet Union?

### ANALYZING PRIMARY SOURCES

1. **ANALYZING TEXT PRESENTATION** In the final sentences of the passage, Wiesel repeats the phrase "eight words." What does his repetition of those words imply in this context?
2. **ANALYZING TEXT** What symbol does the writer use in the first sentence of this excerpt?

Beginning in 1942, Jews from countries occupied by Germany or sympathetic to Germany were rounded up, packed like cattle into freight trains, and shipped to Poland. Six extermination centers were built in Poland for this purpose. The largest was Auschwitz (OWSH • vihts).

> "The cherished objects we had brought with us thus far were left behind in the train, and with them, at last, our illusions.
>
> Every two yards or so an SS man held his tommy gun trained on us. Hand in hand we followed the crowd.
>
> An SS noncommissioned officer came to meet us, a truncheon in his hand. He gave the order: 'Men to the left! Women to the right!'
>
> Eight words spoken quietly, indifferently, without emotion. Eight short, simple words. Yet that was the moment when I parted from my mother."
>
> —Elie Wiesel, *Night* (1956)

About 30 percent of the new arrivals at Auschwitz were sent to a labor camp, where many were starved or worked to death. The remainder of the people went to the gas chambers. Some inmates were subjected to cruel and painful "medical" experiments.

By the spring of 1942, the death camps were in full operation. First priority was given to the elimination of the Polish ghettos. By the summer of 1942, Jews were also being shipped from France, Belgium, and Holland. Even as the Allies were winning the war in 1944, Jews were shipped from Greece and Hungary. In spite of Germany's desperate military needs, even late in the war when Germany was facing utter defeat, the Final Solution often had priority in using railroad cars to ship Jews to the death camps.

Wiesel, Eli. Night. Quoted 2001 by Chametzky, Jules; Felstiner, John; Flanzbaum, Hilene; and Hellerstein, Kathryn. Jewish American Literature: A Norton Anthology. New York: W. W. Norton & Company.

## THE DEATH TOLL

The Germans killed approximately 6 million Jews, more than 3 million of them in the death camps. Even in concentration camps that were not designed specifically for mass murder, large numbers of inmates were worked to death or subjected to deadly medical experiments. Virtually 90 percent of the Jewish populations of Poland, the Baltic countries, and Germany were killed. Overall, the Holocaust was responsible for the death of nearly two out of every three European Jews.

*Japanese troops arrive at Haiphong Port in Indochina*

**UNDERSTANDING CONTEXT**
What was the importance of Indochina to the Japanese war effort?

The Nazis were also responsible for the deliberate death by shooting, starvation, or overwork of as many as another 9 to 10 million non-Jewish people. The Nazis considered the Roma, who are sometimes known as Gypsies, to be an alien race. About 40 percent of Europe's Roma were killed in the death camps. Political activists, homosexuals, and Jehovah's Witnesses were also persecuted and killed by the Nazis.

The leading citizens of the Slavic peoples were arrested and killed. Probably an additional 4 million Poles, Ukrainians, and Belorussians lost their lives as slave laborers. Finally, at least 3 to 4 million Soviet prisoners of war were killed.

The Nazi mass slaughter of European Jews is known as *Shoah*—a Hebrew word meaning "total destruction." Many Jews attempted to resist the Nazis. Friends and strangers aided some Jews, hiding them or smuggling them to safe areas. A few foreign diplomats saved Jews by issuing exit visas. The nation of Denmark saved almost its entire Jewish population.

Some people did not believe the accounts of death camps because, during World War I, Allied propaganda had greatly exaggerated German atrocities to arouse enthusiasm for the war. Most often, people pretended not to notice what was happening. Even worse, **collaborators** helped the Nazis hunt down Jews. Although the Allies were aware of the concentration camps and death camps, they chose to concentrate on ending the war. Not until after the war did the full extent of the horror and inhumanity of the Holocaust impress itself upon people's consciousness.

**DETERMINING MEANING**

The root of the word **collaborator** is *collaborate*. To *collaborate* means "to work together"—literally, to co-labor. How does knowing the meaning of *collaborate* help you determine the meaning of *collaborator*?

### ✓ CHECKING FOR UNDERSTANDING

1. **IDENTIFYING CAUSES** How did Adolf Hitler's views on race influence the New Order?
2. **RELATING EVENTS** How did Hitler view the Holocaust in the context of his plans for the colonization of Europe?

# THE NEW ORDER IN ASIA

**GUIDING QUESTION** *What characterized the New Order in Asia?*

Japan needed its new possessions in Asia to meet its growing need for raw materials, such as tin and oil, and as markets for its manufactured goods. To organize these possessions, Japanese leaders included them in the Greater East Asia Co-Prosperity Sphere. This economic community supposedly would provide mutual benefits to the occupied areas and to Japan.

The Japanese had conquered much of East and Southeast Asia under the slogan "Asia for the Asiatics." Japanese officials in occupied territories promised that local governments would be established under Japanese control. In fact, real power rested with Japanese military authorities in each

**ANALYZING KEY IDEAS AND DETAILS**

1. **SUMMARIZING** How did the New Order develop in Japan and Asia?
2. **CITING TEXT EVIDENCE** What evidence does the text give as the official reason for the foundation of the Greater East Asia Co-Prosperity Sphere? Cite particular text, quoting where necessary.

Keystone-France/Gamma-Keystone/Getty Images

territory. In turn, the Army General Staff in Tokyo controlled the local Japanese military command. Japan used the economic resources of its colonies for its war machine and recruited the conquered peoples, often forcibly, to serve in local military units or in public works projects. In many cases, these policies brought severe hardships on the people subjected to them. In Vietnam, for instance, more than a million people starved in 1944 and 1945 when Japan forcibly took their rice to sell abroad.

At first, many Asian nationalists took Japanese promises at face value and agreed to cooperate. Eventually, the nature of Japanese occupation policies became clear, and sentiment turned against Japan. Japanese officials provoked such attitudes by their contempt for local customs. Like the Germans, Japanese military forces often had little respect for the lives of their subject peoples. The Japanese occupation of China has become notorious for acts of looting, destruction of property, and murder committed against Chinese civilians. Additionally, to help their war effort, the Japanese used labor forces composed of both prisoners of war and local peoples.

This behavior created a dilemma for many nationalists. They had no desire to see the return of the colonial powers, but they did not like what the Japanese were doing. Some turned against the Japanese. Others simply did nothing. Some nationalists tried to have it both ways. Indonesian patriots pretended to support Japan while actually sabotaging them.

### ✓ CHECKING FOR UNDERSTANDING

1. **SUMMARIZING** What characterized the New Order in Asia?

2. **COMPARING** In what ways was the New Order in Asia similar to the New Order in Europe?

3. **DETERMINING CONTEXT** How did Japan's need for new materials and markets contribute to the formation of the New Order in Asia?

## LESSON 4 REVIEW

### Time and Place

1. **DETERMINING CONTEXT** What was the racial perspective of colonizing countries Germany and Japan during World War II?

### Building History-Social Science Analysis Skills

2. **ANALYZING INFORMATION** How did Germany attempt to use other European countries? What were the consequences of these attempts?

3. **EXPLAINING CAUSE AND EFFECT** What effect did nationalism have on the rise of the New Order in Asia?

4. **INFERRING** Describe the reactions of local people to the occupation of German and Japanese forces.

### Writing About History

5. **EXPLANATORY WRITING** Using a variety of sources, research and analyze the causes and consequences of the Holocaust. Be careful to use only sources that are reliable, accurate, and trustworthy. Be sure to include information on the role of anti-Semitism.

### Collaborating

6. **COLLABORATING** With a partner, use your notes to contrast the New Order of Germany with the New Order of Japan.

## ESSENTIAL QUESTIONS

- *Why do political actions often lead to war?*
- *How does war impact society and the environment?*

LESSON 5

# World War II Ends

## THE STORY BEGINS...

When the United States developed the atom bomb, which the government had been developing for years, President Harry Truman realized its importance for the Second World War. He wrote in his diary:

> “This weapon is to be used against Japan between now and August 10. I have told the secretary of war, Mr. Stimson, to use it so that military objectives and soldiers and sailors are the target and not women and children. Even if Japs are savages, ruthless, merciless and fanatic, we as the leader of the world for the common welfare cannot drop this terrible bomb on the old capital or the new. He and I are in accord. The target will be a purely military one and we will issue a warning statement asking the Japs to surrender and save lives. I'm sure they will not do that, but we will have given them the chance. It is certainly a good thing for the world that Hitler's crowd or Stalin's did not discover this atomic bomb. It seems to be the most terrible thing ever discovered, but it can be made the most useful.”

—from the diary of Harry Truman

The Allies brought about a victory over Axis Powers in Europe through traditional battles, but the war in Asia was not ended until Truman decided to drop the atom bomb on Japan. In the years that followed the end of the war, the distrust of Soviets that Truman expressed in his diary grew to such a degree that the tensions between the United States and the USSR received their own name—the Cold War—which would define American foreign policy until the late 1980s and the repercussions of which we still encounter to this day.

*After millions of lives were lost in the Pacific theatre of World War II, the Japanese finally agreed to unconditional surrender.* ▶

PHOTO:World History Archive/Alamy Stock Photo; TEXT:Truman, Harry S. 1945. Reprinted by Baggott, Jim. 2011. The First War of Physics: The Secret History of the Atom Bomb, 1939–1949. Pegasus Books.

| The Final Battles of World War II | |
|---|---|
| Battles | Consequences |
| The invasion of Sicily and mainland Italy | |
| The Normandy invasion on D-Day | |
| Battle of the Bulge | |
| The Iwo Jima and Okinawa offensives | |

**ANALYZING KEY IDEAS AND DETAILS**

**IDENTIFYING CAUSES** Read closely to identify the major consequences of the battles that ended World War II. Explain the major consequences of each battle in a graphic organizer like this one.

# LAST YEARS OF THE WAR

**ANALYZING KEY IDEAS AND DETAILS**

1. **DETERMINING CENTRAL IDEAS** How does the text present and develop central ideas about the end of the war?
2. **CITING TEXT EVIDENCE** What evidence in the text supports the idea that the events at Omaha Beach helped bring about the end of the war?

**GUIDING QUESTION** *How did the tide of battle turn against Germany, Italy, and Japan?*

By the beginning of 1943, the tide of battle had turned against Germany, Italy, and Japan. The land and air campaigns waged by the Allies in North Africa, the Middle East, Italy, and occupied France had weakened the overextended Axis powers. Axis forces in Tunisia surrendered on May 13, 1943. The Allies then crossed the Mediterranean and carried the war to Italy, an area that Winston Churchill, prime minister of Great Britain, called the "soft underbelly" of Europe. After taking Sicily, the Allies began an invasion of mainland Italy in September.

## THE EUROPEAN THEATER

After Sicily fell, King Victor Emmanuel III of Italy arrested Mussolini, but in a daring raid, the Germans liberated him. He was then made the head of a German puppet state in northern Italy as German troops moved in and occupied much of Italy.

The Germans set up defense lines in the hills south of Rome. The Allies advanced up the peninsula with heavy casualties, but they took Rome on June 4, 1944. By then, the Italian war was secondary as the Allied forces opened their long-awaited "second front" in Western Europe.

*On D-Day, June 6, 1944, Allied troops departed landing craft and moved inland.*

**IDENTIFYING EFFECTS** What effect did the Normandy invasion have on Allied progress in World War II?

National Archives and Records Administration

Since the autumn of 1943, the Allies had planned an invasion of France from Great Britain, across the English Channel. Finally, on June 6, 1944 (D-Day), Allied forces under U.S. General Dwight D. Eisenhower landed on the Normandy beaches in history's greatest naval invasion. The Allies fought their way past hidden underwater mines, treacherous barbed wire, and horrible machine-gun fire. Believing the battle was a diversion and the real invasion would occur elsewhere, the Germans responded slowly. This gave the Allied forces time to set up a beachhead. Within three months, the Allies had landed 2 million men and 500,000 vehicles. Allied forces then began pushing inland and broke through German defensive lines.

Allied troops liberated Paris by the end of August 1944. In December, with Allied aircraft grounded, the Germans launched a counteroffensive to regain the seaport of Antwerp in Belgium. The Battle of the Bulge was named for the "bulge" the German attack caused in Allied lines. By January 1945, both sides had suffered heavy losses, but the Allied lines held. In March 1945, the Allied forces crossed the Rhine River and advanced into Germany. At the end of April 1945, Allied armies in northern Germany moved toward the Elbe River, where they linked up with the Soviets.

## WORLD WAR II IN EUROPE AND NORTH AFRICA 1941–1945

The Soviets had come a long way since the Battle of Stalingrad in 1943. The Soviets had soundly defeated the German forces at the Battle of Kursk (July 5 to 12), the greatest tank battle of World War II. Soviet forces now began a steady advance westward. Reoccupying the Ukraine by the end of 1943, they moved into the Baltic states by early 1944. Advancing along a northern front, Soviet troops occupied Warsaw in January 1945 and entered Berlin in April. Meanwhile, Soviet troops along a southern front swept through Hungary, Romania, and Bulgaria.

As the Allied forces advanced into Nazi-occupied Europe, they also liberated the concentration camps and death camps. Although the Nazis tried to destroy some of the evidence, the Allies were able to see for themselves the crimes against humanity carried out by the Nazis.

By January 1945, Adolf Hitler had moved into a bunker 55 feet (almost 17 m) under the city of Berlin. In his final political testament, Hitler, consistent to the end in his anti-Semitism, blamed the Jews for the war. He wrote:

> “Above all I charge the leaders of the nation and those under them to scrupulous observance of the laws of race and to merciless opposition to the universal poisoner of all peoples, international Jewry.”
>
> —from *Hitler's Final Will and Testament,* April 29, 1945

Hitler committed suicide on April 30, two days after Italian **partisans**, or resistance fighters, shot Mussolini. On May 7, 1945, Germany surrendered. The war in Europe was finally over.

### GEOGRAPHIC REASONING

The European theater in World War II included battles in Europe and Africa.

1. **PATTERNS AND MOVEMENT** What are the two major directions of Allied offensives?
2. **SPATIAL THINKING** According to the map, what advantage did the Allies gain in the 1944 Normandy offensive?

### DETERMINING MEANING

Read the paragraph that begins, “Hitler committed suicide. . . .” How does the content of the paragraph help you figure out what **partisans** are?

Hitler, Adolf. April 29, 1945. Quoted 2003 by Brinkley, Douglas. World War II: The Allied Counteroffensive, 1942-1945. The New York Times Company and Agincourt Press. Published by Henry Holt and Company.

WORLD WAR II IN ASIA AND THE PACIFIC 1943–1945

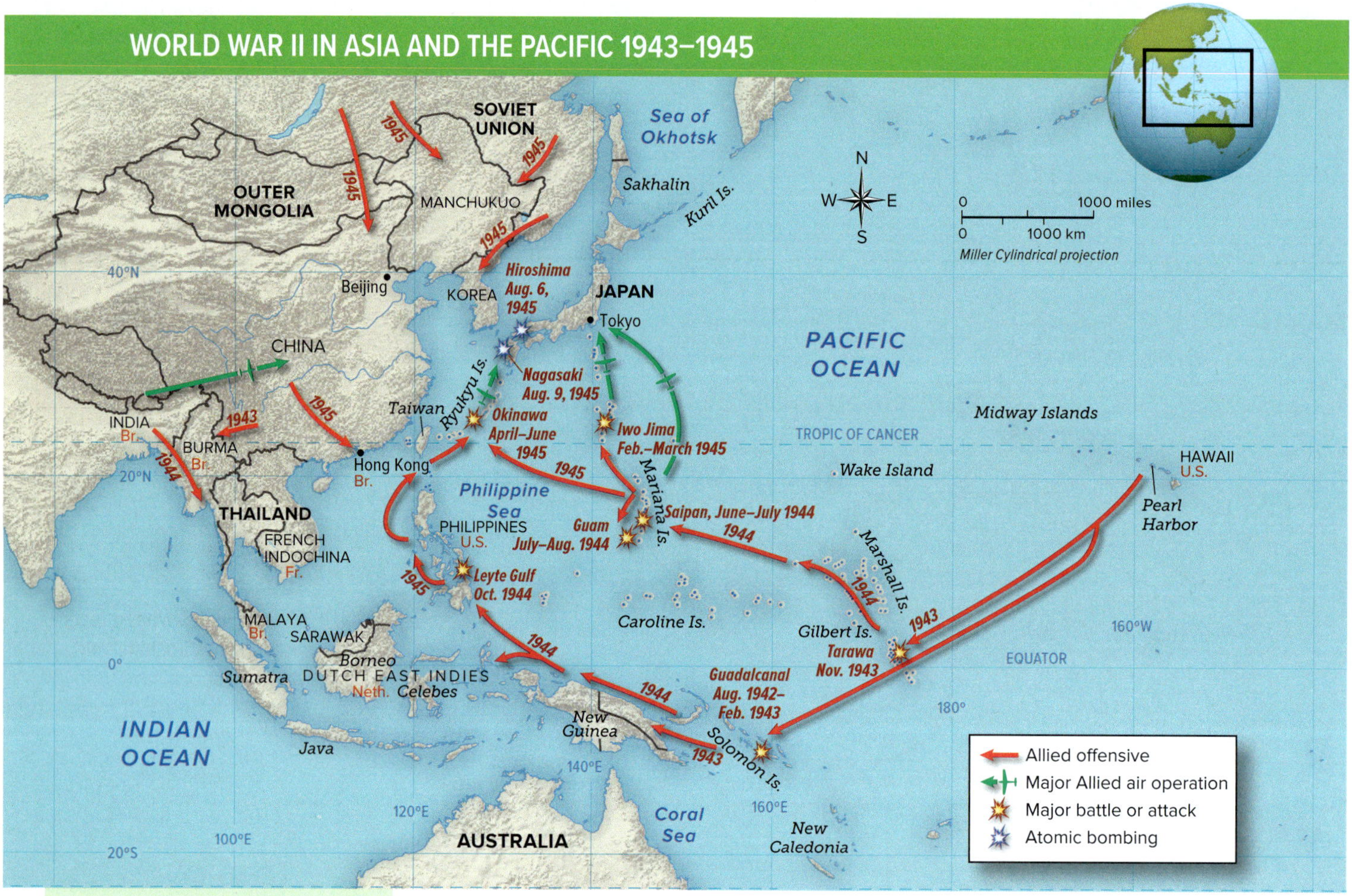

## GEOGRAPHIC REASONING

1. **SPATIAL THINKING** Where did Allied air operations begin?
2. **HUMAN-ENVIRONMENT INTERACTION** What strategy did Allied forces use in fighting the Japanese, and what advantage did this give them?

## THE ASIAN THEATER

The war in Asia continued. Beginning in 1943, U.S. forces went on the offensive and advanced across the Pacific. The United States Armed Forces Far East, which was largely comprised of the Philippine Commonwealth Army, along with Filipino guerrilla forces expelled the Japanese from the Philippines. This would prove important to the further success of the Allies. U.S. forces and its allies continued their island-hopping campaign.

At the beginning of 1945, the acquisition of Iwo Jima and Okinawa helped the Allied military power draw even closer to the main Japanese islands. The islands of Iwo Jima and Okinawa were of great strategic importance. Iwo Jima was essential to the air war on Japan. This small volcanic island had two airfields used by the Japanese to attack Allied aircraft and to support their naval forces. The Allies believed capturing Iwo Jima would lessen the Japanese threat and could aid in the invasion of the Japanese mainland. The Allies hoped that controlling Okinawa would also provide them with a base near the mainland.

The Allies were victorious in both battles, but the victories came at a great cost. Casualties were great on both sides. Fighting in the Pacific between Japanese and American forces was also especially brutal, often due to the prejudices each side had for the other. Many leaders and strategists began to fear even more losses if the war in the Pacific continued. This left Harry S. Truman, who had become president after Roosevelt died in April, with a difficult decision to make.

Scientists, including Enrico Fermi, worked on a top secret project called the Manhattan Project. Their efforts led to the development of the atomic bomb. Should he use newly developed atomic weapons to bring the war to an end? If the United States invaded Japan, Truman and his advisers were convinced that American troops would suffer heavy casualties. There were only two bombs; no one knew how effective they would be.

*Of Hiroshima's 350,000 inhabitants, 190,000 died—some immediately and others after suffering the effects of radiation.*

Truman decided to use the bombs. The first bomb was dropped on the Japanese city of Hiroshima on August 6. Three days later, a second bomb was dropped on Nagasaki. Both cities were leveled. More than 200,000 people died, some immediately and others after suffering the effects of radiation. The devastation led Japanese Emperor Hirohito to accept the Allied forces' demands for unconditional surrender on August 14, 1945.

**IDENTIFYING EFFECTS** What effects did the bombings of Hiroshima and Nagasaki have on Japan's war effort?

World War II was finally over. Seventeen million had died in battle. Perhaps 20 million civilians had perished as a result of ground campaigns, bombings, and other actions against civilians. The Soviet Union alone lost more than 20 million soldiers and civilians combined. Some estimates place total global losses at 60 million, or 3 percent of the total population.

The dropping of the atomic bombs in Japan also marked the beginning of the Nuclear Age. After the world had witnessed the deadly potential of nuclear energy, other countries raced to build their own nuclear weapons. In August 1949, the Soviet Union set off its first atomic bomb, starting an arms race with the United States that lasted for 40 years.

## ✓ CHECKING FOR UNDERSTANDING

1. **IDENTIFYING CAUSES** How did the tide of battle turn against Germany, Italy, and Japan?
2. **RELATING EVENTS** How were the ends of the war in Europe and Asia similar? How were they different?
3. **EXPLAINING CAUSE AND EFFECT** Why did President Truman decide to drop the atom bomb? What were the human and political consequences of this decision?

# PEACE AND A NEW WAR

**GUIDING QUESTION** *What led to the Cold War?*

World War II accelerated the decline of European power worldwide and the rise of the United States militarily, economically, and culturally. A period of political tensions, known as the **Cold War**, followed the total victory of the Allies. An **ideological** conflict between the United States and the Soviet Union, the Cold War dominated world affairs until the end of the 1980s.

Stalin, Roosevelt, and Churchill were the leaders of the Big Three (the Soviet Union, the United States, and Great Britain) of the Grand Alliance. They met at Tehran in November 1943 to discuss strategy. Their major tactical decision had concerned the final assault on Germany—an American-British invasion through France scheduled for the spring of 1944.

**DETERMINING MEANING**

To better understand the term **Cold War**, break down the phrase. What might "cold" mean in this context?

**DETERMINING MEANING**

The root of the word **ideological** is *idea*. How does knowing the meaning of *idea* help you determine the meaning of *ideological*?

**ANALYZING KEY IDEAS AND DETAILS**

1. **SUMMARIZING** Summarize how the events at the end of World War II led to the Cold War.
2. **CITING TEXT EVIDENCE** What evidence does the text give to show society's realization of the severity of the Holocaust in the postwar years?

MAKING CONNECTIONS

## THE DESTRUCTION OF WORLD WAR II

World War II left Japan, the Soviet Union, much of Europe and many other countries with damage to and destruction of historic buildings, monuments, and archeological sites as well as to a vast number of works of art, manuscripts, and books. This great loss of cultural heritage during World War II helped bring about The Convention for the Protection of Cultural Property in the Event of Armed Conflict which was adopted in 1954. The Convention is overseen by the United Nations Educational, Scientific, and Cultural Organization which is known as UNESCO.

The acceptance of this plan had important consequences. It meant that Soviet and British-American forces would meet in defeated Germany along a north-south dividing line. Soviet forces would liberate Eastern Europe. The Allies also agreed to a partition of postwar Germany.

The Big Three powers met again at Yalta in southern Russia in February 1945. By then, the defeat of Germany was **assured**. The Western powers, having once believed that the Soviets were in a weak position, now faced the reality of 11 million Soviet soldiers taking possession of Eastern Europe and much of central Europe.

Stalin was deeply suspicious of the Western powers. He wanted a buffer to protect the Soviet Union from possible future Western aggression. This meant establishing pro-Soviet governments along the Soviet Union's borders. Roosevelt favored the idea of self-determination for Europe. This involved a pledge to help liberated Europe create "democratic institutions of their own choice" through free elections. Roosevelt also agreed to Stalin's price for military aid against Japan: Sakhalin and the Kuril Islands, ruled by Japan, as well as two warm-water ports and railroad rights in Manchuria.

The creation of the United Nations was a major American concern. Both Churchill and Stalin accepted Roosevelt's plans for the establishment of the United Nations and set the first meeting for San Francisco in April 1945.

The issues of Germany and Eastern Europe were treated less decisively. After Germany surrendered, the Big Three agreed to divide Germany into four zones, one each for the United States, Great Britain, France, and the Soviet Union to occupy and to govern. Stalin compromised and agreed to free elections in Poland. However, it was clear that Stalin might not honor this provision for other Eastern European countries. The issue of free elections caused a serious split between the Soviets and Americans.

President Harry S. Truman's assumption of the presidency after Roosevelt's death followed by the use of the atomic bomb in Japan helped accelerate the disintegration of the fragile alliance among the Big Three. During the Potsdam Conference of July 1945, Truman demanded free elections in Eastern Europe. Stalin responded, "A freely elected government in any of these East European countries would be anti-Soviet, and that we cannot allow." Stalin sought absolute security for the Soviets. Free elections would threaten his goal of controlling Eastern Europe. Short of an invasion by Western forces, nothing would undo developments in Eastern Europe. After the war's most destructive conflict had just ended, very few supported a policy of invasion.

The Allies agreed that trials should be held of leaders who had committed crimes against humanity during the war. In 1945 and 1946, Nazi leaders were tried and condemned at war crimes trials in Nuremberg, Germany. War crimes trials were also held in Japan and Italy. The United Nations General Assembly voted unanimously in 1948 to create the United Nations Convention on the Prevention and Punishment of the Crime of Genocide, which criminalized acts committed to destroy ethnic, national, racial, or religious groups.

> "The privilege of opening the first trial in history for crimes against the peace of the world imposes a grave responsibility. The wrongs which we seek to condemn and punish have been so calculated, so malignant, and so devastating, that civilization cannot tolerate their being ignored, because it cannot survive their being repeated. That four great nations, flushed with victory and stung with injury stay the hand of vengeance and

ANALYZING PRIMARY SOURCES

1. **DETERMINING CENTRAL IDEAS** Jackson acknowledges in this opening statement that the trials he is initiating are a departure from the past. In what way does the central idea of this statement support this position?
2. **ANALYZING IDEAS** How does Jackson's presentation of information in the excerpt help to emphasize the legitimacy of the trials at Nuremberg?

voluntarily submit their captive enemies to the judgment of the law is one of the most significant tributes that Power has ever paid to Reason. ”

—Robert H. Jackson, opening statement before the international military tribunal

As the war slowly receded into the past, a new struggle was already beginning. Many in the West thought Soviet policy was part of a worldwide Communist conspiracy. The Soviets viewed Western, and especially American, policy as nothing less than global capitalist expansionism. This conflict between economic and political systems would come to define the post-World War II period.

In March 1946, in a speech to an American audience, the former British Prime Minister Winston Churchill declared that "an iron curtain" had "descended across the continent," dividing Europe into two hostile camps. Stalin branded Churchill's speech "a call to war on the USSR." Only months after the world's most devastating conflict had ended, the world seemed to be bitterly divided once again.

### ✓ CHECKING FOR UNDERSTANDING

1. **EXPLAINING CAUSES** What led to the Cold War?
2. **DETERMINING CONTEXT** What events and factors led the United States and the Soviet Union from being allies to being enemies?
3. **IDENTIFYING EFFECTS** How did the victorious countries agree to deal with Germany?

CITIZENSHIP

### THE UNITED NATIONS

In 1942, Franklin Delano Roosevelt used the term "United Nations" for the first time, in reference to the 26 countries that had pledged to fight against the Axis Powers. When World War II ended, the United States and its allies made the creation of the United Nations (UN) a priority, and representatives from 50 countries drew up the UN Charter in October 1945. The initial goal of the UN was collective security, reinforced by the UN Security Council as well as the General Assembly. Throughout the second half of the twentieth century, the UN worked on maintaining international peace and security, protecting human rights, and providing humanitarian aid. UN peacekeeping efforts included sending missions to war zones, which it continues to do in regions such as the Middle East.

**UNDERSTANDING CONTEXT**
Why was the United Nations an important institution in the years immediately following World War II?

Jackson, Robert H. 1945. International Military Tribunal Opening Statement. November 21, 1945. Nuremberg, Germany.

## LESSON 5 REVIEW

### Time and Place

1. **RELATING EVENTS** What was the connection between the fall of Italy and the end of World War II?

### Building History-Social Science Analysis Skills

2. **EXPLAINING EFFECTS** What were the long-term effects of dropping the atomic bomb in Japan at the end of World War II?
3. **IDENTIFYING CONNECTIONS** What effect did Stalin's suspicion of the Western powers at Yalta have on the negotiations and the postwar world order?
4. **CONTRASTING** Describe at least one difference between World War II and the Cold War, as described in the text.

### Writing About History

5. **ARGUMENTATIVE WRITING** Imagine that you are an adviser to President Truman. Persuade him to use or not to use the atomic bomb. How do you make your case?

### Collaborating

6. **ADAPTING SPEECH** As a class, engage in a Yalta press conference. Divide into groups representing the Soviets, the United States, Great Britain, and the press. What does each group consider important to express? What might the press want to know?

# STUDY GUIDE

## TWO ROADS TO WAR
### LESSON 1

**GERMANY**
- Begins a military draft that expands its army to 550,000 troops
- Sends troops to the Rhineland
- Becomes allied with Mussolini
- Annexes Austria to Germany
- Makes an agreement with Stalin called the Nazi-Soviet Nonaggression Pact
- Invades western Poland
- War declared on by Britain and France

**JAPAN**
- Invades Manchuria
- Withdraws from the League of Nations after the league condemns its actions against Manchuria
- Continues its expansion, with the military now controlling Japanese politics
- Declares war on China
- Attacks the United States and European colonies in Southeast Asia

## EARLY EVENTS OF WORLD WAR II
### LESSON 2

- **1939** Germany attacks Poland.
- **1940** Germany attacks Denmark, Norway, Netherlands, Belgium, and France.
- **1941** Japan attacks Pearl Harbor, and Germany declares war on the United States.
- **1942** Japan is defeated by the United States at the Battle of Midway Island.
- **1943** The Soviet army stops the German advance.

## THE HOME FRONT
### LESSON 3

**MOBILIZATION**

**UNITED STATES**
- New factories created boomtowns
- Produced much of the equipment the Allies needed
- New roles for African Americans led to racial tension

**SOVIET UNION**
- Moved factories inland
- Experienced poverty and food deprivation
- Responsible for producing 78,000 tanks and 98,000 artillery pieces

**GERMANY**
- Citizens not enthusiastic about the war
- Acquired food and raw materials from conquered countries
- Practiced mobilization of the economy near the end of the war

**JAPAN**
- Government controlled all natural resources
- Pilots known as "kamikazes" were encouraged to sacrifice themselves in suicide missions
- Reluctant to mobilize women on behalf of the war effort

## THE HOLOCAUST
### LESSON 4

**Genocide** the deliberate mass murder or physical extinction of a particular racial, political, or cultural group

**The Final Solution** the attempted genocide of the Jewish people by the SS

***Einsatzgruppen*** a special strike force created to carry out The Final Solution

**Death Camps** camps where Jews were contained and worked or starved to death, medically experimented upon, or executed

**Death Toll** The Germans killed more than 6 million Jews, more than 3 million of them in the death camps.

## THE END OF WORLD WAR II
### LESSON 5

**The European Theater**

**Germany** surrendered when the Allies liberated Paris and crossed the Rhine River, advancing into Germany, and when Soviet troops reoccupied the Ukraine and moved into the Baltic states, Warsaw, Hungary, Romania, and Bulgaria.

**The Asian Theater**

**Japan** surrendered after the United States captured the islands of Iwo Jima and Okinawa and then dropped atomic bombs on the Japanese cities of Hiroshima and Nagasaki.

# CHAPTER 11 Assessment

**Directions: On a separate sheet of paper, answer the questions below. Make sure you read carefully and answer all parts of the questions.**

## Short Answer

1. **IDENTIFYING CAUSES** Why did world powers first try to appease or ignore Germany's and Japan's expansionist policies?

2. **RELATING EVENTS** What role did the Munich Conference play in igniting World War II?

3. **UNDERSTANDING CONTEXT** What new technology and strategy of war made Hitler's invasion of Poland so successful?

4. **IDENTIFYING CONNECTIONS** Why was Hitler interested in conquering the Soviet Union early in the war?

5. **SUMMARIZING** What was the effect of new airplane technology on World War II strategies? Was this strategy successful?

6. **EXPLAINING EFFECTS** What was the effect of total mobilization within Germany? When did this occur?

7. **SUMMARIZING** What was the Holocaust? What methods did the Nazis use to carry out the Holocaust?

8. **IDENTIFYING EFFECTS** How did nationalists from Asian countries occupied by the Japanese react to the Japanese presence?

9. **IDENTIFYING CAUSES** What was one major factor in President Truman's decision to drop the atomic bomb?

10. **IDENTIFYING CONNECTIONS** What political tensions, suspicions, and conflict of ideologies led to the Cold War?

## History and Social-Science Analysis

11. **INTERPRETING** What were Germany's and Japan's goals when they expanded? How did they treat the people who lived in occupied regions?

12. **ANALYZING CHANGE** After the Munich Conference, how did Winston Churchill's perspective on Hitler's demands differ from British Prime Minister Neville Chamberlain's perspective?

13. **UNDERSTANDING CHANGE** Explain Stalin's role prior to and during World War II. In your response, explain Stalin's relationship with Hitler before the war, why their relationship changed, and Stalin's response.

14. **SUMMARIZING** How did Churchill perform as prime minister during World War II?

15. **IDENTIFYING CONNECTIONS** What resources was Hideki Tōjō looking for when Japan attacked Southeast Asia? What dilemma did Tōjō face, and how did the bombing of Pearl Harbor seem like a solution? Describe the roles of Tōjō and U.S. President Roosevelt during this period of World War II.

16. **EVALUATING** Define and describe the lasting effects of the Nazis' attempts to implement the Final Solution.

## Analyzing Visuals

*Use the poster to answer the following question.*

17. **UNDERSTANDING CHANGE** This poster from 1942 encouraged American women to participate in the war effort. What message is this propaganda poster sending? What does this poster tell you about the changing roles of women during World War II?

**Need Extra Help?**

| If You've Missed Question | 1 | 2 | 3 | 4 | 5 | 6 | 7 | 8 | 9 | 10 | 11 | 12 | 13 | 14 | 15 | 16 | 17 |
|---|---|---|---|---|---|---|---|---|---|---|---|---|---|---|---|---|---|
| Review Lesson | 1 | 1 | 2 | 2 | 3 | 3 | 4 | 4 | 5 | 5 | 1 | 1 | 1, 5 | 2, 3 | 4 | 4 | 3 |

**18** **DESCRIBING** Create a chart that records the countries Nazi Germany invaded and controlled while World War II raged. Following World War II, many of the same countries fell under Soviet control. Maintain and update this chart as you learn more about the years following the end of the war.

**19** **ANALYZING SOURCES** Using the map from your Place and Time feature, analyze why France was strategically important to an Allied victory.

**20** **EXPLAINING ISSUES** Why was the death toll so high in World War II?

**21** **CONSTRUCTING HYPOTHESES** What was the significance of the Yalta Conference to the beginning of the Cold War?

**22** **USING MAPS** Working with a small group, find a map of the world showing borders after World War II. Mark four borders that changed because of the war, and write labels explaining how political decisions contributed to those changes. Add visuals of some of the people and places affected by them. You may include primary sources.

## Research and Presentation

**23** **RESEARCHING FOR INQUIRY** Research the Sino-Japanese War. How does knowledge of this conflict provide you with context for better understanding the ideologies, goals, and strategies of the Axis Powers? Write an essay in which you compare the two, making sure to include the role of civilians and the horrors of the Rape of Nanjing in your analysis. Then, present your essay to the class.

## Reading and Analyzing Primary Sources

Use the document to answer the following questions.

After the United States dropped the first atomic bomb, the White House released a statement announcing the bombing of Hiroshima.

> "Sixteen hours ago an American airplane dropped one bomb on Hiroshima and destroyed its usefulness to the enemy. That bomb had more power than 20,000 tons of TNT. It had more than two thousand times the blast power of the British 'Grand Slam' which is the largest bomb ever yet used in the history of warfare. The Japanese began the war from the air at Pearl Harbor. They have been repaid many fold. And the end is not yet."
>
> —from a White House press release, August 6, 1945

**24** **DETERMINING MEANING** Why does the White House refer to Japan as "the enemy"?

**A.** To help convince the American people that the United States had the power to defeat Japan
**B.** To help convince the American people that the United States was justified in dropping the atomic bomb
**C.** To make a distinction between the Japanese and the British
**D.** To explain why the war continued even after the atomic bomb was dropped

**25** **DETERMINING CENTRAL IDEAS** What is the White House's belief about the future of the war?

**A.** That the bomb in Hiroshima will stop it
**B.** That it will worsen after the dropping of the bomb
**C.** That it will now improve, though not stop
**D.** That the war will continue to go on

**26** **ANALYZING TEXT PRESENTATION** How does the White House statement shift blame for the dropping of the bomb?

**A.** By implying that the Japanese attack at Pearl Harbor was the reason for the Hiroshima bomb
**B.** By comparing American bomb strength to that of the British
**C.** By stating that the city of Hiroshima will no longer be useful to the Japanese
**D.** By claiming that the United States has already repaid the Japanese several times over

## Writing About History

**27** **EXPLANATORY WRITING** Based on what you read in this chapter, what were the effects of World War II on international relations during the second half of the twentieth century? In your response, analyze not only conflicts but also the formation of alliances.

## Speaking and Listening About History

**28** **PRESENTING** In wartime, ordinary people can do terrible things. Write and present a speech in which you trace how the German machinery of death grew as large as it did and why the Germans were complicit in it.

**Need Extra Help?**

| If You've Missed Question | 18 | 19 | 20 | 21 | 22 | 23 | 24 | 25 | 26 | 27 | 28 |
|---|---|---|---|---|---|---|---|---|---|---|---|
| Review Lesson | 1–5 | 1, 5 | 1–5 | 5 | 5 | 1 | 5 | 5 | 5 | 5 | 4 |

◂ *During an impromptu "kitchen debate," Soviet Premier Nikita Khrushchev and U.S. Vice President Richard Nixon argued about politics at the American National Exhibit in Moscow, 1959. They are pictured here, quarrelling in the kitchen of a model suburban American home.*

**1945 — 1989**

# The Cold War

## CHAPTER 12



**GO DIGITAL**
*It's All online!*

## ASKING AN ESSENTIAL QUESTION

***How does conflict influence political relationships?***

**What Will You Learn?** You will learn how post-World War II rivalries led to the decades-long Cold War and how that conflict played out across the world.

**Why Does This Matter?** For much of the 20th century, a "Cold War" between the United States and the Soviet Union shaped international relations. Although they did not engage in open warfare, their conflict led to uprisings, coups, and wars in Latin America, Africa, and Asia. The relationships and rivalries formed during the Cold War continue to shape international politics and trade today. The modern age also owes much of its scientific advancement, too, to the competition that ensued between the superpowers.

**How Will You Know That You Learned It?** You will be able to identify key figures that shaped Cold War policies as well as to explain the major ideologies and the causes and effects of significant events that played out during the Cold War.

**Using Your Inquiry Journal** As you read this chapter and examine the primary sources, use your Inquiry Journal to help you make notes and expand your list of questions. As you gather information, think about how you will answer the Essential Question above.

Howard Sochurek/The LIFE Picture Collection/Getty Images

# PLACE & TIME U.S. and USSR 1945–1975

The United States and the Soviet Union were allies during World War II but enemies after 1945 until 1989, a period known as the Cold War. The world came to be divided into United States-aligned, Soviet Union-aligned, and nonaligned camps. Although the United States and the Soviet Union avoided direct military confrontation, they intervened in proxy wars and influenced foreign policy in other nations. Especially in the early years of the Cold War, both sides saw the struggle between them as one between communism and capitalism.

## STEP INTO THE PLACE

Read the quotes and look at the information presented on the map.

1. **GLOBAL INTERCONNECTIONS** Where were most U.S.-aligned nations? What about Soviet-aligned nations?

2. **COMPARING POINTS OF VIEW** What does Khrushchev mean when he says that socialism will win over capitalism because "the socialist mode of production possesses decisive advantages over the capitalist mode of production"? How does Eisenhower's advice "to look behind the mask" try to refute such claims?

"When we say that the socialist system will win in the competition between the two systems—the capitalist and the socialist—this by no means signifies that its victory will be achieved through armed interference by the socialist countries in the internal affairs of the capitalist countries. Our certainty of the victory of communism is based on the fact that the socialist mode of production possesses decisive advantages over the capitalist mode of production. Precisely because of this, the ideas of Marxism-Leninism are more and more capturing the minds of the broad masses of the working people in the capitalist countries, just as they have captured the minds of millions of men and women in our country and the People's Democracies."

—Premier Nikita Khrushchev, from the Report to the Twentieth Party Congress, February 1956

"International Communism, of course, seeks to mask its purposes of domination by expressions of good will and by superficially attractive offers of political, economic and military aid. But any free nation, which is the subject of Soviet enticement, ought, in elementary wisdom, to look behind the mask. Remember Estonia, Latvia and Lithuania! . . .

Soviet control of the satellite nations of Eastern Europe has been forcibly maintained in spite of solemn promises of a contrary intent, made during World War II. . . ."

—President Dwight D. Eisenhower, Special Message to the Congress on the Situation in the Middle East, January 5, 1957



## STEP INTO THE TIME

**ANALYZING CHANGE**

Based on the time line, where did violent confrontations unfold during the Cold War?

### THE USSR & THE U.S.

- **1945** World War II ends
- **1947** U.S. President Truman establishes Truman Doctrine
- **1949** NATO forms
- **1954** U.S. backs coup in Guatemala
- **1955** Warsaw Pact forms

**1945** — **1955**

### WORLD EVENTS

- **1946** Civil war erupts in China
- **September 1949** Mao Zedong takes control of China
- **June 1950** Korean War begins
- **July 1954** Geneva Accords divide Vietnam

## THE COLD WAR 1962

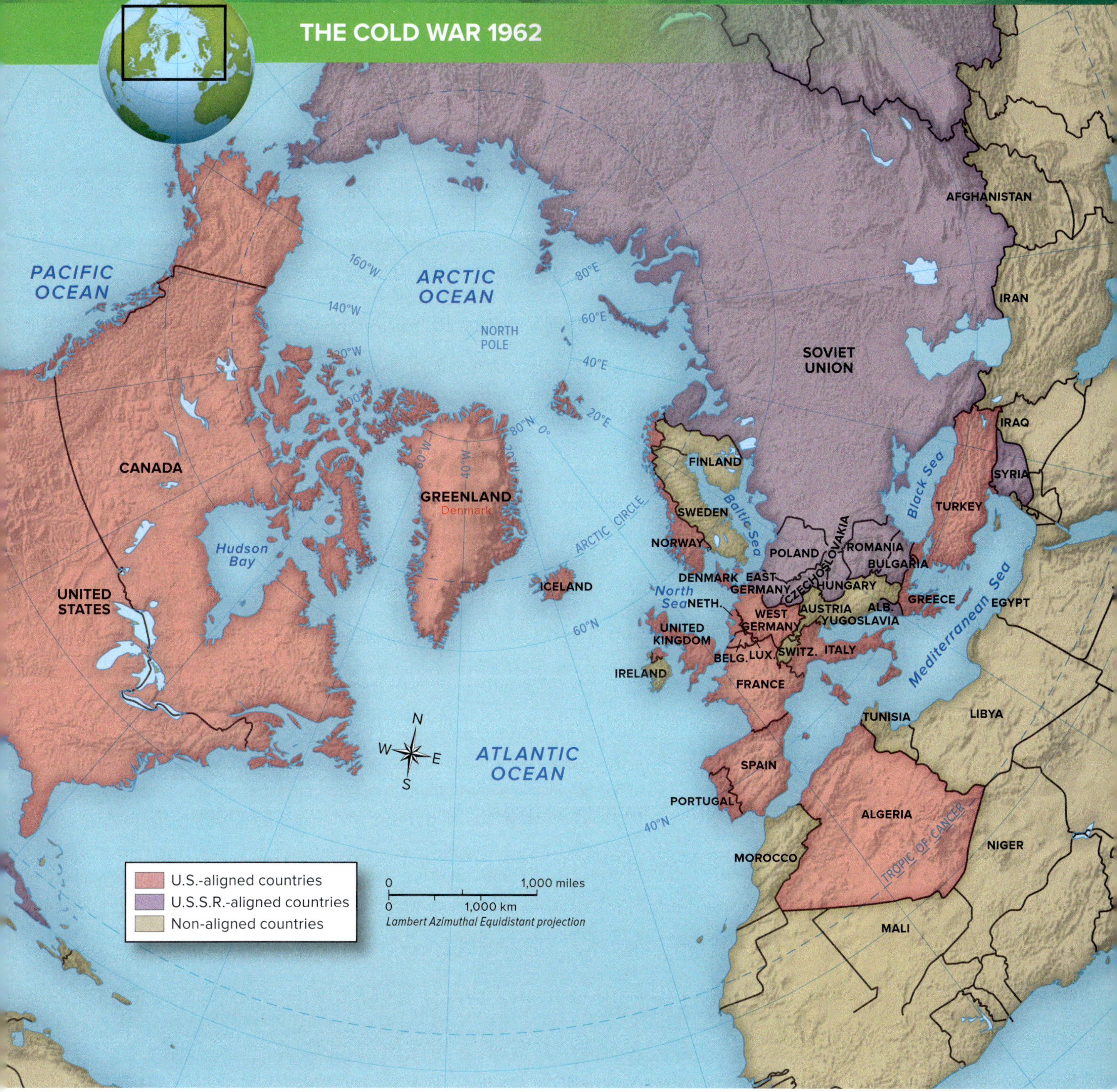


**1957** Soviets launch Sputnik I

**1958** Mao Zedong begins the Great Leap Forward

**1961** Berlin Wall is constructed

**1961** U.S. approves Bay of Pigs invasion in Cuba

**1962** Cuban missile crisis

**1965**

**1965** U.S. troops join combat in Vietnam

**1966** Mao Zedong launches Great Proletarian Cultural Revolution in China

**1972** U.S. President Nixon makes a state visit to China

**1973** U.S. supports coup in Chile

**1975**

**April 17, 1975** North Vietnam defeats South Vietnam; war ends

ESSENTIAL QUESTION

- *How does conflict influence political relationships?*

LESSON 1

# The Cold War Begins

## THE STORY BEGINS...

During the Hungarian uprising in 1956, the revolutionary forces won a brief victory. They succeeded in forming a new government under elected leader Imry Nagy [EEM•ray NAHDJ]. However, Soviet forces returned and captured Budapest. Nagy made this final statement before being seized by the Soviets.

> "This fight is the fight for freedom by the Hungarian people against the Russian intervention, and it is possible that I shall only be able to stay at my post for one or two hours. The whole world will see how the Russian armed forces, contrary to all treaties and conventions, are crushing the resistance of the Hungarian people. They will also see how they are kidnapping the Prime Minister of a country which is a Member of the United Nations, taking him from the capital, and therefore it cannot be doubted at all that this is the most brutal form of intervention. I should like in these last moments to ask the leaders of the revolution, if they can, to leave the country."

—Prime Minister Imry Nagy, November 4, 1956

The violent clashes that resulted from Soviet attempts to suppress discontent among Hungarian workers, students, and others who demanded greater freedoms symbolized the divide between pro-Communist and anti-Communist forces in the Cold War.

*In October 1956, popular discontent led to an uprising against the Soviet-backed Communist government in Hungary. Masses of people protested, burned Communist books, and issued demands. The Soviet Union responded by sending in troops to quell the rebellion.* ▶

| Actions by the United States | Responses by the Soviet Union |
|---|---|
| | |
| | |
| | |

**ANALYZING KEY IDEAS AND DETAILS**

**IDENTIFYING EFFECTS** Read closely to identify actions taken by the United States and responses by the Soviet Union. Record these actions in a graphic organizer like this one. Be sure to include relevant dates.

# BALANCE OF POWER AFTER WORLD WAR II

**GUIDING QUESTION** *Why did the United States and the Soviet Union become political rivals after World War II?*

After the Axis was defeated, the differences between the United States and the Soviet Union became apparent. Stalin still feared the capitalist West, and Western leaders still had a great fear of communism. It was not surprising that these different political and economic systems resulted in conflict.

Because of its need to feel secure on its western border, the Soviet Union was not prepared to give up its control of Eastern Europe after Germany's defeat. Nor were American leaders willing to give up the power and prestige the United States had gained throughout the world. Suspicious of each other's motives, the United States and the Soviet Union soon became rivals.

Eastern Europe was the first area of disagreement. The United States and Great Britain believed the **liberated** nations there should freely determine their own governments. Stalin, however, fearful these nations would be anti-Soviet if they were permitted to have free elections, opposed this idea. Having freed Eastern Europe from the Nazis, the Soviet army stayed in the conquered areas and set up pro-Soviet regimes in Poland, Romania, Bulgaria, and Hungary.

Former British Prime Minister Winston Churchill delivered the following speech at Westminster College in Fulton, Missouri. Some historians argue that Churchill's speech signaled the start of the Cold War.

> "A shadow has fallen upon the scenes so lately lighted by the Allied victory. Nobody knows what Soviet Russia and its Communist international organization intends to do in the immediate future, or what are the limits, if any, to their expansive and proselytizing tendencies. . . ."
>
> —Winston Churchill, "The Sinews of Peace," March 5, 1946

Joseph Stalin responded:

> "In substance, Mr. Churchill now stands in the position of a firebrand of war. . . . Mr. Churchill begins to set war loose, also by a racial theory, maintaining that only nations speaking the English language are fully valuable nations, called upon to decide the destinies of the entire world. . . . Mr. Churchill wanders around the truth when he speaks of the growth of the influence of the Communist parties in Eastern Europe. . . ."
>
> —Joseph Stalin, interview with *Pravda*, March 14, 1946

**UNDERSTANDING CRAFT AND STRUCTURE**

1. **DETERMINING POINT OF VIEW** What point of view does the author express in the first paragraph of the section? How does the section support that point of view?
2. **ANALYZING TEXT PRESENTATION** What does the heading of the section suggest about the rivalry between the United States and the Soviet Union? How do the subheadings organize information to develop that idea?

**ANALYZING PRIMARY SOURCES**

1. **COMPARING POINTS OF VIEW** How do Churchill and Stalin differ in their opinions on the expansion of communism in Eastern Europe?
2. **EVALUATING EVIDENCE** How does Churchill imply that the Soviet Union has escalated tensions in Europe? How does Stalin imply that Churchill is the one escalating tensions?

(t)Churchill, Winston S. 1946. The Sinews of Peace. March 5, 1946. Westminster College, Fulton, Missouri. Reproduced in NATO On-Line Library; (b)Stalin, Joseph. 1946. Stalin's Reply to Churchill. March 14, 1946 (Interview with Pravda). The New York Times.

A civil war in Greece created another area of conflict between the superpowers. The Communist People's Liberation Army and anti-Communist forces, supported largely by Great Britain, fought for control of Greece in 1946. However, Britain was suffering from its own economic problems immediately after the end of World War II. As a result, it needed to withdraw its aid from the anti-Communist forces in Greece.

*Goods sent as part of the Marshall Plan arrive at Royal Victoria Dock in London, England, on February 3, 1949.*

## THE TRUMAN DOCTRINE AND THE MARSHALL PLAN

President Harry S. Truman of the United States, alarmed by British weakness and the possibility of Soviet expansion into the eastern Mediterranean, responded with the Truman Doctrine in 1947. This doctrine said that the United States would provide money to countries (in this case, Greece and Turkey) that were threatened by Communist expansion. If the Soviet Union was not stopped in Greece and Turkey, the Truman argument ran, then the United States would have to face the spread of communism throughout the free world. As Dean Acheson, U.S. undersecretary of state, explained on February 29, 1947:

> “Like apples in a barrel infected by one rotten one, the corruption of Greece would infect Iran and all to the east. It would also carry infection to Africa through Asia Minor and Egypt, and to Europe . . .”

—from *Present at the Creation: My Years in the State Department*

The Truman Doctrine was soon followed by the European Recovery Program. Proposed in June 1947 by General George C. Marshall, then the United States secretary of state, it is better known as the Marshall Plan. Marshall believed that communism was successful only in countries that had economic problems. Thus, to prevent the spread of communism, the Marshall Plan would provided many countries with aid. The Marshall Plan supplied close to $13 billion to rebuild war-torn Europe.

The Marshall Plan did not intend to exclude the Soviet Union or its economically and politically dependent Eastern European **satellite states**, also known as client states. Those states refused to participate, however. According to the Soviet view, the Marshall Plan guaranteed "American loans in return for the relinquishing by the European states of their economic and later also their political independence." The Soviets saw the Marshall Plan as an attempt to buy the support of the smaller European countries.

In 1949 the Soviet Union responded to the Marshall Plan by founding the Council for Mutual Economic Assistance (COMECON) for the economic cooperation of the Eastern European states. COMECON was meant to counteract the Marshall Plan, especially in Eastern Europe. COMECON largely failed, however, because the Soviets were unable to provide much in the way of financial aid.

By 1947, the split in Europe between the United States and the Soviet Union had become a fact of life. In July 1947, George Kennan, a well-known U.S. diplomat with much knowledge of Soviet affairs, argued for a **policy of containment** to keep communism within its existing boundaries and to prevent further Soviet aggressive moves. Containment of the Soviet Union became formal U.S. policy.

**DETERMINING CENTRAL IDEAS**
How did the Marshall Plan try to help European nations recover from World War II? What type of assistance does the photograph show?

**DETERMINING MEANING**

The word *satellite* refers to natural objects, such as moons, and human-made objects, such as *Sputnik I*, that orbit planets. How does this help you understand the meaning of **satellite state**?

**DETERMINING MEANING**

A *policy* is a way of doing something. To *contain* means "to hold, or keep, something inside something else." Use these definitions to explain the U.S. **policy of containment**.

## THE DIVISION OF GERMANY AND THE BERLIN AIRLIFT

The fate of Germany also became a source of heated contention between the Soviets and the West. At the end of World War II, the Allied Powers had divided Germany into four occupation zones, each occupied by one of the Allies—the United States, the Soviet Union, Great Britain, and France. The city of Berlin itself, located deep inside the Soviet zone, was also divided into four occupation zones.

The foreign ministers of the four occupying powers met repeatedly in an attempt to arrive at a final peace treaty with Germany, but they had little success. At the same time, Great Britain, France, and the United States gradually began to merge their zones economically. By February 1948, Great Britain, France, and the United States were making plans to unify the three Western sections of Germany (and their sections of Berlin) and create a West German government.

The Soviets reacted with a blockade of West Berlin, which allowed neither trucks, nor trains, nor barges to enter the city's three Western zones. Food and supplies could no longer get through to the 2.5 million people in these zones. The Russians hoped to secure economic control of all Berlin and force the Western powers to halt the creation of a separate West German state.

The Western powers faced a dilemma. No one wanted to risk World War III. Therefore, an attempt to break through the Soviet blockade with tanks and trucks was ruled out. However, how could the people in the Western zones of Berlin be kept alive when the whole city was blockaded inside the Soviet zone? The solution was the Berlin Airlift—supplies would be flown in by American and British airplanes. For more than 10 months, more than 200,000 flights carried 2.3 million tons (1.4 million t) of supplies. At the height of the Berlin Airlift, 13,000 tons (11,800 t) of supplies were flown daily to Berlin. The Soviets, also not wanting war, finally gave in and lifted the blockade in May 1949.

The blockade of Berlin increased tensions between the United States and the Soviet Union. It also brought the separation of Germany into two states. In September 1949, the Federal Republic of Germany, or West Germany, was formally created. Its capital was Bonn. Less than a month later, a separate East German state, the German Democratic Republic, was set up by the Soviets. East Berlin became its capital. Berlin was now divided into two parts, a reminder of the division between West and East.

*German children cheer an American cargo plane airlifting supplies to Berlin in 1948.*

**UNDERSTANDING CONTEXT** Why do the children in this photograph look so excited? How might their lives have been different had Western powers not conducted the Berlin Airlift?

### ☑ CHECKING FOR UNDERSTANDING

1. **IDENTIFYING CAUSES** Why did the United States and the Soviet Union become political rivals after World War II?
2. **RELATING EVENTS** How did the Greek civil war lead to the Truman Doctrine and the Marshall Plan?
3. **UNDERSTANDING CONTEXT** Why did the blockade of Berlin probably seem like a good strategy to the Soviet Union?

**ANALYZING KEY IDEAS AND DETAILS**

1. **SUMMARIZING** How did the Cold War spread? Summarize the section of text that explains the expansion of Cold War tensions geographically.
2. **CITING TEXT EVIDENCE** What evidence does the text give to justify the stockpiling of nuclear weapons? How does the text explain the reasoning behind this evidence?

**GEOGRAPHIC REASONING**

1. **SPATIAL THINKING** How do geographic factors appear to shape the alliances formed under NATO and the Warsaw Pact?
2. **GLOBAL INTERCONNECTIONS** Draw a T-chart, and list the member nations of NATO and the Warsaw Pact as of 1955.

# THE SPREAD OF THE COLD WAR

**GUIDING QUESTION** *What was the result of increased tensions between the superpowers?*

In 1949 the Cold War spread from Europe to the rest of the world. The Communists' victory in the Chinese civil war created a new Communist regime and strengthened fears in the United States about the spread of communism.

## NEW MILITARY ALLIANCES

The search for security during the Cold War led to the formation of new military alliances. The North Atlantic Treaty Organization (NATO) was formed in April 1949 when Belgium, Luxembourg, France, the Netherlands, Great Britain, Italy, Denmark, Norway, Portugal, and Iceland signed a treaty with the United States and Canada. These powers agreed to provide mutual help if any one of them was attacked. A few years later, Greece and Turkey joined, followed by West Germany.

The Eastern European states soon followed suit with a military alliance. In 1955 the Soviet Union joined with Albania, Bulgaria, Czechoslovakia, East Germany, Hungary, Poland, and Romania in a formal military alliance known as the Warsaw Pact. The alliance operated much like NATO in that member states were required to provide mutual help if any other member was attacked. The Soviet Union also wanted to increase its sphere of influence and to protect its territories in Eastern Europe. The alliance, the Soviet Union hoped, would further its control over the militaries of its Eastern European allies. Europe was once again divided into hostile alliance systems, just as it had been before World War I.

**NATO AND WARSAW PACT MEMBERS 1949–1955**

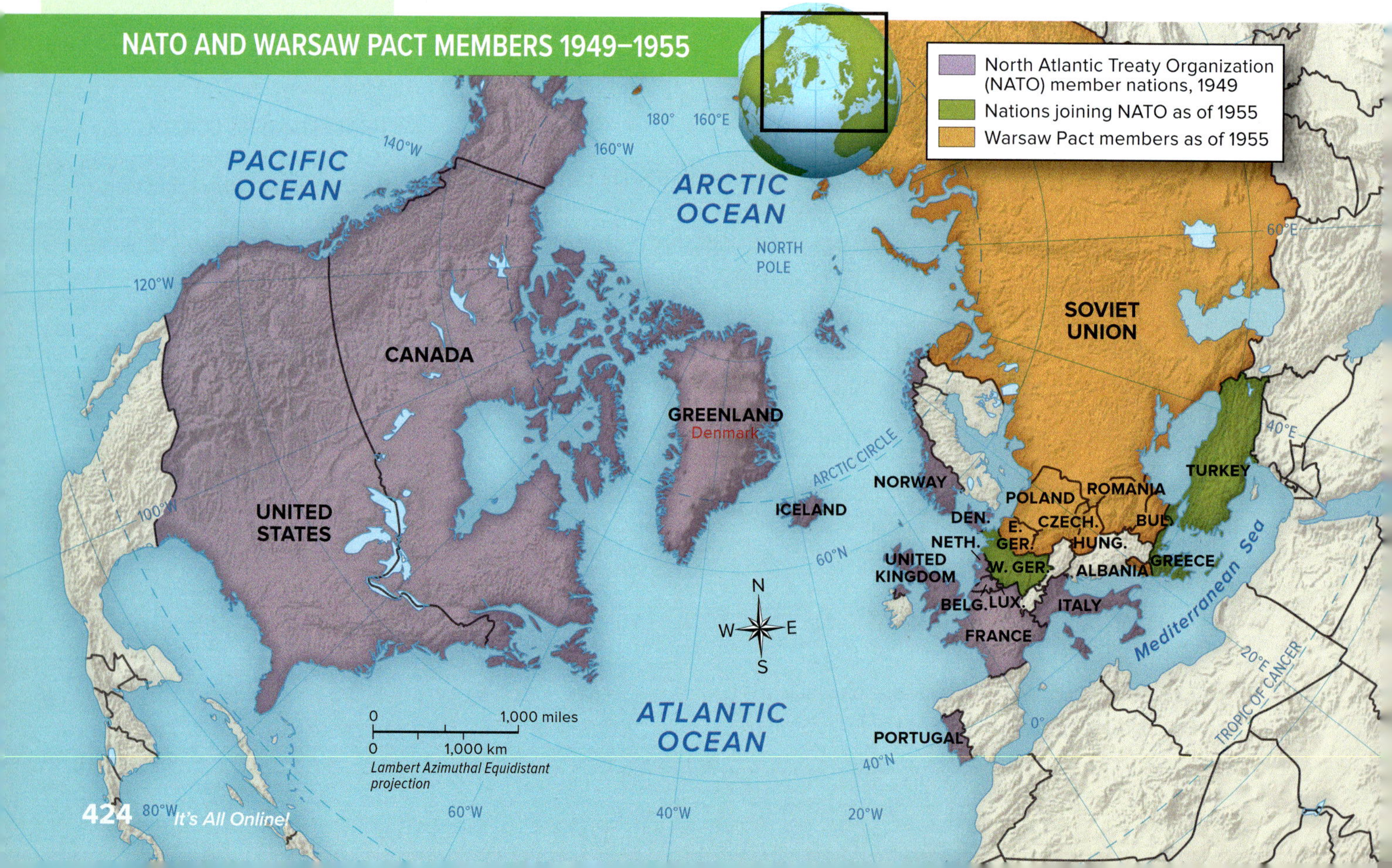

New military alliances spread to the rest of the world after the United States became involved in the Korean War. The war began in 1950 as an attempt by the Communist government of North Korea, which was allied with the Soviet Union, to take over South Korea. The Korean War confirmed American fears of Communist expansion. More determined than ever to contain Soviet power, the United States extended its military alliances around the world. By the mid-1950s, the United States was in military alliances with 42 states around the world.

## THE ARMS RACE BEGINS

By the mid-1950s, the United States and the Soviet Union had become involved in a growing **arms race**, in which both countries built up their armies, increased the size of their weapons arsenal, and competed over advancements in nuclear weapons technology. **Nuclear** weapons added an increasingly frightening element to the arms race as each superpower raced to build deadlier bombs and farther-reaching delivery systems.

Also by the mid-1950s, the United States feared that the Soviet Union was gaining ground in the arms race. The Soviet Union had set off its first atomic bomb in 1949. In the early 1950s, the Soviet Union and the United States developed the deadlier hydrogen bomb. By the late-1950s, both had intercontinental ballistic missiles (ICBMs), which made them capable of sending bombs anywhere.

The United States and the Soviet Union now worked to build up stockpiles of nuclear weapons. The search for security soon took the form of **deterrence**. This policy held that huge arsenals of nuclear weapons on both sides prevented war. The belief was that neither side would launch a nuclear attack, because both knew that the other side would be able to strike back with devastating power.

**DETERMINING MEANING**

To better understand **arms race**, break down the phrase. *Arms* refer to weapons. A *race* is a contest to see which competitor can reach a goal, such as a finish line, fastest. Use these meanings to write a definition for **arms race** in your own words. Use a dictionary or online resource to check your definition.

**DETERMINING MEANING**

To *deter* means to stop someone from doing something because of the threat of punishment. What does **deterrence** mean?

**DETERMINING MEANING** What does "the first artificial satellite" mean? Why is that achievement important?

**MAKING CONNECTIONS TO TECHNOLOGY**

### SATELLITE TECHNOLOGY

When the Soviet Union launched *Sputnik* I into orbit, leaders in the United States were shocked by the engineering success of the Soviets. These leaders were interested in the military applications of satellites. But the civilian applications were equally important. *Sputnik,* for example, was designed to collect information on the density of the atmosphere, to test methods of orbital tracking, and to test how radio waves can travel through the atmosphere.

Since *Sputnik,* many hundreds of satellites have been launched into space. Currently, there are more than 1,400 satellites orbiting Earth. Any one of them is infinitely more powerful than *Sputnik I.* Although we do not see them, these satellites power our modern world. Without them, we would not have GPS mapping, cell phones, accurate weather forecasts, and any number of other communication applications.

1. **CITING TEXT EVIDENCE** What evidence from the passage suggests that the space race was part of the larger arms race that took place during the Cold War?
2. **UNDERSTANDING CONTEXT** How did the launch of *Sputnik I* pave the way toward today's modern digital age?

The Soviet Union launched *Sputnik I,* the first artificial satellite, on October 4, 1957.

NASA

Bridges, Styles. Quoted 2013 by Yanek Mieczkowski. Eisenhower's Sputnik Moment: The Race for Space and World Prestige. Ithaca: Cornell University Press.

In 1957 the Soviets sent *Sputnik I*, the first human-made space satellite, to orbit Earth. New fears seized the American public. Was there a "missile gap" between the United States and the Soviet Union? Could the Soviet Union build a military base in outer space from which it could dominate the world? One American senator said, "The time has clearly come ... [for Americans] to be prepared to shed blood, sweat and tears if this country and the free world are to survive."

## A WALL IN BERLIN

Nikita Khrushchev (kroosh • CHAWF), who emerged as the new leader of the Soviet Union in 1955, tried to take advantage of the American concern over missiles to solve the problem of West Berlin. West Berlin remained a "Western island" of prosperity in the midst of the relatively poverty-stricken East Germany. Many East Germans, tired of Communist repression, managed to escape East Germany by fleeing through West Berlin.

Khrushchev realized the need to stop the flow of refugees from East Germany through West Berlin. In August 1961, the East German government began to build a wall separating West Berlin from East Berlin. Eventually it became a massive concrete block wall 15 feet (4.5 m) high topped with barbed wire. Hundreds of machine-gun watchtowers lined the wall, which stretched 28 miles (45 km) through the city. Another 75-mile- (120.7-km-) long section of wall separated West Berlin from the surrounding East German countryside. The Berlin Wall became a striking symbol of the division between the two superpowers.

### ✓ CHECKING FOR UNDERSTANDING

1. **EXPLAINING EFFECTS** What was the result of increased tension among the superpowers?
2. **EVALUATING** Why did the United States and the USSR form new military alliances? What comparison does the text make with these alliances, and what does that comparison imply?
3. **INTERPRETING** How was the Berlin Wall proof of the tensions in the Cold War?

## LESSON 1 REVIEW

### Time and Place

1. **ANALYZING CHANGE** Explain why the Cold War happened when it did.

### Building History-Social Science Analysis Skills

2. **UNDERSTANDING CHANGE** How did political tensions in the Cold War spur technological change?
3. **EXPLAINING CAUSE AND EFFECT** How did the Soviet Union respond to specific actions taken by the United States? How did the United States respond to Soviet actions?
4. **IDENTIFYING BIAS** Read the primary source quote from Dean Acheson. What bias does he show with his use of the words *infected, rotten, corrupted,* and *infection*? How does his statement reflect a larger sentiment characteristic of the Cold War?

### Writing About History

5. **ARGUMENTATIVE WRITING** Write an essay in which you argue whether using nuclear weapons as a form of deterrence was an effective strategy for preventing conflict between the West and the Soviet Union. Be sure to cite evidence from the text to support your position.

### Collaborating

6. **PRESENTING** You and a partner are members of the team working on the Marshall Plan. What kind of research do you need to do to insure aid goes to locations that need it most? Work together to create a proposal for delivery of aid to a specific country to present to the class.

## ESSENTIAL QUESTION

- *How does conflict influence political relationships?*

LESSON 2

# China After World War II

# THE STORY BEGINS...

In 1921, Mao Zedong attended a meeting of the newly formed Chinese Communist Party. He became leader of the party a decade later. In 1949, he gave a speech in honor of the party's 28th anniversary, just a few months before declaring the formation of the People's Republic of China.

> "China cannot have a bourgeois republic because she is a country suffering under imperialist oppression. The only way is through a people's republic led by the working class. . . . Our present task is to strengthen the people's state apparatus—mainly the people's army, the people's police and the people's courts—in order to consolidate national defense and protect the people's interests. Given this condition, China can develop steadily, under the leadership of the working class and the Communist Party, from an agricultural into an industrial country and from a new-democratic into a socialist and communist society, can abolish classes and realize the Great Harmony. . . . The Communist Party of the Soviet Union is our best teacher and we must learn from it."

—Mao Zedong, June 30, 1949

The victory of Communist guerrillas and the Communist Party in China further hardened U.S. resolve to stop the spread of communism during the Cold War.

*Chinese officials relied in part on the "Little Red Book," a collection of quotations by Chinese Communist leader Mao Zedong, to spread Mao's ideas and to unify and educate China's military forces.* ▶

PHOTO:Rolls Press/Popperfoto/Getty Images; TEXT:Tse-Tung, Mao. 1949. Speech 'In Commemoration of the 28th Anniversary of the Communist Party of China, June 30, 1949'. Selected Works, Vol. 5. New York: International Publishers.

| Changes in Communist China |
| --- |
| |
| |
| |
| |
| |
| |

### ANALYZING KEY IDEAS AND DETAILS

**UNDERSTANDING CHANGE** Read closely to identify changes that took place in China under communist rule. Record these changes in a graphic organizer like this one.

# CIVIL WAR IN CHINA

### ANALYZING KEY IDEAS AND DETAILS

1. **SUMMARIZING** How did Mao Zedong change China? Write a summary of how Mao came to power and what his government did.
2. **CITING TEXT EVIDENCE** What point does the text try to make about the Great Leap Forward? What evidence supports that central idea?

**GUIDING QUESTIONS** *How did Mao use economic policies to try to establish a classless society? Why did Mao believe permanent revolution was necessary?*

At the end of World War II, two Chinese governments existed side by side. The Nationalist government of Chiang Kai-shek, based in southern and central China, was supported by the United States. The Communists, led by Mao Zedong, had built a strong base in northern China. By the end of World War II, 20 to 30 million Chinese were living under Communist rule. The People's Liberation Army of the Communists included nearly 1 million troops.

When efforts to form a coalition government in 1946 failed, a full-scale civil war broke out between the Nationalists and the Communists. In the countryside, promises of land attracted millions of peasants to the Communist Party. Many joined Mao's People's Liberation Army. In the cities, middle-class Chinese, who were alienated by Chiang's repressive policies, supported the Communists. Chiang's troops began to defect to the Communists. Sometimes whole divisions—officers and ordinary soldiers—changed sides.

By 1948, the People's Liberation Army had surrounded Beijing. The following spring, it crossed the Chang Jiang (Yangtze River) and occupied Shanghai. During the next few months, Chiang Kai-shek and 2 million followers fled to the island of Taiwan. On October 1, 1949, Mao Zedong mounted the rostrum of the Gate of Heavenly Peace in Beijing and made a victory statement to the thousands gathered in the square before him. "The Chinese people have stood up," he said, "nobody will insult us again."

## THE GREAT LEAP FORWARD

The Communist Party, under the leadership of its chairman, Mao Zedong, now ruled China. In 1955 the Chinese government launched a new program to build a socialist society. Virtually all private farmland was collectivized. Peasant families were allowed to keep small plots for their private use, but they worked chiefly in large collective farms. The elite members of society were also made to work the collective farms. In addition, most industry and commerce was nationalized.

Chinese leaders hoped collective farms would increase food production, allowing more people to work in industry. Food production, however, did not grow. Meanwhile, China's vast population continued to expand. By 1957, China had approximately 657 million people living within its borders.

Tse-Tung, Mao. 1949. Quoted 1980 by Terrill, Ross. Mao: A Biography. Harper and Row.

In 1958 Mao began a more radical program known as the Great Leap Forward. Under this program, more than 700,000 existing collective farms, normally the size of a village, were combined into 26,000 vast **communes**. Each commune contained more than 30,000 people who lived and worked together. Because they had communal child care, more than 500,000 Chinese mothers worked beside their husbands in the fields by mid-1958.

Mao Zedong hoped his Great Leap Forward program would mobilize the people for a massive effort to speed up economic growth and to reach the **final** stage of communism—the classless society—before the end of the twentieth century. The Communist Party's official slogan promised the following to the Chinese people: "Hard work for a few years, happiness for a thousand."

Despite such slogans, the Great Leap Forward was an economic disaster. Bad weather, which resulted in droughts and floods, and the peasants' hatred of the new system drove down food production. As a result, nearly 15 million people died of starvation. Many peasants were reportedly reduced to eating the bark off trees and, in some cases, to allowing infants to starve. In 1960 the government made some changes. It began to break up the communes and to return to collective farms and some private plots.

**DETERMINING MEANING**

The words *communism, Communist,* **commune**, and *communal* are related words that share the root word *common*. This word means "belonging to all." How does this shared root word help you understand the meaning of **commune** and *communal child care* in *Communist* China?

**DETERMINING MEANING**

The word **source** comes from the Old French noun *sourse*, meaning "the beginning of a river or stream," which derives from the Latin verb *surgere*, meaning "to rise." Use one of these word origins to explain the *Little Red Book* as a source of knowledge in Communist China.

## THE CULTURAL REVOLUTION

Despite opposition within the Communist Party and the commune failure, Mao still dreamed of a classless society. In Mao's eyes, only **permanent revolution**, an atmosphere of constant revolutionary fervor, could enable the Chinese to overcome the past and to achieve the final stage of communism.

In 1966 Mao launched the Great Proletarian Cultural Revolution. The Chinese name literally meant "great revolution to create a proletarian (working class) culture." A collection of Mao's thoughts, called the *Little Red Book*, became a sort of bible for the Chinese Communists. It was hailed as the most important **source** of knowledge in all areas. The book was in every hotel, in every school, and in factories, communes, and universities. Few people conversed without first referring to the *Little Red Book*.

To further the Cultural Revolution, the Red Guards were formed. These were revolutionary groups composed of unhappy party members and discontented young people. They were urged to take to the streets to cleanse Chinese society of impure elements guilty of taking the capitalist road. In June 1966, all schools and universities in China were closed for six months to prepare for a new system of education based on Mao's ideas. Mao had launched China on a new forced march toward communism.

The Red Guards set out across the nation to eliminate the "Four Olds"—old ideas, old culture, old customs, and old habits. The Red Guards destroyed temples, books written by foreigners, and foreign music. They tore down street signs and replaced them with ones carrying revolutionary names. The Red Guards even turned on members of the Communist Party. The city of Shanghai even ordered that red (the revolutionary color) traffic lights would indicate that traffic could move, not stop.

Destruction of property was matched by vicious attacks on individuals who had supposedly deviated from Mao's thought. Those so accused were humiliated at public meetings, where they were forced to admit their "crimes." Many were brutally beaten, often fatally. Intellectuals and artists accused of

*A Chinese woman and child hold up Mao's* Little Red Book *during the Cultural Revolution.*

**DETERMINING CENTRAL IDEAS**
What does the photograph show about the goal of the Cultural Revolution and the role of the *Little Red Book*?

*This poster urges the Chinese people to give energetic support to agriculture.*

**INTEGRATING INFORMATION** What purpose does the poster serve? Why do you think the poster shows the man holding up the *Little Red Book*?

being pro-Western were especially open to attack. Red Guards broke the fingers of one pianist for the "crime" of playing the works of Frederic Chopin, the nineteenth-century European composer. Nien Cheng, who worked for the British-owned Shell Oil Company in Shanghai, was imprisoned for seven years. She told of her experience in *Life and Death in Shanghai*.

From the start of its socialist revolution, the Communist Party had wanted to create a new kind of citizen, one who would give the utmost for the good of all China. In Mao's words, the people should "Be resolute, fear no sacrifice, and surmount every difficulty to win victory."

During the 1950s and 1960s, the Chinese government made some basic changes. Women could now take part in politics and had equal marital rights—a dramatic shift. Mao feared that loyalty to the family would interfere with loyalty to the state. During the Cultural Revolution, for example, children were encouraged to report negative comments their parents made about the government.

Mao found during the Cultural Revolution, however, that it is not easy to maintain a permanent revolution, or constant mood of revolutionary enthusiasm. Key groups, including Communist Party members and many military officers, did not share Mao's desire for permanent revolution. Many people, disgusted by the actions of the Red Guards, began to turn against the movement. In September 1976, Mao Zedong died at the age of 82. A group of practical-minded reformers, led by Deng Xiaoping (DUHNG SHYOW • PIHNG), seized power and soon brought the Cultural Revolution to an end.

**DETERMINING MEANING**

What context clues help you understand that *frontier* refers to a geographic place or region? Use these context clues to explain the meaning of *frontier*.

### ✓ CHECKING FOR UNDERSTANDING

1. **UNDERSTANDING CHANGE** How did Mao use economic policies to try to establish a classless society? Why did Mao believe permanent revolution was necessary?
2. **IDENTIFYING BIAS** How does the poster show bias? What purpose did that bias serve?
3. **ANALYZING CHANGE** Why do you think Mao's consolidation of power in China took place after World War II rather than during the war?

## CHINA AND THE COLD WAR

**GUIDING QUESTION** *How was China affected by the Cold War?*

In 1949 the Cold War spread from Europe to Asia when the Chinese Communists won the Chinese civil war and set up a new Communist regime. American fears about the spread of communism intensified, especially when the new Chinese Communist leaders made it clear that they supported "national wars of liberation"—or movements for revolution—in Africa, Asia, and Latin America. When Communist China signed a pact of friendship and cooperation with the Soviet Union in 1950, some Americans began to speak of a Communist desire for world domination. When war broke out in Korea, the Cold War had arrived in Asia.

China's involvement in the Korean War led to renewed Western fears of China. In turn, China became even more isolated from the major Western powers. The country was forced to rely almost entirely on the Soviet Union for technological and economic aid. Even that became more difficult as relations between China and the Soviet Union began to deteriorate in the late 1950s.

**UNDERSTANDING CRAFT AND STRUCTURE**

1. **ANALYZING TEXT PRESENTATION** How does the text organize information regarding China's role in the Cold War?
2. **DETERMINING MEANING** What did Chinese Communist leaders mean when they said that they supported "national wars of liberation"? Why would this statement heighten tensions with the United States?

Several issues divided China and the Soviet Union. For one thing, the Chinese were not happy with the amount of economic aid provided by the Soviets. A more important issue, however, was their disagreement over the Cold War. The Chinese wanted the Soviets to go on the offensive to promote world revolution. Specifically, China wanted Soviet aid in retaking Taiwan from Chiang Kai-shek. The Soviets, however, were trying to improve relations with the West and refused.

In the 1960s, the dispute between China and the Soviet Union broke into the open. Military units on both sides of the frontier clashed on a number of occasions. Faced with internal problems and a serious security threat from the Soviets on its northern frontier, some Chinese leaders decided to improve relations with the United States. In 1972 President Richard Nixon made a state visit to China. The two sides agreed to improve relations. China's long isolation from the West was coming to an end.

> "One of the gifts that we left behind in Hangchow was a planted sapling of the American redwood tree. . . . Just as we hope that those saplings, those tiny saplings that we left in China, will grow one day into mighty redwoods, so we hope, too, that the seeds planted on this journey for peace will grow and prosper into a more enduring structure for peace and security in the Western Pacific."
>
> —Richard Nixon, remarks at Andrews Air Force Base, February 28, 1972

The end of the Cultural Revolution also affected Chinese foreign policy. In the late 1970s, under Deng Xiaoping, China sought to improve relations with the Western states. Diplomatic ties were established with the United States in 1979. In the 1980s, Chinese relations with the Soviet Union also gradually improved. By the 1990s, China emerged as an independent power and began to play an increasingly active role in Asian affairs.

*In 1970, China invited a U.S. ping-pong team to compete in Peking. Soon after, the Chinese team visited the United States. Then, in 1972, President Nixon visited China to meet with Premier Zhou Enlai. The two leaders discussed many issues and watched a ping-pong match between their nations' teams.*

**DETERMINING MEANING** Why did exchanges between the United States and China during this time become known as "ping-pong diplomacy"? What change did this diplomacy signal?

### ANALYZING PRIMARY SOURCES

1. **DETERMINING POINT OF VIEW** How did Nixon understand the symbolism of leaving the American redwood tree saplings behind in China?
2. **ANALYZING TEXT** How does Nixon use the gift of an American redwood sapling to support his ideas?

### ☑ CHECKING FOR UNDERSTANDING

1. **EXPLAINING EFFECTS** How was China affected by the Cold War?
2. **EVALUATING** How does the text suggest that China has changed since the Cold War?
3. **UNDERSTANDING CONTEXT** Why does it seem reasonable that communism would spread to China and that China would form a pact with the Soviet Union and become involved in the Korean War?

PHOTO:John Dominis/The LIFE Picture Collection/Getty Images; TEXT:Nixon, Richard. 1972. Remarks at Andrews Air Force Base on Returning From the People's Republic of China. February 28, 1972. Peters, Gerhard and Woolley, John T. The American Presidency Project.

## LESSON 2 REVIEW

### Time and Place

1. **ANALYZING CHANGE** How did the Red Guard help sustain Mao's "permanent revolution"?

### Building History-Social Science Analysis Skills

2. **UNDERSTANDING CHANGE** What tactics did Mao use to enforce the Cultural Revolution?
3. **EXPLAINING CAUSE AND EFFECT** Why did Mao focus so much effort on farming? Explain whether Mao achieved his goals.
4. **IDENTIFYING CONNECTIONS** How did communism shape Chinese foreign policy?

### Writing About History

5. **NARRATIVE WRITING** Imagine you are a Chinese peasant who was sent to a commune during the Great Leap Forward. Write an essay describing how this event has affected your life.

### Collaborating

6. **EVALUATING POINT OF VIEW** In small groups, discuss the Cultural Revolution in China. List ways the Cultural Revolution impacted Chinese society. How does it represent extremes?

## POINTS OF VIEW

# The Long Telegram

After World War II, both the United States and the Soviet Union competed for global influence. This contest played out in Europe immediately following the war. However, as time passed, the United States and the Soviet Union would collect allies across the regions of the world, including Southeast Asia, Africa, and in the Middle East.

U.S. diplomat George F. Kennan, in what has come to be known as the "Long Telegram," explained what he believed was the USSR's foreign policy and what he believed should be the U.S. response. Likewise, Soviet ambassador Nikolai Novikov wrote his own telegram decrying U.S. foreign policy and praising Soviet goals.

"[W]e have here a political force committed fanatically to the belief that with U.S. there can be no permanent **modus vivendi**, that it is desirable and necessary that . . . our traditional way of life be destroyed, the international authority of our state be broken, if Soviet power is to be secure. . . . This political force has complete power of . . . one of world's greatest peoples and resources of world's richest national territory. . . . In addition, it has an elaborate and far flung **apparatus** for exertion of its influence in other countries. . . .

We must formulate and put forward for other nations a much more positive and constructive picture of sort of world we would like to see. . . . It is not enough to urge people to develop political processes similar to our own. Many foreign peoples, in Europe at least, are tired and frightened by experiences of past, and are less interested in abstract freedom than in security. They are seeking guidance rather than responsibilities. We should be better able than Russians to give them this. And unless we do, Russians certainly will."

—George Kennan, in a telegram to the U.S. Secretary of State, February 22, 1946

**VOCABULARY**

*modus vivendi:* way of life

*apparatus:* a system of processes by which something is carried out

“The foreign policy of the United States, which reflects the imperialist tendencies of American **monopolistic capital**, is characterized in the postwar period by a striving for world supremacy. This is the real meaning of the many statements by President Truman and other representatives of American ruling circles: that the United States has the right to lead the world. All the forces of American diplomacy—the army, the air force, the navy, industry, and science—are enlisted in the service of this foreign policy. For this purpose broad plans for expansion . . . are being implemented through diplomacy and the establishment of a system of naval and air bases stretching far beyond the boundaries of the United States, through the arms race, and through the creation of ever newer types of weapons. . . .

[T]he preparation by the United States . . . is being conducted with the prospect of war against the Soviet Union, which in the eyes of the American imperialists is the main obstacle in the path of the United States to world domination. This is indicated by facts such as the **tactical** training of the American army for war with the Soviet Union as the future opponent, the siting of American strategic bases in regions from which it is possible to launch strikes on Soviet territory, intensified training and strengthening of Arctic regions as close approaches to the USSR, and attempts to prepare Germany and Japan to use those countries in a war against the USSR.”

—Nikolai Novikov, in a telegram to Moscow,
September 27, 1946

**VOCABULARY**

*monopolistic:* tending toward the complete control of something

*capital:* wealth and goods devoted to production

*tactical:* having to do with combat tactics, or strategies

## What Do YOU Think?

1. **EVALUATING ARGUMENTS** How does Kennan support his claim that the United States “must formulate and put forward for other nations a much more positive and constructive picture of sort of world we would like to see”?

2. **CITING TEXT EVIDENCE** What evidence does Novikov offer to support his claims that the United States is preparing for war with the Soviet Union?

3. **DRAWING CONCLUSIONS** How does Kennan’s description of the Soviet Union compare with the way Novikov describes the United States?

4. **UNDERSTANDING CONTEXT** Novikov suggests that all the military forces of the United States are directed toward the purpose of imperialism. How is this different from the motives Kennan ascribes to the Soviet expansion?

5. **INTERPRETING** What do the differences in these two telegrams indicate about the overall conflict that was the Cold War?

PHOTO:Keystone/Getty Images; TEXT:Novikov, Nikolai. 1946. The Novikov Telegram. Reprinted 1991 by Kenneth M. Jensen. Origins of the Cold War: The Novikov, Kennan, and Roberts 'Long Telegrams' of 1946. Washington, D.C.: United States Institute of Peace.

## ESSENTIAL QUESTION

- *How does conflict influence political relationships?*

# THE STORY BEGINS...

LESSON 3

# Cold War Conflicts

Following World War II, the Soviet Union and the United States each exercised influence in Korea, divided along a line of latitude known as the 38th parallel. The two sides failed to come up with a plan for a unified Korean government. Then, on June 25, 1950, communist guerrilla forces from northern Korea attacked south of the parallel. Two days later, U.S. President Harry S. Truman issued this statement.

> "The attack upon Korea makes it plain beyond all doubt that communism has passed beyond the use of subversion to conquer independent nations and will now use armed invasion and war. It has defied the orders of the Security Council of the United Nations issued to preserve international peace and security. In these circumstances the occupation of Formosa [Taiwan] by Communist forces would be a direct threat to the security of the Pacific area and to United States forces performing their lawful and necessary functions in that area."

—President Harry S. Truman, June 27, 1950

The Korean War was one of several proxy wars in which U.S. and Soviet arms, forces, and ideas clashed.

*During the Korean War between Soviet-backed communist forces in the north and U.S.-backed democratic forces in the south, hundreds of thousands of refugees fled what would become North Korea. The conflict displaced many Koreans throughout the north and the south.* ▶

| Proxy Wars | |
|---|---|
| Causes | Effects |
| | |
| | |
| | |

### ANALYZING KEY IDEAS AND DETAILS

**IDENTIFYING CONNECTIONS** Read closely to identify causes and effects of proxy wars between the Soviet Union and the United States. Record these causes and effects in a graphic organizer like this one.

# THE UNITED STATES AND THE SOVIET UNION

**GUIDING QUESTIONS** *What common factor triggered the "hot" wars in Asia during the Cold War? How did nuclear weapons influence political relationships during the Cold War?*

World War II destroyed European supremacy in world affairs. As the Cold War conflict between the world's two superpowers—the United States and the Soviet Union—grew stronger, the European nations were divided into two armed camps dependent upon one or the other of these two major powers. This division, however, also spread to the rest of the world. The United States and the Soviet Union, whose rivalry brought the world to the brink of nuclear war, seemed to hold the survival of the world in their hands.

Neither power, however, ever went to war directly with the other. Instead, the United States and the Soviet Union fought a series of proxy wars. A **proxy war** occurs when two powers in conflict use substitutes instead of fighting each other directly. Armed with nuclear arsenals, neither the U.S. nor the Soviet Union wanted to fight each other directly. However, both were willing to support opposing sides in local wars in the struggle between their worldviews.

The Truman Doctrine and the Marshall Plan directed the postwar policy of the United States of supplying economic and military aid to stop the spread of communism. Alliance building also played a role. In addition to NATO in Europe, the U.S. also built alliances in other parts of the world. To stem Communist aggression in the East, the U.S., Great Britain, France, Pakistan, the Philippines, Australia, and New Zealand formed the Southeast Asia Treaty Organization (SEATO). The Central Treaty Organization (CENTO), which included Turkey, Iraq, Iran, Pakistan, Great Britain, and the U.S., was meant to prevent Soviet expansion into the Middle East. The Soviet Union also created a series of alliances.

Two major conflicts of the Cold War were the wars that broke out in Korea and Vietnam. The Soviet Union and the United States each sent military support to prevent the other side from expanding its influence. In addition, a Cold War proxy conflict almost turned into a major nuclear war over the small island of Cuba. The United States and the Soviet Union also competed for political influence in Africa, particularly the Congo, and Chile.

### ANALYZING KEY IDEAS AND DETAILS

1. **DETERMINING CENTRAL IDEAS** What is the central idea of this section? How does the text present and develop this idea?
2. **CITING TEXT EVIDENCE** What evidence supports the idea that division of Europe into rival camps, dependent on the United States and the Soviet Union, spread to other parts of the world?

### DETERMINING MEANING

A *proxy* is a substitute, or a person who acts in place of another. How does this explanation help you understand the meaning of **proxy war**?

## ☑ CHECKING FOR UNDERSTANDING

1. **IDENTIFYING CONNECTIONS** What common factor triggered the "hot" wars in Asia during the Cold War?
2. **RELATING EVENTS** How did the Cold War originate? How did it play out geographically?

# THE KOREAN WAR

**GUIDING QUESTION** *What common factor triggered the "hot" wars in Asia during the Cold War?*

Japan controlled Korea until 1945. In August 1945, the Soviet Union and the United States agreed to divide Korea into two zones at the 38th parallel. The plan was to hold elections after World War II to reunify Korea. As American-Soviet relations grew worse, however, two separate governments emerged in Korea—Communist in the north and anti-Communist in the south.

In 1948 Harry S. Truman won re-election as the president of the United States. On January 20, 1949, Truman made these remarks on communism in his inaugural address.

> "Communism is based on the belief that man is so weak and inadequate that he is unable to govern himself, and therefore requires the rule of strong masters. Democracy is based on the conviction that man has the moral and intellectual capacity, as well as the inalienable right, to govern himself with reason and justice. . . .
>
> Communism maintains that social wrongs can be corrected only by violence. Democracy has proved that social justice can be achieved through peaceful change.
>
> Communism holds that the world is so widely divided into opposing classes that war is inevitable. Democracy holds that free nations can settle differences justly and maintain a lasting peace. . . .
>
> I state these differences, not to draw issues of belief as such, but because the actions resulting from the Communist philosophy are a threat to the efforts of free nations to bring about world recovery and lasting peace."
>
> —Harry S. Truman, Inaugural Address, January 20, 1949

Tension between the two governments increased. With the apparent approval of Joseph Stalin, Communist North Korean troops invaded South Korea on June 25, 1950. President Harry S. Truman of the United States, seeing this as yet another example of Communist aggression and expansion, gained the approval of the United Nations (UN) and sent U.S. troops to repel the invaders. Several other countries sent troops as well. In October, UN forces—mostly American—marched across the 38th parallel with the aim of unifying Korea. Greatly alarmed, the Chinese sent hundreds of thousands of troops into North Korea and pushed UN forces back across the 38th parallel.

**UNDERSTANDING CRAFT AND STRUCTURE**

1. **ANALYZING TEXT PRESENTATION** The text states, "With the apparent approval of Joseph Stalin, Communist North Korean troops invaded South Korea on June 25, 1950." Why does the author use *apparent* here? Why is the apparent approval of Stalin significant?
2. **DETERMINING MEANING** Read the paragraph that begins, "The Korean War also confirmed American fears. . . ." How does that paragraph help you figure out what a policy of massive retaliation is?

**ANALYZING PRIMARY SOURCES**

1. **ANALYZING TEXT PRESENTATION** Why does Truman alternate between describing communism and democracy in the first three paragraphs?
2. **ASSESSING** What does Truman claim is his reason for stating these differences? Explain whether you think his argument effectively supports this claim.

*United Nations forces withdraw from P'yŏngyang, North Korea, recrossing the 38th parallel, the dividing line between North and South Korea.*

**INTEGRATING INFORMATION** What is the significance of the sign?

Three more years of fighting led to no final victory. An armistice was finally signed in 1953. The 38th parallel remained, and remains today, the boundary line between North Korea and South Korea. The division of Korea was reaffirmed. To many Americans, the policy of containing communism had succeeded in Asia, just as it had earlier in Europe.

The Korean War also confirmed American fears of Communist expansion. The United States was now more determined than ever to contain Soviet power. In the mid-1950s, the administration of President Dwight D. Eisenhower adopted a policy of massive retaliation. Any Soviet advance, even a ground attack in Europe, would be met with the full use of American nuclear bombs. Moreover, it was after the Korean War that American military alliances were extended around the world. As President Eisenhower explained, "The freedom we cherish and defend in Europe and in the Americas is no different from the freedom that is imperiled in Asia."

### ✓ CHECKING FOR UNDERSTANDING

1. **EVALUATING EVIDENCE** Why did U.S. officials consider the stalemate in Korea to be a successful containment of communism?
2. **EVALUATING EVIDENCE** How might some people argue that the Korean War was a failure for the UN forces?
3. **INTERPRETING** Read the quote from Eisenhower in the last paragraph. How is Eisenhower trying to justify the extension of military alliances around the world?

## THE CUBAN MISSILE CRISIS

**GUIDING QUESTION** *How did nuclear weapons influence political relationships during the Cold War?*

During the administration of John F. Kennedy, the Cold War confrontation between the United States and the Soviet Union reached frightening levels. In 1959 a left-wing revolutionary named Fidel Castro overthrew the Cuban dictator Fulgencio Batista and set up a Soviet-supported totalitarian regime in Cuba. Having a socialist regime with Communist contacts so close to the mainland was considered to be a threat to the security of the United States.

President Kennedy feared that if he moved openly against Castro, then the Soviets might retaliate by moving against Berlin. As a result, the stage might be set for the two superpowers to engage in a nuclear war. For months, Kennedy considered alternatives. He finally approved a plan the CIA had proposed. Exiled Cuban fighters would invade Cuba at the Bay of Pigs. The purpose of the invasion was to cause a revolt against Castro. The invasion, which began on Sunday, April 16, 1961, was a disaster. By Wednesday, the exiled fighters began surrendering. One hundred fourteen died; the rest were captured by Castro's troops.

After the Bay of Pigs, the Soviet Union sent advisers to Cuba. In 1962 Khrushchev began to place nuclear missiles in Cuba, which were meant to counteract U.S. nuclear weapons placed in Turkey. Khrushchev said: "Your rockets are stationed in Turkey. You are worried over Cuba . . . because it lies at a distance of 90 miles across the sea from the shores of the United States. However, Turkey lies next to us."

**MAKING CONNECTIONS TO TECHNOLOGY**

### HELICOPTERS

Although military helicopters had been used as early as the 1930s, it was in the mountainous terrain of the Korean Peninsula that military leaders recognized their true potential. Helicopters such as the Sikorsky HO3S-1 and Bell HTL-4 with its signature clear bubble cockpit were used to evacuate troops, to bring in light supplies, and for reconnaissance and medical evacuations. By the late 1960s, the United States was fighting a new war in Vietnam and using helicopters even more than before. Over the course of that war, a total of 24 different models of helicopters were used. These choppers proved indispensable for getting troops in and out of dense jungle. Today, helicopters are used for a variety of military and civilian tasks. They are used for war, to combat forest fires, to transport the sick, and even to monitor traffic on the highways.

1. **IDENTIFYING CONNECTIONS** Why might the helicopter have proven more useful in the Korean and Vietnamese conflicts than it had in World War II?
2. **ANALYZING CHANGE** What does the history of the military helicopter indicate about the way technology is adopted for both military and civilian applications?

**ANALYZING KEY IDEAS AND DETAILS**

1. **SUMMARIZING** Summarize the series of events that led to a crisis between the United States and the Soviet Union in Cuba.
2. **CITING EVIDENCE** What evidence supports the idea that the blockade of Cuba was a successful strategy? What evidence supports the idea that Kennedy made the right decision by not sending U.S. troops to Cuba?

(t)Eisenhower, Dwight D. 1953. State of the Union Address, 1953. Reprinted 2012 by Lamont Colucci. The National Security Doctrines of the American Presidency - How They Shape Our Present and Future. Volume 2. Santa Barbara, California: Praeger, An Imprint of ABC-CLIO, LLC.; (b)________. 1962. U.S. Department of State, Bulletin XLVII, November 12, 1962.

## ANALYZING PRIMARY SOURCES

*This American political cartoon was published on October 30, 1962. Khrushchev is depicted as a dentist removing Castro's teeth, which appear as missiles.*

### The Cuban Missile Crisis

**The Cuban missile crisis brought the United States and the Soviet Union to the brink of nuclear war. It was, perhaps, the most frightening moment of the Cold War. These sources focus on Khrushchev's agreement to remove Soviet missiles from Cuba.**

"I appreciate your assurance that the United States will not invade Cuba. Hence, we have ordered our officers to stop building bases, dismantle the equipment, and send it back home.

We must not allow the situation to deteriorate, (but) eliminate hotbeds of tension, and we must see to it that no other conflicts occur which might lead to a world nuclear war."

—Letter from Nikita Khrushchev to President John F. Kennedy, October 28, 1962

1. **ANALYZING TEXT** What does the letter to President Kennedy suggest about Khrushchev's reaction to the crisis?
2. **ANALYZING IDEAS** Look at the caption of the cartoon on the left. What point is the cartoonist making about the Cuban missile crisis?

The United States was not willing to allow nuclear weapons within such close striking distance of its mainland. In October 1962, Kennedy found out that Soviet ships carrying missiles were heading to Cuba. He decided to blockade Cuba to prevent the fleet from reaching its destination. This approach gave each side time to find a peaceful solution. Khrushchev agreed to turn back the fleet and remove Soviet missiles from Cuba if Kennedy pledged in return not to invade the island.

The Cuban missile crisis seemed to bring the world frighteningly close to nuclear war. Indeed, in 1992 a high-ranking Soviet officer revealed that short-range rockets armed with nuclear devices would have been used against U.S. troops if the United States had invaded Cuba, an option that Kennedy fortunately had rejected. The realization that the world might have been destroyed in a few days had a profound influence on both sides. A "hotline" system of communication between Moscow and Washington, D.C., was installed in 1963. The two superpowers could now communicate quickly in times of crisis.

### ✓ CHECKING FOR UNDERSTANDING

1. **UNDERSTANDING CHANGE** How did nuclear weapons influence political relationships during the Cold War?
2. **DISTINGUISHING FACT FROM OPINION** Read the paragraph that begins "After the Bay of Pigs. . ." What facts does Nikita Khrushchev use to justify sending nuclear missiles to Cuba?
3. **EVALUATING** What did Kennedy and Khrushchev learn from the experience of the Cuban missile crisis? How did information revealed years later affirm the lessons learned?

# THE VIETNAM WAR

**GUIDING QUESTION** *What common factor triggered the "hot" wars in Asia during the Cold War?*

By 1963, the United States had been drawn into a new struggle that had an important impact on the Cold War—the Vietnam War. After World War II, most states in Southeast Asia gained independence from their colonial rulers. For instance, the Philippines became independent of the United States in 1946. Great Britain also ended its colonial rule in Southeast Asia, beginning in 1948. France refused, however, to let go of its holdings in Indochina. This led to a long war in Vietnam.

Opportunities also arose for nationalist leaders in some of the newly independent countries, or in some countries in the middle of conflicts with their neighbors or in civil wars, to improve their positions by aligning with either the United States or the Soviet Union. However, interventions by these superpowers often complicated internal developments. Additionally, leaders of these states were often compelled to follow development plans for their countries that likely benefited either the United States or the Soviet Union before they benefited their home countries.

Leading the struggle against French colonial rule in Vietnam was the local Communist Party, headed by Ho Chi Minh. In August 1945, the Vietminh, an alliance of Vietnamese rebel forces under Communist leadership, seized power throughout most of Vietnam. Ho Chi Minh was then elected president of a new republic in Hanoi, a large city in northern Vietnam. Refusing to accept this new government, France then quickly reseized the southern part of the country. Vietnam, like Korea before it, had now been divided into northern and southern halves.

### INTEGRATING KNOWLEDGE AND IDEAS

1. **COMPARING AND CONTRASTING** Review the information in the first two paragraphs of this section. How does the writer present the emerging conflict in Vietnam as similar to and different from the conflict in Korea described earlier?
2. **EVALUATING ARGUMENTS** How does the author support the claim that "the domino theory proved to be unfounded"?

### DETERMINING MEANING

The root word of **temporary** comes from the Latin *tempus*, meaning "time." What does knowing the meaning of this root tell you about the meaning of **temporary**? Write a definition in your own words. Check your definition using a dictionary or online resource.

**CITIZENSHIP**

## PROTESTS IN WARTIME

Harold Adler/Underwood Archives/Getty Images

In the late 1960s and early 1970s, some Americans opposed U.S. involvement in Vietnam. Some disagreed with the reasons for U.S. involvement. Many believed that the war had dragged on too long. Most objected to the rising casualties of American soldiers and the progressively destructive campaigns against the Vietnamese. For these and other reasons, thousands assembled on college campuses, at the Pentagon, and in other places across the country to protest the war. They staged marches, rallies, and other nonviolent demonstrations to demand that the United States pull out of Vietnam. Some antiwar protestors also staged acts of civil disobedience in which they burned draft cards or destroyed draft offices. Others wrote letters to their state and federal representatives and signed petitions for peace. Many prominent figures, including civil rights leader Martin Luther King, Jr., spoke out against the war. In 1967, six veterans of the war staged a peaceful protest march through New York City. Together, they formed Vietnam Veterans Against the War, which grew to include more than 30,000 members.

1. **IDENTIFYING CONNECTIONS** What does the antiwar movement in the 1960s and '70s suggest about the challenges of the Cold War?
2. **DETERMINING MEANING** Based on the passage, how do acts of civil disobedience differ from protected forms of free speech and nonviolent protest?

### GEOGRAPHIC REASONING

1. **PATTERNS AND MOVEMENT** How does the map show that the war expanded, geographically, in the early 1970s?
2. **HUMAN-ENVIRONMENT INTERACTION** Where were most U.S. bases? Why do you think that is?

For years, France fought Ho Chi Minh's Vietminh for control of Vietnam, but without success. In 1954, after a huge French defeat at Dien Bien Phu, France agreed to sign the Geneva Peace Accords. Because of the Korean War, China and the Soviet Union wanted to avoid another conflict with the United States. Consequently, they pressured North Vietnam to agree to a **temporary** partition of the country. This was meant to save French pride and satisfy the Americans. Vietnam was divided into two parts. In the north were the Communists, based in their capital city of Hanoi; in the south, the non-Communists were based in their capital city of Saigon.

Both north and south agreed to hold elections in two years to create a single government. Instead, the conflict continued, and Vietnam soon became part of the Cold War. The United States, opposed to the spread of communism, aided South Vietnam under nationalist leader Ngo Dinh Diem. In spite of this aid, the Viet Cong, South Vietnamese Communist guerrillas supported by North Vietnam, were on the verge of seizing control of the entire country by early 1965. Their forces also received military aid from China.

In March 1965, United States President Johnson sent troops to South Vietnam to keep the Communist regime of North Vietnam from gaining control of South Vietnam. U.S. policy makers saw the conflict in terms of a **domino theory** concerning the spread of communism. If the Communists succeeded in South Vietnam, the argument went, all the other countries in Asia that were freeing themselves from colonial domination would likewise fall (like dominoes) to communism.

North Vietnam responded to increased presence of American troops by sending more forces into the south. Despite the massive superiority in equipment and firepower of the American forces, the United States failed to defeat the North Vietnamese. In addition, the growing number of American troops in Vietnam soon produced an antiwar movement in the United States, especially among college students of draft age. The mounting destruction of the conflict, seen on television, also turned public opinion against the war.

#### DETERMINING MEANING

A theory is an idea about how something works. Read the paragraph that begins "In March 1965. . ." What context clues help you understand the **domino theory**?

President Johnson, condemned for his handling of the costly and indecisive war, decided not to run for reelection. Former Vice President Richard M. Nixon won the election with his pledge to stop the war and to bring the American people together.

Finally, in 1973, President Nixon reached an agreement with North Vietnam in the Paris Peace Accords that allowed the United States to withdraw its forces. Within two years after the American withdrawal, Communist armies from the North had forcibly reunited Vietnam.

Despite the success of the North Vietnamese Communists, the domino theory proved to be unfounded. A noisy split between Communist China and the Soviet Union put an end to the Western idea that there was a single form of communism directed by Moscow. Under President Nixon, American relations with China were resumed. New nations in Southeast Asia also managed to avoid Communist governments. Above all, Vietnam helped show the limitations of American power. By the end of the Vietnam War, a new era in American-Soviet relations had begun to **emerge**.

**DETERMINING MEANING**

Synonyms for **emerge** include *arise, come about,* and *surface*. Use one of these synonyms to explain the meaning of **emerge** in the sentence in which it appears in the text.

## ✓ CHECKING FOR UNDERSTANDING

1. **EXPLAINING CAUSES** Why did the domino theory cause the United States to become involved in Vietnam?
2. **UNDERSTANDING CONTEXT** How did the causes of the Vietnam War differ from the causes of the Korean War?
3. **IDENTIFYING CONNECTIONS** How did the Vietnam War help "show the limitations of American power"?

## LESSON 3 REVIEW

### Time and Place

1. **RELATING EVENTS** Why do you think "hot" wars took place in Korea and Vietnam when they did?

### Building History-Social Science Analysis Skills

2. **EVALUATING** What evidence supports the idea that the Bay of Pigs invasion "was a disaster"?
3. **RELATING EVENTS** Would the Cold War have happened had the Soviet Union failed to develop nuclear weapons? Explain.
4. **USING MAPS** Study the map "Vietnam War." How does the map reinforce the idea that North Vietnamese and Viet Cong Communist forces had a great deal of strength and support?

### Writing About History

5. **EXPLANATORY WRITING** Choose one proxy war discussed in the lesson, and write a short paragraph explaining why the United States decided it was important to fight the war.

### Collaborating

6. **USING MULTIMEDIA** Work in a small group to identify how the concept of the domino theory altered America's foreign policy. As a group, design a poster or political cartoon illustrating America's foreign policy during the Cold War.

ANALYZING SOURCES

# POLICIES OF THE COLD WAR

The following excerpts represent Soviet and American viewpoints during the early Cold War period. Read them to learn how each viewed Soviet power.

**VOCABULARY**

*viable:* able to continue

*Kremlin:* seat of government for the USSR

**PRIMARY SOURCE: SPEECH**

## A COMMUNIST'S SPEECH

After the Soviet defeat of Germany on the Eastern Front in World War II, Soviet dictator Joseph Stalin delivered the following speech in February 1946.

> "And so, what is the summation of the war? ... Our victory signifies, first of all, that our Soviet social system was victorious, that the Soviet social system successfully passed the test of fire in the war and proved that it is fully **viable**.
>
> As we know, the foreign press on more than one occasion asserted that the Soviet social system ... was doomed to failure, that the Soviet system was a "house of cards" ... imposed upon the people by the Cheka [secret police], and that a slight shock from without was sufficient to cause this "house of cards" to collapse.
>
> Now we can say that the war has, refuted all these assertions of the foreign press and has proved them to have been groundless. The war proved that the Soviet social system is a genuinely people's system, which grew up from the ranks of the people and enjoys their powerful support . . .
>
> More than that. The issue now is not whether the Soviet social system is viable or not, because after the object lessons of the war, no skeptic now dares to express doubt concerning the viability of the Soviet social system. Now the issue is that the Soviet social system has proved to be more viable and stable than the non-Soviet social system, that the Soviet social system is a better form of organization of society than any non-Soviet social system."

**ANALYZE THE TEXT**

1. **ASSESSING** What evidence does Stalin offer to support his claim that the Soviet system is now much stronger than anyone believed previously?
2. **UNDERSTANDING CONTEXT** Considering what you know about the origins of the Cold War, what can you conclude about the direction Stalin's foreign policy may move following this speech?

**PRIMARY SOURCE: DECLASSIFIED REPORT**

## THE AMERICAN REACTION TO COMMUNISM

This is an excerpt from a once-classified report. Completed in 1950, it discusses American foreign policy during the Cold War.

> "As for the policy of "containment," it is one which seeks by all means short of war to (1) block further expansion of Soviet power, (2) expose the falsities of the Soviet pretensions, (3) induce a retraction of the **Kremlin's** control and influence and (4) in general, so foster the seeds of destruction within the Soviet system that the Kremlin is brought at least to the point of modifying its behavior to conform to generally accepted international standards. . . .
>
> It is quite clear from Soviet theory and practice that the Kremlin seeks to bring the free world under its dominion by the methods of the cold war. The preferred technique is to subvert by infiltration and intimidation. Every institution of our society is an instrument which it is sought to stultify and turn against our purposes. Those that touch most closely our material and moral strength are obviously the prime targets, labor unions, civil enterprises, schools, churches, and all media for influencing opinion. The effort is not so much to make them serve obvious Soviet ends as to prevent them from serving our ends, and thus to make them sources of confusion in our economy, our culture, and our body politic . . ."

**ANALYZE THE TEXT**

1. **CITING TEXT EVIDENCE** What do the two major foreign policies proposed in this document suggest about U.S. intentions abroad? Cite evidence from the text in your answer.
2. **RELATING EVENTS** What does the U.S. policy of "containment" indicate about U.S. perceptions of Soviet power?

(l)Stalin, J. 1946. Speech Delivered by J. V. Stalin at a Meeting of Voters of the Stalin Electoral District, Moscow. February 9, 1946. Reprinted 1950 in J. Stalin Pamphlet Collection. Moscow: Foreign Languages Publishing House.; (r)Lay, Jr., James S. 1950. A Report to the National Security Council by The Executive Secretary on United States Objectives and Programs for National Security. April 14, 1950. Washington: National Security Council.

PRIMARY SOURCE: PHOTOGRAPH

## WOMEN STRIKE FOR PEACE

The group Women Strike for Peace, which worked to put an end to threats of nuclear war, holds a rally on 47th Street near the United Nations Building as tensions rise during the Cuban missile crisis.

PHOTO:World Telegram & Sun photo by Phil Stanziola/Library of Congress Prints and Photographs Division Washington, D.C. 20540 USA

### ANALYZE THE SOURCE

1. **ANALYZING IDEAS** What do the statements on the placards these women hold suggest about their position on the nuclear standoff with the Soviet Union over Cuba?

2. **INTERPRETING** What does this photograph indicate about the challenges U.S. leaders faced in developing Cold War strategies that the USSR did not?

### MULTIPLE PERSPECTIVES

1. **UNDERSTANDING CONTEXT** According to the passages, how would Soviet goals conflict with those of the Americans?

2. **EVALUATING EVIDENCE** In what way do both Stalin and the National Security Council report writers use similar evidence to support their dueling claims about each other's intentions?

# STUDY GUIDE

## THE COLD WAR
### LESSON 1

After World War II, the differences between the **United States** and the **Soviet Union** caused the two countries to come into conflict. The Soviets feared the capitalist West, and Western leaders feared communism. Thus began the **Cold War**, not a conventional war fought with weapons, but a war of political ideologies and a quest for world dominance.

**United States Responses**

**Truman Doctrine**

Created in 1947 to stop the spread of communism in the free world, it said that the United States would provide money to countries (in this case, to Greece and Turkey) that were threatened by Communist expansion.

**Marshall Plan**

Proposed in June 1947, the plan provided $13 billion to rebuild war-torn Europe because it was believed that communism was successful only in countries that had economic problems.

## CHINA AFTER WORLD WAR II
### LESSON 2

**LEADERSHIP UNDER MAO ZEDONG**

- Most industry and commerce was nationalized.
- All private farmland was collectivized.
- The Great Leap Forward combined more than 700,000 existing collective farms into 26,000 vast communes.
- The Great Proletarian Revolution was launched to continue Mao's plans for a classless society.
- Food production did not grow and the population continued to expand.
- The *Little Red Book* became a "bible" for Chinese Communists.
- 15 million people died of starvation.

## COLD WAR CONFLICTS
### LESSON 3

**PROXY WAR**

Two powers in conflict use substitutes instead of fighting each other directly

**DOMINO THEORY**

The idea that if one country falls to communism, neighboring countries will also fall

# CHAPTER 12 Assessment

**Directions: On a separate sheet of paper, answer the questions below. Make sure you read carefully and answer all parts of the questions.**

## Short Answer

1. **IDENTIFYING CONNECTIONS** What was the North Atlantic Treaty Organization? Why was it formed?

2. **UNDERSTANDING CONTEXT** Describe the arms race between the United States and the Soviet Union in the 1950s. Evaluate whether each group was reactionary, strategic, or both.

3. **DESCRIBING** Why did Khrushchev support the building of the Berlin Wall? Describe the military enforcement at the wall.

4. **EXPLAINING CAUSES** What purpose did the Truman Doctrine and the Marshall Plan serve? How did the Soviet Union respond?

5. **IDENTIFYING CONNECTIONS** What steps did Mao Zedong take to increase food production? What were their effects? Why could the outcome be considered politically motivated mass murder?

6. **DESCRIBING** How did the Red Guards assist and harm the Cultural Revolution?

7. **SUMMARIZING** What was Mao's perspective on family loyalty, and how did he encourage children to put the state first?

8. **UNDERSTANDING CHANGE** Did women benefit from changes under Mao? Explain.

9. **SUMMARIZING** What is a proxy war? What two proxy wars were the Soviet Union and the United States involved in during the Cold War?

10. **EXPLAINING EFFECTS** How did the Cuban missile crisis ultimately build common ground between the Soviet Union and the United States?

11. **DESCRIBING** When and how did the Cold War spread from Europe to Asia?

## History and Social-Science Analysis

12. **CONSTRUCTING HYPOTHESES** What was the domino theory? Construct an argument that supports or refutes the viewpoint of the domino theory. Offer reasons to support your argument.

13. **EXPLAINING CAUSE AND EFFECT** What caused the independence movement in Vietnam? What were the effects of the movement?

14. **DETERMINING CONTEXT** How did communism in China differ from communism in the Soviet Union?

*Use the map of Berlin to answer Questions 15 and 16.*

15. **USING MAPS** What does this map tell you about the relationship between geography and the historical development of postwar Berlin? How did this arrangement reflect the division of Germany?

16. **EXPLAINING EFFECTS** How do you think the Berlin Wall's separation of West Berlin from East Berlin and East Germany affected economic life within both parts of the city?

**Need Extra Help?**

| If You've Missed Question | 1 | 2 | 3 | 4 | 5 | 6 | 7 | 8 | 9 | 10 | 11 | 12 | 13 | 14 | 15 | 16 |
|---|---|---|---|---|---|---|---|---|---|---|---|---|---|---|---|---|
| Review Lesson | 1 | 1 | 1 | 1 | 2 | 2 | 2 | 2 | 3 | 3 | 3 | 3 | 3 | 2 | 1 | 1 |

## Research and Presentation

**17 USING TECHNOLOGY** Use appropriate technology to prepare a slide show or interactive time line in which you explain events that led to Mao's rise to power and events as they unfolded under Mao's Communist government.

**18 PRESENTING** Research the construction of the Berlin Wall, and share your findings in a multimedia presentation. If possible, conduct interviews with people who were affected by the wall's construction. Display or post presentations across classrooms, in a school media center, or on a school Web site or blog.

## Reading and Analyzing Primary Sources

*Use the image to answer the following questions.*

*In 1948, the Soviet Union completely blocked all routes into West Berlin. This photograph shows German children in West Berlin waving to an American cargo plane airlifting supplies into the city.*

**19 INTERPRETING** How do the German children in the photograph appear to feel about the arrival of the American cargo plane?

**A.** They are glad to see the plane.
**B.** They are unhappy about the plane.
**C.** They are confused to see the plane.
**D.** They are indifferent to the arrival of the plane.

**20 DESCRIBING** Imagine if the blockade had taken place in the previous century. It would not have been possible then for Britain and the United States to overcome the blockade. What change from the previous century enabled Britain and the U.S. to overcome the blockade?

**A.** Culture had to change.
**B.** Opinions had to change.
**C.** Populations had to grow.
**D.** Technology had to advance.

**21 INTEGRATING INFORMATION** How would this photograph likely have influenced international opinion of communism?

**A.** It would likely have generated criticism.
**B.** It would likely have generated support.
**C.** It would likely have generated confusion.
**D.** It would likely have generated indifference.

## Writing About History

**22 EXPLANATORY WRITING** How did U.S. foreign policies during the Cold War represent both causes and effects of conflict with the Soviet Union and China? Compare and contrast the different foreign policies that evolved under successive administrations.

## Speaking and Listening About History

*Use the primary source excerpt to complete Question 23.*

In April 1971, as public opposition to the Vietnam War mounted, the Senate Foreign Relations Committee held public hearings. John Kerry, a veteran from the war and a future U.S. senator and secretary of state, delivered this testimony.

> "In our opinion, and from our experience, there is nothing in South Vietnam, nothing which could happen that realistically threatens the United States of America. . . . We found that not only was it a civil war, an effort by a people who had for years been seeking their liberation from any colonial influence whatsoever, but also found that the Vietnamese whom we had enthusiastically molded after our own image were hard put to take up the fight against the threat we were supposedly saving them from. We found most people didn't even know the difference between communism and democracy. They only wanted to work in rice paddies without helicopters strafing them and bombs with napalm burning their villages and tearing their country apart."

—John Kerry, in testimony before the Senate Foreign Relations Committee, April 22, 1971

**23 EVALUATING POINT OF VIEW** With a partner, summarize and present John Kerry's point of view by recording his position on the war, his experience of the war, and his purpose in making this statement. Explain why you consider specific reasoning and rhetoric to be strong or weak.

**Need Extra Help?**

| If You've Missed Question | 17 | 18 | 19 | 20 | 21 | 22 | 23 |
|---|---|---|---|---|---|---|---|
| Review Lesson | 2 | 1 | 1 | 1 | 1 | 1 | 3 |

PHOTO:Bettmann/Corbis; TEXT:Kerry, John. 1971. Statement of John Kerry, Vietnam Veterans Against the War. Reprinted 2004. Congressional Record, Volume 150, Part 6. April 20, 2004 to May 4, 2004. Washington: United States Government Printing Office.

▶ *In 1993 Nelson Mandela received the Nobel Peace Prize. He is shown here greeting supporters just after his release from prison in 1990.*

1945 — 1993

# Independence and Nationalism in the Developing World

## CHAPTER 13



**GO DIGITAL**
*It's All online!*

## ASKING ESSENTIAL QUESTIONS

***How can political change cause conflict?***
***How can political relationships affect economic relationships?***

**What Will You Learn?** You will learn about how, following World War II, different countries in Africa, Asia, and Latin America gained independence from colonization and how these countries struggled to develop stable governments and national identities.

**Why Does This Matter?** In the years following World War II, numerous colonial and imperial territories were given their independence. When independent, their struggles did not end, but changed. Citizens of these new countries began to focus not on outside domination but on the contrasts that had developed between the foreign cultures that had been impressed upon them and their own indigenous traditions. This balance remains important today in the context of globalism and nationalism worldwide.

**How Will You Know That You Learned It?** You will be able to identify the cause and effects of independence movements throughout the world during the second half of the twentieth century and the political, cultural, and social implications of these movements.

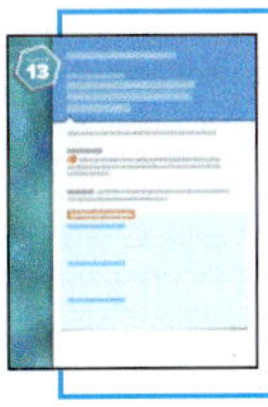

**Using Your Inquiry Journal** As you read this chapter and examine the primary sources, use your Inquiry Journal to help you make notes and expand your list of questions. As you gather information, think about how you will answer the Essential Questions above.

Gallo Images/Alamy

# PLACE & TIME Africa and Asia 1945–1993

Both decolonization and the Cold War, which escalated after World War II, would dramatically change the map of the world with colonies in Africa and Asia winning their independence from European powers. But even after these nations gained their independence, they struggled to maintain balanced economies and political stability.

## STEP INTO THE PLACE

Read the quote and look at the information presented on the map.

1. **EXPLORING REGION** Look at the dates each country gained its independence. Why do you think the first countries to become independent were the larger ones?

2. **DETERMINING CENTRAL IDEAS** What were the goals of nationalist leaders such as Kwame Nkrumah?

## STEP INTO THE TIME

**UNDERSTANDING CHANGE**
According to the information in the time line, how did independence impact the new nations that were founded after World War II?

"For centuries, Europeans dominated the African continent. The white man arrogated to himself the right to rule and to be obeyed by the non-white; his mission, he claimed, was to 'civilise' Africa. Under this cloak, the Europeans robbed the continent of vast riches and inflicted unimaginable suffering on the African people. All this makes a sad story . . . All we ask of the former colonial powers is their goodwill and co-operation to remedy past mistakes and injustices and to grant independence to the colonies in Africa."

—Kwame Nkrumah, from *I Speak of Freedom*, 1961

Nkrumah, Kwame. 1961. I Speak of Freedom: A Statement of African Ideology. Published 1976 by Greenwood Press.

## AFRICA AND ASIA

**1947** India and Pakistan gain independence

**1949** Indonesia gains independence

**1957** Ghana becomes first British colony to gain independence

1945 — 1955 — 1965

## WORLD EVENTS

**1946** Juan Perón is elected president of Argentina

**1948** State of Israel established

**1959** Fidel Castro seizes power in Cuba

**1963** Dr. Martin Luther King, Jr., delivers "I Have a Dream" speech

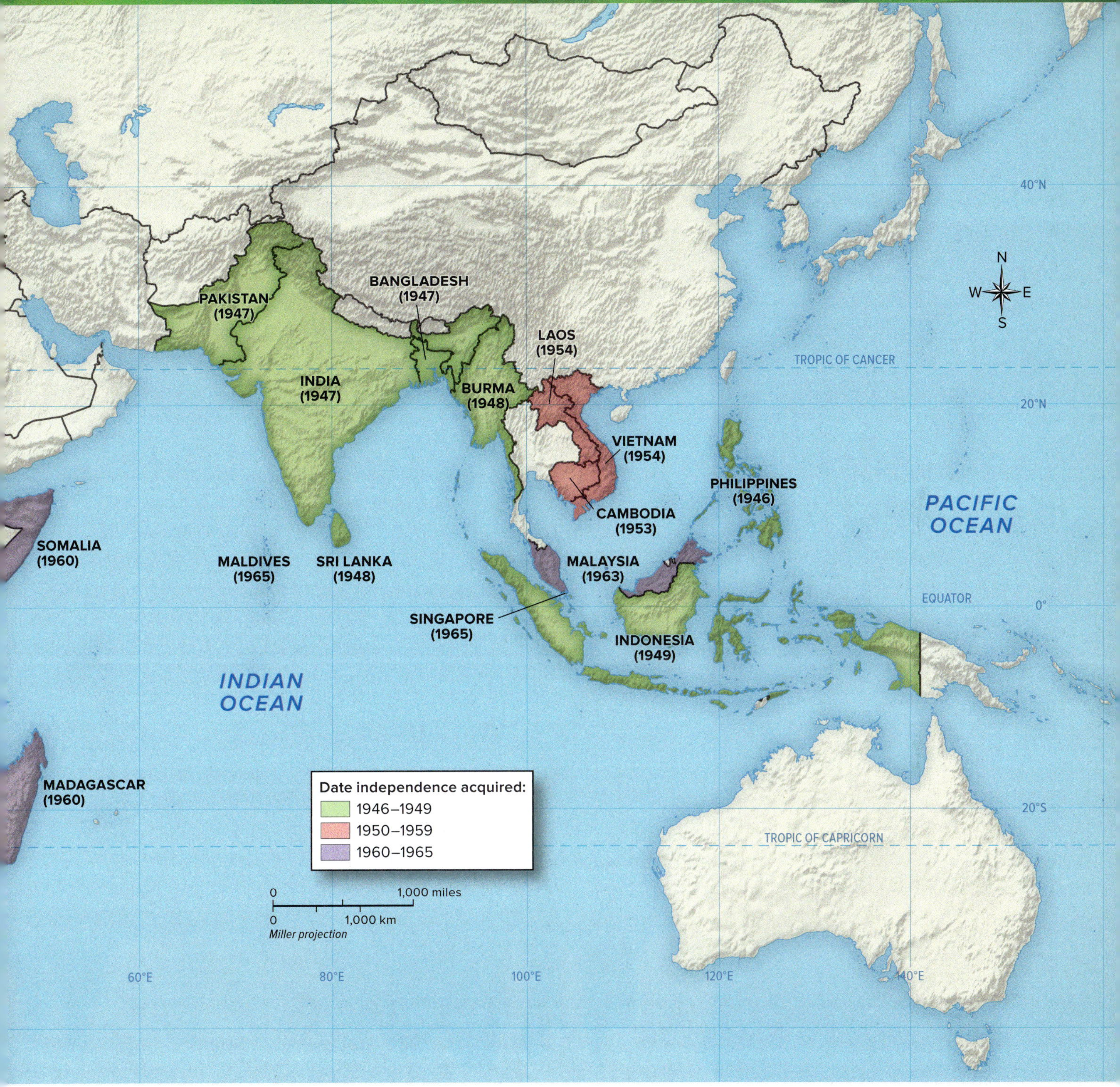


**1966** Indira Gandhi becomes prime minister of India

**1968** Student uprising in France

**1973** U.S. President Richard Nixon signs cease-fire agreement with North Vietnam

**1973** Israeli Prime Minister Golda Meir responds to attacks by Egypt and Syria

**1975**

**1979** Egypt-Israel Peace Treaty signed

**1979** Reza Shah Pahlavi is overthrown in Iranian Revolution

**1980** Poland's Solidarity union is founded

**1985**

**1990** Nelson Mandela is released from prison

**1991** Aung San Suu Kyi wins Nobel Peace Prize for pro-democracy efforts in Myanmar

**1992** Peace settlement ends war in El Salvador

**1993**

**1993** Oslo Accords gives PLO control of semi-independent area

## ESSENTIAL QUESTIONS

- *How can political change cause conflict?*
- *How can political relationships affect economic relationships?*

LESSON 1

# South and Southeast Asia

## THE STORY BEGINS...

After World War II ended, the people of India began putting greater pressure on the British government for independence. These efforts were finally realized on August 15, 1947, when India and Pakistan became independent nations at the stroke of midnight. The previous evening, Jawaharlal Nehru, India's first prime minister gave the following speech:

> "Long years ago we made a tryst with destiny, and now the time comes when we shall redeem our pledge, not wholly or in full measure, but very substantially. At the stroke of the midnight hour, when the world sleeps, India will awake to life and freedom. A moment comes, which comes but rarely in history, when we step out from the old to the new, when an age ends, and when the soul of a nation, long suppressed, finds utterance. It is fitting that at this solemn moment we take the pledge of dedication to the service of India and her people and to the still larger cause of humanity. . . . To the people of India, whose representatives we are, we make an appeal to join us with faith and confidence in this great adventure. This is no time for petty and destructive criticism, no time for ill-will or blaming others. We have to build the noble mansion of free India where all her children may dwell."
>
> —Jawaharlal Nehru, speech on the granting of Indian independence, August 14, 1947

Although India and Pakistan had gained their independence, these new states now faced a number of growing challenges.

*In 1947, India gained its independence from Great Britain and formed its own government. This parade from the time celebrates the event.* ▶

| Challenges in India |
| --- |
| |
| |
| |

**ANALYZING KEY IDEAS AND DETAILS**

**UNDERSTANDING CONTEXT** Read closely to identify the challenges India faced after gaining independence. Record each challenge in a graphic organizer like this one.

## INDIA DIVIDED

**GUIDING QUESTION** *How did India emerge as an independent country?*

At the end of World War II, British India's Muslims and Hindus were divided. The leaders in India decided British India would have to be divided into two countries, one Hindu (India) and one Muslim (Pakistan). Pakistan consisted of two regions separated by India in between them. One section, West Pakistan, was to the northwest of India. The other section, East Pakistan, was to the northeast of India.

On August 15, 1947, India and Pakistan became independent. Millions of Hindus and Muslims fled across the new borders, Hindus toward India and Muslims toward Pakistan. Violence resulted from these mass migrations, and more than a million people were killed. One of the dead was well known. On January 30, 1948, a Hindu militant assassinated Mohandas Gandhi as he was going to morning prayer. India's new beginning had not been easy.

**UNDERSTANDING CRAFT AND STRUCTURE**

1. **ANALYZING TEXT PRESENTATION** In what order does the writer present the facts about India at the end of World War II? Does the way the text is organized help you better understand the information?
2. **DETERMINING MEANING** The text about the "New India" states, "Private enterprise was allowed at the local level. . . ." What does the phrase *private enterprise* mean in this context?

### THE NEW INDIA

> "The future beckons to us. Whither do we go and what shall be our endeavour? To bring freedom and opportunity to the common man, to the peasants and workers of India; to fight and end poverty and ignorance and disease; to build up a prosperous, democratic and progressive nation, and to create social, economic and political institutions which will ensure justice and fullness of life to every man and woman.
>
> We have hard work ahead. There is no resting for any one of us till we redeem our pledge in full, till we make all the people of India what destiny intended them to be."

—Jawaharlal Nehru, *"Tryst with Destiny"* speech, Aug. 14, 1947

**ANALYZING PRIMARY SOURCES**

1. **DETERMINING MEANING** What does Nehru mean by saying, "The future beckons to us"?
2. **ANALYZING IDEAS** How does Nehru emphasize the idea that all Indian people are entitled to civil rights?

Having worked closely with Mohandas Gandhi for Indian independence, Jawaharlal Nehru (juh • WAH • huhr • LAHL NEHR • oo) led the Congress Party, formerly known as the Indian National Congress. Nehru admired the socialist ideals of the British Labour Party. His political goal was a parliamentary government led by a prime minister. His economic goals called for a moderate socialist economy. Under Nehru's leadership, the Indian state took ownership of major industries, utilities, and transportation. Private enterprise was allowed at the local level, and farmland was left in private hands. The Indian government also sought to avoid dependence on foreign investment. India developed a large industrial sector, and industrial production almost tripled between 1950 and 1965.

CITIZENSHIP

## SELECTING A PRIME MINISTER IN INDIA

With more than 1.2 billion people, India is today the world's largest democracy. Unlike in the United States, where the chief executive, the president, is elected through an electoral college, India's prime minister is chosen by the Lok Sahba (the House of the People). This is similar to the way the House of Commons in the United Kingdom selects its prime minister and is a testament to the long influence of Britain in India.

Every five years, India elects representatives from different parties to serve in the Lok Sahba. The party that holds a majority is empowered to select the prime minister. If no single party has a majority of the seats, the parties must create coalitions that can agree on a platform and a prime minister.

1. **DETERMINING CONTEXT** Why are political parties important in the selection of the prime minister?
2. **IDENTIFYING CONNECTIONS** How is the election of India's head of government similar to and different from how the United States elects its own?

**DETERMINING MEANING**

The word *align* comes from the French word meaning "line" and means "to get or fall into line." How does knowing the meaning of the word *align* help you better understand what a **principle of nonalignment** is?

Nehru also guided India's foreign policy according to a **principle of nonalignment**. Concerned about military conflict between the United States and the Soviet Union and about the influence of former colonial powers, Nehru refused to align India with either bloc. Rather, he joined other developing countries in the idea that they should not take sides in the growing Cold War.

After Nehru's death, the Congress Party selected his daughter, Indira Gandhi (not related to Mohandas Gandhi), as prime minister. She held office for most of the time between 1966 and 1984. India faced many problems during this period. In the 1950s and 1960s, India's population grew by 2 percent a year, contributing to widespread poverty. Millions lived in vast city slums. It was in the slums of Kolkata (formerly Calcutta) that Mother Teresa, a Catholic nun, helped the poor, sick, and dying Indian people.

**INFERRING** Examine the photograph. Why do you think these refugees from India and Pakistan are sitting on top of the train cars?

*During partition, nearly 2 million refugees fled to either India or Pakistan.*

Bettmann/Corbis

Growing ethnic and religious strife presented another major problem. One conflict involved the Sikhs. Sikhs are followers of a religion founded in the mid-fifteenth century in northern India. Many Sikhs lived in a region known as Punjab, a northwest Indian province. Militant Sikhs demanded that this province be given its independence from India. Gandhi refused and in 1984 used military force against Sikh rebels. More than 450 Sikhs were killed. Seeking revenge, two Sikh members of Gandhi's personal bodyguard assassinated her later that year.

Conflict between Hindus and Muslims also continued. Religious differences between India and Pakistan fueled a long-term dispute between the two countries over the region of Kashmir. Kashmir is a territory that rests between the two nations along their northern border.

Following the assassination of Indira Gandhi, her son Rajiv replaced his mother as prime minister. As prime minister, Rajiv began to move the government in new directions. Private enterprise was encouraged, as well as foreign investment. His successors continued to **transfer** state-run industries into private hands and to rely on the free market. This led to a noticeable growth in the middle class.

Rajiv Gandhi was prime minister from 1984 to 1989. While campaigning for reelection in 1991, he was assassinated. In the following years, the Congress Party lost its leadership position and had to compete with new political parties. Rajiv's widow, Sonia Gandhi, would become the next leader of the Congress Party in 1998.

### DETERMINING MEANING

Read the text of the paragraph that contains the word **transfer**. One definition of *transfer* is "to cause to pass from one person or entity to another." How does this definition help the reader understand how *transfer* is used in this context?

### GEOGRAPHIC REASONING

1. **EXPLORING REGIONS** Look at Kashmir's position on the map. From the information shown, what can you infer about why this region has experienced conflict until the present day?
2. **HUMAN-ENVIRONMENT INTERACTION** To what areas did India's Muslims flee? Why?

## THE PARTITION OF INDIA 1947

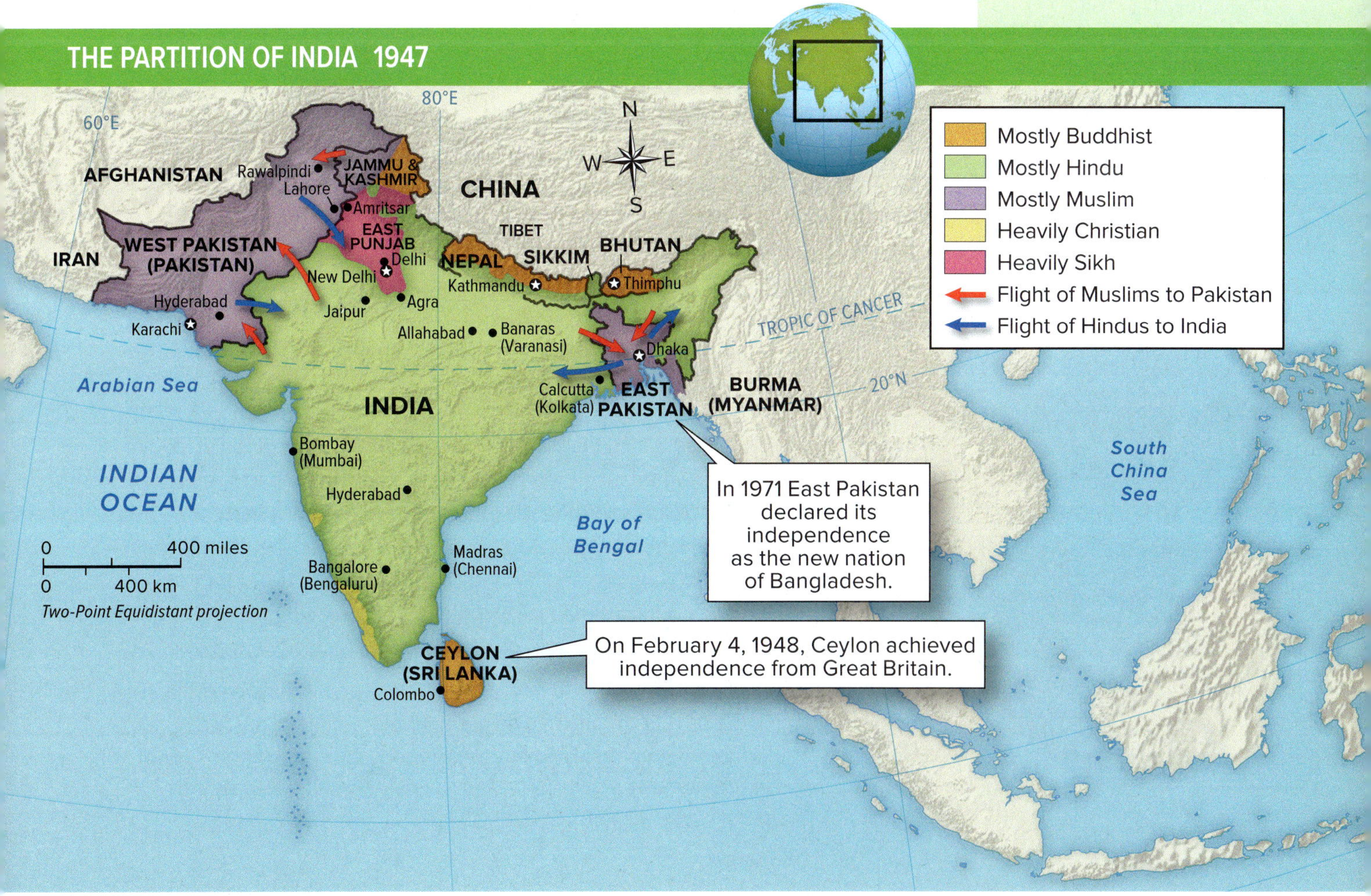

## PAKISTAN AND BANGLADESH

Unlike its neighbor India, Pakistan was a completely new nation when it attained independence in 1947. The growing division between East and West Pakistan, separate regions with different geographical features, caused internal conflicts. Many in East Pakistan believed that the government, based in West Pakistan, ignored their needs. In 1971 East Pakistan declared its independence from Pakistan. After a brief civil war, East Pakistan became the new nation of Bangladesh.

Both Bangladesh and Pakistan (formerly West Pakistan) have remained very poor. They also have had difficulty establishing stable governments. Military officials have often seized control of the civilian government.

### ✓ CHECKING FOR UNDERSTANDING

1. **UNDERSTANDING CHANGE** How did India emerge as an independent country?
2. **UNDERSTANDING CONTEXT** Why did India pursue a principle of nonalignment in the 1950s?
3. **IDENTIFYING EFFECTS** What were the immediate effects of the partition of British India?

# SOUTHEAST ASIA

**GUIDING QUESTION** *What experiences did independence bring to new Southeast Asian countries?*

After World War II, most states in Southeast Asia gained independence from their colonial rulers. The process varied considerably across the region, however. In July 1946, the United States granted total independence to the Philippines. Great Britain was also willing to end its colonial rule in Southeast Asia. In 1948 Burma became independent from Great Britain.

In the beginning, many of the leaders of the newly independent states in Southeast Asia admired Western political and economic practices. They hoped to form democratic, capitalist states like those in the West. By the end of the 1950s, however, hopes for rapid economic growth had failed. Internal disputes weakened the new democratic governments, opening the door to both military and one-party autocratic regimes.

**ANALYZING KEY IDEAS AND DETAILS**

1. **DETERMINING CENTRAL IDEAS** What is a central idea of the section "The Philippines"?
2. **SUMMARIZING** In your own words, summarize the section "Women in South and Southeast Asia."

## INDONESIA AND MYANMAR

The Netherlands was less willing than Great Britain to abandon its colonial empire in Southeast Asia. The Netherlands tried to suppress a new Indonesian republic proclaimed by Achmed Sukarno. When the Indonesian Communist Party attempted to seize power, however, the United States pressured the Netherlands to grant independence to Sukarno and his non-Communist Nationalist Party. In 1949 the Netherlands recognized the new Republic of Indonesia.

In 1950 the new leaders created a parliamentary system and Sukarno was elected the first president. In the late 1950s, however, he dissolved the constitution and tried to rule on his own through what he called "guided democracy." Sukarno also nationalized foreign-owned enterprises and sought economic aid from China and the Soviet Union. Military officers overthrew Sukarno and established a military government under General Suharto. Democracy had failed.

*Aung San Suu Kyi, Myanmar's pro-democracy opposition leader.*

Sandro Tucci/The LIFE Images Collection/Getty Images

Burma, which is now the nation of Myanmar, came under military control in the early 1960s. The people of Myanmar, however, continued to fight for democracy. Aung San Suu Kyi, the daughter of Aung San, who led the Burma Independence Army in 1947, returned to Myanmar in 1988 and became involved in the movement for democracy. Her party won a landslide victory in 1990, but the military rulers refused to hand over power. In 1991 Suu Kyi won the Nobel Peace Prize for her pro-democracy efforts and was appointed state counselor in 2016. She has recently been criticized for the treatment of the Rohingya people, a Muslim minority, within the country.

## VIETNAM AND CAMBODIA

By 1975, North Vietnamese Communist armies had forcibly reunited Vietnam and begun the process of rebuilding that shattered land. The reunification of Vietnam under Communist rule had an immediate impact on the region. By the end of 1975, both Laos and Cambodia had Communist governments. In Cambodia, Pol Pot, leader of the Khmer Rouge, massacred more than 1 million Cambodians. Conflict continued in Cambodia throughout the 1980s. It was not until 1993 that Cambodians held free UN-sponsored elections. Meanwhile, the government in Vietnam remained suspicious of Western-style democracy and repressed any opposition to the Communist Party's guiding **role** over the state.

**DETERMINING MEANING**

The word **role** comes from the French word *rôle*, which means "an actor's script." How does this word origin help a reader better understand how the word *role* is used in this lesson?

**MAKING CONNECTIONS TO TODAY**

### THE CAMBODIAN GENOCIDE

In 1975, Cambodia's Khmer Rouge singled out the rich, the well-educated, and members of ethnic or religious minorities as enemies of the Communist government. The genocide spread to virtually anyone who could not labor on Cambodia's collectivized farms—the elderly, handicapped, ill, and even children and babies. By 2003, when the Cambodian government agreed to prosecute those responsible for the genocide, most of the guilty were dead or disappeared—including Pol Pot, who died of natural causes in 1998 and was never prosecuted. Seeing little action from Cambodia, the United Nations established its own court in 2006 to prosecute the remaining leaders. After 11 years, this court achieved only three convictions, leaving many to fear that the Cambodian genocide will go largely unpunished.

1. **UNDERSTANDING CONTEXT** What role did Cambodia's Communist government have in the genocide that occurred there in the late 1970s?
2. **RELATING EVENTS** How did the genocide hinder democratic progress in Cambodia?

## THE PHILIPPINES

In more recent years, some Southeast Asian societies have shown signs of moving again toward more democratic governments. One example is the Philippines. There, President Ferdinand Marcos came to power in 1965. Fraud and corruption became widespread in the Marcos regime. In the early 1980s, Marcos was accused of involvement in the killing of a popular opposition leader, Benigno Aquino. Corazon Aquino, wife of the murdered leader, became president in 1986 and worked for democratic reforms. Nevertheless, she soon proved unable to resolve many of the country's chronic economic and social problems.

*Filipino students hold a political rally during the funeral procession of Benigno Aquino.*

**DETERMINING CONTEXT** Who are these men, and why are they featured on this poster?

## WOMEN IN SOUTH AND SOUTHEAST ASIA

Across South and Southeast Asia, the rights and roles of women have changed. In India, women's rights expanded after independence. Its constitution of 1950 forbade **discrimination** based on gender and called for equal pay for equal work. Child marriage was also outlawed. Women were encouraged to attend school and to enter the labor market. In Southeast Asia, virtually all the newly independent states granted women full legal and political rights. Women have become more active in politics and occasionally hold senior political and corporate positions.

**DETERMINING MEANING**

The word **discrimination** contains the root word *discriminate*, which means "to divide or separate." How might knowing this root word help a person determine the meaning of *discrimination*?

### ✓ CHECKING FOR UNDERSTANDING

1. **INTERPRETING** What experiences did independence bring to new Southeast Asian countries?

2. **UNDERSTANDING CONTEXT** How was the government of the Philippines different from others in the region?

3. **ANALYZING CHANGE** What challenges did Indonesia and Myanmar confront following independence?

Sandro Tucci/Getty Images News/Getty Images

## LESSON 1 REVIEW

### Time and Place

1. **IDENTIFYING CONNECTIONS** How did the Cold War influence India's principle of nonalignment?

### Building History-Social Science Analysis Skills

2. **ANALYZING CHANGE** What were some differences among the governments that emerged in Southeast Asia in the mid- to late twentieth century?

3. **IDENTIFYING CONNECTIONS** How did the Sikhs respond to Indira Gandhi's use of military force against Sikh rebels?

4. **IDENTIFYING CAUSES** Why did democracy not succeed in Indonesia after it gained independence?

### Writing About History

5. **ARGUMENTATIVE WRITING** Pretend you are a citizen of a South or Southeast Asian country that gained its independence. Write an essay about your experiences.

### Collaborating

6. **COLLABORATING** With a partner, create a list of economic, social, and political issues faced by India after it gained independence.

ESSENTIAL QUESTIONS

- *How can political change cause conflict?*
- *How can political relationships affect economic relationships?*

LESSON 2

# The Middle East

## THE STORY BEGINS...

On New Year's Eve, 1977, Jimmy Carter, president of the United States, was the guest of the Shah of Iran at the Niavaran Palace in Tehran, Iran's capital. During that evening's formal state dinner, President Carter made the following remarks:

> "Iran, because of the great leadership of the Shah, is an island of stability in one of the most troubled areas of the world.
>
> This is a great tribute to you, Your Majesty, and to your leadership and to the respect and admiration and love which your people give to you. . . .
>
> We have no other nation on earth . . . closer to us in planning our mutual military security. We have no other nation with whom we have closer consultation on regional problems that concern us both. And there is no leader with whom I have a deeper sense of personal gratitude and personal friendship."

—President Jimmy Carter, December 31, 1977

However, outside in the streets, demonstrations against the shah's rule had been growing since October. On the 7th of January, 1978, one week after this state dinner, these demonstrations would turn into a revolution that would topple the shah and permanently change the sunny relationship between Iran and the United States.

*The Shah and Queen of Iran, 1971* ▶

| Year | Event |
|---|---|
| | |
| | |
| | |
| | |
| | |

**ANALYZING KEY IDEAS AND DETAILS**

**CITING TEXT EVIDENCE** Read carefully to identify the key events in the history of Arab-Israeli conflicts. List each event along with the year it occurred in a graphic organizer like this one.

# THE MIDEAST CRISIS

**ANALYZING KEY IDEAS AND DETAILS**

1. **DETERMINING CENTRAL IDEAS** What is the central idea of this section, and how does the text present and develop this idea?
2. **CITING TEXT EVIDENCE** How does the writer demonstrate that Nasser supported Pan-Arabism? Cite specific evidence from the text in your answer.

**GUIDING QUESTION** *What key issues underline the Arab-Israeli conflicts?*

In the Middle East, as in Asia and Africa, a number of newly independent states emerged after World War II. Syria and Lebanon gained their independence just before the end of the war. Jordan to their south also achieved its complete self-rule soon afterward. These newly independent states in the Middle East were largely Muslim.

As industry grew around the world, many nations began to rely on the Middle East for its oil resources. This would also serve to put the region on center stage as an area of conflict during the Cold War. Countries within the region used the circumstances of the Cold War to gain political, military, and economic benefits from the United States or the Soviet Union, playing one superpower against the other. Iran's nationalization of its oil industry after World War II would also play a role in conflicts resulting from the rising nationalism in the region.

## THE PALESTINE MANDATE

In the years between the two world wars, many Jews had immigrated to the Palestine Mandate, which is their historic homeland and religious center. Arab immigration to the mandate also increased. Tensions between Jews and Arabs had intensified during the 1930s. After a massive Arab revolt that lasted from 1936 to 1939, Great Britain, which governed the region under the League of Nations' mandate, decided to limit Jewish immigration into the area and rejected proposals for an independent Jewish state.

The Zionist movement wanted the land of ancient Israel to be a home for the Jewish people and had begun building the institutions necessary for statehood. Many people had been shocked at the end of World War II when they learned about the deliberate killing of 6 million European Jews in Nazi death camps. As a result, sympathy for the Jewish cause grew.

In 1947 a United Nations (UN) General Assembly resolution called for the Palestine Mandate to be divided into a Jewish state and an Arab state. As the British Palestine Mandate was set to expire on May 15, 1948, David Ben-Gurion, a Zionist leader who would become Israel's first prime minister, announced the establishment of the State of Israel on May 14th of that year. Around the same time, Arab nations, including Iraq, Syria, Jordan, Lebanon, and areas of Turkey, ended their time as mandates and gained independence.

The Arab states saw the creation of the State of Israel as a betrayal of the Palestinian Arabs and rejected the existence of a Jewish state. In response five Arab countries invaded Israel. The invasion failed, but the Arab states continued to refuse to recognize the State of Israel, leading to ongoing conflict. As a result of these events, hundreds of thousands of Palestinians fled to neighboring Arab countries, as well as the Jordanian-ruled West Bank and Egyptian-ruled Gaza Strip. Many fled at the urging of Arab states who told them they could return after Israel was destroyed. Other Palestinians remained in Israel. Another result of the conflict was that hundreds of thousands of Jews in Muslim countries in the Middle East and North Africa were expelled. Most sought refuge in Israel.

## NASSER AND PAN-ARABISM

In Egypt, a new leader arose who played an important role in the Arab world. Colonel Gamal Abdel Nasser took control of the Egyptian government in the early 1950s. Nasser strongly supported Arab nationalism and also opposed the existence of Israel. He ordered a blockade of the Straits of Tiran to stop ships heading to Israel's southern port of Eliat and supported terrorist attacks on Israel. On July 26, 1956, he seized the Suez Canal Company, which had been under British and French administration since the 1800s.

Great Britain and France were upset by this threat to their world positions. The Suez Canal was an important waterway linking the Mediterranean Sea to Asia. Great Britain and France decided to strike back against Egypt, and Israel quickly joined them. The three nations launched a joint attack on Egypt, starting the Suez War of 1956.

The United States and the Soviet Union joined in supporting Nasser. Both countries opposed French and British influence in the Middle East. They forced Britain, France, and Israel to withdraw from Egypt.

Nasser emerged from the conflict a powerful leader. He began to promote **Pan-Arabism**, or Arab unity. In February 1958, Egypt formally united with Syria in the United Arab Republic (UAR). Nasser was named its first president. Egypt and Syria hoped the union would eventually include all Arab states.

### ARAB-ISRAELI DISPUTES 1947–1993

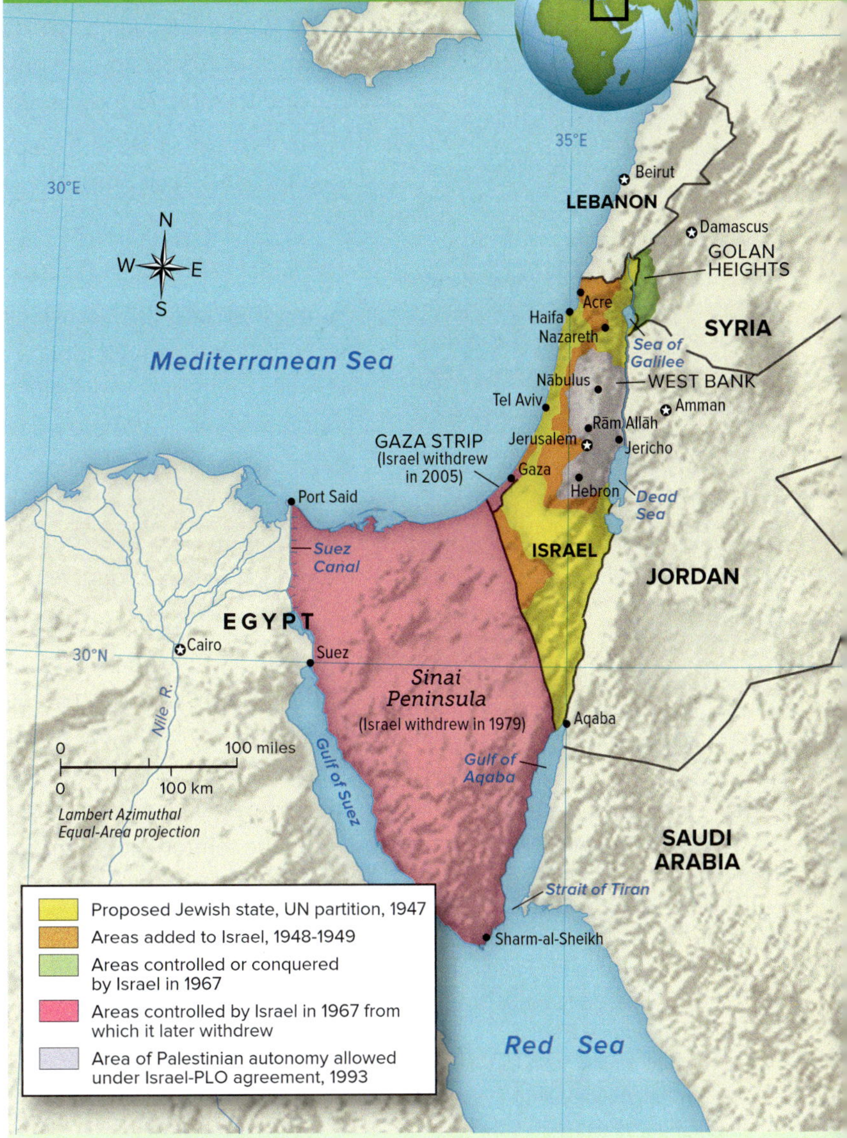


#### GEOGRAPHIC REASONING

1. **SPATIAL THINKING** What makes the Sinai Peninsula strategically important in the Middle East?
2. **HUMAN POPULATION** What was a result of the 1993 Oslo Peace Accords?

#### DETERMINING MEANING

The word **Pan-Arabism** contains the prefix *pan-*, which means "all-inclusive." How does knowing this help the reader understand what *Pan-Arabism* is?

**DETERMINING MEANING**

The word **revenue** comes from the French word *revenir*, which means "to return." How does this word origin help the reader to better understand how the word *revenue* is used in this lesson?

Many other Arab leaders were suspicious of Pan-Arabism. Oil-rich Arab states were concerned they would have to share **revenues** with poorer states in the Middle East. In Nasser's view, Arab unity meant that wealth derived from oil, which currently flowed into a few Arab states or to foreign interests, could be used to improve the standard of living throughout the Middle East.

In 1961 Syrian military leaders took over Syria and withdrew the country from the UAR. Nasser continued to work on behalf of Arab interests.

**BIOGRAPHY**

### GOLDA MEIR
**(1898–1978)**

Golda Meir was born in Kiev, Russia, but immigrated with her family to Milwaukee, Wisconsin, at the age of eight. In her early 20s, she moved to the Palestine Mandate, where she was active in politics and the Zionist movement. Meir signed Israel's declaration of independence in 1948. She was subsequently elected to parliament and later served as both labor and foreign minister. In 1969 Meir became the prime minister of Israel and led her country during the Yom Kippur War. During her career, she attempted to establish peace with neighboring Arab states and fostered diplomacy with foreign powers.

**DRAWING CONCLUSIONS** How do you think Meir's upbringing affected her foreign policy decisions?

## THE ARAB-ISRAELI DISPUTE

During 1956 and 1957, tensions between the Arab states and Israel increased. In 1967 Nasser again imposed a blockade against Israeli shipping and made speeches publicly threatening Israel. He declared, "We are now ready to confront Israel . . . We are [now] ready to deal with the entire Palestine question." In other speeches, he stated that Egypt was "ready to enter a general war with Israel. . ." and ". . . our basic objective will be to destroy Israel." Even as he gave these speeches in the spring of 1967, Arab armies began massing in Syria, Jordan, and Egypt near Israel's borders.

Fearing attack by Egypt and other Arab states, on June 5, 1967, Israel launched air strikes against Egypt and destroyed most of Egypt's air force. When Jordan joined the war, Israel responded again with air strikes. In the Six-Day War, the Israeli army broke the blockade, defeated the Arab forces, and took control of Gaza and the Sinai Peninsula from Egypt. The army also took the West Bank and East Jerusalem from Jordan and the Golan Heights from Syria, tripling the size of the territory under its control. As a result, a million Palestinians now lived in areas under Israeli control, most on the West Bank. Following the war, Israel proposed to return the Sinai and Golan Heights and begin negotiations on the status of Gaza and the West Bank in exchange for Arab recognition of Israel and its right to exist. In the wake of severe defeat and high casualties suffered, the Arab states responded with the Khartoum Resolution: "no peace with Israel, no recognition of Israel, no negotiations with Israel. . ."

Over the next few years, Arab states continued to demand the return of the West Bank and Gaza. Nasser died in 1970, and Anwar el-Sadat succeeded him. On October 6, 1973 (on Yom Kippur, Judaism's holiest day of the year), Egypt and Syria launched a coordinated surprise attack against Israel. Golda Meir, Israel's first female prime minister, had little time to mobilize troops. Soon, however, Israeli forces went on the offensive and pushed into Egypt. A UN-negotiated cease-fire on October 22 stopped the fighting. An agreement in 1974 officially ended the conflict, but tensions remained.

Meanwhile, however, the war was having indirect results in Western nations. In 1960 several oil-producing states had formed OPEC, the Organization of the Petroleum Exporting Countries, to control the price of oil. During the Yom Kippur War, some OPEC nations announced large increases in the price of oil to foreign countries. The price hikes, coupled with cuts in oil production, led to oil shortages and serious economic problems in the West.

In 1977 U.S. President Jimmy Carter began to press for a compromise peace between Arabs and Israelis. In September 1978, President Carter met with President Sadat of Egypt and Israeli prime minister Menachem Begin (BAY • gihn) at Camp David in the United States. The result was the Camp David Accords, an agreement to sign an Israeli-Egyptian peace treaty. The treaty, signed by Sadat and Begin in March 1979, led to a complete Israeli withdrawal from the Sinai Peninsula and ended the state of war between Egypt and Israel. Many Arab countries, however, continued to refuse to recognize Israel.

In 1964 the Egyptians took the lead in forming the Palestine Liberation Organization (PLO) to represent Palestinian interests. The PLO believed that only the Palestinian Arabs should have a state in the Palestine region and called for the destruction of Israel. At the same time, a guerrilla movement called al-Fatah, headed by the PLO political leader Yasir Arafat, began to launch attacks on Israel. These terrorist attacks continued for decades.

During the 1980s, Palestinian Arabs, frustrated by their failure to achieve self-rule, grew more militant. This militancy led to a movement called an **intifada**, or uprising, concentrated on the territories controlled by Israel since the 1967 Arab-Israeli war. Eventually, in the Oslo Accords of 1993, an interim agreement for future negotiations, Israel and the PLO agreed to the establishment of a Palestinian Authority in the West Bank that would exercise considerable autonomy. In return, the PLO recognized Israel and renounced terrorism.

### ✓ CHECKING FOR UNDERSTANDING

1. **DETERMINING CONTEXT** What key issues underline the Arab-Israeli conflicts?
2. **RELATING EVENTS** What was the international reaction to Egypt's seizure of the Suez Canal Company?
3. **EXPLAINING CAUSES** Why was the Palestine Liberation Organization formed?

## IRAN, IRAQ, AND AFGHANISTAN

**GUIDING QUESTION** *How has the move for self-rule led to turmoil among the countries of the Middle East?*

The conflict between Israel and the Palestinians is one of many challenges in the Middle East. As in other parts of the world, a few people are rich while many are poor. Some countries prosper because of oil, but others remain in poverty. A response to these problems is the growth of movements based on Islam. Many of these groups believe that Muslims must return to a pure Islamic culture and values to build prosperous societies. Some are willing to use violence to bring about an Islamic revolution. Such a revolution took place in Iran.

### THE IRANIAN REVOLUTION

Under the leadership of Mohammad Mosaddeq, Iran nationalized its oil industry in 1951. This meant many foreign oil companies, many of them British, lost their control of Iran's oil industry. The international community was alarmed, and Mosaddeq was overthrown in a coup in 1953 led by the Central Intelligence Agency of the United States. The rule of the shah, Reza Shah Pahlavi, was restored. Revenues from oil helped make Iran a rich country.

However, there was much opposition to the shah in Iran. Many Muslims looked with distaste at Iranian society. In their eyes it was based on greed and materialism, which they identified with American influence. Leading opposition to the shah was the Ayatollah Ruhollah Khomeini (ko • MAY • nee), a member of the Muslim clergy. By the late 1970s, many Iranians had begun to respond to Khomeini's words. In

**UNDERSTANDING CRAFT AND STRUCTURE**

1. **ANALYZING TEXT PRESENTATION** In what order does the writer present the facts about the Iranian Revolution? Does the way the text is organized help you better understand the information?
2. **DETERMINING MEANING** Read the paragraph that begins, "After World War II." How does the content of this paragraph help you figure out what *mujahideen* means?

1979 the shah's government collapsed and was replaced by an Islamic republic. Although Iran had been a Shia-controlled nation for centuries, the emergence of a state led by Shia clergy increased regional tensions.

The new government, led by the Ayatollah Khomeini, moved to restore Islamic law. Supporters of the shah were executed or fled Iran. Anti-American feelings erupted when militants seized 52 Americans in the United States embassy in Tehran and held them hostage for more than a year.

> "Xenomaniacs, people infatuated with the West, empty people, people with no content! Come to your senses; do not try to westernize everything you have! Look at the West, and see who the people are in the West that present themselves as champions of human rights and what their aims are. Is it human rights they really care about, or the rights of the superpowers? What they really want to secure are the rights of the superpowers. Our jurists should not follow or imitate them."
>
> —Ayatollah Khomeini, *"The Uprising of Khurdad 15, 1979"* speech

**ANALYZING PRIMARY SOURCES**

1. **DETERMINING CENTRAL IDEAS** What idea is Khomeini trying to impress upon his audience?
2. **ANALYZING IDEAS** What opinion does Khomeini present of Western culture? What does he believe are the motives of the Westerners in the Middle East?

Since the revolution, Iran has been shunned by the international community and by the majority of their neighbors in the Middle East. After Khomeini's death in 1989, a more moderate government allowed some civil liberties. Some Iranians were dissatisfied with the government's economic performance. Others, especially young people, pressed for more freedoms and an end to the rule of conservative Muslim clerics.

## THE IRAN-IRAQ WAR

To the west of Iran was a militant and hostile Iraq, led by Saddam Hussein since 1979. Iran and Iraq have long had an uneasy relationship. Religious differences have fueled their disputes. Although both are Muslim nations, the Iranians are mostly Shia Muslims. The Iraqi leaders under Saddam Hussein, on the other hand, were mostly Sunni Muslims. Iran and Iraq have fought over territory, too, especially over the Strait of Hormuz. Strategically very important, the strait connects the Persian Gulf and the Gulf of Oman.

In 1980 Saddam Hussein launched a brutal war against Iran. During the Iran-Iraq War, children were used to clear dangerous minefields. Saddam Hussein used poison gas against soldiers and civilians, especially the Kurds, an ethnic minority in the north who wanted their own state. In 1988, Iran and Iraq signed a cease-fire without resolving the war's basic issues.

*A pro-Khomeini demonstration during the Iranian Revolution, December 1978*

**ANALYZING INFORMATION** How would you describe the demonstration in this picture?



PHOTO:Alain Keler/Sygma/Corbis; TEXT:Ayatollah Khomeini. 1979. Quoted 2005 by Stephen C. Poulson. Social Movements in Twentieth-Century Iran: Culture, Ideology, and Mobilizing Frameworks. Lanham: Lexington Books, A Division of Rowman & Littlefield Publishers, Inc.

## THE PERSIAN GULF WAR

In August 1990, Saddam Hussein sent his troops across the border to seize Kuwait, an oil-rich country on the Persian Gulf. The invasion began the Gulf War. The United States led the international forces that freed Kuwait. Hoping an internal revolt would overthrow Hussein, the allies imposed harsh economic sanctions on Iraq. The overthrow of Saddam Hussein, however, did not happen.

## AFGHANISTAN AND THE TALIBAN

After World War II, the king of Afghanistan, in search of economic assistance for his country, developed close ties with the Soviet Union. Internal fighting was followed in 1979 by a full-scale invasion of Afghanistan by the Soviets, who occupied the country for 10 years. Anti-Communist Islamic forces (known collectively as the mujahideen), supported by the United States and Pakistan, eventually ousted them. When the Soviets left, the Islamic groups began to fight for control of Afghanistan. One of these, the Taliban, seized the capital city of Kabul in 1996. By the fall of 1998, the Taliban controlled more than two-thirds of the country.

Backed by conservative religious forces in Pakistan, the Taliban provided a base of operations for Osama bin Laden. Bin Laden came from a wealthy family in Saudi Arabia and used his wealth to support the Afghan resistance. In 1988 bin Laden founded al-Qaeda, or "the base," which recruited Muslims to drive Westerners out of nations with a largely Muslim population. After the Taliban seized control of much of Afghanistan, bin Laden used bases there to train al-Qaeda recruits.

### ✓ CHECKING FOR UNDERSTANDING

1. **IDENTIFYING EFFECTS** How has the move for self-rule led to turmoil among the countries of the Middle East?
2. **RELATING EVENTS** What was the outcome of the Persian Gulf War?
3. **SUMMARIZING** How did the Taliban gain control in Afghanistan?

**MAKING CONNECTIONS TO TODAY**

### SHIA ISLAM AND IRAN

Since the seventh century, the two major sects of Islam, Sunni and Shia, have had a hostile relationship. Iran has been a Shia-controlled nation since the Ṣafavid Dynasty took control in Persia in the sixteenth century. One traditional distinction between Sunni and Shia Muslims involves the spiritual connection to the material world. The Shia place a greater emphasis on personal sacrifice for faith, while the Sunni advocate greater participation in the secular world. As a Shia-controlled nation, Iran has been at odds not only with the West but also with Sunni-controlled Islamic countries, such as Saudi Arabia.

1. **UNDERSTANDING CONTEXT** Based on traditional practices, how would a Shia Muslim likely perceive the West as opposed to the way a Sunni Muslim might perceive it?
2. **UNDERSTANDING CONTEXT** As a predominantly Shia nation, why do you think Iran has been so hostile toward outside influences?

# SOCIETY AND CULTURE

**GUIDING QUESTION** *How has Islam influenced society and culture in the Middle East?*

In recent years, conservative religious forces in the Middle East have tried to replace foreign culture and values with Islamic forms of belief and behavior. This movement is called Islamic fundamentalism or Islamic activism. For some Islamic leaders, Western values and culture are based on materialism, greed, and immorality. Extremists want to remove all Western influence in Muslim countries. These extremists give many Westerners an unfavorable impression of Islam.

Islamic fundamentalism began in Iran under the Ayatollah Khomeini. There the return to traditional Muslim beliefs reached into clothing styles, social practices, and the legal system. These ideas and practices spread to other Muslim countries. In Egypt, for example, militant Muslims assassinated President Sadat in 1981.

**INTEGRATING KNOWLEDGE AND IDEAS**

**ANALYZING IDEAS** Reread the paragraph that starts "In recent years. . . ." In what context does the author place the rise of Islamic fundamentalism in the Middle East?

*Women ride an escalator at an upscale shopping center in Dubai.*

**IDENTIFYING PERSPECTIVES**
How does this photograph show the contrast between tradition and modernity in the contemporary Middle East?

At the beginning of the twentieth century, women's place in Middle Eastern society had changed little for hundreds of years. Early Muslim women had participated in the political life of society and had extensive legal, political, and social rights. Cultural practices in many countries had overshadowed those rights, however.

In the nineteenth and twentieth centuries, Muslim scholars debated issues surrounding women's roles in society. Many argued for the need to rethink outdated interpretations and cultural practices that prevented women from realizing their potential. Until the 1970s, the general trend in urban areas was toward a greater role for women. Beginning in the 1970s, however, there was a shift toward more traditional roles for women. This trend was especially noticeable in Iran.

The literature of the Middle East since 1945 has reflected a rise in national awareness, which encouraged interest in historical traditions. Writers also began to deal more with secular themes for broader audiences, not just the elite. For example, *Cairo Trilogy* by Egyptian writer Naguib Mahfouz tells about a merchant family in Egypt in the 1920s. The changes in the family **parallel** the changes in Egypt. Mahfouz was the first writer in Arabic to win the Nobel Prize in Literature (in 1988). Another Middle Eastern writer, Shmuel Yosef Agnon, was the first writer in Hebrew to win a Nobel Prize in Literature (in 1966). The central themes of Agnon's writing explore the relationships among traditional Jewish life, the Hebrew language, and the modern world.

**DETERMINING MEANING**

Read the paragraph that contains the word **parallel**. The word *parallel* describes two objects that are equally side by side. How does this definition help the reader understand how *parallel* is used in this paragraph?

### ✓ CHECKING FOR UNDERSTANDING

1. **SUMMARIZING** How has Islam influenced society and culture in the Middle East?
2. **DETERMINING CONTEXT** How did the Islamic fundamentalists give Westerners an unfavorable view of Islam?
3. **UNDERSTANDING CONTEXT** How did the role of Islam in Middle Eastern society change in the later twentieth century?



## LESSON 2 REVIEW

### Time and Place

1. **IDENTIFYING CAUSES** How has the move for self-rule led to turmoil among the countries of the Middle East?

### Building History-Social Science Analysis Skills

2. **UNDERSTANDING CONTEXT** How did concern over revenue help lead to suspicion of Pan-Arabism?
3. **RELATING EVENTS** Use your notes to list specific events in the Arab-Israeli conflict.
4. **ANALYZING CHANGE** How has Islam influenced society and culture in the Middle East?

### Writing About History

5. **INFORMATIVE WRITING** Research Golda Meir and find out how she became a leader of Israel. What did a woman rising to this position of power say about the State of Israel at that time?

### Collaborating

6. **PRESENTING** With a partner, select one country from the Middle East. Together, create a presentation on this country and its history from 1945 to 1990. Be sure your presentation includes the change this country has experienced in government, economy, and culture and uses proper grammar, usage, and vocabulary terms.

## ESSENTIAL QUESTIONS

- *How can political change cause conflict?*
- *How can political relationships affect economic relationships?*

# THE STORY BEGINS...

LESSON 3

# Africa

A full century after the 1884 Berlin Conference, which inaugurated the era of New Imperialism in Africa, the continent was now largely free of imperialism. But the legacy of that imperialism persisted. In 1984 after receiving the Nobel Prize, the Anglican Bishop and antiapartheid campaigner Desmond Tutu delivered the following address to the Nobel Prize committee:

> "Unrest is endemic, and will remain an unchanging feature of the South African scene until apartheid, the root cause of it all, is finally dismantled. At this time, the Army is being quartered on the civilian population. There is a civil war being waged. South Africans are on either side. When the African National Congress and the Pan-Africanist Congress were banned in 1960, they declared that they had no option but to carry out the armed struggle. We in the South African Council of Church have said we are opposed to all forms of violence - that of a repressive and unjust system, and that of those who seek to overthrow that system. However, we have added that we understand those who say they have had to adopt what is a last resort for them. Violence is not being introduced into the South African situation de novo from outside by those who are called terrorists or freedom fighters, depending on whether you are oppressed or an oppressor. The South African situation is violent already, and the primary violence is that of apartheid, the violence of forced population removals, of inferior education, of detention without trial, of the migratory labor system. . . ."

—Desmond Tutu, *Nobel Lecture,* December 11, 1984

Almost exactly a decade later, black South Africans would finally be able to vote, and when they did, Nelson Mandela was elected South Africa's first black president.

*The rights and freedoms of black South Africans were heavily curtailed under the apartheid system.* ▶

PHOTO:OFF/AFP/Getty Images; TEXT:Tutu, Desmond. 1984. From Nobel Lectures, Peace 1981–1990. Editor-in-Charge Tore Frangsmyr, Editor Irwin Abrams. 1997. Singapore: World Scientific Publishing Co.

| African Leader | Country | Economic Views |
|---|---|---|
| | | |
| | | |
| | | |
| | | |
| | | |

**ANALYZING KEY IDEAS AND DETAILS**

**DETERMINING CENTRAL IDEAS** Read closely to identify the different economic views held by African leaders after independence. List these views in a graphic organizer like this one.

# INDEPENDENCE AND NEW NATIONS

**ANALYZING KEY IDEAS AND DETAILS**

**SUMMARIZING** How does the writer introduce the topic of the Cold War in Africa? How does the writer develop this topic from the beginning of this section to the end of this section?

GUIDING QUESTIONS *What challenges did newly independent African countries face? What challenges have been overcome by African countries?*

Many Africans fought on the side of the Allies during World War II, which only served to intensify their own desire for independent nations. Many nationalist movements across Africa were strengthened by this growing desire, and Europeans began to receive increasing pressure to end colonial rule. The Charter of the United Nations supported this belief. It stated that all colonial peoples should have the right to self-determination. In the late 1950s and 1960s, most African nations achieved independence. However, in many instances, colonial powers still heavily influenced the political and economic systems of newly independent states, and they often played a hand in shaping the governments or economies of these new states.

In 1957 the Gold Coast, renamed Ghana and under the guidance of Kwame Nkrumah, was the first British colony to gain independence. In 1960 the Belgian Congo (now Democratic Republic of the Congo) and Nigeria gained their independence from the Belgians and the British, respectively. Many other nations followed, including Uganda, Kenya, and Botswana. Portugal finally surrendered Mozambique and Angola in 1975.

In North Africa, the French granted full independence to Morocco and Tunisia in 1956. Because Algeria was home to a million French settlers, France chose to keep control there. However, Algerian nationalists began a guerrilla war to liberate their homeland. The French leader, Charles de Gaulle, granted Algeria its independence in 1962.

**DETERMINING MEANING**

The word **goal** comes from an old English root word meaning "boundary." How does this word origin help the reader better understand how the word *goal* is used in this lesson?

## SOUTH AFRICA AND APARTHEID

In South Africa, where whites dominated the political system, the process was more complicated. Blacks began organizing against white rule and formed the African National Congress in 1912. Its **goal** of economic and political reform met with little success.

At the same time, by the 1950s, South African whites (descendants of the Dutch, known as Afrikaners) had strengthened the laws separating whites and blacks. The result was a system of racial segregation known as **apartheid** ("apartness").

**DETERMINING MEANING**

The word **apartheid** comes from a Dutch word meaning "apartness." How does the origin of the word *apartheid* help you better understand its meaning?

Blacks demonstrated against these laws, but the white government brutally repressed the demonstrators. In 1960 police opened fire on people who were leading a peaceful march in Sharpeville, killing 69 people, two-thirds of whom were shot in the back. After the arrest of African National Congress (ANC) leader Nelson Mandela in 1962, members of the ANC called for armed resistance to the white government.

## NELSON MANDELA ON DEMOCRACY

> "During my lifetime I have dedicated myself to this struggle of the African people. I have fought against white domination, and I have fought against black domination. I have cherished the ideal of a democratic and free society in which all persons live together in harmony and with equal opportunities. It is an ideal which I hope to live for and to achieve. But if needs be, it is an ideal for which I am prepared to die."
>
> —Nelson Mandela, statement at the Rivonia Trial, April 20, 1964, from *In His Own Words*

**ANALYZING PRIMARY SOURCES**

**DETERMINING POINT OF VIEW** How did Mandela's words challenge the idea of apartheid?

## THE PAN-AFRICAN MOVEMENT

The African states that achieved independence in the 1950s, 1960s, and 1970s still faced many problems. The leaders of these states, as well as their citizens, dreamed of stable governments and economic prosperity. Many of these dreams have yet to be realized.

Some African leaders believed in the dream of **Pan-Africanism**—the unity of all black Africans, regardless of national boundaries. In the view of Pan-Africanists, all black African peoples shared a common identity. Several of the new African leaders, including Léopold Senghor of Senegal, Kwame Nkrumah, and Jomo Kenyatta, supported Pan-Africanism.

**DETERMINING MEANING**

The word **Pan-Africanism** contains the prefix *pan-*, which means "all-inclusive." How does knowing this help a reader understand what *Pan-Africanism* is?

> "Our objective is African union now. There is no time to waste. We must unite now or perish. I am confident that by our concerted effort and determination, we shall lay here the foundations for a continental Union of African States. . . .
>
> On this continent, it has not taken us long to discover that the struggle against colonialism does not end with the attainment of national independence. Independence is only the prelude to a new and more involved struggle for the right to conduct our own economic and social affairs; to construct our society according to our aspirations, unhampered by crushing and humiliating neocolonialist controls and interference."
>
> —Kwame Nkrumah, speech to the Organization of African Unity, May 24, 1963

**ANALYZING PRIMARY SOURCES**

1. **DETERMINING CENTRAL IDEAS** What is the central idea of Nkrumah's speech?
2. **ANALYZING IDEAS** In Nkrumah's view, what is necessary for African independence?

Nkrumah in particular hoped that a Pan-African union would join all the new countries of the continent in a broader community. His dream never became reality. However, the Organization of African Unity (OAU), founded by the leaders of 32 African states in 1963, was a concrete result of the belief in Pan-Africanism. The OAU gave support to African groups fighting against colonialism. The group also presented a united front against the influence of the United States and the Soviet Union during the Cold War. Some African countries were part of the nonaligned movement and did not take sides in the Cold War.

## THE COLD WAR IN AFRICA

Most leaders of the newly independent states came from the urban middle class. They had studied in Europe or the United States and knew European languages. They believed in using the Western democratic model in Africa. Some, such as Jomo Kenyatta of Kenya, believed in Western-style capitalism.

Leaders in Angola and Mozambique followed Soviet-style communism. Other leaders, such as Julius Nyerere of Tanzania, Kwame Nkrumah of Ghana, Sékou Touré of Guinea, and Patrice Lumumba of the Republic of Congo, preferred an "African form of socialism."

The African form of socialism was not like that practiced in the Soviet Union or Eastern Europe. Instead, it was based on African traditions of community in which ownership of the country's wealth would be put into the hands of the people. As Nyerere declared in 1967, "The basis of socialism is a belief in the oneness of man and the common historical destiny of mankind. Its basis . . . is human equality."

Regardless of political ideology, many people hoped that independence would lead to democratic government. They were soon disappointed. Between 1957 and 1982, more than 70 leaders were violently overthrown. New governments often used force to attempt to integrate the multiple ethnic groups found within its borders into a cohesive group that was loyal to the regime. In the 1980s, either the military or a single party ruled many major African states. In the 1990s, multiparty elections increased, but single-party rule still predominated.

Despite the OAU's push for nonalignment in the Cold War, some African nations were drawn into proxy wars as the United States and the Soviet Union took opposing sides in political struggles in the newly independent countries, notably in Angola, Somalia, and the Congo. This caused prolonged conflict and corruption in some parts of Africa, and it undermined political development.

### GEOGRAPHIC REASONING

1. **GLOBAL INTERCONNECTIONS** Create a table of select African countries that includes the names of the European countries that previously controlled them.
2. **EXPLORING REGIONS** According to the map, the last nations to gain independence in Africa were in which part of the continent?

Nyerere, Julius Kambarage. 1973. Freedom and Development: Uhuru na Maendeleo. A Selection From Writings and Speeches 1968–1973. Oxford University Press.

## INDEPENDENT AFRICA

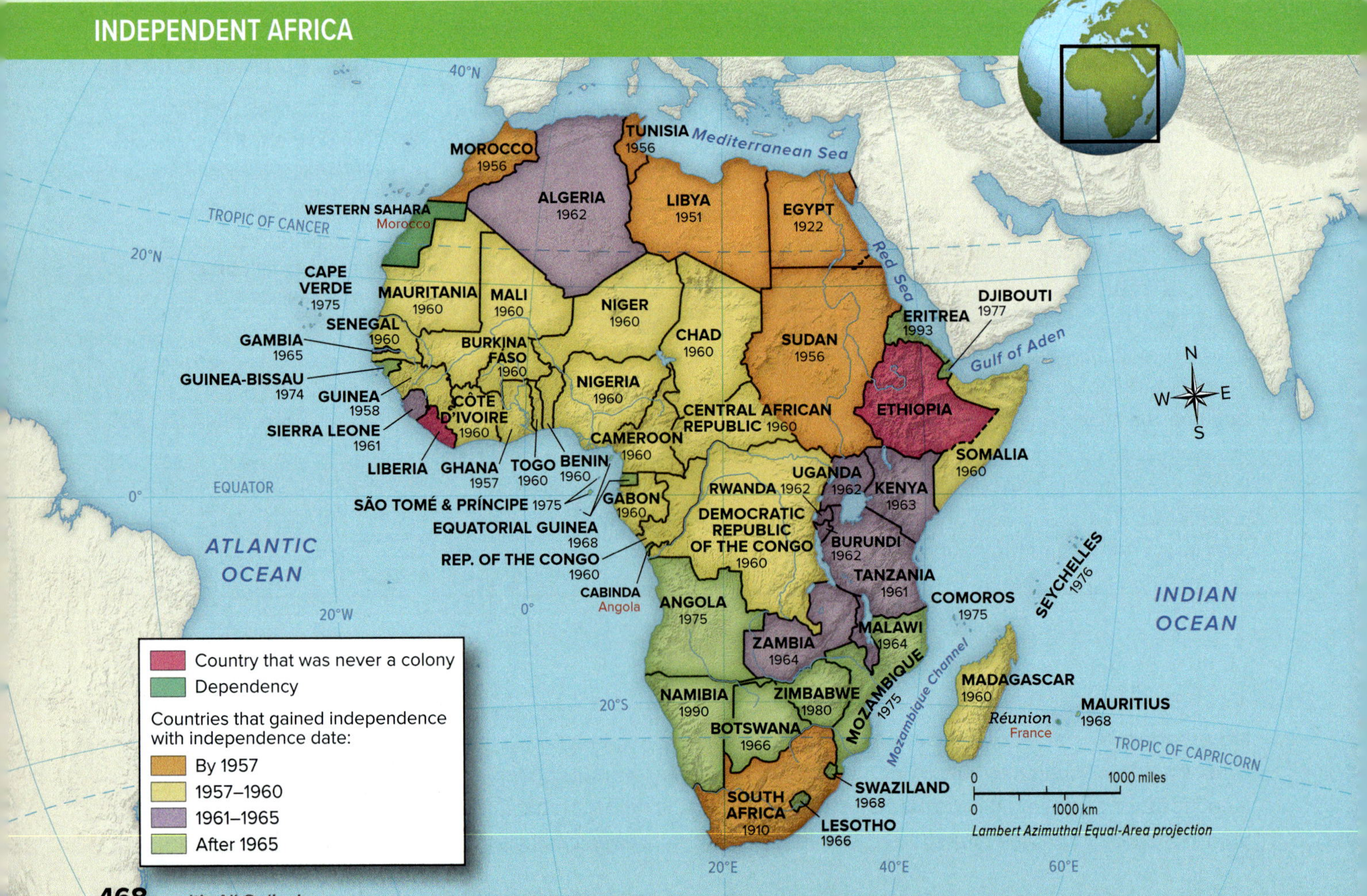

A central example is the Republic of the Congo. After Congo gained its independence from Belgium, the new state was unstable, and its early leaders struggled to keep the southern provinces from breaking away. By 1965, the chief of staff of Congo's armed forces, Joseph Mobutu, gained control of the government in a coup. A firm opponent of communism, Mobutu was supported financially by the United States. It was believed that he would serve as a safeguard against the spread of Soviet influence in central Africa. Mobutu made many authoritarian changes. He outlawed all political parties but his own, elections became rare, and corruption under Mobutu's unchallenged rule became common. When the Soviet Union fell in the early 1990s, relations between Mobutu and the United States cooled.

**MAKING CONNECTIONS**

### PUSH AND PULL FACTORS

Population movement occurs among countries around the world. Some people migrate, or move, from the country of their birth to another country. People may migrate to find better opportunities and employment in wealthier countries. These types of economic factors that attract people to a place are called *pull factors*. Religious and political freedoms are also examples of pull factors. Environmental pull factors make a place a desirable place to live, such as mountains, warm climates, and sea coasts. Other factors of migration, called *push factors,* trigger out-migration. Push factors include lack of economic opportunities, war, religious or political persecution, food shortages, and natural disasters.

## ECONOMIC AND POLITICAL CHALLENGES

Independence did not bring economic prosperity to the new African nations. Most still relied on the export of a single crop or natural resource of which the price could vary greatly on the world market. Liberia, for example, depended on the export of rubber; Nigeria, on oil. When prices dropped, their economies suffered. To make matters worse, Africa depended on foreign investment. Most African states imported technology and manufactured goods from the West and depended on foreign financial aid to develop their countries.

The new states also sometimes created their own problems. Scarce national resources were spent on military equipment or expensive consumer goods rather than on building the foundations for an industrial economy. Corruption was common.

Droughts and rapid population growth have also slowed economic growth and taxed resources. Since the 1980s, recurring droughts in many African countries, including Djibouti, Eritrea, Ethiopia, Kenya, Somalia, and Uganda, have caused starvation and migration.

As a result of these problems, poverty was widespread among both rural and urban dwellers. As cities grew, massive slums populated by displaced rural people surrounded cities, overwhelming sanitation and transportation systems. Pollution and perpetual traffic jams were the result. Millions lived without access to electricity or even clean water. Meanwhile, the fortunate few enjoyed lavish lifestyles. The rich in many East African countries are known as the *wabenzi*, or Mercedes-Benz people.

Diseases, such as **HIV/AIDS**, also presented major challenges to African progress. AIDS is a worldwide epidemic, but Africa is hardest hit. HIV/AIDS has had a serious impact on children and families in Africa. Many children have lost one or both parents to AIDS. Often, relatives are too poor to care for these children. Many orphans thus become heads of households filled with younger siblings. Extended families have been the source of support in difficult times, especially in rural Africa. The HIV/AIDS epidemic, however, has overwhelmed this support system.

*The modern skyline of Nairobi, Kenya, forms a backdrop to one of the slums that surround the city.*

**CONTRASTING** How do the lives of rich and poor African urban dwellers differ?

**DETERMINING MEANING**

The letter "I" in **HIV/AIDS** stands for *immunodeficiency. Immunodeficiency* includes the word *deficiency,* which means "a failing or shortcoming." How does this help you understand what happens when a person contracts HIV/AIDS?

African nations have taken steps to fight the epidemic. It has proved a tremendous burden, however, because many of these countries do not have the money or health facilities to educate their citizens about the disease and how to protect against it. Nor can they purchase the drugs that would extend the lives of those with HIV.

## NATIONALIST CONFLICTS

Within many African nations, warring ethnic groups undermined the concept of nationhood. This is not surprising, because the colonial powers had drawn the boundaries of African nations arbitrarily. Virtually all these states had issues as these borders randomly divided the diverse ethnic, linguistic, and territorial groups.

For example, during the late 1960s, civil war tore Nigeria apart. Conflicts also broke out among ethnic groups in Zimbabwe. Farther north, in central Africa, fighting between the Hutu and Tutsi created unstable governments in Rwanda and Burundi. During the colonial period, Hutu and Tutsi peoples lived together under European control. After independence in 1962, two new countries were created: Rwanda and Burundi. The population in both countries was mixed, but in Rwanda, the Hutu majority ran the government. They resented the position of the Tutsis, who had gotten the best education and jobs under the Belgians. In 1994 a Hutu rampage left some 500,000 Tutsi dead in Rwanda.

Not all the news in Africa has been bad. Popular demonstrations led to the collapse of one-party regimes and the emergence of democracies in several countries. One case was that of Idi Amin of Uganda. After ruling by terror and brutal repression throughout the 1970s, Amin was deposed in 1979. Dictatorship also came to an end in Ethiopia, Liberia, and Somalia. In these cases, however, the fall of the regime was later followed by bloody civil war. Apartheid also ended in South Africa.

*After his release from prison in 1990, Nelson Mandela visits Bishop Desmond Tutu.*

## THE END OF APARTHEID

One of the most remarkable events of recent African history was the 1994 election of Nelson Mandela to the presidency of the Republic of South Africa. Imprisoned in 1962 for his activities with the African National Congress, Mandela spent almost 26 years in maximum-security prisons in South Africa. For all those years, Mandela never wavered from his resolve to secure the freedom of his country.

Mandela was offered freedom in 1985, with conditions. Yet he refused to accept a conditional freedom: "Only free men can negotiate. Prisoners cannot enter into contracts. . . . Your freedom and mine cannot be separated."

Nobel Peace Prize winner (1984) Bishop Desmond Tutu and others worked to free Mandela and to end apartheid. Eventually, worldwide pressure forced the South African government to dismantle apartheid laws. In 1990 Mandela was released from prison. In 1993 the government of F. W. de Klerk agreed to hold democratic national elections—the first in South Africa's history. In 1994 Nelson Mandela became South Africa's first black president. In his presidential inaugural address, he expressed his hopes:

> "We shall build the society in which all South Africans, both black and white, will be able to walk tall, without any fear in their hearts, assured of their inalienable right to human dignity—a rainbow nation at peace with itself and the world."
>
> — from *In His Own Words*

## ✓ CHECKING FOR UNDERSTANDING

1. **EXPLAINING ISSUES** What challenges did newly independent African countries face?
2. **RELATING EVENTS** How did the conflict in Rwanda represent the problems posed by nationalism in Africa?
3. **IDENTIFYING CONNECTIONS** How has the HIV/AIDS epidemic impacted Africa?

# SOCIETY AND CULTURE

**GUIDING QUESTION** *What factors have affected African society and culture?*

Africa is a study in contrasts. Old and new, indigenous and foreign, live side by side. One result is a constant tension between traditional ways and Western culture in most African countries.

In general, the impact of the West has been greatest in the cities. After all, the colonial presence was first and most firmly established in the cities. Many cities, including Lagos, Nigeria; Cape Town, South Africa; Brazzaville, Republic of the Congo; and Nairobi, Kenya, are direct products of colonial rule. Most African cities today look like cities elsewhere in the world.

About 60 percent of the population of Africa lives outside the major cities. Modern influence has had less of an impact there. Millions of people throughout Africa live much as their ancestors did—in thatched dwellings without modern plumbing and electricity. They farm, hunt, and raise livestock by traditional methods, wear traditional clothing, and practice traditional beliefs. Conditions such as drought and flooding affect the ability of rural Africans to grow crops and to tend herds. Migration to the cities for work is one solution. This can be very disruptive to families and villages. Many urban people view rural people as backward. Rural dwellers view the cities as corrupting and destructive to traditional African values.

After independence, women's roles in African society changed. Almost without exception, women were allowed to vote and to run for political office. Some became leaders of their countries. Women still hold few political offices, however. Although women dominate some professions, such as teaching, child care, and clerical work, they do not share in all career opportunities. Most African women are employed in low-paid positions, such as farm laborers, factory workers, and servants. Furthermore, in many rural areas, traditional attitudes toward women, including arranged marriages, prevail.

The tension between traditional and modern and between indigenous and foreign also affects African culture. Africans have kept their local artistic traditions and have adapted them to foreign influences. A dilemma for many contemporary African artists is finding a balance between Western techniques and training on the one hand and the rich heritage of traditional African art forms on the other. In some countries, governments make the artists' decisions. Artists are told to depict scenes of traditional African life. These works are designed to serve the tourist industry.

### ANALYZING KEY IDEAS AND DETAILS

1. **ANALYZING IDEAS** This section of the text begins with the sentence "Africa is a study in contrasts." What clue does this sentence give the reader about the types of ideas that will be presented in the following paragraphs?
2. **CITING TEXT EVIDENCE** The writer claims, "African writers have often addressed the tensions and dilemmas that modern Africans face." What evidence supports this claim?

*South Africans wait in line to vote in the nation's first democratic election.*

BIOGRAPHY

## CHINUA ACHEBE (1930–2013) AFRICAN WRITER AND EDUCATOR

Chinua Achebe was born in Nigeria and studied English at the University of Ibadan. He had a long and industrious career in broadcasting and publishing before entering the academic world. Achebe wrote many novels, but his first work, *Things Fall Apart*, continues to be his most famous. The novel tells the story of the cultural clash between the native people of the Niger River delta and the incursions of Europeans.

Following the publication of *Things Fall Apart* in 1958, Achebe's works address the conflict between traditional and modern ways in African culture, including *No Longer at Ease* (1960), *Arrow of God* (1964), and *A Man of the People* (1966). In the 1970s, Achebe began an academic career that included teaching positions in literature and African studies at the University of Connecticut, Bard College, and Brown University in the United States as well as the University of Nigeria.

1. **DETERMINING CONTEXT** What were Achebe's chief contributions to literature?
2. **ANALYZING INFORMATION** How does Achebe's subject matter represent the idea that Africa is "a study in contrasts"?

African writers have often addressed the tensions and dilemmas modern Africans face. The conflicting demands of town versus country and indigenous versus foreign were the **themes** of most of the best-known works of the 1960s and 1970s. Chinua Achebe, a Nigerian novelist and winner of the Nobel Prize for literature in 1989, writes about the problems of Africans caught up in the conflict between traditional and Western values. In his most famous novel, *Things Fall Apart*, Achebe portrays the simple dignity of traditional African village life.

### ✓ CHECKING FOR UNDERSTANDING

1. **EVALUATING** What factors have affected African society and culture?
2. **DETERMINING CONTEXT** Where in Africa has the impact of the West been the greatest, and why?
3. **SUMMARIZING** What were the themes of the best-known novels written in Africa in the 1960s and 1970s?

## LESSON 3 REVIEW

### Time and Place

1. **IDENTIFYING CONNECTIONS** What are some challenges that have been overcome by African countries since gaining independence?

### Building History-Social Science Analysis Skills

2. **EVALUATING** How successful was the African National Congress in its goal of reforming the South African government and ending apartheid?
3. **SUMMARIZING** Use your notes to summarize post-independence African leaders and their economic views.
4. **ANALYZING CHANGE** What are some of the changes that occurred in African society and culture after its nations received their independence?

### Writing About History

5. **INFORMATIVE WRITING** Research independence movements in two African nations. Evaluate their success and compare how political ideology, ethnicity, and religion shaped their governments.

### Collaborating

6. **EVALUATING POINT OF VIEW** With a small group, imagine you are all citizens of an African nation shortly after it has received its independence. Select a specific country and research its demographics at the time of independence. Then, within your group, make a proposal for a new government. How will your government be structured? Will it be a democracy, a republic, a combination of both, or something entirely different? Explain the reasons for your decision based on the newly independent country you selected.

## ESSENTIAL QUESTIONS

- *How can political change cause conflict?*
- *How can political relationships affect economic relationships?*

LESSON 4

# Latin America

## THE STORY BEGINS...

The Colombian fiction writer Gabriel García Márquez had a first-row seat to the tumultuous transformation of modern Latin America. He worked the themes of this difficult transformation into his celebrated stories. When he accepted the Nobel Prize for literature in 1982, he spoke the following:

> "Why is the originality so readily granted us in literature so mistrustfully denied us in our difficult attempts at social change? Why think that the social justice sought by progressive Europeans for their own countries cannot also be a goal for Latin America, with different methods for dissimilar conditions? No: the immeasurable violence and pain of our history are the result of age-old inequities and untold bitterness, and not a conspiracy plotted three thousand leagues from our home. But many European leaders and thinkers have thought so, with the childishness of old-timers who have forgotten the fruitful excess of their youth as if it were impossible to find another destiny than to live at the mercy of the two great masters of the world. This, my friends, is the very scale of our solitude."

—Gabriel García Márquez, *Nobel Lecture,* December 8, 1982

With these lines, García Márquez was making a plea to Latin Americans to reject the troubling legacies of colonialism and to chart a new course toward a uniquely Latin American future empowered by a uniquely Latin American culture.

*The fantastic themes from this art exhibit in Mexico City match the tones of the magic realism movement in twentieth-century Latin American literature.* ▶

| Country | Significant Events |
| --- | --- |
| | |
| | |
| | |
| | |

**ANALYZING KEY IDEAS AND DETAILS**

**SUMMARIZING** Read carefully to identify significant events that happened in each country during the Cold War. List these events in a graphic organizer like this one.

# GENERAL TRENDS IN LATIN AMERICA

**ANALYZING KEY IDEAS AND DETAILS**

1. **DETERMINING CENTRAL IDEAS** What is the central idea of this section, and how does the text present and develop this idea?
2. **ANALYZING EVENTS** Reread the two paragraphs that begin, "By the 1960s, . . ." What part of these paragraphs states an effect of the economic troubles in Latin America? What words signal this is an effect?

**GUIDING QUESTIONS** *How did the involvement of the United States and the Soviet Union increase instability in Latin American countries? What economic and political challenges did Latin American countries face during the Cold War?*

Since the 1800s, Latin Americans have exported raw materials and bought manufactured goods from industrialized countries. Basing an economy on the export of a limited number of raw materials resulted in many issues for countries in the region as the price paid for raw materials on the world market can vary greatly. For example, the Great Depression caused exports to fall, and revenues to buy manufactured goods declined. In response, Latin Americans developed industries to produce their own goods.

By the 1960s, however, Latin American countries were still experiencing economic problems. They depended on the United States, Europe, and Japan, especially for the advanced technology needed for modern industries. Also, many Latin American countries had failed to find markets abroad to sell their manufactured products.

These economic failures led to political instability. In the 1960s, repressive military regimes in Chile, Brazil, and Argentina abolished political parties and returned to export-import economies financed by foreigners. These regimes also encouraged multinational corporations (companies with divisions in more than two countries) to come to Latin America. This made these Latin American countries even more dependent on industrialized nations. In the 1970s, Latin American countries tried to maintain their weak economies by borrowing money. Between 1970 and 1982, debt to foreigners grew from $27 billion to $315.3 billion. A number of Latin American economies began to crumble. Wages fell, and unemployment and inflation skyrocketed. As the economy declined, people continued to move from the countryside into the cities.

## A MOVE TOWARD DEMOCRACY

Several states endured periods of upheaval and civil war during the 1980s. Although conflicts eased in the 1990s, many of the issues lingered. Discord between indigenous peoples and mestizos as well as political disagreements among conservatives and more left-leaning parties have long plagued the region. Economies reflected the disagreements as many leaders struggled to find footing in either socialist or capitalist economies. However, with the debt crisis in the 1980s, a movement toward democracy emerged. Some military leaders could not deal with their nations' debt problems. Meanwhile, many realized that military power without popular **consent** could not maintain a strong state. As a result, a movement toward democracy was the most noticeable trend of the 1980s and the early 1990s in Latin America.

Even as some states remained under military control, others moved toward civilian governments and held popular, free, multiparty elections. Costa Rica, with its constitution of 1949, is one of the most stable and democratic countries in the region. Likewise, Peru reestablished constitutional rule in 1979 with elections held in 1980. It has maintained a relatively stable democracy despite a number of issues in the 1990s. Through participation in the global economy, both Peru and Costa Rica have continued to achieve economic growth.

The United States has always played a large role in Latin America. In 1948 the states of the Western Hemisphere formed the Organization of American States (OAS), which called for an end to military action by one state in the affairs of any other state.

The formation of the OAS, however, did not end the interference of the United States in Latin American affairs. As the Cold War developed, so too did the anxiety of U.S. policy makers about the possibility of communist regimes in Central America and the Caribbean. As a result, the United States returned to a policy of taking action when it believed Soviet agents were trying to set up governments hostile to U.S. interests.

After Fidel Castro created a Marxist state in Cuba, the desire of the United States to prevent "another Cuba" largely determined U.S. policy toward Latin America. In the 1960s, President John F. Kennedy's Alliance for Progress encouraged social reform and economic development in Latin America. It was hoped that economic growth would keep people happy and less inclined to follow radical leaders. The Alliance for Progress failed to work, however. Much of the money intended for economic development ended up in the pockets of the rich.

When Cuba began to start guerrilla wars in other Latin American countries, the United States reacted by sending massive military aid to anti-Communist regimes, regardless of their nature. In the 1980s and 1990s, the United States returned to a policy of direct intervention in Latin American affairs.

## ✓ CHECKING FOR UNDERSTANDING

1. **EXPLAINING CAUSE AND EFFECT** How did the involvement of the United States and the Soviet Union increase instability in Latin American countries?
2. **UNDERSTANDING CONTEXT** What promoted the movement toward democracy throughout Latin America in the 1980s?

## STRUGGLES FOR DEMOCRACY 1945–1993

SOURCE: Peter Smith, "Cycles of Electoral Democracy in Latin America, 1900–2000," http://repositories.cdlib.org/clas/wp/6; U.S. Department of State.

### GEOGRAPHIC REASONING

1. **EXPLORING PLACE** Of the countries shown on the map, which has experienced the longest period of electoral democracy?
2. **EXPLORING CULTURE** What can be said about the countries with the fewest years of democratic governance on this map?

### DETERMINING MEANING

Read the paragraph that contains the word **consent**. Based on the context of the paragraph, write a definition for the word *consent*. Use a dictionary or online resource to check your definition.

# MEXICO AND THE CARIBBEAN

**GUIDING QUESTION** *What economic and political challenges did Latin American countries face during the Cold War?*

Throughout the twentieth century, Mexico and the Caribbean have experienced political turmoil and economic crises.

## MEXICO

The Mexican Revolution in the early 1900s created a political order that remained stable for many years. The official political party of the Mexican Revolution—the Institutional Revolutionary Party, or PRI—came to dominate Mexico. Every six years, leaders of the PRI chose the party's presidential candidate, who was then elected by the people. During the 1950s and 1960s, steady economic growth led to real gains in wages in Mexico.

At the end of the 1960s, student protests against Mexico's one-party government system led to change. Two presidents, Luis Echeverría and José López Portillo, made political reforms, and new political parties emerged. Greater freedom of debate in the press and universities was allowed.

In the late 1970s, vast new reserves of oil were discovered in Mexico. The government became more dependent on revenues from foreign oil sales. Then, when world oil prices dropped in the mid-1980s, Mexico was no longer able to make payments on its foreign debt. The government adopted new economic policies. One was **privatization**, the sale of government-owned companies to private firms.

President Carlos Salinas de Gortari sped up privatization to relieve the debt crisis. In 1992 de Gortari began working with the U.S. president and the Canadian prime minister to form the North American Free Trade Agreement (NAFTA). It went into effect in 1994.

## THE CUBAN REVOLUTION

In the 1950s, an opposition movement arose in Cuba. It aimed to overthrow the government of the dictator Fulgencio Batista, who had controlled Cuba since 1933. The leader of the movement was a man named Fidel Castro. In 1954 Fidel and his brother Raúl teamed up with a small band of revolutionaries. As the rebels gained more support, the Batista regime collapsed. Castro's revolutionaries seized Havana on January 3, 1959. Many Cubans who disagreed with Castro fled to the United States.

Relations between Cuba and the United States quickly deteriorated when Castro's regime began to receive aid from the Soviet Union. In October 1960, the United States declared a **trade embargo** with Cuba. Just three months later, all diplomatic relations with Cuba were broken.

After the failure of the Bay of Pigs invasion and the Cuban missile crisis, Cuba became less dependent on the Soviet Union and pursued a new strategy of fomenting revolution in the rest of Latin America. Although Cuba's strategy failed, Castro's Marxist regime continued but with mixed results. The Cuban people did secure some social gains, such as free medical services for all citizens. With improvements in education, illiteracy was nearly eliminated.

**ANALYZING KEY IDEAS AND DETAILS**

1. **CITING TEXT EVIDENCE** The section under the heading "Mexico" argues that Mexico suffered economically by relying too much on oil exports. What evidence in the text supports this claim?
2. **ANALYZING EVENTS** Reread the three paragraphs under the heading "The Cuban Revolution." What part of this section states an effect of the failure of the Bay of Pigs invasion?

*Fidel Castro and two guerrillas at their mountain hideout during the insurgency against Cuban dictator Fulgencio Batista*

Corbis

**DETERMINING MEANING**

To better understand the meaning of **trade embargo**, break down the phrase. *Trade* is the "act of buying and selling goods and services." An *embargo* is "an official ban on commercial activity." How does knowing the meaning of each word help a reader understand the meaning of *trade embargo*?

## HAITI

After American troops left Haiti in 1934, the Haitians made several efforts to move toward democracy. In 1957, however, in elections controlled by the military, François Duvalier became president. He created a private militia, established dictatorial rule, and terrorized the country, killing tens of thousands. After his death in 1971, his son continued to rule Haiti with an iron fist. Growing opposition to his rule led to the collapse of his regime in 1986, followed five years later by a return to democracy with the election of Jean-Bertrand Aristide.

### ✓ CHECKING FOR UNDERSTANDING

1. **UNDERSTANDING CHANGE** What economic and political challenges did Latin American countries face during the Cold War?
2. **SUMMARIZING** Describe how Haiti's government returned to democracy.
3. **EXPLAINING EFFECTS** What immediate effects did the Cuban revolution have on Cuba's relationship with the United States?

# CENTRAL AMERICA

**GUIDING QUESTION** *What economic and political challenges did Latin American countries face during the Cold War?*

Central America includes seven countries: Costa Rica, Nicaragua, Honduras, El Salvador, Panama, Belize, and Guatemala. Economically, Central America has historically depended on the export of bananas, coffee, and cotton. Prices for these products have varied over time, however, creating economic crises. In addition, a huge gulf between a wealthy elite and poor peasants has created a climate of instability in the region. The U.S. fear of the spread of communism often led to U.S. support for repressive regimes in Central America. The involvement of the United States was especially evident in the nations of Guatemala, El Salvador, and Nicaragua.

## GUATEMALA

In 1954, with support from the United States, Jacobo Arbenz of Guatemala was overthrown. A series of military or military-dominated dictators then ruled the country for years. Guerrilla forces began forming to oppose the government, which responded in the early 1980s by using military action and economic reforms to defeat the guerrillas. As in El Salvador, right-wing death squads began attacking anyone they believed belonged to the opposition, especially the indigenous people of Guatemala, the descendants of the ancient Maya. The government killed as many as 200,000 people, mostly unarmed Maya.

## EL SALVADOR

After World War II, the wealthy elite and the military controlled the government in El Salvador. The rise of an urban middle class led to hope for a more democratic government. The army, however, refused to accept the results of free elections that were held in 1972.

World attention focused on El Salvador in the late 1970s and the 1980s when the country was rocked by a bitter civil war. Marxist-led, leftist guerrillas and

**BIOGRAPHY**

### OSCAR ROMERO
**(1917–1980)**

Oscar Romero was appointed Archbishop of San Salvador in part because of his moderate political views. But in his weekly radio broadcasts, he soon began to attack the Salvadoran government's violent practices. Romero quickly became, in the words of his personal aide, "the most loved person and the most hated person" in the country. On March 24, 1980, Romero was murdered while he celebrated mass in a private chapel in San Salvador. His death was the most notable in a 12-year-long civil war in which more than 70,000 Salvadorans died.

**UNDERSTANDING CHANGE** How did Oscar Romero's political views change?

**ANALYZING KEY IDEAS AND DETAILS**

1. **DETERMINING CENTRAL IDEAS** Read the text that falls under the heading, "Guatemala." What is the central idea of this section?
2. **CITING TEXT EVIDENCE** This section makes the claim that U.S. intervention in parts of Latin America in the 1970s and 1980s was intended to prevent the spread of communism. What evidence does the section present to support this claim of motive?

right-wing groups battled one another. The Catholic Church became a main **target**, and a number of priests were killed or tortured, among them Archbishop Oscar Romero. The United States began to provide weapons and training to the Salvadoran army to defeat the guerrillas. The hope was to bring stability to the country, but the killings continued until a 1992 peace settlement ended the war.

*This Nicaraguan mural depicts the killing of four students at an anti-Somoza protest on July 23, 1959.*

## NICARAGUA

In Nicaragua, the Somoza family seized control of the government in 1937 and maintained control for the next 43 years. Over most of this period, the Somoza regime had the support of the United States. The Somozas enriched themselves at the expense of the Nicaraguan people and used murder and torture to silence opposition.

By 1979, the United States, under President Jimmy Carter, had grown unwilling to support the corrupt regime. In that same year, Marxist guerrilla forces known as the Sandinista National Liberation Front won a number of military victories against government forces and gained control of the country. Soon, a group opposed to the Sandinistas' policies, called the contras, began to try to overthrow the new government. Worried by the Sandinistas' alignment with the Soviet Union, the United States supported the contras.

The war waged by the contras undermined support for the Sandinistas. In 1990 the Sandinistas, led by Daniel Ortega, agreed to free elections and lost to a coalition headed by Violeta Barrios de Chamorro, who became Nicaragua's first female president.

### ✓ CHECKING FOR UNDERSTANDING

1. **UNDERSTANDING CHANGE** What experiences did Guatemala, El Salvador, and Nicaragua have in common in the post-World War II period?
2. **SUMMARIZING** Why did the United States support the contras over the Sandinistas in Nicaragua?
3. **DETERMINING CONTEXT** Why was so much world attention focused on El Salvador in the late 1970s and 1980s?

# SOUTH AMERICA

**GUIDING QUESTION** *What economic and political challenges did Latin American countries face during the Cold War?*

Throughout the twentieth century, most South American countries experienced political unrest and had economic and social problems.

## CHILE

The history of Chile has mirrored the experience of other Latin American countries. However, it took a dramatic step in 1970 when Salvador Allende (ah • YEHN • day), a Marxist, became president. Allende's election led many to believe it would result in warm relations between Chile and the Soviet Union. This failed to happen. However, relations with the Soviet Union's Cold War opponent, the United States, turned cold.

**ANALYZING KEY IDEAS AND DETAILS**

1. **ANALYZING CENTRAL IDEAS** Summarize the section "Chile" in a single sentence, and explain how the central idea is supported or refuted in the final sentence of the section.
2. **ANALYZING EVENTS** Reread the two paragraphs that begin, "In 1946 Juan Perón was." What part of these paragraphs states a cause of Perón's policy of increased industrialization?

Allende tried to create a socialist society through constitutional means. His first steps were to increase wages and to nationalize the largest corporations. Nationalization of the copper industry angered the companies' owners in the United States, as well as the U.S. government. However, Allende gained support in the Chilean congress. Afraid of Allende's growing strength, General Augusto Pinochet (PEE • noh • CHEHT) moved to overthrow the government. In September 1973, military forces killed Allende and set up a dictatorship.

The Pinochet regime was one of the most brutal in Chile's history. Thousands of opponents were imprisoned, tortured, or murdered. The regime also outlawed all political parties and did away with the congress. These horrible abuses of human rights led to growing unrest in the mid-1980s. Thousands of Pinochet opponents and other civilians were arrested and were never seen again. Pinochet finally lost in 1989 in free presidential elections.

## ARGENTINA

Argentina is Latin America's second-largest country. For years, it had been ruled by a powerful oligarchy whose wealth was based on growing wheat and raising cattle. Support from the army was crucial to the continuing power of the oligarchy.

In 1943, during World War II, a group of army officers overthrew the oligarchy. The new regime was not sure how to deal with the working classes. Juan Perón devised a new strategy. Using his position as labor secretary in the military government, Perón sought to win over the workers, known as the *descamisados* (the shirtless ones). He encouraged them to join labor unions and increased job benefits.

In 1946 Juan Perón was elected president of Argentina, with his chief support coming from labor and the urban middle class. His wife, Eva Perón, was adored by many Argentines and was a major part of the Perón regime. Together, the Peróns brought social reforms to Argentina.

To please his supporters from labor and the urban middle class, Perón followed a policy of increased industrialization. He sought to free Argentina from foreign investors. The government bought the railways and took over the banking, insurance, shipping, and communications industries. Perón's regime, however, was also authoritarian. He created Fascist gangs that used violent means to terrify his opponents.

The military overthrew the Argentinean leader in September 1955. Perón went into exile in Spain. Overwhelmed by problems, military leaders later allowed him to return. He was reelected as president in 1973 but died a year later. In 1976 the military once again took over power. The new regime tolerated no opposition. It is believed that 36,000 people were killed.

In April 1982, the military regime invaded the Falkland Islands off the coast of Argentina. Great Britain, which had controlled the islands since the 1800s, sent ships and troops and took back the islands. The loss discredited the military and opened the door to civilian rule in Argentina. When Raúl Alfonsín was elected president in 1983, he restored democracy and prosecuted the former military leaders.

*The Mothers of the Plaza de Mayo, mothers and grandmothers of the* desaparecidos *(the disappeared) of Argentina's "dirty war," demonstrate outside La Casa Rosada in Buenos Aires.*

## COLOMBIA

Colombia has long had a democratic political system, but a conservative elite led by the owners of coffee plantations has dominated the government. Coffee is an important crop for Colombia, making up about half of the country's legal exports. Yet because the economy relies heavily upon the coffee trade, price fluctuations can have a negative effect on the overall economy.

In addition to economic problems, political problems troubled Colombia in the twentieth century. After World War II, Marxist guerrilla groups began to organize Colombian peasants. The government responded violently. More than 200,000 peasants had been killed by the mid-1960s. Violence continued in the 1980s and 1990s.

**DETERMINING MEANING**

What context clues in the paragraph help you to determine the meaning of **cartel**?

Peasants who lived in poverty turned to a new cash crop—coca leaves, which are used to make cocaine. As the lucrative drug trade grew, two major **cartels** formed in Colombia.

The drug cartels used bribes and violence to force government cooperation in the drug traffic and to dominate the market. Colombia became the major cocaine supplier of the international drug market. Violence increased as rebel guerrillas made deals with the cartels to oppose the government. The government used an aerial eradication program to try to wipe out coca fields, but the program did not have much success. Despite the money earned from drug and coffee exports, the Colombian economy remained weak because of high unemployment and the disruption of civil war.

### ✓ CHECKING FOR UNDERSTANDING

1. **UNDERSTANDING CHANGE** How did the invasion of the Falkland Islands affect Argentina?
2. **SUMMARIZING** What type of government did Salvador Allende try to create?
3. **CONTRASTING** How was Colombia's democratic system different from other democracies?

**DETERMINING MEANING**

The word **megacity** includes the prefix *mega-*, which comes from the Greek word for "great." How does knowing the meaning of this prefix help a reader to better understand what a *megacity* is?

# LATIN AMERICAN SOCIETY AND CULTURE

**GUIDING QUESTION** *How did Latin American society and culture change after World War II?*

Latin America's economic problems have been made worse by its dramatic growth in population. Both Latin America and North America (the United States and Canada) had the same populations in 1950—about 165 million people. By the mid-1980s, however, Latin America's population had exploded to 400 million. That of North America was about 270 million. With the increase in population came a rapid rise in the size of cities. By 1990, there were 29 cities with more than a million people. Mexico City and São Paulo each had over 10 million people. Analysts refer to such cities as megacities. **Megacities** in Latin America have often grown so fast that regular urban services cannot be provided.

**INTEGRATING KNOWLEDGE AND IDEAS**

1. **SUMMARIZING** In your own words, summarize why the rapid growth of megacities in Latin America is a major problem.
2. **CITING TEXT EVIDENCE** The author notes that the genre of **magic realism** became very popular in Latin America. What information from the text supports this conclusion?

Latin American women's roles have changed. Although the traditional role of homemaker continues, women have also moved into new jobs. In addition to farm labor, women have found jobs in industry and as teachers, professors, doctors, and lawyers.

Twentieth-century Latin American writers and artists have played important roles in their society. Their work is seen as expressing the hopes of the people. Because of this, artists and writers hold high status in Latin American society.

In the 1940s, Latin American writers developed a unique form of expression called magic realism. **Magic realism** brings together realistic events with dreamlike or fantasy backgrounds. The rules of ordinary life are suspended in order to comment on a national or social situation. Perhaps the foremost example of magic realism is *One Hundred Years of Solitude*, a novel by Gabriel García Márquez, a Colombian writer, who won the Nobel Prize in literature in 1982. In this story of the fictional town of Macondo, the point of view slips back and forth between fact and fantasy. According to Márquez, fantasy and fact depend on one's point of view.

Latin American art and architecture were strongly influenced by international styles after World War II. Perhaps the most notable example of modern architecture can be seen in Brasília, the capital of Brazil, which was built in the 1950s and 1960s. Brazilian architect Oscar Niemeyer was appointed chief architect for the new capital.

### ☑ CHECKING FOR UNDERSTANDING

1. **ANALYZING CHANGE** How did Latin American society and culture change after World War II?
2. **UNDERSTANDING CHANGE** How have the roles of women changed in Latin America over the last few decades?
3. **IDENTIFYING CONNECTIONS** How has internationalism influenced cities in Latin America?

## LESSON 4 REVIEW

### Time and Place

1. **IDENTIFYING CAUSES** Why did Latin America experience economic problems in the mid-twentieth century?

### Building History-Social Science Analysis Skills

2. **SUMMARIZING** How did the drug cartels in Colombia maintain their control over the cocaine trade?
3. **IDENTIFYING CONNECTIONS** Use your notes to describe the similarities among major events in Latin American countries during the Cold War.
4. **SUMMARIZING** What was NAFTA, and what impact did it have on Latin American trade?

### Writing About History

5. **EXPLANATORY WRITING** Write an essay that explores how the differing principles of communism and capitalism contributed to instability in Cuba, Colombia, Argentina, or Nicaragua that led to violent conflicts, uprisings, and/or changes in political power.

### Collaborating

6. **PRESENTING** With a partner, research the development of art, literature, film, or music in a Latin American country discussed in this lesson. Then, create a presentation about your selection and present it to the class.

# WHAT CHALLENGES DID APARTHEID CREATE FOR SOUTH AFRICANS?

**How did apartheid affect South Africa?** For much of the twentieth century, South Africa's white-run government denied political and economic equality to the country's black majority.

**What progress have South Africans made in overcoming the effects of apartheid?** Despite facing harsh government repression, South Africans carried on a decades-long campaign against apartheid. The nation finally held free elections in 1994, marking the end of apartheid and the beginning of democracy with the election of Nelson Mandela. Apartheid in South Africa attracted international attention.

**PRIMARY SOURCE: SPEECH**

## DESMOND TUTU, SPEECH FROM OCTOBER 23, 1984

*The following passage is from a speech by Desmond Tutu, a black Anglican bishop, to the United Nations Security Council on October 23, 1984.*

> "For my beloved country is wracked by division, by alienation, by animosity, by separation, by injustice, by unavoidable pain and suffering. It is a deeply fragmented society, ridden by fear and anxiety . . . and a sense of desperation, split up into hostile, warring factions. . . .
>
> There is little freedom to disagree with the determinations of the authorities. There is large scale unemployment here because of the drought and the recession that has hit most of the world's economy. And it is such a time that the authorities have increased the prices of various foodstuffs and also of rents in black townships—measures designed to hit hardest those least able to afford the additional costs. . . .
>
> The authorities have not stopped stripping blacks of their South African citizenship. . . . The South African government is turning us into aliens in the land of our birth. White South Africans are . . . scared human beings, many of them; who would not be, if they were outnumbered five to one? Through this lofty body I wish to appeal to my white fellow South Africans to share in building a new society, for blacks are not intent on driving whites into the sea but on claiming only their rightful place in the sun in the land of their birth."

**ANALYZE THE TEXT**

1. **DESCRIBING** According to Bishop Tutu, what problems did South Africa face in 1984?
2. **ANALYZING TEXT** Why does Bishop Tutu believe that the white minority is so obstinate toward giving equal rights to blacks?

**PRIMARY SOURCE: SPEECH**

## NELSON MANDELA, POST-PRISON SPEECH, 1990

*African National Congress leader Nelson Mandela discussed South Africa's past and future in a speech he gave after his release from prison in 1990.*

> "Today, the majority of South Africans, black and white, recognize that apartheid has no future. It has to be ended by our own decisive mass action in order to build peace and security. The mass campaigns of defiance and other actions of our organizations and people can only culminate in the establishment of democracy.
>
> The apartheid's destruction on our subcontinent is incalculable. The fabric of family life of millions of my people has been shattered. Millions are homeless and unemployed. Our economy lies in ruins and our people are embroiled in political strife. . . .
>
> We call on our people to seize this moment, so that the process toward democracy is rapid and uninterrupted. . . . We must not allow fear to stand in our way. Universal suffrage on a common voters roll in a united, democratic and non-racial South Africa is the only way to peace and racial harmony. . . .
>
> I have fought against white domination, and I have fought against black domination. I have cherished the ideal of a democratic and free society in which all persons live together in harmony and with equal opportunity. It is an ideal which I hope to live for and to achieve. But, if need be, it is an ideal for which I am prepared to die."

**ANALYZE THE TEXT**

1. **DETERMINING CENTRAL IDEAS** What do you think Mandela hoped to accomplish with his speech?
2. **DETERMINING POINT OF VIEW** How do you think Mandela's experiences influenced the opinions he expressed in his speech?

(l)Tutu, Bishop Desmond. 1984. "The Question of South Africa". Africa Report, 30 (January/February 1985), Originally a statement to the United Nations Security Council. October 23, 1984;

SECONDARY SOURCE: SUMMARY

In the 1940s, the African National Congress (ANC) formed a Youth League to lead a nonviolent campaign against the apartheid policies of South Africa. In 1960 South African police fired on unarmed demonstrators at Sharpeville, killing 67. A year later the ANC formed an armed wing, Umkhonto we Sizwe, headed by Nelson Mandela to carry out sabotage against government installations. In 1963 the South African government arrested Mandela and, a year later, sentenced him to life imprisonment. In 1990, amidst growing international and domestic pressure, the government released Mandela. Four years later, he was elected president by voters in South Africa. His inauguration marked the end of apartheid.

*Nelson Mandela was sworn in as South Africa's first democratically elected president in 1994.*

**ANALYZE THE SOURCE**

1. **EVALUATING** How does a photograph like this serve as a potent symbol for a country such as South Africa? Why?
2. **UNDERSTANDING CHANGE** Considering the descriptive text, why might some in South Africa have resented the election of Nelson Mandela as president?

## MULTIPLE PERSPECTIVES

1. **COMPARING AND CONTRASTING TEXTS** What similarities exist between the messages conveyed by both text sources?
2. **EVALUATING TEXT EVIDENCE** What challenges did apartheid create for South Africans?

# STUDY GUIDE

## RELIGION IN SOUTH ASIA
### LESSON 1

| | |
|---|---|
| INDIA, SIKKIM | Primarily Hindu |
| PAKISTAN, BANGLADESH | Primarily Muslim |
| EAST PUNJAB | Primarily Sikh |
| NEPAL, BHUTAN, SRI LANKA, JAMMU & KASHMIR | Primarily Buddhist |

## THE IRAN-IRAQ WAR
### LESSON 2

- Religious disputes caused Iran and Iraq to have uneasy relations.
- Iranians are mostly Shia Muslims, while the Iraqis under Hussein were mostly Sunni Muslims.
- In 1980 Iraq, under Saddam Hussein, launched a brutal war against Iran.
- During the war, children were used to clear dangerous minefields.
- Hussein used poisonous gas against soldiers and civilians, especially the Kurds.
- In 1988 Iran and Iraq signed a cease-fire, but the issues of the war were left unresolved.

## CHALLENGES IN NEW AFRICAN NATIONS
### LESSON 3

- Dependence on exports such as rubber or oil
- Dependence on foreign investment
- Using natural resources for uses other than building a foundation for an industrial economy
- Droughts and population growth slowing economic growth and taxing resources
- Poverty widespread among rural and urban dwellers
- Sanitation and transportation systems overwhelmed by massive slums

## CHALLENGES IN LATIN AMERICA
### LESSON 4

| Mexico | Central America | South America |
|---|---|---|
| The Mexican Revolution in the early 1900s created political stability that lasted for many years. | In 1954 with support from the United States, Jacobo Arbenz of Guatemala was overthrown. | Salvador Allende, a Marxist, became president of Chile in 1970. |
| At the end of the 1960s, student protests against the one-party government led to change. | El Salvador was rocked by a bitter civil war in the late 1970s and the 1980s. A peace settlement ended the war in El Salvador in 1992. | Military forces, led by General Augusto Pinochet, killed Allende in 1973 and set up a dictatorship. The Pinochet regime was one of the most brutal in Chile's history. Pinochet finally lost in 1989 in free presidential elections. |
| In the late 1970s, new oil reserves were discovered, which led the government to become more dependent on revenue from foreign oil sales. | The Somoza family, who used murder and torture to silence those who opposed them, controlled Nicaragua for 43 years. They were supported by the United States for most of this period. | In 1946 Juan Perón was elected president of Argentina and, along with his wife, brought many social reforms to Argentina. Perón was overthrown in 1955, and democracy was not restored until 1983. |
| Then-president Carlos Salinas de Gortari began working with the United States to form NAFTA, which went into effect in 1994. | The United States supported the contras against the Sandinistas due to their alignment with the Soviet Union. | Two major drug cartels formed in Colombia, and it soon became the major cocaine supplier of the international drug market. |

# CHAPTER 13 Assessment

**Directions: On a separate sheet of paper, answer the questions below. Make sure you read carefully and answer all parts of the questions.**

## Short Answer

1. **DESCRIBING** Describe the decision that Indian Prime Minister Jawaharlal Nehru made in following the principle of nonalignment after World War II.

2. **SUMMARIZING** Summarize how women's roles changed across South and Southeast Asia after the war.

3. **ANALYZING EVENTS** What events made it difficult to resolve conflict in the Middle East?

4. **UNDERSTANDING CONTEXT** What might have happened if Pan-Arabism had been more widely accepted among Arab states?

5. **ANALYZING EVENTS** In South Africa in 1960, two-thirds of the 69 people killed during a peaceful antiapartheid march were shot in the back. What does this suggest happened?

6. **CONTRASTING** Contrast African cities with rural Africa.

7. **ANALYZING CHANGE** What political changes occurred in the late 1960s in Mexico?

8. **DETERMINING CENTRAL IDEAS** What happened as a result of the Cuban Revolution?

9. **IDENTIFYING CONNECTIONS** Describe the ways in which the postwar independence movements in Asia, Africa, and Latin America were similar.

10. **IDENTIFYING EFFECTS** What were the effects of the changes to the political systems of many European colonial territories in the mid- to late 1900s?

11. **DRAWING CONCLUSIONS** What conclusion can you draw from the attempt by the Netherlands to suppress the Indonesian republic declared by Sukarno?

12. **SUMMARIZING** Summarize how radical Islamic fundamentalism contributed to the growth of al-Qaeda.

13. **IDENTIFYING EFFECTS** What effect did the formation of OPEC have on Western countries?

14. **ANALYZING CHANGE** What were the experiences of the Philippines as a result of the changes following World War II?

15. **DESCRIBING** Explain the impact of the rapid rise in population on Latin American cities.

## History and Social-Science Analysis

16. **EXPLAINING CAUSE AND EFFECT** Create a chart showing the events that led to the rise of independence movements in Southeast Asia and explaining how these movements and new regimes in Southeast Asia created conflict and instability.

Use the graph to answer the following question.

In 1992, Mexican president Carlos Salinas de Gortari began working with the U.S. president and the Canadian prime minister to form the North American Free Trade Agreement (NAFTA). It went into effect in 1994.

**U.S. AGRICULTURAL TRADE WITH NAFTA PARTNERS, 1989–2002**

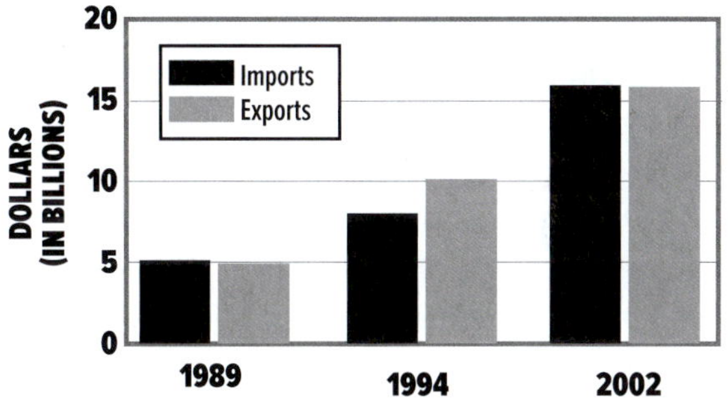


**Source:** U.S. Department of Agriculture

17. **INTERPRETING** Compare and contrast what has happened to the imports and exports among the United States and its NAFTA partners.

## Research and Presentation

18. **USING MULTIMEDIA** Create a cause-and-effect diagram with a partner showing the conflicts two or more African states of your choice have encountered as they struggled to gain independence and how their political relationships have affected economic relationships with other countries or states. Illustrate your diagram using other forms of media.

**Need Extra Help?**

| If You've Missed Question | 1 | 2 | 3 | 4 | 5 | 6 | 7 | 8 | 9 | 10 | 11 | 12 | 13 | 14 | 15 | 16 | 17 | 18 |
|---|---|---|---|---|---|---|---|---|---|---|---|---|---|---|---|---|---|---|
| Review Lesson | 1 | 1 | 2 | 2 | 3 | 3 | 4 | 4 | 1 | 1 | 1 | 2 | 2 | 1 | 4 | 1 | 4 | 3 |

**19** **EXPLANATORY WRITING** Research Gabriel García Márquez's *One Hundred Years of Solitude* and write an essay on how it reflected and transcended the culture in which it was produced.

## Reading and Analyzing Primary Sources

Use the document to answer the following questions.

In the Rivonia Trial, named for a suburb in Johannesburg where a group of African National Congress militants hid, Nelson Mandela and other opponents of South African apartheid were charged with sabotage and conspiracy. Mandela spoke these words at the Palace of Justice in Pretoria:

> "During my lifetime I have dedicated myself to this struggle of the African people. I have fought against white domination, and I have fought against black domination. I have cherished the ideal of a democratic and free society in which all persons live together in harmony and with equal opportunities, It is an ideal which I hope to live for and to achieve. But if needs be, it is an ideal for which I am prepared to die."

— Nelson Mandela, statement at the Rivonia Trial, April 20, 1964, from *In His Own Words*

**20** **ANALYZING IDEAS** Against what two extremes in the fight against apartheid does Mandela stand?

**A.** Forced slavery and voluntary slavery

**B.** Denial of opportunity and coerced opportunity

**C.** Capitalist government and communist government

**D.** White-controlled government and black-controlled government

**21** **ANALYZING TEXT PRESENTATION** How does Mandela uses parallelism and opposition to make his final appeal?

**A.** By offering to die for his beliefs

**B.** By incriminating both blacks and whites

**C.** In explaining how important his vision is to him

**D.** In demonstrating the dangers of all forms of authoritarianism

**22** **DETERMINING POINT OF VIEW** How does Mandela's statement differ from a not-guilty plea?

**A.** He willingly confesses to the crimes with which he is charged.

**B.** He admits that what he has done deserves punishment.

**C.** He takes a stand for what he believes instead of denying guilt.

**D.** He places the blame on himself rather than on others involved.

## Writing About History

**23** **EXPLANATORY WRITING** Write a multiparagraph essay explaining how religious, political, economic, and ethnic reasons have fueled conflicts in South and Southeast Asia, the Middle East, Africa, and Latin America since World War II. Give one or more examples from each of the four lessons in the chapter to illustrate each reason.

## Speaking and Listening About History

**24** **COLLABORATING** Meet in a small group to discuss the following question: What were the short- and long-term effects of colonialism in Africa, Asia, and Latin America? Have one member of your group serve as a moderator of the group discussion.

**Need Extra Help?**

| If You've Missed Question | 19 | 20 | 21 | 22 | 23 | 24 |
|---|---|---|---|---|---|---|
| Review Lesson | 4 | 3 | 3 | 3 | 4 | 4 |

"Duck and cover" drills taught schoolchildren how to protect themselves from a nuclear attack. However, these drills would have provided no real protection from the destruction of a bomb or the resulting nuclear radiation.

1945 — 1989

# Life During the Cold War

## CHAPTER 14



**GO DIGITAL**
*It's All online!*

## ASKING ESSENTIAL QUESTIONS

***How does war result in change?***
***What challenges may countries face as a result of war?***

**What Will You Learn?** You will learn how people lived during the Cold War and how the Cold War shaped politics and ordinary life.

**Why Does this Matter?** The Cold War split not just Europe but much of the world into different camps. The USSR and the United States competed for influence and leadership, leaving a path of proxy wars and installed dictators in their wake. The lines drawn during this cold conflict continue to impact on international politics and to shape the world we live in today.

**How Will You Know That You Learned It?** You will be able to identify the major events that shaped Europe and North America during this period and to explain how the Cold War came to an end.

**Using Your Inquiry Journal** As you read this chapter and examine the primary sources, use your Inquiry Journal to help you make notes and expand your list of questions. As you gather information, think about how you will answer the Essential Questions above.

Bettmann/Corbis

# PLACE & TIME Europe and the U.S. 1945–1989

World War II gave rise to globalization and the Cold War, both of which greatly influenced world affairs during this time period and continue to affect the world today. During the decades of the Cold War, the tension between the United States and the Soviet Union not only colored foreign affairs but also influenced the nature of daily life. Citizens grew increasingly anxious under the threat of nuclear war. In the United States and Western Europe, students protested political and economic conditions. In the Eastern bloc countries, popular discontent increased when the state did not provide political freedoms or economic security. Although the methods of political protest were similar, their goals were different. Furthermore, the level of political freedom in the East and West helped determine the fate of these protest movements.

## STEP INTO THE PLACE

Read the quotes and look at the information presented on the map.

1. **EXPLORING CULTURE** What do you notice in the map about the difference between political movements in free countries and not-free countries?

2. **DETERMINING CENTRAL IDEAS** What were the common goals of the political movements in Czechoslovakia and France (second quote)?

## STEP INTO THE TIME

**ANALYZING CHANGE**

How do the events on the time line show an increase in political freedoms in the United States and Europe after World War II?

"We consider socialist democracy to be a system in which the working man has his own standing and value, his security, his right, and his future. It is based upon human participation, coherence, and cooperation.
We wish to meet people's longing for a society in which they can feel to be human among humans. This active, humane, integrating part of socialism, a society without antagonism, that is what we want to realize systematically and gradually, serving the people."

—First Secretary Alexander Dubček, from a speech to the Central Committee of the Communist Party of Czechoslovakia, April 1, 1968

"We are occupying the faculties, you are occupying the factories. Aren't we fighting for the same thing? Higher education only contains 10 percent workers' children. Are we fighting so that there will be more of them, for a democratic university reform? That would be a good thing, but it's not the most important. These workers' children would become just like other students. We are not aiming for a worker's son to be a manager. We want to wipe out segregation between workers and management."

—the March 22 Movement, "Your Struggle Is Ours," May 21, 1968



### EUROPE AND THE UNITED STATES

- **1945** World War II ends
- **1946** Great Britain passes the National Insurance Act and National Health Service Act
- **1956** Hungarians revolt against Soviets
- **1960** France explodes its first nuclear bomb
- **1963** U.S. passes the Equal Pay Act

1945 — 1955

### THE WORLD

- **1948** UN adopts Universal Declaration of Human Rights
- **1956** Gamal Abdel Nasser takes over Egyptian government
- **1962** Nikita Khrushchev allows publication of *One Day in the Life of Ivan Denisovich*
- **1963** Nelson Mandela delivers speech during Rivonia trial

## POLITICAL FREEDOM 1972

**1964** U.S. president Lyndon B. Johnson signs the Civil Rights Act of 1964

**1968** "Prague Spring" in Czechoslovakia

**1974** Gerald Ford becomes U.S. president after Nixon resigns

**1984** USSR, East Germany, and Cuba boycott Los Angeles Olympics

**1965** **1975** **1985** **1989**

**1964** Creation of the Palestine Liberation Organization (PLO)

**1966** Mao Zedong launches Cultural Revolution

**1978** Camp David Accords negotiate peace between Egypt and Israel

**1979** Soviet Union invades Afghanistan

## ESSENTIAL QUESTIONS

- *How does war result in change?*
- *What challenges may countries face as a result of war?*

# THE STORY BEGINS...

LESSON 1

# Western Europe and North America

During the war, the Red Army made its way across Eastern Europe and took control from the Nazi occupiers just as Great Britain and the United States did in the West. But as the continent settled into peace and the democratic Allies began to encourage the restoration of democracy, the USSR took a different path. It began using its control of territory to expand the reach of communism. Noticing this trend early, former British Prime Minister Winston Churchill gave the following speech at Westminster College in Missouri:

> “From Stettin in the Baltic to Trieste in the Adriatic an iron curtain has descended across the Continent. Behind that line lie all the capitals of the ancient states of Central and Eastern Europe. Warsaw, Berlin, Prague, Vienna, Budapest, Belgrade, Bucharest and Sofia, all these famous cities and the populations around them lie in what I must call the Soviet sphere, and all are subject in one form or another, not only to Soviet influence but to a very high and, in many cases, increasing measure of control from Moscow. . . . The safety of the world, ladies and gentlemen, requires a new unity in Europe, from which no nation should be permanently outcast.”

—Winston S. Churchill, *“Iron Curtain Speech,”* March 5, 1946

This speech introduced the term “Iron Curtain” as a way of describing the separation between the West and the Soviet Union in this speech, and it greatly contributed to a growing sense of opposition to the Soviet Union and the alignment of the United States and Western Europe.

*The Treaty of Rome was signed in 1957. It created the European Economic Community, one of the first steps toward economic globalization.* ▶

| Life During the Cold War | |
|---|---|
| Country | Policies and Events |
| France | |
| West Germany | |
| The United Kingdom | |
| The United States | |

**ANALYZING KEY IDEAS AND DETAILS**

**DETERMINING CENTRAL IDEAS** Read closely to identify the economic policies and events that shaped each country during the Cold War. Record these policies and events in a graphic organizer like this one.

# WESTERN EUROPE

**GUIDING QUESTION** *How did Western Europe recover from World War II?*

With the economic aid of the Marshall Plan, the countries of Western Europe recovered relatively rapidly from the devastation of World War II. By 1950, industrial output in Europe was 30 percent above prewar levels.

## FRANCE AND DE GAULLE

One man—the war hero Charles de Gaulle—dominated the history of France for nearly a quarter of a century after the war. In 1946 de Gaulle helped establish a new government, the Fourth Republic. It, however, was largely ineffective. In 1958 leaders of the Fourth Republic, frightened by bitter divisions caused by a crisis in the French colony of Algeria, asked de Gaulle to form a new government. That year, de Gaulle drafted a new constitution for the Fifth Republic that enhanced the power of the president. The French president would now have the right to choose the prime minister, dissolve parliament, and supervise defense and foreign policy. French voters approved the constitution, and de Gaulle became the first president of the Fifth Republic.

As president, de Gaulle wanted France to be a world power once again. To achieve this, de Gaulle invested heavily in nuclear arms. France exploded its first nuclear bomb in 1960.

During de Gaulle's presidency, the French economy grew at an annual rate of 5.5 percent, faster than the rate of growth in the United States. France became a major industrial producer and exporter, especially of automobiles and weapons. Nevertheless, problems remained. Large government deficits and a rise in the cost of living led to unrest. In May 1968, a series of student protests was followed by a general labor strike. Discouraged, de Gaulle resigned from office in April 1969 and died within a year.

In the 1970s, a deteriorating economic situation caused a political **shift** to the left. By 1981, the Socialists gained power in the National Assembly. Socialist François Mitterrand was elected president. He initiated a number of measures to aid workers—an increased minimum wage, a 39-hour work week, and higher taxes for the rich. The Socialist government also nationalized, or took over, major banks, the steel industry, the space and electronics industries, and insurance firms.

Socialist policies, however, largely failed to work, and France's economic decline continued. In the elections in March of 1993, the Socialists won only 28 percent of the vote. A coalition of conservative parties gained 80 percent of the seats in the National Assembly.

**UNDERSTANDING CRAFT AND STRUCTURE**

1. **ANALYZING TEXT PRESENTATION** In what order does the writer present the facts about the economic recovery of Western Europe after World War II? Does the way the text is organized help you better understand the information?
2. **DETERMINING MEANING** What does it mean to provide a minimal standard of living?

*West German Chancellor Willy Brandt*

## WEST GERMANY: THE ECONOMIC MIRACLE

The three Western zones of Germany were unified as the Federal Republic of Germany in 1949. From 1949 to 1963, Konrad Adenauer (AHD • uh • NAU • uhr), the leader of the Christian Democratic Union (CDU), served as chancellor (head of state). Adenauer sought respect for West Germany. He cooperated with the United States and other Western European nations, especially France—Germany's longtime enemy.

Under Adenauer, West Germany experienced an "economic miracle." This revival of the West German economy was largely guided by the minister of finance, Ludwig Erhard. Unemployment fell from 8 percent in 1950 to 0.4 percent in 1965. After Adenauer resigned in 1963, Erhard succeeded him as chancellor and largely continued his policies.

An economic downturn in the mid-1960s brought the Social Democratic Party into power in 1969. The Social Democrats, a moderate socialist party, were led by Willy Brandt, mayor of West Berlin. In December 1972, Brandt signed a treaty that led to greater contact between East Germany and West Germany. Economic, cultural, and personal ties between the countries were stronger as a result. For his efforts, Brandt received the Nobel Peace Prize for 1971.

> "....The young man who in his time was persecuted, driven into exile in Norway and deprived of his rights as a citizen speaks here today not only in general for the cause of peace in Europe but also most particularly for those from whom the past has exacted a harsh toll. . . . But relaxation of tensions, cooperation between peoples, reduction of forces and arms control, partnership with those who have hitherto been the losers, mutual protection against the danger of mutual destruction - this must be possible, and for this we must work."
>
> —Willy Brandt, *Nobel Prize acceptance speech,* December 10, 1971

### ANALYZING PRIMARY SOURCES

1. **ANALYZING IDEAS** How does Willy Brandt use the recent past in Europe to justify his politics of engagement and diplomacy with the Communist bloc?
2. **DETERMINING POINT OF VIEW** What is Willy Brandt asking his listeners to try to do? What is his goal in regard to European and world politics?

## GREAT BRITAIN

The end of World War II left Great Britain with massive economic problems. In elections held immediately after the war, the Labour Party overwhelmingly defeated Churchill's Conservative Party.

Under Clement Attlee, the new prime minister, the Labour government set out to create a modern **welfare state**, a state in which the government takes responsibility for providing citizens with services and a **minimal** standard of living. In 1946 the new government passed the National Insurance Act and the National Health Service Act. The insurance act provided government funds to help the unemployed, the sick, and the aged. The health act created a system of socialized medicine that ensured medical care for everyone. The British welfare state became the norm for most European states after the war.

Continuing economic problems brought the Conservatives back into power from 1951 to 1964. Although they favored private enterprise, the Conservatives accepted the welfare state and extended it by financing an ambitious building program to improve British housing.

Between 1964 and 1979, power alternated between Great Britain's Conservative Party and Labour Party. In 1979 the Conservatives came to power under Margaret Thatcher, Britain's first female prime minister. Thatcher pledged to limit social welfare, to restrict union power, and to end inflation. Her main focus was privatization. Although she did not eliminate the basic social welfare

### DETERMINING MEANING

To better understand the meaning of the term **welfare state**, break down the phrase. *Welfare* refers to the security, status, and comfort of an individual or group of people, and a state in this context refers to a government. Based on these definitions, write a definition for *welfare state*.

system, Thatcher broke the power of the labor unions and controlled inflation.

Thatcherism, as her economic policy was termed, improved the British economic situation, but at a price. Business investment and the number of small businesses increased substantially. The south of England, for example, prospered. Old industrial areas elsewhere, however, were beset by high unemployment, poverty, and violence. Thatcher dominated British politics in the 1980s, but in 1990 her popularity fell, and she resigned as prime minister.

## THE EUROPEAN ECONOMIC COMMUNITY

The destructiveness of two world wars caused many thoughtful Europeans to consider the need for some form of European unity. National feeling was still too powerful, however, for European nations to give up their political sovereignty. As a result, the desire for unity focused chiefly on the economic arena, not the political one.

In 1957 France, West Germany, the Benelux countries (Belgium, the Netherlands, and Luxembourg), and Italy signed the Rome Treaty. This treaty created the European Economic Community (EEC), also known as the Common Market.

The EEC was a free-trade area made up of the six member nations. These six nations would impose no tariffs, or import charges, on each other's goods. However, as a group, they would be protected by a tariff imposed on goods from non-EEC nations. In this way, the EEC encouraged cooperation among the member nations' economies.

By the 1960s, the EEC had become an important trading **bloc** (a group of nations with a common purpose.) In 1973 Britain, Denmark, and Ireland joined the EEC. With a total population of 165 million, the EEC was the world's largest exporter and purchaser of raw materials. By 1986, Spain, Portugal, and Greece had become members. By 1992, the European Economic Community comprised 344 million people and was the world's largest single trading bloc.

### EUROPEAN ECONOMIC COMMUNITY 1989

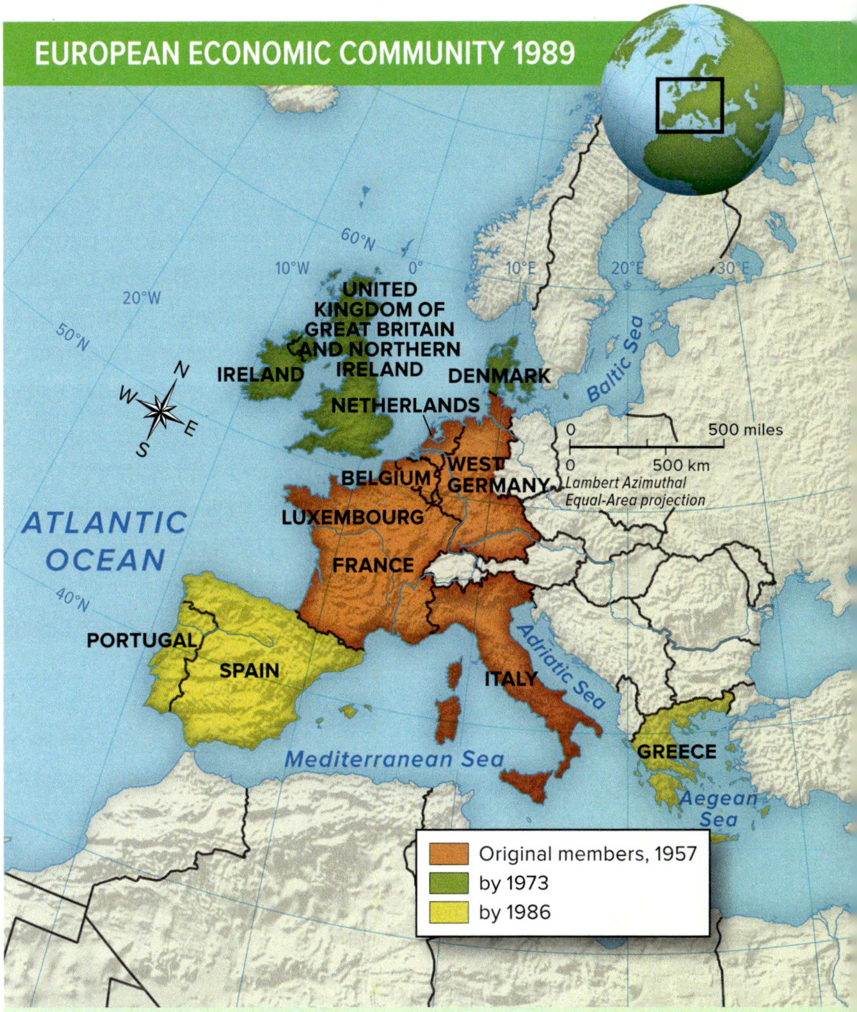


**GEOGRAPHIC REASONING**

1. **GLOBAL INTERCONNECTIONS** Create a map of Europe in 1989 of non-EEC members. How do EEC and non-EEC countries differ?
2. **EXPLORING REGIONS** Create a graph or chart of the expansion of EEC membership.

**DETERMINING MEANING**

A **bloc** refers to a group or collective of some kind, and it usually suggests a group with similar politics and beliefs. What was the common purpose of the EEC bloc?

## ✓ CHECKING FOR UNDERSTANDING

1. **EVALUATING** How did Western Europe recover from World War II?
2. **UNDERSTANDING CHANGE** How did the British commitment to a social welfare state change over time?
3. **COMPARING** How was the Fifth Republic in France different from the Fourth Republic?

# THE U.S. AFTER THE WAR

**GUIDING QUESTION** *What social and political issues challenged the United States during the Cold War?*

Between 1945 and 1970, the ideals of Franklin Delano Roosevelt's New Deal largely determined the patterns of American domestic politics. The New Deal brought basic changes to American society. These changes included a dramatic increase in the role and power of the federal government, the rise of organized labor, the beginning of a welfare state, and a realization of the need to deal fairly with the concerns of minorities, especially African Americans.

The New Deal tradition in American politics was reinforced by the election of Democratic presidents—Harry S. Truman in 1948, John F. Kennedy in 1960, and Lyndon B. Johnson in 1964. Even the election of a Republican president, Dwight D. Eisenhower, in 1952 and 1956, did not change the basic direction of the New Deal.

An economic boom followed World War II. A shortage of consumer goods during the war left Americans with extra income and the desire to buy goods after the war. In addition, the growth of labor unions brought higher wages and gave more workers the ability to buy consumer goods. Between 1945 and 1973, **real wages** grew an average of 3 percent per year, the most prolonged advance ever in American history.

Prosperity was not the only characteristic of the early 1950s. Cold War struggles abroad led to the widespread fear that Communists had infiltrated the United States. This climate of fear produced a dangerous political agitator, Senator Joseph R. McCarthy of Wisconsin. His charges that hundreds of supposed Communists were in high government positions helped create a massive "Red Scare"—fear of Communist subversion. When McCarthy attacked "Communist conspirators" in the U.S. Army, he was condemned by the Senate in 1954. Very quickly, his anti-Communist crusade came to an end.

## THE 1960S AND CIVIL RIGHTS

In August 1963, the Reverend Martin Luther King, Jr., leader of a movement for racial equality, led a march on Washington, D.C., to dramatize the African American desire for equality. King's march and his impassioned plea for racial equality had an electrifying effect on the American people. By the end of 1963, a majority of the American people called civil rights the most significant national issue at that time.

After the assassination of John Kennedy, Lyndon B. Johnson became president. Following his landslide victory in 1964, he pursued the cause of equal rights for African Americans. The Civil Rights Act of 1964 created the machinery to end segregation and discrimination in the workplace and all public places. The Voting Rights Act made it easier for African Americans to vote in Southern states.

**ANALYZING KEY IDEAS AND DETAILS**

1. **ANALYZING CENTRAL IDEAS** Summarize the four paragraphs following "The U.S. After the War" and explain how the central idea explains the section's title.
2. **CITING TEXT EVIDENCE** An important central idea in this section is the struggle for civil rights in the 1960s. Identify two statements in this section that support this idea.

**DETERMINING MEANING**

When we use the term **real wages**, we're not just referring to the amount of money a person makes from wages. The value of money changes over time because of inflation, and by tracking those changes, one can determine how much can be bought with the same amount of money. How is the growth of *real wages* important to a prosperous society?

*The Reverend Martin Luther King, Jr., at the March on Washington, August 28, 1963*

**IDENTIFYING EFFECTS** What do you think was the effect of the March on Washington?

Francis Miller/Time & Life Pictures/Getty Images

## THE VOTING RIGHTS ACT OF 1965

> “This act flows from a clear and simple wrong. Its only purpose is to right that wrong. Millions of Americans are denied the right to vote because of their color. This law will ensure them the right to vote. . . . I pledge you that we will not delay, or we will not hesitate, or we will not turn aside until Americans of every race and color and origin in this country have the same right as all others to share in the process of democracy.”
>
> —President Lyndon B. Johnson, *“Remarks in the Capitol Rotunda at the Signing of the Voting Rights Act,”* August 6, 1965

**ANALYZING PRIMARY SOURCES**

**IDENTIFYING CONNECTIONS**
How was the Voting Rights Act of 1965 important to the civil rights movement?

Laws alone, however, could not guarantee the Great Society that Johnson talked about creating. He soon faced bitter social unrest. In 1968 Martin Luther King, Jr., was assassinated. Riots broke out in more than 100 cities, including Washington, D.C. The riots led to a “white backlash” (whites became less sympathetic to the cause of racial equality) and continued the racial division of the United States. Antiwar protests also divided the United States as some Americans turned against the Vietnam War.

The combination of antiwar demonstrations and riots in the cities caused many people to call for law and order. This was the appeal used by Richard Nixon, the Republican presidential candidate in 1968. With Nixon’s election, a shift to the political right in American politics began.

## THE 1970S AND 1980S

As president, Nixon used illegal methods to gain information about his opponents. This led to the Watergate scandal. After lying to the American public about his involvement in the affair, secret tapes of his conversations in the White House revealed the truth. On August 9, 1974, Nixon resigned rather than face possible impeachment.

**CITIZENSHIP**

### PROTECTING FREEDOM OF THE PRESS

The Watergate scandal was not President Nixon’s first clash with the press. In 1971, *The New York Times* and *Washington Post* began publishing classified documents known as the Pentagon Papers. These revealed that the government was withholding information about the Vietnam War. Nixon’s White House took the newspapers to court, claiming they had violated national security. The U.S. Supreme Court ruled the newspapers had a right under the First Amendment to publish the documents. Under the First Amendment, government is prohibited from determining what the press can and cannot print. Although this right remains strong today, the Internet and changes to news reading habits have driven many newspapers out of business. Those that remain often belong to one of a small list of companies. These changes threaten the ability of the press to perform its function as a check on government power. Although digital publications have helped fill the gaps left by newspapers, these outlets lack the resources that once helped large publications investigate high-profile abuses in government.

*Journalists Bob Woodward and Carl Bernstein, who investigated the Watergate scandal*

1. **UNDERSTANDING CONTEXT** How did the U.S. Supreme Court uphold democratic principles in the Pentagon Papers case?
2. **IDENTIFYING CONNECTIONS** Why is it important for a democracy to have a strong press?

In the 1976 election, the former governor of Georgia, Jimmy Carter, became president. A crisis abroad erupted when the Iranian government of the Ayatollah Khomeini (koh • MAY • nee) held 52 Americans hostage. Carter's inability to gain the release of the American hostages contributed to his loss to Ronald Reagan in the 1980 election.

## CANADA

After the war, Canada began developing electronic, aircraft, nuclear, and chemical engineering industries on a large scale. Under Lester Pearson, the Liberal government laid the groundwork for Canada's welfare state. A national social security system and health insurance program were enacted.

When Pierre Trudeau (TROO • DOH) became prime minister in 1968, he supported a vigorous program of industrialization. He was also dedicated to preserving a united Canada. At the same time, he acknowledged the rights of French-speaking Canadians. His government passed the Official Languages Act, which allowed English and French to be used in the federal civil service.

### ✓ CHECKING FOR UNDERSTANDING

1. **DETERMINING CONTEXT** What social and political issues challenged the United States during the Cold War?
2. **IDENTIFYING CONNECTIONS** How were the elections of Richard Nixon and Ronald Reagan responses to other events?
3. **INTERPRETING** In the United States, how was the decade of the 1970s a reaction to the 1960s?

# WESTERN SOCIETY

**GUIDING QUESTION** *How did Western society change during the Cold War?*

After World War II, Western society witnessed rapid change. New inventions such as computers, televisions, and jet planes altered the pace and nature of human life.

## A NEW SOCIAL STRUCTURE

Postwar Western society was marked by a changing social structure. Especially noticeable were changes in the middle class. Traditional middle-class groups were made of businesspeople, lawyers, doctors, and teachers. A new group of managers and technicians, hired by large companies and government agencies, now joined the middle class.

Changes also occurred among the lower classes. The shift of people from rural to urban areas continued. The number of people in farming declined drastically. By the 1950s, the number of farmers in most parts of Europe dropped by 50 percent. The number of industrial workers declined as white-collar workers increased.

At the same time, a noticeable increase in the real wages of workers made it possible for them to imitate the buying patterns of the middle class. This led to what some observers have called the **consumer society**. Buying on credit

**ANALYZING KEY IDEAS AND DETAILS**

1. **CITING TEXT EVIDENCE** What evidence does the author cite to show change in Western societies during this period?
2. **CITING TEXT EVIDENCE** How do the central ideas of the women's liberation movement compare to the central ideas of the civil rights movement?

**DETERMINING MEANING**

To better understand the meaning of **consumer society**, break down the phrase. *Consumers* are those who buy goods for consumption, and it suggests that they buy more than what they need just to survive. A *society* is a community or group. What might a *consumer society* look like?

MAKING CONNECTIONS TO MUSIC

## ROCK AND ROLL

In the decades after the Second World War, the Western world experienced a degree of affluence that had not been possible before. Because of this affluence, the generations that came of age in the 1950s and '60s had more leisure time and a closer relationship with consumerism than their parents. The effect on popular culture was immense. The classy big bands and cultured jazz music of the prewar period gave way to a new form of pop music—rock and roll. Musicians such as Buddy Holly, Elvis Presley, Chuck Berry, and many others churned out simple, fast-paced songs with catchy lyrics and performed in flashy clothes. This music appealed to these young generations, and the young had the money and time to patronize these performers.

**ANALYZING EVENTS** In what ways was rock and roll a reflection of the political currents and divisions in the Cold War era?

became widespread in the 1950s. Workers could now buy such products as televisions, washing machines, refrigerators, and stereos.

## WOMEN IN THE POSTWAR WORLD

Women's participation in the world wars had resulted in several gains. They had achieved one of the major aims of the nineteenth-century feminist movement—the right to vote.

During World War II, women had entered the workforce in huge numbers. At the war's end, however, they were removed to provide jobs for soldiers returning home. For a time, women fell back into traditional roles. Birthrates rose, creating a "baby boom" in the late 1940s and the 1950s.

By the end of the 1950s, however, the birthrate began to fall and, with it, the size of families. The structure of the workplace changed once again as the number of married women in the workforce increased in Europe and the United States. These women, especially working-class women, faced an old

Barbara Freeman/Hulton Archive/Getty Images

*Men and women march together at an Equal Rights Amendment (ERA) rally in Pittsburgh, Pennsylvania, in 1976.*

**DETERMINING MEANING** Interpret the meaning of the signs carried at the rally.

problem. They still earned less than men for equal work. In addition, women still tended to enter traditionally female jobs. Many faced the double burden of earning income and raising a family. Such inequalities led increasing numbers of women to rebel. In the late 1960s came renewed interest in feminism, or the **women's liberation movement**.

In the 1960s and 1970s, the women's movement emerged in the United States and quickly spread to Western Europe. Supporters of the movement wanted to change the basic conditions of women's lives. The United States passed the Equal Pay Act in 1963. It required women to be paid the same as men for performing the same work.

A controversial issue was abortion. In 1973 the U.S. Supreme Court legalized abortion in *Roe* v. *Wade*. Although national health insurance covered abortion in most of Europe, the procedure was debated in the United States.

## STUDENT REVOLTS

Growing discontent among university students led to an outburst of student revolts in the late 1960s. Many protests were an extension of the revolts in American universities, often sparked by student opposition to the Vietnam War. Some students, particularly in Europe, believed that universities failed to respond to their needs or to the realities of the modern world. Others believed they were becoming small cogs in the large and impersonal bureaucratic wheels of the modern world.

### ✓ CHECKING FOR UNDERSTANDING

1. **ANALYZING CHANGE** How did Western society change during the Cold War?
2. **EXPLAINING CAUSE AND EFFECT** How did the growth of real wages in this period fuel the growth of a consumer society?
3. **SUMMARIZING** What was a goal of the women's liberation movement?

## LESSON 1 REVIEW

### Time and Place

1. **IDENTIFYING CONNECTIONS** Identify and discuss some of the social movements that happened during the Cold War.

### Building History-Social Studies Analysis Skills

2. **RELATING EVENTS** How did France and Great Britain respond to economic downturns that began in the 1970s and 1980s?
3. **RELATING EVENTS** What fed the interest in a united and integrated Europe?
4. **EXPLAINING EFFECTS** What was an effect of the March on Washington?

### Writing About History

5. **INFORMATIVE WRITING** Pick one of the countries discussed in this lesson, and using information from the text and from outside research, write a short essay about the postwar reforms implemented in the country and discuss whether they were successful.

### Collaborating

6. **EVALUATING** With a partner, discuss the major trends going on in Europe after World War II. How were people living? What was going on in their economies? How does this compare to the turmoil of the war years?

## ESSENTIAL QUESTIONS

- *How does war result in change?*
- *What challenges may countries face as a result of war?*

LESSON 2

# Eastern Europe and the Soviet Union

## THE STORY BEGINS...

The cracks in the Soviet Union's domination of Eastern Europe began to show in October of 1956 when a student protest in Budapest demanding the evacuation of Soviet troops from Hungary was violently put down. The violence horrified Hungarians and led to further protests against Soviet influence. The fires of the Hungarian Revolution, as it is now called, were eventually extinguished at a cost of thousands of dead Hungarians. On the first anniversary of the uprising, then Senator John F. Kennedy noted the following:

> "Four thousand four hundred and six miles from here there lies tonight a captive city. While we who are free salute at festive banquets her noble fight for freedom, she weeps for the freedom - and the sons and daughters - that she has lost. While we who acted not deplore the frailties that held us back, she guards the graves of those who gave the last full measure of devotion. While we who only watched and waited seek loudly now to fix the blame and point with shame, she silently waits with ever dimming hope and strength for the keys to her prison door."

—Senator John F. Kennedy, speech on the Hungarian Revolution, October 23, 1957

Three years later, this senator who referred to Eastern Europe as a "prison" would be elected president. Within a few months of his inauguration, the Soviets appeared to turn Kennedy's rhetorical flourish into a reality by beginning construction on the most recognizable artifact of the Cold War—the Berlin Wall.

*In addition to physically dividing the city of Berlin, the Berlin Wall was also a symbol of the political divide between the East and West during the Cold War.* ▶

PHOTO:Bettmann/Getty Images; TEXT: Kennedy, John F. 1957. Remarks of Senator John F. Kennedy at the Annual Freedom Award to the Hungarian Freedom Fighters in New York City, October 23, 1957. Reproduced by John F. Kennedy Presidential Library and Museum website.

| Soviet Leaders and Policies | |
| --- | --- |
| Stalin | |
| Khrushchev | |
| Brezhnev | |

**ANALYZING KEY IDEAS AND DETAILS**

**SUMMARIZING** Read closely to identify the policies of each Soviet leader during this period. Summarize these policies in a graphic organizer like this one.

# POSTWAR SOVIET UNION

GUIDING QUESTION *What political, economic, and social shifts occurred in the Soviet Union during the Cold War?*

World War II devastated the Soviet Union. To create a new industrial base, Stalin returned to the method that he had used in the 1930s. Soviet workers were expected to produce goods for export with little in return for themselves. The incoming capital from abroad could then be used to buy machinery and Western technology.

Economic recovery in the Soviet Union was spectacular in some respects. By 1950, Russian industrial production surpassed prewar levels by 40 percent. New power plants, canals, and giant factories were built. **Heavy industry** increased, chiefly for military benefit. The hydrogen bomb in 1953 and the first space satellite, *Sputnik I,* in 1957 **enhanced** the Soviet Union's reputation as a world power.

Yet the Soviet people were shortchanged. The production of consumer goods did not increase as much as heavy industry, and there was a housing shortage. As a British official in Moscow reported, "Every room is both a living room by day and a bedroom by night."

**ANALYZING KEY IDEAS AND DETAILS**

1. **SUMMARIZING** In two to three sentences, summarize what the Soviet economy was like during the postwar period.
2. **CITING TEXT EVIDENCE** The text makes the argument that Brezhnev was intolerant of dissent. What evidence in the text supports this claim?

**DETERMINING MEANING**

To better understand the term **heavy industry**, look at each word individually. *Heavy* can mean "large or considerable," and *industry* refers to "production of goods." Based on this, what is heavy industry? Name an example of heavy industry.

## THE RULE OF STALIN

Stalin was the undisputed master of the Soviet Union. He distrusted competitors, exercised **sole** power, and had little respect for other Communist Party members or leaders. He is reported to have said to members of his inner circle in 1952, "You are as blind as kittens. What would you do without me?"

Stalin's suspicions added to the regime's increasing repression. In 1946 the government ordered all literary and scientific work to conform to the state's political needs. Along with this anti-intellectual campaign came political terror. The threat of more purges in 1953 disappeared when Stalin died on March 5, 1953.

## THE KHRUSHCHEV ERA

A group of leaders succeeded Stalin, but the new general secretary of the Communist Party, Nikita Khrushchev, soon emerged as the chief Soviet policy maker. After he was in power, Khrushchev took steps to undo some of the worst features of Stalin's regime.

(t)Hilton, Richard. 1949. Military Attache in Moscow. Hollis & Carter.; (b)Leonhard, Wolfgang. 1962. The Kremlin Since Stalin. Oxford University Press.

At the Twentieth Congress of the Communist Party in 1956, Khrushchev condemned Stalin for his "administrative violence, mass repression, and terror." The process of eliminating the more ruthless policies of Stalin became known as **de-Stalinization**.

Khrushchev loosened government controls on literary and artistic works. In 1962, for example, he allowed the publication of *One Day in the Life of Ivan Denisovich*. This novel, written by Aleksandr Solzhenitsyn (SOHL • zhuh • NEET • suhn), is a grim portrayal of life in a Siberian labor camp. Many Soviets identified with Ivan as a symbol of the suffering endured under Stalin.

Khrushchev also tried to place more emphasis on producing consumer goods. He attempted to increase agricultural output by growing corn and cultivating vast lands east of the Ural Mountains. The attempt was unsuccessful and damaged Khrushchev's reputation within the party. This failure, combined with increased military spending, hurt the Soviet economy. The industrial growth rate, which had soared in the early 1950s, now declined sharply from 13 percent in 1953 to 7.5 percent in 1964.

Foreign policy failures also damaged Khrushchev's reputation among his colleagues. His rash plan to place missiles in Cuba was the final straw. While he was away on vacation in 1964, a special meeting of the Soviet leaders voted him out of office (because of "deteriorating health") and forced him into retirement.

**DETERMINING MEANING**

To better understand the meaning of **de-Stalinization,** break down the word. The prefix *de-* refers to reversing or undoing something. *Stalin* was the ruler of the Soviet Union who imposed a very repressive and paranoid government, and *-ation* is a suffix that means "action or process." Putting all of this together, write a definition for *de-Stalinization*.

## THE BREZHNEV ERA

When Nikita Khrushchev was removed from office in 1964, two men, Alexei Kosygin and Leonid Brezhnev (BREHZH • nehf) replaced him. Brezhnev emerged as the dominant leader in the 1970s. He was determined to keep

**ANALYZING PRIMARY SOURCES**

### CONTRASTING DEPICTIONS OF SOVIET SOCIETY

Soviet control over the arts was rigid. Artists had to work within the confines of socialist realist art, which was meant to portray the ideals of Soviet society. Common themes included portraits of Soviet political leaders, people performing manual labor, and industrial progress, such as the sculpture *Worker* and *Kolkhoz [collective farm] Woman* by Vera Mukhina (right).

Not everyone worked within these confines, however. Aleksandr Solzhenitsyn was exiled for writing *The Gulag Archipelago,* which revealed life in the forced labor camps to which many political opponents were sent in the 1950s. "Archipelago" was his metaphor for forced labor camps as they stretched across Siberia like a group of islands. "Gulag" is an acronym for the agency that supervised the camps. A short excerpt from his work:

"But the whole central meaning of their existence was identical for serfdom and the Archipelago; they were forms of social organization for the forced and pitiless exploitation of the unpaid labor of millions of slaves."

— Aleksandr Solzhenitsyn, from *The Gulag Archipelago*

**DETERMINING CONTEXT** How do the text and the sculpture demonstrate differing views of life under the Soviet regime?

*Common themes in socialist realist art included portraits of Soviet political leaders, people performing manual labor, and industrial progress, such as the sculpture* Worker and Kolkhoz [collective farm] Woman *by Vera Mukhina.*

PHOTO:Neil Beer/Getty Images; TEXT:(t)__________. 1966. Thought: A Review of Culture and Idea, Vol. 41. Fordham University Press.; (b)Solzhenitsyn, Aleksandr. 1974. The Gulag Archipelago: 1918-1956, III-IV. Translated 1975 by Thomas P. Whitney. Harper & Row Publishers, Inc.

### DETERMINING MEANING

Read the paragraph that contains the word **détente**. What context clues in the paragraph help a reader understand the meaning of *détente*?

### DETERMINING MEANING

The word **dissident** is related to the word *dissent,* which means "to disagree with opinions or views held by the majority." How does knowing the meaning of *dissent* help a reader understand the meaning of *dissident*?

Eastern Europe under the control of Communist governments and was not interested in reform. Brezhnev insisted on the Soviet Union's right to intervene if communism was threatened in another Communist state (known as the Brezhnev Doctrine).

At the same time, Brezhnev benefited from **détente**, a relaxation of tensions and improved relations between the United States and the Soviet Union. In the 1970s, the two superpowers signed SALT I and SALT II (Strategic Arms Limitation Treaties) and the Anti-Ballistic Missile (ABM) Treaty to limit nuclear arms. Because they felt more secure, Soviet leaders relaxed their authoritarian rule and allowed more access to Western music, dress, and art. Of course, **dissidents**—those who spoke out against the regime—were still suppressed. For example, Andrei Sakharov, father of the Soviet hydrogen bomb, was punished for defending human rights.

### ANALYZING PRIMARY SOURCES

1. **DETERMINING CENTRAL IDEAS** What do the signers believe that the treaty will accomplish?
2. **DETERMINING MEANING** What do the signers mean when they say they are "guided by the principle of equality and equal security"?

> "The United States of America and the Union of Soviet Socialist Republics . . .
>
> *Convinced* that the additional measures limiting strategic offensive arms provided for in this Treaty will contribute to the improvement of relations between the Parties, help to reduce the risk of outbreak of nuclear war and strengthen international peace and security, . . .
>
> *Guided* by the principle of equality and equal security,
>
> *Recognizing* that the strengthening of strategic stability meets the interests of the Parties and the interests of international security,
>
> *Reaffirming* their desire to take measures for the further limitation and for the further reduction of strategic arms, having in mind the goal of achieving general and complete disarmament, . . .
>
> *Have agreed* as follows . . ."

—*Strategic Arms Limitation Treaty (SALT II),* 1972

In his economic policies, Brezhnev continued to emphasize heavy industry. Two problems, however, weakened the Soviet economy. First, the government's central planning led to a huge complex bureaucracy that discouraged efficiency and led to indifference. Second, collective farmers had no incentive to work hard. Many preferred working their own small private plots to laboring in the collective work brigades.

By the 1970s, the Communist ruling class in the Soviet Union had become complacent and corrupt. Party and state leaders, as well as army leaders and secret police (KGB), enjoyed a high standard of living. Brezhnev was unwilling to tamper with the party leadership and state bureaucracy regardless of the inefficiency and corruption the system encouraged.

By the 1970s, détente had allowed U.S. grain and consumer goods to be sold to the Soviet Union. However, détente collapsed in 1979 when the Soviet Union invaded Afghanistan. A new period of East-West confrontation began. The Soviet Union wanted to restore a pro-Soviet regime in Afghanistan. The United States viewed this as an act of expansion. To show his disapproval, President Jimmy Carter canceled U.S. **participation** in the 1980 Olympic Games to be held in Moscow. He also placed an embargo on the shipment of U.S. grain to the Soviets.

Relations became even chillier when Ronald Reagan became president of the United States. Calling the Soviet Union an "evil empire," he began a military buildup and a new arms race. Reagan also gave military aid to the Afghan rebels to maintain a war in Afghanistan, a war the Soviet Union ultimately could not win.

### ☑ CHECKING FOR UNDERSTANDING

1. **SUMMARIZING** What political, economic, and social shifts occurred in the Soviet Union during the Cold War?
2. **IDENTIFYING CAUSES** What factors led to the fall of Nikita Khrushchev from power?
3. **COMPARING AND CONTRASTING** How were U.S.-Soviet relations different during the Khrushchev and Brezhnev regimes?

# EASTERN EUROPE

GUIDING QUESTION *How was Eastern Europe affected by communism after World War II?*

At the end of World War II, Soviet military forces occupied all Eastern Europe and the Balkans (except for Greece, Albania, and Yugoslavia). All the occupied states came under Soviet control.

## COMMUNIST PATTERNS OF CONTROL

The timetable of the Soviet takeover varied from country to country. Between 1945 and 1947, Soviet-controlled Communist governments became firmly entrenched in East Germany, Bulgaria, Romania, Poland, and Hungary. In Czechoslovakia, where there was a tradition of democracy and a multiparty system, the Soviets did not seize control of the government until 1948. At that time, they dissolved all parties but the Communist Party.

Albania and Yugoslavia, however, were exceptions to this pattern of Soviet dominance. During the war, both countries had strong Communist movements that resisted the Nazis. After the war, members of these movements went on to form local Communist parties that took control of the government. Communists in Albania set up a Stalinist-type regime that grew more and more independent of the Soviet Union.

In Yugoslavia, Josip Broz, known as Tito, had been the leader of the Communist resistance movement. After the war, he created an independent Communist state in Yugoslavia. Stalin hoped to take control of Yugoslavia, just as he had done in other Eastern European countries. Tito, however, refused to give in to Stalin's demands. He gained the support of the people by portraying the struggle as one of Yugoslav national freedom. Tito ruled Yugoslavia until his death in 1980. Although Yugoslavia had a Communist government, it was not a Soviet satellite state.

Between 1948 and Stalin's death in 1953, the Eastern European satellite states, directed by the Soviet Union, followed Stalin's example. They instituted Soviet-type five-year plans with emphasis on heavy industry rather than consumer goods. They collectivized agriculture, eliminated all noncommunist parties, and set up the institutions of repression—secret police and military forces.

**ANALYZING KEY IDEAS AND DETAILS**

1. **CITING TEXT EVIDENCE** What evidence in the text suggests that a Czechoslovakian group played a role in Antonín Novotný's fall from power?
2. **ANALYZING CENTRAL IDEAS** What is the central idea of "Communist Patterns of Control"?

## BIOGRAPHY

### ANDREI SAKHAROV (1921–1989)

Andrei Sakharov was a member of a team of scientists working on the Soviet Union's nuclear weapons program following World War II. In the mid-1960s, however, he began to develop concerns about the morality of his work and the Soviet system.

Sakharov would make these concerns public in 1968. As a result, he was removed from the nuclear team and became a target for harassment by the Soviet government. Sakharov then became an activist, calling for an end to repression, democratic reforms, and an end to human rights abuses. He was awarded the Nobel Peace Prize for these efforts in 1976. However, in 1980 the Soviet government exiled him to Gorky, a city foreigners were not allowed to visit.

As the Soviet government implemented reforms in the mid-1980s, Sakharov was allowed to return to Moscow. When there, he returned to activism, dying unexpectedly in December 1989.

Sakharov's tireless efforts did not go unnoticed by the Soviet populace. His work eroded public confidence in the legitimacy of Soviet rule. Reforms he supported in the 1980s also helped bring about the end of the Cold War.

## REVOLTS AGAINST COMMUNISM

Communism did not develop deep roots among the peoples of Eastern Europe. Moreover, the Soviets exploited Eastern Europe economically for their own benefit and made living conditions harsh for most people.

After Stalin's death, many Eastern European states began to pursue a new course. In the late 1950s and 1960s, however, the Soviet Union made it clear—especially in Poland, Hungary, and Czechoslovakia—that it would not allow its Eastern European satellites to become independent of Soviet control.

In 1956 protests erupted in Poland after a strike by factory workers was violently suppressed. Although the strike was centered on better working conditions, the protests introduced the desire of some insurgents for a more moderate form of communism. In response, the Polish Communist Party adopted a series of reforms in October and elected Władysław Gomułka as first secretary. Gomułka declared that Poland had the right to follow its own socialist path. Fearful of Soviet armed response, however, the Poles compromised. Poland pledged to remain loyal to the Warsaw Pact.

Developments in Poland in 1956 led Hungarian Communists to seek the same kinds of reforms. Unrest in Hungary, combined with economic difficulties, led to calls for revolt. To quell the rising rebellion, Imre Nagy, the Hungarian leader, declared Hungary a free nation on November 1, 1956, and promised free elections. It soon became clear that this could mean the end of Communist rule in Hungary.

Khrushchev was in no position at home to allow a member of the Communist group of nations to leave, however. Three days after Nagy's declaration, the Soviet Army attacked Budapest. The Soviets reestablished control over the country. Nagy was seized by the Soviet military and executed two years later.

The situation in Czechoslovakia in the 1950s was different. There, Stalin had placed Antonín Novotný, the "Litte Stalin," in power in 1953. By the late 1960s, however, he had alienated many members of his own party. He was

*The head of a destroyed statue of Stalin in the middle of a Budapest street during the Hungarian revolt of 1956*

**UNDERSTANDING CONTEXT**
What is the symbolic importance of the fallen statue?

especially disliked by Czechoslovakia's writers. A writers' rebellion, which encouraged the people to take control of their own lives, led to Novotný's resignation in 1968.

In January 1968, Alexander Dubček (DOOB • chehk) was elected first secretary of the Communist Party. He introduced a number of reforms, including freedom of speech and press and freedom to travel abroad. He relaxed censorship, began to pursue an independent foreign policy, and promised a democratization of the Czechoslovakian political system. Dubček hoped to create "socialism with a human face." A period of euphoria broke out that came to be known as the "Prague Spring."

*Soviet tanks left Hungary on October 30, 1956, but the Soviets soon returned, crushing the revolt and reestablishing control.*

Keystone-France/Gamma-Keystone/Getty Images

The euphoria proved to be short-lived. As in Poland and Hungary, the Czechoslovakian insurgents varied in their ideals, some wishing to reform the Communist Party into a party that was less restrictive and others that were against communism as a whole. Regardless of the desires of the insurgents, the Soviet Union was fearful of losing control. The Soviet Army invaded Czechoslovakia in August 1968 and crushed the movement. Gustav Husák replaced Dubček, revoked his reforms, and reestablished the old order.

## ✓ CHECKING FOR UNDERSTANDING

1. **EXPLAINING EFFECTS** How were Eastern Europeans affected by communism after World War II?
2. **ANALYZING CHANGE** What political changes took place in Poland and Hungary in 1956?
3. **UNDERSTANDING CONTEXT** Why was Yugoslavia different from other Eastern European countries during the Cold War?

# LESSON 2 REVIEW

## Time and Place

1. **EXPLAINING CAUSE AND EFFECT** How did the period of détente between the United States and the Soviet Union lead to a relaxation of authoritarian rule?

## Building History-Social Studies Analysis Skills

2. **INTERPRETING** How did Yugoslavia manage to be independent of Soviet rule?
3. **EXPLAINING EFFECTS** What were the consequences of Brezhnev's rule in the Soviet Union?
4. **IDENTIFYING EFFECTS** What were some of the effects of Dubček being elected in Czechoslovakia?

## Writing About History

5. **INFORMATIVE WRITING** Research and write an essay about the "Prague Spring." What did it hope to achieve, and why was it unsuccessful? Be sure to include a bibliography of the sources you have consulted.

## Collaborating

6. **INTEGRATING INFORMATION** With a partner, compare and contrast the rules of Khrushchev and Brezhnev. One partner should select the rule of Khrushchev while the other should select Brezhnev. How were their policies similar? How were they different?

POINTS OF VIEW

# The Army-McCarthy Hearings

As part of the "Red Scare" during the early 1950s, Senator Joseph McCarthy of Wisconsin held a series of hearings in which he interrogated and investigated government officials he suspected of having Communist ties. One series of these hearings, held between April and June in 1954 and now known as the Army-McCarthy Hearings, was an investigation of the United States Army. During the course of these hearings, on June 9, 1954, McCarthy questioned special counsel for the army Joseph Welch about another member of his law firm, Fred Fisher, and his possible connections to a Communist organization. This well-known exchange has come to symbolize the animosity displayed during the "Red Scare."

"...in view of Mr. Welch's request that the information be given once we know of anyone who might be performing any work for the Communist Party, I think we should tell him he has in his law firm a young man named Fisher whom he recommended, incidentally, to do work on this committee, who has been for a number of years a member of an organization which was named, oh, years and years ago, as the legal **bulwark** of the Communist Party, an organization which always swings to the defense of anyone who dares to expose Communists. . . . He belonged to that for a sizable number of years, according to his own admission, and he belonged to it long after it had been exposed as the legal arm of the Communist Party. . . .

I don't think you can find anyplace, anywhere, an organization which has done more ... to defend Communists, to defend **espionage** agents, and to aid the Communist cause, than the man whom you originally wanted down here at your right hand . . .

I am not asking you at this time to explain why you tried to **foist** him on this committee. Whether you knew he was a member of that Communist organization or not, I don't know."

—Senator Joseph McCarthy, to Special Counsel Joseph Welch

VOCABULARY

*bulwark:* something that gives support or protection

*espionage:* involving spies or spying, often by governments

*foist:* to impose an unwelcome or unnecessary thing on

PHOTO:Frank Scherschel/The LIFE Picture Collection/Getty Images; TEXT:McCarty, Joseph. 1954. Hearing Before the Special Subcommittee on Investigations of the Committee on Government Operations. United States Senate, Eighty-third Congress, Second Session, Pursuant to S. Res. 189. June 3, 1954. Washington: United States Government Printing Office.

"Until this moment, Senator, I think I never really **gauged** your cruelty or your recklessness. Fred Fisher is a young man who went to the Harvard Law School and came into my firm and is starting what looks to be a brilliant career with us. . . .

Fred Fisher said, "Mr. Welch, when I was in law school and for a period of months after, I belonged to the Lawyers Guild," as you have suggested, Senator. . . .

Little did I dream you could be so reckless and cruel as to do an injury to that lad. It is true he is still with Hale & Dorr. It is true that he will continue to be with Hale & Dorr. It is, I regret to say, equally true that I fear he shall always bear a scar needlessly **inflicted** by you. If it were in my power to forgive you for your reckless cruelty, I will do so. I like to think I am a gentleman, but your forgiveness will have to come from someone other than me. . . .

Let us not assassinate this lad further, Senator. You have done enough. Have you no sense of **decency** sir, at long last? Have you left no sense of decency?"

—Special Counsel Joseph Welch, in response to Senator Joseph McCarthy

---

**VOCABULARY**

*gauged:* measured or estimated

*inflicted:* caused something unpleasant or painful to be suffered

*decency:* behavior that conforms to accepted standards of morality or respectability

## What Do YOU Think?

1. **ANALYZING IDEAS** What is the purpose of McCarthy's final paragraph?
2. **CITING TEXT EVIDENCE** How does Welch's response express his displeasure with McCarthy? Cite evidence from the text.
3. **DIFFERENTIATING** What do the differences between McCarthy's and Welch's descriptions of Fred Fisher suggest about this stage of the Red Scare?
4. **INTERPRETING** Based on Welch's testimony, how might Fisher have responded to McCarthy's accusations about him?
5. **EXPLAINING CAUSES** Public opinion turned against McCarthy after this exchange. Based on both excerpts, why might this have occurred?

## ESSENTIAL QUESTIONS

- *How does war result in change?*
- *What challenges may countries face as a result of war?*

# THE STORY BEGINS...

*In the decades following World War II, Japan experienced impressive economic growth that has made it one of the world's largest economies today.* ▶

LESSON 3

# The Asian Rim

After World War II, Japan was occupied by Allied military forces, which compelled it to draft a new constitution with features similar to Western forms of government. The new constitution began with a statement of peace and a resolution against war:

> "We, the Japanese people, acting through our duly elected representatives in the National Diet, determined that we shall secure for ourselves and our posterity the fruits of peaceful cooperation with all nations and the blessings of liberty throughout this land, and resolved that never again shall we be visited with the horrors of war through the action of government, do proclaim that sovereign power resides with the people and do firmly establish this Constitution. Government is a sacred trust of the people, the authority for which is derived from the people, the powers of which are exercised by the representatives of the people, and the benefits of which are enjoyed by the people. This is a universal principle of mankind upon which this Constitution is founded. We reject and revoke all constitutions, laws, ordinances, and rescripts in conflict herewith."

—The Constitution of Japan, 1946

The constitution was the first step in the transformation of Japan from a military power to the peaceful industrial power it is today. It also set the pace for the expansion of American influence in Asia and the peaceful industrial and economic development of South Korea, Taiwan, Singapore, and Hong Kong.

| Key Areas of Economic Development | |
|---|---|
| South Korea | |
| Taiwan | |
| Singapore | |

**ANALYZING KEY IDEAS AND DETAILS**

**DETERMINING CENTRAL IDEAS** Read carefully to identify the key areas of economic development in South Korea, Taiwan, and Singapore. Summarize these areas in a graphic organizer like this one.

# THE TRANSFORMATION OF JAPAN

**GUIDING QUESTION** *How was Japan transformed after World War II?*

In August 1945, Japan was in ruins, and a foreign army occupied its land. A mere 50 years later, Japan emerged as the second-greatest industrial power in the world.

From 1945 to 1952, Japan was **occupied** by Allied military forces under the command of U.S. General Douglas MacArthur. Under his firm direction, Japanese society was remodeled along Western lines. A new constitution renounced war as a national policy. Japan agreed to **maintain** armed forces sufficient only for self-defense. The constitution established a parliamentary system and reduced the power of the emperor (who was forced to announce that he was not a god). It guaranteed basic rights and gave women the right to vote.

On September 8, 1951, a peace treaty restored Japanese independence. Since then, Japan has emerged as an economic giant. The country's dramatic recovery from the war has been described as the "Japanese miracle." How did the miracle occur?

Modeled on the U.S. Constitution, Japan's new constitution guaranteed basic civil and political rights, and it called for universal suffrage and a balance of power among the executive, legislative, and judicial branches of government. However, it retained some of Japan's nineteenth-century political system under the Meiji. An example involves the distribution of political power. Japan has a multiparty system with two major parties—the Liberal Democrats and the Socialists. In practice, however, the Liberal Democrats have dominated the government. A few party leaders decided key issues such as who should be the prime minister.

The central government plays an active role in the economy. It establishes price and wage policies and subsidizes vital industries. This government role is widely accepted in Japan. Indeed, it is often cited as a key reason for the efficiency of Japanese industry and the emergence of Japan as an industrial giant. Japan's economic system has been described as **state capitalism**.

During their occupation of Japan, Allied officials had planned to dismantle the business conglomerations known as the *zaibatsu*. But with the Cold War, the policy was scaled back. Only the 19 largest companies were affected. Also, the policy did not keep companies from forming ties with each other, which basically gave rise to another *zaibatsu* system.

The occupation administration had more success with its land-reform program. Half the population lived on farms, and half of all farmers were tenants of large

**ANALYZING KEY IDEAS AND DETAILS**

1. **SUMMARIZING** Write a brief summary of the transformation of Japan.
2. **CITING TEXT EVIDENCE** The text claims Japan was transformed into one of the world's greatest industrial powers. What evidence does the text use to support this claim?

**DETERMINING MEANING**

Read the paragraph that contains the word **occupied**. Which words provide context clues you can use to determine the meaning of *occupied*?

**DETERMINING MEANING**

To better understand **state capitalism**, break down the phrase. *State* refers to the central government. *Capitalism* is an economic system concerning the manufacture and sale of goods and services. Based on these definitions, what is state capitalism?

## THE ECONOMY OF MODERN JAPAN

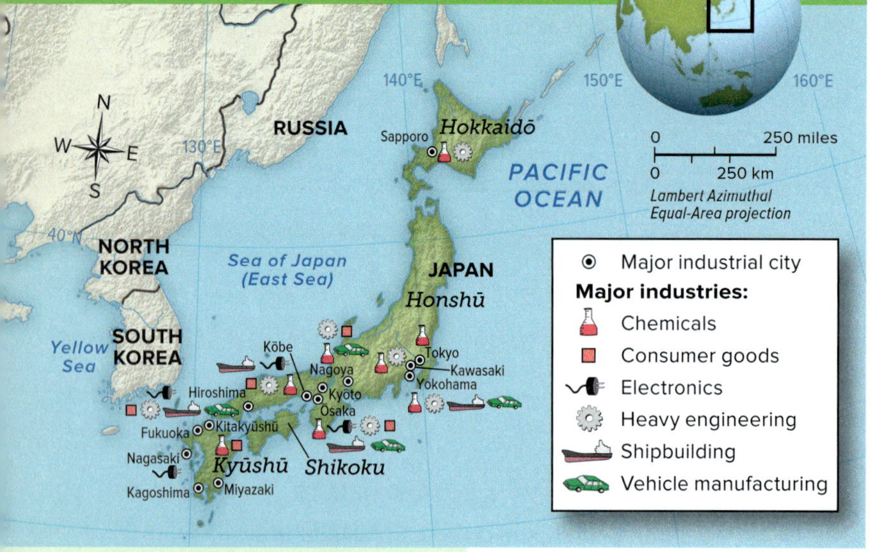


### GEOGRAPHIC REASONING

Japan has one of the world's largest economies.

1. **HUMAN-ENVIRONMENT INTERACTION** How has Japan's geography influenced its economy?
2. **EXPLORING PLACE** What do you think are Japan's major exports and imports?

landowners. Under the reform program, lands were sold on easy credit terms to the tenants. The reform program created a strong class of independent farmers.

At the end of the Allied occupation in 1952, the Japanese gross national product was one-third that of Great Britain or France. By the 1980s, it was larger than both combined. After several decades of impressive growth, Japan was considered a model of economic success.

During the occupation, Allied planners tried to eliminate the aggressiveness that had been part of Japanese behavior. A new educational system stressed individualism and removed references to patriotism and loyalty to the emperor. Efforts to remake Japanese behavior through laws were only partly successful, however. Many characteristics of traditional society have persisted. Emphasis on the work ethic, for example, remained strong. The tradition of hard work is stressed in the educational system.

Women's roles are another example of the difficulty of social change. After the war, women gained the vote and were encouraged to enter politics. However, the subordinate role of women has not been eliminated. Women are legally protected against discrimination in employment, yet very few have reached senior levels in business, education, or politics. Most women are employed in retail or service occupations. Also, their average salary is only about 60 percent that of men.

### UNDERSTANDING CRAFT AND STRUCTURE

1. **ANALYZING TEXT PRESENTATION** How does the writer introduce the topic of the "Asian tigers"? How does the writer develop this topic from the beginning to the end of this section?
2. **DETERMINING MEANING** According to the text, General Park Chung Hee was an autocratic ruler. Based on the text, what might *autocratic* mean?

### DETERMINING MEANING

Read the paragraph that begins, "In 1953 the Republic of Korea. . . ." What context clues in this paragraph help a reader determine the meaning of *coup d'etat*?

### ☑ CHECKING FOR UNDERSTANDING

1. **ANALYZING CHANGE** How was Japan transformed after World War II?
2. **EXPLAINING EFFECTS** What gave rise to a class of independent farmers in Japan?

## THE "ASIAN TIGERS"

**GUIDING QUESTION** *What changes did the Asian Rim countries experience after World War II?*

Sometimes called the "Asian tigers," South Korea Taiwan, Singapore, and Hong Kong have imitated Japan in creating successful industrial societies. Australia and New Zealand, to the south and east of Asia, now have closer trade relations with their Asian neighbors.

In 1953 the Republic of Korea (South Korea) was under the dictatorial president Syngman Rhee. Rhee ruled harshly. In the spring of 1960, demonstrations broke out in Seoul. Rhee was forced to retire. A coup d'état in 1961 put General Park Chung Hee in power. Two years later, Park was elected president and began to strengthen the South Korean economy. South Korea gradually emerged as a major industrial power in East Asia. The key areas for industrial development were chemicals, textiles, shipbuilding, and automobile production.

South Korea was slow to develop a fully democratic government. Park ruled by autocratic means and suppressed protests. However, after his assassination, democratic elections were restored by the early 1990s.

Defeated by the Communists, Chiang Kai-shek and his followers established their capital at Taipei on the island of Taiwan. Chiang Kai-shek said that the Republic of China was the legitimate government of all Chinese people. The Communist government on the mainland claimed to rule all China, including Taiwan. With the protection of American military forces, Taiwan focused on economic growth with no worries about a Communist invasion.

Making good use of foreign aid and the efforts of its people, the Republic of China built a modern industrialized society. A land-reform program, which put farmland in the hands of peasants, doubled food production. Local manufacturing and commerce also expanded. Prosperity did not at first lead to democracy. Chiang Kai-shek ruled by decree and did not allow new political parties to form. After his death in 1975, the Republic of China slowly moved toward a more representative form of government.

Singapore, once a British colony and briefly a part of the state of Malaysia, is now an independent state. Under the leadership of Prime Minister Lee Kwan Yew, Singapore developed a free-market economy based on banking, shipbuilding, oil refineries, and electronics. The authoritarian political system created a **stable** environment for economic growth. Its citizens, however, began to demand more political freedoms.

Like Singapore, Hong Kong became an industrial powerhouse with high standards of living. Having ruled Hong Kong for more than 150 years, Great Britain returned control of Hong Kong to mainland China in 1997. China, in turn, promised that, for the next 50 years, Hong Kong would enjoy a high degree of economic freedom under a capitalist system.

**DETERMINING MEANING**

The word **stable** has the same root as the word *stabilize*. To stabilize something is to make it unlikely to change or fail. How might knowing the meaning of *stabilize* help a reader determine what it means to create "a stable environment for economic growth"?

*The busy port of Singapore, full of containers and container ships, is an international trading hub.*



### ✓ CHECKING FOR UNDERSTANDING

1. **ANALYZING CHANGE** What changes did the Asian Rim countries experience after World War II?

2. **INTERPRETING** How did democratic principles affect economic development in the Asian Rim countries?

## LESSON 3 REVIEW

### Time and Place

1. **EVALUATING** Why was Japan allowed to keep its military?

### Building History-Social Science Analysis Skills

2. **USING MAPS** Based on the map "The Economy of Modern Japan," what conclusions can you draw about Japan's industrial power? Support your conclusions with details from the map.

3. **UNDERSTANDING CHANGE** How did the *zaibatsu* remain an influential factor in Japan after World War II?

4. **IDENTIFYING CONNECTIONS** How did the "Japanese miracle" influence other Asian countries?

### Writing About History

5. **INFORMATIVE WRITING** Do additional research on Japan and the "Asian tigers" and explain in an essay why these countries have been so successful.

### Collaborating

6. **PRESENTING** With a small group, select one of the "Asian tigers" discussed in this lesson. Together, create a brief presentation on the economy of your selected country. Include information on how your country grew its economy after the late 1950s.

# POSTWAR LIFE IN JAPAN

The political, social, cultural, and industrial changes in Japan following the Meiji Restoration turned Japan into a regional power and then into a global power. This growth in power and reach ended in disaster and left Japan in ruins after 1945. Modern Japan emerged from this wreckage and again underwent major political and cultural reforms. These three selections reflect aspects of modern Japanese society in government, education, and gender relations.

**VOCABULARY**

*Diet:* the Japanese parliament

*posterity:* future generations

*consciousness:* awareness, especially of a social or political cause

*garner:* to gather

PRIMARY SOURCE: DOCUMENT

## PREAMBLE TO THE JAPANESE CONSTITUTION

The Preamble to the Japanese Constitution of 1946 was written after Japan's defeat in World War II.

> “We, the Japanese people, acting through our duly elected representatives in the National **Diet**, determined that we shall secure for ourselves and our **posterity** the fruits of peaceful cooperation with all nations and the blessings of liberty throughout this land, and resolved that never again shall we be visited with the horrors of war through the action of government, do proclaim the sovereignty of the people's will and do ordain and establish this Constitution, founded upon the universal principle that government is a sacred trust the authority for which is derived from the people, the powers of which are exercised by the representatives of the people, and the benefits of which are enjoyed by the people; and we reject and revoke all constitutions, laws, ordinances, and rescripts in conflict herewith. Desiring peace for all time and fully conscious of the high ideals controlling human relationship now stirring in mankind, we have determined to rely for our security and survival upon the justice and good faith of the peace-loving peoples of the world. We desire to occupy an honored place in an international society designed and dedicated to the preservation of peace, and the banishment of tyranny and slavery, oppression and intolerance, for all time from the earth. We recognize and acknowledge that all people have the right to live in peace, free from fear and want.”

**ANALYZE THE TEXT**

1. **CITING TEXT EVIDENCE** What phrases in this excerpt indicate Japan was scarred by its experience in World War II?
2. **DETERMINING CENTRAL IDEAS** Based on this excerpt, what role does Japan want to play in international politics?

PRIMARY SOURCE: DOCUMENT

## SCHOOL REGULATIONS IN JAPAN

Japanese children are exposed to a regimented environment. The following are examples of rules for middle school systems in various parts of Japan.

> “1. Boys' hair should not touch the eyebrows, the ears, or the top of the collar.
> 2. No one should have a permanent wave, or dye his or her hair. Girls should not wear ribbons or accessories in their hair. Hair dryers should not be used. . . .
> 3. Keep your uniform clean and pressed at all times. . . .
> 4. Wear your school badge at all times. It should be positioned exactly.
> 5. Going to school in the morning, wear your book bag strap on the right shoulder; in the afternoon on the way home, wear it on the left shoulder.
> 6. When you raise your hand to be called on, your arm should extend forward and up at the angle prescribed in your handbook.
> 7. Your own route to and from school is marked in your student rule handbook; carefully observe which side of each street you are to use on the way to and from school.
> 8. After school you are to go directly home, unless your parent has written a note permitting you to go to another location. . . .
> 9. Before and after school, no matter where you are, you represent our school, so you should behave in ways we all can be proud of.”

**ANALYZE THE TEXT**

1. **CITING TEXT EVIDENCE** What words and phrases in this excerpt show how careful students must be in dress?
2. **ANALYZING IDEAS** What does rule 9 suggest about how the regimented school rules contributed to Japan's sense of national identity?

PRIMARY SOURCE: DOCUMENT

## WOMEN'S RIGHTS IN JAPAN

In 1982 Higuchi Keiko captured new trends for Japanese women in "Japanese Women in Transition."

> "The **consciousness** of Japanese women is now in a state of transition. Their attitude toward the idea that 'men should work outside the home, women inside' has changed greatly in the last 10 years . . . [but] acceptance of sex-differentiated work roles is still deep-rooted in Japan. . . .
>
> Women in Japan are stepping out of the house in ever-swelling numbers. Yet men persist in clinging to the notion that 'women's work is in the home. . . .' It appears inevitable, therefore, that discord will arise between the sexes. . . .
>
> The husband expects his wife to look after the home, and in the home he seeks a place of recreation and relaxation in which to **garner** strength for the coming day's work. This is the view of the wife's role, and of the function of the home, given often in Japanese textbooks of the lower, compulsory levels of school. . . . The wife, however, has begun to entertain misgivings about an existence spent for the most part waiting passively at home for her husband's return. . . .
>
> The new women's liberation movement which spread to Japan in the early 70s brought pressure for change in the lives of both men and women. . . . At the same time, the extremely rapid aging of Japanese society . . . is forcing upon us, willy-nilly, a reevaluation of relationships between the sexes, married and unmarried alike."

ANALYZE THE TEXT

1. **IDENTIFYING CONNECTIONS** What does this excerpt indicate about how Japan was influenced by international trends?
2. **DETERMINING POINT OF VIEW** How does the author view the new trends in women's lives?

### MULTIPLE PERSPECTIVES

1. **COMPARING AND CONTRASTING** Analyzing source 2 and source 3, how would you compare the position of women and of children in traditional Japanese society?
2. **ANALYZING CHANGE** What do sources 1 and 3 indicate about how Japan both embraced and rejected change in the postwar era?

Keiko, Higuchi. 1982. "Japanese Women in Transition". Japan Quarterly, Vol. 29.

# STUDY GUIDE

## EUROPEAN ECONOMIC COMMUNITY (EEC)

### LESSON 1

- A free-trade area made up of member nations
- Original members were France, Germany, Belgium, Netherlands, Luxembourg, and Italy
- Also known as the common market
- Members would impose no tariffs or import charges on each other's goods
- As a group, they were protected by a tariff imposed on goods from non-EEC nations
- Encouraged cooperation among member nations' economies

## POSTWAR SOVIET UNION

### LESSON 2

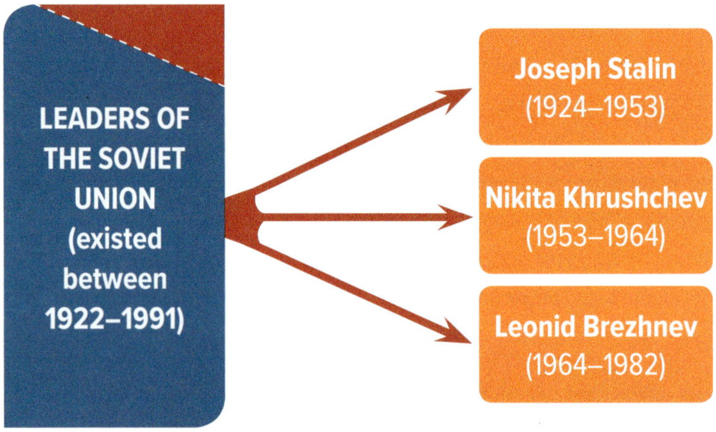


## JAPAN TRANSFORMED

### LESSON 3

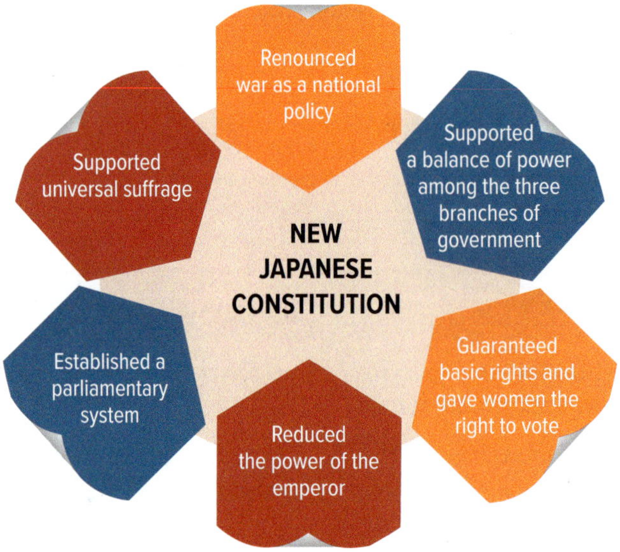

# CHAPTER 14 Assessment

**Directions: On a separate sheet of paper, answer the questions below. Make sure you read carefully and answer all parts of the questions.**

## Short Answer

1. **RELATING EVENTS** What did West Berlin Mayor Willy Brandt receive in 1971? Why?

2. **EXPLAINING CAUSE AND EFFECT** What aspect of Prime Minister Thatcher's economic policy might have caused old industrial areas to suffer?

3. **UNDERSTANDING CHANGE** Explain the formation and purpose of the European Economic Community (EEC) and how it changed from the time of its inception until 1986.

4. **SUMMARIZING** What was Stalin's main goal for the Soviet Union after World War II, and how did he achieve it?

5. **IDENTIFYING EFFECTS** What were the effects of détente in the Soviet Union?

6. **SUMMARIZING** How did the Soviet Union establish control throughout Eastern Europe after World War II?

7. **ANALYZING CHANGE** After World War II, what changes and reforms did the Allied occupation administration lead Japan to make? How successful were these reforms?

8. **UNDERSTANDING CHANGE** How were South Korea, Taiwan, the Republic of China, and Singapore the same as Japan in the years after World War II? How were they different from Japan?

9. **UNDERSTANDING CONTEXT** What special consideration did Hong Kong receive after Britain handed over control to China in 1997, and why might this concession have been made between the two governments?

10. **ANALYZING CHANGE** Identify and explain the effect on Czechoslovakia of the reforms Alexander Dubček introduced after his election in 1968.

11. **IDENTIFYING EFFECTS** What impact did communist movements and struggles elsewhere in the world have on the United States during the Cold War?

12. **EXPLAINING CAUSE AND EFFECT** What were some of the causes of economic changes in the United States after World War II? What impact did these changes have on American society?

13. **IDENTIFYING BIAS** Based on Khrushchev's approval of books published about the years under Stalin's regime, what perspective of his predecessor did Khrushchev have?

14. **DETERMINING MEANING** What is a "welfare state," and why did Great Britain set a trend for most other European states after the war?

15. **UNDERSTANDING CONTEXT** Which events was Richard Nixon taking advantage of when he appealed to "law and order" during his presidential campaign in 1968?

16. **ANALYZING CHANGE** How did the role of women change in the decades following World War II, and how did families change as a result?

17. **EXPLAINING CAUSES** How did the EEC lay the foundations for economic globalization?

## History and Social-Science Analysis

Use the image to answer the following questions.

This photograph shows the Reverend Martin Luther King, Jr., delivering his famous "I Have a Dream" speech at the Lincoln Memorial during the March on Washington on August 28, 1963.

18. **INTERPRETING** What information does this photograph provide about the March on Washington and the role King played in it?

19. **ANALYZING CHANGE** What impact did King's "I Have a Dream" speech have on the civil rights movement and on literary history?

**Need Extra Help?**

| If You've Missed Question | 1 | 2 | 3 | 4 | 5 | 6 | 7 | 8 | 9 | 10 | 11 | 12 | 13 | 14 | 15 | 16 | 17 | 18 | 19 |
|---|---|---|---|---|---|---|---|---|---|---|---|---|---|---|---|---|---|---|---|
| Review Lesson | 1 | 1 | 1 | 2 | 2 | 2 | 3 | 3 | 3 | 1 | 1–3 | 1 | 2 | 1 | 1 | 1 | 1 | 1 | 1 |

# Assessment, continued

**20** **UNDERSTANDING CONTEXT** Write a paragraph in which you analyze how Aleksandr Solzhenitsyn's *The Gulag Archipelago* and *One Day in the Life of Ivan Denisovich* reflect the culture of the Soviet Union during Stalin's regime.

## Research and Presentation

**21** **RESEARCHING FOR INQUIRY** Research the reduction in farming after World War II as tied to population shifts from rural to urban areas. Create a graph showing the shift, designating a starting date and an end date for representation. Identify country or countries researched. Have a peer review the graph and discuss how the data can be interpreted.

**22** **INTEGRATING INFORMATION** Prime Minister Pierre Trudeau passed the Official Languages Act in 1968 making both English and French national languages. Create a map of Canada showing the provinces, and indicate the percentage of French-speaking citizens in each province. Analyze any patterns between geography and language.

**23** **EVALUATING** Choose one or more of the Eastern European national revolts between the mid-1950s and late 1960s, and share the sequence of events from citizen outcry to the Soviet reestablishment of control. Share impressions of the value of the reform efforts even though they ended unsuccessfully. Presentations can combine writing and visual elements.

## Reading and Analyzing Primary Sources

Use the document to answer the following questions.

Bob Dylan expressed the feeling of the younger generation with his song "The Times They Are A-Changin'," released in 1964.

> ***The Times They Are A-Changin'***
> *Come gather 'round people*
> *Wherever you roam*
> *And admit that the waters*
> *Around you have grown*
> *And accept it that soon*
> *You'll be drenched to the bone*
> *If your time to you*
> *Is worth savin'*
> *Then you better start swimmin'*
> *Or you'll sink like a stone*
> *For the times they are a-changin' . . .*

**24** **INTERPRETING** To whom was Bob Dylan most likely directing "come gather 'round people"?

**A.** The Russians
**B.** Soldiers in Vietnam
**C.** The youth of the day
**D.** The politicians in Washington

**25** **DETERMINING MEANING** What did Dylan mean when he wrote "admit that the waters around you have grown"?

**A.** American culture was changing.
**B.** American government was growing.
**C.** The American economy was growing.
**D.** America's overseas interests were changing.

**26** **CITING TEXT EVIDENCE** Which lines from the song suggest Dylan wanted to warn his audience there would be consequences if they did not change with the times?

**A.** *Come gather 'round people / Wherever you roam*
**B.** *And admit that the waters / Around you have grown*
**C.** *If your time to you / Is worth savin'*
**D.** *Then you better start swimmin' / Or you'll sink like a stone*

## Writing About History

**27** **EXPLANATORY WRITING** Explain in one or more paragraphs why Communist rule was met with so much resistance in most Eastern European satellite states.

## Speaking and Listening About History

**28** **COLLABORATING** Meet in a small group to discuss the similarities and differences between the economic and government models of the United States and the Soviet Union. Have one member of your group serve as a moderator for the group discussion.

**Need Extra Help?**

| If You've Missed Question | 20 | 21 | 22 | 23 | 24 | 25 | 26 | 27 | 28 |
|---|---|---|---|---|---|---|---|---|---|
| Review Lesson | 2 | 1 | 1 | 2 | 1 | 1 | 1 | 2 | 1, 2 |

◀ East Germans take sledgehammers to the Berlin Wall, dismantling it piece by piece. The fall of the Berlin Wall reunited Germany and marked the beginning of a new era of diplomacy between the Soviet Union and the West.

1989 — Present

# A New Era Begins

## CHAPTER 15



**GO DIGITAL**
*It's All online!*

## ASKING ESSENTIAL QUESTIONS

***What motivates political change?***
***How can economic and social changes affect a country?***

**What Will You Learn?** You will learn about the major issues facing different regions of the world from 1989 to the present.

**Why Does This Matter?** Within a few years of the fall of the Berlin Wall, the Soviet Union collapsed, ending the Cold War. Many believed democracy and international cooperation would mark the coming age. But the post-Cold War world refused to conform to these hopeful expectations. Beginning in the 1990s, new and violent disputes broke out in the Balkans and parts of Africa. Across the Middle East, popular uprisings changed the political environment in unpredictable ways. And in Asia, China and India began an economic resurgence that would reshape global trade. Understanding these complex challenges and the ways nations have faced them gives you a better understanding of your world.

**How Will You Know That You Learned It?** You will be able to identify, describe, and explain the main global events and trends from the end of the Cold War to the present day.

**Using Your Inquiry Journal** As you read this chapter and examine the primary sources, use your Inquiry Journal to help you make notes and expand your list of questions. As you gather information, think about how you will answer the Essential Questions above.

# PLACE & TIME Eastern Europe 1989–Present

Although the end of the Cold War brought independence for many countries, it also brought new challenges in nation building. Currently the rise in security threats, alterations in the balance of trade, and environmental concerns are changing the global economy as well as political systems in countries around the world. As power shifts, concerns about human rights, support of individual freedoms, and economic inequalities remain.

## STEP INTO THE PLACE

Read the quotes and look at the information presented on the map.

1. **HUMAN-ENVIRONMENT INTERACTION** According to the map, what economic activity is most common near urban areas?

2. **UNDERSTANDING CONTEXT** Using the primary sources, analyze how Khama's statement about the preservation of the environment differs from Merkel's.

"Pioneering programmes have been created and further developed to protect forests and ensure they are used in a climate-friendly way. The global partnership REDD+ is an excellent example of this. It provides funding for measures to protect rain and moist forests in developing countries, with a focus on results. Voluntary initiatives such as the cities alliance Compact of Mayors, in which over 2,000 cities have signed up to ambitious goals and measures, also show us how climate protection can be put into practice locally. And last but not least, wind and solar farm costs have decreased dramatically worldwide, while competitiveness has increased significantly. All countries can make use of the enormous potential."

—German Chancellor Angela Merkel at the Sixth Petersberg Climate Dialogue, 2015

"Going forward we must continue to entrench Democracy and good governance and continue to add our voice with others in the International Community where there is lack thereof, and continue to practise zero tolerance of corruption and self interest. We must strive for even more self reliance and to build further on our developments. We must remain at peace with ourselves and with our neighbours for everlasting stability. We will continue to invest in the dignity and prosperity of our citizens so that each one can sparkle like our diamonds, whilst ensuring we continue to conserve our environment and natural resources."

—Botswanan President Ian Khama, 2016

## STEP INTO THE TIME

**CHRONOLOGICAL THINKING**

What is the significance of the 2001 addition of China to the World Trade Organization?

PHOTO:(t) Peter Cavanagh/Alamy Stock Photo; (b)Karin Duthie/Alamy Stock Photo;
TEXT:(t)Merkel, Angela. 2015. Speech by Federal Chancellor Angela Merkel at the Sixth Petersberg Climate Dialogue. May 19, 2015. Berlin; (b)Khama, Lt. General Dr. Seretse Khama Ian. 2016. Republic of Botswana Independence Day Message. September 30, 2016. Botswana Embassy.

### EASTERN EUROPE AND CENTRAL ASIA

- **1989** Fall of the Berlin Wall
- **1990** Nobel Peace Prize recipient Lech Wałesa elected president of Poland
- **1991** Soviet Union dissolves
- **1992** Yugoslavia disintegrates; Bosnian crisis follows
- **1997** Kyoto Protocol introduced at the UN Convention on Climate Change in Kyoto, Japan

**1990** — **1995**

### WORLD EVENTS

- **1989** Tiananmen Square protests
- **1990** Iraq invades Kuwait
- **1990** Sandinistas defeated in elections in Nicaragua
- **1991** Persian Gulf War
- **1994** North Atlantic Free Trade Agreement goes into effect
- **1995** Terrorists release deadly chemicals in Tokyo subway
- **1995** Fourth World Conference on Women, Beijing

# THE WORLD: NATURAL RESOURCES

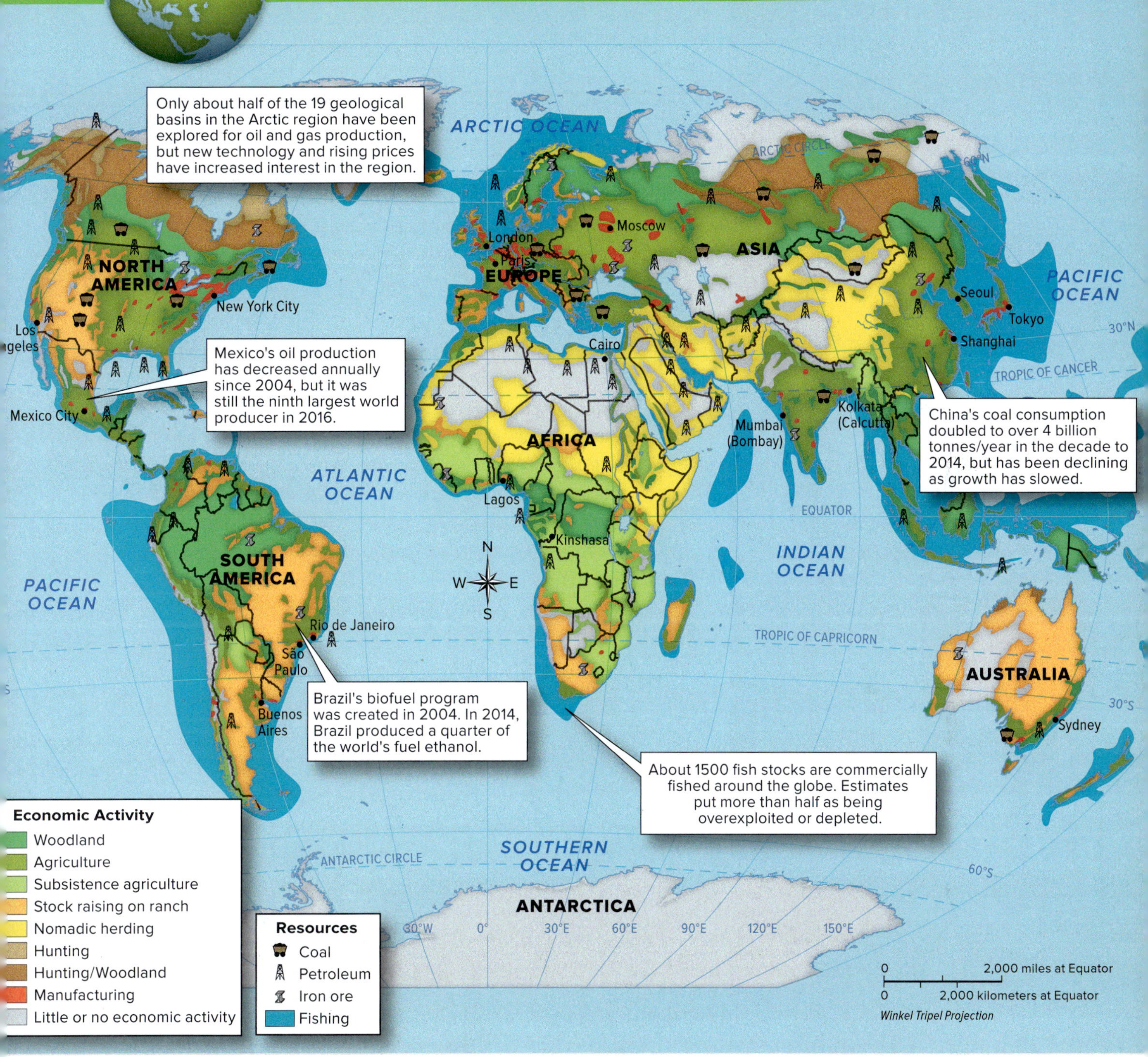


**2000** Vladimir Putin is elected president of Russia

**2001** China joins the World Trade Organization

**2001** Al-Qaeda-led terrorist attacks in the United States on September 11

**2005** Kyoto Protocol officially goes into effect

**2008** Kosovo declares its independence

**2011** Popular uprisings erupt in Tunisia, Egypt, Bahrain, and Libya

**2012** Barack Obama is re-elected president of the United States

**2015** Iran, the United States, and five other world powers reach nuclear deal

**2015** Nearly 200 countries attend UN climate change conference in France

**2016** Donald Trump is elected president of the United States

2000 — 2005 — 2010 — 2017

## ESSENTIAL QUESTIONS

- *What motivates political change?*
- *How can economic and social changes affect a country?*

LESSON 1

# End of the Cold War

## THE STORY BEGINS...

In July 1989, after a few years of pushing liberalization policies in the USSR, the Soviet premier Mikhail Gorbachev announced a new Soviet policy in Europe. He told the Eastern European countries within the Warsaw Pact that they were now free to determine their own futures. This meant the USSR would stop supporting the Communist governments it had propped up for decades.

> "Our perestroika led us to the conclusion that the revolutionary course would not receive the support of the working class if [its] living standards were not improving. But it turned out that the problem of sausage and bread is not the only one. The people demand a new social atmosphere, more oxygen in the society, especially because we are talking about the socialist regime . . . It is important not to miss our chance here. The party should have its own position on these issues, its own clear policy in this respect also. Life will punish us if we are late."

—Mikhail Gorbachev, statement on October 7, 1989

Without necessarily intending to, Gorbachev's speech echoed through the ears of reformists around Eastern Europe. Within just a few months, Germans began taking hammers to the Berlin Wall that had divided that city since the 1960s. By the end of 1991, the Soviet Union itself had collapsed and been dissolved.

*The collapse of Communist regimes was greeted with great excitement by many across Eastern Europe and even in Russia.* ▶

| National Responses Leading to the Dissolution of the USSR | |
|---|---|
| Country/Region | Responses |
| | |
| | |
| | |

**ANALYZING KEY IDEAS AND DETAILS**

**IDENTIFYING CAUSES** Read closely to identify which events or movements in each country or region helped bring about the end of the Soviet Union. Record your responses in a graphic organizer like this one.

# GORBACHEV AND PERESTROIKA

**GUIDING QUESTION** *How did Mikhail Gorbachev's reforms change the Soviet Union?*

By 1980, the Soviet Union was ailing. It had a declining economy, a rise in infant mortality rates, a dramatic surge in alcoholism, and poor working conditions. Within the Communist Party, a small group of reformers emerged. One was Mikhail Gorbachev. When the party chose him as leader in March 1985, a new era began.

From the start, Gorbachev preached the need for radical reforms based on **perestroika** (PEHR • uh • STRAWIH • kuh), or restructuring. At first, this meant restructuring economic policy. Gorbachev envisioned a market economy more responsive to consumers. It was to have limited free enterprise so that some businesses would be privately owned and operated. He realized, however, that reforming the economy would not work without political reform. He hoped to achieve this through **glasnost**, or openness, a policy that encouraged Soviet citizens and officials to discuss openly the strengths and weaknesses of the Soviet Union.

**ANALYZING KEY IDEAS AND DETAILS**

1. **ANALYZING EVENTS** How does the writer draw connections between the Intermediate-Range INF Treaty and the cessation of Soviet military support to Communist governments in Eastern Europe?
2. **ANALYZING IDEAS** This section of the text states Mikhail Gorbachev's policies led to "stunning changes" and that his administration "brought a dramatic end to the Cold War." Why does the text use these words?

**DETERMINING MEANING**

The word **perestroika** comes from the Russian word for "rebuilding." How does knowing the origins of *perestroika* help you determine its meaning?

**DETERMINING MEANING**

Read the paragraph that begins, "From the start. . . ." How does the content of the paragraph help you figure out what **glasnost** means?

**MAKING CONNECTIONS TO MUSIC**

## WESTERN POPULAR MUSIC IN THE USSR

Although Western popular music was not completely banned in the Soviet Union, the Soviet government was careful about what it allowed its citizens to hear. Music from groups such as the Beatles was often permitted because of the anti-imperialist and left-leaning themes. Others such as Van Halen, who embraced materialism and consumption, were dismissed as anti-communist. Despite these considerations, the albums of even acceptable bands often had to be smuggled into the country. This changed with Gorbachev's reforms. The floodgates were opened to Western popular music. In 1984 the heavy metal band Iron Maiden toured the Soviet bloc. Two years later, Billy Joel played in Moscow and St. Petersburg. This open exposure to Western culture made many Soviet people eager for the allowance of even broader freedoms.

1. **IDENTIFYING CONNECTIONS** How does the relationship between the Soviet Union and Western music inform our understanding of the larger political trends at the time?
2. **UNDERSTANDING CONTEXT** What does the information about music tours conducted by musicians in the 1980s tell us about the existing cultural connections between the citizens of Western and communist nations during this period?

At the 1988 Communist Party conference, Gorbachev set up a new Soviet parliament of elected members, the Congress of People's Deputies. It met in 1989. He then created a new state presidency. Under the old system, the first secretary of the Communist Party (Gorbachev's position) had been the most important in the Soviet Union. In March 1990, Gorbachev became the Soviet Union's first—and last—president.

Mikhail Gorbachev's accession to power in 1985 also eventually brought a dramatic end to the Cold War. His willingness to rethink Soviet foreign policy led to stunning changes.

Gorbachev made an agreement with the United States in 1987, the Intermediate-Range INF Treaty, to eliminate intermediate-range nuclear weapons. Both Gorbachev and U.S. President Ronald Reagan wanted to slow down the arms race. They sought to reduce their military budgets to solve domestic problems. Gorbachev hoped to focus resources on social and economic change. The United States wanted to cut its national debt, which had tripled during the Reagan presidency.

Gorbachev also stopped giving Soviet military support to Communist governments in Eastern Europe. This opened the door to the overthrow of Communist regimes. A mostly peaceful revolutionary movement swept through Eastern Europe in 1989. The reunification of Germany on October 3, 1990, was a powerful symbol of the end of the Cold War. In 1991 the Soviet Union itself was dissolved. The long rivalry between the two superpowers was over.

### ✓ CHECKING FOR UNDERSTANDING

1. **INTERPRETING** How did Mikhail Gorbachev's reforms change the Soviet Union?
2. **EXPLAINING CAUSE AND EFFECT** What reasons does the text give for the dissolution of the Soviet Union?
3. **SUMMARIZING** How did Gorbachev's reforms affect Soviet foreign relations?

## REVOLUTIONS IN EASTERN EUROPE

**GUIDING QUESTION** *How did popular revolutions help end Communist regimes in Eastern Europe?*

When Gorbachev decided the Soviets would no longer send troops to support the governments of the satellite countries, revolutions broke out throughout Eastern Europe. A look at four Eastern European states shows how the process worked.

### POLAND

Workers' protests led to demands for change in Poland. In 1980, a worker named Lech Wałesa (lehk vah • LEHN • suh) organized a national trade union known as Solidarity. Solidarity gained the support of the workers and of the Roman Catholic Church, which was under the leadership of Pope John Paul II, the first Polish pope. Even when Wałesa was arrested, the movement continued. Finally, in 1988, the Polish regime agreed to free parliamentary elections—the first free elections in Eastern Europe in 40 years. A new government was elected, ending 45 years of Communist rule.

**ANALYZING KEY IDEAS AND DETAILS**

1. **CITING TEXT EVIDENCE** The text claims that Nicolae Ceauşescu's policies failed in Romania. What evidence does the text present to support this claim?
2. **ANALYZING EVENTS** How does the writer draw distinctions between the mass demonstrations of 1988 and 1989 in Czechoslovakia and the earlier attempts at reform in 1968?

In December 1990, Wałesa was chosen as president. Poland's new path, however, was not easy. Rapid free-market reforms led to severe unemployment. Aleksander Kwasniewski, who succeeded Wałesa, continued Poland's move toward an increasingly prosperous free-market economy and democracy. Recent presidents have emphasized the need to combine modernization with tradition.

**BIOGRAPHY**

### LECH WAŁESA (1943– )

In 1980 during protests at the shipyards in Gdansk, Poland, Lech Wałesa, a former electrician turned labor activist, was elected leader of a strike committee. As a result of his successful negotiations with Poland's Communist government, workers won the right to form the national labor organization known as Solidarity. Although Solidarity was soon outlawed and its leadership arrested, Wałesa won the 1983 Nobel Peace Prize for his efforts. Deteriorating economic conditions later forced the government to accept Solidarity; and in 1990, voters elected Wałesa president.

**IDENTIFYING EFFECTS** What were the effects of Wałesa's negotiations with the government?

## CZECHOSLOVAKIA

The Soviets crushed and then repressed the Czechoslovakian reform movement of 1968. Writers and other intellectuals continued to oppose the government, but they at first had little success. Then in 1988 and 1989, mass **demonstrations** took place throughout Czechoslovakia. By November 1989, crowds as large as 500,000 were forming in Prague.

In December 1989, the Communist government **collapsed**. At the end of that month, Václav Havel (VAHT • slahf HAH • vehl), a writer who had played an important role in bringing down the Communist government, became the new president. Havel was an eloquent spokesperson for Czech democracy and a new order in Europe.

The new government soon faced old ethnic conflicts between the Czechs, in the western half of the country, and the Slovaks, in its eastern half. Avoiding conflict, the Czechs and Slovaks ultimately agreed to a peaceful division of Czechoslovakia, which split into the Czech Republic and the nation of Slovakia. Václav Havel became the first president of the Czech Republic, and Michal Kovác then became the first president of Slovakia.

Under its second president, Václav Klaus, the Czech Republic had one of the most stable and prosperous economies of the post-Communist Eastern European states. Slovakia managed to make the transition from a centrally planned economy to a market economy.

## HUNGARY

The brutal suppression of the 1956 Hungarian Revolution by the Soviet Union brought about a period of retribution for Hungarians who had participated in the uprising. However, conditions began to improve during the 1960s. János Kádár,

Chris Niedenthal/Time & Life Pictures/Getty Images

who had assumed control of the country after the Revolution, loosened restrictions on state-controlled industry and agriculture throughout the 1970s and encouraged contact with the West.

The standard of living steadily increased throughout the 1970s and 1980s as tourism became a viable industry and restrictions on Hungarians traveling abroad were lifted. The 1980s also saw the rise of independent political parties and the creation of a new constitution based on the separation of powers that also guaranteed individual and civil rights.

### ROMANIA

Communist leader Nicolae Ceauşescu (nee • kaw • LY chau • SHEHS • koo) ruled Romania with an iron grip, using secret police to crush all dissent. Nonetheless, opposition to Ceauşescu and Romania's Communist government grew in the late 1980s. By 1989, the government's economic policies had led to a sharp drop in living standards. Food shortages led to government-imposed rationing. Late in the year the Romanian people took to the streets in peaceful protest.

In December 1989, the secret police murdered thousands of people who were peacefully demonstrating. Finally, the Romanian army itself refused to support any more repression. Ceauşescu and his wife attempted to flee the country but were captured and rapidly executed. A new government was then quickly formed.

Former Communists dominated the new government until 1996. Twenty-five years after the end of Communist rule, Romanians elected center-right candidate Klaus Iohannis to succeed Traian Basescu, who was limited from serving another term.

#### ☑ CHECKING FOR UNDERSTANDING

1. **EXPLAINING EFFECTS** How did popular revolutions help end Communist regimes in Eastern Europe?
2. **IDENTIFYING EFFECTS** What was the impact of the 1988 free parliamentary elections in Poland?
3. **EXPLAINING EFFECTS** What role did protesters play in the new governments that formed after the fall of Communism in Eastern Europe?

## END OF THE SOVIET UNION

**GUIDING QUESTION** *How did the Soviet Union fall?*

The Soviet Union, more than twice the size of the United States at its height, was facing serious challenges by the early 1980s. Soviet resources and finances, already taxed by years of proxy wars around the world, struggled with the economic and military burden of supporting such a vast land area. The command economy, too, was faltering. Goods were often produced that were not needed, while desirable and sometimes even basic goods were not manufactured. Consequently, many necessities were often rationed or at times completely unavailable. The pressures of the Cold War, including the arms race with the United States and the associated burden on an already tight state budget, further weakened the Soviet Union.

**ANALYZING KEY IDEAS AND DETAILS**

1. **ANALYZING EVENTS** Why was Putin able to take office in 2012?
2. **DESCRIBING** What challenges did Boris Yeltsin encounter in his early presidency?

## THE FALL OF COMMUNISM 1989–1991

## COLLAPSE

The pressures of the Cold War on the Soviet economy were only increased by the invasion of Afghanistan in 1979. The Soviet Union supported the Communist government in its fight against anti-Communist Muslim guerrillas with troops and money. Meanwhile, the United States was supplying the guerrillas with funds and weapons. The Soviet Union, unable to expend any more resources in the long conflict, finally withdrew its troops in 1989.

The Soviet Union was made of 15 separate republics that included 92 ethnic groups and 112 different languages. As Gorbachev released the iron grip of the Communist Party, centered in Moscow, old ethnic tensions came to the forefront, and people who disagreed with Soviet policies began to push for change. Nationalist movements began. In 1989 and 1990, calls for independence came first in Soviet Georgia and then in the Baltic States (Latvia, Lithuania, and Estonia), Moldova, Uzbekistan, and Azerbaijan.

The conservative leaders of the traditional Soviet institutions—the army, government, KGB, and military industries—were worried the breakup of the Soviet Union would end their privileges. On August 19, 1991, a group of these conservative leaders arrested Gorbachev and tried to seize power. The attempt failed, however, when Boris Yeltsin, president of the Russian Republic, and thousands of Russians bravely resisted the rebel forces in Moscow.

### GEOGRAPHIC REASONING

1. **SPATIAL THINKING** Create a table in which you list the dates of independence from the Soviet Union or the first multi-party elections in former Soviet satellites in chronological order.
2. **EXPLORING REGIONS** How might trade have changed for Russia and former Soviet states and satellite states after the fall of the Soviet Union?

The Soviet republics now moved for complete independence. Ukraine voted for independence on December 1, 1991. A week later, the leaders of Russia, Ukraine, and Belarus announced the Soviet Union had "ceased to exist."

### ✓ CHECKING FOR UNDERSTANDING

1. **SUMMARIZING** How did the Soviet Union fall?
2. **EXPLAINING EFFECTS** What were the effects of the end of the Soviet Union on members of traditional Soviet institutions?
3. **IDENTIFYING CAUSES** Why was President Gorbachev arrested on August 19, 1991?

**THINKING LIKE A HISTORIAN**

### WHAT CAUSED THE COLLAPSE OF THE SOVIET UNION?

International affairs expert Zbigniew Brzezinski attributed the collapse of communism to its failure to "deliver on the material level while its political practices compromised—indeed, discredited—its moral claims." What did Brzezinski mean? How did other factors, such as the weakness of the command economy, nationalism, and increased military spending due to the Cold War, contribute to the collapse? Use Internet resources to find reliable sources about factors that contributed to the collapse.

## THE NEW RUSSIA

**GUIDING QUESTION** *What are political, economic, and social challenges faced by the new Russia?*

Gorbachev resigned on December 25, 1991. He turned over his responsibilities as commander-in-chief to Boris Yeltsin, the new president of Russia. By the end of 1991, one of the largest empires in world history had ended.

**UNDERSTANDING CRAFT AND STRUCTURE**

**ANALYZING TEXT PRESENTATION**
How does the text develop the idea of the Soviet republics' move toward complete independence?

Boris Yeltsin was committed to introducing a free-market economy as quickly as possible, but the transition was not easy. Economic hardships and social disarray were made worse by a dramatic rise in organized crime.

Another problem Yeltsin faced was in Chechnya, a province in the south that wanted to secede from Russia and to become independent. Yeltsin used brutal force against the Chechens (CHEH • chuhnz) to keep the province as part of Russia. Yeltsin did not solve this problem, as fighting continued into the year 2000 under his successor.

At the end of 1999, Yeltsin resigned and was replaced by Vladimir Putin, who was elected president in 2000. Putin, a former KGB officer, was widely seen as someone who wanted to keep a tight rein on government power. In July 2001, Putin launched reforms to boost growth and budget revenues. The reforms included the free sale and purchase of land and tax cuts. In spite of these changes, the business climate remained uncertain, which stifled foreign investment.

Since Putin's reforms, Russia has experienced a budget surplus and a growing economy. Russia can attribute much of its economic growth to its oil and gas exports. The country has an estimated 6 percent of the world's oil deposits and about 30 percent of the world's natural gas deposits.

In 2008 Dmitry Medvedev became president of Russia. Putin could not run for reelection because of limits in Russia's constitution, but he became prime minister. However, since Russia's constitution only limits consecutive terms, Putin won the presidency again in 2012 and in 2018. The term for president was extended to six years in 2008.

Putin's time as president has been witness to controversies that have strained Russia's relationship with much of the world. Russian military interventions in both the Ukrainian revolution of 2014 and the Syrian Civil War of 2015 have been causes for alarm. Russia also faces internal challenges. A drop in the price of crude oil has impacted the Russian economy. Rising alcoholism, criminal activities, and the decline of the traditional family system continue to give Russians concern.

### ☑ CHECKING FOR UNDERSTANDING

1. **SUMMARIZING** What political, economic, and social challenges are faced by the new Russia?
2. **IDENTIFYING CAUSES** What explains Russia's recent economic growth?
3. **IDENTIFYING EFFECTS** What were the effects of Russia's transition to a market economy?

#### ANALYZING KEY IDEAS AND DETAILS

1. **CITING TEXT EVIDENCE** The text in this section argues that Serbia was unwilling to let Yugoslavia disintegrate. What evidence in the text supports this claim?
2. **ANALYZING IDEAS** This section of the text includes the statement that events in Bosnia "revived memories of Nazi atrocities." What does this statement suggest about the information the passage will reveal as to the consequences for Serbia?

## THE DISINTEGRATION OF YUGOSLAVIA

**GUIDING QUESTION** *How did the fall of the Soviet Union impact Eastern Europe?*

Yugoslavia had a Communist government but was never a Soviet satellite state. After World War II, its dictatorial leader, Josip Broz Tito, worked to keep together the six republics and two provinces that made up Yugoslavia. By 1990, however, the Communist Party collapsed.

The Yugoslav political scene was complex. Slobodan Miloševic (slaw • BAW • dahn muh • LOH • suh • vihch), leader of Serbia, rejected efforts toward independence. In Miloševic's view, the borders of the republic first needed to be redrawn to form a new Greater Serbian state. When negotiations failed, Slovenia and Croatia declared their independence in June 1991. In September 1991, the Yugoslav army attacked Croatia. Increasingly, Serbia dominated the Yugoslav army. Serbian forces captured one-third of Croatia's territory before the conflict ended.

The Serbs next attacked Bosnia-Herzegovina and acquired 70 percent of Bosnian territory. Many Bosnians were Muslims. The Serbs followed a policy called **ethnic cleansing** toward Bosnians—killing or forcibly removing

*A police building destroyed during NATO air strikes in Pristina*

them from their lands. Ethnic cleansing revived memories of Nazi atrocities in World War II. In 1995, with support from NATO air attacks, Bosnian and Croatian forces regained considerable territory lost to Serbian forces. The Serbs signed a formal peace treaty that split Bosnia into a Serb republic and a Muslim-Croat federation.

**DETERMINING MEANING**

To better understand **autonomous**, break down the word. *Auto* means "self." *Nomos* means "law." What does it mean for a state to be *autonomous*?

A new war erupted in 1998 over Kosovo, an **autonomous**, or self-governing province within Yugoslavia. After Slobodan Miloševic stripped Kosovo of its autonomy in 1989, groups of ethnic Albanians founded the Kosovo Liberation Army (KLA) and began a campaign against Serbian rule. To crush the KLA, Serb forces massacred ethnic Albanians. The United States and NATO allies worked on a settlement that would end the killing. The Albanians in Kosovo regained their autonomy in 1999. Miloševic's rule ended in 2000. While on trial for his role in the massacre of Kosovo civilians, Miloševic died in 2006.

The last political vestiges of Yugoslavia ceased to exist in 2004 when the government officially renamed the country Serbia and Montenegro. The people of Montenegro voted for independence in 2006; and in 2008, Kosovo declared its independence. Thus, all six republics that formed Yugoslavia in 1918 were again independent nations, and a new one (Kosovo) was born.

## ✓ CHECKING FOR UNDERSTANDING

1. **EXPLAINING CAUSE AND EFFECT** How did the fall of the Soviet Union impact Eastern Europe?

2. **EXPLAINING EFFECTS** What were the effects of Miloševic's removal of Kosovo's autonomy in 1989?

3. **UNDERSTANDING CONTEXT** What role did NATO play in the conflicts in the former Yugoslavia?

## LESSON 1 REVIEW

### Time and Place

1. **COMPARING** How did the end of the Cold War and the dissolution of the Soviet Union affect the politics and economies of Russia and former Soviet states?

### Building History-Social Science Analysis Skills

2. **RELATING EVENTS** Compare and contrast post-Cold War conflicts in Eastern Europe and Yugoslavia.

3. **EXPLAINING CAUSES** What causes does the text provide to explain the dissolution of Yugoslavia?

4. **INFERRING** How did the dissolution of the Soviet Union affect Yugoslavia?

### Writing About History

5. **INFORMATIVE WRITING** Research and write an essay about how life has changed in Russia since the fall of the Soviet Union.

### Collaborating

6. **EVALUATING POINT OF VIEW** Mikhail Gorbachev's rise to power largely brought an end to the Cold War. From what point of view did Gorbachev justify the radical reforms of perestroika and glasnost? With a partner, search the Internet to find examples of reform movements influenced by Gorbachev. Select one of these reform movements and work together to create a short description of this reform policy, what it hoped to change, and whether it failed or succeeded.

## ESSENTIAL QUESTIONS

- *What motivates political change?*
- *How can economic and social changes affect a country?*

LESSON 2

# Western Europe and North America

## THE STORY BEGINS...

The "Rise of the West" had transformed the world as Europe dominated the globe since the early modern era. Now that the colonial era was ending, new solutions were needed to maintain prosperity. British Prime Minister Winston Churchill acknowledged as imperialism must end, Europe would need to look inward to prosper. He stated:

> "[T]here Is a remedy which. . .would in a few years make all Europe. . .free and. . .happy. It is to create the European family, or as much of it as we can, and to provide it with a structure under which it can dwell in peace, in safety, and in freedom. We must build a kind of United States of Europe."

—Winston Churchill, at the University of Zurich, 1946

Churchill's vision of a "United States of Europe" exists today in the form of the European Union. And European imperial holdings, save for a few small islands, no longer exist. Today, Western prosperity depends not on outward expansion but on engaging in trade with its neighbors and with rising global powers such as Brazil, India, and China.

*The formation of the European Union was one response to the declining economic power of individual European nations.* ▶

PHOTO:Dan Kitwood/Getty Images; TEXT: Churchill, Sir Winston. 1946. Quoted by Klos, Felix. 2016. Churchill on Europe: The Untold Story of Churchill's European Project. London and New York: I.B. Tauris & Co. Ltd.

| Major Economic Changes Since 1989 | |
|---|---|
| Country | Economic Changes |
| United Kingdom | |
| United States | |
| Greece | |
| Germany | |
| Ireland | |
| Former Soviet Countries | |

### ANALYZING KEY IDEAS AND DETAILS

**DESCRIBING** Read closely to identify the major shifts in the economies and/or currencies of each of the countries discussed since the end of the Cold War. Explain these changes in a graphic organizer like this one.

# WINDS OF CHANGE IN WESTERN EUROPE

**GUIDING QUESTION** *What were the political and economic trends in Western Europe since the end of the Cold War?*

Western Europe, which began the twentieth century at the pinnacle of global power and influence, found itself losing dominance as the century came to a close. Exhausted after fighting two world wars, Western European nations gradually granted independence to their imperial holdings during the 1950s, 1960s, and 1970s. Along with losing colonies around the world, Western Europeans faced many economic and political challenges. Western European economies found stability in the 1980s, but some problems remained. For instance, unemployment was still high. Despite their economic woes, however, the Western European states seemed quite capable of prospering.

Especially important in that respect was the creation of the European Community, or EC. Begun as an economic union in 1958, it also gradually gave way to a **confederation** known as the European Union, or EU. The EC converted to the EU in 1993. This new organization, comprised of 12 states at its creation, would grow significantly, adding an additional 16 states to its membership by 2013. Many of these new members were states that became independent after the collapse of the Soviet Union.

The EU established a common currency, the euro, which entered circulation in 2002. The euro further helped unify the economies of participating countries. However, public debts in some member countries caused a major crisis for the euro in 2010. Despite such difficulties, the EU largely benefited Western Europe economically as it has helped maintain a relatively high per capita income among its member countries.

### ANALYZING KEY IDEAS AND DETAILS

1. **ANALYZING EVENTS** Reread the paragraph that begins, "Erich Honecker, head of the Communist Party in. . . ." What part of this paragraph states an effect of the fall of the Berlin Wall?
2. **CITING TEXT EVIDENCE** The text states that a federation of European states was "especially important" to the future of Western Europe's economic success. Provide at least three statements from this lesson that explain this statement.

## REUNIFICATION OF GERMANY

In 1982 Helmut Kohl's political party, the Christian Democratic Union, formed a new, more conservative government in West Germany. Kohl was a smart politician who benefited greatly from an economic boom in the mid-1980s. Then events in East Germany led to the unexpected reunification of the two Germanies in 1990.

Erich Honecker, head of the Communist Party in East Germany, ruled harshly. While many East Germans fled their country, others led mass demonstrations against the regime in 1989. When the Communist government opened its entire border with the West, thousands of East Germans swarmed across the border to reunite with their families and friends. The Berlin Wall, long a **symbol** of the Cold War, was torn down. The reunification of Germany took place on October 3, 1990. What had seemed almost impossible became a reality—the countries of West and East Germany had formed one Germany.

With a population of 79 million people, the new Germany became the leading power in Europe. The joy over reunification soon faded as new problems arose. It became clear that the rebuilding of eastern Germany would take far more money than had been thought.

Kohl's government was soon forced to raise taxes. In addition, the virtual collapse of the economy in eastern Germany had led to extremely high unemployment and severe discontent. One result was a return to power for the Social Democrats, who were victorious in the 1998 elections. However, the Social Democrats had little success in solving Germany's economic woes. In 2005 Angela Merkel, leader of the Christian Democrats, became the first female chancellor in German history.

The collapse of the German economy also led to increasing attacks on foreigners. For years, illegal immigrants and foreigners seeking refuge had found haven in Germany because of its very liberal immigration laws. Increased unemployment and economic problems caused tensions between some Germans and immigrant groups.

## GREAT BRITAIN

After Margaret Thatcher resigned as prime minister in 1990, the Conservative Party, now led by John Major, failed to capture the imagination of most Britons. In new elections in 1997, the Labour Party won a landslide victory. Moderate Tony Blair became prime minister. However, his ongoing support of the U.S. war in Iraq, opposed by most Britons, harmed his popularity. Another member of the Labour Party, Gordon Brown, became prime minister in June 2007.

The Conservative Party gained a majority in the 2010 British general election, and David Cameron became prime minister. In 2015 the Conservatives won even more convincingly. Despite the defeat of a Scottish independence referendum in 2014, the pro-independence Scottish National Party also gained a large number of seats in 2015. In 2016 Great Britain held a national referendum, informally known as Brexit, to leave the European Union. Cameron, who opposed the referendum, resigned after the vote narrowly won. Theresa May succeeded him. In a press conference held the day after the referendum, Cameron said:

> "Over 33 million people from England, Scotland, Wales, Northern Ireland and Gibraltar have all had their say. We should be proud of the fact that in these islands we trust the people with these big decisions. We not only have a parliamentary democracy, but on questions about the arrangements for how we're governed. . . Across the world, people have been watching the choice that Britain has made. I would reassure those markets and investors that Britain's economy is fundamentally strong, and I would also reassure Brits living in European countries and European citizens living here that there will be no immediate changes in your circumstances."
>
> —David Cameron, at a press conference, 2016

### ANALYZING PRIMARY SOURCES

1. **DETERMINING POINT OF VIEW** From Cameron's statement, what can you infer about his opinion of the public response to Brexit?
2. **ANALYZING TEXT** What positive words or phrases does Cameron use in the text? What might be the purpose of creating this tone?

Cameron, David. 2016. David Cameron's Resignation Speech in Full. June 24, 2016. Reprinted by CNN.com.

MAKING CONNECTIONS TO TODAY

### THE CENTER OF THE WORLD ECONOMY MOVES EAST

In the Early Modern era, Europe rose as an important location for trade. As the economies of countries bordering the Atlantic Ocean grew due to access to shipping routes and colonies, Western Europe became the worldwide center of trade. The apex of Western Europe as a trade center came at the beginning of the twentieth century. However, by mid-century, Europe had fought in two world wars and was losing colonial territories quickly as they declared independence. At the end of the twentieth century, the center of trade began to shift to Asia, in part because of its rapid industrialization. Today, researchers have found that trade is moving east at an increasingly rapid pace, with many claiming that this is the new center of trade.

1. **COMPARING AND CONTRASTING** How is the rise of the East as a trade center different from the rise of the West?
2. **EXPLAINING CAUSE AND EFFECT** Why would the loss of colonies have affected the Western world's claim to being the center of trade?

## FRANCE

In the elections of 1993, a coalition of conservative parties gained 80 percent of the seats in the National Assembly. Jacques Chirac was president from 1995 to 2007.

By 1995, resentment against foreign-born residents had become a growing political reality. Especially noticeable were the growing tensions between the Muslim community and the remainder of the French population. These tensions helped elect Nicolas Sarkozy president in 2007.

France did not escape the financial woes of the euro crisis. Amid the failing economy and low approval ratings, Sarkozy lost his reelection bid in a runoff election in May 2012. He was defeated by François Hollande of France's Socialist Party.

In the span of one evening in late 2015, Paris was rocked by a series of organized terrorist attacks that killed 130 people at a variety of venues around the city. The following July, a terrorist drove a cargo van into the crowds celebrating Bastille Day in the city of Nice. Militant Islamic groups claimed responsibility for both attacks. These attacks have served to heighten tensions in France around security and immigration. The issues became the focus of a contentious 2017 presidential election campaign.

## NEW ROLE FOR NATO

In part due to the cooperation of EU member states, Western Europe has experienced a long period of peace. Particularly important to the stability of the region is the North Atlantic Treaty Organization (NATO). In 1949, the United States, Canada, and a number of Western European countries formed NATO to offset Soviet forces in Central and Eastern Europe after World War II. The Soviet Union responded by creating the Warsaw Pact in 1955 to strengthen its hold over the satellite states and to increase its power in international negotiations.

Along with the collapse of the Soviet Union came the dissolution of the Warsaw Pact in 1991. This changed the purpose of NATO to more broadly focus on countering threats to global security whether it is an action by a state, organization, or group by using collective forces for defense and managing security risks. NATO continues to expand, adding 12 new member countries throughout the 1990s and 2000s, including Hungary, Poland, Bulgaria, Lithuania, Romania, Slovakia, and Croatia.

Today, NATO utilizes political and military strategies to safeguard the freedom and security of its members. Europe relies heavily on the commitment of the United States to NATO as many member countries are reluctant or incapable of using any substantial military force in other parts of the world.

### ☑ CHECKING FOR UNDERSTANDING

1. **IDENTIFYING CONNECTIONS** What were the political and economic trends in Western Europe since the end of the Cold War?
2. **UNDERSTANDING CONTEXT** What common problems have countries such as Germany, the United Kingdom, and France faced in the post-Soviet era?
3. **EXPLAINING EFFECTS** What happened after the Berlin Wall was dismantled?

# THE UNITED STATES AND CANADA

**GUIDING QUESTION** *What were the political and economic trends in North America since the end of the Cold War?*

As the Cold War was coming to a close, U.S. politics oscillated between the right and left as economic issues became a focus. Canadians were also concerned about economic problems and the status of Quebec.

## THE UNITED STATES

The Reagan Revolution, as it has been called, sent U.S. policy in new directions. Reagan reduced welfare policies by cutting spending on food stamps, school lunch programs, and job programs. At the same time, Reagan oversaw the largest peacetime military buildup in U.S. history.

Total federal spending rose from $631 billion in 1981 to over a trillion dollars by 1987. The spending policies of the Reagan administration produced record government **budget deficits**. A budget deficit exists when the government spends more than it collects in revenues. In the 1970s, the total deficit was $420 billion. Between 1981 and 1987, budget deficits were three times that amount.

George Bush, Reagan's vice president, succeeded him as president. Bush's inability to deal with the federal deficit and an economic downturn, however, allowed Democrat Bill Clinton to be elected president in 1992. Clinton claimed to be a new kind of Democrat, one who favored several Republican policies of the 1980s. A lengthy economic revival won Clinton popular support, but his second term was overshadowed by charges of presidential misconduct. Clinton's problems helped Republican George W. Bush, son of the first President Bush, to win the presidency in 2000.

Bush's administration was largely occupied with the war on terrorism and the U.S.-led war on Iraq. Bush and Congress passed tax cuts to boost the economy, but the cuts also helped produce record deficits. From 2004 to 2008, Bush's popularity fell due to growing discontent over the Iraq War and a significant downturn in the economy caused in part by problems in the home mortgage industry. These key issues in the 2008 presidential race led to a change in American politics with the election of Barack Obama, the first African American president.

In 2009 the Obama administration moved to deal with the worst economic recession since the Great Depression, the passage of national healthcare legislation, and the war in Afghanistan. He was reelected in 2012. In his second term, Obama oversaw the continued rollout of the Affordable Care Act. In foreign policy, a nuclear deal was signed with Iran, and the Trans-Pacific Partnership trade deal was signed with 12 countries in the Pacific Rim.

The 2016 presidential election revealed a deep national divide over political, economic, and social issues. A large field of candidates emerged to vie for the Republican and

### ANALYZING KEY IDEAS AND DETAILS

1. **CITING TEXT EVIDENCE** The text in this section claims deep divisions marked U.S. politics in the last years of the Obama administration. What text evidence supports this claim?
2. **ANALYZING EVENTS** Reread the two paragraphs that begin, "The Reagan Revolution, as it has been called. . . ." What part of these two paragraphs states an effect of the economic problems facing the United States?

### DETERMINING MEANING

Read the paragraph that begins, "Total federal spending rose. . . ." How does the content of the paragraph help you figure out what **budget deficits** are?

*U.S. President Barack Obama served two terms in the White House.*

Official White House Photo by Pete Souza

Democratic Party nominations. Ultimately the race was between Republican candidate Donald Trump, a businessman and television personality, and Democratic candidate Hillary Clinton, a former senator and secretary of state during Obama's first term. Although he lost the popular vote, Donald Trump won the Electoral College, becoming the 45th president of the United States.

CITIZENSHIP

### THE DEBT AND THE DEFICIT

In 2015 the U.S. government spent about $3.7 trillion. However, it took in only about $3.3 trillion in taxes and other revenues. This means that the government ran what is called a deficit, or a shortage. In 2015 the deficit amounted to about $400 billion. Combined with the deficits of previous years, this created a national debt in 2015 equalling $18.2 trillion.

So where is all this money going? There are essentially three types of spending in the U.S. government: mandatory spending, discretionary spending, and interest on the debt. Mandatory spending makes up about 65 percent of all spending and includes things such as Social Security, Medicare, and transportation. Discretionary spending makes up about 30 percent of all spending and includes everything else. The largest single discretionary spending category is the military, which makes up 54 percent of all discretionary spending.

1. **IDENTIFYING CAUSES** What does the breakdown of spending suggest about why George W. Bush ran up such large deficits during his term in office?
2. **IDENTIFYING CONNECTIONS** Getting a budget through Congress that would help get spending under control has proven very difficult in recent decades. Considering what you know about U.S. government spending, what do you think accounts for this difficulty?

## CANADA

In 1993 Canada approved the North American Free Trade Agreement (NAFTA), along with the United States and Mexico, to make trade easier and more profitable. Many Canadians saw the agreement as too favorable to the U.S., and Prime Minister Brian Mulroney lost popularity. Jean Chrétien of the Liberal Party served as prime minister from 1993 to 2003. Most recently, in the 2015 elections, the Conservatives lost, and Prime Minister Stephen Harper stepped down. Justin Trudeau of the Liberal Party became prime minister.

The status of the French-speaking Quebec province has been an issue for decades. In 1995 Quebec voters only narrowly rejected secession. The debate still divides Canadians and was an issue in the 2015 elections.

## CHALLENGES IN THE NEW CENTURY

The United States, although still the most powerful nation in international politics, faces serious economic challenges. With less than a 1 percent population growth rate, the United States will have difficulty maintaining funds to support programs such as Social Security and Medicare as more people retire and there are fewer people entering the workforce. A growing number of economists see the growing inequality between rich and poor as a limit to growth. Adding to these challenges, the United States now imports more manufactured goods than it exports. This imbalance has led to a growing trade deficit.

Over the course of the twentieth century, economic growth in the United States largely served as a trigger for economic growth worldwide. However, the United States will be able to fulfill this function only as long as it is able to borrow funds to cover its trade deficits. Also complicating the economies of the United States and many other countries is the reliance on foreign energy, such as oil from the Middle East. The need to import petroleum products places control of sectors of the economy of many countries in the hands of oil-rich countries, including Iran, Venezuela, and Saudi Arabia.

### ☑ CHECKING FOR UNDERSTANDING

1. **SUMMARIZING** What were the political and economic trends in North America since the end of the Cold War?
2. **RELATING EVENTS** What two major events have proved divisive in Canada in the past 30 years?
3. **DETERMINING CONTEXT** How are U.S. domestic policies being affected by economic conditions around the world and at home in the United States?

## SOCIETY AND CULTURE IN THE WEST

GUIDING QUESTION *What were the cultural trends in Western Europe and North America in the 1990s and 2000s?*

Among the effects of globalization is the spread of culture, and Western culture has expanded to and influenced most parts of the world.

### THE WOMEN'S MOVEMENT

In the 1990s, there was a backlash against the women's movement. Some women urged a return to traditional gender roles. Other women rejected these ideas and continued to look for ways to balance their career and family lives. Although there have been gains in the women's movement in the early decades of the 2000s, women continue to do most of the child rearing and domestic work in most homes.

### ART AND POPULAR CULTURE

The United States dominated the art world after World War II. Abstractionism, especially abstract expressionism, dominated modern art after 1945. Abstract artists focused on conveying emotion and feeling. By the 1980s, a movement known as **postmodernism** had emerged. Postmodern artists often create works that include elements of film, performance, popular culture, and sculpture. Today's artists use digital cameras and computer programs to produce interactive art forms.

Music, movies, television, sports—all are part of what is known as **popular culture**. Known throughout the world, American performers and filmmakers help spread American popular culture. From early post-World War II rock 'n' roll to today's multimillion-dollar musical acts, the world participates in America's musical pop culture. Films also play a big role in spreading Western culture.

#### ANALYZING KEY IDEAS AND DETAILS

1. **CITING TEXT EVIDENCE** The paragraph that begins, "Television and sports have . . ." makes the claim that Europeans are increasingly influenced by American popular culture. What evidence does this paragraph present to support this claim?
2. **ANALYZING IDEAS** Reread the paragraph that begins, "In the 1990s, there. . . ." What clue does this paragraph provide to support the argument that the women's movement still has work to do?

#### DETERMINING MEANING

To better understand **postmodernism**, break down the word. *Post* means "after." *Modernism* means "a style or movement with the goal of breaking away from traditional forms." How do these roots help you understand the meaning of the term *postmodernism*?

(Image at right) Cold Dark Matter: An Exploded View *(1991) by the English sculptor Cornelia Parker is a postmodern art installation.*

**DETERMINING MEANING**

The text about the popularity of American popular culture abroad states, "Some nations worry that American entertainment weakens their own language and culture." What does the term **cultural imperialism** mean in this context?

Television and sports have created a sense that Americans and Europeans share a culture. Europeans watch American shows and become familiar with American brand names—and American attitudes about family, work, and money. As a cultural export, sports have become big business. Some nations worry that American entertainment weakens their own languages and cultures. Critics refer to this as **cultural imperialism**. Although Western music and movies may still dominate, trends in the opposite direction are developing. One trend is that non-Western music has large Western audiences. For example, the reggae music native to Jamaica has an enormous following, and Latin pop has become so popular that there have been Latin Grammy awards since 1999.

### ✓ CHECKING FOR UNDERSTANDING

1. **DETERMINING CONTEXT** What were the cultural trends in Western Europe and North America in the 1990s and 2000s?
2. **DRAWING CONCLUSIONS** What evidence does the text provide that American culture has begun to lose some of its dominance?
3. **EXPLAINING CAUSES** Why has the spread of American popular culture led some critics to be concerned about U.S. cultural imperialism?

## LESSON 2 REVIEW

### Time and Place

1. **IDENTIFYING CONNECTIONS** What was the connection between America's role as a world power and its cultural dominance in the late twentieth and early twenty-first centuries?

### Building History-Social Science Analysis Skills

2. **UNDERSTANDING CONTEXT** How did President Clinton's time in office benefit George W. Bush?
3. **EXPLAINING CAUSE AND EFFECT** What social and economic factors led to the 2008 election of President Barack Obama?
4. **IDENTIFYING EFFECTS** Describe the effects of the spread of American popular culture in Europe.

### Writing About History

5. **NARRATIVE WRITING** Imagine you are a citizen of East Germany. You have been anticipating the reunification of Germany, and it finally happens. Write two letters to a friend, one dated October 3, 1990, and one dated 1998, reflecting on your expectations for reunification and the realities of life in a reunified Germany.

### Collaborating

6. **COLLABORATING** With a partner, discuss possible reasons for the emergence of anti-immigrant sentiment in some Western European nations.

## ESSENTIAL QUESTIONS

- *What motivates political change?*
- *How can economic and social changes affect a country?*

# THE STORY BEGINS...

LESSON 3

# Asia and the Pacific

The story of the early twenty-first century will be the rise of China as an economic superpower. In some ways, this puts China in direct competition with the United States, which dominated the second half of the previous century. Recognizing the reality of this transformation in 2015, President Barack Obama noted the following:

> "Since I took office, American exports to China have nearly doubled and now support nearly one million American jobs. Chinese investment in the United States helps support jobs across our country. We partner to address global challenges, whether it's promoting nuclear security, combating piracy off the Horn of Africa, encouraging development and reconciliation in Afghanistan, and helping to end the Ebola epidemic in West Africa. . . .
>
> So, greater prosperity and greater security—that's what American and Chinese cooperation can deliver. That's why I want to say again, the United States welcomes the rise of a China that is peaceful, stable, prosperous, and a responsible player in global affairs. And I'm committed to expanding our cooperation, even as we address disagreements candidly and constructively."

—President Obama, remarks in a joint press conference with President Xi of the People's Republic of China, September 2015

Following the end of World War II, European states gradually set free their colonies. At the same time, European economies began to stabilize, to stagnate, or even to shrink. This stood in stark contrast with the populations of Asia, which began a period of rapid growth. During the eighteenth century, the growth of Europe's population outpaced the growth of Asia's in a period some historians call the "Great Divergence." Now, with growing population and thriving economies, Asia is slowly returning to the position of global prominence it occupied before the rise of the West.

*Rapid industrialization in Asian countries has turned cities such as Shanghai into powerful centers of global economic activity.* ▶

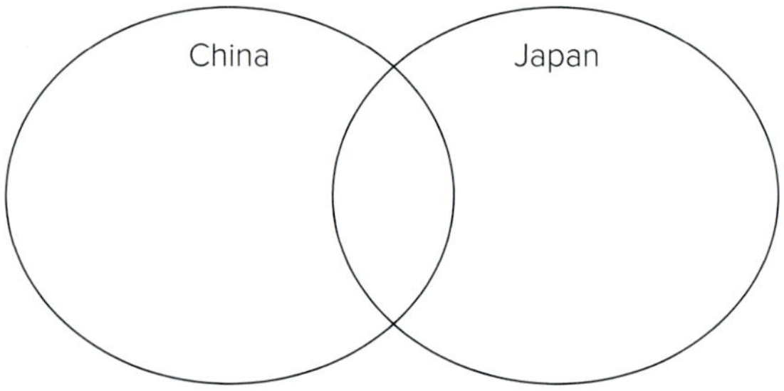


**ANALYZING KEY IDEAS AND DETAILS**

**SUMMARIZING** Read closely to identify the similarities and differences between China's and Japan's economic growth in the post-Cold War era. Summarize these similarities and differences in a Venn diagram like this one.

# CHINA AFTER MAO

GUIDING QUESTION *What political and social changes has China undergone in the late twentieth and early twenty-first centuries?*

After the death of Mao Zedong in 1976, the new government in China under the leadership of Deng Xiaoping (DUHNG SHYOW • PIHNG) called for Four Modernizations—new policies in industry, agriculture, technology, and national defense. For more than 20 years, China had been isolated from the technological advances taking place elsewhere in the world. To make up for lost time, the government invited foreign investors to China. The government also sent thousands of students abroad to study science, technology, and modern business techniques.

A new agricultural policy began. Collective farms could now lease land to peasants who paid rent to the collective. Anything produced above the value of the rent could be sold for profit. Peasants were also allowed to make goods to sell. By adopting this practical approach, China began to make great strides in limiting poverty and engaging in nation building. **Per capita** (per person) income, including farm income, doubled during the 1980s. Housing, education, and sanitation improved. Both agriculture and industrial output skyrocketed.

Despite such achievements, many complained that Deng Xiaoping's program had not achieved a fifth modernization—democracy. People could not directly criticize the Communist Party. Those who called for democracy were often sentenced to long terms in prison.

The problem intensified in the late 1980s. More Chinese studied abroad and learned about the West. As the economy prospered, students and other groups wanted better living conditions and greater freedom. In the late 1980s, rising inflation led to growing discontent among salaried workers, especially in the cities. Corruption and special treatment for officials and party members led to increasing criticism as well. In May 1989, student protesters called for an end to the corruption and demanded the resignation of China's aging Communist Party leaders. These demands received widespread support from people in the cities. Discontent led to massive demonstrations in Tiananmen Square in Beijing.

Deng Xiaoping believed the protesters were calling for an end to Communist rule. He ordered tanks and troops into the square to crush the demonstrators. Between 500 and 2,000 were killed and many more injured. Democracy was a dream.

Throughout the 1990s and into the 2000s, China's human rights violations, determination to **unify** with Taiwan, and increasing military power created

**ANALYZING KEY IDEAS AND DETAILS**

1. **CITING TEXT EVIDENCE** Identify text evidence that supports the following claim made in the lesson: "People could not directly criticize the Communist Party."
2. **ANALYZING EVENTS** Reread the paragraph that begins, "The problem intensified in the. . . ." What part of this paragraph states an effect of rising inflation and a sense that official party members were getting special treatment? What words signal that this is an effect?

**DETERMINING MEANING**

What does the meaning of the term **per capita** indicate about how the wealth described in this paragraph is being measured?

international concern. China's neighbors, especially Japan, India, and Russia, fear the active role China is playing in its area of the world. To Chinese leaders, however, such actions represent China's rightful role in the region.

For now, a strong patriotism seems to be on the rise. This is encouraged by the government as a means of holding together the country. When China was selected to host the 2008 Olympic Games, the Chinese celebrated enthusiastically. The event seemed to symbolize China's emergence as a major national power on the world stage.

Problems remain for China, however, under the leadership of President Xi Jinping. For example, there is continuing unrest among China's national minorities. This is especially true in Tibet, where the Chinese government has violently suppressed Tibetan culture.

*A demonstrator stands in front of the tanks at Tiananmen Square.*

**IDENTIFYING EFFECTS** What were the immediate effects of the Tiananmen Square protests?

### ✓ CHECKING FOR UNDERSTANDING

1. **SUMMARIZING** What political and social changes has China undergone in the late twentieth and early twenty-first centuries?
2. **COMPARING** How do China's neighbors view China's role in the world? How does this differ from the view of the Chinese government?
3. **SUMMARIZING** What is the "fifth modernization," and how has China failed to achieve it?

## CHINESE SOCIETY AND ECONOMY

**GUIDING QUESTIONS** *What political and social changes has China undergone in the late twentieth and early twenty-first centuries? How has modern China become a world economic power?*

From the start, the Communist Party wanted to create a new kind of citizen, one who would give the utmost for the good of all China. In Mao's words, the people should "be resolute, fear no sacrifice, and surmount every difficulty to win victory."

During the 1950s and 1960s, the Chinese government began to allow women to take part in politics and gave them equal marital rights—a dramatic shift. After Mao's death, family traditions returned. People now had more freedom in everyday matters and had better living conditions. Married couples who had been given patriotic names chose more elegant names for their own children. Clothing choices were no longer restricted to a baggy "Mao suit." In contrast, today, wealthy, young Chinese purchase luxury brands from Europe and North America and wear the latest fashion.

**ANALYZING KEY IDEAS AND DETAILS**

1. **ANALYZING IDEAS** Reread the paragraph that begins, "Mao's successors have followed one of his. . . ." Which sentence in this paragraph provides a clue about the reason China abandoned the one-child policy?
2. **ANALYZING EVENTS** Reread the paragraph that begins, "After the Tiananmen Square. . . ." What part of this paragraph states an effect of the Tiananmen Square protests on Chinese policies? What words signal this is an effect?

### CHINESE DOMESTIC POLICIES

Mao's successors have followed one of his goals to the present day—the effort to control population growth. In 1979 the state began advocating a **one-child policy**. Incentives such as education benefits, child care, and housing were offered to couples who limited their families to one child. The policy has successfully decreased China's population growth rate. China's population growth rate has declined from 2.2 percent in 1970–1975 to an estimated 0.5 percent in 2010–2014. An unintended effect has been an aging population. Life expectancy is increasing, but the birth rate remains low. Because of these unintended consequences, Chinese officials announced the end of the one-child policy in 2015. Chinese families are now permitted to have two children instead of one.

## REGIONAL GEOPOLITICS

The Spratly Islands, located in the South China Sea, are claimed by a number of countries in the region, including China, Malaysia, Vietnam, Taiwan, and the Philippines. China attracted attention by installing weapons on the islands in 2016, further staking its claim to the islands. Taiwan's rivalry with China extends beyond claims to these islands. China has viewed Taiwan as a breakaway province since Chiang Kai-shek's government fled to Taiwan in 1949. Some in Taiwan argue that China, who at times has promised to retake Taiwan by force, is unlikely to use military force due to the cost to China's own economy. Tension remains high, however, as China's army is one of the largest military forces in the world.

China has also reached out economically to developing countries in Asia, Africa, the Caribbean, and elsewhere in the world since the 1950s. China has rapidly increased aid to other nations in the twenty-first century. Africa has been the largest recipient, with China supplying aid to fund infrastructure projects, such as the Tan Zam railroad in Zambia, as well as the health, agriculture, and education sectors. China has drawn some criticism for supplying aid to countries that limit civil liberties. Many countries, including the United States, consider the political rights and civil liberties endorsed by a country when making aid determinations.

**DETERMINING MEANING**

The word **sector** has the same root as the word *section*. *Section* means "a smaller part into which something can be divided." How might knowing the meaning of *section* help a person determine the meaning of *sector*?

## ECONOMIC GROWTH

After the Tiananmen Square demonstrations, the Chinese government adopted a policy of promoting rapid economic growth while cracking down harshly on political dissenters. Especially noticeable was the attempt to win middle-class support in the cities by guaranteeing more consumer goods.

During the 1990s, growth rates in industry remained high, leading to predictions that China would become one of the economic superpowers of the twenty-first century. The manufacture of inexpensive consumer goods, such as textiles and electronics, has contributed to China's economic growth.

Domestic capital in China became available to compete with the growing presence of foreign enterprises. The government also shut down inefficient state enterprises. By the early 2000s, the private **sector** accounted for more than 10 percent of the nation's gross domestic product. A stock market opened. At the same time, China was strengthening international trade relations. China joined the World Trade Organization in 2001 and normalized trade relations with the United States in 2002. Some scholars argue that China's adoption of aspects of capitalism may result in a change to its authoritarian government.

Rapid economic change, however, never comes without cost. Workers in Chinese factories complain about poor working conditions and low salaries, leading to labor unrest. Many farmers are also unhappy. They earn only about

*Chinese president Xi Jinping speaking at the Asia-Pacific Economic Cooperation (APEC) conference in the Philippines*

SeongJoon Cho/Bloomberg/Getty Images

half the salary of urban workers. In desperation, millions flee to the big cities, where they are forced to live in pitiful conditions in tenements. Nevertheless, Chinese President Xi Jinping expressed hope for the future, alluding to a concrete plan to improve quality of life for the average Chinese citizen, in a 2015 address to the American people.

> "I know that we must work still harder before all our people can live a better life. That explains why development remains China's top priority. To anyone charged with the governance of China, their primary mission is to focus all the resources on improving people's living standard and gradually achieve common prosperity. To this end, we have proposed the two centenary goals mentioned by Dr. Kissinger, namely to double the 2010 GDP and per capita income of the Chinese and complete the building of a moderately prosperous society by 2020 and to build a prosperous, strong, democratic. . .harmonious, modernist socialist country that realizes the great renew of the Chinese nation by the middle of the century."

—Xi Jinping, from an address to the American people, 2015

### ANALYZING PRIMARY SOURCES

1. **DETERMINING MEANING** In the final sentence of this excerpt, President Xi uses both concrete and abstract language. What are examples of these, and what purpose do they serve in this speech?
2. **EXPLAINING CAUSE AND EFFECT** How does Xi use cause and effect to express his meaning? What does this suggest about progress in China?

### ✓ CHECKING FOR UNDERSTANDING

1. **IDENTIFYING CAUSES** How has modern China become a world economic power?
2. **IDENTIFYING EFFECTS** How has the one-child policy affected the Chinese population?
3. **IDENTIFYING EFFECTS** What negative effects has rapid economic change had on China?

## JAPAN

**GUIDING QUESTION** *What changes have occurred in Japan from the 1990s to the present?*

Between 1950 and 1990, Japan became the greatest exporting nation in the world. It also developed the world's largest economy after that of the United States. Some economists even predicted that Japan would pass the United States as the world's largest economy by 2010. At the end of the 1980s, however, a collapse of the Japanese real estate market sent the economy into a tailspin.

By the 1990s, the Japanese economy had slipped into a recession that has largely continued until the present day. Job security declined as large numbers of workers were laid off. Many older Japanese saw their savings decline. Retirement programs were increasingly strained by the demands of a rapidly aging population. Japan today has the highest proportion of people more than age 65 of any industrialized country in the world—22 percent of the country's total population of about 127 million. Furthermore, the Japanese population started declining in 2004. It is estimated that by 2060, the population will fall to approximately 87 million, and 40 percent of the population will be aged 65 or older.

For more than 20 years, Japan has witnessed slow economic growth and a decline in prices, known as **deflation**. A crisis of confidence has led to deep pessimism about the future and a decline in spending, especially among young Japanese who have now known nothing other than economic decline.

In recent years, Japanese consumers have also complained about a decline in the quality of some domestic products. Even the Japanese automaker Toyota was faced with quality problems in its best-selling fleet of

### ANALYZING KEY IDEAS AND DETAILS

1. **CITING TEXT EVIDENCE** What evidence does the text give as reasons for the discontent of some Japanese citizens? Cite particular text, quoting where necessary.
2. **DETERMINING CENTRAL IDEAS** What were the central ideas of Prime Minister Shinzo Abe's "3 arrows" strategy?

### DETERMINING MEANING

To better understand **deflation**, break down the word. *De-* means "down," and *-flation* is based on the word *inflation,* meaning "expansion." Based on these word parts, what is *deflation*?

Soper, Taylor. 2015. Full text: China President Xi gives policy speech in Seattle, wants to fight cybercrime with the U.S. September 22, 2015. GeekWire.

MAKING CONNECTIONS TO TODAY

## THE JAPANESE AUTOMOBILE INDUSTRY

The *Motor Trend* car of the year in 1973 was the Chevrolet Monte Carlo. It sported a V8 engine, was more than 17.5 feet long, and had a fuel economy of 12 miles per gallon. At that same time, Japanese carmaker Honda was releasing a very different type of car in the United States, the Honda Civic. The earliest Civics were tiny in comparison. But, importantly, they consumed far less gasoline. With the oil crisis of 1973 in full swing, American consumers began looking at the Civic in ways they would not have otherwise. Honda sold about 32,000 in the United States that year. By 1990, that number had reached 220,000. Today, the Civic ranks as the sixth-most popular automobile sold in the United States. Americans bought 366,927 Civics in 2016 alone. This success in the United States has contributed to making Japan the world's third-largest automobile manufacturer in the world and is a big reason Japan remains an economic superpower.

1. **DRAWING CONCLUSIONS** How were the typical American car and the Honda Civic different in the early '70s? Speculate on what accounted for this difference.
2. **IDENTIFYING CONNECTIONS** What does the popularity of the Civic and the oil crisis of the 1970s indicate about changing world markets in this period?

cars. In 2014 and 2015, defective airbags produced by the Japanese supplier Takata were recalled in more than 30 million U.S. vehicles.

The country's economic decline was evident when China passed Japan in the second quarter of 2010 as the world's second-largest economy behind the United States. Despite government attempts to stimulate the economy in 2010, Japan faced a growing government debt and increasing rates of poverty.

## THE TSUNAMI AND FUKUSHIMA

On March 11, 2011, Japan received another crushing blow as a result of a devastating natural catastrophe. An offshore earthquake produced a gigantic tsunami, or tidal wave, that destroyed cities and farmland on the northeast coast. Recorded at 9.0 on the Richter scale, it was the most powerful quake to hit a country that was accustomed to periodic earthquakes. Thousands of people were killed, the overwhelming majority of whom died by drowning, and hundreds of thousands were left homeless. Authorities began a massive rescue and recovery effort.

The tsunami also damaged the nuclear power plant at Fukushima Daiichi and created the worst nuclear disaster since the accident at Chernobyl in Ukraine in 1986. Leaks of radioactive gas into the atmosphere not only endangered the lives of many Japanese but also brought threats of radioactive contamination to Japan's food supplies. Japanese officials worked overtime to contain the damage and created an evacuation zone around the plant where it was deemed unsafe for people to live. Years later, there are still 110,000 evacuees from Fukushima living in other areas of Japan.

*The 2011 tsunami devastated towns such as Natori, Japan. The tsunami also led to rising radiation levels from the damaged Fukushima Daiichi nuclear plant.*

**INFERRING** Do you think the damage at the Fukushima Daiichi nuclear plant has limited the development of new nuclear power plants in the United States? Why or why not?

## SHINZO ABE'S GOVERNMENT

Prime Minister Shinzo Abe has put forth a "3 arrows" strategy to improve the Japanese economy by focusing on bold monetary policy, flexible fiscal policy, and a growth strategy to increase private sector investment. The government has also approved consistent increases in defense spending in the 2000s to coincide with its growing military. Abe has also backed security laws that allow troops to take part in overseas combat missions. This is a concern to some Japanese citizens as it is contrary to the country's pacifist constitution. Although some Japanese support growing the military due to concerns over North Korea's growing militarization and proximity to China, the expansion is increasing tensions among countries within the region.

### ✓ CHECKING FOR UNDERSTANDING

1. **SUMMARIZING** What changes have occurred in Japan from the 1990s to the present?
2. **CONTRASTING** In what ways do the changes in Japan's economy in the late twentieth and early twenty-first centuries contrast with China's?
3. **SUMMARIZING** What factors have contributed to Japan's economic downturn since the 1990s?

# THE KOREAS

**GUIDING QUESTION** *What are the major differences between North Korea and South Korea?*

Although the Korean War ended in 1953, political tensions between North Korea and South Korea continue to threaten the peace between the two countries, primarily due to North Korea's nuclear weapons program. At the same time, South Korea has become one of the strongest economies in Asia.

## NORTH KOREA

North Korea has experienced two leadership transitions since the end of the Cold War. After the death of Kim Il Sung in 1994, his son Kim Jong Il rose to power. Then following Kim Jong Il's death in 2011, his son Kim Jong Un became North Korea's leader at the young age of 29. Under all three leaders in its history, North Korea remained an isolated country with few individual liberties allowed under a communist military dictatorship.

North Korea is plagued by internal social and economic problems. Droughts and famines during the 1990s led North Korea to seek assistance from the United Nations (UN) and the United States. Economic problems forced the North Korean government to devalue its currency in 2009. The UN Food and Agriculture Organization estimates that one in four children in rural North Korea is underweight. In 2015 more than 40 percent of the entire North Korean population was undernourished.

The controversy surrounding North Korea and its nuclear program began in 1994 when Kim Jong Il announced his country's intent to withdraw from the Treaty on the Non-Proliferation of Nuclear Weapons (NPT). Following negotiations, North Korea agreed to freeze its nuclear program in exchange for U.S. foreign aid. This agreement collapsed in 2002. In August 2003,

### UNDERSTANDING CRAFT AND STRUCTURE

1. **DETERMINING MEANING** The text states that "These tensions were exacerbated in 2009 after a North Korean rocket launch." What does the context suggest about the meaning of the word *exacerbated*?
2. **ANALYZING TEXT PRESENTATION** The section describing the economic rise of South Korea begins with a paragraph about the democratization of the country in the late 1980s. Why do you think the writer chose to begin on this topic rather than a topic related to industry, education, or something else more directly related to economic growth?

North Korean and South Korean soldiers guard the demilitarized zone, which is a constant reminder of tensions between the two countries.

multinational negotiations began anew to persuade the regime to suspend its nuclear program, and an agreement was reached in 2005.

North Korea's nuclear program has caused considerable tensions between North Korea and South Korea. These tensions were exacerbated in 2009 after a North Korean rocket launch. There have been other incidents as well. In a 2010 sinking of a military ship that killed 46 soldiers, South Korea blamed North Korea for the attack. Conflict continued in the 2010s as Kim Jong Un's regime continued its rocket launch program and development of nuclear weapons.

## SOUTH KOREA

Unlike North Korea, South Korea has experienced a growing democracy beginning in the late 1980s. National elections held in 1987 removed former military leaders from power, replacing them with civilian leaders, including President Roh Tae-woo. South Korea's democratization process resulted in direct presidential elections, the expansion and increased participation of civil society groups, and civilian control over the military.

There have been several peaceful transfers of presidential power since the 1987 elections. Park Geun-hye became the first female president of South Korea in 2013 but was soon involved in a corruption scandal. Park's administration was accused of coercing businesses into paying large sums of money to charitable foundations with connections to Choi Soon-Sil, a close friend of Park. Choi was arrested and Park was impeached in late 2016. Hwang Kyo-ahn, a previous prime minister of South Korea, became the acting president of South Korea.

South Korea has a strong economy but has faced economic challenges in response to regional and global economic downturns. The country experienced a currency crisis in response to the Asian financial crisis of 1997 following the collapse of Taiwan's banking industry. But South Korea's strong educational institutions and economic policies enabled it to weather the 2008 global economic crisis with an unemployment rate of 3.8 percent in 2009.

Culturally, South Korea is changing rapidly as almost every household has high-speed Internet and cell phones. South Korean television and movies have great popularity throughout Asia, and education remains the number-one priority. The third-largest group of international students in the United States comes from South Korea.

### ☑ CHECKING FOR UNDERSTANDING

1. **COMPARING** What are the major differences between North Korea and South Korea?
2. **IDENTIFYING CONNECTIONS** What does the impeachment of President Park indicate about the current state of South Korean democracy?
3. **DETERMINING CONTEXT** What has led to increased tensions between North Korea and South Korea in recent decades?

## EAST ASIA AND SOUTH ASIA: POLITICS AND ECONOMICS

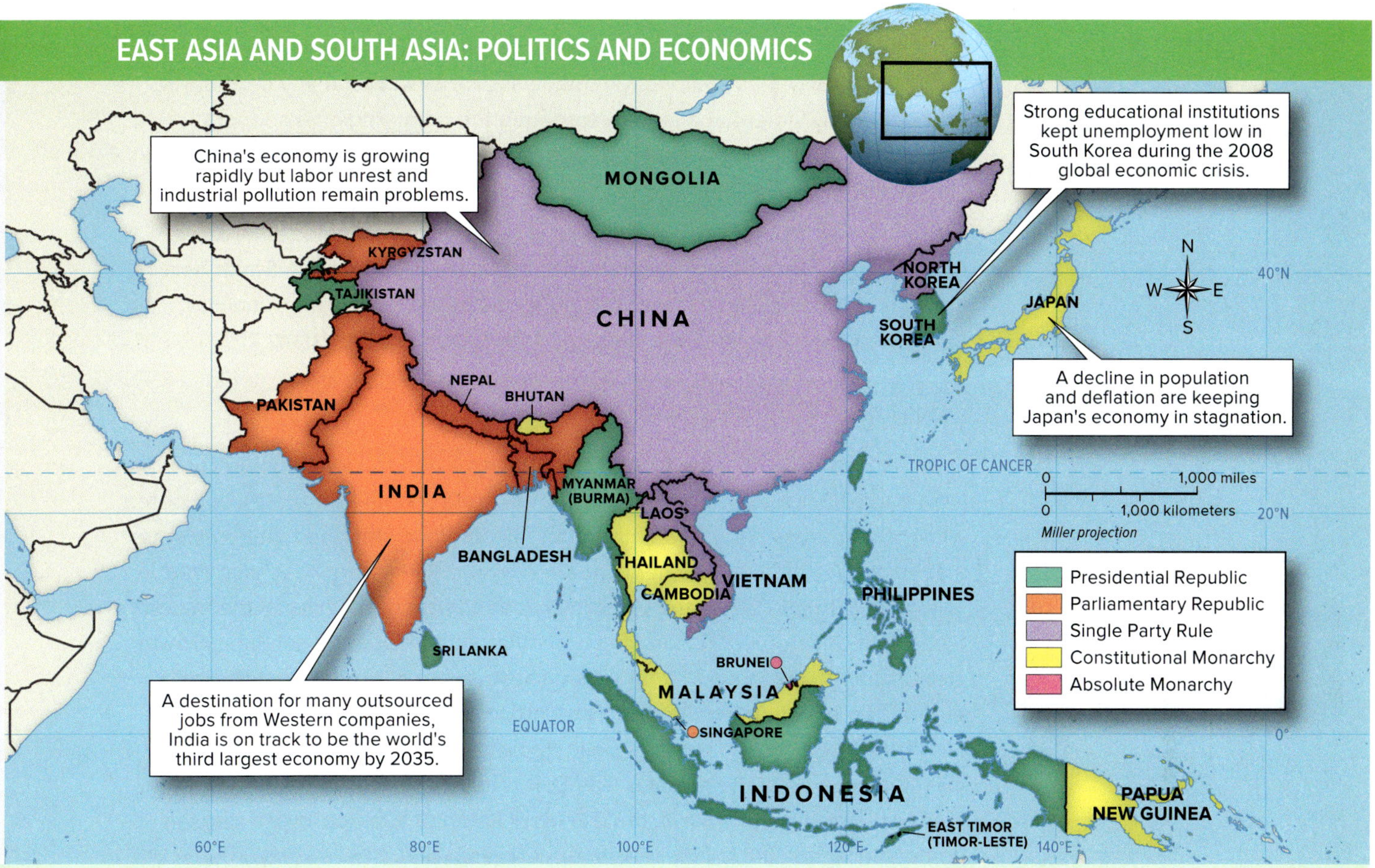


**GEOGRAPHIC REASONING**

1. **EXPLORING REGIONS** Which countries in East and South Asia are republics?
2. **EXPLORING REGIONS** Which of the countries shown are noted as having stable or growing economies?

# SOUTHEAST ASIA AND SOUTH ASIA

**GUIDING QUESTION** *What different economic and political issues have affected the countries of Southeast Asia and South Asia since the 1990s?*

Since 1990, most countries in Southeast Asia have experienced strong and steady economic growth. Especially strong economies are **evident** in the Philippines, Indonesia, Malaysia, Singapore, Thailand, and Vietnam. However, the countries of Myanmar, Cambodia, and Laos have not kept pace. Many of these countries experienced a large financial crisis in 1997, and most took until the early 2000s to fully recover.

Politically, some Southeast Asian societies have once again moved toward democracy in recent years. However, serious troubles remain. For instance, the financial crisis of the late 1990s in Indonesia resulted in the resignation of a president and political unrest. For a long time, too, Myanmar had remained under military rule. However, in the 2015 elections, the League for Democracy party won many seats in parliament, which brought hope for a more democratic government. More recently, the government has been criticized for the treatment of the Rohingya people, a Muslim minority, within the country.

Although the Philippines is democratic, terrorism remains a challenge. Muslim rebels on the island of Mindanao, for example, have used terror to promote their demands for independence.

**ANALYZING KEY IDEAS AND DETAILS**

1. **CITING TEXT EVIDENCE** This section of the text argues that some Southeast Asian countries have struggled to maintain and install democratic governments. What evidence in the text supports this claim?
2. **DETERMINING CENTRAL IDEAS** Read the last paragraph under the heading "India." What is the central idea of this paragraph? Does the last sentence support or contradict the central idea?

Philippine President Rodrigo Duterte, elected in 2016, has raised the concern of the United Nations with his "war on drugs" that many consider to be excessively violent and unfairly targeting the poor. Regional cooperation continues through the Association of Southeast Asia Nations (ASEAN), which fosters trade among Asian states.

South Asia comprises the states of India, Pakistan, Bangladesh, Nepal, Bhutan, Sri Lanka, and the Maldives. Important developments in South Asia since the 1990s are the growing economic power of India, the continuing rivalry between India and Pakistan, and the instability in Pakistan.

## INDIA

During the early 1990s, the Congress Party remained the leading party in India. New parties, such as the militantly Hindu Bharata Janata Party (BJP), competed with the Congress Party for control of the central and state governments. After a series of coalition governments headed by the BJP leader A. B. Vajpayee between 1996 and 2004, the Congress Party returned to power at the head of a coalition government based on a commitment to maintain economic growth and to carry out reforms in rural areas. These reforms included public works projects and hot lunch programs for all primary school children. Manmohan Singh, who had carried out economic reforms in India in 1991 as finance minister, became prime minister. The BJP returned to power in 2014 under the leadership of Narendra Modi. In 2015 Modi had high job approval ratings at home and signed important investment deals abroad.

India's economy has emerged as one of the world's largest and fastest growing. Economic reforms in 1991 fostered foreign investment and began to move India toward a market-based economy. Although agriculture is still the occupation of many Indians, the service and industrial sectors now account for much of India's GDP. Western companies outsource jobs in the information technology, distribution, call centers, and other sectors to India. Many economists believe that India is a rising economic superpower and may have the world's third-largest economy by 2035.

Conflict between Hindus and Muslims has continued, and religious differences have fueled a long-term dispute between India and Pakistan over Kashmir, a territory between the two countries. The danger escalated in 1998 when both countries tested nuclear warheads. Border conflicts in 2002 led to threats of war, but in 2003 the countries agreed to a cease-fire across the line of control that separates Kashmir and restored diplomatic relations. After the 2008 attacks in Mumbai, India, talks between India and Pakistan over Kashmir deteriorated but then improved again briefly in 2010 when the Indian government announced amnesty for fighters from Kashmir. Fighting and shelling across the line of control erupted again in late 2014 and continued into 2017.

## PAKISTAN

After her dismissal by the military on charges of corruption, Benazir Bhutto was reelected as president in 1993. She attempted to crack down on opposition forces but was removed once again in 1997 amid renewed charges of corruption. Her successor, too, was ousted in 1999 by a military coup led by General Pervez Musharraf, who promised to restore honest government.

In September 2001, Pakistan became the focus of international attention when a coalition of forces arrived in Afghanistan to overthrow the Taliban regime. Despite considerable support for the Taliban among the local population, President Musharraf pledged his help in bringing terrorists to justice. By 2003, problems had escalated. As Musharraf sought to fend off challenges from radical Muslim groups, secular opposition figures criticized his regime's authoritarian nature. Exiled, Bhutto planned her return, calling it her "destiny."

She did return to Pakistan early in 2008 to run for president, but she was assassinated. This led to widespread suspicions of official involvement. In September 2008, amid growing political turmoil, Bhutto's widower, Asif Ali Zardari, was elected president of Pakistan. After accusations of **corruption** and misuse of public funds, Mamnoon Hussain of the Pakistan Muslim League was elected into office in 2013. Nawaz Sharif, who had served as prime minister for much of the 1990s, became prime minister in 2013. Terrorism and extremism continue to challenge Pakistan. In December 2014, a horrific terrorist attack on a school killed 140 young children in Pakistan.

**DETERMINING MEANING**

The roots of the word **corruption** are *co-*, meaning "together," and *ruption*, meaning "to damage." How does knowing the meaning of these roots help you determine the meaning of *corruption*?

### ☑ CHECKING FOR UNDERSTANDING

1. **EVALUATING** What different economic and political issues have affected the countries of Southeast Asia and South Asia since the 1990s?
2. **DETERMINING CONTEXT** What was Pakistan's role in the War on Terror?
3. **ANALYZING CHANGE** What political changes has India experienced in recent decades?

## LESSON 3 REVIEW

### Time and Place

1. **IDENTIFYING PERSPECTIVES** How does the Chinese government view its role in the world, and how has this been apparent in its actions in recent decades?

### Building History-Social Science Analysis Skills

2. **ANALYZING INFORMATION** How did the state of the Japanese economy at the end of the twentieth century differ from analysts' earlier predictions for it?

3. **EXPLAINING CAUSE AND EFFECT** What does the success of the South Korean economy suggest about the reasons the North Korean economy continues to stall?

4. **INFERRING** What do the problems Pakistan has struggled with over the last three decades indicate about the future of a stable Pakistan?

### Writing About History

5. **NARRATIVE WRITING** Imagine you are a foreign exchange student attending a Beijing university in 1989. You witness the demonstration at Tiananmen Square. Using proper grammar and usage, write a letter to a friend describing what you saw.

### Collaborating

6. **COLLABORATING** With a partner, identify and discuss the policies of Deng Xiaoping that were intended to help modernize China.

ANALYZING SOURCES

# THE POST-COLD WAR SOVIET UNION

As the Soviet Union neared collapse in the late 1980s and early '90s, there were many opinions about the future of the large state. Then head of state Mikhail Gorbachev believed it was his burden to help Russia make this transition out of the Cold War and into a new environment in which civic life bloomed. Several years later, long-time Soviet critic and writer Aleksandr Solzhenitsyn gave his interpretation of how well the former Soviet Union managed this transition.

**VOCABULARY**

*vanguard:* at the head of an action or movement

*perestroika:* restructuring; Gorbachev's policy of reform

*platform:* plan of political action

*Glasnost:* Soviet policy of openness

*illusory:* deceptive

PRIMARY SOURCE: SPEECH

## GORBACHEV'S COMMUNIST PARTY

Gorbachev spoke to the Central Committee of the Soviet Communist Party on February 6, 1990, about the future of the party in the Soviet Union.

> "... The main thing that now worries Communists and all citizens of the country is the fate of perestroika, the fate of the country and the role of the Soviet Communist Party at the current, probably most crucial, stage of revolutionary transformation. ...
>
> Of no less importance is the understanding of the fact ... that the party will only be able to fulfill the mission of political **vanguard** if it drastically restructures itself, masters the art of political work in the present conditions and succeeds in cooperating with forces committed to **perestroika**. ...
>
> The **platform** says, Our ideal is a humane, democratic socialism, expressing the interests of the working class and all working people and relying on the great legacy of Marx, Engels and Lenin. The Soviet Communist Party is creatively developing socialist ideals to match present-day realities and with due account for the entire experience of the twentieth century.
>
> The platform states clearly what we should abandon. We should abandon the ideological dogmatism that became ingrained during past decades, outdated stereotypes in domestic policy and outmoded view on the world revolutionary process and world development as a whole.
>
> We should abandon everything that led to the isolation of socialist countries from the mainstream of world civilization. ...
>
> The party in a renewing society can exist and play its role as vanguard only as a democratically recognized force. This means that its status should not be imposed through constitutional endorsement.
>
> The Soviet Communist Party ... intends to struggle for the status of the ruling party.
>
> But it will do so strictly within the framework of the democratic process by giving up any legal and political advantages ... cooperating with other social and political forces, always working amidst the masses, living by their interests and their needs."

**ANALYZE THE TEXT**

1. **DETERMINING CENTRAL IDEAS** What does Gorbachev believe the Communist Party must do to stay relevant?
2. **UNDERSTANDING CONTEXT** In what way does Gorbachev attempt to appeal to traditional party members in his speech?

PRIMARY SOURCE: EDITORIAL

## SOLZHENITSYN ON RUSSIAN DEMOCRACY

In a *New York Times* editorial of January 1997, author Aleksandr Solzhenitsyn questioned whether Russia had finally achieved a democracy.

> "What is known today as "Russian democracy" masks a Government of a completely different sort. **Glasnost**—freedom of the press—is only an instrument of democracy, not democracy itself. And to a great extent freedom of the press is **illusory**, since the owners of newspapers erect strict taboos against discussion of issues of vital importance. . . .
>
> Democracy in the unarguable sense of the word means the rule of the people—that is, a system in which the people are truly in charge of their daily lives and can influence the course of their own historical fate. There is nothing of the sort in Russia today.
>
> In August 1991, the "councils of people's deputies," though only window dressing under the rule of the Communist Party, were abolished throughout the country. Since then, the united resistance of the President's machine, the Government, State Duma, leaders of the political parties and majority of governors has prevented the creation of any agencies of local self-government. . . .
>
> There exists no legal framework or financial means for the creation of local self-government; people will have no choice but to achieve it through social struggle. All that really exists is the government hierarchy, from the President and national Government on down. . . .
>
> . . . Russia has been exhausted by crime, by the transfer into private hands of billions of dollars' worth of the nation's wealth. Not a single serious crime has been exposed, nor has there been a single public trial. . . .
>
> The destructive course of events over the last decade has come about because the Government, while ineptly imitating foreign models, has completely disregarded the country's creativity and particular character, as well as Russia's centuries-old spiritual and social traditions. Only if those paths are freed up can Russia be delivered from its near-fatal condition."

### ANALYZE THE TEXT

1. **ANALYZING IDEAS** As presented in this excerpt, what are Solzhenitsyn's views about the effects of *perestroika* and the dissolution of the Soviet Union?
2. **ANALYZING CENTRAL IDEAS** How does Solzhenitsyn distinguish the Russian government from a true democracy?

### MULTIPLE PERSPECTIVES

1. **ANALYZING CENTRAL IDEAS** How do Gorbachev's and Solzhenitsyn's views on the effects of *perestroika* differ?
2. **IDENTIFYING CONNECTIONS** How does Solzhenitsyn's article inform our understanding of the practical implementation of Gorbachev's ideals?

## ESSENTIAL QUESTIONS

- *What motivates political change?*
- *How can economic and social changes affect a country?*

LESSON 4

# Latin America

## THE STORY BEGINS...

Instability in Latin America during the twentieth century often resulted in dictators gaining power. Over the last generation, Latin Americans have worked to rid their countries of dictators, civil wars, cycles of poverty, and other political and social problems. President Obama addressed this shift toward freedom and democracy in the region in 2011:

> "Even now, I know our headlines are often dominated by events in other parts of the world. But let's never forget: Every day, the future is being forged by the countries and peoples of Latin America. For Latin America is not the old stereotype of a region of—in perpetual conflict or trapped in endless cycles of poverty. The world must now recognize Latin America for the dynamic and growing region that it truly is.
>
> Latin America is at peace. Civil wars have ended. Insurgencies have been pushed back. Old border disputes have been resolved. In Colombia, great sacrifices by citizens and security forces have restored a level of security not seen in decades."

—President Obama, remarks on Latin America in Santiago, Chile, March 2011

Despite the optimism of these remarks, many Latin American states continue to face challenges in nation building.

*Modern Mexico City is a huge metropolis of nearly 22 million people and a major player in Latin American economics and politics.* ▶

PHOTO:Gerardo Borbolla/Shutterstock RF/Shutterstock; TEXT:Office of the Press Secretary. 2011. Remarks by President Obama on Latin America in Santiago, Chile. March 21, 2011. The White House: Office of the Press Secretary.

| Issues Facing Latin American Countries | |
|---|---|
| Country | Issue(s) |
| Mexico | |
| Haiti and the Dominican Republic | |
| El Salvador | |
| Honduras | |
| Argentina | |
| Brazil | |
| Chile | |

**ANALYZING KEY IDEAS AND DETAILS**

**DETERMINING CENTRAL IDEAS** Read closely to identify at least one recent issue each of the countries faced. Summarize these issues in a graphic organizer like this one.

# MEXICO

**GUIDING QUESTION** *In what ways did Mexican politics and society change in the 1990s and 2000s?*

Mexico responded to the Cold War differently than many other countries in Latin America that experienced geopolitical influence from the United States and the Soviet Union or internal political revolutions. Mexico had a stable, one-party political system that limited internal opposition. It was not until the Cold War ended that Mexicans' fatigue with one-party rule became evident and opposition parties gained influence.

## END OF PRI DOMINANCE

The Institutional Revolutionary Party, or PRI, dominated Mexican politics for 71 years, from its founding in 1929 until 2000. Every single president and most of the important national and local legislators were members of the PRI. Support for the PRI dropped in the 1990s as the continuing debt crisis, rising unemployment, and corruption scandals increased dissatisfaction with the government.

In 2000 Vicente Fox of the National Action Party, or PAN, unexpectedly defeated Ernesto Zedillo, the PRI candidate for the presidency. The PAN is a center-right political party that had been formed much earlier. A true multiparty system began to emerge in Mexico. Fox's successor, Felipe Calderón, was elected in 2006 and served through 2012. At the same time, the Democratic Revolutionary Party, or PRD, emerged as a weaker third-party challenger to both the PRI and PAN.

The PRI returned to power in 2012 when Enrique Peña Nieto was elected president for a 6-year term in office. PRD candidate Andrés Manuel López Obrador contested the election results with charges of corruption and vote buying by the PRI. Despite these issues, Mexico has maintained a reasonable amount of political stability. Even with the return of the PRI to power, Mexican politics had changed in the 12-year period of its absence from the presidency. Mexico now has a multiparty system with three viable political parties—the PRI, PAN, and PRD.

## MEXICAN SOCIETY AND ECONOMY

The Mexican Revolution of the early twentieth century had a significant effect on Mexican society. Annual celebrations of the revolution and its heroes and artistic movements have promoted the formation of a strong national identity. The PRI also helped elevate the revolution in popular culture, in no small part because it was the official political party of the revolution. Despite some measures to reduce inequality, Mexican society is still largely divided by income and educational levels.

**ANALYZING KEY IDEAS AND DETAILS**

1. **CITING TEXT EVIDENCE** The first paragraph under the heading "Mexico and Its Neighbors" argues that Mexico combined economic liberalization with international trade agreements. What evidence in this paragraph supports this claim?
2. **ANALYZING EVENTS** Reread the two paragraphs that begin with the sentence "In 2000 Vicente Fox of the National Action Party, . . ." What part of these paragraphs states an effect of the rise of PAN on politics in Mexico?

CITIZENSHIP

### HUMAN RIGHTS ORGANIZATIONS

When governments are unable to provide social and economic structures to support the rights of their people, independent organizations may step in. One example of this in Latin America is Covenant House. It was founded in the late 1960s to help support homeless children. For 25 years, Covenant House has operated in Honduras, offering vulnerable children education, aid, and protection. Although Covenant House operates worldwide, it is unique in Honduras in that it fights for juvenile justice in jails and carries out a program for youths who have attempted to move north through Mexico illegally. These actions serve a larger purpose: to advocate for the rights of children and "homeless, addicted and exploited youth" in Honduras. To that end, they have founded a Human Rights Observatory. The Observatory monitors Honduras's children's rights, publishing widely distributed reports about their status.

1. **IDENTIFYING CAUSES** Why did Covenant House Honduras establish the Human Rights Observatory?
2. **ANALYZING EVENTS** Other than through the Human Rights Observatory, how does Covenant House Honduras promote human rights?

Some of Mexico's economic success can be attributed to its location on the Pacific Ring of Fire, which contributes to its vast mineral deposits and natural resources. Development of mineral and natural resources has led to Mexico's becoming a leading exporter of silver, copper, and especially of oil. For much of the twentieth century, Mexico operated as a mixed economy with the government controlling investments and imports as well as having ownership of and tightly regulating businesses. The economy changed dramatically in the 1980s with the deregulation of industries, the encouragement of foreign investment, and dismantling of state industries, encouraging rapid development.

## MEXICO AND ITS NEIGHBORS

As the government loosened its control of the Mexican economy, it began to pursue trade agreements with its neighbors. The North American Free Trade Agreement (NAFTA), approved by the U.S. Congress in 1993, linked Mexico, the United States, and Canada in a free-trade zone. As in the United States, the implementation of NAFTA was not without controversy in Mexico. Family farmers in Mexico found they could no longer compete with the low prices of agricultural imports subsidized by the United States.

As Latin America's second-largest economy, Mexico has strong relationships with other countries in the region. Mexico was the first country to establish relations with and recognize Cuba as a sovereign nation in 1902 and strongly supported its admittance into the Latin American Integration Association (ALADI) in 1999. ALADI encourages free trade and economic cooperation among its members, which also include Argentina, Bolivia, Brazil, Chile, Colombia, Ecuador, Paraguay, Peru, Uruguay, and Venezuela.

Mexican migration, particularly to the United States, was commonplace throughout most of the twentieth century. It increased greatly in the late 1970s as many pursued employment opportunities. In addition, Mexican migration has been influenced by family ties. Familial relations on both sides of the U.S.- Mexican border often prompted Mexicans to either join family already established in the United States or to return to family in Mexico. In addition, the drug war caused many to flee areas where violence is widespread. Immigration to the United States had slowed by the mid-2000s, and many immigrants were returning to Mexico as the U.S. economy declined and the economic situation in Mexico improved.

## DRUG WAR

The emergence of a multiparty political system has helped Mexico remain relatively stable, but it has not solved all of Mexico's problems. High poverty rates, illiteracy, high unemployment, and political corruption have helped fuel the drug trade that has become a violent drug war. This drug war has increasingly challenged the country. When President Felipe Calderón came to office in 2006, he ordered a military response against the country's drug gangs. He hoped to find a way to slow and halt the drug trade and its devastating effects on the country. But the violence and killings only increased. Between 2007 and 2014, more than 164,000 people were killed in this drug war. 2011 saw the most violence, with approximately 27,000 people killed. President Peña Nieto has continued a similar approach to Mexico's drug war since coming to office in 2012, and a number of high-ranking cartel leaders have been arrested. Despite Mexico's ongoing efforts, the violence has continued.

## UNREST IN MEXICO, CENTRAL AMERICA, AND THE CARIBBEAN

### GEOGRAPHIC REASONING

1. **GLOBAL INTERCONNECTIONS** How are the drug trade and violence connected in Mexico, Central America, and the Caribbean?
2. **SPATIAL THINKING** What factors might account for the heightened violence noted in border cities?

The drug trade is a problem not just for Mexico but for all of the Americas. Colombia is the world's biggest producer of cocaine. Mexico serves as the gateway into the United States, which is the largest market for the drug. Mexican drug cartels, or criminal organizations whose chief purpose is to promote and control drug trafficking operations, began to transport drugs for the Colombians. More recently, however, they have taken over the distribution of drugs in the United States. This has led to **considerable** violence on the border of Mexico and the United States.

Mexican drug cartels recruit their members from a pool of soldiers who had served in the armies of several countries, including Guatemala and El Salvador. Increasingly, Mexican drug cartels also rely upon young people of Central America, who are poor and unemployed. These teenagers are willing to transport drugs, to watch kidnap victims, and to perform other low-level tasks.

### ✓ CHECKING FOR UNDERSTANDING

1. **ANALYZING CHANGE** In what ways did Mexican politics and society change in the 1990s and 2000s?
2. **EXPLAINING CAUSE AND EFFECT** In what ways does the Mexican Revolution of the early twentieth century continue to influence modern Mexican society?
3. **IDENTIFYING CAUSES** How has Mexico been able to benefit from its rich mineral deposits and natural resources?

### DETERMINING MEANING

The word **considerable** has the same root as the word *consider,* which means "to think carefully," and the word *considerate,* which means "cautious or careful." How does knowing the meanings of these words help a reader understand the definition of *considerable*?

# THE CARIBBEAN AND CENTRAL AMERICA

**ANALYZING KEY IDEAS AND DETAILS**

1. **CITING TEXT EVIDENCE** The text in this section states that "relations between Cuba and the United States are changing." What evidence does the text provide to support this claim?

2. **ANALYZING IDEAS** This section of the text includes the sentence "Honduras continues to experience internal challenges, including corruption within the national police force, which led to the removal of many high-ranking police officials in 2016." What clue does this sentence give the reader about the future of corruption in Honduras?

**DETERMINING MEANING**

The word **normalization** has the same root as the word *normal*. *Normal* means "standard or expected." How might knowing the meaning of *normal* help a reader understand the definition of *normalization*?

**ANALYZING PRIMARY SOURCES**

1. **UNDERSTANDING CONTEXT** In what way does the modern history of Cuba show the emphasis Castro places on respecting the self-determination of other states?

2. **INTERPRETING** What kinds of changes does CELAC and Castro's speech about it represent?

**GUIDING QUESTION** *How have social and political issues affected Caribbean and Central American countries since the end of the Cold War?*

The distinctive mountains of the Caribbean and Central America were formed by volcanic activity. This activity has also contributed to its mineral resources, such as iron, nickel, and oil, as well as areas of fertile soil for agriculture. Despite these resources, many countries in Central America and the Caribbean are poverty stricken. Some countries in the region have high levels of violence. Others remain extremely poor but have less violence. These challenges have led large numbers of people to emigrate from Central America to Mexico and the United States. Meanwhile, relations between Cuba and the United States are changing.

## CUBA

When the Soviet Union fell in 1989, it was a crushing blow to the Cuban economy, which relied on Soviet aid and the sale of Cuban sugar to Soviet bloc countries. Cuba struggled to find new sources of revenue. Yet the government remained fairly stable. Fidel Castro remained in power until poor health forced him to step down in 2008. His brother, Raúl Castro, then became president of Cuba.

Tense relations between Cuba and the United States began to improve at the end of 2014 when Raúl Castro and U.S. President Obama announced that they would begin restoring diplomatic ties that were severed in 1961. Progress was made in this process of **normalization** throughout 2015. Cuba was removed from the U.S. State Department's list of states that sponsor terrorism in May 2015. Two months later, the United States and Cuba reopened their embassies in Havana and Washington, D.C.

As relations with the United States have normalized, Cuba has also taken a strong role in unifying Latin American and Caribbean countries. In September 2015, Raúl Castro made the following statement to the United Nations.

> "The establishment of the Community of Latin American and Caribbean States (CELAC), and especially the signing by the heads of State and Government in January 2014 of the Proclamation of Latin America and the Caribbean as a Peace Zone, shows that we can move beyond our differences toward unity and the achievement of common goals while respecting our diversity.
>
> In the Proclamation, we reaffirm our steadfast commitment to the principles enshrined in the United Nations Charter and in International Law to settle disputes by peaceful means, and our belief that full respect for the inalienable right of every State to choose their political, economic, social and cultural system is an essential premise to ensure peaceful coexistence between nations. We advocate the application of these principles in other States' relations with our region."
>
> —Raúl Castro, from a statement to the United Nations, 2015

In 2016 travel restrictions were lifted for Americans making educational visits to Cuba. Additionally, as the United States's trade embargo with Cuba requires U.S. congressional approval to end, President Obama issued a presidential directive to lift some restrictions. The directive in part allows online sales of consumer goods to Cubans and lifts the monetary limit on the amount of Cuban products Americans can bring to the United States for personal use.

MAKING CONNECTIONS TO SPORTS

## CUBA AND BASEBALL

Despite the fact that normalization of relations between Cuba and the United States has begun only recently, the two countries have shared a common pastime for centuries: baseball. Baseball arrived in Cuba in 1864, when Cubans studying in the United States were introduced to it. Cuba developed its own professional baseball league, although professional sports were abolished when Fidel Castro came to power and the league turned amateur. Over the years, dozens of Major League Baseball players have defected from Cuba to play professionally in the United States. In recent decades, baseball games have mirrored thawing relations between the countries. In 1999, the Baltimore Orioles played a Cuban baseball team in Havana—the first time the two countries had played against each other on Cuban soil in 40 years.

**ASSESSING** Why might the Orioles have been allowed to play baseball in Havana after a 40-year absence of American teams in Cuba?

## HAITI AND THE DOMINICAN REPUBLIC

The countries of Haiti and the Dominican Republic share the small island of Hispaniola in the Caribbean but are very different countries. Haiti remains an extremely resource-poor nation—one of the poorest in the world. The country, still recovering from the devastating effects of the 2010 earthquake that killed more than 230,000 people and injured more than 300,000 people, faces more obstacles to recovery after Hurricane Matthew devastated crops, destroyed homes, and left towns under several feet of water in 2016.

*Haiti was devastated by the 2010 earthquake. Many structures became uninhabitable and thousands became homeless.*

**DETERMINING CONTEXT** Haiti is the poorest country in the Western Hemisphere. Explain how this affects its recovery from natural disasters such as the 2010 earthquake.

The Dominican Republic has fared better than its western neighbor. The economy of the Dominican Republic relies on tourism and **remittances** from Dominicans abroad. Since the 1990s, democracy has increased in the Dominican Republic.

A recent controversy between Haiti and the Dominican Republic stems from the implementation of an immigration law by the Dominican government. In 2015 the government began deporting Haitians who were unable to prove their Dominican citizenship.

**DETERMINING MEANING**

Read the paragraph that contains the word **remittance**. How does the content of the paragraph help you figure out what *remittance* means?

## EL SALVADOR

Beginning in 1989, conservatives ruled El Salvador. In 2004 President Antonio Saca became El Salvador's fourth-consecutive president from the National Republican Alliance (ARENA) party.

This conservative streak ended in 2009 when the Farabundo Martí National Liberation Front (FMLN) candidate, television journalist Mauricio Funes, became president. He was the first president to acknowledge the crimes committed during El Salvador's bloody civil war, including the murder of Archbishop Oscar Romero. In 2012 El Salvador's high murder rate began to decline following a truce between rival gangs, only to increase again as the truce fell apart. In 2014 Funes's vice president, Salvador Sánchez Cerén, a former schoolteacher and left-wing guerrilla commander during the civil war, became president. Gang violence and poverty continue to challenge the country.

U.S. Air Force photo by Tech. Sgt. James L. Harper Jr.

## RELIGIOUS CHANGE IN LATIN AMERICA

Although Catholicism is the predominant religion in Latin America, Protestantism has increased dramatically in recent decades.

1. **INTEGRATING INFORMATION** Use the information in the bar graph to write a paragraph about the prevalence of different religions in Latin America today. You may use rounded numbers.
2. **ANALYZING CHANGE** What recent trends appear to be taking place in Latin American religion?

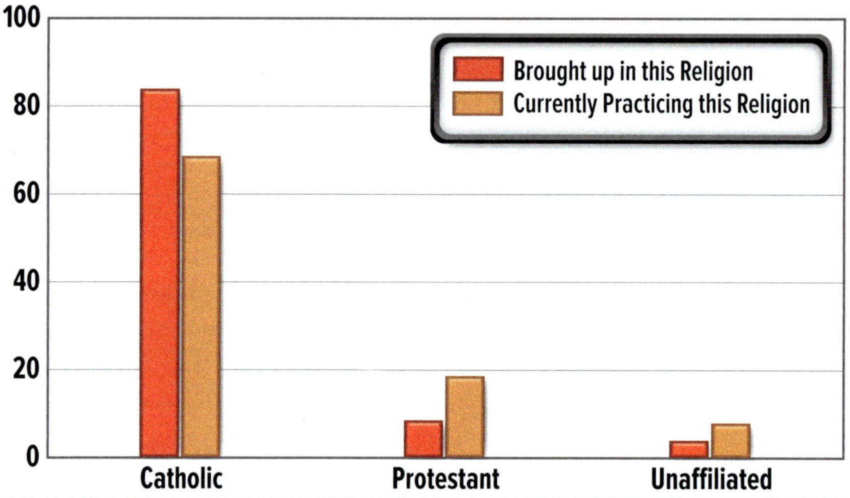


## HONDURAS

After the human rights abuses committed by the armed forces during the 1980s, Honduras began the process of demilitarizing in the 1990s. In 1993 Liberal Party candidate Carlos Reina was elected president and pledged to begin the process of limiting the power of the police forces and armed forces to prevent future abuses. The country was devastated by Hurricane Mitch in 1998. It was a huge economic setback and only increased income inequality and poverty in Honduras. In response, large numbers of migrants left the country.

In 2005 Manuel Zelaya of the Liberal Party became president. In June 2009, Zelaya sought to change the constitution to allow him to serve a second term. The Honduran military forcibly removed him from office in a coup and forced him to go into exile. There was international condemnation of the coup, and many countries temporarily suspended diplomatic ties with Honduras. Porfirio Lobo Sosa of the National Party won the presidential election later that year.

Violence from gangs and police forces continued to be a problem in the 2000s. More than 1,500 homeless children who lived on the streets were murdered—some allegedly with the participation of the police or security forces. Fighting between rival street gangs, including Mara Salvatrucha and the 18th Street gang, has led to escalating violence within the country. Kidnappings for ransom are also frequent. President Juan Orlando Hernández—a conservative—began office in 2014. At the time, Honduras had the highest murder rate in the world. Honduras continues to experience internal challenges, including corruption within the national police force, which led to the removal of many high-ranking police officials in 2016.

### ☑ CHECKING FOR UNDERSTANDING

1. **IDENTIFYING CONNECTIONS** How have social and political issues affected Caribbean and South American countries since the end of the Cold War?
2. **DETERMINING CONTEXT** How has the leadership of Raúl Castro changed the relationship between the United States and Cuba?
3. **EXPLAINING EFFECTS** How has political violence affected El Salvador and Honduras?

## SOUTH AMERICA

**GUIDING QUESTION** *How have economic issues affected South American countries since the end of the Cold War?*

Dominated by the Amazon River and the Andes Mountains, South America contains large amounts of mineral deposits and natural resources. Unfortunately, these resources are highly localized, resulting in great income disparity not only between countries but also within countries as a small percentage of people control the resources. Programs for increased public education and greater economic growth have helped alleviate one of South America's greatest challenges, income inequality, or the large gap between rich and poor.

At the end of the 1990s and first decade of the 2000s, a noticeable political trend has been the election of left-wing governments. Bolivia, Paraguay, and Peru elected populist leaders. Argentina's election of a conservative president in 2015 went against this trend. Most, but not all, of these countries have pushed for democratic freedoms, social reforms, and economic growth.

### PERU

In 1990 Peruvians chose Alberto Fujimoro as president. Fujimoro, the son of Japanese immigrants, promised reforms. However, he later suspended the constitution and congress, became a dictator, and began a campaign against the Shining Path guerrillas. Corruption led to Fujimoro's removal from power in 2000.

**UNDERSTANDING CRAFT AND STRUCTURE**

**DETERMINING MEANING** Reread the first two paragraphs under the heading "Argentina." The word *default* is used a few times in this section. What does the word *default* mean in this context?

**GEOGRAPHIC REASONING**

1. **SPATIAL THINKING** Which South American countries have the highest GDP per capita? Explain the reasons this might be the case for at least two of these countries.
2. **SPATIAL THINKING** Which South American countries have the lowest GDP per capita? Explain the reasons this might be the case for at least two of these countries.

**SOUTH AMERICA: GDP PER CAPITA 2014**

In June 2001, Alejandro Toledo became Peru's first freely elected president of indigenous descent. His successor, Alan García Pérez, sought to increase employment and to decrease poverty to make Peru more economically stable.

Ollanta Humala became president of Peru in 2011. President Humala is a former military officer who led the military revolt against President Fujimoro in 2000 that saw Fujimoro's removal. Humala has taken a moderate stance in office. The Peruvian economy has experienced healthy GDP growth and low inflation. In a close election, Pedro Pablo Kuczynski Godard, who previously served as prime minister of Peru, became president in 2016.

BIOGRAPHY

### MICHELLE BACHELET
**(1951– )**

Michelle Bachelet was born into a political family. Her father was a member of President Salvador Allende's government and was imprisoned and tortured by the regime of Augusto Pinochet. He died in jail. In 1975 she was kidnapped and tortured and then went into exile. She later returned to Chile, completed her studies in medicine, and became a pediatrician. She became involved in government service after becoming active with the Socialist Party. Michelle Bachelet was the first woman to be elected president of Chile. From 2006 to 2010, Bachelet focused on improving the social and health conditions of Chileans. After a few years as head of United Nations Women, she returned as Chile's president in 2014.

**SUMMARIZING** What issues have been prominent in Bachelet's career, political and otherwise?

## ARGENTINA

A severe financial crisis shook Argentina in 2001–2002 that led the Argentine government to default on its debt obligations in 2002. President Néstor Kirchner, a Peronist, served as president from 2003 to 2007. His wife, Cristina Fernández de Kirchner, was elected to two consecutive terms as president. Their politics became known as Kirchnerism—a leftist faction of Peronism.

The economy initially improved under President Kirchner. The government refused to pay creditors the full amount owed and worked with creditors in 2005 and again in 2010 to restructure a large portion of the debt it had defaulted on in 2002. But some U.S. creditors refused the debt restructuring plan, which forced Argentina back into default in 2014. At the same time, inflation began to rise.

In November 2015, in a runoff election, Argentine voters elected Mauricio Macri, the mayor of Buenos Aires and leader of the Republic Proposal, a center-right political party, as president. President Macri is viewed as more supportive of business than his predecessor and in 2016 negotiated settlements of Argentine debts, helping restore stability to the economy.

## BRAZIL

After the Cold War, Brazil began to defer less to foreign powers and moved to become less reliant on imported goods and resources. By using its vast natural resources and improving its industrial sector, Brazil has emerged as the largest economy in Latin America and is a member of G20, an international group focused on issues surrounding the global economy. Brazil plays an increasingly important role in international trade.

Over the last decade, Brazil has played a growing role in both regional and global affairs. Brazil, with the largest military in South America, is seen as the dominant power in the region. However, Brazil's position as the leading economy in the region is the major factor in its dominance. Other countries in South America are somewhat dependent not only on its economy but also its resources. Itaipu Dam, jointly owned by Paraguay and Brazil, provides Paraguay with 75 percent of its electricity. Brazil is also securing dominance on a global level. A leading economist grouped Brazil with Russia, India, and China (BRIC) as poised to become the world's largest suppliers of raw materials and manufactured goods and services by 2050. These countries have the capacity to form a powerful economic alliance, and although no trade agreements have been made, the countries have discussed what would mutually benefit their countries at economic summits.

In 2002 Brazil elected Luiz Inácio Lula da Silva, its first left-wing president in four decades. President Lula da Silva pursued a policy of increased trade and educational reform. He expanded the middle class and created new consumers while continuing to increase exports. Brazil successfully decreased its foreign debt and had record trade surpluses from 2003 to 2007.

His successor, Dilma Rousseff, was elected in 2010 and became the first woman president of Brazil. As President Rousseff began her second term in office, the Brazilian economy went into recession. Political scandals in Rousseff's administration led to her impeachment in 2016. Michel Temer replaced her.

## CHILE

Chile has seen unprecedented economic growth and a low rate of inflation. Chile has signed trade agreements with more than 57 entities, including the United States, China, and the European Union.

President Michelle Bachelet was Chile's first female president. During her first term in office, from 2006 to 2010, she used revenue from copper resources to **fund** social programs for women and children. In her second term, she continued to focus on policies designed to decrease income inequality. However, the issue persists as hundreds of thousands of protesters demanded a reorganization of the country's pension plan in 2016 as pensioners were receiving less than the minimum wage, with nearly half living below the poverty line.

**DETERMINING MEANING**

Reread the paragraph that contains the word **fund**. Write a definition for the word *fund* in your own words, then check your definition, using a dictionary or online resource.

### ☑ CHECKING FOR UNDERSTANDING

1. **EXPLAINING EFFECTS** How have economic issues affected South American countries since the end of the Cold War?
2. **EXPLAINING EFFECTS** Why did Argentina fall back into default after an initial improvement of its economy?
3. **RELATING EVENTS** Which South American countries had female presidents during the 2000s?

## LESSON 4 REVIEW

### Time and Place

1. **RELATING EVENTS** How are recent issues in South American countries similar to or different from those in Central American countries and the Caribbean?

### Building History-Social Science Analysis Skills

2. **EXPLAINING EFFECTS** What have been some of the long-term effects of poverty in Central and South America?
3. **IDENTIFYING CONNECTIONS** How do the economies of Haiti and the Dominican Republic primarily differ?
4. **CONTRASTING** Describe at least one primary difference between Mexico and Cuba in the post-Cold War world, as described in the text.

### Writing About History

5. **INFORMATIVE WRITING** Select one of the Latin American countries discussed in this lesson. Conduct outside research about the current political and economic situation in the country you chose. Write a one-page fact sheet describing the current political administration, the level of democracy in the country, and the state of the economy

### Collaborating

6. **COLLABORATING** With a partner, discuss the movements for democratic freedoms, social reforms, and economic growth in South America in recent decades.

## ESSENTIAL QUESTIONS

- *What motivates political change?*
- *How can economic and social changes affect a country?*

LESSON 5

# The Middle East and Africa

## THE STORY BEGINS...

Although numerous factors in international relations shifted after the Cold War, the peace that would allow for nation building in the Middle East has still proved largely elusive. Conflict and violence are far too common, particularly under the rule of harsh dictatorships. During the Arab Spring, a series of democratic uprisings occurring independently in numerous countries in 2010 and 2011, many citizens rebelled against dictatorships. Some people, such as Deborah A. McCarthy, saw this as a reflection of economic conditions:

> "The Arab Spring was born in part from economic imbalance. Creating the critical infrastructure that facilitates investment, job creation, and entrepreneurial success is an essential part of producing new opportunities to correct this challenge, which countries across North Africa are facing."

—Deborah A. McCarthy, Principal Deputy Assistant Secretary, Bureau of Economic and Business Affairs, National Council on U.S. Arab Relations, Infrastructure and Business Opportunities in North Africa Event, 2012

Nevertheless, inequality and conflict remain present in the Middle East, where many still fight for freedom and democracy today.

*Protests in many parts of the Arab world, like these in Cairo, Egypt's Tahrir Square, characterized the widespread revolutions of the Arab Spring.* ▶

| Causes for Arab Spring Uprisings | |
|---|---|
| Country | Causes |
| Egypt | |
| Libya | |
| Syria | |

### ANALYZING KEY IDEAS AND DETAILS

**IDENTIFYING CAUSES** Read closely to identify the causes of revolutionary actions in each of the countries discussed during the Arab Spring. Record these causes in a graphic organizer like this one.

# THE MIDDLE EAST

**GUIDING QUESTION** *What changes have occurred in the Middle East since the 1990s?*

Arid deserts dominate the landscape of the Middle East. These geographic features continue to play a central role in the development of Middle Eastern countries, second only to the region's vast oil reserves. The Organization of the Petroleum Exporting Countries (OPEC), established in 1960 to organize policies surrounding oil prices and production, has 12 member countries but is dominated by those in the Middle East. Middle Eastern countries hold well over half of all OPEC oil reserves. This dominance as a supplier of oil to countries around the world has led to challenges and conflicts both within and outside the region. The economies of many countries are dependent on the political and economic decisions made by oil-rich Middle Eastern countries. The volatility of the region is also a concern as many countries struggle with internal political issues. There are signs of hope that more countries will move toward democratic societies.

### ANALYZING KEY IDEAS AND DETAILS

1. **SUMMARIZING** Summarize the major causes of recent conflicts in the Middle East in two to three sentences.
2. **CITING TEXT EVIDENCE** The first sentence of the first paragraph under the heading "Iran" states that the country "remains under the control of Muslim clerics." What evidence in this paragraph partially contradicts this assertion?

## ISRAELI-PALESTINIAN CONFLICT

Efforts to reach a peace agreement between the Israelis and the Palestinians, represented by the PLO (Palestine Liberation Organization), have failed due to continued terrorist attacks and disputes over territory, especially Jerusalem. Since the signing of the Oslo Peace Accords in 1993, the peace process has seen more setbacks than not.

In 2000 U.S. President Bill Clinton arranged a meeting at Camp David. The Palestinians rejected a proposal offered by Israel at this meeting, and a second intifada soon erupted. Suicide bombings in the heart of Israel led to Israeli reoccupation of significant areas of the West Bank that had been largely controlled by the Palestinian Authority. Nonetheless, a sign of progress emerged in 2003—the Israeli cabinet formally accepted the principle of a Palestinian state.

PLO leader Yasir Arafat died in 2004, and Mahmoud Abbas, a moderate member of Fatah, the moderate political party that replaced the PLO, succeeded him. In 2005 Israel withdrew from Gaza, and many hoped for real progress toward peace.

In January 2006, however, members of Hamas, a Palestinian resistance movement that rejects Israel's right to exist, won a majority of the seats in parliament. Abbas remained president, but Hamas controlled parliament. In June 2007, Hamas took control of Gaza, and Abbas dissolved the government. With Hamas out of power, Israel resumed peace talks with Abbas. These talks have not borne fruit, and three brief wars ensued between Israel and Hamas in Gaza following rocket attacks on Israeli civilian areas. There have been several attempts for Hamas and Fatah to form a unity government. Israel opposed these efforts because Hamas denies its right to exist, and internal Palestinian differences added additional difficulties.

In 2015 Palestinian Prime Minister Mahmoud Abbas declared before the UN General Assembly that he was no longer bound by past agreements with Israel. He thus cautioned the international community that he was prepared to end the Oslo agreement if steps were not taken toward the establishment of a Palestinian state.

## IRAN

Iran, an oil-rich country, remains under the control of Muslim clerics, who enforce strict adherence to Islamic law. They limit the rights of women and the right to free assembly and a free press. In 2009, following the reelection of Mahmoud Ahmadinejad, hundreds of thousands of Iranians protested the outcome and declared the election a fraud. The violent oppression of the protesters by the Iranian military was captured on cell phones and posted on the Internet. Hassan Rouhani was elected president of Iran in 2013 and began a course of action to improve relations with the West.

In 2015 a nuclear deal was signed among Iran, the United States, the United Kingdom, Russia, France, China, and Germany. The agreement is complex: To simplify, Iran agreed to limit its nuclear development and to accept increased oversight by the international community. The other parties agreed to reduce and eventually remove financial sanctions against Iran.

**GEOGRAPHIC REASONING**

**HUMAN-ENVIRONMENT INTERACTION** How do Saudi Arabia's geography and natural resources benefit it in international trade?

**THE MIDDLE EAST TODAY**

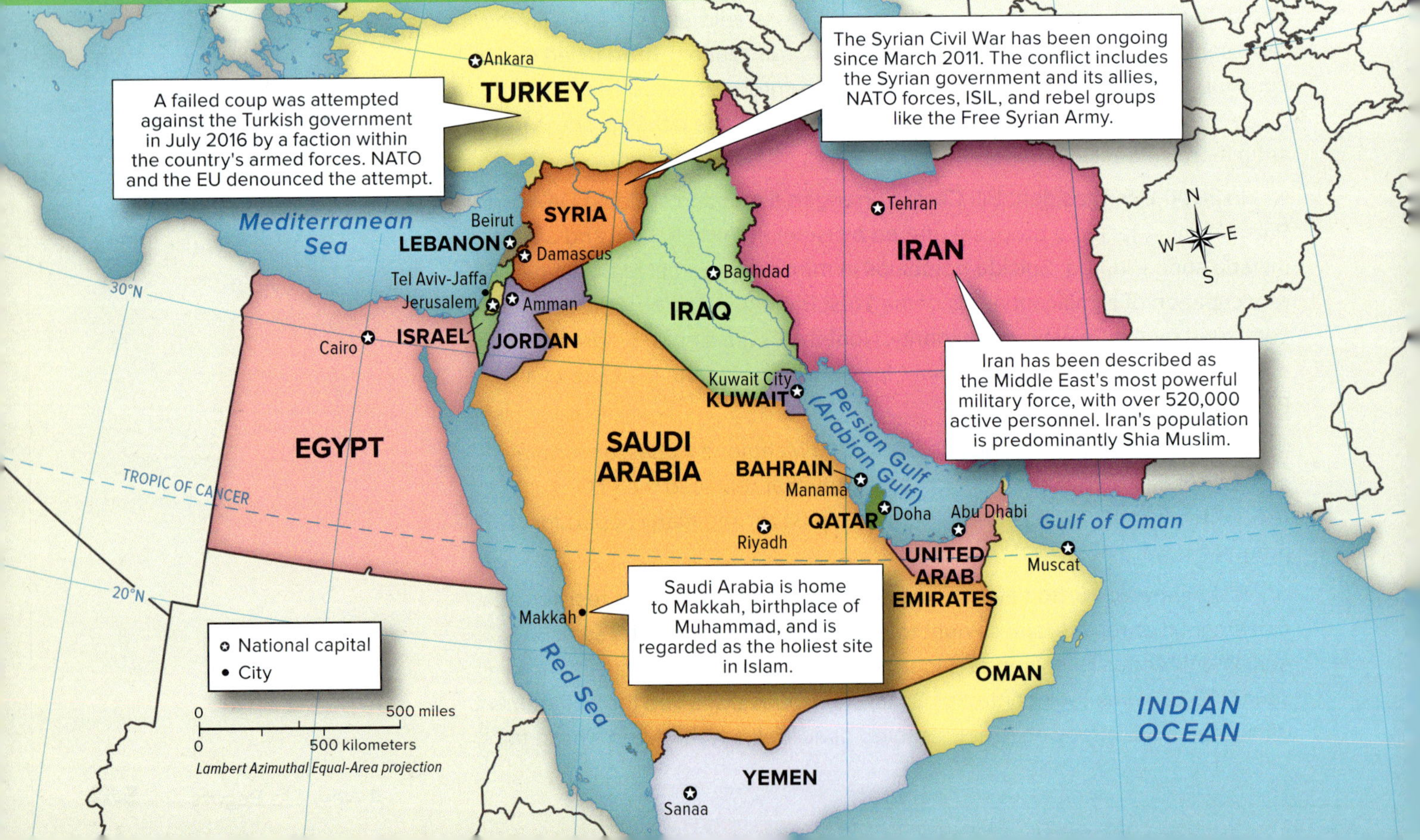

## CRUDE OIL AND NATURAL GAS RESERVES IN THE MIDDLE EAST AND AFRICA

The first bar graph shows the countries in the Middle East and Africa with the highest crude oil reserves. The second bar graph shows the countries in the Middle East and Africa with the highest natural gas reserves. The countries with two asterisks are members of OPEC.

1. **IDENTIFYING CONNECTIONS** How does the oil supply of a country relate to its supply of natural gas? Does an abundance of one signify the presence of the other?
2. **DETERMINING CONTEXT** Explore more resources by researching which countries in the charts are members of OPEC. Create a list of OPEC members in the Middle East and Africa.

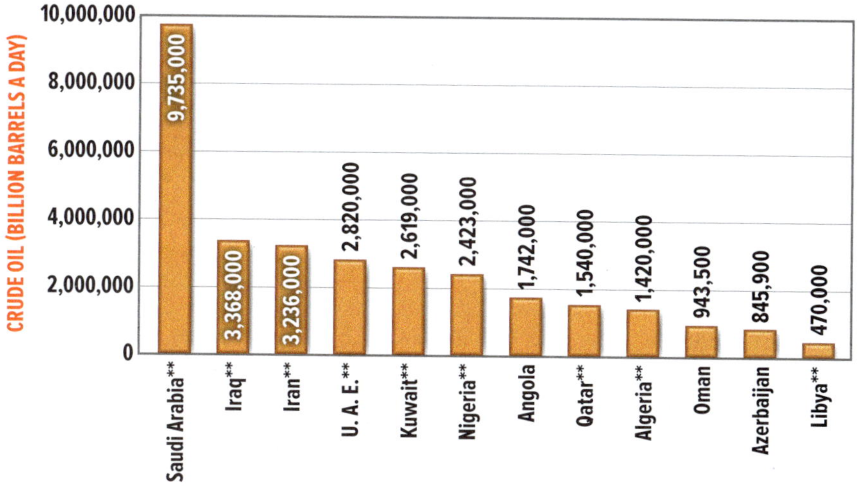


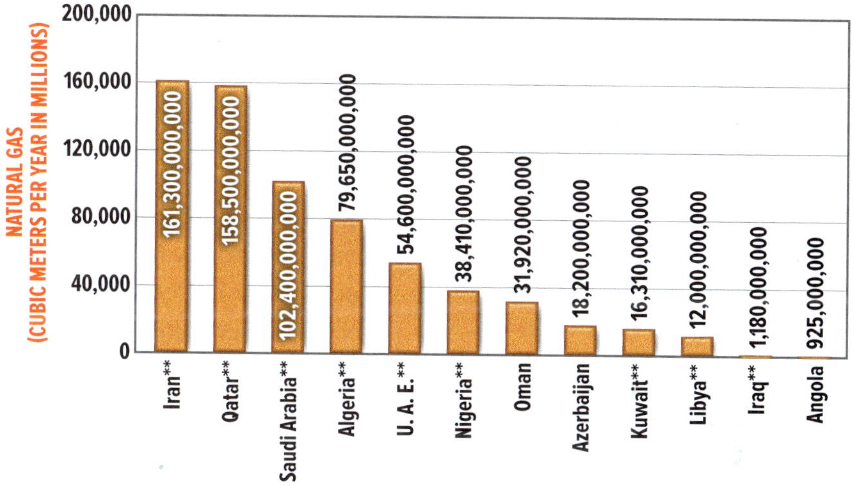


** OPEC Members

**Source:** U.S. Dept. Of Energy Energy Information Administration (Oil & Gas Journal Data)

## AFGHANISTAN AND IRAQ

After the terrorist attacks on the World Trade Center on September 11, 2001, the United States invaded Afghanistan in 2001 and Iraq in 2003. Under the control of the Taliban, Afghanistan was harboring Osama bin Laden, the head of al-Qaeda, who was responsible for the attacks. In 2011 U.S. forces killed bin Laden in Pakistan. A deal was signed between Afghanistan and the United States for thousands of U.S. and NATO troops to remain in the country past 2014. Although the 2014 election results were disputed, there was a high voter turnout, even among women, who were banned from voting under the Taliban.

After the invasion of Iraq by the United States and its allies, the country fell into civil war between the Shia Muslims, who controlled southern Iraq, and the Sunni Muslims, who controlled central Iraq. Elections held in 2010 led to the election of Prime Minister Nuri Kamal al-Maliki, a Shia Muslim, eight months later. U.S. troops withdrew in 2011. Violence intensified in the country in 2013, and in 2014 the military forces of ISIL (Islamic State of Iraq and the Levant) began to seize and occupy parts of Iraq. Thousands were killed. In 2014 Nuri Kamal al-Maliki stepped down, and Haider al-Abadi became prime minister.

## ✓ CHECKING FOR UNDERSTANDING

1. **UNDERSTANDING CHANGE** What changes have occurred in the Middle East since the 1990s?
2. **IDENTIFYING CONNECTIONS** What is similar about the status of women in Iran, Afghanistan, and Iraq, as described in the text?
3. **UNDERSTANDING CONTEXT** What did Iran agree to in the nuclear deal it signed in 2015?

# THE ARAB SPRING

**GUIDING QUESTION** *What were the causes and effects of the Arab Spring?*

An immense uprising rocked North Africa and led to a regime change in Tunisia and Egypt. Most countries in the region have a high percentage of young people; more than half of Egypt's 80 million people are under the age of 25. Most of these young people are unemployed. After 23 years of oppressive government, Tunisian president Zine el-Abidine Ben Ali fled the country following mass protests that began in December 2010. Other protests in the region soon followed. These changes are known as the Arab Spring.

**ANALYZING KEY IDEAS AND DETAILS**

1. **CITING TEXT EVIDENCE** What words and phrases does the text use to signal the common view of President Hosni Mubarak? What impression does this create of the leader?
2. **SUMMARIZING** Summarize how dictatorships in the Middle East and North Africa contributed to events of the Arab Spring.

## EGYPT

In Egypt an oppressive regime under President Hosni Mubarak maintained power through a large security force, which used torture and brutality to suppress any political opposition. By January 28, 2011, hundreds of thousands of Egyptians, including women, from all walks of life flooded Tahrir (meaning Liberation) Square in the downtown section of the city of Cairo. Protesters used social networking and media sites and tools to organize protests. After 18 days of sometimes violent retaliation by Mubarak's secret police forces, the Egyptian army ultimately sided with the protesters, leaving Mubarak with little choice but to leave the country.

*Antigovernment demonstrators in Tahrir Square in Cairo demand the resignation of Egyptian president Hosni Mubarak.*

**UNDERSTANDING CONTEXT** What characterized antigovernment demonstrations of the Arab Spring?

John Moore/Getty Images News/Getty Images

Since the uprising, Egypt has sentenced its former president to life in prison. Elections were held in June 2012, and Egyptians elected Muslim Brotherhood candidate Mohammed Morsi. As president, Morsi suspended much of the Egyptian constitution, resulting in many new unlimited powers for the office of president. Protesters again took to the streets, calling for Morsi's resignation.

Under the leadership of Abdel Fattah el-Sisi, the Egyptian army settled the question by taking over the government in a 2013 coup. In new elections in 2014 that were probably rigged, Sisi was elected president of Egypt. The 2016 swearing in of a new parliament, which supports Sisi's restrictive policies, further dampened prospects for democracy in the country.

## LIBYA

In Libya, protesters rebelled against the authoritarian regime of Colonel Muammar al-Qaddafi. After Colonel Qaddafi's troops began to use force against the protesters, the UN Security Council voted to authorize military action. In March 2011, American and European forces began air strikes against the Qaddafi regime. Libyan rebel forces took control of Tripoli in August, ousting Qaddafi from power. It was not until Qaddafi was killed in October, however, that the creation of a new Libya could begin in earnest. On July 7, 2012, Libya held its first free election since 1952. Mustafa Abushagur was elected prime minister in 2012 but not sworn in. He was quickly removed from office following the terrorist attack by members of the Islamic militant group Ansar al-Sharia on two U.S. government facilities in the city of Benghazi. Fayez Mustafa al-Sarraj currently serves as prime minister, but violence continues as parties struggle for control of the country.

Protests spread throughout the entire region to Algeria, Yemen, Jordan, Bahrain, Oman, Morocco, Saudi Arabia, and Syria. The use of force quickly ended the protests in most of these nations. After decades of conflict, political oppression, and exploitation, the revolutionary upheaval led by young people initially brought hope for a new beginning in the region. Unfortunately, the process of democratization in the region has been halted or even reversed in many countries.

**DETERMINING MEANING**

Reread the paragraph beginning, "In Libya, . . . ." How does this paragraph help you understand the meaning of the word *authoritarian*?

## SYRIA

Many Arab states experienced short-lived violence during the Arab Spring. In Syria this violence erupted into a civil war that continues years after the Arab Spring ended in most of the Arab world. In early 2011, nationwide protests were held against the government of Syrian President Bashar al-Assad. The government responded with brutal crackdowns. As a consequence, the protests shifted into a full rebellion. Different rebel groups have formed, many of which are hostile toward the others. Major rebel groups include the Free Syrian army, who control pockets of territory in the north and west, and the militant group the Islamic State of Iraq and the Levant (ISIL), who control most of eastern Syria. Fighting among these groups and the government continued, although Russian support helped Bashar al-Assad to regain control of most of Syria.

Spencer Platt/Getty Images

*Syrian migrants being assisted by members of the Red Cross as they arrive on the shores of Greece*

**IDENTIFYING CAUSES** What factors have led Syrians to leave their country in large numbers?

## ✓ CHECKING FOR UNDERSTANDING

1. **EXPLAINING CAUSE AND EFFECT** What were the causes and effects of the Arab Spring?
2. **RELATING EVENTS** Where were the first protests of the Arab Spring? What were the effects of these protests?
3. **IDENTIFYING CONNECTIONS** How were the uprisings in Egypt and Libya similar? How were they different?

# AFRICA SOUTH OF THE SAHARA

**GUIDING QUESTION** *What challenges have confronted countries in Africa south of the Sahara since the end of the Cold War?*

The landscape of Africa south of the Sahara changes dramatically from one area to the next, including volcanic mountains, such as Kilimanjaro, the Great Rift Valley, and powerful rivers. The landscape presents unique challenges in development, particularly infrastructure. However, it also houses many natural resources, including oil, gold, and diamonds. Politically, African societies have not yet overcome the challenges they have faced since independence. There are signs of progress toward political stability in some countries. Other nations, however, are still racked by civil war or ruled by brutal dictatorships.

**UNDERSTANDING CRAFT AND STRUCTURE**

1. **DETERMINING MEANING** Reread the paragraph that begins, "Some African nations have mounted an impressive effort to fight AIDS." What does the word *impressive* mean in this context?
2. **ANALYZING TEXT PRESENTATION** How does the writer introduce the topic of religious conflict in Africa south of the Sahara? How does the writer develop this topic from the beginning of this section to the end?

## REGIONAL ORGANIZATIONS

Africans have found ways to address their political problems, to cooperate with one another, and to protect and promote their own interests. In 1991 the Organization of African Unity (OAU) agreed to establish the African Economic Community (AEC). This group is meant to provide greater political and economic integration throughout Africa on the pattern of the European Union. In 2001 the African Union (AU) replaced the OAU. The new organization has sought to mediate several of the conflicts in the region. The AU also promotes democracy and economic growth in Africa.

As Africa evolves, it is important to remember that economic and political change is often a slow and painful process. Introduced to industrialization and ideas of Western democracy only a century ago, African societies are still looking for ways to graft Western political institutions and economic practices onto indigenous structures still influenced by traditional values and attitudes.

**DETERMINING MEANING**

Read the paragraph that begins, "As Africa evolves, . . ." How does the content of the paragraph help you figure out what *evolve* means?

## SOCIAL AND ECONOMIC ISSUES

African countries face many social and economic problems. Rapid population growth has slowed economic growth. In the first decade of the 2000s, Africa's population growth rate was 2.3 percent compared to 1.24 percent in the rest of the world. As a result, poverty remains widespread. Cities have grown tremendously. By 2007, approximately 39 percent of Africans lived in urban areas where there are massive slums and high levels of pollution.

Infrastructure continues to be a problem and requires large amounts of foreign and public investment. Recently, Chinese companies have increased their investment in the region. In 2015 the first light-rail system in Africa south of the Sahara started operations in Ethiopia. Known as the Addis Metro, it opened with 20 miles (32 kilometers) of track and 39 service stations.

*A health counselor teaches South African students about HIV/AIDS prevention.*

Stephane De Sakutin/AFP/Getty Images

Moreover, AIDS remains a serious concern in Africa. More than two-thirds (22.9 million) of all persons infected with HIV are living in Africa south of the Sahara. In this area during 2010, 1.9 million people became infected with HIV and more than 1.2 million died of AIDS.

Some African nations have mounted an impressive effort to fight AIDS. In Uganda, President Yoweri Museveni involved a wide range of national leaders in Ugandan society as well as international health and social service agencies.

> "... through leadership we can overcome the scourge of HIV/AIDS in Africa. The international community has identified Uganda's campaign against HIV/AIDS as one of the world's most successful models in combating the pandemic. In ten years, we have reduced the rate of infection from 30 percent to 6.1 percent, through high profile government solidarity with grass-roots entities to raise awareness, increase prevention and provide treatment for people living with HIV. Across Africa, at least 7,000 people a day are dying of AIDS, and we believe that this urgently demands constructive public-private partnerships to reduce the death rate dramatically through provision of effective anti-retroviral treatments."
>
> —Yoweri Museveni, 2002

Uganda has made significant progress in its fight against AIDS. The number of cases of HIV in Uganda stabilized in the early 2000s.

Despite many challenges, some African nations have seen the standard of living increase moderately since the early 2000s. Countries rich in natural resources have experienced the most growth. Workers in some nations have won wage increases after successful strikes. Continued growth is dependent on many factors, including the price of raw materials on the world market, foreign investment, environmental issues, and the resolution of conflicts within the region.

## POLITICAL TRENDS

Politically, Africa has witnessed a number of women as leaders of their countries. For example, Luisa Diogo became prime minister of Mozambique in 2004. There has also been a trend toward multiparty elections. In Senegal, for example, national elections held in the summer of 2000 brought an end to four decades of rule by the once-dominant Socialist Party. Relatively stable republics, including South Africa, Botswana, and Ghana, help anchor the region. Ghana, one of the first nations to gain independence, experienced tremendous economic growth in the first part of the millennium. Facing economic difficulties, the nation weathered a contentious presidential race in 2016 to elect Anan Akufo-Addo in a successful test of the country's democracy.

The Democratic Republic of the Congo is a vast country with a large number of natural resources, the control of which has contributed to a long civil war and ongoing conflict. Political factors have also contributed to the country's long history of violence. Joseph Kabila became president when his father, Laurent, was assassinated in 2001. He was then elected in 2006 and reelected in 2011, although both elections were controversial.

As Kabila's mandate to rule was set to expire at the end of 2016, Kabila made an agreement with the opposition party to delay the presidential vote until 2018. However, the death of opposition leader Étienne Tshisekedi in 2017 crushed any hopes of Kabila stepping down. Violence within the country continues to escalate as militia groups are clashing with Kabila's military and police forces.

### DETERMINING MEANING

The text about Africa's social and economic issues states, "Infrastructure continues to be a problem. . . ." What does the word *infrastructure* mean in this context?

### ANALYZING PRIMARY SOURCES

1. **IDENTIFYING CONNECTIONS** What approach does President Museveni believe has been most responsible for Uganda's success in its fight against AIDS?
2. **UNDERSTANDING CONTEXT** Based on the words Museveni uses in the final sentence of this excerpt, how does he view the need for further action?

Museveni, Yoweri. 2002. Speech by His Excellency Yoweri Museveni President of the Republic of Uganda. May 14, 2002. Woodrow Wilson International Center for Scholars.

MAKING CONNECTIONS TO TODAY

## CASE STUDY: BOTSWANA

Although many countries in Africa south of the Sahara suffered in the global financial crisis of the 2000s, in Botswana, standards of living continued to rise. Over the last several decades, the per-capita income in Botswana saw a dramatic increase, growing from $70 to $16,900. How has Botswana accomplished this? The answer appears to be a combination of low birthrates and a rapid adoption of new forms of technology. In both cases, engaged citizens have been the key to prosperity.

Botswana has a very active civil society with numerous civil rights, human rights, and youth participation organizations. Furthermore, the combination of valuable natural resources, including diamonds and minerals, and strong leadership led Botswana to an average annual income increase of 6.3 percent annually from 1970 to 2010. In comparison, relatively high-income countries grew at around 1.8 percent in this same time period.

## RELIGIOUS CONFLICT

Religion has played a role in dividing parts of Africa. An Islamic resurgence was evident in a number of African countries. It surfaced in Ethiopia where Muslim tribespeople rebelled against a Marxist regime and eventually established an independent Eritrea.

More recently, in Nigeria and other nations of West Africa, divisions between Muslims and Christians have erupted into violence. In the early 2000s, riots between Christians and Muslims broke out in several northern cities as a result of the decision by Muslim local officials to apply Islamic law throughout their **jurisdictions**. The violence has lessened as local officials managed to craft compromise policies that limit some of the harsher aspects of Muslim law. Nevertheless, the dispute continues to threaten the fragile unity of Nigeria, Africa's most populous country.

**DETERMINING MEANING**

The roots of the word **jurisdiction** are the Latin *juris*, meaning "right or law," and *diction*, meaning "to say." How does knowing the roots of *jurisdiction* help you determine its meaning?

The religious tensions that erupted in Nigeria have spilled over into neighboring states. Under its first president, Felix Houphouet-Boigny, Côte d'Ivoire (Ivory Coast) was often seen as a model of religious and ethnic harmony. But his death in 1993 led to an outbreak of long-simmering resentment between Christians in the south and Muslim immigrants in the north. Elections held in 2000 resulted in the election of a Christian president. Violence and widespread charges of voting irregularities marked the elections.

In 2002, an armed uprising split the nation into a Muslim, rebel-dominated north and a Christian, government-controlled south. A power-sharing deal brought temporary peace in 2007. It was also believed that a presidential election in November 2010 might bring a new unity. Laurent Gbagbo, who had been president since 2000, lost to Alassane Ouattara, who was declared the winner by the United Nations. Gbagbo used the army in an attempt to stay in power, while UN peacekeeping forces guarded Ouattara. Gbagbo's forces terrorized civilians to remain in power. A peaceful march of unarmed women, for example, was stopped by machine gun fire from Gbagbo's armed followers. In November 2011, Gbagbo was arrested for crimes against humanity and placed in detention by the International Criminal Court. His trial, along with that of political leader Charles Blé Goudé, began in March 2017.

A suburb of Abidjan shows the aftermath of the fighting that followed the 2010 election in Côte d'Ivoire.

**IDENTIFYING EFFECTS** What were the consequences of the 2010 election in Côte d'Ivoire?



As in other African countries, civil war devastated the economy of Côte d'Ivoire. Food shortages and massive unemployment were widespread. The peaceful reelection of President Alassane Ouattara in 2015 reinforced the political stability of the country. The government adopted a new National Development Plan in 2016 that is projected to continue the rapid recovery of the economy that began in 2012. However, the nation was rocked by a terrorist attack in 2016 that was carried out by members of al-Qaeda at the beach resort in Grand-Bassam, killing 22 people.

### ✓ CHECKING FOR UNDERSTANDING

1. **UNDERSTANDING CONTEXT** What challenges have confronted countries in Africa south of the Sahara since the Cold War?
2. **RELATING EVENTS** What events make it unlikely that Joseph Kabila will step down from the presidency of the Democratic Republic of the Congo?
3. **EXPLAINING CAUSES** What role has religion played in recent African conflicts?

## LESSON 5 REVIEW

### Time and Place

1. **EXPLAINING EFFECTS** How have unstable governments contributed to social problems in the Middle East and Africa?

### Building History-Social Science Analysis Skills

2. **IDENTIFYING CONNECTIONS** How has the rise of Hamas affected the negotiation of peace talks between Israelis and Palestinians?
3. **INTERPRETING** The text states that "economic and political change is often a slow and painful process." What textual evidence about Africa south of the Sahara supports this claim?
4. **ANALYZING INFORMATION** Describe the attempts of different organizations to fight the spread of AIDS in Africa. How successful have these approaches been?

### Writing About History

5. **ARGUMENTATIVE WRITING** Do you think the uprisings in North Africa in 2009 and 2010 would have been as effective without the use of social networking sites? Why or why not?

### Collaborating

6. **PRESENTING** With a partner, create a 5–10-minute presentation in which you explain the Arab Spring and the events that took place in each country involved.

# STUDY GUIDE

## GORBACHEV'S REFORMS
### LESSON 1

- Urged the need for radical reforms based on **perestroika** (restructuring)
- Set up a new **Soviet parliament** of elected members
- Sought political reform through **glasnost** (a policy that encouraged openness)
- Created a new **state presidency** and became the Soviet Union's first and last president
- Stopped giving **Soviet military support** to Communist governments in Eastern Europe
- Made an agreement with the United States in 1987, the **Intermediate-Range INF Treaty**

## PROBLEMS AFTER THE REUNIFICATION OF GERMANY
### LESSON 2

- More money was needed to rebuild eastern Germany.
- The government was forced to raise taxes.
- The collapse of the economy in eastern Germany led to high unemployment and discontent.
- The Social Democrats were unable to solve Germany's economic problems.
- There were increasing attacks on foreigners, especially immigrant groups.

## THE LEADERS OF NORTH KOREA
### LESSON 3

| Kim Il Sung (1948–1994) | Kim Jong Il (1994–2011) | Kim Jong Un (2011– ) |
|---|---|---|

Under all three leaders in its history, North Korea has been ruled under a **communist military dictatorship** and remained an **isolated country**.

## DRUG TRADE VIOLENCE IN MEXICO
### LESSON 4

- President Felipe Calderón ordered a military response against Mexico's drug gangs in 2006, but the violence only increased.
- Between 2007 and 2014, more than 164,000 people were killed in Mexico's drug war. In 2011, 27,000 people were killed.
- President Peña Nieto has continued Calderón's approach to the drug war since coming to office in 2012. The violence has continued.

## THE MIDDLE EAST
### LESSON 5

**IRAN**

In 2015 the Iran nuclear deal was signed by Iran, the United States, the United Kingdom, Russia, France, China, and Germany. The agreement significantly decreased Iran's ability to develop nuclear weapons, and the countries involved agreed to eventually remove sanctions against Iran.

**IRAQ**

After the United States and its allies invaded Iraq, a civil war began between Sunni Muslims and Shia Muslims. In 2011 U.S. troops withdrew from Iraq, but violence intensified in 2013 and 2014 as the military forces of ISIL (Islamic State of Iraq and the Levant) began to seize and occupy parts of Iraq.

# CHAPTER 15 Assessment

**Directions: On a separate sheet of paper, answer the questions below. Make sure you read carefully and answer all parts of the questions.**

## Short Answer

1. **SUMMARIZING** Explain Gorbachev's role in the fall of communism. Why do you think Gorbachev believed for his economic reforms to be successful, there would also need to be a policy of *glasnost*?

2. **IDENTIFYING CAUSES** What factors led to Russia's economic growth in the early 2000s?

3. **UNDERSTANDING CONTEXT** Why did budget deficits emerge in the United States in the 1980s?

4. **EXPLAINING EFFECTS** How did the reality of German reunification fail to live up to the visions activists had had for it?

5. **SUMMARIZING** Describe the agricultural policy that helped China move into the Industrial Age and improve its economy.

6. **DETERMINING CONTEXT** What challenges confronted President Musharraf when he took control of Pakistan?

7. **DETERMINING CONTEXT** Why was the 2000 election of Vicente Fox in Mexico a significant political shift?

8. **EXPLAINING EFFECTS** Although much changed in Cuba after the fall of the Soviet Union, certain institutions and structures remained stable. How did they do so?

9. **IDENTIFYING CAUSES** Why does infrastructure present a challenge for developing nations in Africa?

10. **IDENTIFYING CONNECTIONS** How did political unrest affect Libya in 2011, and how did the international community respond?

## History and Social-Science Analysis

11. **USING MAPS** Create an illustrated or digital map showing Germany before and after its reunification in 1990. Include former and current capitals and a map key with any population data available.

12. **EXPLAINING EFFECTS** How did the reunification of Germany lead to economic problems? Explain why these challenges were likely inevitable.

13. **DETERMINING CONTEXT** What happened to the territory of Yugoslavia by 2009?

14. **EXPLAINING CAUSES** What led to the breakup of Yugoslavia? In your answer, describe the event that caused NATO to support Bosnian and Croatian forces.

15. **UNDERSTANDING CHANGE** Describe the leadership changes in Pakistan from the years 1993 through 2013. What accounted for these changes in leadership?

16. **ANALYZING CHANGE** Why did China end its one-child policy? What replaced it?

17. **DESCRIBING** With a partner or in a small group, select a country or region discussed in the chapter, and create a chronological multimedia presentation showing political, economic, social, and geographic changes that have occurred in the country or region since the end of the Cold War. Be sure to indicate how the country or region was affected.

Use this table to answer the following question.

**Selected Events in the Middle East and North Africa 2001–2015**

| Date | Event |
|---|---|
| October 2001 | U.S. forces invade Afghanistan |
| March 2003 | U.S. forces invade Iraq |
| December 2006 | The UN imposes economic sanctions on Iran for its nuclear program |
| June 2007 | Hamas takes control of Gaza |
| March 2011 | U.S. and European forces begin air strikes in Libya |
| July 2012 | Libya holds first free election since 1952 |
| July 2013 | Egyptian army takes over government in coup d'état |
| June 2014 | ISIL occupies parts of northern Iraq |
| July 2015 | Iran nuclear deal signed |
| December 2015 | U.S.-led strikes against ISIL in Syria |

**Need Extra Help?**

| If You've Missed Question | 1 | 2 | 3 | 4 | 5 | 6 | 7 | 8 | 9 | 10 | 11 | 12 | 13 | 14 | 15 | 16 | 17 |
|---|---|---|---|---|---|---|---|---|---|---|---|---|---|---|---|---|---|
| Review Lesson | 1 | 1 | 2 | 2 | 3 | 3 | 4 | 4 | 5 | 5 | 2 | 2 | 2 | 2 | 3 | 3 | 1–5 |

 **Assessment,** continued

**18** **ANALYZING CHANGE** Use the information in the table to create an annotated time line with photographs and primary source excerpts. Extend the information in the time line to the present.

**19** **ANALYZING SOURCES** Using the map of South America in Lesson 4, evaluate the three countries with the highest GDP per capita. What might be some of the causes of these high GDPs?

**20** **COMPARING AND CONTRASTING** How are the revolutions of the Arab Spring similar to and different from the independence movements of Eastern European Soviet states?

## Research and Presentation

**21** **COMPARING AND CONTRASTING** Research the 1990s conflicts in the Balkans. How does knowledge of this conflict provide you with context for better understanding the nationalist movements in Europe? Write an essay in which you compare the pre-World War I conflicts in the Balkans to the events that took place in those states in the late twentieth century. Then, present your essay to the class.

## Analyzing Primary Sources

Use the document to answer the following questions.

Boris Yeltsin was president of Russia after Gorbachev stepped down. While in office, Yeltsin grappled with the problems of a post-Soviet Russian economy and society. At the end of his term, he made the following statement. Use the document to answer the questions that follow.

> “I want to ask for your forgiveness for the fact that many of the dreams we shared did not come true. And for the fact that what seemed simple to us turned out to be tormentingly difficult. I ask forgiveness for not justifying some hopes of those people who believed that at one stroke, in one spurt, we could leap from the gray, stagnant, totalitarian past in to the light, rich, civilized future.”
>
> —Boris Yeltsin, December 31, 1999

**22** **ANALYZING IDEAS** How does the structure of Yeltsin's statement reinforce his meaning?

**A.** It indicates sarcasm through his use of abstract language.

**B.** It demonstrates sophistication through the increasingly complex sentences.

**C.** It expresses sincerity through the use of simple sentences building to colorful imagery.

**D.** It provokes confusion through the repetition of words in increasingly convoluted thoughts.

**23** **DETERMINING MEANING** What is the effect of Yeltsin's repetition of "forgiveness"?

**A.** It emphasizes the profundity of his message.

**B.** It undermines his sincerity.

**C.** It places the blame for his failures on the listener.

**D.** It alludes to the uselessness of assigning blame.

**24** **DETERMINING POINT OF VIEW** How does Yeltsin use word choice to emphasize the difficulties of his presidency?

**A.** He explains his failure using complex terminology so that few listeners will understand him.

**B.** He relies on metaphor to avoid addressing his failures directly.

**C.** He attempts to sound more intelligent by using political jargon.

**D.** He uses simple words to create moving imagery to describe an impossible ideal.

## Writing About History

**25** **EXPLANATORY WRITING** Based on what you read in this chapter, what were the effects of the collapse of the Soviet Union on international relations during the 1990s? In your response, analyze not only changes in Europe but also in Asia, Central and South America, and the Middle East and Africa.

## Speaking and Listening About History

**26** **PRESENTING** Over the course of the Arab Spring, revolutions occurred in many countries throughout the Middle East, often with little warning. Research the effects of these revolutions and where the countries' revolutionary movements stand today in terms of what goals they have achieved or failed to achieve. Write and present a speech in which you explain the causes and effects of Arab Spring movements.

**Need Extra Help?**

| If You've Missed Question | 18 | 19 | 20 | 21 | 22 | 23 | 24 | 25 | 26 |
|---|---|---|---|---|---|---|---|---|---|
| Review Lesson | 5 | 4 | 1, 5 | 1 | 1 | 1 | 1 | 2–5 | 5 |

Yeltsin, Boris. 1999. Excerpt from "Boris Yeltsin Resignation Speech, December 31, 1999". Quoted 2003 by Satter, David. Darkness at Dawn: The Rise of the Russian Criminal State. Yale University Press.

▸ *Photographed in 2001, this woman is a Rwandan refugee now living in Nairobi, Kenya. She was able to set up her business as a seamstress with a loan from a microcredit bank.*

1989 — PRESENT

# Contemporary Global Issues

CHAPTER 16



**GO DIGITAL**
*It's All online!*

## ASKING ESSENTIAL QUESTIONS

***What influences global political and economic relationships? How do social and environmental issues affect countries differently?***

**What Will You Learn?** You will learn what political, social, economic, and environmental challenges modern nations face, as well what efforts they are making to address these challenges.

**Why Does This Matter?** The political, social, economic, and environmental challenges faced by the world are problems that impact our everyday lives. It is important that you understand their causes, as well as solutions that are being considered to solve these problems.

**How Will You Know That You Learned It?** You will be able to explain the key challenges that face nations worldwide today and to identify, evaluate, and propose potential solutions to some of the most difficult problems.

**Using Your Inquiry Journal** As you read this chapter and examine the primary sources, use your Inquiry Journal to help you make notes and expand your list of questions. As you gather information, think about how you will answer the Essential Questions above.

# PLACE & TIME The World 1989–Present

One of the most significant parts of the human story has been the growth of cities. Civilization began with the first cities 5,000 years ago. Urbanization greatly accelerated with the Industrial Revolution. If current trends in population growth and economic development continue, the human future will be a story of megacities. A megacity is an urban area with more than 10 million inhabitants. In 1950 there were only two megacities—New York City and Tokyo. In 2015 the United Nations estimated there were 29 megacities.

## STEP INTO THE PLACE

Read the quotation and look at the information presented on the map.

1. **EXPLORING PLACE** What do most of the world's megacities have in common? Why do you think this is?
2. **DETERMINING POINT OF VIEW** What point does the author emphasize about urbanization in Asia?

"Over the next two decades, the world will see a burst of urban expansion at a speed and on a scale never before witnessed in human history. But not all the world will take part. When you hear about the coming urban age, it's really a story about rising Asia and the two countries that will define this new era of the megacity: China and India. Half of Asia will become urbanized, and nearly a billion people will shift from countryside to cityscape. Trillions of dollars will need to be spent on roads, trains, power plants, water systems, and social services. And it's going to happen in less than half the time that it took the West."

—Richard Dobbs, from "Megacities," September/October 2010

## STEP INTO THE TIME

**ANALYZING CHANGE**

Based on the time line, how has the pace of urbanization changed since 1990?

PHOTO:Jess Kraft/Shutterstock; TEXT:Dobbs, Richard. 2010. Prime Numbers: Megacities. August 10, 2010. Foreign Policy online magazine.

## MEGACITIES

**1990** The number of megacities in the world reaches 10

**1995** India has three megacities—Mumbai, Delhi, and Kolkata

**2000** Shanghai becomes China's first megacity

**1989 1990 1995 2000**

## WORLD EVENTS

**1990** World Wide Web created

**1995** World Trade Organization (WTO) begins operations

**2000** Number of international NGOs reaches nearly 37,000

**2001** errorists attack U.S. World Trade Center and Pentagon

**2002** The Euro is launched as a common currency in many Western European nations

**2003** U.S.-led army invades Iraq

**2005** The number of megacities in the world reaches 19

**2007** UN estimates world population at 6.7 billion

**2008** Worldwide recession

**2009** H1N1 flu pandemic outbreak

**2010** Nine percent of the world's population lives in megacities

**2010** More than 1 billion Internet users exist worldwide

**2011** Protests break out in Tunisia, Egypt, Libya, and Bahrain

**2012** The number of megacities in the world reaches 26.

**2015** Deadly terrorist attacks in Paris, France, by members of ISIL

**2016** Deadly terrorist attacks in Nice, France and Grand Bassam, Côte d'Ivoire

2005 2010 2015 2016

## ESSENTIAL QUESTION

- *What influences global political and economic relationships?*

LESSON 1

# Political Challenges in the Modern World

# THE STORY BEGINS...

On March 18, 2014, Russian President Vladimir Putin signed a treaty annexing Crimea to the Russian Federation. That day, he delivered a televised speech at the Kremlin in Moscow. In the speech, he defended the Crimean referendum and Russian annexation and criticized Western powers, particularly the United States, for their opposition.

> "Colleagues, Like a mirror, the situation in Ukraine reflects what is going on and what has been happening in the world over the past several decades. After the dissolution of bipolarity on the planet, we no longer have stability. Key international institutions are not getting any stronger; on the contrary, in many cases, they are sadly degrading. Our western partners, led by the United States of America, prefer not to be guided by international law in their practical policies, but by the rule of the gun. They have come to believe in their exclusivity and exceptionalism, that they can decide the destinies of the world, that only they can ever be right."

—Vladimir Putin, Address by president of the Russian Federation

The United States would naturally dispute Putin's statements. Disagreements like these represent a return to animosities that many hoped would never return after the end of the Cold War.

*In 2014, the people of Crimea and world leaders divided over the Crimean referendum, a vote to leave Ukraine and to join the Russian Federation. Russia annexed the small republic, despite opposition from Crimean Tatars, Ukraine, the United States, and other Western nations.* ▶

| Africa | Asia | Latin America |
| --- | --- | --- |
| | | |

**ANALYZING KEY IDEAS AND DETAILS**

**UNDERSTANDING CHANGE** Read closely to identify important political changes that have taken place in modern Africa, Asia, and Latin America.

# MULTINATIONAL ORGANIZATIONS

**GUIDING QUESTION** *How do the United Nations and the European Union strengthen globalism?*

Since the late Middle Ages, history has largely been the story of the nation-state. Nation-states are sovereign states that are defined by a distinctive language and common institutions and customs. As the world has become more interconnected and interdependent, the nation-state has gradually declined in importance. For instance, global trade has led to the creation of multistate or regional trade agreements. Improvements in communications and the Internet, too, have promoted a rapid exchange of information and ideas between nation-states and their citizens. Finally, multinational organizations such as the European Union and the United Nations have compelled many nation-states to set aside their differences and to pursue common goals and to resolve issues.

**ANALYZING KEY IDEAS AND DETAILS**

1. **SUMMARIZING** Why might some argue that the role of the nation-state is declining? Summarize the reasoning presented in the text.
2. **CITING TEXT EVIDENCE** What evidence in the text supports the conclusion that the United Nations has limitations, or weaknesses? Explain whether you think these qualities hurt the effectiveness of the UN.

## THE EUROPEAN UNION

The European Union had its beginnings in the the European Community (EC), which was largely an economic union. The Treaty on European Union, which went into effect on November 1, 1993, turned the EC into the European Union (EU). This new organization, comprised of 12 states at its creation would grow significantly, adding an additional 16 states to its membership by 2013.

The EU created a common currency, the euro, and also united its states into the world's largest trading bloc. The EU also sets health and safety requirements for the workplace and standards for manufactured products and determines who may and who may not travel freely from one country to another. In 2009 the European Union ratified the Lisbon Treaty, which created a full-time presidential post and a new voting system that reflected each country's population size. It also provided more power for the European Parliament in an effort to promote the EU's foreign policy goals. However, many of the EU's member states still see foreign policy as a national right and are reluctant to give it up. Nevertheless, the EU did create a military force of 60,000 to be used chiefly for peacekeeping purposes.

The EU has taken on many of the tasks that were once the responsibility of individual states. In doing so, the EU has provided many benefits to its members as a whole but has also contributed to the overall decline in the individual power of the nation-state. Over half the legislation passed by national parliaments now has its origins in the EU. However, the nation-states within the EU are still vulnerable to changes in the global economy and the strain of the current influx of refugees throughout Europe.

## THE UNITED NATIONS

Today, the United Nations (UN) is one of the most visible symbols of globalism. The UN was founded in 1945 at the end of World War II as a place for nations to settle disputes and to work together on global issues. In keeping with two of the UN's goals, peace and human dignity, the UN worked hard to establish worldwide standards for human rights. In the Preamble to the United Nations Charter of June 26, 1945, its members pledged "to save succeeding generations from the scourge of war . . . to reaffirm faith in fundamental human rights . . . and to promote social progress and better standards of life in larger freedom."

The General Assembly of the United Nations is made of representatives from all member nations. It has the power to discuss any important question and to recommend action. The Security Council advises the General Assembly and passes resolutions that require the organization to act. Five nations have permanent seats on the Security Council: the United States, Russia, Great Britain, France, and China. Ten other members are chosen by the General Assembly and serve for limited terms. Because each permanent member can veto a decision, deliberations can often end in stalemate. The UN Secretariat, an administrative body, is headed by the secretary-general. The International Court of Justice (or World Court) is the judicial body of the UN.

**DETERMINING MEANING**

How does the word *peacekeeping* help you understand the difference between the UN's **peacekeeping forces** and the military forces of sovereign nations?

UN **peacekeeping forces** settle conflicts and supervise truces in "hot spots" around the globe. However, the UN also provides the main forum for nations to address issues that are transnational, or that cross borders to affect many nations. Transnational issues include sustainable development, peaceful uses of atomic energy, climate change, women's rights, AIDS, and other global health crises. The UN's ability to place rules on its members regarding these issues is limited. However, it has many programs and specialized agencies that organize conferences where nations are able to discuss and make their own agreements on transnational issues.

### ✓ CHECKING FOR UNDERSTANDING

1. **IDENTIFYING CONNECTIONS** How do the United Nations and the European Union strengthen globalism?
2. **ANALYZING CHANGE** How have improvements in technology contributed to the weakening of the power of the nation-state?
3. **INTERPRETING** How do the UN General Assembly and the UN Security Council differ?

**UNDERSTANDING CRAFT AND STRUCTURE**

1. **ANALYZING TEXT PRESENTATION** How does the first paragraph of the section preview the content of the section? How does the structure of the section organize information to support the topical heading?
2. **ANALYZING TEXT** How does the text make clear that human trafficking constitutes a human rights violation? How do the words *exploit* and *exploitation* emphasize this idea?

# INTERNATIONAL SECURITY

**GUIDING QUESTION** *What international security issues confront the post-Cold War world?*

The end of the Cold War in 1989 brought with it the hopes for a lasting peace throughout the world. The terrorist attacks on September 11, 2001, in the United States ended this illusion. Issues of international security, including cross-border crime, weapons of mass destruction, and the challenge of terrorism now play major roles in the domestic and foreign policy decisions of many nations.

## CROSS-BORDER CRIME

As the world has become more interconnected, problems of cross-border or international crime have increased. These crimes include, among others, human trafficking, theft of cultural artifacts, money laundering, and illegal drug and arms trafficking.

Human trafficking, the illegal movement of people most often for the purposes of forced labor, is a human rights violation that has grown in recent decades. Those who traffic in human beings use threats, force, deception, and an abuse of power to exploit individuals. Millions of people, mostly women, are trafficked across international borders each year. These women are subject to sexual and other forms of exploitation. Increasingly concerned, the international community and the UN work to prevent human trafficking and to provide care to its victims through nonprofit organizations and UN.GIFT, the United Nations Global Initiative to Fight Human Trafficking.

The illegal trade in cultural artifacts is the selling of objects that have been unlawfully excavated or removed from their countries of origin. Nations have long been concerned about this illegal trade as it is a loss of cultural heritage and also economic potential as it destroys sites and removes artifacts that are a base for tourism industries. Several conventions have addressed these concerns, such as the United Nations Educational, Scientific and Cultural Organization (UNESCO) Convention on the Means of Prohibiting and Preventing Illicit Import, Export and Transfer of Ownership of Cultural Property, which has been approved by more than 80 countries.

Drug and arms trafficking, or the trade of illegal drugs and weapons, is dependent on money laundering. Money laundering is accomplished by taking funds obtained by criminal actions and moving it through the financial systems at a local, national, or international level. Doing so enables these groups to hide the criminal nature of these funds.

Funds "cleaned" through money laundering allow drug cartels and terrorist groups to operate as well as purchase illegal weapons. These criminal groups work to destabilize countries as governments, particularly in less stable countries, have difficulty maintaining authority. The rise in violence and efforts to combat the problem can also keep economies from growing. As technology advances, making the available weaponry more deadly, arms trafficking becomes an even greater international security concern.

## WEAPONS OF MASS DESTRUCTION

Modern technology has led to frightening methods of mass destruction: nuclear, biological, and chemical weapons. The end of the Cold War reduced the risk of nuclear conflict between the United States and the Soviet Union. However, nuclear weapons still exist, and nuclear conflicts remain possible.

The UN established the International Atomic Energy Agency (IAEA) in 1957. This agency is a safeguard system against **nuclear proliferation**, or the spread of nuclear weapons production technology and knowledge to nations without that capability. Most all countries are parties to the Nuclear Nonproliferation Treaty (NPT), which limits the development of nuclear weapons to the United States, Russia, the United Kingdom, France, and China. The only countries that are not members of the NPT are India, Pakistan, Israel, and North Korea. India

### DETERMINING MEANING

The word *traffic* has many meanings, including "trade." Use this definition to explain *human trafficking, arms trafficking,* and *drug trafficking.*

### MAKING CONNECTIONS

### COSTS OF HUMAN TRAFFICKING

The human and social consequences of human trafficking are immense, from the physical, psychological and emotional trauma of the victims, to the political and economic repercussions of unchecked criminal activity. Human trafficking also influences the domestic and foreign policies of many countries as it can involve the movement of people across borders. Migration policies, human rights issues, national security, and processes for returning victims to their country of origin or for the temporary or permanent residence of victims all have political implications for the countries involved. The economic costs include the amounts spent on its prevention, treatment and support of victims, and the apprehension and prosecution of offenders. Human trafficking also provides criminal networks a stable source of income with little risk, which allows these networks to expand their illegal activities and operate at international levels.

and Pakistan have exploded nuclear devices underground, and North Korea has performed nuclear tests. Israel has never publicly confirmed that it has developed nuclear weapons, although it is widely believed to have done so.

Iran violated the NPT and was subject to international sanctions for years. In 2015 the Joint Comprehensive Plan of Action was signed, limiting Iran's nuclear development in exchange for an easement of international sanctions.

Since the 1990s, there has also been an increased concern of the threat from biological and chemical weapons. Biowarfare, the use of disease and poison against civilians and soldiers in wartime, is not new. For example, chemical weapons were used extensively in World War I and during the Iran-Iraq War in the 1980s. Governments have agreed to limit the research, production, and use of weapons of mass destruction, but these agreements are difficult to enforce. Furthermore, these measures are unable to prevent terrorists from practicing **bioterrorism**, the use of biological and chemical weapons in terrorist attacks.

**DETERMINING MEANING**

The prefix *bio-* refers to living organisms. How does the prefix relate to the meaning of **bioterrorism?**

## THE CHALLENGE OF TERRORISM

Acts of terror have become a regular feature of modern society. Terrorists often kill civilians and take hostages to achieve their political goals. Beginning in the late 1970s and 1980s, many countries placed their concern about terrorism at the top of foreign policy agendas. Terrorist acts have received considerable media attention. When Palestinian terrorists kidnapped and killed 11 Israeli athletes at the Munich Olympic Games in 1972, hundreds of millions of people watched the drama unfold on television.

Some terrorists are militant nationalists who want separatist states. The Irish Republican Army (IRA), for example, wants to unite Northern Ireland with the Irish Republic. IRA leaders now seem more willing to open normal relations with the police of Northern Ireland after decades of violence. The group Basque Fatherland and Liberty (ETA) employs violence as a tool to free the Basque region in the western Pyrenees from Spanish control.

A radical Communist guerrilla group in Peru, known as Shining Path, also used terrorist violence. Aiming to create a classless society, Shining Path killed mayors, missionaries, priests, and peasants across Peru.

One of the most destructive acts of terrorism occurred on September 11, 2001. Al-Qaeda terrorists directed by Osama bin Laden hijacked four commercial jets in Boston, Newark, and Washington, D.C., flying two into the World Trade Center and one into the Pentagon. Almost 3,000 people were killed. President George W. Bush vowed to wage war on terrorism. This process began in Afghanistan in October 2001. President Barack Obama announced a major U.S. victory against al-Qaeda in 2011, when U.S. forces killed bin Laden at his hideout in Pakistan.

Worldwide, one of the most noticeable changes in public policies since September 11, 2001, has been increased security at airports. Many European and Asian governments have also begun working together more closely in their intelligence and police activities to track down terrorists.

*Fire and rescue workers search for survivors amid the rubble of the World Trade Center two days after the September 11, 2001, attacks.*

BETH A. KEISER/AFP/Getty Images

**IDENTIFYING EFFECTS**

What immediate effect did the attacks of September 11, 2001, have on New York City? What was the focus of the city's and country's immediate response?

Despite security upgrades and more international cooperation, terrorist incidents have continued worldwide since September 11, 2001. For example, in July 2005, during the London morning commute, four suicide bombers detonated bombs at three subway stations and on one bus. More than 700 people were injured, and 56 people were killed.

In 2015 alone there have been more than 20 terrorist attacks in which 50 people or more have been killed. The deadliest occurred at the hands of Boko Haram militants in Nigeria in January 2015. More than 2000 civilians were killed in Baga, Nigeria. In November 2015, 130 people lost their lives from terrorist attacks in Paris at the hands of members of the Islamic State of Iraq and the Levant (ISIL), also known as the Islamic State or ISIS.

## FIGHTING THE ISLAMIC STATE

The Islamic State of Iraq and the Levant (ISIL) began as a splinter group of al-Qaeda. It formed and gained strength after the withdrawal of U.S. troops from Iraq in 2011. More extreme than al Qaeda, ISIL has ignored international borders and has rapidly seized control of large areas of northern Iraq and eastern Syria. ISIL has brutally targeted its religious enemies and engaged in public executions. Refugees have fled from ISIL-controlled areas in large numbers.

In June 2014, ISIL advanced further into Iraq, displacing over 1 million Iraqi citizens. The United States increased its advisory troops in Iraq to 800, and in August 2014, U.S. President Obama authorized targeted air strikes within Iraq. Also in August and September, ISIL released public videos of the execution of captured American and British journalists. Obama pledged to increase the number of U.S. troops in Iraq to more than 1,000 and to continue air and drone strikes against ISIL-controlled areas.

In 2015 ISIL stepped up its attacks outside Iraq and Syria. In November 2015, ISIL downed a Russian passenger jet, conducted deadly attacks in Beirut, Lebanon, and claimed responsibility for a deadly attack in Paris.

## CHALLENGES IN THE MIDDLE EAST

The war on terrorism spread to the Middle East when the United States attacked Iraq in March 2003. President Bush claimed Iraq's leader, Saddam Hussein, had chemical and biological weapons of mass destruction and that Saddam had close ties to al-Qaeda. Both claims turned out to be inaccurate, and the United States soon became bogged down in a war in which Hussein's supporters, foreign terrorists, and Islamic militants all battled the American-led forces.

By 2006, Iraq seemed to be descending into a widespread civil war, especially between the Shia, who controlled southern Iraq, and the Sunnis, who controlled central Iraq. An American troop surge in 2007 helped stabilize conditions within a year. The U.S. and Iraqi governments then agreed to a complete withdrawal of American troops by 2011. The withdrawal of ground troops did occur in 2011, but in 2014 the United States returned with air support to Iraq, to combat ISIL.

Much of the terrorism in the Middle East is aimed against the West. One reason Middle Eastern terrorists have targeted Westerners can be traced to the beginning of the UN Mandate system, which began after World War I. This led to Western investment in the Middle East oil industry, which began in the 1920s. This industry brought wealth to ruling families in some Middle

**ANALYZING PRIMARY SOURCES**

**WHAT IS TERRORISM?**

"Terrorism is "any action . . . that is intended to cause death or serious bodily harm to civilians or non-combatants, when the purpose of such an act, by its nature or context, is to intimidate a population, or compel a Government or an international organization to do or to abstain from doing any act."

—UN High-Level Panel on Threats, Challenges and Change, *A More Secure World: Our Shared Responsibility,* December 2004

**DETERMINING MEANING**
According to the United Nations, what two qualities define an act of terrorism?

Eastern kingdoms, but most citizens remained very poor. They often blamed the West, especially the United States, for supporting the ruling families.

The oil business increased Middle Eastern contact with the West. Some Muslims feared this contact would weaken their religion and their way of life. Some Muslims began organizing to overthrow their pro-Western governments. Muslims who support these movements are called fundamentalist militants. They promote their own vision of what a pure Islamic society should be. Although most Muslims do not share this vision and themselves are victims of terror, these ideas have brought great regional instability and violence worldwide.

### ☑ CHECKING FOR UNDERSTANDING

1. **UNDERSTANDING CONTEXT** What international security issues confront the post-Cold War world?
2. **IDENTIFYING CAUSES** How does money laundering further illegal drug and weapons trading?
3. **IDENTIFYING CAUSES** How have governments responded to terrorism since September 11, 2001?

## CIVIL WAR AND ETHNIC CONFLICT

**UNDERSTANDING CRAFT AND STRUCTURE**

1. **ANALYZING TEXT PRESENTATION** How does the organization of the content in this section make the information more accessible?
2. **DETERMINING POINT OF VIEW** What does the use of the word *plagued* in the introductory sentence suggest about the author's point of view?

**GUIDING QUESTION** *How have civil war, ethnic conflict, and genocide affected some nations in the post-Cold War period, and how have governments and nongovernmental organizations responded to them?*

Ethnic and religious conflicts, which often lead to civil war, have plagued many developing nations and some developed nations in Europe.

### EUROPE

In Northern Ireland, Protestants and Catholics have frequently clashed. The Serbs used ethnic cleansing in the 1990s to kill Bosnian Muslims during the war in Bosnia. After Cyprus achieved independence, fighting between Greek and Turkish Cypriots led to a division of the island.

A crisis in Ukraine also led to conflict. In December 2013, many Ukrainians protested against Russia's role in Ukrainian affairs. Pro-Russian protesters began their own demonstrations in the southern Ukrainian peninsula of Crimea, where 60 percent of the population is ethnically Russian. In late February 2014, the Russian military invaded Crimea amid international condemnation. Following the invasion, Crimea overwhelmingly voted to leave Ukraine and to join Russia, but few countries have recognized the legitimacy of that election or Russia's claims.

### AFRICA

Within many African nations, warring ethnic groups undermined the concept of nationhood. This is not surprising because the colonial powers had **arbitrarily** drawn the boundaries of African nations. Virtually all these states included widely different ethnic, linguistic, and territorial groups. In Central Africa, fighting between the Hutu and the Tutsi created unstable governments. In Rwanda, brutal civil war broke out in 1994 as Hutu militias began a campaign of genocide against Tutsis, killing at least 500,000. As thousands of Rwandan refugees died in camps, the United States began a relief operation in conjunction with the UN. In 1997 a UN-sponsored war crimes tribunal began in Tanzania. In 1998 the tribunal sentenced the former Rwandan prime minister to life imprisonment for genocide.

Ethnic violence also plagued Sudan, Africa's largest nation. In the western province of Darfur, Arab militias attacked African ethnic groups with the support of the Arab-led government. Entire villages were burned, more than 200,000 people died, and more than 2 million fled their homes. The UN took over a struggling peacekeeping operation from the African Union at the end of 2007. In 2008 the International Criminal Court issued an arrest warrant for the Sudanese president, Omar Hassan al-Bashir, for genocide, war crimes, and crimes against humanity. In a 2011 referendum, southern Sudan voted to become independent from the north. The country of South Sudan was founded July 9, 2011.

## ASIA

Several areas in Asia and Southeast Asia experienced ethnic and religious conflict, including Tibet, East Timor, and Sri Lanka. Tibet seeks independence from the Chinese government that has suppressed dissent among ethnic minorities. The Dalai Lama led the government of Tibet in exile from India since 1959 but stepped down in 2011.

In Sri Lanka, there has been tension and violence since 1983 between the majority Sinhalese (who are mostly Buddhist) who lead the government and the minority Tamils (who are mostly Hindu). The Tamil Tigers are a terrorist group that has committed violence in the country. A 2002 cease-fire halted the violence temporarily, but it ended with renewed violence in 2008. The military conflict ended in 2010.

### ✓ CHECKING FOR UNDERSTANDING

1. **EXPLAINING EFFECTS** How have civil war, ethnic conflict, and genocide affected some nations in the post-Cold War period, and how have governments and nongovernmental organizations responded to them?
2. **IDENTIFYING CONNECTIONS** How did European colonialism contribute to ethnic strife in Africa? Describe an example of how such conflict developed.
3. **SUMMARIZING** How did governments and international organizations respond to the conflicts in Rwanda and Darfur?

**MAKING CONNECTIONS TO TODAY**

### THE ICC DILEMMA

After the Second World War, the Allies decided the crimes committed by many German and Japanese leaders were so great they should be prosecuted and punished. As a result, two ad hoc tribunals were established to prosecute these leaders. During the Cold War, attempts to create permanent international courts such as these were frequently blocked. But in the years after the collapse of the USSR, the international community created and established the International Criminal Court (ICC), a permanent tribunal to prosecute leaders around the world for crimes against humanity. Since its founding, the court has indicted 39 individuals. However, critics of the ICC have noted the court has focused heavily on African leaders from weak countries for crimes more powerful countries commit with impunity. Some have even called the court a tool of imperialism. As recently as February of 2017, the African Union called for the mass withdrawal of member states from the ICC because of unfair treatment.

**INTERPRETING** Why might the Cold War have made it difficult to establish an International Criminal Court?

# NEW DEMOCRACIES

**GUIDING QUESTION** *Where have new democracies emerged in the late twentieth and early twenty-first centuries?*

Some conflicts that stem from regional, ethnic, and religious differences in the 1990s and 2000s have led to the creation of new countries with fledgling democracies. Several states of the former Yugoslavia and East Timor became independent democratic states in recent years, moving to civilian governments

**UNDERSTANDING CRAFT AND STRUCTURE**

**IDENTIFYING STEPS** How did East Timor gain democratic government? Explain the series of events that unfolded in the country.

A poll worker counts ballots for the 2007 election in East Timor.

INTEGRATING INFORMATION What does the image symbolize about changes in East Timor?

JEWEL SAMAD/AFP/Getty Images

that are freely elected by the people. Other states, such as Eritrea and Uzbekistan, continue to struggle under authoritarian governments with either no elections or token elections with only one candidate able to receive votes by the people.

In 1999 the people of East Timor voted to become free of Indonesian rule, which was followed by violence between Christians and Muslims on the island. Nearly 10,000 died from the conflict. In 2002 East Timor (Timor-Leste) was internationally recognized as an independent country. In 2007, with the help of the UN, East Timor held mostly peaceful democratic elections.

In recent years, democracy has also begun to flourish in Latin America. With the debt crisis in Latin America in the 1980s came a movement toward democracy as people realized military power without popular consent could not maintain a strong state.

### ✓ CHECKING FOR UNDERSTANDING

1. **UNDERSTANDING CONTEXT** Where have new democracies emerged in the late twentieth and early twenty-first centuries?
2. **INTERPRETING** What qualities does the text suggest show a transition to democratic government?
3. **UNDERSTANDING CHANGE** Why does the text say that some nations, such as Eritrea and Uzbekistan, have failed to change from authoritarian to democratic governments?

## LESSON 1 REVIEW

### Time and Place

1. **ANALYZING CHANGE** How has global conflict changed since the end of the Cold War? Cite evidence from the text to support your ideas.

### Building History-Social Science Analysis Skills

2. **RELATING EVENTS** How do resource distribution and scarcity contribute to international security issues today?
3. **ANALYZING CHANGE** How have international bodies, such as the UN, changed the ways in which countries address cross-border crime? Describe benefits and limitations of such international efforts.
4. **RELATING EVENTS** What human characteristic of Crimea do you think encouraged Russian intervention and annexation of the peninsula? How does that characteristic also account for opposition to Russia's actions?

### Writing About History

5. **ARGUMENTATIVE WRITING** Research a place the United Nations has deployed peacekeeping forces, and write an essay on whether or not those forces have been effective at promoting the UN's goals. In your essay, be sure to use proper spelling, capitalization, and grammar and appropriate vocabulary related to the subject.

### Collaborating

6. **PRESENTING** In a small group, discuss whether the world has become a more peaceful place since the end of the Cold War. As a group, explain two to three ways in which the world has or has not become more peaceful. Then, make a recommendation about how you think the United States should promote peace in the world. Present your ideas to the class.

ESSENTIAL QUESTIONS

- *What influences global political and economic relationships?*
- *How do social and environmental issues affect countries differently?*

LESSON 2

# Social Challenges in the Modern World

## THE STORY BEGINS...

The threat presented by global pandemics caused the World Health Organization in 2013 to issue a report calling for greater access to health care and life-saving treatments across the world. Director-General of the World Health Organization Dr. Margaret Chan made this statement when introducing the report:

> "Our world spends more than $100 billion on health research each year. The lion's share of this investment goes to the discovery and development of pharmaceutical and biotechnology products. Research on health systems and service delivery receives only a tiny proportion of this investment. But it is never too late to start research on health systems and delivery. We need to change the research landscape. We need to invest in the science of delivery. We must give more attention to the three Ds: discovery, development, and delivery. What are the roadblocks that prevent delivery? This question needs attention. The report points to a large number of effective and inexpensive interventions that are simply not reaching the people most in need. Many proven interventions are hardly used at all. How can such a potentially life-saving resource be so neglected? This is another clear case of waste and inefficiency. Here is the reality: far more research is invested in developing new technologies than in making better use of existing technologies."

—Dr. Margaret Chan, August 15, 2013

Global health—including diagnosis and the delivery of preventative and treatment services worldwide—poses significant challenges and offers opportunities for global collaboration in the world today.

*In 2014, a deadly strain of the Ebola virus swept across much of West Africa and triggered a large-scale international response.* ▶

| Cause | Effect |
|---|---|
| Global Poverty | |
| | Global Hunger |
| | Global Migration |

**ANALYZING KEY IDEAS AND DETAILS**

**IDENTIFYING EFFECTS** Read closely to identify effects of global poverty and causes of global hunger and global migration.

# GLOBAL POVERTY

**INTEGRATING KNOWLEDGE AND IDEAS**

1. **INTEGRATING INFORMATION** How does the map provide a visual summary of the most important information in this section?
2. **ASSESSING** Read the first paragraph under the heading "Global Poverty." What is the main idea of that paragraph? Explain whether the rest of the section makes an effective argument in support of that main idea.

**GUIDING QUESTION** *What is the social impact of poverty, hunger, and health pandemics in developing nations?*

Developing nations confront many serious problems, not the least of which is extreme poverty. Although global poverty has been decreasing, the number of people living below the international poverty line is staggering. Around 900 million people, mostly in developing nations, live on less than $1.90 per day, which can cause poor health, illness, and even death. Poverty is a complex problem that creates many other challenges for developing nations. It can keep children from attending school, limit access to clean water and sanitation, and cause people to live in unsafe housing and is a primary cause of worldwide hunger.

## WORLD HUNGER

Growing or purchasing enough food for more and more people creates a severe problem in many developing countries. An estimated 795 million people worldwide suffer from hunger. This is slightly more than 1 in 9 people. In developing regions, approximately 13 percent of the population is undernourished.

The effects of hunger and malnutrition are devastating. Every year, more than 10 million people die of hunger and hunger-related diseases. More than 3 million children under age 5 die from poor nutrition annually. The long-term health problems caused by malnutrition are severe. Undernourished infants and children suffer from blindness, intellectual disability, and increased susceptibility to disease.

Among the many causes of worldwide hunger, poverty and economic factors are by far the major ones. The poor do not have enough money to produce or buy an adequate amount of food. For those living in poverty, food is costly.

Natural disasters can also bring about hunger. Droughts, earthquakes, hurricanes, floods, and tsunamis cause many to go without food, at least on a short-term basis. Poor farming practices, deforestation, and overgrazing can also lead to hunger if land becomes depleted and can no longer produce as much food.

Food shortages can also result from civil war. War disrupts normal farming, and warring groups often try to limit their enemies' access to food. For example, in South Sudan in 2015, some 2.5 million people were facing crisis levels of hunger when conflict led to internal displacement and interrupted the food supply.

**DETERMINING MEANING**

To better understand the word **pandemic**, break down its word parts. The prefix *pan-* means "all." The root word *demic* comes from the Greek *demos* for "people." Explain how these word parts reflect the meaning of *pandemic*.

## GLOBAL HEALTH PANDEMICS

The fear of a global swine flu **pandemic** in 2009 made people aware that in a global age, infectious diseases can easily spread as a result of international

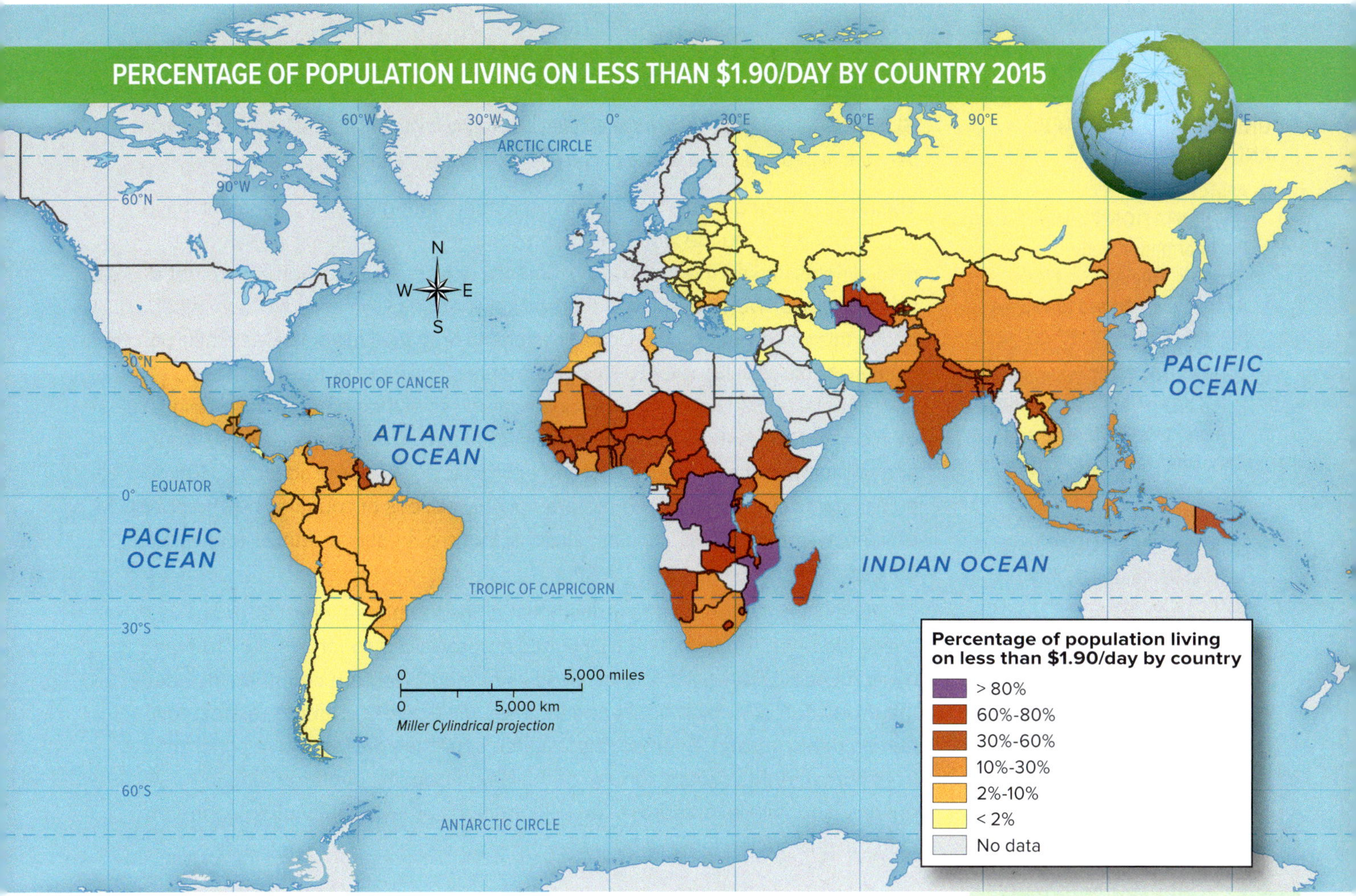


interactions. Global infectious diseases, such as HIV/AIDS, have raised concerns in recent decades. In 2015 approximately 1.2 million people died from AIDS-related illnesses, and Africa has been especially devastated. According to the UN, more than two-thirds of the nearly 37 million people living with HIV are in Africa south of the Sahara. AIDS has had a serious impact on children and families in Africa. Many children have lost one or both parents to AIDS. Often, relatives are too poor to care for these children. Many orphans thus become heads of households filled with younger siblings.

Still, there has been some good news: Global AIDS deaths have declined and the percentage of the world's population living with HIV has stabilized. The decline of AIDS deaths is due in part to the increased availability of antiretroviral therapy (ARV) that has allowed people living with HIV to live longer, productive lives. Organizations, such as UNAIDS, continue to sponsor initiatives to educate the public, to prevent HIV infection, to provide AIDS treatment, and to search for a cure.

## GEOGRAPHIC REASONING

1. **EXPLORING PLACE** Which continent has the most countries with 60–80 percent of the population living on less than $1.90 a day?
2. **GLOBAL INTERCONNECTIONS** How does the map support the conclusion that wealth disparity divides the Global North from the Global South?

## ✓ CHECKING FOR UNDERSTANDING

1. **EXPLAINING EFFECTS** What is the social impact of poverty, hunger, and health pandemics in developing nations?
2. **PREDICTING** What evidence from the text suggests that science might help to prevent future pandemics from occurring?
3. **IDENTIFYING CONNECTIONS** How are problems of poverty and world hunger related?

# HUMAN RIGHTS AND EQUALITY

**UNDERSTANDING CRAFT AND STRUCTURE**

1. **ANALYZING TEXT PRESENTATION** Explain how the information under the heading "Human and Civil Rights" is organized to explain the main concepts.
2. **ANALYZING TEXT** What phrase in the first paragraph under the heading "Mass Violence and Genocide" foreshadows the discussion of genocide in the second paragraph? Why do you think the author begins the second paragraph by referring to the Holocaust?

**GUIDING QUESTION** *How have problems involving human rights and gender inequality been addressed in the late twentieth and early twenty-first centuries?*

The ideas of natural rights and freedoms, formed during the Enlightenment, have since spread around the world. Although some individual nations incorporated natural rights into their governing documents, universal natural rights were not a focus until after World War II. Widespread knowledge of the atrocities committed during this war prompted the United Nations to draft the Universal Declaration of Human Rights (UDHR) in 1948. This document established for the first time fundamental human rights for all people regardless of their gender, class, religion, ethnicity, or race that are to be universally protected. These rights covered legal and political rights as well as social and economic rights. Some advocates for human rights argue that individuals are not only citizens of countries but members of "identity communities," such as religions, that cross national, ethnic, and cultural borders.

It has largely been left to individual nations to choose whether or not to adopt these protections. The UDHR has no provisions to force states to abide by its rules. However, the foreign policies of many Western countries include the protection of human rights and at times will actively promote respect for human rights abroad. Even so, these same countries often receive criticism from human rights groups for use of the death penalty, overcrowding in prisons, and failure to improve social conditions or laws that violate economic, cultural, and social rights at home.

**ANALYZING PRIMARY SOURCES**

**UNIVERSAL DECLARATION OF HUMAN RIGHTS, 1948**

"All human beings are born free and equal in dignity and rights. . . . Everyone is entitled to all the rights and freedoms set forth in this Declaration, without distinction of any kind, such as race, colour, sex, language, religion, political or other opinion, national or social origin, property, birth or other status. . . . Everyone has the right to life, liberty and security of person. . . . Everyone has the right to freedom of movement . . . Everyone has the right to freedom of opinion and expression."

—*from the Universal Declaration of Human Rights, adopted by the UN General Assembly on December 10, 1948*

**DETERMINING CENTRAL IDEAS** Describe the human rights listed above in your own words.

## HUMAN AND CIVIL RIGHTS

Civil rights and human rights have always been connected. At the heart of all civil rights movements are the basic human rights of all individuals and the right to live in freedom with justice and equal opportunity. In the United States, the African American civil rights movement gained momentum rapidly after World War II. Supreme Court rulings, massive protests by civil rights groups, and new federal legislation all combined to make racial segregation illegal, to outlaw discrimination on the basis of race, color, religion, or national origin when selling, renting, or financing housing, and to protect voting rights. Meanwhile, other civil rights movements were also occurring. Movements organizing Latino Americans, Asian Americans, Native Americans, and the LGBT community were also working diligently to gain rights, including legal and social equality, equal protection under the law, and an end to discriminatory practices. These civil rights movements and many others are still actively pursuing civil rights in the United States today.

## MASS VIOLENCE AND GENOCIDE

Governments themselves often carry out the violence. Dictators and military regimes punish people who disagree with their views. In Cuba, Chile, Myanmar, Iraq, Iran, and other countries, people have been persecuted for opposing repressive governments. In other countries, such as Bosnia and Rwanda, ethnic, religious, and racial hatreds have led to the mass murder of hundreds of thousands of people.

Often most closely associated with the Holocaust, genocide—the deliberate and systematic destruction of a group of people because of their ethnicity,

Universal Declaration of Human Rights. Adopted by the General Assembly on the United Nations 10 December 1948.

nationality, religion, or race—has occurred throughout history. Unfortunately, genocide continues to occur today. In 1948 the UN adopted the Convention on the Prevention and Punishment of the Crime of Genocide. All participating countries are to prevent and punish actions of genocide in war and in peacetime. The UN, through a special office on genocide prevention, also monitors situations to assess the risks of genocide occurring with the goal of preventing such events from taking place. Since 2002, the International Criminal Court has been responsible for prosecuting individuals for the international crime of genocide.

#### DETERMINING MEANING

Read the subheading "Human and Civil Rights." What context clues help you understand the meaning of *human rights*? What context clues in the first and second paragraphs help you differentiate *human rights* from *civil rights*?

#### DETERMINING MEANING

*Genocide* comes from the Latin *genus*, meaning "race, or kind," and *cidere*, meaning "to kill." Write a definition for genocide in your own words. Use a dictionary or online resource to check your definition.

## GENDER GAP

In the social and economic spheres of the Western world, the gap that once separated men and women has been steadily narrowing. More and more women are joining the workforce, and they make up half the university graduates in Western countries. Many countries have laws that require equal pay for women and men doing the same work, and some laws prohibit promotions based on gender. Nevertheless, women in many Western countries still do not hold many top positions in business or government.

Gender inequality is more pronounced in developing nations. Women in developing nations face considerable difficulties. They are often unable to obtain education, property rights, or decent jobs. Indeed, one of the UN Millennium Development Goals was to "promote gender equality and empower women." Still, some women in developing nations have become leaders of their countries, such as Ellen Johnson Sirleaf, who became president of Liberia in 2006, and Joyce Hilda Banda, who became Malawi's first female vice president in 2009.

### ✓ CHECKING FOR UNDERSTANDING

1. **DETERMINING CENTRAL IDEAS** How have problems involving human rights and gender inequality been addressed in the late 20th and early 21st centuries?

2. **ANALYZING IDEAS** What effect has the Universal Declaration of Human Rights had on the movement for human rights around the world?

**MAKING CONNECTIONS TO TODAY**

### ACCESS TO EDUCATION

Among the widest disparities between genders is access to education. Studies have shown that where women and girls have greater access to education, rates of poverty go down and economic growth goes up. Education is an important step to sustainable economic development.

However, globally, young women make up more than half of those who do not enter or finish primary school. That disparity increases as the level of education increases. The figures also increase in developing and war-torn regions, particularly in Africa south of the Sahara. To this end, international organizations have made access to education a crucial point of collaboration.

1. **DETERMINING CENTRAL IDEAS** How does access to education reflect the global gender gap?

2. **ANALYZING IDEAS** What wider benefits does the author say result from ensuring women and girls have access to equal education?

# POPULATION AND MIGRATION TRENDS

**ANALYZING KEY IDEAS AND DETAILS**

1. **DETERMINING CENTRAL IDEAS** Read the first two paragraphs under the heading "Population and Migration Trends." What is the central idea of this section? Explain whether subsequent paragraphs support this idea.
2. **ANALYZING IDEAS** Read the sentence that begins, "The issue of global migration. . . ." Given what you have read about population trends, what does this sentence suggest about the impact of global migration?

**GUIDING QUESTION** *How have population and migration trends affected developed and developing nations?*

Estimates by the Population Reference Bureau put the 2015 world population at about 7.3 billion. Their **projections** estimate that the global population could reach 9.8 billion by 2050. The world population is expected to increase approximately one-third over the next four decades.

Almost all population growth is from the developing nations. By 2050, India will have surpassed China in population and will likely remain the most populous country in the world although the government has created a number of policies and initiatives promoting family planning to decrease growth.

Meanwhile, many wealthy regions, such as Western Europe, are declining in population. In fact, by 2050, the United States is expected to be the only wealthy nation with a growing population. Japan recently implemented the Plus One Policy to encourage families to increase their families by one in part by creating parent-friendly working conditions and enhancing daycare services. The developed nations are also "graying"—a larger percentage of the population is reaching retirement age. In the more developed regions, more than one-fifth of the population is aged 60 or over. By 2050, it is expected to reach one-third.

The global age distribution is shifting toward older people because of increases in life expectancies, lower birthrates, and lower death rates. The number of people aged 80 and over and those who live beyond 100 is rising, especially in developed nations. This circumstance is placing increased demands on the economies of developed nations.

Developing countries face different problems. The struggle to develop economically contributes to developing countries having the lowest life expectancy in the world. Between 2015 and 2050, the population in developing countries is expected to grow from 6.1 billion to 8.1 billion. Also, the trend of increased urbanization is expected to continue.

## STAGES OF GROWTH: POPULATION PYRAMIDS

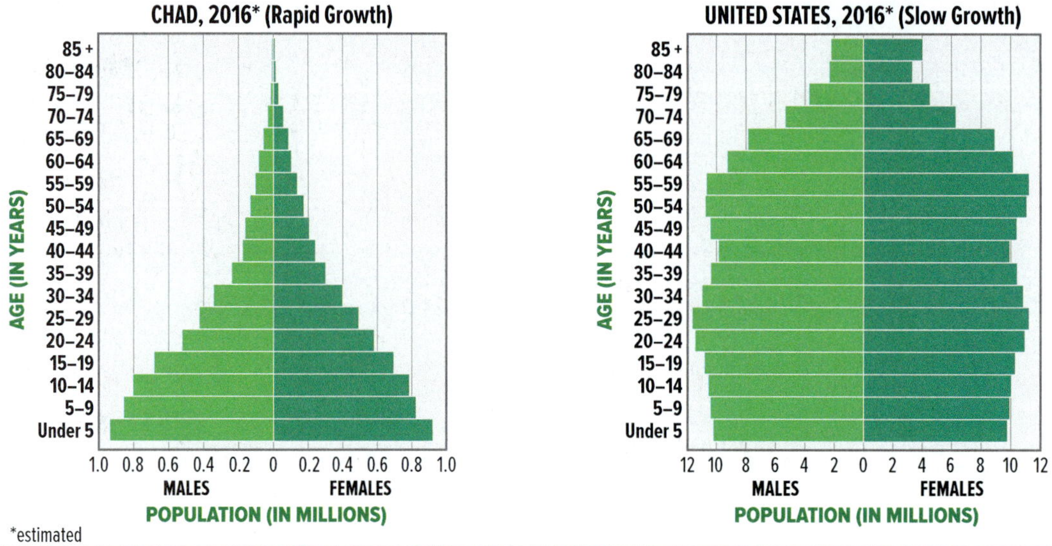


*estimated

Many cities lack the infrastructure to support larger populations than they currently have. As a result, concerns are rising about future international health and environmental problems that may come about with rising population numbers. These are especially of concern in developing nations.

The issue of global **migration** is also connected to population growth. Globally, there are an estimated 232 million international migrants and another 740 million internal migrants, or migrants who move inside a given country. Because most migrants move to urban areas, international migration is also closely tied to urbanization.

There are several reasons people migrate. Persecution for political reasons and brutal civil wars in Asia, Africa, the Middle East, and Europe has led millions of refugees to seek safety in neighboring countries. Starting in the 1960s, the relaxation of some aspects of immigration laws helped spur a new wave of global migration as many people sought new economic opportunities. For example, guest workers from Turkey, India, Pakistan, and North Africa entered more prosperous European countries. Moderate immigration policies reduced the population decline in countries such as Sweden and Germany. But foreign workers often become scapegoats when countries face economic problems. Political parties in France and Norway in the 1990s, for example, called for the removal of blacks and Arabs to protect the ethnic purity of their nations.

## ✓ CHECKING FOR UNDERSTANDING

1. **EXPLAINING EFFECTS** How have population and migration trends affected developed and developing nations?
2. **IDENTIFYING CAUSES** Summarize causes of human migration.
3. **IDENTIFYING CAUSES** Explain the reasons behind the graying of the population in developed countries.

## GRAPH SKILLS

Population pyramids include information about the age and gender distribution of a country's population. The population structure of a country provides insight into population trends. Use the population pyramids of Chad, the United States, and Italy to answer the following questions.

1. **INTEGRATING INFORMATION** How does the shape of the population pyramid for a country undergoing rapid growth differ from a country experiencing decline?
2. **ANALYZING SOURCES** Examine the age groups for those 69 and younger. What does each of these pyramids show about population after the end of World War II?

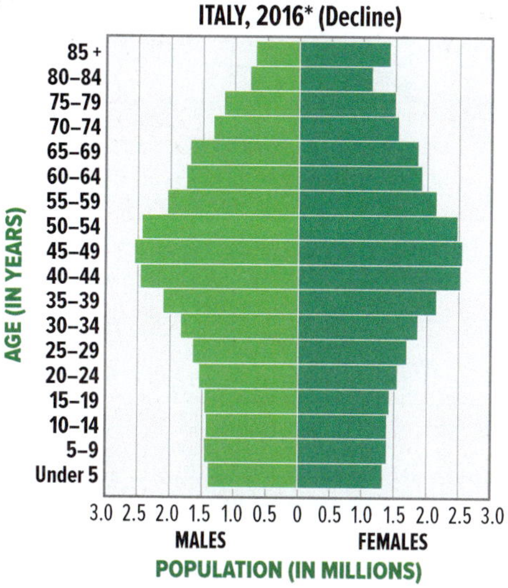


**Source:** U.S. Census Bureau, International Data Base.

UNDERSTANDING CRAFT AND STRUCTURE

1. **DETERMINING MEANING** The prefix *non-* means "not." How does the prefix relate to the meaning of **nongovernmental organizations**? Explain how some nongovernmental organizations might act in opposition to specific governments.

2. **ANALYZING TEXT PRESENTATION** What purpose does the quote from Elise Boulding serve in this section?

**ANALYZING SOURCES** Which countries on this graph currently have the largest populations?

**UNDERSTANDING CHANGE** Why might this graph include the population of the United States alongside the populations of countries such as India, China, and Nigeria?

# TRANSNATIONAL ORGANIZATIONS

**GUIDING QUESTION** *What role do transnational and nongovernmental organizations play in the international arena?*

Global awareness has led to new social movements that focus on problems that nations share. These problems include areas such as the environment, gender inequality, child labor, the appropriate use of technology, and the promotion of peace.

Groups such as the International Red Cross and Red Crescent Movement draw their memberships from different countries. Other groups have members in one country. Many individuals act at the grassroots level, that is, in their own communities. A favorite slogan of grassroots groups is "Think globally, act locally."

Another movement that addresses world problems is the growth of **nongovernmental organizations** (NGOs). NGOs are often represented at the United Nations. They include professional, business, and cooperative organizations, as well as foundations. Also included are religious, peace, and disarmament groups that work to limit the size of military forces and weapons stocks. Some NGOs, such as Greenpeace, work to bring attention to global environmental issues. Other NGOs protect the welfare of women and children or advocate for all human rights.

As interest in human rights grew in the last decades of the twentieth century, NGOs, including Amnesty International, Freedom House, Human Rights Watch, and Doctors Without Borders, were formed. To better inform the

**SELECTED NATIONS - POPULATION GROWTH 2000–2050**

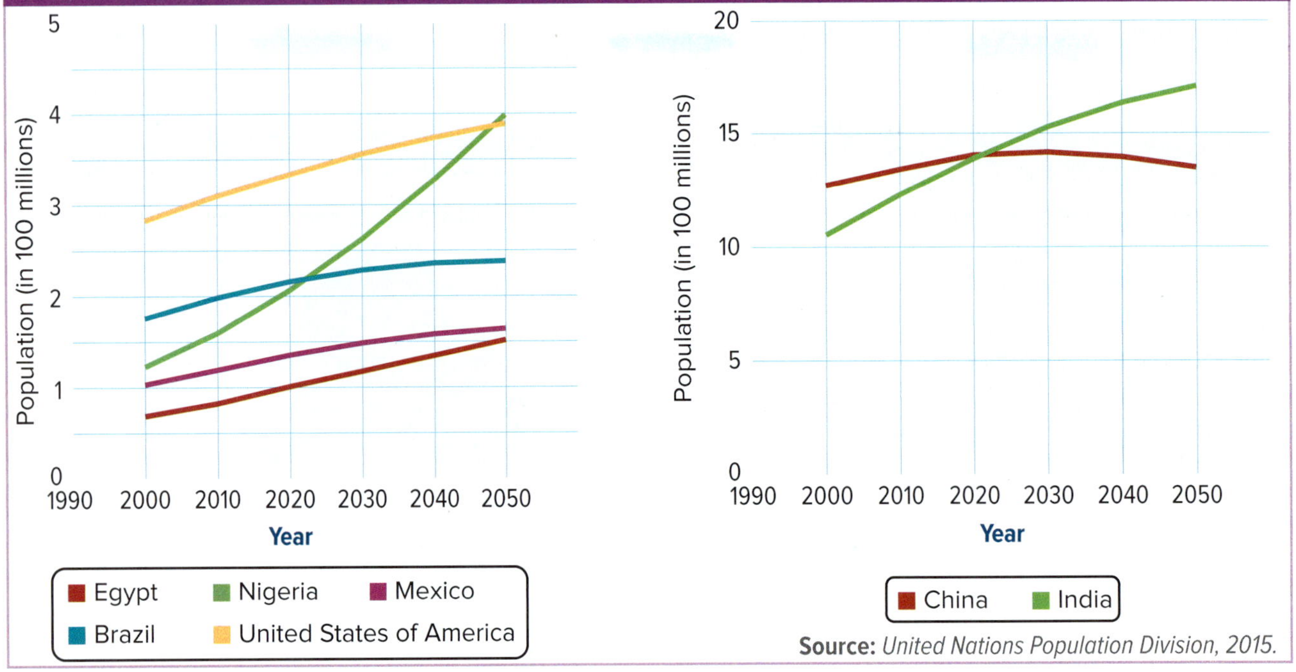


**Source:** *United Nations Population Division, 2015.*

public about human rights, NGOs, such as Human Rights Education Associates were also formed. These NGOs work to expose human rights abuses by all governments and other organizations of the world. The advancements in communications, including the Internet and satellite broadcasting, increase the awareness of human rights violations around the world.

American educator Elise Boulding promoted NGOs. She believed they can educate people to consider problems globally. She said that all NGOs are expected "to define problems in global terms, to take account of human interests and needs as they are found in all parts of the planet." The number of international NGOs increased from 176 in 1910 to nearly 37,000 in 2000.

*An international NGO builds a well to provide safe drinking water for a village in Zimbabwe.*

**ANALYZING INFORMATION** How does the image demonstrate human-environment interaction?

### ☑ CHECKING FOR UNDERSTANDING

1. **IDENTIFYING CONNECTIONS** What role do transnational and nongovernmental organizations play in the international arena?
2. **ANALYZING CHANGE** Read the last sentence under the heading "Transnational Organizations." What global events or conditions do you think account for that change?
3. **IDENTIFYING CONNECTIONS** How are grassroots organizations related to NGOs?

## LESSON 2 REVIEW

### Time and Place

1. **ANALYZING CHANGE** Why are pandemics a concern in an increasingly globalized world?

### Building History-Social Science Analysis Skills

2. **DETERMINING POINT OF VIEW** How does the grassroots slogan "Think Globally, Act Locally" reinforce the mission of transnational and nongovernmental organizations?
3. **IDENTIFYING CONNECTIONS** Why did World War II and the Holocaust lead to international efforts to define and protect human rights?
4. **IDENTIFYING CONNECTIONS** Explain the relationship among geography, population, and social challenges in the modern world.

### Writing About History

5. **EXPLANATORY WRITING** Research global public health policies about polio, malaria, HIV/AIDS, influenza viruses, or Zika. Prepare a report in which you summarize the global impact or threat of the illness; describe policies and efforts undertaken by governments, transnational organizations, and NGOs to address the health concern; and assess the extent to which these policies have promoted public health and the prevention of the transmission of disease.

### Collaborating

6. **USING MULTIMEDIA** With a partner, choose one NGO to research. Find out about the organization's mission, goals, founding, organizational structure, resources, achievements, and challenges. Use what you learn to prepare a multimedia presentation about the organization and its impact in the world. In your presentation, assess whether you consider the NGO to be effective, and explain why or why not.

# Civil Peace from Girls at War and Other Stories

by Chinua Achebe

**BACKGROUND INFORMATION** In 1960 the West African nation of Nigeria gained independence from Britain. However, like many African nations, the borders of the new country did not reflect the territorial claims of ethnic and religious groups. Soon, in 1967, tensions among rival groups erupted into civil war when the eastern province broke away and declared itself the Republic of Biafra. Known as the Biafran War, the conflict and consequent famine resulted in the deaths of more than a million people.

Born Albert Chinualumogu Achebe in Nigeria in 1930, Chinua Achebe experienced the effects of European imperialism in Africa firsthand. He wrote several novels and numerous poems, short stories, and essays about life in Nigeria before and after independence. Many of his works deal with the effects of Western values and culture on African life and society. Through his writing and his travels, Achebe has helped spread the understanding and influence of African literature worldwide. "Civil Peace," excerpted below, is one story from his anthology *Girls at War and Other Stories* in which Achebe responds to the Nigerian civil war.

## Explore the Text

**The Scene:** The short story "Civil Peace" recounts the fictional tale of Jonathan Iwegbu and his family living in Nigeria during the civil war. As the scene begins, the main character, Jonathan, is noting how lucky he is that he still has his bicycle. He decides it is better to think about what he has preserved than what he has lost in the war.

*Chinua Achebe, seen here with one of his best-known works, in the late 1960s.*

Eliot Elisofon/The LIFE Picture Collection/Getty Images

Jonathan Iwegbu counted himself extraordinarily lucky. "Happy survival!" meant so much more to him than just a current fashion of greeting old friends in the first hazy days of peace. It went deep to his heart. He had come out of the war with five **inestimable** blessings—his head, his wife Maria's head and the heads of three out of their four children. As a bonus he also had his old bicycle—a miracle too but naturally not to be compared to the safety of five human heads.

The bicycle had a little history of its own. One day at the height of the war it was **commandeered** "for urgent military action." Hard as its loss would have been to him he would still have let it go without a thought had he not had some doubts about the genuineness of the officer. It wasn't his disreputable rags, nor the toes peeping out of one blue and one brown canvas shoes, nor yet the two stars of his rank done obviously in a hurry in **Biro**, that troubled Jonathan; many good and heroic soldiers looked the same or worse. It was rather a certain lack of grip and firmness in his manner. So Jonathan, suspecting he might be amenable to influence, rummaged in his **raffia** bag and produced the two pounds with which he had been going to buy firewood which his wife, Maria, retailed to camp officials for extra stock-fish and corn meal, and got his bicycle back. That night he buried it in the little clearing in the bush where the dead of the camp, including his own youngest son, were buried. When he dug it up again a year later after the surrender all it needed was a little palm-oil greasing. "Nothing puzzles God," he said in wonder.

He put it to immediate use as a taxi and accumulated a small pile of Biafran money ferrying camp officials and their families across the four-mile stretch to the nearest tarred road. His standard charge per trip was six pounds and those who had the money were only glad to be rid of some of it in this way. At the end of a **fortnight** he had made a small fortune of one hundred and fifteen pounds.

Then he made the journey to Enugu and found another miracle waiting for him. It was unbelievable. He rubbed his eyes and looked again and it was still standing there before him. But, needless to say, even that monumental blessing must be accounted also totally inferior to the five heads in the family. This newest miracle was his little house in Ogui Overside. Indeed nothing puzzles God!

---

**inestimable:** too important to be given a specific value

**commandeered:** seized for military purposes

**Biro:** a British term for a ballpoint pen

**raffia:** fiber of a type of palm tree

**fortnight:** two weeks

#### ANALYZING POINTS OF VIEW

What is Jonathan most grateful for at the end of the war? What does he consider a "bonus"? Explain what his feelings suggest about the experience of the Nigerian civil war.

#### ANALYZING LITERATURE

Jonathan says that he would have let go of his bicycle without a thought had he believed it was really being taken for military use. What does this suggest about Jonathan's character and his feelings about the war?

#### ANALYZING TEXT

Why does Jonathan bury the bicycle?

#### ANALYZING TEXT

How is Jonathan's house a "little miracle"?

Only two houses away a huge concrete edifice some wealthy contractor had put up just before the war was a mountain of rubble. And here was Jonathan's little zinc house of no regrets built with mud blocks quite intact! Of course the doors and windows were missing and five sheets off the roof. But what was that? And anyhow he had returned to Enugu early enough to pick up bits of old zinc and wood and soggy sheets of cardboard lying around the neighborhood before thousands more came out of their forest holes looking for the same things. He got a **destitute** carpenter with one old hammer, a blunt plane and a few bent and rusty nails in his tool bag to turn this assortment of wood, paper and metal into door and window shutters for five Nigerian shillings or fifty Biafran pounds. He paid the pounds, and moved in with his overjoyed family carrying five heads on their shoulders.

**CITING EVIDENCE**

What clues in the story give hints to Nigeria's colonial past and the lasting influence of British rule?

His children picked mangoes near the military cemetery and sold them to soldiers' wives for a few pennies—real pennies this time—and his wife started making breakfast **akara balls** for neighbours in a hurry to start life again. With his family earnings he took his bicycle to the villages around and bought fresh palm-wine which he mixed generously in his rooms with the water which had recently started running again in the public tap down the road, and opened up a bar for soldiers and other lucky people with good money.

At first he went daily, then every other day and finally once a week, to the offices of the Coal Corporation where he used to be a miner, to find out what was what. The only thing he did find out in the end was that that little house of his was even a greater blessing than he had thought. Some of his fellow examiners who had nowhere to return at the end of the day's waiting just slept outside the doors of the offices and cooked what meal they could scrounge together in **Bournvita** tins. As the weeks lengthened and still nobody could say what was what Jonathan discontinued his weekly visits altogether and faced his palm-wine bar.

**ANALYZING POINTS OF VIEW**

Jonathan turns in "rebel money." What does this tell you about his part in the war and about the outcome of the war?

But nothing puzzles God. Came the day of the windfall when after five days of endless scuffles in queues and counter-queues in the sun outside the Treasury he had twenty pounds counted into his palms as ***ex gratia*** award for the rebel money he had turned in. It was like Christmas for him and for many others like him when the payments began. They called it (since few could manage its proper official name) *egg-rasher.*

As soon the palm notes were placed in his palm Jonathan simply closed it tight over them and buried fist and money inside his trouser pocket. He had to be extra careful because he had seen a man a couple of days earlier collapse

---

**destitute:** extremely poor

**akara balls:** fried balls made from blended beans and spices

**Bournvita:** a brand of chocolate malt drink

***ex gratia*:** "as a favor," something done out of kindness or moral obligation into near-madness in an instant before that oceanic crowd because no sooner had he got his twenty pounds than some heartless ruffian picked it off him. Though it was not right that a man in such an extremity of agony should be blamed yet many in the queues that day were able to remark quietly on the victim's carelessness, especially after he pulled out the innards of his pocket and revealed a hole in it big enough to pass a thief 's head. But of course he had insisted that the money had been in the other pocket, pulling it out too to show its comparative wholeness. So one had to be careful.

Jonathan soon transferred the money to his left hand and pocket so as to leave his right free for shaking hands should the need arise, though by fixing his gaze at such an elevation as to miss all approaching human faces he made sure that the need did not arise, until he got home.

**ANALYZING LITERATURE**

Reread the final paragraph. How has Jonathan's character changed over the course of the story, and why does this matter?

## High-Level Critical-Thinking Questions

1. **ANALYZING THEMES** What does Jonathan mean when he says or thinks, "Nothing puzzles God"? How does this phrase relate to the central theme of the story?
2. **ANALYZING TEXT** How does it become clear the bicycle is important to Jonathan and to the story?
3. **ANALYZING POINTS OF VIEW** What is significant about this sentence? What does it show about Jonathan and about Nigeria after the war?
   "He paid the pounds, and moved in with his overjoyed family carrying five heads on their shoulders."
4. **ANALYZING LITERATURE** What part do Jonathan's children play in the story?
5. **ANALYZING LITERATURE** Do you think it is effective for Achebe to discuss the war through an individual account rather than as a direct discussion of the devastation created? Why or why not?

PHOTO:Trinity Mirror/Mirrorpix/Alamy Stock Photo; TEXT:Achebe, Chinua. 1991. 'Civil Peace'. From Girls at War and Other Stories. New York: Anchor Books, A Division of Random House, Inc.

## ESSENTIAL QUESTIONS

- *What influences global political and economic relationships?*
- *How do social and environmental issues affect countries differently?*

# THE STORY BEGINS...

LESSON 3

# Global Economies

Globalization is not new. Those living in the late nineteenth century witnessed the disintegration of international borders as goods and people moved freely around the world. After World War I, Europe and the US retreated to protectionism and nationalism. Following the Second World War, the world again moved in the direction of globalization. This process accelerated after the 1970s with improvements in computer technology and transportation. The overall effects of globalization, however, are seen as mixed. As President Barack Obama said in a speech delivered at the end of his term:

> “The same forces of globalization and technology and integration that have delivered so much progress, have created so much wealth, have also revealed deep fault lines. Around the world, integration and closer cooperation, and greater trade and commerce, and the Internet – all have improved the lives of billions of people – lifted families from extreme poverty, cured diseases, helped people live longer, gave them more access to education and opportunity than at any time in human history. . . .
>
> But trends underway for decades have meant that in many countries and in many communities there have been enormous disruptions. Technology and automation mean that goods can be produced with fewer workers. It means jobs and manufacturing can move across borders where wages are lower or rights are less protected. And that means that workers and unions oftentimes have less leverage to bargain for better wages, better benefits, have more difficulty competing in the global marketplace. . . .
>
> But given the nature of technology, it is my assertion that it's not possible to cut ourselves off from one another. We now are living in a global supply chain. Our growth comes through innovation and ideas that are crossing borders all the time. The jobs of tomorrow will inevitably be different from the jobs of the past. So we can't look backwards for answers, we have to look forward.”

—President Barack Obama, November 16, 2016

*Globalization is a powerful force that shapes everything from politics to human movement and interaction.* ▶

PHOTO:Prasit Rodphan/Shutterstock; TEXT:Obama, President Barack. November 16, 2016. "Remarks by President Obama at Stavros Niarchos Foundation Cultural Center in Athens Greece". The White House: Office of the Press Secretary.

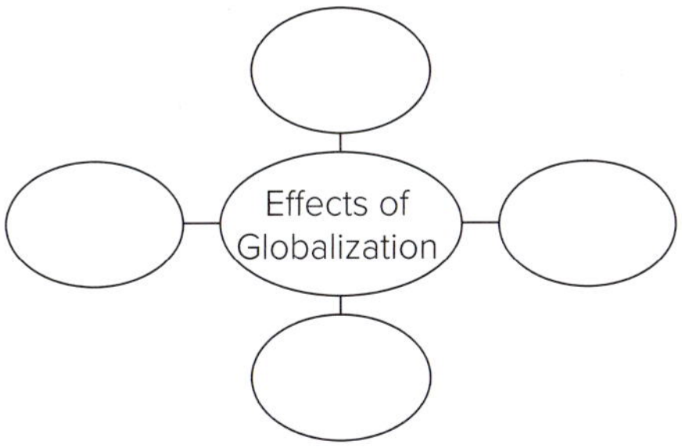


**ANALYZING KEY IDEAS AND DETAILS**

**IDENTIFYING EFFECTS** Read closely to identify effects of globalization.

# GLOBAL ECONOMIC ORGANIZATIONS

**GUIDING QUESTION** *What are the roles of global economic organizations in the world economy?*

**Globalization** is the process by which people and nations have become more interdependent. Politically and socially, globalization has led to the emergence of citizen groups and other transnational organizations that work across national boundaries to bring solutions to common problems. The growing interdependence of people and nations also suggests that the differences among societies and cultures are becoming less distinct as globalization is unifying perspectives of the world.

## THE INTERNATIONAL MONETARY FUND

World War II brought advancements in technology, communication, and transportation that increased globalization. After World War II, the United States and other nations set up the World Bank and the International Monetary Fund (IMF) as a means of expanding global markets and avoiding economic crises. The World Bank is actually a group of five international organizations, largely controlled by developed countries. It provides grants, loans, and advice for economic development in developing countries. The World Bank's stated goal is "a world free of poverty." The IMF, founded in 1945, is now an organization of 188 countries. Its goal is to oversee the global financial system. To achieve its goal, the IMF watches exchange rates and offers financial and technical assistance to developing nations.

## MULTINATIONAL CORPORATIONS

**Multinational corporations** are another reflection of the global economy. Prominent examples of multinational corporations include Siemens, General Motors, Exxon Mobil, Mitsubishi, and the Sony Corporation. These companies are among the 200 largest multinational corporations, which are responsible for more than half the world's industrial production. In addition, these supercorporations dominate much of the world's investment capital, technology, and markets.

A recent comparison of corporate sales and national gross domestic product revealed that only 49 of the world's 100 largest economic entities are nations. The remaining 51 are corporations. For this reason, some believe that economic globalization might best be called "corporate globalization."

**UNDERSTANDING CRAFT AND STRUCTURE**

1. **ANALYZING TEXT PRESENTATION** How do the subheadings in this section relate to the heading "Global Economic Organizations"? How does the text organize and present information relating to the heading and subheadings?
2. **DETERMINING MEANING** Break down the terms *interdependence, modular manufacturing*, and *offshore banking* into their word parts or individual words. Then, write a definition for each term in your own words. Check your definitions in a dictionary or an online resource.

**DETERMINING MEANING**

To better understand globalization, break down the word. The root word *global* means "of or relating to the whole world." The suffix *-ization* means "process." Use these meanings to write a definition for *globalization* in your own words. Check your definition in a dictionary or an online resource.

**DETERMINING MEANING**

The prefix *multi-* means "many." What does this tell you about the meaning of **multinational corporations**?

## WORLD'S LARGEST MULTINATIONAL CORPORATIONS 2015

In 2015 many of the largest multinational corporations were in the banking and the oil and gas operations industries and had their headquarters in the United States or China.

1. **INTEGRATING INFORMATION** Make two bar graphs to compare the sales and profits of the corporations in the chart. Which achieved the highest sales? Which earned the highest profits? Why do you think this is?
2. **INTEGRATING INFORMATION** Make a circle graph to compare the countries of origin of these corporations. Which country has the highest percentage? How might this graph look different if based on the sales of those corporations? What about if based on profits?

| Rank/Company | Country of Origin | Industry | Sales ($bil) | Profits ($bil) |
|---|---|---|---|---|
| 1. ICBC | China | Major Banks | $166.8 | $44.8 |
| 2. China Construction Bank | China | Major Banks | $130.5 | $37 |
| 3. Agricultural Bank of China | China | Major Banks | $129.2 | $29.1 |
| 4. Bank of China | China | Major Banks | $120.3 | $27.5 |
| 5. Berkshire Hathaway | United States | Diversified Financials | $194.7 | $19.9 |
| 6. JPMorgan Chase | United States | Major Banks | $97.8 | $21.2 |
| 7. Exxon Mobil | United States | Oil & Gas Operations | $376.2 | $32.5 |
| 8. PetroChina | China | Oil & Gas Operations | $333.4 | $17.4 |
| 9. General Electric | United States | Conglomerates | $148.5 | $15.2 |
| 10. Wells Fargo | United States | Major Banks | $90.4 | $23.1 |
| 11. Toyota Motor | Japan | Auto & Truck Manufacturers | $252.2 | $19.1 |
| 12. Apple | United States | Computer Hardware | $199.4 | $44.5 |

Source: www.forbes.com

**MAKING CONNECTIONS TO TECHNOLOGY**

### GLOBALIZATION

Computer technology is often recognized as a factor expanding globalization. However, many other technological innovations have increased time-space compression or reduced the relative distance between places and decreased the time it takes to complete tasks. Advances in communications and travel have decreased the barriers in global transactions which, coupled with innovations in manufacturing, have increased production and opened up new markets. This has led to innovations in shipping, such as containerization, in which standardized containers are used. This produces cost savings by allowing goods to be packed once and moved over long distances via a variety of transport modes without being unpacked and repacked.

Multinational corporations have existed since the operation of trading companies like the British East India Company during the seventeenth century. However, today's multinational corporations disperse the production of products to a variety of areas around the world. This is referred to as modular manufacturing or production. For example, a variety of Apple products, including the iPod and the iPad, may be designed in the United States but have parts that are manufactured independently of one another in countries around the world that are then assembled in China. The global economy of today can often be embodied in a single product.

There is also a downside to the growing number of multinational corporations. As they increasingly tie one country to another in a global economy, an economic downturn in one country can create stagnant conditions in other countries. We live in an economically interdependent world.

## GLOBAL TRADE

Global trade is a central component of the global economy. The buying and selling of goods around the world, or the global market, was aided by advancements in transportation that facilitated the rapid movement of goods and greatly decreased international shipping costs. The rise of large international banks and investment companies further developed the global market. However, the vast improvements in communication along with new communication technologies would become a key force in global trade, as these advancements not only allowed money and information to move quickly around the world but are also used to market products to consumers regardless of location. Marketing, through various media, is now used to create global brands for products. This has led to criticism that globalization supplants local cultures by unifying consumer preferences for products around the globe, leading to more Westernized cultures.

Trade agreements among nations or groups of nations have become key components of global trade. Many nations have joined in talks or deals meant to make trade among countries free and easy. These talks led to the General Agreement on Trade and Tariffs (GATT). In 1995 the nations that had signed the GATT treaties agreed to create the World Trade Organization (WTO). Made of 162 member nations, the WTO arranges trade agreements and settles trade disputes.

The Group of Eight (G8) refers to eight industrialized nations in the West that meet annually to discuss global economic and security issues. This is an informal organization. Likewise, the Group of Twenty (G20) is an expanded group of 20 countries that meets to discuss international financial issues. These groups are sometimes criticized for not doing enough to combat global issues, including climate change and alleviating the debt of developing countries. The lack of equitable representation for all regions of the world in these groups is also a common critique as the Caribbean, the Nordic countries, Southeast Asia, and Africa have little to no representation in G8 and G20.

## OFFSHORE BANKS

Offshore banking involves the securing of assets in financial institutions in foreign countries. For people who work internationally or for multinational corporations, the ability to save and use funds in a foreign currency for international transactions saves both time and money. Offshore banking provides a way to access funds in a foreign currency without having to account for rapidly changing exchange rates. There are a number of countries that provide offshore banking services, including the Cayman Islands, Bahamas, Belize, Panama, and Switzerland.

Although offshore banking provides services to meet legitimate business and personal needs, it is also a way to engage in criminal activity. The laundering of money, or moving money gained in illegal activities through the financial system, is often done through offshore banks due to their lack of regulation and secrecy of operation. Offshore banks are also used to hide money received through corrupt or illegal activities, to avoid taxes, and to protect funds from legal action.

### ☑ CHECKING FOR UNDERSTANDING

1. **IDENTIFYING CONNECTIONS** What are the roles of global economic organizations in the world economy?
2. **EXPLAINING EFFECTS** How does marketing promote globalization? Why do some people oppose this trend?
3. **INTERPRETING** How are the World Bank and International Monetary Fund different?

**MAKING CONNECTIONS TO TODAY**

### GLOBALIZATION'S IMPACT ON THE NATION-STATE

Since the Industrial Revolution, nation-states have expanded their authority to assume larger responsibility over the stability of their economies and the welfare of their citizens. However, as globalization has increased, so have the number of "nonstate actors" such as multinational corporations and other transnational groups that reach across borders. These nonstate actors often have the ability to ignore or elude the control of a nation-state. As a consequence, globalization often makes a nation-state appear weak and unable to manage affairs inside its own borders. Many nonstate actors, in comparison, seem more powerful.

**IDENTIFYING CONNECTIONS**
How might a nonstate actor such as a multinational corporation be able to challenge the sovereignty of a nation-state?

ANALYZING KEY IDEAS AND DETAILS

1. **ANALYZING CENTRAL IDEAS** Read the first paragraph under the heading "Regional Trade Organizations." What is the central idea? Predict what you will learn in this section.
2. **CITING TEXT EVIDENCE** What evidence in the text supports the conclusions that NAFTA's free-trade area has hurt some workers?

**GEOGRAPHIC REASONING**

1. **GLOBAL INTERCONNECTIONS** Calculate the percentage of member countries in the EU that have adopted the euro as their currencies. Why might some nations have chosen to keep their own currencies?
2. **EXPLORING REGIONS** In what geographic region are the candidates for EU membership concentrated?

# REGIONAL TRADE ORGANIZATIONS

**GUIDING QUESTION** *What are the effects of regional trade organizations on national and regional economies?*

Groups of nations have also joined together to form trading blocs to foster regional prosperity. Mercosur, for example, is an economic union of Argentina, Brazil, Paraguay, and Uruguay.

## NAFTA

In 1992 Mexican president Carlos Salinas de Gortari began to work with U.S. President George H. W. Bush and the Canadian Prime Minister Brian Mulroney to form the North American Free Trade Agreement (NAFTA). It was ratified and put into effect in the beginning of 1994. It created a free-trade area for Canada, the United States, and Mexico. Some economists have argued it has been beneficial to business owners but harmful to others. Farmers in Mexico, for example, saw prices for their food products drop as cheap American foodstuffs were imported. Industrial workers in the United States lost jobs as American companies outsourced jobs to Mexico to use cheap labor. A similar agreement called the Central America-U.S. Free Trade Agreement (CAFTA) was created by the United States and six Central American nations in the mid-1990s.

## EUROPEAN UNION

The European Community (EC) was chiefly an economic union. By 1992, it comprised 344 million people and was the world's largest single trading bloc.

THE EUROPEAN UNION 2015

SOURCE: European Union, europa.eu

The Treaty on European Union was an attempt to create a true economic and monetary union of all EC members. The EC renamed itself the European Union (EU). One of the EU's first goals was to establish a common **currency**, called the euro, adopted by 12 EU nations early in 1999. On June 1, 1999, a European Central Bank was created, and by January 2010, the euro had officially replaced 16 national currencies. The euro serves approximately 338 million people and has become the world's second-largest reserve currency after the U.S. dollar.

In addition to having a single internal market for its members and a common currency, the European Union also established a common agricultural policy. It provides subsidies to farmers to enable them to sell their goods competitively on the world market. The policy also provides aid to the EU's poorest countries and subsidies for job training, education, and modernization programs.

### OPEC

The Organization of the Petroleum Exporting Countries (OPEC) was founded in 1960 by Iraq, Iran, Saudi Arabia, Kuwait, and Venezuela. OPEC currently has 15 member countries that meet to determine policies on oil prices and production cooperatively. The export of oil is a key factor in the economies of OPEC member countries. In the early 1970s, OPEC placed an embargo on oil shipments to the United States and the Netherlands, which resulted in severe oil shortages and high inflation in the West. OPEC continued to raise prices through the rest of the decade, which increased the political and economic power of OPEC. However, the influence of OPEC on the global oil market is dependent on how much oil they have in reserve and how much they are currently producing. Together, OPEC members own about two-thirds of the world's known petroleum reserves and produce about two-fifths of the world's oil.

### ✓ CHECKING FOR UNDERSTANDING

1. **EXPLAINING EFFECTS** What are the effects of regional trade organizations on national and regional economies?
2. **UNDERSTANDING CHANGE** How did the formation of the EC and then the EU change Europe?
3. **INTERPRETING** Would you describe the European Union as solely an economic entity?

## ASPECTS OF GLOBALIZATION

**GUIDING QUESTION** *What are the costs and benefits of globalization?*

Globalization has increased the exchange of products and ideas and raised the general wealth and welfare of the world as a whole. However, critics believe the cheaper labor costs in less developed countries are used to exploit workers and serve to lower the standard of living. Another challenge to globalization stems from the wide gap between rich and poor nations as well as the income inequality among social classes within societies.

**ANALYZING KEY IDEAS AND DETAILS**

1. **SUMMARIZING** What are key aspects of globalization? How do China and India reflect those aspects? Write a short summary of this section.
2. **CITING TEXT EVIDENCE** What evidence from China and India supports arguments made by environmental critics of globalization?

### PROTESTS

Global economic organizations have come under attack. Both the World Bank and the IMF have been criticized for forcing inappropriate Western economic practices on non-Western nations. The IMF has been the target of particularly strong criticism for requiring countries to privatize public services and to eliminate social services as conditions for receiving loans. Critics also argue that World Bank and IMF policies aggravate the poverty and debt of developing nations. The WTO has been criticized for ignoring environmental and health concerns and for leaving out small and developing countries.

There have also been direct protests against globalization. Critics of globalization have accused multinational corporations of maximizing profits by supporting pitiful workers' wages and working conditions, ignoring the use of child labor, and ignoring environmental concerns. According to one critic, the author Naomi Klein:

> "What we have now is a particular model of globalization that's based on a belief system, and that belief system is how laissez-faire free-market economics, which holds that the pursuit of profit, the pursuit of growth, whether by corporations or by nation states, is essentially the only overarching goal. . . ."
>
> —Naomi Klein, April 21, 2001

**ANALYZING PRIMARY SOURCES**

1. **CITING TEXT EVIDENCE** What evidence does Klein offer that globalization puts the accumulation of wealth, specifically by corporations and nation-states, before human rights and environmental standards?
2. **DETERMINING POINT OF VIEW** How does Klein characterize globalization as it exists today? What alternative model of globalization does she offer, and how does she support her reasoning?

Women's rights have also become an issue in the protests against globalization as women often go unpaid or are engaged only in low-paid labor in many countries. Antiglobalization protesters have clashed with police when trying to disrupt meetings of the IMF and World Bank in cities around the world.

Another challenge to globalization stems from the wide gap between rich and poor nations. Rich nations, or developed nations, are located mainly in the Northern Hemisphere. They include countries such as the United States, Canada, Germany, and Japan, which have well-organized industrial and agricultural systems, advanced technologies, and effective educational systems. The poor nations, or developing nations, include many nations in Africa, Asia, and Latin America. They are often primarily agricultural nations with little technology and income inequality.

*Antiglobalization activists protest outside World Bank headquarters in Washington, D.C.*

**INTEGRATING INFORMATION** What arguments might the people shown in the image make to justify their actions?

Although corporations in developed nations can somewhat easily open manufacturing operations in less developed countries to take advantage of low labor costs, low-wage workers cannot as easily move to more developed countries where wages are higher. This serves only to increase the gap between rich and poor countries as well as individuals. Globalization, in facilitating the spread of information, is also criticized for assisting in the rise of extremist groups who may dislike the largely capitalistic and Western effects of globalization.

## GLOBAL FINANCIAL CRISIS

The global economy experienced worldwide financial troubles beginning in 2007 following the collapse of the U.S. housing market. Spurred by low interest rates in the early 2000s, easily available mortgages drove up housing values. In response, investors began selling financial investments called **collateralized debt obligations** (CDOs), or investments based upon bundled mortgages. Banks in New York sold CDOs to banks in Europe and elsewhere, spreading the wealth and the risk of investment. Many of these mortgages had been to borrowers with low credit ratings and high rates of default. As the initial rates on the mortgages ended, default rates increased, and securities began to lose their value. By September 2008, a number of insurance and mortgage companies, investment firms, and banks fell into bankruptcy. Stock values fell by almost $8 trillion from mid-September to November.

In effect, the crash of the United States housing market in 2008 led to a worldwide recession. As the American economy slowed, trade decreased worldwide because the American consumer, who had been consuming because of higher home values, could no longer do so. Production in Asia decreased and commodity prices fell, especially that of oil, making an impact on both Middle Eastern countries and Russia.

The United States responded to the financial crisis with an emergency program to recapitalize financial institutions and a stimulus package to support growth and to curb unemployment. Europe faced less severe problems than the United States, although European banks with exposure to **subprime investments** required government assistance to recapitalize. In Eastern Europe, recent free-market economies experienced a drastic devaluation of their currencies as investors fled to the stronger dollar and euro. Governmental measures prevented a total failure of the world financial system. However, high unemployment and weak consumption plagued Western nations for years.

### DETERMINING MEANING

The *prime rate* refers to the lowest interest rate at which people and businesses can borrow money. The prefix *sub-* means "under, or beneath." What does **subprime investment** mean? Explain how interest rates in subprime investments compare to those in prime investments.

## EMERGING ECONOMIC POWERS

China and India are experiencing economic growth on a scale rarely seen before. For the past 15 years, China's annual growth rate has been impressive. It has varied from 7.3 to 14.2 percent. India's annual growth rate has also varied; it was 7.3 percent in 2014. Both have the potential for such growth rates to continue for decades. Some economists predict that China's economy will overtake that of the United States by 2050.

The economies of China and India are not the same. China is supreme in industrial concerns and in mass manufacturing. India, on the other hand, is a growing power in design services and software. Multinational corporations have their products built in China and in turn have their software developed in India. One major result of this arrangement is the outsourcing of jobs from the

United States to both India and China, much to the concern of U.S. political leaders who seem helpless to stop the trend.

But both countries have serious problems. Poverty is still prevalent for hundreds of millions of people in India and China. Moreover, environmental problems are growing. Fertile land is in increasingly short supply while the rate of air pollution, especially in China, is 10 times the level in the United States, contributing to growing health concerns. Smog smothers the air in both Shanghai, China, and Mumbai, India. Finally, no one is sure both countries can continue on their **dynamic** rates of economic growth. Per capita income in the United States is six times as high as in China. In India, an estimated 21 percent of the population lives below the international poverty line.

### ✓ CHECKING FOR UNDERSTANDING

1. **SUMMARIZING** What are the costs and benefits of globalization?
2. **PREDICTING** What impact do you predict globalization might have on environmental policies in the United States? What about around the world? Explain your reasoning.
3. **EVALUATING** Why have some individuals protested the practices of global economic organizations?

## LESSON 3 REVIEW

### Time and Place

1. **RELATING EVENTS** How does OPEC demonstrate the value of the geographic distribution of natural resources? How does it reinforce the idea that the world is heading for an oil crisis?

### Building History-Social Science Analysis Skills

2. **COMPARING AND CONTRASTING** One popular slogan among antiglobalization protesters is "people before profits." What do you think critics of globalization mean by this phrase? How might supporters of globalization respond?
3. **UNDERSTANDING CONTEXT** Why did Europe, Asia, and other parts of the world experience financial troubles when the U.S. housing market crashed in 2008?
4. **ANALYZING CHANGE** China and India both have experienced rapid economic growth over the past 15 years. Why do you think that growth happened so long after that of the United States and other developed nations? What impact has this growth had on the United States?

### Writing About History

5. **ARGUMENTATIVE WRITING** Write an essay arguing whether free-trade agreements are a good idea or a bad idea. Be sure to focus on the costs and benefits to both developed and developing countries. In your essay, be sure to use proper spelling, capitalization, and grammar and appropriate vocabulary related to the subject.

### Collaborating

6. **ADAPTING SPEECH** Hold a six-minute debate with a partner around the following prompt: Are the benefits of free-trade agreements worth the costs? Why or why not? Student A should argue in the affirmative while student B argues in the negative for the first three minutes. Then students should switch roles and continue the debate. Students should cite a variety of evidence throughout and adapt their speeches as necessary.

ESSENTIAL QUESTION

- *How do social and environmental issues affect countries differently?*

## THE STORY BEGINS...

*Over the past 20 years, the Internet has transformed the way we work, spend our free time, and communicate.* ▶

LESSON 4

# Science, Technology, and the Environment

In the 1970s and '80s, the world entered a new phase of globalization, an information age. This new age was brought about by great leaps forward in computer and telecommunications technology. By the mid-1990s, the network of interconnections we now call the Internet was already in use. Just a few years later, many were making predictions about this new world. Vint Cerf, an early pioneer of the Internet, noted the following at this transitional moment in time:

> "The number of users of Internet will likely reach over 300 million by the end of the year 2000, but that is only about 5% of the world's population. By 2047 the world's population may reach about 11 billion. If only 25% of the then-world's population is on the Internet, that is nearly 3 billion users or ten times the population estimated at the end of the next year. . . . The Internet is proving to be one of the most powerful amplifiers of speech ever invented. It offers a global megaphone for voices that might otherwise be heard only feebly, if at all. It invites and facilitates multiple points of view and dialog in ways unimplementable by the traditional, one-way, mass media. . . . The Internet is becoming the repository of all we have accomplished as a society. It is becoming a kind of disorganized Boswell of the human spirit. Be thoughtful in what you commit to email, news groups, and other media – it may well turn up in a web search some day. Shared databases on the Internet are acting to accelerate the pace of research progress, thanks to online access to commonly accessible repositories."

—Vint Cerf, Speech to the Computers, Freedom and Privacy Conference, April 7, 1999

Many of Cerf's predictions have become reality. The Internet has transformed how people communicate, work, travel, shop, and generally live their lives. No single invention has done more to create the modern global economy than the Internet.

| Communication, Transportation, and Space | Health Care | Agriculture |
|---|---|---|
| | | |

**ANALYZING KEY IDEAS AND DETAILS**

**DETERMINING CENTRAL IDEAS** Read closely to identify important technological advances today.

**UNDERSTANDING CRAFT AND STRUCTURE**

1. **ANALYZING TEXT PRESENTATION** Use the headings in the section to summarize what you expect to learn.
2. **DETERMINING POINT OF VIEW** What tone does the text have? Use evidence from the text to explain your reasoning.

**MAKING CONNECTIONS TO TECHNOLOGY**

### GEOSPATIAL TECHNOLOGY

Global positioning systems (GPS) and geographic information systems (GIS) are examples of geospatial technology. GPS is used by the military, government, individuals, and businesses in vehicles, space shuttles, aircraft, ships, and for a variety of navigation and location services. Scientists can use GPS to determine the size of an earthquake, which allows them to predict tsunamis. Data from maps, satellite images, text, and statistical databases can be input into GIS, allowing maps to be made and changed quickly. This is useful to city and environmental planners, retail developers, and the military. Geospatial technologies will improve with the advancement of computer, aerospace, and Internet-based technology providing more opportunities for its use with the government, private industry, scientists, and the general public.

# TECHNOLOGICAL REVOLUTION

**GUIDING QUESTION** *How have scientific discoveries and technological innovations transformed society?*

Since World War II, but especially since the 1970s, a stunning array of changes has created a technological revolution. Like the first and second Industrial Revolutions, this revolution is also having a profound effect on people's daily lives and on entire societies. This technological revolution is also closely interrelated with new scientific discoveries.

## COMMUNICATION, TRANSPORTATION, AND SPACE

Global transportation and communication systems are transforming the world community. People are connected and "online" throughout the world as they have never been before. Space exploration and orbiting satellites have increased our understanding of our world and of solar systems beyond our world.

Since the 1970s, jumbo jet airliners have moved millions of people around the world each year. A flight between London and New York took half a day in 1945. Now that trip takes only five or six hours. The Internet—the world's largest computer network—provides quick access to vast quantities of information. The World Wide Web, developed in the 1990s, has made the Internet even more accessible to people everywhere. Satellites, cable television, cellular telephones, and computers enable people to communicate with one another practically everywhere in the world. Communication and transportation systems have made the world a truly global village.

The computer may be the most revolutionary of all technological inventions of the twentieth century. The first computer was really a product of World War II. British mathematician Alan Turing designed the first electronic computer to crack enemy codes. Turing's machine did calculations faster than any human. IBM of the United States made the first computer with stored memory in 1948. These early computers used thousands of vacuum tubes to function and took up considerable space. The development of the transistor and the silicon chip produced a revolutionary new approach to computers.

Then, in 1971, the microprocessor was invented and paved the way for the personal computer. Both small and powerful, the personal computer became a regular fixture in businesses, schools, and homes by the 1990s. The computer made many routine tasks easier and has become important in nearly every area of modern life. Other tools and machines, such as those that help fly airplanes, depend on computers to function.

Through their personal computers, people can access the Internet, a huge web of linked computer networks. The Internet was introduced to the public for the first time in 1972. That same year, electronic mail, or e-mail, was introduced. The system mushroomed, and by the early 1990s, a new way of sending Internet information, called hypertext transfer protocol (http), had been developed. This, combined with the invention of Web browsers, made it easier for people to use the Internet. By 2015, there were more than 3 billion Internet users worldwide.

As Web capabilities increased, new forms of communication began to emerge with Twitter, a communications platform that allows people to send instant updates from their computers or cell phones to their followers. Facebook, a social networking site, and YouTube, an Internet video site that provides instant visual access to many events, are also important.

Advances in telecommunications led to cellular, or mobile, phones. Though cellular phones existed in the 1970s and the 1980s, it was not until the invention of the **microchip**, a small semiconductor used to relay information, that cell phones became truly portable. Cell phones have since become enormously important. Cell phones are everywhere, and their ability to transfer data electronically has made text messaging a standard form of communication. Text and instant messaging have revolutionized written language, as shorthand script has replaced complete sentences for the purposes of relaying brief messages.

## MOBILE PHONE SUBSCRIPTIONS PER 100 PEOPLE

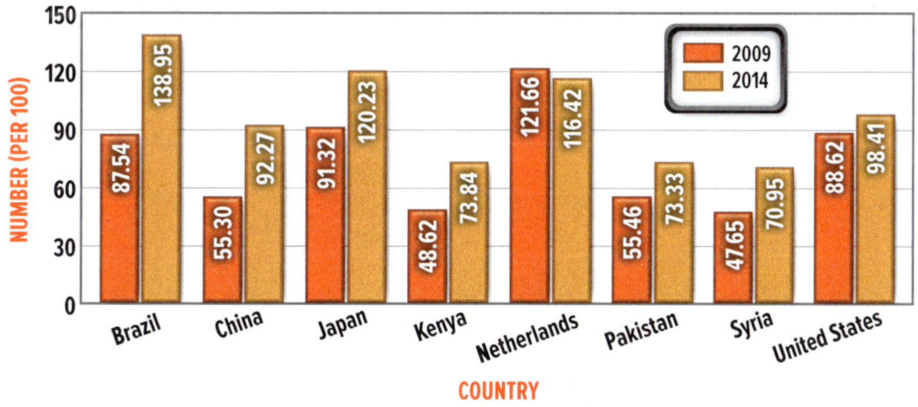


**Source:** International Telecommunications Union, 2015

1. **ANALYZING CHANGE** What overall trend have developed and developing countries seen in mobile phone subscriptions in recent years? What does this suggest about mobile phone usage?
2. **ANALYZING CHANGE** How do developed and developing countries differ in their access to mobile phones? How do they compare in terms of their rate of change between 2009 and 2014?

Technological developments have also improved our ability to explore space. Ever since Neil Armstrong and Buzz Aldrin landed on the moon in 1969, the exploration of space has continued. Space probes have increased our understanding of distant planets.

Today hundreds of satellites orbit Earth. Some are used to predict the weather, and others help navigate ships, aircraft, and cars. Communications satellites are used to relay radio, television, and telephone signals.

Launched in 1990, the Hubble Space Telescope (HST), a large astronomical observatory, orbits about 375 miles (603 km) above Earth's surface. Thus, the HST avoids the distorting effects of the Earth's atmosphere and provides clear views of our solar system and distant galaxies.

INTEGRATING INFORMATION
What does the image suggest about international relations in the fields of science and technology?

The National Aeronautics and Space Administration (NASA) sent two rovers, called *Spirit* and *Opportunity*, to the planet Mars in 2004. Based on the minerals that the rovers found in Mars's rocks, NASA scientists determined that the now-barren planet once had abundant supplies of water. NASA continues its Mars Exploration Program, analyzing data transmissions from rovers to Earth via the *Odyssey* orbiter, which was launched in 2001. Such data includes radiation risks for potential future human exploration of Mars.

## HEALTH CARE

New technologies in health care have allowed people to live longer and more productive lives. For example, doctors use mechanical valves and pumps for the heart and transplant organs. New medicines can treat both physical and mental illness. Scientific research has also led to improvements. From 1990 to 2003, the Human Genome Project unlocked the secrets of DNA, leading to new ways to diagnose and treat genetic diseases. The discovery of DNA itself—the molecule that carries genetic information from one generation to another—was the work of James Watson, Francis Crick, and Maurice Wilkins, who received a joint Nobel Prize for Medicine in 1962. Globalization has aided in the advancement of scientific research and technology by furthering collaboration and communication along with the diffusion of knowledge worldwide. This ability to share knowledge quickly has assisted in international efforts to address challenges presented in time of natural disasters, disease outbreaks, and in tackling environmental issues.

New and improved technologies have broadened the field of bioethics, which deals with moral choices in medical research. There are concerns that genetic engineering, or the altering of genetic information of cells to produce new variations, could create deadly strains of bacteria. The possibility of human cloning, along with stem-cell research (using stem cells from human embryos to research cures for certain diseases), has caused **intense** debate in many countries.

Developing countries, particularly those in parts of Asia and Africa, face many challenges in addressing issues including disease, infant mortality, and longevity. These issues are difficult to address without the availability of funds and resources necessary to meet basic needs such as food and access to clean water. Countries where these resources are readily available have larger issues with health problems related to their abundance, such as obesity, diabetes, and heart disease. Humanitarian aid and relief organizations such as the Red Cross and OXFAM, scientific and medical researchers, and intergovernmental organizations like the United Nations continue to work to address these issues around the world.

MAKING CONNECTIONS TO TODAY

### MEDICAL ADVANCEMENTS

Many medical advancements that have had a major impact on world health today were developed in the mid-20th century. For example, Charles R. Drew, an African American physician, started the American Red Cross blood banking program to assist soldiers. Today, about 6.8 million Americans donate blood each year, less than ten percent of those eligible to do so. Donated blood goes to save both military and civilian lives. Globally, blood donations rates are highest among more developed, wealthy nations. Likewise, Dr. Jonas Salk developed vaccines for flu and polio. Today, mass vaccinations prevent many illnesses each year, and polio is close to being eradicated globally. However, like blood banking, global access to vaccines as well as life-saving medicines reflects another disparity between developed and developing nations. Each year, millions of people—mostly children—die because of inadequate access to vaccines.

## AGRICULTURE

In agriculture, the development of new strains of rice, corn, and other grains, known as genetically engineered (GE) foods, have resulted in greater yields. However, scientists and world leaders disagree over the use of these GE foods, which are created by the **manipulation** of the DNA of plants to improve crops. Some experts see GE foods as a way to solve hunger crises in developing countries, although others worry about the effects GE foods have on the health of individuals and the ecosystem. Huge quantities of chemical fertilizers, which many farmers cannot afford, are needed to grow these new strains of foods.

The growing concern with chemical pesticides has led to an increase in organic farming in industrialized countries and the profitable export of organically grown crops by developing nations. Organic farming rejects the use of chemical fertilizers and pesticides, growth hormones, and livestock feed additives. Its goal is to maintain a healthy and sustainable environment.

*A farmer clears an area of the Amazon rain forest.*

### ✓ CHECKING FOR UNDERSTANDING

1. **UNDERSTANDING CHANGE** How have scientific discoveries and technological innovations transformed society?
2. **INTERPRETING** What does the map "Mobile Phone Subscriptions per 100 People" suggest about technology diffusion?
3. **EXPLAINING ISSUES** What are the arguments for and against the use of GE foods?

# ENVIRONMENTAL CHALLENGES

**GUIDING QUESTION** *What are the environmental challenges of the twenty-first century and how have governments and citizens responded to them?*

In *Silent Spring*, published in 1962, Rachel Carson, an American scientist, argued that the buildup of pesticides—chemicals sprayed on crops to kill insects—was having unforeseen results. Insects were dying, but so too were birds, fish, and other wild animals. Also, the pesticide residue on food harmed humans.

Carson's warnings alarmed many scientists and gave rise to the new science of **ecology**, the study of the relationship between living things and their environment. Since then, scientific research studies have shown that dangers to the environment have many sources.

## ENVIRONMENTAL DEGRADATION

Environmental degradation is the deterioration of the environment through the depletion of resources, including air, water, and soil. Resources are depleted through damage and destruction of the environment, often by pollution, overuse, or unsustainable activities. This destruction of ecosystems and habitats also results in the extinction of plants and animals. **Deforestation** occurs when forests and jungles are removed for firewood, logged for income, or to clear areas for farming and ranching. Deforestation can lead to habitat destruction and loss.

Especially worrisome is the rapid destruction of tropical rain forests near Earth's equator. Although tropical rain forests cover only 6 percent of Earth's surface, they support 50 percent of the world's species of plants and animals. The mass extinction of many species of plants and animals in these areas is a cause of great concern. The loss of plants has dramatic consequences for both animals and humans. For example, the alaotra grebe bird of the Madagascar rain forest was declared extinct in 2009 due to destruction of its habitat. The tropical rain forests are also crucial to human survival because they remove carbon dioxide from the air and return oxygen to it.

### ANALYZING KEY IDEAS AND DETAILS

1. **CITING TEXT EVIDENCE** What evidence in the text supports the conclusion that deforestation can have devastating effects for humans? What evidence supports the conclusion that water pollution poses a serious health concern for many people?
2. **ANALYZING CENTRAL IDEAS** Read the first two paragraphs under the heading "Environmental Challenges." What is the central idea of these paragraphs? How does this central idea tie together the rest of the information in the section?

### DETERMINING MEANING

To better understand **ecology**, break down the word. The root word *eco* comes from the Greek for "habitat." The suffix *-logy* means "study of." Use these meanings to write a definition for *ecology* in your own words. Check your definition in a dictionary or online resource.

DETERMINING MEANING

The words **deforestation** and **desertification** share a common suffix, *-ation*, meaning "process." The prefix *de-*, found in *deforestation*, means "remove, or reduce." Use these meanings to explain *deforestation* and *desertification*. How are the words related?

**Desertification** can be caused by deforestation of land for farming and ranching, uncontrolled fires, and unsustainable practices in cultivating land. More than 250 million people are directly affected by desertification.

Chemical wastes pollute the environment. The release of chlorofluorocarbons—gases used in aerosol cans, refrigerators, and air conditioners—destroys the ozone layer. This thin layer in the upper atmosphere shields Earth from the sun's ultraviolet rays. Acid rain results when air pollution, often sulfur from industries, mixes with moisture in the air. As acid rain falls, it damages buildings and pollutes waterways and soil.

Water, air, and soil pollution caused by ecological disasters can have long-lasting consequences. Toxic fumes from a chemical plant at Bhopal, India, in 1984; a nuclear accident at Chernobyl, Ukraine, in 1986; an oil spill from the *Exxon Valdez* in Alaska in 1989; and an oil platform explosion in the Gulf of Mexico in 2010 caused ecological and health problems that can still be seen today.

## GLOBAL CLIMATE CHANGE

Yet another threat to the environment is global climate change, which has the potential to create a worldwide crisis. Most of the world's scientists agree that the **greenhouse effect**, the warming of Earth due to the buildup of carbon dioxide in the atmosphere, is contributing to devastating droughts and storms, the melting of the polar ice caps, and rising sea levels that could flood coastal regions in the second half of the twenty-first century. These effects have added to political and economic issues in some regions of the world. Migration is fueled by these issues as people look to escape damaged areas to seek employment and flee conflicts. Also alarming is the potential loss of biodiversity. Seven out of ten biologists believe the planet is now experiencing a surprising extinction of both plant and animal species.

In an attempt to reduce carbon emissions, more than 150 nations have signed the Kyoto Protocol, which calls on countries to cut air pollution. The United States did not ratify the treaty, saying that the required changes would be too costly. In December 2015, 196 countries approved a historic climate pact to stabilize global warming, known as the Paris Agreement.

> "This Agreement, . . . aims to strengthen the global response to the threat of climate change, in the context of sustainable development and efforts to eradicate poverty, including by:
>
> (a) Holding the increase in the global average temperature to well below 2°C above pre-industrial levels and pursuing efforts to limit the temperature increase to 1.5 °C above pre-industrial levels, . . . ;
>
> (b) Increasing the ability to adapt to the adverse impacts of climate change and foster climate resilience and low greenhouse gas emissions development, in a manner that does not threaten food production; and
>
> (c) Making finance flows consistent with a pathway towards low greenhouse gas emissions and climate-resilient development."

—Article 2, Paris Agreement, 2015

A number of nations, aware that dependence on fossil fuels is contributing to climate change, have introduced geothermal and hydroelectric power plants. Another clear source of energy is wind. Scientists estimate that one-third of the world's electricity could be supplied by wind generators by 2050.

CITIZENSHIP

### CITIZEN SCIENCE

The Internet, smartphones, and other modern technologies have made possible a new type of citizen activism: citizen science. Citizen science refers to the voluntary participation of citizens across the globe in collaborative projects with professional scientists. Citizen scientists work with professional scientists to find solutions to climate change and wildlife and habitat destruction. These groups do this by making observations in the field, reporting data, and analyzing available data. In recent years, several organizations, including the Citizen Science Association and the Citizen Science Alliance, have formed to help manage the overwhelming demand and interest in such projects. Government institutions have also jumped on board, and several federal agencies in the United States now offer citizen science projects and support. On April 16, 2016, people and institutions across the world celebrated the first Citizen Science Day.

That would be enough to prevent 113 billion metric tons of carbon dioxide from entering the atmosphere each year. Wind farms have sprouted around the world—including in the United States.

## SUSTAINABLE DEVELOPMENT

Economic development that does not limit the ability of future generations to meet their basic needs is known as **sustainable development**. In promoting sustainable development, the United Nations urges countries to work to conserve all natural resources. Many countries have already enacted recycling and water conservation programs, along with curbing the dumping of toxic materials. A limited water supply affects close to 700 million globally. People without access to a source of clean water often get sick with cholera, typhoid, and diarrhea. More than 3 million people die every year from the lack of water or from drinking untreated water.

©Amy Sussman/Corbis

*Rooftop gardens, like the one above, help the environment by insulating the roof, which helps save energy.*

**ANALYZING INFORMATION** How does the activity in the image support the goal of sustainable development?

### ✓ CHECKING FOR UNDERSTANDING

1. **ANALYZING INFORMATION** What are the environmental challenges of the twenty-first century, and how have governments and citizens responded to them?
2. **RELATING EVENTS** How does environmental degradation relate to public health and safety concerns?
3. **SUMMARIZING** How have nations responded to global environmental challenges?

**DETERMINING MEANING**

The root word of *sustainable* is *sustain*. Synonyms for *sustain* include *support, maintain,* and *endure*. Use one of these synonyms to explain **sustainable development**.

## LESSON 4 REVIEW

### Time and Place

1. **ANALYZING CHANGE** Why has access to lifesaving health innovations not been evenly distributed across the world? How has globalization helped address this inequity?

### Building History-Social Science Analysis Skills

2. **ANALYZING INFORMATION** How can sustainable development prevent deforestation and desertification? How can it slow air, water, and ground pollution?
3. **IDENTIFYING CONNECTIONS** Why have some nations responded to climate change by pursuing renewable energy technology?
4. **IDENTIFYING CONNECTIONS** Aside from the knowledge gained about Earth's place in the universe, what benefits do space technologies offer?

### Writing About History

5. **NARRATIVE WRITING** Select one of the technologies discussed in the lesson. Write a narrative essay that demonstrates how that technology has affected your life and discusses how your life might be different without that technology.

### Collaborating

6. **INTEGRATING INFORMATION** In a small group, select one of the environmental challenges discussed in the lesson to research. Investigate the causes and effects of the challenge, and assess how the challenge impacts different parts of the world—and different people—in different ways. Use your findings to write a script for a public service announcement, a podcast, or a documentary about your topic.

ANALYZING SOURCES

# WHAT ROLE SHOULD THE UNITED STATES PLAY IN THE WORLD TODAY?

With the end of the Cold War, the United States emerged as the world's sole superpower. But the victory set the United States foreign policy adrift in the world to seek new goals and to respond to new challenges. Absent the bipolar world of the Cold War period, the United States found itself in a world of religious extremism, ethnic strife, economic disparity, and intractable regional conflicts. In this international environment, it was unclear what role the United States should play. As these excerpts show, U.S. leaders are still grappling with this reality.

### VOCABULARY

*fanatic:* zealous or enthusiastic supporter

*subservience:* a servile or subordinate position

*cede:* to surrender, yield

*dissidents:* people who opposes an established leadership

*aperture:* an opening

*reservoirs:* supplies, places to keep something in store

*eradicate:* to remove, destroy

*bedrock:* lowest point, foundation

PRIMARY SOURCE: SPEECH

## PRESIDENT GEORGE W. BUSH'S FAREWELL ADDRESS

At the end of President Bush's presidency in 2009, he made these remarks about the role of the United States in the world:

> “The battles waged by our troops are part of a broader struggle between two dramatically different systems. Under one, a small band of **fanatics** demands total obedience to an oppressive ideology, condemns women to **subservience**, and marks unbelievers for murder. The other system is based on the conviction that freedom is the universal gift of Almighty God and that liberty and justice light the path to peace. . . .
>
> [A]dvancing this belief is the only practical way to protect our citizens. When people live in freedom, they do not willingly choose leaders who pursue campaigns of terror. When people have hope in the future, they will not **cede** their lives to violence and extremism. So around the world, America is promoting human liberty, human rights, and human dignity. We are standing with **dissidents** and young democracies, providing AIDS medicine to bring dying patients back to life, and sparing mothers and babies from malaria. . . . Freeing people from oppression and despair is eternally right. This Nation must continue to speak out for justice and truth. We must always be willing to act in their defense and to advance the cause of peace.”

—President George W. Bush, January 15, 2009

### ANALYZE THE TEXT

1. **ANALYZING CENTRAL IDEAS** Between what two forces does President Bush make a distinction? How does he use this distinction to justify his foreign policy goals?
2. **DETERMINING POINT OF VIEW** Would you describe President Bush's foreign policy as expressed in this statement “isolationist” or “interventionist”?

PRIMARY SOURCE: SPEECH

## SECRETARY OF STATE HILLARY R. CLINTON ADDRESSES THE COUNCIL ON FOREIGN RELATIONS

Hillary Rodham Clinton served as Secretary of State under President Barack Obama from 2009 to 2013. She went on to run for president in 2016. In this speech, she describes her thoughts on American foreign policy:

> “The State Department now has Twitter feeds in 11 languages, and just this Tuesday, I participated in a global town hall and took questions from people on every continent, including, for the first time, Antarctica. . . . [W]e have to be strategic about all the levers of global power and look for the new levers that could not have been possible or had not even been invented a decade ago. We need to widen the **aperture** of our engagement . . .
>
> The **reservoirs** of good will we built around the world during the 20th century will not last forever. In fact, in some places they are already dangerously depleted. New generations of young people do not remember GIs liberating their countries, or Americans saving millions of lives from hunger and disease. We need to introduce ourselves to them anew, and one of the ways we do that is by looking at and focusing on and working on those issues that matter most to their lives and futures.”

—Secretary of State Hillary Rodham Clinton, January 31, 2013

### ANALYZE THE TEXT

1. **ANALYZING CENTRAL IDEAS** To what purpose do Secretary Clinton and the State Department use social media, such as Twitter, and events such as global town halls? How does Secretary Clinton explain the need for this kind of outreach?
2. **DETERMINING POINT OF VIEW** How would you describe Clinton's approach to foreign policy as expressed in this statement?

PRIMARY SOURCE: SPEECH

## PRESIDENT BARACK OBAMA'S SPEECH IN HAVANA, CUBA

In the spring of 2016, President Barack Obama gave the following speech in Cuba:

> "I've made it clear that the United States has neither the capacity nor the intention to impose change on Cuba. What changes come will depend upon the Cuban people.
>
> We will not impose our political or economic system on you. We recognize that every country, every people must chart its own course and shape its own model. But having removed the shadow of history from our relationship, I must speak honestly about the things that I believe, the things that we as Americans believe. . . .
>
> I believe that every person should be equal. . . .
>
> Every child deserves the dignity that comes with education, health care and food on the table, and a roof over their heads.
>
> I believe citizens should be free to speak their mind without fear. . . .
>
> And yes, I believe voters should be able to choose their governments in free and democratic elections."
>
> —President Barack Obama to the people of Cuba, March 22, 2016

### ANALYZE THE TEXT

1. **ANALYZING CENTRAL IDEAS** What is President Obama insisting should guide U.S. foreign policy toward Cuba?
2. **COMPARING AND CONTRASTING** How is President Obama's stated approach to Cuba similar to and different from that of President Bush's ideas about how the United States should approach international terrorism?

PRIMARY SOURCE: SPEECH

## PRESIDENT DONALD J. TRUMP'S INAUGURAL ADDRESS

President Donald Trump shared his vision for the United States' role in the world at his inauguration:

> "We must protect our borders from the ravages of other countries making our products, stealing our companies, and destroying our jobs. Protection will lead to great prosperity and strength. . . .
>
> We will follow two simple rules: Buy American and Hire American. We will seek friendship and goodwill with the nations of the world—but we do so with the understanding that it is the right of all nations to put their own interests first. We do not seek to impose our way of life on anyone, but rather to let it shine as an example for everyone to follow. We will reinforce old alliances and form new ones—and unite the civilized world against Radical Islamic Terrorism, which we will **eradicate** completely from the face of the Earth.
>
> At the **bedrock** of our politics will be a total allegiance to the United States of America, and through our loyalty to our country, we will rediscover our loyalty to each other."
>
> —President Donald J. Trump, January 20, 2017

### ANALYZE THE TEXT

1. **ANALYZING CENTRAL IDEAS** What central foreign policy goal does President Trump set for the nation? How does he explain his reasoning?
2. **DETERMINING POINT OF VIEW** How would you describe President Trump's foreign policy as expressed in this statement?

### MULTIPLE PERSPECTIVES

1. **COMPARING AND CONTRASTING** How are the foreign policy approaches similar? In what key way do they differ?
2. **IDENTIFYING BIAS** Identify an example of bias in each statement. How does that bias shape the foreign policy expressed by each speaker?

# STUDY GUIDE

## THE RISE OF ISIL (ISLAMIC STATE OF IRAQ AND THE LEVANT)
LESSON 1

- Also known as the Islamic State or ISIS, formed after U.S. troops withdrew from Iraq in 2011
- Targeted religious enemies and committed brutal public executions
- Caused refugees to flee ISIL-controlled areas in large numbers
- Forced over 1 million Iraqi citizens to leave their homes, according to UN estimates
- Began attacks outside Iraq and Syria in 2015
- Downed a Russian passenger jet, conducted deadly attacks in Beirut and Lebanon, and claimed responsibility for a deadly attack in Paris

## SOCIAL CHALLENGES IN THE MODERN WORLD
LESSON 2

### Causes of World Hunger

- Poverty
- Economic factors
- Natural disasters
- Poor farming practices
- Deforestation
- Overgrazing
- Food shortages due to war

### Global Health Pandemics

- International interactions help infectious diseases easily spread.
- 1.2 million people died from AIDS-related illnesses in 2015.
- More than 2/3 of the 37 million cases of HIV come from Africa, which has been devastated by the disease.
- Global AIDS deaths have declined due to the availability of antiretroviral therapy.

## THE EURO
LESSON 3

- The common currency used by members of the European Union (EU)
- Had officially replaced 16 national currencies in 2010
- Second-largest reserve currency after the U.S. dollar
- Serves more than 330 million people
- Adopted by 12 EU nations in 1999

## ENVIRONMENTAL CHALLENGES
LESSON 4

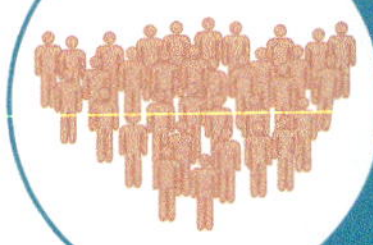

### Impact of Population Growth

**Deforestation** (the clearing of forests)
**Desertification** (formation of degraded soil that turns land into nonproductive desert)

### Chemical Wastes

**Chlorofluorocarbons** (destroys the ozone layer)
**Acid rain** (kills forests and damages buildings)

### Ecological Disasters

**Bhopal, India, 1984** (toxic fumes from a chemical plant)
**Chernobyl, Ukraine, 1986** (nuclear accident)
***Exxon Valdez* in Alaska, 1989** (oil spill)
**Gulf of Mexico, 2010** (oil platform explosion)

# CHAPTER 16 Assessment

**Directions: On a separate sheet of paper, answer the questions below. Make sure you read carefully and answer all parts of the questions.**

## Short Answer

1. **SUMMARIZING** What are the strengths and the weaknesses of the United Nations? Explain how its structure, system of membership, and powers provide benefits and drawbacks.

2. **UNDERSTANDING CONTEXT** What is the nature of the conflict in the Ukraine? Why is it significant for other parts of the world?

3. **EXPLAINING CAUSE AND EFFECT** How did the war in Iraq contribute to the rise of ISIL in the Middle East? What other conditions increased the power of this particular terrorist group?

4. **IDENTIFYING CONNECTIONS** Describe some recent population trends across the world. What challenges do these trends pose for nations today?

5. **EVALUATING** Explain how the prevention of genocide lies in the interest of all nations and why some nations might not act to prevent or stop genocide.

6. **ANALYZING CHANGE** Has the formation of transnational organizations and nongovernmental organizations made the world a more peaceful or secure place? Explain.

7. **EXPLAINING CAUSE AND EFFECT** What led to the development of modern globalization? How has this development changed the world?

8. **COMPARING POINTS OF VIEW** How do proponents and opponents of globalization differ in their perspectives of global economics today?

9. **IDENTIFYING CONNECTIONS** How did the collapse of the U.S. housing market in 2008 contribute to a worldwide recession?

10. **ANALYZING CHANGE** Why do you think social and environmental challenges affect countries differently? Provide specific examples.

11. **UNDERSTANDING CHANGE** How have advances in transportation and communication promoted globalization?

12. **ANALYZING INFORMATION** How have nations responded to share environmental threats, such as global warming and climate change?

## History and Social-Science Analysis

13. **EXPLAINING CAUSE AND EFFECT** What factors affect migration? What are some of the effects of migration?

14. **ANALYZING CHANGE** Why has the influence of Western powers, including the United States, declined since the end of the Cold War?

## Analyzing Visuals

Use the graph to answer Questions 15 and 16.

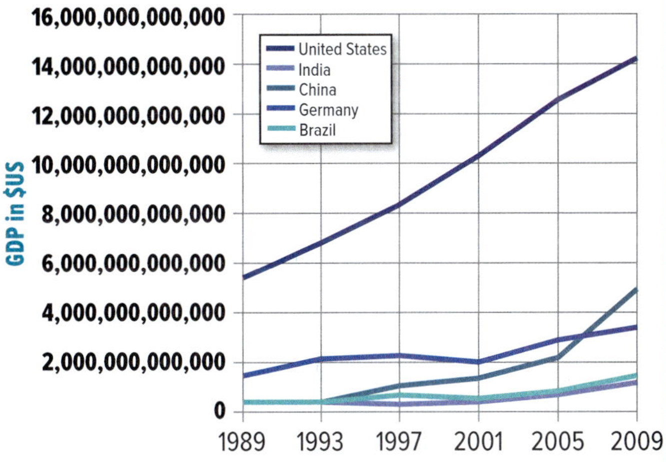


15. **INTERPRETING** Which countries experienced the most GDP growth between 2005 and 2009?

16. **INTEGRATING INFORMATION** How do the economies of Brazil, India, and Germany compare to the economies of the United States and China?

**Need Extra Help?**

| If You've Missed Question | 1 | 2 | 3 | 4 | 5 | 6 | 7 | 8 | 9 | 10 | 11 | 12 | 13 | 14 | 15 | 16 |
|---|---|---|---|---|---|---|---|---|---|---|---|---|---|---|---|---|
| Review Lesson | 1 | 1 | 1 | 2 | 2 | 2 | 3 | 3 | 3 | 4 | 4 | 4 | 2 | 1 | 3 | 3 |

## Research and Presentation

**17** **RESEARCHING FOR INQUIRY** Using what you have learned about the United Nations' efforts as peace-keeping forces, as well as from additional research about the United Nations, write a "white paper"—a short summary of a topic—on the work the United Nations does around the world during times of conflict and unrest. Cite specific examples of its efforts, and evaluate its effectiveness at meeting the goals of the UN. Include evidence from at least one primary source and at least one secondary source in your white paper.

**18** **USING MAPS** Use the text and appropriate resources to identify and investigate five regional free-trade areas or trading blocs. Then, make a map showing the member nations of these trade areas and trading blocs, and identify the year in which each arrangement formed.

**19** **PRESENTING** Use information in the text and additional research to create a multimedia presentation about three democracies that have emerged in the last 30 years. Use visual elements such as photographs, videos, flags, and time lines. Presentations should discuss the basic facts about each country and explain how the country came to exist.

## Reading and Analyzing Primary Sources

Use the document to answer the following questions.

At the United Nations Millennium Summit 2000, world leaders agreed to work together to achieve eight development goals by 2015. These goals included eradicating extreme poverty and hunger, achieving universal primary education, promoting gender equality, reducing child mortality, and combating diseases.

> "We will have time to reach the Millennium Development Goals . . . but only if we break with business as usual. . . . Success will require sustained action. . . . It takes time to train the teachers, nurses and engineers; to build the roads, schools and hospitals; to grow the small and large businesses able to create the jobs and income needed. So we must start now. And we must more than double global development assistance over the next few years. Nothing less will help to achieve the Goals."

—Kofi Annan, former UN Secretary-General, June 7, 2000

**20** **DETERMINING POINT OF VIEW** According to Kofi Annan, how can the goals be achieved?

**21** **ANALYZING IDEAS** What role does the UN play in achieving these goals, and why is this role significant?

**22** **INFERRING** What do these goals tell you about the economies of many countries?

## Writing About History

**23** **EXPLANATORY WRITING** Read the statement from Paul Rusesabagina on the Rwanda genocide below. Rusesabagina is a Hutu man who helped shelter hundreds of Hutus and Tutsis during the Rwanda genocide of 1994. Then, find two to three more primary sources on the conflict between Tutsi and Hutus. Write an analysis of the causes and effects of the conflict. Be sure to cite your sources and to provide specific examples from each.

> "Genocide is not something that comes out of nowhere and finds itself as a certain given place and disappears at a given time. This is not what happens. The Rwandan genocide took place during our civil war."

## Speaking and Listening About History

**24** **COLLABORATING** With a partner, take turns reading aloud the section under the heading "Cross-Border Crime." As you listen, record the main ideas about cross-border crime in a web. What are the three main areas of cross-border crime identified in the text? Which do you consider the most significant challenge for nations today, and why? Write a paragraph in response, and share your ideas with your partner. Together, brainstorm a list of at least five ways citizens, law enforcement, and national leaders can work to address the challenges identified.

**Need Extra Help?**

| If You've Missed Question | 17 | 18 | 19 | 20 | 21 | 22 | 23 | 24 |
|---|---|---|---|---|---|---|---|---|
| Review Lesson | 1 | 3 | 3 | 1 | 1 | 1 | 1 | 1 |

TEXT:(r) Transcrit of the Tavis Smiley Show, "Hotel manager-turned-hero Paul Rusesabagina" (4/3/14). Select "Read the transcript"

# CONTENTS

# World Religions Handbook

## TERMS

**animism**—belief that spirits inhabit natural objects and forces of nature

**atheism**—disbelief in the existence of any god

**monotheism**—belief in one God

**polytheism**—belief in more than one god

**secularism**—belief that life's questions can be answered apart from religious belief

**sect**—a subdivision within a religion that has its own distinctive beliefs and/or practices

**tenet**—a belief, doctrine, or principle believed to be true and held in common by members of a group

A *religion* is a set of beliefs in an ultimate reality and a set of practices used to express those beliefs. Religion is a key component of culture.

Each religion is defined and set apart from other religions by its own special celebrations and worship styles. Most religions also have their own sacred texts, sacred symbols, and sacred sites. All of these aspects of religion help to unite followers of that faith regardless of where in the world they live.

The religions examined in this World Religions Handbook all have these sacred elements, celebrations, and worship styles. Examining these characteristics provides insight into each of these religions.

## World Religions Today

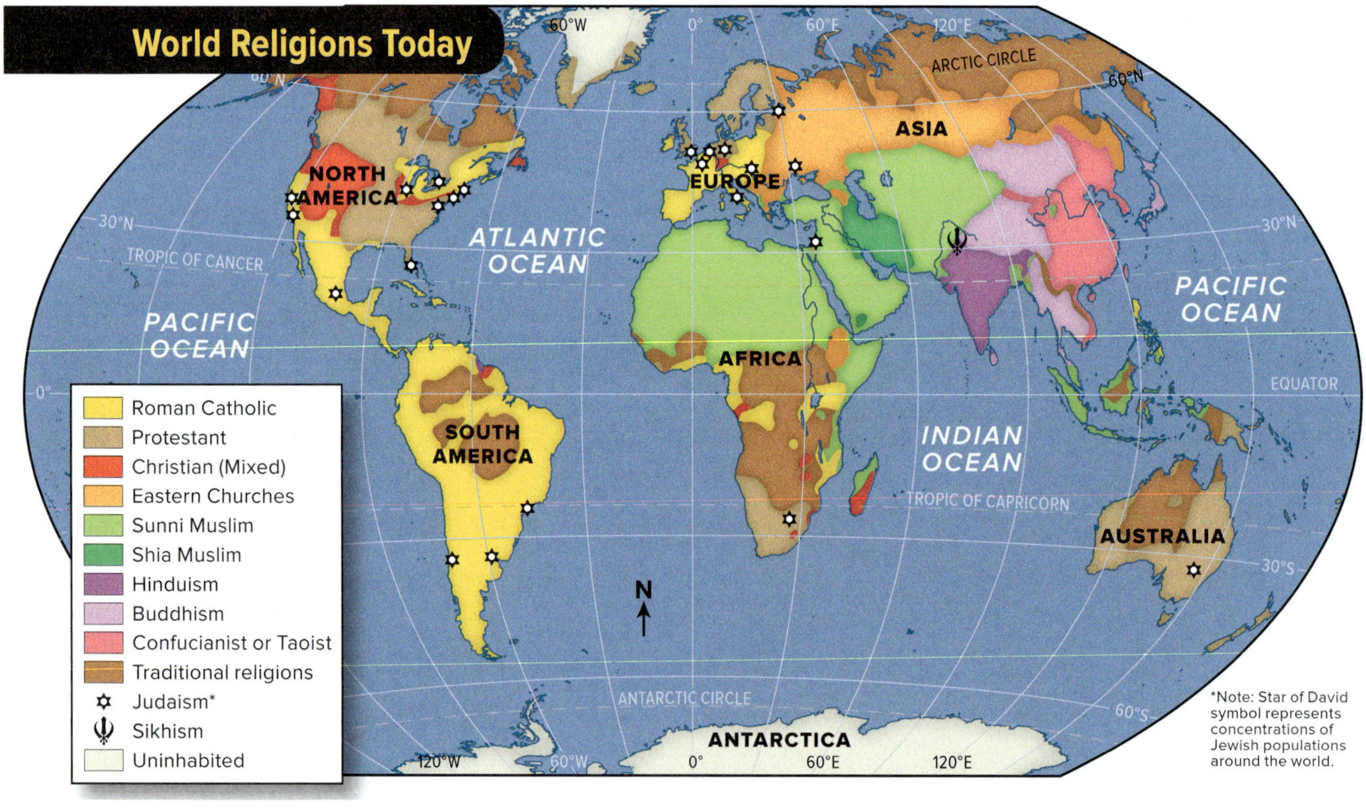


*Note: Star of David symbol represents concentrations of Jewish populations around the world.

*This map shows, on a large scale, where many people of each religion live. This map does not show the diversity of the religions practiced in each region throughout the world. In every region shown on the map, there are people who practice different religions than those shown.*

We study religion because it is an important component of culture, shaping how people interact with one another, dress, and eat. Religion is at the core of the belief system of a religion's culture.

The diffusion of religion throughout the world has been caused by a variety of factors including migration, missionary work, trade, and war. Buddhism, Christianity, and Islam are the three major religions that spread their religion through missionary activities. Religions such as Hinduism, Sikhism, and Judaism are associated with a particular culture group. Followers are usually born into these religions. Sometimes close contract and differences in beliefs have resulted in conflict between religious groups.

**Percentage of World Population**

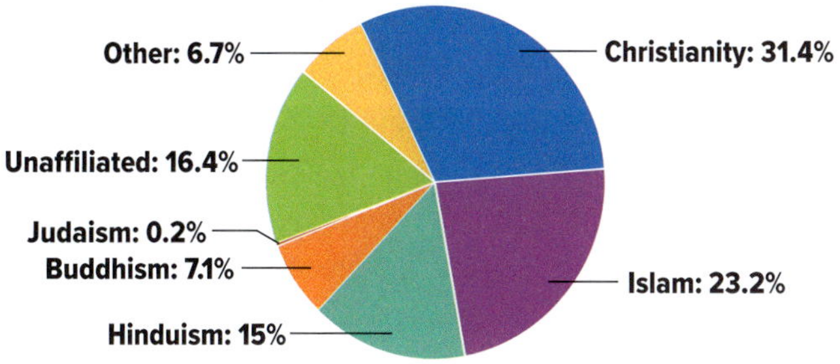


Source: The CIA World Factbook, (2010 estimates)

**Early Diffusion of Major World Religions**

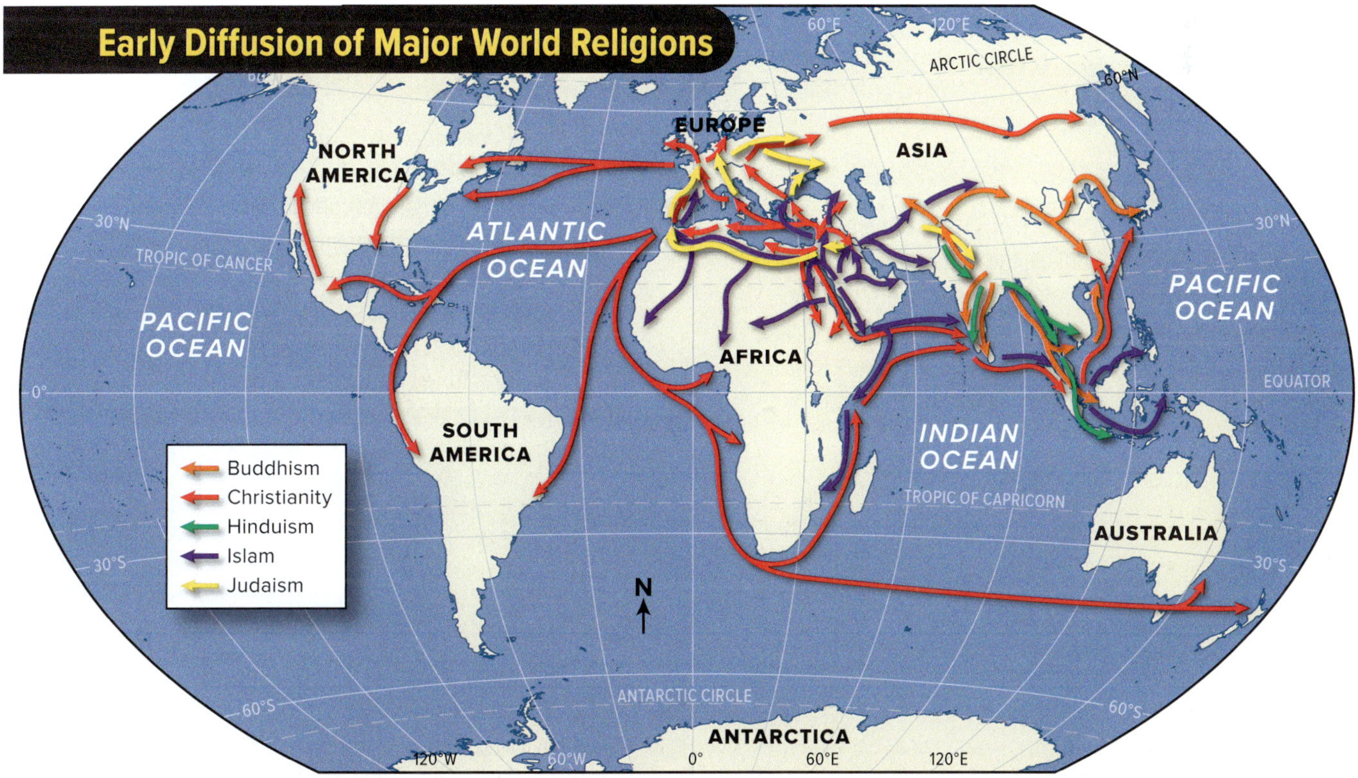

# Buddhism

Siddhartha Gautama, known as the Buddha ("the Awakened") after his enlightenment at the age of 35, was born some 2,500 years ago in what is now Nepal. The Buddha's followers adhere to his teachings (dharma, meaning "divine law"), which aim to end suffering in the world. Buddhists call this goal Nirvana; and they believe that it can be achieved only by understanding the Four Noble Truths and by following the 4th Truth, which says that freedom from suffering is possible by practicing the Eightfold Path. Through the Buddha's teachings, his followers come to know the impermanence of all things and reach the end of ignorance and unhappiness.

Over time, as Buddhism spread throughout Asia, several branches emerged. The largest of these are Theravada Buddhism, the monk-centered Buddhism which is dominant in Sri Lanka, Burma, Thailand, Laos, and Cambodia; and Mahayana, a complex, more liberal variety of Buddhism that has traditionally been dominant in Tibet, Central Asia, Korea, China, and Japan.

*Statue of the Buddha, Siddhartha Gautama*

## Sacred Text

For centuries the Buddha's teachings were transmitted orally. For Theravada Buddhists, the authoritative collection of Buddhist texts is the Tripitaka ("three baskets"). These texts were first written on palm leaves in a language called Pali. This excerpt from the *Dhammapada,* a famous text within the Tripitaka, urges responding to hatred with love:

> *"Never in this world is hate*
> *Appeased by hatred.*
> *It is only appeased by love—*
> *This is an eternal law."*
>
> *—Dhammapada 1.5*

## Sacred Symbol

The *dharmachakra* ("wheel of the law") is a major Buddhist symbol. Among other things, it signifies the overcoming of obstacles. The eight spokes represent the Eightfold Path—right view, right intention, right speech, right action, right livelihood, right effort, right mindfulness, right concentration—that is central for all Buddhists.

[redacted]

## Sacred Site ▲

Buddhists believe that Siddhartha Gautama achieved enlightenment beneath the Bodhi Tree in Bodh Gayā, India. Today, Buddhists from around the world flock to Bodh Gayā in search of their own spiritual awakening.

## Worship and Celebration ▸

The ultimate goal of Buddhists is to achieve Nirvana, the enlightened state in which individuals are free from ignorance, greed, and suffering. Theravada Buddhists believe that monks are most likely to reach Nirvana because of their lifestyle of renunciation, moral virtue, study, and meditation.

(t)Robert Nickelsberg/Getty News Images/Getty Images; (b)Ingolf Pompe/LOOK-foto/Getty Images

# Christianity

Christianity claims more members than any of the other world religions. It dates its beginning to the death of Jesus in 33 C.E. in what is now Israel. It is based on the belief in one God and on the life and teachings of Jesus. Christians believe that Jesus, who was born a Jew, is the son of God and is fully divine and human. Christians regard Jesus as the Messiah (Christ), or savior, who died for humanity's sins. Christians feel that people are saved and achieve eternal life by faith in Jesus.

The major forms of Christianity are Roman Catholicism, Eastern Orthodoxy, and Protestantism. In 1054, disputes over doctrine and the leadership of the Christian Church caused the church to divide into the Roman Catholic Church, headed by the Bishop of Rome, also known as the Pope, and the Eastern Orthodox Churches, led by patriarchs. Protestant churches emerged in the 1500s in an era known as the Reformation. Protestants disagreed with some Catholic doctrines and were critical of the Pope's authority. Despite their different theologies, all three forms are united in their belief in Jesus as savior.

*Stained glass window depicting Jesus*

## Sacred Text

The Christian Bible is the spiritual text for all Christians and is considered to be inspired by God. This excerpt, from Matthew 5:3-12, is from Jesus' Sermon on the Mount.

> *"Blessed are the poor in spirit, for theirs is the kingdom of heaven.*
> *Blessed are those who mourn, for they shall be comforted.*
> *Blessed are the meek, for they shall inherit the earth.*
> *Blessed are those who hunger and thirst for righteousness, for they shall be satisfied.*
> *Blessed are the merciful, for they shall obtain mercy.*
> *Blessed are the pure in heart, for they shall see God.*
> *Blessed are the peacemakers, for they shall be called sons of God.*
> *Blessed are those who are persecuted for righteousness' sake, for theirs is the kingdom of heaven.*
> *Blessed are you when men revile you and persecute you and utter all kinds of evil against you falsely on my account.*
> *Rejoice and be glad, for your reward is great in heaven, for so men persecuted the prophets who were before you."*

## Sacred Symbol

Christians believe that Jesus died for their sins. His death *redeemed* those who follow his teachings. The statue *Christ the Redeemer*, located in Rio de Janeiro, Brazil, symbolizes this fundamental belief.

[redacted]

## Sacred Site ▸

The Gospels affirm that Bethlehem was the birthplace of Jesus. Consequently, it holds great importance to Christians. The Church of the Nativity is located in the heart of Bethlehem. It houses the spot where Christians believe Jesus was born.

## Worship and Celebration ▾

Christians celebrate many events commemorating the life and death of Jesus. Among the most widely known and observed are Christmas, Good Friday, and Easter. Christmas is often commemorated by attending church services to celebrate the birth of Jesus. As part of the celebration, followers often light candles.

(t)©Atlantide Phototravel/Corbis, (b)Remi Benali/The Image Bank/Getty Images

# Confucianism

Confucianism began more than 2,500 years ago in China. Although considered a religion, it is actually a philosophy. It is based upon the teachings of Confucius, which are grounded in ethical behavior and good government.

The teachings of Confucius focused on three areas: social philosophy, political philosophy, and education. Confucius taught that relationships are based on rank. Persons of higher rank are responsible for caring for those of lower rank. Those of lower rank should respect and obey those of higher rank. Eventually his teachings spread from China to other East Asian societies.

*Students study Confucianism, Chunghak-dong, South Korea*

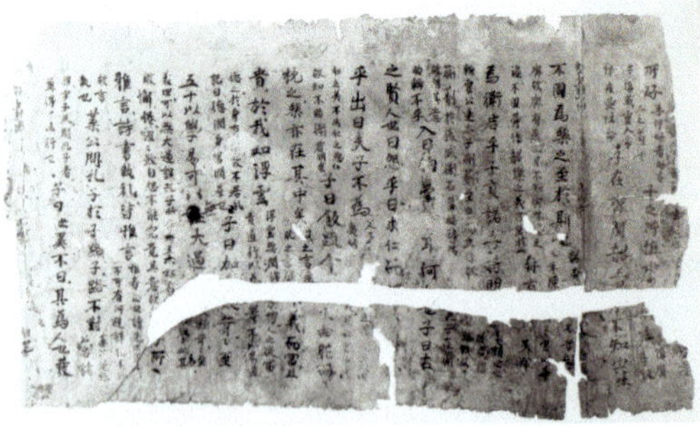

## Sacred Text

Confucius was famous for his sayings and proverbs. These teachings were gathered into a book called the *Analects* (see image above) after Confucius's death. Below is an example of Confucius's teachings:

*Confucius said:*

> *"To learn and to practice what is learned time and again is pleasure, is it not? To have friends come from afar is happiness, is it not? To be unperturbed when not appreciated by others is gentlemanly, is it not?"*

## Sacred Symbol

Yin-yang, associated with both Confucianism and Daoism, symbolizes the harmony offered by the philosophies. The light half represents *yang,* the creative, firm, strong elements in all things. The dark half represents *yin,* the receptive, yielding, weak elements. The two act together to balance one another.

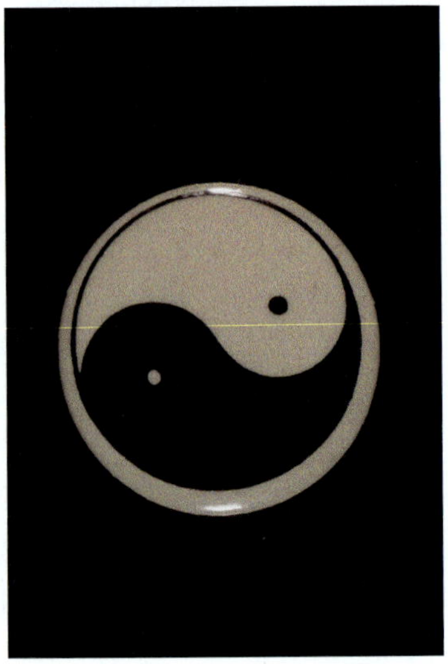

## Sacred Site ▲

The temple at Qufu is a group of buildings dedicated to Confucius. It is located on Confucius's ancestral land. It is one of the largest ancient architectural complexes in China. Every year followers gather at Qufu to celebrate the birthday of Confucius.

## Worship and Celebration ▶

Confucianism does not have a god or clergy, but there are temples dedicated to Confucius, the spiritual leader. Those who follow his teachings see Confucianism as a way of life and a guide to ethical behavior and good government.

(t) STR/Stringer/AFP/Getty Images; (b) Jack Hollingsworth/Photodisc/Getty Images

# Hinduism

Hinduism is the oldest of the world's major living religions. It developed among the cultures in India as they spread out over the plains and forests of the subcontinent. It has no single founder or founding date. Hinduism is complex; it has numerous sects and many different practices among its followers. Most Hindus believe in one god, whose qualities are represented by various divinities. Among the more famous Hindu divinities are Brahma, Vishnu, and Shiva, who represent respectively the creative, sustaining, and destructive forces in the universe. Major Hindu beliefs are reincarnation, karma, and dharma.

Hindus believe the universe contains several heavens and hells. According to the concept of rebirth or reincarnation, which is central to their beliefs, souls are continually reborn. In what form one is reborn is determined by the good and evil actions performed in his or her past lives. Those acts are karma. A soul continues in the cycle of rebirth until release is achieved.

*Statue of Vishnu*

## Sacred Text

The Vedas consist of hymns, prayers, and speculations composed in ancient Sanskrit. They are the oldest religious texts in an Indo-European language. The Rig Veda, Sama Veda, Yajur Veda, and Atharva Veda are the four great Vedic collections. Together, they make up one of the most significant and authoritative Hindu religious texts.

> “*Now, whether they perform a cremation for such a person or not,*
> *people like him pass into the flame,*
> *from the flame into the day,*
> *from the day into the fortnight of the waxing moon*
> *from the fortnight of the waxing moon into the six months when the sun moves north,*
> *from these months into the year, from the year into the sun,*
> *from the sun into the moon, and from the moon into the lightning.*
> *Then a person who is not human—he leads them to Brahman.*
> *This is the path to the gods, the path to Brahman.*
> *Those who proceed along this path do not return to this human condition.*”
>
> —The Chandogya Upanishad 4:15.5

## Sacred Symbol

One important symbol of Hinduism is actually a symbol for a sound. “Om” is a sound that Hindus often chant during prayer, mantras, and rituals.

[redacted]

## Sacred Site ▸

Hindus believe that when a person dies his or her soul is reborn. This is known as reincarnation. Many Hindus bathe in the Ganges and other sacred rivers to purify their soul and to be released from rebirth.

## Worship and Celebration ▾

Holi is a significant North Indian Hindu festival celebrating the triumph of good over evil. As part of the celebration, men, women, and children splash colored powders and water on each other. In addition to its religious significance, Holi also celebrates the beginning of spring.

# Islam

Followers of Islam, known as Muslims, believe in one God, whom they call Allah. The word *Allah* is Arabic for "the god." The spiritual founder of Islam, Muhammad, began his teachings in Makkah (Mecca) in 610 C.E.. Eventually the religion spread throughout much of Asia, including parts of India to the borders of China, and substantial portion of Africa. According to Muslims, the Quran, their holy book, contains the direct word of God, revealed to their prophet Muhammad sometime between 610 C.E. and 632 C.E. Muslims believe that God created nature and without his intervention, there would be nothingness. God serves four functions: creation, sustenance, guidance, and judgment.

Central to Islamic beliefs are the Five Pillars. These are affirmation of the belief in Allah and Muhammad as his prophet; group prayer; tithing, or the giving of money to charity; fasting during Ramadan; and a pilgrimage to Makkah once in a lifetime if physically and financially able. Within Islam, there are two main branches, the Sunni and the Shia. The differences between the two are based on the history of the Muslim state. The Shia believed that the rulers should descend from Muhammad. The Sunni believed that the rulers need only be followers of Muhammad. Most Muslims are Sunni.

*The Dome of the Rock, Jerusalem*

*The Quran*

## Sacred Text

The sacred text of Islam is the Quran. Preferably, it is written and read only in Arabic, but translations have been made into many languages. The excerpt below is a verse repeated by all Muslims during their five daily prayers.

> *"In the Name of Allah, the Compassionate,*
> *the Merciful,*
> *Praise be to Allah, the Lord of the World,*
> *The Compassionate, the Merciful,*
> *Master of the Day of Judgment,*
> *Only You do we worship, and only You*
> *Do we implore for help.*
> *Lead us to the right path,*
> *The path of those you have favored*
> *Not those who have incurred*
> *Your wrath or*
> *Have gone astray."*
>
> —The Quran

## Sacred Symbol

Islam is often symbolized by the crescent moon. It is an important part of Muslim rituals, which are based on the lunar calendar.

[redacted]

## Sacred Site ▸

Makkah is a sacred site for all Muslims. One of the Five Pillars of Islam states that all who are physically and financially able must make a hajj, or pilgrimage, to the holy city once in their life. Practicing Muslims are also required to pray facing Makkah five times a day.

## Worship and Celebration ▾

Ramadan is a month-long celebration commemorating the time during which Muhammad received the Quran from Allah. It is customary for Muslims to fast from dawn until sunset all month long. Muslims believe that fasting helps followers focus on spiritual rather than bodily matters and creates empathy for one's fellow men and women. Ramadan ends with a feast known as Eid-al-Fitr, or Feast of the Fast.

(t)Nabeel Turner/The Image Bank/Getty Images; (b)Fuse/Getty Images

# Judaism

Judaism is a monotheistic religion. In fact, Judaism was the first major religion to believe in one God. Jews trace their national and religious origins back to God's call to Abraham and the revelation of Torah to Moses at Mount Sinai. Jews believe that they have a covenant with God, who expects them to pursue justice and live ethical lives and will one day usher in an era of universal peace.

Over time Judaism has separated into branches, including Orthodox, Reform, Conservative, and Reconstructionist. Orthodox Jews are the most traditional of all the branches.

*El Ghriba Synagogue, Jerba, Tunisia*

*The Magen David*

*The Torah scroll*

## Sacred Symbol

One of the oldest symbols of the Jewish people is the menorah, used in the celebration of Hanukkah, commemorating the re-dedication of the Temple of Jerusalem following the Maccabees' victory over the Syrian Greeks. Another important Jewish symbol is the Star of David, also known as the Magen David, or Shield of David. It has been popular since the 17th century.

## Sacred Text

The Torah is the five books of Moses, which tell the story of the origins of the Jews and explain Jewish laws. The remainder of the Hebrew Bible contains the writings of the prophets, Psalms, and ethical and historical works.

> *"I am the Lord your God, who brought you out of the land of Egypt, out of the house of slavery; you shall have no other gods before me."*
>
> —Exodus 20:2–3

## Sacred Site

The Western Wall is what remains of the structure surrounding the Second Jerusalem Temple, built after the Jews' return from Babylonian captivity. It is considered the most sacred spot in Jewish religious tradition, in the holiest city for Judaism. Worldwide Jews pray facing Jerusalem morning, afternoon, and evening, and within Jerusalem, Jews face toward the Western Wall.

## Worship and Celebration

The day-long Yom Kippur service ends with the blowing of the ram's horn (shofar). Yom Kippur is the holiest day in the Jewish calendar. During Yom Kippur, Jews do not eat or drink for 25 hours. The purpose is to reflect on the past year, repent for one's sins, and gain forgiveness from God. It falls in September or October, ten days after Rosh Hashanah, the Jewish New Year.

(t)Paul Chesley/Stone/Getty Images; (b)Geoff Manasse/Getty Images

# Sikhism

Sikhism emerged in the mid-1400s in the Punjab, in northwest India. Sikhism is a distinct and independent religion that arose out of the teachings of Guru Nanak. Sikh tradition says that Guru Nanak's teachings were revealed directly to him by God.

Sikhs believe in one God who is formless, all-powerful, all-loving, and without fear or hate towards anyone. One can achieve unity with God through service to humanity, meditation, and honest labor. While about 76 percent of the world's 27 million Sikhs live in the Punjab, Sikhism has spread widely as many Sikhs have migrated to new homes around the world.

*Guru Nanak.*

## Sacred Text ▾

The primary scripture for Sikhs is the Guru Granth Sahib. Compiled from the mid-1500s through the 1600s, it includes contribution from Sikh Gurus and from some persons also claimed as saints by Hindus and Muslims, such as Namdev, Ravidas, and Kabir.

> *" Enshrine the Lord's Name within your heart. The Word of the Guru's Bani prevails throughout the world, through this Bani, the Lord's name is obtained. "*
>
> —Guru Amar Das

*Sikh men often wear long beards and cover their hair with turbans.*

## Sacred Symbol

One of the sacred symbols of the Sikhs is the *khanda*. It is composed of four traditional Sikh weapons.

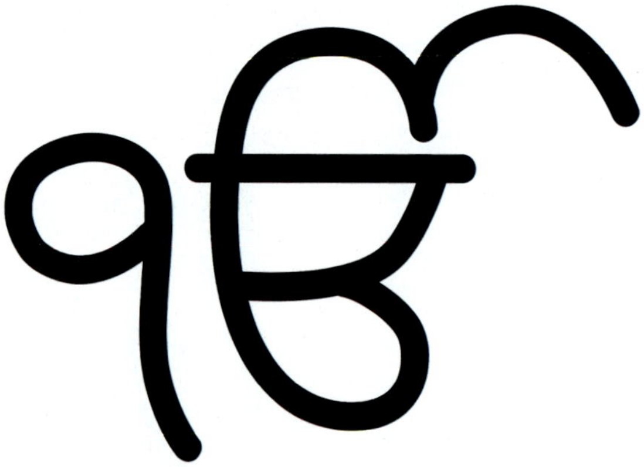

## Central Symbol ▴

Ek Onkar is one of the central Sikh symbols. It represents the belief that there is one God for all people, regardless of religion, gender, race, or culture.

[redacted]

## Sacred Site ▸

Darbar Sahib (also known as the Golden Temple) is located in Amritsar, Punjab. It is one of the most popular Sikh houses of worship because of its historical significance.

## Worship and Celebration ▾

Vaisakhi is a significant Punjabi and Sikh festival in April. Sikhs celebrate Vaisakhi as the day Guru Gobind Singh, the 10th Guru, established the Khalsa, the community of people who have been initiated into the Sikh religion. In Punjab, Vaisakhi is celebrated as the New Year and the beginning of the harvest season.

# Indigenous Religions

There are many varieties of religious belief that are limited to particular ethnic groups. These local religions are found in Africa as well as isolated parts of Japan, Australia, and the Americas.

Most local religions reflect a close relationship with the environment. Some groups teach that people are a part of nature, not separate from it. Animism is characteristic of many indigenous religions. Natural features are sacred, and stories about how nature came to be are an important part of religious heritage. Although many of these stories have been written down in modern times, they were originally transmitted orally.

*These Turkana men from Kenya are performing a traditional jumping dance.*

**Africa** The continent of Africa is home to a variety of local religions. Despite their differences, most African religions recognize the existence of one creator in addition to spirits that inhabit all aspects of life. Religious ceremonies are often celebrated with music and dance.

*Rituals are an important part of African religions. These Masai boys are wearing ceremonial dress as part of a ritual.*

*Masks are a component of ritual and ceremony in many African religions.*

**Japan** Shinto, founded in Japan, is the largest indigenous religion. It dates back to prehistoric times and has no formal doctrine. The gods are known as kami. Ancestors are also revered and worshiped. Its four million followers often practice Buddhism in addition to practicing Shinto.

This Shinto priest is presiding over a ritual at a Japanese temple. These priests often live on shrine grounds.

*Shinto shrines, like this one, are usually built in places of great natural beauty to emphasize the relationship between people and nature.*

**Australia** The Australian Aboriginal religion has no deities. It is based upon a belief known as the Dreaming, or Dreamtime. Followers believe that ancestors sprang from the Earth and created all people, plant, and animal life. They also believe that these ancestors continue to control the natural world.

*These Aborigine women are blessing a newborn with smoke during a traditional ritual intended to ensure the child's health and good fortune.*

*Aborigines, like these young girls, often paint their faces with the symbols of their clan or family group.*

# Indigenous Religions

**Native Americans** The beliefs of most Native Americans center on the spirit world; however, the rituals and practices of individual groups vary. Most Native Americans believe in a Great Spirit who, along with other spirits, influences all aspects of life. These spirits make their presence known primarily through acts of nature.

The rituals, prayers, and ceremonies of Native Americans are often centered on health and good harvest and hunting. Rituals used to mark the passage through stages of life, including birth, adulthood, and death are passed down as tribal traditions. Religious ceremonies often focus on important points in the agricultural and hunting seasons. Prayers, which are offered in song and dance, also concentrate on agriculture and hunting themes as well as health and well-being.

*Rituals are passed down from generation to generation. These Native Americans are performing a ritual dance.*

*There are many different Native American groups throughout the United States and Canada. This Pawnee is wearing traditional dress during a celebration in Oklahoma.*

*Totem poles, like this one in Alaska, were popular among the Native American peoples of the Northwest Coast. They were often decorated with mythical beings, family crests, or other figures. They were placed outside homes.*

# Assessment

## Reviewing Vocabulary

*Match the following terms with their definitions.*

| | |
|---|---|
| 1. sect | a. belief that spirits inhabit natural objects and forces of nature |
| 2. monotheism | b. belief in one God |
| 3. polytheism | c. a subdivision within a religion that has its own distinctive belief and/or practices |
| 4. animism | d. belief in more than one god |
| 5. atheism | e. disbelief in the existence of any god |

## Reviewing the Main Ideas

### World Religions

6. Which religion has the most followers worldwide?
7. On a separate sheet of paper, make a table of the major world religions. Use the chart below to get you started.

| Name | Founder | Geographic distribution | Sacred sites |
|---|---|---|---|
| Buddhism | | | |
| Christianity | | | |
| Confucian-ism | | | |
| Hinduism | | | |
| Islam | | | |
| Judaism | | | |
| Sikhism | | | |
| Indigenous | | | |

### Buddhism

8. According to Buddhism, how can the end of suffering in the world be achieved?
9. What is Nirvana? According to Buddhists, who is most likely to achieve Nirvana and why?

### Christianity

10. In what religion was Jesus raised?
11. Why do Christians regard Jesus as their savior?

### Confucianism

12. What is Confucianism based on?
13. What does yin-yang symbolize?

### Hinduism

14. Where did Hinduism develop?
15. What role do Hindus believe karma plays in reincarnation?

### Islam

16. What are the two branches of Islam? What is the main difference between the two groups?
17. What role does Makkah play in the Islamic faith?

### Judaism

18. What is the Torah?
19. What is the purpose of Yom Kippur?

### Sikhism

20. Where do most Sikhs live? Why?
21. What **is Vaisakhi?**

### Indigenous Religions

22. Why would local religions feature sacred stories about the creation of people, animals, and plant life?
23. Which of the indigenous religions has the largest membership?

## Problem-Solving Activity

24. **Research Project** Use library and Internet sources to research the role of food and food customs in one of the world's major religions. Create a presentation to report your findings to the class.

# DECLARATION OF THE RIGHTS OF WOMAN AND THE FEMALE CITIZEN

Olympe de Gouges composed her own Declaration of the Rights of Woman and the Female Citizen in 1791. Following are excerpts.

**VOCABULARY**

*utility:* something useful or designed for use

*imprescriptible:* cannot be taken away by law

*rigorous:* extremely strict

1. Woman is born free and lives as equal to man in her rights. Social distinctions can be based only on the common **utility**.

2. The purpose of any political association is the conservation of the natural and **imprescriptible** rights of woman and man; these rights are liberty, property, security, and especially resistance to oppression. . . .

4. Liberty and justice consist of restoring all that belongs to others; thus, the only limits on the exercise of the natural rights of woman are perpetual male tyranny; these limits are to be reformed by the laws of nature and reason. . . .

6. The law must be . . . the same for all: male and female citizens. . . .

7. No woman is an exception; she is accused, arrested, and detained in cases determined by law. Women, like men, obey this **rigorous** law. . . .

11. The free communication of thoughts and opinions is one of the most precious rights of woman, since that liberty assured the recognition of children by their fathers. . . .

▲ *Madame Aubry, Olympe de Gouges*

**DBQ ANALYZING HISTORICAL DOCUMENTS**

1. **LISTING** According to Gouges, what are the four “imprescriptible rights” of men and women?
2. **ANALYZING** What does Gouges blame for the limits on the rights of women?
3. **DEFENDING** Olympe de Gouges states that free communication of thoughts is one of the most precious rights of women. Do you agree or disagree? Write a paragraph defending your position.

# THE UNFORTUNATE SITUATION OF WORKING WOMEN

This article was published in *L'Atelier,* a Parisian workingman's newspaper, in 1842.

**VOCABULARY**

*object:* existing in a low state or condition

*repose:* a state of resting

*league:* a measure of distance between approximately 2.4 and 4.6 miles

Although women's work is less productive for society than that of men, it does, nevertheless, have a certain value, and, moreover, there are professions that only women can practice. For these, women are indispensable. . . . It is these very workers in all these necessary trades who earn the least and who are subject to the longest layoffs. Since for so much work they earn only barely enough to live from day to day, it happens that during times of unemployment they sink into **abject** poverty. . . .

▲ *Women worked long hours around heavy equipment for very little pay. This illustration shows a woman examining a power loom in a textile factory.*

Who has not heard of the women silkworkers'. . . –dirty, unhealthy, and badly paid work; of the women in the spinning and weaving factories. . ., working fourteen to sixteen hours (except for one hour for both meals); always standing, without a single minute for **repose**, putting forth an enormous amount of effort. And many of them have to walk a **league** or more, morning and evening, to get home. . . Nor should we neglect to mention the danger that exists merely from working in these large factories, surrounded by wheels, gears, enormous leather belts that always threaten to seize you and pound you to pieces. . . .

The existence of women who work as day laborers, and are obliged to abandon their households and the care of their children to indifferent neighbors is no better. . . [W]e believe that the condition of women will never really improve until workingmen can earn enough to support their families, which is only fair. Woman is so closely linked to man that the position of the one cannot be improved without reference to the position of the other. . . .

**DBQ ANALYZING HISTORICAL DOCUMENTS**

1. **PARAPHRASING** Using your own words, explain what the author meant by "indifferent neighbors." How does this word choice convey the author's opinion about workingwomen?
2. **DESCRIBING** How would you describe working conditions for women?
3. **IDENTIFYING POINTS OF VIEW** What is the attitude of the *L'Atelier* writer toward women and women's work? Is the author of the article likely to be a woman or a man? What makes you think so?

# AN IDEAL FOR WHICH I AM PREPARED TO DIE

Nelson Mandela delivered his speech "I am the First Accused" during the Rivonia Trial in Pretoria, South Africa, on April 20, 1964. Following the trial, he was sentenced to life in prison. The following is an excerpt from his speech.

**VOCABULARY**

*reserves:* a reservation; land set aside for use by a particular group

*squatters:* those who settle on public land without rights or permission

*domination:* the act of holding a commanding position or controlling power over something or someone

. . . The whites enjoy what may well be the highest standard of living in the world, whilst Africans live in poverty and misery. Forty percent of the Africans live in hopelessly overcrowded and, in some cases, drought-stricken **reserves**, where soil erosion and the overworking of the soil make it impossible for them to live properly off the land. Thirty percent are labourers, labour tenants, and **squatters** on white farms . . . The other thirty percent live in towns where they have developed economic and social habits which bring them closer, in many respects, to white standards. Forty-six percent of all African families in Johannesburg do not earn enough to keep them going. . . .

. . . The complaint of Africans, however, is not only that they are poor and whites are rich, but that the laws which are made by the whites are designed to preserve this situation. . . .

. . . During my lifetime I have dedicated my life to this struggle of the African people. I have fought against white domination, and I have fought against black **domination**. I have cherished the ideal of a democratic and free society in which all persons live together in harmony with equal opportunities. It is an ideal which I hope to live for, and to see realized. It is an ideal which I hope to live for and to achieve. But if needs be, it is an ideal for which I am prepared to die.

▲ *Nelson Mandela visits the jail cell where he served a 27-year sentence for opposition to apartheid. He became the first democratically elected president of South Africa in 1994.*

**DBQ ANALYZING HISTORICAL DOCUMENTS**

1. **ANALYZING** According to Mandela, what role does soil play in South Africa's divided society?
2. **IDENTIFYING** What argument do poor South Africans make regarding the country's laws?
3. **EXPLAINING** What ideal does Nelson Mandela discuss?

# FROM "A NEW CHAPTER IN CHINA'S REFORM AND OPENING"

World Trade Organization Director-General Pascal Lamy, in a speech at a forum in Beijing on 11 December 2011 commemorating the 10th anniversary of China's inclusion in the WTO.

### VOCABULARY

*millenary:* relating to 1,000 years

*protectionism:* an economic system that aims to encourage growth of domestic business and industry by placing restrictions on foreign imports

*proactive:* to anticipate and devise plans to solve future problems

Ten years is a long minute in China's **millenary** history. And yet these ten years have witnessed an unprecedented transformation of China's economy and society.

My first trip to China was in the 1980s, accompanying the then President of the European Commission on his first visit to Deng Xiaoping. Bicycles in ChangAn Street were the rule. . . . Ten years later, the streets of Beijing are crowded with family cars, not bicycles. . . . Millions of Chinese farmers have moved to the cities, employed by a rapidly expanding industrial sector, including multinational corporations which have come into China at unprecedented speed since 2001 and played a key part in creating a network of global value chains. . . .

China's accession to the WTO proved decisive in several respects.

The goal to become a WTO member acted as a lever for the process of domestic modernization. . . .

WTO membership also underpinned Chinese export-led growth with a strong insurance policy against **protectionism**.

. . . And yet the lesson learnt from the recent global economic crisis is that the WTO has a significant role to play as a bulwark against protectionism. This is particularly true of China which would have been much more severely affected by protectionist measures, given its prominence in world trade. The WTO has so far protected China against high intensity protectionism during the crisis.

Looking into the future, as a key member of the WTO family, China's role and influence will be vital in our collective endeavour to advance trade opening and global trade regulation. . . .

Today, the Chinese economy and its influence are greater and stronger than ten years ago. As a global power, it is only natural that the expectations of other countries on China have also grown. China's participation and support are vital in any collective action to address global challenges. With today's economic difficulties across the world, resolve and leadership are in desperate need. We all need a **proactive** China. . . .

On this tenth anniversary, and as we look forward for the next decade, I have two wishes that I would like to express.

The first is that China's involvement in the WTO helps us all in keeping this organization on the move towards more open and fairer trade.

The second is that the WTO's relevance for China keeps growing and helps this country to address its reform challenges.

Lamy, Pascal. 2011. "A New Chapter in China's Reform and Opening Up to the World". December 11, 2011. Beijing. Reprinted by World Trade Organization website.

### DBQ ANALYZING HISTORICAL DOCUMENTS

1. **ANALYZING** How does Pascal Lamy view the global role of China now and going forward?
2. **IDENTIFYING** What has changed in China's economy since it was granted admission into the World Trade Organization?

# ANALYZING SOURCES

## FROM TAWAKKOL KARMAN'S NOBEL PEACE PRIZE SPEECH

In 2011, Tawakkol Karman gave her acceptance speech upon receiving the Nobel Peace Prize. She spoke about the democratic movement, known as the Arab Spring, that was affecting her home country of Yemen.

**VOCABULARY**

*rostrum:* a stage or platform for public speaking

*aspiration:* the desire to achieve a goal

"Your Majesties, Highnesses, Excellencies, Distinguished Committee of the Nobel Peace Prize, Arab spring and revolution youth in the arena of freedom and change, and all free people of the world,

Peace upon you from the Nobel Peace **rostrum**.

. . . Alfred Nobel's dream of a world, where peace prevails and wars disappear, has not been achieved yet, but the hope to make it come true has grown large, and the effort to achieve it has doubled. The Nobel Peace Prize still offers this hope spiritual and conscientious momentum. For more than a hundred years, this award has stood as proof of the values of peaceful struggle for rights, justice and freedom, and also as proof of how wrong violence and wars are with all their backfiring and devastating results.

I have always believed that resistance against repression and violence is possible without relying on similar repression and violence. I have always believed that human civilization is the fruit of the effort of both women and men. So, when women are treated unjustly and are deprived of their natural right in this process, all social deficiencies and cultural illnesses will be unfolded, and in the end the whole community, men and women, will suffer. The solution to women's issues can only be achieved in a free and democratic society in which human energy is liberated, the energy of both women and men together. Our civilization is called human civilization and is not attributed only to men or women.

. . . At this moment, as I speak to you here, young Arab people, both women and men, march in peaceful demonstrations demanding freedom and dignity from their rulers. They go forward on this noble path armed not with weapons, but with faith in their right to freedom and dignity. They march in a dramatic scene which embodies the most beautiful of the human spirit of sacrifice and the **aspiration** to freedom and life, against the ugliest forms of selfishness, injustice, and the desire to hold on to power and wealth.

. . . The democratic world, which has told us a lot about the virtues of democracy and good governance, should not be indifferent to what is happening in Yemen and Syria, and happened before that in Tunisia, Egypt, and Libya, and happens in every Arab and non-Arab country aspiring for freedom. All of that is just hard labour during the birth of democracy which requires support and assistance, not fear and caution.

Allow me, ladies and gentlemen, to share my belief that peace will remain the hope of mankind forever, and that the best hope for a better future for mankind will always drive us to speak noble words and do noble deeds. Together, we will push the horizons, one after another, towards a world of true human perfection. . .

**DBQ ANALYZING HISTORICAL DOCUMENTS**

1. **ANALYZING** What is Karman's view about the equality of men and women?
2. **IDENTIFYING** How does Karman believe democracies in the West should react to the protests that made up the Arab Spring movement?

# FROM THE "WORLD ECONOMIC OUTLOOK"

Olivier Blanchard was the Economic Counsellor of the International Monetary Fund, a group of 188 countries whose aim is to encourage stable global economic activity and global economic growth. In this segment of the World Economic Outlook report, Blanchard discusses the economic crisis that hit the European Union economies in the first decade of the twenty-first century.

**VOCABULARY**

*acute:* characterized by severity or size of problem

*tempered:* qualified or moderated

*bank deleveraging:* the action of a bank reducing its amount of debt, in proportion to its amount of fiscal assets

Soon after the September 2011 *World Economic Outlook* went to press, the euro area went through another **acute** crisis. . . . With the value of some of [Spain and Italy's] banks' assets now in doubt, questions arose as to whether those banks would be able to convince investors to roll over their loans. Worried about funding, banks froze credit. Confidence decreased, and activity slumped.

Strong policy responses turned things around. Elections in Spain and the appointment of a new prime minister in Italy gave some reassurance to investors. The adoption of a fiscal compact showed the commitment of EU members to dealing with their deficits and debt. . . .

With the passing of the crisis, and some good news about the U.S. economy, some optimism has returned. It should remain **tempered**. Even absent another European crisis, most advanced economies still face major brakes on growth. . . .

[There are] two main brakes on growth: fiscal consolidation and **bank deleveraging**. Both reflect needed adjustments, but both decrease growth in the short term. . . .

Emerging economies are not immune to these developments. Low advanced economy growth has meant lower export growth. And financial uncertainty, together with sharp shifts in risk appetite, has led to volatile capital flows. For the most part, however, emerging economies have enough policy room to maintain solid growth. . . .

Turning to policies aimed at reducing risks, the focus is clearly on Europe. . . . Measures should be taken to decrease the links between sovereigns and banks, from the creation of euro level deposit insurance and bank resolution to the introduction of limited forms of Eurobonds, such as the creation of a common euro bill market. These measures are urgently needed and can make a difference were another crisis to take place soon.

Taking one step back, perhaps the highest priority, but also the most difficult to achieve, is to durably increase growth in advanced economies, and especially in Europe. . . . For the moment, the focus should be on measures that increase demand. Looking forward, however, the focus should also be on measures that increase potential growth. The Holy Grail would be measures that do both. There are probably few of those. More realistically, the search must be for reforms that help in the long term but do not depress demand in the short term. Identifying these reforms, and addressing their potentially adverse short-term effects, should be very high on the policy agenda.



**DBQ ANALYZING HISTORICAL DOCUMENTS**

1. **ANALYZING** How can bank deleveraging help in the context of the fiscal crisis that was being battled in Europe?
2. **IDENTIFYING** What is meant by the recommendation to "decrease the links between sovereigns and banks"?

# CONTENTS

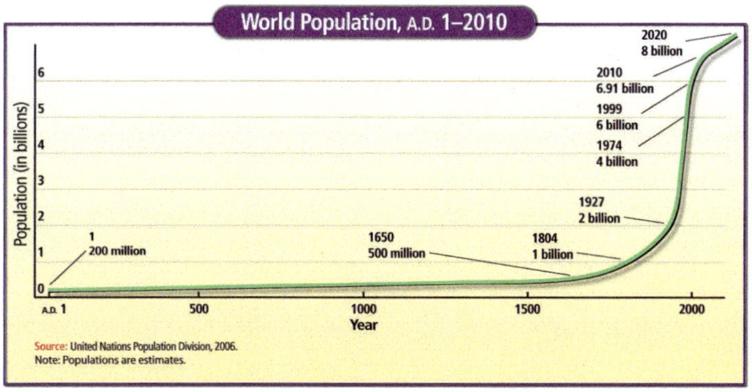


**Population by Continent, 2016**

| Continent | Population, 2010 | Projected Population 2050 |
|---|---|---|
| Asia | 4.367 billion | 5.144 billion |
| Africa | 1.187 billion | 2.306 billion |
| Europe | 746 million | 716 million |
| Latin America and the Caribbean | 625 million | 749 million |
| Northern America | 359 million | 440 million |
| Australia/Oceania | 38 million | 49 million |

**Source:** www.census.gov

**Life Expectancy**

| Country | Years |
|---|---|
| Japan | 85.00 |
| Andorra | 82.80 |
| Israel | 82.40 |
| France | 81.80 |
| New Zealand | 81.20 |
| United Kingdom | 80.70 |
| United States | 79.80 |
| Chile | 78.80 |
| China | 75.50 |
| Brazil | 73.80 |
| Egypt | 72.70 |
| Russia | 70.80 |
| India | 68.50 |
| South Africa | 63.10 |
| Mozambique | 53.30 |

**Source:** *The World Factbook*, 2016, CIA

**Infant Mortality**

| Country | Infant Deaths per 1,000 Live Births |
|---|---|
| Afghanistan | 113 |
| India | 41 |
| Egypt | 20 |
| Brazil | 18 |
| China | 12 |
| Russia | 7 |
| Chile | 7 |
| United States | 6 |
| Canada | 5 |
| United Kingdom | 4 |
| Germany | 3 |
| France | 3 |
| South Korea | 3 |
| Japan | 2 |

**Source:** *The World Factbook*, 2016, CIA

**Most Populous Countries**

| Country | Population |
|---|---|
| China | 1,374,000,000 |
| India | 1,267,000,000 |
| United States | 324,000,000 |
| Indonesia | 258,000,000 |
| Brazil | 206,000,000 |
| Pakistan | 202,000,000 |
| Nigeria | 186,000,000 |
| Bangladesh | 156,000,000 |
| Russia | 142,000,000 |
| Japan | 127,000,000 |

**Source:** *The World Factbook*, 2016, CIA

# MINI ALMANAC

**World's Richest Countries**

| Country | Gross National Income per Capita (in U.S. dollars) |
|---|---|
| Qatar | 132,100 |
| Luxembourg | 99,000 |
| Macau | 98,200 |
| Liechtenstein | 89,400 |
| Bermuda | 85,700 |
| Singapore | 85,300 |
| Isle of Man | 83,100 |
| Brunei | 79,700 |
| Monaco | 78,700 |
| Kuwait | 70,200 |

**Source:** *The World Factbook*, 2016, CIA

**World's Poorest Countries**

| Country | Gross National Income per Capita (in U.S. dollars) |
|---|---|
| Somalia | 400 |
| Central African Republic | 600 |
| Burundi | 800 |
| The Democratic Republic of the Congo | 800 |
| Liberia | 900 |
| Malawi | 1,100 |
| Niger | 1,100 |
| Guinea | 1,200 |
| Mozambique | 1,200 |
| Eritrea | 1,300 |

**Source:** *The World Factbook*, 2016, CIA

**Highest Inflation Rates**

| Country | Rate of Inflation (percent) |
|---|---|
| Venezuela | 480.00 |
| South Sudan | 52.80 |
| Ukraine | 48.70 |
| Syria | 33.60 |
| Yemen | 30.00 |
| Argentina | 27.60 |
| Malawi | 21.90 |
| Ghana | 17.20 |
| Sudan | 16.90 |
| Russia | 15.50 |

**Source:** *The World Factbook*, 2016, CIA

**Lowest Inflation Rates**

| Country | Rate of Inflation (percent) |
|---|---|
| Lebanon | -3.70 |
| Saint Kitts and Nevis | -2.80 |
| Saint Vincent and the Grenadines | -1.70 |
| Cyprus | -1.50 |
| Afghanistan | -1.50 |
| Grenada | -1.30 |
| Greece | -1.10 |
| Switzerland | -1.10 |
| Bulgaria | -1.10 |

**Source:** *The World Factbook*, 2016, CIA

**World's Ten Largest Economies**

| Economy | GDP (Purchasing Power Parity in U.S. Dollars) |
|---|---|
| China | 19.4 trillion |
| European Union | 19.2 trillion |
| United States | 17.9 trillion |
| India | 7.9 trillion |
| Japan | 4.8 trillion |
| Germany | 3.8 trillion |
| Russia | 3.7 trillion |
| Brazil | 3.1 trillion |
| Indonesia | 2.9 trillion |
| United Kingdom | 2.6 trillion |

**Source:** *The World Factbook,* 2016, CIA

**Regional Water and Sanitation**

| Region | Access to Improved Water | Access to Improved Sanitation |
|---|---|---|
| World | 89 | 64 |
| Oceania | 56 | 35 |
| Sub-Saharan Africa | 64 | 30 |
| South-eastern Asia | 89 | 71 |
| Western Asia | 91 | 89 |
| Southern Asia | 91 | 42 |
| Eastern Asia | 92 | 67 |
| Northern Africa | 92 | 91 |
| Latin America and Caribbean | 94 | 82 |
| Caucasus and Central Asia | 86 | 95 |

**Source:** World Health Organization and UNICEF, 2014

**Highest Adult Literacy Rates**

| Country | Rate of Literacy (percent) |
|---|---|
| North Korea | 100 |
| Latvia | 99.9 |
| Ukraine | 99.8 |
| Tajikistan | 99.8 |
| Poland | 99.8 |
| Cuba | 99.8 |
| Estonia | 99.8 |
| Azerbaijan | 99.8 |
| Georgia | 99.7 |

**Source:** *The World Factbook,* 2016, CIA

**Lowest Adult Literacy Rates**

| Country | Rate of Literacy (percent) |
|---|---|
| Niger | 19.1 |
| South Sudan | 27 |
| Guinea | 30.4 |
| Burkina Faso | 36.0 |
| Central African Republic | 36.8 |
| Afghanistan | 38.2 |
| Benin | 38.4 |
| Mali | 38.7 |
| Chad | 40.2 |

**Source:** *The World Factbook,* 2016, CIA

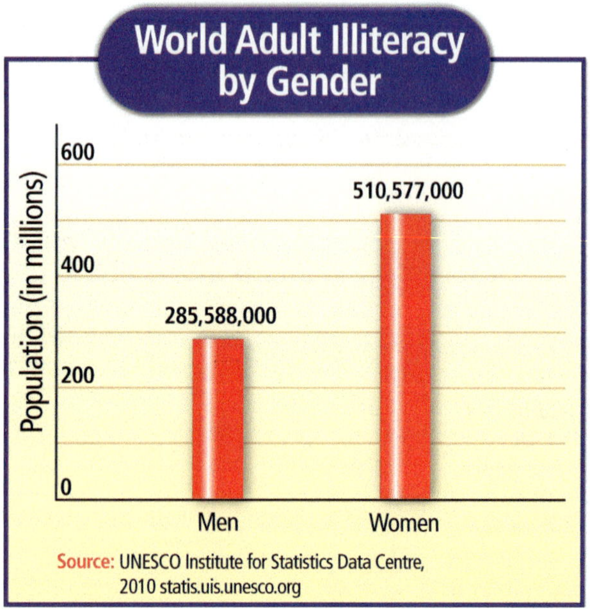


**Years, by Country, in Which Women Gained the Right to Vote**

| Year | Country | Year | Country |
|---|---|---|---|
| 1893 | New Zealand | 1945 | Italy |
| 1902 | Australia | 1945 | Japan |
| 1913 | Norway | 1947 | Argentina |
| 1918 | United Kingdom | 1947 | Mexico |
| 1918 | Canada | 1950 | India |
| 1919 | Germany | 1952 | Greece |
| 1920 | United States | 1956 | Egypt |
| 1930 | South Africa | 1963 | Kenya |
| 1934 | Brazil | 1971 | Switzerland |
| 1944 | France | 1980 | Iraq |

**Source:** *The World Factbook,* 2016, CIA

**Military Spending**

| Country | Billions of U.S. Dollars per Year | as a Percentage of Gross Domestic Product (GDP) |
|---|---|---|
| United States | 780.83 | 4.35 |
| China | 385.86 | 1.99 |
| France | 47.65 | 1.80 |
| Japan | 46.85 | 0.97 |
| United Kingdom | 66.71 | 2.49 |
| Germany | 51.85 | 1.35 |
| Italy | 36.69 | 1.69 |
| South Korea | 51.77 | 2.80 |
| India | 191.16 | 2.40 |
| Saudi Arabia | 134.30 | 7.98 |

**Source:** *The World Factbook,* 2016, CIA

**Nuclear Weapons Capability**

| Country | Date of First Test |
|---|---|
| United States | 1945 |
| Russia (Soviet Union) | 1949 |
| United Kingdom | 1952 |
| France | 1960 |
| China | 1964 |
| India | 1974 |
| Pakistan | 1998 |
| North Korea | 2006 |

**Source:** U.S. Department of State and *TIME* magazine

# REFERENCE ATLAS



## ATLAS KEY

## SYMBOL KEY

- Claimed boundary
- International boundary (political map)
- International boundary (physical map)
- National capital
- State/Provincial capital
- Towns
- Depression
- Elevation
- Dry salt lake
- Lake
- Rivers
- Canal

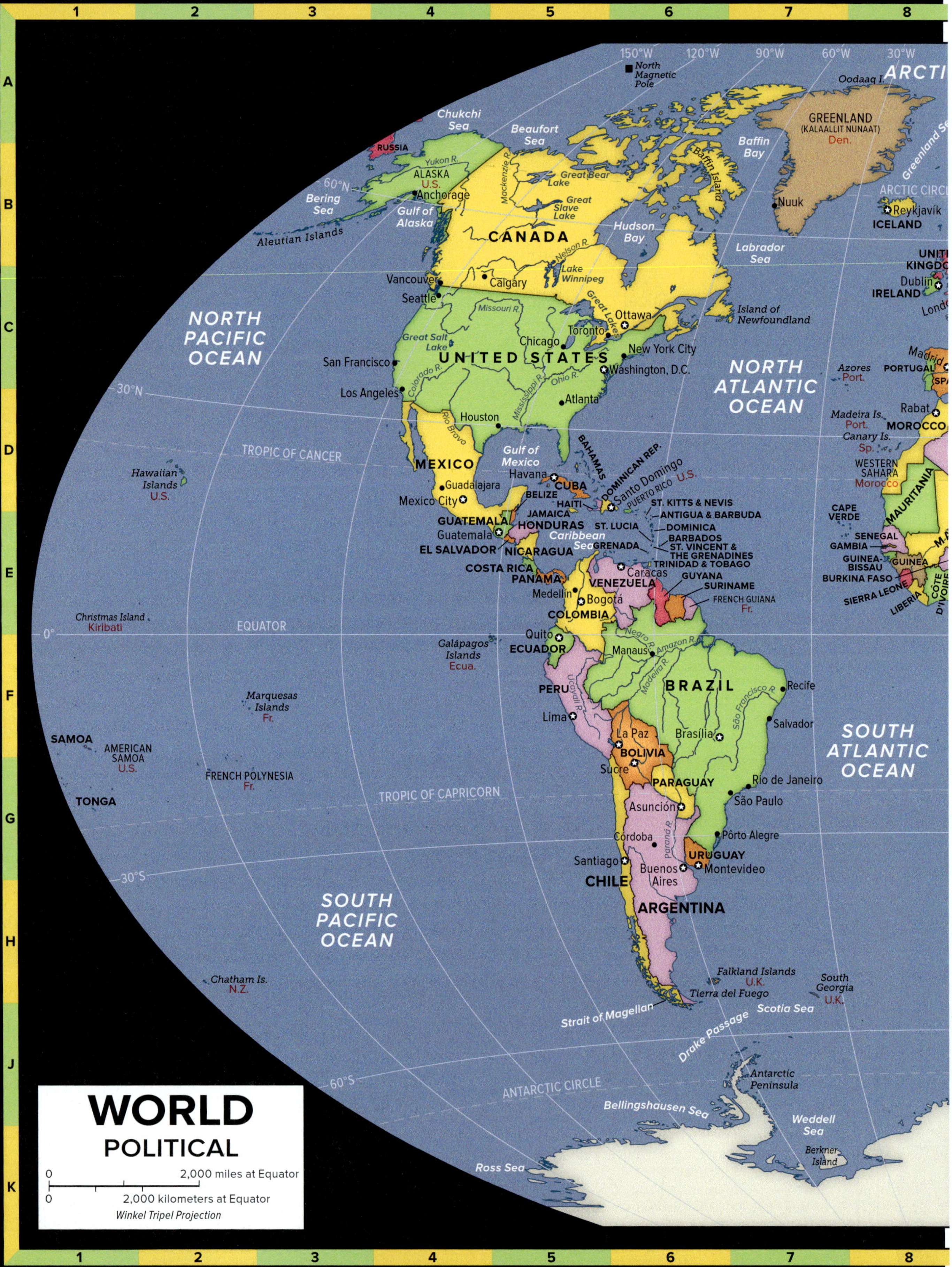

WORLD
POLITICAL
0 2,000 miles at Equator
0 2,000 kilometers at Equator
Winkel Tripel Projection
1
2
3
4
5
6
7
8
A
B
C
D
E
F
G
H
J
K
150°W
120°W
90°W
60°W
30°W
North Magnetic Pole
Oodaaq I.
ARCTI
GREENLAND
(KALAALLIT NUNAAT)
Den.
Chukchi Sea
Beaufort Sea
RUSSIA
Yukon R.
ALASKA
U.S.
60°N
Anchorage
Bering Sea
Gulf of Alaska
Aleutian Islands
Mackenzie R.
Great Bear Lake
Great Slave Lake
Baffin Island
Baffin Bay
Nuuk
ARCTIC CIRCLE
Reykjavík
ICELAND
Hudson Bay
CANADA
Nelson R.
Labrador Sea
Vancouver
Calgary
Lake Winnipeg
Dublin
IRELAND
Seattle
Missouri R.
Great Lakes
Ottawa
Island of Newfoundland
NORTH PACIFIC OCEAN
Great Salt Lake
Chicago
Toronto
San Francisco
UNITED STATES
New York City
Washington, D.C.
Colorado R.
Ohio R.
Mississippi R.
NORTH ATLANTIC OCEAN
Azores
Port.
PORTUGAL
Madrid
30°N
Los Angeles
Atlanta
Houston
Rio Bravo
Madeira Is.
Port.
Rabat
MOROCCO
Canary Is.
Sp.
TROPIC OF CANCER
Gulf of Mexico
BAHAMAS
MEXICO
DOMINICAN REP.
WESTERN SAHARA
Morocco
Hawaiian Islands
U.S.
Havana
CUBA
Santo Domingo
PUERTO RICO U.S.
MAURITANIA
Guadalajara
BELIZE
HAITI
ST. KITTS & NEVIS
CAPE VERDE
Mexico City
JAMAICA
ANTIGUA & BARBUDA
GUATEMALA
HONDURAS
ST. LUCIA
DOMINICA
Guatemala
Caribbean Sea
BARBADOS
SENEGAL
GAMBIA
EL SALVADOR
NICARAGUA
GRENADA
ST. VINCENT & THE GRENADINES
GUINEA-BISSAU
GUINEA
COSTA RICA
TRINIDAD & TOBAGO
PANAMA
Caracas
VENEZUELA
GUYANA
SURINAME
BURKINA FASO
SIERRA LEONE
LIBERIA
CÔTE D'IVOIRE
Medellín
Bogotá
FRENCH GUIANA
Fr.
COLOMBIA
Christmas Island
Kiribati
EQUATOR
0°
Quito
ECUADOR
Negro R.
Amazon R.
Galápagos Islands
Ecua.
Manaus
Madeira R.
PERU
Ucayali R.
BRAZIL
Recife
São Francisco R.
Marquesas Islands
Fr.
Lima
Salvador
SOUTH ATLANTIC OCEAN
SAMOA
AMERICAN SAMOA
U.S.
La Paz
Brasília
BOLIVIA
FRENCH POLYNESIA
Fr.
Sucre
PARAGUAY
Rio de Janeiro
TROPIC OF CAPRICORN
São Paulo
TONGA
Asunción
Paraná R.
Córdoba
Pôrto Alegre
Santiago
URUGUAY
30°S
Buenos Aires
Montevideo
CHILE
ARGENTINA
SOUTH PACIFIC OCEAN
Falkland Islands
U.K.
South Georgia
U.K.
Chatham Is.
N.Z.
Tierra del Fuego
Strait of Magellan
Scotia Sea
Drake Passage
60°S
Antarctic Peninsula
ANTARCTIC CIRCLE
Bellingshausen Sea
Weddell Sea
Berkner Island
Ross Sea

9
10
11
12
13
14
15
16
A
B
C
D
E
F
G
H
J
K
0°
30°E
60°E
90°E
120°E
150°E
C OCEAN
N
Franz Josef Land
Severnaya Zemlya
New Siberian Islands
Svalbard
Nor.
Barents Sea
Kara Sea
Laptev Sea
East Siberian Sea
Novaya Zemlya
Norwegian Sea
NORWAY
SWEDEN
FINLAND
RUSSIA
Yakutsk
60°N
Bering Sea
Sea of Okhotsk
Kamchatka Peninsula
Oslo
St. Petersburg
Yekaterinburg
Omsk
Novosibirsk
Lake Baikal
Sakhalin
DENMARK
NETH.
EST.
LATVIA
LITH.
Baltic Sea
Moscow
Samara
POLAND
BELARUS
Astana
GERMANY
BELG.
CZECH. REP.
Kyiv (Kiev)
KAZAKHSTAN
Ulaanbaatar
MONGOLIA
Harbin
NORTH KOREA
Sea of Japan (East Sea)
Hokkaidō
Sapporo
Paris
SLOVAKIA
UKRAINE
Aral Sea
AUST.
HUNG.
MOLD.
SWITZ.
SLOV.
ROMANIA
AZERBAIJAN
Almaty
Shenyang
Honshū
FRANCE
CROAT.
SERB.
Tashkent
Bishkek
Beijing
P'yŏngyang
NORTH PACIFIC OCEAN
ITALY
BULGARIA
GEORGIA
Black Sea
UZBEKISTAN
KYRGYZSTAN
JAPAN
Rome
KOS.
MACED.
ARMENIA
Caspian Sea
TURKMENISTAN
TAJIKISTAN
Tianjin
Seoul
Tokyo
Ankara
TURKEY
Ashkhabad
Dushanbe
SOUTH KOREA
Osaka
GREECE
CHINA
Kyūshū
Mediterranean Sea
SYRIA
Tehran
Kabul
30°N
Algiers
TUNISIA
CYPRUS
LEBANON
ISRAEL
IRAN
AFGHANISTAN
Islamabad
Shanghai
IRAQ
Baghdad
PAKISTAN
Lahore
Chengdu
Wuhan
Tripoli
JORDAN
Brahmaputra R.
NEPAL
BHUTAN
Delhi
The People's Republic of China claims Taiwan as its 23rd province.
ALGERIA
LIBYA
Cairo
EGYPT
KUWAIT
BAHRAIN
QATAR
Riyadh
New Delhi
East China Sea
Guangzhou
Taipei
Dhaka
BANGLADESH
TAIWAN
Karachi
Masqat
Kolkata (Calcutta)
Hong Kong
Philippine Sea
SAUDI ARABIA
U.A.E.
MYANMAR (BURMA)
Hanoi
OMAN
LAOS
Hainan
Luzon
Red Sea
Mumbai (Bombay)
INDIA
NORTHERN MARIANA ISLANDS
U.S.
NIGER
CHAD
ERITREA
Nay Pyi Taw
South China Sea
Khartoum
Sanaa
Arabian Sea
Hyderabad
Bay of Bengal
THAILAND
VIETNAM
Manila
YEMEN
PHILIPPINES
Niamey
SUDAN
Bangkok
CAMBODIA
N'Djamena
DJIBOUTI
Socotra
Yemen
Bengaluru (Bangalore)
Chennai (Madras)
MARSHALL ISLANDS
NIGERIA
Addis Ababa
Phnom Penh
Ho Chi Minh City
PALAU
SOUTH SUDAN
ETHIOPIA
SRI LANKA
FEDERATED STATES OF MICRONESIA
GHANA
TOGO
BENIN
CAMEROON
Lagos
CENTRAL AFRICAN REPUBLIC
Juba
SOMALIA
Colombo
BRUNEI
Mindanao
MALDIVES
Bangui
Kuala Lumpur
MALAYSIA
EQ. GUINEA
DEM. REP. OF THE CONGO
UGANDA
Mogadishu
EQUATOR
KIRIBATI
GABON
CONGO
KENYA
Borneo
SÃO TOMÉ & PRINCIPE
Nairobi
SINGAPORE
NAURU
Brazzaville
RWANDA
SEYCHELLES
Sumatra
Celebes
Kinshasa
BURUNDI
INDONESIA
New Guinea
CABINDA
Ang.
Dodoma
Dar es Salaam
Jakarta
Java
PAPUA NEW GUINEA
TUVALU
Luanda
TANZANIA
Surabaya
SOLOMON ISLANDS
COMOROS
Arafura Sea
ANGOLA
MALAWI
INDIAN OCEAN
Port Moresby
ZAMBIA
EAST TIMOR (TIMOR-LESTE)
Darwin
Lusaka
MOZAMBIQUE
Antananarivo
Coral Sea
VANUATU
FIJI ISLANDS
NAMIBIA
Harare
ZIMBABWE
MAURITIUS
Windhoek
BOTSWANA
MADAGASCAR
Reunion
Fr.
New Caledonia
Fr.
Gaborone
Maputo
Tshwane (Pretoria)
SWAZILAND
AUSTRALIA
Bloemfontein
SOUTH PACIFIC OCEAN
SOUTH AFRICA
LESOTHO
Brisbane
Cape Town
Perth
Darling R.
30°S
Sydney
North Island
PRIME MERIDIAN (MERIDIAN OF GREENWICH)
Canberra
Murray R.
Melbourne
Tasman Sea
Auckland
Tasmania
NEW ZEALAND
Kerguelen Islands
Fr.
Wellington
South Island
The Atlantic, Indian, and Pacific Oceans merge around Antarctica. Some define this as an ocean, calling it the Antarctic Ocean, Austral Ocean, or Southern Ocean. While most accept four oceans (including the Arctic Ocean), there is little international agreement on the name and extent of a fifth ocean.
SOUTHERN OCEAN
South Magnetic Pole
60°S
Ross Sea
ANTARCTICA

WORLD
PHYSICAL
0 2,000 miles at Equator
0 2,000 kilometers at Equator
Winkel Tripel Projection
NORTH PACIFIC OCEAN
SOUTH PACIFIC OCEAN
NORTH ATLANTIC OCEAN
SOUTH ATLANTIC OCEAN
NORTH AMERICA
SOUTH AMERICA
GREENLAND
ALASKA
ROCKY MOUNTAINS
Canadian Shield
Great Plains
Central Lowland
Appalachian Mountains
AMAZON BASIN
ANDES
Guiana Highlands
Brazilian Highlands
Mato Grosso Plateau
Gran Chaco
Pampas
Patagonia
Atacama Desert
Llanos
North Magnetic Pole
Queen Elizabeth Islands
Ellesmere Island
Oodaaq I.
Banks Island
Melville Island
Victoria Island
Baffin Island
Baffin Bay
Beaufort Sea
Chukchi Sea
Bering Sea
Siberia
Brooks Range
Denali (Mt. McKinley) 20,320 ft. 6,194 m
Alaska Range
Aleutian Islands
Alexander Archipelago
Haida Gwaii (Queen Charlotte Islands)
Vancouver Island
Coast Mountains
Cascade Range
Great Salt Lake
Death Valley -282 ft. -86 m
Baja California
Great Bear Lake
Great Slave Lake
Hudson Bay
Lake Winnipeg
Labrador
Labrador Sea
Island of Newfoundland
Nova Scotia
Iceland
Ireland
Azores
Madeira Islands
Canary Islands
Cape Verde Islands
Gulf of Mexico
Bahama Islands
WEST INDIES
Cuba
Greater Antilles
Hispaniola
Jamaica
Lesser Antilles
Trinidad
Caribbean Sea
CENTRAL AMERICA
Hawaiian Islands
Hawaii
POLYNESIA
Line Islands
Marquesas Islands
Tuamotu Archipelago
Tahiti
Society Is.
Samoa Islands
Cook Islands
Tonga Is.
Fiji Is.
Galápagos Islands
Easter Island
Lake Titicaca
Aconcagua 22,834 ft. 6,960 m
Valdés Peninsula -131 ft. -40 m
Chiloé Island
Falkland Islands
South Georgia
Tierra del Fuego
Scotia Sea
South Sandwich Islands
Strait of Magellan
South Shetland Islands
South Orkney Islands
Antarctic Peninsula
Bellingshausen Sea
Weddell Sea
Ellsworth Land
Ronne Ice Shelf
Berkner Island
Marie Byrd Land
Vinson Massif 16,066 ft. 4,897 m
Ross Sea
Ross Ice Shelf
TRANSANTARCTIC MOUNTAINS
TROPIC OF CANCER
EQUATOR
TROPIC OF CAPRICORN
ANTARCTIC CIRCLE
ARCTIC CIRCLE
30°N
0°
30°S
60°S
60°N
150°W
120°W
90°W
60°W
30°W

OCEAN
Svalbard
Barents Sea
Kara Sea
Severnaya Zemlya
New Siberian Islands
Laptev Sea
East Siberian Sea
Novaya Zemlya
Norwegian Sea
Scandinavia
Central Siberian Plateau
S I B E R I A
West Siberian Plain
Ural Mountains
Sea of Okhotsk
Bering Sea
Kamchatka Peninsula
Aleutian Is.
North Sea
Baltic Sea
Northern European Plain
EUROPE
Lake Baikal
ASIA
The Steppes
Altay Shan
GOBI
Kuril Islands
Hokkaido
Elbrus 18,510 ft. 5,642 m
Aral Sea
Tian Shan
Sea of Japan (East Sea)
Japan
NORTH PACIFIC OCEAN
Alps
Corsica
Sardinia
Black Sea
Caucasus Mts.
Caspian Sea
Taklimakan Desert
Kunlun Shan
Korea
Honshu
Mediterranean Sea
Sicily
Cyprus
Zagros Mountains
Plateau of Tibet
North China Plain
Yellow Sea
30°N
East China Sea
Nampo Shoto
Dead Sea -1,312 ft. -400 m
HIMALAYA
Mt. Everest 29,028 ft. 8,848 m
Ryukyu Islands
SAHARA
Libyan Desert
ARABIAN PENINSULA
Red Sea
INDIA
Taiwan
Philippine Sea
Hainan
Luzon
Arabian Sea
Deccan Plateau
Bay of Bengal
South China Sea
Mariana Islands
SAHEL
Indochina Peninsula
Andaman Islands
Philippine Islands
AFRICA
Gulf of Aden
Ethiopian Highlands
Somali Peninsula
MICRONESIA
Guinea
Sri Lanka
Nicobar Is.
Andaman Sea
Marshall Islands
Gulf of Guinea
Lake Victoria
Maldive Islands
EQUATOR
Malay Peninsula
Borneo
Sumatra
Indonesia
Moluccas
Celebes
Gilbert Islands
Kilimanjaro 19,341 ft. 5,895 m
Congo Basin
Greater Sunda Islands
MELANESIA
Bismarck Archipelago
New Guinea
Lower Guinea
Lake Tanganyika
Seychelles
Java
Solomon Islands
INDIAN OCEAN
Arafura Sea
Madagascar
Coral Sea
Mascarene Islands
Vanuatu
Fiji Islands
Great Sandy Desert
Great Dividing Range
Namib Desert
Kalahari Desert
Drakensberg
AUSTRALIA
New Caledonia
Lake Eyre -52 ft. -16 m
SOUTH PACIFIC OCEAN
Great Victoria Desert
Darling R.
30°S
PRIME MERIDIAN (MERIDIAN OF GREENWICH)
Tasman Sea
Murray
Mt. Kosciusko 7,310 ft. 2,228 m
Tasmania
North Island
NEW ZEALAND
Kerguelen Islands
South Island
The Atlantic, Indian, and Pacific Oceans merge around Antarctica. Some define this as an ocean, calling it the Antarctic Ocean, Austral Ocean, or Southern Ocean. While most accept four oceans (including the Arctic Ocean), there is little international agreement on the name and extent of a fifth ocean.
Auckland Islands
SOUTHERN OCEAN
South Magnetic Pole
60°S
Queen Maud Land
ANTARCTICA
Transantarctic Mountains
Victoria Land
Ross Sea
Ross Ice Shelf
9
10
11
12
13
14
15
16
A
B
C
D
E
F
G
H
J
K

NORTH AMERICA
POLITICAL
ASIA
North Magnetic Pole
N
ARCTIC OCEAN
Chukchi Sea
Bering Sea
Bering Strait
Point Barrow
Beaufort Sea
160°W
Alaska
Yukon R.
Gulf of Alaska
GREENLAND (KALAALLIT NUNAAT) Den.
Greenland Sea
Ellesmere Island
Queen Elizabeth Islands
Parry Islands
Banks Island
Victoria Island
Boothia Peninsula
Baffin Bay
Qeqertarsuaq
Davis Strait
Nuuk (Godthab)
Baffin Island
Labrador Sea
Nunavut
ARCTIC CIRCLE
Great Bear Lake
Mackenzie R.
Yukon
Northwest Territories
Great Slave Lake
Southampton Island
Hudson Bay
Newfoundland and Labrador
CANADA
British Columbia
Alberta
Saskatchewan
Manitoba
Lake Winnipeg
Severn R.
Ontario
Quebec
Gulf of St. Lawrence
St. Pierre and Miquelon Fr.
P.E.I.
N.B.
Nova Scotia
Vancouver Island
ROCKY MOUNTAINS
Lake Superior
Ottawa
Lake Huron
Lake Michigan
Lake Ontario
Lake Erie
ATLANTIC OCEAN
Washington
Oregon
Idaho
Montana
Wyoming
North Dakota
South Dakota
Minn.
Wis.
Michigan
Iowa
Nebraska
Missouri R.
Great Salt Lake
Nevada
Utah
California
Colorado
Kansas
Missouri
Ill.
Ind.
Ohio
UNITED STATES
Arizona
New Mexico
Oklahoma
Ark.
Texas
Rio Grande
Mississippi R.
Miss.
Ala.
Georgia
La.
Florida
Tennessee
Kentucky
W. Va.
Virginia
Washington, D.C.
North Carolina
South Carolina
Maine
Vt.
New Hampshire
Massachusetts
Rhode Island
Connecticut
New York
Pa.
New Jersey
Delaware
Maryland
Bermuda U.K.
PACIFIC OCEAN
Guadalupe I. Mex.
TROPIC OF CANCER
MEXICO
see inset below
Mexico City
Gulf of Mexico
Havana
CUBA
BAHAMAS
Nassau
Turks and Caicos Islands U.K.
Puerto Rico U.S.
San Juan
Hispaniola
Port-au-Prince
HAITI
Santo Domingo
DOMINICAN REPUBLIC
JAMAICA
Kingston
Cayman Is. U.K.
Aruba Neth.
see inset above
BELIZE
Belmopan
Caribbean Sea
HONDURAS
Tegucigalpa
GUATEMALA
Guatemala
San Salvador
EL SALVADOR
NICARAGUA
Managua
COSTA RICA
San José
Panama Canal
Panama
PANAMA
SOUTH AMERICA
EQUATOR
0 1,000 miles
0 1,000 kilometers
Lambert Azimuthal Equal-Area Projection
Virgin Islands U.S.
British Virgin Islands U.K.
Anguilla U.K.
St. Martin Fr.
St. Maarten Neth.
St. Barthélemy Fr.
Saba Neth.
St. Eustatius Neth.
ANTIGUA AND BARBUDA
Montserrat U.K.
Guadeloupe Fr.
ST. KITTS AND NEVIS
DOMINICA
Martinique Fr.
Caribbean Sea
ST. LUCIA
ST. VINCENT AND THE GRENADINES
BARBADOS
GRENADA
TRINIDAD AND TOBAGO
0 200 mi.
0 200 km
1. BAJA CALIFORNIA
2. BAJA CALIFORNIA SUR
3. SONORA
4. CHIHUAHUA
5. SINALOA
6. DURANGO
7. COAHUILA
8. NUEVO LEÓN
9. ZACATECAS
10. TAMAULIPAS
11. NAYARIT
12. AGUASCALIENTES
13. SAN LUIS POTOSÍ
14. JALISCO
15. GUANAJUATO
16. QUERÉTARO
17. HIDALGO
18. COLIMA
19. MICHOACÁN
20. MÉXICO
21. DISTRITO FEDERAL
22. TLAXCALA
23. MORELOS
24. PUEBLA
25. VERACRUZ
26. GUERRERO
27. OAXACA
28. TABASCO
29. CHIAPAS
30. CAMPECHE
31. QUINTANA ROO
32. YUCATÁN

NORTH AMERICA
PHYSICAL
ASIA
EUROPE
ARCTIC OCEAN
ATLANTIC OCEAN
PACIFIC OCEAN
SOUTH AMERICA
North Magnetic Pole
GREENLAND
Gunnbjorn 12,139 ft. 3,700 m
Greenland Sea
Chukchi Sea
Bering Sea
Bering Strait
Beaufort Sea
Baffin Bay
Labrador Sea
Hudson Bay
ALASKA
Denali (Mt. McKinley) 20,320 ft. 6,194 m
Mt. Logan 19,551 ft. 5,959 m
Gulf of Alaska
CANADA
CANADIAN SHIELD
ROCKY MOUNTAINS
GREAT PLAINS
UNITED STATES
CENTRAL LOWLAND
COASTAL PLAIN
Ottawa
Washington, D.C.
Gulf of Mexico
MEXICO
Mexico City
Orizaba 18,700 ft. 5,700 m
Caribbean Sea
WEST INDIES
CUBA
HAITI
DOMINICAN REPUBLIC
JAMAICA
BELIZE
HONDURAS
NICARAGUA
GUATEMALA
EL SALVADOR
COSTA RICA
PANAMA
CENTRAL AMERICA
Mt. Whitney 14,495 ft. 4,418 m
Death Valley -282 ft. -86 m
TROPIC OF CANCER
ARCTIC CIRCLE
EQUATOR
0 1,000 miles
0 1,000 kilometers
Lambert Azimuthal Equal-Area Projection

SOUTH AMERICA
POLITICAL
Lambert Azimuthal Equal-Area Projection
0
1,000 miles
0
1,000 kilometers
N
Caribbean Sea
PACIFIC OCEAN
ATLANTIC OCEAN
EQUATOR
TROPIC OF CAPRICORN
80°W
60°W
40°W
100°W
20°W
0°
20°S
40°S
VENEZUELA
GUYANA
SURINAME
FRENCH GUIANA
Fr.
COLOMBIA
ECUADOR
PERU
BRAZIL
BOLIVIA
PARAGUAY
CHILE
ARGENTINA
URUGUAY
AMAZON BASIN
ANDES
Santa Marta
Barranquilla
Cartagena
Maracaibo
Lake Maracaibo
Caracas
Valencia
Ciudad Guayana
Orinoco R.
Bucaramanga
San Cristóbal
Georgetown
Paramaribo
Cayenne
Medellín
Bogotá
Cali
Malpelo I.
Col.
Boa Vista
Boundary claimed by Suriname
Marajó Island
Esmeraldas
Quito
Guayaquil
Rio Negro
Amazon R.
Manaus
Santarém
Belém
São Luís
Fortaleza
Iquitos
Marañón R.
Teresina
Natal
Purus R.
Madeira R.
Tapajós R.
Xingu R.
Araguaia R.
Tocantins R.
Campina Grande
Recife
São Francisco R.
Ucayali R.
Rio Branco
Pôrto Velho
Callao
Lima
Machu Picchu
Cuzco
Ayacucho
Lake Titicaca
Trinidad
La Paz
Salvador
Brasília
Arequipa
Goiânia
Santa Cruz
Oruro
Sucre
Arica
Paraguay R.
Campo Grande
Uberlândia
Uberaba
Belo Horizonte
Paraná R.
Iquique
Tarija
Londrina
Campinas
Nova Iguaçu
Antofagasta
São Paulo
Rio de Janeiro
Santos
Salta
Asunción
Curitiba
San Félix I.
San Ambrosio I.
Chile
San Miguel de Tucumán
Uruguaiana
Uruguay R.
La Serena
Coquimbo
Santa Maria
Pôrto Alegre
Córdoba
Rosario
Valparaíso
Mendoza
Juan Fernández Is.
Chile
Santiago
Buenos Aires
Montevideo
La Plata
Río de la Plata
Concepción
Colorado R.
Negro R.
Mar del Plata
Bahía Blanca
Puerto Montt
Comodoro Rivadavia
Falkland Islands (Islas Malvinas)
Stanley
Administered by United Kingdom
Claimed by Arg.
Río Gallegos
Punta Arenas
Strait of Magellan
Ushuaia
Cape Horn
South Georgia Island
U.K.

SOUTH AMERICA
PHYSICAL
Caribbean Sea
N
0
1,000 miles
0
1,000 kilometers
Lambert Azimuthal Equal-Area Projection
Caracas
VENEZUELA
Lake Maracaibo
Orinoco R.
LLANOS
GUYANA
SURINAME
Georgetown
Paramaribo
Cayenne
FRENCH GUIANA
Angel Falls
Total drop 3,212 ft. 979 m
Bogotá
Malpelo I.
GUIANA HIGHLANDS
COLOMBIA
Boundary claimed by Suriname
Marajó Island
Río Negro
Quito
EQUATOR
ECUADOR
AMAZON BASIN
Amazon R.
Selvas
Marañón R.
Tapajós R.
Madeira R.
Purus R.
Xingu R.
Ucayali R.
PERU
BRAZIL
Araguaia R.
Tocantins R.
São Francisco R.
ANDES
Lima
Machu Picchu
MATO GROSSO PLATEAU
BRAZILIAN HIGHLANDS
Brasília
Lake Titicaca
La Paz
BOLIVIA
Altiplano
Sucre
Salar de Uyuni
CHACO
Paraguay R.
Paraná R.
20°S
TROPIC OF CAPRICORN
PARAGUAY
GRAN CHACO
Asunción
Iguazú Falls
San Ambrosio I.
San Félix I.
ATLANTIC OCEAN
CHILE
PAMPAS
Uruguay R.
Aconcagua 22,834 ft. 6,960 m
Juan Fernández Is.
Santiago
Buenos Aires
URUGUAY
Montevideo
ARGENTINA
Río de la Plata
Colorado R.
Negro R.
PATAGONIA
Chiloé Island
Valdés Peninsula -131 ft. -40 m
40°S
Gulf of San Jorge
PACIFIC OCEAN
Taitao Peninsula
Falkland Islands (Islas Malvinas)
Laguna del Carbón -344 ft. -105 m
Wellington I.
Stanley
Tierra del Fuego
Strait of Magellan
Cape Horn
South Georgia Island
100°W
80°W
60°W
40°W
20°W
0°

EUROPE
POLITICAL
ICELAND
Reykjavík
Akureyri
ARCTIC CIRCLE
Norwegian Sea
PRIME MERIDIAN
Faeroe Islands
Denmark
Tórshavn
Shetland Islands
Lerwick
Orkney Islands
Isle of Lewis
NORWAY
Trondheim
Ålesund
Bergen
Stavanger
Oslo
SWEDEN
Åre
Sundsvall
Uppsala
Stockholm
Göteborg
Malmö
Skagerrak
North Sea
DENMARK
Århus
Copenhagen
SCOTLAND
Inverness
Aberdeen
Glasgow
Edinburgh
NORTHERN IRELAND
Belfast
UNITED KINGDOM
IRELAND
Dublin
Cork
Irish Sea
Manchester
Liverpool
WALES
ENGLAND
Birmingham
Cardiff
Thames R.
London
Southampton
Celtic Sea
Land's End
ATLANTIC OCEAN
English Channel
NETHERLANDS
Amsterdam
The Hague
Brussels
BELGIUM
Kiel
Hamburg
Elbe R.
Berlin
GERMANY
Rhine R.
Bonn
Frankfurt
POLAND
Gdańsk
Bydgoszcz
Łódź
Oder R.
Wrocław
Prague
CZECH REPUBLIC
Kraków
Luxembourg
LUXEMBOURG
Le Havre
Brest
Rennes
Seine R.
Paris
Nantes
Loire R.
Strasbourg
Danube R.
Munich
La Rochelle
FRANCE
LIECHTENSTEIN
Vaduz
Vienna
AUSTRIA
Bratislava
SLOVAKIA
Budapest
HUNGARY
Bay of Biscay
Limoges
Zürich
Bern
Geneva
SWITZERLAND
Bordeaux
A L P S
Lyon
Milan
Po R.
Ljubljana
SLOVENIA
Zagreb
CROATIA
Venice
Turin
Genoa
Rhone R.
Toulouse
Andorra la Vella
Nice
Marseille
MONACO
SAN MARINO
Adriatic Sea
BOSNIA & HERZEGOVINA
Sarajevo
MONTENEGRO
Podgorica
La Coruña
Vigo
Bilbao
Donostia-San Sebastián
Porto
Valladolid
Ebro R.
Pyrenees
Coimbra
PORTUGAL
Madrid
Zaragoza
ANDORRA
Barcelona
Lisbon
Tagus R.
SPAIN
Valencia
Corsica
France
ITALY
Rome
Tirana
ALBANIA
Cape St. Vincent
Córdoba
Seville
Murcia
Palma
Balearic Islands
Spain
Sardinia
Italy
VATICAN CITY (within Rome)
Naples
Cádiz
Málaga
Cartagena
Cagliari
Strait of Gibraltar
GIBRALTAR
U.K.
Mediterranean
Tyrrhenian Sea
Ionian Sea
Palermo
Messina
Sicily
Italy
Catania
MALTA
Valletta
AFRICA
Tromsø
Gulf
Gotland
Baltic
N
70°N
60°N
50°N
40°N
30°N
30°W
20°W
10°W
0°
10°E
20°E
1
2
3
4
5
6
7
8
A
B
C
D
E
F
G
H
I
J
K

A commonly accepted division between Asia and Europe—here marked by a gray line—is formed by the Ural Mountains, Ural River, Caspian Sea, Caucasus Mountains, and the Black Sea with its outlets, the Bosporus and the Dardanelles.
Europe/Asia boundary
ASIA
RUSSIA
URAL MOUNTAINS
Barents Sea
White Sea
Kola Peninsula
LAPLAND
FINLAND
ESTONIA
LATVIA
LITHUANIA
BELARUS
UKRAINE
MOLDOVA
ROMANIA
SERBIA
KOSOVO
BULGARIA
MACEDONIA
GREECE
TURKEY
GEORGIA
AZERBAIJAN
KAZAKHSTAN
CYPRUS
Black Sea
Caspian Sea
Sea of Azov
Sea of Marmara
Aegean Sea
Bosporus
Dardanelles
Crimea
Caucasus Mountains
Carpathian Mts.
Balkan Mts.
Peloponnese
Crete
Rhodes
Lake Onega
Lake Ladoga
Northern Dvina R.
Volga R.
Don R.
Dnieper R.
Dniester R.
Vistula R.
Ural R.
Bothnia
Murmansk
Kirovsk
Umba
Ivalo
Kiruna
Kemi
Luleå
Umeå
Oulu
Vaasa
Kuopio
Pori
Tampere
Turku
Helsinki
Tallinn
Riga
Daugavpils
Vilnius
Kaunas
Kaliningrad
Minsk
Vitsyebsk
Homyel'
Warsaw
Kem'
Arkhangel'sk
Severodvinsk
Tobseda
Pechora
Syktyvkar
Perm'
Kirov
Ufa
Kazan'
Orenburg
Samara
Oral
St. Petersburg
Novgorod
Yaroslavl'
Nizhniy Novgorod
Tver'
Moscow
Smolensk
Ryazan'
Penza
Saratov
Bryansk
Kursk
Volgograd
Astrakhan
Rostov
Stavropol'
Grozny
Baku
Chernihiv
Sumy
Kyiv (Kiev)
Kharkiv
Poltava
L'viv
Vinnytsya
Donets'k
Dnipropetrovs'k
Chişinău
Odessa
Kerch
Simferopol'
Sevastopol'
Yalta
Bucharest
Constanța
Belgrade
Priština
Sofia
Varna
Skopje
Thessaloniki
Istanbul
Athens
Iraklion
Nicosia
Greece
Sea
0 400 miles
0 400 kilometers
Lambert Azimuthal Equal-Area Projection
30°E
40°E
50°E
60°E
70°E
80°E
60°N
50°N
40°N
30°N
9
10
11
12
13
14
15
16
A
B
C
D
E
F
G
H
J
K

EUROPE
PHYSICAL
ICELAND
Reykjavík
ARCTIC CIRCLE
PRIME MERIDIAN
Norwegian Sea
Faeroe Islands
Shetland Islands
Orkney Islands
Outer Hebrides
British Isles
Highlands
Edinburgh
Belfast
IRELAND
Dublin
Irish Sea
UNITED KINGDOM
Great Britain
Celtic Sea
Cardiff
Thames R.
London
Land's End
North Sea
NORWAY
Oslo
SWEDEN
Stockholm
Skagerrak
Kattegat
Jutland
Zealand
DENMARK
Copenhagen
Gotland
Baltic
ATLANTIC OCEAN
English Channel
NETHERLANDS
Amsterdam
Elbe R.
Berlin
Brussels
BELGIUM
Rhine R.
GERMANY
POLAND
Oder R.
Brittany
Seine R.
Paris
Luxembourg
LUXEMBOURG
Prague
CZECH REPUBLIC
Loire R.
Danube R.
Bratislava
SLOVAKIA
FRANCE
LIECHTENSTEIN
Vienna
Bern
Vaduz
SWITZERLAND
AUSTRIA
Budapest
HUNGARY
Bay of Biscay
Mont Blanc 15,771 ft. 4,807 m
A L P S
Massif Central
Rhone R.
Ljubljana
SLOVENIA
Zagreb
CROATIA
Drava R.
Po R.
Cantabrian Mountains
Pyrenees
Andorra la Vella
MONACO
Riviera
SAN MARINO
Apennines
Adriatic Sea
BOSNIA & HERZEGOVINA
Sarajevo
Douro R.
Ebro R.
IBERIAN PENINSULA
Madrid
ANDORRA
Lisbon
Tagus R.
PORTUGAL
SPAIN
Corsica
ITALY
Rome
MONTENEGRO
Podgorica
Cape St. Vincent
Sardinia
VATICAN CITY (within Rome)
Tiranë
ALBANIA
Balearic Islands
Baetic Mountains
Strait of Gibraltar
GIBRALTAR
Mediterranean
Tyrrhenian Sea
Ionian Sea
Sicily
Etna 10,902 ft. 3,323 m
MALTA
Valletta
AFRICA
70°N
60°N
50°N
40°N
30°N
30°W
20°W
10°W
0°
10°E
N
A
B
C
D
E
F
G
H
J
K
1
2
3
4
5
6
7
8

Barents Sea
North Cape
LAPLAND
Kola Peninsula
White Sea
Pechora R.
URAL MOUNTAINS
Europe/Asia boundary
ASIA
FINLAND
Bothnia
Lake Region
Northern Dvina R.
Lake Onega
Lake Ladoga
EUROPEAN PLAIN
RUSSIA
Helsinki
Gulf of Finland
Tallinn
ESTONIA
LATVIA
Riga
Moscow
Ural R.
LITHUANIA
Vilnius
RUSSIA
Minsk
BELARUS
CENTRAL RUSSIAN UPLAND
Volga R.
Don R.
KAZAKHSTAN
Caspian Depression
Warsaw
Vistula R.
(Kyiv) Kiev
Dnieper R.
Dniester R.
UKRAINE
Carpathian Mts.
Tisza R.
MOLDOVA
Chişinău
Sea of Azov
Crimea
Mt. Elbrus 18,510 ft. 5,642 m
Caucasus Mountains
Caspian Sea
ROMANIA
Belgrade
Bucharest
Danube R.
SERBIA
GEORGIA
AZERBAIJAN
Baku
BALKAN PENINSULA
Balkan Mts.
KOSOVO
Pristina
Sofia
BULGARIA
Black Sea
Skopje
MACEDONIA
Bosporus
TURKEY
Sea of Marmara
GREECE
Dardanelles
Aegean Sea
Athens
Peloponnese
Rhodes
Nicosia
CYPRUS
Crete
Sea
ASIA
0 400 miles
0 400 kilometers
Lambert Azimuthal Equal-Area Projection
30°E
40°E
50°E
60°E
70°E
80°E
60°N
50°N
40°N
30°N
9 10 11 12 13 14 15 16
A B C D E F G H J K

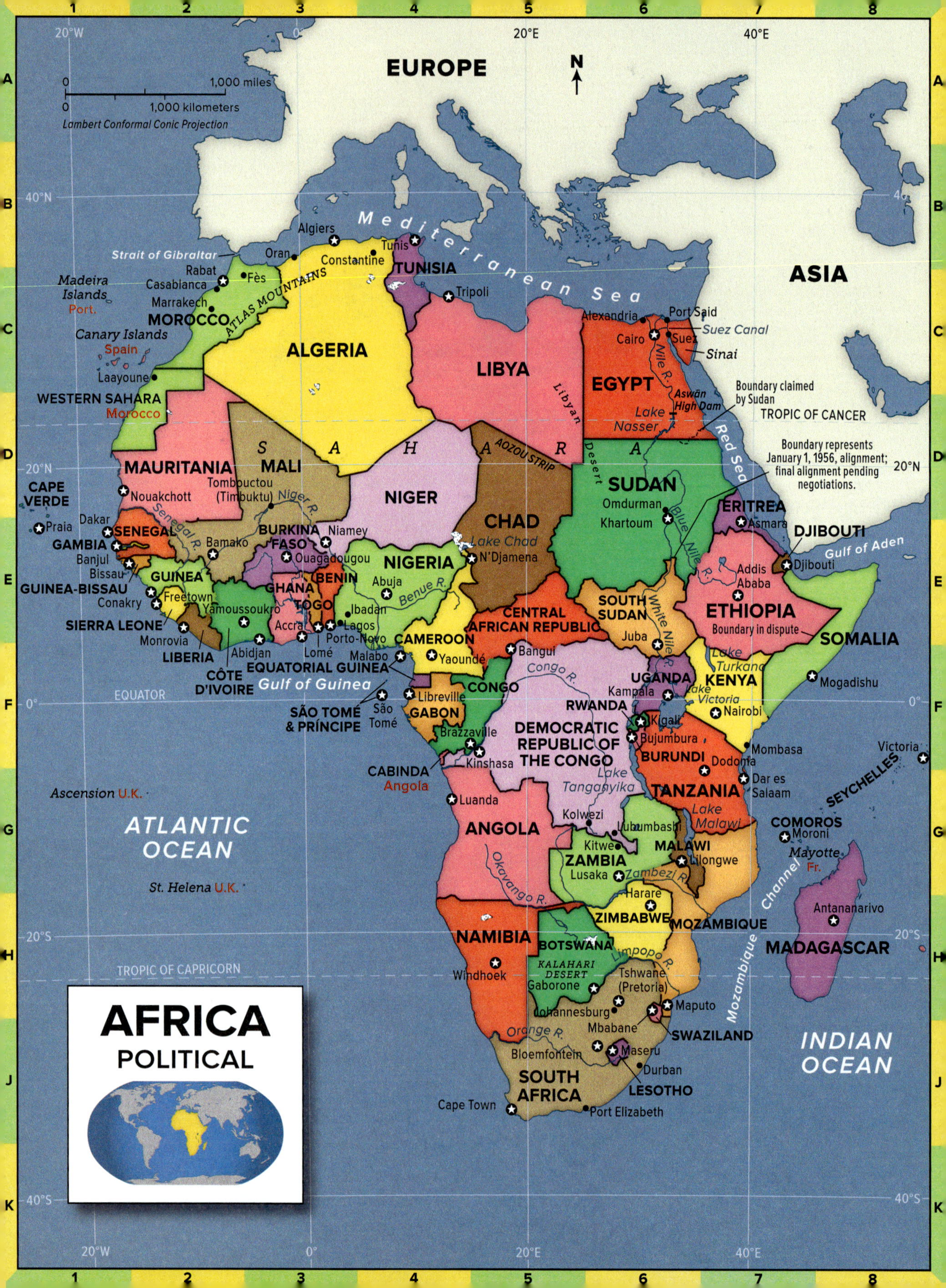

AFRICA
POLITICAL
EUROPE
ASIA
ATLANTIC OCEAN
INDIAN OCEAN
Mediterranean Sea
Red Sea
Gulf of Aden
Gulf of Guinea
Mozambique Channel
N
0 1,000 miles
0 1,000 kilometers
Lambert Conformal Conic Projection
20°W
0°
20°E
40°E
40°N
20°N
EQUATOR
TROPIC OF CANCER
TROPIC OF CAPRICORN
20°S
40°S
Strait of Gibraltar
Madeira Islands Port.
Canary Islands Spain
WESTERN SAHARA Morocco
CAPE VERDE
Praia
Ascension U.K.
St. Helena U.K.
MOROCCO
Rabat
Fès
Casablanca
Marrakech
Laayoune
ATLAS MOUNTAINS
ALGERIA
Algiers
Oran
Constantine
TUNISIA
Tunis
LIBYA
Tripoli
Libyan Desert
SAHARA
AOZOU STRIP
EGYPT
Alexandria
Cairo
Port Said
Suez
Suez Canal
Sinai
Nile R.
Aswān High Dam
Lake Nasser
Boundary claimed by Sudan
Boundary represents January 1, 1956, alignment; final alignment pending negotiations.
MAURITANIA
Nouakchott
MALI
Tombouctou (Timbuktu)
Niger R.
Senegal R.
SENEGAL
Dakar
GAMBIA
Banjul
GUINEA-BISSAU
Bissau
GUINEA
Conakry
SIERRA LEONE
Freetown
LIBERIA
Monrovia
CÔTE D'IVOIRE
Yamoussoukro
Abidjan
BURKINA FASO
Ouagadougou
Bamako
GHANA
Accra
TOGO
Lomé
BENIN
Porto-Novo
NIGER
Niamey
NIGERIA
Abuja
Ibadan
Lagos
Benue R.
CHAD
Lake Chad
N'Djamena
SUDAN
Omdurman
Khartoum
Blue Nile
White Nile
ERITREA
Asmara
DJIBOUTI
Djibouti
ETHIOPIA
Addis Ababa
Boundary in dispute
SOMALIA
Mogadishu
SOUTH SUDAN
Juba
CENTRAL AFRICAN REPUBLIC
Bangui
CAMEROON
Yaoundé
EQUATORIAL GUINEA
Malabo
SÃO TOMÉ & PRÍNCIPE
São Tomé
GABON
Libreville
CONGO
Brazzaville
Congo R.
DEMOCRATIC REPUBLIC OF THE CONGO
Kinshasa
Kolwezi
Lubumbashi
CABINDA Angola
UGANDA
Kampala
Lake Turkana
KENYA
Nairobi
Mombasa
Lake Victoria
RWANDA
Kigali
BURUNDI
Bujumbura
Lake Tanganyika
TANZANIA
Dodoma
Dar es Salaam
Lake Malawi
SEYCHELLES
Victoria
COMOROS
Moroni
Mayotte Fr.
MADAGASCAR
Antananarivo
ANGOLA
Luanda
Okavango R.
ZAMBIA
Kitwe
Lusaka
Zambezi R.
MALAWI
Lilongwe
ZIMBABWE
Harare
MOZAMBIQUE
Maputo
Limpopo R.
NAMIBIA
Windhoek
BOTSWANA
KALAHARI DESERT
Gaborone
Tshwane (Pretoria)
Johannesburg
Mbabane
SWAZILAND
Orange R.
SOUTH AFRICA
Bloemfontein
Maseru
LESOTHO
Durban
Cape Town
Port Elizabeth
1 2 3 4 5 6 7 8
A B C D E F G H J K

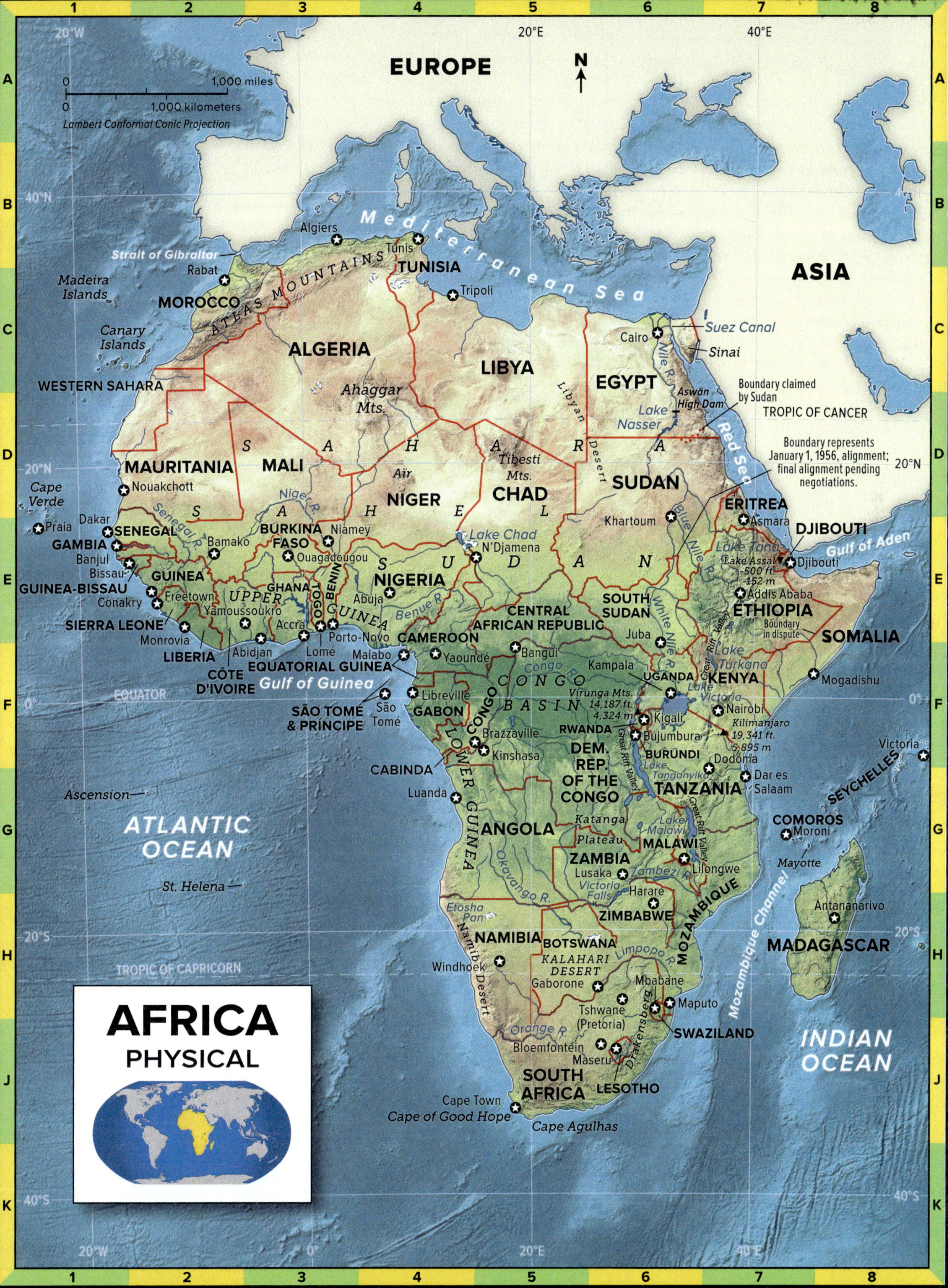
AFRICA
PHYSICAL
0 1,000 miles
0 1,000 kilometers
Lambert Conformal Conic Projection
EUROPE
ASIA
N
Mediterranean Sea
Strait of Gibraltar
Madeira Islands
Canary Islands
Cape Verde
ATLAS MOUNTAINS
Ahaggar Mts.
Tibesti Mts.
Aïr
SAHARA
Libyan Desert
Suez Canal
Sinai
Aswān High Dam
Lake Nasser
Boundary claimed by Sudan
TROPIC OF CANCER
Boundary represents January 1, 1956, alignment; final alignment pending negotiations.
Red Sea
Gulf of Aden
Lake Tana
Lake Assal -500 ft. -152 m
Boundary in dispute
Lake Turkana
Great Rift Valley
Nile R.
Blue Nile R.
White Nile R.
Niger R.
Senegal R.
Benue R.
Lake Chad
SAHEL
UPPER GUINEA
Gulf of Guinea
EQUATOR
CONGO BASIN
Congo R.
Virunga Mts. 14,187 ft. 4,324 m
Lake Victoria
Kilimanjaro 19,341 ft. 5,895 m
Lake Tanganyika
Lake Malawi
LOWER GUINEA
Katanga Plateau
Zambezi R.
Victoria Falls
Okavango R.
Etosha Pan
Namib Desert
KALAHARI DESERT
Limpopo R.
Orange R.
Drakensberg
Mozambique Channel
Cape of Good Hope
Cape Agulhas
TROPIC OF CAPRICORN
ATLANTIC OCEAN
INDIAN OCEAN
Ascension
St. Helena
MOROCCO
Rabat
ALGERIA
Algiers
TUNISIA
Tunis
LIBYA
Tripoli
EGYPT
Cairo
WESTERN SAHARA
MAURITANIA
Nouakchott
MALI
Bamako
NIGER
Niamey
CHAD
N'Djamena
SUDAN
Khartoum
ERITREA
Asmara
DJIBOUTI
Djibouti
ETHIOPIA
Addis Ababa
SOMALIA
Mogadishu
SENEGAL
Dakar
Praia
GAMBIA
Banjul
GUINEA-BISSAU
Bissau
GUINEA
Conakry
SIERRA LEONE
Freetown
LIBERIA
Monrovia
CÔTE D'IVOIRE
Yamoussoukro
Abidjan
BURKINA FASO
Ouagadougou
GHANA
Accra
TOGO
Lomé
BENIN
Porto-Novo
NIGERIA
Abuja
CAMEROON
Yaoundé
Malabo
EQUATORIAL GUINEA
SÃO TOMÉ & PRÍNCIPE
São Tomé
CENTRAL AFRICAN REPUBLIC
Bangui
SOUTH SUDAN
Juba
UGANDA
Kampala
KENYA
Nairobi
GABON
Libreville
CONGO
Brazzaville
Kinshasa
CABINDA
RWANDA
Kigali
BURUNDI
Bujumbura
DEM. REP. OF THE CONGO
TANZANIA
Dodoma
Dar es Salaam
SEYCHELLES
Victoria
COMOROS
Moroni
Mayotte
ANGOLA
Luanda
ZAMBIA
Lusaka
MALAWI
Lilongwe
ZIMBABWE
Harare
MOZAMBIQUE
Maputo
MADAGASCAR
Antananarivo
NAMIBIA
Windhoek
BOTSWANA
Gaborone
SOUTH AFRICA
Tshwane (Pretoria)
Bloemfontein
Cape Town
SWAZILAND
Mbabane
LESOTHO
Maseru
20°W
0°
20°E
40°E
40°N
20°N
20°S
40°S
1 2 3 4 5 6 7 8
A B C D E F G H J K

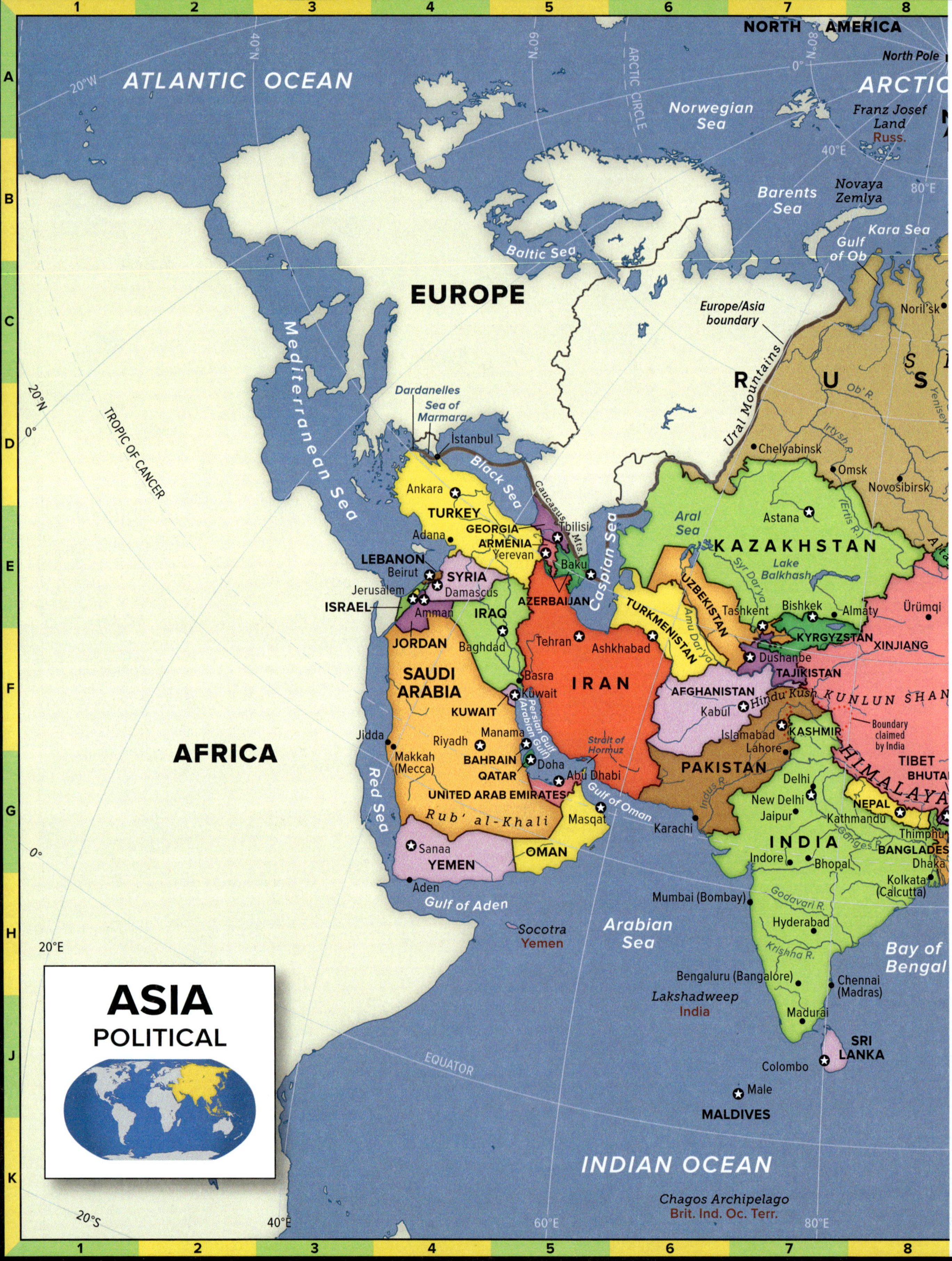
ASIA
POLITICAL
ATLANTIC OCEAN
NORTH AMERICA
North Pole
ARCTIC
Norwegian Sea
Franz Josef Land
Russ.
Barents Sea
Novaya Zemlya
Kara Sea
Gulf of Ob
Baltic Sea
EUROPE
AFRICA
Europe/Asia boundary
Ural Mountains
Noril'sk
Mediterranean Sea
Dardanelles
Sea of Marmara
Istanbul
Black Sea
Caucasus Mts.
Caspian Sea
Aral Sea
Chelyabinsk
Omsk
Novosibirsk
Astana
KAZAKHSTAN
Lake Balkhash
Syr Darya
Amu Darya
Ankara
TURKEY
GEORGIA
Tbilisi
ARMENIA
Yerevan
Baku
AZERBAIJAN
Adana
LEBANON
Beirut
SYRIA
Damascus
Jerusalem
ISRAEL
Amman
JORDAN
IRAQ
Baghdad
Tehran
IRAN
Ashkhabad
TURKMENISTAN
UZBEKISTAN
Tashkent
Bishkek
Almaty
KYRGYZSTAN
Dushanbe
TAJIKISTAN
Ürümqi
XINJIANG
KUNLUN SHAN
Boundary claimed by India
Hindu Kush
AFGHANISTAN
Kabul
Islamabad
KASHMIR
Lahore
PAKISTAN
Indus R.
Karachi
TIBET
HIMALAYA
NEPAL
Kathmandu
Thimphu
BANGLADESH
Dhaka
Delhi
New Delhi
Jaipur
INDIA
Ganges R.
Indore
Bhopal
Kolkata (Calcutta)
Mumbai (Bombay)
Godavari R.
Hyderabad
Krishna R.
Bengaluru (Bangalore)
Chennai (Madras)
Madurai
Bay of Bengal
SRI LANKA
Colombo
Male
MALDIVES
Lakshadweep
India
Arabian Sea
Socotra
Yemen
Basra
Kuwait
KUWAIT
SAUDI ARABIA
Persian Gulf
Arabian Gulf
Strait of Hormuz
Manama
BAHRAIN
Riyadh
Doha
QATAR
Abu Dhabi
UNITED ARAB EMIRATES
Jidda
Makkah (Mecca)
Red Sea
Rub' al-Khali
Masqat
Gulf of Oman
OMAN
Sanaa
YEMEN
Aden
Gulf of Aden
INDIAN OCEAN
Chagos Archipelago
Brit. Ind. Oc. Terr.
EQUATOR
TROPIC OF CANCER
ARCTIC CIRCLE
20°W
40°N
60°N
80°N
0°
40°E
80°E
20°N
20°E
60°E
20°S
1 2 3 4 5 6 7 8
A B C D E F G H J K

NORTH AMERICA
Bering Strait
Chukchi Sea
OCEAN
Wrangel I.
Gulf of Anadyr
Bering Sea
New Siberian Islands
East Siberian Sea
Severnaya Zemlya
Laptev Sea
Taymyr Peninsula
0 1,000 miles
0 1,000 kilometers
Two-Point Equidistant Projection
Kolyma Mts.
Cherski Range
Verkhoyanski Mts.
Lena R.
Commander Is.
Kamchatka Peninsula
Yakutsk
Sea of Okhotsk
Kuril Islands
S I B E R I A
R U S S I A
Sakhalin
Lake Baikal
Irkutsk
Hokkaidō
Sapporo
MANCHURIA
Vladivostok
Honshū
Sea of Japan (East Sea)
JAPAN
Tokyo
MONGOLIA
Ulaanbaatar
Shan
GOBI
Shenyang
NORTH KOREA
P'yŏngyang
Seoul
SOUTH KOREA
Kyōto
Ōsaka
Hiroshima
Shikoku
Kyūshū
Beijing
Yellow Sea
Shijiazhuang
Qingdao
Huang He (Yellow R.)
Lanzhou
Xi'an
Xuzhou
Nanjing
Shanghai
C H I N A
East China Sea
Boundary claimed by China
Chengdu
Chang Jiang (Yangtze R.)
Changsha
Nanchang
Fuzhou
Guiyang
Kunming
Xi R.
Guangzhou
Macau
Hong Kong
Taipei
TAIWAN
Ryukyu Islands
Okinawa
Marcus I. Japan
Bonin Is. Japan
Volcano Is. Japan
Parece Vela Japan
PACIFIC OCEAN
TROPIC OF CANCER
Philippine Sea
Hanoi
Haiphong
Hainan
MYANMAR (BURMA)
Nay Pyi Taw
Yangon (Rangoon)
LAOS
Vientiane
Da Nang
THAILAND
Bangkok
VIETNAM
CAMBODIA
Phnom Penh
Ho Chi Minh City
South China Sea
Luzon
PHILIPPINES
Quezon City
Manila
Mindoro
Samar
Panay
Leyte
Negros
Palawan
Mindanao
EQUATOR
Andaman Islands India
Andaman Sea
Nicobar Islands India
Gulf of Thailand
Bandar Seri Begawan
BRUNEI
SABAH
M A L A Y S I A
SARAWAK
Kuala Lumpur
SINGAPORE
Medan
Borneo
Sumatra
I N D O N E S I A
Mentawai Islands
Greater Sunda Islands
Java Sea
Jakarta
Java
Sulawesi (Celebes)
Halmahera
Morotai
Moluccas
Buru
Ceram
Biak
Jayapura
New Guinea
Aru Is.
Tanimbar Is.
Dolak
Arafura Sea
Dili
EAST TIMOR (TIMOR-LESTE)
Kupang
Timor
Timor Sea
AUSTRALIA

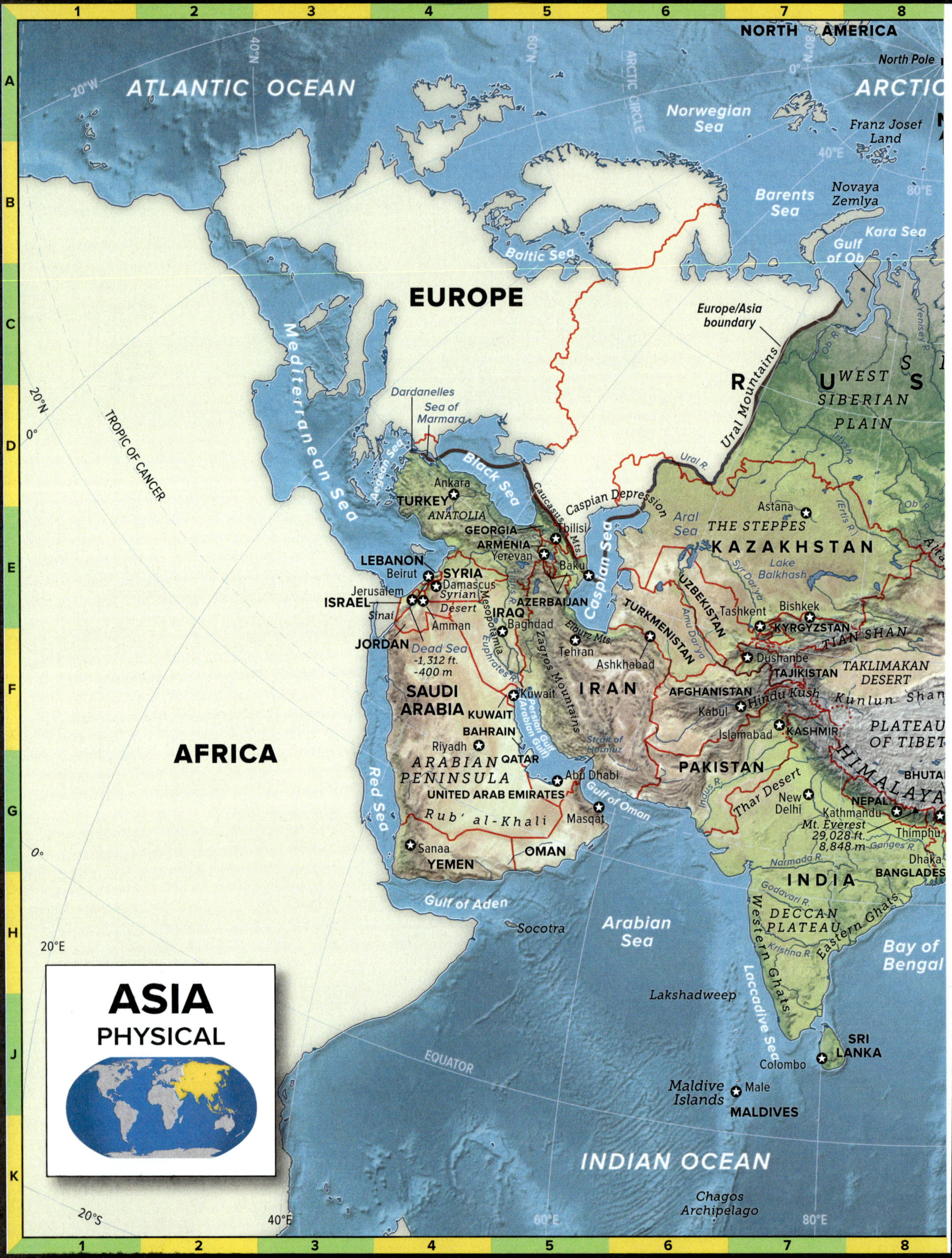
ASIA
PHYSICAL
ATLANTIC OCEAN
ARCTIC
NORTH AMERICA
North Pole
Norwegian Sea
Franz Josef Land
Barents Sea
Novaya Zemlya
Kara Sea
Gulf of Ob
Baltic Sea
EUROPE
Europe/Asia boundary
Mediterranean Sea
Dardanelles
Sea of Marmara
Aegean Sea
Black Sea
Caucasus Mts.
Caspian Depression
Ural Mountains
Ural R.
RUSSIA
WEST SIBERIAN PLAIN
TROPIC OF CANCER
Ankara
TURKEY
ANATOLIA
GEORGIA
Tbilisi
ARMENIA
Yerevan
Baku
Caspian Sea
Aral Sea
Astana
THE STEPPES
KAZAKHSTAN
Lake Balkhash
LEBANON
Beirut
SYRIA
Damascus
Syrian Desert
Jerusalem
ISRAEL
Sinai
Amman
JORDAN
Dead Sea
-1,312 ft.
-400 m
AZERBAIJAN
IRAQ
Baghdad
Euphrates R.
Tigris R.
Mesopotamia
Zagros Mountains
Elburz Mts.
Tehran
TURKMENISTAN
Ashkhabad
UZBEKISTAN
Tashkent
Bishkek
KYRGYZSTAN
TIAN SHAN
Dushanbe
TAJIKISTAN
TAKLIMAKAN DESERT
Kunlun Shan
SAUDI ARABIA
Kuwait
KUWAIT
Persian Gulf
Arabian Gulf
IRAN
AFGHANISTAN
Hindu Kush
Kabul
Islamabad
KASHMIR
PLATEAU OF TIBET
HIMALAYA
BAHRAIN
Riyadh
QATAR
Strait of Hormuz
ARABIAN PENINSULA
Abu Dhabi
UNITED ARAB EMIRATES
PAKISTAN
Indus R.
Thar Desert
New Delhi
NEPAL
Kathmandu
Mt. Everest
29,028 ft.
8,848 m
Thimphu
BHUTAN
Ganges R.
Dhaka
BANGLADESH
Gulf of Oman
Masqat
Rub' al-Khali
Red Sea
Sanaa
YEMEN
OMAN
AFRICA
Gulf of Aden
Socotra
Arabian Sea
Narmada R.
INDIA
Godavari R.
DECCAN PLATEAU
Western Ghats
Eastern Ghats
Krishna R.
Bay of Bengal
Lakshadweep
Laccadive Sea
SRI LANKA
Colombo
Maldive Islands
Male
MALDIVES
EQUATOR
INDIAN OCEAN
Chagos Archipelago
ARCTIC CIRCLE
20°W
40°N
60°N
80°N
0°
20°N
20°E
40°E
60°E
80°E
20°S
1 2 3 4 5 6 7 8
A B C D E F G H J K

NORTH AMERICA
Bering Strait
Chukchi Sea
Chukchi Peninsula
Gulf of Anadyr
Bering Sea
Aleutian Islands
OCEAN
Wrangel I.
New Siberian Islands
East Siberian Sea
Severnaya Zemlya
Laptev Sea
Taymyr Peninsula
Cherski Range
Kolyma Mts.
Verkhoyanski Mts.
CENTRAL SIBERIAN PLATEAU
Commander Is.
Kamchatka Peninsula
Sea of Okhotsk
Sakhalin
Kuril Islands
Hokkaidō
Honshū
JAPAN
Tokyo
Sea of Japan (East Sea)
NORTH KOREA
P'yŏngyang
Seoul
SOUTH KOREA
Sikhote-Alin' Range
Yablonovyy Range
Lake Baikal
Greater Khingan Range
Manchurian Plain
Ulaanbaatar
MONGOLIA
GOBI
Beijing
Yellow Sea
North China Plain
Shikoku
Kyūshū
Nampo Shoto
Qilian Shan
Qaidam Basin
CHINA
Sichuan Basin
Gongga Shan 24,790 ft. 7,556 m
East China Sea
Okinawa
Ryukyu Islands
Taipei
TAIWAN
PACIFIC OCEAN
TROPIC OF CANCER
Mariana Islands
Philippine Sea
Caroline Islands
EQUATOR
Hanoi
MYANMAR (BURMA)
LAOS
Vientiane
Nay Pyi Taw
Hainan
Luzon
South China Sea
Manila
Mindoro
Samar
PHILIPPINE ISLANDS
PHILIPPINES
THAILAND
Bangkok
VIETNAM
CAMBODIA
Phnom Penh
Andaman Islands
Andaman Sea
Gulf of Thailand
Palawan
Sulu Sea
Mindanao
Nicobar Islands
Bandar Seri Begawan
BRUNEI
Celebes Sea
Moluccas
MALAYSIA
Malay Peninsula
Kuala Lumpur
SINGAPORE
Borneo
Sulawesi (Celebes)
Buru
Ceram
Aru Is.
New Guinea
Dolak
Tanimbar Is.
Arafura Sea
INDONESIA
Sumatra
Mentawai Islands
Greater Sunda Islands
Java Sea
Java
Jakarta
Dili
EAST TIMOR (TIMOR-LESTE)
Timor
Timor Sea
AUSTRALIA
0 1,000 miles
0 1,000 kilometers
Two-Point Equidistant Projection

ASIA
N
TROPIC OF CANCER
NORTHERN MARIANA ISLANDS
U.S.
Saipan
Wake Island
U.S.
M I C R O N E S I A
MARSHALL ISLANDS
Bikini Atoll
Ralik Chain
Ratak Chain
Majuro
GUAM U.S.
Agana
Yap Islands
Chuuk Islands
Caroline Islands
Palikir
Pohnpei (Ponape)
Melekeok
PALAU
FEDERATED STATES OF MICRONESIA
INTERNATIONAL DATE LINE
Howland Island
U.S.
Gilbert Islands
Tarawa (Bairiki)
EQUATOR
Yaren
NAURU
New Guinea
Mt. Wilhelm 14,762 ft. 4,500 m
PAPUA NEW GUINEA
New Britain
M E L A N E S I A
Solomon Is.
SOLOMON ISLANDS
Honiara
Santa Cruz Is.
TUVALU
Funafuti
Port Moresby
Torres Strait
WALLIS AND FUTUNA IS.
Fr.
Darwin
Gulf of Carpentaria
INDIAN OCEAN
CORAL SEA ISLANDS TERRITORY
Austral.
VANUATU
Port-Vila
Suva
FIJI ISLANDS
NEW CALEDONIA
Fr.
Nouméa
Coral Sea
Nuku'alofa
Kimberley Plateau
NORTHERN TERRITORY
GREAT DIVIDING RANGE
GREAT SANDY DESERT
AUSTRALIA
Macdonnell Ranges
QUEENSLAND
WESTERN AUSTRALIA
Brisbane
Lake Eyre (dry) -52 ft. -16 m
GREAT VICTORIA DESERT
SOUTH AUSTRALIA
NEW SOUTH WALES
Darling R.
Norfolk Island
Austral.
Lord Howe Island
Austral.
Perth
Great Australian Bight
Adelaide
Murray R.
AUSTRALIAN CAPITAL TERRITORY
Sydney
Canberra
Mt. Kosciusko 7,310 ft. 2,228 m
VICTORIA
Melbourne
Tasman Sea
Auckland
North Island
NEW ZEALAND
Wellington
TASMANIA
Hobart
Mt. Cook 12,349 ft. 3,764 m
Christchurch
Chatham Islands
N.Z.
South Island
Stewart Island
120°E
140°E
160°E
180°
20°N
0°
20°S
40°S

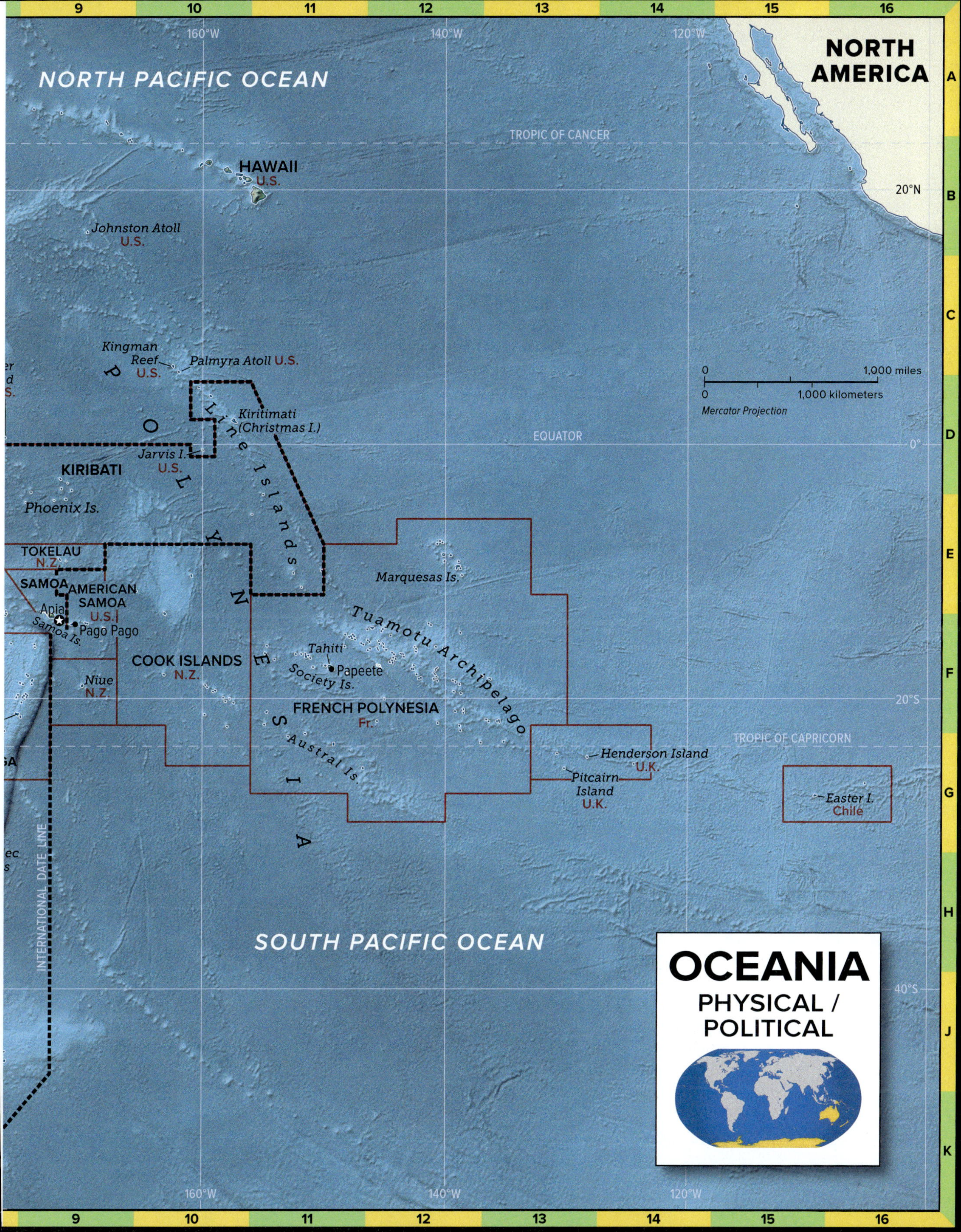
9
10
11
12
13
14
15
16
160°W
140°W
120°W
NORTH AMERICA
NORTH PACIFIC OCEAN
TROPIC OF CANCER
HAWAII
U.S.
20°N
Johnston Atoll
U.S.
Kingman Reef
U.S.
Palmyra Atoll U.S.
Kiritimati (Christmas I.)
Line Islands
0
1,000 miles
0
1,000 kilometers
Mercator Projection
EQUATOR
0°
Jarvis I.
U.S.
KIRIBATI
Phoenix Is.
POLYNESIA
TOKELAU
N.Z.
SAMOA
AMERICAN SAMOA
U.S.
Apia
Samoa Is.
Pago Pago
Marquesas Is.
Tuamotu Archipelago
Tahiti
Papeete
Society Is.
COOK ISLANDS
N.Z.
Niue
N.Z.
FRENCH POLYNESIA
Fr.
Austral Is.
20°S
TROPIC OF CAPRICORN
Henderson Island
U.K.
Pitcairn Island
U.K.
Easter I.
Chile
INTERNATIONAL DATE LINE
SOUTH PACIFIC OCEAN
40°S
OCEANIA
PHYSICAL / POLITICAL
A
B
C
D
E
F
G
H
J
K

RUSSIA
Lake Baikal
Yablonovyy Range
Ulaanbaatar
MONGOLIA
ALTAY SHAN
GOBI
Greater Khingan Range
Manchurian Plain
Amur R.
Sikhote-Alin' Range
KAMCHATKA PENINSULA
Sea of Okhotsk
Sakhalin
Kuril Islands
Bering Sea
ALEUTIAN ISLANDS
Hokkaidō
Sea of Japan (East Sea)
Beijing
P'yongyang
NORTH KOREA
Seoul
SOUTH KOREA
CHINA
Huang He (Yellow R.)
Yellow Sea
Honshū
JAPAN
Tokyo
Shikoku
Kyūshū
East China Sea
Chang Jiang (Yangtze R.)
Nampo Shoto
Ryukyu Islands
Taipei
TAIWAN
NORTH PACIFIC
INTERNATIONAL DATE LINE
Hawaiian
INDIA
MYANMAR (BURMA)
Nay Pyi Taw
Hanoi
LAOS
Vientiane
THAILAND
VIETNAM
Hainan
Bangkok
CAMBODIA
Phnom Penh
South China Sea
Luzon
Manila
PHILIPPINES
PHILIPPINE ISLANDS
Philippine Sea
MICRONESIA
NORTHERN MARIANA ISLANDS
U.S.
GUAM
U.S.
MARSHALL ISLANDS
Ratak Chain
Ralik Chain
Majuro
Andaman Sea
Sulu Sea
Mindanao
Bandar Seri Begawan
BRUNEI
Melekeok
PALAU
Caroline Islands
Palikir
FEDERATED STATES OF MICRONESIA
Kuala Lumpur
MALAYSIA
SINGAPORE
Celebes Sea
Borneo
Sumatra
INDONESIA
GREATER SUNDA ISLANDS
Sulawesi (Celebes)
Moluccas
Tarawa (Bairiki)
Gilbert Islands
KIRIBATI
Phoenix Is.
Yaren
NAURU
POLYNESIA
MELANESIA
Jakarta
Java
Java Sea
Dili
EAST TIMOR (TIMOR-LESTE)
Lesser Sunda Islands
Arafura Sea
New Guinea
PAPUA NEW GUINEA
Port Moresby
Solomon Is.
SOLOMON ISLANDS
Honiara
TUVALU
Funafuti
Tokelau N.Z.
AMERICAN SAMOA U.S.
SAMOA
Apia
Santa Cruz Islands
WALLIS AND FUTUNA IS. Fr.
CORAL SEA ISLANDS TERRITORY Austral.
VANUATU
Port-Vila
Suva
FIJI ISLANDS
TONGA
Nuku'alofa
Niue N.Z.
NEW CALEDONIA Fr.
Coral Sea
AUSTRALIA
Darling R.
Great Australian Bight
Canberra
Norfolk Island Austral.
Lord Howe Island Austral.
Kermadec Islands N.Z.
INDIAN OCEAN
Tasman Sea
NEW ZEALAND
Wellington
Tasmania
Chatham Island N.Z.
0 1,000 miles
0 1,000 kilometers
Mercator Projection
100°E
120°E
140°E
160°E
180°
40°N
20°N
0°
20°S
40°S

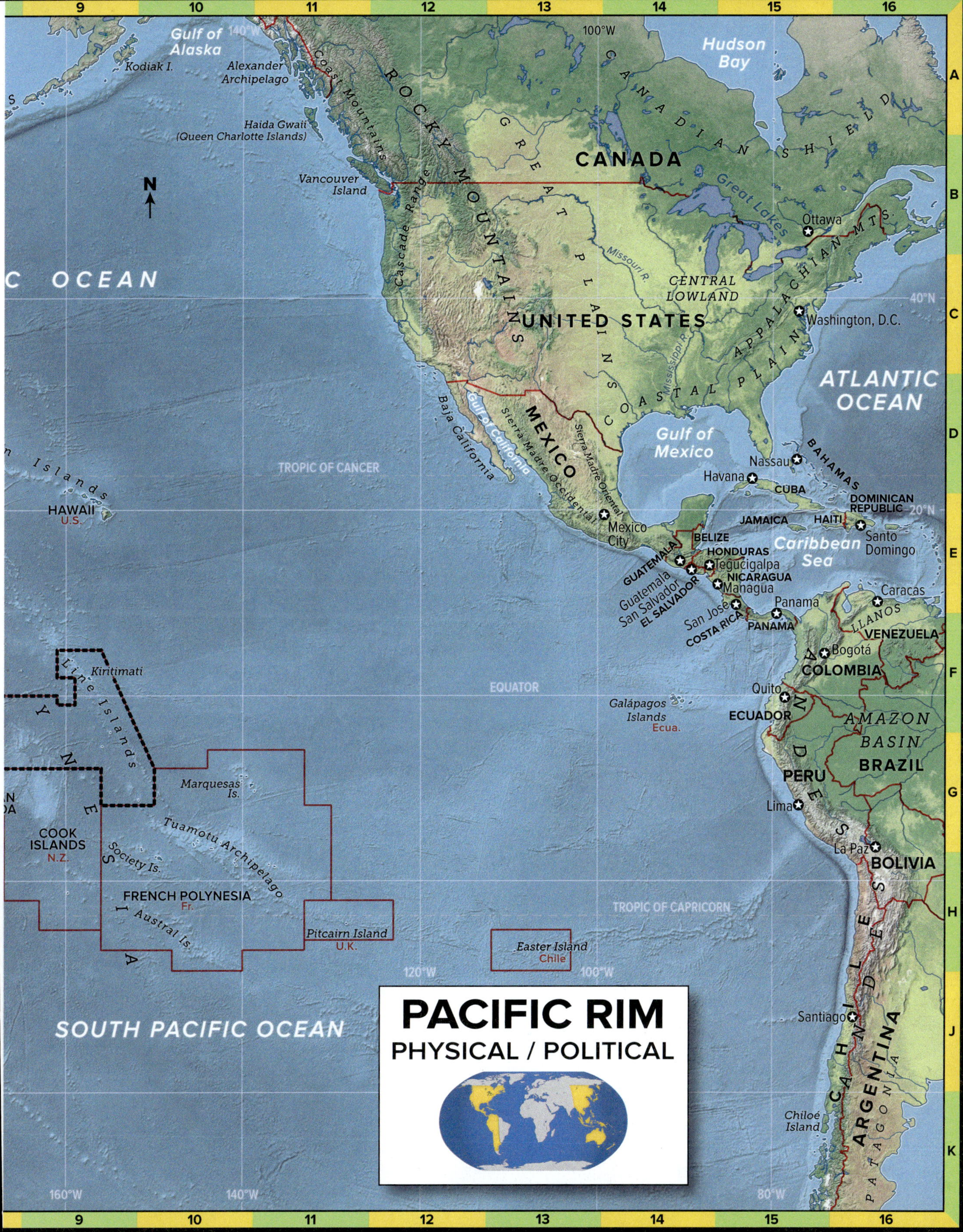
PACIFIC RIM
PHYSICAL / POLITICAL
Gulf of Alaska
Kodiak I.
Alexander Archipelago
Haida Gwaii (Queen Charlotte Islands)
Vancouver Island
Coast Mountains
ROCKY MOUNTAINS
Cascade Range
GREAT PLAINS
CANADIAN SHIELD
Hudson Bay
CANADA
Great Lakes
Ottawa
APPALACHIAN MTS.
CENTRAL LOWLAND
Missouri R.
Mississippi R.
UNITED STATES
Washington, D.C.
COASTAL PLAIN
ATLANTIC OCEAN
OCEAN
Baja California
Gulf of California
Sierra Madre Occidental
Sierra Madre Oriental
MEXICO
Gulf of Mexico
TROPIC OF CANCER
Nassau
BAHAMAS
Havana
CUBA
DOMINICAN REPUBLIC
JAMAICA
HAITI
Santo Domingo
Mexico City
BELIZE
HONDURAS
Caribbean Sea
GUATEMALA
Tegucigalpa
NICARAGUA
Managua
Guatemala
San Salvador
EL SALVADOR
San José
COSTA RICA
Panama
PANAMA
Caracas
LLANOS
VENEZUELA
Bogotá
COLOMBIA
Hawaiian Islands
HAWAII
U.S.
Kiritimati
Line Islands
POLYNESIA
EQUATOR
Galápagos Islands
Ecua.
Quito
ECUADOR
AMAZON BASIN
BRAZIL
PERU
Lima
ANDES
La Paz
BOLIVIA
Marquesas Is.
Tuamotu Archipelago
Society Is.
COOK ISLANDS
N.Z.
FRENCH POLYNESIA
Fr.
Austral Is.
Pitcairn Island
U.K.
TROPIC OF CAPRICORN
Easter Island
Chile
SOUTH PACIFIC OCEAN
Santiago
ARGENTINA
CHILE
PATAGONIA
Chiloé Island
N
140°W
100°W
40°N
20°N
120°W
160°W
80°W
9
10
11
12
13
14
15
16
A
B
C
D
E
F
G
H
J
K

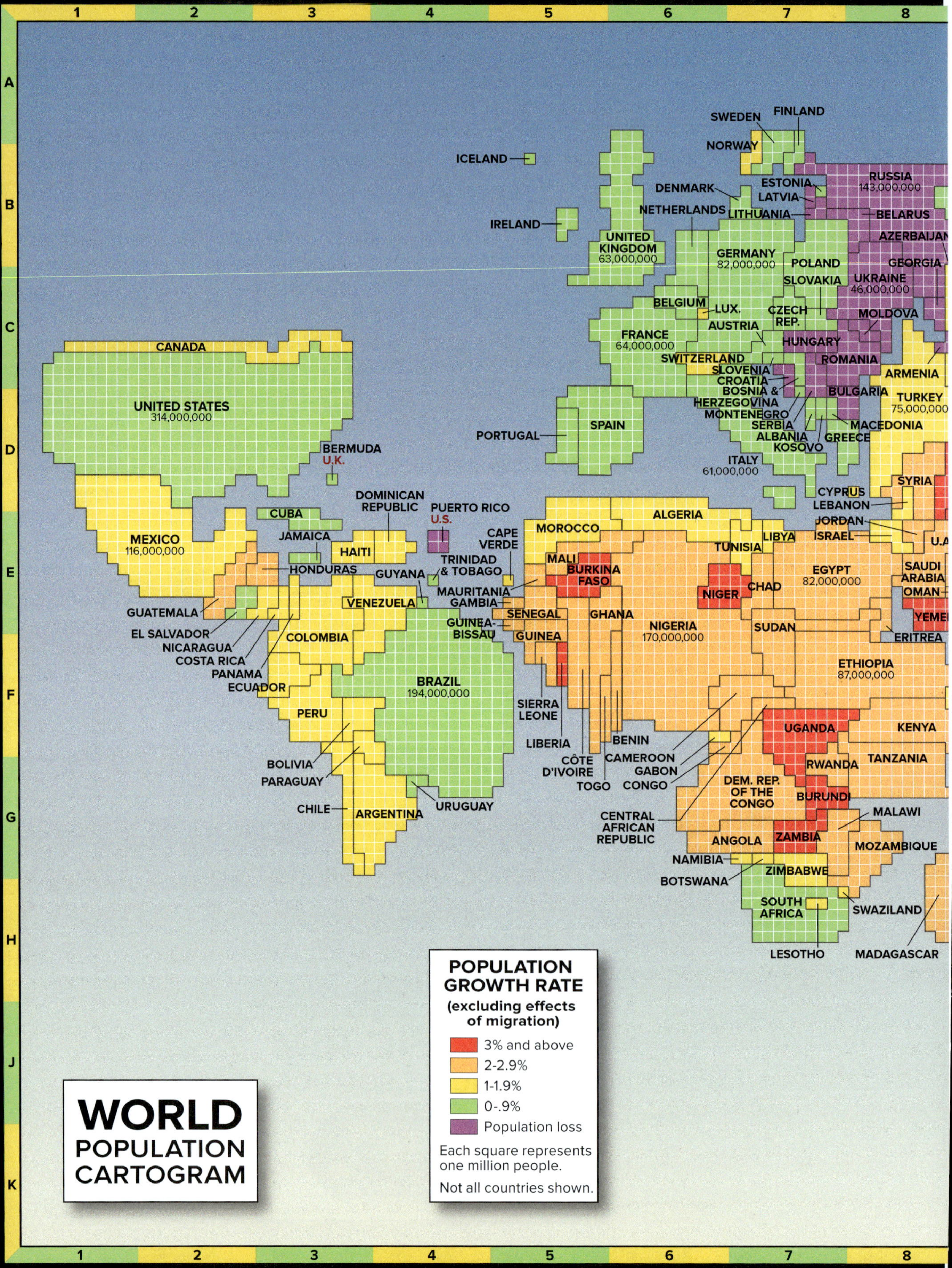
WORLD POPULATION CARTOGRAM
POPULATION GROWTH RATE
(excluding effects of migration)
3% and above
2-2.9%
1-1.9%
0-.9%
Population loss
Each square represents one million people.
Not all countries shown.
1 2 3 4 5 6 7 8
A B C D E F G H J K
CANADA
UNITED STATES 314,000,000
BERMUDA U.K.
MEXICO 116,000,000
CUBA
JAMAICA
HAITI
DOMINICAN REPUBLIC
PUERTO RICO U.S.
HONDURAS
GUATEMALA
EL SALVADOR
NICARAGUA
COSTA RICA
PANAMA
ECUADOR
GUYANA
TRINIDAD & TOBAGO
VENEZUELA
COLOMBIA
PERU
BRAZIL 194,000,000
BOLIVIA
PARAGUAY
CHILE
ARGENTINA
URUGUAY
ICELAND
IRELAND
UNITED KINGDOM 63,000,000
SWEDEN
FINLAND
NORWAY
DENMARK
ESTONIA
LATVIA
LITHUANIA
NETHERLANDS
GERMANY 82,000,000
POLAND
SLOVAKIA
BELGIUM
LUX.
CZECH REP.
AUSTRIA
FRANCE 64,000,000
SWITZERLAND
HUNGARY
SLOVENIA
CROATIA
BOSNIA & HERZEGOVINA
MONTENEGRO
SERBIA
ALBANIA
KOSOVO
GREECE
MACEDONIA
BULGARIA
ROMANIA
MOLDOVA
RUSSIA 143,000,000
BELARUS
AZERBAIJAN
GEORGIA
UKRAINE 46,000,000
ARMENIA
TURKEY 75,000,000
PORTUGAL
SPAIN
ITALY 61,000,000
CYPRUS
LEBANON
SYRIA
JORDAN
ISRAEL
U.A.
SAUDI ARABIA
OMAN
YEMEN
MOROCCO
ALGERIA
TUNISIA
LIBYA
EGYPT 82,000,000
CAPE VERDE
MALI
BURKINA FASO
NIGER
CHAD
MAURITANIA
GAMBIA
SENEGAL
GUINEA-BISSAU
GUINEA
GHANA
NIGERIA 170,000,000
SUDAN
ERITREA
ETHIOPIA 87,000,000
SIERRA LEONE
LIBERIA
CÔTE D'IVOIRE
TOGO
BENIN
CAMEROON
GABON
CONGO
CENTRAL AFRICAN REPUBLIC
UGANDA
KENYA
RWANDA
TANZANIA
DEM. REP. OF THE CONGO
BURUNDI
MALAWI
ANGOLA
ZAMBIA
MOZAMBIQUE
NAMIBIA
BOTSWANA
ZIMBABWE
SOUTH AFRICA
SWAZILAND
LESOTHO
MADAGASCAR

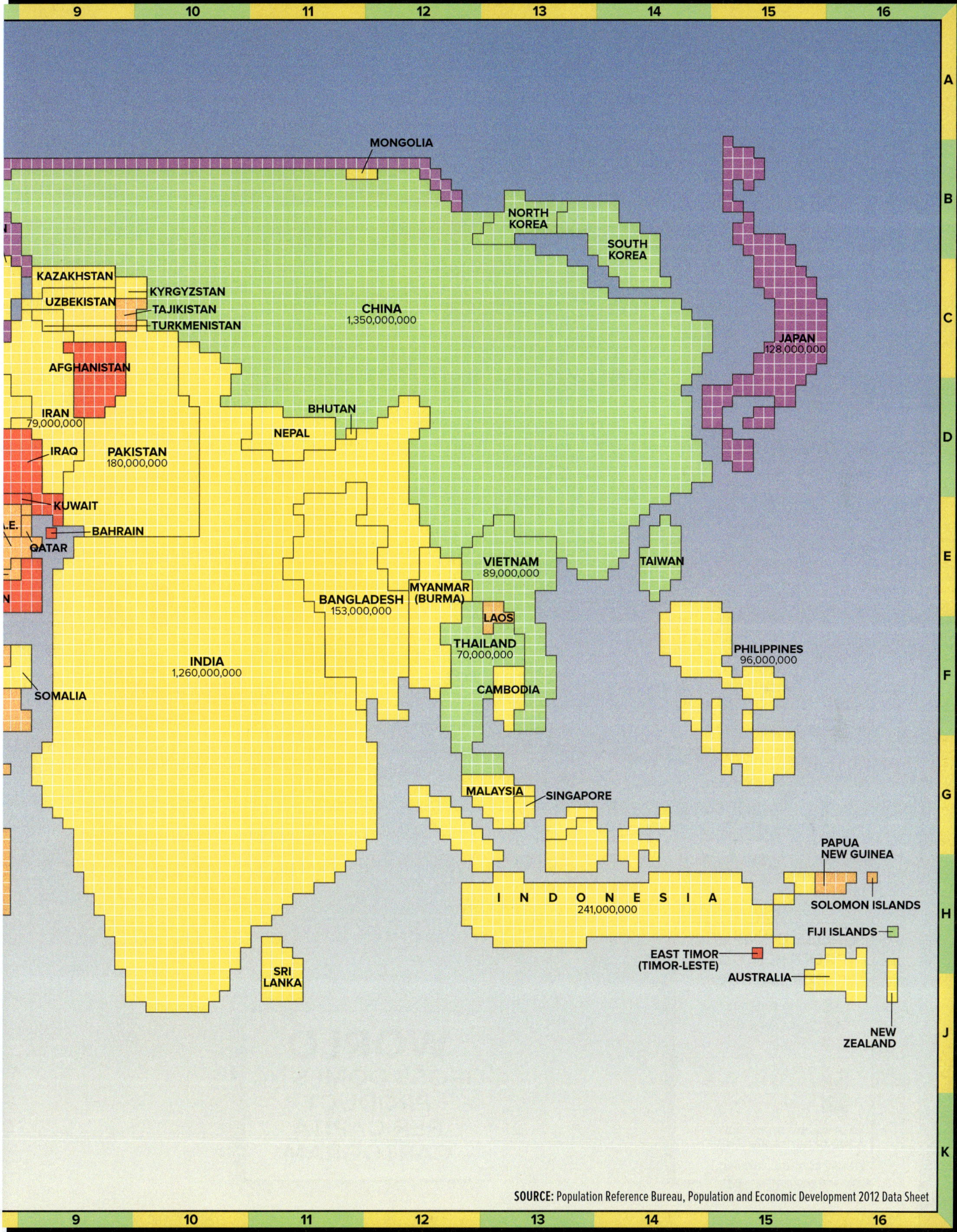
9
10
11
12
13
14
15
16
A
B
C
D
E
F
G
H
J
K
MONGOLIA
NORTH KOREA
SOUTH KOREA
KAZAKHSTAN
KYRGYZSTAN
UZBEKISTAN
TAJIKISTAN
TURKMENISTAN
CHINA
1,350,000,000
JAPAN
128,000,000
AFGHANISTAN
IRAN
79,000,000
BHUTAN
NEPAL
IRAQ
PAKISTAN
180,000,000
KUWAIT
BAHRAIN
QATAR
VIETNAM
89,000,000
TAIWAN
MYANMAR (BURMA)
BANGLADESH
153,000,000
LAOS
THAILAND
70,000,000
PHILIPPINES
96,000,000
INDIA
1,260,000,000
SOMALIA
CAMBODIA
MALAYSIA
SINGAPORE
PAPUA NEW GUINEA
I N D O N E S I A
241,000,000
SOLOMON ISLANDS
FIJI ISLANDS
EAST TIMOR (TIMOR-LESTE)
SRI LANKA
AUSTRALIA
NEW ZEALAND
SOURCE: Population Reference Bureau, Population and Economic Development 2012 Data Sheet

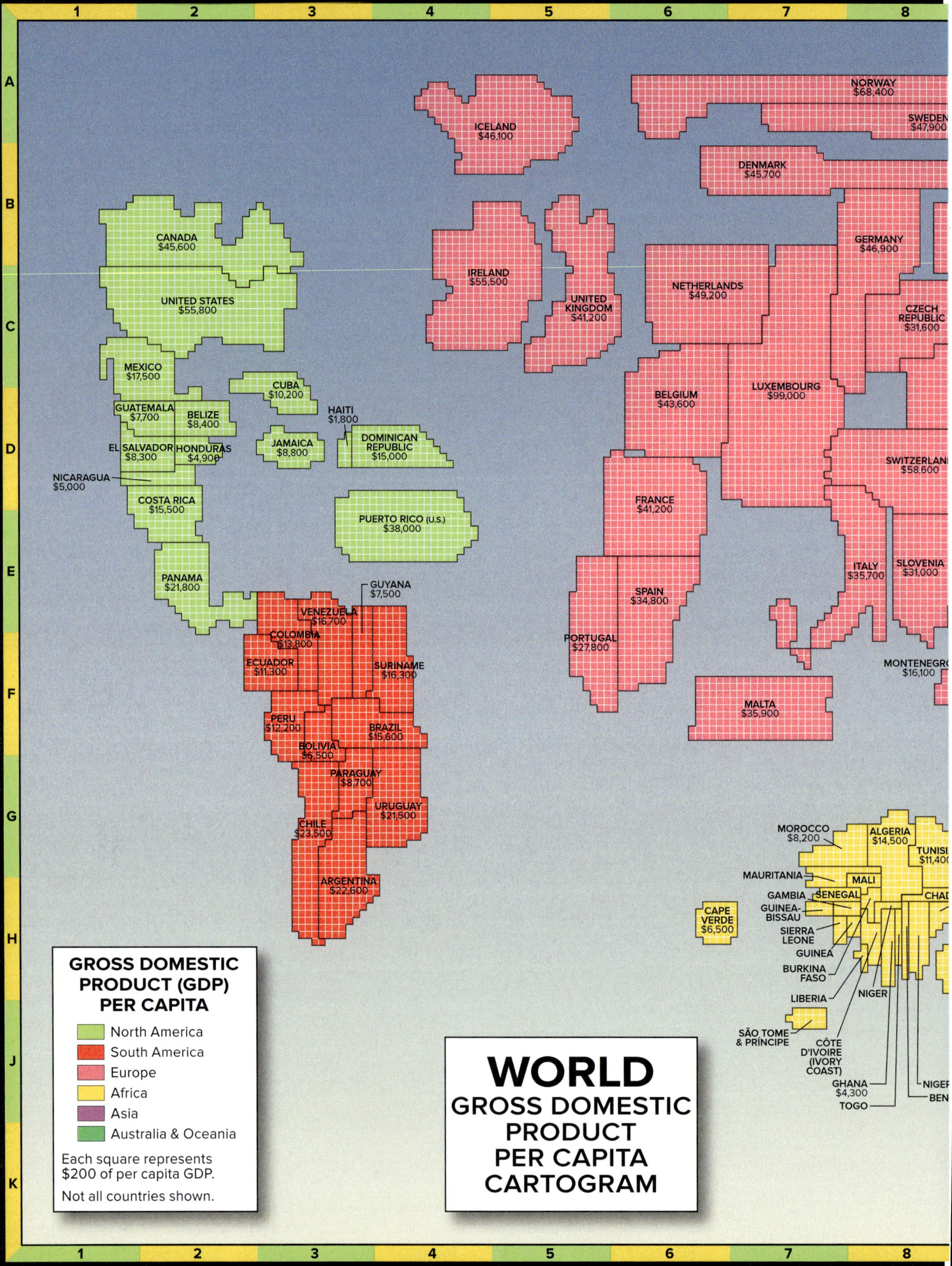
1 2 3 4 5 6 7 8
A B C D E F G H J K
ICELAND $46,100
NORWAY $68,400
SWEDEN $47,900
DENMARK $45,700
CANADA $45,600
UNITED STATES $55,800
IRELAND $55,500
UNITED KINGDOM $41,200
GERMANY $46,900
NETHERLANDS $49,200
CZECH REPUBLIC $31,600
MEXICO $17,500
CUBA $10,200
HAITI $1,800
GUATEMALA $7,700
BELIZE $8,400
JAMAICA $8,800
DOMINICAN REPUBLIC $15,000
EL SALVADOR $8,300
HONDURAS $4,900
NICARAGUA $5,000
COSTA RICA $15,500
PUERTO RICO (U.S.) $38,000
BELGIUM $43,600
LUXEMBOURG $99,000
SWITZERLAN $58,600
FRANCE $41,200
PANAMA $21,800
GUYANA $7,500
VENEZUELA $16,700
COLOMBIA $13,800
ECUADOR $11,300
SURINAME $16,300
SPAIN $34,800
PORTUGAL $27,800
ITALY $35,700
SLOVENIA $31,000
MONTENEGR $16,100
MALTA $35,900
PERU $12,200
BRAZIL $15,600
BOLIVIA $6,500
PARAGUAY $8,700
URUGUAY $21,500
CHILE $23,500
ARGENTINA $22,600
MOROCCO $8,200
ALGERIA $14,500
TUNISI $11,40
MAURITANIA
MALI
GAMBIA
SENEGAL
CHAD
GUINEA-BISSAU
CAPE VERDE $6,500
SIERRA LEONE
GUINEA
BURKINA FASO
LIBERIA
NIGER
SÃO TOME & PRINCIPE
CÔTE D'IVOIRE (IVORY COAST)
GHANA $4,300
TOGO
NIGEF
BEN
GROSS DOMESTIC PRODUCT (GDP) PER CAPITA
North America
South America
Europe
Africa
Asia
Australia & Oceania
Each square represents $200 of per capita GDP.
Not all countries shown.
WORLD
GROSS DOMESTIC PRODUCT PER CAPITA CARTOGRAM

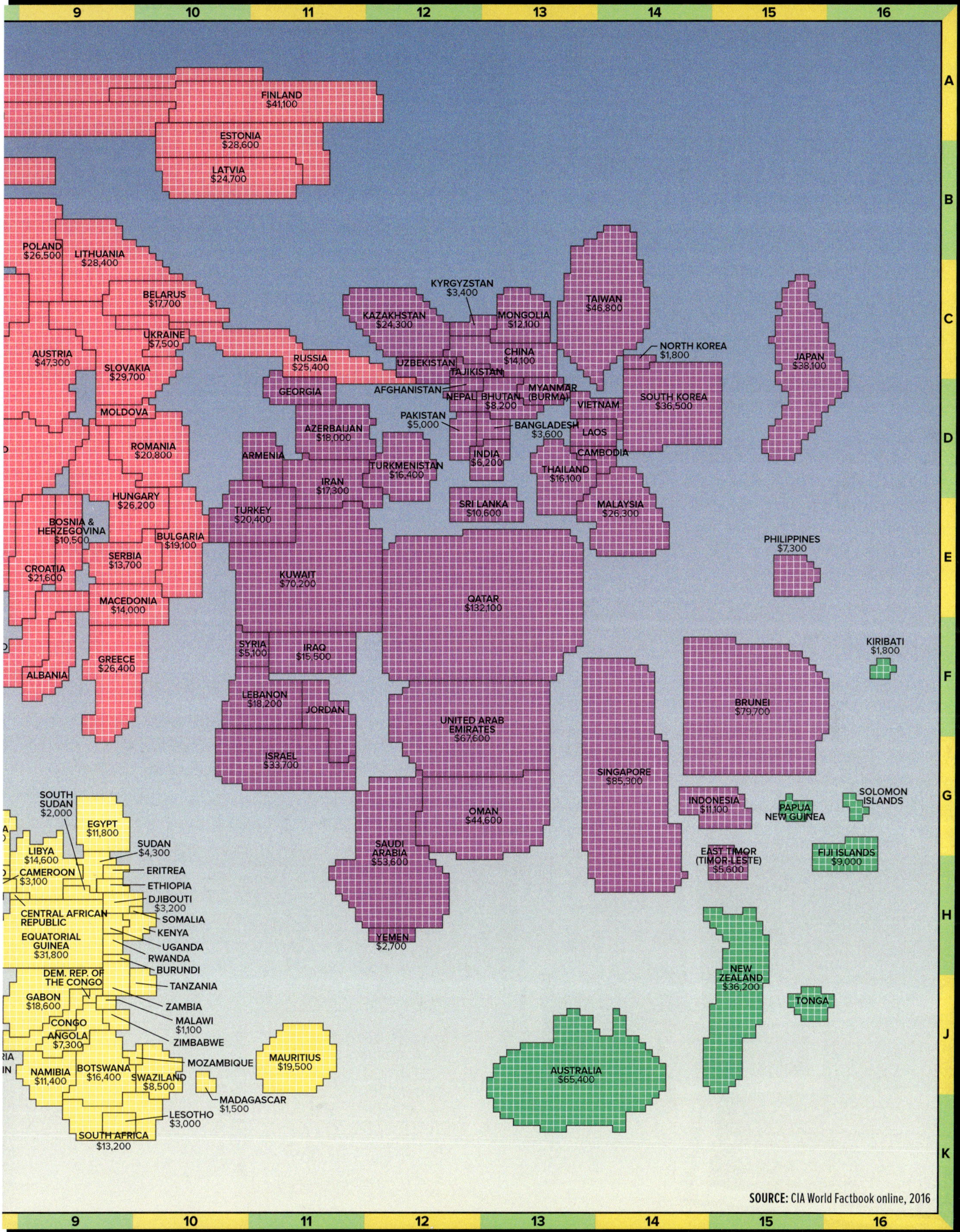
9
10
11
12
13
14
15
16
A
B
C
D
E
F
G
H
J
K
FINLAND $41,100
ESTONIA $28,600
LATVIA $24,700
POLAND $26,500
LITHUANIA $28,400
BELARUS $17,700
UKRAINE $7,500
AUSTRIA $47,300
SLOVAKIA $29,700
RUSSIA $25,400
MOLDOVA
ROMANIA $20,800
HUNGARY $26,200
BOSNIA & HERZEGOVINA $10,500
BULGARIA $19,100
SERBIA $13,700
CROATIA $21,600
MACEDONIA $14,000
GREECE $26,400
ALBANIA
KYRGYZSTAN $3,400
KAZAKHSTAN $24,300
MONGOLIA $12,100
TAIWAN $46,800
CHINA $14,100
NORTH KOREA $1,800
JAPAN $38,100
UZBEKISTAN
TAJIKISTAN
AFGHANISTAN
GEORGIA
NEPAL
BHUTAN $8,200
MYANMAR (BURMA)
VIETNAM
SOUTH KOREA $36,500
PAKISTAN $5,000
BANGLADESH $3,600
LAOS
AZERBAIJAN $18,000
ARMENIA
INDIA $6,200
CAMBODIA
TURKMENISTAN $16,400
THAILAND $16,100
IRAN $17,300
SRI LANKA $10,600
MALAYSIA $26,300
TURKEY $20,400
PHILIPPINES $7,300
KUWAIT $70,200
QATAR $132,100
SYRIA $5,100
IRAQ $15,500
KIRIBATI $1,800
LEBANON $18,200
JORDAN
BRUNEI $79,700
UNITED ARAB EMIRATES $67,600
ISRAEL $33,700
SINGAPORE $85,300
SOUTH SUDAN $2,000
EGYPT $11,800
INDONESIA $11,100
PAPUA NEW GUINEA
SOLOMON ISLANDS
OMAN $44,600
SUDAN $4,300
LIBYA $14,600
SAUDI ARABIA $53,600
EAST TIMOR (TIMOR-LESTE) $5,600
FIJI ISLANDS $9,000
CAMEROON $3,100
ERITREA
ETHIOPIA
DJIBOUTI $3,200
CENTRAL AFRICAN REPUBLIC
SOMALIA
KENYA
EQUATORIAL GUINEA $31,800
UGANDA
YEMEN $2,700
RWANDA
BURUNDI
NEW ZEALAND $36,200
DEM. REP. OF THE CONGO
TANZANIA
GABON $18,600
ZAMBIA
TONGA
CONGO
MALAWI $1,100
ANGOLA $7,300
ZIMBABWE
MAURITIUS $19,500
MOZAMBIQUE
AUSTRALIA $65,400
NAMIBIA $11,400
BOTSWANA $16,400
SWAZILAND $8,500
MADAGASCAR $1,500
LESOTHO $3,000
SOUTH AFRICA $13,200
SOURCE: CIA World Factbook online, 2016

# How do I study **Geography?**

Geographers have tried to understand the best way to teach and learn about geography. In order to do this, geographers created the *Five Themes of Geography*. The themes acted as a guide for teaching the basic ideas about geography to students like yourself.

People who teach and study geography, though, thought that the Five Themes were too broad. In 1994, geographers created 18 national geography standards. These standards were more detailed about what should be taught and learned. The Six Essential Elements act as a bridge connecting the Five Themes with the standards.

These pages show you how the Five Themes are related to the Six Essential Elements and the 18 standards.

## 5 Themes of Geography

### 1 Location
Location describes where something is. Absolute location describes a place's exact position on the Earth's surface. Relative location expresses where a place is in relation to another place.

### 2 Place
Place describes the physical and human characteristics that make a location unique.

### 3 Regions
Regions are areas that share common characteristics.

### 4 Movement
Movement explains how and why people and things move and are connected.

### 5 Human-Environment Interaction
Human-Environment Interaction describes the relationship between people and their environment.

# 6 Essential Elements

# 18 Geography Standards

## I. The World in Spatial Terms

Geographers look to see where a place is located. Location acts as a starting point to answer "Where is it?" The location of a place helps you orient yourself as to where you are.

1 How to use maps and other tools.

2 How to use mental maps to organize information.

3 How to analyze the spatial organization of people, places, and environments.

## II. Places and Regions

**Place** describes physical characteristics such as landforms, climate, and plant or animal life. It might also describe human characteristics, including language and way of life. Places can also be organized into regions. **Regions** are places united by one or more characteristics.

4 The physical and human characteristics of places.

5 How people create regions to interpret Earth's complexity.

6 How culture and experience influence people's perceptions of places and regions.

## III. Physical Systems

Geographers study how physical systems, such as hurricanes, volcanoes, and glaciers, shape the surface of the Earth. They also look at how plants and animals depend upon one another and their surroundings for their survival.

7 The physical processes that shape Earth's surface.

8 The distribution of ecosystems on Earth's surface.

## IV. Human Systems

People shape the world in which they live. They settle in certain places, but not in others. An ongoing theme in geography is the movement of people, ideas, and goods.

9 The characteristics, distribution, and migration of human populations.

10 The complexity of Earth's cultural mosaics.

11 The patterns and networks of economic interdependence.

12 The patterns of human settlements.

13 The forces of cooperation and conflict.

## V. Environment and Society

How does the relationship between people and their natural surroundings influence the way people live? Geographers study how people use the environment and how their actions affect the environment.

14 How human actions modify the physical environment.

15 How physical systems affect human systems.

16 The meaning, use, and distribution of resources.

## VI. The Uses of Geography

Knowledge of geography helps us understand the relationships among people, places, and environments over time. Applying geographic skills helps you understand the past and prepare for the future.

17 How to apply geography to interpret the past.

18 How to apply geography to interpret the present and plan for the future.

# GEOGRAPHY SKILLS HANDBOOK

## CONTENTS



### Geography Skills Handbook

Throughout this text, you will discover how geography has shaped the course of events in history. Landforms, waterways, climate, and natural resources all have helped or hindered human activities. Usually people have learned either to adapt to their environments or to transform them to meet their needs. The resources in this Geography Skills Handbook will help you get the most out of your textbook—and provide you with skills you will use for the rest of your life.

*Geographers use a wide array of tools to collect and analyze information to help them understand the Earth. The study of geography is more than knowing a lot of facts about places. Rather, it has more to do with asking questions about the Earth, pursuing answers, and solving problems. Thus, one of the most important geographic tools is inside your head: the ability to think geographically.*

BananaStock/PictureQuest

# Globes and Maps

A **globe** is a scale model of the Earth. Because Earth is round, a globe presents the most accurate depiction of geographic information such as area, distance, and direction. However, globes show little close-up detail. A printed **map** is a symbolic representation of all or part of the planet. Unlike globes, maps can show small areas in great detail.

## From 3-D to 2-D

Think about the surface of the Earth as the peel of an orange. To flatten the peel, you have to cut it into segments that are still connected as one piece. To create maps that are not interrupted, mapmakers, or **cartographers**, use mathematical formulas to transfer information from the three-dimensional globe to the two-dimensional map. However, when the curves of a globe become straight lines on a map, distortion of size, shape, distance, or area occurs.

## Great Circle Routes

A straight line of true direction—one that runs directly from west to east, for example—is not always the shortest distance between two points. This is due to the curvature of the Earth. To find the shortest distance, stretch a piece of string around the globe from one point to the other. The string will form part of a *great circle*, an imaginary line that follows the curve of the Earth. Ship captains and airline pilots use these **great circle routes** to reduce travel time and to conserve fuel.

The idea of great circle routes is an important difference between globes and maps. A round globe accurately shows a great circle route, as indicated on the top right map. However, the flat map below shows the great circle distance (dotted line) between Tokyo and Los Angeles to be much shorter than the true direction distance (solid line). In fact, the great circle distance is 314 miles (505 km) shorter.

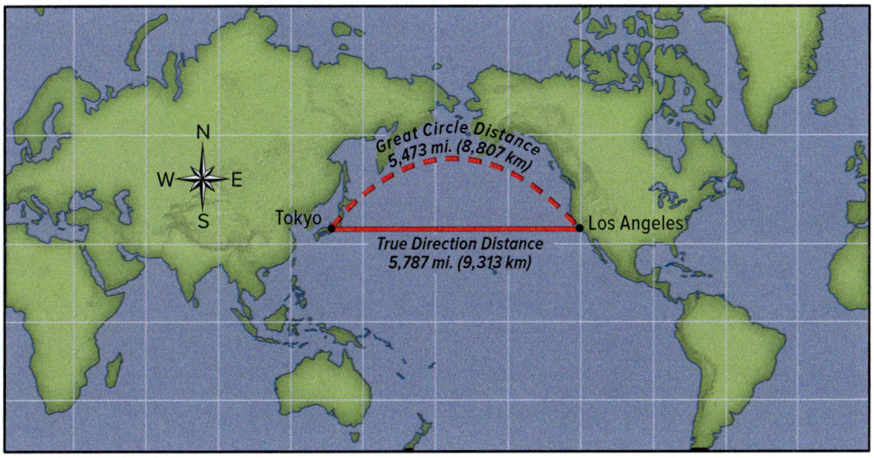


### VOCABULARY

*globe:* a scale model of the Earth

*map:* a symbolic representation of all or part of the planet

*cartographers:* mapmakers

*great circle route:* an imaginary line that follows the curve of the Earth and represents the shortest distance between two points

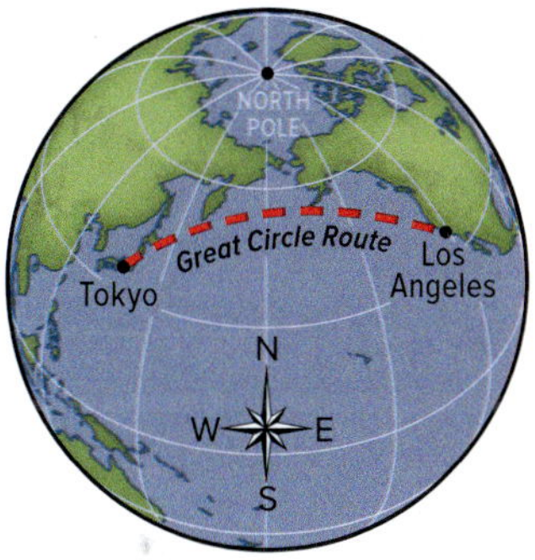


### GEOGRAPHIC REASONING

1. Explain the significance of the following: globe, map, cartographer, great circle route.
2. Describe the problems that arise when the curves of a globe become straight lines on a map.
3. Use a Venn diagram like the one below to identify the similarities and differences between globes and maps.

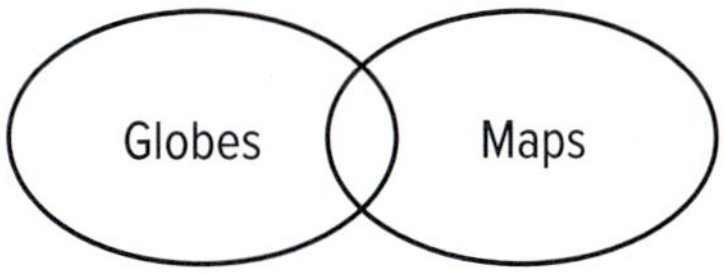

# Projections

To create maps, cartographers project the round Earth onto a flat surface—making a **map projection.** Distance, shape, direction, or size may be distorted by a projection. As a result, the purpose of the map usually dictates which projection is used. There are many kinds of map projections, some with general names and some named for the cartographers who developed them. Three basic categories of map projections are shown here: **planar, cylindrical,** and **conic**.

### Planar Projection

A planar projection shows the Earth centered in such a way that a straight line coming from the center to any point represents the shortest distance. Also known as an azimuthal projection, it is most accurate at its center. As a result, it is often used for maps of the Poles.

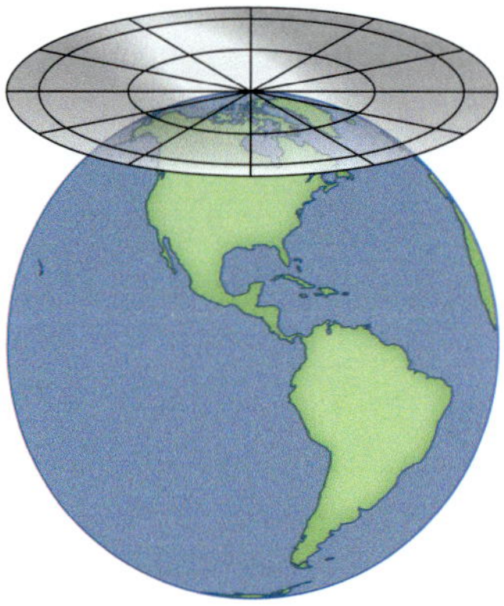

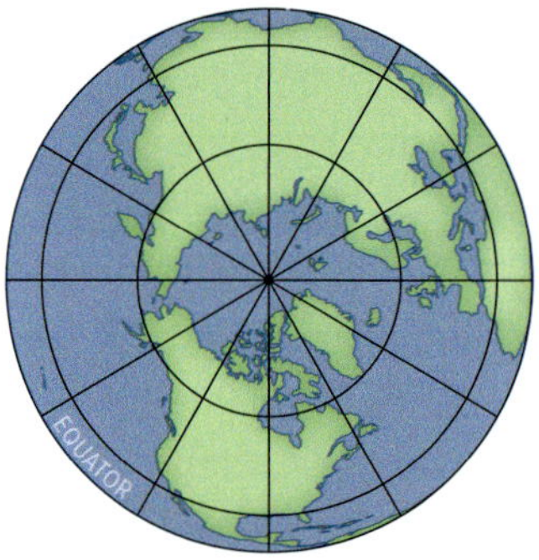


### Cylindrical Projection

A cylindrical projection is based on the projection of the globe onto a cylinder. This projection is most accurate near the Equator, but shapes and distances are distorted near the Poles.

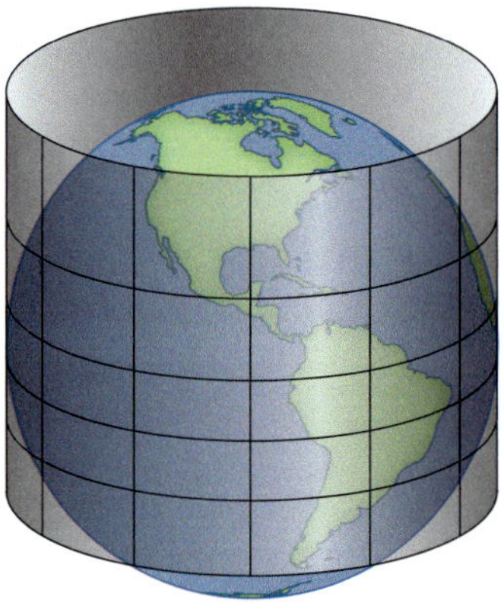

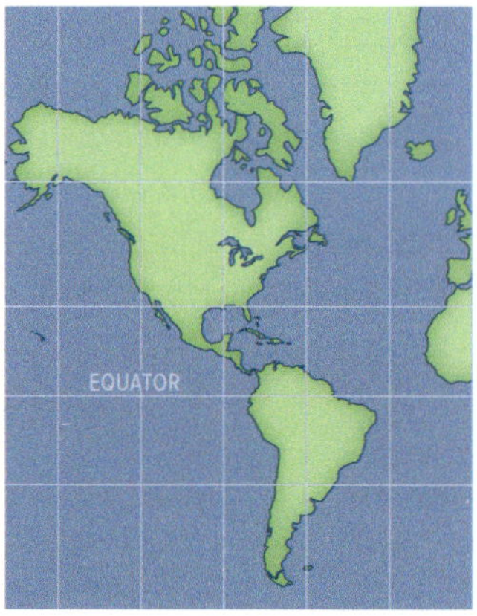


### Conic Projection

A conic projection comes from placing a cone over part of the globe. Conic projections are best suited for showing limited east-west areas that are not far from the Equator. For these uses, a conic projection can indicate distances and directions fairly accurately.

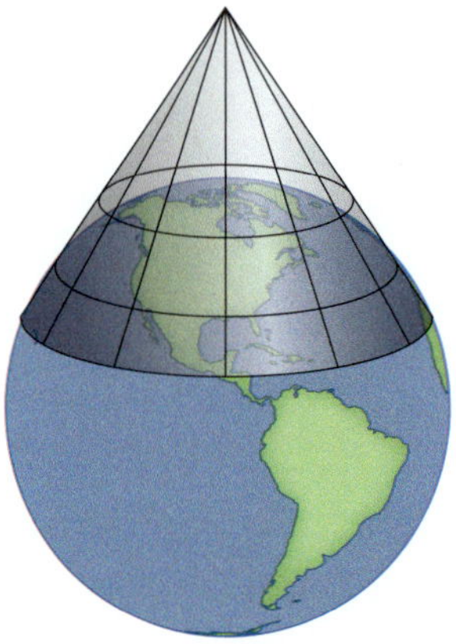

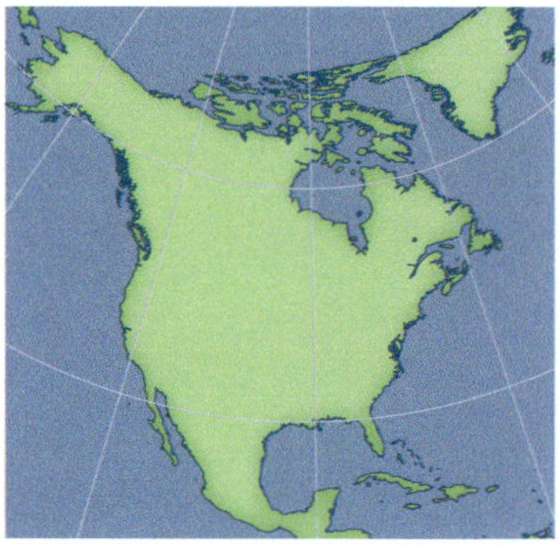

# Common Map Projections

Each type of map projection has advantages and some degree of inaccuracy. Four of the most common projections are shown here.

### VOCABULARY

*map projection:* the image of round Earth projected onto a flat surface

*planar:* a map projection that is most accurate at the center

*cylindrical:* a map projection that is most accurate near the Equator

*conic:* a map projection that accurately shows east-west areas near the Equator

## Winkel Tripel Projection

Most general reference world maps are the Winkel Tripel projection. It provides a good balance between the size and shape of land areas as they are shown on the map. Even the polar areas are depicted with little distortion of size and shape.

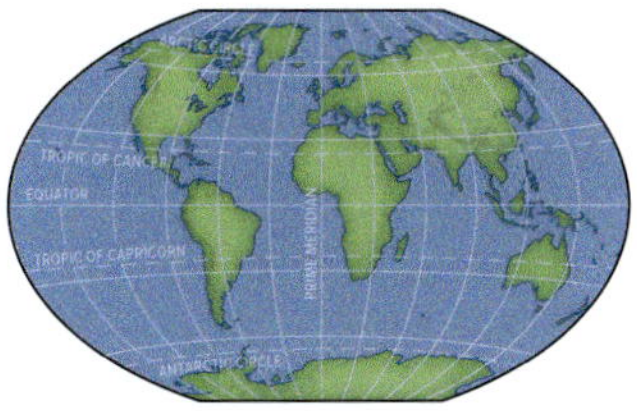


## Robinson Projection

The Robinson projection has minor distortions. The sizes and shapes near the eastern and western edges of the map are accurate, and outlines of the continents appear much as they do on the globe. However, the polar areas are flattened.

## Goode's Interrupted Equal-Area Projection

An interrupted projection looks something like a globe that has been cut apart and laid flat. Goode's Interrupted Equal-Area projection shows the true size and shape of Earth's landmasses, but distances are generally distorted.

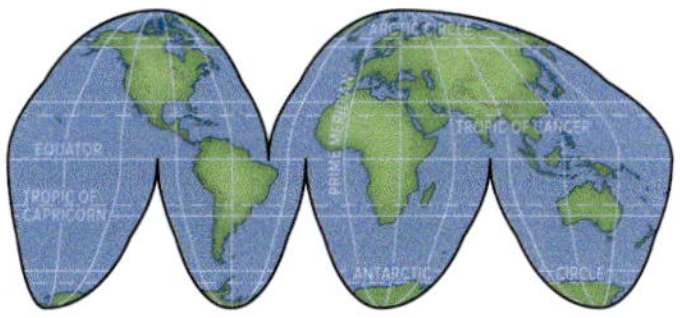

## Mercator Projection

The Mercator projection increasingly distorts size and distance as it moves away from the Equator. However, Mercator projections do accurately show true directions and the shapes of landmasses, making these maps useful for sea travel.

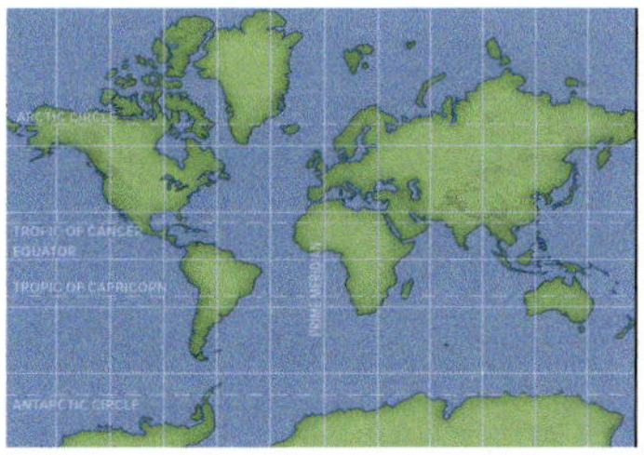

### GEOGRAPHIC REASONING

1. Explain the significance of the following: map projection, planar, cylindrical, conic.
2. How does a cartographer determine which map projection to use?
3. How is Goode's Interrupted Equal-Area projection different from the Mercator projection?
4. Which of the four common projections described above is the best one to use when showing the entire world? Why?
5. Use a Venn diagram like the one below to identify the similarities and differences between the Winkel Tripel and Mercator projections.

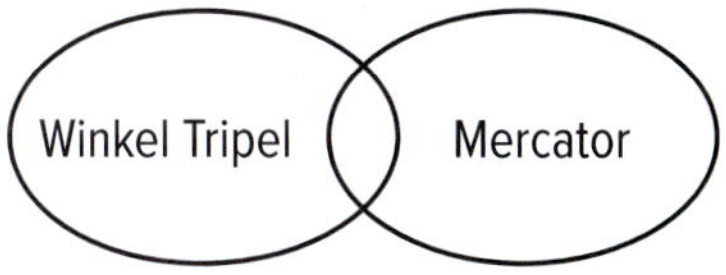

**VOCABULARY**

*grid system:* a pattern of lines on a map or globe that determine exact locations on Earth's surface

*hemisphere:* one of the halves that geographers divide the Earth into

*latitude:* lines that circle the Earth parallel to the Equator

*longitude:* lines that circle the Earth from Pole to Pole

*Prime Meridian:* the line of longitude set at 0°

*absolute location:* a global address determined by the intersection of longitude and latitude lines

# Determining Location

Geography is often said to begin with the question *Where?* The basic tool for answering the question is *location*. Lines on globes and maps provide information that can help you locate places. These lines cross one another forming a pattern called a **grid system**, which helps you find exact places on the Earth's surface.

A **hemisphere** is one of the halves into which the Earth is divided. Geographers divide the Earth into hemispheres to help them classify and describe places on Earth. Most places are located in two of the four hemispheres.

## Latitude

Lines of **latitude**, or parallels, circle the Earth parallel to the Equator and measure the distance north or south of the Equator in degrees. The Equator is measured at 0° latitude, while the Poles lie at latitudes 90°N (north) and 90°S (south). Parallels north of the Equator are called north latitude. Parallels south of the Equator are called south latitude.

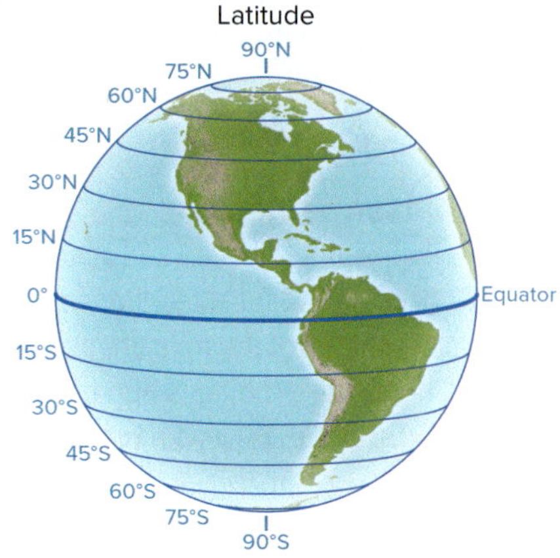


## Longitude

Lines of **longitude**, or meridians, circle the Earth from Pole to Pole. These lines measure distance east or west of the **Prime Meridian** at 0° longitude. Meridians east of the Prime Meridian are known as east longitude. Meridian west of the Prime Meridian are known as west longitude. The 180° meridian on the opposite side of the Earth is called the International Date Line.

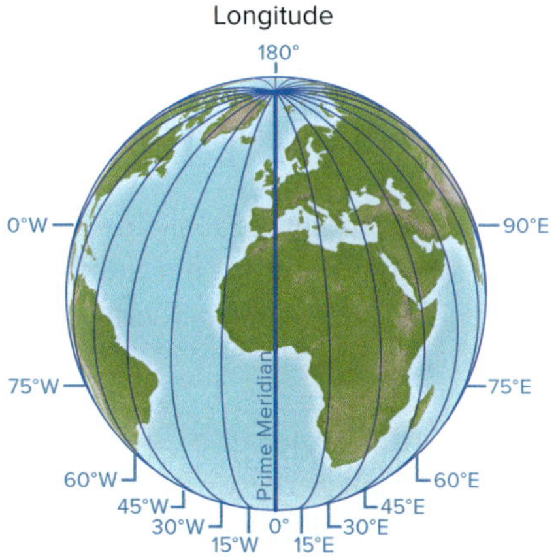


## The Global Grid

Every place has a global address, or **absolute location**. You can identify the absolute location of a place by naming the latitude and longitude lines that cross exactly at that place. For example, Tokyo, Japan, is located at 36°N latitude and 140°E longitude. For more precise readings, each degree is further divided into 60 units called minutes.

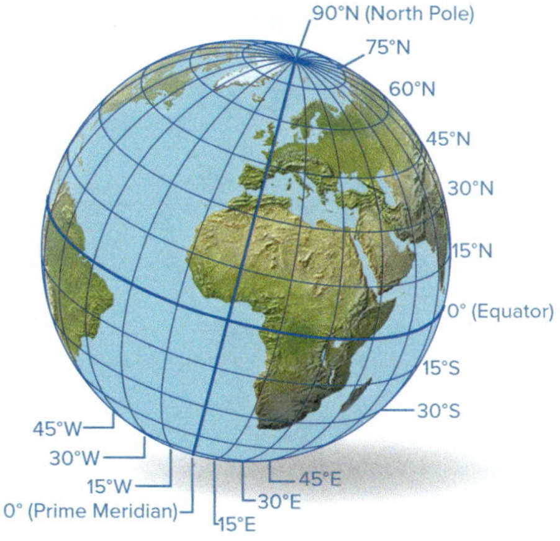

## Northern and Southern Hemispheres

The diagram below shows that the Equator divides the Earth into the Northern and Southern Hemispheres. Everything north of the Equator is in the **Northern Hemisphere**. Everything south of the Equator is in the Southern Hemisphere.

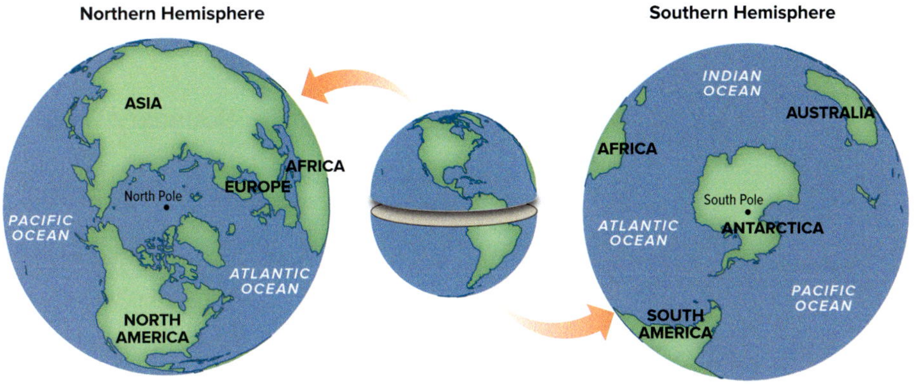


## Eastern and Western Hemispheres

The Prime Meridian and the International Date Line divide the Earth into the Eastern and Western Hemispheres. Everything east of the Prime Meridian for 180° is in the **Eastern Hemisphere**. Everything west of the Prime Meridian for 180° is in the **Western Hemisphere**.

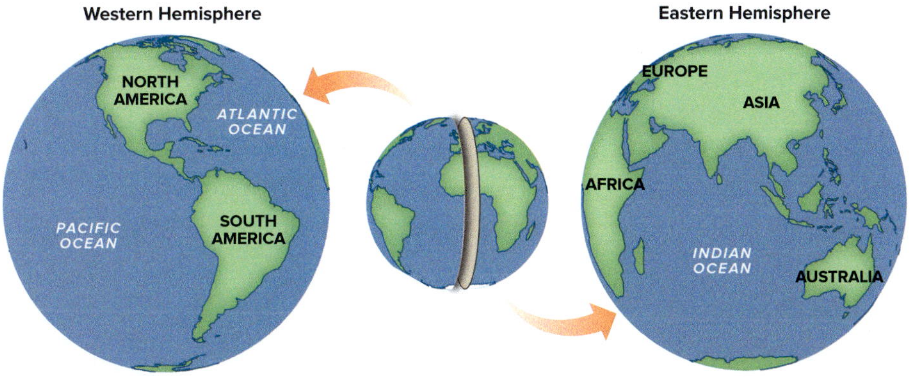


### VOCABULARY

*Northern Hemisphere:* the half of the globe north of the Equator

*Southern Hemisphere:* the half of the globe south of the Equator

*Eastern Hemisphere:* the half of the globe east of the Prime Meridian for 180°

*Western Hemisphere:* the half of the globe west of the Prime Meridian for 180°

### GEOGRAPHIC REASONING

1. Explain the significance of the following: location, grid system, hemisphere, Northern Hemisphere, Southern Hemisphere, Eastern Hemisphere, Western Hemisphere, latitude, longitude, Prime Meridian, absolute location.
2. Why do all maps label the Equator 0° latitude and the Prime Meridian 0° longitude?
3. Which lines of latitude and longitude divide the Earth into hemispheres?
4. Using the Reference Atlas maps, fill in a chart by writing the latitude and longitude of three world cities. Have a partner identify the cities listed in your chart.
5. Use a chart like the one below to identify the continents in each hemisphere. Some may be in more than one hemisphere.

| Hemisphere | Continents |
|---|---|
| Northern | |
| Southern | |
| Eastern | |
| Western | |

# Reading a Map

In addition to latitude and longitude, maps feature other important tools to help you interpret the information they contain. Learning to use these map tools will help you read the symbolic language of maps more easily.

### Key
The key lists and explains the symbols, colors, and lines used on the map. The key is sometimes called a legend.

### Title
The title tells you what kind of information the map is showing.

### Boundary Lines
On political maps of large areas, boundary lines highlight the borders between different countries or states.

### Compass Rose
The compass rose indicates directions. The four cardinal directions—north, south, east, and west—are usually indicated with arrows or the points of a star. The intermediate directions—northeast, northwest, southeast, and southwest—may also be shown.

### Scale Bar
The scale bar shows the relationship between map measurements and actual distances on the Earth. By laying a ruler along the scale bar, you can calculate how many miles or kilometers are represented per inch or centimeter. The map projection used to create the map is often listed near the scale bar.

### Cities
Cities are represented by a dot. Sometimes the relative sizes of cities are shown using dots of different sizes.

### Capitals
National capitals are often represented by a star within a circle.

# Using Scale

All maps are drawn to a certain scale. **Scale** is a consistent, proportional relationship between the measurements shown on the map and the measurements of the Earth's surface.

**Small-Scale Maps** A small-scale map, such as this political map of France, can show a large area but little detail. Note that the scale bar on this map indicates that about 1 inch is equal to 200 miles.

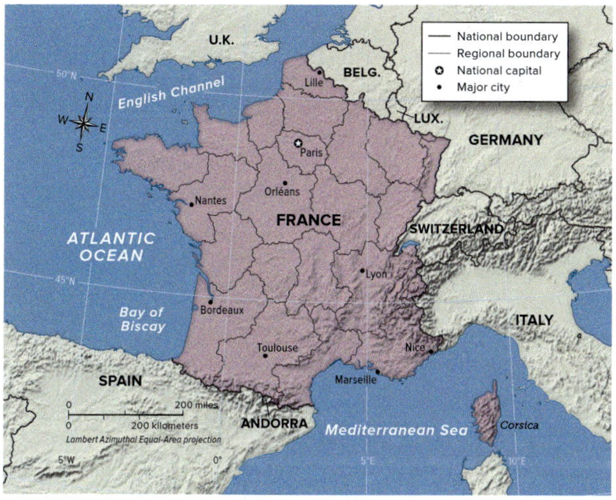


**Large-Scale Maps** A large-scale map, such as this map of Paris, can show a small area with a great amount of detail. Study the scale bar. Note that the map measurements correspond to much smaller distances than on the map of France.

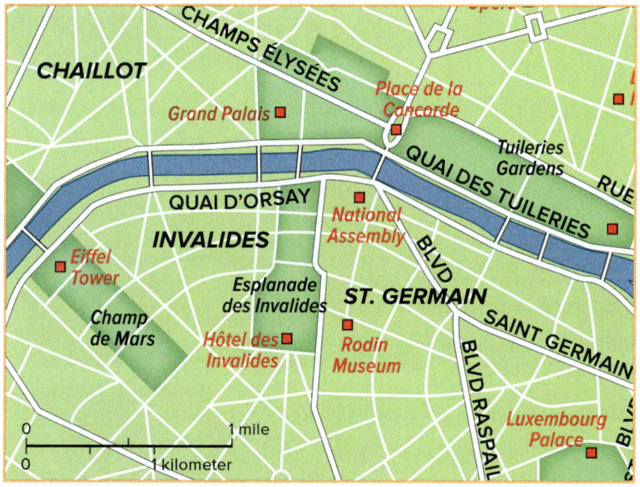


## Absolute and Relative Location

Absolute location is the exact point a line of latitude crosses a line of longitude. Another way to indicate location is by **relative location**, or the location of one place in relation to another. To find relative location, find a reference point—a location you already know—on a map. Then look in the appropriate direction for the new location. For example, locate Paris (your reference point) on the map of France above. The relative location of Lyon can be described as southeast of Paris.

### VOCABULARY

*scale:* a consistant, proportional relationship between measurements shown on a map and measurements of the Earth's surface

*relative location:* the location of one place in relation to another

### GEOGRAPHIC REASONING

1. Explain the significance of the following: key, compass rose, cardinal directions, intermediate directions, scale bar, scale, relative location.
2. Describe the elements of a map that help you interpret the information displayed on the map.
3. How does the scale bar help you determine distances on the Earth's surface?
4. Describe the relative location of your school in two different ways.
5. Use a Venn diagram to identify the similarities and differences of small-scale maps and large-scale maps.
6. Using the scale provided on the map at left, determine the distance in miles between the Eiffel Tower and the Grand Palais. Then, determine the distance in miles between the Eiffel Tower and the National Assembly, walking along the Quai D'Orsay.

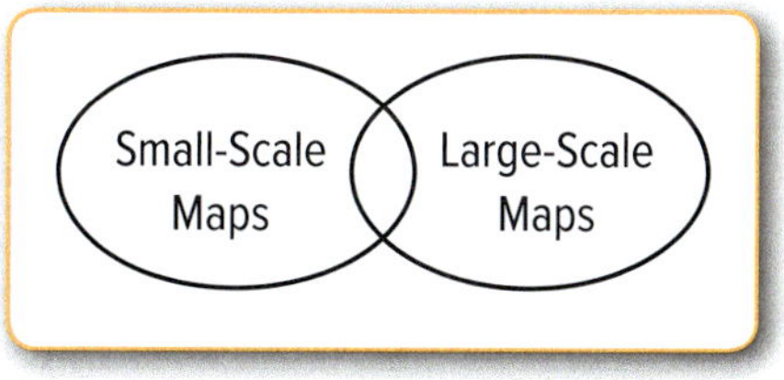

**VOCABULARY**

*physical map:* a map that shows the location and shape of the Earth's physical features

*political map:* a map that shows the boundaries and locations of political units such as countries, states, and cities

# Physical and Political Maps

Physical and political are the two main types of maps in this book. A **physical map** shows the location and the topography, or shape, of the Earth's physical features. A study of an area's physical features often helps explain its historical development. A **political map** shows the boundaries and locations of political units such as countries, states, and cities. Nonsubject area is usually shown in a different color to set it apart from the main area of the map. This nonsubject area gives you a context for the region you are studying.

## Physical Maps

Physical maps use shading and texture to show general relief—the differences in elevation or height—of landforms. Landforms are physical features such as plains, mountains, plateaus, and valleys. Physical maps show rivers, streams, lakes, and other water features.

## Political Maps

Many features on a political map are human-made, or determined by humans rather than by nature. Some human-made features are boundaries, capital cities, and roads. Political maps may also show physical features such as mountains and rivers.

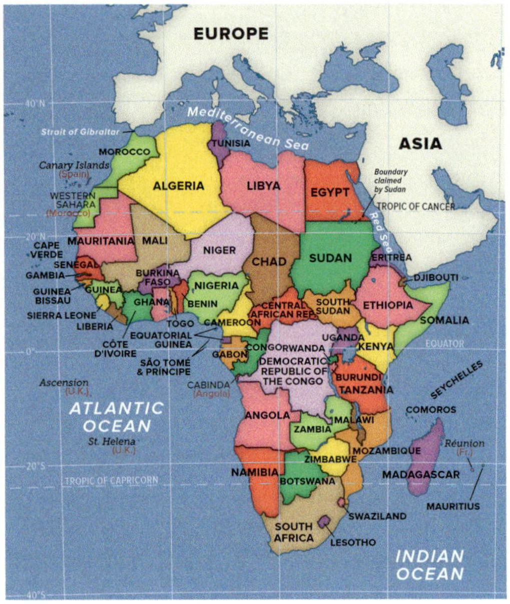

# Thematic Maps

Maps that emphasize a particular kind of information or a single idea are called **thematic maps**. This textbook includes thematic maps that show civilizations, migrations, natural resources, war, trade, and exploration.

VOCABULARY

*thematic maps:* maps focused on a kind of information or a single idea

## Qualitative Maps

Maps that use colors, symbols, lines, or dots to show information related to a specific idea are called qualitative maps.

## Flow-Line Maps

Maps that use arrows to show the movement of people, ideas, or physical systems are called flow-line maps.

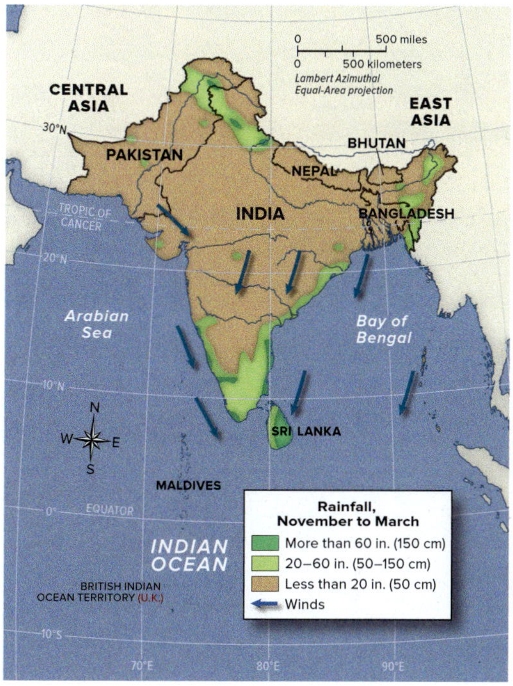


### GEOGRAPHIC REASONING

1. Explain the significance of the following: physical map, political map, thematic map, qualitative map, flow-line map.
2. Complete a Venn diagram like the one below to compare physical and political maps.
3. Select an area near you to use as a focus for a qualitative map you will create. You can select your home region, state, or county or the city where you live. Next, select the kind of qualitative map you would like to create, such as a land use or natural resources map or a map displaying information about the population, such as density or zoning districts. Then, using the Internet, research the information you would like to display. Create your map using the data you collect on the Internet.

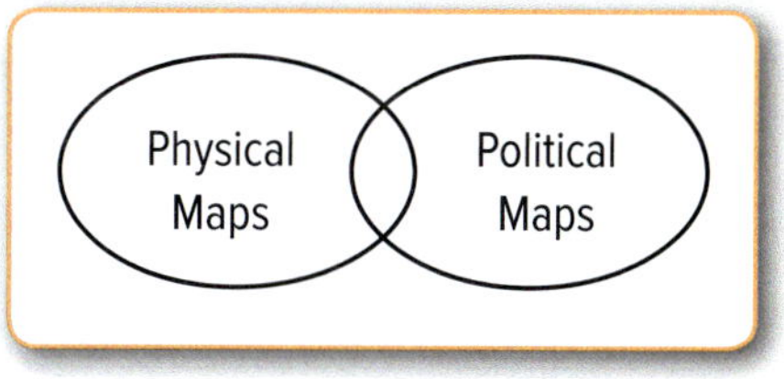

**VOCABULARY**

*ecosystem:* a community of plants and animals that depend upon one another and their surroundings for survival

*Biodiversity:* the variation of life-forms within an ecosystem

# Ecosystems and Biodiversity

An **ecosystem** is a community of plants and animals that depend upon one another and their surroundings for survival. There are many different ecosystems on Earth. Plants, animals, and microorganisms interact within an ecosystem. **Biodiversity** is the variation of life-forms within an ecosystem.

Rain forests are one type of ecosystem. Nowhere is biodiversity more apparent than in tropical rain forests, which harbor at least half of all animal and plant species on Earth. Although the world's largest remaining tropical rain forests are in Brazil, there are temperate rain forests from North America to Australia, as seen in the photograph.

Desert climates occur in just under one-third of the Earth's total land area. The natural vegetation of a desert ecosystem consists of scrub and cactus, plants that tolerate low and unreliable precipitation, low humidity, and wide temperate ranges. This arid landscape is in Arizona.

**Biodiversity at Risk** As the human communities expand, they threaten natural ecosystems. Because the Earth's land, air, and water are interrelated, what affects one part of the system affects all the other parts—including humans and other living things. The photograph shows deforestation, in this case clear-cutting of the Brazilian rain forest.

**GEOGRAPHY CONNECTION**

1. Explain the significance of the following: ecosystem, biodiversity.

2. Complete a table like the one below to list some of the types of interactions in the physical systems.

| *Hemisphere* | *Interactions* |
|---|---|
| Atmosphere | |
| Hydrosphere | |
| Lithosphere | |

(t to b)Digital Vision/PunchStock; MedioImages/Punchstock; Digital Vision/PunchStock

# Geographic Information Systems

Modern technology has changed the way maps are made. Most cartographers use computers with software programs called **geographic information systems** (GIS). A GIS is designed to accept data from different sources—maps, satellite images, printed text, and statistics. The GIS converts the data into a digital code, which arranges it in a database. Cartographers then program the GIS to process the data and to produce maps. With GIS, each kind of information on a map is saved as a separate electronic layer.

**VOCABULARY**

*geographic information systems:* software programs used by cartographers that arranges a variety of data in a database and uses those data layers to produce maps

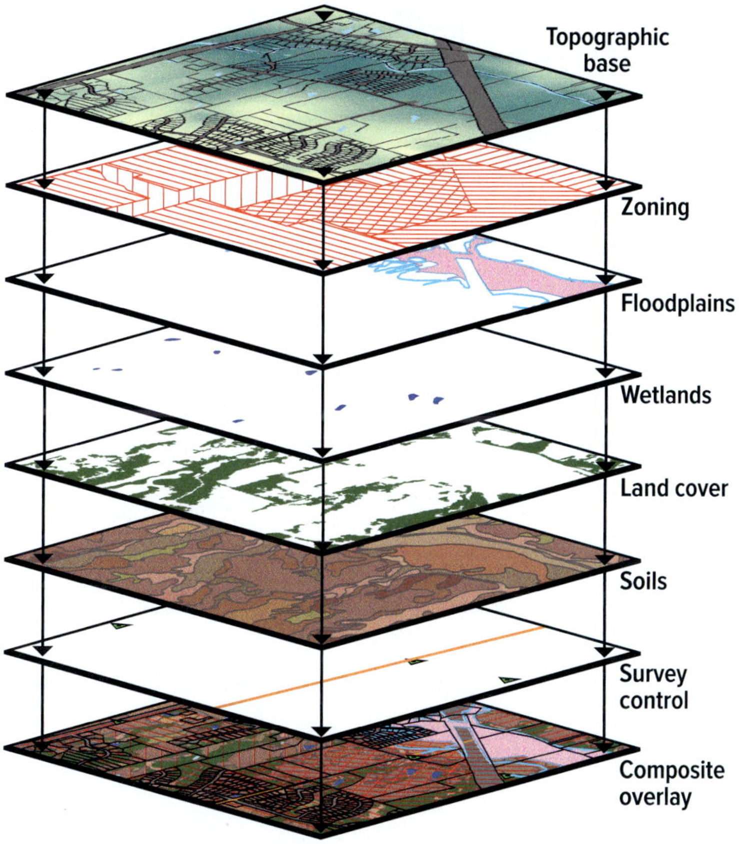


**GEOGRAPHIC REASONING**

1. How does GIS allow cartographers to create maps and to make changes to maps quickly and easily?
2. Complete a chart like the one below by identifying the different types of layers available in a GIS to make more informative maps.

| *Layers* |
| --- |
| |
| |
| |
| |

**archipelago** a group of islands

**basin** area of land drained by a given river and its branches; area of land surrounded by lands of higher elevations

**bay** part of a large body of water that extends into a shoreline, generally smaller than a gulf

**canyon** deep and narrow valley with steep walls

**cape** point of land that extends into a river, lake, or ocean

**channel** wide strait or waterway between two landmasses that lie close to each other; deep part of a river or other waterway

**cliff** steep, high wall of rock, earth, or ice

**continent** one of the seven large landmasses on the Earth

**delta** flat, low-lying land built up from soil carried downstream by a river and deposited at its mouth

**divide** stretch of high land that separates river systems

**downstream** direction in which a river or stream flows from its source to its mouth

**escarpment** steep cliff or slope between a higher and lower land surface

**glacier** large, thick body of slowly moving ice

**gulf** part of a large body of water that extends into a shoreline, generally larger and more deeply indented than a bay

**harbor** a sheltered place along a shoreline where ships can anchor safely

**highland** elevated land area such as a hill, mountain, or plateau

**hill** elevated land with sloping sides and rounded summit; generally smaller than a mountain

**island** land area, smaller than a continent, completely surrounded by water

**isthmus** narrow stretch of land connecting two larger land areas

**lake** a sizable inland body of water

**lowland** land, usually level, at a low elevation

**mesa** broad, flat-topped landform with steep sides; smaller than a plateau

**mountain** land with steep sides that rises sharply (1,000 feet or more) from surrounding land; generally larger and more rugged than a hill

**mountain peak** pointed top of a mountain

**mountain range** a series of connected mountains

**mouth** (of a river) place where a stream or river flows into a larger body of water

**oasis** small area in a desert where water and vegetation are found

**ocean** one of the four major bodies of salt water that surround the continents

**ocean current** stream of either cold or warm water that moves in a definite direction through an ocean

**peninsula** body of land jutting into a lake or ocean, surrounded on three sides by water

**physical feature** characteristic of a place occurring naturally, such as a landform, body of water, climate pattern, or resource

**plain** area of level land, usually at low elevation and often covered with grasses

**plateau** area of flat or rolling land at a high elevation, about 300 to 3,000 feet (90 to 900 m) high

**reef** a chain of rocks, coral or sand at or near the surface of the water

**river** large natural stream of water that runs through the land

**sea** large body of water completely or partly surrounded by land

**seacoast** land lying next to a sea or an ocean

**sound** broad inland body of water, often between a coastline and one or more islands off the coast

**source** (of a river) place where a river or stream begins, often in highlands

**strait** narrow stretch of water joining two larger bodies of water

**tributary** small river or stream that flows into a large river or stream; a branch of the river

**upstream** direction opposite the flow of a river; toward the source of a river or stream

**valley** area of low land usually between hills or mountains

**volcano** mountain or hill created as liquid rock and ash erupt from inside the Earth

- Content vocabulary are words in the lessons that relate to world history content.
- All vocabulary words are **boldfaced or highlighted in yellow** in your textbook.

| ENGLISH | | ESPAÑOL |
|---|---|---|
| | **A** | |
| **abdicate** to formally give up control of a country or state (p. 284) | | **abdicar** renunciar formalmente al control de un país o Estado (pág. 284) |
| **abolitionism** a movement to end slavery (p. 139) | | **abolicionismo** movimiento para acabar con la esclavitud (pág. 139) |
| **absolutism** a political system in which a ruler holds total power (p. 18) | | **absolutismo** sistema político en el que el gobernante mantiene un poder total (pág. 18) |
| **abstract** a style of art, emerging around 1910, that spoke directly to the soul and avoided visual reality by using only lines and color (p. 178) | | **abstracto** estilo artístico que surgió alrededor de 1910; hablaba directamente al alma y evitaba la realidad visual usando sólo líneas y colores (pág. 178) |
| **advocate** to support; to speak in favor of (p. 163) | | **defender** apoyar; hablar en favor de (pág. 163) |
| **aid** assistance such as money or supplies (p. 284) | | **ayuda** asistencia económica o en especie (pág. 284) |
| **amendment** an alteration proposed or effected by parliamentary or constitutional procedure (p. 60) | | **enmienda** alteración propuesta o realizda por el parlamento o un procedimiento constitucional (pág. 60) |
| **annex** to incorporate into an existing political unit, such as a city or country (p. 199) | | **anexar** incorporar a una unidad política existente, como una ciudad o un país (pág. 199) |
| **annual** yearly (p. 303) | | **anual** que sucede una vez al año (pág. 303) |
| **apartheid** "apartness"; the system of racial segregation in South Africa from the 1950s until 1991 (p. 466) | | **apartheid** "separación"; sistema de segregación racial que se dio en Suráfrica desde la década de 1950 hasta 1991 (pág. 466) |
| **appeasement** the process of satisfying reasonable demands of dissatisfied powers in an effort to maintain peace and stability (p. 380) | | **apaciguamiento** satisfacer demandas razonables de potencias insatisfechas en un esfuerzo por mantener la paz y la estabilidad (pág. 380) |
| **appropriate** suitable or compatible; fitting (p. 308) | | **apropiado** adecuado o compatible; que encaja (pág. 308) |
| **arbitrarily** (adverb form of *arbitrary*) at one's discretion; randomly (p. 582) | | **arbitrariamente** (adverbio de arbitrario) a discreción propia; al azar (pág. 582) |
| **arbitrary** at one's discretion; random (p. 40) | | **arbitrario** a discreción personal; al azar (pág. 40) |
| **armada** a fleet of warships (p. 6) | | **armada** flota de barcos de guerra (pág. 6) |
| **armistice** a truce or an agreement to end fighting (p. 289) | | **armisticio** tregua o acuerdo para poner fin a un combate (pág. 289) |
| **arms race** the act of building up armies and stores of weapons to keep up with an enemy (p. 425) | | **carrera armamentista** acumulación de ejércitos y reservas de armas para hacer frente al enemigo (pág. 425) |
| **Aryan** a term used to identify people speaking Indo-European languages; Nazis misused the term, treating it as a racial designation and identifying the Aryans with the ancient Greeks and Romans and twentieth-century Germans and Scandinavians (p. 320) | | **ario** término usado para identificar a los hablantes de alguna lengua indoeuropea. Los nazis tergiversaron el uso del término empleándolo como una designación racial e identificaron a los arios con los antiguos griegos y romanos, y con los germanos y escandinavos del siglo (pág. 320) |

**assembly line** pioneered by Henry Ford in 1913, a manufacturing method that allowed much more efficient mass production of goods (p. 154)

**cadena de montaje** método de producción instaurado por Henry Ford en 1913, que permitía una producción masiva de bienes más eficiente (pág. 154)

**assure** made certain of something; guaranteed (p. 412)

**asegurar** cerciorarse de algo; garantizar (pág. 412)

**attitude** a mental position regarding a fact or state (p. 312)

**actitud** posición mental con respecto a un hecho o un estado (pág. 312)

**authoritarian** favoring or enforcing strict obedience to authority, especially that of the government, at the expense of personal freedom (pp. 38, 315)

**autoritario** que favorece o fuerza la estricta obediencia a una autoridad, especialmente la de un gobierno, a expensas de las libertades individuales (págs. 38, 315)

**authority** power; person in command (p. 18)

**autoridad** poder; persona a cargo (pág. 18)

**autonomous** self-governing (p. 528)

**autónomo** que se gobierna a sí mismo (pág. 528)

## B

**bioterrorism** the use of biological and chemical weapons in terrorist attacks (p. 580)

**bioterrorismo** uso de armas biológicas y químicas en ataques terroristas (pág. 580)

**blitz** the British term for the German air raids on British cities and towns during World War II (p. 399)

**bombardeo aéreo** término con que los británicos designaron los ataques aéreos alemanes sobre las ciudades y los pueblos británicos durante la Segunda Guerra Mundial (pág. 399)

**blitzkrieg** German for "lightning war"; a swift and sudden military attack; used by the Germans during World War II (p. 386)

***blitzkriegk*** en alemán, "guerra relámpago"; ataque militar rápido y sorpresivo; usado por los alemanes durante la Segunda Guerra Mundial (pág. 386)

**bloc** a group of nations with a common purpose (p. 493)

**bloque** grupo de naciones con un propósito común (pág. 493)

**bourgeoisie** the middle class, including merchants, industrialists, and professional people (pp. 72, 156)

**burguesía** la clase media, que incluye comerciantes, industriales y profesionales (págs. 72, 156)

**boyar** a Russian noble (p. 22)

**boyar** noble ruso (pág. 22)

**budget deficit** the state that exists when a government spends more than it collects in revenues (p. 533)

**déficit presupuestario** estado que tiene lugar cuando los gastos de un gobierno superan los ingresos que recauda (pág. 533)

## C

**caliphate** the office or dominion of a caliph (p. 335)

**califato** gobierno o jurisdicción de un califa (pág. 335)

**capable** having or showing ability (p. 90)

**capaz** que tiene o demuestra habilidad (pág. 90)

**capital** money available for investment (p. 115)

**capital** dinero disponible para invertir (pág. 115)

**cartel** a group of drug businesses (p. 479)

**cartel** grupo dedicado al narcotráfico (pág. 479)

**cash crop** a crop that is grown for sale rather than for personal use (p. 145)

**cultivo comercial** cultivo destinado a la venta, no para el uso personal (pág. 145)

**caudillo** in post-revolutionary Latin America, a strong leader who ruled chiefly by military force, usually with the support of the landed elite (p. 144)

**caudillo** en la América Latina posrevolucionaria, líder fuerte que gobernaba principalmente mediante la fuerza militar, por lo general con el apoyo de la élite latifundista (pág. 144)

## ENGLISH

**Cavaliers** supporters of King Charles I in the English Civil War (p. 13)

**cease** to come to an end (p. 352)

**circumstance** a state of affairs (p. 399)

**citizenship** the qualities a person is expected to have as a responsible member of a community (p. 39)

**civil** involving the general public or civic affairs (pp. 98, 210)

**civil disobedience** refusal to obey laws that are considered to be unjust (p. 346)

**Cold War** the period of political tension following World War II and ending with the fall of Communism in the Soviet Union at the end of the 1980s (p. 411)

**collaborator** a person who assists the enemy (p. 405)

**collapse** to break down completely; to suddenly lose force or effectiveness (p. 523)

**collateralized debt obligation** a security guaranteed by a pool of bonds, loans, and other types of debt (p. 605)

**collective bargaining** the right of unions to negotiate with employers over wages and hours (p. 306)

**collectivization** a system in which private farms are eliminated and peasants work land owned by the government (p. 314)

**commodities** agricultural, mined, and mass-produced marketable goods (p. 245)

**commonwealth** a nation, state, or other political unit founded on law and united by agreement for and by the people (p. 13)

**commune** in China during the 1950s, a group of collective farms that contained more than 30,000 people who lived and worked together (p. 429)

**compensation** payment (p. 343)

**complex** having many intricate parts (p. 263)

**concentration camp** a camp where prisoners of war, political prisoners, or members of minority groups are confined, typically under harsh conditions (p. 319)

**concession** a political compromise (p. 248)

**condemn** to declare to be reprehensible, wrong, or evil usually after weighing evidence and without reservation (p. 51)

**confederation** a group of people, countries, organizations, etc., that are joined together in some activity or effort (p. 530)

## ESPAÑOL

**caballeros** partidarios del rey Carlos I durante la Guerra Civil Inglesa (pág. 13)

**cesar** terminar (pág. 352)

**circunstancia** estado de un asunto (pág. 399)

**ciudadanía** cualidades que se espera que una persona tenga como miembro responsable de una comunidad (pág. 39)

**civil** que implica asuntos relacionados con el público o los asuntos cívicos (pág. 98, 210)

**desobediencia civil** negativa a obedecer leyes que se consideran injustas (pág. 346)

**Guerra Fría** periodo de tensión política posterior a la Segunda Guerra Mundial, que terminó con la caída del comunismo en la Unión Soviética, a finales de la década de 1980 (pág. 411)

**colaborador** persona que ayuda al enemigo (pág. 405)

**colapsar** desplomarse por completo; perder fuerza o efectividad de manera repentina (pág. 523)

**obligaciones de deuda garantizada** valor garantizado por obligaciones, créditos y otro tipo de deudas (pág. 605)

**negociación colectiva** derecho de los sindicatos a negociar con los empleadores los salarios y horarios de trabajo (pág. 306)

**colectivización** sistema en el cual se eliminan las granjas privadas y los campesinos trabajan la tierra que pertenece al gobierno (pág. 314)

**bienes de consumo** bienes comercializables agrícolas, mineros y de producción masiva (pág. 245)

**mancomunidad** país, Estado u otra unidad política que se funda en la ley y mantiene su cohesión por acuerdo popular (pág. 13)

**comuna** en la China de la década de 1950, grupo de granjas colectivas donde vivían y trabajaban juntas más de 30,000 personas (pág. 429)

**compensación** pago (pág. 343)

**complejo** que tiene muchas partes intrincadas (pág. 263)

**campo de concentración** campo donde se confinaba a los prisioneros de guerra, prisioneros políticos o miembros de grupos minoritarios, por lo general en condiciones inhumanas (pág. 319)

**concesión** compromiso político (pág. 248)

**condenar** declarar ser reprehensible, malo o malo generalmente después de sopesar pruebas y sin reservas (pág. 51)

**confederación** grupo de personas, países, organizaciones, etc., que se unen en alguna actividad o esfuerzo (pág. 530)

**conflict** opposition; a fight, battle, or war (p. 5)

**conscription** military draft (p. 263)

**consent** approval (p. 475)

**conservatism** a political philosophy based on tradition and social stability, favoring obedience to political authority and organized religion (p. 97)

**considerable** large in amount or quantity (p. 553)

**constitution** the basic principles and laws of a nation, state, or social group that determine the powers and duties of the government and guarantee certain rights to the people in it (p. 98)

**consulate** the government established in France after the overthrow of the Directory in 1799, with Napoleon as first consul in control of the entire government (p. 89)

**consumer** someone who uses economic goods (p. 71)

**consumer society** a society preoccupied with buying goods (p. 496)

**containerization** shipping method in which material is packed into large standardized size containers (p. 600)

**context** the circumstances surrounding a situation or event (p. 251)

**controversy** a dispute or quarrel (p. 175)

**convert** to change from one belief to another (p. 13)

**cooperation** a common effort (p. 290)

**corporation** an association of employers and employees in a basic industry (p. 155)

**corruption** impairment of integrity, virtue, or moral principle (p. 547)

**cottage industry** a method of production in which tasks are done by individuals in their rural homes (p. 116)

**coup d'état** a sudden overthrow of the government (p. 86)

**creole** a person of European descent born in Latin America and living there permanently (p. 141)

**cultural diffusion** the spread of culture traits, both material and non-material, from one culture to another (p. 189)

**cultural imperialism** referring to Western nations' control of other world cultures similar to how they had controlled colonial governments (p. 536)

**currency** coins, for example, that are in circulation and used as a medium of exchange (p. 603)

**czar** Russian for *caesar;* the title used by Russian emperors (p. 22)

**conflicto** oposición; lucha, batalla o guerra (pág. 5)

**conscripción** reclutamiento military (pág. 263)

**consentimiento** aprobación (pág. 475)

**conservadurismo** filosofía política basada en la tradición y la estabilidad social, que apoya la obediencia a la autoridad política y la religión organizada (pág. 97)

**considerable** de gran tamaño o cantidad (pág. 553)

**constitución** principios y leyes básicos de una nación, Estado o grupo social, que determinan los poderes y deberes del gobierno y garantizan algunos derechos a sus habitantes (pág. 98)

**Consulado** el gobierno establecido en Francia después del derrocamiento del Directorio en 1799, con Napoleón como el primer cónsul a cargo de todo el gobierno (pág. 89)

**consumidor** alguien que usa bienes económicos (pág. 71)

**sociedad de consumo** sociedad que se preocupa por comprar bienes (pág. 496)

**containerization** transporte en contenedores (pág. 600)

**contexto** circunstancias que rodean una situación o evento (pág. 251)

**controversia** disputa o discrepancia (pág. 175)

**convertirse** cambiar de una creencia a otra (pág. 13)

**cooperación** esfuerzo común (pág. 290)

**corporación** asociación de empleadores y empleados en una industria básica (pág. 155)

**corrupción** falta de integridad, virtud o principios morales (pág. 547)

**industria artesanal** método de producción en el cual los individuos realizan el trabajo en sus hogares rurales (pág. 116)

**golpe de Estado** derrocamiento repentino de un gobierno (pág. 86)

**criollo** persona de ascendencia europea nacida en América Latina y que vive allí permanentemente (pág. 141)

**difusión cultural** la propagación de rasgos culturales, tanto materiales como no materiales, de una cultura a otra (pág. 189)

**imperialismo cultural** relativo al control que ejercen las naciones occidentales sobre otras culturas, semejante a la manera en que estas naciones controlaban los gobiernos de las colonias (pág. 536)

**moneda** billetes y monedas, por ejemplo, que están en circulación y se usan como medio de intercambio (pág. 603)

**zar** "césar" en ruso; título adoptado por los emperadores rusos (pág. 22)

## ENGLISH — D — ESPAÑOL

**deficit spending** when a government pays out more money than it takes in through taxation and other revenues, thus going into debt (p. 306)

**gasto deficitario** cuando un gobierno paga más dinero del que recibe por concepto de impuestos y otros ingresos, y por lo tanto se endeuda (pág. 306)

**deflation** a contraction in the volume of available money or credit that results in a general decline in prices (p. 541)

**deflación** reducción en el volumen de dinero o crédito disponible que lleva a una caída general en los precios (pág. 541)

**deforestation** the clearing of forests (p. 611)

**deforestación** devastación de los bosques (pág. 611)

**deism** an eighteenth-century religious philosophy based on reason and natural law (p. 36)

**deísmo** filosofía religiosa del siglo XVIII basada en la razón y la ley natural (pág. 36)

**demilitarized** relating to the elimination or prohibition of weapons, fortifications, and other military installations (p. 379)

**desmilitarización** eliminación o prohibición de usar armas, fortalezas u otras instalaciones militares (pág. 379)

**demonstration** a public display of group feeling toward a person or cause (p. 523)

**manifestación** expresión pública de los sentimientos de un grupo hacia una persona o causa (pág. 585)

**depression** a period of low economic activity and rising unemployment (p. 304)

**depresión** periodo de baja actividad económica y aumento del desempleo (pág. 304)

**desertification** formation of degraded soil, turning semi-arid lands into nonproductive deserts (p. 611)

**desertificación** formación de suelo degradado que transforma tierras semiáridas en desiertos improductivos (pág. 611)

**de-Stalinization** the process of eliminating Stalin's more ruthless policies (p. 501)

**desestalinización** proceso de eliminación de las políticas más despiadadas de Stalin (pág. 501)

**détente** a phase of relaxed tensions and improved relations between two adversaries (p. 502)

**détente** fase de alivio de las tensiones y mejoramiento de las relaciones entre dos adversarios (pág. 502)

**deterrence** during the Cold War, the U.S. and Soviet policies of holding huge arsenals of nuclear weapons to prevent war; each nation believed that neither would launch a nuclear attack since both knew that the other side could strike back with devastating power (p. 425)

**disuasión** durante la Guerra Fría, política de Estados Unidos y la Unión Soviética que consistía en poseer enormes arsenales de armas nucleares para evitar la guerra; cada nación creía que ninguna de ellas lanzaría un ataque nuclear porque ambas sabían que la contraparte podría responder con una fuerza devastadora (pág. 425)

**direct rule** colonial government in which local elites are removed from power and replaced by a new set of officials brought from the colonizing country (p. 193)

**gobierno directo** gobierno colonial en el cual se retira del poder a las élites locales y las reemplaza un nuevo grupo de funcionarios del país colonizador (pág. 193)

**discrimination** prejudicial treatment usually based on race, religion, class, sex, or age (p. 456)

**discriminación** tratamiento que va en detrimento de las personas por razones de raza, religión, clase social, sexo o edad (pág. 456)

**dissident** a person who speaks out against the regime in power (p. 502)

**disidente** persona que habla en contra del régimen en el poder (pág. 502)

**divine right of kings** the belief that the kings receive their power from God and are responsible only to God (pp. 12)

**derecho divino de los reyes** creencia de que los reyes reciben su poder de Dios y son responsables solo ante Él (págs. 12)

**dollar diplomacy** the diplomacy that seeks to strengthen the power of a country or to effect its purposes in foreign relations by the use of its financial resources (p. 217)

**diplomacia del dólar** diplomacia que busca fortalecer el poder de un país o alcanzar sus propósitos en las relaciones internacionales mediante el uso de sus recursos financieros (pág. 217)

**domestic** relating to or originating within one's country (p. 82)

**interno** relativo al país de una persona o que se origina allí (pág. 82)

**dominate** to influence or control (p. 379)

**dominar** influir o controlar (pág. 379)

**domino theory** the idea that if one country falls to communism, neighboring countries will also fall (p. 440)

**teoría del efecto dominó** idea según la cual si un país cede al comunismo, los países vecinos también lo harán (pág. 440)

**Duma** the Russian legislative assembly (p. 172)

**duma** Asamblea Legislativa de Rusia (pág. 172)

**dynamic** an activity or change that is continuous and productive (p. 606)

**dinámica** actividad o cambio que es continuo y productivo (pág. 606)

## E

**ecology** the study of the relationships between living things and their environment (p. 611)

**ecología** estudio de las relaciones entre los seres vivos y su medioambiente (pág. 611)

**elector** an individual qualified to vote in an election (p. 85)

**elector** un individuo calificado para votar en una elección (pág. 85)

**element** a distinct group within a larger group (p. 335)

**elemento** un grupo distinto dentro de un grupo más grande (pág. 335)

**emancipation** the act of setting free (p. 138)

**emancipación** acción de poner en libertad (pág. 138)

**emerge** to come into being through evolution; to develop (pp. 20, 441)

**emerger** surgir por evolución; desarrollar (págs. 20, 441)

**empiricism** the theory that says knowledge is achieved through observation (p. 34)

**empirismo** teoría según la cual el conocimiento se adquiere por medio de la observación (pág. 34)

**enhance** to improve (p. 500)

**aumentado** mejorado (pág. 500)

**enlightened absolutism** a system in which rulers tried to govern by Enlightenment principles while maintaining their full royal powers (p. 49)

**despotismo ilustrado** sistema en el cual los gobernantes trataron de dirigir siguiendo los principios de la Ilustración, pero en el que conservaban todas sus facultades reales (pág. 49)

**entrepreneur** a person who finds new business opportunities and new ways to make profits (p. 115)

**empresario** persona interesada en hallar nuevas oportunidades comerciales y formas de obtener ganancias (pág. 115)

**epidemic disease** a widespread occurrence of an infectious disease at a particular time (p. 159)

**enfermedad epidémica** aparición generalizada de una enfermedad infecciosa en un momento determinado (pág. 159)

**erupt** to suddenly become active or violent (p. 144)

**estallar** entrar en actividad o tornarse violento repentinamente (pág. 144)

**establish** to set up permanently; to found (p. 362)

**establecer** instalar permanentemente; fundar (pág. 362)

**estate** a landed property with a large house (p. 213); one of the three classes into which French society was divided before the revolution: the clergy (First Estate), the nobles (Second Estate), and the townspeople (Third Estate) (p. 71)

**latifundio** propiedad de tierra con una casa grande (pág. 213); una de las tres clases en las que se dividía la sociedad francesa antes de la revolución: el clero (Primer estado), los nobles (Segundo estado) y el pueblo (Tercer estado) (pág. 71)

**ethnic** relating to people who have common racial, religious, or cultural origins (p. 402)

**étnico** relativo a las personas que tienen un origen racial, religioso o cultural común (pág. 402)

## ENGLISH

**ethnic cleansing** a policy of killing or forcibly removing an ethnic group from its lands; used by the Serbs against the Muslim minority in Bosnia (p. 527)

**eventually** in the end (pp. 50, 353)

**evident** apparent (p. 545)

**exclusion** barred from inclusion or participation in (p. 75)

**exclusive** limited to a single individual or group (p. 232)

**exploit** to make use of meanly or unfairly for one's own advantage (p. 193)

**export** to send a product or service for sale to another country (p. 193)

**extraterritoriality** living in a section of a country set aside for foreigners but not subject to the host country's laws (p. 230)

## F

**fascism** a political philosophy that glorifies the state above the individual by emphasizing the need for a strong central government led by a dictatorial ruler (p. 310)

**federal system** a form of government in which power is shared between the national and state governments (p. 59)

**feminism** the movement for women's rights (p. 163)

**final** the last in a series, process, or progress (p. 429)

**fossil fuel** a fuel (such as coal, oil, or natural gas) formed in the earth from plant or animal remains (p. 117)

**fund** to give money for a specific purpose (p. 559)

## G

**generation** a group of individuals born and living at the same time (p. 40)

**genocide** the deliberate mass murder or physical extinction of a particular racial, political, or cultural group (pp. 273, 403)

**glasnost** a Soviet policy permitting open discussion of political and social issues (p. 521)

**globalization** the movement toward a more integrated and interdependent world economy (p. 599)

## ESPAÑOL

**limpieza étnica** política que consiste en asesinar o sacar a la fuerza de sus tierras a un grupo étnico; la usaron los serbios contra la minoría musulmana en Bosnia (pág. 527)

**con el tiempo** al final (págs. 50, 353)

**evidente** aparente (pág. 545)

**exclusión** prohibición de incluir o participar (pág. 75)

**exclusivo** limitado a un individuo o grupo (pág. 232)

**explotar** hacer uso de manera cruel o injusta para beneficio propio (pág. 193)

**exportar** enviar un producto o servicio para venderlo en otro país (pág. 193)

**extraterritorialidad** vivir en una sección de un país destinada a las personas extranjeras, pero que no está sujeta a las leyes del país anfitrión (pág. 230)

## F

**fascismo** filosofía política que exalta al Estado por encima del individuo, poniendo énfasis en la necesidad de un gobierno central fuerte liderado por un dictador (pág. 310)

**sistema federal** forma de gobierno en la cual el poder se comparte entre los gobiernos nacional y estatal (pág. 59)

**feminismo** movimiento que lucha por los derechos de las mujeres (pág. 163)

**final** último en una serie, proceso o progreso (pág. 429)

**combustible fósil** combustible (como carbón, petróleo o gas natural) formado en la tierra a partir de restos vegetales o animales (pág. 117)

**financiar** dar dinero con un propósito definido (pág. 559)

## G

**generación** grupo de individuos que nacen y viven durante la misma época (pág. 40)

**genocidio** asesinato masivo o exterminio físico deliberado de un grupo racial, político o cultural específico (págs. 273, 403)

**glasnot** política soviética que permitió el debate abierto de temas políticos y sociales (pág. 521)

**globalización** movimiento hacia una economía mundial más integrada e interdependiente (pág. 599)

**goal** an aim or a purpose (p. 466)

**meta** objetivo o propósito (pág. 466)

**greenhouse effect** global warming caused by the buildup of carbon dioxide in the atmosphere (p. 612)

**efecto invernadero** calentamiento global ocasionado por la acumulación de dióxido de carbono en la atmósfera (pág. 612)

**guarantee** to assure fulfillment of a condition (p. 60)

**garantizar** asegurar el cumplimiento de una condición (pág. 60)

**guerrilla tactics** the use of unexpected maneuvers such as sabotage and subterfuge to fight an enemy (p. 354)

**táctica de guerrillas** uso de maniobras inesperadas como el sabotaje y el uso de subterfugios para combatir a un enemigo (pág. 354)

**gunboat diplomacy** diplomacy backed by the use or threat of military force (p. 190)

**diplomacia de la cañonera** diplomacia respaldada por el uso o la amenaza de la fuerza militar (pág. 190)

## H

**heavy industry** the manufacture of machines and equipment for factories and mines (p. 500)

**industria pesada** manufactura de maquinaria y equipo para fábricas y minas (pág. 500)

**heretic** one who does not conform to established doctrine (p. 5)

**hereje** persona que no acepta la doctrina establecida (pág. 5)

**highlight** to center attention on (p. 229)

**destacado** algo sobre lo cual se centra la atención (pág. 229)

**HIV/AIDS** human immunodeficiency virus/acquired immunodeficiency syndrome; any of the strains of HIV-1 and HIV-2 that infect and destroy the immune system's helper T cells, causing a large drop in their numbers, and become AIDS when a person has 20 percent or less than the normal level of helper T cells (p. 469)

**VIH/sida** virus de inmunodeficiencia humana/síndrome de inmunodeficiencia adquirida; cualquiera de las cadenas de VIH-1 y VIH-2 que infectan y destruyen las células T cooperadoras del sistema inmunológico, lo que ocasiona una gran disminución de las mismas. Se convierte en sida cuando el número de células es igual o inferior al 20 por ciento del recuento normal de células T cooperadoras (pág. 469)

## I

**ideological** based on a set of beliefs (p. 511)

**ideológico** que se basa en una serie de creencias (pág. 511)

**illegitimate** not sanctioned by law (p. 39)

**ilegítimo** no sancionado por la ley (pág. 39)

**imperialism** the extension of a nation's power over other lands (p. 189)

**imperialismo** extensión del poder de una nación sobre otras tierras (pág. 189)

**indemnity** the payment for damages (p. 235)

**indemnización** pago para compensar un daño (pág. 235)

**indigenous** native to a region (p. 203)

**indígena** nativo de una región (pág. 203)

**indirect rule** a colonial government in which local rulers are allowed to maintain their positions of authority and status (p. 193)

**gobierno indirecto** forma de gobierno colonial en la cual se permitía a los gobernantes mantener sus cargos de autoridad y su estatus (pág. 193)

| ENGLISH | ESPAÑOL |
|---|---|
| **inductive reasoning** the doctrine that scientists should proceed from the particular to the general by making systematic observations and carefully organized experiments to test hypotheses or theories, a process that will lead to correct general principles (p. 34) | **razonamiento inductivo** doctrina según la cual los científicos deben ir de lo particular a lo general haciendo observaciones sistemáticas y experimentos organizados cuidadosamente para probar hipótesis o teorías, un proceso que llevará a los principios generales correctos (pág. 34) |
| **industrial capitalism** an economic system based on industrial production or manufacturing (p. 121) | **capitalismo industrial** sistema económico basado en la producción o manufactura industrial (pág. 121) |
| **inflation** a rapid increase in prices (p. 8) | **inflación** aumento rápido de los precios (pág. 8) |
| **insecure** uncertain, shaky; not adequately covered or sustained (p. 173) | **inseguro** incierto, flojo; que no está cubierto o sostenido adecuadamente (pág. 173) |
| **intense** marked by great zeal, energy, determination, or concentration (p. 610) | **intenso** marcado por gran fervor, energía, determinación o concentración (pág. 610) |
| **intensity** extreme degree of strength, force, energy, or feeling (p. 181) | **intensidad** grado extremo de resistencia, fuerza, energía o sentimiento (pág. 181) |
| **intervention** the involvement in a situation to alter the outcome (p. 143) | **intervención** participación en una situación para alterar el resultado (pág. 143) |
| **intifada** "uprising"; a militant movement that arose during the 1980s among supporters of the Palestine Liberation Organization living in Israel (p. 461) | **intifada** movimiento militante que se generó en la década de 1980 entre quienes apoyaban a la Organización para la Liberación de Palestina, y que Vivian en Cisjordania y Gaza (pág. 461) |
| **investor** a person or an entity that commits money to earn a financial return (p. 360) | **inversionista** persona o entidad que compromete dinero para obtener un rendimiento financiero (pág. 360) |
| **involvement** a commitment or a connection to (pp. 387, 389) | **participación** compromiso o conexión con algo (págs. 387, 389) |
| **isolationism** a policy of national isolation by abstention from alliances and other international political and economic relations (p. 387) | **aislacionismo** política de aislamiento nacional llevada a cabo absteniéndose de establecer alianzas y otras relaciones políticas y económicas internacionales (pág. 387) |
| **isolationist** a person who avoids involvement in alliances (p. 303) | **aislacionista** una persona que evita involucrarse en alianzas (pág. 303) |



## J

| ENGLISH | ESPAÑOL |
|---|---|
| **joint-stock company** a business where stocks, or a share of ownership in a company, are bought and owned by shareholders (p. 109) | **sociedad por acciones** negocio en el cual los beneficiarios compran y poseen acciones, o cuotas porpropiedad en una compañía (pág. 109) |
| **jurisdiction** the limits or territory within which authority may be exercised (p. 568) | **jurisdicción** límites o territorio dentro del cual se puede ejercer autoridad (pág. 568) |

## K

**kaiser** German for "caesar"; the title of the emperors of the Second German Empire (p. 136)

**kamikaze** Japanese for "divine wind"; a suicide mission in which young Japanese pilots intentionally flew their airplanes into U.S. fighting ships at sea (p. 398)

**káiser** en alemán, "césar"; título de los emperadores del Segundo Imperio Alemán (pág. 136)

**kamikaze** en japonés, "viento divino"; misión suicida en la cual jóvenes pilotos japoneses estrellaban sus aviones intencionalmente contra los barcos de combate estadounidenses que estaban en el mar (pág. 398)

## L

**labor** work performed by people that provides the goods or services in an economy (p. 115)

**laissez-faire** the concept that the state should not impose government regulations but should leave the economy alone (p. 37)

**legislature** an organized body that makes laws (p. 333)

**liberal** broad-minded; associated with ideals of the individual, especially economic freedom and greater participation in government (p. 92)

**liberalism** a political philosophy originally based largely on Enlightenment principles, holding that people should be as free as possible from government restraint and that civil liberties—the basic rights of all people—should be protected (p. 98)

**liberated** freed (p. 421)

**mano de obra** trabajo realizado por personas, que proporciona los bienes y servicios en una economía (pág. 115)

***laissez-faire*** concepto según el cual el Estado no debe imponer regulaciones gubernamentales, sino que debe haber libertad en la economía (pág. 37)

**Legislativo** cuerpo organizado que hace las leyes (pág. 333)

**liberal** de mente abierta; asociado con ideales de los individuos, en especial la libertad económica y una mayor participación en el gobierno (pág. 92)

**liberalismo** filosofía política basada originalmente en los principios de la Ilustración, que sostiene que las personas deben estar tan libres como sea posible de las restricciones impuestas por el gobierno y que las libertades civiles, es decir los derechos fundamentales de las personas, se deben proteger (pág. 98)

**liberar** poner en libertad (pág. 421)

## M

**magic realism** a form of expression unique to Latin American literature; it combines realistic events with dreamlike or fantasy backgrounds (p. 481)

**maintain** to keep in an existing state; to preserve from failure or decline (p. 509)

**mandate** a territory temporarily governed by another nation on behalf of the League of Nations (p. 293)

**manipulation** skillful or artful management (p. 610)

**realismo mágico** forma de expresión propia de la literatura latinoamericana; combina sucesos reales con trasfondos irreales o fantásticos (pág. 481)

**mantener** conservar en estado de existencia; preservar del malogro o el deterioro (pág. 509)

**mandato** territorio gobernado temporariamente por un país en nombre de la Liga de las Naciones (pág. 293)

**manipulación** manejo hábil o astuto (pág. 610)

## ENGLISH

**mass production** production of goods in quantity usually by machinery (p. 154)

**media** channels or systems of communication (p. 311)

**megacity** a very large city (p. 480)

**mercantilism** a set of principles that dominated economic thought in the seventeenth century; it held that the prosperity of a nation depended on a large supply of gold and silver (p. 109)

**mestizo** a person of mixed European and indigenous descent (p. 142)

**microchip** also called an integrated circuit; a tiny assembly of electronic components and their connections that is produced in or on a tiny bit of material, usually silicon (p. 609)

**Middle Passage** the forced voyage of enslaved Africans across the Atlantic Ocean to the Americas (p. 112)

**migration** the movement of people from one country, place, or locality to another (p. 591)

**militarism** the reliance on military strength (p. 135)

**military** relating to the armed forces or to soldiers, arms, or war (p. 263)

**minimal** barely adequate (p. 492)

**ministerial responsibility** the idea that the prime minister is responsible to the popularly elected legislative body and not to the king or president (p. 169)

**mobilization** the process of assembling troops and supplies and making them ready for war (pp. 266, 395)

**modernism** a movement in which writers and artists between 1870 and 1914 rebelled against the traditional literary and artistic styles that had dominated European cultural life since the Renaissance (p. 177)

**motive** a reason to take action (p. 243)

**multinational corporation** a company with divisions in more than two countries (p. 599)

**multinational empire** an empire in which people of many nationalities live (p. 130)

## ESPAÑOL

**producción masiva** producción de bienes en cantidad por lo general mediante el uso de maquinaria (pág. 154)

**medios de comunicación** canales o sistemas de comunicación (pág. 311)

**megaciudad** una ciudad muy grande (pág. 480)

**mercantilismo** conjunto de principios que dominaban el pensamiento económico en el siglo XVII. Planteaba que la prosperidad de una nación dependía de una abundante acumulación de oro y plata (pág. 109)

**mestizo** persona que desciende de un europeo y un indígena americano (pág. 142)

**microchip** conocido también como circuito integrado; diminuto ensamblaje de componentes electrónicos y sus conexiones, producido en (o sobre) un trozo pequeño de material, por lo general silicio (pág. 609)

**travesía intermedia** viaje obligado de los africanos esclavizados a través del océano Atlántico hasta América (pág. 112)

**migración** movimiento de personas de un país, lugar o área a otra (pág. 591)

**militarismo** dependencia del poderío militar (pág. 135)

**militar** relativo a las fuerzas armadas o a los soldados, las armas o la guerra (pág. 263)

**mínimo** apenas adecuado (pág. 492)

**responsabilidad ministerial** idea según la cual el primer ministro es responsable ante el órgano legislador elegido popularmente y no ante el rey o el presidente (pág. 169)

**movilización** proceso de reunir tropas y provisiones y prepararlas para la guerra (págs. 266, 395)

**modernismo** movimiento en el cual los escritores y artistas entre 1870 y 1914 se rebelaron contra los estilos literarios y artísticos tradicionales que predominaban en la vida cultural de Europa desde el Renacimiento (pág. 177)

**motivo** razón para actuar (pág. 243)

**empresa multinacional** compañía con divisiones en más de dos países (pág. 599)

**imperio multinacional** imperio en el cual viven personas de muchas nacionalidades (pág. 130)

## N

**nationalism** the unique cultural identity of a people based on common language, religion, and national symbols (p. 93)

**national sovereignty** the independence of a state combined with the right and power of regulating itself without foreign interference (p. 10)

**natural rights** rights with which all humans are born, including the rights to life, liberty, and property (p. 16)

**Nazi** shortened form of the German *Nazional,* or the National Socialist German Workers' Party; a member of such party (p. 318)

**neutrality** the refusal to take sides or become involved in wars between other nations (p. 387)

**nongovernmental organization** an organization that has no government ties and works to address world problems (p. 592)

**normalization** the act of bringing something back to a normal condition (p. 554)

**nuclear** being a weapon whose destructive power comes from a nuclear reaction (p. 425)

**nuclear proliferation** the spread of nuclear weapons production technology and knowledge to nations without that capability (p. 579)

**nacionalismo** identidad cultural exclusiva de un pueblo que comparte su lengua, su religión y sus símbolos nacionales (pág. 93)

**soberanía nacional** autonomía de un Estado y su derecho y potestad para regularse sin intromisión extranjera (pág. 10)

**derechos naturales** derechos con los cuales nacen los seres humanos, como el derecho a la vida, la libertad y la propiedad (pág. 16)

**nazi** abreviatura del alemán *Nazional*, relativo al Partido Nacional Socialista Obrero Alemán; miembro de ese partido (pág. 318)

**neutralidad** negativa a tomar partido o involucrarse en guerras entre otras naciones (pág. 387)

**organización no gubernamental** organización que no tiene vínculos con el gobierno y que trabaja para tratar problemas mundiales (pág. 592)

**normalización** retornar a las condiciones normales (pág. 554)

**nuclear** arma cuyo poder destructivo proviene de una reacción nuclear (pág. 425)

**proliferación nuclear** expansión de la tecnología de producción y los conocimientos de armas nucleares a naciones que no tienen esa capacidad (pág. 579)

## O

**occupation** the military force occupying a country or the policies carried out by it (p. 402)

**occupied** held by a foreign power (p. 509)

**oligarchy** "the rule of the few"; a form of government in which a select group of people exercises control (p. 362)

**one-child policy** China's effort, between 1979 and 2015, to control population growth; incentives such as education benefits, child care, and housing were offered to couples who limited their families to one child (p. 539)

**Open Door policy** a policy, proposed by U.S. Secretary of State John Hay in 1899, that stated all powers with spheres of influence in China would respect equal trading opportunities with China and not set tariffs giving an unfair advantage to the citizens of their own countries (p. 234)

**ocupación** cuando las fuerzas militares se apoderan de un país; políticas derivadas de esta acción (pág. 402)

**ocupado** en poder de una potencia extranjera (pág. 509)

**oligarquía** "gobierno de pocos"; forma de gobierno en la cual un grupo selecto de personas ejerce control (pag. 362)

**política de un solo hijo** iniciativa de China, del año 1979 al año 2015, para controlar el aumento de su población; las parejas que limitaban sus familias a un solo hijo reciben incentivos como beneficios educativos, cuidado de los niños y vivienda (pág. 539)

**política de Puertas Abiertas** política propuesta por el Secretario de Estado estadounidense John Hay en 1899, según la cual las potencias con esferas de influencia en China debían respetar las mismas condiciones comerciales con ese país y no fijar aranceles que dieran una ventaja desleal a los ciudadanos de su país (pág. 234)

## ENGLISH

# P

**Pan-Africanism** the unity of all black Africans, regardless of national boundaries (pp. 345, 467)

**Pan-Arabism** Arab unity, regardless of national boundaries (p. 458)

**pandemic** a widespread outbreak of a disease (p. 586)

**parallel** to correspond to; to have the same direction or course (p. 464)

**participation** having a part in or sharing in something (p. 502)

**partisan** a resistance fighter in World War II (p. 409)

**peacekeeping forces** military forces drawn from neutral members of the United Nations to settle conflicts and supervise truces (p. 578)

***peninsulare*** a person born on the Iberian Peninsula; typically, a Spanish or Portuguese official who resided temporarily in Latin America for political and economic gain and then returned to Europe (p. 141)

**per capita** per person (p. 538)

**percent** a part of a whole divided into 100 parts (p. 83)

**perestroika** the fundamental restructuring of the Soviet economy; a policy introduced by Gorbachev (p. 521)

**permanent revolution** an atmosphere of constant revolutionary fervor favored by Mao Zedong to enable China to overcome the past and achieve the final stage of communism (p. 429)

**phase** a part in the development cycle (p. 241)

**philosophe** French for "philosopher"; applied to all intellectuals during the Enlightenment (p. 35)

**planned economy** an economic system directed by government agencies (p. 275)

**plantation** a large agricultural estate (p. 110)

**plebiscite** a popular vote (p. 137)

**pogrom** the organized massacre of a minority group, especially Jews (p. 181)

**policy** an overall plan embracing the general goals and acceptable procedures of a governmental body (p. 6)

**policy of containment** a plan to keep something, such as communism, within its existing geographical boundaries and prevent further aggressive moves (p. 422)

## ESPAÑOL

**panafricanismo** unión de todos las personas africanas negras sin importar sus fronteras nacionales (págs. 345, 467)

**panarabismo** unión de todos los pueblos árabes sin importar sus fronteras nacionales (pág. 458)

**pandemia** brote generalizado de una enfermedad (pág. 586)

**paralelo** que tiene la misma dirección o curso; semejante (pág. 464)

**participación** que tiene parte en algo o comparte la propiedad de algo (pág. 502)

**partisano** combatiente de la resistencia durante la Segunda Guerra Mundial (pág. 409)

**fuerzas de paz** fuerzas militares conformadas por miembros neutrales de las Naciones Unidas para resolver conflictos y supervisar las treguas (pág. 578)

**peninsular** persona nacida en la Península Ibérica; por lo general, un funcionario español o portugués que vivía temporalmente en América Latina para obtener beneficios políticos y económicos y luego regresaba a Europa (pág. 141)

**per cápita** por persona (pág. 538)

**porcentaje** parte de un todo dividido entre 100 (pág. 83)

**perestroika** reestructuración de los fundamentos de la economía soviética; política introducida por Mijaíl Gorbachov (pág. 521)

**revolución permanente** atmósfera de fervor revolucionario constante promovida por Mao Tse-Tung para permitir que China superara el pasado y llegara a la etapa final del comunismo (pág. 429)

**fase** parte en el ciclo de desarrollo (pág. 241)

***philosophe*** término francés para "filósofo"; se aplicaba a todos los intelectuales durante la Ilustración (pág. 35)

**economía dirigida** sistema económico dirigido por agencias del gobierno (pág. 275)

**plantación** gran propiedad agrícola (pág. 110)

**plebiscito** voto popular (pág. 137)

**pogromo** masacre organizada de una minoría, especialmente los judíos (pág. 181)

**política** plan general que comprende los objetivos generales y los procedimientos aceptables de un organismo gubernamental (pág. 6)

**política de contención** plan para mantener algo, como el comunismo, dentro de los límites geográficos existentes y evitar movimientos radicales en el futuro (pág. 422)

**popular culture** entertainment created for a profit and for a mass audience (p. 535)

**popular sovereignty** the right to govern through the consent of the people (p. 58)

**postmodernism** an artistic movement that emerged in the 1980s; its artists do not expect rationality in the world and are comfortable with many "truths" (p. 535)

**prefecture** in the Japanese Meiji Restoration, a territory governed by its former daimyo lord (p. 249)

**principle of intervention** the idea that great powers have the right to send armies into countries where there are revolutions to restore legitimate governments (p. 97)

**principle of nonalignment** Jawaharlal Nehru's refusal to align India with any bloc or alliance (p. 452)

**privatization** the sale of government-owned companies to private firms (p. 476)

**prohibit** to prevent or to forbid (p. 321)

**proletariat** the working class (p. 156)

**propaganda** ideas spread to influence public opinion for or against a cause (p. 269)

**protectorate** a political unit that depends on another government for its protection (p. 191)

**provincial** local; of or relating to a province (p. 241)

**proxy war** a war in which the powers in conflict use third parties as substitutes instead of fighting each other directly (p. 435)

**psychoanalysis** a method by which a therapist and patient probe deeply into the patient's memory; by making the patient's conscious mind aware of repressed thoughts, healing can take place (p. 179)

**psychological** mental; directed toward the will or mind (p. 288)

**puddling** the process in which coke derived from coal is used to burn away impurities in crude iron to produce high-quality iron (p. 117)

**Puritans** English Protestants who believed the Church of England needed further reform and sought to simplify and regulate forms of worship (p. 12)

**cultura popular** entretenimiento creado con fines de lucro y dirigido a una audiencia masiva (pág. 535)

**soberanía popular** derecho a gobernar por consentimiento del pueblo (pag. 58)

**posmodernismo** movimiento artístico surgido en la década de 1980; los artistas que lo practican no esperan encontrar racionalidad en el mundo y están a gusto con muchas "verdades" (pág. 535)

**prefectura** durante la Restauración Meiji en Japón, territorio gobernado por su antiguo señor daimio (pág. 249)

**principio de intervención** idea según la cual las grandes potencias tienen derecho a enviar ejércitos a países donde se presenta una revolución para restaurar los gobiernos legítimos (pág. 97)

**principio de no alineación** negativa del líder Jawaharlal Nehru a alinear India con ningún bloque o alianza (pág. 452)

**privatización** venta de compañías del gobierno a firmas privadas (pág. 476)

**prohibir** evitar o impeder (pág. 321)

**proletariado** clase trabajadora (pág. 156)

**propaganda** ideas difundidas con el fin de influenciar a la opinión pública a favor o en contra de una causa (pág. 269)

**protectorado** unidad política que depende de otro gobierno para su protección (pág. 191)

**provincial** local; de una provincia o relativo a ella (pág. 241)

**guerra subsidiaria** guerra en la cual las potencias en conflicto usan a terceros como sustitutos en lugar de combatir entre ellos directamente (pág. 435)

**psicoanálisis** método por el cual un terapeuta y un paciente exploran en lo profundo de la memoria del paciente; se puede obtener una cura trayendo al consciente del paciente los pensamientos reprimidos (pág. 179)

**psicológico** mental; que se dirige a la voluntad o la mente (pág. 288)

**pudelación** proceso en el cual se usa coque derivado del carbón para quemar las impurezas del hierro bruto para producir hierro de alta calidad (pág. 117)

**puritanos** protestantes ingleses que sentían que la Iglesia de Inglaterra necesitaba una reforma más profunda y buscaban simplificar y regular las formas de culto (pág. 12)

ENGLISH

R

**racism** the belief that race determines a person's traits and capabilities (p. 189)

**radical** relating to a political group associated with views, practices, and policies of extreme change (p. 128)

**rationalism** a system of thought expounded by René Descartes based on the belief that reason is the chief source of knowledge (p. 33)

**real wages** the actual purchasing power of income (p. 494)

**redistribution of wealth** the shifting of wealth from a rich minority to a poor majority (p. 357)

**regime** the government in power (p. 137)

**remittance** money sent (p. 555)

**reparation** a payment made to the victor by the vanquished to cover the costs of war (p. 290)

**require** to demand as being necessary (p. 321)

**resolve** determination; a fixed purpose (p. 387)

**restoration** the process of bringing back to a former position or condition (p. 13)

**revenue** the yield of sources of income a nation or state collects and deposits into its treasury for public use (p. 460)

**revisionist** a Marxist who rejected the revolutionary approach, believing instead in evolution by democratic means to achieve the goal of socialism (p. 157)

**revolution** an overthrow of government (p. 282)

**rivalry** a state or situation in which people or groups are competing with each other (p. 52)

**rococo** an artistic style that replaced baroque in the 1730s; it was highly secular, emphasizing grace, charm, and gentle action (p. 42)

**role** a socially expected behavior pattern (p. 455)

**Roundheads** supporters of the Parliament in the English Civil War (p. 13)

**rule of law** a situation in which the laws of a country are obeyed by everyone (p. 14)

ESPAÑOL

**racismo** creencia de que la raza determina los rasgos y capacidades de una persona (pág. 189)

**radical** relativo a un grupo político asociado con opiniones, prácticas y políticas de cambio extremo (pág. 128)

**racionalismo** sistema de pensamiento expuesto por René Descartes, que se basa en la creencia de que la razón es la fuente principal del conocimiento (pág. 33)

**salario real** poder adquisitivo real de los ingresos (pág. 494)

**redistribución de la riqueza** paso de la riqueza de una minoría rica a una mayoría pobre (pág. 357)

**régimen** gobierno que está en el poder (pág. 137)

**remesa** dinero enviado (pág. 555)

**reparación** pago que el vencido hace al vencedor para cubrir los gastos de la guerra (pág. 290)

**exigir** demandar como algo necesario (pág. 321)

**resolución** determinación; propósito fijo (pág. 387)

**restauración** regreso a una posición o condición anterior (pág. 13)

**renta** producto de diversas fuentes de ingresos que una nación o Estado recauda y deposita en su tesoro para destinarlo al gasto público (pág. 460)

**revisionista** marxista que se oponía al enfoque revolucionario, y en cambio, creía en la evolución por medios democráticos para alcanzar los objetivos del socialismo (pág. 157)

**revolución** derrocamiento de un gobierno (pág. 282)

**rivalidad** estado o situación en la que personas o grupos compiten entre sí (pág. 52)

**Rococó** estilo artístico que reemplazó al Barroco en la década de 1730; altamente seglar, con énfasis en la gracia, el encanto y las acciones gentiles (pág. 42)

**conducta** patrón de comportamiento socialmente esperado (pág. 455)

**cabezas redondas** partidarios del Parlamento durante la Guerra Civil Inglesa (pág. 13)

**imperio de la ley** situación en la que las leyes de un país son obedecidas por todos (pág. 14)

## S

**salon** an elegant urban drawing room where, in the eighteenth century, writers, artists, aristocrats, government officials, and wealthy middle-class people gathered to discuss the ideas of the philosophes (p. 41)

**salón** elegante recinto urbano donde, durante el siglo XVIII, escritores, artistas, aristócratas, funcionarios del gobierno y personas acaudaladas de la clase media se reunían a analizar las ideas de los filósofos (pág. 41)

**sanction** restriction intended to enforce international law (p. 384)

**sanciones** restricciones cuyo propósito es hacer cumplir las leyes internacionales (pág. 384)

**sans-culottes** "without breeches"; members of the Paris Commune who considered themselves ordinary patriots (in other words, they wore long trousers instead of the fine, knee-length breeches of the nobles) (p. 77)

***sans-culottes*** "sin pantalón corto"; miembros de la comuna de París que se consideraban patriotas comunes (es decir, usaban pantalones largos en lugar de los finos pantalones hasta la rodilla que usaban los nobles) (pág. 77)

**satellite state** a country that is economically and politically dependent on another country (p. 422)

**nación satélite** país que dependen política y económicamente de otro país (pág. 422)

**scientific method** a systematic procedure for collecting and analyzing evidence that was crucial to the evolution of science in the modern world (p. 33)

**método científico** procedimiento sistemático para recolectar y analizar evidencias, que fue fundamental para la evolución de la ciencia en el mundo moderno (pág. 33)

**sector** a sociological, economic, or political subdivision of society (pp. 220, 540)

**sector** subdivisión sociológica, económica o política de la sociedad (págs. 220, 540)

**self-strengthening** a policy promoted by reformers toward the end of the Qing dynasty under which China would adopt Western technology while keeping its Confucian values and institutions (p. 232)

**autofortalecimiento** política promovida por los reformistas hacia el final de la dinastía Qing, en la cual China adoptaba la tecnología occidental, pero mantenía sus valores e instituciones confucianos (pág. 232)

**separation of powers** a form of government in which the executive, legislative, and judicial branches limit and control each other through a system of checks and balances (p. 35)

**separación de poderes** forma de gobierno en la cual las ramas ejecutiva, legislativa y judicial se limitan y controlan entre sí mediante un sistema de equilibrio de poderes (pág. 35)

**sepoy** an Indian soldier hired by the British East India Company to protect the company's interests in the region (p. 209)

**cipayo** soldado indio contratado por la Compañía Británica de las Indias Orientales para proteger sus intereses en la región (pág. 209)

**shift** a change in direction (p. 491)

**desplazamiento** cambio de dirección (pág. 491)

**social contract** the concept proposed by Rousseau that an entire society agrees to be governed by its general will, and all individuals should be forced to abide by the general will because it represents what is best for the entire community (p. 39)

**contrato social** concepto planteado por Rousseau según el cual una sociedad accede a ser gobernada por su voluntad general, y todos los individuos deben ser obligados a acatar la voluntad general ya que esta representa lo que es mejor para toda la comunidad (pág. 39)

**Social Darwinism** theory used by Western nations in the late nineteenth century to justify their dominance; it was based on Charles Darwin's theory of natural selection, "the survival of the fittest," and applied to modern human activities (p. 180)

**darwinismo social** teoría de finales del siglo XIX con la cual las naciones occidentales justificaban su dominación; se basaba en la teoría de la selección natural de Charles Darwin, "la supervivencia del más fuerte", aplicada a las actividades humanas modernas (pág. 180)

**socialism** a system in which society, usually in the form of the government, owns and controls the means of production (p. 122)

**socialismo** sistema en el cual la sociedad, por lo general representada por el gobierno, posee y controla los medios de producción (pág. 122)

**sole** being the only one (p. 500)

**exclusivo** que es único (pág. 500)

| ENGLISH | ESPAÑOL |
|---|---|
| **source** a document or primary reference book that gives information (p. 429) | **fuente** documento o libro usado como referencia primaria para aportar información (pág. 429) |
| **soviets** Russian councils composed of representatives from the workers and soldiers (p. 282) | **sóviets** consejos rusos conformados por representantes de los obreros y los soldados (pág. 282) |
| **sphere of influence** area in which foreign powers have been granted exclusive rights and privileges, such as trading rights and mining privileges (p. 232) | **esferas de influencia** áreas en las cuales se concede a las potencias extranjeras derechos y privilegios exclusivos, como derechos comerciales y privilegios para la explotación minera (pág. 232) |
| **stability** the state of being stable; strong enough to endure (p. 18) | **estabilidad** propiedad de estable; suficientemente fuerte como para resistir (pág. 18) |
| **stable** not changing or fluctuating; steady (p. 511) | **estable** que no cambia ni fluctúa; invariable (pág. 511) |
| **state capitalism** an economic system in which the central government plays an active role in the economy, establishing price and wage policies and subsidizing vital industries (p. 509) | **capitalismo de Estado** sistema económico en el cual el gobierno central desempeña un rol activo en la economía, estableciendo las políticas de precios y salarios, y subsidiando las industrias vitales (pág. 509) |
| **subprime investments** investments based on loans that have interest rates that are higher than prime rates and are extended especially to low-income borrowers (p. 605) | **inversiones de alto riesgo** inversiones basadas en préstamos que tienen una tasa de interés más alta que la tasa preferencial y se otorgan especialmente a prestatarios de bajos ingresos (pág. 605) |
| **subsidy** a payment made to support an enterprise that a government thinks is beneficial (pp. 109, 250) | **subsidio** pago que se hace para respaldar una iniciativa considerada beneficiosa por un gobierno (pags. 109, 250) |
| **successor** one who follows, especially one who takes over a throne, title, estate, or office (p. 50) | **sucesor** el que sigue, especialmente el que asume el trono o un título, una propiedad, o recibe una herencia o un cargo (pág. 50) |
| **suffrage** the right to vote (p. 164) | **sufragio** derecho al voto (pág. 164) |
| **surrealism** an artistic movement that seeks to depict the world of the unconscious (p. 308) | **Surrealismo** movimiento artístico que busca representar el mundo del inconsciente (pág. 308) |
| **sustainable development** an economic development that does not limit the ability of future generations to meet their basic needs (p. 613) | **desarrollo sostenible** desarrollo económico que no limita la capacidad de las generaciones futuras de satisfacer sus necesidades básicas (pág. 613) |
| **symbol** something that stands for something else by way of association; a visible sign of something invisible (p. 531) | **símbolo** algo que representa otra cosa por asociación; signo visible de algo invisible (pág. 531) |

## T

| | |
|---|---|
| **taille** an annual direct tax, usually on land or property, that provided a regular source of income for the French monarchy (p. 71) | **talla** impuesto directo anual, usualmente sobre la tierra o las propiedades, que proveía una fuente habitual de ingresos a la monarquía francesa (pág. 71) |
| **target** something or someone marked for attack (pp. 272, 478) | **objetivo** algo o alguien marcado para un ataque (págs. 272, 478) |
| **temporary** lasting for a limited time; not permanent (pp. 128, 440) | **temporal** de duración limitada; que no es permanente (págs. 128, 440) |
| **tenant farmer** a farmer who works land owned by another and pays rent either in cash or in shares of produce (p. 217) | **agricultor arrendatario** agricultor que trabaja en tierras de propiedad de otra y paga renta en efectivo o en acciones de producción (pág. 217) |

**theme** a subject or topic of artistic work (p. 472)

**tema** materia o asunto de una obra artística (pág. 472)

**totalitarian state** a government that aims to control the political, economic, social, intellectual, and cultural lives of its citizens (p. 310)

**Estado totalitario** gobierno que intenta controlar la vida política, económica, social, intelectual y cultural de sus ciudadanos (pág. 310)

**total war** a war that involved the complete mobilization of resources and people, affecting the lives of all citizens in the warring countries, even those remote from the battlefield (p. 275)

**guerra total** guerra que implica la movilización total de recursos y personas, y afecta la vida de todos los ciudadanos de las naciones en conflicto, aun aquellas alejadas del campo de batalla (pág. 275)

**trade embargo** a policy prohibiting trade with a particular country (p. 476)

**embargo comercial** política que prohíbe comercializar con un país en particular (pág. 476)

**traditions** the established customs of a people (p. 204)

**tradiciones** costumbres establecidas de un pueblo (pág. 204)

**transfer** to take over the control of (p. 453)

**traspasar** asumir el control (pág. 453)

**transition** changeover; the move from one form, stage, or style to another (p. 156)

**transición** conversión; pasar de una forma, etapa o estilo a otra (pág. 156)

**trench warfare** fighting from ditches protected by barbed wire, as in World War I (p. 270)

**guerra de trincheras** combatir desde zanjas protegidas por alambre de púas, como en la Primera Guerra Mundial (pág. 270)

## U

**uncertainty principle** the idea put forth by Werner Heisenberg in 1927 that the behavior of subatomic particles is uncertain, suggesting that all of the physical laws governing the universe are based on uncertainty (p. 308)

**principio de incertidumbre** idea planteada por Werner Heisenberg en 1927 según la cual el comportamiento de las partículas subatómicas es incierto, lo cual sugiere que las leyes físicas que gobiernan el universo se basan en la incertidumbre (pág. 308)

**uncharted** not mapped; unknown (p. 200)

**inexplorado** no cartografiado; desconocido (pág. 200)

**unification** the act, process, or result of making into a coherent or coordinated whole; the state of being unified (p. 133)

**unificación** acción, proceso o resultado de conformar un todo coherente o coordinado; estar unificado (pág. 133)

**unify** to make into a unit or whole; to unite (p. 538)

**unificar** hacer un todo; unir (pág. 538)

**universal male suffrage** the right of all males to vote in elections (p. 128)

**sufragio universal masculino** derecho de todos los hombres a votar en las elecciones (pág. 128)

**unrestricted** having no restrictions or bounds (p. 274)

**irrestricto** que no tiene restricciones o límites (pág. 274)

## V

**viceroy** a governor who rules as a representative of a monarch (p. 210)

**virrey** gobernante que regía como representante de un monarca (pág. 210)

**violation** a disregard of rules or agreements (p. 379)

**violación** desprecio de las reglas o acuerdos (pág. 379)

**volunteer** one who enters the military voluntarily (p. 343)

**voluntario** persona que entra al ejército voluntariamente (pág. 343)

| ENGLISH | ESPAÑOL |
| --- | --- |

## W

**war communism** in World War I Russia, the government control of banks and most industries, the seizing of grain from peasants, and the centralization of state administration under Communist control (p. 285)

**comunismo de guerra** durante la Primera Guerra Mundial en Rusia, control gubernamental de bancos y la mayoría de industrias, la incautación de los granos y la centralización de la administración del Estado bajo el control comunista (pág. 285)

**war of attrition** a war based on wearing down the other side with constant attacks and heavy losses, such as in World War I (p. 271)

**guerra de desgaste guerra** que consiste en desgastar a la contraparte con ataques constantes y pérdidas numerosas, como en la Primera Guerra Mundial (pág. 271)

**welfare state** a state in which the government takes responsibility for providing citizens with services such as health care (p. 492)

**estado de bienestar** estado en el cual el gobierno asume la responsabilidad de proveer a los ciudadanos servicios como la atención en salud (pág. 492)

**whereas** although (p. 217)

**en tanto que** aunque (pág. 217)

**widespread** widely extended or spread out (pp. 395, 400)

**generalizado** muy ampliado o difundido (págs. 395, 400)

**women's liberation movement** the renewed feminist movement of the late 1960s, which demanded political and economic equality with men (p. 498)

**movimiento de liberación femenina** movimiento feminista renovado de finales de la década de 1960, que exigía la igualdad política y económica con los hombres (pág. 498)

## Z

***zaibatsu*** in the Japanese economy, a large financial and industrial corporation (p. 348)

***zaibatsu*** en la economía japonesa, sociedad financiera e industrial grande (pág. 348)

**Zionism** an international movement originally for the establishment of a Jewish national homeland in Palestine, where ancient Israel was located, and later for the support of modern Israel (p. 181)

**sionismo** movimiento internacional que apoyaba inicialmente el establecimiento de un territorio judío en Palestina, donde se ubicaba el antiguo Israel, y luego se convirtió en fundamento del Israel moderno (pág. 181)

# INDEX



The following abbreviations are used in the index: *m* = map; *f* = feature (photograph, picture, painting, cartoon, chart); *t* = table; *q* = quote.

## A

## B



Index

## C

## D

## G

## H

Index

## K



## L

Index

## N



## O

Index

## X



## Y



## Z